NEW TESTAMENT APOCRYPHA

New Testament Apocrypha

More Noncanonical Scriptures

VOLUME ONE

Edited by

Tony Burke and Brent Landau

WILLIAM B. EERDMANS PUBLISHING COMPANY

GRAND RAPIDS, MICHIGAN

Wm. B. Eerdmans Publishing Co.
2140 Oak Industrial Drive N.E., Grand Rapids, Michigan 49505
www.eerdmans.com

Printed in the United States of America

22 21 20   3 4 5 6 7

ISBN 978-0-8028-7289-0

Library of Congress Cataloging-in-Publication Data

Names: Burke, Tony, 1968– editor. | Landau, Brent, editor.
Title: New Testament apocrypha : more noncanonical scriptures / edited by Tony Burke, Brent Landau.
Other titles: Bible. Apocrypha. English. 2016.
Description: Grand Rapids, Michigan : William B. Eerdmans Publishing Company, 2016– |
    Includes bibliographical references and index.
Identifiers: LCCN 2016009263 | ISBN 9780802872890 (hardback : vol. 1)
Subjects: LCSH: Apocryphal books (New Testament)
Classification: LCC BS1692 2016 | DDC 229/.92052—dc23
    LC record available at https://lccn.loc.gov/2016009263

Biblical citations in this volume follow the New Revised Standard Version unless otherwise noted.

Dedicated to

Montague Rhodes James and James Keith Elliott,
editors and translators of *The Apocryphal New Testament* (1924 and 1993)

Contents

I. GOSPELS AND RELATED TRADITIONS OF NEW TESTAMENT FIGURES

Contents

II. APOCRYPHAL ACTS AND RELATED TRADITIONS

Foreword: The Endurance of the Christian Apocrypha

"Of making many books there is no end" in Ecclesiastes 12:12 may be a fair judgment about the seemingly interminable stream of writings concerned with the events and personages of the New Testament commonly gathered together under the umbrella title "The Christian Apocrypha." The King James Version of the rest of that verse, ". . . and much study is a weariness of the flesh," however, may be sensibly glossed over as an inappropriate sentiment to cite in this scholarly book.

Defining "New Testament Apocrypha"

The so-called apocryphal writings are an amorphous and flexible collection of writings that do not constitute an agreed or settled entity, nor are they a body of literature from a defined timeframe. There is no agreed set number of books as there is in the so-called Old Testament Apocrypha, usually printed separately in many Protestant Bibles. Such an enormous, yet unspecified, number of such texts is the reason why *more* Christian apocrypha need to be published.

The titles given to collections may vary. All the words in the title "The Apocryphal New Testament" are wrong, and "Early Noncanonical Christian Literature," although preferred by many academics, is not precise or ideal. We study not only early texts, not all of them are Christian (one in the current collection here is Jewish in origin), and "noncanonical" in such a title is as anachronistic as "apocryphal" (in the literal sense). At least "New Testament Apocrypha" is a well-known, if less than perfect, title, which most readers and prospective readers recognize; they know the sorts of writings that may be found in a book with this name on its spine.

Early Christian Apocrypha Collections

Some apocryphal Christian texts have been known for centuries and are among the earliest books printed. The *Arabic Infancy Gospel* was first printed in 1697 and the *Protevangelium of James* in 1552. The *Infancy Gospel of Thomas* and the *History of Joseph the Carpenter* were published in the eighteenth century. A Latin version of the *Acts of Timothy*, included here, was published in Leuven in 1485 and later revised by the Bollandists in 1643.

Printed collections containing, admittedly, only a limited number of apocryphal texts, as commonly designated, can be traced to the volumes edited by Fabricius (1719), Jones (1726–1727), Birch (1804), Thilo (1832), or Giles (1852). Modern translations of some of these texts into Western languages have been edited over the past century by Walker, Cowper, Vouaux, Amiot, de Santos Otero, and others. A strange but very popular collection containing not only conventional apocryphal texts but some of the Apostolic Fathers was edited by William Hone in 1820 and went through many editions; the editor is now rightly criticized for peddling the false belief that the apocryphal writings were deliberately and wilfully excluded from the canon by its compilers.

Modern Christian Apocrypha Collections

Those of us who have had the privilege, and problem, of making a meaningful, representative, and manageable selection of the New Testament apocryphal texts have an *embarras de richesses* to work with. When I was asked in the late 1980s to revise M. R. James's classic collection *The Apocryphal New Testament*, first published in 1924, Oxford University Press gave me *carte blanche* over what to include. For the most part I obviously followed James's lead, but I added texts unknown in his day and expanded or changed others where newer or better manuscripts had been published. In the end there was no trouble filling a volume of roughly 700 pages with what I judged to be the most important and influential apocryphal texts, although not necessarily including only the oldest such writings. I made reference to the many subordinate and secondary apocryphal acts such as the *Acts of John in the City of Rome* or the *Acts of John* according to Prochorus. I also had knowledge of the many apocryphal apocalypses over and above those I included, which were the apocalypses of Paul, of Peter, and of Thomas.

I was all too aware that at the time the multi-volume editions by Mario Erbetta and by Luigi Moraldi included many more texts than I was willing or able to use. *The Investiture of Abbaton* found in English in the present book had previously appeared in Italian in Moraldi's and in Erbetta's collections. I knew that the various editions of the German collection of apocrypha begun by Edgar Hennecke and continued by Wilhelm Schneemelcher had also made a somewhat different selection. The first volume of the latest, seventh edition of Hennecke (-Schneemelcher), *Neutestamentliche Apokryphen*—edited by Christoph Markschies and Jens Schröter and published in 2012—greatly expanded its predecessors' collection of texts relating to the gospels. The first volume alone totals 1468 pages, compared with the 442 pages of volume one of Hennecke-Schneemelcher. The editors of Hennecke-Schneemelcher decided that a new title was needed, and they came up with what they hoped would be the more accurate and inclusive *Antike christliche Apokryphen*. Its editors have restricted themselves to early texts, setting John of Damascus (d. 749 CE) as their *terminus*.

The latest French-language selection of apocryphal texts has also adopted a similar title, *Écrits apocryphes chrétiens* (= *EAC*). These are published as two volumes in the prestige series Bibliothèque de la Pléiade, an extensive multi-volume library of the classics of world literature. In them are several Christian apocrypha that have previously seldom seen the light of day, for instance the *Encomium on John the Baptist, On the Priesthood of Jesus,* the *Acts of Titus,* the *Epistle of Christ from Heaven* (although the latter is in de Santos Otero's and in Erbetta's collections of apocryphal books), and the *Dialogue of the Paralytic with Christ,* all of which are now to be found in English in our current book, *New Testament Apocrypha: More Noncanonical Scriptures* (= *MNTA*). Several other collections in French are more popular in approach, some of them trying to satisfy a readership interested in the Cathars or other "fringe" movements—for example, Charles Mopsik, *Les Évangiles de l'ombre: apocryphes du Nouveau Testament* (Paris: Lieu commun, 1983) or France Quéré, *Évangiles apocryphes* (Paris: Seuil, 1983).

Some apocryphal texts that have been identified or catalogued have not yet been published. Others, again, have been discovered, recovered, or uncovered in the last few decades in libraries and monasteries or in archaeological excavations with the scholarly world at large being exposed to them only in recent times. The *Gospel of Judas* in the Codex Tchacos was studied only this millennium; the complete *Gospel of Thomas* in Coptic with all 114 logia was found in only 1945; the *Gospel of Peter* came to light in the 1880s; previously unknown portions of the *Acts of Paul* became known to scholars in the twentieth century. It was in 1974 when François Bovon and Bernard Bouvier found Xenophontos 32, a hitherto unexamined but crucially important witness to the *Acts of Philip.* The *Discourse of the Savior* included in *MNTA* was found only in 1965.

When Is Enough Enough?

One may ask: With Erbetta, Moraldi, and now *HS*[7] and *EAC,* do we not have enough apocrypha to satisfy scholarship? Why ask for more? Apart from a natural human curiosity to find, to assemble, and (*pace* Ecclesiastes 12:12b) to study as much as there is, the (re)quest for "more" (texts) is greeted now with a greater understanding than that exhibited by Mr. Bumble and Mr. Limbkins in Charles Dickens's *Oliver Twist* when Oliver begged for "more" (gruel).

Scholarly appetite for this literature has grown recently. Not only is there a learned journal, *Apocrypha,* dedicated to publishing essays on this discipline, but there is also an increased publication of critical editions, translations, and studies of this body of literature. One need look only at the growth of the compendious bibliographical listings of the annual *Bulletin de l'AELAC,* published since 1991 by the active research group, the Association pour l'étude de la littérature apocryphe chrétienne (= AELAC; the group is itself a significant symptom of the academic hunger for this work), to recognize that this is an area of great scholarly industry within theological studies. AELAC is a body of, mainly, European scholars that is encouragingly active, editing and translating as well as aiding research into the whole general area. Whereas previously such study was typically restricted to a few antiquarians, personified by the likes of M. R. James himself in the early twentieth century, nowadays we do not dub such research "recherché." Predominantly, but certainly not exclusively, North American in membership, the Society of Biblical Literature hosts a number of significant seminars and study groups in the whole area of early Christian apocrypha, and its annual jamborees see a healthy number of younger scholars presenting their innovative work on these noncanonical texts. Some of these academics' work bears fruit in the present book.

Much of this recent and increased interest is doubtless fueled by a healthy desire to understand the origins and growth of Christianity within the widest geographical and literary contexts. Whatever uniqueness the pious may claim for the 27 New Testament books, many apocryphal writings also acquired a literary and theological life of their own. Work on the apocrypha (to be pedantic, books that were "*apokryph gewordene*"—i.e., books described later as apocryphal—to adopt a neat German description) shows that these later, oftentimes pioneering books, may indeed have a history ultimately influenced by the biblical canon (again, to speak more accurately, "writings that were to become canonical") but that thereafter the apocryphal texts themselves went on to influence other writings, sometimes as pervasively as had the authorized Scriptures.

Unlike the British novelist Kingsley Amis who coined the tag "More means worse" (albeit originally relating to the increasing numbers of students in higher education), scholars of Christian apocrypha do not use the word "more" pejoratively. Far from it. An increased awareness of apocryphal literature in all its variety enhances our understanding of Christian history, theology, and culture. There is more still to be read. Taking

Maurice Geerard's *Clavis Apocryphorum Novi Testamenti* (Turnhout: Brepols, 1992) as a convenient register, we can look through its titles to see just how many have already been identified but have not yet been edited or published in a critical edition, let alone translated into a familiar Western language. The extensive Old and Middle Irish apocrypha are a case in point. There are several valued texts in these corpora, which only recently have been receiving the attention they deserve, in many cases thanks to Brepols's Corpus Christianorum Series Apocryphorum (= CCSA), which to date has three volumes devoted to apocryphal literature in the language once called Erse. Coptic fragments of allegedly apocryphal material also, perhaps inevitably, keep emerging—not least in ongoing publication from the Oxyrhynchus hoard. Georgian and Armenian texts deserve more prominence, and it is rewarding to see one such apocryphon here in *MNTA*: the *Dialogue of the Paralytic with Christ*. Further newly edited Armenian texts are to be found in two other CCSA volumes. Those whose interests lie not only in apocryphal texts in general but in those from particular language areas are well catered for by newly edited texts: the *Acts of Cornelius the Centurion* here survives substantially in Ethiopic. The *Life of John the Baptist by Serapion* is an Arabic text; the *Revelation of the Magi* is in Syriac, as is the *History of Simon Cephas*, and as too is the version included here of the *Infancy Gospel of Thomas*.

More New Testament Apocrypha

This present collection, *MNTA*, is the first of a projected multi-volume series. We owe a great debt of gratitude to the editors, Tony Burke and Brent Landau. This first volume contains some thirty texts newly introduced and translated by a distinguished panel of contributors, all of whom have been active in their research on these texts. The whole scholarly enterprise has been scrupulously and carefully edited. *MNTA* shows splendid examples of how this increased number of publications can enhance our understanding. In some cases the texts here add to our repertoire of stories about New Testament worthies: Mary of Nazareth, Simon Cephas, a paralytic, Barnabas, the Good Thief, Judas, Mary Magdalene, Timothy, Cornelius, Titus, John the Baptist (about whom there are three examples here), and the Magi (the focus of two texts). As stated above, sometimes a study of the apocryphal texts is undertaken to examine the literature of a particular language group. At other times one may wish to undertake further study into a particular genre, for example apocalypses; one finds here apocalypses of John and of the Virgin Mary (now with her own tour of hell). This genre has been acquiring attention recently and further work needs to be done. The underrepresented genre of epistle writing is enhanced here by two texts written as letters. Again, more texts are required in this field of study.

At yet other times research may use reception history *(Wirkungsgeschichte)* to plot how ideas, characters, storylines, or events were received by later generations of writers. Once again, this present collection helps shed new light on how key figures like Mary Magdalene or Peter were later understood. The texts here on the Magdalene and on Simon Cephas, for example, have many helpful allusions to and quotations from earlier sources such as the Pseudo-Clementine writings, the *Acts of Peter*, and, of course, the New Testament itself, which are themselves of interest. The *Hospitality of Dysmas* has fascinating textual and literary links to other Christian apocrypha, especially the *Acts of Pilate*.

The expanding, and occasional contracting of stories, such as we find in, say, the *Dysmas* apocryphon are characteristic of much apocryphal literature, partly because writers were not constrained; they felt freer to rewrite texts that were not treated as authorized Scripture. We may wish to plot theological or biographical details about stories of Mary's early life from the *Protevangelium* through to the *Gospel of Pseudo-Matthew* and on to the ninth-century *Nativity of Mary,* the last only recently studied in depth. Without that last writing, any investigation into the onward march of the traditions about Mary would be truncated. In those stories relating to Mary's early life there is a more realistic chance to plot the reception history and/or literary development of the stories from their origins onwards the more evidence we can draw upon. Each new text, like the *Hospitality of Dysmas,* provides us with further pieces of the jigsaw in this expanding picture.

Many a dissertation awaits the writing on the multifarious accounts of the Virgin Mary's dormition (or "transitus" or "falling asleep" or "obsequies" or "assumption") in the various ancient Christian languages and, although it seems well nigh impossible to consider there could ever be a synopsis of all the accounts or a Diatessaron-like retelling of them all in one narrative, nonetheless possible influences, recurrent concerns and teachings, may become apparent and will need careful unraveling as new texts emerge and familiar ones are reexamined.

To those whose interest may primarily be in ancient Christian art or medieval drama or poetry the study of written apocrypha may provide helpful parallels with, potential sources of, and developments from iconographic expressions. Many a fresco or stained glass may show an awareness of a story known to us in written form. The English medieval mystery plays often include tales drawn from the apocrypha, such as the so-called Harrowing of Hell, paralleling the *Descensus ad inferos. Saint John* by the eighteenth-century German poet Herder draws on the Story of the Partridge from *Acts of John* 56–57. Among earlier poets, Milton and Dante seem to have been influenced by apocryphal apocalypses. The Hymn of Jesus in *Acts of John* 94–95 inspired Gustav Holst's music performed at the English Three Choirs Festival in 1921. Even Hollywood failed to escape the biblical apocrypha, as evidenced by the blockbuster film *Quo Vadis?* As more apocrypha are published we are likely to recognize further parallels with the creative or plastic arts, whichever way the direction of such influence be.

Excuses for a publication like *MNTA* are unnecessary. The texts here and others awaiting future publication are apocrypha that need not and ought not remain apocryphal in the sense of "hidden away." The *richesses* within these writings, great literature though they seldom are, nevertheless need exposure.

On Writing Christian Apocrypha
It is often said that the Christian apocrypha began life with the filling-in of perceived gaps in the biblical narratives because human curiosity quite naturally wanted fuller accounts of what the founders of the faith had done and said. More complete biographies were demanded of all its heroes. Thus deeds and deaths, typically martyrdoms of the eponymous heroes, were written. Likewise, parallel tales about a church's or a region's founding fathers were concocted; later, hagiographies followed similar lines. As far as Jesus was concerned, tales about his mother's and Joseph's early life were invented; imaginative and sometimes bizarre childhood tales about Jesus were created that filled in some of his "missing" years; Jesus' three-day absence in the underworld between the crucifixion and resurrection also fueled imaginative deeds of derring-do. But not all the "silent" times in Jesus' career gave rise to imaginative retellings. For instance, very few apocrypha deal with gaps in the period of his earthly ministry, although a few agrapha and some of the logia in the *Gospel of Thomas* may best be planted in that time. By contrast, the creative writers of the apocrypha seemed strangely satisfied by the canonical Gospels' Easter stories, even though these

amount to very few events allegedly occurring during the forty days that Jesus remained on earth being gainfully occupied prior to his ascension. As far as I know, no further confections beyond those in our canonical writings seem concerned about where Jesus went, who else observed or met him, or what other things he did in his newly acquired and transient resuscitated state, despite the tantalizing absence of a running commentary on such a unique stage in his career. However, it is still true to a great extent that expansions of the sparseness characteristic of many biblical sequences were sometimes the reasons behind later rewritings.

Jacob of Voragine's famous and popular *Golden Legend* is not an apocryphal writing as such—it is a collection of hagiographies—but many of his accounts of the lives of the saints, especially those of the disciples, the apostles, and Jesus' family, drew on stories found in Christian apocrypha. The inspiration of characters from the New Testament has also continued to fuel many a modern literary re-creation; Lazarus, the Prodigal Son, and Salome all readily come to mind, and the Christian apocrypha themselves have inspired modern stories about the descent of Jesus to the underworld, for instance. Rewritten biblical events and enhanced details about the *dramatis personae* of the New Testament are still being composed; some could perhaps be styled "modern apocrypha." E. J. Goodspeed in 1931 collected together and discussed eight such compositions under the title *Strange New Gospels.* Further such compendia have been published of late.

On a proper literary level, many novels—some of which are surveyed by Susan Haskins (*Mary Magdalene: Myth and Metaphor* [San Francisco: HarperCollins, 1993]), Richard C. Trexler (*The Journey of the Magi: Meanings in History of a Christian Story* [Princeton: Princeton University Press, 1997]), and Kim Paffenroth (*Judas, Images of the Lost Disciple* [Louisville, Ky.: Westminster John Knox, 2001])—adapt stories from the New Testament, often to subvert them, although in some cases a new narrative is merely being grafted onto a biblical theme, type, or character. Anthony Swindell's *Reworking the Bible: The Literary Reception-History of Fourteen Biblical Stories* (Sheffield: Sheffield Phoenix, 2010), appropriately published in the series The Bible in the Modern World, investigates many such compositions. These literary creations themselves should also not be confused with apocrypha proper.

One of the current book's co-editors, Tony Burke, published the results of a symposium held at York University in Canada in 2011 on the so-called *Secret Gospel of Mark* under the title *Ancient Gospel or Modern Forgery: The Secret Gospel of Mark in Debate* (Eugene, Ore.: Cascade, 2012). Many scholars now see this apocryphon as an elaborate and clever hoax perpetrated by Morton Smith; it is in no sense an ancient apocryphal text with anything to do with an alternative contemporary version of canonical Mark or with the historical Clement of Alexandria. Several scholars have been sidetracked by the modern forgery, but they may gain comfort that "Secret" Mark may still be called an apocryphon, albeit one composed in 1973 rather than one emerging from antiquity. In that sense the *Secret Gospel of Mark* should be treated like those writings in Goodspeed's book; all such modern forgeries are superfluous to the normal concerns of a serious academic study of Christian apocrypha.

Nevertheless, we are alert to the ongoing fascination that apocryphal stories hold for modern generations. We may even compare the insatiable lust for ancient stories about biblical and early Christian events and characters with comparable yarns inspired by twentieth-century Marian apparitions and their associated legends—the incredible examples at Fatima in Portugal readily coming to mind. We are obviously not considering such modern confections in this book, but it is worth recalling that Christian apocryphal writings, the origins of many of which were in the earliest Christian centuries, still demand re-dressing in modern garb, just as they always have done throughout their colorful and variegated histories. An unquenchable human desire for ever more details about the past, more manifestations of allegedly divine occurrences and, indeed, more tangible supporting evidence of these phenomena could perhaps be explained by sociologists, especially sociologists of religion—and maybe particularly convincingly analyzed by psychologists—but, whatever the motives behind this relentless desire for *more* and our plotting the progression of such stories and events, we have in books like the present further exposés of previously submerged older written evidence from a gradually reducing iceberg.

Of Apocrypha There Is No End

The books in Geerard's *Clavis* belong to an ongoing stream of writings that for convenience's sake ends with the invention of printing. It is those that *MNTA* and biblical scholars concentrate on, i.e., Christian texts from the earliest centuries, through the "dark ages" and up to the Renaissance. The writing of books and articles about the seemingly endless ancient texts whose existence may hitherto have been merely noted fleetingly and tantalizingly in, say, Geerard's *Clavis* is itself also boundless. The growing number of these new publications means that, in the context of the Christian apocrypha, there is a fuller and increasingly comprehensive set of evidence on which scholars can establish a better, more rounded picture of Christian literature and history. Additional volumes of *MNTA* are promised by the present editors and we wish all power to their collective elbows as they prepare other significant but largely neglected texts to present not only to their academic peers but ultimately to a readership with a healthy appetite for such writings. The endurance of the traditions deriving from the earliest Christian apocrypha is impressive; the commendable endurance of modern scholars in editing and interpreting surviving texts facilitates a greater understanding of Christian history and theology.

J. K. ELLIOTT
The University of Leeds, U.K.
St. Thecla's Day, 2014

Preface

Collections of Christian apocrypha hold particular allure for those of us who work in the field. Our romance with this fascinating literature began by seeking out one of these indispensable tomes in search of insight about a particular text; one text led to another and before long we had fallen in love, seduced by their promise of revealing forbidden secrets. Certainly apocrypha collections are not the only resource for reading and researching these texts, but having them gathered together into one book lent them a magical quality—a canon of literature like the Bible, but not the Bible at all.

As we delved further into the literature it soon became clear that one collection alone is not enough. Because no anthology contains all the apocryphal texts known to us, and not every entry represents the best and most recent work. So, more collections are needed, in more languages, both ancient and modern. And before long our personal libraries contained a collection of collections, each one capturing the state of the art in its time and location.

As with other apocrypha collections, *New Testament Apocrypha: More Noncanonical Scriptures* reflects the trends in scholarship current in its time and place. Its primary goal is to present to English readers a broad assortment of texts, much as Italian, French, and German anthologies have done before it. And its editors and most of its contributors reside in North America, and are thus influenced by approaches that are particular to American and Canadian scholarship. Multi-author apocrypha collections have appeared in English before but this is the first such initiative to come from North America. We hope that, like previous anthologies, it too will capture the hearts and minds of its readers.

Together the editors would like to thank all of our contributors for their work and for their patience in bringing this project to realization. We have learned much from reading their texts. In particular, we thank Alin Suciu, David Eastman, and Slavomír Čéplö for going above and beyond the call by reading over other contributions in the volume and offering their insights. It is an honor to have J. Keith Elliott contribute a foreword and we thank him for his willingness to be "supplemented." Keith is one among many giants in our field who have inspired us in our work; we acknowledge particularly Walter Bauer†, François Bovon†, Bart Ehrman, Jean-Daniel Kaestli, Helmut Koester†, Christoph Markschies, Marvin Meyer†, James Robinson†, and Pierluigi Piovanelli.

This project would not have been possible without the inspiration and support of Jim Davila, co-editor of our sister publication *Old Testament Pseudepigrapha: More Noncanonical Scriptures*. A special thank you goes to the staff at Eerdmans including Allen Myers, Andrew Knapp, David Cottingham, Jim Chiampas, David Bratt, and Vicky Fanning. And we each thank our co-editor for putting up with us through the long process of seeing this book through to publication; any errors that remain are his fault. Now, on to volume two!

Individually, Tony acknowledges the personal and professional support of his teachers Harold Remus, Michel Desjardins, Robert Sinkewicz, Peter Richardson, and John Kloppenborg. And he has benefitted much from collaboration with members of the Canadian Society of Biblical Studies, the Canadian Society of Patristic Studies, the Society of Biblical Literature Christian Apocrypha Section, the North American Society for the Study of Christian Apocryphal Literature, and participants in the 2011–2015 York University Christian Apocrypha Symposium Series. Most importantly, Tony wishes to thank his wife Laura Cudworth for her unfaltering support and encouragement.

Brent is especially grateful to the late François Bovon, his *Doktorvater* and guide into all things apocryphal. He is also very grateful to the following teachers, colleagues, and friends: George W. E. Nickelsburg, Ralph Keen, Ellen Aitken†, Helmut Koester†, Karen King, Charles Kimball, Tom and Barbara Boyd, Geoff Smith, Steve Friesen, and L. Michael White. Financial support for the research necessary to complete this project was provided by Harvard Divinity School, the Religious Studies Program of the University of Oklahoma, the Department of Religious Studies of the University of Texas at Austin, and the Institution for the Study of Antiquity & Christian Origins at the University of Texas at Austin. He is most thankful to his wife, Elizabeth, and his two children, Zack and Charlie, for their love, patience, and generally for putting up with a daddy who was sometimes grumpy as this project neared completion.

Introduction

In the pages that follow, the reader will learn about: a heavenly letter sent by Christ himself promising dire consequences for those who do not attend Sunday services; a luminous Jesus who appears to the Magi in the form of the Star of Bethlehem; a fearsome child Jesus who has no need of repentance, rehabilitation, or education; a Mary Magdalene who is not Jesus' love interest, but his great-aunt; the nightmarish flying severed head of John the Baptist; a Jesus who harasses incognito a paralyzed man in order to test the man's faith; one of the thieves who was crucified with Jesus meeting Jesus' family thirty years prior to his execution and showing them hospitality during their stay in Egypt; the angel Muriel and how he became Abbaton, the Angel of Death; two apocalypses that, in medieval times, were vastly more popular than the canonical Book of Revelation; and a trove of other largely forgotten tales that were written over one thousand years ago to preserve communal memories, to function as religious propaganda, to provide edification and entertainment for Christians, and yes, to serve as authoritative and inspired Scriptures.

When it comes to giving a name to the types of writings described above, specialists in this literature immediately are confronted with vexing terminological difficulties. What should we call such writings? The broadest, and perhaps fairest, approach would be to call them simply "early Christian writings." But such a neutral designation immediately demands further clarification. What *kind* of writings are these, what *genre?* Narratives, homilies, epistles, treatises? Is the *author* of each work an identifiable historical figure? Or is their authorship a pious (or possibly duplicitous) fiction, or completely anonymous and unknown? To which *generation* or *timeframe* do these writings belong—to the very beginnings of Christianity, the first few centuries, or much, much later?

So "early Christian writings" raises many more questions than it answers. May we instead define them, as has often been done, by what they are not? That is, as "writings not included in the New Testament"? Or similarly, "noncanonical writings"? No, because this presupposes that all of these writings existed at the time—if such a moment can even be ascertained—that the New Testament was being assembled as a set of authoritative writings. In fact, based upon the best current scholarly understandings of the canonization process, a great many writings in the present volume came into being long after a canonical New Testament had solidified (roughly in the fourth century). It also presumes, potentially erroneously, that those responsible for the creation of such writings uniformly desired them to be on par with the four canonical Gospels, the letters of the apostle Paul, and the like. Perhaps some authors sought such a status for their text, but it is just as likely that many of these writings were intended as supplements to the canonical New Testament (hereafter NT, for short).

Instead of "noncanonical," an even more popular descriptor for this literature is "apocryphal"—the precise valences of which we will say more about later. The term appears in *The Apocryphal New Testament,* the most venerable anthology of such writings in English. Published in 1924 by M. R. James and overhauled more than twenty years ago by J. K. Elliott,[1] who has generously written the foreword for this volume, *The Apocryphal New Testament* is one of the chief predecessors of the present work. Yet Elliott and even James himself were ambivalent about such a title, since it implies that these writings were considered for inclusion within the NT and rejected. Worse yet, it suggests that such texts constituted a sort of sinister anti–New Testament, a heretical mockery designed by enemies of Christianity. But no such conspiracy was indeed present in the production of nearly all the writings included here (save for the Jewish parody of the life of Jesus, the *Toledot Yeshu*). Not only was there no conspiracy, but there is also not a fixed number of writings that would constitute such an "apocryphal New Testament." The existence of the present volume demonstrates that previous "apocryphal New Testaments" have not managed to exhaust the storehouse of this literature. Indeed, even if the two volumes in this series continue into three or even more, it would still be impossible to include everything produced by ancient, medieval, and modern Christians that should be regarded as apocryphal literature—a scenario anticipated by John 21:25 ("But there are also many other things that Jesus did; if every one of them were written down, I suppose that the world itself could not contain the books that would be written").

The term "New Testament apocrypha," which has been adopted as the title of the present volume, at least has the advantage over "apocryphal New Testament" of less strongly implying a numerically fixed canon of writings. It also stands in continuity with the venerable Hennecke-Schneemelcher anthology, translated into English as *New Testament Apocrypha*—though the new incarnation of this anthology, spearheaded by Christoph Markschies, has opted instead for the title *Antike christliche Apokryphen* ("ancient Christian apocrypha").[2] Moreover, although the title still compares this category of writings with the canonical NT, one benefit of this comparison is that it reveals that these writings are largely the same genres found in the NT: gospels, acts, epistles, and apocalypses. Yet it is dangerous to insist too strictly on a continuity of genre between the NT and these writings, since one encounters in the present collection an array of genres much broader than those found in the canon.

The designation for this literature most preferred among scholars at present is not, in fact, "New Testament apocrypha," but "Christian apocrypha."[3] One reason for this current scholarly preference is that it is thought to be more free from an unfair and potentially anachronistic comparison to the NT writings, and it allows for broader chronological parameters and flexibility of genres. Yet even many of its proponents will admit that it is still inadequate, since it employs as part of its title a word that in common parlance is synonymous with "false" or "fictitious." There are, however, some reasons to retain the term "apocrypha" in spite of its baggage, as we will soon see. But it is still preferable, at least as concerns the title of an anthology, to use the descriptor "New Testament" instead

---

1. Montague Rhodes James, *The Apocryphal New Testament* (Oxford: Clarendon, 1924; 2nd ed. 1953); J. Keith Elliott, ed. and trans., *The Apocryphal New Testament: A Collection of Apocryphal Christian Literature in an English Translation* (Oxford: Clarendon, 1993; updated paperback ed. 2005).

2. For a history of the Hennecke-Schneemelcher-Markschies anthology tradition see "Collecting Christian Apocrypha" below.

3. The program unit within the Society of Biblical Literature devoted to the study of this literature is called "Christian Apocrypha," a designator that has been in place for more than fifteen years.

of "Christian" for these writings, both because of the former's established usage in early collections and because it is still very unclear how much of an improvement the latter is, given its retention of the highly problematic word "apocrypha."

Terminology

Two interrelated terms and concepts must be addressed in order to properly contextualize the writings contained in this anthology. The first of these is "apocrypha," and the second is "canon."[4] We will take them in order.

Apocrypha

The term "apocrypha" has become the standard way of referring to early Christian texts that were not included in the NT of the Christian Bible. But what is the origin of this term? The Greek adjective *apokryphos* means, first and foremost, "secret" or "hidden." This can have a positive sense, such as an authoritative teaching that has been restricted for sophisticates, or a revelation that was lost but has now been found. At least two CA texts do intend this meaning in their titles: the *Apocryphon of James* and the *Apocryphon of John*, both found among the texts of the Nag Hammadi library (though the *Apocryphon of John* is also extant in the Berlin Gnostic Codex).[5] Furthermore, although not extant in the original Greek, the prologue of the *Gospel of Thomas* likely used the term *apokryphoi* to describe the "secret sayings" of Jesus.[6]

But these uses of *apokryphos* are not confined to texts outside of the canon, since the adjective and its cognate verb are used seven times in NT writings, all with positive connotations.[7] Consider, for example, the use of *apokryphos* and *apokryptō* in Paul's Letter to the Colossians, regarded by a significant majority of scholars as pseudepigraphic. In Col 1:26, Paul refers to the "word of God" *(ton logon tou theou)* as "the mystery hidden *(apokekrymmenon)* from the ages and the generations." The theme of secret teachings or hidden wisdom is continued in Col 2:3, where Christ is said to be the one "in whom are hidden *(apokryphoi)* all the treasures of wisdom and knowledge." Given the valorization of esoteric understandings of Christ in this discussion, it should not be surprising that there were Christian groups in the second century that positively described their communities' sacred texts as *apokrypha*.

Despite the positive associations for this term among some Christian groups, over time *apokryphos* took on a more negative connotation. The second-century heresiologist Irenaeus of Lyons mocks the sect of the Marcosians for using a number of "apocryphal and spurious writings" *(apokryphōn kai nothōn graphōn)*, among them a story about the child Jesus learning the alphabet found also in the *Infancy Gospel of Thomas* (*Haer.* 1.20.1). Similarly, Tertullian uses the Latin terms *apocrypha* and *falsa* interchangeably in *Pud.* 10.12 to

---

4. For both of these terms, the "General Introduction" by Wilhelm Schneemelcher (in Schneemelcher, ed., *New Testament Apocrypha* [trans. from the corrected 6th ed. of *Neutestamentliche Apokryphen in deutscher Übersetzung* by Robert McLachlan Wilson; 2 vols.; Louisville, Ky.: Westminster John Knox, 1991–1992]), 1:9–75) remains helpful.

5. See the introductions to and translations of these texts in Marvin Meyer, ed., *The Nag Hammadi Scriptures: The International Edition* (San Francisco: HarperCollins, 2007), 19–30 and 103–32.

6. See the reconstruction by Harold W. Attridge, "The Gospel According to Thomas. Appendix: The Greek Fragments," in *Nag Hammadi Codex II,2–7* (ed. Bentley Layton; 2 vols.; NHS 20; Leiden: Brill, 1989), 1:95–128 at 113.

7. Mark 4:22; Luke 8:17; 10:21; 1 Cor 2:7; Eph 3:9; Col 1:26; 2:3.

criticize those who would regard the *Shepherd of Hermas* as an authoritative book. The fact that Tertullian refers to *Hermas,* usually numbered among the "Apostolic Fathers,"[8] as an apocryphal book is noteworthy and indicates that the precise contours of the category of what came to be called apocrypha were rather uncertain in antiquity, as they are today. But it was the fourth-century champion of orthodoxy, Bishop Athanasius of Alexandria, who was responsible for drawing the line between apocryphal and canonical writings most sharply. In his 39th Festal Letter for the year 367, Athanasius not only advances for the first recorded time the same 27-book NT canon used by most Christian communities today, but he also characterizes the "apocrypha" as writings that are entirely the recent product of heretics wishing to ascribe some ancient origin to their ideas.[9] It is apparently due to the efforts of such polemicists that when the term "apocryphal" first appears in English literature in the late sixteenth and seventeenth centuries, it has the clear meaning, "[o]f doubtful authenticity; spurious, fictitious, false; fabulous, mythical."[10]

Despite this modern connotation of "apocryphal," most specialists intend the term "Christian apocrypha" as a neutral designation for a particular body of ancient Christian texts. In his popular introduction to this literature, Tony Burke describes the category as follows:

> The term 'Christian Apocrypha' designates non-biblical Christian literature that features tales of Jesus, his family and his immediate followers. They are similar in content and genre to texts included in the New Testament; the essential difference is that they were not selected for inclusion in the Bible, either because those who decided on the Bible's contents did not approve of them, or because they were composed after the time of this selection process.[11]

Notice, however, that Burke does not specify chronological parameters for this literature. The question of a timeframe for the CA has been controversial among specialists, and by using the title "New Testament Apocrypha" for the present collection of writings, the co-editors have taken a definite position on this issue. Wilhelm Schneemelcher had proposed restricting the category of the CA to writings produced in the first three centuries of Christianity; writings produced thereafter about NT figures are better understood as hagiography (that is, accounts of the life and miracles of saints or other ecclesiastical figures). Schneemelcher argues that this is not an arbitrary cut-off; rather, "As is clear from our survey of the history of the canon, it makes a considerable difference whether a work of this kind originated before or after the middle of the 4th century."[12] This is because, he contends, that "[w]hether the canon included twenty-two or twenty-six or twenty-seven books, all that is important here is the fact that a firmly closed collection of recognised texts, invested with the highest authority, now existed everywhere."[13]

---

8. For the most recent discussion of the origins of this term, see David Lincicum, "The Paratextual Invention of the Term 'Apostolic Fathers,'" *JTS* 66 (2015): 139–48.

9. See the translation of the relevant section of his letter in Schneemelcher, "General Introduction," 49–50.

10. "apocryphal, adj. and n.," *OED Online*, released March 2015, http:// http://www.oed.com/.

11. Tony Burke, *Secret Scriptures Revealed: A New Introduction to the Christian Apocrypha* (Grand Rapids, Mich.: Eerdmans; London: SPCK, 2013), 6.

12. Schneemelcher, "General Introduction," 54.

13. Schneemelcher, "General Introduction," 57.

Although Schneemelcher exaggerates when he says that a "firmly closed collection . . . existed everywhere," he is certainly correct to notice that it is in the fourth century that there arises a more widespread concept of a fixed number of texts constituting the NT. Nevertheless, the co-editors side with Éric Junod in this debate,[14] preferring to leave the chronological parameters for the production of the CA completely open, given that CA are still being produced today. Many of the writings in the present volume were indeed produced after the fourth century, which would theoretically disqualify them as CA by Schneemelcher's standards. Yet it is not necessarily the case that, on the whole, CA define themselves in relationship to a fixed canon. A few seem to perceive themselves as replacing canonical writings, others as complementing them. Many others, however, do not articulate any sort of relationship with the canon, positively or negatively. Although we cannot, at present, dispense with describing the CA with some degree of juxtaposition to the writings of the NT, it does not seem obvious to us that the fourth-century development of a fixed canon had the sort of clear and definitive effect on the production of CA that Schneemelcher supposes it did.

Canon

Although the use of the term "canon" to describe a fixed group of Christian writings only occurs for the first time in the fourth century, a move toward privileging certain works above others certainly arose prior to this time. It will be helpful, however, to describe briefly the etymology of the term "canon" and how it came to mean what it did,[15] before addressing the more complicated issue of the relationship between the formation of the NT canon and the CA.

The Greek word *kanōn* is apparently a loanword from the Hebrew *qāneh,* meaning "reed." Although it originally meant a kind of measuring stick, over time it took on the meaning of a fixed standard. For example, 4 Macc 7:21 speaks of living one's life by the rule *(kanona)* of philosophy, and Epictetus *(Diatr.* II.11.24) claims that philosophy is simply the investigating and establishing of standards *(kanones).* Most of the uses of the term in early Christian literature are in keeping with this idea of a normative rule. This is not, of course, necessarily the same as having a firmly fixed group of writings, but one can certainly see how the idea of the former might have contributed to a desire for the latter. However, an additional usage of *kanōn* that may have been relevant is the notion of a list, chart, or table. This is what Eusebius uses to describe his set of tables for the Synoptic Gospels, and it was used also to describe astrological or chronological data in a non-Christian context. Presumably, we should not think of either the "rule" or the "list" meaning of *kanōn* as being exclusively determinative for its eventual use in Christian discourse about the shape of the biblical canon. At any rate, it was not until the fourth-century Council of Laodicea and its directives about "noncanonical books" *(akanonista biblia)* not being permitted to be read in church that we find this terminology deployed to denote the idea of books being inside or outside of the Bible.[16]

---

14. See his "Apocryphes du NT ou Apocryphes chrétiens anciens," *ETR* 58 (1983): 408–21. For an overview of the subsequent debate over redefining the category see Péter Tóth, "Way Out of the Tunnel? Three Hundred Years of Research on the Apocrypha: A Preliminary Approach," in *Retelling the Bible: Literary, Historical and Social Contexts* (ed. Lucie Dolezalová and Tamás Visi; Frankfurt am Main: Peter Lang, 2011), 45–84 at 74–80.

15. This brief overview follows Schneemelcher, "General Introduction," 10–13.

16. Cited in Schneemelcher, "General Introduction," 10. Text in Erwin Preuschen, *Analecta: Kürzere*

When discussing the formation of the NT canon in the context of the CA, five inter-related observations are key. First, our knowledge of the process by which the form of the NT became fixed has significant gaps, and in many cases we can only make an educated guess about why a given CA text was not included in the NT canon. Second, however, only a few CA texts should be regarded as being of comparable age as the most prominent of the writings found in the NT—that is, the letters of Paul and the four canonical Gospels (plus Acts)—so it is unwise to posit an overarching conspiracy that unfairly removed the CA from inclusion in the NT. Third, there is regional and temporal variation in what constituted canonical writings: the situation in Rome in the fourth century was not the same as that of Syria in the third, or that of Alexandria in the fifth, etc. Fourth, many ancient Christian discussions of the canon do not simply say which texts are in and which are out, but instead operate with a third category, in which appear texts whose canonicity is in dispute or that are suitable for private but not public reading. Fifth, although the influence of the canonical writings on the formation of Christian beliefs and practices is no doubt enormous, the persistent roles that CA text played in this development as well must not be overlooked.

First of all, there is much we simply do not know about how the NT canon came together. We cannot provide here a thorough presentation of the chief textual witnesses for the canonization process; let it suffice to say that there are a number of sources (for example, the Muratorian Canon or the *Decretum Gelasianum*) that provide a snapshot of what a given group of Christians in a certain place at a certain time thought should be inside and outside of the canon. However, even these fragments rarely give us any information about *why* a writing was accepted or rejected. For the apocryphal gospels that have been the subject of the most scholarly attention, such as the *Gospel of Thomas* or the *Gospel of Peter,* we have nothing like a series of deliberations about whether a writing should be included or not. In the case of the *Gospel of Peter,* we do have a very interesting piece of correspondence (preserved by Eusebius in *Hist. eccl.* 6.12) from around the year 200 between Serapion, the bishop of Antioch, and a church at Rhossus that was experiencing divisions over the status of this text. But this data point is highly puzzling in a number of respects: Serapion says that he has never read the *Gospel of Peter,* nevertheless, he is comfortable with the community reading it; when problems arose, Serapion did not perceive there to be objectionable characteristics in the text itself, but in the faith of those who were reading it; and Serapion's concluding verdict seems to be that the *Gospel of Peter* was unproblematic with the exception of a few passages that he points out, perhaps thereby allowing the community to continue to read it. In the case of the *Gospel of Thomas,* its rejection was due in part probably to its use by groups that were scorned by proto-orthodox branches of the church. But the Gospels of John and Luke were both favorites of "heretics," and yet this did not ultimately lead to their rejection. Why the *Gospel of Thomas* suffered this fate, we simply do not know.

Second, even if we cannot be certain why a writing like the *Gospel of Thomas* was rejected, it would be highly inaccurate to say that the canonization process was on the whole a bald power-play by the proto-orthodox church to include and exclude texts based on the church's positions on Christology, doctrine, community organization, and so forth. When we look carefully at the writings that appear to have been the most authoritative and the

---

Texte zur Geschichte der alten Kirche und des Kanons (2 vols.; 2nd ed.; Tübingen: J. C. B. Mohr, 1909–1910), 2:70.

least disputed in canon lists, we find the letters of the apostle Paul and, quite often, the four Gospels of Matthew, Mark, Luke, and John. In other words, we find most of the very earliest Christian compositions. No Christian writings earlier than Paul's letters have survived or are even known to have existed. Similarly, with the exception of the Q document used by Matthew and Luke, there is remarkably little evidence of any other gospels as ancient as those that would be included in the NT canon. The *Gospel of Thomas* may well be very old; it is possible that the lost gospel preserved in Papyrus Egerton 2 is early as well, though its fragmentary nature precludes definitive statements. The *Gospel of Peter* and several of the Jewish Christian Gospels (though not the *Gospel of the Hebrews*) are best understood as harmonizations of the early second century, even if they do, on occasion, preserve very archaic traditions not found in the canonical writings. In the case of the infancy gospels, the earliest of which probably came into being prior to 150, virtually all of their materials are best understood as creative expansions upon the infancy narratives of Matthew and Luke—instances like the *Protevangelium of James's* possibly independent tradition of a cave as the birthplace of Jesus are exceptions that prove the rule. Thus, the impression created by popular treatments of early Christianity, like Dan Brown's novel *The Da Vinci Code,* that the gospels and other core writings of the NT were chosen over a multitude of equally early CA simply does not comport with what we know about the earliest of the Christian writings.

Regarding the third point, about the diversity of canons by place and time in ancient Christianity, there is an incorrect impression in nonspecialist circles that there was a single definitive moment, generally identified as the Council of Nicea in 325, when the church as a whole "decided" what would be in its Bible. But some variety in church canons persisted beyond the fourth century. This variety is illustrated particularly well by the Syriac-speaking branch of the ancient Christian church. Well into the fifth century, the standard format in which the Gospels appeared in Syriac was the *Diatessaron,* a gospel harmony that blended the four canonical Gospels with additional extracanonical traditions. Moreover, the pseudepigraphic Pauline epistle embedded within the *Acts of Paul,* commonly known as *3 Corinthians,* was regarded as authoritative by patristic writers like Ephrem and Aphrahat. Finally, Revelation was, as in other Eastern Christian communities, not accepted in the Syriac church until much later than in the West.[17] All of these features of the canon in Syriac Christianity are found *after* Athanasius's famous festal letter of 367 CE. Clearly, the letter did not lead automatically to the adoption of a standard twenty-seven-book New Testament throughout the ancient Christian church. Even in the West, the Muratorian Canon, which is perhaps a fourth-century Roman product,[18] demonstrates that apart from the four Gospels and the Pauline corpus, the periphery of the Western canon was somewhat fuzzy—texts that would later become securely canonical or apocryphal mingled at the edges. Also, it is important to recognize that Athanasius is not simply passing on a previous tradition, but is instead actively striving to impose his vision of a sharp binary between canonical and apocryphal upon an Egyptian Christianity that in many places still regarded Athanasius's category of the "apocryphal" to contain

---

17. For an overview, see Sebastian Brock, *The Bible in the Syriac Tradition* (Piscataway, N.J.: Gorgias, 2006).

18. On recent reevaluations of the origins of the Muratorian Fragment see Geoffrey Mark Hahneman, "The Muratorian Fragment and the Origins of the New Testament Canon," in *The Canon Debate* (ed. Lee Martin McDonald and James A. Sanders; Peabody, Mass.: Hendrickson, 2002), 405–15.

many valuable writings.[19] Indeed, it has sometimes been suggested that the Nag Hammadi writings were placed in jars and buried, perhaps by a community of monks, in order to protect them from Athanasius's push for a definitive canon.[20] This effort, however, was not entirely successful, as Christian communities for centuries thereafter continued to advance different canon lists. The Armenian Church, for example, included 3 *Corinthians* and the *Repose of John* (a portion of the Greek *Acts of John*) in their biblical manuscripts, and the thirty-five-book Ethiopic canon still in use today includes the *Book of the Rolls*, the *Didascalia,* and several church orders. Consider also the modifications to the canon advocated by Martin Luther, who acquiesced to tradition by including the Epistle of James in his translation of the Bible, but nevertheless refused to grant it page numbers in the first edition.[21]

A fourth point of importance concerning the canon in antiquity is that Athanasius is somewhat unusual in his attempt to create a binary division between those texts that are clearly in and those that are out. In many of our ancient sources for the history of the canon, we frequently see a tripartite division consisting of texts that are "accepted" *(homologoumena)*, texts that are "false," "forged," or "spurious" *(notha* or *pseudē)*, and a third category of texts that are "disputed" *(antilegomena* or *amphiballomena*, meaning that some communities approve of their use and some do not). These disputed texts are sometimes said to be allowable for private but not public reading, or are "useful for the soul" *(psychophelē)*, or some other description that does not permit an easy classification as canonical or apocryphal.[22] In this third category appear writings that would later be regarded as canonical, as apocryphal, or as something else entirely. Depending on which canon list is consulted, considered disputed are the Epistle of James, Jude, 2 Peter, Revelation, *Shepherd of Hermas,* the *Acts of Paul,* and the *Apocalypse of Peter,* as well as the *Wisdom of Solomon,* categorized today among the apocrypha of the Old Testament. Thus, while Athanasius may have attempted to draw the line between canonical and apocryphal quite sharply, and much of later Christian tradition followed his lead, the situation was far more fluid than this for many early Christians. In fact, even Athanasius himself concedes that the *Shepherd of Hermas* and the *Didache* can be read privately by newcomers to the faith, undermining his sharp distinction between canonical and apocryphal.

Fifth and finally, in part because of this continuum between universal acceptance and almost complete rejection of writings, it is important to recognize that the designation of a given text in antiquity as apocryphal did not immediately relegate it to the dustbin of history. In numerous instances, an apocryphal writing has had a far greater impact on the development of Christian tradition—narratives, doctrines, art, music, and so forth—than many writings contained in the Bible. To provide one such example of an extremely impressive reception history, consider the second-century infancy gospel known as the *Protevangelium of James,* which tells of Mary's life from her childhood up through the birth of Jesus. In contrast to apocryphal texts that are extant in a single fragmentary manuscript,

---

19. On this, see most recently David Brakke, "A New Fragment of Athanasius's Thirty-Ninth *Festal Letter:* Heresy, Apocrypha, and the Canon," *HTR* 103 (2010): 47–66.

20. This theory is recounted, and challenged, in Nicola Denzey Lewis and Justine Ariel Blount, "Rethinking the Origins of the Nag Hammadi Codices," *JBL* 133, no. 2 (2014): 399–419.

21. See Albert Maichle, *Der Kanon der biblischen Bücher und das Konzil von Trient* (Freiburg: Herder, 1929), 6–7.

22. See François Bovon, "Beyond the Canonical and the Apocryphal Books, the Presence of a Third Category: The Books Useful for the Soul," *HTR* 105 (2012): 125–37.

the *Protevangelium of James* is preserved in over 150 Greek manuscripts, to say nothing of its attestation in other ancient languages. Such a remarkably rich manuscript record greatly undermines any suggestion that Christians did not pay attention to this text because it was not in the biblical canon. The contributions of the *Protevangelium of James* to the development of Mariology are very well known, as this text provides the names of Mary's parents, the idea of Joseph as an older widower, and an early articulation of the concept of Mary's perpetual virginity. But the influence of another, often-overlooked element may indeed be even more impressive: the *Protevangelium of James* is the first text to depict Mary as traveling to Bethlehem riding on a donkey, with Joseph walking alongside of it. The early history of this element's reception has not yet been entirely clarified, but it has become an absolutely unquestioned part of the visual representation of the Christmas story. A Christmas card, storybook, children's pageant, motion picture, or any other medium containing a depiction of the Holy Family's journey to Bethlehem would appear quite strange without the presence of the *Protevangelium of James*'s donkey.

Collecting Christian Apocrypha

The writing of noncanonical Christian texts began, as with canonical Christian texts, in the first century, though at the time no distinction was made between the two categories of literature. The separation originated late in the second century when Christians established their own collections of Scripture distinct from Jewish Scripture. Marcion, often credited with creating the first Christian-only Scripture collection, is said to have considered only the Gospel of Luke and ten of the letters of Paul (all edited to cohere with Marcion's theology)[23] to be authoritative, though there is evidence that his later followers also valued Matthew and two additional (perhaps falsely attributed) letters of Paul: one to the Laodiceans and one to the Alexandrians. To Marcionite Christians, all other texts would have been considered "apocryphal." Writers in the proto-orthodox tradition favored a more expansive collection, with four gospels, fourteen letters of Paul, and Acts. Opinion differed over other texts, with some championing letters by other apostles (1 and 2 Peter, 1–3 John, James, and Jude), apocalypses (Revelation and the *Apocalypse of Peter*), and other texts (the *Shepherd of Hermas,* the *Acts of Paul, 1* and *2 Clement,* the *Epistle of Barnabas*) in a variety of combinations. Some of these combinations are particularly puzzling. Does the presence of 1 and 2 Peter and Jude along with the *Protevangelium of James, 3 Corinthians,* and a portion of the *Odes of Solomon* in Papyrus Bodmer V indicate an elevation of these apocryphal texts to canonical status or a devaluation of the epistles? Are the placements of *Hermas* and the *Epistle of Barnabas* at the end of Codex Sinaiticus and *1–2 Clement* and the *Psalms of Solomon* at the end of Codex Alexandrinus indicative that they were valued on par with the rest of these collections or are they meant to be understood as appendices?

Several additional early texts achieved a similar esteem, despite ecclesiastical efforts to discourage their circulation. For example, the *Protevangelium of James* and the *Infancy Gospel of Thomas,* both in circulation by the latter half of the second century, were widely copied and translated into numerous languages. So valued were these texts that many later writers expanded them with the addition of other texts or traditions (as with the

---

23. Note, however, that the conventional wisdom that Marcion "mutilated" Luke's Gospel recently has been subject to increasing scrutiny. See Jason BeDuhn, *The First New Testament: Marcion's Scriptural Canon* (Salem, Ore.: Polebridge, 2013) and Dieter Roth, *The Text of Marcion's Gospel* (Leiden: Brill, 2015).

Gospel of Pseudo-Matthew, the *Arabic Infancy Gospel,* and the Syriac Life of Mary collections), or reused them in homilies,[24] or drew upon them as authoritative resources to craft new texts, such as the *Life of John the Baptist* attributed to Serapion. Similarly, the earliest apocryphal acts circulated widely, though for the most part in condensed forms, shorn of the apostles' teachings and much of the activities that precede their martyrdoms; and, like the second-century infancy gospels, the apocryphal acts were used in the creation of other accounts of the apostles, such as the Syriac *History of Simon Cephas,* which combines portions of the *Acts of Peter,* the Pseudo-Clementine *Recognition,* and the *Preaching of Simon Cephas in the City of Rome.* Perhaps all of these esteemed early texts could be considered part of another middle category between canonical and noncanonical—something akin to hagiography—or perhaps they demonstrate that the boundary between scripture and apocrypha was more porous than the creators of the various canon lists suggest.

Formal declarations of the shape of the canon seem to have done little to stop the creation of new apocrypha. Coptic Christians in post-Chalcedonian Egypt created a genre of literature known today as "pseudo-apostolic memoirs."[25] These feature tales of various early Christian figures in texts that, the authors claim, were hidden away in a house or library in Jerusalem until they were rediscovered by illustrious fourth-century homilists—though these attributions too are fictions. The *Berlin-Strasbourg Apocryphon,* the *Investiture of Abbaton,* and the encomia on John the Baptist and Mary Magdalene are all examples of this literature. Alin Suciu believes they were written to create a distinct identity for Coptic Christianity; indeed, many of them institute festivals for particular saints or angels and promise rewards for their proper worship. Similar motives lie behind a number of late-antique Greek and Latin apocrypha, such as the *Acts of Cornelius* and the *Acts of Barnabas,* composed, at least in part, to provide warrant for the acceptance of saints' relics in local churches. Other late-antique texts, such as the *Apocalypse of the Virgin* or the *Epistle of Christ from Heaven,* were written to regulate behavior, and whenever tragedy affected the church, new apocalypses, like the *Tiburtine Sibyl,* appeared to address the anxiety of the times. Despite church officials' calls to avoid, even destroy, apocryphal texts, sometimes churches created their own apocrypha when it served their interests. It is unlikely that any of the writers of these texts expected their work to be added to their church's canon, though such a development would not be impossible; changes to the canon were made over the centuries, including the late addition of Revelation to the Greek canon and the occasional inclusion of the *Epistle to the Laodiceans* in Vulgate manuscripts,[26] and many of these apocryphal texts did enjoy a popularity that, at times, surpassed that of canonical works.

---

24. See the homilies on the Passion attributed to Eusebius of Alexandria surveyed in John A. McCulloch, *The Harrowing of Hell: A Comparative Study of an Early Christian Doctrine* (Edinburgh: T.&T. Clark, 1930), 174–91; and the use of an early translation of *Prot. Jas.* in Latin homilies discussed in Jean-Daniel Kaestli, "Le Protévangile de Jacques latin dans l'homélie: Inquirendum est pour la fête de la Nativité de Marie," *Apocrypha* 11 (2001): 99–153.

25. The texts that conform to this genre are described by Alin Suciu in "Apocryphon Berolinense/ Argentoratense (Previously Known as the Gospel of the Savior). Reedition of P. Berol. 22220, Strasbourg Copte 5–7 and Qasr el-Wizz Codex ff. 12v–17r with Introduction and Commentary" (PhD diss., Université Laval, 2013), esp. 75–91. See also the introduction to Suciu's entry on *B-S Ap.* in this volume.

26. The manuscript sources (more than 100 in all) are provided in Samuel Berger, *Histoire de la Vulgate pendant les premiers siècles du Moyen-Age* (Nancy, 1893) and summarized in Irena D. Backus, "Renaissance Attitudes towards New Testament Apocrypha. Jacques Lefèvre d'Étaples and His Epigones," *Renaissance Quarterly* 51 (1998): 1169–97 at 1172–73.

The value placed on apocryphal texts is evident also in efforts made to compile the material; such compendia circulated long before the era of printed apocrypha collections. For example, the Nag Hammadi codices and other books of "gnostic" texts—the Coptic Bruce, Askew, Berlin, and Tchachos codices—testify to collectors' interests in assembling noncanonical texts, as does Codex Panopolitanus from Akhmim (collecting portions of the *Gospel of Peter,* the *Apocalypse of Peter, 1 Enoch,* and some Psalms), and numerous miscellanies created in monastic contexts that contain various combinations of apocryphal and hagiographical texts. Efforts were made also to collect texts with generic, not just thematic, affinities. The five great apocryphal acts were circulated as a group by Manicheans as early as the fifth century, and Latin apocryphal acts of the entire college of apostles (save for Judas) were combined around the sixth century to form the ten-volume collection *Virtutes apostolorum* attributed to Abdias of Babylon, said to be one of the seventy-two disciples mentioned in Luke 10:1.[27] Christians in Egypt could read a similar collection of texts—which includes not only apocryphal acts but also the *Letter of Pseudo-Dionysius on the Deaths of Peter and Paul*—in Arabic and Ethiopic.[28] Gospels also were brought together in collections. Latin infancy gospels, such as the various iterations of the *Gospel of Pseudo-Matthew,* are found alongside the *Gospel of Nicodemus* in many manuscripts, thus forming an apocryphal Life of Jesus.[29] Similarly, Syriac Life of Mary collections use the *Protevangelium of James* and the *Dormition of Mary* as bookends to additional apocryphal traditions, including the *Infancy Gospel of Thomas* and the *Vision of Theophilus.*[30] Sometimes canonical and noncanonical stories were combined into sprawling gospels, such as the Arabic *Apocryphal Gospel of John* and its Ethiopic translation, the *Miracles of Jesus,* the latter of which was employed in Ethiopic liturgy.[31] Apocryphal traditions were assembled also to provide material for liturgical readings of the saints in *menologia* and *synaxaria* and for popular lives of saints collections such as Jacob of Voragine's *The Golden Legend.*[32] Each of these examples illustrate, once again, that Christians continued to value certain noncanonical texts and traditions long after their church leaders declared them "apocryphal." Indeed, some of these combinations

---

27. For recent work on the collection see the essays collected in Els Rose, ed., *The Apocryphal Acts of the Apostles in Latin Christianity: Proceedings of the First International Summer School on Christian Apocryphal Literature (ISCAL), Strasbourg, 24–27 June 2012* (Turnhout: Brepols, 2014).

28. The Arabic and Ethiopic witnesses are numerous (over fifty in total). The most recent edition of the Ethiopic collection is that of Ernest A. W. Budge, *The Contendings of the Apostles* (2 vols.; London: Henry Frowde, 1899–1901; repr. Amsterdam: APA Philo, 1976); for the Arabic see Agnes Smith Lewis, *Acta Mythologica Apostolorum* and *The Mythological Acts of the Apostles* (Horae Semiticae 3–4; London: Clay, 1904). French translations of select chapters (on Matthew, Bartholomew, Luke, and James the Less) can be found in *EAC* 2:867–978.

29. Zbigniew Izydorczyk's *Manuscripts of the Evangelium Nicodemi: A Census* (Toronto: Pontifical Institute of Mediaeval Studies, 1993) lists seventy-one manuscripts containing Gos. Nic. with an account of Jesus' childhood (whether *Ps.-Mt.,* the Latin version of *Inf. Gos. Thom.,* or an unidentified text).

30. Some of these Life of Mary collections are found in Syriac manuscripts as early as the fifth century. For a comprehensive overview of the available evidence see Tony Burke, "The Infancy Gospel of Thomas from an Unpublished Syriac Manuscript. Introduction, Text, Translation, and Notes," *Hugoye* 16, no. 2 (2013): 225–99, at 232–37; and the entry on *Inf. Gos. Thom.* in this volume.

31. On the liturgical use of the text see Witold Witakowski, "The Miracles of Jesus: An Ethiopian Apocryphal Gospel," *Apocrypha* 6 (1995): 279–98 at 280–81.

32. For a detailed discussion of the use of apocryphal texts and traditions in the *Golden Legend* see Rémi Gounelle, "Sens et usage d'*apocryphus* dans la Légende dorée," *Apocrypha* 5 (1994): 189–210.

of texts may have been regarded as supplementary volumes to be read and appreciated alongside the canonical writings.

As the age of manuscript production merged into the era of printing, apocryphal texts began to be published in *incunabula*—early printed books that bear some of the characteristics of handwritten manuscripts. Some of the more popular texts—such as the *Gospel of Nicodemus,* the *Gospel of Pseudo-Matthew,* and the *Life of Judas*—appear in *incunabula* of the fifteenth and sixteenth centuries, demonstrating the continued attraction these texts held for Christian laity and, at the same time, providing scholars today with print copies of otherwise-lost manuscripts.[33] One of the first "rediscovered" apocryphal texts from the East, the *Protevangelium of James,* was first published as an *incunable* in 1552.[34] The edition, published by Theodore Bibliander, features a translation of the text into Latin made by Guillaume Postel along with the Gospel of Mark and other materials. The goal of the publisher was to demonstrate that the text was the lost introduction to Mark; such arguments for the historical value of newly found apocrypha often attended their publication, as did contrary arguments that maintained the superiority of the canonical texts over the noncanonical. Other apocryphal texts soon appeared, though published somewhat sporadically, utilizing whatever manuscripts each editor happened to have at hand.[35] The most significant of these are the *incunabula* of the *Virtutes apostolorum,* the first published in 1531 by Friedrich Nausea,[36] and the small collection included in the second and third editions of Michael Neander's Latin translation of Martin Luther's *Shorter Catechism.* By its third edition in 1567, Neander's collection had grown to encompass the *Protevangelium of James* (this time in Greek), the Abgar Correspondence, several Letters of Pilate, and a series of Sybilline books.[37] Not long after, the Bollandists in Belgium began to systematically collect lives of saints and apply to them the scholarly techniques that were being applied to classical works.[38] The

---

33. As yet no systematic study has been made of CA in early printed books, though there has been some discussion of *incunabula* of the three texts listed here. In addition, Backus ("Renaissance Attitudes," 1181–82) mentions a 1514 edition of *Ep. Lao.* and *Ep. Paul Sen.* printed along with Paul's canonical epistles.

34. Guillaume Postel, *Protevangelion, de seu de natalibus Iesu Christi et ipsius matris Virginis Mariae sermo historicus divi Iacobi Minoris. Evangelica historia quam scripsit B. Marcus. Vita Marie evangelistae collecta per Theodorum Bibliandrum* (Basel: Ioannis Oporini, 1552).

35. The early history of scholarship on the CA is a growing area of interest in the field. See particularly Justin Champion, "Apocrypha, Canon and Criticism from Samuel Fisher to John Toland, 1650–1718," in *Judaeo-Christian Intellectual Culture in the Seventeenth Century: A Celebration of the Library of Narcissus Marsh (1638–1713)* (ed. Allison P. Coudert et al.; Dordrecht: Kluwer, 1999), 91–117; and works by Irena D. Backus, including the monograph *Historical Method and Confessional Identity in the Era of Reformation (1378–1615)* (Studies in Medieval and Reformation Thought 94; Leiden: Brill, 2003); also helpful is Tóth, "Way Out of the Tunnel?"

36. Friedrich Nausea, *Anonymi Philalethi Eusebiani in vitas, miracula passionesque Apostolorum Rhapsodiae* (Cologne: Peter Quentel, 1531).

37. Michael Neander, *Catechesis Martini Lutheri parua, Graecolatina, postremum recognita* (3rd ed.; Basel: Ioannis Oporini, 1567). For detailed discussion of Neander's editions see Irena D. Backus, "Les apocryphes néo-testamentaires et la pédagogie luthérienne des XVIe-XVIIe siècles: les recueils de Michael Neander (1564, 1567) et Nicolas Glaser (1614)," in *Apocryphité. Histoire d'un concept transversal aux religions du livre. En hommage à Pierre Geoltrain* (ed. Simon Claude Mimouni; Bibliothèque de l'École des Hautes Études. Sciences religieuses 113; Turnhout: Brepols, 2002), 263–76; eadem, "Early Christianity in Michael Neander's Greek-Latin Edition of Luther's *Catechism,*" in *History of Scholarship. A Selection of Papers from the Seminar on the History of Scholarship Held Annually at the Warburg Institute* (ed. Christopher Ligota and Jean-Louis Quantin; Oxford: Oxford University Press, 2006), 197–230.

38. For a brief history of the Bollandists see David Knowles, *Great Historical Enterprises. Problems in Monastic History* (London: Thomas Nelson & Sons, 1963), 1–32.

first volume of their *Acta Sanctorum,* featuring saints commemorated in January, appeared in 1643. The initial twelve volumes include a number of medieval lives of early Christian figures, including the *Acts of Barnabas* and the *Acts of Timothy.* And to our benefit, the Bollandists continue to revise and supplement the collection.

The same urge to compile and examine nonbiblical Christian texts gave birth to the first substantial scholarly CA collection: *Codex apocryphus Novi Testamenti* by the celebrated bibliographer Johann Albert Fabricius, published in three volumes between 1703 and 1719.[39] Fabricius's collection was valuable, and remains so, because it compiles much of what had appeared before his day, including the manuscripts published in *incunabula,* along with a comprehensive range of ancient testimonies, and liturgies under the names of apostles, all accompanied by extensive commentary. The material is arranged intentionally as a mirror of the New Testament canon: separated into gospels, acts, letters, and apocalypses. This strategy was often imitated in subsequent collections, thus forming, in a sense, a canon of New Testament apocrypha.[40] Like other scholars of his day, Fabricius was far from dispassionate about the subject of his collection; indeed, his dislike for the CA, and the Catholic traditions reflected in them, is captured in the subtitle to his volumes, translated as "[texts] collected, castigated, and illustrated with testimonials, censures and critical notices."

Fabricius's collection quickly became established as the standard resource for the CA and remained so for over a century. All of the first modern-language compilations are translations of the texts collected by Fabricius, including the English translations presented in Jeremiah Jones's *A New and Full Method of Settling the Canonical Authority of the New Testament* (1726),[41] the French collection by Voltaire and Simon Bigex published in 1769,[42] and the 1832 German volume prepared by J. G. Bartholmä.[43] Additional texts and manuscripts of texts became known, but aside from a supplement by Andreas Birch in 1804,[44] no effort was made to supplant Fabricius until 1832, with the first (and only) volume of Johann Karl Thilo's *Codex Apocryphus Novi Testamenti.*[45] Thilo's plans for subsequent volumes is not known, but the first, focusing on apocryphal gospels, trimmed down

---

39. Johann A. Fabricius, *Codex apocryphus Novi Testamenti: Collectus, Castigatus, Testimoniisque, Censuris & Animadversionibus illustratus* (3 vols.; rev. ed.; Hamburg: Schiller & Kisner, 1719). The first volume appeared in 1703 and the second followed in 1719, along with a revision of the first and a third volume containing corrections and supplements.

40. Fabricius's other well-known collection, *Codex pseudepigraphus Veteris Testamenti, collectus castigatus testimoniisque, censuris et animadversionibus illustratus* (Hamburg & Leipzig: Sumptu Christiani Liebezeit, 1713) is credited with doing much the same for Old Testament pseudepigrapha. For an evaluation of the author's impact on the field see Annette Yoshiko Reed, "The Modern Invention of 'Old Testament Pseudepigrapha,'" *JTS* 60, no. 2 (2009): 403–36. The separation of apocryphal texts between Old Testament pseudepigrapha and New Testament apocrypha began with Fabricius's volumes, though some Christian-authored pseudepigrapha occasionally appear in CA volumes.

41. Jeremiah Jones, *A New and Full Method of Settling the Canonical Authority of the New Testament* (2 vols.; Printed for J. Clark and R. Hett at the Bible and Crown in the Poultrey near Cheapside, 1726); a third volume was added in 1727. Jones's translations were later used in the often-reprinted volume by William Hone: *The Apocryphal New Testament* (London: Printed for William Hone, 1820).

42. Voltaire and Simon Bigex, *Collection d'anciens Évangiles, ou monuments du premier siècle du christianisme, extraits de Fabricius, Grabius et autres savants* (Amsterdam: M. M. Rey, 1769).

43. Johann Georg Bartholmä, *Die Apogryphen (sic) des neuen Testamentes* (Dinkelsbühl: Walther, 1832).

44. Andreas Birch, *Auctarium Codicis apocryphi Novi Testamenti Fabriciani* (Copenhagen: Arntzen et Hartier, 1804).

45. Johann Karl Thilo, *Codex apocryphus Novi Testamenti* (Leipzig: Vogel, 1832).

the material from Fabricius by focusing on the texts Thilo believed to be most important; he also endeavored to carefully compare and adjudicate between readings from newly published sources rather than simply reprint earlier editions based on single manuscripts. Thilo's gospels became the basis for a new string of vernacular collections: in English by John Allen Giles,[46] in French by Jacques-Paul Migne and Pierre Gustave Brunet,[47] and in German by Richard Clemens and Karl Friedrich Borberg.[48]

Thilo's introduction of philological principles to the study of the Christian apocrypha was continued and refined by Constantin Tischendorf, well known as a hunter of biblical manuscripts, in particular the Codex Sinaiticus, which he acquired from St. Catherine's monastery in the Sinai. Tischendorf also found manuscripts of apocryphal texts in his travels and several of these were used in his three volumes of texts, one each on gospels *(Evangelia Apocrypha)*, acts *(Acta Apostolorum Apocrypha)*, and apocalypses *(Apocalypses Apocryphae)*.[49] Tischendorf's collection of apocryphal gospels replaced Thilo as the standard resource for scholars seeking to work with CA in their original languages. Even today, some of Tischendorf's texts have yet to be supplanted by new editions.

But anyone in Tischendorf's day seeking CA in ancient languages other than Greek and Latin had to look elsewhere. Texts extant in oriental languages—such as Syriac, Arabic, and Coptic—became available to scholars as early as the seventeenth century with Henry Sike's edition of the *Arabic Infancy Gospel*,[50] but the publication of oriental manuscripts accelerated in the nineteenth century, first with Paul de Lagarde's 1861 edition of an early Syriac manuscript of the *Pseudo-Clementines*. Soon after, three collections of Syriac texts appeared, all based primarily on manuscripts from the British Library: William Cureton's *Ancient Syriac Documents Relative to the Earliest Establishment of Christianity in Edessa*, published posthumously in 1864; and William Wright's two publications: *Contributions to the Apocryphal Literature of the New Testament* in 1865, focusing on gospels, and his two-volume *Apocryphal Acts of the Apostles* in 1871.[51] Additional texts appeared in Paul Bedjan's seven volumes of Syriac martyrologies, including the *History of Simon Cephas, the Chief of the Apostles*, published between 1890 and 1897;[52] and the so-called sisters of Sinai, Agnes Smith and Margaret Gibson, published their acquisitions and discoveries in

46. John Allen Giles, *Codex Apocryphus Novi Testamenti: The Uncanonical Gospels and other Writings referring to the first ages of Christianity in the original languages: collected together from the editions of Fabricius, Thilo and others* (2 vols.; London: D. Nutt, 1852).

47. Jacques-Paul Migne, *Dictionnaire des Apocryphes ou, Collection de tous les livres apocryphes relatifs à l'Ancien et au Nouveau Testament* (2 vols.; Paris: Ateliers catholiques, 1856–1858); Pierre Gustave Brunet, *Les Évangiles apocryphes. Traduits et annotés d'après l'édition de J. C. Thilo* (Paris: A. L. Herold, 1848).

48. Richard Clemens, *Die geheimgehaltenen oder sogenannten Apokryphen Evangelien* (Stuttgart: J. Scheible, 1850); Karl Friedrich Borberg, *Bibliothek der neutestamentlichen Apokryphen, gesammelt, übersetzt, und erläutert* (Stuttgart: Literatur-Comptoir, 1841).

49. Constantin Tischendorf, ed., *Evangelia Apocrypha* (Leipzig: Mendelssohn, 1853; 2nd ed. 1876); idem, *Acta apostolorum apocrypha* (Leipzig: Mendelssohn, 1851); idem, *Apocalypses apocryphae* (Leipzig: Mendelssohn, 1866).

50. Henry Sike, *Evangelium Infantiae; vel, Liber Apocryphus de Infantia Salvatoris; ex manuscripto edidit, ac Latina versione et notis illustravit Henricus Sike* (Trajecti ad Rhenum: Halman, 1697).

51. William Wright, ed., *Apocryphal Acts of the Apostles: Edited from Syriac Manuscripts in the British Museum and Other Libraries* (2 vols.; London: Williams & Norgate, 1871); idem, *Contributions to the Apocryphal Literature of the New Testament* (London: Williams & Norgate, 1865); William Cureton, *Ancient Syriac Documents Relative to the Earliest Establishment of Christianity in Edessa and the Neighbouring Countries* (London: Williams & Norgate, 1864).

52. Paul Bedjan, *Acta Martyrum et Sanctorum* (7 vols.; Paris: Otto Harrassowitz, 1890–1897).

several volumes of Syriac and Arabic texts between 1902 and 1904.[53] A few decades later, Alphonse Mingana published a number of Arabic (Garšūnī) texts in the series *Woodbrooke Studies*.[54] As for Coptic, pages from manuscripts produced at the White Monastery were published at the turn of the century by Oscar von Lemm,[55] Pierre Lacau,[56] Eugène Revillout,[57] and Forbes Robinson.[58] At first some of these pages were believed to derive from apocryphal gospels, but recent efforts to reunite the pages has revealed that many of the texts are pseudo-apostolic memoirs, such as the *Encomium on John the Baptist*. Additional Coptic texts, including the *Investiture of Abbaton* and the *Mysteries of John*, appeared in three collections assembled by E. A. W. Budge between 1913 and 1915.[59]

Translators of CA were slow to integrate the oriental texts and manuscripts into modern-language collections. Paul Peeters is a notable exception. He worked with Charles Michel on a two-volume CA collection in 1911 and 1914,[60] contributing translations of Coptic, Arabic, and Armenian texts, including the lengthy *Armenian Infancy Gospel* published by Esayi Tayets'i in 1898.[61] Also noteworthy is the expansive assortment of translations combined as volume 8 of the *Ante-Nicene Fathers*, containing republished material from the Ante-Nicene Christian Library—Alexander Walker's 1873 volume of *Apocryphal Gospels, Acts, and Revelations*, the *Pseudo-Clementines*[62]—along with some Jewish pseudepigrapha and Cureton's Syriac texts.[63] Most collections in translation, how-

---

53. Margaret Dunlop Gibson, *Apocrypha Sinaitica* (Studia Sinaitica 5; Cambridge: C. J. Clay & Sons, 1896); eadem, *Apocrypha arabica* (Studia Sinaitica 8; Cambridge: C. J. Clay & Sons, 1901); Agnes Smith Lewis, *Apocrypha Syriaca: The Protevangelium Jacobi and Transitus Mariae* (Studia Sinaitica 11; Cambridge: C. J. Clay & Sons, 1902); eadem, *Acta mythologica apostolorum/The Mythological Acts of the Apostles* (Horae Semiticae 3–4; Cambridge: C. J. Clay & Sons, 1904). For a popular account of these women's work, see Janet Soskice, *The Sisters of Sinai: How Two Lady Adventurers Discovered the Hidden Gospels* (New York: Vintage, 2009).

54. Alphonse Mingana, *Woodbrooke Studies: Christian Documents in Syriac, Arabic, and Garshuni* (7 vols.; Cambridge: Cambridge University Press, 1927–1934). The first three volumes of the series include the *Life of John the Baptist* by Serapion, the *Vision of Theophilus*, the *Book of the Rolls* (under the title "Apocalypse of Peter"), the *Lament of Mary*, and the *Martyrdom of Pilate*.

55. Oscar von Lemm, "Koptische apocryphe Apostelakten 1," *Bulletin de l'Académie Impériale des Sciences* 33 (1890): 509–81; idem, "Koptische apocryphe Apostelakten 2," *Bulletin de l'Académie Impériale des Sciences* 35 (1892): 233–326.

56. Pierre Lacau, *Fragments d'apocryphes coptes* (Mémoires publiés par les membres de l'Institut français d'archéologie orientale, 9; Cairo: Imprimerie de l'IFAO, 1904).

57. Eugène Revillout, *Apocryphes coptes du Nouveau Testament* (Études Égyptologiques 7; Paris: F. Vieweg, 1876); idem, *Les apocryphes coptes. Première partie: Les Évangiles des douze apôtres et de Saint Barthélemy* (PO 2/2; Paris: Firmin Didot, 1904).

58. Forbes Robinson, *Coptic Apocryphal Gospels. Translations Together with the Texts of Some of Them* (TS 4.2; Cambridge: Cambridge University Press, 1896).

59. Ernest A. W. Budge, *Coptic Apocrypha in the Dialect of Upper Egypt* (Coptic Texts 3; London: Oxford University Press, 1913); idem, *Coptic Martyrdoms in the Dialect of Upper Egypt* (2 vols.; Coptic Texts 4; London: Oxford University Press, 1914); and idem, *Miscellaneous Coptic Texts in the Dialect of Upper Egypt* (Coptic Texts 5; London: Oxford University Press, 1915).

60. Charles Michel and Paul Peeters, eds., *Évangiles apocryphes* (Textes et documents pour l'étude historique du Christianisme 13 and 18; Paris: Librairie Alphonse Picard & Fils, 1911–1914).

61. Esayi Tayets'i, *Ankanon girk' Nor Ktakaranats'* (T'angaran haykakan hin ew nor dprtu'eants' 2; Venice: S. Ghazar, 1898).

62. Alexander Walker, *Apocryphal Gospels, Acts and Revelations* (The Ante-Nicene Christian Library 16; Edinburgh: T.&T. Clark, 1873); Thomas Smith, Peter Peterson, and John Donaldson, *The Clementine Homilies* (The Ante-Nicene Christian Library 17; Edinburgh: T.&T. Clark, 1870).

63. Arthur Cleveland Coxe, ed., *The Ante-Nicene Fathers*, vol. 8 (Buffalo, N.Y.: Christian Literature

ever, remained focused on Greek and Latin sources, except for those texts extant only in other languages (e.g., the *History of Joseph the Carpenter,* the *Epistula Apostolorum,* and the *Book of Bartholomew*) or for texts preserved better in oriental manuscripts (e.g., the Ethiopic version of the *Apocalypse of Peter,* and portions of the *Infancy Gospel of Thomas* available at that time only in Syriac).

The same neglect affected a number of late-antique texts in Greek. As the CA collections narrowed their focus to texts of the first three centuries, it became difficult for newly published texts to find a place in the emerging apocryphal "canon." The materials in Athanasius Vasiliev's *Anecdota graeco-byzantina* (the *Decapitation of John the Forerunner,* a *Dialogue between Jesus and the Devil,* and manuscripts of the *Legend of Aphroditianus,* the *Epistle of Christ from Heaven,* the *Apocalypse of the Virgin,* and others)[64] and the first volume of M. R. James's *Anecdota Apocrypha* (with the *Life and Conduct of Xanthippe and Polyxena,* the *Apocalypse of the Virgin,* a *Description of the Anti-Christ in Latin,* and others),[65] both published in 1893, rarely make an appearance in subsequent apocrypha collections. Also largely disregarded are the three volumes of Jacques-Paul Migne's *Patrologia Graeca* that feature Simeon Metaphrastes's lives of the saints (the *Acts of Cornelius* among them; see *PG* 114–16) and a smattering of texts included in the companion series *Patrologia Latina* (e.g., the *Discovery of John the Baptist's Head* in *PL* 67). After the nineteenth century, wide-ranging collections of apocrypha in their original languages became exceedingly rare. Except for the update of Tischendorf's volume of apocryphal acts by Richard Adelbert Lipsius and Maximilien Bonnet (*Acta Apostolorum Apocrypha,* published 1891–1903),[66] there have been few efforts to supplant and expand the great collections; instead scholars have slowly replaced these early authorities with new editions of individual texts.

Modern-language CA collections were plentiful in the twentieth century, with editions in Afrikaans, Czech, Dutch, English, French, German, Italian, Polish, Norwegian, and Spanish.[67] Three of these became so influential that they established publishing legacies that continue to today. The first is Edgar Hennecke's *Neutestamentliche Apokryphen* and accompanying *Handbuch* in 1904.[68] The collection follows the earlier convention of including the Apostolic Fathers and some Christian-authored pseudepigrapha (*5 and 6 Ezra*), but innovates with the delegation of texts or subgenres of texts to individual scholars. The second edition in 1924[69] updates and combines the two 1904 volumes into one, while the third, in 1959/1964 (edited with Wilhelm Schneemelcher),[70] narrows its focus to just the CA, a tem-

Publishing Co., 1886).

64. Athanasius Vasiliev, *Anecdota graeco-byzantina, pars prior* (Moscow: Imperial University, 1893).

65. Montague Rhodes James, *Apocrypha Anecdota: A Collection of Thirteen Apocryphal Books and Fragments Now First Edited from Manuscripts* (TS 2.3; Cambridge: Cambridge University Press, 1893). The texts in the second collection (*Apocrypha Anecdota.* Second Series [TS 5.1; Cambridge: Cambridge University Press, 1897]) have received more attention.

66. Richard A. Lipsius and Maximilien Bonnet, eds., *Acta Apostolorum Apocrypha* (3 vols. in 2; Leipzig: Mendelssohn, 1891–1903).

67. For more information on the collections not discussed below see the bibliographical references in *ANT,* xx.

68. Edgar Hennecke, *Neutestamentliche Apokryphen in deutscher Übersetzung* and *Handbuch zu Neutestamentlichen apokryphen in deutscher Übersetzung* (Tübingen: J. C. B. Mohr, 1904).

69. Edgar Hennecke, *Neutestamentliche Apokryphen in deutscher Übersetzung* (2nd ed.; Tübingen: J. C. B. Mohr, 1924).

70. Edgar Hennecke and Wilhelm Schneemelcher, *Neutestamentliche Apokryphen in deutscher Übersetzung* (3rd ed.; Tübingen: J. C. B. Mohr, 1959–1964); English trans.: *New Testament Apocrypha* (trans. Robert McLachlan Wilson; 2 vols.; Philadelphia: Westminster John Knox, 1963–1966).

plate continued for the revised fifth edition of 1987/1989 (edited by Schneemelcher alone).[71] Hennecke's pioneering work is so esteemed among German scholars that the major revision currently in progress by Christoph Markschies and Jens Schröter is nicknamed the "new Hennecke."[72] In England M. R. James worked alone on his collection, *The Apocryphal New Testament*, published in 1924 and again in 1953 with a small update.[73] The volume features the texts that have become standard but notably also includes descriptions of several Coptic, Armenian, and Ethiopic texts, along with discussions of a number of later apocryphal acts (including the *Virtutes apostolorum*), and a handful of medieval and modern apocrypha. Much of this abbreviated material was omitted in the "new James" edited by J. K. Elliott in 1993,[74] but the descriptions of later apocryphal acts remained, and a few newly discovered texts from the Nag Hammadi library were added. By Elliott's time, however, the English translations of Hennecke-Schneemelcher had become the standard resource even among English-language scholars. Spanish readers encountered the texts first in a three-volume collection of gospels by Edmundo González-Blanco in 1934[75] and, beginning in 1956, in successive editions of Aurelio de Santos Otero's bilingual (Greek and Latin texts with Spanish translations) *Los Evangelios Apócrifos*, which has yet to be superseded.[76] Two other bilingual editions appeared in the first half of the century, one in French (by Michel and Peeters, mentioned above) and one in Italian (Giuseppe Bonaccorsi's *Vangeli apocrifi* from 1948)[77] but neither of these attained the levels of success enjoyed by the German, English, and Spanish scholarly traditions.

By the 1960s the Hennecke-Schneemelcher selection of texts had become entrenched; unfortunately, as noted above, the progressive narrowing of the corpus brought with it a rather narrow definition of "Christian apocrypha." In the introduction to the 1959 edition, Schneemelcher characterized the CA as texts that "lay claim to be in the same class with the writings of the canon, and which from the point of view of Form Criticism further develop and mould the kinds of style created and received in the NT, whilst foreign elements certainly intrude."[78] But the number of texts that could be considered for inclusion kept increasing, resulting in a challenge to Schneemelcher's definition. A number of Irish apocrypha began to see publication in the 1920s; much of it was collected and translated into English for Máire Herbert and Martin McNamara's 1989 compilation of *Irish Biblical Apocrypha*,[79] which includes, among other works, excerpts from two miscellanies: the *Liber Flavus* and the *Leabhar Breac*. Georgian versions of the apocryphal acts were collected by Korneli Kekeliże in 1959.[80] And Aurelio de Santos Otero drew

---

71. Wilhelm Schneemelcher, *Neutestamentliche Apokryphen in deutscher Übersetzung* (5th ed.; 2 vols.; Tübingen: Mohr Siebeck, 1987–1989); English trans.: *New Testament Apocrypha* (trans. from the corrected 6th ed. by Robert McLachlan Wilson; 2 vols.; Louisville, Ky.: Westminster John Knox, 1991–1992).

72. Christoph Markschies and Jens Schröter, eds., *Antike christliche Apokryphen in deutscher Übersetzung* (Tübingen: Mohr Siebeck, 2012).

73. James, *Apocryphal New Testament*.

74. Elliott, ed. and trans., *Apocryphal New Testament*.

75. Edmundo González-Blanco, ed., *Los Evangelios Apócrifos* (3 vols.; Madrid: Bergua, 1934).

76. Aurelio de Santos Otero, ed., *Los Evangelios Apócrifos: Colección de textos griegos y latinos, versión crítica, estudios introductorios y comentarios* (Madrid: Biblioteca de Autores Christianos, 1956[1], 2006[13]).

77. Giuseppe Bonaccorsi, ed., *Vangeli apocrifi* (Florence: Libreria Editrice Fiorentina, 1948).

78. Schneemelcher, "General Introduction," 59.

79. Máire Herbert and Martin McNamara, *Irish Biblical Apocrypha: Selected Texts in Translation* (Edinburgh: T.&T. Clark, 1989).

80. Korneli Kekeliże, ed., *Kartuli versiebi apokripebisa mocikulta sesaxeb: IX–XI ss. xelnacerta mixedvit.*

Western scholars' attention to the large body of Slavonic apocrypha in a two-volume study published in 1978 and 1981.[81] Unfortunately, de Santos Otero did not include texts and translations in his study and very few of these texts have since been published. The biggest change in the field came with the publication of the Coptic texts from Nag Hammadi, which began to appear in 1956, with a complete collection published by James Robinson in 1977.[82] Within the thirteen codices can be found fourteen apocryphal Christian texts, including a complete copy of the *Gospel of Thomas,* the *Gospel of Philip,* and the *Acts of Peter and the Twelve Apostles.*

Two Italian scholars fully integrated these new developments into their expansive CA collections. Mario Erbetta's four volumes, published between 1966 and 1981,[83] incorporated the recently published texts from Nag Hammadi and other gnostic texts, such as the *Pistis Sophia,* along with a wide range of infancy gospels and Dormition traditions, and some rarely seen apocalypses (the *Investiture of Abbaton* and the apocryphal apocalypses of John) and epistles (the medieval letters of the Virgin Mary). Luigi Moraldi's 1971 collection is notable particularly for its broad assortment of apocryphal acts, including the entire *Virtutes apostolorum* corpus.[84] The broad scope of the Italian compendia gave rise to the debate by Junod, Picard, Rordorf, and others about redefining and relabeling the literature.[85] Out of this discussion came the creation of a scholarly organization, the Association pour l'étude de la littérature apocryphe chrétienne (AELAC), with a mandate to create a French collection of texts with a scope similar to those of their Italian colleagues. The group specifically sought to broaden the CA corpus to include texts composed after the fourth century and texts written by Christians that focus on Old Testament figures and events. The principle is reflected in the title of their two-volume collection *Écrits apocryphes chrétiens* (published in 1997 and 2005) and in its contents, which feature the standard early texts along with later, rarely seen material (e.g., *On the Priesthood of Jesus,* the *Book of the Rooster,* and the *Martyrdom of Luke*), and Christian-authored Pseudepigrapha (e.g., *Lives of the Prophets, 5 Ezra*).[86] The AELAC is responsible also for a series of critical editions (Corpus Christianorum Series Apocryphorum) focusing on individual texts (such as the *Acts of John* and the *Infancy Gospel of Thomas*) and also collections of texts in lesser-studied languages: to date the series has included compendia on texts in Armenian, in two volumes by Louis Leloir,[87] and Irish, in multiple volumes published in association with the Irish Biblical Association and edited, once again, by Martin McNamara.[88]

Teksti gamosacemad moamzada, gamokvleva da leksikoni daurto ("Georgian Versions of the Apocryphal Acts of the Apostles"; Tblisi: Sakartvelos SSR mecnierebata akademiis gamomcemloba, 1959).

81. Aurelio de Santos Otero, *Die handschriftliche Überlieferung der altslavischen Apokryphen* (2 vols.; PTS 20 and 23; Berlin: De Gruyter, 1978–1981).

82. James M. Robinson, *The Nag Hammadi Library in English* (San Francisco: Harper & Row, 1977).

83. Mario Erbetta, ed. and trans., *Gli Apocrifi del Nuovo Testamento* (3 vols. in 4; Turin: Marietti, 1966–1981).

84. Luigi Moraldi, ed. and trans., *Apocrifi del Nuovo Testamento* (2 vols.; Classici delle Religioni 24.5; Turin: Unione Tipografico-Editrice Torinese, 1971; 2nd ed. in 3 vols. 1994).

85. Summarized in Tóth, "Way Out of the Tunnel?" 74–80.

86. François Bovon, Pierre Geoltrain, and Jean-Daniel Kaestli, eds., *Écrits apocryphes chrétiens* (2 vols.; Bibliothèque de la Pléiade 442 and 516; Paris: Gallimard, 1997–2005).

87. Louis Leloir, *Acta Apostolorum Armeniaca: Écrits apocryphes sur les apôtres: Traduction de l'édition arménienne de Venise* (2 vols.; CCSA 3–4; Turnhout: Brepols, 1986 and 1992).

88. Martin McNamara et al., eds., *Apocrypha Hiberniae. Part 1: Evangelia infantiae* (2 vols.; CCSA 13–14; Turnhout: Brepols, 2001); John Carey, *Apocrypha Hiberniae. Part 2, vol. 1: In Tenga Bithnua—The Ever-New Tongue* (CCSA 16; Turnhout: Brepols, 2009). Two volumes of apocalypses are currently in production.

Despite the AELAC's call for the examination of texts written after the fourth century, the group has stopped short of including modern apocrypha, such as Nicolas Notovitch's *Unknown Life of Christ* and the *Letter of Benan,* in their projects. Many of these texts are surveyed in Edgar J. Goodspeed's *Strange New Gospels* published in 1931 and later expanded as *Modern Apocrypha and Famous "Biblical" Hoaxes* in 1956.[89] A larger group of texts was covered by Per Beskow in 1983 and recently revisited in a 2011 essay.[90] Neither Goodspeed nor Beskow had much sympathy for the material; Goodspeed, for example, said they were of "baseless character," were "dredged up from obscure depths mostly beyond the ken of educated people," and he only examined them to show that they were not "genuine documents of Christian antiquity." But in 2005 one prominent AELAC member, Pierluigi Piovanelli, called for expanding CA collections to include modern texts.[91] So far the only person who has been willing to take up this challenge is Laurie Maffly-Kipp who published a collection of *American Scriptures* in 2010,[92] which includes selections from the *Aquarian Gospel of Jesus the Christ,* the *Archko Volume,* the *Book of Mormon,* and others. Examined objectively, there really is little difference between the modern texts and those produced at other times in history. They all claim to be written either by an esteemed early Christian figure or their disciple, they all draw upon canonical Christian Scripture (variously reinterpreting and augmenting it), and they all seek to speak to contemporary situations in ways that canonical texts do not. All of these texts are worthy of study as reflections of the interests, beliefs, practices, and knowledge of their time—whether that time is ancient history, the recent past, or even today.

With the resurgence of interest in the CA occasioned by Dan Brown's bestselling novel *The Da Vinci Code* and the rediscovery of the *Gospel of Judas,* publishers rushed to satisfy the public's curiosity with new CA collections, though most of these take little account of current discussion of what constitutes "Christian apocrypha." The best of these is Bart Ehrman and Zlatko Pleše's *Apocryphal Gospels* from 2011—one of the few collections in ancient and modern languages to appear in a century, and the first ever in English.[93] It combines the standard infancy and ministry gospels with a number of "gnostic" texts (the *Gospel of Thomas,* the *Gospel of Mary,* the *Gospel of Judas*), and a broad selection of texts from the Pilate Cycle. But even this edition focuses only on early texts, the ones most useful for understanding pre-Constantinian Christianity. The Italian and French collections, and now the "new Hennecke" by Markschies and Schröter, have left Schneemelcher's defi-

---

89. Edgar J. Goodspeed, *Strange New Gospels* (Chicago: University of Chicago Press, 1931); idem, *Modern Apocrypha and Famous "Biblical" Hoaxes* (Grand Rapids, Mich.: Baker Book House, 1956).

90. Per Beskow, *Strange Tales about Jesus: A Survey of Unfamiliar Gospels* (Philadelphia: Fortress, 1983); idem, "Modern Mystifications of Jesus," in *The Blackwell Companion to the New Testament* (ed. Delbert Burkett; London: Wiley-Blackwell, 2011), 458–74.

91. Pierluigi Piovanelli, "What Is a Christian Apocryphal Text and How Does It Work? Some Observations on Apocryphal Hermeneutics," *Nederlands theologisch tijdschrift* 59 (2005): 31–40.

92. Laurie F. Maffly-Kipp, *American Scriptures: An Anthology of Sacred Writings* (New York: Penguin, 2010).

93. Bart D. Ehrman and Zlatko Pleše, *The Apocryphal Gospels: Texts and Translations* (Oxford and New York: Oxford University Press, 2011). Other bilingual editions have appeared but these are much less comprehensive, focusing only on infancy gospels (e.g., Gerhard Schneider, *Evangelia infantiae apocrypha—Apokrype Kindheitsevangelien* [Fontes christiani 18; Freiburg: Herder, 1995]) and fragmentary texts (e.g., Dieter Lührmann and Egbert Schlarb, *Fragmente apokryph gewordener Evangelien in griechischer und lateinischer Sprache* [Marburg: Elwert, 2000]; Andrew E. Bernhard, *Other Early Christian Gospels: A Critical Edition of the Surviving Greek Manuscripts* [London: T.&T. Clark, 2007]).

nition far behind, advocating for the examination of noncanonical texts for their own sake as valid and fascinating expressions of Christian belief and not merely as texts that aid in understanding the origins of the New Testament. The same spirit has guided the creation of *New Testament Apocrypha: More Noncanonical Scriptures.*[94]

This Collection

The present collection is related to and was inspired by our sister project *Old Testament Pseudepigrapha: More Noncanonical Scriptures (MOTP)* edited by Richard Bauckham, Jim Davila, and Alexander Panayotov. The first volume of *MOTP* was published in November 2013; a second is set to appear in the next few years. The *MOTP* volumes are intended to be a supplement to the highly regarded collection of pseudepigrapha assembled by James H. Charlesworth in the 1980s. Bauckham, Davila, and Panayotov saw a need to publish additional texts and manuscripts of texts not included in Charlesworth but, recognizing the enduring value of Charlesworth's volumes, the editors decided it was better to create a supplement to Charlesworth, rather than a replacement. They opted also not to include texts that are sufficiently and more appropriately covered in other English collections, such as the texts found among the Dead Sea Scrolls or the Nag Hammadi library. *MNTA* plays a similar role for the CA, supplementing the most recent comprehensive collection of the texts in English: J. K. Elliott's *The Apocryphal New Testament,* published in 1993. The title, *New Testament Apocrypha: More Noncanonical Scriptures,* was chosen to illustrate both its relationship to Elliott's collection (as well as a nod to the Hennecke-Schneemelcher tradition) and to *MOTP.* Some readers may think the title was chosen in ignorance or defiance of the current trend in the field that advocates studying apocryphal Christian texts for their own sake, not for what can be learned from them about the origins and development of canonical texts. Clearly this is not the case, as many of the texts included in this collection were composed long after those in the New Testament, and one of the reasons for the creation of the *MNTA* series was to bring attention to texts that have been neglected by scholars because they have little bearing on the study of early Christianity. The chosen title also is more recognizable to a wide readership, a benefit recognized by Elliott when considering candidates for his own collection. After noting such alternatives as "Early Non-Canonical Christian Writings" and "Christian Apocrypha," Elliott concluded, "most readers turning to a book with this title are usually aware of the sort of literature they expect to find within its covers. Having become a conventional title it is now difficult to substitute for it another that would be more accurate yet still be recognized for what it is."[95]

The texts featured in this volume, and future volumes in the series, were chosen based on the following criteria.

First, *ANT* was conceived as an update to the 1924 compilation by James; thus Elliott added a few texts that had been published in the intervening decades, though he chose to include only two of the Christian texts from the Nag Hammadi library (the *Gospel of Thomas* and the *Apocryphon of James*) since these texts were already widely available in other compilations. *MNTA* follows in the James-Elliott tradition by including texts not available to Elliott—specifically, the fragment P. Oxy. 5072 (published in 2011), the *Berlin-Strasbourg*

---

94. The creation and scope of the project are described in the preview article by Tony Burke, "More Christian Apocrypha," *BSR* 41, no. 3 (2012): 16–21.

95. *ANT,* xii.

Apocryphon (first published as the *Gospel of the Savior* in 1999), and the *Dance of the Savior* and *Discourse of the Savior* from Qasr el-Wizz (published in 2006). The remaining texts in the volume have been available to scholars for a considerable amount of time.

Second, Elliott's collection, like many other CA compilations, focuses primarily on texts believed to have been composed in the first three centuries. Some later texts do appear in his volume—the *Epistle of Lentulus,* the *Epistle to the Laodiceans,* several apocalypses, some *Dormition* texts (relegated to an appendix), and descriptions or excerpts of later apocryphal acts and texts from the Pilate Cycle—but, despite Elliott's assertion that his collection "does not limit itself exclusively to early writings," on the whole, it does, but perhaps more for pragmatic concerns: to limit the collection to a single volume.[96] *MNTA* is less restricted. Currently, a second volume of *MNTA* is in development, and additional volumes are in consideration. The number of texts that could be included is staggering—Maurice Geerard's 1992 *Clavis (CANT)* alone lists 346 texts, and there are more besides, particularly if one includes modern apocrypha, such as the *Unknown Life of Christ* and the *Archko Volume.* It seemed prudent, therefore, to adopt a temporal limit for the series. The *MOTP* editors settled on a time of composition before the rise of Islam in the seventh century, though with a few exceptions. Roughly the same limit has been followed for the *MNTA* series; a few texts push that boundary—such as the *(Latin) Revelation of John about Antichrist* (composed, likely, no earlier than the tenth century)—but are included for their intrinsic value and in awareness of the difficulties of dating texts known for their tendency to be altered, sometimes considerably, in the course of their transmission.

Third, the *MNTA* series appears at a time in scholarship when CA collections in other modern languages are less bound by the generic categories of texts within the canon. The most recent Italian, French, and German compendia surveyed above feature a much broader variety of texts, including dialogues, martyrdoms, Christian-authored pseudepigrapha, and apocryphal traditions embedded in other literature, such as chronicles and homilies. Apocrypha extant in lesser-known languages, such as Armenian and Georgian, are also incorporated. *MNTA* similarly casts its net wide, incorporating selections from medieval apocalypses, tales of relic invention, free-floating stories, patristic references to apostles, recycled apocryphal acts, and the growing corpus of Coptic pseudo-apostolic memoirs. Though the *MNTA* volumes follow Elliott in arranging the texts into the broad categories of gospels, epistles, acts, and apocalypses, it is with the awareness that some texts ill-fit these categories and that the boundaries between the genres are somewhat porous—for example, the *Encomium on Mary Magdalene* is placed within gospel texts, since it narrates some events from the life of Jesus, but it also has affinities with apocryphal acts (since it focuses on the life and mission of a prominent early Christian figure), and with apocalypses, since it concludes with a revelation discourse from an angel. Similarly, the *Letter of Pseudo-Dionysius* is placed among the epistles but it reports events surrounding the martyrdoms of Peter and Paul, events typically related in apocryphal acts.

Fourth, a number of texts in this first volume have appeared previously in English translation but needed to be reexamined in light of new manuscript discoveries and new trends in scholarship. This is particularly the case with the *Life of John the Baptist* by Serapion, which was published almost a century ago on the basis of two manuscripts; the new translation draws upon a significantly broader manuscript base and the accompanying introduction is the first significant discussion of the text. Another text, the *Infancy Gospel*

---

96. Elliott discusses his motivations in organizing the volume in his introduction to *ANT,* ix-x.

of Thomas appears in Elliott's volume, but not in its Syriac form; indeed the Syriac version of the text, believed to be very important for the establishment of the gospel's original form, has not been sufficiently utilized in any CA collection since its *editio princeps* in 1865. Another curious entry in the volume is the Aramaic fragment of the *Toledot Yeshu,* a Jewish satire of Christian gospel literature. The *Toledot Yeshu* rarely appears in CA collections but it certainly fits the definition (stories about Jesus and his contemporaries that are not officially part of the canon of the Western church) and, in some of its versions, incorporates traditions found in Christian-penned apocrypha, such as the story of Jesus animating the birds from the *Infancy Gospel of Thomas* and several other texts. The *MOTP* collection features several Christian-authored Jewish pseudepigrapha; it is fitting, therefore, for *MNTA* to include an apocryphon about Jesus composed and transmitted by Jews.

And finally, many CA texts are not included in the collection because they are readily available in recently published English translations. The Christian texts from Nag Hammadi, for example, can be read in the update of Robinson's Nag Hammadi library collection edited by Marvin Meyer.[97] The lengthy *Armenian Infancy Gospel,* published in a critical edition in 1898 and translated into French in 1914, finally appeared in English translation less than a decade ago;[98] and Ps.-Cyril of Jerusalem's *On the Life and the Passion of Christ,* another pseudo-apostolic memoir, debuted in a critical edition by Roelof van den Broek in 2014.[99] The only exception to this rule is the *Revelation of the Magi,* which was published in a popular market translation by Brent Landau in 2010;[100] however, the entry included in this volume features only a summary of the text, and the introduction includes additional details about the text more appropriate for a scholarly reader.

Importance of This Collection

Generally speaking, the CA are of value in several different respects. In the case of the earliest apocryphal gospels, they provide us with otherwise-unknown traditions about Jesus, as well as materials also found in the canonical Gospels, but perhaps preserved in a more archaic form in the CA. But the number of CA texts that can be reasonably dated as contemporaneous with the NT writings is extremely small; thus, if the CA are to be considered of interest, it must be primarily on the basis of other considerations. Indeed, there are numerous reasons for regarding the CA as valuable for specialists in the field of ancient Christianity and other academic areas, as well as for interested general readers. In what follows, we will refer both to well-known CA texts as well as to those texts from this volume that are much less familiar to most readers.

First and foremost, the CA provide insight into the diversity of ancient Christian beliefs about Jesus Christ, God, humanity, religious diversity, salvation, repentance, martyrdom, and a host of other theological considerations. If we, for the sake of space, restrict our examples to Christology,[101] the *Gospel of Thomas* promotes the view that Jesus' sig-

---

97. Meyer, ed., *Nag Hammadi Scriptures.*

98. Abraham Terian, *The Armenian Gospel of the Infancy with Three Early Versions of the Protevangelium of James* (Oxford and New York: Oxford University Press, 2008).

99. Roelof van den Broek, *Pseudo-Cyril of Jerusalem, On the Life and the Passion of Christ. A Coptic Apocryphon* (Supplements to Vigiliae Christianae 118; Leiden: Brill, 2013).

100. Brent C. Landau, *Revelation of the Magi: The Lost Tale of the Wise Men's Journey to Bethlehem* (San Francisco: HarperCollins, 2010).

101. For a helpful overview of this topic, see Einar Thomassen, "Jesus in the New Testament Apocrypha," in *Alternative Christs* (ed. Olav Hammer; Cambridge: Cambridge University Press, 2009), 33–50.

nificance is not primarily (if at all) in his death, but in his saving words, which the reader of the gospel must interpret. The *Acts of John,* the *Acts of Peter,* and the *Revelation of the Magi* all depict Jesus as being capable of altering his appearance at will, an ability that scholars term "polymorphy."[102] The *Infancy Gospel of Thomas* imagines a child Jesus who does not hesitate to maim or kill those who fail to show him proper reverence, going far beyond instances of Jesus' anger in the canonical Gospels. The *Dialogue of the Paralytic with Christ* features a similarly cold-blooded Jesus who, in disguise, relentlessly mocks a paralyzed man for his misfortune before finally restoring him to health. All of these emphases found in the CA have some analogues with incidents reported in the canonical Gospels, but there they are somewhat muted. In the case of the many apocryphal gospels written after the canonical Gospels, it is possible to view such depictions of Jesus as instances where a later writer "walked through a door" that was "opened" by one of the earliest narratives about Jesus.

A second reason for the significance of this literature dovetails with this notion of the canonical Gospels as an "opened door." The CA are extremely valuable witnesses to the practice of biblical interpretation by ancient Christians. No less than the commentaries on biblical books produced by patristic writers, the CA demonstrate a desire to know more about events that the NT writings mention only in passing. For example, in Romans 15 Paul expresses a desire to travel to Spain after he delivers his collection to Jerusalem; no NT source indicates whether Paul fulfilled this desire, but the ending of Acts would seem to imply that he did not. Yet the idea of Paul reaching the farthest western part of the inhabited world was too tempting a scenario for the author of the *Life and Conduct of Xanthippe and Polyxena* to pass up. As another instance of biblical interpretation, the infancy narrative of Luke's Gospel implies that Jesus has Levitical ancestry through his mother Mary. *On the Priesthood of Jesus* takes this data and spins it into a fascinating story of Jesus' election to the Jerusalem priesthood that the Jews conspired to hide. Also taking a page from Luke's infancy narrative, the *Infancy Gospel of Thomas* builds upon the intriguing story of Jesus as a twelve-year-old prodigy in the temple to imagine what Jesus would have been like if he was truly a divine being throughout his entire childhood. Finally, infancy gospels like the *Legend of Aphroditianus* and the *Revelation of the Magi* demonstrate how intriguing Matthew's brief and laconic story of the mysterious foreigners who visited the child Jesus was for Christian exegetes.

A third significance of the CA is that they are creative literary products in their own right. Despite the fact that an overwhelming percentage of CA texts are dependent upon NT writings, many of them are remarkably imaginative nonetheless. The *Dialogue of the Paralytic with Christ* and the *Revelation of the Magi* have been mentioned already, but these two narratives should be noted again here for their bold and surprising narrative innovations. The *Legend of the Thirty Silver Pieces* develops an elaborate backstory in which the money that Judas received for betraying Jesus passed through the hands of many other important biblical figures. The *Hospitality of Dysmas* explains how the "good thief" from Luke's passion narrative came to the aid of Jesus' family during their sojourn in Egypt long before the crucifixion. The *Investiture of Abbaton* describes how the angel Muriel was the sole angel who did not shrink at the name of God and played an essential role in the creation of humanity; as a result, God appointed him as the Angel of Death (Abbaton), who protects the

---

102. For the best discussion of this christological development, see Paul Foster, "Polymorphic Christology: Its Origins and Development in Early Christianity," *JTS* 58 (2007): 66–99.

dead from the clutches of the devil. Although not a Christian composition, the *Toledot Yeshu* creates an "anti-narrative" of Jesus' life that draws on elements from the canonical Gospels and apocryphal traditions but repurposes them to present Jesus as a nefarious false prophet.

Fourth, the CA go beyond simply fashioning new narratives or new interpretations of details found in the NT. Instead, they both create and reflect new doctrines and ideas that develop in Christian thought. In terms of more familiar CA texts, the *Protevangelium of James* is a very noteworthy instance of such innovation, with its immense contributions to the early development of Mariology. Also, the *Apocalypse of Peter*, which was considered an authoritative book by numerous early Christian communities, provides us with the first detailed "tour of hell," in which sinners are subject to all manner of awful tortures. This notion of hell as a place of eternal torment is very difficult to find in canonical writings, but it evolves into the standard Christian teaching about hell, informing such later works as Dante's *Inferno*. Regarding the texts found in the present collection, the *Epistle of Christ from Heaven* presents a communiqué from Christ himself enjoining Christians to attend church on Sundays. More study would be needed to see whether this inspires or attests to the notion of "holy days of obligation"—mandatory times, including every Sunday, when the faithful must be present; nevertheless, such an idea is not found in the earliest Christian writings, and its official articulation may be relatively late. Combining these elements, the *Apocalypse of the Virgin* envisions sinners burning in hell for sleeping in instead of attending Sunday services.

Fifth and finally, the CA do function as "history," insofar as many of them give us valuable information about historical events. Whether the apocryphal gospels and the apocryphal acts tell us much of anything reliable about the historical Jesus or the first apostles is very unlikely, to be sure. Nevertheless, we are sometimes able to triangulate the CA with other historical data to determine to what events a given writing was responding. The *Life of John the Baptist* by Serapion and the *Life and Martyrdom of John the Baptist* both provide information about the circumstances under which the relics associated with John the Baptist came to light in mid-fifth-century Syria. The *Acts of Titus*, which describes the role played by Titus in the foundation of the Christian community on Crete, is itself a production of Cretan Christianity and reflects the ecclesiastical structure and historical circumstances of this community during the fifth to seventh centuries. But CA texts do not only reflect history; in some cases, they also help to create it. The *Revelation of the Magi* describes a community of Christians living at the furthest reaches of the inhabited earth, and this text was one of several that early explorers of the Americas drew on to make sense of the civilizations they discovered in the "new world."

Thus far we have described the importance of the CA in general, both familiar and unfamiliar writings. But there are several ways in which this present anthology and the texts contained within it are noteworthy compared with previous CA collections. To start, this is the first major anthology of the CA that is based in North America. Until now, Elliott and the English translations of Hennecke-Schneemelcher have been the only major anthologies of the CA available in English. *MNTA* thus marks nothing less than a watershed moment in the study of the CA in North America, which has long lagged far behind the state of research in Europe. Coinciding with the publishing of *MNTA*, its co-editors have also begun a series of biennial symposia on the CA, the first three of these held at York University in Toronto, with plans to hold future symposia at other institutions in North America. These continuing symposia are one of the chief initiatives of a new scholarly organization devoted to the study of the CA: the North American Society for the Study of Christian Apocryphal Literature (NASSCAL).

A second important feature of *MNTA* is that the majority of the texts within its covers have never been translated into any modern scholarly language, let alone discussed even in passing in the existing anthologies. For example, only six of the texts presented in *MNTA* are explicitly mentioned in Elliott's *ANT* (the Syriac *History of Simon Cephas*, the *Acts of Barnabas*, the *Acts of Titus*, the *Life and Conduct of Xanthippe and Polyxena*, the Strasbourg fragment of the *Berlin-Strasbourg Apocryphon*, and the Syriac version of the *Infancy Gospel of Thomas*), and most of these amount to only several sentences of summary. Even the comprehensive two-volume *EAC* collection, in which several of these texts also appear *(Dialogue of the Paralytic with Christ, On the Priesthood of Jesus, Acts of Timothy, Acts of Titus, Epistle of Christ from Heaven,* and *Encomium on John the Baptist)*, lacks many of the texts found in *MNTA*. Although an anthology of the standard CA texts produced by a team in North America remains a desideratum, it is nevertheless more urgent to introduce new texts to the field, which is what *MNTA* has as its top priority.

Third, the texts assembled in *MNTA* are impressive in terms of their range of dates. Some texts included are quite early, dating from the second century, while a few are very late, written perhaps early in the second millennium CE. An average date for all of the texts would probably fall around the fifth century. Among the most ancient texts are the two fragments of apocryphal gospels, Papyrus Oxyrhynchus 210 and 5072. P. Oxy. 210 has been dated to the third century, while P. Oxy. 5072 may be from the late second century, which would make it the second earliest fragment of an apocryphal gospel, behind Papyrus Egerton 2. The Syriac version of the *Infancy Gospel of Thomas* is certainly much older than the "Greek A" recension usually found in anthologies, probably quite close to the original second-century form of the text. Two texts, one about the apostle John and a robber and the other about the death of Judas, are respectively found in the writings of Papias and Clement of Alexandria, both of whom lived during the second century. And the editors of the *Legend of Aphroditianus* and the *Revelation of the Magi* have each proposed third-century dates for these infancy gospels. So, it is simply not the case that so many of the texts featured in *MNTA* are of a very late date. Rather, there is certainly a continuum present from quite early to very late, with most of the texts falling somewhere between these two poles.

Fourth, although an average date around the fifth century places many of these texts outside of the chronological parameters adopted by Hennecke-Schneemelcher and Elliott, scholars of the CA have begun to move beyond a fixation on only the very earliest of the CA, rejecting the premise that an early text was inherently more valuable and interesting than a later one. Rather, an increasing number of scholars believe that all examples of CA are inherently worthy of study, and that a given text can be significant and challenging regardless of its date of origin; in this regard, CA scholars align themselves more with the basic principles of the humanities and less with the traditional theologically motivated study of the foundational Christian writings.

Finally, it is worth noting two particularly striking attributes found in a number of the *MNTA* texts. First, several of these texts have been extremely popular, even outstripping other CA or even canonical writings. The *Epistle of Christ from Heaven*, an ancient instance of a "chain letter," exists in such a multiplicity of versions and recensions that reconstructing a transmission stemma would be a hopeless endeavor. The apocalyptic *Tiburtine Sibyl* has had a far greater influence on Western Christian eschatology than the canonical Book of Revelation, with more than 130 extant manuscripts of the Latin version alone. Another apocalyptic text, the *Apocalypse of the Virgin,* had a very similar level of popularity in the Greek East, with manuscripts of it being copied well into the nineteenth century. A second attribute is that a number of texts belong to a genre that has no precise equivalent in the NT: the pseudo-apostolic memoir. In this volume, the *Encomium on Mary Magdalene,* the *Encomium on John the Baptist,* and the *Investiture of Abbaton* are all examples of this genre. Moreover, the *Berlin-Strasbourg Apocryphon,* which was introduced to the scholarly world as the *Gospel of the Savior* in 1999 and regarded by its editors as a new second-century apocryphal gospel, is yet another example of a pseudo-apostolic memoir, most likely composed no earlier than the fifth century. Thus, while we may have "lost" an extremely early apocryphal gospel, the *Berlin-Strasbourg Apocryphon* has helped to establish the existence of a distinctive and frequently employed genre used by Coptic Christians in late antiquity.

Future Volumes
The expansion of the definition of "Christian apocrypha" has broadened the scope of the field to such an extent that one volume alone cannot contain all the apocryphal texts that have been written. One additional volume of *New Testament Apocrypha* is planned, but if the initial two volumes are successful, then a third or possibly even a fourth volume may appear in the years ahead. Certainly there are still plenty of candidates for inclusion. The following is the current list of texts to be included in volume two.

On the Star, by Pseudo-Eusebius of Caesarea
The Infancy of the Savior (Arabic Infancy Gospel)
The Rebellion of Dimas
The Hospitality and Perfume of the Bandit
The Vision of Theophilus
A Homily on the Life of Jesus
The Book of the Rooster
The Life of Judas
The Life of Mary Magdalene
The Life of Joseph of Arimathea
The Decapitation of John the Forerunner
The Martyrdom of Zechariah
The Discovery of John the Baptist's Head
The Rood-Tree Legend
The Dream of Nero
The Cure of Tiberias
The Pseudo-Clementines
The Preaching of Simon Cephas in the City of Rome
The Voyages of Peter
The Acts of John in the City of Rome
John and Cerinthus (Irenaeus, *Haer.* 3.3.4; Eusebius, *Hist. eccl.* 3.28)
The Epistle of James to Quadratus
The Martyrdom of James
The Martyrdom of Luke
The Acts of Nereus and Achilleus

The Acts of Peter (Rome, Angelicus graecus 108)
The History of Philip in the City of Carthage
The Teaching of the Apostles
The Epistle of Pelagius
An Encomium on the Apostles
The Dialogue between Jesus and Andrew
The Catechesis of Ps.-Basil of Caesarea/Letter of Luke
1 Apocryphal Apocalypse of John
2 Apocryphal Apocalypse of John (Questions of James)
3 Apocryphal Apocalypse of John
The Mysteries of John (Coptic Apocalypse of John)
The Apocalypse of John Chrysostom

Conclusion

Apocrypha have been part of the Christian tradition almost from the time of Christ. Indeed, so ubiquitous is apocryphal literature that it should be more fully embraced, by historians and theologians, as a fundamental aspect of Christian thought and expression. These texts are not just the ramblings of heretics, often characterized as working to undermine and transform the gospel taught by Jesus and bequeathed to the church by his apostles. Indeed, the expansion of the CA corpus represented by the *MNTA* volumes demonstrates that CA come in many forms and play many roles: to fill in gaps in the gospel record, to counter or correct the views of other Christians, to establish festivals, to guarantee the authenticity of relics, to ensure compliance with rules of practice, to educate, frighten, and entertain. Despite calls to destroy early apocrypha, Christians, sometimes even so-called orthodox Christians, continued to compose new texts when the need arose. Some of these new creations achieved a high level of popularity, so much that they were valued alongside, perhaps even above, canonical texts. Some would have been lost to history were it not for scholars such as those who have contributed to this volume. Each of them has embraced the goal of bringing awareness to texts that often have been neglected by other scholars eager to use the CA simply for reconstructing the life and teachings of Jesus. But there is far more value to these texts and much to offer scholars and readers interested in any of the myriad aspects of Christian history. Expanding the CA corpus brings added complexity to the study of this literature, breaking the boundaries between what is canonical and noncanonical, between the concepts of orthodoxy and heresy, the temporal divisions of early and medieval Christianity, and such scholarly constructs as Coptic Studies, Gnostic Studies, and Patristic Studies. What once seemed a clearly marked path is now a labyrinth. Fortunately, the *MNTA* volumes are here to help guide the way.

Abbreviations

Unless listed below, all abbreviations used in this volume are found in *The SBL Handbook of Style* (ed. SBL Press; 2nd ed.; Atlanta, Ga.: SBL Press, 2014).

AG   *The Apocryphal Gospels: Texts and Translations.* Edited and translated by Bart Ehrman and Zlatko Pleše. Oxford: Oxford University Press, 2011.

ANT   *The Apocryphal New Testament: A Collection of Apocryphal Christian Literature in an English Translation.* Edited and translated by J. Keith Elliott. 1993; rev. ed. Oxford: Clarendon, 2005.

CANT   *Clavis apocryphorum Novi Testamenti.* Edited by Maurice Geerard. Corpus Christianorum. Turnhout: Brepols, 1992.

CPC   Clavis Patrum Copticorum. Online at http://cmcl.aai.uni-hamburg.de/.

EAC   *Écrits apocryphes chrétiens.* Vol. 1 edited by François Bovon and Pierre Geoltrain. Bibliothèque de la Pléiade 442. Paris: Gallimard, 1997. Vol. 2 edited by Pierre Geoltrain and Jean-Daniel Kaestli. Bibliothèque de la Pléiade 443. Paris: Gallimard, 2005.

Abd. Pass. Pet.	*Passion of Peter (Ps.-Abdias)*
Acts Barn.	*Acts of Barnabas*
Acts Corn.	*Acts of Cornelius the Centurion*
Acts Pet. Paul	*Acts of the Apostles Peter and Paul*
Acts Tim.	*Acts of Timothy*
Acts Titus	*Acts of Titus*
Apoc. Ps.-Meth.	*Apocalypse of Ps.-Methodius*
Apoc. Vir.	*Apocalypse of the Virgin*
(Apocr.) Gos. John	*Apocryphal Gospel of John*
Arator	
Act. apost.	*De actibus apostolorum*

Augustine
  Ep. 237   *Epistle to Ceretius*

Birth Sav.   *Book about the Birth of the Savior (Liber de Nativitate Salvatoris)*

Bk. Bart.   *Book of the Resurrection of Christ by Bartholomew the Apostle*

Bk. Rooster   *Book of the Rooster*

B-S Ap.   *Berlin-Strasbourg Apocryphon* (aka *Gospel of the Savior*)

Chron. Zuq.   *Chronicle of Zuqnin*

Dance Sav.   *Dance of the Savior*

Dial. Par.   *Dialogue of the Paralytic with Christ*

Disc. Head Bapt.   *Discovery of John the Baptist's Head*

Disc. Sav.   *Discourse of the Savior*

Doctr. Addai   *Doctrina Addai*

Egeria
  Itin.   *Itinerarium*

Encom. Bapt.   *Encomium on John the Baptist*

Encom. Mary   *Encomium on Mary Magdalene*

Ep. Chr. Heav.   *Epistle of Christ from Heaven*

Ep. Herod Pil.   *Epistle of Herod to Pilate*

Ep. Tim. Dion.   *Epistle of Pseudo-Dionysius the Areopagite to Timothy*

Ephrem
  Comm. Diat.   *Commentary on the Diatessaron*

Epiphanius
  Ancor.   *Ancoratus*

Eusebius
  Supp. Quaest.   *Supplementa ad quaestiones ad Stephanum*

Gregory of Nyssa
  Eun.   *Contra Eunomium*

Gregory of Tours
  Glor. mart.   *Liber in gloria martyrum*

  Hist. Franc.   *Historia Francorum*

Hist. patr. Alex.   *History of the Patriarchs of Alexandria*

Hist. Sim. Ceph.   *History of Simon Cephas, the Chief of the Apostles*

Hist. Virg.   *(East Syriac) History of the Virgin*

Hom.   Pseudo-Clementine *Homilies*

xlviii

Hom. Rock	*Homily on the Church of the Rock*
Hosp. Dysmas	*Hospitality of Dysmas*
Hosp. Oint. Band.	*Hospitality and Ointment of the Bandit*
Hosp. Perf. Band.	*Hospitality and Perfume of the Bandit*
Invest. Abbat.	*Investiture of Abbaton*
Jos. Arim.	*Narrative of Joseph of Arimathea*
JSol	*Judgments of Solomon*
Julius Africanus *Chron.*	*Chronographiae*
Leg. Aphr.	*Legend of Aphroditianus*
Leg. Sil.	*Legend of the Thirty Pieces of Silver*
Liber Requiei	*Liber Requiei Mariae*
Life Bapt. Serap.	*Life of John the Baptist* by Serapion
Life Mart. Bapt.	*Life and Martyrdom of John the Baptist*
Lin. Mart. Pet.	*Martyrdom of Blessed Peter the Apostle (Ps.-Linus)*
Mart. Head Paul	*Martyrdom of Paul the Apostle and the Discovery of his Severed Head*
Maximus of Turin *Serm.*	*Sermones*
Michael Glykas *Quaest.*	*Quaestiones in sacram scripturam*
Miracles Bapt.	*Five Miracles of John the Baptist*
Obseq. Virg.	*Obsequies of the Virgin*
Op. Imperf.	*Imperfectum in Matthaeum*
Pass. Apost. Pet. Paul	*Passion of the Apostles Peter and Paul*
Pass. Holy Pet. Paul	*Passion of the Holy Apostles Peter and Paul (Pseudo-Marcellus)*
Pass. Mark	*Passion of Mark*
Philip of Side *Hist. Christ.*	*Historia Christianae*
Photius of Constantinople *Bib.*	*Bibliotheca*
Pre. Pet. Rome	*Preaching of Simon Cephas in the City of Rome*
Priest. Jes.	*On the Priesthood of Jesus*

Prudentius
Perist. — *Peristephanon*

Quest. Bart. — *Questions of Bartholomew*

Reb. Dimas — *Rebellion of Dimas*

Rec. — Pseudo-Clementine *Recognition*

Rev. John Ant. — *Revelation of John about Antichrist*

Rev. Magi — *Revelation of the Magi*

Socrates Scholasticus
Hist. eccl. — *Historia ecclesiastica*

Solomon of Basra
Bk. Bee — *Book of the Bee*

Sozomen
Hist. eccl. — *Historia ecclesiastica*

Theodorus Lector
Hist. eccl. — *Historia ecclesiastica*

Theodosius
Pan. Bapt. — *Panegyric on John the Baptist*

Thomas Aquinas
ST — *Summa Theologiae*

Tib. Sib. — *Tiburtine Sibyl*

Vis. Theo. — *Vision of Theophilus*

Xanth. — *Life and Conduct of the Holy Women Xanthippe, Polyxena, and Rebecca*

Sigla

[text] — Square brackets indicate damaged, illegible, or missing text, whether restorable or unrecoverable.

(text) — Parentheses or round brackets indicate words added by the translator for clarity.

<text> — Pointed brackets indicate a correction or emendation made to a text by the translator.

{text} — Braces enclose dittographies (double writings) or other erroneous readings in a manuscript or text.

{. . .} — Braces containing three ellipsis points indicate that a textual tradition (i.e., involving more than one manuscript) has lost one or more words in transmission and that the original reading cannot be reconstructed with any confidence.

I. Gospels and Related Traditions of New Testament Figures

The Legend of Aphroditianus
A new translation and introduction

by Katharina Heyden

The *Legend of Aphroditianus* (*Leg. Aphr.*; *CANT* 55) is a supplement to the pericope of the adoration of the Magi in Matthew 2:1–12. It first explains how the Magi knew about the birth of the Messiah in Bethlehem and then describes their journey and their encounter with Christ and Mary in more detail than the canonical account. In the Slavic cultures, especially in medieval Russia, *Leg. Aphr.* was a popular text that was read during the Christmas liturgy. In consequence, all modern Russian collections of Christian apocrypha contain *Leg. Aphr.*[1] In the West, however, the legend has remained almost completely unknown, for in Greek manuscripts it is rarely transmitted on its own,[2] but is usually embedded in larger literary works that were themselves long-neglected by scholars, even though they are preserved in many manuscripts. *Leg. Aphr.* is also known in scholarship as the "Narrative of Events Happening in Persia on the Birth of Christ," falsely attributed to Julius Africanus.

Contents

In its first part (chaps. 1–6), *Leg. Aphr.* describes a miracle in the temple of Hera in Persia (1) at the time of Christ's birth. In the presence of the Persian king and a priest, the statues of the temple dance and sing, announcing that Hera has been made pregnant by Zeus and will give birth to a child (2). Then a star appears above the statue of Hera. A voice proclaims the birth, and all the other statues fall down upon their faces (3). The wise men of Persia interpret the miracle as an announcement of the birth of the Messiah in Judah (4). In the evening, the god Dionysus appears to confirm this interpretation and to proclaim the end of the worship of the pagan gods (5). Then the king sends the Magi to Judea with gifts, the star pointing them along their way (6). The second part of *Leg. Aphr.* (chaps. 7–9) is a report of the Magi about their journey to Jerusalem and Bethlehem, including a discussion between the Magi and the Jewish leaders (7), and their meeting and encounter with Mary and the two-year-old Jesus (8). Of interest here are the precise description of Mary's appearance (8:4) and the remark that the Magi brought back to Persia a likeness of the mother and child, which they placed in the temple where the star originally appeared. The report of the Magi concludes with the appearance of an angel who, warning the Magi of a plot against them, advises them to return home (9).

---

1. For an overview of these editions see Heyden, *"Erzählung des Aphroditian,"* 32–39.

2. Bringel, *"Une polémique religieuse,"* 134–226, lists 15 Greek manuscripts that transmit *Leg. Aphr.* on its own; the other 43 present the legend as part of *De gestis in Perside*.

Transmission and Editions

Leg. Aphr. has a complex and fascinating history of transmission. The oldest written version is found in an anonymous Greek work entitled *De gestis in Perside (Pers.)*, a fifth- or sixth-century fictional religious dispute between pagans, Christians, Jews, and a Persian magus at the court of the Sasanian Empire,[3] in which *Leg. Aphr.* plays an important part. In *Pers.*, Aphroditianus is a pagan philosopher appointed by the king of Persia as an independent arbitrator in the dispute, but Aphroditianus turns out to be a defender of the Christian position, quoting *Leg. Aphr.* as the main argument in favor of the Christian truth.

Traces of *Leg. Aphr.* can be found in later literature, though these hint too of an earlier origin for the text. In the eighth century, John of Damascus included the legend in a *Homily on the Incarnation of Christ (Homilia in nativitatem Domini)*,[4] presenting it to the audience as a pagan oracle explaining why the Magi knew about the birth of Christ. Inserting biblical texts, omitting certain passages, and altering some formulations, John modified the text of *Leg. Aphr.* to harmonize the legend with the Gospels. Two illustrated Byzantine manuscripts of this homily from the second half of the eleventh century (Jerusalem, Greek Orthodox Patriarchate, Taphou 14 and Mount Athos, Esphigmenou 14) contain splendid miniatures accompanying the homily, bearing witness to the popularity of *Leg. Aphr.* at the time of the Macedonian dynasty of the Byzantine Empire (867–1056).[5]

The Slavonic versions of *Leg. Aphr.* are excerpts of the legend from *Pers.* translated from Greek. The first of these translations (Slav I) was made, probably in Bulgaria, in the tenth century.[6] Through the southern Slavs, *Leg. Aphr.* was transmitted to Russia during the twelfth century, where it became very popular and was revised several times.[7] In the

---

3. On *Pers.* see Bratke, *Das sogenannte Religionsgespräch*, 46–271; Bringel, "Une polémique religieuse," 13–133; Déroche, "La polémique anti-judaique"; Heyden, "Erzählung des Aphroditian," 116–70; Külzer, *Disputationes*, 112–27.

4. Bonifatius Kotter, ed., *Die Schriften des Johannes von Damaskos* (5 vols.; PTS 7, 12, 17, 22, 29; Berlin: De Gruyter, 1969–1988), 5:324–47. Even though the homily is preserved in 58 manuscripts, it was neglected by scholars because its authenticity was denied for a long time (see Kotter, *Schriften des Johannes*, 307–10). A historical and theological analysis of the homily is given by Heyden, "Erzählung des Aphroditian," 94–115.

5. The miniatures of Esphigmenou 14 are published in Stylianos M. Pelekanidis et al., *The Treasures of Mount Athos. Illuminated Manuscripts*, vol. 2: *The Monasteries of Iveron, St. Pantaleimon, Esphigmenou, and Chilandari* (Athens: Ekdotike Athenon, 1975), 223–52, tabl. 344–407; the 17 miniatures from *Leg. Aphr.* are reproduced in Heyden, "Erzählung des Aphroditian," 333–41, tabl. 14–30; the nine folios with miniatures on *Leg. Aphr.* from Taphou 14 were first completely published by Heyden, "Erzählung des Aphroditian," 344–52, tabl. 38–48. For iconographical and historical analyses see Heyden, "Erzählung des Aphroditian," 67–93.

6. The most ancient Old Bulgarian manuscript of *Leg. Aphr.* dates from the thirteenth century, but it is likely that the first translation was made already during the reign of King Simeon the Great (893–927), who ordered many translations of Greek Christian works.

7. Of the 92 Slavonic manuscripts of *Leg. Aphr.* 78 come from Russia, most of them being part of liturgical collections. An examination of *Leg. Aphr.* and its various redactions in medieval Russia is given in Heyden, "Erzählung des Aphroditian," 20–56. In the sixteenth century, the Greek monk Maksim Grek published a polemical essay in Russian entitled "Speech of the monk Maksim Grek from the Holy Mountain on accusation and conviction of the lying writing of the erroneous Persian Aphroditianus" (see Heyden, "Erzählung des Aphroditian," 20–25). Maxim formulated three conditions to accept ancient Christian works within the Orthodox Church: first, that the author is well known and highly esteemed by the ancient authorities; second, that it corresponds with apostolic doctrines and traditions; and third, that it does not contain self-contradictions. In his polemics, Maxim tries to show that *Leg. Aphr.* does not meet these

sixteenth century, Aphroditianus was regarded as one among other pagan figures—such as the Sibyl, Hermes, Homer, and Plato—who are said to have announced the coming of Christ; this association is reflected in Aphroditianus's representation on the bronze portals of Kremlin cathedrals.[8] The second Slavonic translation (Slav II) was made in the fourteenth century, probably by Serbian monks of Mount Athos, but based on a different Greek text.[9] This version was translated later into Romanian.[10] It differs from Slav I in some respects, two details being especially remarkable. First, the names of the Magi are given—Elimelech, Elisur, and Eliav—together with etymological explanations (see the note to *Leg. Aphr.* 6). Second, in the title of this version the legend is attributed to "the presbyter Philippus who was syncellus of the great John Chrysostom." This attribution deserves attention because it provides clues as to how *Leg. Aphr.* came to be incorporated into *Pers.*

The title of Slav II corresponds to an addendum to *Pers.* that clarifies the identity of the historian Philippus whose *History*, according to the initial sentences of *Pers.*, caused the dispute between pagans and Christians in the Sasanian kingdom. The note reads:

> This Philippus was a presbyter and syncellus of John, the archbishop of Constantinople. He wrote the whole [history] organizing it in periods in such an admirable way that no other of the historiographers can compare with him. The same presbyter narrated that from the day on which the star appeared in the temple, every year on the same day until the ascension of the Lord, all statues were uttering their own characteristic voices so that the whole city remained there to watch the great miracles and the annual appearance of the star.[11]

This note identifies the Philippus of *Pers.* with Philip of Side, a Christian historian who, in the fifth century, compiled a monumental *Historia Christianae* in Constantinople, of which only a few fragments have survived.[12] Moreover, mentioning the report of the annual repetition of the miracle in the temple of Hera, the addendum shows that *Leg. Aphr.* was a part of Philip's *Hist. Christ.*, possibly of a book entitled "Hellenic Oracles."[13] But was Philip the author of the legend? This seems improbable for two reasons. First, his *Hist. Christ.* is a monumental work composed of many sources.[14] Second, *Leg. Aphr.* contains

---

criteria. Unintentionally, with this polemic Maksim Grek bears witness to the popularity of *Leg. Aphr.* at his time.

8. Aphroditianus stands beside Homer on the north-portal of the Blagoveschenskij Sobor and on the south-portal of the Usbenskij Sobor, in both cases accompanied by the inscription, "For God was born from the immaculate virgin Mary, in him is the origin of faith." Of course, Aphroditianus differs from these other pagan figures in that he did not live prior to Jesus. For pictures of the portals see Heyden, *"Erzählung des Aphroditian,"* 304–7, tabl. 1–4.

9. The Greek pattern of this version is preserved in Mount Athos, Vatopedi, gr. 10 (14th cent.), which contains the entire text of *Pers.*

10. For a German translation of the Romanian version, which survives in a single manuscript of the seventeenth century, see Gaster, "Die rumänische Version."

11. The Greek text can be found in Bratke, *Das sogenannte Religionsgespräch,* 45; and Bringel, "Une polémique religieuse," 488–90.

12. A descriptive catalogue of the fragments is given in Heyden, "Christliche Geschichte."

13. This title is mentioned in *Pers.* 5.5 (Bratke), where Aphroditianus asks a slave to read out a passage of Philip's *Hist. Christ.* entitled "Hellenic Oracles." According to Socrates Scholasticus (*Hist. eccl.* 7.27.4), *Hist. Christ.* was divided into 36 books that were thematically arranged.

14. This is evident from the polemics of Socrates (*Hist. eccl.* 7.27) and Photius (*Bib.*, cod. 35).

some elements that point to a place of origin other than Constantinople and to a time earlier than the fifth century.[15]

In 1804, the German scholar Johann Freiherr von Aretin published for the first time a Greek text of *Leg. Aphr.* using two manuscripts from Munich (Bayerische Staatsbibliothek, Monac. gr. 61 and 199); the text was accompanied by a translation into Latin.[16] Athanasius Vassiliev published the entire text of *Pers.* in 1893 from two manuscripts: Moscow, State Historical Museum, Synod. gr. 252 (11th cent.) and Vatican, Biblioteca apostolica, Palat. gr. 364 (14th/15th cent.).[17] This manuscript base was expanded dramatically by Eduard Bratke in 1899,[18] and Pauline Bringel in her unpublished thesis from 2007.[19] Bratke compared 29 manuscripts of *Pers.* and chose Paris, Bibliothèque nationale de France, gr. 1084 (11th cent.) as the base text for his edition. Bratke mentioned also an Armenian version of the text, but this has not yet been published.[20] Bringel included 14 more manuscripts and divided the evidence into two redactions: a short one that is preserved in Vatican, Biblioteca apostolica, Palat. gr. 4 (10th/11th cent.) and a long one found in all other manuscripts, of which Bringel favored Munich, Bayerische Staatsbibliothek, Ms. gr. 467 (11th cent.) as the best witness. In 2009, Katharina Heyden published a monograph on the transmission of *Leg. Aphr.* in the East and the West, discussing the literary, theological, and historical aspects for every stage of the text's transmission as well as the origin of the legend.[21] In this study, *Leg. Aphr.* was presented as an independent apocryphal writing for the first time to readers in the Western world.

Date and Provenance

The miracle in the temple of Hera that is narrated in the first part of *Leg. Aphr.* (chaps. 1–6) has its parallels in the cult of the Syrian goddess Atargatis in Hierapolis, as described by the Roman author Lucian of Samosata in his satirical work *De Dea Syria* in the second century.[22] According to Lucian, the goddess was called "Syrian Hera," and her statue

---

15. See the discussion of all pre-Constantinian elements in *Leg. Aphr.* in Heyden, *"Erzählung des Aphroditian,"* 226–94.

16. Aretin, *Beyträge,* 49–69, published again in PG 10:97–108. The manuscripts of Munich attribute the legend to an "Africanus." Therefore, the legend was considered to be a work of the second-century Christian historian Julius Africanus. This attribution was accepted by the editors of the *Patrologia Graeca* as well as by those of the *Ante-Nicene Fathers* (ANF 6:127–30), even though Aretin himself in his introduction doubted it. Most likely, the attribution to Julius Africanus is based on a misunderstanding of the Greek abbreviation *Aphr* that actually does not refer to "Africanus" but to "Aphroditianus." Bringel, however, does not totally abandon the attribution to Julius Africanus (cf. Bringel, "Une polémique religieuse," 13–14). But, there is information in *Aphr.* that clearly contradicts a note in the *Chronography* of Julius Africanus. According to *Leg. Aphr.* 8:4, Christ was nearly two years old when the Magi came to Bethlehem, whereas Julius Africanus notes that the child was only seven days old. Cf. Julius Africanus, *Chron.,* fragment T 91 in the edition of Martin Wallraff, *Iulius Africanus: Chronographiae. The Extant Fragments* (trans. William Adler; GCS NF 15; Berlin-New York: De Gruyter, 2007), 274–75.

17. Vassiliev, *Anecdota graeco-byzantina,* 73–125, with manuscript details on pp. xxvii–xxxii.

18. Bratke, *Das sogenannte Religionsgespräch.*

19. Bringel, "Une polémique religieuse," 44–61. Bringel presented a detailed introduction to *Pers.,* a new critical edition, and a translation into French.

20. Bratke, *Das sogenannte Religionsgespräch,* 128.

21. Heyden, *"Erzählung des Aphroditian."*

22. Edition and commentary in Jane L. Lightfoot, ed., *Lucian, On the Syrian Goddess* (Oxford: Oxford University Press, 2003), 247–86. Other sources for the cult of Hierapolis are Plutarch, *Crassus;* Macrobius, *Saturnalia;* Athenaeus Grammaticus, *Deipnosophistae;* Aratus Latinus, *Phaenomena,* as well as iconographic and archaeological evidence.

combined characteristics of other goddesses, such as Athena, Aphrodite, Selene, Rhea, Artemis, and Nemesis. Her statue was adorned with the belt and the crown of the goddess Urania. By night, a precious stone above the statue of the goddess lit up the temple. In addition to the goddess in the cella, the temple also featured a statue of Zeus-Helios and another mysterious statue identified by many people as Dionysus, who was regarded as the founder of the temple. The temple was sumptuously adorned with gold and silver, and the statues would move and give oracles of their own accord. Near the temple, there was a pool of spring water with fish that were regarded as holy to the goddess. Iconographical evidence shows that Atargatis, the Syrian goddess par excellence, was adored as "Source" and "Virgin." All these elements suggest that the origin of *Leg. Aphr.* can be located in the environment of the cult in Hierapolis—i.e., in western Syria. The Christian author of *Leg. Aphr.* presumably intended to offer his audience an *interpretatio christiana* of this popular pagan cult.[23]

The argument for a Syrian origin is plausible also with regard to the second part of *Leg. Aphr.* (chaps. 7–9). The notice that the Magi at their return placed a portrait of Mary and the child in the royal temple recalls the Abgar Correspondence, according to which Hannan, the courier of King Abgar, made a likeness of Jesus that was placed in the royal palace of Edessa (*Doctr. Addai* 6). Pauline Bringel supposes that, in composing *Leg. Aphr.*, a west Syrian author intended to compete with the Christians of Edessa, claiming the existence of an older image of Christ.[24] Provided that these parallels are accurate, *Leg. Aphr.* was probably composed in the third century, because the cult of Hierapolis prospered in the first three centuries of CE, and the Abgar Correspondence also originated at this time— Eusebius of Caesarea (*Hist. eccl.* 1.13) refers to the legend, without mentioning, however, the portrait of Christ.[25] In addition, the eucharistic use of the Christian symbol of the fish in combination with the mention of a "source" (see, e.g., *Leg. Aphr.* 2:2 where Hera is named Pege, meaning "source" or "spring") appears also in the epitaph inscriptions of Abercius and Pectorius that date from the early third century.[26] The original language of *Leg. Aphr.* was certainly Greek.

Literary and Theological Importance

Leg. Aphr. combines the characteristics of two literary forms that were very popular in the pre-Constantinian era. In its first part, the text presents "hellenic oracles" in favor of Christianity similar to those attributed by Christians to the Sibyllines, Hermes Trismegistos, Zoroaster, Hystaspes, and other pagan authorities from the East. In comparison with other early Christian collections of oracles, however, the special feature of *Leg. Aphr.* is its literary form, for here the hellenic oracles are presented within a narrative frame.

The second part of *Leg. Aphr.* can be compared to other apocryphal retellings of the

---

23. See Heyden, "Erzählung des Aphroditian," 261–70. The location in Syria, however, seems to contradict the first paragraph of *Leg. Aphr.* (1:1), where the temple is localized in the capital of Persia. Perhaps the author already knew a tradition according to which the Magi came from Persia, or perhaps the first sentences of *Leg. Aphr.* were missing in the original legend and were added only by Philip of Side or by the unknown author of *Pers.*

24. Bringel, "Une polémique religieuse," 54–55.

25. Bratke (*Das sogenannte Religionsgespräch*, 151–57) places *Leg. Aphr.* within the context of the mariological controversy of the fifth century. In my view, however, this is not conclusive because the characteristic term of this time, *theotokos*, does not appear in the text.

26. Text and brief commentary on the inscriptions in Margherita Guarducci, *Epigrafia greca* (4 vols.; Rome: Istituto Poligrafico e Zecca dello Stato, 1967–1978), 4:380–81 (Abercius) and 4:487–88 (Pectorius).

infancy of Christ, such as the second-century *Protevangelium of James* or the *Liber de Nativitate Salvatoris* (also known as the *J Composition*). But while *Prot. Jas.* was designed to defend the virginity of Mary before a Jewish or Jewish-Christian audience, *Leg. Aphr.* was addressed to pagans and gentile Christians, drawing on the pagan myth of the holy wedding of male and female gods and combining it with the Magi pericope of Matt 2:1–12.

The manifold transmission of *Leg. Aphr.* testifies to the popularity of such a positive use of pagan elements in support of Christianity in various times and contexts. Unfortunately, this openness toward pagans comes alongside polemics against the Jews (see the encounter between the Magi and the Jewish leaders in Jerusalem in *Leg. Aphr.* 7).

It is impossible to assign *Leg. Aphr.* clearly to a specific theological school. Composed in an epoch that was rightly called the "laboratory of Christian theology,"[27] the legend combines elements of various theological doctrines. Thus, the rejection of the idea that Pege-Mary was made pregnant by an earthly carpenter (2:3) seems to be a reaction to Jewish-Christian groups that denied the divinity of Jesus and the virginity of Mary and emphasized that the carpenter Joseph was the father of Mary's child.[28] The phrase "bride of the triple-named single divinity" (3:1) recalls the doctrine of the Sabellians, who used the term *triōnumos* to express the hypostatical unity of the divine persons.[29] On the other hand, the humanity of Christ is emphasized in the interpretation of the miracle by Persian interpreters of prodigies who proclaim "the son of the Omnipotent, carried in bodily form in the bodily arms of a woman" (4:2) and in the report of the Magi who mention that Jesus looked like his mother and that he "smiled and leaped" (8:7). In addition, *Leg. Aphr.* 7 contains soteriological statements that are known from Jewish-Christian writings, especially from the eighth book of the *Sibylline Oracles* (see *Leg. Aphr.* 5 and *Sib. Or.* 8:265–70).

Altogether, the main intention of *Leg. Aphr.* seems to be the defense of the divinity of Christ against Jewish Christians on the one side, and of the humanity of Christ against monarchianistic tendencies on the other. These tendencies, which work to emphasize the unity of divinity and humanity in Christ, is expressed in *Leg. Aphr.* 4:2, in the interpretation of the miracle given by the wise men of Persia: "a divine and royal root has risen, bearing the stamp of a heavenly and earthly king." From the perspective of the history of religions, the mixture of pagan and Christian elements in favor of a popular mariology and Christology is striking, since it shows that the differentiation between pagans and Christians was actually not as clear as many Christian apologists tried to suggest. The positive representation of the Persian interpreters of prodigies and of the Magi who, according to *Leg. Aphr.*, recognize the meaning of the miracle immediately and of their own accord, points to a certain affinity of *Leg. Aphr.* and *Rev. Magi.*[30]

Translation

The accompanying translation of *Leg. Aphr.* is based on the critical editions of *Pers.* established by E. Bratke in 1899 and P. Bringel in 2007.[31] The relevant differences between Bratke and Bringel and my own text-critical decisions are documented in the notes. Fur-

---

27. Christoph Markschies, "Alte Kirche," *RGG*3 (1998): 1:344–60 at 353.

28. Cf. Eusebius, *Hist. eccl.* 3.27; Origen, *Comm. Matt.* 16.12.

29. Cf. Gregory of Nyssa, *Eun.* 3.8.23; Eusebius, *Eccl. theol.* 3.6; Socrates, *Hist. eccl.* 3.7.15.

30. On early Christian traditions on the Magi see Heyden, "Erzählung des Aphroditian," 287–93; and Thomas Holtmann, *Die Magier vom Osten und der Stern: Mt 2,1–12 im Kontext frühchristlicher Traditionen* (Marburger Theologische Studien 87; Marburg: Elwert, 2005).

31. *Leg. Aphr.* previously appeared in English translation in *ANF* 6:128–30 as a work of Julius Africanus.

thermore, the notes document the productive reception of *Leg. Aphr.* in the *Homily* of John of Damascus and in the Slavonic tradition. The *Homily* of John of Damascus is translated from the critical edition by Kotter; Slav I. from the text established by Veder,[32] and Slav II from the edition by Bobrov.[33] The chapter numbering is newly established. It enables one to reference *Leg. Aphr.* without recourse to the writings in which the legend was embedded during its long history of transmission.

Sigla

A   *Pers.* from Paris, Bibliothèque nationale de France, gr. 1084
C   *Pers.* from Munich, Bayerische Staatsbibliothek, gr. 467
J   *Pers.* from Vatican, Biblioteca apostolica, Palat. gr. 4
JD   John of Damascus, *Homilia in nativitatem Domini*
Slav I   First Slavonic translation
Slav II   Second Slavonic translation

Bibliography

EDITIONS AND TRANSLATIONS

Aretin, Johann Freiherr von. *Beyträge zur Geschichte und Literatur, vorzüglich aus den Schätzen der pfalzbaierischen Centralbibliothek zu München.* 2 vols. Munich: Scherer, 1804. (The *editio princeps* of *Leg. Aphr.* as an independent text.)

Bobrov, Alexander G. *The Apocryphal Legend of Aphroditianus in the Literature and Bookmaking of Old Russia. Dissertation and Edition* (in Russian). St. Petersburg: Nauka, 1994.

Bratke, Eduard. *Das sogenannte Religionsgespräch am Hof der Sassaniden.* TU N.F. 4/3. Leipzig: Hinrichs, 1899.

Bringel, Pauline. "Une polémique religieuse à la coeur perse: le *De gestis in Perside*. Histoire du téxte, édition critique et traduction." 2 vols. PhD diss., Université de Paris I, Panthéon-Sorbonne, 2007. (A comprehensive edition and translation of *Pers.*)

Gaster, Moses. "Die rumänische Version der Legende des Aphroditian." *Byzantinisch-Neugriechische Jahrbücher* 14 (1938): 119–28.

Vassiliev, Athanasius. *Anecdota graeco-byzantina, pars prior.* Moscow: Imperial University, 1893.

Veder, William R. "The Slavonic Tale of Aphroditian: Limitations of Manuscript-Centred Textology." *Tărnovska knižovna škola* 9 (2009).

STUDIES

Bringel, Pauline. "Interprétation et réécritures dans la tradition manuscrite du Récit d'Aphroditien." Pages 285–96 in *Entre Actes. Regards croisés en sciences humaines. Réalités et représentations: les pistes de la recherche. Actes du Ier Colloque international des jeunes chercheurs en sciences humaines et sociales de Strasbourg, 10 et 11 mai 2004.* Edited by Laurent Angard. Strasbourg: Université Marc Bloch, 2005.

Déroche, Vincent. "La polémique anti-judaique au VIe et au VIIe siècle. Un mémento inédit, les Képhalaia." *Travaux et Mémoires* 11 (1991): 275–311.

Heyden, Katharina. *Die "Erzählung des Aphroditian." Thema und Variationen einer Legende im*

---

32. Veder, "Slavonic Tale."
33. Bobrov, *Apocryphal Legend* (Russian), 127–32.

Spannungsfeld von Christentum und Heidentum. Studien und Texte zu Antike und Christentum 53. Tübingen: Mohr Siebeck, 2009. (Further bibliography may be found here.)

————. "Die Christliche Geschichte des Philippos von Side. Mit einem kommentierten Katalog der Fragmente." Pages 209–43 in *Julius Africanus und die christliche Weltchronistik.* Edited by Martin Wallraff. TU 157. Berlin/New York: De Gruyter 2006.

Külzer, Andreas. *Disputationes graecae contra Iudaeos. Untersuchungen zur byzantinischen antijüdischen Dialogliteratur und ihrem Judenbild.* Byzantinisches Archiv 18. Leipzig/Stuttgart: Teubner, 1999.

The Legend of Aphroditianus[a]

Part one: The miracle in the temple of Hera
Introduction: The temple of Hera

1 [1]To Persia, Christ was known from the beginning, for nothing escapes the learned lawyers of that country, who investigate all things with eagerness. Therefore, I will announce what is inscribed upon the golden tablets and laid up in the royal temples: that the name of Christ has first been heard of in the temples there and by the priests connected with them.[b]

2There is a temple of Hera, which surpasses the royal palace and in which King Cyrus, the expert of all piety, built and erected golden and silver statues and he adorned it[c] with precious stones—not to digress into describing the ornamentation.

The miracle of the dancing statues

2 [1]In those days—as the inscribed tablets teach—when the king came to get a dream-interpretation in the temple, the priest Proupippus[d] said to him, "I rejoice with you, master, for Hera has conceived." The king, smiling, said to him, "The dead one has conceived?" And he said, "She who was dead has come to life again and gives birth to life." The king said, "What is this? Explain it to me!"

---

a. The original title of the legend is unknown. The Greek manuscripts witness various ascriptions either to Aphroditianus—e.g., "From the Legend of Aphroditianus the philosopher on the Magi and the star" (Berlin, Königliche Bibliothek, gr. 77); "The Legend of Aphroditianus the philosopher on the incarnation of our Lord Jesus Christ" (Paris, Bibliothèque nationale de France, gr. 897)—or to an "Africanus" (as to that attribution see the introduction, p. 6 n. 16) as in, e.g., Vienna, Österreichische Nationalbibliothek, Theol. gr. 48: "The Legend of Africanus on the things that happened in Persia during the incarnation of the Lord and our Savior Jesus Christ." Slav I has: "The Legend of Aphroditianus on the miracle that happened in the land of Persia," and Slav II: "The Legend of Aphroditianus the Persian, written down by the presbyter Philip, who was syncellus of the great John Chrysostom, on the birth of Christ and on the star and on the adoration of the Magi from Persia."

b. C (and Bringel) omits the phrase "and the priests connected with them." In Slav I the first sentences differ slightly: "To Persia, Christ was known from the beginning, for nothing escapes the learned men of that country, who diligently investigate all things that are inscribed upon golden tablets and laid up in the royal temples. Here I announce something that was heard by the priests there: There is a temple of Hera etc." JD begins the narration with "Cyrus, the king of the Persians, built a temple and erected golden and silver statues in it and adorned it with precious stones."

c. C (and Bringel) has "adorned them (i.e., the statues)."

d. The manuscripts give several different variants of the priest's name: e.g., Proupipos, Proupiptos, Proupippios (see Bringel, "Une polémique religieuse," 332)

[2]He said, "Indeed, master, you have come here at the right time.[a] For over the whole night the images were dancing, both the males and the females, saying to each other, 'Come, let us rejoice with Hera.' And they said to me, 'Prophet, come and rejoice with Hera, for she has been loved.' And I said, 'Who was able to be loved, she who does not exist?'[b] They said, 'She has come to life again and is no longer called Hera, but Urania (i.e., "queen of heaven"). For the mighty Helios (i.e., "great sun") has loved her.' And the females said to the males, obviously to disparage the matter, 'Pege (i.e., "source" or "spring") is she who was loved, for Hera did not marry a carpenter!'[c]

[3]"And the males said, 'That she was rightly called Hera, we admit. But her name is Myria (i.e., "the thousandfold"),[d] for she bears in her womb, as in the sea, a vessel burdened with a myriad. If she is also called Pege, let it be understood thus: a spring of water continuously sends forth a spring of spirit[e] containing a single fish, which is taken with the hook of divinity and which sustains with its own flesh the whole world, dwelling there as though in the sea.[f] You have well said: "she has a carpenter,"[g] but the carpenter whom she bears does not come from a marriage-bed. For this carpenter who is born, the child of the chief carpenter, has built the triple-constructed celestial roof[h] with most-wise skill, establishing this triple-habitated dwelling by the Logos.'[i]

[4]"Thus, the statues continued to dispute with each other concerning Hera and Pege and unanimously they said, 'When the day is brought to completion, we all, male and female, shall come to know the matter clearly. Therefore now master, remain for the rest of the day, for the matter will certainly receive full clarity. For what has emerged is no accident.'"[j]

[5]When the king remained there and was watching the statues, the harpers began to strike their harps of their own accord, and the Muses began to sing.[k] And all four-legged animals and birds of silver and gold within (the temple) were uttering their own characteristic voices. And as the king shuddered and was filled with great fear so that he was about to withdraw, for he could not endure the

---

a. Slav I: "Indeed, master, the time has come."

b. JD: "By whom could she be loved—for she is mine?"; Slav I: "Who can love her, who does not exist?"

c. J lacks "for Hera did not marry a carpenter."

d. J and Slav I: "Maria." Slav II: "Karia."

e. Slav II: "A spring of water fluently flows."

f. From the Greek text, it is not clear whether the phrase "dwelling there as though in the sea" refers to "a single fish" or to the "whole world."

g. Some manuscripts add the phrase: "She married a carpenter—for she has a carpenter, but etc."

h. C (and Bringel) has: "framed the triple-constructed sky as a roof." JD has: "has built the triple hypostatic roof of the heavens."

i. Slav II: "You have well said that Hera is engaged to a carpenter, but the carpenter is not descended from a male sperm, but the one to whom she gives birth is the everlasting Word and the son of the everlasting creator, who created the triple roof out of nothing with the utmost wisdom and who established this triple heaven with a word."

j. C (and Bringel) lacks this phrase.

k. Slav I: "The king remained there and saw the statues predicting the future and playing harps, and the singers sang." Slav II: "The king remained, and every statue moved of its own accord, the females played harps and the singer began to sing."

spontaneous tumult, the priest said to him, "Remain,[a] O king, for the full revelation is at hand, which the God of the gods had decided to make plain to us."

The appearance of the star above the statue of Pege

3 [1]When these things had been said, the roof was opened, and a bright star descended and stood above the statue of Pege, and a voice was heard as follows: "Mistress Pege, the Mighty Helios has sent me to announce to you and at the same time to serve you in your giving birth, for he produces a blameless childbirth for you, who is becoming mother of the first of all ranks, bride of the triple-named single divinity.[b] And the unbegotten new-born is called Beginning and End—the beginning of salvation, the end of destruction."

[2]When this voice had been given, all the statues fell down upon their faces.[c] Pege alone remained standing, upon whom a royal diadem was found fastened, having on its upper side a star made of precious stones—carbuncle and emerald. And above her the star rested.

The interpretation of the miracle by the wise men of Persia

4 [1]Immediately the king gave an order[d] to bring together all wise interpreters of prodigies who are under his dominion. When the heralds urged them on with their trumpets, they all came into the temple.

[2]When they saw the star above Pege, and the diadem with the starry stone, and the statues lying on the floor, they said, "O king, a divine and royal root has risen, bearing the stamp of a heavenly and earthly king.[e] For Pege is the daughter of Karia[f] the Bethlehemite, and the diadem is a royal sign, and the star is a heavenly announcement of marvels on earth. Out of Judah a kingdom has arisen which will abolish all the memorials of the Jews.[g] The prostration of the gods upon the floor prefigured the end of their honor. For he who comes is of more ancient dignity and will shake those who are new in it. Therefore, o king, send to Jerusalem! For you will find the son of the Omnipotent, carried in bodily form in the bodily arms of a woman."

[3]The star remained above Pege, who has been called Urania, until the Magi went forth, and then it went with them.[h]

---

a. Slav I: "Rise!"

b. JD: "bride of the autocrat with three names"; Slav I: "As an uncorrupted message I serve you, mother of the oldest of all ranks, you appear as the bride of the triple-named and single divinity."

c. JD adds: "and shattered."

d. C (and Bringel) has: "Having watched these things, the king gave order etc."

e. Slav II adds: "Therefore, we request your authority to hear this."

f. The name Karia remains obscure; some manuscripts have *Kyria* ("Mistress"), others *Maria* ("Mary").

g. J replaces "of the Jews" with "of the kings," thus omitting the anti-Jewish tendency.

h. Slav II: "The star remained above the statue that has been called the Heavenly One, until the Magi were sent forth from Cyrus, the Persian king, and it went with them."

The apparition of Dionysus[a]

5 [1]Then in the late evening, Dionysus appeared in the same temple, without the Satyrs,[b] and said to the statues, "Pege is no longer one of us, but she stands far above us, since far above us she gives birth to a human being, the fetus of the divine Tyche (i.e., Fortune). O priest Proupippus, what are you doing sitting here? An action, indicated in writing, has proceeded against us, and we are going to be exposed as false by an acting person. That which we imagined, we have imagined. That which we commanded, we have commanded.[c] No longer do we give oracular responses. Removed from us is the honor. Inglorious and unrecompensed we have become, because one, and one only, has received his proper honor.

[2]"Say (to the king): 'Do not be disturbed!'[d] No longer do the Persians demand tributes of earth and air. For he who established these things is present, and he brings tribute of actions to him who sent him. He re-creates the ancient image, and puts together image with image, and the unlike he brings to likeness.[e]

Gen 1:26–27

[3]"Heaven rejoices with earth, and the earth boasts the heaven's boast that it received. That which has not happened above, has happened below. He whom the order of the blessed has not seen, at him looks (the order of) the miserable. For those whom a flame threatens, the dew has come.[f] It is the fortune of Karia

---

a. Chap. 5 is missing in JD.

b. Slav I: "with a flag"; Slav II: "with the Satyrs."

c. Slav II: "That which we dreamed, we misleadingly dreamed; that which we hoped, we illusively hoped."

d. The Greek text seems corrupt here. I follow the edition of Bringel: *"eipon: mē throbadei,"* according to the majority of the Greek manuscripts. The Greek verb *eipon* can be understood either as a third-person aorist "they said," referring to the statues, or as a first-person aorist ("I said"), or as an imperative singular ("Say!"). The verb *throbadei,* however, is not attested elsewhere. Slav I has the equivalent of the Greek *mē thorybei.* I assume that this translation represents the meaning of the original Greek verb. However, Bringel supposes *eipon* to be a third-person plural, interpreting the following sentences as the answer of the statues to Dionysus (see n. e below), and translates as "They said: 'Do not grumble!'" But this does not fit with the phrase below: "rightly do the females dance and say," for in the speech of the statues this statement should be given in the first-person plural. Therefore, the *eipon* is to be understood as an imperative "say!" and is addressed to the priest Proupippus who—instead of "sitting here"— shall deliver the following message to the king. The call "Do not be disturbed" is the reaction to the statement on the king's emotional condition in *Leg. Aphr.* 2:5 ("And as the king shuddered and was filled with great fear so that he was about to withdraw, for he could not endure the spontaneous tumult etc."). Bratke follows a small group of Greek manuscripts, including A, that read: "*eipon Mithrobadē*" ("say to Mithrobades"). Mithrobades appears twice in *Pers.* (37.26 and 44.12 Bratke) as the son or a high official of the king Arrinatos who presided over the dispute. This fact may explain why some writers replaced the corrupted text inserting this name. Even if Bratke's reconstruction of the text were right, the mention of Mithrobades could not help to date the Legend, because we do not know any historical person of this name.

e. Slav I: "They said: Do not grumble! No longer will the Persians demand tributes of earth and air. For he who established these things has come and he brings tribute to him who sent him. He rebuilds the first image and renews the new one, he came at the right time with his spirit." Slav II: "I say to you, Proprie, do not be wrong! No longer will the Persians demand tributes of earth and air, for the word of God, that brings all from nothing to being, comes and brings effective tributes to the Father who has sent it, and it re-creates the ancient image and impresses the image and brings the unlike back to the likeness."

f. Slav II: "For those there are flame and forgiveness, for these dew and happiness."

to give birth to Pege in Bethlehem. It is Pege's grace to become heaven-desired and to conceive grace of grace.

4"Judea has bloomed, but now it is withering.[a] To gentiles and foreigners salvation has come, to the miserable there is more than enough refreshment. Rightly do the females dance and say, Lady Pege, Spring-bearer, you who have become mother of the heavenly light-giver, you are the cloud that after the heat brings dew to the world; remember your servants, dear mistress."[b]

Part two: The narration of the Magi
The king sends the Magi to Judea

6 Then the king, without delay, sent the Magi who were under his dominion[c] with gifts, and the star showed them the way. And then they returned, and they narrated to their contemporaries those things that were written also on golden plates and that were to the following effect:[d]

The conversation between the Magi and the Jews

7 ¹When we came to Jerusalem, the sign,[e] together with our arrival, disturbed everyone. "What is this?" they said. "Wise men of the Persians arrive, and along with them an appearance of a star?" Matt 2:1–2

²The leaders of the Jews asked us what was going to happen and the reason for our coming. And we said, "He whom you call Messiah is born." They were confounded and dared not oppose us. But they said to us, "By the heavenly Justice, tell us what you know!" Matt 2:3–4

³We said to them, "You labor under unbelief, and neither without an oath nor with an oath do you believe, but you follow your own thoughtless goal.[f] For

---

a. Bratke has: "Judea has bloomed, and immediately our affairs are withering." I follow the text of Bringel, who in accordance with the majority of the manuscripts omits the phrase "our affairs" (*ta hēmetera*) that is found only in A and—as a supralinear correction—in one other manuscript (Paris, Bibliothèque nationale de France, gr. 1538).

b. Slav II adds "o unmarried mother, mistress!"

c. Bringel has "sent some Magi of those under his dominion." In content, this is more logical than the *lectio difficilior* of Bratke given above.

d. JD who lacks the entire speech of Dionysus, introduces the second part of *Leg. Aphr.* as follows: "The king of the Persians then did not think and hesitate for long, but called all kings-Magi who were under his dominion and sent them with gifts to honor the newborn king, bringing him the primal offering of the gentiles." After this introduction, JD inserts the text of Matt 2:2–7, the conversation of the Magi and Herod. JD then continues with, "And they said to him, 'We have observed the star for days—since we departed for our journey, until we were led by him over here.' For Herod wanted to learn the time of the birth of Christ—not to honor him, but because he wanted to kill him." The same text is given in a copy of *Pers.* in Vienna, Österreichische Nationalbibliothek, gr. 307 (13th cent.). Both put the entire narration of the Magi in the third-person plural. Mount Athos, Vatopedi, gr. 10 (14th cent.) and Slav II have another insertion: "When the king saw and heard these things, he did not tremble and sent Magi of his kingdom with gifts. They were called Elimelech, Elisur, and Eliav. Elimelech means in Assyrian divine mercy and divine kingdom; to him he gave gold; Elisur (means) divine salvation and joy, to him he gave incense; Eliav (means) my God is my father and protector, to him he gave myrrh. The star led them on the right way to Jerusalem. Then they returned, they narrated all that they had heard and seen, as it was written on golden tablets as follows."

e. C (and Bringel) adds "of the star."

f. Slav II. has "your foolish reason."

the Christ, the son of the Most High is born, annulling your law and your synagogues. And for this reason, struck by a most excellent oracle,[a] you do not hear with pleasure this name which has come upon you unexpectedly."

[4]When they had taken counsel together, they implored us to accept their gifts and to conceal this[b] from their country, lest a revolt rise against us.[c] But we said, "Gifts we have brought in his honor, with the aim of proclaiming those great things that had happened in our country on the occasion of his birth. And you say we should take the gifts and conceal the things that have been manifested by a celestial divinity and neglect the orders of our own king? Or do you not know what an experience you had once with the Assyrians?"[d] They became afraid and after beseeching us repeatedly, they gave the matter up.

2 Kgs 16; 17:3–6; 2 Chr 28:16–25

[5]But then the one who was ruling over Judea[e] sent for us and spoke with us and asked us, and we said to him (things) at which he was thoroughly disturbed.[f] And we departed from him without giving any greater heed to him than to any worthless person.

Matt 2:7–8

The Magi in Bethlehem

8 [1]We went to the place to which we had been sent, and we saw her, the one who had given birth, and the one who had been born, the star indicating to us the lordly infant.[g]

Matt 2:9–10

[2]We said to the mother, "What is your name, O renowned mother?"

She said, "Mary, masters."

"Where do you come from?"

"From this district," she said, "of the Bethlehemites."

"Do you not have a husband?"

She said, "I have only been engaged; the pre-nuptial arrangements have been concluded,[h] but my thought is divided, for I did not want to come to this affair at all. But while I was giving little concern to it, at the dawn of the Sabbath, at the rising of the sun, an angel came to me announcing suddenly to me a childbirth. I was disturbed and cried out, 'By no means can this happen to me, Lord! I do not have a husband.' And he assured me that it was God's will that I would have the child."

Matt 1:18; Luke 1:27

Luke 1:26–38

---

a. C (and Bringel) has "struck by madness"; J: "struck by rage"; Slav II has "struck by jealousy."

b. C (and Bringel) adds "important matter."

c. Slav I: "Then they had taken counsel together, and they implored us to accept their gifts and to conceal this matter. So they did with foreigners lest the shame would not take themselves."

d. This is an allusion to the conflict between the Judean kings Ahaz and Hoshea and the Assyrians. JD lacks this sentence.

e. Slav II: "But then Herod, who ruled Judea."

f. JD lacks this sentence.

g. JD: "And they saw the mother and the newborn. They opened their treasuries, bowed to the earth and gave him as gifts gold and incense and myrrh—gold [for him] as king, incense [for him] as god, myrrh [for him] as a mortal being. Thus was fulfilled what is said by the prophet (cf. Ps 72:10): 'The kings of Arabia and Saba shall offer gifts. The kings of Tarshish and of the isles shall bring presents. And to him will be given the gold of Arabia.'"

h. JD concludes the verse here.

³We said to her, "Mother of Mothers, all the gods of the Persians have called you blessed. Your glory is great. For you are better than all renowned women and you have become manifestly more queenly than all queens."ᵃ

⁴The child, moreover, sat on the ground, being, as she said, nearly two years old and having in part the likeness of her who bore him. For she was small in stature even when she stood upright, and had a delicate body, wheat-colored; and she had her hair bound with a simple, very beautiful hairstyle.

⁵As we had along with us a servant quite skilled in painting,ᵇ we brought back with us a likeness of them both to our country. And it was placed in the temple in which the oracle was given,ᶜ with the inscription: "In the heaven-sent temple,ᵈ the power of Persia dedicated this to Zeus Helios, the great God, King Jesus."

⁶Taking the child up and bearing him in our arms, each of us saluted and worshiped him and presented to him goldᵉ and said to him, "(We give) to you what is your own. We lavish you, O heavenly power.ᶠ In no other way could the unordered things be ordered than by your presence; in no other way could things above be compounded with things below than by your descent. For a service is not carried out to such a degree if someone sends a servant, as when he (i.e., the master) himself is present; nor when the king sends the satraps to war, as when he himself departs.ᵍ It is quite fitting for your wise method to deal in this manner with rebels."ʰ

⁷The child smiled and leaptⁱ during our flattery and our words. When we had bidden the mother farewell, and when she had shown us honor, and we had glorified her properly, we went to the place in which we lodged.ʲ

Luke 1:48

Matt 2:11

---

a. Slav I lacks "and you have become manifestly more queenly than all queens."

b. Slav I lacks "and as we had along with us a servant quite skilled in painting."

c. JD replaces "in which the oracle was given" with "for it would be honored by all."

d. Slav II: "in the divine temple of Dionysus and Hera."

e. Slav I and Bringel: "gold and myrrh and incense." Slav II: "gifts—gold, incense and myrrh."

f. Slav I and Bringel: "We honor you in love, heavenly Jesus." Slav II: "We brought to you what is your own, heavenly Jesus."

g. JD and Slav I lack "nor . . . departs."

h. JD: "It was quite fitting for your wise method to face the rebels in such a body through your incarnation"; Slav II: "It was quite fitting for your wise prudence to defeat and to overthrow your adversaries this way."

i. C (and Bringel) omits "smiled."

j. JD adds the interesting passage: "And they told each other about the child and how he appeared to them. The first of them said, 'I saw him as a child.' The second one said, 'I saw a thirty-year-old man.' And the third one, 'I saw him as a man who had grown old.' And they were surprised at the varying appearance of the child.'" With this passage, JD inserts the idea of the "polymorphy" of Christ into *Leg. Aphr.* The idea of the varying appearance of Christ has its origin in the pagan theologumenon of the polymorphy of a divinity and can be already found in Christian gnostic texts of the second to fourth centuries. It is present even in *(Arm.) Gos. Inf.* 11 and in *Rev. Magi* 14:3–8; 28:1–3. The theological point of the polymorphy of Christ is that human beings are not in the condition to look at Christ in his divine form. Therefore, Christ appears to everyone in an appropriate form. The concept of the polymorphy of Christ was controversial, because orthodox theologians—such as the patriarch Photius in the ninth century—associated with it the risk of a docetic Christology. Therefore, it is surprising that John of Damascus in his homily refers to this idea without any comment. A very interesting iconographical realization of the concept of Christ's trimorphy we find, however, in a miniature of Jerusalem, Greek Orthodox Patriarchate, Taphou 14 (fol. 106v; 11th cent.) that illustrates the

The departure of the Magi

9 [1]In the evening, there came to us someone terrible and awesome[a] saying to us, "Get away quickly, lest you fall prey to a plot." And we said with fear,[b] "Who is it who is plotting against such an embassy, o general of God?" And he (said), "Herod.[c] But get up immediately and depart, so you will be preserved in peace!" We hurried and mounted our strong horses and departed from there in all earnestness; and we reported all that we had seen in Jerusalem.

Matt 2:12

[2]Behold then, such great things we have told you[d] regarding Christ and we know that Christ has become our Savior.[e] But you, by your ways, are opposed to him, all the time slandering his pain. For speaking unworthy things, and doing still more unworthy things, are a mark of hatred.[f]

---

meeting of the Magi and Mary in the homily of John of Damascus. The child is depicted three times: the oldest, white-bearded Magi bends down to Christ as a child, which is depicted in the iconographical character of Emmanuel; the second, brown-bearded Magi bears an adult Christ-Pantocrator in his arms; and the youngest Magi holds an old man with a white beard and a blue himation. Obviously, Christ is depicted in these three characters as a representation of the whole history of salvation. For a convincing interpretation of this miniature, see Tamar Avner, "The Impact of Liturgy on Style and Content: The Triple-Christ Scene in Taphou 14," *Jahrbuch für Österreichische Byzantinistik* 32, no. 5 (1982): 459–68. For the trimorphism of Christ see Jacques Duchesne-Guillemin, "Die drei Weisen aus dem Morgenlande und die Anbetung der Zeit," *Antaios* 7 (1965): 234–52.

a. C (and Bringel): "a certain terrible angel."

b. C (and Bringel) omits "with fear."

c. JD lacks the entire following passage and concludes the legend with the words: "When the Magi had heard this and received the order of the angel they mounted the strong horses and went back to their country on another way."

d. These last sentences of the report given by the Magi address the people of Jerusalem.

e. For liturgical reasons, the end of the legend differs in the Slavonic tradition. Slav I has: ". . . that Christ has become our Savior and for all who believe in him. To him be honor and glory to the end of time. Amen." Slav II: "He could not stand it any longer, that the unharmed image was trampled on with sinful feet. Thus, he who was in the form of God took upon him the form of a servant (cf. Phil 2:6–7) in order to redeem the slaves from sin and to save them from death. Through his death he leads back to the first heritage and creates sons of the heavenly Father, who form themselves according to his image. Therefore, the son of justice lighted up in the last times, in order to renew the entire human creature in the light of his grace. To him be honor to the end of time. Amen."

f. C (and Bringel) adds: "And these are the frightening accounts of the inspired Magi."

The Revelation of the Magi
A summary and introduction

by Brent Landau

The *Revelation of the Magi* (*Rev. Magi*) is a pseudepigraphical early Christian writing purporting to be the personal testimony of the Magi (better known as the "Wise Men" or the "Three Kings") on the events surrounding the coming of Christ. It is by far the longest apocryphon devoted to these figures, and contains several unique interpretations of the biblical Magi story (Matt 2:1–12) not seen elsewhere in early Christian biblical interpretation. In *Rev. Magi* there are twelve Magi, or possibly more, in contrast to the traditional enumeration of three. They reside in a semi-mythical land in the Far East called "Shir"; and perhaps most startlingly, the Magi's star is actually Jesus Christ himself, who transforms from star to human and back again throughout the course of the narrative. Although the only complete version of *Rev. Magi* is preserved in Syriac, a much briefer Latin summary of the same basic narrative exists in an ancient commentary on the Gospel of Matthew.

Contents
Rev. Magi is a lengthy text—about 6,500 words in Syriac. The narrative will be summarized briefly here, and a much more detailed summary will follow the introduction. *Rev. Magi* is summarized in this volume instead of translated because it was published recently in English by a trade press in a format designed primarily for a general audience.[1] The chief goals of this entry are twofold. First, it provides a fuller introduction to the text and its interpretative problems than that found in the trade press version. Second, because of the length and complexity of *Rev. Magi*, a detailed summary provides readers with a convenient and accessible overview of the text's content.

According to *Rev. Magi*, the Magi are an ancient order of mystics residing in a land called "Shir," located at the extreme eastern edge of the inhabited world (1–2). They are descendants of Adam's son Seth, who received a prophecy from his father Adam about the coming of a star that would signify the birth of God in human form (2). This prophecy is written down by Seth in the world's first book, and is transmitted through the generations by his offspring, the Magi (3–4). In expectation of the star's coming, every month the Magi immerse themselves in a sacred spring, ascend their country's most sacred mountain (the "Mountain of Victories"), pray to God in silence, and enter a cave (the "Cave of Treasures of Hidden Mysteries") atop the mountain to read Seth's prophecies (5). At last, the star appears to the present generation of Magi (who serve as the story's narrators), descends to the peak of the Magi's mountain, and transforms into a small, luminous human being (11–13). Then, in star form once more, it guides them on a miraculously brief journey from

---

1. See Landau, *Revelation of the Magi*. For more detailed discussion of the text, consult the author's dissertation, "Sages and the Star-Child."

Shir to Bethlehem, during which it relieves their fatigue and multiplies their food (16). When they reach Bethlehem, the star enters a cave, transforms into a luminous infant, and commissions the Magi to return to their country to spread his gospel with his other disciples (18–21). After meeting Mary and Joseph (22–25), the Magi return to Shir with the star's assistance (26). They tell the inhabitants of their country about their journey, and explain that the people of Shir also can experience the presence of Christ if they partake of the food that the star multiplied (27). The people eat, immediately have visions of the heavenly and earthly Jesus, and convert to the faith proclaimed by the Magi (28). Finally, the apostle Judas Thomas arrives in the land of Shir, meets the Magi, and baptizes them and commissions them to preach throughout the entire world (29–32).

Manuscripts and Versions

The full text of *Rev. Magi* is preserved only in Syriac, in a single eighth-century manuscript housed in the Vatican Library (Biblioteca apostolica, syr. 162). The manuscript contains a world-chronicle known as the *Chronicle of Zuqnin* (named for the monastery in southeastern Turkey where it was produced, henceforth *Chron. Zuq.*) or, less accurately, as the *Chronicle of Pseudo-Dionysius of Tell-Mahre*.[2] In its recounting of the history of the world from Creation to the late eighth century, *Chron. Zuq.* embeds a number of previously independent documents, such as a legend about Alexander the Great, the legend of the Seven Sleepers of Ephesus, and *Rev. Magi*. Based on the way that the compiler of *Chron. Zuq.* has handled other literary sources that he incorporated, there is no reason to think that he has altered the text in any substantial respect.[3] A critical edition of Vat. syr. 162 was produced by the Swedish scholar Otto Tullberg and his pupils in 1851.[4] In 1927 J.-B. Chabot edited the text again for the CSCO and translated *Chron. Zuq.* into Latin,[5] though by the time of Chabot's edition the manuscript had become increasingly illegible (the cause of the deterioration remains unclear) and Chabot was forced to rely on Tullberg's readings at several points.[6] The present author is preparing a new edition of the Syriac as part of his CCSA volume on *Rev. Magi;* the new edition utilizes high-resolution digital photographs of the manuscript taken under ultraviolet light, in addition to direct observation of the manuscript at the Vatican Library.

Although the only witness to the complete text of *Rev. Magi* is Vat. syr. 162, a much shorter summary of the same basic narrative appears in the *Opus Imperfectum in Matthaeum* (henceforth *Op. Imperf.*), a Latin commentary on the Gospel of Matthew that was wrongly attributed to John Chrysostom.[7] Some scholars have regarded the summary

---

2. See the comments of Amir Harrak, *The Chronicle of Zuqnin, parts III and IV: A.D. 488–775* (Toronto: Pontifical Institute of Mediaeval Studies, 1999), 3–4.

3. See Witakowski, *Syriac Chronicle of Pseudo-Dionysius*, 124–36.

4. Tullberg, *Dionysii Telmahharensis Chronici liber primus*.

5. Chabot, *Chronicon anonymum Pseudo-Dionysianum*.

6. See Witakowski, *Syriac Chronicle of Pseudo-Dionysius*, 32 n. 20.

7. In Migne, PG 56:637–38. A critical edition of *Op. Imperf.* is apparently underway, though the prefatory volume appeared more than twenty years ago; see van Banning, *Opus Imperfectum*. The portion related to *Rev. Magi* is translated in Landau, *Revelation of the Magi*, 103–5; for a detailed comparison of the *Op. Imperf.* version of the legend with the Syriac form of *Rev. Magi*, see Landau, "Sages and the Star-Child," 137–74. An introduction to and translation of the summary has been published recently by Alexander Toepel, "The Apocryphon of Seth," in *Old Testament Pseudepigrapha: More Noncanonical Scriptures* (ed. Richard Bauckham, James R. Davila, and Alexander Panayotov; Grand Rapids, Mich.: Eerdmans, 2013), 33–39. For a complete translation of *Op. Imperf.*, see James A. Kellerman, trans., *Incomplete Commentary on Matthew (Opus Imperfectum)* (2 vols.; Downers Grove, Ill.: InterVarsity, 2010).

found in *Op. Imperf.* as a witness to a shorter, more succinct version of *Rev. Magi* that was later expanded into the form contained in the extant Syriac text from *Chron. Zuq.*[8] But there has been no consensus about which portions of the Syriac might be secondary, and the version in *Op. Imperf.* possesses the same basic narrative structure found in the Syriac. Therefore, it seems preferable to regard *Op. Imperf.* as a witness to a form of *Rev. Magi* very similar in content and length to that found in the received Syriac.

Original Language, Date, and Provenance

If we assume, as does the most recent scholarship, that *Op. Imperf.* was written in the fifth century by an Arian theologian who had spent some time in Constantinople, then a Greek version of *Rev. Magi* must have been in existence at this time.[9] Nevertheless, it is highly likely that *Rev. Magi* originally was written in Syriac. Several plays on words only make sense in Syriac,[10] and Judas Thomas was the apostle *par excellence* for Syriac-speaking Christian communities.

The Syriac form of *Rev. Magi* must have existed by some time in the fourth century in order to account for its translation into Greek. However, there are several reasons to suspect an origin earlier than the fourth century.[11] Chief among these is the fact that the concluding episode about Judas Thomas's visit to the Magi's homeland in *Rev. Magi* 29–32 appears to be an interpolation. The narrative abruptly switches from first-person narration by the Magi to third-person narration just prior to Thomas's arrival. The Thomas episode also uses vocabulary not previously seen in the narrative, including Syriac ascetical terminology and the proper name "Jesus Christ," which is steadfastly avoided in the first-person plural narration by the Magi. In addition to these textual markers of interpolation, on a literary level the Judas Thomas episode shows a concern for officially integrating the Magi into the broader Christian church through an apostolic visit and baptism, whereas the earlier part of the text has the Magi receive revelation directly from Jesus Christ despite his never being identified to the Magi by this specific name.

A comparison between the Judas Thomas interpolation and the *Acts of Thomas* helps to determine the date of composition for the interpolation. The Thomas story shows no awareness of the storyline of *Acts Thom.*, particularly its setting in India. Yet the baptismal hymn sung by Thomas in *Rev. Magi* 30:2–9 has strong formal similarities to several of the epicletic prayers in *Acts Thom.*[12] These factors suggest that the Judas Thomas interpolation was composed in an environment where liturgical forms similar to those in *Acts Thom.* were in use, but at a time when traditions about the precise places Thomas evangelized were still somewhat in flux. Therefore, a third-century date for the composition and interpolation of the Judas Thomas episode seems appropriate.[13]

The original form of *Rev. Magi,* as a pseudepigraphon with only the Magi as its pur-

---

8. See the discussion of the relationship between these witnesses in Landau, "Sages and the Star-Child," 165–73.

9. See van Banning, *Opus Imperfectum,* v–vi.

10. For example, the play on the words "divide/division" and "doubt" (7:2), both of which have the same root in Syriac.

11. For a broader discussion of the evidence see Landau, "Sages and the Star-Child," 176–90.

12. This was noted independently of my own research by Sebastian P. Brock, "An Archaic Syriac Prayer over Baptismal Oil," in *Studia Patristica: Papers Presented at the Fourteenth International Congress on Patristic Studies Held in Oxford 2003* (ed. Francis M. Young, Mark J. Edwards, and Paul M. Parvis; Leuven: Peeters, 2006), 3–12.

13. See Landau, "Sages and the Star-Child," 190–200.

ported authors, likely was composed in the early third or late second century, based on the affinities of this work with other Christian literature of this time period. Other Christian pseudepigraphic compositions attributed to "pagans," such as the Abgar Correspondence and the earliest forms of the Pilate literature, probably originated in the second or third century as apologetic pieces illustrating the truth of Christianity through the testimony of outsiders.[14] Also, the ability of Christ in *Rev. Magi* both to transform his appearance and to appear in several different forms simultaneously is quite similar to the depictions of the polymorphic Christ found in the *Acts of John* and other second-century texts.[15]

There is one other early Christian writing with which *Rev. Magi* has a substantial amount in common, though the literary relationship between the two writings is far from clear. This is the little-studied but potentially quite ancient infancy gospel incorporated in a branch of the manuscript tradition of *Ps.-Mt.* and in several Irish witnesses.[16] First discussed by M. R. James in 1927[17] and recently christened the *Liber de nativitate salvatoris* ("Book about the Birth of the Savior," abbreviated henceforth as *Birth Sav.*) by Jean-Daniel Kaestli,[18] this work is an expansion and harmonization of Matthew's and Luke's infancy narratives. In Kaestli's opinion, the *Protevangelium of James* may be dependent upon *Birth Sav.*,[19] which would necessitate an origin for *Birth Sav.* sometime in the middle of the second century or earlier. *Birth Sav.*'s account of the Magi's visit shares a number of striking details with the contents of *Rev. Magi*—for example, in both texts only the Magi can see the star, a tradition found nowhere else in early Christian literature.[20] It appears that one text is dependent upon the other, though it is not certain in which direction the relationship goes. We may provisionally say that *Rev. Magi* is more likely to be dependent on *Birth Sav.* than the other way around, because in terms of genre *Birth Sav.* is a harmony and expansion of the canonical infancy narratives, and gospel harmonies appear to be some of the earliest apocryphal compositions that exist,[21] whereas narratives that focus on one specific biblical character or group of characters seem to be a slightly later development in the tradition. Moreover, given that *Birth Sav.* may date from the mid-second century or

---

14. See Landau, "Sages and the Star-Child," 214–18. See also Landau, "The Christian Production of 'Pagan' Pseudepigrapha" (paper presented at the annual meeting of the SBL, Boston, Mass., November 24, 2008).

15. For a comparison of the polymorphic Christ in *Rev. Magi* with that found in the *Acts of John,* see Landau, "Polymorphy, Metamorphosis, or Something Else? The Plasticity of Christ in the Syriac *Revelation of the Magi* and the *Apocryphal Acts of John*" (paper presented at the annual meeting of the SBL, Chicago, Ill., November 18, 2012).

16. For text and translation of the Irish witnesses and text of the Latin Arundel and Hereford recensions, see Jean-Daniel Kaestli and Martin McNamara, "Latin Infancy Gospels: The J Compilation," in *Apocrypha Hiberniae 1: Evangelia Infantiae* (ed. Martin McNamara et al.; 2 vols.; CCSA 13–14; Turnhout: Brepols, 2001), 2:619–880. See also the translation of the Latin Arundel recension in *AG*, 115–55.

17. Montague Rhodes James, *Latin Infancy Gospels* (Cambridge: Cambridge University Press, 1927).

18. See the recent study by Kaestli, "Mapping."

19. See Kaestli, "Recherches nouvelles."

20. The similarities between *Rev. Magi* and *Birth Sav.* were recognized first by Alois Kehl, "Der Stern der Magier: Zu §94 des lateinischen Kindheitsevangeliums der Arundel-Handschrift," *JAC* 18 (1975): 69–80. For more detailed comparisons of these two texts, see Landau, "Sages and the Star-Child," 202–14, and Kaestli, "Mapping," 528–33.

21. Although they probably contain some traditions independent of the canonical Gospels, the *Gospel of Peter* and at least some of the so-called Jewish-Christian Gospels may profitably be described as gospel harmonies, all of which likely originated in the first half of the second century.

earlier, dependence upon *Rev. Magi* would mean that *Rev. Magi* is earlier than any other Syriac Christian literature we possess, and this seems inherently unlikely.[22]

In sum, a date for *Rev. Magi* in the late second or early third century appears warranted. There are no compelling reasons to believe that the Syriac text is a translation of an originally Greek work. As the strongest center of early Syriac Christianity, Edessa would be a very likely candidate for this text's place of birth. At any rate, the popularity of Judas Thomas in Edessa would indicate that at least the redaction of the text took place there. Determining the characteristics of the individual or the community that produced this pseudepigraphic composition is quite speculative. Nevertheless, it is tempting to read some elements of *Rev. Magi*'s narrative—in particular, ingesting a particular food that facilitates visionary experience—as the religious experiences of some early Christians who adopted the personae of the Magi in order to give expression to such experiences.[23]

Literary Context

As mentioned above, *Rev. Magi* may have been directly or indirectly dependent on the traditions about the Magi found in *Birth Sav.* Apart from this work, several other definite and potential influences on *Rev. Magi* may be noted. Obviously, it is indebted to the story of the Magi in Matt 2:1–12 above all; yet *Rev. Magi* is not slavish in its devotion to this source text. It shows little interest in the Magi's interaction with the inhabitants of Jerusalem; it never even alludes to King Herod's slaughter of the innocents; and the gifts brought by the Magi to Jesus are neither specified as the familiar gold, frankincense, and myrrh, nor as anything else. As for other NT texts, the Gospel of John is as important as Matt 2:1–12, if not more so. *Rev. Magi* is replete with Johannine terminology, often describing Christ as the "Son" who "was sent" by the "Father," and its depiction of Christ as a star may be influenced by the Fourth Gospel's well-known description of Christ as "the light of the world" (John 8:12; 9:5).

Two geographical locations found in *Rev. Magi* also appear in the Syriac work known as the *Cave of Treasures* (*Cav. Tr.*), dated in its final form to the sixth or seventh century but doubtlessly preserving earlier traditions.[24] In *Rev. Magi*, the "Cave of Treasures of Hidden Mysteries" is where Seth's books of revelation are kept, along with (unspecified) gifts that the Magi are to offer to Christ when the star appears; in *Cav. Tr.*, the cave is the burial place of Adam and his offspring, as well as the repository of the Magi's gifts. Additionally, in *Rev. Magi*, the Magi's sacred mountain is named the "Mountain of Victories" and the "Cave of Treasures" is located at its summit; the "Mountain of Victories" is mentioned also in *Cav. Tr.*, as the residence of Methuselah, Lamech, and Noah (14:1). These commonalities are intriguing; however, *Cav. Tr.*'s narrative about the Magi has very little in common with the content of *Rev. Magi*. In *Cav. Tr.*, the Magi live in Persia, are startled by the unexpected appearance of the star, and consult the "revelations of Nimrod"—not Seth—to understand the meaning of the star (45:11). It is often thought that *Cav. Tr.* had

---

22. The earliest Syriac Christian writings are probably the *Odes of Solomon* (often dated to the early second century) and Tatian's *Diatessaron* gospel harmony (second half of second century).

23. See my "Under the Influence (of the Magi): Did Hallucinogens Play a Role in the Inspired Composition of the Pseudepigraphic *Revelation of the Magi?*" Forthcoming in *Fakes, Forgeries, and Fictions: Writing Ancient and Modern Christian Apocrypha* (Eugene, Ore: Cascade).

24. See the new introduction to and translation of this work by Alexander Toepel, "The Cave of Treasures," in *Old Testament Pseudepigrapha: More Noncanonical Scriptures* (ed. Richard Bauckham, James R. Davila, and Alexander Panayotov; Grand Rapids, Mich.: Eerdmans, 2013), 531–84.

access to earlier Christian (and perhaps Jewish) exegetical traditions; in the case of the Magi traditions it is probable that both works had access to similar sources, but that neither work utilized the other. *Rev. Magi* also knows earlier traditions about a revelation or testament of Adam written down by Seth and about the great virtue of Seth and his progeny. It is intriguing that Josephus (*Ant.* 1.70–71) names the land of Seth's descendants as "Seiris," though Josephus apparently envisions this land as being somewhere in Transjordan, whereas *Rev. Magi* is dependent upon a widespread ancient geographical tradition that designated "Shir" or "Seiris" as the land known today as China.[25] In its use of the figure of Seth, *Rev. Magi* does not show any resemblance to the speculation about Seth as a salvific figure that appears in some works from the Nag Hammadi library.[26]

One final alleged antecedent (or group of antecedents) must be mentioned, since it dominated earlier scholarship on *Rev. Magi* and is still cited as authoritative by some recent scholars. Beginning in the late nineteenth century, scholars associated with the "History-of-Religions" School claimed that *Rev. Magi* was a product of indigenous Iranian religious thought.[27] Most notably, it was held that the appearance of Christ to the Magi atop the Mountain of Victories was a lightly Christianized version of an Iranian legend about the coming of the Saoshyant (a Zoroastrian savior figure) or the birth of the god Mithras.[28] Even scholars who were critical of the most thoroughgoing forms of this "Iranian thesis" have conceded that *Rev. Magi* has some Iranian elements.[29] As alluring as it may be to regard *Rev. Magi* as a window into the beginnings of Christianity in Iran and pre-Christian Iranian religion, the alleged parallels between *Rev. Magi* and Iranian religion are indeed quite meager and rely heavily on inference. It is important to note also that the genealogical approach to religious thought espoused by the "History-of-Religions" School, wherein all religions are merely replicating the ideas of earlier, primitive religions in disguised form, has largely fallen out of favor among scholars because it posits a very simplistic view of interaction between religious systems. Finally, it must be kept in mind that the scholars who put forth the most detailed versions of this thesis wrote in the 1950s and 1960s, when there was an obsession with establishing Iran as the cradle of Jewish, Christian, and gnostic thought—a notion few scholars today accept.[30] Thus, there is little need to resort to more exotic influences than earlier Christian and Jewish texts and traditions in order to explain the religious worldview found in *Rev. Magi*.

Literary and Theological Importance

Although *Rev. Magi* was virtually unknown and/or ignored by specialists in early Christian apocryphal literature until quite recently, the text contains several distinctive and intriguing elements. First, and most obviously, it is by far the longest and most detailed apocryphon relating to the enigmatic figures of the Magi to have survived from antiq-

---

25. See Reinink, "Das Land 'Seiris.'"

26. For contextualization of *Rev. Magi* among other traditions about Seth, see Albertus F. J. Klijn, *Seth in Jewish, Christian and Gnostic Literature* (Leiden: Brill, 1977), 48–60.

27. See the (favorable) overview of this scholarship by Hultgård, "Magi and the Star."

28. The most famous and committed proponent of this viewpoint was the Swedish scholar Geo Widengren. For the fullest exposition of Widengren's thesis, see his *Iranisch-semitische Kulturbegegnung in parthischer Zeit* (Cologne and Opladen: Westdeutscher Verlag, 1960), 62–86.

29. See the evaluation of Mary Boyce and Frantz Grenet, *Zoroastrianism under Macedonian and Roman Rule* (vol. 3 of *A History of Zoroastrianism;* Leiden: Brill, 1991), 449–53.

30. See the criticisms of these tendencies of the "History of Religions" School in Karen L. King, *What Is Gnosticism?* (Cambridge, Mass.: Harvard University Press, 2003), 71–109.

uity. The Magi do make appearances in the *Protevangelium of James* and other infancy gospels,[31] and there are several shorter compositions in which the Magi play a major role.[32] Yet *Rev. Magi* tells the story of Christ and, indeed, the entire history of salvation, from the perspective of the Magi themselves with a level of detail found nowhere else.

Second, the text surprisingly places the Magi in the legendary far-eastern land of Shir, ignoring the most popular homelands imagined for the Magi by other early Christian commentators: Persia, Babylon, and Arabia. In a number of ancient sources, the land of Shir seems to be roughly equivalent to China, and its inhabitants are said to possess extraordinary virtues and abilities.[33] No other ancient Christian writing locates the Magi in this land,[34] and the author of *Rev. Magi* presumably intended to appropriate for the figures of the Magi the sorts of qualities elsewhere ascribed to the inhabitants of China.

Third, the text is strongly invested in the notion of a polymorphic Christ, which, as mentioned above, demonstrates an affinity with writings of the second and third centuries.[35] *Rev. Magi* contains several instances of Christ appearing simultaneously to people in a multiplicity of forms (see chaps. 14 and 28), but the most distinctive instance of Christ's shape-shifting is his transformation from a star into human form and back again during the narrative.[36] Although there was a great deal of debate in ancient Christian circles about what the mysterious "Star of Bethlehem" was,[37] *Rev. Magi* is the only known writing to claim that this star was Jesus in a celestial, pre-incarnational form. The precise background for the idea of Jesus being a star still remains unclear, though it is certainly possible that the well-known statement of Christ that he is "the light of the world" in John 8:12 and 9:5 has played a role. In any case, *Rev. Magi* suggests in 13:1–2 that it is actually Christ's luminous appearance as a star that is closest to his true form, with his human form merely being an accommodation for the purposes of fragile human beings. Beyond these instances of polymorphy or metamorphosis, it is also notable that *Rev. Magi* depicts Christ as being able to appear in two places simultaneously—both with the Magi in Shir and in Bethlehem (13:9, see also 23:2).

These extraordinary bodily properties of Christ are relevant also for the fourth and

---

31. See *Prot. Jas.* 21, *(Arm.) Gos. Inf.* 10–11 (see n. 39 below), *(Arab.) Gos. Inf.* 7, and *Birth Sav.* (see the discussion above).

32. For other substantial (but still significantly shorter than *Rev. Magi*) compositions featuring the Magi, see the *Legend of Aphroditianus* elsewhere in this volume, and Pseudo-Eusebius's *On the Star* in William Wright, "Eusebius of Caesarea on the Star," *Journal of Sacred Literature* 9 (1866): 117–36 (Syriac text); 10 (1866): 150–64 (English translation).

33. See Reinink, "Das Land 'Seiris.'" Attributing such exalted status to peoples on the edges of the civilized world was a common trope in Greek and Roman literature; see James S. Romm, *The Edges of the Earth in Ancient Thought: Geography, Exploration, and Fiction* (Princeton: Princeton University Press, 1992).

34. Though some later Syriac Christian texts, probably under the influence of *Rev. Magi*, place the apostle Thomas's missionary work in China. See Jürgen Tubach, "Der Apostel Thomas in China: Die Herkunft einer Tradition," *ZKG* 108 (1997): 58–74.

35. The best discussion of this phenomenon is Paul Foster, "Polymorphic Christology: Its Origins and Development in Early Christianity," *JTS* 58 (2007): 66–99; see also Landau, "Polymorphy."

36. *Rev. Magi* is also one of the only Christian texts to depict Jesus appearing in nonhuman form (though cf. the strange statement in 1 Cor 10:4 that "the rock was Christ").

37. See the discussions in Dale C. Allison, "The Magi's Angel (2:2, 9–10)," in his *Studies in Matthew: Interpretations Past and Present* (Grand Rapids, Mich.: Baker, 2005), 17–41, and Nicola F. Denzey, "A New Star on the Horizon: Astral Christologies and Stellar Debates in Early Christian Discourse," in *Prayer, Magic, and the Stars in the Ancient and Late Antique World* (ed. Scott B. Noegel, Joel T. Walker, and Brandon M. Wheeler; University Park: Pennsylvania State University Press, 2003), 207–21.

final distinctive feature of *Rev. Magi*: the text's surprisingly tolerant attitude toward religious diversity. Since Christ can appear to anyone, in any place, at any time, *Rev. Magi* holds him to be the source of most—if not all—of humanity's religious systems. In an extremely important passage, Christ (who is not named as such until the redactional Judas Thomas ending) tells the Magi:

> And I am everywhere, because I am a ray of light whose light has shone in this world from the majesty of my Father, who has sent me to fulfill everything that was spoken about me in the entire world and in every land by unspeakable mysteries, and to accomplish the commandment of my glorious Father, who by the prophets preached about me to the contentious house, in the same way as for you, as befits your faith, it was revealed to you about me. (13:10)

According to this statement, Christ has been spoken of throughout the entire world, not just through Israel's prophets and the Magi's books of revelation (see also the Magi's similar statements at 17:5 and 23:4). This belief is quite unusual in early Christian literature, as most early Christian writers regarded the gods of other peoples as either imaginary or demonic. This more tolerant attitude perhaps has its origins in the fact that Syriac Christians had far more exposure to well-established religious traditions of Central and Southeast Asia—Zoroastrianism, Buddhism, and Hinduism, most notably—than did their Christian counterparts within the Roman Empire. As a consequence of this inclusive attitude regarding religious diversity, the Magi in *Rev. Magi* become followers of Christ despite never actually knowing him *by* the name "Jesus Christ"—a situation that the more theologically conservative redactor of the text who added the concluding Judas Thomas episode sought to remedy.[38]

Later Influence

There are two distinct trajectories for the reception history of *Rev. Magi*: the use of the original Syriac form of the text in Eastern Christian communities, and the use of *Rev. Magi*'s narrative as preserved in *Op. Imperf.* in medieval Europe. The former trajectory is somewhat sparse, while the latter is surprisingly rich. We will examine each trajectory in turn.

The earliest Eastern Christian text to show awareness of the Syriac *Rev. Magi* is not in Syriac; rather, it is the sixth-century *Armenian Infancy Gospel,* which is based upon a lost Syriac original. The gospel references *Rev. Magi*'s notion that the Magi are in possession of an ancient prophetic writing by Seth; in fact, they bring this writing with them to present it to Jesus (*[Arm.] Gos. Inf.* 10–11 and 22–23).[39] In the late eighth century, about the same time as *Chron. Zuq.* was written, the Syriac writer Theodore bar Konai mentions that the Magi arrived in Jerusalem "in the month of flowers" (i.e., April), and that they laid their crowns at his feet.[40] Both of these elements also appear in *Rev. Magi* (at 17:1 and

---

38. For more detailed analysis of *Rev. Magi*'s understanding of divine revelation, see Landau, "'One Drop of Salvation"; and Landau, "Sages and the Star-Child," 244–66.

39. See the translation by Abraham Terian, *The Armenian Gospel of the Infancy* (New York: Oxford University Press, 2008), 51–52.

40. Theodore bar Konai, *Book of Scholia*, 7.17. For a French translation of the passage, see Theodore bar Koni, *Livre des Scholies (recension de Séert) II. Mimrè VI-XI* (trans. Robert Hespel and René Draguet; CSCO 432, Syr. 188; Leuven: Peeters, 1982), 51.

18:5, respectively), and the tradition about Jesus being born during the month of April is quite unusual, so it is highly probable that Theodore was familiar with *Rev. Magi*. Because Theodore lived in Ira and *Chron. Zuq.* was compiled in southeastern Turkey, this suggests that *Rev. Magi* had been disseminated rather widely by the end of the eighth century.

In the thirteenth century, Solomon, the bishop of Basra, wrote a compendium of biblical and extrabiblical lore known as the *Book of the Bee,* which demonstrates some knowledge of *Rev. Magi.* Solomon mentions that some Christians say that the gifts brought by the Magi were deposited in the Cave of Treasures by Adam, and that he commanded his son Seth to hand them down through the generations (*Bk. Bee* 39; cf. *Rev. Magi* 4:7). Solomon also states that some say that it was at the time of Seth that writing was invented (*Bk. Bee* 18), and *Rev. Magi* 3:3 claims that Seth wrote the first book in the history of the world. Both of these traditions, Solomon says, are not accepted by the church. This suggests that Solomon viewed *Rev. Magi* as heterodox in some respects, but he does not elaborate further.[41]

It is also worth mentioning that the list of the names of the twelve Magi and their fathers in *Rev. Magi* 2:3 is found in works by a number of other Syriac writers. However, the names from this list are never referenced again in the narrative of *Rev. Magi,* and they are so widespread throughout Syriac literature that they are likely not to have originated in *Rev. Magi,* but instead were added to the text at some point after its creation.[42] Indeed, there are hints scattered throughout *Rev. Magi* that the Magi constituted a group much larger than twelve: the text uses the Syriac term *mashritha* to describe them on several occasions, a word found in the Syriac NT to translate the Greek *parembolē,* used almost exclusively for large assemblies of people (e.g., Acts 21:34; Heb 11:34; 13:11).

Although there are some clear indications that *Rev. Magi* remained known in Syriac Christian communities for several centuries after its inclusion in *Chron. Zuq.,* the references to it are rather meager overall. In contrast, *Op. Imperf.*'s summary *of Rev. Magi's* narrative was extremely influential for understandings of the Magi in medieval Europe. *Op. Imperf.* was attributed, incorrectly, to John Chrysostom, and thus it was copied along with his other works. Its story about the Magi was incorporated into Jacob of Voragine's *Legenda Aurea* (the "Golden Legend"), an extremely popular thirteenth-century compendium of saints' lives.[43] In the fourteenth century, the German priest John of Hildesheim used *Op. Imperf.*'s narrative (along with other sources) in the composition of his enormously popular *Historia Trium Regum* ("History of the Three Kings"), which stands as the most detailed medieval account of the Magi.[44] The Magi legend was referenced also by Thomas Aquinas, Peter Abelard, and other medieval theologians.[45]

---

41. For an English translation of the relevant passages see Solomon of Basra, *The Book of the Bee* (trans. Ernest A. W. Budge; Oxford: Clarendon, 1886), 28 and 85.

42. See the helpful tables of the names of the Magi in Syriac sources in Witakowski, "Magi in Syriac Tradition," 839–43.

43. For an English translation of the material in the *Golden Legend* pertaining to the Magi, see Jacobus de Voragine, *The Golden Legend: Readings on the Saints* (trans. William G. Ryan; 2 vols.; Princeton: Princeton University Press, 1995), 1:40, 78–84.

44. The most accessible version of the *Historia Trium Regum* is a Middle English recension; see Frank Schaer, *The Three Kings of Cologne: Edited from London, Lambeth Palace MS 491* (Heidelberg: Universitätsverlag Winter, 2000).

45. See Thomas Aquinas, *ST* III, Q. 36, Art. 5, ad. 4, and Peter Abelard, *Sermo IV in Epiphania Domini.* For the latter, see Paola de Santis, *I sermoni di Abelardo per monache del Paracleto* (Leuven: Leuven University Press, 2002), 198–99.

Artistic representations of *Rev. Magi*'s narrative exist as well: Vincent of Beauvais's *Speculum Humanae Salvationis* ("Mirror of the Salvation of Humankind") contains a drawing of the Magi bowing before a star containing a small child, an unmistakable reference to *Rev. Magi*'s understanding of the Magi's star as Christ himself.[46] Moreover, two fifteenth-century paintings by the Flemish artist Rogier van der Weyden and his school show the Magi looking in awe at the star-child hovering over a mountain; one of these shows the Magi bathing in their sacred spring.[47] It is also remarkable that the *Rev. Magi* traditions were known by some of the early explorers of the Americas: one Spanish Augustinian was so impressed by the similarities between Incan religious practices and Christianity that he surmised that the Incans were the descendants of those evangelized by the Magi and the apostle Thomas.[48] Thus, the narrative of *Rev. Magi* became a valuable resource during the Age of Exploration for fitting the indigenous cultures of the Americas into the traditional Christian schematization of the world.

About the Summary

Because *Rev. Magi* is easily accessible in English through the present author's HarperCollins translation and his dissertation, it is unnecessary to reproduce that translation here. Instead, what follows is a detailed summary of the text (with explanatory footnotes for difficult passages) that will help readers to become aware of the specific content of *Rev. Magi* without having to read a translation of a Syriac text that is not infrequently verbose, repetitive, and stylistically awkward.

Bibliography

EDITIONS AND TRANSLATIONS

Chabot, Jean-Baptiste. *Chronicon anonymum Pseudo-Dionysianum vulgo dictum*, I. CSCO 91, 121, Syr. 3.1–2. Paris: E Typographeo Reipublicae, 1927. (Edition and Latin translation of *Chron. Zuq.*)

Landau, Brent C. *Revelation of the Magi: The Lost Tale of the Wise Men's Journey to Bethlehem*. San Francisco: HarperCollins, 2010. (English translation and commentary.)

———. "The Sages and the Star-Child: An Introduction to the *Revelation of the Magi*, An Ancient Christian Apocryphon." ThD diss., Harvard Divinity School, 2008. (Comprehensive study of the text; further bibliography may be found here.)

Tullberg, Otto F. *Dionysii Telmahharensis Chronici liber primus. Textum e codice ms. Syriaco Bibliothecae Vaticanae*. Uppsala: Regiae Academiae Typographi, 1850. (*Editio princeps* of *Chron. Zuq.*)

---

46. See the plate in Landau, *Revelation of the Magi*, 40–41; two other versions of this image are found in Hugo Kehrer, *Die heiligen drei Könige in Literatur und Kunst* (2 vols.; Leipzig: Seemann, 1908), 2:211, 213.

47. See the plates in Landau, *Revelation of the Magi*, ii, 51. These paintings today reside, respectively, in the Gemäldegallerie in Berlin and the Cloisters Museum in New York. For discussion of these artistic witnesses to the Magi narrative of *Op. Imperf.*, see Jacques Duchesne-Guillemin, "The Wise Men from the East in the Western Tradition," in *Papers in Honour of Professor Mary Boyce* (ed. Jacques Duchesne-Guillemin and Pierre Lecoq; 2 vols.; Leiden: Brill, 1985), 1:149–57.

48. See the discussion of the Spanish search for the Magi and the apostle Thomas in Trexler, *Journey of the Magi*, 135–52.

STUDIES

Banning, Joop van. *Opus Imperfectum in Matthaeum. Praefatio.* CCSL 87b; Turnhout: Brepols, 1988.

Hultgard, Anders. "The Magi and the Star: The Persian Background in Texts and Iconography." Pages 215–25 in *"Being Religious and Living through the Eyes": Studies in Religious Iconography and Iconology.* Edited by Peter Schalk and Michael Stausberg. Uppsala: Uppsala University Library, 1998.

Kaestli, Jean-Daniel. "Mapping an Unexplored Second Century Apocryphal Gospel: The *Liber de Nativitate Salvatoris (CANT* 53)." Pages 506–33 in *Infancy Gospels: Stories and Identities.* Edited by Claire Clivaz et al. Tübingen: Mohr Siebeck, 2011.

Landau, Brent C. " 'One Drop of Salvation from the House of Majesty': Universal Revelation, Human Mission and Mythical Geography in the Syriac *Revelation of the Magi.*" Pages 83–103 in *The Levant: Crossroads of Late Antiquity.* Edited by Ellen B. Aitken and John M. Fossey. Leiden: Brill, 2014.

———. "The *Revelation of the Magi* in the *Chronicle of Zuqnin.*" *Apocrypha* 19 (2008): 182–201.

Monneret de Villard, Ugo. *Le leggende orientali sui Magi evangelici.* Studi e Testi 163. Vatican City: Biblioteca Apostolica Vaticana, 1952.

Reinink, Gerrit J. "Das Land 'Seiris' (Šir) und das Volk der Serer in jüdischen und christlichen Traditionen." *JSJ* 6 (1975): 72–85.

Trexler, Richard C. *The Journey of the Magi: Meanings in History of a Christian Story.* Princeton: Princeton University Press, 1997.

Witakowski, Witold. "The Magi in Syriac Tradition." Pages 809–43 in *Malphono w-Rabo d-Malphone: Studies in Honor of Sebastian P. Brock.* Edited by George Kiraz. Piscataway, N.J.: Gorgias, 2008.

———. *The Syriac Chronicle of Pseudo-Dionysius of Tel-Mahre: A Study in the History of Historiography.* Uppsala: Uppsala University Press, 1987.

The Revelation of the Magi (Summary)

Introduction (chap. 1)

The compiler of *Chron. Zuq.* has provided his own descriptive title for the work that follows: "About the revelation of the Magi, and about their coming to Jerusalem, and about the gifts that they brought to Christ" (1:1). The text presents itself as the personal testimony of the Magi; these Magi are called by that name because they pray in silence.[a] In their silent prayer, they glorify the Father of Heavenly Majesty, who is above all human thought. The only way in which the lower and upper worlds can speak about him is if the Father wills to reveal himself to them by means of a gift.

The Magi: Their names and lineage (chap. 2)

The connection of the name "magi" to their practice of silent prayer is restated and, once again, the object of their prayer is the Father of Heavenly Majesty. The text supplies the names of the twelve current Magi and the names of their fathers. The Magi are described as wise men and kings who live in the land of Shir, which is on the eastern edge of the inhabited world, at the shore of the great Ocean, east of the land of Nod, in which Adam dwelt. The Magi have handed down from generation to generation books of laws and commandments, which go back to Seth, who received these revelations from his father Adam.

The transmission of the Magi's mysteries (chap. 3)

Seth listened to the instructions of Adam with a virtuous heart, and he wrote them down in a book, the first book ever written. Seth gave the book to his descendants, and his descendants passed it down to Noah, who took the books (hereafter described in the plural) with him in the Ark during the Flood, and then passed it down to his descendants. The books continued to be handed down by Seth's progeny until the present generation of Magi—who narrate this writing—receive them from their fathers. In accordance with the teachings of their fathers, the present Magi pray in silence, bowing their knees and stretching their hands forth toward the heavens.

The prophecy of the star (chap. 4)

Seth's books are placed in a cave, known as the Cave of Treasures of Hidden Mysteries, that is atop the Mountain of Victories, located in the eastern part of the land of Shir. Re-

---

a. Although the text suggests that there is an etymological relationship between the words "magi," "silence," and/or "prayer" in the Magi's language, there is no obvious resemblance between these words in any of the relevant ancient languages. Since the Magi are said to live in a semi-mythical country, this alleged wordplay may simply be an exoticizing device intended to provide realism for the narrative.

citing the prophecy that they received from their own fathers, the fathers of the present generation of Magi instruct them to wait for a star that will appear over the Mountain of Victories, then descend to the mountain, and sit upon a pillar of light in the Cave of Treasures. The Magi are instructed also to tell their own sons about this coming star, whose great light will obscure the sun, moon, and stars. The star is a "mystery" of the Son, a being who is the visible counterpart of the Father of Heavenly Majesty. When the Magi see this star, they are to take the gifts deposited in the Cave of Treasures and follow where the star leads. They will see God appearing in the lowly human form of an infant, and they shall offer their gifts to the child and worship him. The Magi, in turn, will receive salvation from the child. Finally, their fathers exhort the present Magi that if the star does not come during their lifetime, they are to instruct their sons to pass along the prophecy to future generations until the prophecy is fulfilled.

The Magi's monthly ritual (chap. 5)

The Magi come together at the Mountain of Victories from their own dwelling places every month. On the twenty-fifth day of each month, they purify themselves in a spring on the foothills of the mountain. The "Spring of Purification" has seven diverse trees around it, and the smell of sweet spices effuses from the beautiful mountain. On the first day of the month, the Magi climb to the top of the mountain and stand before the Cave of Treasures, bowing their knees and stretching forth their hands in silent prayer. On the third day of the month, they enter the cave, see the gifts that have been prepared for the star's coming, and recite from Seth's books of revelation. Then they descend from the mountain and instruct their families and anyone else who wishes to learn. When any of the Magi die, one of his sons or other relatives is raised up in his place. The Magi present their teachings to the people of Shir, though some do not wish to learn from the Magi because of their practice of silent prayer.[a]

An excerpt from Seth's books of revelation about Adam's fall (chaps. 6–10)

The narration about the Magi, their prophecy, and their ritual is interrupted by an extended quotation from Seth's books of revelation, mainly consisting of a speech of Adam to Seth about the circumstances of his fall, a prediction of apostasy in the end times, and an exhortation to Seth to seek after righteousness.[b] The speech of Adam is prefaced by the explanation that Adam was able to prophesy about the coming star because the same star hovered over the Tree of Life in the Garden of Eden. When Adam sinned, the star disappeared from his sight and he was expelled from Eden. Adam tells Seth that he was deceived by Eve, and that Seth should take care not to let himself be deceived by her as well. Despite Eve's complicity in his downfall, Adam admits that he did not sufficiently recognize how exalted he was above all of God's other creations. Adam states that God was

---

a. The passage from 5:11 that apparently describes the opponents of the Magi is confusing and may be corrupt, since it seems to lack an apodosis: "And those who did not wish to learn and distanced themselves from help because they saw our quiet way of life, that we prayed in silence, and we said our mysteries to them with honor."

b. Although this "excerpt" probably contains some earlier Jewish traditions, there is no evidence that chapters 6–10 had a prior written existence independent of *Rev. Magi*. That said, its subject matter pertains very little to the narrative of *Rev. Magi*. From a narratological point of view, however, these chapters do serve the function of giving the impression of some passage of time between the first time that the present generation of Magi has performed their monthly ritual (in chap. 5) and the occasion upon which the star appears to them (in chap. 11).

indeed merciful in his punishment, since he did not take away from Adam the authority he possessed over all creation. In contrast, the snake was treated harshly by God, losing both its ability to speak and its feet.

Adam then predicts that the generations that come forth from him will be the venerable possessors of the ritual practices connected with the worship of the Father of Heavenly Majesty. Despite their great honor, however, they will rebel against the Father at the end of time.[a] They shall blaspheme the Father, make idols, worship the sun and moon, and desire the pleasures of the world. Adam concludes his instructions to Seth by reiterating his own failure to understand the Father's ways, and encourages Seth and his generations to seek mercy from the Father when they stray. Seth writes down these instructions and other commandments of Adam in the books, which are then placed in the Cave of Treasures, and the reading of these books continues throughout the ages until the present generation of Magi.

The star's appearance to the Magi (chap. 11)

After this "flashback" to the instruction of Seth by Adam, *Rev. Magi* then resumes its narrative, with the present generation of Magi revealing that it was in their time that the star and its wondrous visions finally appeared. As is their custom, the Magi come together to wash in the Spring of Purification, but a pillar of light suddenly appears and hovers over the spring, terrifying the Magi. The star[b] that the Magi see is unspeakably bright, far brighter than the sun, which becomes as faint as the daytime moon in the star's presence. Yet, it is only the Magi themselves who are able to see this star, since they alone are deemed worthy by the Father to hand down the prophecy through the generations.

The star descends to the Mountain of Victories (chap. 12)

The Magi finish bathing in their spring, climb the Mountain of Victories, and find the pillar of light standing in front of the Cave of Treasures. In their usual way, they kneel before the cave and pray in silence, praising God for the wonders they are seeing. Then, the heavens are opened, and two glorious men carry the star down from heaven and place it upon the pillar, filling the mountain with ineffable light. A small hand emerges from the pillar and star to comfort the terrified Magi. The star enters the cave, and a friendly voice bids the Magi to enter as well.

Epiphany in the Cave of Treasures (chap. 13)

The star gradually transforms itself into a small, humble human being, and says to the astonished Magi, "Peace to you." The being then begins a lengthy discourse about the form he has taken, what the Magi are to do, and what his mission upon the earth is. The being has taken the form of a humble human because it is impossible for humanity to see the true glory of the Son of the Father. He has humbled himself in this form and will even die upon a cross in order to bring salvation to humanity. The being instructs the Magi to

---

a. Presumably, Adam refers here to the Magi, but this is never made explicit. The apparent prediction of the Magi's apostasy is found only here in *Rev. Magi*. It may be a coded reference to schisms in the community in which *Rev. Magi* was produced.

b. The Magi begin to describe the star in 11:5, but the star does not actually seem to appear in the narrative until 12:3, when it is carried down from heaven by two glorious men. There is a lacuna of one word in 11:3 before the phrase "in the form of an ineffable pillar of light," but "star" is probably not the missing word, since *Rev. Magi* seems to regard the star and the pillar of light as separate entities.

take the treasures deposited in the cave and to bring them in worship to the place[a] where the being will be born in human form. Indeed, even as the being is speaking now with the Magi atop the Mountain of Victories, he is also present in the place where he will be born and in the presence of the Father. The being is actually everywhere in the entire world, because he is a ray of light from the Father of Majesty. The Father has sent him in order to fulfill everything spoken about him throughout the entire world, which includes both the prophets of Israel and the Magi's own books of revelation. The being will be a guide for the Magi on their miraculous journey to Jerusalem, where their prophecies will be fulfilled at last. The humble and frail human form that the being takes will cause the people of the world to do evil to him, but this will lead both to their own destruction and to the salvation that the Father intended.

The Magi realize Christ's polymorphy (chap. 14)

After the being has said these things to the Magi, they exit the cave with the treasures that were set aside for the coming of the star and begin to descend the mountain, rejoicing at all they have seen and heard. As they speak to one another about the revelations of the star, they realize that they each saw something different in the cave. One of the Magi saw a light with many images; another, an infant with indescribable forms; another, a youth with an otherworldly form; another, an ugly and humble human being; another, a cross and a person of light upon it, taking away the sins of the world; another saw the being powerfully descend into Sheol and receive worship from the dead; another, his ascension (from Sheol?) and his opening of the graves; and another, his ascension into heaven, accompanied by throngs of praising angels. The Magi rejoice greatly at the sharing of these numerous visions and the fact that they, among all the righteous people of the earth, were deemed worthy to see them.

The Father speaks to the Magi (chap. 15)

As the Magi rejoice, they suddenly hear a voice from the heavens that reveals itself eventually to be that of the Father himself. In a lengthy speech, the Father describes the manifold attributes of the Son.[b] He tells the Magi that everything they have just experienced is merely "one drop of salvation from the house of majesty" (15:1), a tiny fraction of the Son's activities and attributes. The Son is the only being who knows the Father, and it is the Son himself who created everything in the heavenly and earthly worlds. He reveals the Father's secrets to his believers and he becomes a human being in order to destroy death and grant eternal life. He is the "bread of life," the "shepherd of truth," and the "great priest who by his blood absolves the worlds" (15:9). In spite of the Son's multiplicity of forms, he is nevertheless one with the Father.

The miraculous journey (chap. 16)

As the Father speaks to the Magi, the star is present with them also. The entire company[c] gathers its provisions for the lengthy journey and the star's gifts, and sets out with the star

---

a. Two lacunae in 13:8 make it unclear whether or not the being specifically states the location of his birth (which is, of course, Bethlehem).

b. The detailed and extravagant speech of the Father is difficult to summarize succinctly; I have only mentioned some of its most noteworthy elements here.

c. In 16:2 we have the first of several instances of the Syriac term *mashritha* ("encampment") used to describe the Magi. Since this term is used in the Syriac versions of the NT to describe large groups of

as their guide. In the extraordinary journey that follows, the Magi walk day and night in the light of the star, having no need of the sun or the moon. Despite their continuous travel, the Magi miraculously experience no fatigue. The star also provides a sort of dwelling-place for them to rest on the journey.[a] Moreover, the Magi's provisions increase whenever the star's light shines upon them. Mountains and other rugged terrain are made level for the Magi by the star, they cross rivers by foot, and trample beasts and snakes underfoot. The star appears to the Magi in a multiplicity of forms throughout the journey, a journey that seems incredibly swift to the Magi despite the great distances.

The Magi in Jerusalem (chap. 17)

After a journey of unspecified duration, the Magi arrive in Jerusalem in the month of April. The star leads them into the city, but its inhabitants apparently cannot see the star and mistakenly regard these Magi as practicing "Magianism."[b] The Magi inform the Jerusalemites about their prophecy and what they have seen, and Herod calls the "elders of the city" and asks where the Messiah and savior of the world will be born. As soon as the elders reveal that it will be in Bethlehem, the Magi see their star (again?), rejoice greatly, and set forth to Bethlehem. The Magi remark that the foolish scribes fail to believe what is written in their own sacred writings. They also state that Herod had asked them to return to tell him where the Messiah is found, but that the star told them not to obey him.[c]

Arrival in Bethlehem (chap. 18)

When the Magi enter Bethlehem, they see a cave just like the Cave of Treasures of Hidden Mysteries in their own country. As with the star's initial epiphany, the pillar of light descends and stands in front of the cave, and the star with its accompanying angels descends upon the pillar. The star, angels, and pillar enter the cave, and a voice bids the Magi to enter. The Magi enter, place their crowns under the child's feet, kneel and worship before him, and offer their treasures to him.

Epiphany in the Bethlehem cave (chap. 19)

As with the epiphany in the Cave of Treasures, here again the luminous infant[d] gives a lengthy discourse to the Magi. He declares that their ancient mysteries have now been completely fulfilled with his bringing of them from Shir to Bethlehem. He tells them that

---

people, it may be that the earliest form of *Rev. Magi* envisioned the Magi as a group much larger than the list of twelve found in 2:3.

a. The author of *Rev. Magi* apparently does not regard the star's removal of the Magi's fatigue and its providing of a resting place for them as being contradictory.

b. The text at 17:2 reads: "'On account of what cause have you come here? Perhaps because of the mysteries of your Magianism?' because they saw us looking up at heaven, and worshiping our sign, and praying to our guide, because they did not understand our mysteries, and they reckoned us as Magi." Obviously this is a quite difficult passage, since it implies that the central protagonists of the narrative are somehow *not* Magi. Presumably *Rev. Magi* is attempting to make a distinction between the Magi who are Seth's descendants from the land of Shir and more "common" magi who are simply astrologers and/or magicians.

c. There is no reference here or elsewhere in *Rev. Magi* to the "slaughter of the innocents" (Matt 2:16–18). The text simply states that Herod "was not worthy for the worship of the light that was born, because he was a dwelling of error . . ." (17:9). Whereas Matthew's Gospel is more concerned with the consequences that the arrival of the Magi and their star produce for the inhabitants of Judea, *Rev. Magi* is interested instead in the identity of the Magi and their star; so, its retelling of this part of the Matthean narrative seems almost perfunctory.

d. Unlike in chapter 13, there is no explicit narration here of the star's transformation into human form.

they will be his witnesses in the East, along with his disciples. The being will return to his Father when he has completed everything commanded by the Father, yet he is never actually separated from him. The being tells the Magi that when they see the sun darkened during the daytime, a great earthquake, and the dead rising from their graves, they will know that the end of the ages has come and they will see him ascending into the heavens.[a]

Angels praise Christ (chap. 20)
As the star-child speaks with the Magi, the cave shines so much that it becomes like some other world. Suddenly, the voices of many (apparently invisible angelic) beings offer praises to him. They praise his creation of the worlds, his complete unity with the Father, and the salvation that he provides.

The commissioning of the Magi (chap. 21)
At the sound of these angelic praises, the Magi fall to the ground terrified. The star-child puts his hand upon them forcefully and comforts them. He tells them that as powerful as these angelic beings might seem to the Magi due to their human frailty, they are insignificant to him. There are, in fact, other things that even the angels are incapable of hearing or speaking about. Because the Magi's ancient mysteries have been completed, the star-child now dismisses them to return to their own land. They will be witnesses to him along with his disciples, and once he has ascended to heaven, he will send disciples to them. The Father and the Son are completely inseparable.[b] The Son has been sent to redeem the world from Adam's sin, and will give eternal life to the Magi through water and the giving of the Holy Spirit. Unseen voices praise the Son once more.

The Magi meet Mary and Joseph (chap. 22)
The Magi go forth from the cave to begin the return journey to their homeland. Joseph and Mary, who were appointed to be the parents of the star-child, go out with the Magi.[c] They see the light traveling along with the Magi, the same light that had been born in their house, and so Mary and Joseph are upset by the prospect that the Magi are taking their child away from them.

The Magi's revelation to Mary (chap. 23)
The Magi praise Mary for being chosen to give birth to the Son in human form. They tell her that her child is still inside of her[d] and is in her house, even though he is also present with the Magi. This great gift does not belong to Mary alone, but is for the salvation of all the heavenly and earthly realms. The Magi urge her to look up and see that he is present

---

a. The events predicted by the star-child seem to be the Passion, particularly its Matthean version with the earthquake and the raising of the saints (cf. Matt 27:51–53). It is curious, however, that this prediction never actually comes to pass in the form of *Rev. Magi* that we possess. If the Judas Thomas episode is indeed an interpolation, it is possible that the fulfillment of this prediction did actually take place in the narrative, but was obliterated when the Judas Thomas redactional material was added.

b. Much of the content of this speech is slightly rephrased from the speech of the star-child in chapter 19 (and to some degree, the speeches in chaps. 13 and 15).

c. The appearance of Mary and Joseph is quite abrupt: were they in the cave with the Magi, or were they simply in the general vicinity?

d. It is surprising that the text claims that the child is still inside of Mary, since the birth would seem to have already taken place. But this is best interpreted as another case of *Rev. Magi*'s strong insistence on Christ's omnipresence throughout the entire world.

throughout the entire creation, and he appears in every land, since he has been sent for the redemption of all human beings.

Mary speaks to Christ (chap. 24)

After the Magi explain to Mary and Joseph the true nature of their child, the couple returns to their house.[a] They find their luminous child laughing and speaking about his great mysteries. Mary and Joseph worship him, and Mary praises the child who has been given to her because of her obedience. She explains to the child that she had supposed that he was going with the Magi because of the gifts that they had offered him.

Christ blesses Mary (chap. 25)

The child praises Mary for being worthy to conceive the one who would bring salvation into the world; her deed will bestow blessing and remembrance upon her in this world, and reward in the world to come. She has redeemed Eve and her offspring, and all the worlds have peace because of her. He is now turning to his believers throughout the world, for whom he will fulfill everything promised by the Father.

The return journey home (chap. 26)

During the journey back to Shir, the star again appears to the Magi, and they worship it. The star tells the Magi that he is everywhere, and that he is even greater than the sun. When the time comes to eat, the Magi see that their provisions are now even more full than when they departed from their homeland, a miracle that causes them fear and awe. As they eat their provisions, the visions and wonders that they see in the presence of their guide do not resemble one another.[b]

The Magi address the people of Shir (chap. 27)

The Magi complete their journey back to Shir under the guidance of the star, and when they arrive at the border of their land, their families and many other inhabitants of the land come to greet them and marvel at their health despite the length of their journey. The Magi narrate for the people the journey that they undertook. They mention the visions of the star that accompanied them, their visit to Jerusalem, and the epiphany of the star-child at Bethlehem in the cave that resembled the Cave of Treasures. When they began the journey back to their homeland, the Magi say, they found their provisions to be more full than what they initially had brought, and now these overflowing bags of provisions are sitting before the people of Shir. The Magi invite the people to partake of these provisions, because when they eat them, they too will be able to experience the visions and revelations that the Magi have seen.

---

a. In chapters 24 and 25, which take place in the house of Mary and Joseph, there is no indication that the Magi are present. If they are not, this would be the only interruption in the first-person narrative perspective of the Magi between the formal commencement of first-person narration in 3:6 (or possibly 2:6) and the clear termination of first-person narration in 28:4, just prior to the beginning of the Judas Thomas material.

b. This statement that the Magi have diverse visions is similar to what was stated about the epiphany in the Cave of Treasures in chapter 14. However, the fact that these visions take place for the Magi in the context of eating their provisions foreshadows the visions of the inhabitants of Shir in chapter 28, which are clearly connected with the people's eating of the same food (though the Magi's visions here are not expressly said to be the result of the eating of the provisions).

The people eat the Magi's food (chap. 28)

Some of the people eat from the Magi's provisions, and as soon as they do, they begin rejoicing because of the visions that they immediately see. One of the people sees a great light unlike anything in the world; another sees God giving birth to himself; another, a star of light that darkens the sun; another, a man uglier than any other human being, saving the world through his blood and his appearance; another, a lamb hanging upon a tree of life, redeeming the world through his blood; and another, a pillar of light diving down inside the earth, with the dead rising and worshiping it. The ones who eat of the provisions see many other things beyond these, and the people of the entire land come to hear the revelations of the Magi.[a] Day by day, the revelations increase, all sorts of miracles are performed by the Magi, and the faith of the Lord Jesus Christ grows in the land of Shir.

Judas Thomas arrives in Shir (chap. 29)

The faith increases even more when the apostle Judas Thomas arrives in the land, sent there by the Lord. When the Magi hear of his arrival, which the star-child had promised to them, they go to meet him. Thomas[b] rejoices when they come, and after they tell him about the journey that they underwent, he recognizes "that the gift of our Lord had overflowed upon them" (29:4). He tells them, in turn, about his own experiences with Christ during the Lord's earthly ministry, including his ever-changing appearances. When the Magi hear this, they glorify God and ask Thomas to give them "the seal of our Lord," baptism (29:5).

The hymn of Judas Thomas (chap. 30)

Early on Sunday, while still night, Thomas takes the Magi to a spring of water. He takes oil and sings a hymn over it. He praises Christ for the gift of the oil, which gives salvation and takes away darkness, and he praises the oil, which hovers over the water as the Holy Spirit did. Using a number of epithets for Christ, Thomas asks him to be present and come upon the believers for their salvation.

The Magi receive the Eucharist and commission to preach (chap. 31)

After singing this hymn, Thomas baptizes them, and when they come out of the water, a luminous child descends to them from heaven. The Magi fall upon the ground, terrified, and when they stand up, the child has become a glorious young man. He takes a loaf of bread, gives praise, and breaks it, giving it first to Thomas and then to them. The being then ascends into heaven once more. Thomas glorifies the amazing and diverse images in which this being appears, stating that none of the names that he is called is his true name, which only he and the Father know. Thomas thanks the Son for enduring all the suffering on humanity's behalf, despite "being exalted above all sufferings and being a kinsperson of that one who does not suffer" (31:6). The Magi echo Thomas's praise, confessing that the Son's majesty is beyond their ability to describe. As they give thanks and praise, a great

---

a. At 28:4 the first-person narration definitively ceases, the Magi are spoken about here as if they are new characters not previously introduced into the narrative, and we have the first use of the familiar Christian terminology "our Lord." The text reads: "And there was great joy in the entire land of the East, and the nobles, and the poor, and women, and children from the entire land were gathered together in the love of our Lord before those nobles who were called Magi."

b. The text refers to this individual mostly as "Judas." Because the name "Thomas" is more familiar to many readers, I use that name here instead.

many are added to the faith day by day. Thomas tells the Magi that they must fulfill the commandment of the Lord to preach the gospel throughout the entire world, just as the other apostles have done.

The preaching of the Magi (chap. 32)

The Magi go out from there, preach about the coming of Jesus Christ, and perform miracles and healings through his name. They preach to everyone, urging all to flee from the "fearsome judgment of fire that will come suddenly to purify the entire earth from error" (32:2). By faith in Jesus Christ, all will be delivered from the fire and shall enter the eternal rest prepared for believers in his kingdom. At the end of the Magi's missionary speech, the compiler of *Chron. Zuq.* adds, "The story about the Magi and their gifts has finished" (32:4).

The Hospitality of Dysmas
A new translation and introduction

by Mark Glen Bilby

The *Hospitality of Dysmas* (*Hosp. Dysmas; BHG* 2119y) is a short tale interpolated into manuscripts of the *Acts of Pilate*. It describes the devotion and kind welcome that a bandit named Dysmas, the so-called "good thief" of Luke 23:40–43,[1] and his wife show Mary (frequently honored in the text as the Theotokos) during her sojourn in Egypt with Joseph and the infant Jesus. Through Mary two rewards are bestowed: the bandit's child is instantly healed from leprosy by bathing in water first used to bathe Jesus, and the bandit is blessed such that he will providentially share in the death and destiny of Jesus. The title given here is not attested in any manuscripts, but instead is proposed in view of the ambiguity of titles and incipits among the manuscripts containing this story, as well as to avoid confusion with several other stories about a bandit who shows Jesus hospitality. Of these stories, *Hosp. Dysmas* appears to be the earliest. In previous scholarship all of these stories are collectively entitled "The Good Thief" ("Le bon larron," "Der gute Schächer").

Contents
The story opens (v. 1) as a narrative aside from the passion account from *Acts Pil.* into which the story is inserted. The scene shifts backwards in time, "thirty-three years prior" to the Passion. The Holy Family makes its way to Egypt, where hunger prompts Mary to command a ripe date-palm to bow down and feed them (2). Soon after, they meet the "bandit . . . Dysmas" (3). At the sight of Mary he is stunned by her beauty—even more so when she takes Jesus to her breast. He then bows down before her, finds himself confessing her as the mother of God, and invites them to his home. When they arrive (4), Dysmas commands his wife to give them hospitality fit for a noblewoman such as Mary, then he leaves to hunt wild game. Next, the bandit's wife prepares a bath for Jesus (5). After Mary bathes her child, the bandit's wife bathes her own child—leprous and given to wailing from the time of its birth—in the leftover water. Instantly, the child is healed of its leprosy and becomes quiet. When the bandit returns (6), everyone sits down to eat. The unusual silence prompts the bandit to ask about his child. His wife explains the miracle and echoes her husband's earlier confession of Mary's nobility due to her mediation of the miraculous healing of their child. Upon hearing this (7), the bandit explains his question: he had thought his child was dead. The splendid miracle prompts him to laud Mary as a conduit of divine answers to prayers. He submits himself to become her devotee and protector

---

1. This customary and somewhat problematic title is not attested in ancient sources. See Bilby, *As the Bandit*, 296. Medieval apocryphal literature has played no small part in the transformation of this Lucan character into the proverbial "good thief."

during her stay in Egypt. He goes so far as to lead Mary on the dangerous roads back to Judea, ensures the safety of her path before saying farewell, and begs her to return some-day to his home (8). His extraordinary hospitality and devotion to Mary finally meet with a reward (9). Through the favor of Mary and Jesus, he will become a witness (or martyr!) with Christ and share in his destiny.

Manuscripts and Editions

The text of *Hosp. Dysmas* as we have it is bound up with the extremely complicated history of the *Acts of Pilate,* titled the *Gospel of Nicodemus* in its Latin form. *Acts Pil.* is represented by two forms: Greek A and B;[2] *Gos. Nic.* is known in three: Latin A, B, and C. Rémi Gounelle, who is currently preparing a critical edition of *Gos. Nic.* in the Corpus Christianorum Series Apocryphorum, has proposed a revision to Tischendorf's sigla so that the Byzantine manuscript tradition designated as Greek B, which is pluriform and dependent on *Gos. Nic.* Latin A (not Latin B), is now referred to as Greek M (for "Medieval") and divided into three distinct recensions: M1 (created 9th–10th cent.), M2 (12th–14th cent.), and M3 (14th–15th cent.).[3] *Hosp. Dysmas* appears in two witnesses to the M2 recension—Paris, Bibliothèque nationale de France, gr. 808, fol. 270r–271r (= B; 15th cent.) and Vatican, Biblioteca apostolica, Ottoboni gr. 411, fol. 152v–153v (= Tb; early 15th cent.)—and most of the manuscripts of M3.[4]

The copyist of B inserted *Hosp. Dysmas* into the Passion account (*Acts Pil.* 10) after the quotation of Luke 23:43, where it is found also in M3. Tb, on the other hand, incorporates *Hosp. Dysmas* into an appendix, a brief collection of four short texts together introduced as the "Lament of Mary."[5] The first two texts in this appendix, both laments attributed to Mary Magdalene, are found also in the M2 recension. Then follows a unique story about Veronica and the crucifixion, and the collection finishes with *Hosp. Dysmas.*

Tischendorf excluded *Hosp. Dysmas* from his edition of *Acts Pil.*, perhaps because of its poor Greek; however, he does mention some elements of the story in the apparatus.[6] Huidekoper's edition of *Acts Pil.*, based only on B, includes *Hosp. Dysmas,*[7] as do the late nineteenth-century devotional texts produced by Kokorelis and Panagopoulos, though

---

2. Edited by Constantin Tischendorf in *Evangelia Apocrypha* (1853; 2nd ed. Leipzig: H. Mendelsohn, 1876), 210–86 (Greek A), 287–332 (Greek B).

3. Gounelle first proposed the sigla B1, B2, and B3 in the article "Acta Pilati grecs B (*BHG* 779u-w). Traditions textuelles," *Recherches Augustiniennes* 26 (1992): 273–94. Later, he revised them to M1 (formerly B1), M2 (formerly B3), and M3 (formerly B2). See Gounelle, *Les recensions byzantines;* see also idem, "Une légende apocryphe," 247.

4. The most important witness to M3 is D (Oxford, Bodleian Library, Holkham gr. 24, 14th/15th cent.), the common ancestor of the entire family (CILMOPXY). However, M (Venice, Biblioteca Nazionale Marciana, gr. app. II, 97; 15th cent.) does not contain the story, but only apparently because the extant text starts with *Acts Pil.* 12.4.2 (in Gounelle's numbering). Nor is the story present in O (Oxford, Bodleian Library, Holkham gr. 9; 16th cent.), perhaps because its ancestor—one held in common with I (Mount Athos, Iveron 692; 16th cent.)—placed *Hosp. Dysmas* after the conclusion of *Acts Pil.*, and the copyist of O opted not to include this additional material. Another M3 MS recently came to light, but not soon enough to be included in the critical edition of M3: St. Petersburg, National Library of Russia, RAIK 166 (ca. 1760–1770). See Gounelle, *Les recensions byzantines,* 9.

5. Gounelle, *Les recensions byzantines,* 122; idem, "Une légende apocryphe," 251.

6. Tischendorf, *Evangelia apocrypha,* 308; see also the discussion in Gounelle, "Une légende apocryphe," 252 and n. 38.

7. Gounelle, "Une légende apocryphe," 252 and n. 39, citing Huidekoper, *Acts of Pilate,* iii-iv.

these rely apparently on a single descendant of D (MS X).[8] The first proper edition of *Hosp. Dysmas* was made by Gounelle in 2003.[9]

Gounelle opted to publish two separate editions of *Hosp. Dysmas* alongside each other: Tb (on its own) and a hyperarchetype for D and B, to which I have assigned the siglum H2.[10] He argued also that H2 and Tb have a common ancestor (which I designate as H1). In his explanation of this approach, he notes the complicated relationships among the manuscripts. B and D mostly agree with one another and their common text is apparently the most ancient in most cases. Sometimes B preserves the most ancient reading by itself, but this is also occasionally true of Tb. Sometimes D and Tb even agree against B. While all three texts reflect reworkings of some kind, in general B shows a tendency to make brief expansions and abridgements, D abridges often and sometimes quite considerably, and Tb abridges occasionally.[11] Both D and Tb make various grammatical corrections not made by the copyist of B. D especially stands out for its pious emendations.

Literary and Theological Importance

Hosp. Dysmas is one of a number of elaborations of the story of the "good thief" found in apocryphal literature.[12] These include:

1. *Birth Sav.* 111–25 (= CANT 78.1; hereafter the *Hospitality and Ointment of the Bandit [Hosp. Oint. Band.]*): describes how the hospitable bandit receives healing and wealth from the magical bathwater of Jesus.[13]

2. Namur, Seminary Library, Lat. 80, fol. 13v–15v, 17r–17v (12th cent.) (= CANT 78.2; hereafter the *Rebellion of Dimas [Reb. Dimas]*): an interpolation into a manuscript of *Ps.-Mt.* between chapters 19 and 20, it features the bandit as a procurator's son who facilitates the escape of the Holy Family from Israel.[14]

3. London, British Library, Harley 3199, fol. 104v–106r (14th cent.) (= CANT 78.3, hereafter the *Hospitality and Perfume of the Bandit [Hosp. Perf. Band.]*): a second, distinctive interpolation into a manuscript of *Ps.-Mt.* after chapter 17, this story connects the hospitable bandit's miraculous bathwater to the eventual conversion of Mary Magdalene.[15]

4. *Leabhar Breac* from Dublin, Royal Irish Academy, 23 P 16 (1230), 131–32 (ca. 1408–1411): an interpolation into this Irish infancy narrative known as the "Speckled

---

8. Gounelle, "Une légende apocryphe," 252.

9. Gounelle, "Une légende apocryphe." Gounelle later published separate editions of *Hosp. Dysmas* from B (in the footnotes as a M2 interpolation) and D (as the main text of M3); see *Les recensions byzantines,* 244–48 (even pages) for the B text of the story, and 247–51 (odd pages) for the D text.

10. Gounelle, "Une légende apocryphe," 262–69.

11. Gounelle, "Une légende apocryphe," 253–58; see the many examples in the translation footnotes below.

12. The reader may refer to Gounelle, "Une légende apocryphe," for a section-by-section discussion of many of the possible parallels with the text.

13. Martin McNamara et al., *Apocrypha Hiberniae I. Evangelia Infantiae* (CCSA 14; Turnhout: Brepols, 2001), 866–71; available also in *AG* 147–55.

14. Gounelle, "Une légende apocryphe," 247 and n. 25; see also the critical edition of the story in Geerard, "Le bon larron." Gounelle ("Une légende apocryphe," 246 and n. 20) notes a possible connection to a sermon of Pseudo-Ephrem (*BHG* 415p = *CPG* 4145.22/4162.3) whose dual Georgic/Arabic edition is introduced and edited by Michel van Esbroeck, "Une homélie inédite éphrémienne sur le bon larron en grec, géorgien et arabe," *AnBoll* 101 (1983): 327–62. Unlike its Greek forebear (*CPG* 4877), this text lacks a proper backstory, but it still makes some brief claims about the bandit's past.

15. Latin text in Geerard, "Gute Schächer."

Book," its story of the bandit as a child who encounters Jesus in Egypt is close to that recounted by Aelred of Rievaulx.[16]

5. *(Arab.) Gos. Inf.* 23 (= *Hist. Virg.*, pp. 59–60): a story of the good bandit (Titus) bribing the bad bandit (Dumachus) to prevent the robbery of the Holy Family in Egypt.[17]

6. *Jos. Arim.*: chapter 1 expands the backstories of both bandits and pins the blame for the execution of Jesus on the good bandit's righteous (!) theft of relics from the Jerusalem temple; chapter 3 has an expanded dialogue between Jesus and Demas during the crucifixion; chapter 5 depicts the resurrected Jesus appearing to Joseph of Arimathea with Demas, carrying his cross.[18]

7. *Vis. Theo.* pp. 19–20, 26–29: two bandits, one Jewish, one Egyptian, take the Holy Family's clothes, but the Egyptian (the "good thief" of the account) repents and returns them.[19]

8. The Coptic/Arabic *Homily on the Church of the Rock* 31–32 (in the Coptic and Arabic recensions; 17–18 in the Ethiopic recension; hereafter *Hom. Rock*); this story is quite similar to that in *Vis. Theo.*, except that the bad bandit steals not only the Holy Family's clothes, but also the baby Jesus![20]

9. The Ethiopic *Miracles of Jesus* 7:1–4 (= Arabic *[Apocr.] Gos. John* 10:1–4): the Ethiopic version adds a third bandit character because of a mistranslation; the basic plot represents a selective combination of elements from *Hist. Virg.* and *Vis. Theo.*[21]

Hosp. Dysmas is closely associated with *Hosp. Oint. Band.* and *Hosp. Perf. Band.* All three texts, while distinct from each other in many ways, share several features that appear in none of the other legends: their bandit 1) has a wife, 2) has a child (children in *Hosp. Oint. Band.*), 3) welcomes the Holy Family into his home, 4) and receives a healing miracle as a result of Jesus taking a bath.[22]

---

16. The Irish text and English translation appear in Martin McNamara et al., *Apocrypha Hiberniae I. Evangelia Infantiae* (CCSA 13; Turnhout: Brepols, 2001), 404–7. On the idea of its interpolation, see 405 n. 168. For the similar story by Aelred of Rievaulx, see his work *De institutione inclusarum* 30 (comp. 1160–1162 CE) in Anselm Hoste and Charles H. Talbot, eds., *Aelredi Rievallensis Opera omnia 1: Opera ascetica* (CCCM 1; Turnhout: Brepols, 1971), 664.

17. An English translation of the relevant section appears in *ANT*, 105. The Syriac *Hist. Virg.*, the precursor to *(Arab.) Gos. Inf.*, is available in the edition of Ernest A. W. Budge, *The History of the Blessed Virgin Mary and the History of the Likeness of Christ* (London: Luzac & Co., 1899).

18. Text in Tischendorf, *Evangelia Apocrypha*, 459–70; English translation in *AG*, 572–85.

19. Alphonse Mingana, "Woodbrook Studies 5: *Vision of Theophilus,*" *BJRL* 13 (1929): 383–474 (repr. in *Woodbrooke Studies: Christian Documents in Syriac, Arabic and Garshūni, Edited and Translated with a Critical Apparatus,* vol. 3 [Cambridge: W. Heffer & Sons Limited, 1931], 1–92).

20. Anne Boud'hors and Ramez Boutros, *L'homélie sur l'Église du Rocher* (PO 49.1; Turnhout: Brepols, 2001), 38–47 (Coptic text and translation), 132–37 (Arabic text and translation). The Ethiopic text and translation appear in Gérard Colin, *L'homélie sur l'Église du Rocher* (PO 49.2; Turnhout: Brepols, 2001), 248–53.

21. Sylvain Grébaut, *Les Miracles de Jésus* (PO 12.4; Paris: Firmin-Didot, 1919), 618–23. The Arabic *(Apocr.) Gos. John,* the precursor to the *Miracles of Jesus,* is available in the edition of Giovanni Galbiati, *Iohannis Evangelium apocryphum arabice* (Milan: In aedibus Mondadorianis, 1957), 52–55 (the Arabic page numbers are matched in the Latin translation). The Ethiopic translation introduces a number of significant errors and changes. Most notable for our purposes is the addition of the third bandit character ("Gamhour") because of a mistranslation of the Arabic word for "multitude" (*gamhur*).

22. *(Arab.) Gos. Inf.* (= *Hist. Virg.*) features a number of stories about Jesus' bathwater healing various people from leprosy (*[Arab.] Gos. Inf.* 17–18, 27, 28, 31, 32, 33); see Gounelle, "Une légende apocryphe," 245.

While this cluster of three texts apparently endeavors to clean up the bandit's story and reputation, *Hosp. Dysmas* is the ultimate expression of this effort. Among all the legends of the bandit encountering the Holy Family during the flight to Egypt, only *Hosp. Dysmas* leaves out any reference to the bandit participating in banditry! Other texts lack mention of the bandit actually robbing the Holy Family (*Hom. Rock* and ostensibly with the child bandit of Aelred, *Leabhar Breac,* and *Reb. Dimas*), or portray him as being reluctant to do so (*Vis. Theo.*), but in *Hosp. Dysmas* he is a bandit in title only.[23] Thus, there is no need for a conversion in the bandit's character. *Hosp. Dysmas* is also unique among these stories in that it makes no reference to anyone at all trying to rob the Holy Family, as well as its lack of mention of any bad bandit, other bandit, or gang of bandits. There is no tangible or obvious threat to the Holy Family, only a brief allusion to the potential danger on the road along which the good bandit leads Mary and her family (v. 8). Nothing evil ever approaches to tarnish the story or reputation of Dysmas or of the All-pure Theotokos whom he venerates.

Hosp. Dysmas belongs to a slightly broader cluster of five stories that share two unique features. Of all the extant legends of the bandit, only these are self-contained texts interpolated into major apocryphal collections, and they all tie the miracle of the bending date-palm to the story of the bandit, in effect mentioning the palm tree just before the encounter with the bandit. In *Hosp. Dysmas* and *Hosp. Oint. Band.,* the story of the palm tree is included within the interpolation itself, and the *Leabhar Breac* interpolation alludes to it as well. In *Reb. Dimas* and *Hosp. Perf. Band.,* the bandit's story is interpolated immediately after the *Ps.-Mt.* account of the palm tree. This consistent structuring points to a dedicated effort to draw a parallel between the bending palm and the prostrating bandit. Both pay homage to the Madonna with Child, both nourish the Holy Family, and both are ultimately planted in paradise. The likening of the bandit to the palm tree resonates with early Christian horticultural typologies,[24] as well as a wider range of typologies based on the key intertext between Gen 2–3 and Luke 23:43.[25]

Several stories about the bandit exalt Mary and give her a central role in the bandit's story (such as *Vis. Theo., Hom. Rock,* [*Arab.*] *Inf. Gos.,* and *Hosp. Perf. Band.*); *Hosp. Dysmas* stands out as the most rigorous effort to do so.[26] While it is Jesus who performs the miracle of the palm in *Ps.-Mt.* 20–21 and the *Leabhar Breac* (and probably implicitly in *Hosp. Oint. Band.* as well), in *Hosp. Dysmas* it is Mary who does so. Most of the stories set during the flight to Egypt describe the bandit being taken with the sight of Jesus during their initial encounter, even if his mother is holding him. But *Hosp. Dysmas* shifts the awe from Jesus to the Theotokos.[27] At the encounter, the bandit's first glance is taken up with the beauty of the Theotokos

---

23. Gounelle notes this as one of "deux traits remarquables" about this story, that "Dysmas mérite à peine sa désignation de larron," showing no evil characteristics whatsoever. He further notes its unique lack of a bad bandit character or any "gang" of bandits. See "Une légende apocryphe," 242.

24. See Bilby, *As the Bandit,* 269–79. Ancient interpreters described the bandit as a tree transplanted into paradise, as a partaker of the fruit and sap of the tree of life, and as foliage of that tree.

25. Bilby, *As the Bandit,* 279–303. By entering into the paradise from which Adam was expelled, the bandit becomes a second Adam together with Christ. Where Adam fell prey to Satan, the bandit was liberated by Christ and along with Christ defeats Satan. Perhaps drawing on the idea that the first Adam was the thief, ancient interpreters also play with the idea of the bandit stealing paradise.

26. Gounelle makes a similar observation, regarding it as the second remarkable trait of this story: "le récit se concentre entièrement sur la personne de Marie; Joseph et Jésus n'y jouent aucun rôle actif et le narrateur omet souvent de les mentionner." See "Une légende apocryphe," 242.

27. Gounelle comes to the same conclusion. See "Une légende apocryphe," 244.

alone—"like a star shining from heaven" (3).[28] Even when *Hosp. Dysmas* has Mary complete her own icon, as it were, by bringing the infant to her bosom, it is the Theotokos herself who remains the focus of his reverence and praise. At the miraculous healing of the leprosy of the bandit's child, *Hosp. Perf. Band.* describes the bandit bowing down to Jesus to worship him as the "Son of God." But in *Hosp. Dysmas* all of the credit and praise is given to Mary, both by the bandit's wife (6) and the bandit himself (7). As in *(Arab.) Gos. Inf.*, the infant becomes a holy object and instrument with which Mary does miracles. A similar shift is found in the blessing of the bandit: typically the blessing comes from Jesus, but in both *Hosp. Dysmas* and *(Arab.) Gos. Inf.*, Mary gives the blessing. In *(Arab.) Gos. Inf.*, however, Mary's blessing is the forgiveness of sins, and appended to this blessing is Jesus' own prediction of the bandit's future beatitude whereas in *Hosp. Dysmas* Mary promises the bandit a reward at an indefinite time in the future—a reward that turns out to be his shared death and eternal life with Jesus—and the infant Jesus is silent. Mary's centrality in *Hosp. Dysmas* becomes even more striking when contrasted with her role in other, roughly contemporaneous stories about the bandit: the *Leabhar Breac* has no named part or action for Mary at all in regard to its story of the bandit's friendship with Jesus, Aelred notes Mary's presence but reserves no active role for her, and in *Reb. Dimas* Mary is too afraid even to speak.

Original Language, Date, and Provenance

The only known forms of the text are Greek, and there is no reason to doubt that Greek was the original language. Gounelle situates its composition between the last half of the twelfth century (the creation of M2) and the fourteenth or fifteenth century (the dates of the *Hosp. Dysmas* MSS).[29]

A comparison of *Hosp. Dysmas* with other legends about the bandit provides additional support for Gounelle's postulated range of dates. On the one hand, Eastern legends supply a variety of potential influences. While *Hosp. Dysmas* does not share the pilgrimage features of *Vis. Theo.* (ca. 6th cent.),[30] it does share a similar preoccupation with hospitality—in *Vis. Theo.* the Holy Family cannot find hospitality in Egypt in anyone's home. *Hosp. Dysmas* (as well as *Hosp. Oint. Band.* and *Hosp. Perf. Band.*) resolves this problem by making the bandit into a family man and agent of hospitality. *Hosp. Dysmas* may very well rely upon the Syriac *Hist. Virg.* (ca. 8th cent.) for its repeated trope of the leprosy-healing bath as well as for its precedent of Mary giving the bandit a blessing. *Hosp. Dysmas* may borrow from *(Apocr.) Gos. John* (ca. 10th/11th cent.) the idea of the bandit accompanying Mary to protect her. These parallels suggest that *Hosp. Dysmas* had a Byzantine Greek provenance and a close affinity to other Eastern Christian communities. It also confirms the plausibility of Gounelle's *terminus a quo* in the last half of the twelfth century, though an earlier date for the original story is worth consideration.

---

28. Cf. *Vis. Theo.*, in which the pseudonymous narrator (Theophilus of Alexandria) mentions that he was utterly "bewildered" by a vision of Mary coming to him, "so dazzling that I believed that the sun itself was shining on me"; see Mingana, "*Vision of Theophilus*," 18. The vision begins Mary's account to Theophilus of the flight to Egypt, only a little before the story of their first encounter with the bandits (pp. 19–20).

29. Gounelle, "Une légende apocryphe," 247–48.

30. Mingana, "*Vision of Theophilus*," 3–4, and Gounelle ("Une légende apocryphe," 244) place *Vis. Theo.* in the eleventh century. More recent scholarship places Cyriacus, the possible author of the text, in the sixth century. See René-Georges Coquin, "Cyriacus," *The Coptic Encyclopedia* (ed. Aziz S. Atiya; 8 vols.; New York: Macmillan, 1991), 2:669b–671a. My research shows a close proximity between *Vis. Theo.* and *Hom. Rock*, thus reinforcing the plausibility of a sixth-century date.

The relationship of *Hosp. Dysmas* to Western legends may allow for a firmer *terminus ad quem*. The tradition that the bandit was a child when he encountered the infant Jesus (as in Aelred, the *Leabhar Breac*, and *Reb. Dimas*) is well in evidence by the twelfth century. While *Hosp. Dysmas* does not recall this motif, it may reflect a related effort to assert the bandit's innocence and good character. Accounts of the hospitality of the bandit as a family man appear concurrently in fourteenth-century manuscripts in the other two texts that belong to this cluster: *Hosp. Oint. Band.* and *Hosp. Perf. Band.*, and both stories seem to rely upon *Hosp. Dysmas*. Indeed, *Hosp. Oint. Band.* significantly expands and intensifies certain aspects of the common storyline, narrating two encounters with the bandits (thus two occasions of hospitality), making the bandit personally oversee this hospitality, and weaving in an extra story about miraculous ointment. *Hosp. Perf. Band.* also presumes the same basic plot, but it weaves in a story about special perfume given to the bandit and ties it to the story of Mary Magdalene. The Western witnesses provide a date range from the late eleventh century to the early fourteenth century, with a twelfth-/thirteenth-century setting most likely.

Translation

Despite the complicated nature of the relationships of the major manuscripts, there is a reasonable basis to attempt to establish an *editio princeps*. The translation and notes below reflect such an attempt, based on a fresh collation of those manuscripts. This is the first published translation of *Hosp. Dysmas* into English, but the second translation into a modern language, Gounelle's French translation being the first. The text is divided into nine short verses with the numbering of Gounelle's Byzantine *Acts Pil.* M2 recension given in parentheses.

Sigla

B	Paris, Bibliothèque nationale de France, gr. 808
D	Oxford, Bodleian Library, Holkham gr. 24
Tb	Vatican, Biblioteca apostolica, Ottoboni gr. 411
H1	The postulated common ancestor of BD and Tb
H2	The postulated common ancestor of B and D reconstructed by Rémi Gounelle

Bibliography

EDITIONS AND TRANSLATIONS

Gounelle, Rémi. "Une légende apocryphe relatant la rencontre du bon larron et de la sainte famille en Égypte (*BHG* 2119y)." *AnBoll* 121 (2003): 241–72.
Huidekoper, Frederic. *Acts of Pilate from a Transcript of the Codex Designated by Thilo as Paris D.* Cambridge: Cambridge University Press, 1887.

STUDIES

Bilby, Mark Glen. *As the Bandit Will I Confess You: Luke 23:39–43 in Early Christian Interpretation.* Cahiers de Biblia Patristica 13. Strasbourg: University of Strasbourg; Turnhout: Brepols, 2013. (Further bibliography may be found here.)
Geerard, Maurice. "Gute Schächer: Ein neues unediertes Apokryphon." Pages 85–89 in *La spiritualité de l'univers byzantin dans le verbe et l'image.* Edited by Kristoffel Demoen and Jeannine Vereecken. Instrumenta Patristica 30. Steenbrugis: In Abbatia S. Petri; Turnhout: Brepols, 1997.

————. "Le bon larron, un apocryphe inédit." Pages 355–63 in vol. 2 of *Philologia Sacra: Biblische und patristische Studien für Hermann J. Frede und Walter Thiele zu ihrem siebzigsten Geburtstag*. Edited by Roger Gryson. 2 vols. Vetus Latina: Aus der Geschichte der lateinischen Bibel 24. Freiburg: Herder, 1993.

Gounelle, Rémi. *Les recensions byzantines de l'Évangile de Nicodème*. CCSA Instrumenta 3. Turnhout: Brepols, 2008.

The Hospitality of Dysmas[a]

Introduction

[1](10.2.2a)[b] At the (time of) the birth of Christ—which was thirty-three years prior[c]—a voice went out through[d] an angel to Joseph for him to take the infant and his mother, the supremely holy[e] Mistress[f] Theotokos, and for them to flee Jerusalem[g] of Judea, to leave[h] to Egypt for fear of Herod, when[i] he had ordered that all[j] the infants found who were three years old and below be killed.[k] All this took place in order for them to kill Jesus.[l] At that time, Joseph took[m] the infant and his mother, and he went[n] to Egypt, while a donkey trotted alongside them to carry them by turns down the road.

Matt 2:13

Matt 2:16

Matt 2:14

A date-palm bows to Mary

[2](10.2.2b) As he drew near to the area of[o] Egypt, both Joseph and the Theotokos were hungry. Immediately, they saw a fruitful and fully ripe date-palm.[p] Then the Theotokos said,[q] "Bend, my good tree, and grant us[r] some of your

---

a. B and D share the title "About the bandit on the right," while Tb is more descriptive: "It is still said that such a wonder happened in regard to the faithful bandit Dysmas."

b. B adds a hortatory preface: "Now listen to yet another story concerning this bandit on the right." D identifies the main character and his name at the outset: "This is the bandit Dysmas."

c. Tb omits the reference to Christ's birth and the thirty-three years between the birth and crucifixion.

d. Tb: "from."

e. Tb: "all-holy."

f. D lacks *despoina* (mistress, lady, queen, princess), which seems odd in view of its repeated, unique appearances in D later. In the interest of consistency, subsequent uses of this title will be translated as "Mistress," while *kuria* will be translated "Lady."

g. Tb lacks "Jerusalem."

h. D: "to depart," conforming the lemma to Matt 2:13–14.

i. D: "because."

j. B and Tb opt for *hola,* while D conforms to the Matthean use of *pantas* (here *panta*).

k. B adds "by tarring (them)."

l. B adds "Christ." Tb piously substitutes "the infant of the Theotokos."

m. Instead of saying that "Joseph took the infant and his mother," B recounts that "after being warned by the angel to do this, Joseph led the infant and his mother."

n. B: "they went."

o. D lacks "the area of."

p. Tb adds "tree" after "date-palm," using the latter as an adjective rather than a noun.

q. In the parallel tale from *Ps.-Mt.* 20 it is Jesus who orders the tree to bend down.

r. D: "me."

Ps.-Mt. 20; *Birth Sav.* 111

ripe[a] fruit." After (she spoke) this word, the tree immediately bent,[b] and they took of its fruit as much as they needed to eat.[c] And[d] again the tree stood up just as before. Then they again traveled[e] the road.[f]

Dysmas bows to Mary

3(10.2.2c) When they had passed a little farther,[g] they met this bandit, that is to say,[h] Dysmas. When the bandit saw the Theotokos, he was amazed by her beauty—like a star shining from heaven.[i] And when she held the infant on her breast,[j] the bandit also came near[k] and bowed down to her, even though he did not know that she was the Theotokos. He said,[l] "In truth, (my) Lady, if God had a mommy,[m] I would want to say[n] that it is you."[o] And he invited her, along with Joseph,[p] to come to his house.

Birth Sav. 117

Dysmas shows hospitality to Mary

4(10.2.2d) He brought them to his house and entrusted them to his wife,[q] saying, "Wife, I am leaving for the hunt.[r] As for you, show them hospitality—as much as you can to do them honor—until I am recalled[s] from the hunt[t] and we pay

---

a. D: "most ripe."

b. D has only "And it immediately bent."

c. D: "as much as they wanted."

d. Tb instead starts this sentence with, "Now after they had eaten."

e. Tb: "moved to travel."

f. D lacks this sentence. Tb restates, "Then they again started to travel the road."

g. Tb lacks this transitional clause.

h. Tb: "whose name was."

i. Tb piously clarifies that Mary herself was "shining like a star giving light from heaven." The construction in B and D is ambiguous about whether Mary or her beauty is the antecedent of the participial phrase.

j. D: "in her elbows/arms," apparently a pious emendation.

k. B: "the bandit was again amazed by this wonder, and he drew near." D instead says, "As the bandit came with fear and trembling," a stock biblical phrase found in Mark 5:33, 1 Cor 2:3, and elsewhere.

l. B adds "of the Theotokos." Tb clarifies that he spoke "to her."

m. Following the vulgarism in B, *manna*, which D and Tb both emend (whether for reasons of piety, clarification, or both) to *mētera* (mother).

n. D and Tb read "I would have said," though in different forms.

o. Tb: "that you are the mother of God."

p. D adds "and their entourage," though it makes no mention of any other characters elsewhere in the narrative, nor gives any indication as to their identity. The idea that others joined the Holy Family during the sojourn to Egypt also appears in *Vis. Theo.* (Salome), *Hom. Rock* (Salome and Dionius the carpenter), *Hosp. Oint. Band.* (a "large group"), and *Leabhar Breac* 124 (a company of twelve, all named).

q. D lacks most of this sentence, abruptly transitioning the scene to the bandit's house by introducing his speech to his wife: "And the bandit said to his spouse."

r. D lacks this prefatory remark, starting the speech with the following command, "Wife, show them hospitality." Tb only lacks "Wife."

s. D simplifies: "I come."

t. Tb entirely lacks this sentence up to this point. D relocates here the references to the hunt being "of wild animals" and "according to custom" that conclude this section in B and Tb.

the noblest honor to this noble foreigner.[a] For, as it would appear, she[b] is from the noblest lineage." Then the bandit departed to hunt wild animals, according to custom.[c]

The healing of the bandit's child

[5](10.2.2e) Now he had a child,[d] and it was leprous from birth. It was inconsolable; that is to say,[e] it never stopped crying.[f] Now this wife of the bandit made hot (water)[g] to bathe the infant of the Theotokos.[h] After she had first bathed the child Jesus,[i] she also bathed her own leprous[j] child from the water left over from Jesus.[k] And immediately the child was healed from leprosy and all manner of its infirmity, and it ceased from crying.[l]

Birth Sav. 117

(Arab.) Gos. Inf. 17–18, 27, 28, 31, 32, 33

The bandit's wife explains the miracle

[6](10.2.2f) Now, when the bandit came from the hunt,[m] they arranged[n] a table and honored her.[o] Now, after they had sat down at the table[p] and had eaten, the bandit remembered[q] his child and said to his wife, "Where is our child?"[r] And

---

a. D lacks "and we pay the noblest honor to this noble foreigner"; and Tb reads "you must do the noblest honor to this noble foreign woman."

b. D piously elaborates: "This same Lady and my Mistress."

c. Tb: "his custom"; B: "just as he had learned." D relocates the rest of this line and attaches it to the previous reference to the hunt (see p. 48 n. t).

d. B expands and clarifies: "The same bandit also had his own child." D has "And the bandit had an infant." The child's sex is never specified in any of the Greek MSS.

e. D and Tb lack the sentence up to this point.

f. D: "and it did not stop crying both day and night." Tb: "always crying and not being quiet."

g. Tb has "hot water."

h. Tb clarifies this as the moment when Mary entered the bandit's house and has Mary, rather than the bandit's wife, prepare the hot bath: "After the blessed Theotokos came into the house, she made hot water."

i. Tb substitutes "it" for "the child Jesus." The context of B and its "first . . . also" (*proteron . . . kai*) construction suggests that the bandit's wife, not Mary, bathes Jesus. This raises the problem of a contradiction with the story of the bandit's wife in verse 6, wherein she describes Mary giving Jesus a bath. In Tb, however, Mary not only clearly prepares the bath for Jesus (see above), but also bathes Jesus herself. D removes the entire phrase as well as the reference to Mary giving Jesus a bath in verse 6.

j. D omits "leprous."

k. Tb clarifies that "the bandit's wife" takes over from Mary here in order to wash her own child: "The bandit's wife thoroughly bathed her leprous child in the water left over from the Lord."

l. After the word "immediately," the three MSS vary considerably. Here the reconstruction (H1) follows Gounelle's H2. B is most faithful to H1, but B reverses the order of the reports of healing and silence: "that child ceased from crying and was healed from leprosy and all manner of its infirmity." D adds visual drama and makes the afflictions the subject of the sentence: "his leprosy, along with every infirmity he had, fell off of him, and he ceased from crying." Tb simplifies: "the child was healed from leprosy and ceased from weeping."

m. B has "came to his house"; Tb has only "the bandit arrived."

n. Tb: "prepared."

o. D: "the Mistress."

p. D lacks "at the table."

q. B: "thought about" or "considered."

r. D adds a second question for dramatic effect: "Did he perhaps die?"

she told him,[a] "Know in truth that, just as you enjoined[b] me to show hospitality to this noble woman, I prepared hot (water)[c] in order for her to wash her infant, just as is customary for children.[d] And she bathed her infant, and I washed our child in the afterwash from her son.[e] Immediately, it was healed from every infirmity.[f] And it was at peace, by God's favor,[g] and never wailed much,[h] as had been its custom. As it appears, I think (that)[i] this noble woman[j] is favored by God Most High, and through her favor our child was healed." She brought forth the healed child, peaceful and bright-eyed.[k]

Luke 1:28, 30

The bandit devotes himself to Mary

[7](10.2.2g) When the bandit saw it,[l] he was amazed from[m] this wonder. And he said, "(I swear) by the Most High, because I did not hear its crying,[n] I thought[o] that it had passed away from this world.[p] And I think in truth that this (is a) noble woman[q] who has come to us[r] to keep[s] many prayers from God Most High." He bowed down to her and thanked her profusely, and he did whatever he could through her[t] for as long as she[u] was[v] in the area of Egypt.

The bandit's protection and Mary's reward

Matt 2:21

[8](10.2.2h) Now after[w] her sojourn, in order for her to come[x] again to Judea, that is to say, to Jerusalem,[y] the bandit accompanied her[z] with all exceeding joy and

---

a. D: "His wife said what happened."

b. Tb: "commanded."

c. Tb has "hot water."

d. Tb: "so that she might bathe her child, as is the custom of infants."

e. Tb: "After she had washed it, I also washed our child in that water of the afterwash."

f. B ends with: "as has been said."

g. D lacks the wife's entire speech and states only: "His wife said what happened. For this reason it was at peace, by God's favor."

h. Tb: "did not wail altogether."

i. Tb improves the syntax: "Therefore, as it appears to me, . . ."

j. Tb simplifies: "this woman."

k. Again abbreviating the narrative, D omits most of this sentence and combines it with the previous one: "through her our child will be bright-eyed." Tb shortens this sentence a little: "Then she brought it forth, bright-eyed and healthy."

l. D: "saw it thus happy and healthy." B: "saw his child healthy."

m. Tb: "by."

n. B adds "as always." Tb restates: "on account of not hearing it crying."

o. Tb relocates the initial oath formula ("by the Most High") here.

p. D lacks this entire sentence from the bandit's direct speech.

q. Tb: "this woman"; D: "this Mistress and Lady."

r. D lacks "who has come to us."

s. Tb: "has procured."

t. Tb: "for her."

u. D: "the Theotokos."

v. B: "patiently endured."

w. B: "And on."

x. To this point, D reads: "Now after the Theotokos turned back."

y. In keeping with its omission of Jerusalem as the journey's origin (v. 1), Tb entirely omits the reference to Jerusalem as the specific destination. It significantly abbreviates the opening sentence of this section to this point, reading only: "Now after her return."

z. BD: "the Theotokos." The narrative's intent to focus on Mary displaces any stated role for

honor. And he scouted ahead of her[a] to see her away from every treacherous, dangerous, and difficult area.[b] When they drew near to a good[c] area, he penitently begged[d] her to return to his house. And he thanked her with a completely honorable thanksgiving. And the All-Pure said,[e] "Go in peace. I wish that at the proper moment the reward for what you did for us will return to you."[f]

Birth Sav. 118, 124

Conclusion

[9](10.2.2i) Now behold such a bandit![g] The one who did such things—whatever things were commanded him—was made worthy through the favor of the merciful Christ and his mother so that he would become a martyr[h] on the cross together with Christ.[i] And he spoke as it was said,[j] "*Remember me*, Lord, *when you come in your kingdom.*" Then Jesus said,[k] "*Truly*[l] *I tell you, today you will be with me in paradise.*"[m]

Birth Sav. 125

Luke 23:42–43

Joseph even in this return narrative, which has its originating impulse in Matthew's Joseph-focused story.

a. B: "And he led and was her advance-party."

b. Tb: "to guard her away from every treacherous and difficult thing." D: "to guard her away from a treacherous and uneven and wooded place."

c. BD: "good and straight."

d. BD lit. "he made penance of her." Tb: "he bowed down to her."

e. D: "And the all-pure Theotokos replied."

f. D clarifies that Mary herself will give the reward: "I will recompense the reward to you." Tb replaces her words with indirect speech: "to go in peace but her only-begotten son would give the reward to him at the proper moment indeed." But then Tb shifts to direct speech adding, "just as you did for us."

g. D begins with a different sort of brief summary: "For this reason he was made worthy even at this (time)," i.e., the time of the crucifixion. Tb omits this phrase.

h. Or "bear witness."

i. Tb significantly reframes this entire sentence, and thereby the conclusion to the whole story: "Therefore, the bandit who did so many and such evil things." It turns the laudatory reference to his good deeds into an occasion to substantiate the bandit's evil past. It thus apparently conforms the bandit's story to the criminal's confession in Luke 23:41, but in doing so departs considerably from the bandit's consistently positive character portrayal in the rest of this story. It also removes any mention of the bandit being made worthy of his reward.

j. D clarifies: "as the Scripture said." Tb attributes the bandit's confession to his recognition and accompanying confession of Christ, "And, since he recognized him on the cross, he cried out in a clear voice."

k. B may describe Jesus responding antiphonally to the bandit, or else it clarifies the fulfillment of Mary's wish: "And Jesus spoke to him about what was set forth." Tb rephrases, "Therefore, he heard from the Savior."

l. Tb adds a second "truly."

m. Tb adds a concluding reference to 1 Tim 6:12, an intertext that may evoke the traditional trope of the bandit as a martyr: "Therefore, through such a good confession, he became a partaker of the divine kingdom."

The Infancy Gospel of Thomas (Syriac)
A new translation and introduction

by Tony Burke

The *Infancy Gospel of Thomas* (*Inf. Gos. Thom.*; *CANT* 57) is a collection of tales of wonders, some destructive, performed by Jesus from the ages of five to twelve. Because of its attribution to the apostle Thomas, scholars believed for centuries that the text was the "Gospel of Thomas" labeled as gnostic by early church writers. Since the gospel did not contain any of the readings from the "Gospel of Thomas" cited in antiquity, it was thought that *Inf. Gos. Thom.* originally must have been a much longer text, filled with gnostic sayings and cosmogonic myths expurgated by orthodox editors. With the discovery of the actual *Gospel of Thomas* in 1945, *Inf. Gos. Thom.* was set free from its association with Gnosticism; nevertheless, some readers and scholars continue to confuse the texts. Such problems would be alleviated to some degree if greater attention is paid to the Syriac tradition of the text. The Syriac is an extremely early version of the gospel, far closer to the original, shorter form of this writing than the version appearing in most collections of the Christian apocrypha. This form of the gospel is not ascribed to the apostle Thomas—it bears the title, "The Childhood of the Lord Jesus"—nor can it be regarded as "gnostic" in any meaningful sense.

Contents
Inf. Gos. Thom. is most widely known in the nineteen-chapter form referred to as the Greek A recension. In this longer version, the gospel begins with an introduction ascribing the text to "Thomas the Israelite Philosopher," presumably intended to be the apostle of the same name. Then Jesus appears, playing with other children by a stream. From the mud he creates twelve birds and brings them to life (2). The son of Annas "the scribe" disturbs Jesus' work and is maimed as a result (3). Then Jesus murders another boy in the marketplace (4) and, when some villagers criticize him for it, Jesus blinds them (5). Seeking to correct his unruly behavior, a teacher named Zacchaeus tries to teach him letters (6) but he is humbled by Jesus' superior knowledge (7). When Zacchaeus admits his ignorance, Jesus restores to health those he cursed (8). Jesus then performs a series of beneficent miracles: he revives a boy who dies after falling from a roof (9), and heals a young man's foot (10); at the age of seven he carries water to his mother in a cloak (11) and reaps a miraculous harvest after sowing only a handful of seeds (12); then, at eight years old he helps his father by stretching a beam for a bed (13). Jesus returns to his maleficent ways when Joseph once again takes him to learn letters. At the school, another teacher becomes frustrated with Jesus and, like Zacchaeus, strikes him on the head; in response, Jesus kills him and returns to his home (14). A third teacher tries to teach Jesus, but once he recognizes that the boy does not need instruction, the teacher defers to Jesus' greater knowledge and the boy revives the previous teacher (15). Three more healings follow: Je-

sus saves his brother James from a snakebite (16), and then he revives a dead baby (17) and a housebuilder (18). The text concludes with a retelling of the story of the twelve-year-old Jesus in the temple from Luke 2:41–52 (19).

Many scholars have seen in the nineteen-chapter form of *Inf. Gos. Thom* a progression in Jesus' behavior from cursing to blessing. The Syriac tradition, however, features a number of significant departures from the longer form of the text—most notably the absence of the introduction ascribing the text to Thomas and several of the healing miracles (chaps. 10, 17, and 18). The study of the various early versions of the gospel has shown that the Syriac text's arrangement of the stories is more representative of the gospel's original contents. If so, the author of *Inf. Gos. Thom.* does not regard Jesus' curses as a defect in his behavior in need of rehabilitation. Instead, they are one of several ways the text demonstrates the power, authority, and wisdom possessed by Jesus even when only a child.

Manuscripts and Versions

Inf. Gos. Thom. is extant in a number of languages and forms.[1] Several of these forms have become entrenched in scholarship through the critical edition of Constantin Tischendorf, who published four versions of the text:

1. Greek A, based on four manuscripts: Bologna, Biblioteca Universitaria, 2702 (15th cent.); Dresden, Sächsische Landesbibliothek, A 187 (16th cent.); and two fragmentary witnesses: Paris, Bibliothèque nationale de France, ancien fonds gr. 239 (1422/1423) and Vienna, Österreichische Nationalbibliothek, Philos. gr. 162 (144) (before 1455).[2]
2. Greek B, a shorter text containing only chapters 1–11 and 13, based on Mount Sinai, St. Catherine's Monastery, gr. 453 (14th/15th cent.).[3]
3. The First Latin version from a fragmentary palimpsest, Vienna, Österreichische Nationalbibliothek, lat. 563 (5th cent.) and in an appendix to later manuscripts of the *Gospel of Pseudo-Matthew.*[4]
4. The Second Latin version, which prefaces the nineteen-chapter form with three chapters on the Holy Family in Egypt, based on Vatican, Biblioteca apostolica, lat. 4578 (13th/14th cent.).[5]

Greek A, B, and the Second Latin version have been very popular in scholarship; Elliott's collection, for example, follows the common practice of including translations of the two Greek forms and the Second Latin's Egyptian prologue.[6]

Tischendorf and his contemporaries were surprised that *Inf. Gos. Thom.*, then known simply as the "Gospel of Thomas," contained no observable gnostic elements. They assumed

---

1. For comprehensive discussion of all presently known forms of the text see Burke, *De infantia Iesu,* 127–71.

2. Tischendorf, *Evangelia Apocrypha,* 140–57.

3. Tischendorf, *Evangelia Apocrypha,* 158–63.

4. Tischendorf, *Evangelia Apocrypha,* xliv–xlvi, 93–112. Additional lines from the palimpsest were restored by Guy Philippart in "Fragments palimpsestes latins du Vindobonensis 563 (Ve siècle?): Évangile selon S. Matthieu, Évangile de Nicodème, Évangile de l'Enfance selon Thomas," *AnBoll* 90 (1972): 391–411. The determination that the palimpsest was related to *Ps.-Mt.* was made by Voicu, "Verso il testo primitivo," 29–34.

5. Tischendorf, *Evangelia Apocrypha,* 164–80.

6. *ANT,* 68–71.

as a result that the text had been edited of these elements over the centuries. This "expurgation theory" was eventually called into question with the publication of additional versions of the text. The first of these was the Syriac tradition. W. Wright published the first Syriac manuscript in 1865: a sixth-century manuscript from the British Library in London (Add. 14484, fol. 14v–18v; =W).[7] Despite the antiquity of W, the manuscript initially made little impact on scholarship because it contains a shorter text—chapters 1, 10, 17, and 18 are missing, and many of the extant chapters are shorter, except for chapter 6 which contains material absent from Tischendorf's Greek texts—and therefore looked to be even more expurgated than the Greek and Latin versions. Nevertheless, the extra material from chapter 6 often appears in Christian apocrypha collections as an appendix to translations of Tischendorf's Greek A text. A second Syriac source appeared in E. A. W. Budge's 1899 edition of the East Syriac *Hist. Virg.* (= Se). Budge published this text from two manuscripts, one of which (a copy of a 13th-/14th-century MS from Alqoš; now lost) contains several chapters from *Inf. Gos. Thom.* (4, 6–8, 11–16) based on the same Syriac translation as W, though with some developments. A third witness, Göttingen Universitätsbibliothek, Syr. 10, fol. 1v–4v (5th/6th cent.; =G) first came to light in a brief notice by H. Duensing in 1911.[8] Some readings from the manuscript were subsequently used by A. Meyer to construct his translation of *Inf. Gos. Thom.* for the 1924 edition of E. Hennecke's *Neutestamentliche Apokryphen.*[9] The full text of G did not see publication until a 1993 article by W. Baars and J. Heldermann.[10] A reading of their collation shows that G is very similar to W and, though it has some omissions (5:2, 6:1, 6:2d–2e, 7:2, and chaps. 14 and 15), it is valuable because it contains some material missing from W (most notably parts of 7:1, 3). Finally, a fourth Syriac manuscript was noted in P. Peeters's 1914 discussion of infancy gospels.[11] He found a Garšūnī manuscript of the *Arabic Infancy Gospel* (Vatican, Bibliotheca apostolica, syr. 159, fol. 237r–239v; dated 1622/23; =P) with *Inf. Gos. Thom.* appended in Syriac. Unfortunately, Peeters presented only chapters 5–8 of the text and only in French translation.[12]

As the various new Syriac sources were appearing in scholarship, a number of other versions of *Inf. Gos. Thom.* also saw publication:

1. Greek D, based on Athens, Ethnike Bibliotheke, gr. 355 (15th cent.). This third Greek recension includes the Egyptian prologue, thus situating it as the antecedent of the Second Latin form.[13]
2. The Slavonic tradition, comprised of sixteen manuscripts and ultimately originating in a tenth/eleventh-century translation from Greek A.[14]

---

7. Wright, *Contributions*, 11–16 (in Syriac page-numbering; text), 6–11 (translation).

8. Hugo Duensing, "Mitteilungen 58," *TLZ* 36 (1911): 637.

9. Arnold Meyer, "Kindheitserzählung des Thomas," in *Neutestamentliche Apokryphen* (ed. Edgar Hennecke; 2nd ed.; Tübingen: J. C. B. Mohr, 1924), 93–94.

10. Baars and Heldermann, "Neue Materielen," 194–97. Additional pages from the same MS have surfaced among the new finds from St. Catharine's Monastery; see Alain Desreumaux, "Deux anciens manuscrits syriaques d'oeuvres apocryphes dans le nouveau fonds de Sainte-Catherine du Sinaï: La *Vie de la Vierge* et Les *Actes d'André et Mathias*," *Apocrypha* 20 (2009): 115–36.

11. Peeters, *Évangiles apocryphes*, i–lix.

12. Peeters, *Évangiles apocryphes*, 304–8.

13. Published by Armand Delatte, "Évangile de l'enfance de Jacques: Manuscrit No. 355 de la Bibliothèque Nationale," in *Anecdota Atheniensia*, vol. 1, *Textes grecs inédits relatifs à l'histoire des religions* (ed. Armand Delatte; Paris: Edouard Champion, 1927), 264–71.

14. For an overview of the manuscripts and scholarship on the text see the edition of Thomas Rosén,

3. A version in Irish verse created ca. 800 from the First Latin text.[15]
4. The Ethiopic tradition, found in twenty-five manuscripts of the seventeenth-nineteenth centuries.[16]
5. A Georgian manuscript: Tblisi, National Center of Manuscripts, Cod. A 95 (10th cent.).[17]
6. An Arabic translation in Milan, Biblioteca Ambrosiana, G 11 sup. (undated).[18]

The latter four versions, along with the Syriac, became important for the study of *Inf. Gos. Thom.* when L. van Rompay compared their readings and demonstrated effectively that they were witnesses to an earlier, and better, form of the text that lacked chapters 1, 10, 17, and 18.[19] With this determination, it looked as if the Greek tradition would recede into the background in text-critical work on the text. But yet another discovery, Jerusalem, Bibliotheke tou Patriarcheiou, 259 (11th cent.=Greek S), provided us with a Greek text in a position intermediary between the early versions and the later Greek, Latin, and Slavonic traditions.[20] Like the early versions, this new Greek recension lacks chapters 17 and 18 but contains chapter 1 and places chapter 10 between 16 and 19. Many of its readings also agree better with those of the early versions than the later traditions.[21]

Of all these early versions, the Syriac is perhaps the most important. Two of the manuscripts are of considerable antiquity (5th/6th cent.) and, unlike the Georgian and First Latin traditions, it provides us with a complete text of the gospel. The text of the Syriac tradition also has been much improved recently with the editing and publication of several additional manuscripts. In 2013, T. Burke published Peeters's Vatican manuscript and compared its readings against those of W, G, and a fourth witness (Edgbaston, University of Birmingham, Mingana Syr. 105, fol. 27v–29v; 1832/1833; =M).[22] Burke also provided a list of additional sources for the East Syriac *Hist. Virg.*, two of which contain the *Inf. Gos. Thom.* material: Edgbaston, University of Birmingham, Mingana Syr. 502 (1836), and

---

The Slavonic Translation of the Apocryphal Infancy Gospel of Thomas (Acta Universitatis Upsaliensis, Studia Slavica Upsaliensia 39; Uppsala: Almqvist & Wiksell, 1997).

15. For the most recent translation see Máire Herbert and Martin McNamara, "A Versified Narrative of the Childhood Deeds of the Lord Jesus," in *Apocrypha Hiberniae*, vol. 1, *Evangelia Infantiae* (ed. Martin McNamara et al.; CCSA 13; Turnhout: Brepols, 2001), 443–83.

16. Published on the basis of three manuscripts by Sylvain Grébaut, "Les miracles de Jésus: Texte éthiopien publié et traduit," *PO* 12, no. 4 (1919): 555–652.

17. Gérard Garitte, "Le fragment géorgien de l'Évangile de Thomas," *RHE* 51 (1956): 511–20.

18. Sergio Noja, "L'Évangile arabe apocryphe de Thomas, de la 'Biblioteca Ambrosiana' de Milan (G 11 sup)," in *Biblische und Judistische Studien: Festschrift für Paolo Sacchi* (ed. Angelo Vivian; Judentum und Umwelt 29; Paris: Peter Lang, 1990), 681–90; idem, "À propos du texte arabe d'un évangile apocryphe de Thomas de la Ambrosiana de Milan," in *YAD-NAMA: in memoria di Alessandro Bausani* (ed. Biancamana Scarcia Amoretti and Lucia Rostagno; 2 vols.; Rome: Bardi Editore, 1991), 1:335–41.

19. Lucas van Rompay, "De ethiopische versie van het Kindsheidsevangelie volgens Thomas de Israëliet," in *Enfant dans les civilisations orientales* (ed. Aristide Théodoridès, Paul Naster, and Julien Riesl; Leuven: Peeters, 1980), 119–32.

20. The manuscript was first mentioned in scholarship by Jacques Noret ("Pour une édition de l'Évangile de l'enfance selon Thomas," *AnBoll* 90 [1972]: 412); its significance for the study of the text was recognized by Sever J. Voicu in "Notes sur l'histoire du texte de l'*Histoire de l'enfance de Jésus*," *Apocrypha* 2 (1991): 119–32. An edition and translation is available in Burke, *De infantia Iesu*, 301–37, and another in Aasgaard, *Childhood of Jesus*, 219–41. Burke's volume also contains new editions and translations of the Greek A, B, and D recensions incorporating additional manuscript discoveries.

21. Burke, *De infantia Iesu*, 196–97; *contra* Voicu, "Verso il testo primitivo," 26–27.

22. Burke, "Unpublished Syriac Manuscript."

Mingana Syr. 122 (1670).[23] The second of these contains also chapters 5 and 19, making it a better witness to the branch of the tradition than Budge's Alqoš Ms. Burke also called attention to another group of witnesses: a West Syriac *Life of Mary* compilation (= Sw) containing the complete *Inf. Gos. Thom.* as the fourth of six books.[24] This collection is extant in a number of manuscripts:[25]

Cambridge, University Library, Add. 2001, fol. 57r–65r (1480–1481)
Cambridge (Mass.), Harvard Houghton Library, Syr. 35, fol. 60r–67r (16th/17th cent.)
Cambridge (Mass.), Harvard Houghton Library, Syr. 39, fol. 155v–162v (1857)
Cambridge (Mass.), Harvard Houghton Library, Syr. 59, fol. 86r–94r (1857)
Cambridge (Mass.), Harvard Houghton Library, Syr. 82, fol. 74v–84r (17th/18th cent.)
Cambridge (Mass.), Harvard Houghton Library, Syr. 129, fol. 20r –25r (17th cent.)
Edgbaston, University of Birmingham, Mingana Syr. 5, fol. 18v–26v (1479)
Edgbaston, University of Birmingham, Mingana Syr. 48, fol. 29r–32v (1906, but copied
    in part from a manuscript of 1757)
Edgbaston, University of Birmingham, Mingana Syr. 560, fol. 60v–67v (1491)
Lebanon, Syro-Catholic Monastery of Charfet, Fonds Rahmani 42, fol. 56v–63v (1495)
Mardin, Za'faran Monastery, 393, p. 78–88 (20th cent.)
Paris, Bibliothèque nationale de France, syr. 377, fol. 145r–154v (1854/1855)
Vatican, Bibliotheca apostolica, syr. 537, fol. 64r–71r (16th cent.)

An additional manuscript—Diyarbakir, Meryem Ana Syriac Orthodox Church, 99 (1728–1731)[26]—has been catalogued but today its whereabouts are unknown. The text is extant also in four Garšūnī manuscripts:

Edgbaston, University of Birmingham, Mingana Syr. 39, fol. 70v–73r (1773)
Edgbaston, University of Birmingham, Mingana Syr. 114, fol. 56–67 (1901)
Lebanon, Syro-Catholic Monastery of Charfet, Fonds Rahmani 48 (15/16th cent.)
Vatican, Bibliotheca apostolica, syr. 561, fol. 33r (1683; fragmentary)

The Syriac *Inf. Gos. Thom.* has a rich, but rather uncomplicated manuscript tradition. The most important witnesses remain W, G, P, and M. These can be used to establish with some certainty the original form of the Syriac text, an extremely valuable resource for establishing the earliest form of the gospel.

---

23. An earlier list of several unpublished MSS is found in Mimouni, "Vies de la Vierge," 241 n. 135.

24. See also Naffah, "Les 'histoires' syriaques de la Vierge," 161–66; Mimouni, "Vies de la Vierge," 239 n. 128.

25. Four additional *Life of Mary* manuscripts are known to scholars but these all lack book four: Syro-Catholic Monastery of Charfet, Fonds Rahmani 60 (19th cent.; contains book five only); Cambridge (Mass.), Harvard Houghton Library, Syr. 36 (16th/17th cent.; contains only books five and six); Edgbaston, University of Birmingham, Mingana Syr. 184 (1637; contains only the end of book six); and Vatican, Bibliotheca apostolica, Borgia syr. 128 (1720; book four alone is missing).

26. This seems to be identical to Mardin, Chaldean Bishopric, 80 (also considered lost), which shares the same folio numbers and dimensions.

Literary and Theological Importance

Before the publication of the *Gospel of Thomas*, *Inf. Gos. Thom.* was believed to have been a product of gnostic Christianity. For the most part, scholars have abandoned this identification and have begun examining the text in new and interesting ways. Attention to the Syriac tradition, along with the other early versions, has also helped to determine the author's inspirations and intentions.

Modern readers of *Inf. Gos. Thom.* are troubled often by its portrayal of Jesus as a miscreant who curses those around him. Medieval copyists seem to have felt a similar discomfort and transformed the text in a variety of ways in order to rehabilitate the young wonderworker. This is seen most dramatically in a series of additions to the text, including an expansion of the curse of the son of Annas (chap. 3) in which the villagers reproach Joseph for having "such a child," two additions to chapters 11 and 13 in which Joseph and Mary praise Jesus, an epilogue to the third teacher story in which Jesus restores the second teacher to life, and three new chapters (10, 17, and 18) in which Jesus heals a variety of villagers in stories reminiscent of Synoptic-Gospel pericopae. The weight of these additions has contributed to a view that the gospel shows a development in Jesus' character—from one who curses to one who blesses. But without these transformations, *Inf. Gos. Thom.* appears less interested in rehabilitating Jesus than in effecting change among those around Jesus, from a lack of understanding of his divinity to a recognition that "this one is something great—either a god, or an angel" (7:4). The later Greek (and related) traditions also alter the text's Christology by adding Johannine phrases to several of the chapters (such as miracles as "signs" and God as "the one who sent me to you"), particularly in the speech of Jesus from chapter 6. But the original text appears to have been indebted primarily to Luke-Acts, a text that particularly celebrates the image of the Christian holy man as one who curses as well as blesses (e.g., Acts 5:1–11; 13:6–11; and perhaps even the woes from the Sermon on the Plain in Luke 6:24–26). This reliance on Luke-Acts contributes to the argument for an early dating for *Inf. Gos. Thom.*, before the blending of the Christology of the four canonical Gospels in Christian theology.

The abandonment of the theme of character development aids also in situating *Inf. Gos. Thom.* in its appropriate literary context. R. Hock demonstrated effectively that the gospel is an example of ancient biography.[27] The goal of these biographies was to illustrate that the given text's subject displayed the same abilities in youth for which he or she is known in adulthood. To the ancients, character was static; it did not change over the course of one's lifetime. Therefore, the Jesus of *Inf. Gos. Thom.* curses as a child because the author must have felt the adult Jesus did the same; and such behavior is not unprecedented—in the canonical Gospels, Jesus curses a fig tree (Mark 11:12–14, 20–21//Matt 21:18–21) and utters woes (Luke 6:24–26; Luke 10:13–15//Matt 11:21–23).[28] This determination helps to understand better the gospel's relationship to Luke. With its view of Jesus as an irascible young holy man and its culmination in Luke 2 in chapter 19, *Inf. Gos. Thom.* may have been written specifically to fill in details in the life of Jesus considered "absent" in Luke.[29]

---

27. Hock, *Infancy Gospels*, 95–97 and developed further by Burke, *De infantia Iesu*, 268–84.

28. Early readers of *Inf. Gos. Thom.* seem to have been less sensitive to the text's portrayal of a cursing Jesus than modern readers. John Chrysostom (*Hom. Jo.* 17), the earliest writer to comment on the text, objects only that Jesus performing childhood miracles seemingly contradicts John 1:31 (how could John "not know him" if Jesus performed such wonders?), and other writers (e.g., Anastasius Sinaita, *Hodegos* 13) reject the text because it contradicts John 2:11, which states that Jesus' first miracle was as an adult in Cana.

29. For more on the relationship between *Inf. Gos. Thom.* and Luke see Tony Chartrand-Burke, "Com-

The combination of the two texts thus presents Christians with a biography of Jesus more consistent, and more competitive, with typical birth-to-death biographies in antiquity.

Though never considered a candidate for inclusion in any known canon of Christian texts, *Inf. Gos. Thom.* was still a popular enough text to be transmitted over the centuries in a variety of languages and locations. In the West, it was translated into Latin and achieved its widest circulation as an appendix to a number of manuscripts of *Ps.-Mt.* This tradition was translated subsequently into European vernacular languages. In the Greek East and Slavic lands, *Inf. Gos. Thom.* remained an independent text but was combined with additional stories (such as the Egyptian prologue in the Second Latin version). Further east, the Syriac tradition was joined to *Prot. Jas.* and other infancy traditions to form the West Syriac *Life of Mary* compilation and the East Syriac *Hist. Virg.*, which in turn was translated into Arabic to form the *Arabic Gospel of the Infancy.* And in Ethiopia, the text was incorporated into the *Miracles of Jesus,* an expansive biography of Jesus drawing upon canonical and noncanonical tales.

Original Language, Date, and Provenance

Scholars are largely in agreement that *Inf. Gos. Thom.* was composed in Greek in the second century. Irenaeus (*Haer.* 1.20.1) and the *Epistula Apostolorum* (chap. 4) draw upon the story of Jesus and the Teacher (from either chap. 6 or 14), suggesting that the text was in evidence by the end of the second century. When Syriac manuscripts of *Inf. Gos. Thom.* began to be published, some scholars entertained the theory that the gospel was composed in Syria, based primarily on the perceived low quality of the Greek and the text's apparent attribution to the apostle Thomas. P. Peeters was the first to unequivocally claim the text was written in Syriac.[30] Unfortunately, he stated this conclusion without offering any evidence in its support. S. Voicu and T. Burke each presented their own arguments against Syriac composition;[31] and in any case a Syriac original is inherently quite unlikely, given that Christian texts of the second century are overwhelmingly, if not entirely, written in Greek. Also, without the attribution to Thomas (which is absent in the early versions), there is no reason to place the text in Syria. But that leaves no other secure indications of provenance. A few scholars have suggested Palestine as its place of origin, perhaps even among the Palestinian Jewish-Christian group the Ebionites.[32] But there is no compelling evidence to support these conclusions. The best that can be said is that it likely was composed by a gentile Christian in a location in which the Gospel of Luke was held in high regard. Asia Minor is a possibility, as is Syrian Antioch where John Chrysostom, the earliest writer to refer to the *paidika* of Jesus (see *Hom. Jo.* 17), came into contact with *Inf. Gos. Thom.* in the late fourth century.

Translation

The accompanying translation of the Syriac *Inf. Gos. Thom.* is based on the four principal manuscripts of the independently transmitted text of the gospel: W, G, P, and M. The com-

---

pleting the Gospel: The *Infancy Gospel of Thomas* as a Supplement to the Gospel of Luke," in *The Reception and Interpretation of the Bible in Late Antiquity. Proceedings of the Montréal Colloquium in Honour of Charles Kannengiesser, 11–13 October 2006* (ed. Lorenzo DiTommaso and Lucian Turcescu; Bible in Ancient Christianity 6; Leiden: Brill, 2008), 102–19.

30. Peeters, *Évangiles apocryphes*, xvii–xxii.

31. Burke, *De infantia Iesu*, 174–88; Voicu, "Verso il testo primitivo," 53–55.

32. See the discussion in Burke, *De infantia Iesu,* 205–12.

pilations Sw and Se are employed when required to adjudicate between readings in the other manuscripts. The notes indicate where the Syriac differs from the Greek tradition, and variants from the early versions are provided where these may point to more original readings. The chapter numbering and verse divisions are those used by Tischendorf for Greek A, except for the additional material in chapter 6 which uses the convention established by Voicu.

Sigla

W	London, British Library, Add. 14484
G	Göttingen, Universitätsbibliothek, Syr. 10
P	Vatican, Biblioteca apostolica, syr. 159
M	Edgbaston, University of Birmingham, Mingana Syr. 105
Sw	The West Syriac *Life of Mary* manuscripts
Se	The East Syriac *Hist. Virg.* manuscripts
Ga	Greek A
Gb	Greek B
Gd	Greek D
Gs	Greek S
LM	The First Latin text
LT	The Second Latin text
Slav	The Slavonic tradition
Geo	The Georgian manuscript
Eth	The Ethiopic tradition

Bibliography

EDITIONS AND TRANSLATIONS

Baars, Wilhelm, and Jan Heldermann. "Neue Materielen zum Text und zur Interpretation des Kindheitsevangeliums des Pseudo-Thomas." *OrChr* 77 (1993): 191–226; 78 (1994): 1–32.

Budge, Ernest A. W. *The History of the Blessed Virgin Mary and the History of the Likeness of Christ.* 2 vols. London: Luzac & Co., 1899.

Burke, Tony. "An Unpublished Syriac Manuscript of the *Infancy Gospel of Thomas:* Introduction, Text, Translation, and Notes." *Hugoye* 16, no. 2 (2013): 225–99.

Peeters, Paul. *Évangiles apocryphes.* Vol. 2. Textes et documents pour l'étude historique du Christianisme 18. Paris: Librairie Alphonse Picard & Fils, 1914.

Wright, William, *Contributions to the Apocryphal Literature of the New Testament.* London: Williams & Norgate, 1865. (*Editio princeps* based on manuscript W.)

STUDIES

Aasgaard, Reidar. *The Childhood of Jesus: Decoding the Apocryphal Infancy Gospel of Thomas.* Eugene, Ore.: Cascade Books, 2009.

Burke, Tony. *De infantia Iesu euangelium Thomae graece.* CCSA 17. Turnhout: Brepols, 2010. (Further bibliography may be found here.)

Desreumaux, Alain. "Les apocryphes syriaques sur Jésus et sa famille." Pages 51–69 in *Les apocryphes syriaques.* Edited by M. Debie, A. Desreumaux, C. Jullien, and F. Jullien. Études syriaques 2. Paris: Geuthner, 2005.

Hock, Ronald F. *The Infancy Gospels of James and Thomas.* The Scholars Bible 2. Santa Rosa, Calif.: Polebridge, 1995.

Horn, Cornelia B., and Robert R. Phenix. "Apocryphal Gospels in Syriac and Related Texts Offering Traditions about Jesus." Pages 527–55 in *Jesus in apokryphen Evangelienüberlieferungen*. Edited by Jörg Frey and Jens Schröter. WUNT 254. Tübingen: Mohr Siebeck, 2010.

Mimouni, Simon Claude. "Vies de la Vierge. État de la question." *Apocrypha* 5 (1994): 211–48.

Naffah, Charles. "Les 'histoires' syriaques de la Vierge: traditions apocryphes anciennes et récentes." *Apocrypha* 20 (2009): 137–88.

Tischendorf, Constantin. *Evangelia Apocrypha*. 2nd ed. Leipzig: H. Mendelsohn, 1876 (1853).

Voicu, Sever J. "Verso il testo primitivo dei Παιδικὰ τοῦ Κυρίου Ἰησοῦ 'Racconti dell'infanzia del Signore Gesù.'" *Apocrypha* 9 (1998): 7–95.

The Infancy Gospel of Thomas (Syriac)[a]

Jesus animates the clay sparrows

2 [1]Now when the boy Jesus Christ was five years old, he was playing at the ford of streams of water. And he was catching and confining the waters and directing them in channels and making them enter into pools. He was making the waters become pure and bright.[b] [2]He took soft clay from the wet ground and molded twelve birds. It was the Sabbath and many children were with him.

[3]But one of the Jews saw him with the children making these things. He went to his father Joseph and incited him against Jesus, and said to him, "On the Sabbath he molded clay and fashioned birds, something that is not lawful on the Sabbath."

John 9:14–16; Mark 2:24 par.

[4]Joseph came and rebuked him, and said to him, "Why are you making these things on the Sabbath?" Then Jesus clapped his hands and made the birds fly away before these things that he said.[c] And he said, "Go, fly, and be mindful of me, living ones." And these birds went away, twittering. [5]But when that Pharisee saw (this) he was amazed and went and told his friends.[d]

Quest. Bart. 2:11

The curse on the son of Hannān

3 [1]The son of Hannān the scribe[e] also was with Jesus. He took a willow branch and leaked out and broke down the pools and let the waters escape that Jesus had gathered together, and dried up their pools. [2]When he saw what had happened, Jesus said to him, "Without root shall be your shoot[f] and your fruit shall dry up

---

a. The title in the Syriac MSS is "The Childhood of the Lord Jesus" (W and G, though G adds "Christ"). M and P have the more elaborate, "A story about the childhood and upbringing of Jesus Christ and about the wonders which he performed in his time." The titles in the Greek and related traditions derive from chapter 1, which attributes the text to a certain Thomas, presumably the apostle.

b. W and G: "pure and virtuous." Both words share the same root, suggesting perhaps that the second is a corruption. Therefore, the reading from P and M, and shared with Sw, has been adopted here.

c. Gs and Geo: "in front of everyone"; similarly, Sw: "before all the people."

d. This verse is absent in all Sw MSS.

e. Several witnesses—Gs, one Greek A manuscript, Geo, and LM—identify Hannān (Annas) as the High Priest. This is presumably the same Annas who will become high priest (in Luke 3:2, John 18:13, 24, Acts 4:6, *Prot. Jas.* 15:1, and *Acts Pil.* 1).

f. P and M: "branches."

John 15:6 like a branch that is broken[a] by the wind and is no more."[b] ³Suddenly, that boy withered.[c]

Jesus kills a boy in the marketplace

4[d] ¹Again Jesus was going with his father, and a boy (was) running and struck him on the shoulder. Jesus said to him, "You shall not go on your way." And suddenly he fell down and died. Those who saw him cried out and said, "From where was this boy born, that all his words are a deed?" ²The family of that boy who died approached Joseph his father and were blaming him[e] and saying to him, "As long as you have this boy[f] you cannot dwell with us in the village, unless you teach him to bless."[g]

Joseph rebukes Jesus

5 ¹Joseph approached the boy and was lecturing him and saying to him, "Why do you do these things? For what reason do you say these things? These (people) suffer and hate us." Jesus said, "If the words of my Father were not wise, he would not know (how) to instruct children." He spoke again, "If these were children of the bedchamber,[h] they would not be receiving a curse. These shall not see their torment." At that moment, those who were accusing him were blinded.[i]

²Joseph[j] became angry and took hold of his ear and pulled it hard.

Matt 7:7//Luke 11:9–13;
John 7:34 ³Jesus answered and said to him, "It is enough for you, that you should be commanding me and finding me; for you have acted ignorantly."[k]

Jesus before the teacher Zacchaeus

6 ¹A teacher, whose name was Zacchaeus, heard him speaking with his father and said, "O wicked boy!"[l] ²He said to Joseph,[m] "How long will you not wish to hand over this boy, so that he may learn to love children his age and honor old

---

a. P and M: "torn apart," a reading shared with Sw.

b. P and M lack "and is no more," but the reading is found also in Sw.

c. The Greek and related traditions (except for Gs) expand this verse. The parents of the boy appear, take him home, and reproach Joseph for having "such a child."

d. The *Inf. Gos. Thom.* material in Se begins here after a shortened version of the encounter with Zacchaeus (6:1 and 6:3).

e. W lacks "and they were blaming him."

f. W and G have only "you have this boy." P and M are supported here by Sw.

g. P and M lack "unless you teach him to bless," but this clause is found in Sw and Se along with Gs, Geo, Eth, and LM. The other versions (except Eth) also add "and not to curse."

h. Only in the Syriac tradition do we have this reference to the bed or bridal chamber. The other witnesses differ widely here.

i. In G the episode finishes here; the story continues at 6:2.

j. The Greek and related witnesses (except for Gs) begin the verse differently. Ga has "And when they saw, they were very afraid and disturbed, and they said about him that every word he happened to say, whether good or bad, has become a deed" (cf. 4:1).

k. The Greek and related witnesses continue with, "You have not seen me clearly, why I am yours. Behold! You know to not make me upset, for I was yours, and I have been subdued before you" (Gs), "You do not know that I am yours. Do not make me upset, for I am yours" (Ga), "You do not know who I am and that I am with you" (Gd).

l. P and M: "O stubborn boy!," agreeing with Se. Zacchaeus does not speak here at all in Gs and the early versions.

m. G begins the chapter here with "Zacchaeus the scribe began to say to his father."

age[a] and to be in awe of elders,[b] in order that the love of children may be with him and, moreover, so that he may teach them?"[c] [2a]Joseph said, "Who is able to teach a boy like this? Do you not think that he is equal to a small cross?"

[2b]Jesus answered and said to him, "Teacher, these words that you have now spoken and these names that you name,[d] I am a stranger to them; for I am outside of you, yet I dwell among you. Honor of the flesh I have not. You (live) by the law and by the law you remain.[e] For when you were born, I was.[f] But you think that you are my father.[g] You shall learn from me that teaching that no one else knows nor is able to teach. As for that cross you mentioned, the one to whom it belongs shall bear it. For when I am greatly exalted I shall lay aside what is mixed in your race. For you do not know where I was born nor where you are from;[h] for I alone know you truly—when you were born and how much time you have to remain here."

John 8:58

[2c]When they heard,[i] they were astounded[j] and cried out greatly and said, "O wonderful sight and sound! Words like these we have never heard anyone speak—neither the priests, nor the scribes, nor the Pharisees. Where was he born, who is five years old and speaks such words? Such a one has never been seen among us." [2d]Jesus answered and said to them, "You are amazed by me and you do not believe me concerning what I have said to you.[k] I said that I know when you were born;[l] and I have even more to say to you."[m]

[2e]When they heard (these words), they were silent and unable to speak.[n] He approached them again and said, laughing, "I laughed at you because you are amazed at trifles and you are becoming small in your minds."

The teaching of the Aleph

[2f]When they were comforted a little, Zacchaeus the teacher said to the father of Jesus, "Bring him to me[o] and I will teach him what is proper for him to learn."

---

a. W finishes the sentence at this point.

b. G lacks "to be in awe of elders," likely due to homoeoarcton.

c. The MSS used by Tischendorf for Greek A lack verses 2a–2f, but they are present in other Greek A MSS as well as Gs and Gd.

d. W has only "and these names."

e. G lacks this sentence. P and M finish the sentence with "you search," a reading shared by Sw.

f. G lacks this sentence.

g. Jesus has switched his attention to Joseph. This shift is made explicit in Gs with the statement "And he said to Joseph."

h. P and M: "from where I am"; the entire sentence in W reads only "For you do not know where you are from," likely as a result of homoeoarcton.

i. G breaks off here and continues in the middle of 6:2e.

j. Se interrupts the story here and moves on to chapters 14, 15, 16, 19:1–2 and then resumes at 6:3.

k. W has only "You wonder at what I have said to you." Sw shares this reading but ends the verse entirely here. P and M's longer reading is supported in Gs and LM.

l. W lacks "born," but the reading is supported in Gs, Geo, Eth, and LM.

m. This "even more" is not extant in the Syriac MSS but is supplied in various ways by the other witnesses.

n. The verse ends here in W.

o. W lacks "bring him to me" but the reading is supported in Sw and the non-Syriac witnesses.

He coaxed him[a] and made him go into the school. Yet, going in, he was silent. But Zacchaeus the scribe was beginning to teach him (starting) from Aleph, and repeating to him many times the whole alphabet. He said to him that he should answer and speak after him, but he was silent. Then the scribe was angry and struck him with his hand upon his head. And Jesus said, "The smith's anvil, when struck repeatedly,[b] may be instructed, yet is unfeeling.[c] I can say those things spoken by you[d] *like a noisy gong or a clanging cymbal.* These do not respond with any sound nor do they have the power of knowledge and understanding."[e]

[margin: 1 Cor 13:1]

[3] Then Jesus said all the letters from Aleph to Tau with much wisdom. He answered again and said, "Those who do not know the Aleph, how do they teach the Beth? Hypocrites! First, teach what is the Aleph and then I will believe you concerning the Beth."[f] [4] Then Jesus began to enquire concerning the form of each character. He began with the letters. Concerning the first, why it has many angles and characters, pointed, thick and prostrate and projected and extended; their summits gathered together and sharp and ornamented and erect and squared and inverted; and transformed and folded over and bent at their sides, and fixed in a triangle and crowned and clothed in life.[g]

[margin: *Ep. Apos.* 4; Irenaeus, *Haer.* 1.20.1; *Acts Thom.* 79]

Zacchaeus's lament

7 [1] Then Zacchaeus the scribe, astounded and amazed on account of all these names and the greatness of his speech, cried out and said,[h] "I have brought this <matter>[i] on myself. [2] Take him away from me, I beg of you. It is not right for him to be this (way) on the earth; truly this one is worthy of a great cross. He is able to even set fire to fire. And I think that he was born before the flood of Noah.[j] What womb carried him? Or what mother reared him? For I cannot bear him. I am in a great stupor because of him; and I am out of my mind.

[margin: Luke 11:27; *Gos. Thom.* 79; *Prot. Jas.* 3:2]

---

a. W lacks "he coaxed him" but the reading is supported in Sw as well as Gs, Eth, and Geo.

b. W and Sw lack "repeatedly."

c. The anvil aphorism is found only in the Syriac and other early versions. The Greek recensions have instead, "I wish to teach you rather than be taught by you, for I know the letters which you are teaching more accurately and far better than you" (Gs, and similarly in Ga and Gd).

d. G breaks off here, resuming at 7:1.

e. W shortens this exchange, reading ". . . those things spoken by you, with knowledge and understanding." The longer reading in P and M is supported by Sw and the non-Syriac witnesses. W terminates here, resuming at 7:4.

f. The MSS (except for Se) have Aleph and Beta, though likely Beth is intended. The majority of the other non-Syriac versions use the Greek letters (Alpha and Beta) throughout. Only the Syriac tradition, LM, and one Greek MS use the Semitic letters.

g. "And clothed in life" does not appear in Se; Sw has just "and clothed." Neither reading is supported in the non-Syriac versions.

h. W and G lack much of this chapter. G continues from Zacchaeus's dialogue at 6:2f with "'. . . and the greatness of his speech.' He cried out and said" and then resumes again at 7:3. W has "The scribe answered and said" and moves to 7:4. The Greek recensions begin Zacchaeus's lament with "Woe is me! Woe is me! I am at a loss, wretch that I am"; the other early versions begin simply with "Woe is me."

i. "Matter" is an emendation. P and M, as well as Sw, have an indecipherable word here. The entire sentence is absent in Se.

j. The Greek recensions have "before the creation of the world."

Wretched am I to think I had acquired a student; and, although I considered him a student, he was my teacher.[a]

[3]"O my friends! I cannot bear it. I am fleeing from the village; I cannot look upon him. By a little child I, an old man, am defeated. But what can I, who was defeated, say? How, even from the beginning, I did not understand a thing he was saying. Have mercy on me! I am dying.[b] My soul is clearly before my eyes because of the order of his voice and the beauty of his words.[c] [4]He is something great—either a god, or an angel, or what I should say I do not know."

Jesus restores those cursed

8 [1]Then the boy Jesus laughed and said, "Let those in whom there is no fruit, produce fruit; and let the blind see the living fruit of judgement."[d] [2]Those who had fallen under his curse came alive and rose up. No one was daring to anger him again.[e]

The fall of Zeno

9[f] [1]One time, on the day of the Sabbath,[g] Jesus was playing with children on a roof. One of the children fell and died. When those other children saw (what had happened), they ran away, and Jesus remained alone. [2]The family of the one who was dead seized him and said to him, "You threw the boy down." And Jesus said, "I did not throw him down." They were accusing him.

[3]Then he came down to the dead one[h] and said in a loud voice,[i] "Zeno, Zeno"—for thus indeed was his name—"did I throw you down?"[j] Immediately, he leaped up and stood and said to him, "No, my Lord." [4]All of them were astounded. Even the boy's parents[k] were praising God for this wonder that had happened.[l]

---

a. Se inserts here 6:2e.

b. The prior three sentences are based primarily on M. At this point, P has two lines struck out, obscuring the text. The Greek recensions have: "What can I say or tell anyone concerning the lines of the first element which he imposed on me? For I understand neither the beginning nor the end" (Gs, and similarly in Ga and Gd).

c. This sentence has no parallel in the non-Syriac witnesses.

d. The Greek recensions add here the following: "Because I am here from on high so that I may deliver those below and call them to the heights just as the one who sent me to you commanded me" (Gs, and similarly in Ga and Gd). In Se, Jesus says only "Indeed, I laugh with you" and omits 8:2.

e. This entire verse is missing in W, thus leaving all of Jesus' previous victims injured or dead. The verse is likely original, as it is present in all other Syriac witnesses as well as the Greek recensions and other versions.

f. This episode is absent in Se.

g. Only the Syriac tradition and LM place this episode on the Sabbath.

h. P and M preface this sentence with: "The boy Jesus answered and said to them, 'Leave now, so that I may go down to the dead boy and I will ask him, and immediately he will declare to us the truth who really threw him down.'"

i. W and G lack "in a loud voice" but it finds support in Sw and the early versions.

j. P and M add "as your family is accusing me."

k. P and M add "who were accusing Jesus."

l. Ga, Gd, and Gb (along with Slav and LT) follow this chapter with the story of the young man who cut his foot with an axe. The same story occurs in Gs following chapter 16.

Jesus carries water in his cloak

11 [1]Again, when Jesus was seven years old, his mother sent him to fill[a] water. And in the press of a great crowd, his pitcher struck (against something) and was broken. [2]Then Jesus spread out the cloak with which he was covered and he collected and brought (home) that water.[b] His mother Mary was amazed and she was keeping in her heart all that she was seeing.[c]

Luke 2:18, 52

The miraculous harvest

12[d] [1]Once again Jesus was playing. He sowed one measure of wheat. [2]And he harvested 100 cors and gave them to the people of the village.

Jesus stretches a beam

13 [1]Jesus was eight years old. Joseph was a carpenter and made nothing else but ploughs and yokes. A man had ordered from him a bed of six cubits. One plank did not have the (proper) length on one side, for it was shorter than the other. The boy Jesus said to his father, "Take hold of the end of the one shorter than the other."[e] [2]Jesus took the measure of the wood and pulled and stretched it and made it equal to its other. Jesus said to Joseph his father, "Do henceforth what you wish."

The second teacher

14[f] [1]When Joseph saw his intelligence, he wished to teach him writing,[g] and he brought him to the school.[h] The scribe said to him, "Say Aleph." And Jesus said <it>. Again the scribe added that he should say Beth. [2]Jesus said to him, "Tell me first what Aleph is, and then I will tell you about Beth."[i] The scribe was furious and struck him, and immediately (the scribe) fell down and died.

cf. *Ep. Apos.* 4;
Irenaeus, *Haer.* 1.20.1;
Acts Thom. 79

[3]Jesus went back to his family. Joseph called Mary his mother and spoke to her and commanded her not to permit him to go out of the house, so that those who strike him will not die.[j]

A third teacher

15[k] [1]But another scribe said to Joseph, "Hand him over to me. I will teach him by flattery."[l] [2]Jesus entered the school.[m] He took a scroll and was reading, not what

Luke 4:16–21

---

a. G: "to draw."

b. P and M, along with Sw, state that Jesus' cloak was a hood (Sw explicitly identifies this hood as his *sticharion*, a clerical garment). They add that Jesus "poured the water into his hood" and then carried it home.

c. W has "His mother Mary was astonished at all that she was seeing." The longer reading is supported by Sw, Se, and the non-Syriac witnesses.

d. Se transposes chapters 12 and 13 and then concludes the *Inf. Gos. Thom.* material.

e. W, G, and Sw lack this sentence but it is supported by Se and several versions (Gs, LM, and the related Irish MS).

f. This chapter is absent in G.

g. P and M: "learning."

h. "School" can also be translated as "house of the scribe." P and M have only "to a scribe."

i. Gs and LV reverse the order of the letters. The exchange is missing in Eth.

j. In P and M, as well as Sw and Se, Joseph's command is in direct speech.

k. This chapter is absent in G.

l. W lacks "by flattery," but the reading is supported by Sw and Se and is present also in Gs.

m. "School" can be translated also as "house of a/the scribe."

was written, but he opened his mouth and spoke in the spirit,[a] so that that scribe sat with him on the ground[b] and beseeched him.[c] Great crowds, hearing his words, assembled and stood there. Jesus thus opened his mouth and was speaking, so that all who arrived and stood there might be astounded and amazed.

[3]When Joseph heard, he ran <and> came because he was afraid lest the scribe also would die. The scribe said to Joseph, "You have delivered to me not a student but a master." [4]And Joseph took him and led him back to his home.[d]

James is bitten by a snake

16 [1]Again Joseph had sent his son James to gather sticks. Jesus was going with him. While they were gathering sticks, a deadly viper bit James on his hand. [2]When Jesus came near to him, he did to him nothing more than stretch out his hand and blow on the bite. And it was healed, the viper died, and James lived.[e]

Jesus in the temple

Luke 2:41–52

19 [1] When Jesus was twelve years old, they had gone to Jerusalem, as it was custom for Joseph and Mary to go to the festival of Passover. When they had made Passover, they returned to their home.[f] When they had turned to come <home>, Jesus remained in Jerusalem. Neither Joseph nor Mary his mother knew <it>, but they thought that he was with their companions.

[2]When they came to the rendezvous of that day, they were seeking him among their kinsfolk and among those whom he knew. When they did not find Jesus, they returned to Jerusalem and were seeking him. After three days they found him in the temple, sitting among the teachers, and listening to them[g] and questioning them. All those hearing were amazed at him, because he was silencing those teachers,[h] for he was expounding to them the parables of the prophets and the mysteries and allegories of the law.[i]

[3]His mother said to him, "My son, why have you done this to us so? We were distressed and agitated and searching for you. Jesus answered and said, "Why were you searching for me? Do you not know that it is fitting for me to be in my Father's house?"[j] [4]The scribes and the Pharisees answered and said to Mary,

---

a. W: "not what was written but great miracles" and the chapter ends here.

b. For "sat" (found also in Se), P has "wrote"; Sw has "fell," which is consistent with Gs, Eth, and LM.

c. A second verb is required here. Sw has "and he was beseeching him that he would teach him."

d. The Greek recensions (and related versions) add an epilogue in which Jesus restores the teacher from chapter 14 to life.

e. W and G have only "and it was healed." The longer reading is supported by Sw, Se, and several versions (Gs, LM, and in part by Eth). Ga and Gd (as well as Slav and LT) continue with two additional chapters: the resurrection of a dead child (chap. 17) and the resurrection of a housebuilder (chap. 18).

f. Sw lacks this sentence.

g. G finishes the verse here.

h. P and M, along with Sw, have "elders and teachers." The other remaining witnesses have "elders" (Gs) and "priests" (Eth).

i. Se moves here to chapter 6:3 and continues on through to chapter 13, though omitting chapter 9.

j. Jesus' response to his mother is lacking in G, likely due to homoeoteleuton.

Luke 1:42; 11:27 · "Are you the mother of this boy? The Lord has blessed you in your fruit, for the glory of wisdom such as this in children we have neither seen nor heard that anyone has spoken."

⁵He rose and went with them and was obedient to his parents. But his mother

Luke 2:19, 51 was preserving all these words in her heart.ᵃ Jesus was excelling and growing in wisdom and stature and grace before God and before men.

Here <ends> the Childhood of our Lord Jesus.ᵇ

---

a. W lacks "in her heart." The reading is supported by Sw, Gs, and Eth. The entire sentence is lacking in G.

b. G adds "Christ." P and M do not include this title and end instead with a short prayer.

On the Priesthood of Jesus
A new translation and introduction

by William Adler

On the Priesthood of Jesus (*Priest. Jes.*; CANT 54), known also as the *Confession* or *Apology of Theodosius*, recounts the story of a secret registry jealously guarded in the city of Tiberias and recording Jesus' admission into the Jerusalem priesthood.[1] Preserved in numerous languages and versions (some of them unpublished), the story is most notable for its account of the priests' confirmation of Jesus' Levitical ancestry and divine sonship, following a grueling interrogation and physical examination of Mary, and a thorough investigation into Mary's background.

Contents
Set during the reign of the emperor Justinian (r. 527–565), the longer version of *Priest. Jes.* recounts the earnest efforts of a Christian money dealer (*arguropratēs*) named Philip to convince his friend Theodosius, a well-regarded Jewish leader and teacher, to become a Christian (1–3). While wavering in his decision to formally convert, Theodosius assures Philip of his privately held belief in Jesus' divine sonship (4). Jesus' realization of the promises of the prophets was only part of the reason for this belief; Theodosius was also party to a "secret" (*mystērion*) known only to the Jews (6). During the time of the Second Temple, he says, Jewish priests had conducted an exhaustive search to fill a position vacated by a recently deceased member of their ranks (8–11). Following an unavailing search for a suitable replacement, a priest, prompted by the Holy Spirit, finally nominated Jesus, who at the time was residing in Judea. Although he had not yet begun his public ministry, the council agreed that Jesus satisfied the moral and scholastic requirements for the position (12).[2]

Once the priest advocating for Jesus resolved a genealogical objection raised by a dissenting faction (13–15), a final requirement had to be satisfied. Custom dictated that the name of the newly appointed priest be entered into the registry along with the names of his father and mother; for that reason, the priests had to obtain direct testimony from Jesus' parents. But only Mary was alive and available to provide a deposition (16–17). When asked to disclose the names of Jesus' parents, she described (albeit reluctantly, out of fear of ridicule and disbelief) how the angel Gabriel revealed to her that she would give birth

---

1. Unless otherwise indicated, citations from the work in the ensuing discussion refer to the longer Greek recension. I would like to acknowledge with gratitude the very helpful suggestions and improvements of the editors.

2. Although Jesus' age at the time is not given, the version of the story later known to Michael Glycas states that Jesus was twenty-five years of age at the time of his election (*Quaest.* 54, 94.10–12); see Sophronios Eustratiades, ed., *Michaēl tou Glykas, Eis tas aporias tēs Theias Graphēs kephalia* (2 vols.; Athens: P. D. Sakellariou, 1906–1912).

69

to a son from the Holy Spirit (18–28). Initially skeptical but overwhelmed by the mountain of evidence in support of her claim, the priests admit Jesus into the ranks of the priesthood, adding to the registry the following notice: "On this month and this indiction, by a unanimous vote we have appointed as priest Jesus, the son of the living God and Mary the virgin" (29:2). The registry of priests was rescued from the temple before its destruction in 70 and hidden in Tiberias, where it remained until the author's day (30–35).[3]

Manuscripts and Versions

Priest. Jes. was composed in Greek and now is attested in several languages and versions. The longer recension of *Priest. Jes.* (= GrL) survives in three Greek manuscripts: L (Mount Athos, Lavra Γ 37, fol. 176v–187r); T (Turin, Biblioteca Nazionale, gr. 185, fol. 289r–294r) and V (Vatican, Biblioteca apostolica, gr. 687, fol. 245r–259r). Other witnesses to the longer recension include the Georgian translation and an Arabic version of the story (= Arab) found at the beginning of the *History of the Patriarchs of Alexandria* (10th cent.).[4] A shorter recension (= GrS) is preserved in several Greek manuscripts; the two Paleoslavic versions also derive from the shorter recension.[5] In the *Suda* lexicon (= *Suda*), a Byzantine encyclopedia dating to the tenth century, the lemma *Iēsous ho Chistos kai theos hēmōn* contains an even more abbreviated recension.[6] The first Latin translation of the work, done by Robert Grosseteste, bishop of Lincoln, in the thirteenth century, is based on the *Suda* text. Until recently, all subsequent translations of the text in the West were likewise based on the *Suda,* including one in Anglo-Norman.[7]

In his *Anecdota Graeco-Byzantina,* Athanasius Vassiliev published the Greek text of the *Suda*'s version alongside a very similar text preserved in a twelfth-century Moscow manuscript (Russian State Library, gr. 443, fol. 85–88). He also published the text of Vatican, Biblioteca apostolica, Ottoboni gr. 408, fol. 170–72, a much shorter account lacking the framing narrative about Theodosius and Philip.[8] The Arabic text with accompanying English translation can be found in B. Evetts's edition of the *History of the Patriarchs of Alexandria.*[9] The Georgian version was initially published by S. J. Q'ubaneišvili. In

---

3. On the location of the hidden codex in Tiberias, see further below, pp. 78–79.

4. For discussion of the Georgian witnesses, see Michel van Esbroeck, *Les plus anciens homéliaires géorgiens. Étude descriptive et historique* (Publications de l'Institut Orientaliste de Leuven 10; Leuven-la-Neuve: Institut Orientaliste, Université Catholique de Leuven, 1975), 201–2, 279. The Arabic text, described in the prologue to the *History of the Patriarchs of Alexandria* as a translation from Coptic, is at least one step removed from the Greek original.

5. See Ziffer, "Contributo allo studio della tradizione slava." Because Ziffer's thesis was unavailable to me, the contents and manuscript witnesses to the shorter recension could not be ascertained. But cf. Nuvolone (*EAC* 2:80–81), who states that the shorter text is similar to the entry in the *Suda.* It is thus likely that Ziffer's GrS is based, at least in part, on Moscow gr. 443 (translated below).

6. Adler, ed., *Suidae Lexicon,* 2:620–25 (#229).

7. See Ruth J. Dean, "An Anglo-Norman Version of Grosseteste: Part of His Suidas and Testamenta XII Patriarcharum," *PMLA* 51 (1936): 607–20. For discussion of early translations of the *Suda* lemma, see Giovanni Mercati, *Ultimi contributi alla storia degli umanisti* (2 vols.; Studi e testi 90–91; Vatican City: Biblioteca Apostolica Vaticana, 1939), 1:70–85. For an early French translation of the *Suda* text, see Jacques-Paul Migne, ed., *Dictionnaire des Apocryphes* (2 vols.; 1856–1858; repr. Turnhout: Brepols, 1989), 2:383–87. For critical editions of six Latin translations of the *Suda* text, see Jeroen De Keyser, "Early Modern Latin Translations of the Apocryphal *De Sacerdotio Christi,*" *Lias* 40 (2013): 29–82.

8. Vassiliev, *Anecdota Graeco-Byzantina,* 58–72. For Vassiliev's discussion of these witnesses, see his introduction, xxv–xxvii.

9. Evetts, ed. and trans., *History of the Patriarchs,* 120–34.

his unpublished MA thesis, G. Ziffer reedited and translated (into Italian) the Georgian and Paleoslavic versions.[10] He also published editions and Italian translations of the longer and shorter Greek recensions.[11] In the 2005 French edition of Christian apocrypha, F. Nuvolone published a new French translation of the longer Greek recension. Although mostly based on Ziffer's edition, he also incorporated readings from the recently discovered Athos manuscript (L).[12]

Literary Context

One of the more notable features of *Priest. Jes.* is its assertion of Jesus' genealogical qualifications for the Jewish priesthood. After the priests offer their tentative support for Jesus' appointment, some object to his nomination on the grounds that "he is not from our tribe" (13:1). To meet this objection, the priest advocating for Jesus claims that his mother Mary was the product of a pattern of intermarriage between the tribes of Judah and Levi extending all the way back to the time of Aaron. That claim is strikingly different from the representation of the priesthood of Jesus in the Epistle to the Hebrews. "For it is evident," writes the author of Hebrews, "that our Lord was descended from Judah, and in connection with that tribe Moses said nothing about priests" (7:14). Here the priesthood of the Judahite Jesus is both distinct from and superior to its Levitical counterpart.

Though categorically opposed to the viewpoint of Hebrews, the representation of Jesus in *Priest. Jes.* as a priest of mixed Judahite and Levitical ancestry nevertheless is deeply rooted in Christian tradition. It is already attested in the *Testaments of the Twelve Patriarchs*, a work which in its final Christian form originated ca. the second century CE. Although its provenance and textual prehistory remain highly contested, *T. 12 Patr.* draws heavily on Second Temple Jewish tradition.[13] In the five passages from the work that look forward to a Messianic high priest and king arising from the tribes of Judah and Levi, three of them identify Jesus as this awaited Messiah of mixed pedigree.[14] Thus, what we see in *Priest. Jes.* is a narrative exposition of a much older Jewish/Christian expectation of the Messiah as combining in one person the dual role of Levitical high priest and Judahite king.[15] It is striking that proponents of Jesus as the perfect and eternal Levitical priest sometimes interpreted this as a fulfillment of the well-known verse from Ps 110:4: "The Lord has sworn and will not change his mind, 'You are a priest forever according to the order of Melchizedek.'"[16] The fact that Hebrews 7:1–17 quotes the same verse to prove the

---

10. Ziffer, "'La Confessione di Teodosio.'"

11. Ziffer, "Una versione greca."

12. Nuvolone, "Sur le sacerdoce du Christ."

13. For discussion of the date and provenance of the *Testaments*, see most recently R. Kugler, *Testaments of the Twelve Patriarchs* (Sheffield: Sheffield Academic, 2001), 31–38.

14. See *T. Sim.* 7:1–3: "And now, my children, be obedient to Levi and Judah . . . [because from them will arise the Savior come from God]. For the Lord will raise up from Levi someone as high priest and from Judah somone as king [God and man]. He will save all the gentiles and the tribe of Israel" (trans. Howard Clark Kee, in *The Old Testament Pseudepigrapha* [ed. James H. Charlesworth; Garden City, NY: Doubleday, 1983], 1:778–828); see also *T. Levi* 2:11; *T. Dan* 5:10; *T. Naph.* 8:2–3; *T. Gad* 8:1; *T. Jos.* 19:11. For the Greek text of the *Testaments*, see Marinus de Jonge, ed., *The Testaments of the Twelve Patriarchs* (Leiden: Brill, 1978). For discussion, see Harm Wouter Hollander and Marinus de Jonge, *The Testaments of the Twelve Patriarchs: A Commentary* (Leiden: Brill, 1985), 125–26; and, in the context of *Priest. Jes.*, Dagron, "Jésus prêtre du judaïsme," 21–22.

15. Already suggested by Thilo, *Codex apocryphus Novi Testamenti*, 376, who traced the ideology to "Christians of Jewish origin (*Christiani e Judaeis*)."

16. See, for example, Origen, *Adnot. Num.* (PG 12:584C): God deliberately exempted the Levites and

opposite (namely, Jesus' superiority to the temporal Levitical priesthood) at least raises the possibility of two co-existing and competing understandings of the meaning of Jesus' fulfillment of the terms of Psalm 110—the former stressing Jesus' continuity with the hereditary temple priesthood, the latter stressing discontinuity and separation.[17]

In Christian exegesis, the representation of Jesus as Levitical priest and Judahite king also appears in conjunction with a Messianic interpretation of two other much-discussed verses from Jewish Scriptures. One is Jacob's prophecy to Judah in Gen 49:10 (LXX): "a ruler (*archōn*) shall not be wanting from Ioudas and a leader (*hēgoumenos*) from his thighs until the things stored up for him come." The other is Gabriel's revelation to Daniel of the "cutting off" of "an anointed ruler" (*christou hēgoumenou*; Dan 9:25–26). Because both passages, taken together, suggested to Christian interpreters that a precondition for the coming of the Messiah was the cessation of Judahite kings and high priests, the collapse of the Hasmonean dynasty, not long before the birth of Jesus, was said to have satisfied the terms of both prophecies. Proponents of this intepretation held that the succession of post-exilic high priests involved, like Jesus himself, rulers of mixed Levitical and Judahite ancestry.[18] The fall of the Hasmonean dynasty with the accession of Herod the Great to power thus signaled the cutting off of the anointed ruler, the cessation of Judahite rule, and the coming of the Messiah in the person of Jesus, the eternal Levitical high priest and Judahite king. Already attested in the fourth century, this older exegetical tradition survived into the Byzantine age.[19] It is also found in modified form in *Priest. Jes.* After

---

Judahites from the prohibition against intertribal marriage, so that Christ would be able to satisfy the terms of his dual office as "king and priest after the order of Melchizedek." The same proof text appears in versions of *Priest. Jes.* See, for example, the title of the text of Vatican, Otto. gr. 408: "Exposition of how Christ became a priest. For the prophet David says of him, 'You are a priest forever according to the order of Melchizedek' "; see also Arab 131; John of Euboea, *In conceptionem Deiparae* 18.2.

17. As noted by Dagron, "Jésus prêtre du judaïsme," 23.

18. For Christian discussion of the dual Levitical/Judahite ancestry of the Hasmonean dynasty, see in particular the very detailed exposition in Basil of Caesarea, *Ep.* 236.3 (to Amphilochius) (*Saint Basile. Lettres* [ed. Yves Courtonne; 3 vols.; Paris: Les Belles Lettres, 1957–1966]). For this claim as an aspect of Hasmonean political ideology, see Victor Aptowitzer, *Parteipolitik der Hasmonäerzeit im rabbinischen und pseudoepigraphischen Schrifttum* (Vienna: Verlag der Kohut-Foundation, 1927), 87–91. Aptowitzer ascribes its origins to partisans of the Hasmoneans, who made this claim in order to justify the assertion of royal prerogatives by the Hasmonean high-priesthood. The representation of the Messiah of mixed Judahite and Levitical ancestry found in *T. 12 Patr.* was thus a projection of Hasmonean political ideology. For a good summary and critique of Aptowitzer's thesis, see Marshall D. Johnson, *The Purpose of Biblical Genealogies: With Special Reference to the Setting of the Genealogies of Jesus* (2nd ed.; Cambridge: Cambridge University Press, 1989), 131–38.

19. Elements of this exegetical tradition even appear in the writings of the church fathers. See, for example, Basil of Caesarea, *Ep.* 236.3. After the return from captivity, Basil writes, rule over the Jewish nation transferred to the priesthood "because of the mixing of the priestly and royal tribes (*dia to anamigēnai tēn hieratikēn kai basilikēn phylēn*). Hence the Lord is both king and high priest in matters respecting God. And the royal tribe did not cease until the coming of Christ." See further Epiphanius, *Pan.* 29.1.3.5; 51.22.18– 21: ". . . Judea was entirely handed over and became subject to them (the Romans), when the rulers from Judah ceased (*lēxantōn tōn apo Iouda archontōn*) and Herod, a gentile, was appointed as ruler, even though he was a proselyte. Then Christ was born in Bethlehem of Judea and came to proclaim the gospel, when anointed rulers descended from Judah and Aaron (*lēxantōn tōn apo Iouda kai Aarōn christōn hēgoumenōn*) came to an end; they had lasted until Alexander, an anointed ruler (*christou hēgoumenou*), and Salina, also called Alexandra. Thus was fulfilled the prophecy of Jacob: 'A ruler shall not fail from Judah . . . (Gen 49:10)." For discussion, see Aline Pourkier, *L'hérésiologie chez Epiphane de Salamine* (Christianisme antique 4; Paris: Beauchesne, 1992), 420–30. For Byzantine witnesses, see George Syncellus, *Ecloga Chronographica* (ed. Alden A. Mosshammer; Leipzig: Teubner, 1984), 383.10–15; George Monachus, *Chronicon* (ed. Carolus

documenting for Philip the enrollment of Jesus in the registry of pre–70 Jerusalem priests, Theodosius tells him of his discovery of "something even greater": no other name appears in the registry of priests after the name of Jesus. It is thus clear, Theodosius says, that Jesus, the eternal high priest and Judahite king, and seal of Jacob's prophecy, was the "one who was reserved as savior of the world, at which time kings and priests have ceased in Israel" (30:2–3).

In his analysis of its origins, Theodor Zahn theorized that the tradition about Jesus' mixed royal and priestly lineage originated in the primitive Jerusalem Christian community.[20] One piece of evidence in support of his argument involves the priestly role played by James, the brother of Jesus and leader of the early Jerusalem church. On the authority of Hegesippus, a second-century Jewish convert to Christianity, Eusebius's *Ecclesiastical History* recalls how James used to make regular intercession with God in the Holy of Holies on behalf of the Jewish nation (*Hist. eccl.* 2.23.6). Although Eusebius fails to explain how James claimed entitlement to the office of high priest, other sources provide a more satisfactory justification. In his *Panarion,* Epiphanius reports the same tradition as Eusebius; but he adds another critical explanatory detail lacking in Eusebius. James, he writes, was a "distinguished member of the priesthood, because the two tribes were linked exclusively to one another, the royal tribe to the priestly one and the priestly to the royal, just as earlier, in the time of the exodus, Nahshon the phylarch took as his wife the Elisheba of old, [the] daughter of Aaron (*sic*)" (78.11.13.5–6).[21] This symmetry with Jesus' putative ancestry suggests an underlying theory of dynastic succession in the Jerusalem leadership: Jesus and his successor James had inaugurated a new dynastic line of priests/kings of mixed Judahite and Levitical stock.[22]

Already by the third century, there were scattered attempts to domesticate the tradition through harmonization with the Gospel genealogies and the emerging consensus of Jesus as the Davidic Messiah. In the first and fragmentarily preserved part of his epistle to Aristides, the Christian scholar Julius Africanus (ca. 160–ca. 240) speaks scornfully of certain unnamed Christians who, in their interpretation of the Gospel genealogies of Christ, appealed to the same argument as the priest advocating for Jesus' appointment to the priesthood: namely the practice of intermarriage between the tribes of Levi and Judah beginning with Aaron's marriage to Elisheba, the daughter of the Judahite Amminadab and sister of the Judahite phylarch Nahshon (Exod 6:23). Understood in this context, the apparent discrepancies in the genealogies of Jesus in Matthew and Luke revealed a deeper truth about Jesus' dual function as priest and king (*Ep. ad Arist.* 1–9).[23] Although harmo-

---

de Boor; Leipzig: Teubner, 1904), 299.22–301.2. For other witnesses, see William Adler, "Exodus 6:23 and the High Priest from the Tribe of Judah," *JTS* 48 (1997): 24–47 at 36–38, and n. 46.

20. Theodor Zahn, *Forschungen zur Geschichte des neutestamentlichen Kanons* (10 vols.; Leipzig: Deichert, 1981–1926), 6:329 n. 2.

21. Epiphanius, *Panarion* (ed. Karl Holl; vol. 3; GCS 37; Leipzig: Hinrichs, 1933). Epiphanius makes this claim in response to a question from heretics as to how Mary could be both from the tribe of Judah and the line of David, and a kinswoman of the Levite Elizabeth at the same time. Epiphanius's identification of the Judahite phylarch Nahshon (not Aaron) as Elisheba's husband is obviously in error. For detailed discussion of the passage, see Pourkier, *L'hérésiologie,* 432–40; also Zahn, *Forschungen,* 6:211–12.

22. On this idea that James and the leaders of the church inherited the eternal high priesthood and kingship, see Epiphanius, *Pan.* 29.4.8.

23. Christophe Guignard, ed., *La lettre de Julius Africanus à Aristide sur la généalogie du Christ* (TU 167; Berlin: De Gruyter, 2011). Apparently, Africanus's adversaries speculated that the non-royal Davidic line of Nathan through which Luke traces Jesus' genealogy establishes his priestly pedigree. For his part,

nization with the Gospel genealogies traced Jesus' Levitical ancestry through the line of both Joseph and Mary, Mary was the one most often said to be of mixed lineage. Probably this was because Luke had already connected her at least indirectly with the line of Aaron.[24] The rather convoluted genealogy of Mary set forth in *Priest. Jes.* validates Zahn's observation about the distortions produced by integrating Mary's Davidic lineage with her mixed Levitical and Judahite ancestry.[25] In response to the objection from some of the Jerusalem priests that Jesus lacked the proper pedigree, the priest advocating for him invites his colleagues to explore the issue more thoroughly. "Conduct an investigation," he tells them, "and you will see that during the time of Aaron the priest, there was a mixing between Aaron and Judah, *that is to say from David.* . . . After having examined the facts for myself, I have discovered that Mary as well, by her genealogy, descends from both tribes" (14:1–2, emphasis mine).

The tradition of Jesus, the priest/king Messiah of mixed Levitical and Judahite lineage, has a complex and still largely unexplored history. Eusebius, on the authority of an "untitled commentary," states that many "men of renown" *(polloi . . . tōn dokimōn)* knew and endorsed the idea (*Supp. Quaest.* 14 [PG 22:973AB]).[26] But the tradition probably received its biggest boost once it began to circulate in the form of a narrative.

Date and Provenance

In his very thorough analysis of the several versions of the work, Flavio Nuvolone sets out a compelling case for the chronological priority of the longer recension.[27] In general outline, the narrative of *Priest. Jes.* in the longer version consists of three segments: a) an account of the friendship between Philip and Theodosius, and the former's appeal to

---

Africanus, while not denying Jesus' dual role as priest and king, dismisses attempts to prove this from the gospel genealogies as "hairsplitting" (*Ep. ad. Arist.* 3).

24. Cf. Luke 1:36, which refers to John the Baptist's mother Elizabeth, one of the "daughters of Aaron" (1:5), as a "kinswoman" of Mary. For the use of this passage in support of the view that Mary was of mixed royal and priestly lineage, see Eusebius, *Supp. Quaest.* 14 (PG 22:974). For the view that Mary was a Levite, see, for example, the claim of Faustus the Manichaean that Jesus could not be legitimately called a Davidic king of the tribe of Judah, because Mary was the daughter of a priest named Joachim (in Augustine, *Faust.* 23.4.9). For the tradition that Jesus' father Joseph was himself a priest (of Davidic lineage!), see *Hist. Jos. Carp.* 2 and 7. For discussion of Mary's Levitical ancestry and its bearing on Jesus' own mixed lineage, see Walter Bauer, *Das Leben Jesus in Zeitalter der neutestamentlichen Apokryphen* (Tübingen: Mohr, 1909), 9–17.

25. Zahn, *Forschungen*, 6:329 (n. 2). Conceivably, the conflation was somehow suggested by David's descent from Miriam, the sister of Moses and Aaron; for the idea that David was of priestly lineage through Miriam, see *Sifra Num*, par. 78.

26. For pre-Eusebian witnesses to this genealogy of Jesus, see, for example, Hippolytus, *Ben. Is. Jac.* 15 (*Hippolyte de Rome. Sur les bénédictions d'Isaac, de Jacob et de Moise* [ed. Maurice Brière, Louis Mariès, and Benoît-Charles Mercier; PO 27.1–2; Paris: Didot, 1954], 72.8–11): Jesus was "tribally mixed" in order that as a "descendant of both tribes he might be shown to be both king and priest of God." For discussion, see Louis Mariès, "Le Messie issu de Levi chez Hippolyte de Rome," *RSR* (Mélanges J. Lebreton) 39–40 (1951–1952): 381–96. Eusebius himself appears to have found elements of the underlying exegetical tradition appealing. See, for example, *Hist. eccl.* 1.6–11 and *Dem. ev.* 8.1.32, which incorporate all the elements of the exegesis of Gen 49:10 and Dan 9:24–27 except for its genealogical presuppositions. According to Eusebius, the "only consistent" understanding of the word "Judah" in Jacob's prophecy is the "Jewish race," not the tribe of Judah. Cf. also Eusebius, *Supp. Quaest.* 14 (PG 22:973), who, in disputing their tribal kinship, maintained that the word *syngenis* in Luke implied only that Mary and Elizabeth were both Jews, not that they were from the same tribe.

27. Nuvolone, "La Légende du Christ," esp. 206–12.

his friend to convert to Christianity; b) Theodosius's revelation of the existence of the secret codex, and the circumstances that result in Jesus' registration as priest; and c) a concluding section describing the preservation of the codex in Tiberias. In this final section, Theodosius pleads with Philip not to pass this information on to Justinian in a spasm of religious zeal. The only outcome of a futile campaign to recover the codex would be needless conflict and bloodshed. While heeding his advice, Philip does inform friends and Christian officials, the latter of whom subsequently confirm Theodosius's claims about Jesus' priesthood.

Both internal and external evidence provide some clues, however imprecise, about the time of the work's composition. When the priests enter Jesus' name into the registry, they date the event according to the number of the indiction (29:2). Since the indiction, a fifteen-year fiscal cycle, was a chronological convention unknown before the reign of Constantine, the story at least in its preserved version must have been composed no earlier than the fourth century.[28] A précis of the story by John of Euboea in his *In conceptionem Deiparae* 18 (*Sermon on the Conception of the Mother of God;* PG 96:1489–92) shows that the work was already known in some form by the mid-eighth century. Although the exchange between Theodosius and Philip takes place during the reign of Justinian, the story is told from the standpoint of an anonymous third-person narrator. In the Greek witnesses to the longer recension, the narration later shifts to Philip himself, who, after learning about the codex from Theodosius, describes how he communicated the story to friends and authorities in the church. But this is for dramatic effect only. The shorter version found in the *Suda* puts the narrative entirely into the mouth of an unnamed third party who had, by his own testimony, learned about the codex only indirectly. From the standpoint of the narrator, Justinian is in either case a figure of the past, the "emperor of pious memory" (*Priest. Jes.* 1:1; *Suda* 1:1). Theodosius's concerns about the violence bound to occur if Justinian were to attempt to recover the "codex" also raises the possibility that the story was composed at a time when Palestine was no longer under the control of the Byzantines (seventh century). The approximate date of the composition of the work in its original form would thus fall somewhere between the seventh and eighth centuries.

Sharp twists in the narrative, unexplained details, discrepancies, and questionable claims are pervasive in *Priest. Jes.* If the word "codex" refers to the physical appearance of the registry, this, like the reference to the indiction number, would be an obvious anachronism.[29] Strikingly, Jesus never appears to make a deposition or even to speak in his own defense. The council summons Mary only. From the standpoint of the narrative, this means that, after recounting the assembly of the priests, the storyline transitions to a highly fraught account of the interrogation of Mary and the tests to validate her virginity. According to Theodosius, the reason why the temple priests were under such pressure to find an immediate replace-

---

28. On the origins of the indiction cycle, see Bonnie Blackburn and Leofranc Holford-Strevens, *The Oxford Companion to the Year: An Exploration of Calendar Customs and Time-Reckoning* (Oxford: Oxford University Press, 1999), 769–71.

29. Cf. Nuvolone, "Sur le Sacerdote," 83 (note to title), who suggests that, by the time of the composition of the work, the term "codex" may have meant only an official registry, without implying anything about its actual physical form. Some later versions describe the registry differently; cf., for example, John of Euboea, *In conceptionem Deiparae* 18.2, 4 (*tomos*). In his own description, Michael Glycas typically refers to the registry as a *chartēs* ("papyrus"); see 92.5; 93.7; 94.5; 94.11; 96.6; 96.22; 99.15; 100.2; 102.12; 103.16; 103.23; 105.16. On occasion, however, he calls it a "codex" (96.1; 105.17–18) and a "scroll" (*eilitarion*): 105.12; 105.19; 105.25; 107.17.

ment for the deceased priest was because of a custom requiring that the number of priests be fixed at 22, in line with the number of books of the Hebrew Bible (7:1). In later versions, this symmetry is extended to include the 22 letters of the Hebrew alphabet (see, for example, *Suda* 3:1–2). The source for this tradition about a fixed quota of 22 priests is unknown, and is most likely an extension of the symbolism associated with that number found in other patristic and Byzantine sources.[30] Theodosius implies that he had learned about the circumstances of Jesus' enrollment in the priesthood from the witness of the secret codex. But we would hardly expect to find these details recorded in what was, by Theodosius's own description, a simple registry of the names of the priests and their parents, and the date of their appointment. What this suggests is that the story of the hidden codex was only one element of a much more developed secret tradition about Jesus' enrollment as priest. The reason for its prominence was that it served both as a physical witness to Theodosius's account of events and a tangible reminder, maintained by the Jews themselves, of their refusal to accept the truth of Jesus' divine sonship.

The subsequent verification of Theodosius's testimony from other authorities presents its own problems. The Christian bishops and monks to whom Philip passes on the information are said to have verified Theodosius's story of Jesus' priesthood from the Gospels, Josephus, and the "Memoirs" of Eusebius's *Ecclesiastical History* (34:1–3). Since nothing about Jesus' service in the Jerusalem temple priesthood survives in the writings of Josephus, this is likely one of many documented instances in which Josephus, a highly regarded authority in the Byzantine Church, has been turned into an independent witness to the truth of Christian doctrine.[31] Philip's mention of the "Memoirs" in the *Ecclesiastical History* presumably means the memoirs of Hegesippus, a second-century Jewish convert to Christianity and one of Eusebius's principal authorities for the history of the early Jerusalem church. In his *History,* Eusebius does credit Hegesippus as the source for his notice about James's officiating as Jerusalem high priest. But there is nothing in Eusebius's excerpts from him describing "how Jesus, along with the priests, used to enter into the temple and perform sacred rites" (34:2).

The two passages from the New Testament Gospels that the author cites as independent verification of Jesus' priesthood are his cleansing of the temple and Luke's account of the beginning of his ministry in Galilee (34:3). According to Luke 4:16–19, the first official act of Jesus' public ministry was to enter a synagogue in Galilee and read a passage from the prophet Isaiah. The opening verses of this passage contain the words: "The Spirit of the Lord is upon me, because he has anointed me to preach good news to the poor" (Isa 61:1). In the older interpretive tradition, this was cited often as evidence of Jesus' anointing by

---

30. There is no ancient authority for the existence of a fixed number of 22 priests; cf. 1 Chr 24:7–18, which speaks of 24 priestly courses organized during the reign of David; see also Josephus, *Ant.* 7.365, who speaks of 24 courses, each consisting of six priestly families. The number 22 may have been derived from a reference in the book of Nehemiah to the names of 22 post-exilic priests, who came up to Jerusalem with Zerubbabel and Jeshua (12:1–7, 12–21). On the enumeration of the 22 books of Jewish Scriptures, see Josephus, *Ag. Ap.* 1.37–38. See also *Jub.* 2:23, which also numbers 22 acts of creation and 22 patriarchs from Adam to Jacob. Patristic and Byzantine authors also note some of the numerical symmetries; cf. Georgius Syncellus, *Chron.* 3.14–18, who on the authority of *Jubilees,* numbers 22 works of creation, 22 Hebrew books, and 22 patriarchs from Adam to Jacob; see also Epiphanius, *De mens. et pond.* 22; *Pan.* 8.6, according to which the 27 books of the Hebrew should be counted as 22, equal to the number of letters in the Hebrew alphabet, the works of creation.

31. According to the *Suda*'s version (14:2), Josephus supplied the corroborative information in his "Capture of Jerusalem" (*ton syngraphea tēs halōseōs Hierosolymōn*), ostensibly in reference to his *Jewish War.*

God as priest (see Eusebius, *Hist. eccl.* 1.3.13–14). But the narrator of our story has understood its significance differently. Situating the episode in the Jerusalem temple and reasoning analogically from his own knowledge of Byzantine practice, the author concludes that Jesus must have been a priest at the time; otherwise, he would have been prohibited from publicly reading sacred Scripture in a house of worship. That anachronistic explanation suggests that the author had not always fully grasped the significance of the assorted testimonies to Jesus' priesthood that he had received from older tradition.

In his brief introduction, Vassiliev traces the authorship of *Priest. Jes.* to a "Christianus e Iudaeis."[32] Van der Horst saw the presence of extraneous, "non-functional" details in the narrative as possibly suggestive of a "kernel of historicity" embedded in an otherwise highly fictionalized dialogue.[33] Nuvolone, for his part, maintained that behind *Priest. Jes.* lay an older version, composed by a Jewish Christian sometime before its current setting during the reign of Justinian. One of its purposes was to present a "Jewish Jesus," the perfect embodiment of the eternal priest-king of Jewish messianic expectation. The Jewish-Christian author also hoped to explain to his readers why, in spite of his personal convictions, he could not sever his ties with his ancestral customs and submit to baptism. A later editor then reshaped this *apologia* into a self-condemning exposé of the author's more venal underlying motives.[34] While there are certainly enough internal tensions in the preserved version to justify this reconstruction of the text's prehistory, more precise analysis of the work's provenance and literary and textual history must await further study. What we can say in any case is that especially in the earlier, longer versions of *Priest. Jes.*, the treatment of the dilemma facing "secret believers" in the Jewish community is, while hardly complimentary, at least forgiving.[35]

Although the anti-Jewish element of the story is more pronounced in some later versions, vilification of the Jews is at best a secondary interest of this complex and multifaceted work.[36] There are, to be sure, caricatures of Jewish leaders. In their inquisition of Mary, the conduct of the temple priests is by turns officious, deceitful, argumentative, condescending, cajoling, suspicious, and ultimately desperate. But these men are literary foils to Mary, their villainous behavior mainly serving to dramatize her virtue and plight in the face of badgering adversaries. Offsetting the subsequent conspiracy devised by Jewish elites to keep Christians and their co-religionists from knowing the truth is the intimate and mutual friendship between a well-meaning Christian and a Jew under pressure to convert. Theodosius's spiritual well-being is not the only reason why Philip pleads with him to convert; it would also enable the two of them to strengthen the bonds of friendship. Philip's counterpart emerges as a genuinely sympathetic character, torn by inner conflicts. Even if he cannot publicly affirm what he privately knows, Theodosius decides, for the sake of their friendship, to tell his Christian friend about the secret codex (6:3). He admits

32. Vassiliev, *Anecdota graeco-byzantina*, xxv.

33. Cf. also Pieter W. van der Horst, "Jesus and the Jews according to the Suda," *ZNW* 84 (2009): 268–77 at 275 n. 24, who, as an example, cites the description of Philip as a money-dealer.

34. Nuvolone, "La Légende du Christ," 213–15.

35. In the context of official policy towards the Jewish community of the middle Byzantine age, Theodosius's confession could be understood as an appeal for a relaxation of the practice of involuntary baptism; see further below, p. 79.

36. Note, however, that Heinz Schreckenberg does include the work in his inventory of Christian *adversus Judaeos* literature; see his *Die christlichen Adversus-Judaeos-Texte und ihr literarisches und historisches Umfeld (1.–11. Jh.)* (4th ed.; Europäische Hochschulschriften. Reihe XXIII, Theologie 172; Frankfurt am Main: Peter Lang, 1999), 404.

that loyalty to ancestral customs is only a pretext masking the more selfish reasons lying behind his refusal to convert. While acknowledging his fear of losing his privileged standing in the Jewish community, Theodosius rues this as a character flaw born of "human reasoning," and one that endangers his life in the world to come. And he pins much of the blame for his reluctance on Christians themselves. Christians, he complains, have forgotten the debt they owe to the Jews; "Christ and the apostles, *your masters*," he points out "belong to our race" (5:4, emphasis mine). Why convert to Christianity, Theodosius asks, when Christians conduct themselves so shamefully, heaping abuse upon Jewish converts to Christianity, and likening their baptism to "giving water to an ass" (4:5–5:4)?

In Speyer's judgment, Theodosius's conspiratorial talk of a hidden codex was little more than a ruse to account for a work that existed "only in the imagination of the forger."[37] While that might be true, the motif functions here more than as a cover story. After learning about the registry, the impetuous Philip, "moved by divine zeal," warns Theodosius that his continued silence about its existence is an affront to God (31:1). Theodosius's response to this charge is made to appear more sober, self-reflective, and ultimately more compelling. God, he says, will not judge him for his silence; rather he will hold Philip and the emperor to account for instigating a failed campaign to recover the document, resulting only in needless bloodshed and the permanent loss of the object itself (32:1). Because Christians are already convinced of Jesus' divine sonship, he says to Philip, they hardly require more proof. On the other hand, the existence of a hidden registry, carefully (and ironically) guarded by the Jews themselves in Tiberias, will serve as an eternal rebuke to their unbelief. However counterintuitive it may appear to Philip, its existence must therefore remain a "true *mystērion* hidden by them (the Jews) forever" (32:1; 35:1).

For Christian readers frustrated by the failure of the mission to the Jews, it might be reassuring to learn that status anxiety, not religious principles, kept a respected and well-compensated Jewish leader like Theodosius from disowning Judaism and formally entering the Christian community through baptism. So would the story of inaccessible and jealously guarded books, corroborative of Christianity but known only to religious insiders. If there were such books, Tiberias, the home of the leading rabbinic academy until the Arab conquest of Palestine, was the obvious place to conceal them.

From at least as early as the fourth century, synagogues in Tiberias were said to have preserved documents potentially supportive of Christian doctrines. Although these documents were closely guarded, Jewish insiders occasionally leaked out information about them. According to Epiphanius (*Pan.* 30.8.1–12.10), Jewish converts had spoken to him at length about Hebrew versions of Christian books stored in the treasuries (*gazophylakiois*) of the synagogues of Tiberias. One of his Jewish informants was Joseph of Tiberias, a Christian convert who went on to attain high standing as a "count" (*comes*) in Constantine's court. After becoming progressively more interested in and troubled by Christianity, Joseph witnessed the deathbed baptism of the Jewish patriarch. Later, to satisfy his curiosity, he opened a sealed treasury in Tiberias, and found there Hebrew versions of Matthew, John, and the Acts of the Apostles. Yet, he remained obstinate, even after experiencing two visions of Jesus and curing an insane man of his afflictions by performing Christian rites. The parallels between the stories of Joseph and Theodosius are arresting. Like Theodosius, Joseph is a man of high station, who in his capacity as "apostle" had served as

---

37. Wolfgang Speyer, *Bücherfunde in der Glaubenswerbung der Antike* (Hypomnemata, vol. 24; Göttingen, Vandenhoeck & Ruprecht, 1970), 139.

adviser to the Jewish patriarch in Tiberias. Even in the face of overwhelming evidence of the truths of Christianity, his high office in the Jewish community of Tiberias of the fourth century initially deterred him from converting. The critical difference between him and Theodosius lies in the resolution of their spiritual conflicts. Theodosius, unlike Joseph, never formally converts to Christianity; even so, the revelation of the secret codex by an influential and respected Jewish leader could only enhance its credibility.

Forcible baptism of Jews, conspiracy theories involving Jewish elites, the existence of crypto-Christians in the Jewish community, and suspicions about the motives of Jewish proselytes, are also common topics in Byzantine literature from the seventh to ninth centuries.[38] *Priest. Jes.*, in its generous description of the moral and spiritual crisis of a Jewish leader and close friend of a Christian, its call for Christian self-scrutiny, its representation of Jesus as a Jewish priest of certifiable Levitical ancestry, and its assertion of Christianity's debt to and continuity with Judaism, stakes out a singularly benevolent position on topics of ongoing interest in Byzantium.

Literary and Theological Influence

In a brief gloss appended to the end of the entry in the *Suda* lexicon, an editor, somewhat unexpectedly, upends the whole narrative with a brief closing verdict: "But Chrysostom categorically rejects the priesthood attributed to Christ" (15:7).[39] The Byzantine historian Michael Glycas (12th cent.), a writer with a deep distrust of "apocryphal" books, was far more scathing in his assessment. In his *Annales* and in a lengthier exposition addressed to the monk Chariton, he forcefully denounces any secret document propounding Jesus' appointment as Levitical priest.[40] When pitted against the collective opposing testimony of John Chrysostom, Athanasius, Cyril, Maximus, Gregory, Basil, and the New Testament itself, Michael writes, the lone witness of "that Jew" (*tou Ioudaiou ekeinou*) Theodosius should be straightaway discounted as an absurdity.[41] The requirements of such an important and publicly visible office would hardly square with the Gospel presentation of Jesus as a relatively obscure and unknown figure before his baptism by John.[42] If the priestly registry had in fact named God as his father, then Jewish leaders would not have continued challenging the authority of the "son of Joseph."[43] Granted, a book of the Bible was given to him to read in the synagogue of Galilee; but this was in recognition of his gifts

---

38. For these motifs in Byzantine literature, see Vincent Déroche, "Regards croisés des hérésiologues, des canonistes et des hagiographes sur les Juifs à Byzance," in *Orthodoxy and Heresy in Byzantium: The Definition and the Notion of Orthodoxy and Some Other Studies on the Heresies and the Non-Christian Religions* (ed. Antonio Rigo and Pavel Ermilov; Quaderni di Nea Rhome 4; Rome: Università degli Studi di Roma Tor Vergata, 2010): 61–78 at 67–68; Gilbert Dagron and Vincent Déroche, "Juifs et Chrétiens dans l'Orient du VIIe siècle," *Travaux et Mémoires* 11 (1991): 260–63, 354–57.

39. For Chrysostom's views on Jesus' non-Levitical priesthood, see n. 11 to *Suda* 15:7.

40. Michael Glycas, *Annales* (ed. Immanuel Bekker; CSHB 21; Bonn: Weber, 1836), 394.12–16. Glycas's more detailed exposition of the question, addressed to Chariton, has the title: "If it is necessary to pay attention to those who say that Christ was elected priest by the Jews" (*Quaest.* 54, 92–107, ed. Eustratiades). For Glycas's views on apocryphal books, see, for example, his *Annales*, 206.21–22, where he dismisses the contents of *Jub.* as a "joke and a farce." This is exactly the same language that he applies to *Priest. Jes.* (*Quaest.* 54, 93.13–14).

41. *Quaest.* 54, 105.18. See also 54, 93.5–13, where Glycas doubts the reliability of a Jewish informant willing to betray self-incriminating secrets and ridicules the gullibility of tradesmen like Philip.

42. *Annales*, 394.12–16; *Quaest.* 54, 94.23–95.4. Later versions seem to have recognized the difficulty; see below, p. 80 and n. 54.

43. *Quaest.* 54, 95.6–12; 95.19–96.4.

as a teacher, not of his priestly office.[44] Above all, Glycas recognized the inconsistency of the whole story with the epistle to the Hebrews (7:13–14), and the latter's representation of Jesus as eternal non-Levitical high priest.[45]

But in spite of these expressions of doubt and even the opposing testimony of the estimable John Chrysostom, *Priest. Jes.* experienced what Gilbert Dagron has rightly termed a "partial success" in the churches of the East.[46] Glycas himself acknowledges as much when he states that the story of Jesus' enrollment as temple priest was so "widely spoken of" (*polythryllēton*) that it demanded of him a thorough refutation. Its inclusion in the popularly known *Suda* lexicon obviously was one reason for its standing and subsequent dissemination in the West.[47] In a work attributed to "Neophytus the Recluse," the author, apparently on the authority of the *Suda* version, retells the story to buttress and explain Byzantine eucharistic theology.[48] Granted, he writes, it might seem strange for Jesus to have accepted consecration from "lawless and murderous priests"—it would have seemingly been more fitting had the roles been reversed—but this was an act of humility on Jesus' part, and one necessary to the divine economy. In addition to ratifying him as eternal priest after the order of Melchizedek and authorizing his acts against the money-changers in the temple, it enabled him to play the role of both priest and sacrificial lamb in the mystery of the Eucharist.

Equally, if not more, important was the story's contribution to the cult of the Theotokos in the Eastern Church.[49] In the longer recension, Theodosius's account of Jesus' appointment as priest features a dramatic and extended account of Mary's interrogation from the council of priests, who demand to learn from her the name of Jesus' true father. Like Susanna, another virtuous biblical heroine falsely accused of sexual infidelity, she despairs at being "hemmed in on all sides (*stena moi pantothen*)" (20:1).[50] Mary's recollection of the trial of bitter waters and the subsequent physical examination by midwives recalls similar traditions found in the *Protevangelium of James,* another work central to the developing cult of Mary. If her own husband Joseph insisted that she submit to the test of bitter waters and remained unconvinced until the angel Gabriel appeared to him, how, Mary asks, could she possibly dispel the suspicions of strangers (21:1)?[51] But in spite of the priests' best efforts to coax from her an admission of adultery, ultimately her honor is vindicated through an elaborate regimen of tests; these include the gynecological exami-

---

44. *Quaest.* 54, 98.12–28.

45. *Quaest.* 54, 101.3–8. See also similar criticisms of the story by Maximus the Greek, a scholar and translator working in Russia during the sixteenth century; for discussion and Italian translation of his critique, see Ziffer, "Contributo allo studio della tradizione slava," 349–51.

46. A position encapsulated in the title of Dagron's essay, "Jésus prêtre du judaïsme: le demi-succès d'une légende."

47. See above, p. 70 and n. 7.

48. See Ioannes P. Tsiknopoullos, "The Minor Works of Neophytus, Priest, Monk, and Recluse" (in Greek), *Byzantion* 39 (1969): 344–48; see further Dagron, "Jésus prêtre du judaïsme," 20.

49. On the use of the tradition of her mixed lineage in the veneration of Mary, see, for example, Andrew of Crete (7th cent.), *De nativitate beatae Virginis* (PG 97:812BC). Here, Mary, the woman of mixed royal and priestly ancestry, becomes the conduit through which the lines of Aaron and David were channeled into the eternal high priesthood and kingship of Jesus. For discussion, see René Laurentin, *Maria. Ecclesia. Sacerdotium,* vol. 1: *Essai sur le développement d'une idée religieuse* (Paris: Nouvelles Éditions Latines, 1952), 67–69.

50. Cf. Sus 1:22: *Stena moi pantothen.*

51. On the trial of bitter waters, see Num 5:11–31; cf. *Prot. Jas.* 16, and note 19 to 21:1.

nation and testimony from eyewitnesses at the time of her birth (26:2).[52] The influence of this tradition on Byzantine Mariology is most evident in John of Euboea's *In conceptionem Deiparae* 18. He cites the story of the secret registry more for the purpose of establishing Mary's purity than to prove Jesus' fitness for priesthood.

In the course of the transmission of this many-sided narrative, the story has undergone numerous omissions, revisions, and adaptations.[53] To forestall Glycas's objection that the Jerusalem priesthood would never have considered a figure as obscure as Jesus was at the time of his appointment, the version of the story attested in Moscow gr. 443 states that Jesus' ministry had actually already begun when the priests decided to consider him for the office (7:1).[54] According to the *Suda,* the anonymous narrator of the story, not the bishops and monks, verifies the accuracy of Theodosius's account from his own investigations of Eusebius, Josephus, and the Gospels. For reasons that are unclear, the *Suda* traces Jesus' mixed lineage through Joseph, not Mary (7:2). Witnesses to the story also take contradictory positions on the extent of Jewish collusion in concealing the secret codex. In the longer recension, Theodosius's statement that "a great number of our community" (32:3) were familiar with the codex amounts to an acknowledgment that awareness of its existence was not confined to a Jewish inner circle. According to the *Suda,* however, Theodosius confides in Philip that the secret was made known only to "a very few and the trustworthy of our nation" (15:2). Underlying this inconsistency is an unresolved tension between two opposing tendencies in the tradition: 1) the codex as a carefully protected secret (*mystērion*) entrusted to the custody of a select few with a vested interest in concealing its existence from others; and 2) the codex as proof that the Jewish refusal to publicly acknowledge Jesus' divine sonship stood in direct defiance of conclusive and recognized testimony from their own temple records.

Later retellings also supplement the Gospel proof texts adduced as evidence of Jesus' admission into the priesthood. One of them is the *Pericopae Adulterae* about the woman caught in adultery and Jesus' bold challenge to her accusers (John 8:2–11). When asked for a legal opinion from the scribes and Pharisees, Jesus bends over and writes something in the sand (8:6, 8). In the reprise of the incident recorded in Vatican, Ottoboni gr. 408 (5:4–12), the scribes and Pharisees are now priests. Over the course of several days, Jesus records in the sand a transgression each of them had committed, which he then privately reveals to him. At the end of this discreetly executed exercise, none of the priests is able to proclaim publicly that he is without sin. Only a member of their own ranks, the author concludes, could claim the authority to condemn his fellow priests in this way.

Some of the most extensive rewriting involves the portrayal of Judaism. While largely following the Greek text of the longer recension, the Arabic translation sets the dialogue between Philip and Theodosius during the reign of the "unbelieving emperor Julian," not Justinian; the site of their meeting is changed to a harbor city of Syria where Philip had recently disembarked to carry on commerce. In the narrative, which takes pains to stress their mutual affection, Theodosius acknowledges that the "greater part of our Jewish com-

---

52. For a similar account of a gynecological test by the midwife Salome at the time of Jesus' birth, see *Prot. Jas.* 19–20; see further note 21 to 26:2.

53. For detailed discussion of later reworkings of the story, see Nuvolone, "La Légende du Christ," 211–12.

54. See also John of Euboea, *In conceptionem Deiparae* 18.2, who points to Luke 2:52 ("And Jesus increased in wisdom and in years, and in divine and human favor") as proof that Jesus' wisdom was recognized well before the beginning of his ministry.

munity" actually accepts Jesus' messiahship; and his critique of the failings of Christians is even more severe than that of the parallel Greek text (*Hist. patr. Alex.* 122). There is also an edifying resolution to the strains on the friendship created by their religious differences. After revealing the story of the hidden codex, Theodosius accepts baptism and proves to be a sound expositor of the faith. Inspired by the actions of a Jewish leader willing to act against interest and forfeit his honor and prestige in exchange for his religious convictions, many other Jews follow suit (*Hist. patr. Alex.* 133–34).

The sharp invective against the Jews found in some of the later, shorter versions pulls the story in the opposite direction. Theodosius's critique of Christians for their abuse of Jewish proselytes and their failure to appreciate Christianity's debt to Judaism is either muted or disappears altogether. In later retellings, the codex is no longer merely a silent rebuke of the Jews; the final public reading of the registry now becomes one of the eschatological judgments against the Jews.[55] At the conclusion of the version found in Vatican, Ottoboni gr. 408, the author speaks triumphantly of having demonstrated Jesus' priesthood from the very testimony of "the prophet-killing and lawless Jews" (6:4). Pro-forma language like this is mild compared to John of Euboea's intemperate denunciation of the Jews in his own rendition of the story. Omitting the framing narrative about the friendship between Theodosius and Philip, he begins with an outburst against the "folly, obtuseness, and arrogance" of the Jews (1). Scores will be settled when, at the second coming, the secret registry is at last opened and read, and the Jews are condemned by the written deposition of their own priests: "Jesus, the son of God, and son of Mary, by a vote from on high, will be priest forever" (2).

Translations

Five texts are presented here. The longer Greek version is based on Ziffer's published edition. Chapter numbers follow Ziffer's divisions; verse numbers are my own.[56] Then follows a synopsis of the better-known text of the *Suda* based on A. Adler's edition alongside Vassiliev's edition of the similar text in Moscow, Russian State Library, gr. 443 (chapter and verse divisions are my own). Also featured is Vassiliev's other manuscript, Vatican, Ottoboni 408 (chapter and verse divisions are my own), and finally, a précis of the story by John of Euboea from J.-P. Migne's edition of *In conceptionem Deiparae* 18 (verse divisions are my own).

Sigla

Arab	Arabic version in the *History of the Patriarchs of Alexandria*
K	Georgian version
GrL	Longer Greek recension
L	Mount Athos, Lavra Γ 37
T	Turin, Biblioteca Nazionale, gr. 185
V	Vatican, Biblioteca apostolica, gr. 687
GrS	Shorter Greek recension

---

55. The belief that the registry would be read in condemnation of the Jews in the final judgment must have later become well integrated into the tradition. At the conclusion of his refutation of the story, Glycas denounces this idea at length (*Quaest.* 54, 106.4–107.9).

56. Because I did not have access to the Greek text attested in the unpublished MS L, I have generally not included readings from this manuscript. References to the Georgian version in the notes to the text are derived from readings in Ziffer's apparatus (from "Una versione greca").

Mosc.   Moscow, Russian State Library, gr. 443
Ottob.   Vatican, Biblioteca apostolica, Ottoboni gr. 408
S   Text in the *Suda* lexicon

Bibliography

EDITIONS AND TRANSLATIONS

Adler, Ada, ed. *Suidae Lexicon*. 5 vols. Leipzig: Teubner, 1928–1938.

De Keyser, Jeroen. "Early Modern Latin Translations of the Apocryphal *De Sacerdotio Christi*." *Lias* 40 (2013): 29–82. (Critical editions of six Latin translations of the *Suda* text).

Evetts, Basil Thomas Alfred, ed. and trans. *History of the Patriarchs of the Coptic Church of Alexandria (Saint Mark to Theonas)*. PO 1.2. Paris: Firmin-Didot, 1948.

Nuvolone, Flavio G., trans. "Sur le sacerdoce du Christ ou Confession de Théodose." Pages 77–99 in *EAC* 2. (French translation of the longer Greek recension.)

Qubaneišvili, Solomon, ed. *Zveli k'art'uli literaturis krestomathia*. Tbilisi, 1946. (Edition of Georgian translation of the longer recension.)

Vassiliev, Athanasius. *Anecdota graeco-byzantina, pars prior*. Moscow: Imperial University, 1893. (Includes three Greek witnesses to the story.)

Ziffer, Giorgio. " 'La Confessione di Teodosio' nella sua tradizione orientale." MA thesis, Rome: La Sapienza, Facolta di lettere e filosofia, 1985.

———. "Una versione greca inedita del 'De Sacerdotio Christi.'" Pages 141–73 in *Studi per Riccardo Ribuoli. Scritti di filologia, musicologia, storia*. Edited by Franco Piperno. Rome: Edizioni di storia e letteratura, 1986. (Edition and Italian translation of the longer Greek recension.)

STUDIES

Adler, William. "Exodus 6:23 and the High Priest from the Tribe of Judah." *JTS* 48 (1997): 24–47.

Dagron, Gilbert. "Jésus prêtre du judaïsme: le demi-succès d'une légende." Pages 1–24 in *Leimôn. Studies Presented to Lennart Rydén on His Sixty-Fifth Birthday*. Edited by Jan O. Rosenqvist. Acta Universitatis Upsaliensis, Studia Byzantina Upsaliensia 6. Uppsala: Uppsala University, 1996. (Close analysis of the *Suda* lemma, along with a French translation of a portion of the text.)

Horst, Pieter W. van der. "Jesus and the Jews according to the Suda." *ZNW* 84 (1993): 268–77.

Külzer, Andreas. *Disputationes graecae contra Iudaeos*. Stuttgart and Leipzig: Teubner, 1999. (Inventory of witnesses, and brief summary of the story, pp. 129–34.)

Nuvolone, Flavio G. "La Légende du Christ, XXIIe et dernier prêtre du temple de Jérusalem: priorité du texte long." Pages 203–32 in *Anthropos Laïkos: mélanges Alexandre Faivre à l'occasion de ses 30 ans d'enseignement*. Edited by Marie-Anne Vannier, Otto Wermelinger, and Gregor Wurst. Fribourg, Switzerland: Éditions Universitaires, 2000.

Thilo, Johann Karl. *Codex apocryphus Novi Testamenti*. Leipzig: Vogel, 1832. (Dated but highly learned discussion of the Levitical lineage of Jesus motif in the *Suda* text, pp. 375–76.)

Ziffer, Giorgio. "Contributo allo studio della tradizione slava della 'Confessione di Teodosio.'" *OCP* 54 (1988): 331–51.

On the Priesthood of Jesus
Longer recension (GrL)

Introduction

Apology[a] of Theodosius, schoolmaster[b] and teacher of the Jews, to Philip, a money-dealer,[c] concerning the divine incarnation, and the fact that Jesus, son of Mary, the mother of God, was registered as priest in the hidden codex[d] existing in Jerusalem.

Philip urges Theodosius to convert

1 [1]In the time of Justinian,[e] the emperor of pious memory, there was a man, a prince of the Jews,[f] by the name of Theodosius. [2]He was known not only by a very great number of Christians, but even by the aforementioned emperor. [3]There was also in that time a Christian named Philip, a money-dealer who owned a money-dealing business called the "Payments."[g] [4]Because he considered Theodosius not only an acquaintance and a client, but also a very true friend, he would constantly urge him to become a Christian.

2 [1]So one day, with even greater persistence, he began to say to him: [2]"I marvel that you, a man who is a true scholar and one who knows especially well what the prophets have proclaimed about Christ, are not a believer. [3]Please become

---

a. Title from V. T has: "Discussion (*dialexis*), or the agreement (*synkatathesis*), of Theodosius a Jew with Philip, a Christian silversmith (*arguroplatēn*) of Constantinople, regarding the divine incarnation of God the Logos, his priesthood, and his registration." For "apology (*apologia*)" L has "confession (*homologia*)"; K: "Confession of Theodosius prince of the Jews written by Philip about the incarnation of Christ and how he became a priest." For Theodosius's description of his revelation to Philip as a "confession," see further below, 4:3.

b. Text: *archipherekitou*, a word possibly derived from the Aramaic *ryshy prq'* (lit. "heads of the chapter"). The word first appears in Justinian, *Novella 146, Peri Hebraiōn* which prohibits the "archipherecites, the elders, and the teachers" from preventing by anathema the reading of the Septuagint text of Jewish Scriptures. For discussion of the meaning of the word, see most recently David Goodblatt, *The Monarchic Principle: Studies in Jewish Self-government in Antiquity* (Tübingen: Mohr Siebeck, 1994), 274–76. Later in the narrative (30:1), Theodosius is identified as a priest; in the Arabic version, Theodosius is also twice called a priest (120, 121).

c. Text: *arguropratēs*, which could mean both "money-dealer" and "silversmith." In Byzantium, the two occupations overlapped; see Dagron, "Jésus prêtre du judaïsme," 11 n. 5. Philip's occupation as silversmith is more clearly suggested in the title of MS T, which calls him *arguroplatēs*.

d. Text: *kōdix*. Nuvolone translates as "registre," in the sense of a state registry; for explanation see his note on the title (*EAC* 2:82) and the introduction, p. 75.

e. Arab 121, which sets the dialogue during the reign of the "unbelieving prince Julian" in a port city of Syria, where Philip had docked his ship.

f. Arab 120: "a priest of the Jews."

g. Text: *ta apodosima*, the meaning of which is uncertain.

a Christian, and we will rejoice not only in the spirit, but in the flesh as well, by spending time and eating together."

3 [1]After Philip uttered these words in his endeavor, as far as he was able, to persuade him to believe in Christ, Theodosius welcomed Philip and said to him, "I am well aware that you hold a great love for me. [2]And even if what you are saying to me was not truthful, I would have had to welcome your affection for me. [3]Because I welcome this affection, I will also reveal to you my innermost thought, so that if you depart without accomplishing anything, you might not be thoroughly affronted by me.

Theodosius confesses his secret Christian faith

4 [1]"Thus, in the sight of God, I commence my discourse to you without any falsehood, but I entreat you, out of respect for our perfect love, to keep this to yourself. [2]The Christ proclaimed by the prophets, the one who is worshipped by you, has come. [3]This I confess as true and I have complete assurance of it. [4]I also have confidence in you, as a genuine friend, that it is for my benefit that you persist in doing all these things. [5]But because I am under the sway of purely human reasoning, I do not become a Christian. [6]In this, even if I am under judgment, at least I am for the time being a prince of my people, and I enjoy great honor, glory, and everything that is necessary for this life. [7]But were I to become a Christian, I would be deprived of this.

5 [1]"And not only would I give offense to my people, I would also be abused by you Christians, just as I see other Jews, after their baptism, being disparaged by you and hearing, 'If you baptize a Jew, you are giving water to an ass!'[a] [2]What incentive do I have to become a Christian? [3]I know that Christians, in doing this, are sinning and provoking God's wrath, because in failing to discern that salvation has come to them from us, they are offending those whom they ought further to encourage. [4]For Christ and his apostles, your masters, belong to our race. [5]If they had wanted to edify us immediately, they would have provided for all of us collectively to become Christians.[b]

John 4:22

6 [1]"For this reason, to avoid being deprived of what are deemed the pleasures of life and so that I will not be abused by you Christians, I too disdain Christianity, and rather content myself with the ancestral customs, which I plead as an excuse. [2]Certainly, more than you, many of us know both from the documents and the very facts, that we are committing a sin in refusing our salvation. [3]And now, lest by chance you suppose that I am mocking you, see, I am confirming it for you by my acts as well: I will reveal to you the secret[c] hidden by us for a long time. [4]From it, even more than you, we have received complete certainty

---

a. Arab 121–22: "When a Jew is baptized, it is as if one baptized an ass." The shorter Greek recensions do not include Theodosius's critique of Christian abuse of Jewish converts.

b. The meaning is uncertain. Cf. Arab 122: "But you neglect the good tidings that they brought to you, and the doctrine that they taught you." On the basis of the Georgian text, Nuvolone ("La Légende du Christ," 209) conjectures that the original Greek text may have read: "Accordingly, they wanted to build on our foundation and to prepare us collectively, and by mutual agreement, to become Christians." That is to say, Christ and the apostles intended to create a unified church of Jews and gentiles by building on their Jewish heritage.

c. Text: *mystērion*, translated as "secret" throughout.

that this man is truly the Christ, the one who has already come and who reigns. [5]Here is the story of the secret kept by us.

The priests assemble to select a new member

7 [1]"In ancient times, when the temple of Jerusalem was still standing, there was a custom among the Jews to appoint 22 priests in the temple, in accordance with the number of our books.[a] [2]A codex was deposited in the temple. [3]When someone was appointed among the number of the priests, his name was recorded in it, as well as the names of his father and mother, so that it would be clear that he belonged to those who were pleasing to God.

8 [1]"As this, then, was the prevailing custom among the ancients, it happened that, at that time in which Jesus was living in Judea, before he had manifested himself,[b] one of the 22 priests died. [2]The others assembled to vote on the one person who ought to take the place of the deceased. [3]After a while, the priests were unable to reach an agreement among themselves, since they disagreed on the persons being nominated. [4]For the custom among them was not only that the one elected be blameless, but that his family also be above reproach. [5]And even if perhaps he led a virtuous life, but happened to lack knowledge of the law and the prophets, he was prevented from becoming a priest.

9 [1]"In a word, divine providence was orchestrating it in this way, so that in continuing to countermand one another, they would remain at an impasse until they came to Jesus, the one they needed.[c]

10 [1]"After considering all the candidates for election and all their selectors, and when the person they needed remained undiscovered, one of them, moved by the Holy Spirit, and not by human zeal, stood up in their midst and said to them: [2]'Look, it has been already so many days since we assembled, and we have been unable to achieve anything more. [3]Therefore, I gather from this that, unless the priestly order receives the appropriate person, preordained by God, He will not allow us to reach a mutual agreement. [4]And in our attempt to find him, we are not accomplishing anything; but once we do find him, let us keep silent.[d] [5]Then the divine plan will be revealed to us.'

11 [1]"They said to him, 'If you know of anyone worthy of the priestly order, reveal him to us, and all of us will acknowledge you with the greatest gratitude.' [2]He answered them, 'If you do not give me your word that you will submit to impartial persuasion and do not contradict and quarrel with me, it is not possible for you to learn from me the one who it is. [3]For I know that no one will be reasonably able to reproach the one whom I nominate.' [4]When the priests heard

---

a. Other versions also draw a parallel with the 22 letters of the Hebrew alphabet; see below, *Suda* 3:1–2. See the introduction, p. 76, n. 30.

b. The text implies that before his public ministry Jesus was living in Judea, not Galilee. See also 12:3, where the priest advocating for Jesus states that his high character was recognized by all the inhabitants of Jerusalem.

c. For God's control of the chain of events, see also 15:1; 28:1.

d. Reading with the L manuscript. Other Greek manuscripts read *mē siōpēsōmen* ("Let us not keep silent"). In preferring the text attested in L, Nuvolone (note *ad loc.*) suggests that the priest supporting Jesus' candidacy appeals for silence in order that God might reveal his will to the council, whose deliberations up to that time had resulted only in deadlock.

this and agreed, they orally swore an oath that in fear and justice[a] they would accept and put forward for election the man being made known to them, on the sole condition that he be above reproach.

Jesus is nominated for priesthood

12 [1]"When that priest was fully satisfied with the assurance that he desired, he said to them, 'As for me, with God, I nominate Jesus, the one called son of Joseph;[b] he is, to be sure, of a young age, but he is distinguished by his speech, his conduct, and morals. [2]And I believe that no one has ever appeared on the earth so impartial and irreproachable in every way. [3]For all the inhabitants of Jerusalem, this is an undeniable fact.' [4]When they heard these and similar words, and in particular out of great respect for the oath that they had pronounced, the other priests said to him, 'Truly, we know that you have made a nomination that is good and useful.'

13 [1]"Now because they wanted to refute him on reasonable grounds, they said, 'But he is not from our tribe. [2]Moreover, even his birth is a subject of dispute among us, because it has become well known to everyone that his birth was responsible for a slaughter of a multitude of children.'[c] [3]The priest replied, 'Let us submit patiently to the truth, and I myself will guide you to the discovery of the true story about him. [4]Only let us not transgress against God and prefer convoluted ideas. [5]I know for a fact that if you investigate, with the aid of God, and with circumspection, we can discover the truth.' [6]They responded to him, 'As for you yourself, based on your belief, assure us with total certainty on the subject of his childhood and of his tribe, and you will have us in complete agreement with you.'

Matt 2:16

The priestly ancestry of Jesus revealed

14 [1]"He then said, 'Conduct an investigation, and you will see that during the time of Aaron the priest, there was a mixing between Aaron and Judah, that is to say from David, and that for this reason, I marvel at the life of Jesus.[d] [2]After having examined the facts for myself, I have discovered that Mary as well, by her genealogy, descends from both tribes.[e] [3]In carrying out my investigation,[f]

---

a. Arab 124: "So when all the priests heard this, they swore an oath by Truth and Sincerity that, if one who was worthy was shown to them, they would accept and appoint him."

b. Arab 124: "O my brethren, the most high God has put it into my mind that he who is worthy of this place is Jesus, who is called the son of Joseph."

c. The priest's response does not address this concern.

d. In reference to the marriage of the high priest Aaron to Elisheba, the latter of the tribe of Judah (Exod 6:23). The words "that is to say from David" obviously are meant to establish Jesus as Davidic king and Levitical priest. But how Jesus' Davidic ancestry is connected with the intermarriage between Aaron and Elisheba is unclear. Cf. Arab 125: "Enquire and you will learn that in the days of Aaron the priest there was an alliance by marriage between Aaron and the tribe of Judah, *to which the prophet David bore witness*"; K: "from which descends king David." For the underlying tradition, see the introduction, pp. 72–74.

e. Cf. *Suda* and Mosc. 11:1–2, both of which say that Joseph, not Mary, was of mixed Levitical and Judahite lineage. See the introduction, p. 81.

f. Presumably, this is an allusion to the priest's discovery of Mary's virginity. The word *psēlaphaō*, translated here as "investigate," literally means "feel," possibly in anticipation of the physical examination later performed by the midwives.

I discovered another secret, and I am delighted that you also will conduct an investigation and that after having made the discovery you will further confirm me, or else, if you do not make this finding, you will set me straight.'

15 ¹"Emboldened at the thought of invalidating the nominee, consider how thoroughly they began to inquire into his family; and driven by a divine force they discovered that Mary, in her lineage, was part of the two tribes at the same time. ²Thereupon, spurred by their oath and out of deference for the priest who was pressing them on, they ceased investigating the subject of the contested birth. ³In fact, all of them jointly decided to lead Mary into the interior of the temple, and in the presence of the Law, to give to her a guarantee by oath that she would not suffer anything, in order that, without any fear or hesitation, and without incurring any danger, she would explain to them the origin of her conception and birth to Jesus."

Mary appears before the priests

16 ¹"So after conducting Mary into the interior of the temple and before the Law, they said to her: 'As you see, O woman, all of us who are assembled here are mutually of one opinion on the subject of Jesus. ²Because we see that he is not only agreeable to God, but also because he is esteemed by men and because he has a brilliant reputation in Israel, we give glory to God for seeing fit to send us such a man in the place of Solomon, son of David and the wife of Uriah.ᵃ ³That is also why we have appropriately decided to propose him as priest among us.'

Matt 1:6

17 ¹"'But we are in doubt on only one point. ²For we wish to learn from you from what origin and from whom you have conceived and given birth to him. ³We do this, lest, having been corrupted as a result of a sudden impulse, you drive us from the truth, and that in the end you are perhaps judged guilty anyway.ᵇ ⁴Here, with the utterances of the law lying before us, we make an agreement with you, as in the presence of the invisible God, that you will absolutely undergo no harm from any one of us, and that you will not incur even the slightest word of blame regarding whatever you might declare to us truthfully. ⁵To the contrary, by overlooking it, we will repudiate the offense that you have perhaps committed. ⁶And we will acknowledge our utmost gratitude to you provided only that you put an end to our dispute over this.'

Mary is afraid to discuss Jesus' origins

18 ¹"Mary, in a quandary, wondered whether, in revealing the hidden secret of her childbirth, she might not generate more disbelief and sink into deeper trouble. ²She thus said to them, 'Even supposing that I want to say something, I do

---

a. For Jesus' superiority to Solomon, cf. also Matt 12:42//Luke 11:31. The reference to Solomon here as son of "the wife of Uriah" is apparently meant to contrast Solomon's questionable birthright as son of David with the subsequent discovery of the purity of Mary.

b. Although the precise meaning is uncertain, the priests seem to be suggesting that speaking the truth now, however unpleasant, is preferable to deception. As long as Mary speaks truthfully, the priests promise leniency, even if she admits to adultery. But if Mary lies to the council and the true circumstances of her pregnancy are discovered anyway, the punishment might well be much worse.

not know how to describe to you that which is ineffable. ³And I fear that, were I to speak, you will regard what I say as undeserving of belief, and I will be sorry for not having kept silent on the subject.'

19 ¹"They hastily interrupted her and, after hearing her words, said, 'No danger will come your way if you confess to us the truth. ²Mary, please know this: we ourselves also know whose son Jesus is. ³And even though Joseph has died, we can also fully assure ourselves of these things about him, even without having to trouble you. ⁴But when we hear such things truthfully from you, we have been mutually constrained by oaths and writings to accept and submit to them. ⁵Accordingly, we urge and entreat you to set yourself straight at once and declare the truth to us. ⁶Do not, out of doubt or shame, push us away from truth and lead us astray. ⁷For while believing that you are freeing yourself from your action, you will make yourself liable to the law for ages.'

20 ¹"After they had said this to her and more, Mary said in dismay, 'I am hemmed in on all sides. ²In the first place, I am under judgment to defend myself today regarding him to whom I have given birth in a way that defies comprehension. ³What will I do? If I speak the truth, I would probably not be believed. ⁴But if I do not wish to speak, I would be coerced by you. ⁵Furthermore, this I know: this birth that you ask me to reveal, you could not believe it when you hear it, nor could you as a result give your consent to my words, as you say.'   *Sus 1:22*

21 ¹"'For Joseph was thrown into turmoil and rejected what I had said to him as nonsense, and led me to the water of accusation, until, after receiving confirmation from an angelic vision, he was awestruck by the birth and glorified God.ª   *Prot. Jas.* 16
²So how could that which had appeared impossible to Joseph, who was with me, be acceptable to you?

22 ¹"'Therefore, if you have decided to hear from me from what origin I conceived Jesus, remain quiet and do not give me trouble. ²You have previously admitted to me that I have, without doubt, given birth to Jesus. ³So then, if this question has perhaps been shown to you as problematic, why are you pressuring me to declare from what origin I conceived him, when you often are fond of arguing that I did not give birth to him?'

23 ¹"They said to her, 'It is a fact known to us and beyond dispute and acknowledged in the presence of the divine oracles before us that you are the one who gave birth to Jesus. ²For a woman who has conceived a child cannot ever conceal it. ³Nor does a woman who has experienced labor pains voluntarily offer another woman her joy about the child who has been born. ⁴Therefore, from now on, have confidence in us, and value nothing more than the truth. ⁵For there is no need for us either to ensnare you after so much time, especially since you are a woman, or to condemn you for a blunder. ⁶As we have stated previously to you, we need only to hear truthfully and to accede in good faith to what you say.'

---

a. On the ordeal of bitter waters for a woman suspected of adultery, see Num 5:11–31. According to *Prot. Jas.* 16, it was the temple priest who insisted that both she and Joseph undergo the test. While submitting to the test, Joseph's misgivings had already been allayed by the angel (14).

The virgin birth is revealed and proven

24 [1]"The Virgin Mary, while taking heart, hesitated, tilted her head, and, her eyes filled with tears, said to them, 'I have given birth to Jesus—this I know, just as you yourselves already acknowledge. [2]But I do not know a man; as natural proof of this I offer the seal of my virginity.'

Luke 1:34;
Prot. Jas 13:8

25 [1]"Upon hearing this, and at a loss and in state of confusion, they were reduced to utter paralysis. [2]Then after recovering themselves, they said to her, 'It is not possible for us, nor is it without risk to register in the divine codex the child born from you in violation of accepted practice, unless you reveal his father as well. [3]So that we might persuade you by our action, here, the codex is set before you as proof. [4]Examine it, and you will see how, based on ancient custom, each priest reports his patronymic and tribal lineage from Levi. [5]So do not hinder us, and your son as well, regarding the question under consideration and what by mutual agreement we have resolved to do about him.'

26 [1]"Holding fast once more to her words, she said, 'As I have said, I do not know a man. Do what you deem right.' [2]Then after deliberating among themselves at length, they fetched midwives and after conducting every test and careful examination, they found that she truly was a virgin. [3]And as they were no longer able to resist her on the grounds that she was not the mother of Jesus, because of the oath they swore to the law, and their promise, they interrogated the neighbors and the family, secretly believing that they would find some outsiders[a] to discredit her maternity.

Prot. Jas. 20

27 [1]"But, quite the opposite, they found everyone of one accord in confirming that not only did Mary give birth to Jesus at that time, but that the infant appeared fully formed, as if it were two years of age. [2]All those who saw the newborn child thus were beside themselves, saying, 'This infant was born for the salvation of Israel.' [3]Then, defeated on all sides, and in a real dilemma, they then became, by necessity, even more cautious. [4]And they brought Mary and said to her, 'See we have conducted every test, and discovered things just as you said. [5]But because it is necessary for us to register him after hearing from your living voice, we adjure you by the almighty God to tell us truthfully who is the father of your son Jesus, whom we are required to register in the codex set before your eyes.'

28 [1]"And she, filled by the Holy Spirit, answered them in the words of God, 'I say that it is none other than the God, whom, in a prophetic way, you have just invoked under oath.' [2]And thereupon she began to explain to them the vision of Gabriel and the assurance that Joseph received from the angel, and her own response to the angel.

Luke 1:26–38; Matt
1:20–21

Jesus is brought before the assembly

29 [1]"When they heard this, they were struck with fear and awe, and immediately brought Jesus and led him up to the temple. [2]And they appointed him priest, enrolling him in the codex in the customary way, as follows: 'On this month, and

---

a. Text: *exōtikous*. The meaning is unclear; it could either refer to "foreigners" or those from another family or (non-Levitical?) tribe.

this indiction,[a] by a unanimous vote we have appointed as priest Jesus, the son of God and the Virgin Mary.'"

Philip demands to see the codex

30 [1]After fully assuring Philip the money-dealer of these things, Theodosius swore to him, "As a priest and teacher of the law, this is what I have found recorded in this codex.[b] [2]And I have found something else, even greater, with the power to compel belief that the son of Mary is himself the Christ, who also sealed the prophecy of the patriarch Jacob. [3]For since that time, no one else has come forward after Jesus and been enrolled in the codex as priest; it is thus clear that he was the one who was reserved as savior of the world, at which time kings and priests have ceased in Israel."[c]

31 [1]Upon hearing this, Philip, moved by divine zeal, said to Theodosius, "If you choose to remain silent, you are willing to incur condemnation. [2]But for my part, I am immediately referring what you have said to the faithful emperor. [3]And he will send for the box[d] to be brought where the codex is kept, and he will reveal it for the reproof of the unbelieving Jews." [4]But Theodosius said to him, "You fail to understand that the judgment you inflict is rather on your own soul, since you will be unable to obtain the desired object.[e] [5]For if this only becomes known to the Jews, they will incite a great war and much bloodshed will occur.[f] [6]When they see themselves overpowered, they will set fire to the place where the codex is kept rather than consent to surrender their secret chest. [7]And he will find himself at odds with God, depriving both sides of the codex.

32 [1]For it has been hidden from you up to this time, seeing that you have no need for it; rather it exists just as it is, as a rebuke to us. [2]And what we had to reveal to you today is no small thing; for there would be no man or book able to persuade me to believe in your Christ, except that, apart from a personal decision,[g] I am completely convinced from the codex. [3]And for a great num-

---

a. The indiction, a fifteen-year cycle originally used for assessing taxes, did not become a standard for dating documents until the fourth century; see the introduction, p. 75. The Arabic version mentions only the day, the month, and the year.

b. In other witnesses, Theodosius describes here how the codex survived the destruction of the temple and was secretly removed to Tiberias. The omission of this information in the longer Greek recension at least raises the possibility that the removal of the registry to Tiberias was a secondary addition.

c. In reference to Jacob's prophecy in Gen 49:10 (LXX): "A ruler shall not be wanting from Ioudas (*archōn ex Iouda*) and a leader from his thighs (*hēgoumenos ek tōn mērōn autou*), until the things stored up for him come, and he is the expectation of nations." Like other Christian interpreters, the author understood this passage to mean that with the coming of Jesus, the final priest and king, the succession of Jewish high priests and kings had come to an end. For discussion, see the introduction, pp. 72–73.

d. Text: *arklan*, from Latin.

e. For discussion, see the introduction, pp. 75, 78. In the more extended account in Arab 132, Theodosius also warns Philip not to bring judgment on himself by violating their promise of confidentiality.

f. Lit. "And many murders (will) fall." Cf. T: "And much bloodshed will ensue, and many will fall."

g. Text: *dicha haireseōs*. The meaning of this phrase, omitted in L and T, is unclear. Cf. Nuvolone (*EAC* 2:97): "regardless of any doctrine (indépendamment d'une quelconque doctrine)."

ber of our community this is actually clear and acknowledged—that which you yourself intend to destroy if you put your words into action."

The existence of the codex is confirmed

33 [1]Appealing to me with these and many other words, he exhorted me, after disclosing this information, to exercise discretion, considering it sufficient to protect this testimony about Christ as a judgment against the Jews. [2]But I, Philip, described these matters at length to many of my closest friends, and I wrote to the bishops and monks, encouraging them to travel to Jerusalem to learn the truth.[a] [3]The latter were astonished at this, and took great care to put it to the test and determine if in fact what Theodosius said was actually true. [4]And it was in this way that they discovered in Tiberias that Jesus, after being enrolled among the priests, was registered in the codex.[b]

34 [1]And after examining and reading many ancient books, they discovered that what was said by Josephus is truthful and indisputable.[c] [2]And Eusebius Pamphili in his *Ecclesiastical History* says clearly in the *Book of Memoirs* concerning Jesus that he, along with the priests, used to enter into the temple and perform sacred rites.[d] [3]And Luke the evangelist agrees with this when he states that when Jesus entered into the temple, the book of Isaiah was given him, and he read for the hearing of the people: "*The Spirit of the Lord is upon me, because he has anointed me.*"[e] [4]And again after making a whip he expelled in his zeal all the orators[f] from the temple.[g] [5]This is clear, that a book would

Luke 4:16–21 (Isa 61:1)

John 2:15; Mark 11:15 par.

---

a. The first-person narrative from Philip and the important details about his communication of the secret to religious authorities and their confirmation of its veracity are lacking in the shorter recensions. How these authorities confirmed the truth about the codex in Jerusalem is not explained.

b. On Tiberias as the home of secret works preserved by Jews and confirming Christian doctrine, see Epiphanius, *Pan.* 30.6.7. See the introduction, pp. 78–79.

c. Arab 133 identifies Josephus's work as the "books of the Captivity." According to the *Suda* (see below, 18:2), the tradition about Jesus' priestly office was found in Josephus's *Conquest of Jerusalem*, presumably in reference to the *Jewish War*. Information about Jesus' enrollment in the Jerusalem priesthood is lacking in the latter work.

d. Because Eusebius is not credited with writing the *Book of Memoirs*, this is probably a reference to the Jewish Christian writer Hegesippus, the author of a work entitled *ta hupomnēmata* (the "Memoirs"), excerpts from which survive in Eusebius's *Ecclesiastical History*. Although Eusebius's excerpts from Hegesippus do not mention Jesus' performance of rites in the temple, he does ascribe high-priestly functions to James, "the brother of the Lord" (*Hist. eccl.* 2.23). See the introduction, pp. 73, 76.

e. Cf. Arab 130, according to which Theodosius himself cites the passage from Luke in his account of Jesus' appointment as priest. According to Luke, Jesus spoke these words in the synagogue of Nazareth, not the Jerusalem temple. For the interpretation of this passage as a sign of Jesus' priesthood, see Eusebius, *Dem. ev.* 4.15, who understands Jesus' words about being "anointed" as a sign of his consecration as God's eternal priest.

f. The words *tous agorētas* ("the orators") are probably a corruption of *tous agorazontas* ("those who buy"); cf. Matt 21:12: "(Jesus) drove out all who were selling and buying (*agorazontas*) in the temple."

g. In the shorter recensions, the anonymous narrator, after learning about the secret codex from Philip, confirms Jesus' priesthood for himself from the testimony of Josephus, Eusebius, and Luke.

not have been given him to read in the assembly, unless he was enrolled in the priestly office.[a]

35 [1]From all these things, therefore, we know that Theodosius neither lied nor fabricated anything, but revealed as to a very true friend and with sound intention a true secret, and hidden by them forever. [2]Glory forever to Christ the son of the living God, born from the Virgin Mary.

---

a. K adds: "and even more on Sunday before the assembly, and secondly so that the prophecy of David would be fulfilled, in which he says: You are a priest forever according to the order of Melchisedek; and he who, over him, was a priest and high-priest forever and for all times has taken upon himself this temporal priesthood." The analogy drawn between Jesus' reading from Jewish Scriptures in the synagogue and the role of the Byzantine lector/priest is a misunderstanding of the original intention of the citation. See the introduction, pp. 76–77.

On the Priesthood of Jesus
from the Suda/Moscow gr. 443

Suda, pp. 620–24 (#229)

Moscow, Russian State Library, gr. 443

Philip urges Theodosius to convert

1 [1]In the time of the most pious emperor Justinian there was a certain man, a leader of the Jews, whose name was Theodosius. [2]He was actually known to a great many of the Christians, including the aforementioned faithful emperor himself.

2 [1]At that same time, there was a certain man, a Christian, named Philip, a money-dealer by trade.[a] [2]He was aware of Theodosius's situation; and as he maintained a very intimate friendship with him, he kept urging and admonishing him to become a Christian. [3]One day, then, the aforementioned Philip said something like the following to this Theodosius: "How can it be that you, a man who is truly wise and possessed of an unerring understanding of what the law and the prophets have proclaimed in advance about Christ the Lord, not believe in him and become a Christian? [4]For I am convinced concerning you that it is not out of ignorance of what divinely inspired Scriptures have foretold about the advent of our universal Lord Christ that you refrain from becoming a Christian.

1 [1]In the time of the reign of the faithful emperor Justinian of blessed memory, there was a certain man, a prince of the Jews, whose name was Theodosius. [2]He was actually known to the Christians for a great many years, including even the most pious emperor himself.

2 [1]At that same time, there was a certain man, a Christian, named Philip, a money-dealer by trade. [2]He was well acquainted with the aforementioned Theodosius the Jew, and associated with him quite often; as he had a genuine affection for him, he kept counseling him to become a Christian. [3]One day, then, the aforementioned Philip said the following to Theodosius: "I know that you are a wise man and possess an unerring understanding of what the law and the prophets have proclaimed about our Lord, Jesus Christ; why do you not believe in him and become a Christian? [4]For I am convinced about you that you are not ignorant of what divinely inspired Scriptures have foretold about our universal Savior and Lord Christ. [5]Make haste, then, to save your own soul, and do not refrain from becoming a Christian, but

---

a. For the meaning of *arguropratēs,* see note to GrL 1:3.

⁵Make haste, then, to save your own soul, by believing in the Savior and our Lord Jesus Christ, lest by continuing in unbelief you might make yourself liable for eternal judgment."

3 ¹Upon hearing these words spoken to him by the Christian, the Jew received him with favor, expressed his gratitude to him for his words, and answered him in the following way: ²"I welcome your act of love according to God, because, by encouraging me to become a Christian, you strive earnestly for the salvation of my soul. ³Therefore, as in the presence of God who knows and sees the secrets of the hearts, I will make this assertion to you without guile and dissembling and with all truthfulness:

Theodosius confesses his secret Christian faith

4 ¹"Christ, the one who was foretold by the law and the prophets, the one who is worshipped by you Christians, has come." ²Of this I am fully assured, and I confess it boldly, as to my true friend, and one who is also always earnest in his kindness to me. ³But because I am swayed by human thinking, I do not become a Christian and for this I condemn myself. ⁴For I, a Jew by origin, am at this time a prince of the Jews, and enjoy great honor and many gifts and all the necessities for this life. ⁵Now I imagine that if I were to become a patriarch of the catholic church or receive even greater powers and dignities from you, I would not be deemed worthy of such consideration.

5 ¹To keep from losing, then, what are held to be pleasures in this life, I disdain the life to come and fare ill in

believe in the Savior and our Lord Jesus Christ, lest by continuing in unbelief you might make yourself liable for eternal judgment."

3 ¹Upon hearing these words spoken to him by the Christian, the Jew received the Christian with favor, expressed his gratitude to him for his words, and answered him with the following: ²"I welcome your act of love according to God, because you strive earnestly for the salvation of my soul and encourage me to become a Christian. ³Therefore, as God knows and discloses the secrets of the hearts, I will make this assertion to you without guile and dissembling and with all truthfulness:

4 ¹"Christ, the one who was proclaimed by the law and the prophets, and the one who is worshipped by you Christians, has come." ²Of this I am fully assured and I confess it boldly to you, as you are my true friend, and one who is also always earnest in doing things for my benefit. ³But because I am swayed by human thinking, I do not become a Christian and for this I condemn myself. ⁴For at this time I am a Jew and a prince of the Jewish nation, and enjoy great honor and many gifts and all the necessities for this life. ⁵Now if I were to become a Christian, I would receive none of these things. For I suppose that were I to become a patriarch of the catholic church, neither would I receive from you greater powers or exceeding honors, nor even if I were to become a king, which is impossible.

5 ¹To keep from losing, then, the pleasures of this life, I disdain the life to come. For I fare ill, by not paying

doing so.[a] [2]But in order that I might show that my words in response to your love are truthful, I am entrusting to you a secret, which has been kept hidden by us Hebrews. [3]From it we know full well that the Christ who is worshipped by you Christians is the very one who has been foretold by the law and the prophets; this we know not only from what has been publicly written, but from the secret that has been registered by us and hidden. [4]The story of this secret is as follows:

The priests assemble to select a new member

6 [1]"In ancient times, when the temple used to stand[b] in Jerusalem, there was a custom among the Jews to appoint priests in the temple equal in number with the 22 letters comprising our alphabet. [2]For this reason, we also number 22 divinely inspired books. [3]There was, then, a codex stored in the temple, in which was recorded the name of each of the 22 priests, and the name of his father and that of his mother. [4]Thus, when one of the priests died, the remaining priests would convene in the temple, and by common vote would appoint another priest in place of the priest who had died, thereby completing the number of the 22 priests. [5]And it would be recorded in the codex, that on that day priest 'so and so' had passed away, the son of 'such and such' man and woman, and in his place priest 'so and so' was appointed.

------

a. In the longer recension, Theodosius also blames his refusal to become a Christian on the church's treatment of baptized Jews; see above, GrL 5:1–3. On the suppression of this motif in later versions of the story, see the introduction, p. 82.

b. Text: *ektizeto.* Lit. "was being built."

heed to what is to come. [2]It is thus for this reason that I am not becoming a Christian. But in order that I show that my words in response to your love are truthful, I will entrust to you a secret, which has been kept hidden by us Jews. [3]From it we know full well that the Christ who is worshipped by you Christians is the very one who is proclaimed by the law and the prophets; of this we are fully assured not only from the very things written about this in the law and the prophets, but also from the secret that has been hidden by us. [4]It is the following:

6 [1]"In more ancient times, when there was the temple in Jerusalem, a custom existed among the Jews to appoint priests in the temple according to the number of the 22 letters that are in our alphabet. [2]For this reason, we also number 22 divinely inspired books and we appoint 22 priests for the temple according to the number, as was said, of the 22 letters of our alphabet. [3]And a codex was stored there, in which was recorded the name of the 22 priests, and the name of the father and the mother of each priest. [4]Thus, when one of the 22 priests died, the remaining priests would convene in the temple, and after making a common vote would appoint another priest in place of the priest who had died, so as to complete the number of the 22 priests. [5]And they registered in the codex, that on that day priest 'so and so' had passed away, the son of 'such and such' man and woman.

7 [1] "Now as this was the prevailing custom in the Jewish nation, it so happened that in those times, when Jesus was residing in Judea, one of the 22 priests died, before Jesus began to make himself known and to teach men to believe in him. [2]So the remaining priests assembled to appoint another priest in place of the priest who had died. [3]When each priest proposed someone he believed worthy of becoming a priest, the others rejected him for being deficient in virtue, which is required to appoint a priest. [4]For if he was wise, and worthy both in his moral character and mode of life, but proved to be ignorant of the law and the prophets, he was judged unsuitable for the priesthood.

8 [1]"So when many priests were in this way voted on and all were rejected, a certain priest stood up in their midst and said to the others: [2]'Look, many were nominated by us and found unfit for priesthood. [3]Accept, then, what I have to say about one man who ought to be appointed in place of the priest who died. [4]For I suppose that none of you will be displeased by my nomination.'

Jesus is nominated for priesthood

9 [1]"When the remaining priests granted him permission, he said, [2]'It is my wish that Jesus, the son of Joseph the carpenter, replace the priest who died. Granted, he is a young man, but he is highly well equipped in speech, mode of life, and excellent moral character. [3]And I suppose that there has never appeared a man such as him in speech, mode of life, or morals. [4]And I think also that for

7 [1]"Now as this was the prevailing custom among people of old in the Jewish nation, it so happened that at that time, when Jesus was residing in Judea, one of the 22 priests died. Now Jesus had begun to make himself known and to teach men to believe in him. [2]So the priests assembled to appoint another priest in place of the priest who had died. [3]When each priest nominated someone and proposed him as one who ought to become priest, the others rejected him for being deficient in virtue, which is required to appoint a priest. [4]For if he was of sound mind, he was not suitable in character and mode of life; or being equipped in character and mode of life, he was uncultivated in speech and knowledge.

8 [1]"When many priests were in this way voted on and found unfit for the priesthood, a certain priest got up and stood in their midst and said to them: [2]'Look, many were nominated by us and shown to be unfit for priesthood. [3]Accept, then, what I have to say about one man, so that he might be appointed priest in place of the priest who died. [4]For I suppose that none of you, nor any one else, will repudiate the nomination that I am making public.'

9 [1]"When the remaining priests granted him permission to name whom he wanted to become priest in place of the deceased, he said to them, [2]'Jesus, the son of Joseph the carpenter is, granted, a young man, but he is well prepared in speech, mode of life, and moral character. [3]And I suppose that no man on earth has shown to be like him in speech, deed, mode of life, or moral character. [4]And if this is recog-

all of you who live in Jerusalem, this is recognized and undeniable.'

10 [1]"When they heard this statement, the other priests responded favorably to the man and confirmed the nomination, after having · said that Jesus was fit for priesthood more than any other man. [2]But some began to say of him that he was not from the tribe of Levi, but actually from the tribe of Judah.[a] And under the assumption that he was a son of Joseph (for this was the way he was known by name among the Jews), everyone bore witness that Joseph was from the tribe of Judah, not from the tribe of Levi. [3]For this reason, because it was thought that he was not from the Levitical tribe, they prevented him from becoming a priest.

The priestly ancestry of Jesus revealed

11 [1]"Then the priest who nominated him replied to them that he was of mixed ancestry. [2]For long ago, among the generations of old, there was intermingling of the two tribes, and it was from this that the lineage of Joseph traced its ancestry.[b] [3]So upon hearing this, the other priests consented to the nomination. And by common consent all the priests who assembled determined to appoint Jesus as a replacement for the priest who had died.

12 [1]"Now since there was a custom not only to register the name of the new priest in the codex, but the name of his father and mother as well, some of them said that they had first to summon his parents and learn

nized and incontrovertible also to all of you living here, let him be the one.'

10 [1]"When they heard this statement, the other priests approved of the man and confirmed it by a vote. And they concurred that Jesus was fit for priesthood more than everyone else. [2]Now some began to say that he was not from the tribe of Levi, but that Joseph was actually from the tribe of Judah. [3]For this reason only, because he was not from the Levitical tribe, they were preventing him from becoming a priest.

11 [1]"Then the priest who nominated him said that his lineage was mixed. [2]For before the giving of the law, there was intermingling of the two tribes, during the time of the high priest Aaron, and Joseph was from that lineage. [3]When he had said this, the other priests consented to a vote, and by joint decree the priests who had convened saw fit to appoint Jesus as a replacement for the priest who had died.

12 [1]"Now from ancient times, this was the custom among them: to register in the codex not only the name of the priest-to-be, but the names of the father and mother as well, and to receive their deposition that the one being appointed to the priesthood was their son. [2]As, then, this was the opinion of all the priests, the priest who had selected Jesus said, 'Joseph, the father of Jesus, has died, but his

---

a. For discussion, see the introduction, pp. 71–74.

b. Cf. GrL 14:2, which traces Jesus' mixed ancestry through Mary.

from them their names, and to get a deposition from them that the one being appointed to the priesthood was their son. [2]This was acceptable to all of them. The priest, then, who had previously nominated Jesus to be priest, said that his father Joseph had died, and that only his mother was still alive. [3]All of them thus came to an agreement to bring his mother to the council[a] and learn from her if she was in fact the mother of Jesus and if she gave birth to him, and to hear the name of her husband, from whom she gave birth to Jesus. [4]When, moreover, this was accepted by everyone, they summoned the mother of Jesus and said to her. [5]'Priest so-and-so, the son of such-and-such father and mother has died. We wish to replace him with your son. [6]But there is a custom that the name of the mother and father be registered. [7]Tell us, therefore, if Jesus is your son, and if you gave birth to him.'

mother is still alive.' [3]All of them then resolved to summon Jesus' mother to the council and learn from her <if> she was the <mother> of Jesus and if she gave birth to him, and to learn the name of her husband as well, from whom she gave birth to Jesus. [4]When, moreover, this was resolved upon by all the priests, they summoned the mother of Jesus and said to her. [5]'Since priest so-and-so, the son of such-and-such man and woman has died, we wish to replace him with Jesus, your son. [6]But there is a custom that not only the name of the priest be registered, but the names of his father and mother as well. [7]Tell us, then, if Jesus is your son, and if you gave birth to him, and the name of the father by whom you gave birth to him, so that there might be registered in the codex the name of Jesus, your name, and that of your husband, by whom you gave birth to him.'

Mary appears before the priests

13 [1]"Now Mary heard this and answered the priests, 'Jesus is my son, this I avow. [2]For I gave birth to him, and both men and women can be found who will attest that I gave birth to him. [3]But he does not have a father on this earth—let me assure you of this, seeing that you want to know.[b] [4]For I was a virgin and living in Galilee; and an angel of God, when I was awake and not sleeping, came into the house where I was, and

13 [1]"Now Mary heard this and answered the priests, 'He is my son, this I avow. [2]And that I gave birth to him, both men and women are to be found who will testify to this. For I gave birth to him. [3]But he does not have a father on this earth—you can be completely assured of this, seeing that you might want to know this. [4]For I was a virgin and living in Galilee; and I saw an angel of God, when I was awake and not sleeping. He entered the place where

---

a. Text: *synedrion*. In pre–70 Judaism, the full cohort of the Great Sanhedrin probably consisted of 71 members, overseen by the high priest, but not exclusively comprised of priests.

b. Text: *labete par' emou, hōs boulesthe*. A possible alternative translation: "receive this assurance from me as you will."

proclaimed the good news to me that I would give birth to a son from the Holy Spirit. [5]And he instructed me to call him by the name Jesus. [6]So then, even though I was a virgin, after seeing this vision I conceived and gave birth to Jesus, remaining a virgin up to this day, and after I gave birth.'

I was, and proclaimed the good news to me that I would give birth to a son from the Holy Spirit. [5]And it was he who instructed me to call him by his name Jesus. [6]So then, even though I was a virgin, after seeing this vision I conceived and gave birth to Jesus.'

Mary is tested

14 [1]"Upon hearing this, the priests ordered trustworthy midwives to come and directed them to conduct an examination to determine whether Mary was still really a virgin. [2]Fully assured by the evidence, they confirmed that she was in fact a virgin. [3]Now other women were also discovered who came forth as having witnessed her giving birth, attesting that Jesus was her son. [4]The priests were astonished at what was being said by Mary and those who had testified about the birth of her child. [5]And they replied to Mary, 'Tell us forthrightly, that we might hear from your mouth, of which father and mother is he the son, so that we might thereby register him. [6]Whichever parents you tell us, these we will register, and no one else.' [7]And she answered, 'I was the one who really did give birth to him. I did not know his father on this earth, rather I heard from the angel that he is son of God. [8]So he is son of me, the one named Mary, and son of God, and I am in fact an unmarried virgin.' [9]When they heard this, the priests brought out the codex and subjoined the following: [10]'On this day, priest so-and-so died, the son of such-and-such man and woman, and by common vote of all of us, Jesus has become a priest in his place, Jesus the son of the living God and Mary the virgin.'

14 [1]"Upon hearing this, the priests ordered trustworthy midwives to come and directed them to conduct an examination of her, and determine whether Mary was still really a virgin. [2]And after receiving complete confirmation of this, they assured the priests that Mary was really a virgin. [3]Now other women were also discovered who came forth, and had witnessed her giving birth, and attested that Jesus was her son. [4]The priests were astonished at what was being said about Mary and those who were giving testimony about her childbirth. [5]And they replied to Mary, 'You have given to us a clear statement and an explanation to justify making Jesus, without condition, a priest. [6]Therefore, tell us by your own mouth, whose son Jesus is, so that we might thereby register him accordingly.' [7]And she answered forthrightly, 'I heard from the angel that the one to whom I was giving birth, he is a son of God, and that the one whom I gave birth to is the son of God and my son. [8]My name is Mary, and I am in truth a virgin.' [9]When they heard this, the priests brought out the codex and made the following entry: [10]'On this day, priest so-and-so died, the son of such-and-such man and woman, and by common vote of all of us, Jesus has become a priest in his place, Jesus the son of the living God and Mary the virgin and Mother of God.'

Luke 1:24–35

Luke 1:31

Prot. Jas. 20

Philip demands to see the codex

15 [1]"And this codex was rescued from the temple through the exertion of those among the Jews who were taking out the primary objects at the time of the capture of the temple and Jerusalem, and it was deposited in Tiberias.[a] [2]This secret was made known to a very few and the trustworthy of our nation. [3]Therefore, it was also revealed to me, since I am a leader and teacher of the Jewish nation. [4]For it is not only from the law and the prophets that we are assured that the Christ who is worshipped by you Christians is himself the son of the living God, who came to earth for the salvation of the world; [5]but we also have this assurance from the register, which is preserved even up to this very day and is deposited in Tiberias."

16 [1]After hearing what was said to him by the Jew, the Christian was moved by divine zeal and said to the Jew, "I am reporting what you said at once and without delay to the believing and pious emperor, so that he might send to Tiberias and make known the codex of which you speak, so as to refute the unbelief of the Jews." [2]But the Jew said to the Christian, "Why do you want to bring judgment on your own soul and report this to the emperor and then not obtain the sought-after object? [3]For if something like this were to happen, a great war is bound to occur, and bloodshed will immediately ensue. [4]And then, if they see themselves being subdued, they will set fire to the place in which the codex is stored, and we will labor in vain in not succeeding in obtaining that which we seek; rather we shall only be the cause

15 [1]"And this codex was carried out of the temple through the effort of those among the Jews who were taking out the primary objects at the time of the capture of Jerusalem, and it was deposited in Tiberias. [2]This secret was made known to a very few trustworthy people and those of our nation.[a] [3]Therefore, it was also revealed to me, since I am a leader and teacher of the Jews. [4]It is not only from the law and the prophets that we are completely assured that the Christ who is worshipped by you Christians is himself the son of the living God, who came to earth for the salvation of the world; [5]but it is also preserved even up to this very day in a register and is deposited in Tiberias."

16 [1]The Christian, after hearing this from the Jew, was moved by divine zeal and said to the Jew, "I am reporting what you said at once to the emperor, so that he might send to Tiberias and make known the codex of which you speak, so as to refute the unbelief of the Jews." [2]But the Jew said to the Christian, "Why do you want, my good sir, to bring judgment on your own soul and report this to the emperor and then not obtain the sought-after object? [3]For if this were to happen to the Jews, a great war is bound to occur. For the Jews will mass together, and great slaughter will immediately ensue. [4]And if they see it being overpowered, they will set fire to the place where the codex is also stored. And this will be in vain, in that the desired object will not be obtained; and you might become for

---

a. On Tiberias as a repository of hidden books, see the introduction, pp. 78–79.

a. Text: *oligois panu pistois kai tois tou ethnous hēmōn.* The meaning is somewhat unclear.

of bloodshed.[a] [5]For since you are a true friend, and because of your love, I have revealed these things to you, so that I might assure you that I do not reject Christianity out of ignorance, but out of empty glory."

17 [1]After hearing this from the Jew, the Christian was also confident that what he said was true. [2]But he did not reveal this story to the emperor Justinian, a believer; this was so that, incited by zeal, that great and faithful emperor might not cause bloodshed, without the sought-after object then being successfully obtained. [3]But to many of his acquaintances and friends, he did reveal this story.[b]

The existence of the codex is confirmed

18 [1]We have learned the story from those who heard it from the aforementioned Philip the money-dealer, and have expended not a little care in our desire to know if in fact the Jew spoke the truth in his story about such a registry. [2]We have thus found that Josephus, the author of the Capture of Jerusalem,[c] whom Eusebius Pamphili recalls at length in his *Ecclesiastical History,* says clearly in his memoirs of the captivity that Jesus performed sacred rites in the temple with the priests.

19 [1]Having thus discovered that Josephus, a man of antiquity, who was

me a cause of destruction. [5]For since you are a true friend, I have revealed this, so that I might assure you that I do not reject Christianity out of ignorance, but for the sake of empty glory and luxury."

17 [1]After hearing this from the Jew, the Christian believed that what the Jew said was true. [2]But he did not reveal this story to the emperor Justinian, lest, incited by divine zeal, that great and faithful emperor might cause blood to be shed, without the sought-after object then <being successfully obtained>. [3]But to many of his friends and acquaintances, he did make this story known.

18 [1]We have thus learned the story from the aforementioned Philip, and we have expended not a little care in our desire to know if in fact the Jew's story about the priesthood of Jesus and the registry that existed among the Jews is true. [2]We have found confirmation in the Book of the Memoirs of Josephus[a] in the *Ecclesiastical History* of Eusebius Pamphili. The aforesaid Eusebius himself makes mention of these things when he clearly states that Jesus went into the temple with the priests and performed sacred rites.

19 [1]Having thus discovered that Josephus, a man of antiquity, wrote

---

a. By using the first-person plural, Theodosius assumes some responsibility for the outcome of a failed campaign to recover the codex, even though he previously advises Philip against the plan (16:2). In other versions, Theodosius more explicitly distances himself from Philip's proposal.

b. Cf. GrL 33:2–4, according to which Philip passes Theodosius's information on to Christian officials.

c. An alternative title of Josephus's *Jewish War* already known to Origen.

---

a. The reference in Mosc. to the Memoirs of Josephus probably confuses Josephus with Hegesippus, the author of the Memoirs. See further above, GrL 34:1–2, notes c, d, and the introduction, p. 78.

not long after the time of the apostles, says this, we searched to find this story confirmed as well from divinely inspired Scriptures. [2]So we found in the Gospel according to Luke that Jesus entered into the Jewish synagogue and a book was given to him, and he read the prophet Isaiah which says, "The Spirit of the Lord is upon me, because he has anointed me to bring good news to the poor." [3]Now I have deduced by analogy that if the Christ Jesus did not have some ministerial service among the Jews, a book would not have been given to him in the synagogue to read for the hearing of the people. [4]For among us Christians, it is not possible for someone to read in the churches books of divinely inspired Scriptures to the laity, unless he is enrolled in the clergy.[a] [5]And from what was written by Josephus and recorded by the evangelist Luke, we know that Theodosius the Jew, when he told the preceding story to the aforementioned Philip the money-dealer, did not fabricate it. [6]Rather, he truthfully confided in Philip, since he was a true friend, the secret hidden among the Jews. [7]But Chrysostom categorically rejects the priesthood attributed to Christ.[b]

this, we have come to believe that Jesus was a priest. And so we have set forth these things in writing after a long time, because of our concern to know if, in fact, it is possible to find confirmation for this story in divine Scriptures. [2]And after doing an investigation, we found it recorded in the Gospel according to Luke that Jesus entered into the Jewish synagogue and there was given to him a book of the prophet Isaiah, which says, "The Spirit of the Lord is upon me, because he has anointed me." [3]Now when we had discovered this in the Gospel according to Luke, we deduced by analogy that if Jesus had not had some ministerial role service among the Jews, a book would not have been given to him in the synagogue to read for the hearing of the people. [4]For among us Christians, it is not possible (for someone) to read in the churches a book of divinely inspired Scriptures at the pulpit, unless he is enrolled in the clergy. [5]And we discover from his Memoirs that Josephus has recorded this. And we also came to know from what would be said by the evangelist Luke that Theodosius the Jew told a truthful account to the aforementioned Philip the money-dealer. [6]And since he was a true friend, he entrusted to him the secret hidden among the Jews. [7]For God arranged this, who having spoken among the fathers of earlier time and from the beginning, induced Theodosius the Jew to tell of what had been written beforehand, in order that we might glorify the Father and the Son and the Holy Spirit, the one divinity for whom all glory, honor, and power is fitting for all ages. Amen.

Luke 4:16–21 (Isa 61:1)

---

a. See intro, p. 76.

b. This editorial gloss is found only in the *Suda*. For Chrysostom's views on the non-Levitical priesthood of Jesus, see his *Hom. Heb.* 7.1 (PG 63:101–3), on Heb. 7:11–14; and *Adv. Jud.* 7.5 (PG 48:923–25). In these passages, however, Chrysostom does not reveal any direct awareness of the alternative tradition about Jesus' enrollment as Levitical priest.

On the Priesthood of Jesus
from Vatican, Biblioteca apostolica, Ottoboni gr. 408

Introduction

Exposition of how Christ became a priest. For the prophet David says of him,
Ps 110:4 (Heb 7:17) *"You are a priest forever according to the order of Melchizedek."*[a]

The priests assemble to select a new member

1 [1]Many are unaware of this. [2]Among the Hebrews there was a prescribed form for their priesthood: 22 priests were appointed to serve in the priesthood. [3]If one of them died, they would inquire where they might discover a member of the Levitical tribe so that they might appoint a twenty-second priest in place of the one who died.

Jesus is nominated for priesthood

2 [1]After inquiring at length and reaching an impasse, they failed to find a member of the Levitical tribe. [2]As they found themselves at a loss, one of the priests called to mind Christ and said to them, "All of you have spoken and your nominees were found to be unsuitable.[b] [3]So I too will speak once for all, if, that is, it pleases you." [4]They said to him, "Please speak." [5]And he said, "Hearken to me; let us establish as priest Jesus, the son of Joseph the carpenter from Nazareth." [6]The high priests said, "But Joseph is not from Levi, and Mary is descended from David." [7]For the Mother of God used to be called "*exotonos.*"[c] [8]The aforementioned priest said, "The codex states that among the people of old, there was a mixing of Levi and Judah and the Levitical tribe was combined."[d]

---

a. Entitled an "exposition (*apodeixis*)," this highly condensed version of the story lacks the framing dialogue between Theodosius and Philip and the former's revelation of the priestly codex hidden in Tiberias. On Jesus' election as priest as fulfillment of the eternal priesthood of Melchizedek, see also Arab 131.

b. Lit. "And you were found unsuitable."

c. Text: *exotonos*. The meaning of this *hapax legomenon* is obscure. The prepositional prefix *exo* (*exō?*) may suggest the idea that Mary was an "outsider." It could possibly be a corruption of *exōtikos* ('outside the tribe'). Cf. GrL 26:3, where the priests seek out "outsiders (*exōtikous*)" to discredit Jesus' lineage.

d. Text: *katalēphthē*. The translation "was combined" is only a conjecture based on the context. This is the only witness that states that the mixing of the two tribes was recorded in the priestly registry.

Mary appears before the priests

3 [1]The high priests[a] and the whole council said, "This is correct. [2]Call his father and mother and let us question them." [3]And they said, "But Joseph has died." [4]They summoned Jesus' mother. [5]After she arrived and stood up, they say to her, "Tell us: Of what father is your son?" [6]And she said in response, "Believe me, my son does not have a father on this earth. [7]While I was awake, not sleeping, an angel of God came into my house and said to me, '*Greetings, favored one! The Lord is with you!* [8]*You will conceive in your womb and bear a son, and you will name him Jesus.*' [9]I said to him, 'How shall this be, since I do not know a man?' [10]And he said to me, '*The Holy Spirit will come upon you, and the power of the Most High will overshadow you.*' [11]I gave birth to him and to this very day am a virgin, under the protection of God. [12]As the angel was withdrawing, he said to me, 'I am Gabriel the archangel of God.' [13]He said this to me (and) then withdrew from me."

Luke 1:28

Luke 1:31

Luke 1:34–35

The virgin birth is revealed and proven

4 [1]Upon hearing this, the high priests and all the council were astonished and at once brought trustworthy midwives to examine her.[b] [2]After examining her they found her more pure than the pure one when he was born.[c] [3]They assured the council and all the people that she was really a virgin. [4]Everyone was astounded, and they said to her, "Tell us so that we might register him." [5]And the Mother of God said in response, "I, Mary, gave birth to him. He does not have a father on this earth; rather he is son of God and son of me, the virgin." [6]After hearing this, the priests brought the codex and wrote the following: [7]"We the priests of the Jewish people write as follows: 'Priest of the temple so-and-so has died on such-and-such day, and in his place we register as priest Jesus, son of the living God and son of Mary the virgin, so that he may serve as priest forever.'"

Prot. Jas. 20

Jesus' priesthood is confirmed

5 [1]If he were not a priest, he would not have been given a book and have read from the prophet Isaiah, "*The Spirit of the Lord is upon me, because he has anointed me.*" [2]If he were not a priest, he would not have thrown out the utensils of worldly business from the temple and said to the priests, "Do not make the house of my father a house of utensils." [3]If he were not a priest, he would not have sat in the synagogue, and he would not have silenced whoever was unreasonable in judgment. [4]A certain young girl was a sinner among the people, and they brought her to the tribunal to pass judgment on her. [5]In a word, she was condemned to be stoned.[d] [6]The priests then determined the time. [7]They said to Jesus, "What do you say, Jesus, about the girl who sinned?" [8]And Jesus said to the people and the priests, "Let whoever has not sinned cast a stone at

Luke 4:16–21 (Isa 61:1)

John 2:16

---

a. The other versions refer to them only as priests.

b. Text: *schēmatisai*. Lit. "to position her."

c. The reference to the "pure one (*tou katharou*)" is unclear.

d. The use of the story about the woman caught in adultery to establish Jesus' priestly office is unique to this version. Although the officials accusing the woman were "scribes and Pharisees," not priests (John 8:3), the setting of the episode in the temple may have inspired the author to see Jesus' actions as proof of his priestly office.

her." ⁹He wrote to them each day the following: "You have committed this sin today." ¹⁰And to another, "See what you have done," and likewise to another.ᵃ ¹¹Simply put, he told the whole company of the high priests of their sins, not openly, but in private. ¹²And no one was found to throw a stone at the girl. ¹³In the synagogue of the Jews, Jesus (said) more things besides this. ¹⁴If Jesus were not a priest, it would not have been reasonable for him to judge and speak boldly among the people.

John 8:2–11

Jesus' priesthood foretold by David

6 ¹Have you heard, brethren, how many years earlier the prophet David foretold the priesthood of Christ? ²In this believe that Christ was made a priest by the Jews. ³Fittingly the prophet David says about him: "*You are a priest forever according to the order of Melchizedek.*" ⁴See, I have demonstrated to you how by the prophet-killing Jews and lawless Hebrews, they made our Lord Jesus Christ priest. ⁵Glory to him forever and ever, Amen.

Ps 110:4 (Heb 7:17)

---

a. At John 8:8, some later manuscripts add "the sins of each of them" to the words "and once again he bent down and wrote on the ground." The story found here about Jesus' reproof of the priests seems to develop this theme.

Appendix:
John of Euboea, *In conceptionem Deiparae* 18[a]

¹Alas for the obtuseness of the Jews! Alas for their folly! Alas for the blasphemy of heretics! Alas for their darkened heart! For those who crash with strife and jealousy, like a pot against a kettle, are no worse than the arrogance of the Jews. They crash and they shatter. Did not the prophets belong to them? Even now they profess the prophets as their kinsmen; yet they do not heed their words. Over all the ages, how did they not see[b] that the maiden[c] was raised in the holy of holies, or, again, that she was a virgin after giving birth?

Prot. Jas. 8:1

²When the Lord became high priest,[d] did not some of them, writing with their own hands, acknowledge that the holy Mary was a virgin? For some of them elected the Lord as high priest, in order to fulfill the Scripture which had been written: "*You are a priest forever according to the order of Melchizedek.*" This occurred because "he was advancing in wisdom with God and man,"[e] and because Mary, the blessed Mother of God, was from the royal and high priestly tribes. They did this in accordance with custom. For with the priests standing by,[f] they would ask the father and the mother and record their names in the election to the priesthood. And they asked the holy virgin: "Is Jesus your son?" And she said, "Yes." They said, "Who is his father?" And this unblemished woman replied, "He does not have a father on this earth. But I did give birth to him, as he himself knows. For his father is God." And they said, "Are we to record him in the registry roll as son of God?"[g] She said, "Do so." And they recorded in the roll the following, "Jesus the son of God, and son of Mary by a vote from on high will be priest forever."

Ps 110:4 (Heb 7:17)

Luke 2:52

---

a. Although John retains elements of the older tradition about Jesus' enrollment as priest, his highly condensed rendition of the story, in conformity with the broader purpose of his treatise, is mainly concerned with establishing Mary's virginity at the time she gave birth to Jesus. More hostile to the Jews than the older versions, John's account also omits the framing narrative about the friendship between Theodosius and Philip, Theodosius's disclosure of the existence of the codex, and his confession of Christ's divine sonship; see the introduction, p. 82.

b. Text: *pou oun eidon.* Emended to *pou ouk eidon.*

c. *korēn* in reference to Mary.

d. In most of the other witnesses, Jesus is elected as priest, not as high priest.

e. This proof text from Luke, lacking in the other versions, was probably included to explain how Jesus came to be recognized by the Jerusalem priesthood even before his public ministry. Cf. Michael Glycas, *Annales,* 394.20–395.5, who denies that Jesus' precocity would have gained him any enduring recognition in Jerusalem.

f. Text: *probainontōn.* Lit. "stepping forward."

g. Notice that here the document is called a *tomos* ("roll" or "tome"), not a "codex."

³And thus was fulfilled what was written, as was mentioned above, "*You are a priest forever according to the order of Melchizedek.*" For after the Lord returned from the wilderness, "*he came to Nazareth, where he had been brought up,* and *he went to the synagogue, on the sabbath day, as was his custom. He stood up to read, and the scroll of the prophet Isaiah was given to him. He unrolled the scroll and found the place where it was written, 'The Spirit of the Lord is upon me, because he has anointed me, and so forth.'*"

⁴This very roll is, then, preserved among them up until the present day. And this book will be opened at his second coming for the condemnation of the Jews. For prophets did not persuade them, nor did they pay heed to the Lord himself. But from the very writings composed by the hands of their priests, they will be condemned. For as they are always both deceiving and deceived, they used to shout that the truth is error, and embrace error, with which they will depart for eternal punishment.[a] For the Lord himself said to them: "*I have come in my Father's name, and you do not accept me; if another comes in his own name, you will accept him.*"

Ps 110:4 (Heb 7:17)

Luke 4:16–21 (Isa 61:1)

John 5:43

---

a. While lacking in other witnesses, John's prediction that the book would be opened at Christ's second coming as judgment upon the Jews was apparently not John's own editorial addition. In Glycas's own retelling of the story, he also mentions this motif, only to reject it (*Quaest.* 54, 106.4–107.9).

Papyrus Oxyrhynchus 210
A new translation and introduction

by Brent Landau and Stanley E. Porter

Papyrus Oxyrhynchus II 210 (henceforth P. Oxy. 210) is a single fragmentary leaf from a third-century papyrus codex containing a text that may or may not be an apocryphal Christian gospel. Due in large part to its very fragmentary condition, this text has not been included in any of the standard anthologies of Christian apocrypha until very recently, nor is it listed in Geerard's *CANT*. Previous editors of the manuscript have disagreed markedly about its reconstruction and identity. All that can be said for certain about its contents is that it includes sayings or narratives about: an angel, good things (fruits? people?), Jesus, an image, and the form of God; some of the sayings are in the format of "I am" statements. Thus P. Oxy. 210 contains an intriguing blend of Synoptic, Johannine, and Pauline elements, but further determining its character remains difficult.

Contents
Although P. Oxy. 210 is quite fragmentary, its text has been reconstructed to varying degrees by several scholars. There has been a general consensus that the side of the manuscript with the writing along the fibers (henceforth "recto"[1]) contains an infancy narrative story involving Joseph receiving instructions about Mary from an angel (recto, lines 4–7). This supposition may not be warranted, however, given the lack of any other clear references to an infancy context apart from the mention of an angel. The side of the manuscript with the writing against the fibers (henceforth "verso") appears to contain at least two pericopes in which Jesus is the primary speaker. The first pericope (verso, lines 4–17) resembles the teaching about good trees and fruit and bad trees and fruit (cf. Matt 7:17–19//Luke 6:43–44). The second pericope (verso, lines 17–20) contains a series of "I am" statements similar to those of John's Gospel, though with terms like "image" and "form of God" that are familiar from the Pauline tradition.

Manuscript Details
P. Oxy. 210 is a single fragmentary piece of papyrus with writing on both sides, measuring approximately 17.2 cm high and 9.4 cm wide.[2] Because the same scribe wrote both sides, it is very probably a leaf from a codex, rather than a roll or a sheet. P. Oxy. 210 is currently housed in the University Library at Cambridge, under the shelfmark Add. MS 4048. Included in the same plate is a very small fragment that apparently was placed in the same

---

1. This usage of recto and verso follows the language set forth by Tobias Nicklas, "Eine neue alte Erzählung im Rahmen antiker Jesustraditionen: Reste eines Exorzismus auf P.Oxy. lxxvi 5072," *Annali di Storia dell'Esegesi* 29 (2012): 13–27.

2. For images of the fragment, see Wayment, *Text of the New Testament Apocrypha*, 402–3 (color), and Bernhard, *Other Early Christian Gospels*, plates 24 and 25 (black and white).

envelope as P. Oxy. 210 at some point after its excavation. However, the form of the one visible letter, an *eta,* on the small fragment is quite different from the formation of *etas* on P. Oxy. 210; therefore this small fragment should not be regarded as part of the same text contained on the larger fragment.

The fact that the letters of the verso are somewhat thinner than those on the recto is probably due, at least in part, to the difficulty of writing against the fibers, and is not evidence of a different hand. A very small section of the top edge of the leaf remains, but the bottom of the leaf has not survived. For the first six lines of the recto, the top layer of the papyrus has broken away, so that no writing remains legible. Leaving aside the missing six lines at the top of the leaf, there are a total of seventeen lines on the recto, although lines 14–16 are no longer extant due to the top layer of the papyrus breaking away in this section. On the recto, the best-preserved line (line 5) has thirteen letters, whereas the worst-preserved lines (lines 12 and 13) have only three letters extant. Only the beginnings of lines 7–13 and 17 are preserved, so it remains uncertain how many letters were in a typical line on the recto. On the verso, there are a total of twenty-eight lines, with at least one partial letter preserved per line. Lines 1 and 2 are the worst preserved, each containing a single partial letter; the best preserved is line 17 with sixteen letters. The ends of lines 16–23 are preserved, but not the beginnings.

Determining the typical number of characters per line would help significantly in attempting a reconstruction of the contents of P. Oxy. 210, but arriving at an appropriate methodology for calculating this figure is difficult. As said, no full lines are preserved on either the recto or verso, but several pieces of data could help to arrive at an estimate. First, at line 15 on the verso, there is a rather large space before the first extant letter, which could indicate that it was the beginning of the line. Taking this in combination with the extant endings of lines 16–23 suggests an approximate length of 16–18 letters per line, at least on the verso. However, this would mean that line 15 had been indented significantly farther than the other surrounding lines, and it is unclear why a fairly competent scribe would have destroyed the symmetry of the beginnings of the lines in such a fashion. Furthermore, although the space before the initial letter in line 15 is relatively large, one can find other instances of generous spacing between letters elsewhere in the fragment. Therefore, relying heavily on line 15 for estimating the average number of letters per line seems quite hazardous. Moreover, as will be discussed momentarily, 16–18 letters per line would be significantly shorter than is typical of early Christian papyri, making this estimate even more unlikely.

Second, it may be possible, at several places on the recto of the fragment, to estimate the number of missing letters by means of an attempted reconstruction. In the most detailed reconstruction of P. Oxy. 210 to date, Stanley E. Porter reconstructed the number of letters per line in recto lines 4–7 as 21, 24, 22, and 18, respectively.[3] Additionally, for recto lines 6–7, Landau suggests tentative reconstructions of 25 and 26 letters, respectively.[4] These letters-per-line counts would suggest that P. Oxy. 210 had an average of 20–25 letters per line. The counts would also square with many other early Christian papyri, which frequently have 20–30 characters per line.[5] Given how difficult it is to make sense of the

---

3. Porter, "POxy II 210," 1101.
4. See p. 120 n. c below on these lines in the reconstructed translation.
5. The following numbers of letters per line are taken from papyrus manuscripts of the second through fourth centuries: P46, f. 20r, line 3 has 32 letters; P47, f. 7r, line 6 has 30 letters; P66, f. 30r, line 2 has 24 let-

text as we have it, it seems probable that even the most well-preserved lines are missing approximately 5–10 letters. The prospects for fully reconstructing such a fragmentary text, of course, remain quite slim, and thus any hypotheses about the precise contents of this text are very tentative. Nevertheless, a key precondition of any future reconstructions is a plausible and well-reasoned argument about the extent of the text missing.

P. Oxy. 210 was dated to the third century by its first editors, Grenfell and Hunt, and later commentators (Roberts, Lührmann, and Porter) have not contested this dating. This quite early date, combined with its use of familiar terminology from the NT, merited its inclusion in Lührmann's survey of apocryphal gospel fragments, the first such collection of Christian apocrypha to include an entry on P. Oxy. 210. In the view of the present editors, the third-century dating still appears quite probable, though it may be possible to date the fragment with a bit more precision: the best comparanda to the hand of this manuscript are found in dated documentary papyri from the mid- to late-third century. The scribe wrote this text in a mostly majuscule hand, though several ligatures do appear; it is a competently executed hand overall, but certainly not elegant. There are also several punctuation marks present in the manuscript: *trema* marks at recto line 1 and verso lines 6 and 25, and *diastrophes* at recto line 6 and verso lines 11 and 14.[6] As Wayment observes, "The large margins lend the impression of a well-executed codex,"[7] so we seem to possess in P. Oxy. 210 the remnant of a literary document produced with a certain degree of care and professionalism.

History of Research

The first critical edition of P. Oxy. 210 appeared in the second volume of Grenfell and Hunt's *The Oxyrhynchus Papyri* in 1899. The edition is very brief, with only two paragraphs of introduction and the transcription.[8] Moreover, Grenfell and Hunt did not label the text from the outset as an apocryphal gospel, instead giving it the title "Early Christian Fragment." In the first sentence of their edition, they are similarly equivocal, stating that it is "a theological work, the nature of which, whether historical [by which they probably mean 'narrative'] or homiletic, is doubtful." Yet several sentences later, they suggest that because Jesus appears to be speaking, "this points to the work having been an apocryphal gospel, possibly the 'Gospel according to the Egyptians.'" They then qualify this by stating that the text may have only quoted *Gos. Eg.*, since "the recto contains no indication that the book was of a narrative character." Apart from these statements, they also call attention to the fact that lines 11–17 on the recto begin farther to the left than the previous lines, which might indicate, intriguingly, the presence of a quotation.

Overall, Grenfell and Hunt have relatively little to say about this fragment, but several of their statements are open to question. The interpretation of lines 11–17 on the recto as a quotation is very reasonable, and they are certainly correct to express uncertainty about whether this is truly an apocryphal gospel, as opposed to some other theological work.

---

ters; P75, f. 44r, line 3 has 31 letters; P. Ryl. 463 (the *Gospel of Mary*), ↓5 has 25 letters; P. Oxy. 1 (the *Gospel of Thomas*), ↓20 has 19 letters; P. Bodmer 5 (the *Protevangelium of James*), p. 1, line 7 has 24 letters.

6. For discussion of such punctuation marks, see Eric G. Turner, *Greek Manuscripts of the Ancient World* (2nd ed.; rev. Peter J. Parsons; Bulletin of the Institute of Classical Studies Supplement 46; London: Institute of Classical Studies, University of London, 1987), 11, 19.

7. Wayment, *Text of the New Testament Apocrypha,* 188.

8. Grenfell and Hunt, *Oxyrhynchus Papyri,* 9–10. All subsequent quotations from Grenfell and Hunt derive from page 9 of this study.

Yet they do not offer any reasons for suggesting that it was specifically part of *Gos. Eg.*,[9] rather than some other apocryphal gospel. Furthermore, it is the recto that contains the references to an angel, which would seem more explicable as a narrative of some sort than a discourse.

In any case, unlike other fragments of apocryphal gospels discovered at the end of the nineteenth century (e.g., the Fayyum Fragment, *Gos. Pet.*, and the *Logia* from Oxyrhynchus later identified as *Gos. Thom.*), the publication of P. Oxy. 210 did not generate an enthusiastic flurry of scholarship.[10] The fragment was not included in M. R. James's 1924 *The Apocryphal New Testament,* and, until quite recently, was not to be found in any anthologies of Christian apocrypha: Elliott, the two volumes of *Écrits apocryphes chrétiens,* Erbetta's Italian anthology, and de Santos Otero's Spanish anthology all omit it, as does Maurice Geerard's *Clavis Apocryphorum Novi Testamenti.* The only mention it receives in Hennecke-Schneemelcher (until the very recent overhaul by Christoph Markschies and Jens Schröter) is in the entry for *Gos. Eg.*, and then only to dismiss Grenfell and Hunt's argument.[11]

More recent collections of Christian apocrypha have included the text, though often in quite brief treatments. This trend seems to have been initiated in 2000 by D. Lührmann and E. Schlarb in their survey of apocryphal gospel fragments, which helpfully provides a proposed reconstruction of the text (with a critical apparatus of the two previous editions) and an accompanying German translation.[12] A. Bernhard's critical edition of gospel fragments also provides a text and translation, papyrological details, and black and white plates of the recto and verso (Grenfell and Hunt did not include plates of the fragment in their edition).[13] Although the *Gospel Fragments* volume of the Oxford Early Christian Gospel Texts series does not include a dedicated section on P. Oxy. 210, co-editor T. Kraus notes the potential affinities between the "good and bad fruits" discourse in P. Mert. 51 and the "good" language found on the verso of P. Oxy. 210.[14] B. Ehrman and Z. Pleše's *Apocryphal Gospels: Texts and Translations* includes a modest introduction to the text, along with a reproduction of Lührmann's reconstruction of the Greek and Ehrman's own English translation.[15] Thanks to the prominence of its lead author and its affordable price, this volume has contributed significantly to awareness of this fragment's existence. The recently published and completely reconfigured seventh edition of Hennecke-Schneemelcher by Markschies and Schröter includes an introduction and German translation of P. Oxy. 210 by Stanley Porter,[16] based upon his previous reconstruction of the Greek text (see further below). Porter's presentation of P. Oxy. 210 in Markschies/Schröter marks the first ap-

---

9. For a succinct and up-to-date discussion of *Gos. Eg.*, see *AG,* 223–29.

10. Save for the brief comments by Adolf Deissmann, "Review of Grenfell and Hunt, *Oxyrhynchus Papyri* 2," *TLZ* 26 (1901): col. 72, in which he rejects Grenfell and Hunt's hypothesized connection of the text with *Gos. Eg.*

11. In the 1963 English translation of Hennecke-Schneemelcher[3], P. Oxy. 210 is briefly discussed on pages 92 and 174. In the 1991 English translation of Hennecke-Schneemelcher[4], only the mention from page 92 is retained (now on pp. 92–93), while the mention from page 174 is omitted from the discussion on page 214.

12. Lührmann and Schlarb, *Fragmente Apokryph Gewordener Evangelien,* 159–63.

13. Bernhard, *Other Early Christian Gospels,* 100, 108–13, Plates 24 and 25.

14. Thomas J. Kraus, Michael J. Kruger, and Tobias Nicklas, *Gospel Fragments* (Oxford Early Christian Gospel Texts; New York/Oxford: Oxford University Press, 2009), 261–63.

15. *AG* 259–65.

16. Porter, "Der Papyrus Oxyrhynchus II 210," 387–89.

pearance of this fragment in one of the standard anthologies of the Christian Apocrypha. Finally, in 2013, Thomas Wayment included in *The Text of the New Testament Apocrypha (100–400 CE)* his own transcription and brief paleographical analysis of P. Oxy. 210 and, most helpfully, color plates of the manuscript.[17]

The most significant contributions to the study of P. Oxy. 210, however, have come from four scholars who have produced the most detailed transcriptions of the fragment, since many of its readings have been disputed. The first transcription was by Grenfell and Hunt in 1899, but then in more recent years transcriptions were made by the late eminent papyrologist Colin Roberts (1987)[18] and Stanley Porter (2000),[19] whose study of the text is by far the most extensive. Roberts's study of P. Oxy. 210 is relatively brief. It summarizes the observations of Grenfell and Hunt, demonstrates a preference for understanding the text as a homily (because of its evident quotations), presents his own transcription with an apparatus listing divergent readings from Grenfell and Hunt, and includes a series of notes with several possible reconstructions and scriptural parallels.

Porter's study goes significantly farther than any of the others, providing a wealth of transcriptional observations and a hypothesis about the Egyptian Christian context in which the apocryphal gospel represented by P. Oxy. 210 was produced. His article begins with a review of the meager amount of previous scholarship, and he stresses how divergent the transcriptions of Grenfell/Hunt and Roberts are: a total of 25 different readings in 45 lines of text.[20] He then describes the papyrological characteristics of the fragment, and suggests that originally there were around 21 characters per line, though he does not explain in his article the basis for this calculation.[21] His diplomatic transcription follows. What is especially valuable about his contribution is that he includes commentary explaining the observational evidence (such as the typical ways in which letters are formed in the fragment) for those places where previous editions differ and offers his own adjudication.[22] He then provides a reconstructed version of the Greek text, once more with commentary discussing grammatical and exegetical decisions and difficulties. Given how significantly reconstruction and transcription can affect the interpretation of a papyrus fragment's content, Porter's approach should be emulated for future studies of P. Oxy. 210 and other fragmentary texts, apocryphal or otherwise.

Because Porter is the only scholar thus far to have attempted a reconstruction of the Greek text detailed enough to allow for the identification of specific narratives and sayings, it is worthwhile to describe those reconstructed narratives here in some detail. On the recto, Porter reconstructs an infancy narrative scene about Joseph taking Mary as his wife upon the instructions of an angel (recto, lines 4–6; cf. Matt 1:24).[23] The angel seems to speak of a sign given to the people (recto, line 7; cf. Luke 2:10–12). The righteous behavior of Joseph may have been introduced with a paraphrase of the Pauline teaching about the inadequacy of human standards of wisdom from 1 Cor 1:26–27 (recto, lines 1–3). This infancy narrative scene may have been followed by a quotation of some OT text, since lines 11–17 of the recto are farther to the left than the lines above them, as Grenfell and Hunt

---

17. Wayment, *Text of the New Testament Apocrypha*, 187–89, 402–3.
18. Roberts, "Early Christian Papyrus," 293–96.
19. Porter, "POxy II 210," 1095–1108.
20. Porter, "POxy II 210," 1096–97.
21. Porter, "POxy II 210," 1097.
22. Porter, "POxy II 210," 1098–1101.
23. Porter, "POxy II 210," 1101–2.

had observed. On the verso, Porter believes that we have a narrative of a person approaching Jesus with a question about what is good, to which Jesus responds that God alone is good (verso, lines 4–8; cf. Mark 10:17–18).[24] Rather than continuing the discussion about the keeping of commandments from Mark 10, however, Jesus next paraphrases the parable about good and bad trees and fruit (verso, lines 9–17; Matt 7:17–19//Luke 6:43–44). After this, Jesus uses Johannine "I am" language to describe himself as the "image" (verso, lines 18 and 20; cf. 2 Cor 4:4 and Col 1:15) and as the "form of God" (verso, line 19; cf. Phil 2:6), phrasing found not in the canonical Gospels, but present in the Pauline and deutero-Pauline literature. Thereafter may have followed more self-disclosure from Jesus, with allusions to Pauline language about God's unseen attributes (verso, line 23; cf. Rom 1:20) and the powers of this age (verso, line 24; cf. 1 Cor 2:6–8).[25]

Literary Context
Since the fragmentary state of P. Oxy. 210 makes any reconstruction quite tentative, it is not surprising that almost no one has attempted to find a suitable historical and literary context for its production. The one exception to this is Porter. On the basis of the reconstruction just described, Porter suggests that this fragment may provide us with several insights into Egyptian Christianity, the character of which is quite shadowy in earliest Christianity. First, he argues that P. Oxy. 210 provides evidence for a quite robust scriptural "canon" in third-century Egypt, with three or four of the canonical Gospels and five Pauline and deutero-Pauline epistles. This is a much larger scriptural repertoire than other apocryphal gospel fragments, and is particularly noteworthy for its Pauline elements.[26] Second, Porter suggests that the use of the parable of good and bad fruit, which is also found in the apocryphal gospel fragment P. Mert. 51,

> indicates that there was less concern within this Egyptian Christian community for struggling for differentiation of Christianity from . . . Judaism, and more concern for encouraging continued productive fidelity to the Christian faith, as indicated in the call for right behavior that is at the heart of this parable.[27]

This situation would reflect the circumstances of Christians in Egypt after the decimation of Jewish communities during the revolt under Trajan. Third and finally, this text presents an extremely high Christology, essentially fusing the most spectacular claims about Jesus from the Johannine and Pauline traditions. The language used may be on the road to gnostic Christian formulations, but, as Porter maintains, "at this point the language is all biblically based, and at best reflects the plurality of belief and expression of Egyptian Christianity at the time, some of which later figured into significant divisions of Egyptian Christianity from other expressions of Christianity in the fifth century."[28]

As is evident, Porter has devoted extensive effort to deciphering and contextualizing this tantalizing but puzzling fragment. However, there are several potential problems with his results. First, on the textual level, at some places his transcription of the manuscript is

---

24. Porter, "POxy II 210," 1102–4.
25. The reconstruction from 1 Cor 2:6–8 is actually Roberts's, which Porter seems inclined to follow; see Roberts, "Early Christian Papyrus," 296.
26. Porter, "POxy II 210," 1104–5.
27. Porter, "POxy II 210," 1106.
28. Porter, "POxy II 210," 1107.

probably incorrect, based upon Landau's own in-person analysis of the fragment in July 2014. Of course, all of the previous transcriptions are inaccurate at points, and Landau intends to publish a revised transcription of the fragment in the near future—though undoubtedly it too will be incorrect in some of its readings. Second, at several places in his reconstructed Greek text, the letters that he has conjectured do not match the extant versions of these letters found in the fragment; thus, these restorations are very unlikely to be correct. For examples of these instances, consult the notes to the translation below. In some cases, these unlikely restorations undercut the evidence for allusions to specific biblical authors or narratives.

Third, the restoration of the recto as an infancy narrative scene is, although plausible, still highly speculative. The interpretation is not unique to Porter; Lührmann also reconstructed the text in this fashion, and the origins of this interpretation apparently go back to Roberts's study. It is true that there are two undisputed occurrences of the Greek word "angel" on the recto (perhaps a third is present as well), and there are a significant number of references to a singular angel in the infancy narratives of Matthew and Luke. Yet a singular angel also appears in (some of) the resurrection narratives, during Jesus' agony in Gethsemane at Luke 22:43, and in a quotation from the *Gospel of the Hebrews* in which an angel carries Jesus to the top of Mount Tabor, perhaps during his temptation (cited by Origen, *Comm. Jo.* 2.12). So the infancy narratives do not exhaust the gospel mentions of a single angel, and if we count those stories and sayings from the gospels in which multiple angels appear (for which it would be easy for there to be a variant tradition with a single angel), the number of possible scenes expands dramatically. Ultimately, a "smoking gun," such as the presence of the name "Joseph" or "Mary," would make an infancy context much more secure. Apart from this, there is also the related problem of an infancy scene appearing so closely to teachings of Jesus in a gospel narrative (which is what the verso of P. Oxy. 210 almost certainly is). Of course, this fragment may not be a gospel text at all, but instead something like a homily, in which case this objection is moot. But given that the verso very likely contains direct discourse by Jesus, it still seems most probable to view P. Oxy. 210 as a fragment of a lost gospel.[29]

The fourth and final criticism concerns Porter's utilization of P. Oxy. 210 as a source for early Christianity in Egypt. Obviously, one could fault Porter in general for drawing conclusions from this text about the shape of the scriptural canon in Egypt and the sociological concerns of this Christian community, but Porter himself admits that drawing insights from a fragmentary document such as this is highly speculative.[30] More problematic than any of these speculations is Porter's unquestioned assumption that P. Oxy. 210 is a product of Egyptian Christianity simply by virtue of it being discovered there. For example, no one would argue that the Gospels of John and Luke, or the Pauline epistles, give us extensive insight into Egyptian Christianity simply because that is where P46 and P75 were produced. Porter, however, responds to this last criticism with the following observations: 1) we have no evidence of this text being in circulation outside of Egypt; 2) the text coheres with what we know of developments within Egyptian Christianity; and 3) the text is consistent with the development of a Christian corpus of sacred texts in the third century, a development for which Egypt provides extensive evidence. Therefore, Porter contends

---

29. Even if P. Oxy. 210 is not actually an apocryphal gospel, but a homily, it still either uses apocryphal traditions or cites canonical material in an extremely free way.

30. Porter, "POxy II 210," 1104.

that until we find another copy of this text or something like it somewhere else that fits as well within its environment, we should presume that it reflects Egyptian Christianity.

Despite the criticisms enumerated above, Porter's study clearly represents a quantum leap forward in the deciphering and interpretation of this enigmatic gospel fragment. Apart from his very thorough discussion of the transcriptional possibilities for the fragment, he also has recognized how unusual it is to have thoroughly "Pauline" elements appearing within sayings ascribed to Jesus. For example, one part of the fragment unambiguously reads: "I am an image" (verso, line 18),[31] in an apparent blending of the Johannine "I am" sayings with a Christology from Col. 1:15 that is possibly even more elevated than that of John's Gospel. Whether such a blending could have taken place at a quite early date in the Jesus tradition,[32] or instead indicates an origin for the text at a somewhat later date, remains a topic for future examinations.

Translation

Because P. Oxy. 210 is so fragmentary, it seems advisable to present here two translations in parallel columns. The translation on the left side of the page (designated the "diplomatic translation") represents an extremely conservative appraisal of the fragment's contents: only words that are complete or so nearly complete that their identity is certain are translated. The translation on the right side of the page (designated the "reconstructed translation"), in contrast, represents the most thoroughly reconstructed version of P. Oxy. 210, utilizing the reconstructions of Landau, Porter, Lührmann, and Roberts. The intended effect of presenting these two translations will be to demonstrate, side by side, *what is definitely there* versus what scholars who have studied the fragment think *might have originally been there*. In those cases where the reconstructions of scholars diverge, we have placed the most plausible reconstruction in the main text and the other reconstruction(s) in footnotes. Also indicated in the footnotes are places where a given reconstruction seems implausible on the basis of the traces of letters that remain. In one or two cases, the reconstruction in the main text is two different words separated by a slash; these are instances where two different words are conceivable on the basis of the Greek text that remains, and are discussed in the footnotes. Readers should be cautioned that the reconstructed text does not present anything like a complete, intelligible text: too much of P. Oxy. 210 is missing to allow for that.

Although the present anthology only presents texts in English translation, we have also included additional information in parentheses and brackets that we gain from the specifics of Greek grammatical structure. If enough of a noun or adjective is preserved that its case is clear but its function in the sentence is not, then abbreviations for the nominative, genitive, dative, or accusative case follow in parentheses. In addition, in instances where an adjective seems to have modified a noun that is not extant, after the adjective we have placed in brackets "*something*" to indicate that a noun is missing. If there is doubt about whether an adjective modifies a noun or acts on its own as a substantive (for example, "good person" versus "I am good"), we refrain from inserting "*something*" after the adjec-

---

31. At the very least, this passage reads *eimi eikōn,* though it is possible that the previous word, which ends in an omicron, is actually a scribal error for omega, in which case the passage would be a very Johannine/Pauline *egō eimi eikōn.*

32. See, for example, Helmut Koester's arguments for an early dating of Papyrus Egerton 2 on the basis of its interweaving of Synoptic and Johannine materials in *Ancient Christian Gospels* (Harrisburg, Pa.: Trinity, 1990), 205–16.

tive. Readers who desire greater specificity about what is present or absent in the manuscript should consult the available transcriptions and plates.

In the conservative translation, we use a system to describe what is missing or illegible in the fragment that requires some explanation. Although the translation does not present any of the Greek text, it nonetheless borrows some conventions from notation used in the editing of papyrus documents:

- The presence of dots <u>without brackets</u> denotes letters in the manuscript that are extant and legible, but that do not permit a confident reconstruction of the word in question.[33] Each dot corresponds to a single letter (<u>not</u> to an entire word).
- The presence of dots <u>inside brackets</u> denotes letters in the manuscript that are illegible or missing, but for which we can be reasonably certain how many letters were present. Again, each dot corresponds to a letter.
- If there are more than five letters in a row that cannot be reconstructed confidently, or are missing or illegible, these are denoted by a plus/minus sign and a number (for example, ±6), either without or inside of brackets.
- If an uncertain number of letters is missing, this is denoted by the abbreviation "*lac*" (for "lacuna") in brackets.

A few sample lines from the conservative translation illustrate how to interpret these different symbols and abbreviations:

- Line 1 of the recto reads: [. .] . . . . [. . . . .] [*lac*]. This means that two letters at the beginning of the line are missing;[34] then, four letters are present, but cannot be reconstructed into intelligible words with certainty; then, approximately five letters are missing; and finally, an indeterminate number of letters are missing at the end of the line.
- Line 12 of the verso reads: [*lac*] God (nom.) . [. . .] but [±6]. This means that an indeterminate number of letters at the beginning of the line are missing; then, the word "God" appears in the nominative case; then, one letter is extant; then, approximately three letters are missing; then, the word "but" appears; and finally, approximately six letters are missing.
- Line 27 of the verso reads: [*lac*] [±14] ±5. This means that an indeterminate number of letters at the beginning of the line are missing; then, approximately 14 letters are missing; and finally, five letters are present, but cannot be reconstructed into intelligible words with confidence.

As a final point, note that in the reconstructed translation we do not carry over the dots from the conservative translation, since in a number of cases it would be difficult to give a precise number of letters missing in addition to the reconstructed portion of the text.[35] Rather, we use a single bracket to denote places where some text, which could not be satis-

---

33. Note that this is a different use of an underdot from that found in critical editions of papyri, where an underdot by itself indicates that a letter is present but is so fragmentary that it cannot be identified. Here, a dot indicates a letter that is legible but cannot be confidently reconstructed to form a word, and letters that are so fragmentary that they cannot be identified instead are enclosed within brackets.

34. In a number of cases, the number of missing letters can be discerned by comparing the missing space to the place where a line with an intact beginning commences.

35. The one exception to this is in verso 12, where a set of double brackets with four dots appears in

4 to endure [.] . . . [*lac*]

Matt 1:24 5 angel commanded . . [*lac*]

6 [. . .] . angel (gen.) . . . [*lac*]

John 8:39 7 [. . .] . . . [±7] [*lac*]

4 to endure them.[a] He did the things that [

5 as the angel commanded, to take Mary.[b] But

6 the things spoken about the angel [

7 our sins. The children of Abraham][c]

---

possibilities in the reconstructed translation, separated by slashes.

a. "Them" reconstructed by Porter.

b. "He . . . Mary," first reconstructed by Roberts on the analogy of Matt 1:24, followed by Lührmann and, with slight modifications, by Porter.

c. Recto 7 is extremely difficult to reconstruct, and previous editions of P. Oxy. 210 have shown a remarkable amount of diversity in their transcriptions. In addition, the two co-editors of this piece have come to quite different conclusions in their reconstructions, so it is worthwhile to go into some detail here about this line. Landau's reconstruction has been retained in the reconstructed translation, though more will be said below about this decision. Porter (expanding upon Roberts's reconstruction) reconstructs it as "it is a sign for the people," echoing Luke 2:10. Whereas Porter and Roberts reconstruct the first four letters as *esti* ("it is"), Landau finds the reading *tias* more probable, especially regarding the partially preserved initial letter. In this case, it may have been the end of *hamartias* ("sins" in the accusative; "sin" in the genitive singular is also possible). Next, Porter and Roberts have read *sēmeion* ("sign," Lührmann has read this word as a plural), while Grenfell and Hunt, Bernhard, and Wayment have read *hēm(e)in* ("to/for us"). Landau, however, regards the letter after eta-mu as an *omega*, both because it lacks the middle stroke found in *epsilons* and because it resembles the incrementally rising *omegas* found elsewhere in the manuscript; this would yield the word *hēmōn* and the reconstructed sequence "our sins." Moving to the end of the line, Landau is of the opinion that Grenfell and Hunt are almost certainly correct in reading the final extant letter as a *beta*; it is worth noting that they did not underdot this letter in their edition, indicating that they were quite confident about its identity. The top of the letter looks nothing like any of the other extant letterforms in the papyrus and Landau clearly

8 ±7 [*lac*]
9 this . . [*lac*]
10 he will still have . [*lac*]
11 . . . . [*lac*]
12 . . . [*lac*]
13 . . . [*lac*]
14–16 [*lac*]
17 . . . [. .] [*lac*]

8 it is not possible [
9 this [
10 he will still have [
(Lines 11–16 too fragmentary for any reconstruction)

17 saying/he said[a] [

---

observed the beginning of a second loop below the top one in his in-person autopsy. The *beta* was probably preceded by two *alphas* in a row (the one immediately before the *beta* was not underdotted by Grenfell and Hunt, but the first of the two did receive an underdot). Prior to the *alphas,* only the smallest portion of a letter-top remains, but Grenfell and Hunt probably are correct also that this is a *tau* (which they have underdotted). Hence, the reconstructed sequence preferred by Landau is: *tias hēmōn ta ab.* Words beginning with the sequence *alpha-beta* are quite uncommon, but two possibilities from the NT are *Abba* and *Abraam.* Given the presence of the neuter plural article *ta, Abraam* (in the genitive case) seems more likely, perhaps sandwiched in the middle of a noun like *ta tekna* to yield "the children of Abraham" (cf. John 8:39). Porter, however, has significant doubts about the identity of both the *beta* and the *alpha* immediately preceding it; he believes that the surviving letter fragments are too ambiguous to permit reconstruction. The reconstruction of Landau has been placed in the reconstructed translation, however, due both to his strong insistence on the correctness of Grenfell and Hunt's reading of the final two letters, and to the fact that his reconstruction of the beginning of this line is more probable than Porter's. Readers, however, should be cautioned that the editors are very much at loggerheads over the reconstruction of this line, and so extreme caution should be taken in accepting either reconstruction as definitive.

a. Landau's reconstruction; the first three letters are almost certainly *sei,* with a *pi* likely after this. The final visible letter seems either to be *omicron* or *omega,* so *eipōn* ("saying") or *eipon* ("he said") is a probable reconstruction.

Verso: Against the Fibers (↓)

Diplomatic Translation

1 [*lac*] . [±10]
2 [*lac*] . [±10]
3 [*lac*] [. .] . . . [±6]
4 [*lac*] good[a] [±6]
5 [*lac*] he said [±7]
6 [*lac*] . Father (gen.)[b] . [±7]
7 [*lac*] . . . . [±7]
8 [*lac*] . . [±7]

9 [*lac*] [. .] . . [±8]
10 [*lac*] . . . . . [±6]
11 [*lac*] brings forth [±6]
12 [*lac*] God[c] (nom.) . [. . .] but [±6]

Reconstructed Translation

(Lines 1–3 too fragmentary for any reconstruction)

4] of the good[a] [*something*] [
5] he said to them[b] [
6] of your Father[c] [
7] the good [*something*] (acc.) [
(Line 8 too fragmentary for any reconstruction)
9] prophet[d] [
10] the good tree[e] [
11] brings forth [
12] God [. . . .][f] but [

a. So Porter, reading the word as a genitive because of the presence of a verb of speaking in the next line. No traces of any letters remain after *agatho,* so it might also be nominative or accusative.

b. "To them" is reconstructed by Porter, who reads the final fragmentary letter as an *alpha,* commencing the word *autois.* It is possible, though less likely, that the letter is instead a *nu,* in which case it would be the end of *elegen* ("he said").

c. So Porter, taking the final letter *upsilon* as the beginning of *humōn* ("your"). Alternatively, Roberts considers the reconstruction "son [*huios*] of the Father" more likely, on the basis of the *trema* mark above the *upsilon.*

d. Landau's reconstruction; the only certain letters are the sequence *rho-omicron.* After this pair, a *phi* seems likely. Before the pair, there may be a *pi,* though this is still quite uncertain. In any case, if the sequence *roph* can be read, the most probable word including this sequence is, by far, *prophētēs;* its grammatical case, however, cannot be determined.

e. So Porter. The noun is neuter in gender, so it may be either the subject or the object.

f. Verso 12 contains a missing portion that is very difficult to reconstruct. All that is certain is that the *nomen sacrum* "God" is followed by an *omicron,* then by a gap of three or four letters, then the word *alla* ("but"). Landau has suggested that there may be the smallest end of a *nomen sacrum*

a. The last letter of "good" is missing, so the case of the word is uncertain.

b. "Father" is abbreviated as a *nomen sacrum.*

c. "God" abbreviated as a *nomen sacrum.*

13 [*lac*] . Jesus[a] [. . .] ±6 [±6]

14 [*lac*] . . . . [.] brings forth . [±6]
15 [*lac*] . . . [. .] good (nom.) [±6]
16 [*lac*] . . . . [. . .] . . . a good (gen.) [*something*]
17 [*lac*] . . . . [. .] good (acc.) I am
18 [*lac*] [±6] I am an image of
19 [*lac*] [±7] . . . in a form of God[b]

20 [*lac*] [±6] . . . . . images (nom.) . .
21 [*lac*] [±9] to God, to God[c] . .
22 [*lac*] [±11] . . . to be
23 [*lac*] [±11] . . . . . visible things

13] the things which Jesus will also say[a]: [

14] "God brings forth good fruits.[b] [
15] But the good fruit (nom.) [
16] of a good tree brings forth

                          Matt 7:17–19//Luke 6:43–44

17] under the good. I am
18] I am an image

                          2 Cor 4:4; Col 1:15

19 of his goodness,[c] which in a form of God

                          Wis 7:26

                          Phil 2:6

20] as his image
21] to God, to God the
22] to be[d]
23] visible things

                          Rom 1:20

line just after the gap in the manuscript; if so, then another *nomen sacrum* might have followed "God," perhaps "Father." But it is quite possible that this is a shadow from a hole in the manuscript, and not a *nomen sacrum* line at all. Moreover, the phrase "God the Father" with the presence of an article before "Father" (*theos ho patēr*) is quite unusual in the NT, occurring only at 1 Cor 8:6 and 2 Thess 2:16, so Landau's reconstruction is extremely conjectural.

a. This reconstruction is shared by all previous editors. However, there are two potential difficulties with it. First, reconstructing *kai* ("also") is problematic, since the *iota* and the letter that has been regarded as an *alpha* are not connected, and elsewhere in the fragment they are almost always joined with a ligature (the one exception may be at the end of verso 24). Second, [*ka*]*i erei* ("he will also say") could possibly be read as "to the priest" (*ierei*), so that Jesus would be having some sort of debate with a priest. If "he will say" is indeed the correct reading, Roberts regards this discourse as being "set in the context of the Last Judgment."

b. So Porter, who rightly recognizes the beginning of a *nomen sacrum* at the end of the line, probably to be read as "God."

c. "Of his goodness" (*tēs agathotētos autou*) echoes Wis 7:26; it was first suggested by Roberts and subsequently adopted by Porter as his reconstruction.

d. The verb *einai* ("to be") is preceded by the article *tou*, which may indicate that this is part of an infinitive absolute construction, though it is difficult to reflect this possibility in the translation.

a. "Jesus" abbreviated as a *nomen sacrum*. Because the last letter of the *nomen sacrum* is missing, it is uncertain what case "Jesus" is; however, it is reasonable to suppose that Jesus is the subject of the sentence.

b. "Of God" abbreviated as a *nomen sacrum*.

c. Both instances of "to God" are abbreviated as *nomina sacra*.

1 Cor. 2:6–8   24 [*lac*] [±12] . . . of the . . [.]   24] the rulers (nom.) of this age[a]
                25 [*lac*] [±12] ±5 that   25] he saw that
                26 [*lac*] [±14] . . . he saw   26] if he saw
                27 [*lac*] [±14] ±5   (Line 27 too fragmentary for any re-
                                                             construction)
                28 [*lac*] [±13] a human being[a] (nom.) .   28] a human being (nom.)

---

a. "Human being" abbreviated as a *no-men sacrum*, though there is disagreement among previous editors as to the identity and quantity of letters in the *nomen sacrum*.

---

a. So Roberts, on the analogy of 1 Cor 2:6–8.

Papyrus Oxyrhynchus 5072
A new translation and introduction

by Ross P. Ponder

Papyrus Oxyrhynchus LXXVI 5072 (hereafter P. Oxy. 5072), although a small piece of just twenty-four fragmentary lines, looms large as one of the most recent apocryphal gospels published. It contains writing on both sides—thus, likely it was part of a codex—with material both similar to and distinct from the canonical Gospels. One side preserves an exorcism account, recording parts of a conversation between Jesus and a demon-possessed person. The other side includes a dialogue between Jesus and another party about the meaning of discipleship. Analysis of the fragment's handwriting dates the text between the late second and early third centuries, making P. Oxy. 5072 one of the earliest apocryphal gospel fragments.

Contents
The recto[1] of the papyrus includes an account of Jesus casting out a demon from a possessed person. The demoniac is brought before a crowd, but falls down on account of something, likely a spirit, overpowering him (*katelabē auton;* lines 2–3). Reproaching Jesus in lines 3–5, the demoniac cries, "Son of God, what have you to do with us? Did you come here before the time to destroy us?"[2] Jesus then rebukes and casts out the demon. This exorcism scene, while recalling several familiar stories from the canonical Gospels, appears similar to the healing of the so-called lunatic boy (Mark 9:14–29 par.) and the miracle story performed at Gadara/Gerasa (Mark 5:1–20 par.).[3] The latter miracle of Jesus famously includes the demon self-identifying as "Legion; for we are many" (Mark 5:9). In the synoptic account Jesus expels the demons into swine, which become crazed, run off the side of a cliff, and drown in the lake below. However, the expulsion of the demons into swine does not appear in P. Oxy. 5072.[4] The remainder of the narrative is difficult to discern, as the scene appears to switch and the papyrus is incomplete.

The verso depicts a conversation between Jesus and another party on the nature of

---

1. Recto refers here to the side with writing along the fibers of the papyrus, and verso refers to the side with writing across the fibers. This usage of recto and verso follows the language set forth by Nicklas, "Eine neue alte Erzählung."

2. All of the English translations are my own. For the Greek text used here, see "Reconstruction and Textual Parallels."

3. Another similar scene is the healing of a boy with an unclean spirit in Capernaum (Mark 1:21–28 par.). For more on these similarities, see "Reconstruction and Textual Parallels" below.

4. P. Oxy. 5072 is not as closely linked to the miracle performed at Gadara/Gerasa as others have suggested. Tobias Nicklas, for instance, cites P. Oxy. 5072's supposed connection to the miracle performed at Gadara/Gerasa as evidence of how some apocryphal gospels made New Testament stories less sensational ("Christian Apocrypha and the Development of the Christian Canon," *Early Christianity* 5 [2014]: 220–40 at 223).

discipleship. Jesus apparently speaks the entirety of this portion of the fragment to several addressees, expressly noting, "I myself will deny" (line 3) the addressee who shall be treated shamefully.[5] Discussions of whom and what Jesus will accept or deny bear similarities to some statements in the Synoptic Gospels (cf. Matt 10:32–33//Luke 12:8–9; Mark 8:38//Luke 9:26). The verso continues with mention of scribes, wise men and/or women, Jerusalem, the kingdom (of God), as well as concealing things from the intelligent (cf. Matt 11:25–26//Luke 10:21; Isa 29:14 LXX).

Manuscript Details

P. Oxy. 5072, a small fragment of just 7 × 7 cm and 24 fragmentary lines, contains writing on both sides; thus, it was likely part of a codex.[6] The letters are formed in a cursive-like script with numerous ligatures. The handwriting on the verso, written across the fibers of the papyrus, is less readable than the recto. On the whole, the handwriting looks to be the work of a single scribe, with several aids for ancient readers added later either by the same or another scribe.

Scholars are unable to calculate definitively the actual size of the original page and the extent of the missing text due to the disappearance of the margins at the beginning and end of lines. The papyrus is cracked vertically in two places, rendering several letter-forms difficult to discern. In spite of these difficulties, scholars have made estimates about the papyrus's size. For example, Chapa, the initial editor of the fragment, determined the size of the page (approx. 12 cm × 15–25 cm) and the number of letters per line (33–34) based on a plausible reconstruction of lines 5–6 on the verso side. Thus, P. Oxy. 5072 could represent up to half a page of a codex.[7] Line 5 in Chapa's more complete reconstruction has 31 letters, and other reconstructions offered, such as those for lines 8 and 9 on the verso, have as few as 29 letters.[8]

Analysis of the handwriting establishes the earliest possible date for the manuscript as the early second century CE. However, several of the cursive letter-forms adhere more closely to documentary texts from the late second century, such as P. Oxy. 4068 (200 CE) or P. Flor. II 278 (203–204 CE).[9] Chapa locates the handwriting anywhere between writings from the second half of the second century, like P. Oxy. 842, and the middle of the third century, such as P. Ryl. III 463 (the *Gospel of Mary*). Intriguingly, Chapa concludes

---

5. Even though the name Jesus does not appear on the verso, similarities with the canonical Gospels strongly suggest that this side of the papyrus contains a conversation between Jesus and someone who followed him, as well as sayings of Jesus addressed to different parties.

6. Readers can consult the Oxyrhynchus Papyri webpage for high-resolution and low-resolution images of P. Oxy. 5072 ("POxy Online: Oxyrhynchus Online," accessed on December 15, 2014, http://www.papyrology.ox.ac.uk/POxy/).

7. Chapa, "Uncanonical Gospel?" 3.

8. Not all early Christian manuscripts have an entirely uniform range of letters per line. For example, P75, f. 44v has a difference of up to nine letters per line (lines 4, 19, and 43 each have 26 letters, whereas line 28 has 35 letters), excepting cases of superlinear or marginal notation (line 16 has 22 letters). Lines 27 and 29 each have 30 letters, sandwiching the longest line of 35 letters. The number of letters per line has been determined by comparing images with the transcription of Victor Martin and Rodolphe Kasser (*Papyrus Bodmer XIV-XV: Evangiles de Luc et Jean*, Vol. 1, *Papyrus Bodmer XIV: Evangile de Luc chap. 3–24* [Cologny-Geneva: Biblioteca Bodmeriana, 1961]).

9. Chapa cites these examples ("Uncanonical Gospel?" 2).

that P. Oxy. 5072 might just "be the second earliest [apocryphal] gospel fragment, after P. Egerton 2."[10]

Several interesting "sacred names" (*nomina sacra*) are attested in the fragment: *hue* in recto line 3 for "son," and *baleia* in verso line 9 for "kingdom." A common *nomen sacrum* for "son" appears in a less common form, the Greek vocative case: "O Son of God" (*hue th[u]*) in line 3 of the recto.[11] An uncommon abbreviation for "kingdom" (*basileia*) appears in line 9 of the verso, abbreviated as *baleia*. While the word's contraction is sparsely attested compared to some other *nomina sacra* (i.e., *Iēsous, Kyrios*), P. Egerton 2 attests another early use of a *nomen sacrum* not unlike that of P. Oxy. 5072: *baleusin*.

Readers' aids within the papyrus likely indicate how and in what manner to read and study it. Six punctuation marks—a diagonal bar above the line—can be identified within the papyrus: two on the recto side at lines 5 and 7; and four on the verso side at lines 4, 5, 7, and 9.[12] The precise meaning of these is difficult to discern, but they appear at the end of sense units.[13] Further, the Greek *paragraphos* marker, a common diacritical mark in Greek literary texts, appears between lines 8 and 9 of the recto. The *paragraphos* marker—the Greek word from which we get the English paragraph—is a marginal notation, typically signaling the beginning or end of a thought. Ancient scribes marked paragraphs with ink marks and punctuation to clue readers in to when to have shorter or longer pauses when reading aloud, perhaps in public readings.[14] The scribe(s) of P. Oxy. 5072 employed the Greek *paragraphos* marker between lines 8 and 9 of the recto to indicate that the exorcism story had ended.[15]

History of Research

The first critical edition of P. Oxy. 5072, by Juan Chapa, appeared in volume 76 of *The Oxyrhynchus Papyri* in 2011. Chapa's edition offers a diplomatic transcription, a limited reconstruction of the text, and a thick commentary evaluating many possibilities for reconstructing the text. Intriguingly, Chapa did not offer a definitive identity for the text, instead raising a question about its contents: "Uncanonical Gospel?" However, Chapa relabeled the text as "gospel fragment" in a subsequent publication in 2012.[16] In the same 2012 publication Chapa prophesies about the future of research on the fragment: "[T]he newly published fragment will no doubt be the object of numerous studies and in years

---

10. Chapa, "Newly Published," 382. For a fuller explanation of the relationship between P. Oxy. 5072 and P. Egerton 2, see the history of research below.

11. For instance, Paap only includes two instances of the Greek vocative case (*hue*) being used for son (*huios*): *hue david* for "O, Son of David" in P46 (= P. Chester Beatty II, no. 21 in Paap); and *hue thu* for "Son of God" in P. Berol. 11858 (no. 420 in Paap). A. H. R. E. Paap, *Nomina Sacra in the Greek Papyri of the First Five Centuries A.D.: The Sources and Some Deductions* (Leiden: Brill, 1959).

12. Chapa identifies all of the punctuation marks except for recto line 5 and verso line 9, as well as the *paragraphos* marker between lines 8 and 9 of the recto ("Uncanonical Gospel?" 2, 17–18).

13. A sense unit coheres roughly to a complete thought or idea. The readers' aid of the diagonal bar would then function to mark complete or nearly complete thoughts.

14. William A. Johnson, "The Function of the Paragraphus in Greek Literary Prose Texts," *ZPE* 100 (1994): 65–68; Eric G. Turner, *Greek Manuscripts of the Ancient World* (2nd ed.; rev. Peter J. Parsons; Bulletin of the Institute of Classical Studies Supplement 46: London: Institute of Classical Studies, University of London, 1987), 9–14 and plates 14, 16, and 22.

15. I am grateful to Prof. Dirk Obbink for first pointing out the *paragraphos* marker in P. Oxy. 5072.

16. Chapa, "Newly Published."

ahead we will perhaps be able to situate it better in relation to other texts."[17] Yet little research has appeared on the fragment thus far.

After Chapa's two publications, the gospel fragment appeared in Rick Brannan's collection of Greek apocryphal gospels.[18] The stated goal of Brannan's collection is to allow nonspecialists to trace the development of heresies within ancient Christianity.[19] Brannan reproduced most of Chapa's reconstructed text, added a brief introduction, and produced the first English translation of the fragment. Brannan importantly makes P. Oxy. 5072 available to a wider audience.

In the same year as Brannan's collection of apocryphal gospels, Charles E. Hill made some passing references to P. Oxy. 5072 in an article on gospel traditions and the canon of the New Testament. Hill summarizes Chapa's research on the use of *nomina sacra* in P. Oxy. 5072 and P. Egerton 2 and uses these corresponding features to hypothesize why the texts used nonstandard abbreviations.[20] The presence of a nonstandard *nomen sacrum* for kingdom, according to Hill, underscores the fact that these gospels are noncanonical; thus, they stand outside of the norms of early Christianity, bearing witness to an early fourfold gospel tradition in the second century. Hill's discussion of P. Oxy. 5072, while clearly driven by Christian apologetic concerns, is to be commended for bringing it into conversation with other material from the late second and early third centuries.

One ensuing scholarly conversation places P. Oxy. 5072 in the context of early Christians reciting familiar gospel stories from memory. Appealing to social memory and orality studies, both Tobias Nicklas and Juan Chapa have argued that some apocryphal gospels, rather than redacting or harmonizing a single account from the canonical Gospels, function as reenactments of familiar gospel stories. Nicklas first developed the idea working on P. Egerton 2, noting the manner in which the text seems loosely related to the Gospel of John.[21] Also, P. Egerton 2 (1 A, lines 11–13) appears to recount the healing of a leper in language similar to the synoptic accounts (Mark 1:40–44 par.). Chapa cites Nicklas's work on P. Egerton 2, extending the idea that memory and orality might have played an important role in the production of early apocryphal gospels. Chapa describes P. Oxy. 5072 in this manner:

---

17. Chapa, "Newly Published," 387.

18. Brannan, *Greek Apocryphal Gospels*. It is not possible to provide precise page numbers for Brannan's treatment of P. Oxy. 5072, since this is an electronic book.

19. Logos Bible Software describes the apologetic goals of the collection this way on its website: "The documents in this resource are primary sources that show the religious context around the early church. Written after the ministry of Christ and the apostles, these collections of writings are not considered to be divinely inspired and were considered by many early Christian to be heretical. These writings were never included in a Bible but were used by some heretical groups. They are useful in tracing the history of non-Christian understandings of Jesus and the teachings of the apostles" ("Greek Apocryphal Gospels, Fragments, and Agrapha," accessed October 17, 2014, https://www.logos.com/product/17854/greek-apocryphal-gospels-fragments-and-agrapha).

20. For Hill's overarching research agenda on this topic, see Charles E. Hill, *Who Chose the Gospels? Probing the Great Gospel Conspiracy* (Oxford: Oxford University Press, 2010). He cites the papyrus also in his article "Four-Gospel Canon," 317, 318, 322, esp. 326–27.

21. Tobias Nicklas, "The 'Unknown Gospel' on Papyrus Egerton 2," in *Gospel Fragments* (ed. Thomas J. Kraus, Michael J. Kruger, and Tobias Nicklas; Oxford Early Christian Gospel Texts; New York/Oxford: Oxford University Press, 2009), 11–120, esp. 107 and 113. Raymond E. Brown made a similar argument for the composition of the *Gospel of Peter* earlier than the work of Nicklas and Chapa ("The Gospel of Peter and Canonical Gospel Priority," *NTS* 33 [1987]: 321–43 at 337).

Thus, if P. Oxy. LXXVI 5072 was not composed (i.e. more or less directly paraphrased) from the canonical Gospels themselves, it may have originated from traditions orally transmitted which were familiar to the author, based on the accounts (i.e. the narratives of exorcisms) of Matthew, Luke, and less obviously, Mark, and perhaps on other non-canonical writings or traditions of sayings of Jesus. Thus, it might have been an abridged version (e.g. for private or instructional use) of more than one canonical gospel, or an account of gospel stories and sayings recounted from memory.[22]

After Chapa published P. Oxy. 5072, Nicklas returned to his theory about memory and orality in the production of apocryphal gospels. Nicklas further elaborated on Chapa's suggestion that memory and orality might have been a factor in the production and circulation of P. Oxy. 5072.[23] Nicklas argues (more forcefully than Chapa) that P. Oxy. 5072 should be understood as a "re-enactment" of the notion that Jesus performed exorcisms, even as other extant stories circulated; however, not all communities had access to such texts, nor were they as important as stories told about Jesus orally.[24] In the end, the scholarly conversation about the composition of the fragment came full circle: Nicklas elaborating on Chapa elaborating on Nicklas.

While the notion that some apocryphal gospels were composed from memory seems attractive, a recent critique of performance criticism in New Testament studies casts serious doubt on the idea. Larry W. Hurtado has argued that the performative arguments appear to rest upon simplifications of Roman reading patterns without a firm grasp of the relevant sources in early Christianity and the Roman Empire. Hurtado raises several provocative questions for canonical texts, using manuscripts dated to the late second and early third centuries, the time of P. Oxy. 5072, to describe first-century scribal habits.[25]

Placing Hurtado's critique of performance criticism alongside parts of Chapa and Nicklas's work on memory and orality in P. Oxy. 5072 reveals two significant shortcomings. First, Chapa's work has a static perception of how memory and orality informed Roman reading practices. Any attempt to substantiate his intriguing claims need to be backed up with robust references to primary and secondary sources; unfortunately, this has not yet happened. Second, Nicklas incompletely situates his study of P. Oxy. 5072 in Roman culture while citing the work of Jan Assmann.[26] Historical study of memory ought to be culturally specific. Assmann remains one of the leading Egyptologists in the world,

---

22. Chapa, "Newly Published," 389 quoting himself verbatim without attribution from "Uncanonical Gospel?" 7.

23. Nicklas, focusing only on lines 1–7 of the recto ("Eine neue alte Erzählung"), leaves aside Chapa's suggestion that P. Oxy. 5072 "might have just been an abridged version of more than one canonical gospel for private or catechetical use" (Chapa, "Uncanonical Gospel?" 1). Nicklas restated some of his work on P. Oxy. 5072 at the Kenneth Willis Clark Lectureship at Duke Divinity School in a lecture titled "Apocryphal Gospel Fragments and Our Images of Early Christianity," on April 9, 2014.

24. Nicklas comments on the goals of his work on P. Oxy. 5072: "Since I am unable even for technical reasons to add something to Chapa's precise paleographic analysis, I will hereafter focus on the reconstructed text of P. Oxy. lxxvi 5072. Again, my own contribution is modest" ("Eine neue alte Erzählung," 19). It is my own English translation of the German.

25. Larry W. Hurtado, "Oral Fixation and New Testament Studies? 'Orality', 'Performance' and Reading Texts in Early Christianity," *NTS* 60 (2014): 321–40. Claiming that scribes typically followed what they copied precisely, Hurtado wants to make a genealogical argument from third-century texts to possible first-century exemplars (337).

26. Nicklas ("Eine neue alte Erzählung," 15 n. 8) cites Jan Assmann's famous work, *Das kulturelle Gedächtnis: Schrift, Erinnerung und politische Identität in frühen Hochkulturen* (Munich: Beck, 1997).

and his take on cultural memory is most noticeably shaped by and relevant to ancient Egypt. A priestly caste maintained control of writing for centuries in Egyptian civilization, ensuring a relatively stable view of memory (i.e., tradition and cultural practices). Transferring Assmann's model to another society, even Roman Egypt in the late second/early third centuries CE, yields mixed results. Nicklas's intriguing study would have benefited from noting cross-cultural limitations. What, then, can the second- and third-century evidence, which Hurtado presents in his article, teach us about ancient Christian reading and writing practices in the second and third centuries?

Instead of looking at how P. Oxy. 5072 might have been composed (i.e., from memory), a more productive research direction could be the exploration of the readers' aids within the papyrus. A recent proposal analyzes the visual and physical features of early gospel manuscripts in order to determine whether a certain manuscript was intended for liturgical (i.e., public) reading versus private study.[27] The presence of readers' aids (i.e., the *paragraphos* marker, six punctuation markers [diagonal bars], diaeresis) in P. Oxy. 5072 could mean that the text was intended for liturgical (i.e., public) reading. However, Chapa advocates the view that P. Oxy. 5072 was probably intended for private or instructional (i.e., catechetical) use.[28] Research on the readers' aids within the papyrus itself would be a welcome addition to the growing body of secondary literature.[29]

Reconstruction and Textual Parallels

Since the edges of P. Oxy. 5072 are no longer extant, scholarly reconstructions remain quite provisional. Chapa's two studies abound in their use of the subjunctive voice to offer a plausible reconstruction for the fragmentary text. Indeed, while Chapa's careful scholarship is to be commended, two problems exist with his work. First, Chapa's transcription is most likely incorrect in some places, using Ponder's own in-person analysis of the papyrus in July 2014 as a point of comparison.[30] Second, in several places of his reconstructed Greek text, Chapa misreads certain letter-forms that appear elsewhere in the fragment.[31] The totalizing effect of these misreadings of certain letter-forms, it is argued, undercut

---

27. Scott D. Charlesworth, "Public and Private Second and Third-Century Gospel Manuscripts," in *Jewish and Christian Scripture as Artifact and Canon* (ed. Craig A. Evans and H. Daniel Zacharias; London: T.&T. Clark, 2009), 148–75. However, the concepts of public and private are used with some hesitations, since modern conceptions of public and private do not map onto the Roman context coherently. For instance, reading aloud is often thought to be public in modernity, but in Roman antiquity our data tells us that most, if not all, reading happened aloud; cf. Catherine Hezser, "'Privat' und 'öffentlich' im Talmud Yerushalmi und in der griechisch-römischen Antike," in *The Talmud Yerushalmi and Graeco-Roman Culture*, vol. 1. (ed. Peter Schäfer; TSAJ 71; Tübingen: Mohr Siebeck, 1998), 423–579. Similarly the space a human body moves through was not necessarily just public or private, as work on ancient houses and the cubiculum has demonstrated. Cf. Andrew Wallace-Hadrill, *Houses and Society in Pompeii and Herculaneum* (Princeton: Princeton University Press, 1994); John H. D'Arms, "Between Public and Private: The Epulum Publicum and Caesar's Horti trans Tiberim," in *Horti Romani: Atti del Convegno Internazionale, Roma, 4–6 Maggio, 1995* (ed. Maddalena Cima and Eugenio La Rocca; Rome: L'Erma di Bretschneider, 1998): 32–43; and Andrew M. Riggsby, "'Private' and 'Public' in Roman Culture: The Case of the Cubiculum," *JRA* 10 (1997): 36–56.

28. Chapa, "Uncanonical Gospel?" 7.

29. See, for example, William A. Johnson, *Readers and Reading Culture in the Early Roman Empire* (New York: Oxford University Press, 2010), 179–99; idem, "Toward a Sociology of Reading in Classical Antiquity," *AJP* 121 (2000): 593–627.

30. Ponder intends to publish a revised critical edition in the near future.

31. For particular examples, refer to the notes in the following translation.

some of the biblical parallels that Chapa identifies, chief among them being the connection to the demoniac at Gerasa/Gadara.

Beginning with the recto, several lines are very fragmentary and difficult to reconstruct, but it is not an impossible task. Chapa tentatively suggests that lines 1–3 should be reconstructed as: "they brought him (the demon-possessed person) before Jesus. And he did not [*lac*], but he tore apart as much as he was able."[32] However, based on recent in-person examination, the lines are better read as: "they brought him (the demon-possessed person) before the crowd, but he (the demon-possessed person) fell down as often as it (the demon) overtook him."[33] The phrases "before the crowd" (*enantion tou ochlou*) and "they brought" (*p[rosēnenkan*) fit the ink traces of the papyrus and the context.[34] The Greek verb "to bring before" (*prospherō*), commonly used in miracle stories of Jesus, can designate a disabled person who is brought before Jesus.[35] Further, the reconstruction between lines 2 and 3—"as often as it (the demon) overtook him (the demon-possessed person)"—employs language not unlike the healing of the lunatic boy in Mark 9:18, which reads: "and whenever it seizes him, it dashes him down" (*kai hopou ean auton katalabē rēssei auton*). Both texts employ uncommon etymologically related words: *katarrēssō* and *rēssō*. Chapa notes the parallelism of language between Mark 9:18 and P. Oxy. 5072 here, but finds the connection not helpful for reconstructing the text of the papyrus.[36]

Lines 3–5 present the demoniac speaking in language similar to two miracle stories. The first part of the speech recalls parts of the demoniac's question at Gerasa/Gadara: "Son of God, what have you to do with me?" (Mark 5:7 par.). Interestingly, the second part of the sentence in the fragment—"have you come before the time to destroy us?"—is closely paralleled in Matt 8:29, particularly a textual variant found in Codices Sinaiticus and Washingtonianus. The textual variant of these two codices employs the Greek word *apolesai* ("to destroy") instead of *basanisai* ("to torment"). The reconstructed text of the papyrus employs a verb (*parapollymi*) related etymologically to the word for "destroy" (*apollymi*) used in the textual variants of Matt 8:29.[37]

Lines 7–9 are also difficult to reconstruct. Chapa suggests that the text might have read, "When it left, the person sat in the middle of them, embracing the feet of Jesus."[38] However, it is difficult to resolve Chapa's suggestions with the residual ink traces. The remaining lines, unfortunately, are too damaged to restore with any degree of certainty. Chapa suggests the following reconstruction for lines 9–11: "but Jesus wrapped him up,

---

32. The abbreviation "*lac*" designates a hole in the manuscript. The reconstruction of lines 1–3 offered by Chapa reads: *enantion [to]u i(ēso)u k[ai] ouk [. . .] |. . .] alla katerrēssen hosa ischue kai idōn auto]n* ("Uncanonical Gospel?" 9–10).

33. Ponder's reconstruction: *enantion [t]ou o[chl]ou p[rosēnenkan | auton] alla katerrēssen hosa[kis katelabe | auto]n.* The verb *katarrēssō* is taken as intransitive, meaning to "fall to the ground."

34. The letter-form of *p* at the end of line 1 looks very similar to the *p* in line 4 on the same side of the papyrus.

35. For similar uses of *prospherō*, see Matt 4:24; 8:16; 9:2, 32; 12:22; 14:35; 17:16; Mark 2:4.

36. Chapa, "Uncanonical Gospel?" 10.

37. Luke 4:34 also uses *apolesai* similarly. The reconstructed text in lines 5–6 differs from Chapa's suggestion "*parapolesai ho de i]s*" ("Uncanonical Gospel?" 11–12). Chapa mistook a punctuation marker just before *epitimēsen* in line 5 as a superlinear stroke. The superlinear strokes designating sacred names (*nomina sacra*) in this papyrus fragment do not float over the following letter, as the diacritical mark does over the epsilon here (i.e., compare the markers over epsilon in recto line 7).

38. Chapa reconstructs the Greek text: *elthōn ekathisen ho [anthrōpos en mesō a]utōn per[i]pt[usa]s to[us podas iu* ("Uncanonical Gospel?" 12–13).

and he (Jesus) ordered him to put on clothes . . . someone to him."[39] This reconstruction is problematic due to line spacing. Chapa's suggestion for line 9 only has 25 letters, which coincidently is one of the more fragmentary lines of the papyrus and also one of Chapa's shortest reconstructions for an entire line. An additional problem is the lack of literary parallels. However, on account of the fragmentary nature of the lines, a more viable reconstruction has not been put forth.

Turning from the recto, the verso depicts a conversation between Jesus and another party on the nature of discipleship, a conversation that has some affinities with Matt 10:32–33//Luke 12:8–9. Jesus apparently speaks the entirety of the fragment.[40] The addressees change at several points, since the narrative employs both the second-person singular in lines 3–4 (*esē*, and *se*) and the second-person plural in line 5 (*hymin*). The beginning of the extant text presents Jesus asking somebody to confess him as a teacher (*didaskalon* in line 3). Chapa notes the beginning of the Greek word "confess" (*homol . . .*) at the end of line 2, but the translation below suggests a specific verbal form for confess (*homologeō*). The presence of "confessing" (*homol . . .* in line 2) and "denying" (*aparnēsomai* in line 3) reflects the language of Matt 10:32–33//Luke 12:8–9. Chapa notes that the presence of the first-person singular subject "I" (*ego* in line 3) "brings the text of the papyrus closer to the Gospel of Matthew, although the verb *aparneomai* ['to deny'] occurs in Luke."[41] Jesus raises the honor/shame stakes by claiming that the one who does not recognize him shall experience shame eternally (*esē aischynomenos | eis ta eschata*, lines 4–5; cf. Mark 8:38//Luke 9:26). Another saying of Jesus in the reconstructed text of lines 5–7 demands detachment from worldly bonds so as to become Jesus' worthy disciple. This much can be deduced from echoes of language from Matt 10:37–39//Luke 14:26–27. Thus, a plausible reconstruction for lines 5–7 is: "the one who loves his soul above me is not worthy to be my disciple."[42]

Unfortunately, the remaining lines of the verso of the papyrus are too poorly preserved to find precise parallels within biblical and parabiblical literature. All hope is not lost for restoring the text, though, as there are two important clues. First, the proximity of two conditional phrases in lines 8 ("if then you are a scribe" [*ei oun grammatikos ei*]) and 9 ("although, if you are a wise person" [*kai ei sophistēs ei*]) suggests a corresponding relationship between them. The second and more important clue occurs at the beginning of line 9, where the word "Jerusalem" occurs in order to complete the thought of the first conditional statement. In the New Testament, when "Jerusalem" is spelled this way (*Hierosolyma*), it almost always includes the preposition "to" (*eis*) with a verb of motion (such as "to go up" [*anabainō*]). Thus, it is reasonable to expect an imperative command such as: "Go up to Jerusalem!" (*anabaine eis Hierosolyma*).[43] Just as an imperative verb of motion

---

39. Chapa reconstructs the Greek text: *ho de iēsous periest[eilen auton kai | himat]ion endus[ai ekeleusen [lac] ei tis autō[i* ("Uncanonical Gospel?" 13).

40. Even though the name Jesus does not appear on the verso, similarities with the canonical Gospels strongly suggest that this side of the papyrus contains a conversation between Jesus and someone who followed him, as well as a saying of Jesus addressed to a different party.

41. Chapa, "Newly Published," 386.

42. Chapa cautiously suggests this reconstruction: *ho philōn tēn psychēn autou huper eme ouk estin mou axios einai mathētēs* ("Newly Published," 386).

43. *Hierosolyma* occurs 37 times in the New Testament, and 35 of them include the preposition "to" (*eis*). Fifteen of the 35 combine the imperative command to go up to Jerusalem (*anabainō*). Chapa, "Uncanonical Gospel?" 16–17.

and location follows a conditional statement in lines 7–8, so too does one expect the pattern to continue to complete the thought of the second conditional statement in lines 8–9.

The text of line 9 is badly preserved between the definite article "the" (*tas*) and the phrase "but the kingdom" (*hē de baleia*), but recent in-person examination of the ink traces and letter spacing allows for the reconstruction of the text as "the courts (of heaven)" (*tas aulas*). While Chapa suggested this as a possibility, he dismissed it in favor of "Athens" (*Athēnas*) for three reasons. First, he saw a parallelism between the scribes (*grammatikos*) and Jerusalem of lines 7–8 with the wise people (sophists) and Athens in lines 8–9.[44] Just as Jerusalem was the center of scribal life and learning for Jewish culture, so was Athens for the Roman world of the Second Sophistic. Unfortunately, recent scholarship on intellectuals within the Roman Empire does not support Chapa's intriguing connection between Athens and Jerusalem as antithetical centers of learning for intellectuals. Kendra Eshleman has demonstrated that geography—i.e., in the city of Athens or Rome—did not separate insiders from outsiders for Roman and Christian intellectuals.[45] Philosophers, sophists, and Christian intellectuals policed their group's boundaries from outsiders and teachers within the movement. Access into groups of Roman or Christian intellectuals, according to Eshleman, relates to conceptions of "public" and "private" teaching, where insiders arrive at true knowledge that is available to a select few.[46] Such negotiations often left a group, like ancient Christians, both to perceive and to fear the threat of an invasion by impostors.[47] All in all, Eshelman's work has shown that Roman intellectuals determined insiders from outsiders not by contrasting centers of learning (e.g., Athens vs. Jerusalem) but through the "common set of culturally available strategies of self-definition."[48]

Chapa's second objection to the "courts (of heaven)" concerns line spacing for individual letters. Chapa correctly noted the tight spacing of letters, as well as the initial letter alpha. However, the reading would fit the 22-mm hole in the papyrus. Chapa's preferred reconstruction of Athens (*Athēnas*) would have required even more space than court (*aulas*).[49] In addition to the concern of line spacing, Chapa's third objection concerned the absence of parallel examples for lines 7–9.[50] Yet a similar semantic range occurs at a few points in biblical and parabiblical literature. Within the canonical Gospels, both the kingdom and Jerusalem occur at Luke 19:11. The Alexandrian Jewish writer Philo employs the language of personified wisdom, the court of heaven, and the kingdom to describe the attributes of a monarch: "and wisdom is the court and kingdom of the all-governing, absolute, and independent king" (*Congr.* 116).[51] Other examples could also be cited. In the end,

---

44. Chapa, "Newly Published," 386–87; idem, "Uncanonical Gospel?" 17. I suspect that Chapa, even though he does not cite it, made this argument with Tertullian's famous quote in mind: "What has Athens to do with Jerusalem?" (*Praescr.* 7). Tertullian's comment occurs in the context of arguing that philosophical inquiry does not undercut scriptural authority and its modes of learning.

45. Kendra Eshleman, *The Social World of Intellectuals in the Roman Empire: Sophists, Philosophers, and Christians* (Cambridge: Cambridge University Press, 2012), 21–66.

46. Eshleman, *Social World*, 25–34.

47. 2 Tim 3:6–7; Titus 1:1. Eshleman, *Social World*, 49–54.

48. Eshleman, *Social World*, 261.

49. To be fair, Chapa acknowledges this much, yet insists that Athens is the better reading: "[H]owever, the restoration can only be tentative, for, although the traces do not rule it out, it must be admitted that the space for the missing *as* is probably too narrow" ("Uncanonical Gospel?" 17; idem, "Newly Published," 387 n. 5).

50. Chapa, "Uncanonical Gospel?" 15–18.

51. Greek text derives from Monique Alexandre, *Philon d'Alexandrie: De Congressu Eruditionis Gratia. Introduction, Traduction et Notes* (Paris: Cerf, 1967). It is my own English translation.

Chapa's suggestion of "Athens" (*Athēnas*) for the lacuna in line 9, while an intriguing possibility, does not work, for it is too long and does not match the ink traces of the papyrus.

Lines 10–12 can be reconstructed as: "My father conceals these things from the wise and intelligent ones."[52] Intriguingly, Chapa does not remark on the similarity of language between these verses and Isa 29:14 LXX: "Then I will destroy the wisdom of the wise, and will conceal the understanding of the intelligent" (*kai apolō tēn sophian tōn sophōn kai tēn sunesin tōn sunetōn krupsō*, my trans.).[53] Both passages have a remarkably similar semantic range: concealing (*apek[rupse* in P. Oxy. 5072; *krupsō* in Isa 29:14b LXX), wisdom (*sophōn* in P. Oxy. 5072; *sophian* in Isa 29:14b LXX), and intelligent ones (*sunetōn* in both P. Oxy. 5072 and Isa 29:14b LXX).

The new reconstruction of the papyrus fragment allows for more precise evaluation of the text's parallels to biblical and parabiblical literature. The episode on the recto, instead of cohering to a single episode from the New Testament gospels, contains elements with affinities to several different canonical exorcism stories: the casting out of a demon at Gadara/Gerasa (Mark 5:1–20 par.), the healing of a man with an unclean spirit in Capernaum (Mark 1:21–28 par.), and the so-called lunatic boy (Mark 9:14–29 par.). In line 2 the possessed person falls down after a spirit overtakes him. The use of *ekathisen* ("to sit down" in line 7; cf. Luke 8:35) and *endu* (line 10; cf. *enedusato* in Luke 8:27) recalls the changes to the text made in Luke's redaction of Mark. The expression "before the time" (*pro kairou;* line 4), only present at two places in the New Testament, occurs in Matthew's version of the exorcism at Gadara (8:29). The phrase "Yes, I say to you" (*nai legō hymin;* line 5) occurs four times in the New Testament, but mostly in the Gospel of Luke.[54] Additionally, the narrator's phrase in line 3, "He cried out, saying," as well as "he rebuked him, saying: 'Come out of the human!'" in lines 5–6 cohere not only to the exorcism scene at the lake in Matthew, but also to Jesus healing a man with an unclean spirit in a Capernaum synagogue (Mark 1:25//Luke 4:35). Similarly, the verb for cry out (*epitimeō*) and the command for a demon to leave a person occur in the healing of the lunatic boy (Mark 9:25). Thus, the recto appears to employ Greek words and language from all three of the Synoptic Gospels. While one expression can be found in Mark ("he cried out, saying" [*anekraxe legōn*] in line 3), the majority of the similarities are with Matthew and Luke, though there is no clear indication of dependence upon one account.[55]

The verso of the papyrus treats the topic of discipleship with similar statements occurring in biblical and parabiblical literature. The speaker, who is most likely Jesus, exclaims, "I myself will deny" the addressee, who will suffer shameful treatment eternally. The presence of "confessing" and "denying" in these initial lines of the verso coheres nicely with Matt 10:32–33//Luke 12:8–9. Another important similarity between P. Oxy. 5072 and the canonical Gospels occurs in lines 5–7. The papyrus fragment employs a saying of Jesus (Mark 8:38//Luke 9:26) about those who love their own life above Jesus' as not being wor-

---

52. Chapa reconstructs as: *ho pr mou | apo sophōn kai sunetōn apek[rupse tauta* ("Uncanonical Gospel?" 19).

53. I am grateful to Geoffrey S. Smith for suggesting this parallel.

54. Matt 11:9; Luke 7:26; 11:51; and 12:5. Chapa also makes this observation ("Uncanonical Gospel?" 5).

55. Curiously, one of the more memorable features of the exorcism at Gerasa/Gadara remains absent from P. Oxy. 5072: the expulsion of the demons into swine that drown in the lake. Assuming a width of 30–35 letters per line, there is not enough space in lines 6–7 to restore the drowning of the pigs, strongly suggesting that the papyrus is not merely a harmonization of the demoniac story in Mark, but depends on multiple sources.

thy of discipleship. Lines 7–9 contain striking similarities in language with Luke 19:11 and Philo's *Congr.* 116. Lines 10–12 tend to cohere with the language of Isa 29:14 LXX. Other sections of the verso of the papyrus fascinate interpreters: Why do scribes go up to Jerusalem, and wise people go to the courts (lines 8–9)? Does it have something to do with the need to conceal things from the intelligent (lines 10–12)?

Finally, the aforementioned comparisons between P. Egerton 2 and P. Oxy. 5072 may indicate something about the origins of the two untitled gospels. Both texts have been invoked (by Nicklas and Chapa) as possible examples of secondary orality. More specifically, both texts employ unusual but similar abbreviations for kingdom (*baleia,* P. Oxy. 5072, verso line 9; *baleu[sin,* P. Egerton 2, 2, line 7), and use the word "teacher" (*didaskalos* in P. Oxy 5072 verso line 3, P. Egerton 2, 1A, line 12; and 2A, line 4) to refer to Jesus. The comparison has limits, as P. Egerton 2 appears similar to the Synoptic Gospels and Gospel of John, whereas P. Oxy. 5072 has points of contact with up to three different episodes from the Synoptic Gospels.[56]

Translation[57]

Due to the fragmentary nature of P. Oxy. 5072, the translation is presented in two parallel columns. The lefthand column presents a diplomatic translation of words that can definitely be reconstructed.[58] The righthand column presents the most fully reconstructed translation of the papyrus possible, drawing upon the reconstructions of Chapa and Ponder. The purpose of the two columns is to alert readers to the interpretative decisions made by scholars to show *what is actually there* on the lefthand side as well as *what most likely had been there* on the righthand side.

The diplomatic translation uses a system to describe what is missing or illegible in the fragment that borrows some conventions from notation used in the editing of Greek papyrus documents:

- The presence of dots <u>without brackets</u> denotes letters in the manuscript that are extant and legible, but that do not permit a confident reconstruction of the word in question.[59] Each dot corresponds to a single letter (<u>not</u> to an entire word).
- The presence of dots <u>inside brackets</u> denotes letters in the manuscript that are illegible or missing, but for which we can be reasonably certain how many letters were present. Again, each dot corresponds to a letter.
- If there are more than five letters in a row that cannot be reconstructed confidently, or are missing or illegible, these are denoted by a plus/minus sign and a number (for example, ±6), either without or inside of brackets.
- If an uncertain number of letters is missing, this is denoted by the abbreviation "*lac*" (for "lacuna") in brackets.

---

56. For P. Egerton 2's relationship with the four canonical Gospels, see Nicklas, "Unknown Gospel," 107 and 113. Chapa provides other citations ("Uncanonical Gospel?" 7; idem, "Gospel Fragment," 388).

57. The presentation of the translation here closely follows the guidelines set forth by Brent Landau and Stanley E. Porter for their work on P. Oxy. 210 elsewhere in this volume.

58. This includes complete words or fragmentary words whose identity can be reconstructed definitively.

59. Note that this is a different use of an underdot from that found in critical editions of papyri, where an underdot by itself indicates that a letter is present but is so fragmentary that it cannot be identified. Here, a dot indicates a letter that is legible but cannot be confidently reconstructed to form a word, and letters that are so fragmentary that they cannot be identified instead are enclosed within brackets.

- The presence of an open bracket marker at the beginning or end of a line indicates the edges of the papyrus fragment.
- The presence of a diagonal slash / indicates a readers' aid within the papyrus fragment. For instance, the diagonal bar in line 5 of the recto could indicate that the narrative voice has switched from the first-person of the demoniac to the third-person voice of the narrator describing Jesus' actions.
- Underlined text indicates the presence of a *paragraphos* marker. The *paragraphos* marker typically occurs between two lines as a horizontal slash.
- When the subject of a noun is unclear, parentheses specify the person taken as the subject.

The following examples from the diplomatic translation illustrate the ways to interpret the symbols and abbreviations just described.

- Line 1 of the recto reads: [*lac*] before [.] ... [. .] ... [*lac*]. This means an indeterminate number of letters are missing at the beginning of the line. The first (and only) legible word is "before" (*enantion*). The following letter is missing; next, three letters are present; then, two letters are missing; after that, three letters are extant; and finally, an indeterminate number of letters at the end of the line are missing.
- Line 4 of the recto reads: [*lac*] did you come before the time us (acc.) . . [*lac*]. The beginning of the line is missing. The words occur precisely in this order in the Greek; therefore, an infinitive verb probably followed the first-person plural pronoun "us."
- Line 8 of the recto reads: [*lac*] them ... [.] .. [. . .] ... [*lac*]. This means that the beginning of the line is missing. Four of the five letters for the word "them" occur, allowing for its reconstruction. Underneath the first two letters of the extant line rests the *paragraphos* marker. Next, three letters occur; then, one letter is missing; then, two letters occur; then, approximately three letters are missing; and finally, there are about three letters that cannot be confidently reconstructed before the text breaks off.

The reconstructed translation does not use the dots from the diplomatic translation, since it would often be impossible to give a precise number of missing letters alongside the hypothetical reconstructed text. The readers' aids within the papyrus are not marked in the full reconstruction, but readers can readily locate them in the diplomatic translation. Curious readers should consult the above section on reconstructing the papyrus fragment as well as the footnotes to the translation below, in addition to other transcriptions and plates, for information regarding the manuscript's contents.

Bibliography

Brannan, Rick. *Greek Apocryphal Gospels, Fragments and Agrapha*. Bellingham, Wash.: Lexham, 2013.

Chapa, Juan. "A Newly Published 'Gospel Fragment.'" *Early Christianity* 3 (2012): 381–89.

———. "Uncanonical Gospel?" Pages 1–20 in vol. 76 of *The Oxyrhynchus Papyri*. Edited by Daniela Colomo and Juan Chapa. Graeco-Roman Memoirs 97. London: The Egyptian Exploration Society, 2011. (*Editio princeps* of the manuscript.)

Hill, Charles E. "A Four-Gospel Canon in the Second Century?" *Early Christianity* 4 (2013): 310–34.

Nicklas, Tobias. "Eine neue alte Erzählung im Rahmen antiker Jesustraditionen: Reste eines Exorzismus auf P.Oxy. lxxvi 5072." *Annali di Storia dell'Esegesi* 29 (2012): 13–27.

Papyrus Oxyrhynchus 5072

Recto: With the Fibers (→)

Diplomatic Translation	*Reconstructed Translation*	
1 [*lac*] before [.] . . . [. .] . . . [*lac*]	1] they brought him (the demon-possessed person) before the crowd,[a]	
2 [*lac*] but he fell down [*lac*]	2 But he (the demon-possessed person) fell down as often as it (the demon) overtook	Mark 9:18
3 [*lac*] . He cried out, saying, "Son . [*lac*]·	3 him.[b] He (the demoniac) cried out, saying, "Son of God, what have you to do with me?[c]	Mark 5:7 par.
4 [*lac*] did you come before the time us (acc.) . . [*lac*]	4 Did[d] you come here[e] before the time to destroy us?"[f]	Matt 8:29

a. *Contra* Chapa's tentative reconstruction ("before Jesus, and not ["; *enantion [to]u iu k[ai] ouk* [; Chapa, "Uncanonical Gospel?" 9), Ponder's transcription fits the ink traces more closely: *enantion [t]ou o[chl]ou p[rosēnenkan | auton.*

b. *Contra* Chapa's tentative reconstruction at the end of line 2 and the beginning of line 3 (*i[schue kai idōn | autō]n*), Ponder's transcription works better: *hosakis katelabē | auto]n.* See above "Reconstruction and Textual Parallels."

c. The reconstructed text between lines 3 and 4 (*ti emoi kai | soi*) follows the synoptic parallels (Mark 5:7 par.); cf. Chapa, "Uncanonical Gospel?" 11; Nicklas, "Eine neue alte Erzählung," 21.

d. The end of line 3 and the start of line 4 can be reconstructed as: *th[u, ti emoi kai | soi ēl]thes.*

e. The Greek word for "here" (*hōde*) technically occurs at the beginning of line 5 in Ponder's reconstruction. But the word has been moved in the translation for the sake of clarity.

f. The present reconstruction expands

The Dialogue of the Paralytic with Christ
A new translation and introduction

by Bradley N. Rice

The *Dialogue of the Paralytic with Christ* (*Dial. Par.*; CANT 85) is a little-known apocryphon that circulated widely in Georgia and Armenia during the late Middle Ages. It recounts a lively and often provocative conversation between the resurrected Jesus and a paralytic in Jerusalem. The dialogue is unique among Christian apocrypha in that the roles played by Jesus and the paralytic are completely the opposite of what the reader expects. The paralytic shines forth as the faithful hero of this story, unwavering in his belief that he will be healed; Jesus, on the other hand, is cast as something of a gadfly, challenging and provoking the hapless paralytic at every turn. *Dial. Par.* thus turns out to be a kind of dark comedy in which a paralytic, steadfast in his faith that Christ will heal him, is contradicted and challenged by a most unexpected disbeliever: Christ himself.

Contents
The text of *Dial. Par.* exists in multiple forms, found in a number of Georgian and Armenian manuscripts from the thirteenth century onwards. The popularity of the dialogue in the Caucasus and Anatolian plateau eventually led to its inclusion in some early recensions of the Armenian menologium, and it is this form of *Dial. Par.* that became most widespread. In this version of the apocryphon (here identified as the recension ArmD), the resurrected Jesus makes an appearance in disguise to a certain paralytic who sits in the streets of Jerusalem begging for alms (1). Jesus inquires about his condition, and the paralytic answers that he has been lying there afflicted for thirty-eight years, despite his fervent belief that Christ will heal him (2-3). Jesus responds with citations of Scripture on the suffering of the righteous, causing the paralytic to wonder about the identity of this strange man (3-4). Jesus replies that he is a wanderer who has just been to India and has studied with Athanagines the physician (5). Jesus then asks the paralytic why he has not yet been made well, given his faith in Christ and his familiarity with the preaching of the apostles (6). Jesus presses the paralytic on why he suffers, and suspects that some grievous sins must have brought this condition upon him. The paralytic counters that given his condition, he cannot have sinned (7), and then informs Jesus about what he learned from Christian preachers (8). This again makes Jesus wonder why the paralytic was not also sent out to preach the gospel (9).

Jesus tells the paralytic once more that his suffering is deserved, while the paralytic assures Jesus that he too shall be judged (10). Jesus proceeds to request gold and silver from the paralytic in return for a healing, yet the paralytic avers, to Jesus' disbelief, that he has no more than a few coins and a piece of bread (11-12). Jesus and the paralytic then dispute how judgment is meted out, exchanging condemnations (13-14). The paralytic becomes exasperated with Jesus and begs him to go away (15). After a final challenge from Jesus, the paralytic once more proclaims his faith in Christ in no uncertain terms. At last moved to compassion, Jesus finally heals him (16). The dialogue then concludes with an *apologia* confirming the veracity of the tale (17).

Manuscripts and Versions

Dial. Par. is extant in a wide number of Armenian and Georgian manuscripts of the thirteenth to nineteenth centuries. Several different forms of the apocryphon are attested, often varying significantly from one another. The Armenian version of *Dial. Par.* found in the menologium, for example, is nearly three times as long as the earliest attested Georgian version. A preliminary foray into this complex manuscript tradition has been made by Bernard Outtier, who has detected as many as eight different recensions of *Dial. Par.*, five in Armenian and three in Georgian:[1]

ArmA: represented by the earliest Armenian manuscript of *Dial. Par.*, a fourteenth-century miscellany found in the collection of the Collegio Leoniano Armeno in Rome (ROL 24).[2]

ArmB: represented by at least two manuscripts, one of which is a miscellany dated to 1582, found in the Matenadaran in Yerevan (M6686).

ArmC: an abridged version of ArmB, represented by several manuscripts from the fifteenth to eighteenth centuries, one of which is a miscellany housed in the Matenadaran (M9220).

ArmD: version incorporated into some recensions of the Armenian menologium (*haysmawurkʿ*),[3] with a note on the veracity of the tale appended (17:1–3 in the present translation).

ArmE: versions adapted from the menologium (ArmD) for private use.

GeoA: represented by six manuscripts, the earliest of which is from the thirteenth century.

GeoB: translation of the Armenian version of the menologium (ArmD).

GeoC: another translation of the Armenian version of the menologium (ArmD).

Except for the three Armenian manuscripts mentioned above (ROL 24, M6686, M9220), Outtier unfortunately has not indicated which manuscripts belong to which of the eight recensions he has outlined. But several preliminary observations are in order, pending a more detailed examination of the manuscripts. The Georgian tradition is less complicated and the manuscripts far fewer. If Outtier is correct that GeoA is represented by six manuscripts, they would appear to be the following:

---

1. Outtier, "Paralytique et ressuscité," 113–14; idem, "Dialogue du paralytique," 64.

2. Armenian manuscripts are cited according to the system established by Bernard Coulie, *Répertoire des bibliothèques et des catalogues de manuscrits arméniens* (Corpus Christianorum; Turnhout: Brepols, 1992); idem, *Répertoire des manuscrits arméniens / Census of Armenian Manuscripts. Liste des sigles utilisés pour désigner les manuscrits* (Association Internationale des Études Arméniennes, n.p., n.d.). The transliteration of Armenian and Georgian words follows the system established by the Library of Congress: www .loc.gov/catdir/cpso/roman.html.

3. For the various recensions of the Armenian menologium, see especially Paul Peeters, "Pour l'histoire du synaxaire arménien," *AnBoll* 30 (1911): 5–26; Sirarpie Der Nersessian, "Le synaxaire arménien de Grégoire VII d'Anazarbe," *AnBoll* 68 [*Mélanges Paul Peeters*, vol. 2] (1950): 261–85; Ugo Zanetti, "Apophtegmes et histoires édifiantes dans le synaxaire arménien," *AnBoll* 105 (1987): 167–99.

Tbilisi, National Center of Manuscripts, A–70, fol. 242r–243v (13th cent.)
Tbilisi, National Center of Manuscripts, A–153, fol. 293r–296v (17th cent.)[4]
Tbilisi, National Center of Manuscripts, H–433, fol. 148r–150r (1842)
Tbilisi, National Center of Manuscripts, H–881, fol. 112r–122v (1853)[5]
Tbilisi, National Center of Manuscripts, S–300, fol. 119r–120r (1779)
Tbilisi, National Center of Manuscripts, S–1345, fol. 9v–12v (1833)[6]

Several other late Georgian manuscripts appear to be translations of ArmD, and therefore belong to Outtier's second and third Georgian recensions (GeoB and GeoC):[7]

Tbilisi, National Center of Manuscripts, Q–608, fol. 21r–24r (1822)
Tbilisi, National Center of Manuscripts, Q–750, fol. 1r–6v (19th/20th cent.)
Tbilisi, National Center of Manuscripts, Q–961, fol. 268–279 (19th cent.)[8]
Tbilisi, National Center of Manuscripts, S–12, fol. 66v–73r (1833–1836)[9]

The Armenian manuscript tradition is more complicated. Outtier is probably correct to suggest that the earliest Armenian version of *Dial. Par.* (ArmA) is represented by ROL 24.[10] Far less clear is which manuscripts should be reckoned to Outtier's second (ArmB), third (ArmC), and fourth (ArmD) recensions. In the introduction to his translation of *Dial. Par.*, Outtier indicated that ArmB is represented by M6686 and ArmC by M9220;[11] other manuscripts belonging to these recensions remain unidentified. It is also not clear whether ArmC and ArmD should be considered separate recensions. Outtier suggests that when ArmC was integrated into the menologium, an *apologia* for its authenticity (17:1–3) was appended, thus constituting a fourth recension of *Dial. Par.* (ArmD). Yet the *apologia* may also be found in recensions of the dialogue preserved in certain miscellanies (e.g., P65, M9220), indicating that it might have been added before *Dial. Par.* entered the menologium. Clearly much work remains to be done in elucidating the Armenian manuscript tradition; in the meantime, the designation "ArmD" will be used to indicate Outtier's third (ArmC) and fourth (ArmD) recensions.

---

4. Tʻamar Bregaże, Mixeil Kʻavtʻaria, and Lili Kʻutʻatʻelaże, *Kʻartʻul xelnacertʻa ağceriloba: Qopʻili saeklesio muzeumis (A) kolekʻcʻiisa* (5 vols.; Tbilisi: Gamomcʻemloba mecʻniereba, 1955–1985), 1.2:214. The authors of this more recent catalogue seem to have overlooked the apocryphon in their description of Tbilisi A–70 (1.1:243–51). The presence of a certain *apokrificheskoe skazanie o razslablennom i Gospode* is described, however, in the earlier catalogue by Fëdor D. Zhordanïia, *Opisanïe rukopiseĭ Tiflisskago Tserkovnago muzeia Kartalino-Kakhetniskago dukhovenstva* (Izdanïe Tserkovnago muzeia 12; Tipografïia "Gutenberg," 1903), 70.

5. Simon Janašia and Ilia Abulaże, *Sakʻartʻvelos saxelmcipʻo muzeumis kʻartʻul xelnacertʻa sazogaderebi (H kolekʻcʻia)* (6 vols.; Tbilisi: Sakʻartʻvelos SSR mecʻnierebatʻa akademiis gamomcʻemloba, 1946–1953), 1:322 (for H–433), 2:252 (for H–881).

6. Tʻamar Bregaże and Elene Metreveli, *Kʻartʻul xelnacertʻa ağceriloba: Qopʻili Kʻartʻveltʻa šoris cerakitʻxvis gamavrcʻelebeli sazogadoebis (S) kolekʻcʻiisa* (7 vols.; Tbilisi: Sakʻartʻvelos SSR mecʻnierebatʻa akademiis gamomcʻemloba, 1959–1973), 1:336 (for S–300), 2:156 (for S–1345).

7. In a correspondence of November 12, 2012, Outtier mentioned to me that there are also Georgian manuscripts from Kutaisi, though I have been unable to locate them.

8. Elene Metreveli, Kʻristine Šarašiżi, and Ilia Abulaże, *Sakʻartʻvelos saxelmcipʻo muzeumis kʻartʻul xelnacertʻa ağceriloba: Muzeumis xelnacertʻa axali (Q) kolekʻcʻia* (2 vols.; Tbilisi: Sakʻartʻvelos SSR mecʻnierebatʻa akademiis gamomcʻemloba, 1957–1958), 2:66 (for Q–608), 2:198 (for Q–750), 2:373 (for Q–961).

9. Bregaże and Metreveli, *Kʻartʻul xelnacertʻa ağceriloba*, 1:18.

10. See the discussion of this important manuscript below.

11. Outtier, "Dialogue du paralytique," 64.

There is not yet a census of all the Armenian manuscripts containing *Dial. Par.*, and many of the important collections remain inadequately or only partially catalogued.[12] The following is a preliminary inventory of Armenian manuscripts containing the dialogue, although there are undoubtedly many others:

- J25, fol. 687v ff. (1435)[13]
- LOB Harl. 5459, fol. 77v ff. (1689)
- LOB Or. 4787, fol. 269v ff. (1701)
- LOB Or. 6555, fol. 430v ff. (1488)[14]
- M639, fol. 293r–301v (1409)
- M1533, fol. 316v–317r (1725–1730)[15]
- M3854, fol. 73v–77v (1471)
- M4547 (1709)
- M6686 (1582)
- M6952 (16th cent.)
- M9220, fol. 3v ff. (18th cent.)
- M10245 (1609)[16]
- OXL Arm. c. 3, fol. 342r–344r (16th cent.)
- OXL Arm. f. 17, fol. 4v–7v (18th cent.)[17]
- P65, fol. 128r–134r (1684)[18]
- ROL 24, fol. 15v ff. (14th cent.)[19]

12. On this problem, see Valentina Calzolari Bouvier, "Un projet de répertoire des manuscrits arméniens contenant les textes apocryphes chrétiens," in *Apocryphes arméniens: Transmission, traduction, création, iconographie (Actes du colloque international sur la littérature apocryphe en langue arménienne, Genève, 18–20 septembre, 1997)* (ed. Valentina Calzolari Bouvier, Jean-Daniel Kaestli, and Bernard Outtier; Publications de l'Institut romand des sciences bibliques 1; Lausanne: Éditions du Zèbre, 1999), 53–70.

13. Norayr Bogharean, *Mayr tsʻutsʻak dzeṙagratsʻ Srbotsʻ Hakobeantsʻ* (9 vols.; Calouste Gulbenkian Foundation Armenian Library; Jerusalem: Armenian Convent Printing Press, 1966–1979), 1:128.

14. Frederick Cornwallis Conybeare, *A Catalogue of the Armenian Manuscripts in the British Museum* (London: British Museum, 1913), 216. Further discussion of LOB Harl. 5459 may be found in Michael E. Stone, "Two Armenian Manuscripts and the *Historia sacra*," in *Apocryphes arméniens*, 21–36.

15. Ōnnik Eganyan et al., *Mayr tsʻutsʻak hayerēn dzeṙagratsʻ Mashtotsʻi Anvan Matenadarani* (7 vols.; Yerevan: Haykakan SSH GA Hratarakchʻutʻyun, 1984–2012), 3:157 (for M639), 5:375 (for M1533).

16. Ōnnik Eganyan, *Tsʻutsʻak dzeṙagratsʻ Mashtotsʻi anvan Matenadarani* (2 vols.; Yerevan: Haykakan SSṘ Gitutʻyunneri Akademiayi Hratarakchʻutʻyun, 1965–1970), 1:1097 (for M3854), 1:1233 (for M4547), 2:372 (for M6686), 2:428 (for M6952), 2:890–91 (for M9220), 2:1078 (for M10245).

17. Sukias Baronian and Frederick Cornwallis Conybeare, *Catalogue of the Armenian Manuscripts in the Bodleian Library* (Catalogi codd. mss. bibliothecae Bodleianae Pars 14; Oxford: Clarendon, 1918), §64 (p. 144) and §90 (p. 199).

18. Frédéric Macler, *Catalogue des manuscrits arméniens et géorgiens de la Bibliothèque nationale* (Paris: Imprimerie nationale, 1908), 159, and more recently Raymond H. Kevorkian and Armen Ter-Stepanian, *Manuscrits arméniens de la Bibliothèque nationale de France: Catalogue* (Paris: Bibliothèque nationale de France, 1998), 893.

19. Nersēs Akinean, *Tsʻutsʻak hayerēn dzeṙagratsʻ hṙomi hayotsʻ hiwranotsʻi i S. Vlas ew kʻah. Lewonean hay varzhani / Katalog der armenischen Handschriften des armenischen Hospitals zu S. Blasius in Rom und des Pont. Leoniano Collegio Armeno, Roma* (Vienna: Mkhitʻarean tparan, 1961), 24–25. Akinean's description of these manuscripts may also be found in the monthly review published by the Mekhitarists in Vienna: "Tsʻutsʻak hayerēn dzeṙagratsʻ hṙomi hayotsʻ hiwranotsʻi i S. Vlas," *Handes Amsorya: Zeitschrift für armenische Philologie* 8–10 (1957): 432–35. ROL 24 was formerly MS 24 of the Catholic Armenian church of St. Blaise; it is no. 33 in Akinean's catalogue, which describes the collections of both St. Blaise and the Levonian College in Rome.

W214, fol. 44r ff. (16th/17th cent.)
W224, fol. 427r (1428)
W427, fol. 59v–73v (15th/16th cent.)
W437, fol. 485v ff. (1603)[20]
W536, fol. 127r ff. (16th/17th cent.)[21]

The title "Dialogue of the Paralytic with Christ" is taken from the earliest Armenian manuscript of the apocryphon (ROL 24), and it was the one preferred by Outtier for his initial publications on *Dial. Par.* The similar title "Dialogue of Jesus and the Paralytic" is favored by the Georgian manuscript tradition (e.g., Tbilisi A–153, H–433, H–881). Many other titles are attested by the Armenian manuscript tradition, including "Story of the Paralytic," "Healing of the Paralytic," "Life and Story of the Paralytic," "Story of the Healing of a Paralytic by Christ," "Commemoration of the Paralytic, whom Christ healed," and "Disputation of Christ and the Paralytic." One manuscript even attests the apposite title, "Interrogation of the Paralytic, whom Christ tested by way of a ruse" (M6952).

Editions and Translations

Only two of the recensions outlined by Outtier are found in published editions. The Georgian version (GeoA) of *Dial. Par.* was published by Solomon Qubaneišvili in 1946.[22] Qubaneišvili's edition is based on the two earliest-known Georgian manuscripts of the dialogue: Tbilisi A–70 and Tbilisi A–153. The first of these, Tbilisi A–70, represents the earliest attested of all forms of *Dial. Par.*, dating to the thirteenth century. In his edition, however, Qubaneišvili neglects to indicate which readings are derived from which of the two manuscripts. This is curious, for he also mentions that the text of A–153 is shorter than that of A–70 and lacks some of its episodes.

The later Armenian version (ArmD) of *Dial. Par.* was published by Karapet Melikʻ-Ōhanjanyan in 1957.[23] His edition is based on a single and relatively late Armenian manuscript, M9220, a miscellany dating to the eighteenth century. Melikʻ-Ōhanjanyan seems to have overestimated the value of this manuscript, classifying it as part of a menologium belonging to the sixteenth century.[24] He did not offer the complete text of *Dial. Par.*, and part of the list of Jesus' miracles (chap. 8) as well as the appended *apologia* (chap. 17) have been omitted.

Thus far the only published translation of *Dial. Par.* is Outtier's French translation of the Armenian text edited by Melikʻ-Ōhanjanyan.[25] Outtier has supplied the missing portions in Melikʻ-Ōhanjanyan's edition using M4547, a menologium of 1709.

---

20. Hakovbos Tashean, *Tsʻutsʻak hayerēn dzeṟagratsʻ Mkhitʻarean Matenadaranin i Vienna / Catalog der armenischen Handschriften in der Mechitaristen-Bibliothek zu Wien* (Mayr tsʻutsʻak hayerēn dzeṟagratsʻ 1.2; Vienna: Mkhitʻarean tparan, 1891), 105 [Ger] and 545 [Arm] (for W214), 116 [Ger] and 583 [Arm] (for W224), 202 [Ger] and 879 [Arm] (for W427), 207 [Ger] and 898 [Arm] (for W437).

21. This manuscript preserves a form of the dialogue written in Armeno-Turkish, and was briefly described by Tashean as a "Lives of the Saints in the Tatar language, but in Armenian script, all slavishly translated from the Armenian" ("Heiligenleben in tatarischer Sprache, aber in arm. Schrift, alle sclavisch aus dem Arm. übersetzt"; *Catalog der armenischen Handschriften*, 241).

22. Qubaneišvili, *Żveli kʻartʻuli literaturis*, 26–27.

23. Melikʻ-Ōhanjanyan, *Ējer hay mijnadaryan*, 208–14.

24. Melikʻ-Ōhanjanyan, *Ējer hay mijnadaryan*, 278.

25. Outtier, "Dialogue du paralytique," 67–74.

Original Language, Date, and Provenance

The origins of *Dial. Par.* remain uncertain. In his masterful overview of Old Georgian literature, Korneli Kekeliże offers a terse description of the Georgian version as found in Qubaneišvili's edition.[26] He was persuaded that a version of the apocryphon had been translated into Georgian no later than the ninth century; why he offers this assessment is not explained. Kekeliże's position was followed by Michael Tarchnišvili in the latter's German revision of Kekeliże's *Istoria*.[27] Neither Tarchnišvili nor Kekeliże gives any indication of the apocryphon's original language. Outtier postulates a Greek *Vorlage* for the Georgian version,[28] but why he does so is not explained.

On the other hand, Outtier does offer good reason to believe that the Armenian version was based on an Arabic exemplar. In an earlier study treating the translation of Arabic literature into Armenian and Georgian, Outtier mentions having come across *Dial. Par.* in ROL 24, a fourteenth-century manuscript presently kept in the Pontificio Collegio Armeno in Rome.[29] This important manuscript, the earliest extant Armenian version of the apocryphon, was reported as stolen in the 1990s but resurfaced in 2005.[30] It begins with the following title: "Tales and discourses before kings and sovereigns, which were translated into Armenian from the Arabic language for David the Curopalate."[31] What follows is none other than an Armenian translation of the "City of Bronze" from the famed Arabic collection *One Thousand and One Nights* (beginning at fol. 3v). *Dial. Par.* follows immediately thereafter at fol. 15v. The remainder of the manuscript contains certain other tales of Arabic or Persian origin, such as the "Questions of the Maiden" and the "Story of Farman-i Asman," as well as certain hagiographica, including a "Life of John" and a "Life of St. Alexios."[32]

Outtier therefore concluded that the Armenian version of *Dial. Par.* probably had an Arabic *Vorlage*.[33] The Georgian version probably also should be traced to this Arabic exemplar. The David mentioned in ROL 24, called *kouropalates* ("curopalate"), was governor of the Iberian theme (military unit) of Tayk' during the late tenth century.[34] His court was known to be bilingual, and the district of Tayk' (Georgian *Tao*) was the center of a literary renaissance during which many literatures of the East were translated into Armenian as well as Georgian; the tale of the "City of Bronze," for instance, was also translated into Georgian during this time.[35] Thus, it is not hard to imagine

---

26. Kekeliże, *K'art'uli literaturis istoria*, 1:444.

27. Tarchnišvili, *Geschichte der kirchlichen georgischen Literatur*, 339. For an overview of the early period to which Tarchnišvili would date the text, see pp. 24–34.

28. Outtier, "Dialogue du paralytique," 64.

29. Outtier, "À propos des traductions," 63.

30. Outtier, "Paralytique et ressuscité," 113. Outtier reports having attempted to obtain this manuscript for some years when, in 2005, he was finally informed that the manuscript had resurfaced, whereupon he went to Rome to make a copy (private correspondence, November 12, 2012). On the rediscovery of the manuscript, see also Anna Sirinian, "Le nuove accessioni manoscritte armene del Pontificio Collegio Armeno di Roma: Un primo *report*," *Le Muséon* 116 (2003): 71–90.

31. Akinean, *Ts'uts'ak hayerēn dzeṛagrats'*, 24.

32. Further description of the contents of the manuscript may be found in Jean-Pierre Mahé, "Philologie et historiographie du Caucase chrétien," *École pratique des hautes études. Section des sciences historiques et philologiques: Livret-Annuaire* 15 (1999–2000): 50.

33. Outtier, "Dialogue du paralytique," 64.

34. On David the Curopalate see Karen N. Yuzbashian, "L'administration byzantine en Arménie aux Xe-XIe siècles," *Revue des Études Arméniennes* 10 (1973–1974): 154–56.

35. Paruyr Muradyan, "Patmut'iwn pghndzē k'aghak'i zruyts'i haykakan ev vrats'akan patumneri u

that an Arabic version of *Dial. Par.*, otherwise unknown and of which no traces now remain, was translated into different Georgian and Armenian versions sometime during the tenth century.

Literary and Theological Contexts

The paralytic in *Dial. Par.* is only loosely based on the paralytics healed by Jesus in the New Testament (Mark 2:1–12 par.; John 5:1–15). The reference to "thirty-eight years" of infirmity in the text of ArmD (3:2) has led some to identify the paralytic with the one healed by Jesus in John 5:1–15.[36] But whereas John's paralytic waits by the pool of Bethesda for the stirring of the waters, the paralytic in *Dial. Par.* lies in the streets of Jerusalem to ask for alms (GeoA 1:1; ArmD 1:2); and while the Johannine pericope is set during Jesus' ministry, the episode in *Dial. Par.* is set after the resurrection (ArmD 1:3–2:1). The Georgian lacks mention of the thirty-eight years, and its concluding doxology (GeoA 4:8) tends rather to identify the paralytic with the lame man who lay at the Beautiful Gate in Jerusalem (Acts 3:1–10). But unlike all those healed by Jesus in the New Testament, the paralytic of *Dial. Par.* is easily infuriated and has a very sharp tongue. His pointed questions to Jesus on the suffering of the righteous recall the protests of Job against the God of Israel, even as Jesus' acerbic answers echo the clichéd theodicy of Job's friends. Jesus in *Dial. Par.* comes across as a ruthless character, not wholly unlike the menacing young Jesus in the *Infancy Gospel of Thomas.*

Perhaps it is not surprising, then, that the closest literary parallel to *Dial. Par.* is found among the infancy gospels. In particular, the dialogue bears a remarkable resemblance to certain healing episodes in the *Armenian Gospel of the Infancy.*[37] In these episodes a young Jesus encounters someone in need of healing and asks him several questions about his background and situation; Jesus' identity, on the other hand, remains unknown to his interlocutor. Then, in a fashion quite similar to *Dial. Par.*, Jesus requests an exorbitant payment in return for a cure, such as gold, silver, and precious gems—costly items of which the poor person has never heard. This leads to further questioning, testing, and probing by Jesus. The ailing person does not hesitate to talk back, and wonders why this annoying stranger is making fun of him. But above all there is a bitter sense of irony: the one about to be cured takes offense at his bothersome conversation partner, not realizing that he is the very one able to heal him.

While Jesus' mischievous behavior in *(Arm.) Gos. Inf.* might readily be excused as the product of a tempestuous adolescence, it is much more difficult to account for the conduct of Jesus in *Dial. Par.* Medieval readers were clearly troubled by this portrait of Jesus, as shown by the Armenian *apologia* which confirms its authenticity (ArmD 17). Other medieval readers found the *apologia* itself unacceptable and crossed it out altogether.[38] Early modern reactions to *Dial. Par.* were no more favorable; one of the earliest French

---

nrants' p'okhharaberut'yan shurj," *Banber Matenadarani* 6 (1962): 249–60 (with summaries in Russian [p. 261] and French [p. 262]).

36. Thus Outtier, "Dialogue du paralytique," 63; Tarchnišvili, *Geschichte der kirchlichen georgischen Literatur,* 339.

37. See the recent translation by Abraham Terian, *The Armenian Gospel of the Infancy* (Oxford: Oxford University Press, 2008), 113–15 (chap. 24) and 120–22 (chap. 27).

38. In the manuscript OXL Arm. c. 3, for example, the first verse of the *apologia* (17:1) has been crossed out: "Now let nobody doubt that what was said actually happened. This really happened. And it is not too much for the compassion of the will of God" (fol. 344r).

readers of *Dial. Par.*, the abbot Guillaume de Villefroy (1690–1777), had the following to say about the dialogue:

> The brazen author of this ridiculous fable has Jesus descend from heaven and situates him in Jerusalem beside a paralytic with whom he is made to have the most outland-ish conversation in the world, even having Jesus say that the evangelists put whatever they wanted in their gospel . . . the paralytic becomes furious and sends Jesus to the depths of hell; and when Jesus asks the sick man how much gold or silver he would give him to heal him, the paralytic answers that he is evidently a relative of Judas. This ungodly conversation makes up the contents of nearly the entire story . . .[39]

Villefroy's comments notwithstanding, *Dial. Par.* continued to be copied in the Caucasus until the early twentieth century. Although the origins of the apocryphon remain a mystery, perhaps the enduring appeal of the dialogue may be explained not by its portrayal of Jesus, but that of the paralytic. *Dial. Par.* reveals a broken man who is steadfast in his Christian faith and resolute in his belief that Christ will heal him. Since Jesus' taunts and even denial of Christian orthodoxy often elicit from the paralytic both fearless condemnations as well as bold statements of faith, it may be that *Dial. Par.* was meant to encourage Christians to remain steadfast in contexts of persecution and/or apostasy. The tumultuous history of Armenia and Georgia after the twelfth century is filled with such moments, and Christian readers of *Dial. Par.* may well have seen in the paralytic a reflection of their own experiences during difficult times.

Translation

Translated below are two forms of *Dial. Par.*: the shorter Georgian version published by Qubaneišvili (GeoA) and the longer Armenian version of the menologium (ArmD). GeoA is the earliest attested textual form of *Dial. Par.* and is therefore presented first. My translation of this Georgian version is based on Qubaneišvili's edition of Tbilisi A–70 and A–153. As mentioned above, Qubaneišvili's edition does not clearly indicate which readings are derived from which of the two manuscripts. His edition appears to print the text of A–70 and then includes several readings from A–153 within square brackets (at 1:5, 1:6, 1:8, and 3:5 in the present translation).[40] Some of these readings only add further confusion to the text; therefore, I have proposed several corrections and emendations in the notes. I have also introduced a system of chapters and verses.

My translation of the Armenian version is based on an unpublished sixteenth-century manuscript of the menologium presently housed in the Bodleian Library at Oxford, OXL Arm. c. 3 (fol. 342r–344r). This manuscript is earlier and generally superior to the single manuscript used by Melikʿ-Ōhanjanyan for his edition, M9220, and has helped to clarify some of the more difficult and occasionally faulty readings found in that edition (indicated in the notes). The Oxford manuscript also contains a slightly longer text than M9220, with additional content at 10:4–6 and 16:2–6. Finally, chapter divisions follow those established by Outtier, though I have now also introduced a system of verses.

---

39. Villefroy's text (here translated from the French) and further discussion are found in Outtier, "Paralytique et ressuscité," 111. See also idem, "Guillaume de Villefroy, un arméniste méconnu," *Revue du monde arménien moderne et contemporain* 5 (1999–2000): 45–54.

40. At the time of writing, I have only been able to consult Tbilisi A–153.

Bibliography

EDITIONS AND TRANSLATIONS

Melikʻ-Ōhanjanyan, Karapet. *Ējer hay mijnadaryan gegharvestakan ardzakitsʻ.* Yerevan: Haykakan SSR GA hratarakchʻutʻyun, 1957. (*Editio princeps* of the Armenian recension D text.)

Outtier, Bernard. "Dialogue du paralytique avec le Christ." Pages 63–74 in *EAC* vol. 2.

Qubaneišvili, Solomon. *Żveli kʻartʻuli literaturis kʻrestomatʻia.* Tbilisi: Stalinis saxelobis Tʻbilisis saxelmcipʻo universitetis gamomcʻemloba, 1946. (*Editio princeps* of the Georgian recension A text.)

STUDIES

Kekeliże, Korneli. *Kʻartʻuli literaturis istoria.* 6 vols. 4th ed. Saxelmcipʻo gamomcʻemloba "Sabčotʻa Sakʻartʻvelo," 1960.

Outtier, Bernard. "Paralytique et ressuscité (*CANT* 85 et 62): Vie des apocryphes en arménien." *Apocrypha* 8 (1997): 111–19.

———. "À propos des traductions de l'arabe en arménien et en géorgien." *ParOr* 21 (1996): 57–63.

Tarchnišvili, Michael. *Geschichte der kirchlichen georgischen Literatur, auf Grund des ersten Bandes der georgischen Literaturgeschichte von K. Kekelidze.* Studi e testi 185. Vatican City: Biblioteca apostolica vaticana, 1955.

The Dialogue of the Paralytic with Christ
(Georgian A Recension)

Jesus enters Jerusalem and encounters a paralyzed man

1 [1]As Jesus was entering Jerusalem, there was a paralyzed man who was lying upon his mat and continually[a] groaning in agony.[b] [2]When Jesus had drawn closer, he said to him, "What ailment do you have?" [3]The paralytic said, "To begin with, I am paralyzed, a leper, bedridden,[c] my eyes are sore, my liver aches—I have 360 ailments."[d]

Jesus requests unimaginable wealth from the paralytic

[4]Jesus said to him, "If someone cured you, what would you give him?" [5][The paralytic answered:] "What request would you make of me, young man?"

[6]Jesus said to him, "First I want [from you] precious stone; second, the fifth heaven;[e] third, the sixth heaven.[f] This is worth eighteen thousand gold coins."[g] [7]The paralytic said to him, "Young man, you must be someone wealthy, saying such grand things. I swear by my Lord Jesus Christ, neither in this city nor any other have I heard of the jewels[h] you speak of.[i] If you do not cure me, my Lord will cure me on the last day."

---

a. Lit.: "without resting and without falling silent."

b. Geor. *gančrili* is an unusual word; the lexica tend to construe it as based on the root *čar* (*čr*), "to cut." In this context, however, it is probably based on the root *čir*, "to need, be afflicted."

c. Geor. *ganborkilebuli*, a rare word. It could be another form of the more common *ganboklebuli*, "leper, leprous," in which case two different words are used to describe the paralytic's leprous condition, *ket'rovani* and *ganboklebuli*. It is more likely, however, that *ganborkilebuli* is based on the root *borkil*, "fetters," in which case *ganborkilebuli* could be read similarly to *šeborkilebuli*: "bound, shackled, fettered." This seems to be the meaning here, thus "bedridden" in the present translation.

d. Tbilisi A–153 has "365" (Qubaneišvili, *Żveli k'art'uli literaturis*, 26 n. 1). This is the only instance where Qubaneišvili has specified a difference in the readings of Tbilisi A–70 and A–153. Here the Armenian has "seven afflictions" (3:4; 13:1).

e. Geor. *čimčimelsa* and *kimkimelsa*. These two words are highly obscure, and generally refer to the planetary orbits of Mars and Jupiter, respectively (see Tarchnišvili, *Geschichte der kirchlichen georgischen Literatur*, 233 n. 2). Of course, this would make Jesus' request most peculiar indeed. It may be that *čimčimeli* and *kimkimeli* should be understood as otherwise unattested words for precious stones.

f. Omitting Qubaneišvili's restoration of "and" from Tbilisi A–153.

g. Geor. *drahkan*, a gold coin weighing about four grams.

h. Or perhaps "pearls." The Georgian word *mżive* generally refers to "pearls" or "beads" as found on a necklace, and it may be that *čimčimeli* and *kimkimeli* at 1:6 should be understood as types of pearls.

i. The syntax of this clause is most peculiar, though this would appear to be the sense.

Jesus conceals his true identity

[8]Jesus said to him, "I am familiar with the son of Joseph, who wandered from city to city.[a] The Jews apprehended him, hung him upon a tree, and laid him in a tomb and sealed it. His disciples came during the night, saying 'The Lord is risen,' and stole him."[b]

Matt 28:13

2 [1]The paralytic said to him, "Where do you come from, young man?" [2]Jesus said to him, "I come from India."[c] [3]The paralytic said to him, "Have you not heard the news about Athanasius the physician?"[d] [4]Jesus said to him, "I am not a disciple of Athanasius the physician.[e] I know another practice, better than his."

[5]The paralytic said to him, "You are ignorant and are speaking out of your ignorance. May the Lord[f] open your blind eyes." [6]Jesus said to him, "What do you know about the opening of blind eyes? It was I who brought the dry land[g] its very first nourishment[h] and the good of fertility. It was I who, when King Nebuchadnezzar threw those three servants into the furnace, then cooled them with dew."

Dan 3:49–50 LXX

The paralytic appeals to Jesus for healing

3 [1]"Young man, you seem like one of the saints—and if you are able to heal me, heal me!" [2]Jesus said to him, "And what will you give me? Tell me." [3]The paralytic said to him, "I have one piece of wheat bread, which a lady[i] gave me today, and two barley loaves. Take this and heal me, and our Lord Jesus Christ will reward you a hundredfold and grant you eternal life."

Disputing the resurrection of the dead

[4]Jesus said to him, "Do you really believe in the resurrection of the dead?" [5]The paralytic said to him, "Ignorant man, you do not know what you are saying! When the Lord comes with ten thousand angels, then they will come out—those who have done good, to the [good] resurrection,[j] [while those who have done evil, to the resurrection] of condemnation."

1 En. 1:9

John 5:29

---

a. Omitting Qubaneišvili's restoration of "and" from Tbilisi A–153. Qubaneišvili's punctuation of the following text is awkward, with commas instead of periods after "wandered" and "sealed it." It seems likely that this section should be divided rather into three separate sentences, as reflected in the present translation.

b. This is the first of several instances in which Jesus effectively turns orthodox Christian belief on its head; cf. 3:4; 3:6; and ArmD 10:4.

c. Or "Ethiopia." The Georgian word *hindoeti* may refer to India or Ethiopia; see also ArmD 5:2.

d. The Armenian has "Athanagines the physician" (5:5). There is no mention of Athanasius in Tbilisi A–153 (Qubaneišvili, *Žveli k'art'uli literaturis*, 26). See also the note at ArmD 5:5.

e. Here the Armenian reads "I am his student" (5:6).

f. Lit.: "He himself."

g. Lit.: "dead land."

h. Lit.: "dung" or "fertilizer."

i. For this sense of the Georgian word *dedop'ali*, often glossed as "queen," see Davit' Č'ubinovi, *Gruzinsko-russko-frantsuzskiĭ slovar' / Dictionnaire géorgien-russe-français* (Saint Petersburg: V tipografii Imperatorskoĭ Akademii Nauk, 1840), 186; I. Abulaże, *Žveli k'art'uli enis lek'sikoni* (Tbilisi: Gamomc'emloba mec'niereba, 1973), 139.

j. Qubaneišvili's edition indicates a haplography at 3:5 in Tbilisi A–70, and supplies the missing text from A–153.

[6]Jesus said to him, "It is not as you say. They will inherit the kingdom of heaven, and their storehouses will be filled[a] with wheat and wine and all sustenance."

The paralytic rebukes Jesus and proclaims his faith

4 [1]The paralytic said to him, "You appear to be a heretic, young man. The Lord God has saved judgment for you. He will lead you into the unfathomable darkness and will cast you into the bottomless pit." [2]Jesus said to him, "I praise the one[b] who is able to cast me into the darkness and throw me into the bottomless pit."

[3]The paralytic said to him, "If, then, you praise him, you are a friend of Jesus." [4]Jesus said to him, "You, who are a friend of Christ, for this reason lie here and groan."

[5]The paralytic said to him, "Young man, why do you mock me?[c] Although here I groan, there I shall rejoice. Although here my soul is wasting away, there my soul will shine again. Although here I am afflicted, there I look forward to eternal life. I swear by the name of my Lord Jesus Christ, if I could stretch out my arm and take a sword, I would bring a terrible thing upon you."

Jesus heals the paralytic at last

[6]Jesus then smiled and asked, "Paralyzed man, have I embittered you?" Jesus said to him: *"Stand up, take your mat, and walk."* [7]He then immediately stood up and began leaping about and was saying, "I have seen many physicians, but not one like this."

John 5:8; Mark 2:11 par.

[8]Behold how that paralytic, who lay at the gates of Jerusalem, was healed by <our>[d] Lord Jesus Christ, to whom belongs the glory, now and always and forever and ever. Amen.

---

a. The syntax of this clause is peculiar, though this appears to be the sense.

b. Lit.: "the young man."

c. Qubaneišvili's punctuation of the text is awkward, with a comma instead of a question mark after *rasa maquedreb* ("Why do you mock me?").

d. Emending *č'emman* ("my") to *č'uenman* ("our").

The Dialogue of the Paralytic with Christ
(Armenian D Recension)

A paralyzed man in Jerusalem asks for alms

1 [1]There was a certain paralyzed man, poor and forlorn, weak and helpless, without friends[a] or family,[b] handicapped and deprived of all use of his members, for his eyes were blind and his arms feeble, his legs crippled and his body covered with sores. [2]And so he lay in a street in the city of Jerusalem, to receive the alms which people would give him. [3]And this was during the era of Christianity, after the ascension of Christ in glory to his Father in heaven, from whom he had not been separated.

Luke 24:51; Acts 1:10

Jesus appears to the paralytic in disguise and asks about his condition

2 [1]Christ descended to earth out of his love for humanity and, like a person under the pretext of some matter or other, was passing through that street in which the paralytic lay. [2]Christ came and approached the paralytic, greeted him and said, "Why are you sitting here?" [3]The paralytic said, "To ask for alms, for I am lame and blind, crippled and abandoned, as you can see."

3 [1]Jesus said, "How long have you been lying here?" [2]The paralytic said, "I have been sitting here for 38 years, not knowing what else to do." [3]Christ says, "What illness do you have?" [4]The paralytic said, "I am just what you see: a stump,[c] lying upon the ground and fully laden with seven[d] afflictions."

John 5:5

[5]Jesus says, "Do you have any kin?"[e] [6]The paralytic said, "I have someone, Christ; and as kin, my sores; as parents, my hunger and want; and as an inheritance, the blindness of my eyes and the frailty of my body."

[7]Jesus says, "The one who endures to the end will live." [8]The paralytic said, "How long must I endure? Christ has made me the laughing-stock of all peoples." [9]Jesus said, *"The Lord disciplines those whom he loves."*

Mark 13:13//Matt 24:13; Matt 10:22

Job 17:6; Ps 44:14

Heb 12:6 (Prov 3:12)

---

a. Melik'-Ōhanjanyan's edition has "unable to walk" (lit.: "without legs").

b. This understanding of the unusual word *ankarewor* is based on the use of *karewor* in 3:5 (see comment).

c. The Armenian word *kochgh* generally has to do with the deprivation of limbs or branches. Here it could be interpreted in several different ways, and all of them are fitting: a tree trunk rooted in the ground, a heavy log fixed in place, the bust of a shattered statue, a prisoner whose arms and legs are shackled, etc.

d. Emending *i* to *ē* (= *ewt'n*, "seven"), based on Jesus' statement later in the dialogue: "You said that you have seven afflictions" (13:1). Here the Georgian has "360 ailments" (1:3).

e. Lit.: "anyone close (to you)." This use of *karewor* to indicate "closeness" or "intimacy" is supported by the mention of "parents" and "inheritance" in 3:6.

Jesus conceals his true identity

4 [1]The paralytic said, "Christ has disciplined me; this is what I deserve. But I would like to ask you: Who are you, you who say all of this to me?" [2]Christ says, "I am a man, just like you. Ask whatever you like."

[3]The paralytic said, "Are you a priest or a teacher?" [4]Jesus says, "I am neither a priest nor a teacher." [5]The paralytic said, "What is your occupation,[a] then? Your scent is that of a priest, and your words are those of a teacher." [6]Jesus says, "I am a traveling man, a wayfarer."

5 [1]The paralytic said, "Where are you coming from?" [2]Jesus says, "From the country of the Indians."[b]

[3]The paralytic said, "Have you been to school?" [4]Jesus says, "I have studied a little, and I am still striving to learn, for I have an iron will and am eager to attain, if possible,[c] correct teaching." [5]The paralytic said, "Have you not heard about Athanagines the physician?[d] Or where he might be?" [6]Christ says, "I am his student,[e] but I know a practice better than his."

[7]The paralytic said, "You are a young man and talk like a young man.[f] How can a student know more than his teacher?" [8]Jesus says, "Goodness and greatness is recognized in deeds."

Matt 10:24//Luke 6:40

Matt 7:16–20; Matt
12:33–35//Luke 6:43–45

The paralytic reveals his knowledge of Christ

6 [1]The paralytic said, "Have mercy upon me,[g] so that you also may receive mercy at the coming of Christ." [2]Jesus says, "How do you know about Christ?" [3]The paralytic said, "I have heard the reports about him, for his apostles have proclaimed everywhere the power of his miracles, of which the holy gospel also tells." [4]Christ says, "Since you are so familiar with Christ, his holy gospel and the apostles, why have you not been made well?" [5]The paralytic said, "I did not have anyone to bring me to the feet of the apostles, that they would heal me."[h]

Sin as the reason for suffering

7 [1]Jesus says, "What would you give me to heal you?" [2]The paralytic said, "But who else could heal me, what other than the right hand of Christ?" [3]Jesus says, "If you have put so much trust in Christ, why will he not cure you? Could it be that you are faithless, and guilty of some unspeakable sins?"

---

a. Lit.: "What kind of man are you?"

b. Or "From the country of the Ethiopians." The Armenian word *hndik* may refer to India or Ethiopia; see also GeoA 2:2.

c. Lit.: "if it be."

d. The Georgian has "Athanasius the physician" (2:3). Outtier identifies this Athanagines with a certain Athenogenes of Pedachthoe, who was martyred under Diocletian and whose cult was widespread in Armenia and Georgia ("Dialogue du paralytique," 69, n. 5). This identification seems only to have been made in the Armenian version; the identity of "Athanasius the physician" is otherwise unknown.

e. Here the Georgian reads "I am not a student of Athanasius the physician" (2:4).

f. Lit.: "and speak according to your understanding," i.e., the understanding of a young man. The Georgian reads "you are ignorant and speak out of your ignorance" (2:5).

g. Or "Give me alms." The word *oghormut'iwn* may denote both "alms" and "mercy."

h. Melik'-Ôhanjanyan's edition lacks "me," which led Outtier to translate *or bzhshkēin* somewhat improbably as an imperfect, "qui guérissaient" ("who were doing healings").

⁴The paralytic then became angry and said, "How could I have sinned, since I do not have the means of sinning? My eyes are blind and my arms are frail, my legs are feeble and covered with these sores. This is my activity:[a] day and night I pray to Christ for the peace and prosperity of this world, and especially for those who offer alms, and for my own afflictions."

⁵Christ says, "Then why do you suffer in this way, if you are not a sinner? For Christ loves the righteous and hates the sinner, heals the righteous and afflicts the sinner." ⁶The paralytic said, "You wouldn't happen to be one of his disciples, would you?" ⁷Jesus says, "I am not one of his disciples and I have not heard his preaching."

Ps 11:5; Prov 15:9

The paralytic informs Jesus about the message of the gospel

8 ¹The paralytic said, "Have you not heard about his incarnation that redeems the world, that he descended from heaven and became incarnate from the holy Virgin Mary? He was born in the cave, received offerings from the Magi, was honored by the shepherds, worshipped by angels, glorified by kings, and served by celestial beings. ²At the age of forty days he came to the temple and opened the temple door that had shut by itself, was cradled[b] by the old man[c] and proclaimed God. He loosened the old man[d] from the bonds of the body and brought him from death to life. He fled to Egypt and destroyed the idols.

³"He was baptized by John in the Jordan river, was borne witness by the Father's voice and the descent of the Holy Spirit in the form of a dove. He fasted for forty days and vanquished the tempter in three forms of combat, walked upon air[e] and tread upon the waves of the sea, turned water into wine and the desires of the flesh into the continence of the spirit. ⁴He[f] cast out demons, cleansed lepers, made the lame walk, gave sight to the blind, multiplied the loaves, raised the dead, forgave the adulteress, absolved the tax collector.

⁵"He was crucified and buried, rose from the dead and ascended to heaven in glory. He was seated at the right hand of the Father on high, and will come again to judge the living and the dead, and repay each according to their deeds."

Prot. Jas. 18:1; Justin,
1 Apol. 1.33

Matt 2:11; Luke 2:8–20;
Mark 1:13//Matt 4:11

Luke 2:22–35

Ps.-Mt. 23; (Arab.)
Gos. Inf. 10–11

Mark 1:9–11 par.;
John 1:32–33; Matt
4:1–11//Luke 4:1–13;
Mark 6:45–51//Matt
14:22–33; John 2:1–11

Mark 6:30–44 par.;
Mark 8:1–9 par.; John
6:5–14; 11:38–44;
8:2–11; Luke 19:1–10

Recompense comes according to merits

9 ¹Jesus says, "Where did you learn all this?" ²The paralytic said, "I learned it from teachers and heard it from preachers." ³Christ says, "Since you are such an expert, why did Christ not send you to preach his gospel?" ⁴The paralytic said, "As my lot he has given me the aches of my body and the blindness of my eyes." ⁵Jesus says, "This is what you deserve."

10 ¹The paralytic then became angry and said, "I do indeed deserve this. But you will not go unpunished." ²Jesus says, "It is because of your tongue that you

---

a. Lit.: "this is my word and work."

b. Arm. *ggwetsʾaw*. The reading *zguetsʾaw* in Melikʿ-Ōhanjanyan's edition is presumably a misprint.

c. Arm. *tseroyn*. Melikʿ-Ōhanjanyan's edition has the plural *tserotsʾn*.

d. Arm. *tsern*. Melikʿ-Ōhanjanyan's edition has the plural *tsersn*.

e. Possibly a reference to the "flying Jesus" of the *Diatessaron;* see Tjitze Baarda, "'The Flying Jesus': Luke 4:29–30 in the Syriac Diatessaron," *VC* 40 (1986): 313–41.

f. Melikʿ-Ōhanjanyan's edition omits the final part of the eighth chapter (8:4–5).

are in this condition."[a] [3]The paralytic said, "I have received mine[b] according to my merits, and yours will come[c] according to your merits."

Jesus asks the paralytic for silver and gold

[3]Jesus says, "You must be used to telling lies.[d] Your tongue is sly and your face is unblushing. You are blind[e] in order that your face would turn red with embarrassment. [4]You[f] say that Christ brings resurrection and grants immortality. Yet he prevents[g] the resurrection of humankind, while the immortality of the son is neither here nor there. And the kingdom of humankind is this: who eats and drinks and fulfills the needs of the body."[h]

Rom 14:17

[5]The paralytic said, "Alas! You are a wily man and a heretic worse than Arius.[i] Be gone! Get away from me, for God will judge you alongside Satan!" [6]Jesus says, "This is not your concern. I know this, as does God. [7]But if you want to be made well, give me what you have and I will heal you."

11 [1]The paralytic said, "What do you wish to receive from me in return for my health?"[j] [2]Jesus says, "I know that you have many gold *dekans* wrapped up in your sack. Give these to me, and I will cure you of your terrible afflictions."

[3]The paralytic said, "You surely make a living;[k] how could I have gold *dekans?*" [4]Jesus says, "If you do not have any gold, give me some silver." [5]The paralytic said, "I do not have any silver." [6]Jesus says, "You have some, but you are tightfisted and unable to hand it over." [7]The paralytic said, "I said that you surely make a living,[l] and you have your days ahead of you. How could I have silver and gold?"

Acts 3:6

The paralytic offers the little he has to Jesus

12 [1]Jesus says, "What do you have then?" [2]The paralytic said, "God is my witness,[m] I have four copper *poghs* and a piece of bread and two *lumays*. Here, take these for yourself and cure me."

[3]Jesus says, "When the house is swept, two or three *lumays* and even more are carried off with the broom, and the piece of bread is thrown to the dog." [4]The

Luke 15:8

Mark 7:27–28//Matt 15:26–27

---

a. Or perhaps "You have such a tongue because you are in this condition." The syntax of this clause is unusual; cf. 13:5.

b. I.e., "my condition" or "what I deserve."

c. Arm. *galotsʿ*. The reading *galoy* in Melikʿ-Ōhanjanyan's edition seems to be a misprint.

d. Melikʿ-Ōhanjanyan's edition has "talking too much."

e. Lit.: "Your eyes have not seen."

f. 10:4–6 are not found in the manuscript used by Melikʿ-Ōhanjanyan.

g. The meaning of Arm. *kinnē* is uncertain, though this would appear to be the sense.

h. Here Jesus essentially reverses orthodox Christian belief, alluding to Rom 14:17; cf. GeoA 1:8; 3:4; 3:6.

i. A reference to Arius of Alexandria (d. 336), often reviled as the most loathsome of heretics by later Christian orthodoxy. This is an anachronistic blunder added by a later scribe, and certainly does not belong to earlier forms of the dialogue.

j. Melikʿ-Ōhanjanyan's edition has "What do you wish to receive from me? For I have nothing."

k. Lit.: "You have such a life" or "such a living." This unusual expression seems to imply that Jesus appeared to be a person of some means; see comment at 11:7.

l. Lit.: "You have such life and days." The addition of "days" presumably refers to Jesus' appearance as a young man (5:7). See also the comment at 11:3.

m. Melikʿ-Ōhanjanyan's edition has "Christ is my witness."

paralytic said, "Two *lumays* is the hire of a donkey,[a] and the servant[b] eats the piece of bread."

13 [1]Jesus says, "You said that you have seven afflictions.[c] For such wages as you offer, who would take away all these afflictions from you?" [2]The paralytic said, "You are an intolerably greedy and grasping man. Would you happen to be a relative of Judas?"

Disputing punishment for sins

[3]Jesus says, "Do you not know that every human being is descended from Adam,[d] and that we are all one family? But each one will be requited according to his or her deeds." [4]The paralytic said, "If requital is according to one's deeds, then I will not perish." [5]Jesus says, "It is because of your thoughts that you have such afflictions."[e]

14 [1]The paralytic said, "Although in body I am an object of ridicule, in spirit I am invited into the bosom of Abraham. [2]And[f] here you are tormented for your misdeeds, and there too you will be tormented. For you believe yourself greatly beloved of God, yet God[g] has prepared for you utter darkness and the fire of gehenna." [3]Jesus says, "I do not serve the one who would cast me into the outer darkness and the pit of gehenna."[h]

Luke 16:22

Matt 8:12; 13:50; 22:13; 25:30

The paralytic rebukes Jesus

15 [1]The paralytic then became angry and said, "Step aside and get away from me, a crippled man! Move aside and go away! Just look at how you have disavowed Christ! Step aside from me, a beggar—today you have distracted me from begging! [2]If you were to speak before the royal court with this rhetoric,[i] you would bring the whole country to ruin.[j] Go on, get away from me, wretch that I am, and find yourself someone to talk with in the city square."

[3]Jesus says, "You boast so much in Christ that it seems you must be a relative of Christ or otherwise highly favored. What are you, that your merits are anything next to Christ?"

---

a. Or "beast of burden" more generally (Arm. *grast*). Outtier offers the less probable translation "c'est le salaire d'un imbécile" ("these are the wages of an idiot") understanding *grast* in the pejorative sense of "dullard" or "fool." It is unlikely that this sense is intended here, however, since the paralytic is attempting to *contradict* what Jesus just said.

b. Arm. *muk'erik*. This rare word apparently refers to a cook's assistant or apprentice. According to Acharean, this person would have been responsible for lighting the oven *(tandoor)*, cleaning out ashes, bringing water, etc. (Hrach'eay Acharean, *Hayerēn armatakan baṛaran* [4 vols.; Yerevan: Erevani Hamalsarani Hratarakch'ut'yun, 1971–1979], 3:365).

c. See note at 3:4.

d. Lit.: "is a son of Adam."

e. Or perhaps "You have these thoughts because you are burdened by these afflictions." The syntax of this clause is unusual; cf. 10:2.

f. In Melik'-Ōhanjanyan's edition this sentence is understood as Jesus' retort, with the paralytic's response resuming with "For you believe yourself greatly beloved of God," etc.

g. Melik'-Ōhanjanyan's edition has "Christ."

h. Here the Georgian reads "I praise the one who is able to throw me into the darkness and cast me into the bottomless pit" (4:2).

i. Lit.: "with this declamatory tongue that you have."

j. The syntax here is peculiar, though this appears to be the sense.

The paralytic proclaims his faith

16 ¹The paralytic said, "I have faith in Christ my God and in him I have hopes of finding mercy. Although I am a sinner, he atones for sins. Although I am lost, he is finder of the lost. Although I am scorned, he honors those scorned. Although I am flawed, he is the renewer. Although I am dead, he gives life. ²But[a] for a renegade like yourself awaits the fire of gehenna and the outer darkness, the weeping of eyes and gnashing of teeth within the icy depths of Tartarus."

Matt 8:12; 13:50; 22:13; 25:30

³Jesus says, "I am no renegade, but speak the truth. But you are ignorant and foolish. If you were wise or had any understanding, you would have been healed by now. You must have had no faith, and the apostles no power to do healings." ⁴The paralytic said, "The apostles of Christ performed mighty miracles, as the gospel of Christ and the story of the holy apostles demonstrate."

⁵Jesus says, "The apostles were stupid and lazy men, who wrote whatever they wished with a great deal of paper and ink," whereupon the paralytic became angry and said, "Why has this day dawned upon me? Just look at this unbelieving man! Get away from me, blasphemer! ⁶Will the all-powerful right hand of Christ not overtake you as well as me? I am faithful, and I believe in Christ God, who was incarnate of the holy Virgin Mary. He will heal me. ⁷The one who healed the wounds of Adam by his suffering on the cross, he will heal me. The one who raised up Lazarus, who was dead for four days, he himself will pity me and grant me health."

John 11:38–44

Jesus heals the paralytic at last

⁸Jesus then had compassion for him, and said to him in a gentle voice, "*Stand up, take your mat, and walk.*" ⁹And at that instant the man stood up with healthy limbs, agile feet, nimble hands, sturdy arms, and bright eyes. He began to walk with a sturdy gait,[b] and gave thanks to God. And then he no longer saw Jesus.

John 5:8; Mark 2:11 par.

Truth of the tale

17 ¹Now[c] let nobody doubt that what was said actually happened. This really happened. And it is not too much for the compassion of the will of God. ²For he who wrestled with Jacob from evening until dawn was also joined and united with this sinful nature without confusion, and our corruptible flesh, which he received from the holy Virgin Mary, he made incorruptible, and the sinful he made sinless. ³It was he who in his mercy spoke with the paralytic and granted him health—that is, Christ our God.

Gen 32:24

---

a. Verses 2–6 are not found in the manuscript used by Melikʻ-Ōhanjanyan.

b. Melikʻ-Ōhanjanyan's edition has "with sturdy limbs."

c. Melikʻ-Ōhanjanyan's edition omits the concluding *apologia* (17:1–3).

The Toledot Yeshu (Aramaic Fragment)
A translation and introduction

by F. Stanley Jones

The *Toledot Yeshu* ("Life of Jesus") is the predominant name for an ancient Jewish life of Jesus that portrays Jesus in anything but flattering terms. Although this story is enormously fascinating, for various reasons it has not been a subject of interest for broader swaths of scholarship. Readers may be surprised that there is a Jewish story of Jesus and may wonder why they have never even heard of it. New Testament scholars generally seem to consider it too late for their study. It has not been customary to include the *Toledot Yeshu* in collections of Christian apocrypha.[1] Rabbinic scholars are perhaps uncertain about the place and relevance of this tale in the rabbinic tradition. In general, there has perhaps been a desire to try to ignore this salacious story, even though it is evidenced in Jewish folklore throughout the ages. Consequently, many questions about the historical origin and evolution of the *Toledot Yeshu* have not been adequately addressed. The text is preserved principally in Hebrew, but extant also are several very important Aramaic fragments. One of these, Cairo Genizah, Taylor-Schechter Misc. 35.88 is translated into English here for the first time. It is perhaps the earliest available continuous narrative from the *Toledot Yeshu*. Thus, the translation provides the reader with perhaps the best starting point for a historically oriented appreciation of the many later elaborations.

Contents
The basic story[2] that underlies all the various versions of the *Toledot Yeshu* is a tale about a bastard son of Pandera, Jesus, who uses the *Shem ha-Meforash* (the divine name) to perform miracles. He gathers five disciples. Eventually, Jesus is captured and put to death. Then, a rabbi named Jehuda buries Jesus in a pit under a water canal in his garden. When the claim is made that Jesus has ascended to heaven, Jehuda is able to display Jesus' actual corpse. The various versions contain additional details, along with more specific identifications of the characters. Only this meager outline is shared by the main traditional strands.

In the Aramaic fragment translated here we find an account of the arrest of Jesus "the

---

1. Two versions were translated in full in Richard Clemens, *Die geheimgehaltenen oder sogenannten apokryphischen Evangelien*, vol. 5 (5 vols.; Stuttgart: J. Scheible, 1850). Summaries of two versions are found among other Christian apocrypha in Sabine Baring-Gould, *The Lost and Hostile Gospels: An Essay on the Toledoth Jeschu, and the Petrine and Pauline Gospels of the First Three Centuries of Which Fragments Remain* (London: Williams & Norgate, 1874), 76–115. More recently, it is discussed among "anti-gospels" in Klauck, *Apocryphal Gospels*, 211–20.

2. The standard edition of the text is Krauss, *Das Leben Jesu*, which features nine different versions of the text. For an accessible summary (based on a very late version of the text in Schichtling, *Ein jüdisches Leben Jesu*), see Klauck, *Apocryphal Gospels*, 212–18.

wicked" and John the Baptist. John is executed but Jesus escapes through flight like a bird to the cave of Elijah, which he seals by using the divine name. Jesus is found by Rabbi Jehuda and recaptured (in the form of a bird) and executed. He is buried under a stream by Jehuda. When his followers arrive the next day, they do not see Jesus' body and thus declare that he has ascended to heaven. The text ends with the beginning of an account of the excavation and display of the corpse to refute the claim of ascension.

Manuscripts and Versions

The *Toledot Yeshu* is preserved in Hebrew manuscripts, Aramaic fragmentary manuscripts, medieval Jewish and Christian writers, Judeo-Arabic texts, and later vernacular versions such as German (Yiddish), Italian, and Slavonic. Scholarship has distinguished three groups among the extant sources: the Herod-group, the Helen-group, and the Pilate-group.[3] As the names indicate, each group is distinguished by the presence of the indicated figure presiding at the trial of Jesus as well as by various episodes that may also appear in one of the other groups.[4] Only further study can lead to overall characterizations of these groups.

The Herod-group, which opens with a mention of King Herod, is represented chiefly by the 1705 publication of a (now lost) Hebrew manuscript by Johann Jakob Huldreich. This version calls Mary's betrothed "Pappos" and mentions the flight to Egypt. It states that the boy Jesus dropped his ball in a valley, threw his head covering off in anger, refused to put it back on, and told the sons of the priests that wearing a head covering was not prescribed by Moses in the Torah and that the words of the wise have no substance. Later, Jesus kills his father in a rage.

---

3. Translations of representatives of the Helen-group are most readily accessible. The Strasbourg manuscript was translated by George Robert Stow Mead for his *Did Jesus Live 100 B.C.? An Enquiry into the Talmud Jesus Stories, the Toldoth Jeschu, and Some Curious Statements of Epiphanius—Being a Contribution to the Study of Christian Origins* (London and Benares: Theosophical Publishing Society, 1903), 258–80; this translation has also been reproduced variously. Hugh J. Schonfield, *According to the Hebrews* (London: Duckworth, 1937), 35–61, translates the same manuscript. Another representative of the Helen-group (ed. Johann Christopherus Wagenseil in his *Tela Ignea Satanæ* [Altdorf: Joh. Henricus Schönnerstædt, 1581], 3–24) was translated by George W. Foote and Joseph M. Wheeler, *The Jewish Life of Jesus* (London: Progressive Publishing, 1885), 13–38. This translation and Mead's translation are reproduced in Frank R. Zindler, *The Jesus the Jews Never Knew* (Cranford, N.J.: American Atheist, 2003), 365–407, 423–50. An English translation of most of an edition of a Herod-group representative (ed. Johann Jacob Huldreich, *Historia Jeschuae Nazareni* [Leiden: Apud Johannem du Vivie, Is. Severinum, 1705]) is found in Baring-Gould, *Lost and Hostile Gospels*, 102–15. Translations of the Pilate-group are more difficult to locate. Herbert W. Basser ("The Acts of Jesus," in *The Frank Talmage Memorial Volume* [ed. Barry Walfish; 2 vols.; Haifa: Haifa University Press, 1992–1993], 1:274–83, esp. 277–80) translated what he calls "the eclectic edition" by Louis Ginzberg ("Ma'aseh Yeshu," 324–38), but Ginzberg did not produce an eclectic edition and Basser's translation renders Taylor-Schechter Misc. 35.87 (pp. 329–36 in Ginzberg). William Horbury's unpublished dissertation ("Critical Examination") contains translations of fragments from this group (Taylor-Schechter Misc. 35.87, Adler 2102, and a text published by A. Harkavy) and from the other groups, though not a translation of Taylor-Schechter Misc. 35.88.

4. This system of classification was developed by Riccardo Di Segni, *Il vangelo del ghetto* (Magia e religioni 8; Rome: Newton Compton, 1985). Peter Schäfer has been promoting a project to study the issue anew, but he seems to have correctly accepted Di Segni's classification scheme. See, e.g., his "Introduction," in Schäfer et al., *"Toledot Yeshu" Revisited*, 1–11, esp. 2–4. Schäfer writes here of "preparing an edition of all the available manuscripts" and of "an electronic database on a CD" (2). This edition (*"Toledot Yeshu": The Life Story of Jesus*), along with its translation of many manuscripts, appeared after the present work was prepared for publication.

The Helen-group, which features a Queen Helen and calls Mary's betrothed "Jochanan," is most widely witnessed by Hebrew and vernacular manuscripts. Here, Jesus forms birds out of clay and makes them fly (cf. *Inf. Gos. Thom.* 2) through use of the divine name. Jesus engages in a flying competition with Juda Ishcariota, who brings Jesus down by ejaculating or urinating on him. This version contains the explicit account that Jesus, having foreseen the manner of his death, employed the divine name to cause all trees to break under his weight; thus, a cabbage stalk had to be used to hang him up.

The Pilate-group, in which Pilate's appearance is distinctive, is documented primarily in the fragmentary Aramaic manuscripts from the Cairo Genizah. There are five major fragments: three in Cambridge (Cambridge Genizah Library, Taylor-Schechter Misc. 35.87, 35.88, and Taylor-Schechter NS 298.56) and two in New York (both catalogued as Jewish Theological Seminary of America, MS 2529 [Adler 2102]).[5] Tiberius Caesar also appears in this version of the text, as does an account of an impregnation of his virgin daughter by Jesus through the use of magical words. Jesus initially escapes execution by flying away to the cave of Elijah and then transforming himself into a bird.

The oldest elements of the story could be isolated by collating these three groups for items shared by all three (see above on the contents). Further determination of the antiquity of elements of the story can be gained through comparison with Celsus, Justin and other early Christian writings, and the Talmud. There are good reasons to believe that the earliest version of the story is generally best represented by the Aramaic fragments and that the tale initially gained currency in Aramaic. Most importantly, parallels from the early church fathers correspond most with the details in these fragments, and recent studies have disclosed distinctive Palestinian Aramaic traits in Taylor-Schechter Misc. 35.88.[6] The date of the manuscript is uncertain; perhaps it can be ascribed to approximately the eleventh century, which is exceptionally early for manuscripts of the *Toledot Yeshu* (most date to the sixteenth to nineteenth centuries).[7]

Genre

In genre, the *Toledot Yeshu* may be considered a parody or satire. Aristophanes and Lucian are perhaps the best-known Greek satirists from antiquity; Apuleius's *Metamorphoses (The Golden Ass)*, the *Life of Aesop*, and Petronius's *Satyricon* are Latin exemplars. Among Jewish literature, Esther, Judith, Tobit, and the *Testament of Abraham* have been identified as containing parody or satire, particularly of foreigners. The *Toledot Yeshu* also incorporates folkloristic elements of the same general sort as do Christian apocrypha (miracles and magic, heroes and villains, animistic views of plants and animals). Thus, the basic structure of the old story allowed many openings for the addition of a variety of episodes.

---

5. For details (editions) see Smelik, "Aramaic Dialect(s)," 41 n. 4. Something of a compiled republication of the main Aramaic texts is found in Deutsch, "New Evidence."

6. See Smelik, "Aramaic Dialect(s)." Sokoloff ("Date and Provenance," 16), though dismissive of Smelik's larger conclusions, admits that he "cannot give a plausible explanation at present for the occurrence of occasional JPA [sc. Jewish Palestinian Aramaic] morphological forms found in" Taylor-Schechter Misc. 35.88.

7. For the dating, see an opinion of J. Leveen that the similar manuscript Taylor-Schechter Misc. 35.87 is "of about the eleventh century" mentioned by William Horbury, "The Trial of Jesus in Jewish Tradition," in *The Trial of Jesus* (ed. Ernst Bammel; SBT 2/13; London: SCM, 1970), 103–21 esp. 118 n. 6.

Date and Provenance

The date and provenance of the *Toledot Yeshu* have not been adequately determined. While one branch of scholarship views the entire tale as very late (Middle Ages), an alternative branch has argued for a much older date, sometimes as early as the second century. Parallels from known early church fathers (Justin, Tertullian, Origen as a witness for Celsus) document the antiquity of at least certain motifs and have led some scholars to postulate a continuous early story.[8] Grammatical and dialectical analysis of the Aramaic fragments has suggested a "provenance in Palestine in the third-fourth century CE."[9]

Literary Context

The relationship of the *Toledot Yeshu* with early Christian texts is fascinating and largely unexplored. The image of Jehudah and his garden, or Jehudah the gardener, recalls Mary Magdalene's mistaken identification of the risen Jesus as a gardener in John 20:15 and is emblematic of many, often surprising resonances with the gospel narratives. The notion of a flying Jesus is found in Syriac-speaking Christianity in its interpretation of the *Diatessaron*.[10] Jesus' transformation into a bird or rooster is reminiscent of the *Book of the Rooster*, in which Jesus resurrects a rooster that had been cooked in order that it might follow Judas (*Bk. Rooster* 4:1–8).[11] Emphasis on the scriptural commandment not to leave a body hanging when the sun goes down parallels *Gos. Pet.* 5. Interestingly, it is not entirely clear how the *Toledot Yeshu* tradition conceived of the mode of Jesus' death; the following translation takes something of a neutral approach and translates, in accord with the other recensions, words for "hanging" that could possibly be interpreted as "crucifying."[12] The text translated below also speaks of stoning Jesus. The *Toledot Yeshu* employs also a variety of Jewish Scriptures and traditions. In particular, Esther (and its later interpretations, especially within the context of the festival of Purim and its revelry) provided a storehouse of imagery and motifs dealing with the hanging of the villain Haman and his ten sons (Esth 7:10; 9:14).[13]

Translation

The accompanying translation of Taylor-Schechter Misc. 35.88 is based on the edition by Louis Ginzberg[14] with consideration taken of the corrections from a more recent collation by William Horbury.[15] The fragment comprises a single page; folio side and line numbers are indicated.

---

8. See, e.g., Horbury, "Critical Examination," 427–44.

9. Smelik, "Aramaic Dialect(s)," 71. Sokoloff ("Date and Provenance," 25) decides for "the provenance of the Aramaic *Toledot Yeshu* as being Jewish Babylonia, and its time of composition toward the middle of the first millennium CE."

10. See Tjitze Baarda, "'The Flying Jesus': Luke 4:29–30 in the Syriac Diatessaron," in his *Essays on the Diatessaron* (CBET 11; Kampen: Kok Pharos, 1994), 59–85 (originally published in *VC* 40 [1986]: 313–41).

11. *Bk. Rooster* may be consulted in a French translation by Pierluigi Piovanelli in *EAC* 2:153–203.

12. See the discussion and literature in Chapman, *Ancient Jewish*, 13–38.

13. See, e.g., a recent discussion and documentation of the Jewish texts by Sarit Kattan Gribetz, "Hanged and Crucified: The Book of Esther and *Toledot Yeshu*," in Schäfer et al., *"Toledot Yeshu" Revisited*, 159–80.

14. Ginzberg, "Ma'aseh Yeshu."

15. Horbury, "Critical Examination," 90–91.

Bibliography

EDITIONS AND TRANSLATIONS

Ginzberg, Louis. "Ma'aseh Yeshu." Pages 324–38 in vol. 1 of *Ginze Schechter*. 3 vols. New York: Jewish Theological Seminary, 1928–1929. (*Editio princeps* of Taylor-Schechter Misc. 35.88.)

Horbury, William. "A Critical Examination of the Toledoth Jeshu." PhD diss., University of Cambridge, 1970. (Features a new collation of Taylor-Schechter Misc. 35.88.)

STUDIES

Chapman, David W. *Ancient Jewish and Christian Perceptions of Crucifixion*. WUNT 2/244. Tübingen: Mohr Siebeck, 2008.

Deutsch, Yaacov. "New Evidence of Early Versions of *Toldot Yeshu*" (in Hebrew). *Tarbiz* 69 (2000): 177–97.

Di Segni, Riccardo. *Il vangelo del ghetto*. Magia e religioni 8. Rome: Newton Compton, 1985.

Huldreich, Johann Jacob. *Historia Jeschuae Nazareni*. Leiden: Apud Johannem du Vivie, Is. Severinum, 1705.

Klauck, Hans-Josef. *Apocryphal Gospels: An Introduction*. London: T.&T. Clark, 2004.

Krauss, Samuel. *Das Leben Jesu nach jüdischen Quellen*. Berlin: S. Calvary, 1902. (The standard edition of the entire text of *Toledot Yeshu*.)

Schäfer, Peter, Michael Meerson, and Yaacov Deutsch, eds. *"Toledot Yeshu" ("The Life Story of Jesus") Revisited: A Princeton Conference*. TSAJ 143. Tübingen: Mohr Siebeck, 2011.

Schäfer, Peter, and Michael Meerson, eds. and trans. *"Toledot Yeshu": The Life Story of Jesus*. 2 vols. and database. TSAJ 159. Tübingen: Mohr Siebeck, 2014.

Schichtling, Günter. *Ein jüdisches Leben Jesu. Die verschollene Toledot-Jeschu-Fassung Tam ū-mū`ād. Einleitung, Text, Übersetzung, Kommentar, Motivsynopse, Bibliographie*. WUNT 24. Tübingen: Mohr Siebeck, 1982.

Smelik, Willem F. "The Aramaic Dialect(s) of the Toledot Yeshu Fragments." *AS* 7 (2009): 39–73.

Sokoloff, Michael. "The Date and Provenance of the Aramaic *Toledot Yeshu* on the Basis of Aramaic Dialectology." Pages 13–26 in *"Toledot Yeshu" ("The Life Story of Jesus") Revisited: A Princeton Conference*. Edited by Peter Schäfer, Michael Meerson, and Yaacov Deutsch. TSAJ 143. Tübingen: Mohr Siebeck, 2011.

The Toledot Yeshu
from Taylor-Schechter Misc. 35.88

(fol. 1r)[a] [1]They put them in irons, and he brought them to Tiberias. And they took [2]John the Baptist and hung him up in the fifth hour [3]of the day, and afterwards they buried him. And after him, [4]they brought Jesus the wicked and sought to hang him up. [5]And as soon as he saw that the stake was standing for hanging him up, [6]he spoke a word of magic and flew from their hand [7]in the air of the heaven like a bird.

Jehuda [8]the gardener said to Rabbi Jehoshua the son of Periah, "What shall I do? [9]I shall go after him." Jehoshua the son of Periah answered and said [10]to him, "Go after him and do not delay!" In that hour [11]he recalled, reconsidered, and spoke the word of the Name [12]that is special and flew after him. And when he saw (that Jehuda had come after him), Jesus [13]went and hid in the cave of Elijah and spoke [14]words of magic and closed the opening of the cave. [15]And Jehuda the gardener came and spoke the words of the Name [16]that is special and opened the opening of the cave. And Jesus [17]transformed himself into a bird until there came

(fol. 1v) [1]Rabbi Jehuda the gardener, and he captured him in his cloak [2]and brought him before Rabbi Jehoshua the son of Periah. [3]And they brought Jesus the wicked and hung him up on [4]a stalk of cabbage, and before they brought him, [5]Jesus knew what was written in the Law: "You shall not [6]keep his corpse overnight on the stake." He sent and called [7]the people he had deceived and said to them, "When you come [8]tomorrow and do not find me or my body on the stake, [9]know that I have ascended to the firmament of heaven." And they hung (him) up [10]and stoned him with stones and he died on the stake, and they did not [11]want to take him down from the stake.

Deut 21:23

---

a. Since the text is fragmentary and consists of merely this one page, it is not entirely certain what narrative preceded and what followed. The best guide is likely to be Taylor-Schechter Misc. 35.87, which is a larger fragment and contains a section that generally runs parallel to Taylor-Schechter Misc. 35.88. In Misc. 35.87, essentially a new development in the story begins at this point. Prior to the decision to kill John and Jesus, there is an account in which Jesus has used magical words to cause a virgin (Tiberius Caesar's daughter) apparently to become pregnant; Pilate binds Jesus and John for nine months to await the birth, while Israel is in distress and proclaims a three-day fast. God answers by turning the embryo into a stone. After twelve months and no birth, Jesus is allowed to tear open the womb, but he finds only a stone, and even with prayer he is unable to carry out Caesar's command to make the stone live. Prior to the story of Jesus and the virgin, the manuscript has an account of the trial and execution of Jesus' five disciples: Matthai, Naqi, Buni, Nezer, and Todah.

Rabbi Jehoshua the son [12]of Periah said to them, "On account of Jesus the wicked shall we change the statute of the Law where it is written, [13]'You shall not keep his corpse overnight on the stake'?" So said to them Rabbi Jehoshua the son [14]of Periah. They took him down from the stake, and they took him down and buried him in a stream [15]of water of the garden of Rabbi Jehuda the gardener. And when those people came [16]and did not find him on the stake, they said, "He told us the truth, Jesus [17]our Lord. The Jews deal in deceit. If he was hung on the stake, [18]where has his body gone? In truth, he has ascended to heaven."

And Pilate [19]the governor called Jehuda the gardener and said to him, "The man you hung up . . ."[a]

---

a. In Taylor-Schechter Misc. 35.87, Jehuda the gardener then digs up the corpse and drags it through all the streets of Tiberias; Pilate then orders Jehuda to rebury the corpse.

The Berlin-Strasbourg Apocryphon
A new translation and introduction

by Alin Suciu

The *Berlin-Strasbourg Apocryphon* (*B-S Ap.*; *CPC* 0870) is a Christian writing that is preserved only fragmentarily in the Sahidic dialect of Coptic. The surviving parts of the text form an apocryphal account of the events that preceded the arrest of Christ. Although the revelation dialogue genre seems to prevail, the text is punctuated by narrative episodes. *B-S Ap.* incorporates a long hymn of the cross sung by Jesus, while the apostles are gathered around him and answer "Amen" to his utterances. The hymn has some literary connections with the well-known "Dance of the Cross" from the *Acts of John* (*CANT* 215).[1]

As the two manuscripts that preserve *B-S Ap.* are acephalous (see below), the original title and authorship remain unknown. The text is largely known today as the *Gospel of the Savior*[2] or the "Unbekanntes Berliner Evangelium" ("Unknown Berlin Gospel"). However, these titles label the text inadequately. *B-S Ap.* belongs in fact to a well-defined, albeit little-known, genre of Coptic literature, formed of apocryphal stories allegedly written by the apostles and their disciples, which can be conventionally called "pseudo-apostolic memoirs."[3] Some of these Coptic memoirs are incorporated into homilies attributed to church fathers. The pretended authors claim to have found the memoirs in the library of Jerusalem.

As the text cannot presently be identified more precisely, I have decided to designate it according to the location of the two manuscripts that preserve it, hence the *Berlin-Strasbourg Apocryphon*.

Manuscripts and Editions
B-S Ap. is attested in two incomplete Sahidic manuscripts. The first of them, P. Berol. 22220, is a fragmentary parchment codex of unknown provenance kept in the papyrus collection of the Egyptian Museum in Berlin. Thirty fragments of various sizes have survived of this manuscript. Paleographical data suggest that it might have been copied during the seventh or eighth centuries CE. The Berlin manuscript was published for the first time in 1999 by Charles Hedrick and Paul Mirecki.[4] However, this edition does not order properly the sequence of the fragments, which affects the order of the narrative. The fragments have been reordered according to the principles of the codicology of parchment

---

1. On the connection between the two hymns of the cross see Piovanelli, "Thursday Night Fever"; Yingling, "Singing with the Savior," 260–61, 271–75; Dilley, "*Christus Saltans*" and his entry on the *Discourse of the Savior* and the *Dance of the Savior* in this volume.

2. The editors opted for this title because Jesus is called "the Savior" throughout much of the surviving fragments; see Hedrick and Mirecki, *Gospel of the Savior,* 17.

3. The expression "memoirs of the apostles" was coined by Piovanelli, "Thursday Night Fever," 238.

4. Hedrick and Mirecki, *Gospel of the Savior.*

manuscripts by Stephen Emmel.[5] In the same article, Emmel proposed a number of emendations of the *editio princeps*.[6] Hans-Martin Schenke worked independently from Hedrick and Mirecki and produced about the same time a German translation of P. Berol. 22220.[7] An unpublished concordance of the Sahidic text has been prepared by Wolf-Peter Funk and is privately circulating.

Fragments of a papyrus codex containing the same text are preserved in the Strasbourg University Library as Copte inv. no. 5–7 (*CANT* 6). These fragments have been known for a long time as the "Strasbourg Coptic Gospel." The *editio princeps* was published by Adolf Jacoby at the turn of the twentieth century.[8] Because datable comparanda are lacking, the Strasbourg fragments cannot be dated paleographically. The connection between the Berlin and Strasbourg manuscripts was made by Stephen Emmel in an article published in 2002.[9] A few years later, Emmel reedited the Berlin manuscript, restoring many lacunae on the basis of the Strasbourg fragments.[10]

Finally, a manuscript discovered in 1965 by the archaeological mission of the Chicago Oriental Institute at Qasr el-Wizz in Nubia features an abridged version of *B-S Ap.*'s hymn of the cross. This manuscript, a well-preserved codex of small dimensions, is currently kept in the Nubian Museum in Aswan (Special Number 168). The text was published for the first time by Peter Hubai.[11] The Qasr el-Wizz codex is roughly datable to around 1000 CE.

In my PhD thesis, which I defended in 2013 at Laval University, Québec, I provide new editions of all three manuscripts.[12]

Contents

Most of the extant portions of *B-S Ap.* represent a dialogue between Jesus and the apostles. From time to time, the dialogue is punctuated by some narrative episodes, although the succession of the events is difficult to understand because of the numerous lacunae. The text features many verbatim quotations, allusions, or paraphrases of various biblical verses. Throughout the text, the narrative voice belongs to the apostles as a group or to an individual apostle who refers to the apostolic group using the first-person plural. This is a very common rhetorical device in the Coptic pseudo-apostolic memoirs.

Neither manuscript preserves the beginning of the work. The text starts on page 97 of the Berlin manuscript, with Christ addressing the apostles. Given that the previous sentences are missing, the topic of the dialogue is difficult to establish. The surviving text suggests that this portion might have contained a series of sayings about the kingdom of

---

5. Emmel, "Recently Published *Gospel of the Savior*."

6. Other important suggestions concerning the Coptic text are found in Nagel, "'Gespräche Jesu.'"

7. Schenke, "'Unbekannte Berliner Evangelium' (UBE)."

8. Jacoby, *Evangelienfragment*. Many corrections and restorations of lacunae were proposed in Carl Schmidt, review of Jacoby, *Evangelienfragment*, *Göttingische gelehrte Anzeigen* 162 (1900): 481–506; and Walter Ewing Crum, "Notes on the Strassburg Gospel Fragments," *Proceedings of the Society of Biblical Archaeology* 22 (1900): 72–76.

9. Emmel, "Unbekanntes Berliner Evangelium."

10. Emmel, "Preliminary Reedition and Translation."

11. Hubai, *Koptische Apokryphen aus Nubien* (German translation of *A Megváltó a keresztrol*). An English translation has appeared recently in Tsakos et al., "The Wizz Codex," and another translation is provided by Paul C. Dilley elsewhere in this volume.

12. Suciu, "Apocryphon Berolinense/Argentoratense." The dissertation will soon appear with Mohr Siebeck in the WUNT 1st series.

heaven, since the first lines refer to it no less than three times (1:1–2). Christ's discourse is followed by a question of the apostle Andrew, of which only the introductory words "My [Lord]" have survived (1:5). It is possible that Christ's reference to the Harrowing of Hell, which occurs after the lacuna, is part of Christ's answer to Andrew (1:6). The text continues with what seems to be a discussion about sin and free will. This assumption is based on the fact that the Greek word *autexousios* is mentioned twice (2:3–4).

A colon inserted by the scribe on page 98, col. B,14 indicates that here a new section begins. This is further ascertained by the fact that Christ resumes his speech addressing the apostles with, "Arise, let us leave this place. For the one who shall hand me over has approached" (3:1; cf. Mark 14:42; Matt 26:46).

At 3:2–8, the Savior anticipates his Passion, explaining to the disciples the importance of self-sacrifice. This portion represents a gospel-like section that blends several quotations from the New Testament:

> You shall all flee and be offended because of me. You shall all flee and leave me alone, but I do not remain alone for my Father is with me. I and my Father, we are a single one. For it is written: "I shall strike the shepherd and the sheep of the flock will be scattered." I am the good shepherd. I shall lay down my soul for you. You, yourself, lay down your souls for your companions to be pleasing to my Father, for there is no commandment greater than this: that I lay down my soul for people. This is [why] my Father loves me, because I fulfilled [his] wish. (3:2–8)

At 4:1 a question is addressed to Jesus by one of the apostles. Unfortunately, the parchment is damaged so that the question can be read only partly. It is possible that the apostles enquire of Christ about their mission on earth after his death.

It seems that a new section starts after this because the Savior asks his disciples to arise and pray. The setting of the dialogue has also changed, because at 4:4 Christ and the apostles are now said to be on a mountain. As this section is partly an elaboration of the Ascension scene, it is possible that the text refers to Mount Tabor, although the Mount of Olives, the favorite setting of the dialogues between Christ and the disciples in the Coptic pseudo-apostolic memoirs, cannot be completely ruled out. Jesus ascends to heaven on the mountain, while the apostles are mystically transformed by a vision of the seven heavens, which open in order to reveal the tabernacle of the Father. During the ascent of Christ, the heavens tremble and the angels run away fearing that the commotion will destroy them (4:7–8). As the heavens remain open after the ascent of Christ, the apostles are able to see what happens in the uppermost heaven—i.e., the seventh, where the tabernacle of the Father is situated. They recount that the heavenly beings welcome the Savior in his Father's throne room (4:14–19). They see the Son bowed down in front of his Father, saying to him in distress, "O my Father, if it is possible, let this cup pass from me!" (cf. Matt 26:39). The author evidently has transferred the Gethsemane scene to heaven (5:2–14). Unfortunately, much of the text of this section is lost.

At 6:4–9, possibly in a new section, there appears an anaphora of the wood of the cross. This anaphora can be compared with a similar composition included in Ps.-Theophilus of Alexandria's homily *On the Cross and the Good Thief* (*CPG* 2622; *CPC* 0395), which has survived only in Sahidic Coptic.[13] Unfortunately, the hymn in *B-S Ap.* is heavily damaged.

---

13. Alin Suciu, "Ps.-Theophili Alexandrini *Sermo de Cruce et Latrone* (*CPG* 2622): Edition of Pierpont

B-S Ap.	Ps.-Theophilus, *On the Cross*[14]
[The] wood of [. . .]	The wood of incorruptibility,
The wood of [. . .]	The wood of forgiveness of sins,
The wood of [. . .]	The wood of the healer,
The wood [. . .]	The wood of the life-giver,
[The wood of] strength	The wood of the fruit-giver,
[The wood of forgiveness] of sins	The wood of relief,
	The wood of gladness,
	The wood of joy,
	The wood of salvation,
	The wood of blessing,
	The wood of life,
	The wood of the grace

In both *B-S Ap.* and Ps.-Theophilus manuscripts each verse fills one line, showing that the copyists were aware that they were transcribing hymnic sections. The anaphora of *B-S Ap.* appears shorter than that of Ps.-Theophilus in the table above, but this is probably because the Berlin parchment is damaged and some verses are lost in the preceding lacuna. The fragmentary state of P. Berol. 22220 hampers the comparison between the two anaphoras. However, one of the two verses that can be fully reconstructed in the Berlin manuscript, "[the wood of forgiveness] of sins," appears as well in Ps.-Theophilus, but also in a Sahidic antiphonary that belonged to the Monastery of the Archangel Michael, in the Fayyum, kept today in the Pierpont Morgan Library, New York (M575, fol. 9v).[15] This might indicate that the anaphora of the wood of the cross was fairly widespread in the Coptic church and probably served as a liturgical text.

Pages 103–106 of the Berlin manuscript are heavily damaged. The text continues on page 107, apparently with a dialogue about the nature of Christ's body after the resurrection. Jesus affirms that his resurrected body will be unbearable to humans. In order to argue that Jesus' body will be fiery after the resurrection, the author puts into his mouth two sayings: the *Noli me tangere* statement (John 20:17) and the agraphon of the fire ("The [one who is close] to me [is] close to [the] fire. The one who is far from me is far from life," 7:6–8), well known from other early Christian sources.[16] One must note that although apocryphal material is used here, the interpretation is altered in order to sound orthodox. According to Pierluigi Piovanelli, the agraphon of the fire "has been not only reemployed, demetaphorized (in spite of his human nature, the risen Christ will truly burn), and contextualized into a new narrative framework, but also adapted to the Johannine perspectives of its new environment."[17]

Morgan M595 with Parallels and Translation," *ZAC* 16 (2012): 181–225. Cf. also Suciu, "Apocryphon Berolinense/Argentoratense," 198–99.

14. Coptic text and English translation in Suciu, "Ps.-Theophili Alexandrini," 211, 222.

15. Maria Cramer and Martin Krause, *Das koptische Antiphonar* (Jerusalemer Theologisches Forum 12; Münster: Aschendorf, 2008), 90.

16. *Gos. Thom.* 82, but also in Origen, *Hom. Jer.* 3.3, Didymus the Blind, *Comm. Ps.* (PG 39:1488D) and in a Syriac anti-Marcionite commentary on the Gospel parables attributed to Ephrem, which is preserved only in an Armenian translation.

17. Pierluigi Piovanelli, "The Reception of Early Christian Texts and Traditions in Late Antiquity Apocryphal Literature," in *The Reception and Interpretation of the Bible in Late Antiquity. Proceedings of the*

At 8:8 begins a long hymn of the cross in which the disciples encircle Christ while he sings (8:1–4); the apostles clap their hands and reply "Amen" to the utterances of the Savior. The hymn resembles the hymn of the Father that appears in *Acts John* 94–95,[18] but also the Manichaean "Amen hymn."[19]

The Berlin manuscript breaks off before the end of the hymn of the cross, but the continuation can be found on the recto of Strasbourg Copte 5 (S14–21). The verso of this fragment features a new textual unit, which demonstrates that Jesus' dialogue with the disciples continues after the hymn. Here Christ encourages the apostles to remain and watch with him (S24; cf. Mark 14:37; Matt 26:41).

Unfortunately, the end of *B-S Ap.* is lost. We do not have evidence about the content of the missing portions after Strasbourg Copte 5, but it is possible that the text mentioned also the Passion and, possibly, the resurrection.

Literary Context

B-S Ap. has often been included among the ancient Christian gospels in the modern collections of apocrypha, together with texts such as the *Gospel of Thomas,* the *Gospel of Philip,* the *Gospel of Mary,* the *Gospel of Peter,* and others.[20] However, although the text can be categorized as apocryphal, it does not belong to the ancient gospel genre. As I have already mentioned, *B-S Ap.* has obvious literary connections to a group of little-known Coptic apocryphal writings that can be designated as pseudo-apostolic memoirs. These writings are late productions, none of them earlier than the fifth century CE.

The pseudo-apostolic memoirs were probably composed directly in Coptic. They survive either in one or more of the major dialects of Coptic—Sahidic, Bohairic, and Fayyumic—or in the other languages that preserve extensive portions of the Coptic literary her-

---

Montréal Colloquium in Honour of Charles Kannengiesser, 11–13 October 2006 (ed. Lorenzo DiTommaso and Lucian Turcescu; Bible in Ancient Christianity 6; Leiden: Brill, 2008), 429–39, at 437.

18. In addition to the scholarship provided in note 1 above, one may consult Max Pulver, "Jesu Reigen und Kreuzigung nach den Johannes-Akten," *Eranos-Jahrbuch* 9 (1942): 141–77; Willem C. van Unnik, "A Note on the Dance of Jesus in the *Acts of John,*" *VC* 18 (1964): 1–5; Arthur J. Dewey, "The Hymn in the *Acts of John*: Dance as Hermeneutic," *Semeia* 38 (1986): 67–80; Jean-Daniel Kaestli, "Response to A. J. Dewey," *Semeia* 38 (1986): 81–88; Paul G. Schneider, *The Mystery of the Acts of John: An Interpretation of the Hymn and the Dance in Light of the Acts' Theology* (San Francisco: Mellen Research University Press, 1991); Barbara Ellen Bowe, "Dancing into the Divine: The Hymn of the Dance in the *Acts of John,*" *JECS* 7 (1999): 83–104; Melody Gabrielle Beard-Shouse, *The Circle Dance in the Acts of John: An Early Christian Ritual* (M.A. thesis; Graduate Faculty of the University of Kansas, 2009) (available online at http://kuscholarworks.ku.edu/handle/1808/6462; accessed November 2014).

19. Charles R. C. Allberry, *A Manichaean Psalm-Book: Part II* (Manichaean Manuscripts in the Chester Beatty Collection, 2; Stuttgart: W. Kohlhammer, 1938), 189–91.

20. Until Emmel revealed that the Berlin and the Strasbourg manuscripts contain the same work ("Unbekanntes Berliner Evangelium"), they were published and studied separately. For P. Berol. 22220, see Uwe-Karsten Plisch, *Verborgene Worte Jesu—verworfene Evangelien. Apokryphe Schriften des frühen Christentums* (Berlin: Evangelische Haupt-Bibelgesellschaft und von Cansteinsche Bibelanstalt, 2000), 27–34; Bart D. Ehrman, *Lost Scriptures: Books That Did Not Make It into the New Testament* (New York: Oxford University Press, 2003), 52–56; Hans-Martin Schenke, "Das Unbekannte Berliner Evangelium, auch 'Evangelium des Erlösers' genannt," in *Antike christliche Apokryphen in deutscher Übersetzung* (1 vol. in 2 parts; ed. Christoph Markschies and Jens Schröter; Tübingen: Mohr Siebeck, 2012), 1.2:1277–89; Bart D. Ehrman and Zlatko Pleše, *The Other Gospels: Accounts of Jesus from Outside the New Testament* (Oxford: Oxford University Press, 2014), 217–25. For the Strasbourg fragments, see Wilhelm Schneemelcher, "The Strasbourg Coptic Papyrus," in *New Testament Apocrypha* (2 vols.; ed. Wilhelm Schneemelcher; Knoxville: Westminster John Knox, 1991), 1:103–5; Daniel A. Bertrand, "Papyrus Strasbourg copte 5–6," in *EAC* 1:425–28.

itage: Arabic, Ethiopic and, more rarely, Old Nubian. As it is well known, these traditions represent a literary continuum. When the Coptic language fell into oblivion, a significant number of Coptic texts were translated into Arabic in order to be used by the Arabophone Christians. As the Ethiopic church was under the control of the Alexandrian Patriarchate, the Christianity of Ethiopia was deeply influenced by the Copto-Arabic culture; thus, numerous Coptic texts passed into Gəʿəz via Arabic. Consequently, although some of the pseudo-apostolic memoirs are lost or only fragmentarily preserved in Coptic, they can sometimes be recovered in complete Arabic and Ethiopic versions. As for the Old Nubian versions, they are translations from Coptic but, unfortunately, the manuscripts in this language are rare and generally even more damaged than those in Coptic. An exception is the Serra East codex (Berlin, Staatsbibliothek MS Or. 1020), which contains the Nubian version of the *Discourse of the Savior*.[21]

The pseudo-apostolic memoirs are a group of texts variously attributed to the apostles Peter, John, Bartholomew, and James the Just, or to the disciples Stephen the Protomartyr, Evodius, Gamaliel, and Prochorus, or to the apostles as a group. They allegedly contain apostolic testimonies concerning the deeds and words of Christ, written in a gospel-like style. The texts often mention that the apostles wrote down the revelation of Christ in a book and deposited it in a library in Jerusalem; the book was discovered later by one of the church fathers during a pilgrimage to the Holy Land.[22]

Because many pseudo-apostolic memoirs have survived in Coptic only fragmentarily, they have sometimes been identified erroneously as apocryphal gospels or apocalypses.[23] However, these labels are misnomers for our texts. The Berlin and Strasbourg fragments of the "Gospel of the Savior" went through a similar process of apocryphization, through which a new ancient gospel has imaginarily been created.

The pseudo-apostolic memoirs can be broadly divided into two categories:

A. Included in a patristic homily.

Ps.-Cyril of Jerusalem, *On the Life and the Passion of Christ* (CPG 3604; CPC 0113)

Ps.-Cyril of Jerusalem, *On Mary Magdalene* (CANT 73; CPC 0118)[24]

Ps.-Cyril of Jerusalem, *On the Virgin Mary* (CPC 0119)

Ps.-Cyril of Jerusalem, *On the Dormition of the Virgin* (no clavis number)

Ps.-Bachios of Maiuma, *On the Apostles* (CPC 0067)

Ps.-Bachios of Maiuma, *On the Three Children in the Fiery Furnace* (CPC 0068)

Ps.-Cyriacus of Behnesa, *On the Flight of the Holy Family to Egypt* (no clavis number)

Ps.-Cyriacus of Behnesa, *On the Dormition of the Virgin* (CANT 147; 153)

Ps.-Cyriacus of Behnesa, *Lament of Mary* (CANT 74)

Ps.-Cyriacus of Behnesa, *Martyrdom of Pilate* (CANT 75)

---

21. Francis L. Griffith, *The Nubian Texts of the Christian Period* (Abhandlungen der Königlich Preussischen Akademie der Wissenschaften Philosophisch-historische Klasse 1913,8; Berlin: Reimer, 1913), 41–53; reedited in Gerald M. Browne, "Griffith's Stauros-Text," *SPap* 22 (1983): 75–119.

22. This topos is documented in Suciu, "Apocryphon Berolinense/Argentoratense," 75–91.

23. For example, Eugène Revillout published several fragments of the Sahidic apostolic books (including Strasbourg Copte 5–6) under the misleading title the *Gospel of the Twelve Apostles;* see his "L'Évangile des XII Apôtres récemment découvert," *RB* 1 (1904): 167–87, 321–55. For a criticism of Revillout's method, see Enzo Lucchesi, "Un évangile apocryphe imaginaire," *OLP* 28 (1997): 167–78. Adolf von Harnack and Carl Schmidt translated into German a Berlin fragment from the *Book of Bartholomew* as a Moses-Adam apocalypse; see "Ein koptisches Fragment einer Moses-Adam Apokalypse," *SDAW* 51 (1891): 1045–49.

24. Translated by Christine Luckritz Marquis in this volume.

Ps.-Archelaos of Neapolis, *On the Archangel Gabriel* (*CPC* 0045)
Ps.-Basil of Caesarea, *On the Building of the Church of the Virgin* (*CPG* 2970; *CPC* 0073)
Ps.-John Chrysostom, *On the Four Bodiless Creatures* (*CPG* 5150.11; *CPC* 0177)
Ps.-John Chrysostom, *On John the Baptist* (*CPG* 5150.3; *CANT* 184; *CPC* 0170)[25]
Ps.-John Chrysostom, *Revelation on the Mount of Olives, 40 Days after the Crucifixion* (no clavis number)
Ps.-Cyril of Alexandria, *On the Dormition of the Virgin* (no clavis number)
Ps.-Timothy Aelurus, *On the Archangel Michael* (*CPG* 2529; *CPC* 0404)
Ps.-Timothy Aelurus, *On Abbaton* (*CPG* 2530; *CPC* 0405)[26]
Ps.-Theodosius of Alexandria, *On the Dormition of the Virgin* (*CPG* 7153; *CPC* 0385)

B. Without homiletic framework.
History of Joseph the Carpenter (*BHO* 532–33; *CANT* 60; *CPC* 0037)
Investiture of Michael (*CPC* 0488)
Investiture of Gabriel (*CPC* 0378)
Mysteries of John (*CPC* 0041)
Book of Bartholomew (*CANT* 80; *CPC* 0027)
Discourse of the Savior (no clavis number)[27]
Ps.-Evodius, *On the Dormition of the Virgin* (*CANT* 133; *CPC* 0151)
Ps.-Evodius, *On the Passion 1* (*CPC* 0149)
Ps.-Evodius, *On the Passion 2* (*CANT* 81; *CPC* 0150)

Three other fragmentary texts seemingly belong to the group of the pseudo-apostolic memoirs, but they remain unidentified: 1) a Sahidic Miaphysite christological extract;[28] 2) a Sahidic fragment from Bala'izah;[29] and 3) the *Berlin-Strasbourg Apocryphon*.

In the writings of the first category, the alleged apostolic records are found by a church father in the library of the house of Mary, mother of John Mark (cf. Acts 12:12), but other locations, like the library of Jerusalem, or the house of Prochorus, the disciple of the apostle John, are mentioned as well as repositories of the apostolic memoirs. The incorporation of these apocrypha in sermons attributed to the great figures of Coptic Miaphysite orthodoxy, such as Cyril of Alexandria, John Chrysostom, Basil of Caesarea, Timothy Aelurus, Theodosius of Alexandria, etc., assured their success in Coptic monasteries.

The analysis of the texts suggests that they were elaborated in the milieu of post-Chalcedonian Coptic Egypt.[30] This assertion is based on several elements that are found in the pseudo-apostolic memoirs. For example, the Christology of the texts is influenced by the fifth-century debates concerning the person of Christ. In some memoirs, the Miaphysite position is explicitly defended, which demonstrates that the texts must be dated after the council of Chalcedon (451 CE).[31] It is possible that the pseudo-apostolic memoirs

---

25. Translated by Philip L. Tite in this volume.
26. Translated by me in this volume.
27. Translated by Paul C. Dilley in this volume.
28. Charles W. Hedrick, "A Revelation Discourse of Jesus," *JCoptS* 7 (2005): 13–15.
29. Paul E. Kahle, *Bala'izah. Coptic Texts from Deir el-Bala'izah in Upper Egypt* (2 vols.; London: Oxford University Press, 1954), 1:403–4; the fragment was translated for the first time by Walter E. Crum in William Matthew Flinders Petrie, *Gizeh and Rifeh* (London: School of Archaeology in Egypt, 1907), 39.
30. See Suciu, "Apocryphon Berolinense/Argentoratense," 7, 118–21 et passim.
31. See Suciu, "Apocryphon Berolinense/Argentoratense," 121–29.

and other similar pseudo-patristic writings represent an attempt of Coptic Christianity to develop a new identity after the schism. The myth of the apostolic library of Jerusalem and the attribution of the texts to the church fathers granted to the pseudo-apostolic memoirs a double legitimization. In this way, Coptic Christians could show that their faith is founded both on apostolic and patristic grounds.

B-S Ap. as a Pseudo-Apostolic Memoir

B-S Ap. contains features that allow us to place it confidently among the pseudo-apostolic memoirs. These features include similar themes and rhetorical devices, identical expressions and precise textual parallels.[32]

For example, the pseudo-apostolic memoirs are usually written in the first-person plural, the narrators being the apostles. The same applies to *B-S Ap.*, in which the narrative voice belongs to the apostolic group. Thus, expressions such as "he said to us" (4:3), "we, too" (4:5), "we saw" (4:6, 9), "us, the apostles" (4:11) are common throughout the text.

Another literary connection between *B-S Ap.* and the pseudo-apostolic memoirs is the very peculiar form of address, "O my holy members." Jesus calls his disciples using this vocative three times in *B-S Ap.*:

The Savior said to us, "O my holy members, my blessed seeds" (4:3);
"But now gather to me, O my holy members, dance and [answer to me]" (8:1);
He said to us, "O my holy members, [blessed are you]" (P. Berol. 22220 Frag. 9F).

This expression is based on Pauline ecclesiology, where Christians are seen as members of Christ's body.[33] "O my holy members" and other derived vocatives ("O my honored members," "O my holy fellow-members" etc.) are standard formulae in numerous pseudo-apostolic memoirs, such as *Disc. Sav.*; *Bk. Bart.*; *Hist. Jos. Carp.*; the *Investiture of Michael*; the *Investiture of Gabriel*; Ps.-Chrysostom, *On the Four Bodiless Creatures*; Ps.-Timothy Aelurus, *On Abbaton*; Ps.-Theodosius of Alexandria, *On the Dormition of the Virgin*; Ps.-Evodius, *On the Passion 2*; Ps.-Evodius, *On the Dormition*; Ps.-Bachios of Maiuma, *On the Apostles*; Ps.-Cyriacus of Behnesa, *Martyrdom of Pilate*; the Bala'izah Sahidic fragment published by Kahle; and the Miaphysite fragment edited by Hedrick.[34] The fact that this expression is used so often in the Coptic books attributed to the apostles seems to suggest that they were composed in the same milieu and probably around the same date.

Outside the pseudo-apostolic memoirs, the expression "O my holy members" has a meager attestation. It appears, however, in several other Coptic texts.[35] We may thus conclude that this form of address is restricted to Coptic literature and that it features prominently in the pseudo-apostolic memoirs.

In his first article on the *Berlin-Strasbourg Apocryphon*, Stephen Emmel showed that the scene of Christ's ascent to heaven (chap. 4) is found also in *Bk. Bart.*[36] Christ is depicted here as a gigantic figure, with his feet standing on the mountain where the apostles

---

32. For *B-S Ap.* as a pseudo-apostolic memoir see Hagen, "Ein anderer Kontext," and Suciu, "Apocryphon Berolinense/Argentoratense."

33. See Hedrick and Mirecki, *Gospel of the Savior*, 95–96.

34. The complete references can be found in Suciu, "Apocryphon Berolinense/Argentoratense," 103–15.

35. See Suciu, "Apocryphon Berolinense/Argentoratense," 112–15, where I conclude that the expression has a monastic background.

36. Emmel, "Recently Published *Gospel of the Savior*," 54–55.

are found, while his head reaches the sky. The parallel is so close that Emmel was able to restore P. Berol. 22220 100, col. B, 20–24 on the basis of the parallel passage in *Bk. Bart.*[37] Moreover, Joost Hagen has supplied yet another parallel to the same passage, which appears in the book of the apostles included in the homily of Ps.-Cyril of Jerusalem *On the Life and the Passion of Christ.*[38]

B-S Ap. 4:9	*Bk. Bart.* 18:1	Cyril of Jerusalem, *On the Passion* 78
We saw our Savior traversing all the heavens, [his] feet [being fixed with us] on the [mountain], while [his head] pierced [the seventh] heaven.	We looked (and) saw our Savior as his body went up to heavens, his feet being fixed with us on the mountain.	We looked and saw the Savior like a column of fire, and his feet were with us on the mountain but his head reached to the heaven.

The same scene includes a vision of the apostles, who see the heavens opening up one after another. In another pseudo-apostolic memoir, the *Investiture of Michael,* the apostles experience a similar vision of the opened heavens: "And immediately, we, the apostles, looked and we saw the heavens opening. The heavens were revealed, our eyes perceived, we saw the Paradise and we saw the Tree of Life."[39] The apostles are mystically transformed after the vision because their bodies now shine like the sun.[40] In *B-S Ap.*, the apostles similarly testify that "we, too, became like spiritual bodies" (4:5). Remarkably, in both texts the narrative voice belongs to the group of the apostles ("we, the apostles").

What is more, the vision of the apostles in *B-S Ap.* has certain verbatim correspondences with the parallel episode from the *Investiture of Michael.*[41]

B-S Ap. 4:11	Strasbourg Copte 6	*Investiture of Michael* 13 (Sahidic)	*Investiture of Michael* 13 (Fayyumic)
our [eyes] penetrated [all] the heavens	our eyes penetrated everywhere (and) we perceived the glory of his divinity	Our eyes perceived and we saw the Paradise	Our eyes penetrated and we saw the Paradise

In this passage, P. Berol. 22220, Strasbourg Copte 6 and the Fayyumic version of the *Investiture of Michael* use the verb "to penetrate" (*jōte/jōti*). The Sahidic version of the *Investi-*

---

37. The passage in question can be found in Matthias Westerhoff, *Auferstehung und Jenseits im koptischen "Buch der Auferstehung Jesu Christi, unseres Herrn"* (Orientalia Biblica et Christiana 11; Wiesbaden: Harrassowitz, 1999), 152; chapter and verse divisions follow the French translation of Jean-Daniel Kaestli and Pierre Cherix in *EAC* 1:299–356.

38. Hagen, "Ein anderer Kontext," 362–63. Since Hagen's article, the homily of Ps.-Cyril of Jerusalem has been published; see the passage in question in Roelof van den Broek, *Pseudo-Cyril of Jerusalem, On the Life and the Passion of Christ. A Coptic Apocryphon* (Supplements to Vigiliae Christianae 118; Leiden: Brill, 2013), 150–52.

39. Sahidic text in Caspar Detlef G. Müller, *Die Bücher der Einsetzung der Erzengel Michael und Gabriel* (2 vols.; CSCO 225–26, Copt. 31–32; Leuven: Sécretariat du CorpusSCO, 1962), 1:40.

40. Müller, *Die Bücher der Einsetzung,* 1:59.

41. Müller, *Die Bücher der Einsetzung,* 1:40–41.

ture of Michael employs instead the verb "to perceive" *(eiōrah)*, which is also found in the Strasbourg fragment of *B-S Ap.*

Dating

B-S Ap. does not contain any detail on the basis of which we could date the text with a high degree of accuracy. The authors of the *editio princeps* thought that the author of *B-S Ap.* shows familiarity with a form of the sayings of Christ prior to the canonization of the gospels and dated it not later than the end of the second century CE.

> [. . .] the Gospel of the Savior was composed at a time when Christian oral traditions were still influential as written gospel texts. Thus the latest date for the composition of the Gospel of the Savior that best fits these conditions is the latter half of the second century before the canonical Gospels had consolidated their influence over the church and at which time the oral tradition remained a viable competitor to the written texts.[42]

This view was accepted uncritically soon after the publication of the *editio princeps,* but it can hardly be defended today.[43] For example, Jörg Frey and Titus Nagel have convincingly argued that the text depends on the canonical Gospels rather than on oral traditions.[44] In an important article on *B-S Ap.*, Peter Nagel subscribes to the view that the text can be explained best as a genuinely Coptic composition, not earlier than the fifth century CE.[45] Similar theories have been expressed by Hagen, Piovanelli, and myself.[46]

While it is true that *B-S Ap.* cannot be dated precisely on internal evidence, its age can be roughly estimated through inference, given that none of the related pseudo-apostolic memoirs can be assigned a date before the fifth century CE. Therefore, we do not have any reason to date *B-S Ap.* earlier than the other texts of the category to which it belongs.

Translation

The translation below is based on my own collation of P. Berol. 22220, which I had the opportunity to examine several times in the Berlin papyrus collection. However, many useful lacunae restorations have already been proposed by Charles Hedrick in the *editio princeps* and by Stephen Emmel in his *Harvard Theological Review* article. The translation of the fragments of Strasbourg Copte 5–7 was made from the color photographs kindly supplied to me by Stephen Emmel. As the order of the Strasbourg fragments does not coincide here with Emmel's 2003 translation of *B-S Ap.* in the journal *Apocrypha,* his verse divisions could not be retained. Therefore, I have introduced a new division of the text into chapters and verses.

---

42. Hedrick and Mirecki, *Gospel of the Savior,* 23. Hedrick maintained the early dating in his latest contribution to the topic, "Dating the *Gospel of the Savior*," 235–36.

43. On the history of the research on *B-S Ap.*, see Suciu, "Apocryphon Berolinense/Argentoratense," 53–69.

44. Frey, "Leidenskampf und Himmelsreise"; Nagel, "Das 'Unbekannte Berliner Evangelium.'"

45. Nagel, "'Gespräche Jesu,'" 234–38. Nagel's view is based on the use of the Bible in *B-S Ap.*, which follows the Sahidic version, and on the Christology of the text.

46. Hagen, "Ein anderer Kontext"; Piovanelli, "Thursday Night Fever," 237; Suciu, "Apocryphon Berolinense/Argentoratense," esp. 128–29.

Bibliography

EDITIONS AND TRANSLATIONS

Emmel, Stephen. "Preliminary Reedition and Translation of the *Gospel of the Savior*: New Light on the *Strasbourg Coptic Gospel* and the *Stauros-Text* from Nubia," *Apocrypha* 14 (2003): 9–53.

———. "The Recently Published *Gospel of the Savior* ('Unbekanntes Berliner Evangelium'): Righting the Order of Pages and Events." *HTR* 95 (2002): 45–72.

———. "Unbekanntes Berliner Evangelium = The Strasbourg Coptic Gospel: Prolegomena to a New Edition of the Strasbourg Fragments." Pages 353–74 in *For the Children Perfect Instruction: Studies in Honor of Hans-Martin Schenke on the Occasion of the Berliner Arbeitskreis für koptisch-gnostische Schriften's Thirtieth Year*. Edited by Hans-Gebhard Bethge et al. Nag Hammadi and Manichaean Studies 54. Leiden: Brill, 2002.

Hedrick, Charles W., and Paul A. Mirecki. *Gospel of the Savior: A New Ancient Gospel*. California Classical Library. Santa Rosa, Calif.: Polebridge, 1999. (*Editio princeps* of the Berlin manuscript.)

Hubai, Péter. *Koptische Apokryphen aus Nubien. Der Qasr el-Wizz Kodex*. TUGAL 163. Berlin/New York: Walter de Gruyter, 2009. Translation by Angelika Balog of *A Megváltó a keresztről: Kopt apokrifek Núbiából (A Kasr El-Wizz kódex)*. Cahiers Patristiques, Textes Coptes. Budapest: Szent István Társulat, 2006. (*Editio princeps* of the Nubian text.)

Jacoby, Adolf. *Ein neues Evangelienfragment*. Strasbourg: Karl J. Trübner, 1900. (*Editio princeps* of the Strasbourg fragment.)

Schenke, Hans-Martin. "Das sogenannte 'Unbekannte Berliner Evangelium' (UBE)." *ZAC* 2 (1998): 199–213.

Suciu, Alin. "Apocryphon Berolinense/Argentoratense (Previously Known as the Gospel of the Savior). Reedition of P. Berol. 22220, Strasbourg Copte 5–7 and Qasr el-Wizz Codex ff. 12v–17r with Introduction and Commentary." PhD diss., Université Laval, 2013.

Tsakos, Alexandros, Christian Bull, Lloyd Abercrombie, and Einar Thomassen. "*Miscellanea Epigraphica Nubica IV*: A New Edition of the Wizz Codex with an English Translation." *Collectanea Christiana Orientalia* 10 (2013): 193–209.

STUDIES

Dilley, Paul C. "*Christus Saltans* as Dionysos and David: The Dance of the Savior in Its Late-Antique Cultural Context." *Apocrypha* 24 (2013): 237–54.

Frey, Jörg. "Leidenskampf und Himmelsreise. Das Berliner Evangelien-Fragment (Papyrus Berolinensis 22220) und die Gethsemane-Tradition." *BZ* 46 (2002): 71–96.

Hagen, Joost L. "Ein anderer Kontext für die Berliner und Straßburger 'Evangelienfragmente.' Das 'Evangelium des Erlösers' und andere 'Apostelevangelien' in der koptischen Literatur." Pages 339–71 in *Jesus in apokryphen Evangelienüberlieferungen. Beiträge zu außerkanonischen Jesusüberlieferungen aus verschiedenen Sprach- und Kulturtraditionen*. Edited by Jörg Frey and Jens Schröter. WUNT 254. Tübingen: Mohr Siebeck, 2010.

Hedrick, Charles W. "Dating the *Gospel of the Savior*. Response to Peter Nagel and Pierluigi Piovanelli." *Apocrypha* 24 (2013): 223–36.

Nagel, Peter. "'Gespräche Jesu mit seinen Jüngern von der Auferstehung'—Zur Herkunft und Datierung des 'Unbekannten Berliner Evangeliums.'" *ZNW* 94 (2003): 215–57.

Nagel, Titus. "Das 'Unbekannte Berliner Evangelium' und das Johannesevangelium." *ZNW* 93 (2002): 251–67.

Piovanelli, Pierluigi. "Thursday Night Fever: Dancing and Singing with Jesus in the *Gospel of the Savior* and the *Dance of the Savior Around the Cross*." *Early Christianity* 3 (2012): 229–48.

Suciu, Alin. "Apocryphon Berolinense/Argentoratense (Previously Known as the Gospel of the Savior). Reedition of P. Berol. 22220, Strasbourg Copte 5–7 and Qasr el-Wizz Codex ff. 12v–17r with Introduction and Commentary." PhD diss., Université Laval, 2013.

Yingling, Erik. "Singing with the Savior: Reconstructing the Ritual Ring-Dance in the *Gospel of the Savior*." *Apocrypha* 24 (2013): 255–79.

The Berlin-Strasbourg Apocryphon

P. BEROL. 22220

The Savior's discourse on the kingdom of heaven and the descent to hell

(P. 97) **1** ¹"[. . . *9 lines broken* . . .] for the kingdom of heaven [. . .] by the glory [. . .] with the kingdom of heaven on your right. ²Blessed is the one who shall eat with me in the kingdom of heaven. ³You are the salt of the earth, you are the lamp that illuminates the world. ⁴Do not sleep nor slumber [until you] put on the garment of the kingdom, the one that I bought with the blood of the grape."

⁵Andrew replied and said: "My [Lord]" ‖ [. . . *24 lines broken* . . .]

⁶"If I healed those of the world, it is also necessary for me to descend into Amente for the others that are bound there. ⁷So then, that which is necessary [

(P. 98) **2** ¹"[. . . *23 lines broken* . . .] everything with certainty. ²I, for my part, shall gladly reveal to you, for I know that you are able to do everything with joy. ³For the man is in his own power ‖ [. . . *7 lines broken* . . .] ⁴[own power] [. . .] [master yourself]. So then, while you are in the body, do not let matter master you!

Luke 14:15; 22:29–30; Matt 8:11//Luke 13:29

Matt 5:13–14; John 8:12; Gos. Thom. 10

Mark 14:23–25 par.

1 Pet 3:19

The Savior's final words before his arrest

3 ¹"Arise, let us leave this place. For the one who shall hand me over has approached. ²You shall all flee and be offended because of me. ³You shall all flee and leave me alone, but I do not remain alone for my Father is with me. ⁴I and my Father, we are a single one.

⁵"For it is written: 'I shall strike the shepherd (P. 99) and the sheep of the flock will be scattered.' ⁶I am the good shepherd. I shall lay down my soul for you. ⁷You, too, lay down your souls for your companions to be pleasing to my Father, for there is no commandment greater than this: that I lay down my soul for people. ⁸This is [why] my Father loves me, because I fulfilled [his] wish, ⁹for I am God (and yet) I became human because [. . . *12 lines broken* . . .] ‖

Mark 14:42//Matt 26:46; John 14:31

Mark 14:27//Matt 26:31

John 10:30; 17:21

Mark 14:27//Matt 26:31 (Zech 13:7)

John 10:11, 15–18

John 15:13; Mark 12:31

The journey to the seventh heaven

4 ¹"[. . .] after how long time, or else, remember us, send for us, take us out of the world so that we may come to you?" [. . . *25 lines broken* . . .] ²(P. 100) the Savior.

³He said to us: "O my holy members, my blessed seeds, get up [. . .] pray [. . . *24 lines broken* . . .] ‖

1 Cor 6:15; 12:27; Rom 12:4–5

STRASBOURG COPTE 6 + 7,7 RECTO

The Savior appears to the disciples in glory

[1]"[I will] (P. 157) reveal to you my entire glory and I will instruct you concerning all your power and the mystery of your apostleship." [2]Immediately, he revealed to us [. . .] give us [. . .] on the mountain [. . . *3 broken lines* . . .] power [. . .]

P. BEROL. 22220

[4][. . .] on the mountain. [5]We, too, became like spiritual bodies. Our eyes opened in every direction (and) everything was revealed to us. [6]We saw the heavens opening up one after another. [7]Those who guard the gates were disturbed. [8]The angels were afraid and they ran to this side and that, thinking [that] they would all be destroyed. [9]We saw our Savior traversing all the heavens, [his] feet [being fixed with us] on the [mountain], while [his head] pierced [the sev-

Bk. Bart. 18:1   enth] heaven. [10][. . . *8 lines broken* . . .]

(P. 101) [. . .] from all the heavens. [11]Then, this world became like darkness before us, the apostles. [12]We became like those in the immortal aeons, with

P. BEROL. 22220

our [eyes] penetrating [all] the heavens, while the power of our
John 1:14   apostleship was upon us. And we saw our Savior when he reached the seventh heaven [. . . *6 lines broken* . . .]

STRASBOURG COPTE 6 + 7,7 VERSO

(P. 158) [3]our eyes penetrated everywhere (and) we perceived the glory of his divinity and the entire glory of [his] lordship. [4]He clothed us with the power of our apostleship [5][. . .] they became like [. . .] light [. . .]

P. BEROL. 22220

[13]The [heavens] were disturbed,
[14][The] angels and the archangels prostrated on [their faces],
[15][The Cherubs prostrated] before his [. . .],
[16]The Seraphs let down their wings,
[17]The [angels] ‖ that are [outside the veil of the Father sang],
[18]The elders [seated] on their [thrones] cast [down their] crowns before the
Rev 4:10   [throne] of the Father,
[19]All [the saints took a] robe [and] after [they rolled it, the] Son [bowed] to
Rev 6:11   [the feet of his Father] [. . . *6 broken lines* . . .] [20]then why are you crying and grieving so that the entire angelic host is disturbed?" [21]He answered [thus]: [. . . *5 lines broken* . . .] (P. 102)

Agony at the throne of the Father

5 [1]"[. . .] I am greatly [grieved] [. . .] killed [. . .] by the [people of] Israel. [2]O my
Matt 26:39   [Father], if it is [possible], let this [cup] pass me by. [3]Let them [. . .] through another [. . .] if they [. . .] Israel [. . . *7 lines broken* . . .] [4][so that] salvation may come to the entire world."

Matt 26:42; Mark   [5][Then] again, the Son [bowed] to the feet [of] his Father, saying: [6]"[O my]
14:39   Father, [. . . *4 lines broken* . . .] [7]I [want] ‖ to die with joy and to shed my blood for the human race, [8]but I cry only because of my beloved, these being [Abra-

ham], Isaac [and] Jacob, for [they shall] stand [on] the day of Judgment, [while] I shall sit on [my] throne to judge the world. ⁹[They shall] say to me: [. . . *7 lines broken* . . .] ¹⁰[for] the glory that has been given to me on earth. ¹¹O my [Father, if it is possible, let this cup] pass from me."

Matt 25:31–33

Matt 26:39

¹²[The Father said] to him for [the] second [time]: ¹³"[O my son [. . .] (P. 103) [. . . *28 lines broken* . . .]

¹⁴The Son replied for the [third] time: ¹⁵"O [my] Father, if the [. . .] ‖ [. . . *32 lines broken* . . .]

Matt 26:44

Anaphora of the wood of the cross

(P. 104) **6** ¹[. . . *32 lines broken* . . .] ‖ [. . . *29 lines broken* . . .] he completed the service until [he] went to them.

(P. 105) ²[. . .] all [. . .] in the [. . . *24 broken lines* . . .] prophet. ³[The Savior] said to us: "There is no lot that surpasses yours, [nor] glory more exalted ‖ than [yours] [. . . *27 broken lines* . . .]

⁴[The] wood of [. . .]

⁵The wood of [. . .]

⁶The wood of [. . .]

⁷The wood [. . .]

(P. 106) ⁸[The wood of] strength

⁹[The wood of forgiveness] of sins

¹⁰[. . .] the kingdom [. . .] unless [. . .] king [. . . *25 broken lines* . . .] ¹¹shadow [. . .] ¹²O entirety ‖ [. . .] good [. . .] ¹³O [. . . *18 broken lines* . . .] the cross [. . . *6 broken lines* . . .]

The apostles ask Jesus about the form he will take upon his return

7 ¹"[. . .] three [days I shall] take you [to heaven] with me to instruct you about the things that you desire (P. 107) [to] see. ²So [do not be disturbed] when [you] see me."

³We said to him: "Lord, in what form will you appear to us? Or in what kind of body will you come? Tell us." ⁴John spoke up and said: "Lord, when you come to us, do not reveal yourself to us in all your glory but turn your glory into another glory so that we may be able to bear it, lest we see [you] and despair [because of] fear."

1 Cor 15:35–44

Phil 3:21

⁵[The Savior answered]: "I [shall take away] from you [the fear] that you are afraid [of], so that you might see and believe. ⁶But do not touch me until I go ‖ up to [my] Father who [is your] Father, [my God] who is your God, and my Lord who is your Lord. ⁷If someone approaches me, he will [burn]. I am the [fire that] blazes. ⁸The [one who is close] to me [is] close to [the] fire. The one who is far from me is far from life.

John 20:29

John 20:17

Gos. Thom. 10

The first dance of the cross

8 ¹"But now gather to me, O my holy members, dance and [answer] to me." ²The Savior [. . .], he [stood up] (and) [we made a circle surrounding] him.

Acts John 94–95; Dance Sav. 1

1 Cor 6:15; 12:27; Rom 12:4–5

³[He] said to us: "I am [in] your midst [like] a child." He said: "Amen! ⁴A little while I am in your midst." [We] answered: "Amen!"

Mark 9:33–37 par.

(P. 108) ⁵[Those who] want [to set the] world against me are taking counsel

John 7:33 against me because I am stranger to it. ⁶Behold then now, I grieve because of the sins of the world, [but] I rejoice for [you] because you [have fought] well in [the world]. ⁷Know [yourselves] so that you might profit from me and I shall rejoice over your work.

⁸"I am the King, Amen!

⁹I [am] the [Son] of the King, [Amen]!

¹⁰I am the [straight] travelling [road], [Amen!

John 6:35; Matt 26:26;
Dance Sav. 3 ¹¹I am the immortal] bread. Eat and [be satiated], Amen!

¹²I fight [for] you. You, too, make war, Amen!

John 17:18; 20:21 ¹³I am sent. I, myself, want to send you, ‖ Amen!

¹⁴[Why], O men, [. . .] yourself? [. . .] ¹⁵I would like [to bring] you joy in the world, but grieve instead for the world as if you have not entered it, Amen!

¹⁵Do not weep from now on, but rejoice instead, Amen!

John 16:33 ¹⁶I vanquished the world. You, do not let the world vanquish you, Amen!

John 8:36 ¹⁷I became free from the world. You, too, [be] free of [it], Amen!

Mark 15:36 par.; John
19:29–30 ¹⁸[They] shall give [me] [vinegar and gall] to drink, but [you], acquire [for yourself] life and [rest], Amen!

John 19:34 ¹⁹They shall [pierce] me with a lance [in my] side. The one who saw, let him

John 19:35; 21:24 bear witness. And his testimony is true, Amen!

(P. 109) ²⁰[. . . *4 broken lines* . . .] The one who shall [. . .] I shall [. . .] Amen!

²¹The one who has [. . .] me, I, [myself], I shall make him [. . .] with me, Amen!

Mark 14:22–24 par.;
John 6:54–55 ²²The one who does not [receive] my body [and] my blood, this one is a stranger to me, Amen!"

²³When he finished [his dance, we answered] after [him]: "Amen!" [. . . *4 broken lines* . . .]

²⁴"[. . .] to you [. . .], Amen!

²⁵"[. . . *6 broken lines* . . .] Cross, Amen!

²⁶I [shall] approach you, Amen!

²⁷A ‖ dispensation [. . . *3 broken lines* . . .] Cross [. . . *3 broken lines* . . .]

²⁸you are the [. . .] from the beginning [. . .]

P. BEROL. 22220

Cross [. . .], Amen!

²⁹[. . .] those on the right [shall] take shelter [under you], [apart from] those on [the left, O] Cross [. . .] shall destroy [. . . *3 broken lines* . . .]. ³⁰Rise up, [rise], O [Cross. Lift] yourself [up] [and] lift up to the [heaven] [if] this is your wish. ³¹O Cross, do not be afraid. I am rich. I shall fill you with my wealth.

Dance Sav. 1:9; 4:4 ³²[I] shall climb [upon] you, O Cross.

Mark 13:9; Dance Sav.
1:9; 3:4 They shall hang me upon you (P. 110) [as a testimony against them, Amen!

STRASBOURG COPTE 7,2.6.4.3 RECTO

⁶Cross [. . .] [Amen].

⁷These [that] are [on] the right [shall] take [shelter under you, apart] from [those on the left, O Cross] [. . . *few missing lines* . . .] ⁸[O Cross, rise up], O [holy Cross, lift yourself] and [lift] [. . .] to the [sky] [. . . *few missing lines* . . .]

⁹O Cross, [they shall hang me] upon you as a [testimony against them], Amen. [. . .]

P. BEROL. 22220

³³Receive me to yourself], O [Cross, do not reveal my] body, [Amen!] *Dance Sav.* 1:10

³⁴[. . . *3 broken lines* . . .] the generation.

³⁵[Do not] weep, O [Cross], but rejoice instead and know that [your] Lord who is coming [to] you is [gentle] and [humble], Amen!" *Dance Sav.* 1:7–11

The second dance of the cross

9 ¹The second dance of [the cross].

²"[. . .] [I am] not [poor] but [I am rich]. I shall [fill you] with my [wealth]. *Dance Sav.* 1:8; 4:2

³A little longer, O Cross, that which is lacking is perfected and that which is diminished is full.

⁴A little longer, O Cross, the one that has fallen rises.

⁵[A little longer], O Cross, the entire fullness is perfected. ‖

P. BEROL. 22220

⁶[. . . *5 broken lines* . . .] [I see you, I] laugh.

⁷[Many] people [also] looked for you, one [laughing] and rejoicing, another one weeping, [mourning] and smiting.

⁸You are eager for me, O Cross. I, [myself], I shall be eager for you.

⁹[You and me], O [Cross], [we are . . .]. [We are strangers and] [. . . *9 broken lines* . . .]

¹⁰[me and you], O Cross, truly, [the one who is] far from [you] is far [from (P. 111) me] [. . . *unknown number of lines missing* . . .]

STRASBOURG COPTE 7,2.6.4.3

(VERSO) ¹⁰[. . .] also, I [see] you, [I laugh. ¹¹Many] people [also looked for] you, there is one [laughing,] rejoicing, [and another one] [. . .]

¹²[you] and me, [O Cross, we are] [. . .] [we are] strangers [and] [. . .] [. . . *few lines missing* . . .]

¹³[me] and you, [O Cross, truly the one] who is far [from you is far] from [me] [. . .]

10 ¹"[Glory] to you, [tree] whose fruit appeared so that it might be known in the lands of the foreigners and might be glorified because [. . .] (P. 112) [. . .] shame. ²Your names were written on your robes, which are coming down spreading [. . .].

STRASBOURG COPTE 5 + 7,9

(RECTO) ¹⁴"[. . .] [so that] it might be known in [the lands of the] foreigners and they might [glorify] it because of its fruit, because [he] [. . .] a multitude of [. . .], Amen.

STRASBOURG COPTE 5 + 7,9

¹⁵Give me your [force, O] my Father, so that [it] shall endure with me [on the cross], Amen.

¹⁶[I] accepted [for myself the] crown of the Kingdom [from the wood. The] Isa 62:3 diadem [. . .] destroys them [. . .] [in] humiliation, without their having [. . .].

Matt 22:44

[17]I became king from [the wood. O] Father, you shall make [my enemies] submit to me, [Amen. [18]The] enemy shall be [vanquished through] whom? Through the [cross], Amen.

[19]The claw of death [shall be destroyed] through whom? [Through the] Only-Begotten, Amen.

[20]Whose is [the] kingdom? It is [of the Son], Amen.

Dance Sav. 4:10–18

[21]From [where is his Kingdom? It is from the wood, Amen]. [. . .]"

The Savior comforts his disciples

(VERSO) [22][When he] finished the entire [hymn] of the [cross], he turned to us. He told [us]: [23]"The hour has approached when I shall be taken from [you].

Mark 14:41//Matt 26:45; Mark 2:20 par.

[24]The spirit [is eager but] the [flesh is] weak. So [remain] and watch [with me]."

Mark 14:26//Matt 26:41; Mark 14:34// Matt 26:38

[25][And] we, the apostles, [we] cried saying: "But [if] you are [afraid], [you, the Son] of God, what [. . .]?" [26]He answered (and) [told us]: "Do not be afraid [that you shall be] destroyed, but rather [rejoice] greatly. [27][Do not be afraid] of the power of death. [28]Remember all [the things that I told] you: if they perse-

John 15:20

cuted [me, they shall] persecute you. [29]So [you] be glad that I [vanquished the]

John 16:33

world. I [. . .]

UNPLACED P. BEROL. 22220 FRAGMENTS

FRAG. 9 (HAIR SIDE)

(COL. A) [. . .] of wisdom [. . .] [power]. The wood [. . .] entirety [. . .] (COL. B) [. . .] the multitudes, unless the one who shall [. . .] image [. . .]. When he [finished to] sing [. . .] [to the] cross [. . .]

FRAG. 9 (FLESH SIDE)

1 Cor 6:15; 12:27; Rom 12:4–5

(COL. A) [. . .] established it/him among us. He said to us, "O my holy members, [blessed] are you for my Father has [. . .] you [. . .] (COL. B) [. . .] after the [patriarchs] and prophets, [these being] Abraham, [Isaac and Jacob] [. . .]

FRAG. 10 (HAIR SIDE)

(COL. B) [. . .] [Abraham, Isaac,] Jacob [and Moses] the [. . .]

FRAG. 14

(HAIR SIDE) [. . .] the [disciples] [. . .] in that city. [We asked the] Savior: "[What] is this city?" He said to us: "[This] is Jerusalem [. . .] [the] city [. . .] [my] beloved [. . .] (FLESH SIDE) [. . .] no one [. . .] We [asked him saying]: "[What is] this place that [. . .] to heaven [. . .]?" He said: "[This is] the tent [of my] Father from the [beginning], that a [wonder] [. . .]

FRAG. 15 + 17

(HAIR SIDE) [. . .] son(s) [. . .] prophet(s) [. . .] death [. . .] righteous [. . .] them [. . .] (FLESH SIDE) [. . .] while you are [sitting at the] right of [the Father upon] your [throne] [. . .]

FRAG. 19

(HAIR SIDE) [. . .] the book of life. His [generation] will not be remembered, for his wife [will] become widow [and his] sons [will be orphans] [. . .] (FLESH SIDE) [. . .] gives milk, another one gives honey. Rest yourselves [by] the source of [the water] of life [. . .]

FRAG. 20

(HAIR SIDE) [. . .] the Savior. He [. . .] just like he became weak [. . .] he ran away. The Savior said [to him]: "O Judas [. . .] weak [. . .] (FLESH SIDE) [. . .] woman [. . .] faithful [. . .] penitence [. . .]

FRAG. 21

(HAIR SIDE) [. . .] and you give shadow [. . .] to the Adversary, this being [. . .] according [. . .]

FRAG. 22

(FLESH SIDE) [. . .] a proclamation [. . .] proclaim [. . .] in the entire world, or because [. . .]

FRAG. 24

(FLESH SIDE) [. . .] pound of [. . .] pound of [. . .] pound [. . .] pound [. . .]

FRAG. 25

(HAIR SIDE) [. . .] Behold, [they] take counsel [against me] [. . .] kill [. . .] So then [. . .] (HAIR SIDE) [. . .] So [then], O my [. . .] you in a [. . .] and [. . .]

The Discourse of the Savior and the Dance of the Savior
New translations and introduction

by Paul C. Dilley

The Coptic Qasr el-Wizz Codex (Aswan, Nubian Museum, Special Number 168; former-ly Cairo, Coptic Museum inv. 6566) was an instant media sensation upon its discovery in 1965. The *New York Times* declared it one of the "great finds" and "treasures" of the UNESCO salvage excavations conducted before the flooding from the Aswan High Dam.[1] However, four decades passed before the first critical edition appeared in 2006; so its true significance is only now becoming apparent. The manuscript contains two treatises in Coptic: the *Discourse of the Savior on the Mystery of the Cross (Disc. Sav.)* featuring a post-resurrection dialogue between Jesus and the disciples about the nature of the cross; and the *Dance of the Savior (Dance Sav.)*, in which Jesus leads the apostles in a hymn to the cross as they dance around it. Both texts attest to the major significance of cross piety; the second suggests that Christian ritual dancing, already attested in the second-century *Acts of John*, was practiced through the early medieval period. *Dance Sav.* is closely related to the *Gospel of the Savior*, an unprovenanced late-antique Coptic text now in Berlin, as well as the Strasbourg fragments of the same work.[2] *Disc. Sav.* has appeared in scholarship also under the name of the "Stauros-Text" and the "Discourse upon the Cross"; *Dance Sav.* is also known as the "Hymn to the Cross."

Contents
Both texts in the Qasr el-Wizz Codex are set on the Mount of Olives, and both are related to the cross and its veneration. The first, *Disc. Sav.* (fol. 2r–12r), is a dialogue between Jesus and the apostles four days before his ascension. Peter's initial question to the "Savior," a frequent title for Christ in both texts, sets the stage for the entire discourse: "Why will you bring (the cross) with you on the day when you will judge in righteousness, namely the sign of the cross that is honored?" (5). The Savior responds with a series of common stau-rological teachings on the eschatological and soteriological function of the cross, which will accompany Jesus at the Resurrection and, at the Final Judgment, will take root in the Valley of Josaphat (7–8), presumably to serve as a witness, before ascending back to heaven. There is an anti-Jewish section, in which the Savior asserts various wrongs done against him, including placing the crown of thorns on his head (6), an action attributed to Pilate's soldiers in the canonical Gospels (Mark 15:17 par.; John 19:2). At the end, the apostles glorify the Holy Trinity (16).

---

1. Sanka Knox, "Old Coptic MS. Unearthed Near Abu Simbel," *New York Times,* 24 December 1965, 15. Another such object was the temple of Dendur (which also contains a Coptic inscription recording its dedication as a church), moved and reassembled at the Metropolitan Museum of Art in New York.

2. This text has been prepared for this volume by Alin Suciu, under the title *Berlin-Strasbourg Apoc-ryphon.*

Dance Sav. is a modern title for the second text (fol. 12v–17r), which lacks a title in the manuscript. It consists of four hymns that Jesus sings to the cross as he dances around it, while the apostles encircle him, responding "Amen." This scene occurs on the Mount of Olives before the crucifixion (here ascribed to "the lawless Jews," 4:1), and is presumably an expansion of the brief notice in Mark 14:26//Matt 26:30, according to which Jesus and the apostles sing a hymn before going up to the Mount of Olives. The hymn includes various christological exclamations ("I am the immortal bread. Eat and be satisfied," 2:3); exhortations to the cross to fulfill the soteriological mission ("Receive me to you, O Cross," 3:5); and words of praise ("O Cross, which is full of light," 3:2). The text ends abruptly after the fourth hymn, with a brief description, as in *Disc. Sav.*, of the apostles glorifying God. Like the *Disc. Sav.* which it follows, the *Dance Sav.* glorifies the cross and Jesus for their key role in salvation history (4:12).

Manuscripts and Versions

Unlike many manuscripts containing apocryphal literature, the Qasr el-Wizz Codex has a secure archaeological provenance, which helps immensely in understanding how it was used and by whom. It was excavated in a monastery on November 18, 1965 by George Scanlon, a freelance archaeologist working on behalf of the Oriental Institute at the University of Chicago, which was participating in the UNESCO rescue excavations in advance of the Aswan High Dam's flooding of the region, which became Lake Nasser. Qasr el-Wizz is about a half-hour walk north from Faras (Pachoras), the capital of the medieval Christian Kingdom of Nobadia in modern Sudan. In his preliminary report on the excavations, Scanlon states that the manuscript was discovered "complete in seventeen folios, but with the cover missing, found on the floor of cell E at the NW. corner below the platform."[3] Cell II-E was part of a "cell-bloc" on the ground floor, a standardized living area with "a small, raised platform which went round the cell . . . and which was used for sitting and for sleeping pallets; and a series of arched niches in the walls, which were used for lamps, books, utensils, and clothing, and which are generally referred to in the archaeological sources as 'cupboards."[4] In addition to four wall niches, cell E had one floor-level niche, which would have been used for storing objects such as clothing, lamps, or books. Artur Obluski, who is publishing the results of the Oriental Institute's campaigns at Qasr el-Wizz, suggests, based on the detailed documentation in the excavation's notes, that the book was discovered in the fill of a floor-level niche.[5]

The Qasr el-Wizz manuscript is a complete parchment codex with 17 leaves, or 34 pages, with 31 containing Coptic text, and two depictions of the cross at the beginning and end. At 10 cm in width and 16.7 cm in height, it can be considered a large example of the miniature codex format.[6] The size of the codex indicates it was made for personal use, whether in a monastic or a church setting. The manuscript is not dated but the script

---

3. Scanlon, "Excavations at Qasr el-Wizz," 18. For a picture of the "Platform in cell II-E from above," see Plate IX.1.

4. Scanlon, "Excavations at Qasr el-Wizz," 16–17. For a plan of the church and monastery, see p. 8, Figure 1.

5. In the object card (Reg. No. 65-11-106) at the University of Chicago's Oriental Institute, it is recorded that the manuscript was discovered on 18 November 1965; under "Area" is the following note: "II-E Fill Towards N.W. Corner Flooring."

6. For an extensive codicological and paleographical analysis, including a discussion of the varied, almost whimsical miniatures, see Hubai, *Koptische Apokryphen aus Nubien*, 22–47.

provides some clues about its origins. The same scribe wrote both works in the codex, in a large hand (only 12 or 13 lines per page), tentatively assigned by Alin Suciu to "around the year 1000 CE," based on a comparison with dated manuscripts from the monastery of Mercurius in Edfu, southern Egypt.[7]

A critical edition and translation of both texts was prepared by Péter Hubai and published in Hungarian in 2006, which was made more widely available by Angelika Balog's 2009 German translation.[8] The texts have appeared in English in an unpublished translation by George Hughes made shortly after the discovery and now held among Hughes's work at the Oriental Institute in Chicago, and alongside a new edition of the codex by Alexandros Tsakos, Christian Bull, Lloyd Abercrombie, and Einar Thomassen.[9] *Dance Sav.* alone was translated by Pierluigi Piovanelli in a 2012 article,[10] and by Alin Suciu in his 2013 dissertation.[11]

There is also an Old Nubian version of the *Disc. Sav.*, in a manuscript (Staatsbibliothek zu Berlin–Preussischer Kulturbesitz, Orientabteilung, Ms. orient. quart. 1020, fol. 1–18) found in nearby Serra East, a Christian settlement in a Pharaonic-era fort, and purchased by the German scholar Carl Schmidt on the Cairo antiquities market in 1906. In this manuscript, first edited by F. L. Griffith in 1913,[12] *Disc. Sav.* is followed not by *Dance Sav.* but by a similar set of addresses to the cross taken from Ps.-Chrysostom's Greek homily *In venerabilem crucem,* the full version of which was found in another Old Nubian manuscript at Serra East during the 1963–1964 excavations of the University of Chicago. Like the Qasr el-Wizz Codex, the Old Nubian manuscript is also a "handbook," measuring approximately 12 cm in height and 18.1 cm in length. Although the manuscript is without archaeological context, the scribal colophon notes that its donors had it placed in the Jesus Church of Serra East.[13]

The Qasr el-Wizz and Serra East manuscripts reflect the complex linguistic situation of the Christian kingdoms of medieval Nubia. Old Nubian was spoken by most inhabitants of Nobadia, Makuria, and Alodia; a relatively small corpus of texts, mostly biblical, apocryphal, and homiletic, have been recovered in southern Egypt and Nubia since the late nineteenth century. Greek was still used in the liturgy, as was Coptic, the language of many monks who had arrived from southern Egypt.[14] While both *Disc. Sav.* and *Dance Sav.* are developments of literary traditions originating ultimately in Greek texts (see below), in their current form they are best understood as Coptic compositions; the *Disc.*

---

7. Suciu, "Apocryphon Berolinense/Argentoratense," 32. Note, however, the ninth-century date proposed in Hubai, *Koptische Apokryphen aus Nubien,* 36.

8. Hubai, *Koptische Apokryphen aus Nubien.*

9. Tsakos et al., "*Miscellanea Epigraphica Nubica IV.*"

10. Piovanelli, "Thursday Night Fever," 240–41.

11. Suciu, "Apocryphon Berolinense/Argentoratense," 170–71.

12. Griffith, *Nubian Texts,* 41–53; reedited by Browne, "Griffith's Stauros Text."

13. Gerald M. Browne, *Chrysostomus Nubianus: An Old Nubian Version of Ps. Chrysostom, In venerabilem crucem sermo* (Papyrologica Castroctaviana 10; Rome and Barcelona: Papyrologica Castroctaviana, 1984), 97–98.

14. A trilingual inscription (Greek and Old Nubian, with a signature in Coptic) of Dan 3:57–81 in the church baptistry at Qasr el-Wizz demonstrates the complex linguistic environment in the northern Nubian kingdom of Makuria: see John Barns, "A Text of the 'Benedicite' in Greek and Old Nubian from Kaṣr el-Wizz," *JEA* 60 (1974): 206–11. For more on monasticism in Makuria, see Włodzimierz Godlewski, "Monastic Life in Makuria," in *Christianity and Monasticism in Aswan and Nubia* (ed. Gawdat Gabra and Hany Takla; Cairo: American University in Cairo Press, 2013), 157–74.

Sav., at least, was later translated from Coptic into Old Nubian. The inclusion of both texts in the same codex with no explicit demarcation between them, no doubt because of similarities in content, shows how malleable was the structure of these noncanonical compositions.

Genre, Structure, and Prosody

Disc. Sav. and *Dance Sav.* were placed together by the scribe of the Qasr el-Wizz Codex because they both contain exchanges between Jesus and the apostles about the cross. *Disc. Sav.* is a brief post-resurrection revelation dialogue between Jesus and the apostles, a literary form that was widely used in early Christian literature from the beginning of the second century.[15] Peter is the only speaker throughout, although the Savior also addresses the apostles as a group. After a preface setting the scene on the Mount of Olives, the Savior discusses several "mysteries" about the cross, ending with an apostolic commission. The concluding doxology and prayer for mercy situate these topics in the context of worship: "may we find mercy and grace on the day when he will judge in righteousness, now and in every time, forever and ever, amen." Indeed, the Savior notes that anyone copying a book praising the cross will be rewarded at the Last Judgment (7), and the "handbook" size of the Qasr el-Wizz Codex suggests that it was commissioned and read by worshippers.

This liturgical connection is shared with *Dance Sav.*, which contains a four-part hymn to the cross delivered by Jesus (again called "the Savior"), as the apostles form a moving circle around him on the Mount of Olives. Jesus addresses the cross by various titles ("O Cross which is full of light," 3:2), commands it ("receive me to you, O Cross," 3:5), and at the same time reveals aspects of his own identity in phrases that recall the Johannine gospels ("I am rich, amen. I will climb up on you, O Cross," 1:8–9). At one point, Jesus explicitly mentions that he is dancing ("I will dance for the Cross the third time," 3:1). The subsequent, final section is called the "fourth dance of the cross." The text is probably adapted from a liturgical hymn to the cross, with Jesus featured as the primary speaker, followed by a series of "amen" responses from the audience, represented by the apostles. Similar glorifications of the cross are found throughout the late-antique Mediterranean world. In Italy, for example, Paulinus of Nola's *Carmina* 19, a poetic work likely designed for the liturgy, contains a similar series of epithets for, and addresses to, the cross. Such addresses are also found in homilies, which might have been accompanied by periodic acclamations of "amen" from the audience—for example, they are embedded in the Pseudo-Athanasian Easter sermon, *De passione domini* (PG 28:1056B). Pseudo-Chrysostom's *In venerabilem crucem,* which accompanies *Disc. Sav.* in the Old Nubian manuscript from Serra East, is less a homily than a series of addresses to the cross.[16]

Literary Context

Immediately after the discovery of the Qasr el-Wizz Codex, an article in *Time Magazine* likened the texts within it to "apocryphal gospels composed by the Gnostics."[17] However, despite similarities in literary form to second-century texts such as the *Sophia of Jesus*

---

15. For a good overview, see, e.g., Pheme Perkins, *The Gnostic Dialogue: The Early Church and the Crisis of Gnosticism* (New York: Paulist, 1980).

16. The homily was already attributed to John Chrysostom by the early fifth century, and was known by Augustine (Suciu, "Apocryphon Berolinense/Argentoratense," 64–65, with notes).

17. "New Words of Jesus?" *Time Magazine* 87, no. 1 (7 January 1966): 32. See also Emmel, "Preliminary Reedition," 22–24 for a summary of the discovery of the codex.

Christ and the *Apocryphon of James* (sometimes described as "gnostic"), *Dance Sav.* and *Disc. Sav.* were composed several centuries later. As such, they are developments of older apocryphal traditions, and, as I will argue, were sometimes deliberately positioned in opposition to certain themes that had been deemed heretical, including secret revelations.

Like other late-antique apocryphal texts, *Dance Sav.* and *Disc. Sav.* were frequently copied and redacted. Indeed, Alin Suciu has argued that *Dance Sav.* is a slightly abbreviated excerpt from a larger work, the *Berlin-Strasbourg Apocryphon,* of which substantial fragments have been published under the modern name the *Gospel of the Savior.*[18] He situates this text within a group of late-antique Coptic apocryphal texts usually attributed to famous bishops, who are said to have discovered memoirs of the apostles detailing their dialogues with Jesus; these dialogues are then embedded in the bishop's homily.[19] While the Qasr el-Wizz Codex does not contain this homiletic framework, Suciu notes certain characteristics that *B-S Ap.* shares with these "apostolic books," especially the phrase "O my holy members" to refer to the apostles, a term also used by monks in late-antique Egypt.[20]

In his largely synchronic study, Suciu argues that the purpose of the "apostolic memoirs" genre was to provide legitimacy for Egyptian liturgical usage (including feasts) through appeal to Christ's teachings. But diachronic analysis is also important, especially given earlier developments in late-antique apocryphal literature. Athanasius of Alexandria, one of the most significant of all Egyptian saints, ordered the use of a fixed canon of twenty-seven books for authoritative teaching from the apostolic era in his famous *Festal Letter* 39 of 367 CE. Were the apostolic memoirs, then, in violation of his proclamation?

The frequent assertion in Coptic homilies of discovering a book at the apostolic library in Jerusalem is best understood as an apologetic response to the canon established by Athanasius. Indeed, this *topos* of discovery is related to an earlier development of the fourth and fifth centuries: apocryphal texts, such as the Abgar Correspondence and the *Apocalypse of Paul,* came to be employed by bishops, and even legitimated by emperors.[21] This was justified by what I have called the "invention of Christian tradition": apocrypha were presented as newly discovered apostolic autographs that either had languished in archives or were buried with other relics. Just as the discovery of martyrs' relics was gradually accepted, so too was the invention of Christian tradition for use in the liturgy. The *topos* of secret oral transmission, found in many writings deemed heretical by late-antique orthodoxy, was thus effectively contrasted with the claim to have official documents written in the apostles' own hands, which (like many relics) were discovered or authenticated by a famous bishop.

While the texts from the Qasr el-Wizz Codex are not presented as "apostolic mem-

---

18. See Alin Suciu's entry on *B-S Ap.* in this volume; Piovanelli 2012 also stresses this literary relationship. Suciu offers a synoptic table of the related texts in "Apocryphon Berolinense/Argentoratense," 45–47. For an argument against the theory that *Disc. Sav.* was a part of the *Gospel of the Savior* (Emmel, "Preliminary Reedition," 27–28), see "Apocryphon Berolinense/Argentoratense," 63–64. The name "Gospel of the Savior" was assigned to the text in the *editio princeps* published by Hedrick and Mirecki *(Gospel of the Savior)*.

19. See also the entries on the *Encomium on John the Baptist* and the *Investiture of Abbaton* in this volume. Hagen ("Ein anderer Context") independently reached a similar conclusion; he describes the genre of Coptic apocrypha embedded in homilies as "diaries of the apostles."

20. Another key formal similarity is the location of the revelation dialogue between the risen Jesus and his disciples on the Mount of Olives.

21. For the following, see Dilley, "Invention of Christian Tradition."

oirs," their orthodoxy is asserted in other ways, despite important similarities to earlier noncanonical works with "heretical" tendencies. For example, the Bruce Codex and the Askew Codex, both textual miscellanies, also contain revelation dialogues between the resurrected Jesus and the disciples; in *Pistis Sophia,* the dramatic setting is on the Mount of Olives, just as in *Disc. Sav.* and *Dance Sav.* There are more specific connections: in both *Pist. Soph.* 358 and the *Books of Jeu* (2 *Bk. Jeu* 66), the apostles gather in a circle around Jesus as he prays, just as in *Dance Sav.*; and various hymns are interspersed throughout the manuscripts, either as free-standing compositions (after 1 *Bk. Jeu* 32 and 2 *Bk. Jeu* 52), or as amen-responsories featuring the apostles (1 *Bk. Jeu* 41). Yet the Qasr el-Wizz Codex reverses one major convention of these "gnostic" texts: while the mysteries that Jesus reveals in the Bruce and Askew codices are secret, in *Disc. Sav.* he urges the apostles to proclaim the mystery of the cross to the entire world.[22] Similarly, Jesus assures Peter that he has not given other disciples a privileged, esoteric revelation: "I have never hidden from you a single word which you have asked me about, have I? Nor will I hide it from you" (4). Finally, there are significant differences in content: the Bruce and Askew codices contain esoteric information about cosmology and the ascent of the soul, in contrast to the eschatological imagery of the cross with Jesus at the Last Judgment in the Qasr el-Wizz Codex.[23]

A similar pattern of selective appropriation is found with respect to the second-century apocryphal acts of the apostles. In *Acts Pet.* 38, for example, the "hidden mystery" of the cross is a sign for the repentance of humanity, an association with clear affinities to the theological concerns of *Disc. Sav.* The literary structure of *Dance Sav.* also resembles the famous passage in the second-century *Acts of John,* in which Jesus hymns the cross as he dances with the apostles, who respond "amen" as he exhorts them not to reveal his mysteries (*Acts John* 94–95).[24] Yet there is almost no overlap in content with the earlier hymn, which famously includes invocations of the Ogdoad and the Twelve. *Dance Sav.* should also be seen in the context of various other literary allusions to the *Christus Saltans* in early Christian literature, not all of them esoteric. Many of these citations employ the Platonic image of the cosmic dance as a symbol of divine order. Already at the beginning of the second century, Ignatius of Antioch described the dance of the stars around Christ's star at his birth (*Eph.* 19.2). Clement of Alexandria, in his *Protrepticus,* an exhortation for polytheists to become Christians, moves the scene from the firmament to the heavenly court, in an extended comparison with Dionysian mysteries: "You will dance with the angels around the unbegotten and indestructible, one and only true God, while the Logos of God sings the hymn with us" (*Protr.* 12).[25] Here, the singing Logos replaces *Acts John*'s earthly Christ, and it is the angels who dance, not the apostles. Gregory of Nazianzus also

---

22. Other "apostolic memoirs," such as the *Mysteries of John the Apostle and the Holy Virgin,* copied at the monastery of Saint Mercurius in Edfu (southern Egypt), similarly emphasize that the apostles will preach their new teachings throughout the world: see Ernest A. W. Budge, *Coptic Apocrypha in the Dialect of Upper Egypt* (London: British Museum, 1913), 74. Another popular apocryphal text, the *Epistula Apostolorum,* was probably an attempt to provide "orthodox" content for the gnostic revelation dialogue, as argued in Manfred Hornschuh, *Studien zur Epistula Apostolorum* (PTS 5; Berlin: De Gruyter, 1965).

23. Despite these differences, it is interesting to note that the Bruce codex, like the Qasr el-Wizz manuscript, has a large image of the cross on its flyleaf (though the former is in the form of an ankh).

24. Much ink has been spilled on the dance scene in *Acts John;* for an extended commentary on the hymn, see Eric Junod and Jean-Daniel Kaestli, eds., *Acta Iohannis,* vol. 1: *Praefatio - Textus;* vol. 2: *Textus alii - Commentarius - Indices* (CCSA 1–2; Turnhout: Brepols, 1983), 2: 621–27 and 642–55.

25. Otto Stählin and Ursula Treu, eds., *Clemens Alexandrinus,* vol. 1: *Protrepticus und Paedagogus* (GCS 12; Berlin: Akademie-Verlag, 1972), 84 lin. 28–29.

employs this image in his *Theological Orations,* declaring that "Angels and Archangels," along with other heavenly powers, dance around the "first cause" (*Or.* 28.31).[26] Pseudo-Hippolytus, in his homily *De Pascha,* might be alluding to either the earthly or the heavenly dance in this address to Christ: "O Crucified One, leader of the mystical dances!" (*De Pascha Homilia* 6; PG 59, 744). Like *Dance Sav.,* which was read by monks many centuries later at Qasr el-Wizz, this work attributed to Hippolytus was "orthodox" and associated with the public liturgy, in this case Easter.

Date and Provenance

It is difficult to identify precisely the date and place of composition of either *Disc. Sav.* or *Dance Sav.* Both texts are preserved in a medieval Coptic manuscript from Nubia (with another version of the former in an unprovenanced Old Nubian manuscript), with no earlier attestations. At the same time, *Dance Sav.* is part of a long tradition of Jesus and the apostles dancing and hymning to the cross, first attested in the *Acts of John,* a text usually dated to the second century. No features of either text clearly point to a specific geographical provenance. Indeed, the *topos* of the dance of Christ and his apostles, with accompanying hymn, was known beyond Egypt and Nubia: an epistolary exchange between Augustine and Ceretius (*Ep.* 237) demonstrates that a Latin version was read in early-fifth-century Gaul.

The developing scholarly consensus is that the texts in the Qasr el-Wizz Codex must be understood in the context of late antiquity. Hubai, for example, dates the text to the end of the fourth century, citing such evidence as a short-lived Trinitarian phrase in the doxology of *Disc. Sav.* ("Father who is in the Son, Son who is in the Father, with the Holy Spirit," v. 10), which is otherwise only attested by Amphilochius of Iconium and Epiphanius of Salamis.[27] While this feature is certainly noteworthy, highlighting it has the effect of situating *Dance Sav.* primarily in relation to the discourse of orthodoxy and the development of normative theology. Hubai's brief foray into the role of dance is more promising, but here too he stays within the terms of early Christian polemics, appealing to patristic criticism of dance, which he argues intensified during the fourth century.[28]

This approach obscures *Dance Sav.*'s affinities with two major aspects of post-Constantinian Christianity—namely, public worship and imperial symbolism, for which the figure of the dancing Christ could serve as a legitimating example.[29] The martyr cult in particular seems to have involved dancing as part of the all-night revelry, with both lay and monastic participants in evidence. Similarly, the imperial *adventus* ceremony, in which a visiting or returning emperor was welcomed by the community, often included dance. David's celebration before the ark remained a powerful model for emperors: Heraclius (r. 610–641) is said to have danced in front of the True Cross when it was returned, after its capture by the Persians, to Jerusalem in 628 CE. More generally, the focus on cross piety in the Qasr el-Wizz Codex is especially understandable in light of the discovery of the cross in the reign of Constantine, a key moment in the development of Christian pil-

---

26. Paul Gallay and Maurice Jourjon, eds., *Gregory Nazianzen: Discourse 27–31* (SC 250; Paris: Cerf, 1978), 172 lin. 16–20.

27. Hubai, *Koptische Apokryphen aus Nubien,* 112.

28. Hubai, *Koptische Apokryphen aus Nubien,* 113. Hubai also sensibly notes that the emphasis on the cross suggests a date after Constantine, and in particular, the legend of the discovery of the True Cross by Helena (111).

29. For the following, see Dilley, "*Christus Saltans.*"

grimage, the cult of relics, and even the liturgy. Indeed, the Qasr el-Wizz texts were likely read at Easter, and/or one of the major festivals of the cross in the late antique period (The Exaltation and Adoration of the Cross), commemorating Helena's discovery of the cross or its return by Heraclius.

There is substantial evidence for such festivals in honor of the cross in late-antique monasticism: for example, at the monastery of Apa Jeremias at Saqqara (near the Old Kingdom pyramids), an inscription listing feast days includes the commemoration of the cross, the celebratory nature of which is underscored by its allotment of wine.[30] And the numerous paintings of the cross in the monks' cells, often with accompanying inscriptions, attest to its popularity as an object of personal piety.[31] One of these inscriptions is the invocation *staure boēthison:* "cross, help (us)," the same personification and address of the cross as found in *Dance Sav.*[32] The Qasr el-Wizz Codex itself was found in a Nubian monastery. However, liturgies of the cross were equally at home in non-monastic churches; the Old Nubian version of the *Disc. Sav.*, after all, was deposited by its donors in the church of Serra East.

Translations

The following translations are based on Hubai's *editio princeps* of the Qasr el-Wizz Codex for the Coptic text of *Disc. Sav.* and *Dance Sav.*, with a few minor emendations, also proposed by Tsakos, Bull, Abercrombie, and Thomassen. I have consulted their new edition and translation, as well as the earlier translations of Hughes *(Disc. Sav.* and *Dance Sav.)*, Piovanelli *(Dance Sav.)*, and Suciu *(Dance Sav.)*. The variant readings from the Old Nubian (Old Nub.) version of *Disc. Sav.* are placed in the notes, following the text of Griffith and the corrections of Browne, both of whose English translations I have consulted; I cite page number in Browne when following his construal of longer sentences. Key biblical allusions and citations (which can be difficult to distinguish) largely follow Hubai's list.[33] There is no versification schema in previous editions and translations of the Qasr el-Wizz texts, so I have introduced basic chapter divisions.

Bibliography

EDITIONS AND TRANSLATIONS

Browne, Gerald M. "Griffith's Stauros Text." *SPap* 22 (1983): 75–119.

Griffith, Francis L. *The Nubian Texts of the Christian Period*. Abhandlungen der Königlich Preussischen Akademie der Wissenschaften Philosophisch-historische Klasse 1913,8; Berlin: Reimer, 1913. *(Editio princeps* of the Old Nubian version of *Disc. Sav.)*

Hubai, Péter. *Koptische Apokryphen aus Nubien. Der Qasr el-Wizz Kodex*. TUGAL 163. Berlin/New York: Walter de Gruyter, 2009. Translation by Angelika Balog of *A Megváltó a keresztről: Kopt apokrifek Núbiából (A Kasr El-Wizz kódex)*. Cahiers Patristiques, Textes Coptes. Budapest: Szent István Társulat, 2006. *(Editio princeps* of the Qasr el-Wizz texts.)

---

30. James E. Quibbel, *Excavations at Saqqara (1908–1909, 1909–1910)* (Cairo: IFAO, 1912), inscr. 226, 69–71.

31. For an overview, see Paul van Moorsel, "The Worship of the Holy Cross in Saqqara: Archaeological Evidence," in *Theologia Crucis—Signum Crucis: Festschrift für Erich Dinkler zum 70. Geburtstag* (ed. Carl Andresen and Günter Klein; Tübingen: Mohr Siebeck, 1979), 409–15.

32. Quibbel, *Excavations at Saqqara*, 108, pl. 38,3.

33. Hubai, *Koptische Apokryphen aus Nubien*, 85–87.

Tsakos, Alexandros, Christian Bull, Lloyd Abercrombie, and Einar Thomassen. "*Miscellanea Epigraphica Nubica IV*: A New Edition of the Wizz Codex with an English Translation." *Collectanea Christiana Orientalia* 10 (2013): 193–209.

STUDIES

Dilley, Paul C. "*Christus Saltans* as Dionysos and David: The *Dance of the Savior* in its Late-Antique Cultural Context." *Apocrypha* 24 (2013): 237–53.

———. "The Invention of Christian Tradition: Apocrypha, Imperial Policy, and Anti-Jewish Propaganda." *GRBS* 50.4 (2010): 586–614.

Emmel, Stephen. "Preliminary Reedition and Translation of the Gospel of the Savior: New Light on the Strasbourg Coptic Gospel and the Stauros-Text from Nubia." *Apocrypha* 14 (2003): 9–53.

Hagen, Joost L. "Ein anderer Context für die Berliner und Straßburger 'Evangelienfragmente'. Das 'Evangelium des Erlösers' und andere 'Apostelevangelien' in der koptischen Literatur." Pages 339–71 in *Jesus in apokryphen Evangelienüberlieferungen. Beiträge zu außerkanonischen Jesusüberlieferungen aus verschiedenen Sprach- und Kulturtraditionen*. Edited by Jörg Frey and Jens Schröter. WUNT 254. Tübingen: Mohr Siebeck, 2010.

Hedrick, Charles W., and Paul A. Mirecki. *Gospel of the Savior: A New Ancient Gospel*. California Classical Library. Santa Rosa, Calif.: Polebridge, 1999.

Heid, Stefan. *Kreuz, Jerusalem, Kosmos: Aspekte frühkristlicher Staurologie*. Münster: Aschendorff, 2001.

Hughes, George R. "A Coptic Liturgical Book from Qasr el-Wizz in Nubia," in *The Oriental Institute Report for 1965/66* (Chicago: Oriental Institute, 1966), 10–13.

Piovanelli, Pierluigi. "Thursday Night Fever: Dancing and Singing with Jesus in the Gospel of the Savior and the Dance of the Savior Around the Cross." *Early Christianity* 3 (2012): 229–48.

Scanlon, George T. "Excavations at Qasr el-Wizz: A Preliminary Report. II." *JEA* 58 (1972): 7–42.

Suciu, Alin. "Apocryphon Berolinense/Argentoratense (Previously Known as the Gospel of the Savior). Edition of P. Berol. 22220, Strasbourg Copte 5–7 and Qasr el-Wizz Codex ff. 12v–17r with Introduction and Commentary." PhD diss., Université Laval, 2013.

The Discourse of the Savior on the Mystery of the Cross

[1]A discourse, which our Savior and our Lord Jesus Christ spoke to his glorious apostles, before he was taken up, concerning the power and the frank speech and the way of life of the glorious, life-giving cross. In the peace of God.[a]

Acts 1:2

Jesus gathers the apostles on the Mount of Olives

[2]My beloved, it happened one day, while our Savior was walking on the Mount of Olives, four days before he was taken up in the heavens, while his apostles gathered with him.[b] He spoke to them the incomprehensible mysteries,[c] those that are in heaven, and those that are on earth; and the way he will judge the living and the dead; and the resurrection of the dead.

Rom 12:19
Acts 1:2

Peter asks about the mystery of the cross

[3]Peter answered and said to him, "Our Lord and Our God, and the Savior of the souls, and of everyone who hopes in you, and the healing of souls which have been wounded in sin: You have revealed to us all the mysteries, and also now, may you reveal to us the mystery which we will ask you!"

John 20:28

[4]The Savior answered and said, "O my chosen, Peter, and you, my fellow inheritors,[d] I have never hidden from you a single word which you have asked me about, have I? Nor will I hide it from you. But may you (pl.) ask me everything that you have wanted to understand. I will reveal it you."

Matt 14:28
Rom 8:7; Heb 11:9

[5]Peter answered and said, "Our Lord, and Our God, and Our Savior,[e] we want you to tell us the mystery of the cross—why will you bring it with you on the day when you will judge in righteousness, namely the sign of the cross that is honored?—so that we will hear from you concerning it, and preach it in the whole world."

John 20:28

Acts 17:31

---

a. Old Nub.: "A discourse of our Savior and Lord Jesus Christ, which he spoke concerning his passion and his future coming in glory and the glorious, life-giving cross, and which he caused the apostles to know, when he was going to ascend to the heavens. Let the peace of God, our Savior, and his life-giving cross be with all of us. Amen, amen" (Browne, "Griffith's Stauros Text," 82).

b. Old Nub.: "forty days."

c. Old Nub.: "us."

d. Old Nub.: "heirs and my servants."

e. Old Nub.: "Our Lord and our God."

Jesus recounts the crucifixion

Matt 28:10; John 20:17

Mark 15:29 par.

Matt 26:67; Luke 22:63

Mark 15:17–19; Matt 27:29–20; John 19:2

[6]The Savior answered and said, "O my chosen, Peter, and you, my brothers, you know everything which the law-breaking Jews did to me, and the blasphemies that they spoke to me on the cross. They spit on me, they hit me, they placed the crown of thorns on me; and the words of rebuke that they spoke to me. On account of this I will bring the cross with me so that I might reveal their shame; and I will place their lawlessness upon their head.

Rewards for standing under the cross

[7]But now, listen to me further; I will tell you another great honor of the cross. When I sit on my throne of glory, so that I might judge the whole world, the

Joel 4[3]:2, 12

cross will stand at my right in the valley of Josaphat.[a] While, on the one hand, its roots are under the earth; on the other, its branches will shoot up again, as at first. But its branches have hidden it on the earth, three parts of the earth.[b] Everyone who has believed in the cross with their whole heart will go and stand under the shadow of the cross, whether he has fed the hungry, caused the thirsty

Matt 25:35–38

to drink, or clothed the naked; and all the more to those who have written books of praise of the cross[c]—until I finish judging the whole world.

[8]After I judge the entirety of the just and the sinners, again the cross <will rise and go up> to the heavens.[d] Everyone who believed in it will <return?> with it,

Matt 19:23; 19:29

going into the kingdom of the heavens. They will inherit eternal life.[e] I will not judge anyone among them, whether through a word or through a deed. But they will live through the power of the cross.

Jesus commissions the apostles

1 Cor 6:15; 12:27; Rom 12:4–5

Matt 28:19

[9]But now, O my holy members, go and proclaim to the whole world, so that they will follow the cross, so that they will possess this great glory on the day which is under that fear.

John 14:13

Heb 4:16

Acts 17:31

[10]After we listened to these things, we, the apostles, answered the Savior, saying to him, "Glory to you, Father who is in the Son, Son who is in the Father, with the Holy Spirit. Forever and ever. Amen. You have always given those who have loved you glory. May it happen to us that we find mercy and grace on the day he will judge in righteousness, now and always, forever and ever, amen."

---

a. Likely intending "Jehoshaphat" as in Joel.

b. The Coptic text here is probably corrupt; Old Nub.: "Its roots will irrigate the earth, and its branches will overshadow the third part of the earth" (Browne, "Griffith's Stauros Text," 87).

c. Old Nub.: "If he fed the hungry in his name or clothed the naked or wrote a book of praise and gave it to the church, believing in it, as is appropriate, with his whole heart, when he comes to those who have followed it, he will rest under the shadow of the Cross, until I cease judging the world" (Browne, "Griffith's Stauros Text," 87–88).

d. The Coptic verbs are in the perfect tense, which is inexplicable in the narrative context, so I have emended the text.

e. Old Nub.: "paradise of joy."

The Dance of the Savior

Jesus gathers the apostles on the Mount of Olives

1 ¹It happened one day that the Savior was sitting on the Mount of Olives, before the law-breaking Jews had crucified him.[a] We all gathered with him. ²He answered,[b] saying, "O my holy members, gather to me and I will hymn the cross; and you answer me." And we made a crown, and we circled around him.

Mark 14:26; Matt 26:30

1 Cor 6:15; 12:27; Rom 12:4–5; *B-S Ap.* 8:1–2

The first hymn of the cross

³He said to us,

"I am in your midst like these little children." He said "Amen."[c]
⁴"A little while I am with you in your midst.
⁵They are taking counsel concerning me now.
⁶Do not keep me back, O Cross.
⁷Get up, get up, O Holy Cross, and lift me, O Cross.
⁸I am rich, amen.
⁹I will climb up on you, O Cross. I will be called to you, as a witness for them.
¹⁰Receive me, O Cross.
¹¹Do not weep, O Cross, but all the more, rejoice."
¹²After he completed the hymn, we all answered him, saying, "Amen."

Acts John 94–95

Mark 9:33–37 par.

John 7:33

B-S Ap. 8:3–5

B-S Ap. 8:5

Mark 13:9

B-S Ap. 8:30–35

The second hymn of the cross

2 ¹The second hymn of the cross:[d]
²"I am the honored way of life
³I am the immortal bread. Eat and be satiated."
⁴We answered after him, "Amen."

John 14:6

Matt 26:26; John 6:35; *B-S Ap.* 8:11

---

a. According to the two Gospel accounts, the disciples and Jesus go to the Mount of Olives after singing a hymn.

b. The lack of a question is a sign of redaction, already at the beginning of the text.

c. This is the beginning of the unmarked first hymn. Jesus himself declares "Amen" in this introductory line, whereas later it is the apostles who answer "Amen"; in many cases, the speaker is unspecified.

d. The use of titles in *Dance Sav.* is inconsistent, further highlighting the text's heavily redacted nature. Although this section is described as a hymn, another section similar in form is called the "Fourth Dance," suggesting that the entire scene with Jesus and the encircling apostles was choreographed.

The third hymn of the cross

1 Cor 6:15; 12:27; Rom 12:4–5

3 [1]He said to us again, "Gather to me, O my holy members, and I will dance for the cross the third time; and answer after me, 'Amen.'"[a]

[2]"O Cross, which is full of light. Again also it will carry the light."—"Amen."

[3]"I will give my light to you, O Cross.

Mark 13:9

[4]I will climb upon you as a testimony to them.

B-S Ap. 8:32–33

[5]Receive me to you, O Cross. Do not reveal my body."—"Amen."

The fourth hymn of the cross

4 [1]The fourth dance of the cross:

[2]"I am not poor, O light-giving Cross."—"Amen."

B-S Ap. 8:31; 9:2

[3]"I will fill you with my richness."—"Amen."

[4]"I will climb up upon you.

B-S Ap. 8:32–33

[5]Receive me to you, O Cross.

Matt 26:39

[6]Glory to you because you have listened to your father."—"Amen."

[7]"Glory to you, the entire sweetness."—"Amen."

[8]"Glory to the divinity."—"Amen."

[9]"Open your grace, O my Father, so that I might hymn the Cross."—"Amen."

Isa 62:3

[10]"I received for myself the crown of the kingdom in wood."—"Amen."

Matt 22:44

[11]"I will cause my enemies to be subordinated to me."—"Amen."

[12]"The enemy will be destroyed through the Cross."—"Amen."

1 Cor 15:55–56; John 3:16, 18

[13]"The sting of death will be destroyed through the only-begotten son."—"Amen."

[14]"To whom does the kingdom belong?"—"Amen."

[15]"It belongs to the son."—"Amen."

B-S Ap. (Stras.) 16–21

[16]"Where is the kingdom from? It is from the wood."—"Amen."

[17]"Who is it who has sent him to the Cross? It is the Father."—"Amen."

[18]"What is the Cross? Where is it from? It is from the Spirit."—"Amen."

Matt 25:30

[19]"It is forever, from all time, from the foundation of the world."—"Amen."

[20]"I am the Alpha."—"Amen."

Rev 21:6

[21]"And the Omega. The beginning and the end."—"Amen."

[22]"I am the unutterable beginning, and the unutterable end."—"Amen."

Matt 9:8

[23]After we listened to these things, we glorified the Father, to whom is the glory, forever and ever. Amen.

---

a. This is presumably the beginning of the unmarked "third hymn."

An Encomium on Mary Magdalene
A new translation and introduction

by Christine Luckritz Marquis

The *Encomium on Mary Magdalene* (*Encom. Mary; CANT* 73; *CPC* 0118) is a homily attributed to Cyril, bishop of Jerusalem (ca. 350–386) and theologian, though its author is more properly referred to as Pseudo-Cyril. The text is fragmentary, portraying Mary Magdalene's life and a revelation received from the archangel Gabriel. The text is valuable as a rare witness to Christian attempts to explicate more fully Mary Magdalene's life and role in the development of the church. Beyond the importance of unique material about Mary, Gabriel's revelation is also noteworthy, as it is a Coptic rendering of passages from the *Cave of Treasures* (*Cav. Tr.*; *CAVT* 11).

Contents
The first fragment of the text (1:1–2:11) introduces Cyril as the source of the homily and frames the Magdalene's importance by highlighting how her continual virginity inclined Jesus to love her and convey the mysteries to her (2:7–8). Just as Cyril is about to explain how he found Mary's "Life" in a library in Egypt, the text breaks off. The second fragment (3:2–22) picks up during the Magdalene's youth, indicating the names of her parents (3:2–5) and how, when they died, she came to live with her half-sister, Anna (3:17). Anna is also the Virgin Mary's mother,[1] making the Magdalene the aunt of the Virgin Mary (3:18). The fragment abruptly ends as Cyril begins to explain how the Magdalene served as a nurse, presumably to the Virgin (3:22).

When the text continues in the third fragment (6:1–21:21), the author recounts the feeding of the 5,000 (6:1–19) before telling of an incident between Mary's custodian, Theophilus (perhaps to be identified with the Theophilus of Luke and Acts),[2] and King Herod that resulted in Mary sending a letter to the Emperor Tiberius (7:1–8). It seems that King Herod had attempted to seize animals that belonged to the Magdalene, and may also have extorted three gold coins from Theophilus. Emperor Tiberius sends a reply to

---

1. Cf. *Prot. Jas.*, where Anna is also named as the Virgin Mary's mother. The conflation of Marys occurs also in Ps.-Cyril's *On the Virgin Mary* (CPC 0119) where the Virgin is called also Mary Magdalene, Mary of Cleopas, and Mary of James. Other Ps.-Cyril homilies, such as *On the Passion and the Resurrection* (CPS 0116) and *On the Resurrection* (CPC 0117), as well as Ps.-Cyriacus's *Lament of Mary* (CANT 74), also of Egyptian provenance, portray the Virgin as the Mary who sees the empty tomb and informs the apostles that Jesus has risen. For descriptions of the Ps.-Cyril texts see van den Broek, *Pseudo-Cyril*, 77–81, 93–97.

2. For this identification, see Ri, *Commentaire*, 68–69; and Paul-Hubert Poirier, "Note sur le nom du destinataire des chapitres 44 à 54 de la *Caverne des Trésors*," in *Christianisme d'Égypte. Hommages à René-Georges Coquin* (ed. René-Georges Coquin and Jean-Marc Rosenstiehl; Cahiers de la bibliothèque copte, 9; Leuven/Paris: Peeters, 1995), 115–22. Note also the identification of the boy with the loaves and fishes as Philemon (6:5); is the reader supposed to believe this is the Philemon of Paul's letter? or are both Theophilus and Philemon simply a playful repurposing of names known in Christian tradition?

Judea, stating that if anyone should resist Mary in anything, they will be beheaded and their property confiscated (7:9–13). The episode continues with a retelling of Jesus' feeding of the 4,000, ending with Mary Magdalene keeping the left-over food to serve to the disciples (8:1–3). The story then shifts to Mary requesting that Nicodemus and Joseph of Arimathea (identified in the text as Nicodemus's brother) ask Pilate for Jesus' body following his crucifixion (10:1–3). While the two initially protest that Mary, having the emperor's letter, ought to ask Pilate, they eventually concede after Mary insists and sends them with money for Pilate (10:4–6). Pilate hands over the body and refuses the money. They prepare Jesus' body and bury it in Joseph's garden tomb (10:7–13). A blending of the canonical Gospels' resurrection appearances then follows, though aspects of the narratives are changed. So, Mary Magdalene and the Virgin Mary both return to Jesus' tomb, and it is the Virgin Mary who confuses Jesus for the gardener, while the Magdalene waits at the tomb's mouth until Jesus calls for her. The vignette ends when Mary Magdalene runs and tells the disciples about Jesus' resurrection (11:1–37).

The homily then begins to narrate what happened when the Virgin Mary was about to die, claiming that the Virgin appointed Mary Magdalene as her replacement among the disciples (12:1–4). The disciples then wait in Jerusalem before heading out to evangelize. While they wait, the apostles compose the Gospels; the text lists all four canonical Gospels and Paul's letters as well as gospels of Peter and Paul (13:1–13). Then, the text moves forward to a later time when Mary is sitting with her custodian, Theophilus, discussing Scripture. When Theophilus confesses confusion about its meaning, Mary prays for understanding, and immediately the archangel Gabriel appears, promising to convey to Theophilus everything that he wishes to know. At this point, Mary seems to fall out of view as a character. Gabriel asks Theophilus what precisely he wants to understand, and Theophilus responds he would like to know everything from the creation of Adam to the present (14:1–23). The remainder of the text, in which Gabriel narrates the creation of Adam and Eve (15:1–16:18), their fall and expulsion from paradise (17:1–18:18), the births and struggles of Cain and Abel (19:1–20), the birth of Seth (20:1–7), and the death of Adam (21:1–21) shares material found in the *Cave of Treasures*.[3] The last two fragments also parallel content from *Cav. Tr.*: the first contains a genealogy from Adam to Nachor (78:11–13), and the second describes Herod's death (81:9–18) before ending abruptly in the midst of a discussion about John, the son of Zachariah, baptizing Jesus (82:1–5).

Manuscripts, Date, and Provenance

Encom. Mary survives only in three Coptic fragments:

> Fragment 1: Cairo, Institut français d'archéologie orientale (IFAO), Copt. inv. no. 186–87; 190–97 (also catalogued as IFAO, Copt. 27)[4]
>
> Fragment 2: a manuscript that once belonged to Sylvestre Chauleur[5]

---

3. For an updated introduction and translation of *Cav. Tr.* see Alexander Toepel, "The Cave of Treasures," in *Old Testament Pseudepigrapha: More Noncanonical Scriptures*, vol. 1 (ed. Richard Bauckham et al.; Grand Rapids, Mich.: Eerdmans, 2013), 531–84.

4. For a description of the IFAO folia, see Catherine Louis, "Catalogue raisonné des manuscrits littéraires coptes conservés à l'IFAO du Caire. Contribution à la reconstitution de la bibliothèque du Monastère Blanc" (PhD diss., École Pratique des Hautes Études, Section des Sciences Religieuses, Paris, 2005), 285–87.

5. Published in Chauleur, "Deux pages." The manuscript is now in the possession of Gérard Godron.

Fragment 3: New York, Pierpont Morgan Library, Ms. 665(4), consisting of two folia, numbered 2 and 7, with folia 3–6 missing[6]

R.-G. Coquin and G. Godron recognized the relationship of these three fragments and sorted them into two codices.[7] The IFAO codex is clearly distinguishable, as several leaves are still joined together (e.g., folia 5 and 8). The Chauleur and PPM Ms. 665(4) folia were determined, based on evidence of a common scribal hand and content, to constitute a second codex. While the two codices do not contain overlapping material, Coquin and Godron made the plausible presumption that Chauleur and PPM Ms. 665(4)'s content fit into missing intervening pages from the IFAO manuscript. IFAO 186–87 promises that in what follows the Magdalene's childhood will be described. Such a description is extant in Chauleur. But, the relationship between the two codices more reliably hinges on the relationship between the second section of the IFAO manuscript, 190–97, which contains material related to the *Cav. Tr.* tradition, and the PPM Ms. 665(4) pages, which as Poirier noted, also contains material from *Cav. Tr.* Coquin and Godron's edition of the text features a Coptic transcription of the IFAO folia and Chauleur with French translations as well as a French translation of P.-H. Poirier's Coptic transcription of PPM Ms. 665(4).[8]

PPM Ms. 665(4) and, with it, the Chauleur fragment (assuming they both come from the same codex) are part of a collection of manuscripts and manuscript fragments dated by H. Hyvernat to the ninth century.[9] Coquin and Godron saw his dating as a little too early, though not impossible. The provenance of PPM Ms. 665(4) is contested. While its discoverers asserted that it was part of a cache of ninth-/tenth-century codices found near the village of al-Hāmūlī in the Fayyum,[10] Hyvernat was not convinced. Hyvernat based his claim on a comparison of PPM Ms. 665(4) (and other folia in its lot) with Pierpont Morgan codices purchased a few years earlier with a firm al-Hāmūlī provenance. Thus, PPM Ms. 665(4)'s provenance is possibly the Fayyum, but little more can be asserted.[11] The manuscript does seem to be earlier than the IFAO folia, which Coquin and Godron date to the eleventh or twelfth century.[12]

The actual text of *Encom. Mary* is undoubtedly older. A probable date may be determined in light of the text's relationship to other versions of the *Cav. Tr.* tradition. The narrative extant here in Coptic is very close to the West Syriac version of *Cav. Tr.* but contains multiple deviations that are closer to the East Syriac version.[13] Although Su-Min Ri thinks that the Coptic is often most similar to the Garšūnī manuscript Edgbaston, University of Birmingham, Mingana Syr. 32, he does concede that the names found in our Coptic text

---

6. For a description of the two extant folia, see Depuydt, *Catalogue*, 213 (no. 110).

7. Coquin and Godron, "Un encomion copte," esp. 170–71.

8. For the Coptic transcription, see Poirier, "Fragments."

9. Henry Hyvernat and John Pierpoint Morgan, *A Checklist of Coptic Manuscripts in the Pierpont Morgan Library* (New York: Private Printing, 1919), xiv.

10. Depuydt, *Catalogue*, lxv.

11. For a description of the Askren lot, as PPM Ms. 665(4)'s lot was known, see Depuydt, *Catalogue*, lxxiv–lxxvii. The manuscript bears all scribal features of the codices inscribed in the scriptorium of Touton, in the Fayyum. For some discussion of these features see Chièmi Nakano, "Indices d'une chronologie relative des manuscrits coptes copiés à Toutôn (Fayoum)," *Journal of Coptic Studies* 8 (2006): 147–59.

12. Coquin and Gordon, "Un encomion copte," 170–72.

13. Ri, *Commentaire*, 67–68. See also Coquin and Godron, "Un encomion copte," 212.

occasionally differ, with no parallel in any other tradition.[14] Thus, the version of *Cav. Tr.* witnessed here underscores the problematic nature of a simple binary of Eastern and Western Syrian transmission histories. Nevertheless, given the text's close relationship to *Cav. Tr.*, whose variant traditions are often dated between the fourth and sixth centuries, we can offer a rough date for *Encom. Mary* of the mid-fifth to early sixth century.[15]

The original language of *Encom. Mary* has also been a source of debate. Poirier originally viewed PPM Ms. 665(4) as perhaps a Coptic translation of a Syriac version of *Cav. Tr.*[16] Coquin and Godron, for their part, argued for an underlying Greek source (based on the biblical names being closer to Septuagint spellings than Peshitta renderings), from which our extant Coptic versions were translated.[17] More recently, van den Broek has discussed the issue, noting that unusual syntax does not necessitate a Greek original. Furthermore, the text's claim to be based upon documents "Cyril" found in "the Egyptian language" (that is, Coptic), should be taken seriously.[18] Given that *Encom. Mary* participates in enthusiasm for Cyril, a figure who would become popular among Miaphysite Christians, it seems plausible that its original language may have been Coptic, with the passages from *Cav. Tr.* witnessing to a complicated translation history from one (or multiple?) Syriac versions.

Authorship, Genre, and Literary Context

While Cyril of Jerusalem is given as the author of *Encom. Mary*, I follow previous scholars in recognizing that this attribution is a later, spurious claim. The presence of portions from *Cave Tr.* in *Encom. Mary* indicates that Cyril cannot have been its author, as he was already deceased. Nor, other than in its introduction, is there any further reference to Cyril in the extant fragments.[19] As Roelof van den Broek has noted, assertions of Cyril's authorship occur in several texts, and attributing the miraculous discovery of an ancient text to Cyril helps to establish the authenticity of the apocryphal (and potentially heretical) claims that would follow in such texts.[20] Cyril, as bishop of Jerusalem in the fourth century, was a well-known and prominent figure. In particular, his instructions for new Christians *(Catecheses)* were known and mentioned by Jerome (*Vir. ill.* 112) and others, and were widely copied, including extant translations into Coptic.[21] Thus, Cyril's own prestige as author coupled with his location at the increasingly important See of Jerusalem made him an ideal candidate for pseudonymous authorship.[22]

---

14. A notable difference is that the addressee of the Syriac versions is a certain Namosaya, while *Encom. Mary*'s addressees are Theophilus and Mary (Ri, *Commentaire*, 502).

15. Such a dating is particularly probable in light of C. Leonhard's arguments for a fifth- to sixth-century date for *Cav. Tr.* See Clemens Leonhard, "Observation on the Date of the Syriac *Cave of Treasures*," in *The World of the Aramaeans III: Studies in Language and Literature in Honor of Paul-Eugene Dion* (ed. P. M. Michèle Daviau, John W. Wevers, and Michael Weigl; Sheffield: Sheffield Academic, 2001), 255–94 at 287–88. This date range also aligns well with Alin Suciu's situating of P. Berol. 22220 in a fifth-century milieu concerned with Christ's humanity ("Apocryphon Berolinense/Argentoratense," 74).

16. Poirier, "Fragments," 417.

17. Coquin and Godron, *Un Encomion*, 173.

18. Van den Broek, *Pseudo-Cyril*, 111.

19. This is a point also noted by van den Broek, *Pseudo-Cyril*, 112.

20. Van den Broek, *Pseudo-Cyril*, 11.

21. Suciu, "Apocryphon Berolinense," 91–92.

22. Suciu, likewise, notes the importance of Cyril's location at Jerusalem as part of his appeal, "Apocryphon Berolinense," 92.

The "Life of Mary" found by Cyril appears to be attributed to a certain Simon, "a eunuch and scribe" (3:10), who makes his authorial presence known early in the text. Several uses of the personal pronouns "we" and "us" in the feeding accounts (6:15–19; 8:3) and the post-resurrection portion of the text (13:1, 9, 13) suggest that Simon is presented as a witness, not only to Mary's early life, but also to the career of Jesus and the post-resurrection instruction to write and transmit Scripture.

The actual author of *Encom. Mary* is unidentifiable, but the text's claim to Cyril's legacy as well as its use of a fictive book from the library of Jerusalem are tropes found in several other Coptic writings. Alin Suciu terms such texts "pseudo-apostolic memoirs."[23] In these "memoirs," the purported genre of the entire text is often that of a homily, though in fact what follows rarely is homiletic in nature. *Encom. Mary* follows this rule, with the exception perhaps of a few earlier sections that engage in expansion on canonical passages about the Magdalene. In the past, scholars have identified fragmentary texts such as *Encom. Mary* as apocryphal gospels, largely due to the texts' claims to be a revelation received by one of Jesus' early apostles, here Mary Magdalene and Theophilus. As Suciu and others note, however, these relationships are based upon partial texts whose pieces are sometimes situated in multiple locales, making genre statements difficult to ascertain.[24] It seems that Suciu offers the best expression of *Encom. Mary*'s genre, situating it among other pseudepigraphic memoirs attributed to Cyril of Jerusalem, and so I follow him in this genre attribution. Suciu notes that one of the most common shared attributes of these pseudo-memoirs is the incorporation of anti-Jewish sentiments, and this phenomenon is observable in several portions of the text (7:12; 11:32–36; and 14:15).[25] *Encom. Mary* also may have some association with the *Lament of Mary* as this text also has the Virgin Mary confuse Jesus with the gardener at his tomb, allowing Mary the Magdalene to be an eyewitness to their interaction.[26]

Encom. Mary resonates with other Christian apocryphal texts that seek to explain the relationships of Jesus to Mary Magdalene and to the Virgin Mary, as well as the relationship between the two Marys. Multiple early Christian texts make mention of the Magdalene as a prominent figure in the early Christian movement.[27] One of the most important witnesses to such traditions regarding the Magdalene is the *Gospel of Mary of Magdala*. Here, Mary is situated as the only one of the disciples who understood Jesus' teachings correctly. Further, she then reveals secret teachings that Jesus shared with her alone. Thus, much like *Encom. Mary*, the text makes Mary a recipient of a divine revelation. The no-

---

23. Suciu, "Apocryphon Berolinense," 91. See also the contributions in this volume on the *Berlin-Strasbourg Apocryphon*, the *Discourse of the Savior*, the *Dance of the Savior*, the *Investiture of Abbaton*, and the *Encomium on John the Baptist*.

24. Suciu, "Apocryphon Berolinense," 89–90. Here he cites the warnings of Paulino Bellet and Tito Orlandi.

25. Suciu, "Apocryphon Berolinense," 211.

26. See n. 1 above. For further discussion of the *Lament of Mary*, see Tedros Abraha and Daniel Assefa, "Apocryphal Gospels in the Ethiopic Tradition," in *Jesus in apokryphen Evangelienüberlieferungen: Beiträge zu außerkanonischen Jesusüberlieferungen aus verschiedenen Sprach- und Kulturtradtionen* (ed. Jörg Frey und Jens Schröter; Tübingen: Mohr Siebeck, 2010), 611–53 at 643–45.

27. *Gospel of Mary, Gospel of Thomas, Gospel of Philip, Sophia of Jesus Christ, Dialogue of the Savior*, and the *First Apocalypse of James* are all texts that mention the Magdalene within the Nag Hammadi corpus. For a full list of texts beyond Nag Hammadi that also mention the Magdalene, see Jane Schaberg, *The Resurrection of Mary Magdalene: Legends, Apocrypha, and the Christian Testament* (New York: Continuum, 2002), 357–60.

table difference between the two revelations is that, in *Gos. Mary,* Mary alone receives the revelation, whereas *Encom. Mary* has Mary accompanied by Theophilus in the reception of knowledge. This slight demotion of Mary's authority stands in contrast to the Virgin Mary's appointing of the Magdalene as the leader of the other disciples on her deathbed (12:1–4). Another Pseudo-Cyril homily, *On the Virgin Mary* (CPC 0119),[28] similarly has the Virgin Mary call the Magdalene to her deathbed, but here she is charged not with leadership of all the disciples, but only of the virgins in the community. Both pseudo-Cyril homilies stand as witnesses to attempts to locate the Magdalene's role within the early Christian community by routing her authority through the Virgin Mary. As Stephen Shoemaker has argued, the Mary of apocryphal and "gnostic" literature is a complicated mixture of traditions surrounding both Mary Magdalene and the Virgin Mary.[29] *Encom. Mary* indicates such a desire to understand the relationship between the two Marys: first by negotiating their relationship as familial, portraying the Magdalene as the Virgin's aunt and childhood nurse, and later by having the Virgin appoint the Magdalene as her replacement.

Translation

The following translation is based upon Coquin and Godron's transcription of IFAO Copt. 186–87, 190–97 and of the Chauleur fragment, and upon Poirier's transcription of PPM Ms. 665(4). I have tended to follow the previous editors' emendations, noting in the footnotes when I have disagreed with them and why. In constructing a chapter and verse system, I have attempted to leave space for the possible discovery of intervening material—both the absent passages surrounding the Chauleur fragment and the missing sections between the last IFAO folio and PPM Ms. 665(4). In regard to the portions corresponding to the *Cav. Tr.* recensions, I have attempted to estimate how many intervening chapters might be missing. Thus, when IFAO fol. 197 ends at *Encom. Mary* 21 (*Cav. Tr.* 6), I have estimated fifty-six intervening chapters are lost, and began numbering PPM Ms. 665(4) at *Encom. Mary* 78 (*Cav. Tr.* 44). Although the two traditions are related, I have not followed the chapter breaks of *Cav. Tr.*, but have broken the text into narrative units. Lacunae in the manuscript are indicated by square brackets; three dots within the brackets signal lacunae of up to one or two lines, and a single dot is used for one word or a partial word that cannot be reconstructed.

Bibliography

EDITIONS AND TRANSLATIONS

Chauleur, Sylvestre. "Deux pages d'un manuscrit sur la sainte Vierge." *Cahiers Coptes* 12 (1956): 3–5.

Coquin, René-Georges, and Gérard Godron. "Un encomion copte sur Marie-Madeleine attribué à Cyrille de Jérusalem." *BIFAO* 90 (1990): 169–212. (Edition and French translation of the IFAO manuscript along with the previous manuscript discoveries.)

Poirier, Paul-Hubert. "Fragments d'une version copte de la caverne de tresors." *Orientalia* 52 (1983): 415–23. (Edition and translation of the Pierpont Morgan Library manuscript.)

---

28. For references to manuscripts of this text and a description, see van den Broek, *Pseudo-Cyril,* 93–97.
29. Stephen Shoemaker, "Rethinking the 'Gnostic Mary': Mary of Nazareth and Mary of Magdala in Early Christian Tradition," *JECS* 9, no. 4 (2001): 555–95.

STUDIES

Broek, Roelof van den. *Pseudo-Cyril of Jerusalem, On the Life and the Passion of Christ: A Coptic Apocryphon.* Supplements to Vigiliae Christianae 118. Leiden: Brill, 2013.

Depuydt, Leo. *Catalogue of Coptic Manuscripts in the Pierpont Morgan Library.* Corpus of Illuminated Manuscripts 4, Oriental Series 1. Leuven: Peeters, 1993.

Grypeou, Emmanouela, and Helen Spurling. *The Book of Genesis in Late Antiquity: Encounters between Jewish and Christian Exegesis.* Leiden and Boston: Brill, 2013.

Ri, Su-Min. *Commentaire de la Caverne des Trésors: Étude sur l'histoire du texte et de ses sources.* CSCO 581. Subsidia 103. Leuven: Peeters, 2000.

———. *La Caverne des Trésors: Les deux recensions syriaques.* 2 vols. CSCO 486–87, Syr. 207–8. Leuven: Peeters, 1987.

Suciu, Alin. "Apocryphon Berolinense/Argentoratense (Previously Known as the Gospel of the Savior). Reedition of P. Berol. 22220, Strasbourg Copte 5–7 and Qasr el-Wizz Codex ff. 12v–17r with Introduction and Commentary." PhD diss., Université Laval, 2013.

An Encomium on Mary Magdalene

IFAO COPT. 186–87

Introduction and opening prayer

1 [1]A homily of the wise in divine matters and archbishop, Abba Cyril of Jerusalem, that he preached concerning the noble saint, Mary the Magdalene, beginning from her infancy until her death, revealing her whole life, from which family she came. [2]He spoke about the seven unclean spirits that dwelt in her, revealing how God guarded her, a holy virgin, (from) sin[a] before she came to the world. [3]He also spoke about her conduct before the savior and her six other cousins. [4]And he spoke about how the crown was placed on her, (how) she went down to Egypt,[b] and about the wonders God performed through her, and that she resembled[c] the holy God-bearer Saint Mary, who bore God truly, and she was her sister.[d] [5]The day of her rest is the twenty-third of the month Paone.[e] [6]In the peace of God, may holy blessings come down upon us together. Amen.

Luke 8:2

---

a. Van den Broek (*Pseudo-Cyril*, 105 n. 38) sees *nabi* as a corruption. I suggest that it could be read as "from sin" due to the copyist or author accidently dropping or eliding the expected preposition *n-* with the first letter of the Fayyumic word for sin *(nabi)*. Although the text seems to be of the Sahidic dialect, given the lexical complexities/problems of the text, the possibility of occasional Fayyumic spellings seems plausible and renders sensible the extant text. However, we should note that Depuydt (*Catalogue*, lxv) sees the use of Fayyumic fragments in bindings for Sahidic codices as evidence for the waning of the Fayyumic dialect in the eighth century.

b. Van den Broek suggests that the Coptic should be corrected to read *ayeine* ("was brought") rather than the *aceine* ("went down") present in the text (*Pseudo-Cyril*, 105–6 n. 39). His correction presumes that the author is listing narrative items chronologically, which I am not sure is the case. So, for example, the miracles wrought by Mary and her relationship to the Virgin need not refer to incidents after her death. He also notes that no other early tradition has the Magdalene go to Egypt. It is worth noting that by the ninth century the ascetic, Mary of Egypt, had been elided with the Magdalene in certain medieval Christian traditions. For a discussion of this, see Erich Poppe and Bianca Ross, eds., *The Legend of Mary of Egypt in Medieval Insular Hagiography* (Dublin: Four Courts, 1996).

c. The Coptic words here are *teco nprosopon*. The presence of the Greek term *prosopon* is worth noting, as it would become one of the terms used by Nestorius, bishop of Constantinople, and contested by Cyril, bishop of Alexandria, in the course of their exchanges leading up to the Council of Ephesus in 431 CE. Such a historical contextualization is especially noteworthy if one accepts Suciu's suggestions that many of the pseudo-Cyrillian texts emerged within the context of fifth-century debates about Christ's humanity.

d. Note that here the text refers to the Marys as sisters. This is probably meant to convey their familial relationship loosely, as the Magdalene will later, more precisely, be described as the Virgin's aunt (see 3:17–18).

e. From the end of May to the end of June.

Cyril's discovery of the "Life of Mary Magdalene"

2 ¹For God works for our salvation, us men, guarding those who are good. He searches and examines the kidneys and the heart of each one. ²Truly, I desire to move the organ of my tongue and cry out with the holy temple singer, our father, David: "The virgins will be brought in to the king after her." ³Who are the virgins who will be brought in after her? ⁴O holy psalmist, David, let your pity come down upon me and teach me the interpretation of this passage. ⁵"Listen," heᵃ said. "It is I who will teach you . . . I am speaking," he said, "about the queen, the mother of the king of kings, Jesus Christ. ⁶After her death, a crowd of women will emulate her and become virgins, and they will be brought after her and they will be given to the temple of the king, which is to say, the heavenly Jerusalem."

⁷Now, as the Magdalene was a virgin from her birth until her death, because of this he loved her. ⁸He joined her to him, revealing to her the hidden mysteries, as (he had to) his mother, the Virgin. ⁹Just as it says in the Gospel, when they announced to him, "Look, your mother and your brothers are standing outside," he said to the one who asked him, "Who is my mother, and who are my brothers?" ¹⁰"For," he said, "whoever does the will of my father in heaven is my brother and sister and mother." ¹¹(While) I desire also to say many words regarding the words of our Savior who is sweet, for they are unattainable, yet I desire to reveal to you the life of this chaste noblewoman, Saint Mary the Magdalene, and the way that I found it in the library of the holy city (Jerusalem), written in Egyptian.

*A lacuna follows of an undetermined number of pages.*ᵇ

CHAULEUR FOLIO

Mary's lineage and childhood

3 . . . ²his name is David. ³[Wh]en Anna'sᶜ mother died, she laid down her body as all humans (do). ⁴After remaining (alone) for a year, he took for himself a wife, whose name was Syncletica, the daughter of an important, wealthy man of the palace, who was from [Ma]gdala. ⁵[Syncletica bore a daughter,]ᵈ her father named her Mary. ⁶Her mother gave the name of the city to her, Magdalene. ⁷And the day on which she was born was the third of the month Koyahk.ᵉ

⁸When she was four years old her father died and afterwards her mother [. . .]. ⁹For, before her father died, he gave everything into my hands. ¹⁰I am Simon.ᶠ ¹¹I am a eunuch and scribe. ¹²And the names [. . .]ᵍ are the three children of Aminadab. ¹³The other three are the children of Syncletica. ¹⁴And he gave them into

Ps 7:9; Jer 11:20; 20:12

Ps 45:14–15

Matt 12:46–50 par.

---

a. Exactly who "he" is here is uncertain, but it seems to be David.

b. What would have been pages 3 to 14 are missing between IFAO Copt. 186 and 187. I follow Coquin and Godron in placing the Chauleur folio somewhere within this lacuna.

c. Anna is considered the mother of the Virgin Mary in several apocryphal texts, probably based on *Prot. Jas. Encom. Mary* is the only text that has Anna as the Magdalene's half-sister.

d. Coquin reconstructs the next four lines. His conjecture seems reasonable given the space on the folio and what follows in the beginning of the next column.

e. From the end of November to the end of December.

f. It is unclear precisely who Simon is, but he seems to be the purported author of the "Life of Mary" that Cyril found, or at least of this portion of the "Life."

g. The lacuna presumably lists the names of David's three children by Aminadab.

my hands with all of his property. ¹⁵And the little Magdalene, he entrusted her to God, with me, in order that I might continue caring for her. ¹⁶Then, after he had died, Syncletica died also. ¹⁷Anna, the sister of Magdalene from the children of (her) father, took her in with her [. . .] ¹⁸Wh[en] my [mi]stress, the Magda-lene, was thirteen years old,[a] Anna herself begat the Theotokos, Mary. ¹⁹She gave (the name) Mary to her. ²⁰Anna said, "An angel of the Lord said to me, 'Name her Mary.'" ²¹And great prophecies were (fulfilled) because of her. ²²As the little Magdal[en]e was acting as nurse for [. . .]

Prot. Jas. 5:2

The Chaleur folio ends here and it is not known how many intervening pages are missing.

IFAO COPT. 190–97

The feeding of the 5,000

6 [. . .] ¹bring to us those things that we need according to custom. ²I did not know what happened to them, my Lord." ³But Jesus, knowing everything, re-peated the word, "There is not bread here [.] at all." ⁴They sought out and found a young boy who had five barley loaves and two fish, namely, two *bore*.[b] ⁵And the name of that young boy was Philemon. ⁶It was his custom to eat in the purity of his heart [.] ⁷God gave him a voice that was pleasant for anyone who heard it. ¹⁰And then, so that I might not speak for too long,[c] Christ took the five loaves and two fish. ¹¹He gave thanks over them and he commanded that the crowd recline themselves. ¹²He divided the bread and the fish, and he gave them to my fathers,[d] the apostles. ¹³They placed (the bread and fish) before the crowd. ¹⁴And they ate and they were filled. ¹⁵We collected the pieces that remained and we filled twelve baskets.¹⁶And when we had seen the great miracle that occurred, it pleased us thus to count the crowd. ¹⁷We found 5,000 children. ¹⁸And the wom-en, we did not know their number, because when they saw what had happened, they arranged themselves in groups on the mountain, running to one another, glorifying God, saying, "Glory to God in the highest, his peace upon the earth." ¹⁹Jesus commanded us to take the remainder of the blessing, and we gave it to Saint Magdalene so that she could serve it to us at mealtime.

Mark 6:38–43 par.;
John 6:8–14

Mark 6:44//Matt 14:21

Luke 2:14

Theophilus informs Mary that Herod has stolen her animals

7 ¹And inside of a month, the animals arrived, laden with goods. ²The servants who came brought her a letter from master Theophilus, written thus: "Theophi-lus, this unworthy one, he who governs over the property of the Magdalene, I inform your ladyship that when the animals came to me, I did not neglect to send them to you except for those that had been seized. ³I gave three gold coins

---

a. The Coptic literally says "After thirteen years since the birth of my mistress, the Magda-lene."

b. *Bore* is an uncommon word for fish. Coquin and Godron suggest in their translation that it is a word indicating two mullet fish ("Un encomion," 201).

c. The Coptic literally reads "so that we might not increase the word greatly." Here we have an interjection from "Cyril."

d. The voice here may be that of "Cyril" or "Simon."

to him. [4]Behold, I sent (the animals) to you." [5]When she had read the letter, she said, "Your judgments are true, Lord. [6]As this fox, Herod,[a] being praised throughout the land of Judea, afterwards[b] set out to seize the animals."

Luke 13:32

Mary writes to Tiberius

[7]It seemed good to Saint Magdalene to write to the emperor, Tiberius, about those things Herod had done to her. [8]She gave the writings to John, the son of Zebedee, and she sent him to the emperor. [9]When the emperor Tiberius received the writings of the Magdalene, he read them and he wrote to the land of Judea, "Let no one oppose Mary the Magdalene [.]. [10]For, whoever opposes her or knows any word (against her),[c] his head shall be taken with a sword and his belongings confiscated for the treasury of the emperor." [11]God put it upon John's heart to request from the emperor writings on his behalf, "Lest," he said, "when the Jews hear that I brought writings to you, they kill me." [12](Tiberius) also wrote to Herod: "Look after John, son of Zebedee. [13]Let no one oppose him before John comes to it (home?) [.]"

The feeding of the 4,000

8 [1]Christ came upon the sea of Tiberias. He blessed seven loaves and 4,000 men ate and they were sated. [2]Seven baskets remained. [3]We took them to our lady the Magdalene and she continued to serve us from them.

Mark 8:1–9//Matt 15:32–38

Herod receives Tiberius's letter

9 [1]When John had brought the writings of the emperor to Herod, he [. . . John . . . emperor . . . Emperor Caesar . . . the Magdalene . . .][d] concerning the command of the emperor Caesar.

Jesus' burial

10 [1]When our Savior gave up his spirit upon the cross, the Magdalene quickly ran to the home of Nicodemus. [2]She found Joseph, his brother, from Arimathea, sitting with him. [3]She requested that they go to Pilate and take the body of the Lord and place it in a tomb. [4]They said, "Our lady Magdalene, if you go to him, it is possible for you to do this rather than us because the order of the emperor is in your hands."

Mark 15:37 par.; John 19:30

[5]She said, "It is not right that a woman go to the governor so that he give (the body). [6]But take money, give it to him, and he will give (the body) to you." [7]So, they went to Pilate and he gave them the body of Jesus and he did not take the money from them. [8]He brought (the body) down. [9]The sun rose when they

Mark 15:42–45 par.; John 19:38–39

---

a. Note that Herod's name is written above the line on the folio.

b. The text here has Herod's name on the line, but for clarity I have omitted it.

c. I have attempted to make some sense of the Coptic here, which is very confusing. In particular, it is not clear how to understand the term *nidosepos*. My translation above suggests that perhaps the Coptic combines *eidos* ("knowing") with *epos* ("a word"), but this is very tentative. Coquin and Godron, likewise, had trouble rendering this section. Their French translation reads "que personne soit?" ("Un encomion," 202).

d. The following twelve lines are largely destroyed or illegible. I have given the few words that are possibly decipherable.

had brought the body down because, when he had given up his spirit, a great
earthquake had occurred. ¹⁰They[a] gave him many perfumes. ¹¹Saint Magdalene
poured upon his body the oil that remained from Lazarus's sister,[b] which Christ
had commanded him (to keep) until the day that he was buried. ¹²They prepared
him, placing him in Joseph's new tomb with a garden. ¹³They rolled a great stone
and placed it upon the mouth of the tomb, and they went away.

Matt 27:54
John 11:2

Mark 15:46 par.; John
19:39–41

Jesus' resurrection and appearance to the Marys

11 ¹But the saint, she told everything to her sister,[c] Mary, his mother. ²On the
evening of the Sabbath, at the dawn of Sunday, the Magdalene came to the tomb
with some women. ³When they reached the tomb, they saw an angel sitting upon
the stone that they had rolled before the mouth of the tomb. ⁴He told them, "The
Lord has risen, go to his disciples and say this to them." ⁵They ran away, being
afraid, and they did not say a word to anyone.

Mark 16:1–8 par.

⁶Afterwards, Saint Magdalene returned to the tomb. ⁷She looked into the
tomb and she saw two angels sitting, the one at [his head] and the other at
[his feet] in the place where [the body] of Jesus had been. ⁸[They said to her,
"Woman], O M[ary . . .] he r[ose . . .][d] [¹¹the V]irgin, [.] "My sister saying these
things, I would not believe, if she had not seen it and come to me." ¹²Peter arose
with John and they ran to the tomb. ¹³They saw the linens lying there. ¹⁴They
came to the Theotokos and said to her, "Truly, the Lord has risen." ¹⁵But they
were not able to persuade her heart, (since) she (was) waiting for the return
of her sister.

John 20:11–13

John 20:3, 7

¹⁶Afterwards, when Mag[da]lene came, the Virgin said, "My sister, do you
say my son is raised?" ¹⁷(Magdalene replied), "I, myself, have not seen him."
¹⁸When the mother of Jesus heard this, she ran to the tomb, being disturbed,
uttering words of grief. ¹⁹Her sister (i.e., the Virgin Mary) placed herself at the
rear of the tomb, because of the guards. ²⁰The Magdalene came herself and
stood at the mouth (of the tomb). ²¹After a little while, Jesus appeared to his
mother at the rear of the tomb. ²²He spoke with her, she thinking that he was
the gardener.

Matt 27:65–66

²³Then, the time came and he was going to his father. ²⁴While the Magdalene
was still at the mouth of the tomb, he called her name, "Mariham." ²⁵She recognized his voice and came, being persuaded. ²⁶And his mother said, "Rabbouni.
²⁷You have risen, truly you have risen!" ²⁸His mother reached toward him in
order to embrace him. ²⁹He stopped her, "Do not touch me!"

---

a. Who these individuals are is not certain, but it would seem the "they" here may still be
Nicodemus and Joseph, though the Magdalene also reappears in the subsequent line.

b. It is worth noting that in the Johannine version of the anointing of Jesus, Lazarus' sis-
ter, another Mary, is the one who anoints Jesus with perfume. But some late ancient, Western
Christians came to interpret the Lukan version (7:37–50), where the woman is anonymous, as
Mary the Magdalene, based perhaps on mention of her in the following chapter (Luke 8:2).
The early Christian eliding of the Lukan woman and the Magdalene first appears in Gregory
the Great's *Homily 33* (PL 76:1239). For a discussion of this "composite saint," see Katherine L.
Jansen, *The Making of the Magdalen: Preaching and Popular Devotion in the Later Middle Ages*
(Princeton: Princeton University Press, 2001), 32–35.

c. See p. 205 n. c above.

d. The rest of the line and the next twelve lines are destroyed or illegible.

³⁰And she began to cry, "Why, my lord and my son, do you make me a stranger to yourself today?" ³¹The Savior said, "I do not make you a stranger to me, but because you have not listened. ³²You are of the house of John, you who are in the midst of the Jews, being so polluted[a] that the dust from their feet[b] falls from your garments, those that I did not permit, being filthy, ever. ³³It is impossible for the dust of those impious ones to touch the clothing that I have placed upon myself until I ascend up to my father. ³⁴But go to my brothers and tell them that I have risen. ³⁵Let them wash their garments, come to Galilee, and I will reveal myself to them and I will give them my peace. ³⁶Do you not know, my mother, that I suffered everything because of the disobedience that has occurred since the beginning?" ³⁷The Magdalene went and told the disciples that she had seen the Lord and that he had said these things to her.

John 20:11–18

The Virgin Mary's Dormition

12 ¹It happened after these things, in the fifteenth year after the resurrection from the dead of our Savior, the holy Theotokos, Saint Mary, died on the twenty-first of the month Tobe.[c] ²She called all the apostles and appointed her sister, Magdalene, among them. ³She commanded them, saying to them, "Listen to her as [if] she is me."[d] ⁴And she died.

The writings of the disciples

13 ¹Before the apostles dispersed to preach, we stayed in Jerusalem a short while until Paul, the man of Tarsus, came into the congregation, and the apostles wrote the Gospels, and the Paraclete descended and they learned the language of every land. ²Christ came to them daily, teaching them the canons and the rule of the offering. ³{Matthew}[e] wrote the Gospel, speaking about the birth of the Savior. ⁴Paul wrote the Gospel. ⁵The Holy Spirit was given to Luke, speaking the good news of Christ. ⁶Peter wrote the Gospel. ⁷The Spirit was given to Mark, speaking in his beginning about the baptism of John. ⁸John wrote his Gospel, speaking about the word that became enfleshed. ⁹I received the Psalter. ¹⁰Paul wrote also all the fourteen epistles. ¹¹One by one, the apostles wrote them. ¹²They brought them with them for preaching in Egypt, because they preached to the lands that were near them, still being in Jerusalem and Egypt and the other lands that are in the south. ¹³We remained in Jerusalem, when the Savior came to Saint Magdalene, visiting her and teaching her the many hidden mysteries.

Acts 8:1; 11:19–21

Acts 9:26–28

Acts 2:1–4

---

a. The Coptic literally reads "polluted until the point that."

b. The first three lines on the verso side of the folio repeat the following phrasing from the recto side: "of the Jews, being polluted until the point that the dust of their feet."

c. From the end of December to the end of January.

d. Compare to Ps.-Cyril, *On the Virgin Mary*, where the Virgin Mary appoints Mary Magdalene as the new mother over the virgins she leads. See the introduction, p. 202.

e. I disagree with Coquin's translation here of "disciples." I believe we have here a scribal error. While the Coptic does seem to have the word *mathētēs*, i.e., "disciples," the passage also contains a singular masculine verb modifying the main phrase, paralleling similar constructions to describe the Gospels of Mark and John. Moreover, the emendation renders the larger context more understandable, as Matthew's is the only canonical Gospel lacking in the list, and this change would resolve that absence.

Gabriel's revelation to Mary and Theophilus[a]

14 [1]It happened one day, she was sitting with Lord Theophilus, her custodian, and they were talking about all the Scriptures of God. [2]Theophilus said, "Truly, my thoughts confuse me and I do not understand the fullness of the Scriptures and the genealogies of the first ones because we find much in the Scriptures, each refuting the other."

[3]When she heard these things, she rose and turned her face toward the east. [4]She prayed in Hebrew. [5]Immediately, the holy archangel Gabriel stood in her presence. [6]He said, "Behold, I have come, O Saint. [7]That which you desire, request, because the Savior commanded me to fulfill everything that you request from me."

[8]She said, "My Lord, I desire for you to tell me and Theophilus completely about the fullness of the Scriptures and the dispensation of my Savior." [9]The archangel said to Theophilus,[b] "All the things you desire to know fully, I will tell you completely about all of them because it is I in whom the counsel of the Father is hidden since the creation of Adam until the end of the age."

[10](Theophilus) prostrated himself and greeted him, saying, "Your grace, I have received now, my Lord, the archangel." [11]They sat together like two men talking to one another. [12]Theophilus said, "My Lord, my thoughts confuse me and I do not know the fullness of the Scriptures."

[13]Gabriel said, "Which ones?" [14]Theophilus said, "From the creation of Adam until now [.] possible for those who will seek further after this, because everything you said to blessed Daniel truly happened. [15]But educate me, for a time, about the fullness of the first ones and the dispensation of my Savior, from which tribe he came, (and) why the Hebrews oppos[e] the Christians. [16][I] desire for you to tell me about the flo[o]d and the sku[ll] of Adam, namely, where it [is] on Golg[o]tha.[c] [17]For some s[a]y that the flood brought it (there), while others, in different words, could not establish the truth concerning it. [18]Tell us how the worship of idols came to be, and on which day Adam and Eve were created, and how she came into being, since the Hebrews quarreled whether she existed alone or, as others say, she is from the devil,[d] while in Genesis, God said, 'He brought a sleep upon Adam, he took one of his ribs, and he created Eve.'"

Gen 2:21–22

---

a. This section serves as a preface to the *Cav. Tr.* material that follows, beginning at *Encom. Mary* 15:1. While no precise parallel to this preface exists, Su-Min Ri (*Commentaire*, 89) suggests that a similar type of preface is found in the Arabic recension of *Cav. Tr.*, though the circumstances, the recipient, and the source of the revelation are different between the Coptic and Arabic versions.

b. From this point forward the Magdalene is rarely referenced. What follows seems to be a revelation primarily directed at Theophilus.

c. The tradition of Adam's skull being buried at Golgotha is first attested by Origen of Alexandria in the third century. In *Comm. Matt.* 27.32 (PG 13:1777; cf. John Chrysostom, *Hom. Jo.* 85.1), Origen claims to have received a Hebrew tradition about Adam's skull being buried at Golgotha. However, there is no extant rabbinic witness to such a tradition. Here, the reference probably points to the *Cav. Tr.* tradition, which also locates Adam's skull at Golgotha (23:17–18; cf. 48:15–49:10; see also *Encom. Bapt.* 9:1 in this volume). For a discussion of the complicated traditions surrounding Adam's skull, Golgotha, and early Christianity, see Grypeou and Spurling, *Book of Genesis*, 71–79.

d. Although I know of no tradition where Eve was "from the Devil," at least as early as Tertullian she was deemed "the devil's gateway" (*Cult. fem.* 1.1).

[19]The ar[cha]ngel said, "Truly, [you] seek after higher percept[io]ns. [20]These things have n[o]t been revealed to all the wise. [21]Observe their fullness. [22]Give your heart and your mind [t]o me and I will speak with you because there are many inquiries there before the fullness of all these things. [23]But I will take my leisure and speak with you until I have filled you.

[24]"God created Adam from the virgin earth and he left him without giving him the spirit for forty days. [25]He ascended to heaven, the choir of angels going before him. [26]He sat upon his throne and the angels went to their dwelling places. [27]The quarrel-loving Devil rose and went to Paradise, the place in which Adam was before his existence. [28]He struck him with his finger on his right side, saying, 'Arise, man, and I will give the spirit to your mouth and you will be a slave with your sons.' [29]He suffered, consorting with him, but he did not move him. [30]He placed this curse of shame upon him: that this would be the first of the bad things that would come from his mouth. [31]Immediately, when (the curse) was given, the Father cried upon his throne. [32]He said, 'I repent that I have made man wholly, except that my only-begotten son was grasped, since he was left without having been given the spirit.[a] [33]Because of this, every man who will curse me, cursing his God who created him, God shall come upon him in his anger. [34]Since the word of Genesis is true: 'God brought a sleep upon Adam and he brought Eve from him.'"

Gen 2:21-22

Creation of Adam and Eve

Cav. Tr. 2

15 [1]"In the beginning, God created Adam, on the sixth of Parmoute, Friday, on the first hour of the day. [2]God brought a great quiet upon all the angelic host on high. [3]God said, 'Let us create man according to our likeness and our image.' [4]When the angels heard the voice, they were in a great fear and trembling, (saying), 'A great wonder has been revealed to us today because Go[d] created one in his likene[ss].' [5]W[he]n they said these things, they looke[d] and they saw the right ha[nd] of God, s[tr]etching over the earth. [6]The whole earth was enclosed in his right hand. [7]They saw, behold, from all the elements of the earth, he took a little dust, from every nature of waters, he took a drop, from the nature of the air, a little breath, from every nature of fire, a little from its heat. [8]The angels saw the four elements that God lifted in his right hand. [9]They were astonished that God created Adam from the four humble elements, exc[ep]t is not the entirety [su]bjected to him? [10][.] he was created from the earth so that [eve]ry nature on earth would be [s]ubjected to Adam. [11][F]rom the nature of [w]ater, a drop[.], so that those in the se[a] and the rivers would be under his power, [a] little from the air so that [h]e would be master [o]ver the birds, [a] little from fire so that the flames of fire and the powers of heaven would be a help to him.

Gen 1:26

Gen 2:7

[12]"Then, God created Adam in his holy hands according to his likeness and his image. [13]The angels saw the likeness of Adam, as he had been made in this great glory. [14]They were disturbed, seeing the likeness of his beautiful face, shining like the sun, the lights of his eyes like rays. [15]His body was luminous

---

a. This sentence seems to imply that God leaving Adam without a spirit made him susceptible to the devil's graspings.

and he shone like a crystal. [16]He stood in the middle of the earth. [17]He put his feet upon the place where they fixed the cross of Jesus Christ. [18]He wore royal garments and he placed upon himself the crown of glory. [19]He was king and priest and prophet. [20]He sat upon the throne of his glory there. [21]They brought Adam the birds and the beasts. [22]He named them and they bowed their heads to him. [23]They worshipped the Lord saying, 'Behold, I have set you as king and priest and prophet. [24]It is to you alone that I have given the power over everything that I created.' [25]The angels worshipped God and they adored the work of his hands."

Gen 2:19–20

Satan's fall and the creation of Eve

Cav. Tr. 3

16 [1]"When Satan, the one who is appointed over the last things, saw the height and the glory that God had granted Adam, he became jealous from that moment and he did not want to worship him. [2]When the jealousy overtook him, he fled. [3]He and his whole order with him fell, on Friday, on the sixth of Parmoute at the second hour of the day. [4]When the fall of the devil occurred, he and his whole order removed the garments of glory. [5]He was called 'Satan,' the interpretation of which is 'the one who turned away from God.' [6]He was called 'the Devil' because he caused disorder [.]. [7]He was called 'd[e]mon' because he was cut o[ff] from the garments of his glo[ry] since th[at] day they were removed and he [fled] from the glory of Go[d].

[8]"To Adam, God [descended] in a chari[ot] of fire to par[a]dise. [9]The angels hymned him with the cherubim [and] the seraphim, praising and worshipping God, rejoicing over Adam because he was placed i[n] Paradise. [10](God) commanded him concerning the tree. [11]It was on the third hour of the day, on Friday, that he was placed in Paradise. [12]God brought a sleep upon Adam and he slept. He took his right rib and he formed Eve. [13]When he had awoke, he saw her and he rejoiced over her. [14]Adam was with Eve in Paradise, they were bearing glory and honor and joy. [15]Paradise was in the heights [of] the air, being high [a]bove the mountains and the hi[ll]s of 100 spans according to [the] measure of the spirit. [16][G]od planted a [p]aradise in Eden in the east. [17]He placed man in paradise, paradise surrounding the whole earth,' as the great Moses said. [18]Eden—namely, the inheritance of the saints of the church—is the mercy of God, which has been ordained to spread over all humanity, because God has foreknowledge."

Gen 2:16

Gen 2:21–22

Gen 2:8

Adam and Eve in paradise

Cav. Tr. 4

17 [1]"He foreknew Satan's thoughts, which (Satan) pondered concerning Adam because (God) had made (Adam) a king and priest and prophet. [2](God) placed (Adam) in paradise to work in Eden. [3]God planted the tree of life in the middle of the paradise, namely, the cross of our salvation. [4]When the Devil saw Adam and Eve rejoicing, he was filled exceedingly with jealousy. [5]He settled upon the snake and he flew with him into the air. [6]He settled with him nearby in the paradise, to the side of Adam.

Gen 2:9

[7]"Why did he settle on the snake? [8]Because he knew that there was an ugliness in his likeness and also because, if Eve saw his face, being shameful and frightening, she would tremble and run from him. [9]Like those who take birds,

named 'parrots,'[a] and teach them the Greek language and bring some others and place them in their presence, when one speaks secretly in front of them, then the birds, immediately, hear the voice of those who cry out behind them and they see those who resemble them in their presence, and they rejoice, thinking that those they speak with are their brothers. [10]Immediately, they incline their ears secretly and joyously and they receive the voice that speaks with them. [11]And they become accustomed to learning Greek words.

[12]"It was in this way that the Devil entered. [13]He settled upon the snake and he remained (there) until he found the opportunity and saw Eve resting alone. [14]He called her name so that she would come to him. [15]When she turned, she saw his likeness. [16]He spoke with her and he deceived her with his soft words so that she believed every word. [17]When she listened to him concerning the tree, she ran hastily and she harvested the tree in paradise. [18]She called Adam and he came to her. [19]She stretched herself toward the fruit and she ate it. [20]He ate also. [21]The two were naked and they ma[de] for themselves apron[s] of fi[g] leaves. [22]They remained in the apron[s] of shame for thre[e] hours. [23]I[n] the evening, they received the condemnation of their transgression. [24]God made tunic[s] of skin and he gave them to them, which is mortality and belongs to the [fl]esh of the tomb."

Gen 3:1–7

Gen 3:21

Adam and Eve's punishment

Cav. Tr. 5:1–13

18 [1]"[At] the third hour of the day, Adam was placed in paradise. [2]For three hours, he was joyous in good things; for three hours he was naked. [3]And it was in the ninth hour of the day, in the evening, that his exile from paradise (occurred); they came out in sadness, crying. [4]God spoke with Adam, giving him cour[a]ge, 'Take cou[r]age, Adam. Do not [fe]ar nor be [faint]-hearted. [5][I will] return you to your inhe[rit]ance aga[in]. [6]Look to my [lov]e for you, [.] who I cursed the earth because of you and the [sna]ke who deceived [you.] [7]You, I redeem, you who are not cur[se]d. [8]But, I have made him with[out] feet and I have caused him to move upon his heart and upon his belly. [9]He will eat earth all his days. [10]I set the yoke of submission upon him so that he would remain submitting to men. [11]Now inasmuch as you transgressed my commands, run now from paradise and do not grieve.

Gen 3:17

Gen 3:14

[12]"After this time of exile that I have commanded upon you and the earth that I have cursed, I will send my word and he will redeem you, he having been made flesh from the holy Virgin Mary, from the house of David. [13]At that time, I will redeem you and I will return your inheritance again. [14]Command your children and they will prepare you for burial and they will anoint you with myrrh and cassia and oil and they will bury (your body) in the cave that I will show you on the mountain, because you are the one who is worthy of remaining in it for days until the day when a separation will occur and your sons will be far from paradise. [15]Those who shall remain in those days, I will command them to take your body and they will bury it in the middle of the earth and in that place I will save you and your children. [16]God revealed to Adam all the mysteries of his son: [17]'It is necessary for him to suffer on account of you.' [18]When Adam left paradise, the cherubim took swords of fire and kept watch over it."

Gen 3:24

---

a. Here I follow Coquin and Godron in reading *teitakos* as *psittakos* ("Un encomion," 208).

Cav. Tr. 5:14–32

Adam and Eve beget a family

19 [1]"Adam left Paradise with Eve and he dwelt in the Cave of Treasures; both of them were virgins. [2]After the completion of forty days, Adam and Eve came down from the mountain, from that place. [3]Adam [kne]w Eve, his wife. [4]She conceived and she bore Cain and Elioupeida, his sister. [5]When the children were big, Adam said to Eve, who had borne Abel and Kalmia, his sister, 'Let Cain take Kalmia, the sister of Abel, and Abel himself take Elioupeida, the sister of Cain.'[a] [6]Cain said to Eve, his mother, 'I shall take my sister, let Abel himself take his sister,' because Elioupeida was very beautiful, resembling Eve, her mother. [7]Wh[e]n Adam heard his words, he grieved gr[ea]tly, saying, 'It is a transgression to [take] your sister who was [born] with you.' [8]Afte[r these things], Adam said to them, '[.] take from the fruit[s] of the earth and from the first of the sheep [.] and go up [the] holy mountain. [9]Go [i]nto the Cave of [Tr]easures. [10]Offer up y[o]ur sacrifices and give [.] and pray to God. [11]Afterwards, join with your women.' [12]And Adam, the first priest, went with Cain and Abel up the holy mountain.

Gen 4:1–2

[13]"The Devil had mastery over Cain, who killed Abel, his brother, because of Elioupeida, his sister. [14]When the evil was revealed in his heart, God rejected his sacrifice because he did not bring it in righteousness. [15]And the sacrifice of Abel, God received it. [16]When Cain saw that [Go]d accepted the sacrifice of Abel, jealousy [overtook him] completely. [17][Cain] said [to] Abel, his brother, '[Le]t us go to the fie[ld].' [18]Then [it] happened, they [. in] the field and their [.], Cain raised [against A]bel, his brother, (his hand) and he [killed] him with a stone [.]. [19]He received the [sentence] of the curse. [20][A tremb]ling and mourning came upon him all the days of his life. God reject[ed] his face and caused him to dw[el]l in the forest [and] the marsh."

Gen 4:3–11

Cav. Tr. 6:1–5

The birth of Seth

20 [1]"[Adam a]nd Eve mourned A[bel], their son for one hundred [y]ea[r]s. [2]Then, A[dam] knew Eve, his [wife], and she conceived and she bore [Seth], who was very beautiful in his likeness. [3]He was a man of strength, being perfect like Adam, his father. [4]And he is the one who became the father of the strong ones. [5]Seth [w]as with his [wif]e and he begat [E]nosh. [6]Enosh begat Kenan, Kenan begat Mahalalel. [7]These were those who were born during Adam's lifetime."

Gen 4:25

Gen 5:6

Gen 5:9, 12

Cav. Tr. 6:6–24

Adam's death and the division of the land

Gen 5:5

21 [1]"And Adam lived 930 years. [2]When Mahalalel himself was 130 years old, the day of our father Adam's death drew near. [3]Our fathers, Seth, Enosh, [a]nd Mahalalel, gathered and came to (Adam) an[d] they [al]l received a blessing [from] him. [4]He prayed over them and he commanded Seth, saying, 'Look, my son, what I command you (to do) today, you [comm]and it of En[osh], and Enosh command it of Kenan, and Kenan command it of Mahalalel. [5]Practice this word among your tribes. [6]Prepare [m]y body with myrrh [and c]assia and oil. [7]Take

---

a. *Jub.* 4:8 also contains a tradition of Adam and Eve having two daughters, though their names are instead listed as Awan and Azura. For a discussion of the marriage of Abel and Cain to their sisters, see Grypeou and Spurling, *Book of Genesis,* 122–26.

me and bury me in the Cave of Treasures. [8]And the one who remains from your tribes, at that time, he will take with him my body, and set it in the middle of the earth, namely, that place where God will listen to our entire race. [9]You yourself, my s[o]n, Seth, [b]ecome a [lea]d[er o]ver your peo[ple]. [10]Shepherd them in fear of God. [11]Separate the sons of Cain, the murderer, from your people.'

[12]"When he had ceased to command him, he went limp and he died. [13]All his children gathered to him. [14]Adam died, being 930 years old, at the fourteenth moon, on the fourteenth of Parmoute, on Friday. [15]On that day, the Son of God came and he gave up his so[ul] for our salvation. [16]And he gave [hi]s spirit into the hands of the [fat]her. [17]When [A]dam had died, Seth and his [children] pre-pared [him] for burial and they set him in the C[ave] of Treasures becau[se his death] was the first on earth. [18]They [grieved] him with mour[ning] and they were mourning beca[use of him] for 140 day[s. [19]Af]ter the death of Adam, those begotten from Seth separated from the sons of Cain. [20]Seth took his sons and he wen[t] with them upon [. the] mountain, alone, i[n the place] of the tomb of Ad[am]. [21]Cain, himself, with [his] sons, he remained in [the place] where he killed [Abel]."

An unknown number of pages are missing.[a]

PIERPONT MORGAN LIBRARY, MS. 665(4)

Genealogy from Adam to Nachor

Cav. Tr. 44:12–31

78 [11]"... them, nor also were the sons of the church, those who were historians, able to show how the body of Adam had come to Golgotha, nor also concerning Melchizedek, who were his parents, nor the parents of the holy Virgin Mary. [12]I, also, am the one who will fill you, O Theophilus. [13]And I will not hide anything from you about it, and also because no part of [the ch]urch exists in vai[n]:[b]

1. Adam took Eve, he begat Seth
2. Seth took Kalmia, the sister of Abel, he begat Enosh
3. Enosh took Halot, the daughter of Iobel, he begat Kenan
4. Kenan took Pharit, the daughter of Kattour, she bore Mahalalel
5. Mahalalel took Thather, the daughter of Enosh, she bore Jared
6. Jared took Happit, [the] daughter of Chnithou, she [b]ore [En]o[ch]
7. Enoch to[ok] Gagan, the dau[ght]er of Touna, the son of Mahalalel, she bore Methuselah
8. Methuselah took Sakout, the daughter of Chousin, the son of Enoch, she bore Lamech
9. Lamech took Ichas, the daughter of Chouppa, the son of Methuselah, she bore Noah

---

a. While it is unclear how many intervening pages have been lost, if the text continues to follow *Cav. Tr.*, then roughly 38 chapters of *Cav. Tr.* are missing.

b. For the male members listed in 1–9, cf. Gen 5; for those listed in 10–13, cf. Gen 10:21–25. No corresponding biblical passage exists for the men of 14–16. None of the women's names are biblical. Ri (*Commentaire*, 68) notes that the spellings in the Coptic here for the women's names are quite different from their Syriac counterparts.

9.[a] And Noah took Hecher, the daughter of Omosa, the son of Enoch, she bo[re] Shem

10. [Sh]em took O[.]r, the daugh[ter] of Narna [.] she bore Arpa[ch]shad

11. Arpachshad took Artout, the daughter of Seoul, the son of Iaphet, she bore Shelah

12. Shelah took Morthath, the daughter of Gahenech, the son of Sem, she bore Eber

13. Eber took Salpita, the daughter of Lamech, she bore Peleg

14. Peleg took Ahithit, the daughter of Shelah, she bore Hragau

15. Hragau took Mhat, the daughter of Eber, she bore Serouch

16. Serouch took Hiel, the daughter of Peleg, she bore Nachor"

Four intervening pages have been lost.

Herod and John the Baptist

81 [9]"... the land of Egypt until all that was written was completed. [10]But when the ungodly Herod saw that the Magi laughed at him, he sent (for) and he killed every child who was in Bethlehem and all those who were on its limits, from two years of age and under. [11]When John, the son of Zacharias, was hidden, he was not found. [12]Herod said, 'Truly, John is the king of Jerusalem because the angel spoke with his father in the temple.' [13]And when he did not find John, he also ordered that Zacharias, his father, be killed in the temple. [14]And the anger of God also came upon Herod, the lawless one. [15]And (Herod) was eaten, while living, by worms and his entire body (became foul), and he commanded Archelaus, his son, and Salome, his d[au]ghter, '[If] I die, [do] not place [.] do [.] on it [.] also upon you. [16]But if I die, seize a man from each house in all of Judea. [17]Bring them and kill them so that if I die, all will grieve, so that they will not rejoice over my death.'[b] [18]When Herod, the lawless one, died, behold, the angel of the Lord revealed himself [to J]oseph, say[in]g, '[C]ome out [of] Egypt and [dw]ell in Na[z]areth.'"

Cav. Tr. 47:10–27
Matt 2:13

Matt 2:16

Prot. Jas. 23

Acts 12:23

Matt 2:19–20

John the Baptist baptizes Jesus

82 [1]"[A]nd also when Christ was thirty years old, he was baptized by John, the holy Forerunner, the son of Zacharias. [2]John passed all of his life eating locusts and wild honey. [3]In the nineteenth year of Tiberius, they crucified our Savior, Jesus Christ. [4]Realize for yourself, O Theophilus, that in the fortieth year of Jared, the first 1,000 years was completed. [5]In the fourteenth [. . .]"

Cav. Tr. 48:1–5
Mark 1:9–11 par.; John 1:19–34

Mark 1:6 par.

---

a. The copyist accidentally doubled number nine in the list, so all numbers henceforth are off by one.

b. Cf. Josephus, *Ant.* 17.6.5, where Herod, on his deathbed, requests that the most important Jewish men from each village be gathered in the hippodrome before his death is announced so that they might not rejoice in his passing.

An Encomium on John the Baptist
A new translation and introduction

by Philip L. Tite

The *Encomium on John the Baptist* (*Encom. Bapt.*; *CANT* 184; *CPC* 0170; *CPG* 5150.3) is a collation of traditions revolving around the figure of John the Baptist, extant in two Coptic manuscripts produced in monastic contexts in tenth-century Egypt. The homily on Matt 11:7 that begins *Encom. Bapt.* is attributed to John Chrysostom (1:1–3); however, this attribution is most likely erroneous, based perhaps on a similar homily addressing Matt 11:7 that comes from the hand of John Chrysostom *(Hom. Matt. 37)* or on a more general tendency to incorporate apostolic memoirs into Coptic pseudo-Chrysostom homilies. *Encom. Bapt.* has appeared also in scholarship as *On John the Baptist* by Pseudo-John Chrysostom. Care must be taken to distinguish the text from two works titled *Panegyric on John the Baptist,* one attributed to Patriarch Theodosius of Alexandria (*CANT* 185; *CPC* 0513) and the other anonymous.[1]

Contents
If the text is indeed composite, then there are at least four sets of redactional material that can be identified within it. There are two previously unknown texts brought together—a Homily on John the Baptist and the Apocalypse of the Third Heaven—connected via scribal and transitional material:

A. Scribal Preface (1:1–3): Introducing *Encom. Bapt.* and its key themes; includes the mistaken attribution to John Chrysostom.

B. Homily on John the Baptist (2–8, 21): A sermon in praise of John the Baptist, based on Matt 11:7.

C. Transitional Section of Miscellaneous Material (9–11): Traditions on the fate of Adam's bodily remains, the dead in Amente (the Underworld), the commissioning of the apostles, and the flight of the child John and his mother Elizabeth into the desert.

D. The Apocalypse of the Third Heaven (12–20): Following a post-resurrection appearance, the apostles are given a tour of the seven heavens, particularly the third heaven, which has been given to John the Baptist.

Several consistent themes tie these otherwise disparate and stylistically distinct texts together. In the scribal introduction, John is declared as greater than any "born of women"; he is also "above the holy ones" and even "excels the angels" (1:1–2). The scribe establishes a key theme for *Encom. Bapt.*: John the Baptist has been given honor and glory both on

---

1. See the references to these works in the entry on *Life Bapt. Serap.* in this volume.

earth and in heaven that excels that given to anyone else. The closing of the *Encom. Bapt.* (which either is the conclusion to the Homily or is a colophon added by the scribe) returns to this very theme: "Truly, my dear beloved, there is no one like John the Baptist in heaven and on earth, nor more exalted in glory" (21:1; cf. 21:6). This motif arises throughout the text (e.g., 7:3; 10:4; 13:2; 18:6). This heaven/earth distinction is effectively accomplished by reading the Homily and the Apocalypse of the Third Heaven beside each other: the latter demonstrating the glory given in heaven, while the former upon earth. Both the Homily and the Apocalypse of the Third Heaven closely connect John to Jesus through the affectionate and kinship relationship as well as John's role in Jesus' redemptive work. There are also strong cultic and ethical motifs in these two underlying texts. Those who are allowed into the third heaven are those who have given proper honor to John on earth (again evoking the earthly/heavenly distinction). In the Homily such cultic honoring is exemplified by Jesus. This cultic role extends to being compassionate and merciful, a motif that also arises in the transitional material at 10:1–3. Thus, the reader or congregation is exhorted to embody the charitable nature of both Jesus and John the Baptist.

These connective themes suggest that *Encom. Bapt.* has a greater literary coherence than may be evident upon first reading. Such coherence could indicate that the final redactor (perhaps the scribe) did not randomly stitch traditions together. The overarching theme of honor given to John the Baptist in the scribal preface (1:1–2) may have been a coherent theme that prompted the scribe to join these various sources. Alternatively, such coherence could also call into question source-critical analysis of *Encom. Bapt.* The fact that both of the Coptic manuscripts of the text contain material from the Homily and the Apocalypse supports an argument in favor of literary integrity. However, the internal content and the stylistic features of the Homily and the Apocalypse suggest that we have two separate sources sharing certain thematic motifs.

Manuscripts and Editions

Encom. Bapt. survives in two Sahidic Coptic manuscripts. The more complete of these manuscripts—London, British Library, Or. 7024 (fol. 1a–17b)—based on the colophon (fol. 49b), was produced in 987 CE by the scribe Theopistos (the son of Severus, an archpresbyter of St. Mercurius in Snê) on behalf of one Michael of the city of Snê, and subsequently offered as a gift to the Monastery of St. Mercurius near Edfu. In a different hand a short note follows the colophon mentioning Abba Nicodemus, who perhaps was the one to receive the book on behalf of the monastery. The colophon states that the donation of the book was for "the salvation of his [Michael's] soul" and the edification of the monks (cf. *Encom. Bapt.* 16:5). British Library, Or. 7024 also includes a second text, *The Instructions of Apa Pachomius the Archimandrite* (fol. 18a–49b). A transcription (and only other English translation to date) was published by E. A. W. Budge in 1913.[2] The other manuscript—Paris, Bibliothèque nationale de France, Copte 12918 fol. 116–20—also dated to the tenth century, survives in only four leaves from the White Monastery. E. O. Winstedt published an edition and English translation of the Paris fragments in 1907.[3] The four leaves come from a larger codex that likely included a full version of *Encom. Bapt.* The first three leaves contain material from the Homily—the feeding of the five thousand (6:1–7:1a) and

---

2. Budge, *Coptic Apocrypha*, l–lvi (introduction), 128–45 (text), 335–51 (translation). Budge mistakenly dates the manuscript to 985 CE.

3. Winstedt, "Coptic Fragment."

Jesus' discussion of the reed flute (8:1–3)—followed by a portion of the Apocalypse of the Third Heaven (13:2–17:2). The fourth leaf comes from a later section of the codex and recounts a story of a demon-possessed police officer, exorcised through the power of the martyred Baptist. Winstedt suggests that the codex may have been a "book of the miracles of John."[4] Other possible manuscript evidence includes three sixteenth-century manuscripts of an Arabic *Homily of John Chrysostom on John the Baptist and Matthew 11:7* and an Ethiopic version.[5] To my knowledge, the Arabic and Ethiopic versions have not been edited and translated.

The Paris fragments only offer stylistic variances to the better-preserved British Library, Or. 7024; however, its value lies in presenting us with an independent witness to the circulation of *Encom. Bapt.* with both the Homily and the Apocalypse already together. Stylistic differences suggest that the two Coptic manuscripts are independent productions. The scribal note and transitional material are not extant in the remains of the Paris manuscript. Otherwise, identification of the underlying sources has to be based solely on internal evidence (i.e., content and style).

Encom. Bapt. may have been known to Jacob of Voragine in the thirteenth century, either as a work attributed to John Chrysostom or, more likely, as a set of traditions now contained in *Encom. Bapt.* There are strong thematic (though not structural) ties between the *Golden Legend* 86[6] and *Encom. Bapt.*, along with several references to Chrysostom's treatment of John the Baptist "as more than a prophet" (including at the meeting of Elizabeth and Mary, p. 330; cf. *Encom. Bapt.* 7:2).

Encom. Bapt. has been sorely neglected in previous scholarship. Along with Budge's and Winstedt's editions and translations, there is Walter Till's German translation (1958), which also identified the fragments published by Winstedt with the text translated by Budge,[7] and Anne Boud'hors's French translation (1997). Both Boud'hors and Till offer several corrections to Budge's reading of the Coptic, and Till demonstrates the heavy presence of Greek loanwords in *Encom. Bapt.* As for the text's contents, Budge's introduction to his edition draws a close correlation between the Apocalypse and Egyptian myths of the afterlife. Beyond the English, German, and French translation projects, there has only been a smattering of references to *Encom. Bapt.* in scholarship and no substantial analysis of the text. Occasionally, it has been suggested that the journey into the third heaven is a separate source. Winstedt made the unpersuasive suggestion that *Encom. Bap.* might be related to the Naasene Gnostics described by Hippolytus (*Haer.* 9).

Literary and Theological Significance

Given the possible underlying sources for *Encom. Bapt.*, questions of genre and literary structure need to be addressed first for each section and then as a composite text.

A. *The Homily on John the Baptist*

The Homily is an encomium (a speech offered in praise of someone, usually within a funerary context), likely designed for a liturgical setting in honor of John the Baptist. Situ-

---

4. Winstedt, "Coptic Fragment," 240.

5. See Boud'hors, "Éloge de Jean-Baptiste," 1558. On a possible Ethiopic version, see Gianfrancesco Lusini, "Appunti sulla patristica greca di tradizione etiopica," *SCO* 38 (1988): 469–93 esp. 488.

6. For a modern translation see Jacobus de Voragine, *The Golden Legend: Readings on the Saints* (trans. William Granger Ryan; 2 vols.; Princeton: Princeton University Press, 1993), 1:328–36.

7. Till, "Johannes der Taüfer."

ating this text within the (especially Eastern) liturgical calendar, this sermon likely was delivered early in January (January 7 being the celebration of John the Baptist, following the marking of the baptism of Jesus during Epiphany; see "the eleventh day of the month of Tobe," in 7:3). The material falls into two literary blocks: (1) the life and death of John the Baptist, ending with the funerary love-feast in his honor (chaps. 2–6); and (2) questions from John while in prison to Jesus, who is performing miracles with the crowd, closing with an interpretation of the "reed flute" in the desert (chaps. 7–8). The combination of these two blocks of material is peculiar. Not only is there a shift from John's death, burial, and funeral/love-feast to an indirect exchange between John and Jesus (while John is in prison and Jesus is performing healings), but the preacher then uses this exchange to launch into an exposition of Matt 11:7. The exposition does not follow John Chrysostom's exposition of the "reed flute" (*Hom. Matt. 37,* 1). For John Chrysostom, the concern is whether John the Baptist, in posing his question to Jesus, was like a reed wavering in the wind (Matt. 11:3–7)—i.e., Chrysostom worries that readers could wonder if John the Baptist was losing his faith while in prison. For the preacher of the Homily, however, the focus falls on the reed flute in the desert, reading the flute not as something that should not be identified with John the Baptist, as Chrysostom reads it, but as something that should be read as a positive metaphor for John the Baptist. Likely the preacher has picked up on the lack of a follow-up statement to the reed flute, such as there is to those "in fine clothes" (a negative statement, as those people are "in royal palaces" rather than in the desert) and going to see "a' prophet" (a positive statement, though elevating John beyond what was expected). The reed flute is taken as literally something that draws people out to the desert, just as the preaching of John the Baptist does for the crowds. Despite the awkward combination, both blocks of material work together to praise John the Baptist.

As an encomium, the Homily focuses on praising John the Baptist. Ancient education included training in the production of such speeches as part of epideictic rhetoric. Jerome Neyrey presents five standard conventions that are found in the progymnasmata exercises.[8] Of the five conventions, only one is absent from the Homily—i.e., his second convention "Nurture and Training: Education (teachers, arts, skills, laws, mode of life)." Given the rustic background of John the Baptist and his divine appointment as Jesus' forerunner, this absence is not surprising. The following four conventions from Neyrey's list are present:

1. Origin: Geography and Generation (country, race, ancestors, parents); Birth (special phenomena at birth)

Encomia mention origins in order to highlight noble lineage (land and family) as well as supernatural indicators of the person's specialness. In praising John the Baptist, the sermon places special emphasis on the family relationship between Jesus and John (2:1; 5:3, 4; 6:1, 2; 7:2). This familial bond opens the Homily by elevating John the Baptist beyond the bounds of human praise (2:1). The preacher's modesty is reinforced by John being praised by such eminent figures as Athanasius, Theophilus, Cyril, and Innocent. Drawing upon the Lukan infancy narrative, John's special relationship to Jesus and his function in being a witness to Jesus are reinforced at 7:2 where John leaps in his mother's womb at the meeting of Elizabeth and Mary. The preacher even identifies Jesus as the cause of the miraculous

---

8. Jerome H. Neyrey, "Encomium versus Vituperation: Contrasting Portraits of Jesus in the Fourth Gospel," *JBL* 126, no. 3 (2007): 529–52 at 533.

birth of John. Miracles attached to John's birth arise when the sermon identifies John as "a priest and son of a priest" (2:2), recounting Zechariah's ability to speak being taken from him until John's birth and naming (3:1). A strong affection connects Jesus to John (5:3), a familial bond that explains Jesus' funerary love-feast for his dear cousin (5:4; 6:1). Thus, John's genealogy and birth justifies the praise given to him both in the narrative (i.e., the love-feast) and in the liturgical calendar, as these elements of praise support the scriptural claim that "among those born of women, none greater has arisen than John the Baptist" (2:1; 8:1).

2. Accomplishments: Deeds of the Body (beauty, strength, agility, might, health); Deeds of the Soul (justice, wisdom, temperance, courage, piety); Deeds of Fortune (power, wealth, friends, fame, fortune)

The accomplishments of the person being praised demonstrate his or her virtues—whether physical features, virtues, or societal honors. In an honor/shame culture where the perception of one's society determines one's value, extolling such accomplishments is necessary in offering praise. In the Homily, John the Baptist's primary accomplishment is being the forerunner (2:1) and witness of Jesus (7:1–2) as well as the one deemed worthy enough to baptize Jesus (7:3). While the preacher claims that there are a "great number of his mighty deeds" (3:2) that could be recounted, the other significant deeds of John include fettering and opening his father's mouth (3:1) and being "a medicine and remedy that heals every sickness" (2:2). These accomplishments are directly connected to the name "John" (see 3:2, where the preacher declares: "the name 'John' is one that is worthy of being marveled at, for it is the lamp of the whole world"; cf. John 5:35), thereby directly tying the name to acts of (spiritual) benefaction. John's healing role is tied into such benefaction through the "name" and "the remembrance" of John. Even the narrative function of Zechariah is the naming of John (and the miracle attached to that naming). By stressing both John's role in Jesus' ministry and the benefits attached to his very name, the preacher sets up the benefaction offered by Jesus on behalf of John for the crowds (note, e.g., that Jesus also performs healings among the crowd; 7:2). A funerary feast in honor of John is a logical and appropriate extension of the accomplishments of the honoree.

3. Comparison

In encomia, comparison serves to elevate someone by setting side-by-side either states of equal honor (thus, assigning greatness to the honoree through comparison) or a greater and lesser contrast (with the honoree elevated through discussion of things worthy/unworthy or smaller/greater). In the Homily, the latter approach is used. Framing the entire sermon is the claim that "among those born of women, none greater has arisen than John the Baptist" (2:1; 8:1). The entire sermon is designed to demonstrate the validity of this claim. At 7:3, the preacher directly ties this honoring of John to his kinship relationship to Jesus. John is "most favored" and has "attained greatness above all those honored" because he was "deemed worthy" to baptize Jesus and, thereby, participate in Jesus' soteriological role (cf. John being the "lamp of the whole world"; 3:2; cf. John 5:35).

4. Noble Death and Posthumous Honors

Like other encomia, the Homily offers praise as a memorial for an important person now deceased. Encomia were designed to extol the noble death of the honoree. In antiquity, how one died was as important as one's life for determining the nobility of that person.

This was particularly true in accounts of the philosopher's death and, by extension in early Christian circles, the martyr's death. While many such speeches were funeral orations, the Homily likely was designed for a feast day in honor of John the Baptist. Sermons of this sort were not uncommon in the cult of the saints. *Encom. Bapt.* has two major blocks of material commemorating the noble death of and posthumous honors given to John.

The first block of material, which comes immediately after the preacher declares the "great number of his mighty deeds" (3:2), recounts the death of John at the hands of Herod's executioner due to the ploy of Herodias and her dancing daughter (who remains unnamed in this account) (4). The arrest of John, the hesitation and remorse of Herod, and the accusations by John on the royal family's immorality are all absent from the narrative—the reader is assumed to already know the full story. John plays no active role as a character here, except as the victim of the actions of others. Those actions are presented as a chain of activity linking Herod to John via Herodias, her daughter, and the guard who beheads John (note in the Coptic the repeated use of "then" to link these characters and their actions). Although absent as an active character, John remains the central focus. His death is unjustified, does not follow a trial, and directly leads to both his burial by his disciples and a report to Jesus, and thus the funerary feast in his honor. John's death, therefore, is that of a martyr (see 2:2, where he is explicitly called a martyr).[9] It is perhaps significant that John's death is tied to Herod's birthday, as it is common for a martyr's celebrated "birthday" to be his or her date of death. Note also Serapion's *Life of John the Baptist,* where John's mother, Elizabeth, dies on the same day as Herod (7:2). The contrast between a noble and ignoble death in Serapion's account may also underlie the death/birthday motif here in the Homily. John's death is a noble death.

The second block of material shifts from John's noble death to the posthumous honors bestowed upon John. From 5:3 to 6:2, we have the miraculous feeding of the crowd, understood in *Encom. Bapt.* as a funeral feast for John. Such feasts, according to the Homily, are common and appropriate cultural customs, justified here using the biblical example of Joseph offering such a feast for his deceased father Jacob/Israel (6:2). Thus, what Jesus does for his relative is not only culturally appropriate but is grounded within a biblical example of the founding of the nation of Israel. The feast is tied also to mourning. Upon hearing the news of John's death, Jesus is so moved that he withdraws from the public sphere to enter into private mourning (5:1). When the crowd follows him, they share in his grief (5:4). Furthermore, the feast extends John's noble deeds posthumously. Jesus' rebuke of the disciples intersects both the needs of the crowd ("If they are sent away in such hunger, they will faint along the way") and the ethics of commensality ("What sort of thanksgiving [*eucharist*] is being offered before my relative?" 6:1). Thus, just as John offered benefaction to the people during his life (e.g., 2:2), so also does his death offer benefit to the crowds. Thus, Jesus' compassion and mercy (6:1) mirrors John's noble character. Such posthumous benefaction nicely evokes the liturgical significance of the feast in honor of John ("the remembrance of you" at 2:2). As a sermon, this praise invites the congregation to join in the memorial feast, to be one of "the crowd" and thus to participate in the benefits offered by John the Baptist via Jesus (and now via the preacher/church). Such benefits are contingent on joining the preacher in praising the nobility of John here at the close of Epiphany.

---

9. Compare with *Golden Legend* 86, where John the Baptist is also called a martyr.

B. The Apocalypse of the Third Heaven

The Apocalypse of the Third Heaven demonstrates common apocalyptic literary motifs found elsewhere in early Christian apocalypses.[10] Specifically, this apocalypse follows a spatial axis, where the visionary is swept up or ascends into the heavenly realms, receives special revelations about heavenly things, and descends back to earth with a divine commission. The text is comprised of five literary sections:

    I. Discovery of a Secret Apostolic Book (12)
   II. Post-Resurrection Scene and Ascent in a Luminous Cloud (13:1–14:1)
  III. General Tour of the Totality of the Heavens (14:2–3a)
  IV. Specific Tour of the Third Heaven (14:3b–19)
   V. Conclusion: Descent to Earth (20)

The most developed section is the fourth one. The author's primary concern is with the honor given to John the Baptist in the heavens, specifically his function with regard to the fate of the dead and the wondrous or exotic nature of the third heaven. The other sections of material nicely frame this central presentation of the third heaven.

An apocalyptic vision is supposed to be a secret. Only those worthy to receive the revelation are allowed to be informed. Occasionally, the revelation is said to be written in a book where it is hidden away until the time when it can be read (e.g., Rev. 1:11; 22:7–10; *Herm. Vis.* 1.3.3; 5.5; *Ap. Jas.* 1.29–2.21; *Ap. John* 1.1–4; 31.32–32.5; *2 Apoc. Jas.* 44.14–17; 63.30–32; *Zost.* 1.1–7; 130.1–5; the *Book of Elchasai* fragment 1 [= Hippolytus, *Haer.* 9.13.1–3]; and especially *Apoc. Paul* 1–2).[11] The Apocalypse of the Third Heaven exhibits this secrecy theme in the first section. The author claims to have found an ancient book written by the apostles in Jerusalem while he or she was attending a religious festival. What follows is supposed to be a transcription of the book's contents. From a narrative perspective, the Apocalypse of the Third Heaven is characterized as a lost apostolic text with a secret revelation. Unlike the Homily in the *Encom. Bapt.*, the Apocalypse of the Third Heaven is not an exposition on sacred texts, it *is* sacred text. The antiquity, location, and apostolic authorship all serve, for the author, as literary devices to add credibility to the text.

The Apocalypse proper opens with section two, where we have a post-resurrection appearance of the Savior on the Mount of Olives. Like other texts (e.g., Matt 28:10–20; Acts 1:6–9; *Ep. Pet. Phil.* 132.16–133.8), the appearance occurs when the apostles have "gathered together" (13:1). This restoration of the apostles (though there is no reference to replacing Judas as in the New Testament book of Acts) immediately leads into a global missionary commission ("Go into the whole world, proclaiming to them the gospel of the kingdom"; 13:1). The apostolic commission seems to have no other function in the narrative beyond an excuse for the visionary experience. The text immediately shifts to the topic of John

---

10. John J. Collins, "Introduction: Toward the Morphology of a Genre." See also Collins, *Apocalyptic Imagination,* 1–42. Furthermore, this apocalypse fits Collins's type IIc: "Otherworldly Journeys with Only Personal Eschatology" ("Morphology," 15).

11. See also the discussion in Roelof van den Broek, *Pseudo-Cyril of Jerusalem on the Life and the Passion of Christ: A Coptic Apocryphon* (Supplements to Vigiliae Christianae 118; Leiden: Brill, 2013), 10, where van den Broek briefly mentions *Encom. Bapt.* as one of many Coptic examples of a secret book from the apostles being discovered. For a more detailed overview of this genre of literature ("Pseudo-Apostolic Memoirs" or "Diaries of the Apostles") see Suciu, "Apocryphon Berolinense/Argentoratense," 71–129. Note also the chapters on *B-S Ap.*, *Encom. Mary,* and *Invest. Abat.* in this volume.

the Baptist "and the honors that he (the Savior) bestowed on him in heaven," specifically the third heaven (13:2). The apostles request more precise or in-depth knowledge about the third heaven. They identify this honor granted John the Baptist as payment for his martyrdom (and martyrdom motifs are not uncommon in apocalyptic works; e.g., Mark 13; Rev 6:9–11; 20:4–6; *Apoc. El.* 4; *1 Apoc. Jas.* 27.14–21; 32.13–33.5). The apostles ask for three specific things, all of which are granted in the heavenly journey that follows: (1) to be shown the third heaven; (2) to be shown the "good things" in the third heaven; and (3) to be shown John. In response to their request, the Savior immediately brings a "cloud of light" down and together they ascend in the cloud. The cloud of light appears in other revelatory accounts (e.g., *1 En.* 14:8; *Gos. Judas* 57.16–26; *Allogenes* 62.9–18; *Apoc. Paul* 51; *Zost.* 4.20–24; note also *Life Bapt. Serap.* 7:6–8, 20–21; cf. *Acts Andr. Mth.* 21).

The opening of the Apocalypse is balanced by the closing (section V). Once again the cloud functions as transportation, this time for the descent back to the Mount of Olives. The descent follows the completion of the revelation ("When the good Savior had said these things"; 20:1). Unlike with some texts, such as the *Acts of Peter and the Twelve Apostles, Letter of Peter to Philip,* and the Gospel of Matthew, the commissioning of the apostles is not openly stated once again, though given the location (Mount of Olives) and the earlier commissioning (13:1; cf. 16:4 where an explicit commission does occur) we can assume that the apostles were now ready for their missionary endeavors. Rather than a repeated commissioning, the Apocalypse of the Third Heaven closes with a worshipful tone as the Savior ascends. We have angelic hymns in worship of the Savior as well as a peace wish given to the apostles. The text closes, therefore, on a tone of reverence and awe.

The third section is a brief transition into the main section of the Apocalypse (section IV). Here the Savior gives the apostles a complete tour of the heavens, which, for this text, are comprised of seven heavens. The narrator does not indicate whether or not the apostles entered any of the heavens, but simply that they were shown "everything." The emphasis, therefore, falls not on the content of the seven heavens but on the completeness of the tour. This emphasis serves two literary functions. First, it fits with other visionary tours, such as in the *Book of the Watchers* (*1 En.* 1–36), where the visionary is shown the totality of the universe. Thus, the revelation is complete and absolute. Nothing is missing. Second, by first seeing all the other heavens, the apostles, and thus the readers, are assured of the greater quality of the third heaven. There is no doubt in the comparison. John truly has been given greater "glory and honor" than any other in the heavens (13:2b).

The revelation of the third heaven breaks down into four subsections: an initial tour of the third heaven and then three discourses by the Savior. Once the apostles have entered (or reentered) the third heaven, they are immediately struck by its beauty, opulence, and magnificence (15:1). This wonder is mirrored in the presentation of John the Baptist and his parents, Zechariah and Elizabeth—all three dressed in magnificent clothing embellished with precious stones or gems. This opening subsection (15) technically fulfills all three of the apostles' requests while adding John's family (this is one of the few familial elements in the Apocalypse of the Third Heaven) and a hierarchal presentation of the apostles with Peter at the head and Matthias or Matthew at the end (15:1). An awkward shift occurs at 15:3, where James, the brother of the Lord, takes on the first-person narrative voice. The first-person intrusion of James has led some scholars to label this section of *Encom. Bapt.* as an Apocalypse of James (implicitly suggesting a separate source from the rest of *Encom. Bapt.*) or an Apocalypse of John (the latter due to a mistranslation by

Budge).[12] Both before and after 15:3 the voice is first-person plural (the apostles). Furthermore, James plays no role in the rest of the text (indeed, it is Peter that stands at the head of the apostles in this text). Added to this awkward shift in voice is the unnecessary redundancy of the promise of good things to those "who remember him (John the Baptist) on earth" (15:3b; cf. 15:2b). It is possible that 15:3 is an interpolation intended to identify the visionary so as to grant a first-person oath to support the veracity of the revelation. It is also possible that 15:3 is designed to reinforce the earlier statement by means of redundancy (and thus is not an interpolation).

The main body of the Apocalypse of the Third Heaven is comprised of three discourses by the Savior. The first and third discourses focus on the fiery river through which the dead must pass and the golden boat that is given to John the Baptist to ferry the souls of the dead into the third heaven. The central discourse offers a description of the wonders of paradise in the third heaven. The first discourse opens by establishing the apostolic and angelic witnesses for the revelation (both according to a hierarchal ranking) (16:1-2). Just as they were witnesses to the Savior's life on earth, so also now they are to function as witnesses to the heavenly honors bestowed upon John the Baptist. Furthermore, the explicit missionary commissioning is directly connected to "remembering" John the Baptist.

The discourses on the fiery river and the golden boat focus on the fate of those dead who have given honor to John the Baptist on earth. Emphasis on "remembrance" of John the Baptist dominates these discourses. Indeed, the explicit commission at 16:4 identifies the content of missionary preaching as calling people to such remembrance. The theme of remembrance carries cultic and ethical implications. The giving of offerings, love-feasts, charitable gifts, or preserving such remembrance in "the holy book" or precious fabrics "in (John's) place" are all acts in support of the veneration of John the Baptist, specifically within the cult of the saints (16:5; 19:2; cf. *Golden Legend* 86).[13] As in the Homily, these acts—and the subsequent benefits—are connected to John's "name" (cf. 3:2). Ethical acts comprise feeding the hungry, giving drink to the thirsty, and clothing the naked (16:5; 17:2; cf. Luke 3:10-14; *Apoc. Paul* 40).[14] Passage into the third heaven is directly linked to such reverence of John through the lampstands of the boat's magical oars ("Any person who kindles a lamp at the place . . ."; 19:2).[15] Thus, actions in life have an impact on the soul's fate in the afterlife.[16] As with the Homily, social ethics are directly linked to John

---

12. I have decided to name this apocalypse the Apocalypse of the Third Heaven, in part to distinguish it from other apocalypses attributed to James, to which the Apocalypse of the Third Heaven has no relationship, and partly due to the internal content of the apocalypse and the possible interpolation of 15:3.

13. The offering of "a holy book" at 16:5, especially with spiritual benefits, parallels the motivation for the production of British Library, Or. 7024 and its being given to the Monastery of St. Mercurius (as indicated in the colophon).

14. Note Theodosius, *Pan. Bapt.* 2:9-3:1 attributes such ethical activity to John's parents, Zechariah and Elizabeth.

15. Budge (*Coptic Apocrypha*, ix, lvi; cf. lxxi) sees the oars and lampstands indicating a second boat in *Encom. Bapt.* 19. Given the symmetry between the first and third discourses to bracket the second discourse, as well as the lack of any indicators that a second boat is being introduced into the narrative, it is more likely that the boat of 19 is the same golden boat of 17.

16. The lampstands may also be metaphors in honor of John the Baptist, perhaps derived from John 5:35. Such an understanding arises in *Golden Legend* 86, where the celebration of John's death both praises him and lowers him in relation to Christ: "Lighted torches are also carried around this bonfire, because John was a burning and shining torch, and a wheel is spun because the sun begins to be lower in its cycle. This signifies the decline of Saint John's fame, by which he was thought to be Christ, as he himself testified when he said: 'I must decrease, but he must increase'" (trans. Ryan, p. 336). Gregory of Tours, *Glor. mart.*

the Baptist (cf. 2:2; 7:2): just as Jesus embodied the compassion of John, so also must those who wish to enter the third heaven.

These two discourses describe the role that John the Baptist plays in the afterlife. John is the ferryman of the dead and is given a golden boat for conveying these souls across the fiery river. At the end of the crossing, the Savior will baptize these souls in the river, where it will be like a hot bath (cf. *3 En.* 36). The ferryman of the dead is a motif that is certainly at home in Egyptian mythology of the afterlife.[17] As Egyptian cemeteries were commonly located on the west side of the Nile, the place of the dead was often referred to as "the West" and the dead themselves "Westerners" (with Osiris as "foremost of the West" or "foremost of the Westerners"). Thus, the term Amente ("the West") could be used in reference to both the western side of the Nile, where the dead would be buried, and to the realm where the dead dwell. The term nicely taps into the journey of the sun in the transportation of the dead to this realm, where the sun sets in the west. In Egyptian views of the afterlife, the dead (or their *ba*) are often portrayed as being ferried on a celestial boat by the ferryman Anubis or Herfhaf. This boat can be portrayed as a solar boat (the bark or boat of Ra). For example, a very popular text regarding the afterlife from Roman Egypt reads:

> Hail Osirius of the god's father, god's servant of Amun-Re king of the gods, god's servant of Min-Amun, Osoeris, justified, son Spotous, justified. You will enter the underworld in great purity. The two truths will purify you in the great hall. Cleansing will be performed for you in the hall of Geb. Your body will be purified in the hall of sunlight. You see Re when he sets and Atum in the evening. Amun is with you, giving you breath. Ptah fashions your body. You will enter the horizon together with Re. Your *ba* will be taken to the *neshmet*-bark in company with Osiris. Your *ba* will be divinized in the house of Geb. You are justified forever and ever.[18]

Here we find not only the use of a sun boat, but also a purification process for the dead to enter into the underworld. Similarly, P.Parma 183, a papyrus from the first century CE, states: "Your *ba* will soar skywards into the presence of Re." P.Parma 183 further describes bodily rejuvenation as an act of purity and blessing.[19] As in the Apocalypse of the Third Heaven, the dead must be purified. One of Osiris's key functions was to judge the dead, allowing only the righteous access to the afterlife.[20] Consequently, preparing the deceased

---

14, tells the tale of a young girl who, while lighting lamps with a candle in the oratory housing the relics of John the Baptist, miraculously receives a spark to light her candle so she could find her way. See also the healing miracle in *Glor. mart.* 15.

17. Budge (*Coptic Apocrypha*, lxi–lxxii, especially lxi–lxvi on Amente) makes a strong link between Egyptian mythology and the Coptic texts he translates, including *Encom. Bapt.* However, he does not identify any connections with Greco-Roman myth. See also Barry, "Magic Boat," 195–98 for further parallels. Barry briefly mentions *Encom. Bapt.*, following Budge's connection of the ferryman motif to Egyptian myth.

18. Text 25: "The Letter for Breathing Which Isis Made for Her Brother Osiris" 3.19–20 (Smith, *Traversing Eternity*, 470). See also, P.BM Ea 10507 (= Text 12, Smith, *Traversing Eternity*, 262–63).

19. P.Parma 183 Recto 1.19–20 (= Text 35, Smith, *Traversing Eternity*, 539).

20. Furthermore, Osiris served as moral exemplar for the dead. See Smith, *Traversing Eternity*, 6: "The god Osiris was not only the ruler of the realm of the dead and the chief of its tribunal. He was also a model for emulation by the deceased. . . . Subsequently, Osiris was revivified by her [Isis], with the help of other gods and goddesses, and justified in a tribunal against his murderer."

for the afterlife was vitally important.[21] Sinfulness and morality are shared concepts between Egyptian motifs of the afterlife and *Encom. Bapt.* In both cases, actions in life affect existence in the afterlife. During the Ptolemaic and Roman periods, a negative view of the West spread in afterlife texts. Amente was seen as a gloomy place of darkness and suffering from which the dead need liberation.[22] For an Egyptian reader of *Encom. Bapt.*, such a view of the realm of the dead may fit nicely the promise that Christ will not abandon the righteous to Amente (10:1–2; and esp. 16:5, 7). This view of a solar boat conveying the dead may have been the inspiration for the golden boat in the Apocalypse of the Third Heaven and the *Apocalypse of Paul* (if these Christian texts were produced in Egypt). Significant is that only worthy or moral souls would be ferried to the land of Osiris (cp. the Apocalypse of the Third Heaven 16:5–7).

The concept of the ferryman is found also in Greco-Roman mythology. Plato's *Phaedo* 107B–115C, for example, presents, in Socrates' voice, a view of the world of the afterlife that closely parallels what we find in the Apocalypse of the Third Heaven. The *Phaedo* describes hot and cold rivers connecting the various regions of the world (111E), not unlike the fiery river in our apocalypse. Of these, there are four great rivers, three of which flow into the Acherusian lake (112E–113D): Oceanus, Acheron (directly flowing to the lake), Pyriphlegethon (via the Mediterranean to Tartarus and then to the Acherusian lake), and the Stygian (via the Styx to Tartarus and then to the Acherusian lake). The dead that are ferried along the Acheron are purified when they reach the Acherusian lake (113D-E). Such purification is similar to what we find in the Savior's first discourse on the golden boat (17:3). As in the Apocalypse of the Third Heaven, the journey of the dead in the *Phaedo* leads them to a paradise.

A common mythical figure is Charon, the Greek ferryman of souls, who transports the dead for a coin (note the accusation of avarice in Apuleius, *Metam.* 6.18). Unlike Virgil's rugged presentation of Charon (*Aeneid* 6.290–322), the Apocalypse of the Third Heaven dresses John the Baptist in splendor (15:1; perhaps as a heavenly contrast to the rugged apparel he had on earth; cf. Mark 1:6//Matt 3:4). As with Charon in Euripides, *Alcestis* 252–57, the boat of John the Baptist has oars; yet the oars of the golden boat in the Apocalypse of the Third Heaven are evidently not manned by John but are magical oars that seem to work on their own (or by angelic means, if the lampstands are taken as symbols for angels, perhaps guardian angels for the souls; cf. *Apoc. Paul* 7; Plato, *Phaedo* 108C, 113D). The cult of Charon as described by Strabo (*Geogr.* 14.1.44) ties Charon (along with Pluto and Kore) to healing, a motif that nicely parallels John the Baptist's function in the Homily (2:2; cf. 7:2).

The crossing of a river or lake to a heavenly paradise is also found in early Christian traditions, such as the apostles' journey to the city of Habitation in the *Acts of Peter and the Twelve Apostles.* Just as the journey to Habitation is fraught with dangers, so also is the fiery river potentially threatening here in the Apocalypse of the Third Heaven. A golden boat is also mentioned in *Apoc. Paul* 23, when Paul enters the golden city of Christ, a city with golden gates through which only pure souls can pass (cf. *Apoc. Paul* 12). *Apoc. Paul* has a river of fire where lukewarm souls are punished, thus offering a negative function of the river in contrast to the positive, baptismal function found in the Apocalypse of the Third Heaven.

---

21. Smith (*Traversing Eternity,* 6) refers to this as "moral mummification."
22. Smith, *Traversing Eternity,* 9.

The central discourse describes the wonders of paradise with agricultural images. Paradise is a place of great abundance, with fruits that are huge and satisfying (18:2–4) (cf. *Apoc. Paul* 21). The spices listed are exotic and expensive items, thereby reinforcing the image of a realm of splendor (18:2; cf. *Apoc. Peter [Eth.]* 16 where such a garden is also presented; in the parallel Greek fragment, the text adds the shining raiment worn by those living there, such as the "wings of light" at *Encom. Bapt.* 16:5). These are the "good things" that are promised to those who remember John the Baptist on earth. Again, there is a strong parallel with the *Phaedo,* where the true upper heaven or real earth is described, in good Platonic terms, as an uncorrupted realm of which the earth and lower heavens are "injured and corroded" reflections (110A). This upper world is filled with an abundance of precious stones as well as beautiful trees and fruits (110C-D). No disease exists in this upper realm (111B). And this is the realm where the dead can converse with the gods (111C). All these characteristics apply to the third heaven: John and his parents are clothed with precious stones and clothing (15:1); paradise is filled with exotic and abundant fruits, trees, and spices (18:2–4); the apostles stand in the presence of wondrous beings (John, his parents, the angels) (15:1; 16:1–3); and healing elements in the Homily may nicely parallel what arises in Socrates' description of the upper world (direct references to healing do not arise in the Apocalypse of the Third Heaven, though satisfaction, plenty, and not being abandoned to Amente are key motifs). This description of paradise also fits within an Islamic context, where the Qur'an describes paradise as a garden through which rivers flow (e.g., 2:25, 3:15, 4:57, 85:11), sometimes with a direct reference to Eden (9:72, 18:31; cf. Gen 1:11), and as a place of plenty (43:68–73) and adornments for the righteous (gold and silver bracelets and silk clothing; 18:31 and 76:21; cf. *Encom. Bapt.* 15:1).

This discourse also presents the reason for John being worthy of such honor using Trinitarian language. According to the Apocalypse of the Third Heaven, when John baptized Jesus he became a witness to all three members of the Trinity (18:6). Not only does the description of the third heaven demonstrate the great honor given to John the Baptist (see 18:6a), but it is designed to motivate the reader to fulfill her or his ethical and cultic obligations within the veneration or remembrance of John (19:2).

C. Transitional Material: Miscellaneous Traditions

Between the Homily and the Apocalypse of the Third Heaven, the scribe or author has inserted a series of seemingly random traditions loosely related to John the Baptist. These traditions fall into three literary blocks. The first two blocks close with a transitional section that returns to the theme of honoring John the Baptist (9:2; 10:4).

The first block relates a tradition about the bodily remains of Adam (9). Adam's body is transplanted and reburied in Jerusalem by the Noahic flood. Later the Savior stands on the head of Adam while teaching. Although the narrator does not explain this legend, nor how it relates to John the Baptist, it fits into a rich tradition about Adam's bodily remains and especially his skull that was widespread in the Eastern Christian areas (e.g., Armenia, Ethiopia, Romania, Russia, and Bulgaria), but also can be found in Irish apocryphal legends and Italian Renaissance art. These traditions, which still persist today, may go back to at least the third century (as Origen is aware of an earlier version of this legend).[23] In

---

23. Origen, *Comm. Matt.* 27.32 (PG 13:1777; Caten. Mss Graec). The attribution of this tradition to "the Hebrews" (either Jews or Jewish Christians) only appears in the Greek and not the later Latin version. John Chrysostom (*Hom. Jo.* 85.1) also knew of this tradition.

the Irish *Saltair na Rann,* it is also by means of the Noahic flood that Adam's remains are brought to Jerusalem.[24] Artistic and literary imagery have Jesus' blood dripping onto the skull of Adam at the base of the cross, thus indicating the salvation of humanity through the crucifixion. In legends of the Holy Rood, which build on the *Life of Adam and Eve* and the *Apocalypse of Moses,* it is from seeds or a branch planted in the skull of Adam by his son Seth that a tree grows, the same tree used for Jesus' cross. In the tenth-century Bulgarian *Tale of the Tree of the Cross,* which is a compilation of Byzantine Greek legends, we find a well-developed tale of this legendary tree along with a reference to the head of Adam being found in the Jordan River by the child Jesus and later buried at Golgotha. These traditions suggest that the bodily parts of Adam are tied to salvation history, specifically the reversal of the fall of the first Adam by the second Adam (= Christ).[25] *Encom. Bapt.* 9 intersects four temporal or spatial periods within such a salvation history along a temporal apocalyptic axis: (1) the body of Adam, (2) Noah's flood, (3) Jerusalem as the center or mother of Judaism or Israel, and finally (4) the coming of the Savior. All elements come together in the fourth period, bringing history to a soteriological climax.[26]

The second block taps into traditions of Christ's descent into the underworld between his crucifixion and resurrection as well as offering another commissioning of the apostles (10). This block emphasizes the mercy and goodness of Christ and contains no direct reference to John the Baptist until the transitional section (10:4). Although the *Descensus ad inferos* is perhaps most well known from the *Acts of Pilate,* the motif of a liberating Christ figure is both widespread and enduring. Whereas the *Acts of Pilate* presents Jesus as extending redemption to biblical figures who had died before the coming of the messiah, *Encom. Bapt.* extends that temporal quality to an ethic of inclusivity. Christ "gathers all sinners," including those "who have been in Amente since the beginning" (10:2). The inclusive offering of redemption includes those who are of the lowest social strata—i.e., tax collectors and prostitutes (10:2–3). Four New Testament figures in particular are mentioned (though not identified by name): a "prostitute you made a virgin" (= either Mary Magdalene or the woman caught in adultery in John 8:2–11); "a bandit you brought into Paradise" (= the Lukan bandit crucified with Jesus who was saved); "a tax collector you made an Evangelist" (= Levi/Matthew); and "a persecutor you made an apostle" (= Paul). A strong restorational theology arises here with the phrases "all these abounding mercies you have gathered to you this day" and "you rounded up those who had been scattered" along with "I will give you rest" (10:2). This ingathering may evoke the diaspora and restorational motif of Acts 1–2. The commissioning of the apostles at 10:3 extends Christ's redemptive work to the activity of the apostles. Unlike other instances of apostolic commissioning in *Encom. Bapt.,* 10:3 does not relate the content of preaching to honoring John the Baptist. Rather, the apostles are to "proclaim . . . the redemption for the forgiveness of sin." Here sinfulness, and not the cult of the saints, is central.

The third block returns the reader to John the Baptist, specifically the Massacre of the Innocents in Matt 2:16–18 and the flight of Elizabeth and her child, John, into the desert. The narrative explains how John ended up in the desert before appearing at the Jordan

---

24. A similar motif appears in the *Cave of Treasures* 18:6, 23:17–18 (cf. 48:15–49:10), where Adam's body is placed on the ark and transported to Golgotha where it is buried.

25. Theodosius, *Pan. Bapt.* 22:12 presents John the Baptist (like Christ) as a second Adam and Adam as the first forerunner.

26. Tite, "Body Parts Abound!" offers a more thorough discussion of these Adam traditions in connection to *Encom. Bapt.*

River. Divine providence is a central theme here, as is indicated not only in the saving of baby Jesus from Herod's massacre, but in Elizabeth and John eluding Herod's executioners, finding shelter miraculously in the rock (along with heating and air conditioning!), obtaining a supply of food and other necessities, and living amicably with wild animals. Beyond Matt 2, this material either draws upon or parallels traditions found in *Prot. Jas.* 22 and *Life Bapt. Serap.* 3.

Original Language, Date, and Provenance

As with many early Christian texts that survive only in Coptic, *Encom. Bapt.* could be interpreted as a translation of an earlier Greek version no longer extant. The prominence of Greek loanwords running throughout *Encom. Bapt.* would seem to lend weight to such a suggestion.[27] If an earlier Greek version underlies the Coptic, then *Encom. Bapt.* could have originated outside of Egypt or it could have been produced within a Greek-speaking community within Egypt. However, as scholarship on Coptic manuscripts is increasingly recognizing, Greek words in Coptic texts need not indicate a translation from Greek into Coptic. Coptic texts often use Greek terms, especially within Christian liturgical contexts or when dealing with Christian traditions.[28] The stylistic differences between the Paris and London manuscripts, however, could suggest independent translation from a Greek original. The internal evidence, however, is not strong enough to argue either way. External evidence offers a strong argument for Coptic as the original language of *Encom. Bapt.*; specifically that the Pseudo-Chrysostom encomia preserved in Coptic do not have a Greek manuscript tradition.[29] Thus, the *Encom. Bapt.* seems to fall within a Coptic-Arabic-Ethiopic continuum with the Greek loanwords being Coptic lexemes rather than clues to an underlying Greek original.

If *Encom. Bapt.* originated in Greek, then the text could have circulated from outside of Egypt and thus may reflect non-Egyptian motifs. If the text circulated within Roman Egypt's urban context, even if originally in Coptic, then Hellenistic ideas may have been picked up by the earliest readers. Such an implication is especially relevant with regard to concepts of the afterlife where Greco-Roman and Christian myths of the journey of the dead (in particular the ferryman motif) may have as much a bearing on the reading of the Apocalypse as would those Egyptian myths identified by Budge.

The *terminus ante quem* of *Encom. Bapt.* is established by the manuscript evidence as the tenth century. At the earliest, the text may go back to the latter half of the sixth century, given the reference to John with the title "Chrysostom" ("golden mouth") (1:1), a title not attributed to him until over a century after his death. This reference, however, only offers a *terminus post quem* for the scribal note in the final version of *Encom. Bapt.* and not for the rest of the text (either as a complete text or as independent texts/traditions). Most likely the scribal note was written in the tenth century when the manuscript was produced. *Encom. Bapt.* does demonstrate knowledge of earlier Christian traditions, such as the fate of Adam's body parts (suggesting a date of the third or fourth century), the flight of Elizabeth and John into the desert (e.g., in *Prot. Jas.* 22:3, end of the second century), the *Descensus ad inferos* traditions (from the second century onwards; e.g., in the *Acts of Pilate* and the *Interpretation of Knowledge*), and the apocalyptic traditions of Paul's journey into the third heaven (see the

---

27. Till, "Johannes der Taüfer," *passim.*
28. So also Boud'hors,. "Éloge de Jean-Baptiste," 1557.
29. See Lucchesi, "Trois éloges coptes," 323–24.

two independent *Apocalypses of Paul;* again, fourth century—though the influence could be 2 Cor 12:2–5). These parallels would suggest a date no earlier than the beginning of the fifth century, though some of these traditions may pre-date those parallel texts (e.g., *Encom. Bapt.* 11 or its material could pre-date Serapion). There is also an odd mention at 18:2 of an exotic spice. The Coptic is *mouschatōn,* which Till (followed by Boud'hors) has suggested might be nutmeg (identifying this term with the Greek *moschos,* as an earlier variant of the modern Greek word *moschokaruon* for nutmeg). This translation is speculative, of course, and we should be careful not to put too much weight on such a reading, but if correct then it would suggest a date no earlier than the eighth century as nutmeg was not introduced into the Mediterranean world until that time.[30] Comparing *Encom. Bapt.* to other Coptic memoirs of the apostles, furthermore, reinforces a dating of no earlier than the fifth century (though the christological polemics of such memoirs are not evident in the *Encom. Bapt.*).[31] Consequently, *Encom. Bapt.* could be dated anytime from about the late fourth/early fifth century to the tenth century (though a date closer to the tenth century seems more plausible) and it could have originated either in Egypt (in Coptic or Greek) or, less likely, it could have circulated to Egypt where it was then translated into Coptic.

Translation

The following translation is the first English translation published since Budge's edition from over a century ago. This fresh translation is based on the critical edition prepared by Budge in consultation with the Paris manuscript edited by Winstedt. The chapter/verse system is offered in place of the recto/verso page numbering found in Budge, in order to highlight thematic blocks of material for the reader as well as to suggest editorial transitions between the sources. Quotations of Scripture, in most cases, have not been harmonized with the NRSV in an effort to best preserve the particular readings of the Coptic text.

Bibliography

EDITIONS AND TRANSLATIONS

Boud'hors, Anne. "Éloge de Jean-Baptiste." Pages 1553–59 in *EAC* vol. 1.

Budge, Ernest A. W. *Coptic Apocrypha in the Dialect of Upper Egypt.* London: Oxford University Press, 1913. (Edition and translation of the London manuscript, pp. 128–45, 335–51.)

Till, Walter C. "Johannes der Taüfer in der koptischen Literatur." *Mitteilungen des Deutschen Archäologischen Instituts Abteilung Kairo* 15 (1958): 128–45, 335–51.

Winstedt, Eric O. "A Coptic Fragment Attributed to James the Brother of the Lord." *JTS* 8 (1907): 240–48. (Edition and translation of the Paris fragment.)

STUDIES

Barry, Phillips. "The Magic Boat." *Journal of American Folklore* 28, no. 108 (1915): 195–98.

Collins, John J. "Introduction: Toward the Morphology of a Genre." *Semeia* 14 (1979): 1–20.

———. *The Apocalyptic Imagination: An Introduction to Jewish Apocalyptic Literature.* 2nd edition. Biblical Resource Series. Grand Rapids, Mich.: Eerdmans, 1998.

---

30. See Andrew Dalby, *Food in the Ancient World from A to Z* (London/New York: Routledge, 2003), 89 and references listed.

31. Suciu, "Apocryphon Berolinense/Argentoratense," 121–29.

Kuhn, Karl H. *A Panegyric on John the Baptist attributed to Theodosius Archbishop of Alexandria.* CSCO 269, Copt. 34. Leuven: Secrétariat du CorpusSCO, 1966.

Lucchesi, Enzo. "Trois éloges coptes de Jean-Baptiste attribués à Athanase, Théophile et Cyrille d'Alexandrie." *VC* 53 (1999): 323–24.

Neyrey, Jerome H. "Encomium versus Vituperation: Contrasting Portraits of Jesus in the Fourth Gospel." *JBL* 126, no. 3 (2007): 529–52.

Smith, Mark. *Traversing Eternity: Texts for the Afterlife from Ptolemaic and Roman Egypt.* Oxford: Oxford University Press, 2009.

Suciu, Alin. "Apocryphon Berolinense/Argentoratense (Previously Known as the Gospel of the Savior). Reedition of P. Berol. 22220, Strasbourg Copte 5–7 and Qasr el-Wizz Codex ff. 12v–17r with Introduction and Commentary." PhD diss., Université Laval, 2013.

Tite, Philip L. "Body Parts Abound! The Soteriological Significance of Adam's Traveling Head in the Coptic *Encomium of John the Baptist*," paper presented at the AAR/SBL Pacific Northwest Regional meeting, Seattle University, Seattle WA, 2013.

An Encomium on John the Baptist

Scribal preface

1 [1]An encomium, which our holy father Saint Apa[a] John, archbishop of Constantinople—who was glorious in every respect—the holy Chrysostom, proclaimed to the glory and honor of the holy John the Baptist, the holy forerunner and relative of the Christ,

[2]Who, *among those born of women, none greater has arisen;*   Matt 11:11//Luke 7:28
Who, above the holy ones, God exalted in honor and glory;
Who, in purity, excels the angels.

[3]He[b] proclaimed this encomium in connection with the passage written in the Gospel of Matthew, explaining to us the meaning of the words which are written: "*What did you go out into the desert to look at?*" In God's peace may his   Matt 11:7
holy blessing come upon us, so that we may all attain salvation. Amen.

HOMILY ON JOHN THE BAPTIST

The author's humility and the praiseworthiness of John

2 [1]My beloved, I wish to proclaim to you some of the exalted words and right judgments of the Baptizer, who is pure, and the Forerunner, who is glorious—that is, the holy John, the relative of Christ. But I find myself in serious trouble, for my tongue falters, incapable of declaring his might and his honor in the manner that they deserve. Furthermore, our holy fathers, the God-fearing bishops who lived before our time—Athanasius, Theophilus, Cyril, and Innocent—declared many exalted words about you, O John the Baptist, who, *among those born of women, none greater has arisen.*   Matt 11:11//Luke 7:28

[2]Who of our forbearers has not uttered words of praise about you, O you priest and son of a priest, prophet and son of a prophet, virgin and martyr, equal of any angel, and, dear holy John the Baptist, the friend of the true bridegroom who is the Christ? Truly your name and the remembrance of you have become a medicine and remedy that heals every sickness.[c]

---

a. "Apa" is a title of reverence.

b. That is, John Chrysostom.

c. Linking the name of John to these various titles serves a hagiographic function. Compare with a similar linking of titles to names in *Golden Legend* 86. Like *Encom. Bapt.*, the birth of John the Baptist in *The Golden Legend* begins with a brief discussion of the name of John prior to the actual birth and naming narrative. See also *Encom. Bapt.* 7:3.

The naming of John the Baptist

Luke 1:5–25

3 [1]I now speak about John, who fettered the tongue of his father through the act of his conception, and who again made the mouth of his father to be opened through his birth. For when Zechariah was asked, "What do you want him to be called?" he made a sign with his hand by which he asked for a writing tablet. He wrote these three letters that are wonder-worthy: namely, Iota and Omega and Alpha. In the very act of writing, his mouth suddenly opened, and, his tongue now set free, he spoke and he gained strength. He cried out with a loud voice,

Luke 1:59–63

"John is his name!"

John 5:35

[2]For in truth the name "John" is one that is worthy of being marveled at, for it is the lamp of the whole world. But my tongue falters greatly, and it will fail in recounting the great number of his mighty deeds; nevertheless, I desire to set out on my journey upon the sea of understanding.

Matt 14:6–12//Mark 6:21–29

The death of John the Baptist

4 [1]When the birthday of the accursed Herod arrived, the daughter of Herodias came forth and she danced, pleasing Herod and those dining with him.[a] Then he promised to give her anything she asked for. She went to her mother to report this to her. (Herodias) said to her, "Ask for the head of John the Baptist, and have them present it upon a platter."

[2]She returned to the king and said to him, "Give me at this very moment the head of John the Baptist upon a platter." The king ordered that it be given to her. He sent a guard to the prison with orders to fetch John's head. (The guard) brought it back on a platter. He gave it to the girl and she brought it to her mother. [3]Then his disciples[b] came and took his body and they buried it. And they conveyed the news to Jesus.

Jesus' reaction and the feeding of the crowds

5 [1]Upon hearing the news, Jesus withdrew into the desert, to a solitary location by himself. When the crowd heard of this, they followed after Jesus. When Jesus saw the crowd, he felt sorry for them. When evening came, his disciples came to him and said, "This is a desert place. Dismiss the crowd so that they may go buy food to eat in the nearby villages."

[2]But Jesus said to them, "Do you have nothing to give to them to eat?" And they said to him, "We have nothing but five barley loaves and two fish." Then Jesus said, "Bring them here." Commanding the crowd to sit down upon the grass, he took the five barley loaves and two fish, and, looking up to heaven, he blessed, broke, and gave them to the disciples. The disciples then gave them to the crowd, and all were well fed. And the remnants that were collected filled five baskets. And the number fed were about five thousand, not counting women

Matt 14:13–21 par.

and children.

[3]My beloved, I want to tell you about the honor given to John as well as what

---

a. Literally, "seated with" or "reclining with" him, which suggests a feasting context (which would be appropriate given the celebratory occasion).

b. That is, John's disciples. There is a shift from this point in the text from John's disciples to those of Jesus.

a love-feast *(agapē)* Christ held for him—oh, how he loved him, for he was his friend and relative. For with these five barley loaves and two fish he fed; the number of those fed being about 5,000, not counting women and children.

[4]For the crowd had gathered together to weep for John, and Jesus wept and mourned for John. And he distributed the love-feast *(agapē)* for him, for he was his relative and his friend. For this reason, when the disciples had said to him, "Dismiss the crowd so that they may go and buy something to eat," he refused, not wanting them to go away in such hunger.

Matt 14:15–16 par.

6 [1]Take note of the word here![a] To begin, when Jesus had received the news about John the Baptist, he withdrew and the crowd hurriedly followed after him. Furthermore, when the compassionate and merciful Jesus had seen them, he felt sorry for them, just as a good shepherd always does. And when the disciples requested of him to "Dismiss the crowd so that they may go and buy something to eat," the Savior said to them, "No!" as he thought, "What sort of thanksgiving *(eucharist)* is being offered before my relative, if those who have come to me on his account are troubled in this way? If they are sent away in such hunger, they will faint along the way."

[2]Just as Joseph the patriarch distributed a love-feast *(agapē)* upon the death of his father Jacob, so also did Jesus. He distributed a love-feast *(agapē)* for his relative John. Furthermore, the custom of giving a love-feast *(agapē)* is preserved by all people, distributing a love-feast *(agapē)* in honor of their family members when they die.

Gen 50:1–14

Jesus responds to the questions from John's disciples

7 [1]Now I wish to tell you another noble and profound thought. The holy Evangelist[b] said: While he was in prison, John heard about the activities of the Christ. He called two of his disciples and sent them to the Lord to ask, "*Are you the one who is to come, or are we to wait for another?*"

Matt 11:2–3; cf. Luke 7:18–19

[2]When they came before Jesus, they said to him, "John the Baptist sent us to you to ask, '*Are you the one who is to come, or are we to wait for another?*'" At that moment, he had been doing healings among the crowd. Then he said to the messengers from John, "Go and tell John what you have seen and what you have heard: that the blind see, the paralyzed walk, the dead are resurrected, to the poor the gospel is declared, and blessed is he who does not try to scandalize me. I am the one who graciously gave you your father Zechariah and Elizabeth your mother. I am he who came to you when you were in the womb of Elizabeth your mother and when I myself was in the womb of Mary my mother—I greeted you and there inside you jumped.

Matt 11:4–6; cf. Luke 7:22–23

Luke 1:5–6

Luke 1:39–41

[3]"I am also the one who came to you at the tenth hour of the night, on the eleventh day of the month of Tobe, to receive baptism from your holy hands.[c]

Mark 1:9//Matt 3:13

---

a. Budge connects *pshaij* ("the word") with "Scripture," which is certainly correct. The preacher is drawing the congregation's attention back to the text in order to draw out the lesson of the passage. As the shift is somewhat abrupt, and transitions into a summary and explanation, I have marked it as emphatic (as does Till) and set it as a new paragraph.

b. The preacher refers here to the author of the Gospel of Matthew.

c. The baptism of Jesus on the eleventh day of the month of Tobe (December 27 to January 25) is part of the Coptic liturgical calendar for Epiphany and appears in other Coptic apocry-

Luke 1:25

Matt 11:11//Luke 7:28

Mark 1:9//Matt 3:16

John 1:29

Truly, dear John, whose name means 'grace,'[a] you have attained greatness above all those honored, because you were deemed worthy to baptize me. I am the one who is to come and I have received baptism from you. I am the one who will take away the sin of the world.

Mark 1:2–3 par.

Matt 3:2

Hab 1:5

[4]"Dearest John, you are the one I have chosen; I along with my father who is in heaven as well as with the Holy Spirit. I have sent you forth as my forerunner and as the one to prepare the way for me. Thus, speak to the crowd, calling them to repent, for the kingdom of heaven draws near. People cannot contemplate it, for it has been declared, 'Behold, I will do a wondrous work in your days, and even if you hear of it, you will not believe it.'"

Matt 11:4–6; cf. Luke 7:22–23

[5]And Jesus said to the messengers sent from John, "Go and tell John what you have seen and what you have heard: that the blind see, the paralyzed walk, the dead are resurrected, to the poor the gospel is declared, and blessed is he who does not try to scandalize me."

Jesus' declaration regarding John and the preacher's exposition

8 [1]After they had departed, he spoke to the crowd about John: "What did you go out into the desert to see? A reed blown about by the wind? But what did you go out to see? Someone in fine clothing? Behold, those in fine clothes are found in the houses of royalty. But did you go out to see a prophet? Yes, and I say to you, more than a prophet! For it is written concerning him: 'Behold, I will send my messenger[b] before you to make straight your way.' Amen, I say to you that among those born of women, none greater has arisen than John the Baptist. Yet the one who is much lesser than him is far greater in the kingdom of heaven."

Matt 11:7–11; cf. Luke 7:24–28

[2]It is now necessary to elucidate this passage for you. For there are many, not being proficient in the Scriptures, who think that it is a real reed blown about by the wind, as it is with all other plants upon the earth: the date-palm tree, the fig tree, the sycamore tree, the persea tree, or the thorn (acacia) tree, even the crops of the field; if they grow then they are blown back and forth by the wind—as is obvious to any weak-minded person, but even more to those who are learned. But what the Savior spoke of was the reed flute in an empty place where there is nobody; when it makes a loud sound, those who hear it from far away say, "What has happened? We hear this reed flute."

Matt 3:3 par.

[3]Immediately they gathered together to see what has happened, to discover that such-and-such a son has been victorious in a competition and, specifically, that such-and-such a son has been well schooled.[c] That is the reason why the

---

pha—e.g., in Pseudo-Cyril of Jerusalem, *On the Life and the Passion of Christ* 12 (see van den Broek, *Pseudo-Cyril*, 129).

a. Compare with *Encom. Bapt.* 3:2. By indicating that "John" means "grace," the preacher highlights the "most favored" status attributed to John, thereby reinforcing the greatness and honor given to John. The name may also relate to Luke 1:25, where John's birth brings favor from God to counter Elizabeth's shame due to her barrenness. Similarly, Theodosius, *Pan. Bapt.* 8:1 directly links the meaning of John's name to God being gracious.

b. Literally "angel" (cf. earlier references to "angel" in *Encom. Bapt.*). This statement perhaps merges John's elevated status as a forerunner of Christ and his status in relation to the angels and prophets. This entire declaration regarding John is evoked in the Scribal Preface.

c. The phrasing here is unclear and awkward (literally, "and lettered by/in the school"). The translation offered attempts to resolve the problems of the sentence by directly relating the

reed flute was heard where the prophet was prophesying and all of them gathered together to receive instruction. This is why the Savior said, "What did you go out into the desert to see? A reed blown about by the wind? But what did you go out to see? Someone in fine clothing? Behold, those in fine clothes are found in the houses of royalty."

Matt 11:7–8; cf. Luke 7:24–25

⁴Therefore, my dear beloved ones, having clarified this matter, I shall, by the will of God, explain to you a further account.

TRANSITIONAL SECTION: MISCELLANEOUS TRADITIONS

The Noahic flood and the body of Adam

9 ¹When the great flood waters washed over the earth in the days of Noah, the surging waters raised the body of Adam; they carried him and placed him in the middle of Jerusalem. Washing over him, the waters of the earth covered him with mud. When the Savior came and walked in that area while teaching, he said, "If anyone will serve me, my father will honor that one. My *father, save me from this hour!*" At the moment the Savior said this, the heel of his right foot rested on Adam's head.ᵃ ²The narrative has come thus far. Surely this subject is of great value for us to discuss, but this is not the moment to look further into it, for the feast of the relative of the true bridegroom, Christ, is before us.

John 12:26–27

The dead in the "West" and the commissioning of the Apostles

10 ¹For if you are so disposed as to look, you will see a throng of people crying out to Christ in Amente:ᵇ "Have mercy on us, Lord, have mercy on us!" Also you will hear many shouting, "Lord, awaken your power and save us,ᶜ our good godᵈ and philanthropic Christ."ᵉ

Ps 80:2

²By your abounding mercies you have gathered all these to you this day. You have rescued those who have been in Amente since the beginning; you have

---

competition to being well schooled, a connection that relates back to the preacher's concern about being "proficient in the Scriptures" (the *graphē* at 8:2).

a. See the introduction pp. 228–29 for a discussion of Adam's body parts, including textual parallels and potential sources for this motif here in *Encom. Bapt.*

b. *Amente* could also be translated as "the West" or "the underworld," but is left as a place name in the translation given the Egyptian ideas about the place of the dead. See introduction pp. 226–27.

c. There is a possible allusion here to Matt 8:25//Luke 8:24, given the "raising" (or "awakening") in this sentence in connection to the need for being saved. If such an allusion is being evoked, then the imperative *pjs ma tounec tekgom* would better follow the translation "awaken your power" rather than the "raising up" translations found in Budge, Till, and Boud'hors. The basic idea is to prompt God to "stir up" or activate his "power" for the purpose of effecting deliverance or salvation from some danger. This is exactly the context in the Synoptic parallels to which this line may allude.

d. It is unclear if the text uses "god" as a title for Christ or is a separate entity "God" (i.e., the Father). Cf. 18:6 in support of the titular reading.

e. The dialogue shifts at this point from those in Amente to the voice of the preacher, who now directly addresses and praises the Lord for fulfilling the request of those in the realm of the dead. This praiseful section likely evokes the belief that Christ descended into the underworld between his crucifixion and his resurrection in order to rescue those righteous people in the underworld who had died prior to the resurrection.

John 8:11

Luke 23:43; Matt 9:9

Acts 9:1; 1 Cor 15:9

Ps 146:7–8

Matt 11:28

Luke 24:47–48;
Acts 1:8

Luke 2:7

Matt 2:16

Matt 2:13–15

Prot. Jas. 22:3; Life
Bapt. Serap. 5:1

gathered all sinners to you in life: A prostitute you made a virgin, you forgave her sins; a bandit you brought into Paradise; a tax collector you made an Evangelist; a persecutor you made an apostle. You rescued those who were captives. You lifted up those who had fallen. You rounded up those who had been scattered. With the mouth of God,[a] you cried out to everyone: *"Come to me, all you that are weary[b] and are carrying heavy burdens, and I will give you rest."*

[3]This is the very day when you commanded your holy apostles, saying to them: "Beginning from Jerusalem, you are to go to the ends of the world.[c] It is you who are witnesses about what the Jews/Judeans did to me. Go and proclaim to them redemption for the forgiveness of sin.[d] Do not cast away the sinners from yourselves, but embrace them into repentance. Give repentance to the tax collectors. Forgive the sins of the prostitutes."[e] [4]My dearly beloved ones, you have now seen how Christ honored his relative, the forerunner who is the holy John the Baptist. (Christ) gave him honor in heaven. He gave him even greater honor upon the earth.[f]

Elizabeth and the child John flee into the desert

11 [1]And when the time came that our Lord Jesus was born on the earth at the inn in Bethlehem, the massacre of the little children by the wicked Herod occurred. So when the archangel Gabriel warned Joseph in a dream, (Joseph) took the child Jesus with his mother and they went down to Egypt. Furthermore, when Elizabeth was seized by fear, she took John and fled with him into the desert.

[2]So when Herod's executioners chased after her and her son in order to kill them, she looked back and saw them closely approaching. Then when she and her son arrived at the rock of the mountain, she cried out, "Rock, receive me inside of you along with my son!" And at that very moment, the rock opened its mouth, split and accepted them into itself. It became for her a sequestered[g] and restful[h] place.

---

a. Or: "a divine mouth."

b. Or: "who are troubled/distressed" or "who are suffering from toil."

c. Or: dispensation/civilized world/inhabited world (*oikoumena*).

d. The text seems to suggest that those to whom the apostles are to preach are the very people who did harmful things to Jesus in the preceding sentence. Thus, the beginning of a worldwide apostolic commission is to begin in Jerusalem with the Jewish or Judean people who rejected Jesus and, subsequently, that mission is to extend to the "ends of the world." Cf. Acts 2, which this author may have had in mind.

e. Note the parallel with 10:2, where Jesus forgives the sin of the prostitute and transforms the tax collector into an Evangelist (i.e., a gospel writer). Here at 10:3, the author, now using Jesus' voice, extends that transformative acceptance of sinners to the work of the apostles and, by implication, the work of the universal church. This extension adds a further inclusion of those Jews/Judeans who rejected Jesus and either gentiles or apostates.

f. The honor given points back to the love-feast given to John by Jesus at 5:3–4. The "honor upon the earth" is certainly the funerary meal that Jesus gives on behalf of John in the Homily, while the "honor in heaven" refers back to the opening exaltation of John in the heavens at 2:1 and also foreshadows the contents of the Apocalypse. Thus, this section likely was composed by the scribe who wrote the preface as he or she attempts to interweave the various materials that comprise *Encom. Bapt.*

g. The Greek loanword, *monasterion*, literally means a solitary place, as in a monastic or cloistered place. While the narrative may be evoking an image of Christian monasticism, such a connection is not necessarily intended.

h. The Greek loanword, *ēsuchazein* ("to rest" or "to be still"), carries the sense of not only

³As the need arose, they went to the place of the rock, which would open up for them and then close up again, by means of the providence of God. It was an expansive place for their coming and going. And if they requested anything that they had need of, it was there; such as if they needed locusts or wild honey it came to them that way. And the door to the cave opened for them and closed for them by itself. ⁴During the summer days the air was rendered cool, so that the burning heat did not oppress them; whereas during the winter days the air was rendered warm, so that the cold did not give them any distress. This is also how they co-existed amicably with the wild animals up to the day that the holy John appeared at the Jordan.

Matt 3:4//Mark 1:6

THE APOCALYPSE OF THE THIRD HEAVEN

Transition into the apocalypse

12 ¹Yet now let us return to speaking about some of the honors bestowed by God to his beloved John, according to what we found in the ancient books that our fathers, the apostles, wrote and placed in the library of the holy city, Jerusalem.ᵃ ²Being myself there in Jerusalem, I resided in a church that an old godly presbyter managed, staying there so that I could celebrate the festival of the resurrection of the Lord Jesus Christ along with the festival of the holy cross. ³Now I was looking through these books and to my great encouragement I found a small, ancient book that the apostles had written. This is what it said:

Encom. Mary 2:11;
Invest Abbat. 3:1–6.

Post-resurrection appearance

13 ¹It happened that when we apostles had gathered together with our Savior on the Mount of Olives after he had been raised from the dead, he spoke to us, entrusting us with this task: "Go out into the whole world, proclaiming to them the gospel of the kingdom."ᵇ ²He also spoke to us about John the Baptist and the honors that he bestowed on him in heaven. And we said to him, "Surely it is fitting for us to be well informed about your beloved relative, John, as you have attested: 'I will bestow to him the third heaven, a gift along with the good things in it, in exchange for the blood that he shed for me.' So now, our Lord, precisely inform us about him and show us the heaven that you have bestowed to your beloved John, along with the good things you have prepared for it. And show us John, about whom you have said, 'Not one in the heavens matches him in the glory and honor bestowed to him by the Father.'"

Mark 16:15; Luke
24:47–48; Acts 1:8

---

a place of rest but a quiet, still place. This term effectively contrasts the fleeing and chasing danger with the secure, safe place of rest or nonmotion.

a. See introduction p. 223 for a discussion of this motif.

b. Compare with 10:3, which parallels the more concise commissioning of the apostles here at 13:1. Note a few differences, such as (1) the apostles are commanded to go "to the ends of the (civilized) world" (*oikoumena*) (10:3), whereas here it is to "the whole world" (*pkosmos tēref*; lit. "all the world"); (2) the concern over the Jews/Judeans in 10:3 is dropped at 13:1; (3) there is no concern at 13:1 over social relations, as we see at 10:3; and (4) the object of proclamation is a bit different—"the gospel of the kingdom" at 13:1 versus "the redemption for the forgiveness of sin" at 10:3.

Ascent into the heavens

14 [1]Right away, at our Savior's command, he brought down a cloud of light. He entered into it and directed us, the apostles, to enter with him into the cloud. [2]He took us up to the first heaven, and then to the second. When he arrived at the third heaven, he would not let us enter but instead took us on to the fourth heaven, and to the fifth, and to the sixth, as well as to the seventh.[a] And he would not let us enter.[b] [3]After he had shown us everything, he brought us back into the third heaven.

Tour of the third heaven

15 [1]We marveled at its beauty, its opulence, and its magnificence. And we saw John the Baptist there along with his father Zechariah and his mother Elizabeth. They were dressed in such magnificence, wearing[c] precious stones of scarlet[d] and stones of every color. Our Savior had us stand before John and he placed John among us, with Zechariah on his right and his mother Elizabeth on his left. And we, the apostles, he placed according to our rank, from our father Peter down to Matthias (or Matthew).[e]

---

a. The cosmology of the Apocalypse of the Third Heaven only includes seven heavens, unlike some other early Christian cosmologies that have an eighth or ninth (i.e., those that break beyond the earthly cosmos). The seven heavens in the Apocalypse of the Third Heaven evoke a common planetary motif in late antiquity of seven planetary bodies, comprising therefore the totality of the heavens. In other words, by showing the apostles the seven heavens, the Savior has shown them everything, and it is this totality that the third heaven excels (thus fulfilling the claim that John the Baptist is the most honored in heaven and on earth).

b. It is unclear if the apostles are not allowed to enter any of the seven heavens, or only those above the second heaven, or are barred entry only into the third heaven. Given the exact parallel "he would not let us enter" *(mp efkaan e bwk e hoyn)* at the end of the journey and when they arrived at the third heaven, it seems more likely that the apostles were not allowed to enter the third heaven during this tour of heaven. Such a reading also makes sense with the summary statement, "after he had shown us everything" (though this could mean simply that the Savior only showed them the heavens but did not let them enter them, especially the third, which becomes the focal point of the journey from this point on).

c. That is, they are wearing magnificent clothing that has been embellished with these precious stones or gems.

d. Till ("Johannes der Taüfer," 328 n. 5) correctly identifies the Greek loanword *kokkos*, best translated as "scarlet" in this context (contra Budge), which works well with the other precious stones that the three characters wear. The specification of scarlet likely evokes wealth and prestige, whereas the other stones may suggest an abundance of wealth. Thus, these three characters are as opulent as the third heaven itself.

e. The Coptic name could be rendered as Matthias (so Budge and Boud'hors) or Matthew, as Till suggests. In early Christian texts the two names are occasionally conflated or confused. Given the descent in order from Peter, if we follow the Matthias reading then we are likely seeing an allusion to Acts 1 (thus the order is set according to when someone became an apostle, with Matthias being the last of the twelve as he fills Judas's place). If we follow the Matthew reading, then we may be seeing the apostolic arrangement following the type of sinfulness from which the apostle was called (i.e., Matthew as a tax collector). The latter reading nicely picks up on the "tax collector you made an Evangelist" at 10:2 (and thus integrates the Apocalypse of the Third Heaven with the transitional material, thereby suggesting that the redactor identified the character with Matthew). The former reading fits nicely with the commissioning of the twelve apostles at 13:1 (when they had gathered together). Not uncommon is the reestablishment of the entire twelve in such commissioning accounts (e.g., *Acts of Peter and the Twelve Apostles*), a restoration motif that Matthias fulfills in the opening of Acts

²Going on before us, our Savior revealed the entirety of the heaven.[a] He revealed to us all the good and pleasurable things that had been prepared in advance for it. These things he granted as gifts to his beloved John, so that they may be granted to any who remember John while on earth, as (John) is his relative and his forerunner.[b]

³I James,[c] the brother of the Lord, swear to you that I will not conceal any of the good things that were revealed to me, things which have been prepared in the third heaven; the things God has bestowed upon the holy John so that these may in turn be given to any who remember him on earth.[d]

2 Cor 12:2; *Apoc. Paul* 20

The Savior's first discourse on the golden boat and the fiery river

16 ¹Moreover, Paul and Luke, as well as Mark, were with us. Then the good Savior summoned the seven archangels, starting with Michael—the greatest archangel and chief military commander of the powers of heaven—down to Sedekiel.[e] ²(The Savior) summoned us, the apostles, according to rank and according to name, starting with our father Peter—the greatest of the apostles—down to Mark the Evangelist.[f]

---

prior to the coming of the Spirit that inaugurates the Lukan age of the church. Perhaps a shift occurs from Matthias to Matthew through the redactional incorporation of the Apocalypse with the Homily.

a. That is, of the third heaven. While the text could refer to heaven in its totality, the narrative journey motif clearly fits a reference to just the third heaven (as the Savior has already shown the apostles the other heavens at 14:2–3 and the narrative focuses on the third heaven).

b. This discussion of gifts is very rich in a liturgical or ritual sense. The Greek loanwords used here link the Savior's grace with the gifts, the latter of which is an offering of divine benefaction given to mortals. The remembrance on earth motif likely evokes ritual devotion granted to John the Baptist, such as we find in the cult of the saints. Budge has translated this motif in order to convey just such a sense ("who celebrated upon the earth the festival of the Commemoration of John . . ." and again with "who kept the festival of his commemoration upon earth"). This translation perhaps overtranslates the Coptic, but the likely cultic motif is certainly alluded to in the text. Perhaps the "to remember" evokes a eucharistic motif, thus connecting the benefaction in heaven to motifs found in the Homily (e.g., 5:2–4 to 6:1–2) and especially in the transitional material (10:4). The symmetry between earthly benefaction ("remembering" John) and heavenly benefaction ("good and pleasurable things" in the third heaven) nicely parallels the earthly/heavenly honor granted John the Baptist at 10:4.

c. Budge mistranslates *jakköbos* as "John" instead of "James." The statement is an apocalyptic motif identifying the visionary, here identified as James, the brother of the Lord. This identification may be interlinking the family dynamics so prevalent in *Encom. Bapt.*

d. This line repeats the statement just before the shift to the declaration of James. This redundancy either adds emphasis to the earlier statement by reinforcing the claim by means of the first-person oath or, less likely, it indicates a redactional addition of a common apocalyptic formula. The latter suggestion is supported by James playing no other role in the Apocalypse. Indeed, without this oath statement, the Apocalypse would read as a revelation to all the apostles (see 14:3) and not a particular individual. Regardless, these two parallel statements set the stage for the soteriological role that John the Baptist will play later in the Apocalypse.

e. The cosmological landscape shifts here with the singular "heaven." Either this indicates a slip on the part of the author, an underlying source or influence (such as Revelation), or "heaven" is being used to encompass all seven heavens of the Apocalypse of the Third Heaven.

f. Note the parallel presentation of the archangels and the apostles along identical hierarchal lines, thus suggesting a heavenly and earthly balance in the Savior's forces. Furthermore, Mark's position at the lower end of the scale, while grouped together with Paul and Luke at 16:1, is set in contrast with Peter's higher status at 16:2 thereby suggesting a possible juxtaposing of

³And (the Savior) said to us, "O my archangels and holy servants[a] as well as my apostles. You are witnesses of my birth, my suffering[b] and my crucifixion. Therefore, I appoint you as witnesses once more. For behold I have given the third heaven as a gift to John the Baptist, my friend and my relative.[c] ⁴Therefore, proclaim throughout the entire world that any person who keeps in remembrance the beloved John upon the earth—whether by means of an offering or by means of a love-feast *(agapē)* or by means of a charitable gift that is given to the poor—either at his place in his name,[d] or written down in the holy book as a remembrance of him and kept within the church, or by covering with precious fabrics the table in your[e] place, you[f] will lead them into the third heaven, which I have bestowed to you, and clothe them in heavenly garments.

⁵"I say to you, my dear beloved John—who was deemed worthy to baptize me with his holy hands[g]—if anyone makes an offering of first fruits in your place in your name, or feeds one who is hungry in your name, or gives drink to one who is thirsty, or covers one who is naked[h] in your name, I will not abandon them to Amente;[i] rather, you will lead them into eternal life[j] and I will let my angels clothe them in wings of light and I will bestow on them all the good things that

Apoc. Paul 40

Matt 25:34–46; 10:42

the gentile and Jewish missions. With the mention of John and Matthew/Matthias at 15:1, we have all four NT gospel writers presented, with the mention of Peter and Paul offering apostolic status to Luke and Mark.

a. As there are only two sets of beings (archangels and apostles) who have been summoned, I am taking the conjunction *ayō* as epexegetical for the first set of beings (thus identifying the "holy servants" with the "archangels") with the conjunction *mñ* distinguishing and coordinating this first set of beings with the second set (i.e., the apostles).

b. "Suffering" here likely refers to Jesus' Passion leading up to the crucifixion (so also Budge) rather than the Savior's suffering in general. The three elements in this sentence (birth, suffering, crucifixion) encompass the basic plot progression in the New Testament gospels, especially the Synoptic Gospels. What is missing, of course, is a witness to the resurrection. Rather than finishing with the glorification of Jesus, the Apocalypse of the Third Heaven shifts that climactic glorification to John the Baptist in the third heaven.

c. Cf. 5:3–4 where John the Baptist is referred to as Jesus' "friend and relative." Here at 16:3 we have this relationship stated overtly by Jesus rather than by the narrator.

d. The "place" *(topos)* mentioned twice here (see 16:5) likely refers to a sacred space dedicated to honoring John the Baptist, such as a martyr shrine, tomb, or specific space within a sanctuary or church.

e. The shift to the second-person singular *(pek-)* when one would expect a third-person singular or plural *(pef-* or *pey-)* does not refer to any of the apostles or archangels nor to those who might keep remembrance on earth. Rather, the text transitions awkwardly into a direct address to John the Baptist in the next sentence. This identification is almost certain given that the person addressed has been given the third heaven, which, as we already know, was given to John the Baptist.

f. That is, John the Baptist.

g. The shift to third-person singular suggests that this is an aside comment directed to the reader/hearer of the Apocalypse by the narrator, rather than a part of the dialogue between the Savior and John the Baptist.

h. Or to "clothe" or "give covering" to one who is naked. The translation "to cover one who is naked" suggests a possible allusion to Gen 9:20–27, especially 23. Such a biblical allusion would shift the statement from ethical behavior (directed toward the less fortunate) to the soteriological or ontological (sinful) condition.

i. See 10:1–2.

j. Most likely alluding to Matt 25:34–46, where hunger, thirst, nakedness, and entering into either eternal punishment or eternal life are all present. Another possible allusion could be Matt 10:42. If there is a direct influence of Matt 10:42 here in the Apocalypse of the Third Heaven,

are in my kingdom. [6]My father will bless your right hand, which you placed upon my head. My tongue will bless your mouth and your tongue, with which you said: '*Here is the Lamb of God who takes away the sin of the world.*'

John 1:29

[7]"For I am in the truth. And any person who remembers you on earth, truly I say to you, my relative John, I will not abandon that one to Amente eternally[a] nor to its punishments, even to the river of fire that every person must cross over whether righteous or a sinner. Behold, I bestow as a gift for the crossing of this river of fire a golden boat. Any who remembers you on earth will be carried over this river of fire by you."

2 En. 10; Apoc. Paul 31; Bk. Bart. 21:5

Apoc. Paul 23

17 [1]Then we the apostles said to him, "Our Lord, what is the breadth and depth of this river of fire? Teach us so that we may teach people how terrifying it is." [2]Our Savior said to us, "I will let you know its dimensions and the dimensions of the golden boat that I have given to my beloved John. The depth of the river of fire is thirty wave lengths from shore to shore, and from crest to crest it is thirty stadia by wave.[b] But I have given the golden boat to my relative John for crossing over the river of fire, so that he may ferry over all who have remembered him on earth, even if just by a small piece of bread or a cup of cold water.[c]

Matt 10:42

[3]"When they reach the final wave, there I baptize them in the river of fire. When they come to be baptized, for those who have kept the remembrance of John the river of fire will be like bath waters and the waters will be hot as when a person washes, such will be the river of fire. [4]Therefore, anyone who remembers you upon earth, dearest John, my friend and relative, whether through an offering, first fruits, or any gift given in remembrance of your holy name, I order you to ferry that one over the waters of the river of fire in the golden boat that I have bestowed to you, taking them into the third heaven so that they may enjoy all the eternal good things that have been prepared."

The Savior's discourse on the paradise of the third heaven

18 [1]And when our good Savior had told us all these things, we rejoiced over the great honors bestowed upon John the Baptist. [2]He then said to us, "Come, I will instruct you regarding everything in the paradise of the third heaven." And he had us wander in fields full of fruits each according to their own kind and exuding fragrant smells. And all the trees of the fields, according to season,[d] produced fruit consistent with its own kind, from their roots to their heights: cinnamon, amomon,[e] mastic, and nutmeg(?)[f]—exuding fragrant smells, each one distinct.

Gen 1:11

---

then the latter has qualified "the name of a disciple" as John the Baptist. See also Matt 5:3–6// Luke 6:20–21. A strong ethical motif arises in this soteriological statement by the Savior.

    a. It is unclear if the author is saying that the person will not spend eternity in Amente or will not be in Amente for all of eternity (i.e., if there is a period spent in Amente, such as a type of purgatory process for the soul).

    b. That is, about three or four miles across the river as well as three or four miles in depth. Compare with John 6:19, to which the author may be alluding. Cf. Plato, *Phaedo* 112A-B.

    c. The Matthean allusion suggests an ethical rather than sacramental activity.

    d. Or "fruits."

    e. An Indian spice, perhaps a type of cardamom. The same Greek term is used in Rev 18:13 also alongside cinnamon.

    f. Identifying the last of the exotic spices listed as nutmeg is a conjecture proposed by Till and followed by Boud'hors. The exact meaning of the term, however, remains unclear; though,

³Thomas said to the Savior, "Lord, behold, you have instructed us about all the fragrant trees in Paradise, the seasons[a] and the date-palms.[b] Now instruct us as to how large is the yield of dates, how large is each piece of fruit per each tree's yield, how large is the cluster of each tree's yield."

⁴The Savior said, "I will not withhold anything about which you (pl.)[c] have asked. As to the yield, which you (pl.) inquired about, there are ten thousand fruit clusters on it, with each cluster overflowing with six measures.[d] Now as to the date-palms of Paradise, their yield is ten thousand, each the length and measure of a person. So also with figs there are ten thousand per branch. If three people eat a single fig, they will be sated. A sole ear of wheat grain from Paradise has ten thousand clusters of grain and so also is the height of the citrus trees[e] which bear ten thousand each. The apple and peach(?)[f] trees are of the same height, each bearing ten thousand and if three people eat a single piece then they will be sated.

Apoc. Paul 22; *1 En.* 10:19

⁵"These are the good things that I have prepared for anyone who remembers my beloved relative John on earth. Blessed are all those who are deemed worthy to inherit these good things, which the eye has not seen, nor the ear heard,

---

given the context, it is undoubtedly an exotic spice that, in Mediterranean cultures of late antiquity, would have been imported from the East. See introduction p. 231.

a. Or "fruits."

b. Literally, date-palm or its fruit (dates), which makes sense given the clusters of fruit that follow. As the date-palm has not been mentioned up to this point, the text could also be indicating simply the yield or product of the trees (i.e., their fruit) that have been mentioned. If the latter reading is correct, then this phrase could be translated: "the seasons and the yield" (i.e., of the fragrant trees). However, given the specific Coptic term used here *(bñne)*, whereas the author uses the more general Greek term for "fruit" elsewhere *(karpos)*, it is more likely that the date-palm and dates are meant. A parallel to date-palms in the garden of Paradise is found in the Qur'an 55:68.

c. The shift to the second-person plural indicates that the Savior responds to all of the apostles and not just Thomas.

d. The Greek is *metrētēs*, a liquid measurement. This suggests (so Budge, Till, and Boud'hors) that the fruit clusters are grapes hanging on vines for wine production. Cf. Babylonian Talmud, *Ketubbot* 111b. See discussion in Henk J. de Jonge, "BOTPYC BOHCEI: The Age of Kronos and the Millennium in Papias of Hierapolis," in *Studies in Hellenistic Religions* (ed. Maarten Jozef Vermaseren; Leiden: Brill, 1979), 37–49 at 38–41 for further parallels, including a reference to *Encom. Bapt.* The clearest parallel to 18:4 is Papias, Fragment 1: "The days are coming when vines will come forth, each with ten thousand boughs; and on a single bough will be ten thousand branches. And indeed, on a single branch will be ten thousand shoots and on every shoot ten thousand clusters; and in every cluster will be ten thousand grapes, and every grape, when pressed, will yield twenty-five measures of wine" (translation from Bart Ehrman, *The Apostolic Fathers* [2 vols.; LCL; Cambridge, Mass.: Harvard University Press, 2003], 2:93–95; see alternative translation with discussion in de Jonge, "BOTPYC BOHCEI," 40). If *metrētēs* is read in connection to wine production, then, like Papias, the author of the Apocalypse of the Third Heaven has used grapes to describe the abundance of the afterlife (though with Papias, this abundance is tied less to a spatial apocalyptic model than to a future apocalyptic period).

e. The Greek is *kitrion* and correctly translated by Till and Boud'hors as "citrons." Budge mistakenly translates this term as "cedars."

f. The Coptic is *thourakion,* the meaning of which is unknown. Boud'hors suggests a possible relation to the rare Greek term *dōrakion* from the Latin *duracinum* (a type of peach). But the meaning remains uncertain.

nor instilled within the human heart. These things God has prepared for those who love him[g] and love John, his[h] friend and relative. [6]There is none who have received the honor he attained in heaven and on earth. He was deemed worthy to baptize the Son of God with his holy hands and to look upon the holy Trinity: the Son he baptized with his hands; the voice of the Father he heard saying, '*You are my Son, the Beloved, with whom I am pleased*';[i] and the Holy Spirit who came down from heaven, settling upon him like a dove."

1 Cor 2:9 (Isa 64:4)

Mark 1:10–11 par.

The Savior's second discourse on the golden boat and the fiery river

19 [1]Peter said again to the Savior, "Our Lord and our God,[j] let us know the purpose of these oars and these lampstands." [2]The Savior said, "There is a lampstand for each oar and seven holes[k] per lampstand burning brightly. Any person who kindles a lamp at the place of the holy John, even if before his image, will be ferried across the river of fire in the golden boat that I have bestowed to my beloved John. These lampstands will illuminate the way before them, shining forth until they have passed through the dark paths, carrying them into the third heaven, which I have given as a gift to my beloved John, where they will inherit for eternity the good things that are there."

John 20:28

Rev 1:12

The conclusion of the apocalypse and descent from the heavens

20 [1]When the good Savior had said these things, he went up onto the cloud. He ordered us to go up with him. He brought us down and set us on the Mount of Olives. [2]He stood praying with us and he said, "*Peace be with you.*" When he said this, he went up to heaven in great glory where the angels sang hymns to him.

John 20:21; cf. 14:27
Luke 24:50–51; Acts 1:9

HOMILY ON JOHN THE BAPTIST: CONCLUSION

21 [1]Truly, my dear beloved (pl.),[l] there is no one like John the Baptist in heaven and on earth, nor more exalted in glory. According to the mouth of Christ, which cannot lie, "*Among those born of women, no one has arisen greater than John the Baptist.*" [2]Behold, you (pl.) now know the glory and honor that God has bestowed on John the Baptist.[m] You should devote yourselves to the giving

Matt 11:11; cf. Luke 7:28

---

g. That is, God.

h. The use of the pronoun *pef-* ("his") rather than *pa-* ("my") relates "friend" and "relative" back to God rather than the Savior, which is an odd shift in the text that may prepare the reader for the Trinitarian theology vis-à-vis John the Baptist that follows.

i. More literally: "You are my son, my beloved, to whom my love/pleasure is directed."

j. Cf. 10:1 where we read "our good god and philanthropic Christ."

k. These are likely for candles or wicks.

l. Here the text returns to the Homily on John the Baptist, with the congregation being called "beloved."

m. It is unclear if Christ continues speaking here or if the voice shifts back to the preacher. The former is possible, as it fits with the Apocalypse that precedes this section. Most likely it is the preacher who now speaks with "Behold" rather than Christ given the exhortations that follow (and such a reading allows this closing section to remain as part of the Homily, with the Apocalypse of the Third Heaven remaining a separate source). Therefore, the plural "you" at this point refers directly to the congregation.

of charitable gifts, love-feasts, and offerings in his holy name. My dear brethren, you know that the human life on earth is nothing.

³If you would be saved[a] and inherit eternal life, then hurry to redeem your sins by means of charitable gifts and your lawless acts by means of merciful acts for the poor and the needy, so that you may have enjoyment in the good things in the joyful place of rejoicing. Even if you have sinned, turn and repent and he will set you free from your sin, for God is compassionate and his mercy counteracts the wickedness of the person who turns to him.

⁴For he said regarding the prophet Ezekiel, "I do not wish the death of the impious, rather that that one turn back from his way, repent, and live." Now again: "If the lawless turn back from their wickedness and do righteous deeds, I will not remember their lawlessness," the Lord says, "but by doing righteousness they shall live." And he says in another place, "Turn to me, children who have wandered off, and I will heal your fractures." In yet another place, he says,[b] "*I have come to call not the righteous but sinners to repentance.*"

⁵You know, my dear beloved (pl.), that charitable gifts are good and that love-feasts are splendid. Let none neglect in giving charitable gifts and love-feasts for the poor and needy, according to his power.[c] And you should also make offerings for the church in the name of the saints. ⁶On account of all these things,[d] let us give glory to God and his holy forerunner John the Baptist, the virgin, the martyr, and the relative of our Lord Jesus Christ. This is the one who bestowed such great honors on (John), (and) who is due all glory and honor with his good Father and the Holy Spirit forever and forever. Amen.

Margin references:
Ezek 33:11
Ezek 18:21–22, 27
Jer 3:22
Luke 5:32; cf. Mark 2:17//Matt 9:13

---

a. Or: "made whole."

b. The preacher most closely follows the Lukan saying where "repentance" is mentioned.

c. It is unclear if "according to his power" *(kata tefchom)* is best read as the giver's ability (i.e., "according to his means") or as an external force or power that enables the person to give (i.e., either the power of God or the power of John the Baptist). Both readings are possible and both would fit the context of the Homily.

d. It is unclear if these gifts (i.e., the charitable acts, love-feasts, and offerings) are the means by which glory is given to God and John the Baptist or are the reward for giving glory to God and John the Baptist. With the Apocalypse of the Third Heaven in mind, the latter option is possible (thus, the congregation is promised the blessings of the third heaven), but in the context of the Homily, especially the immediate context (of actively giving charitable gifts, love-feasts, and offerings), it is more likely the former. A third option is to read the sentence as "concerning these things." Thus the glory given to God and John the Baptist is due to all the things preceding this sentence as a way to pull the sermon to a close.

The Life and Martyrdom of John the Baptist
A translation and introduction

by Andrew Bernhard

The *Life and Martyrdom of John the Baptist* (*Life Mart. Bapt.*; CANT 181) is a chronological narrative about key events in the earthly life of John the Baptist. The text deals primarily with the Baptist's activity during adulthood, but it also includes a brief introduction about his birth and a concise conclusion about his burial. It is especially focused on John—no details are given about the fate of any notable character associated with John's life—and is strikingly lacking in fantastic elements—it describes no miracles performed by John nor on his behalf. As one of many Baptist-related apocryphal writings, *Life Mart. Bapt.* is a testament to enduring Christian interest in the enigmatic figure of John and relics associated with him.

Modern scholars have given *Life Mart. Bapt.* various titles, all indicating that the text was attributed to Mark the Evangelist.[1] These titles have had the unfortunate consequence of obscuring the fact that the text in its original form was almost certainly attributed to an anonymous disciple of John the Baptist; only later manuscripts containing a major revision of the text actually ascribe it to Mark. The new title adopted here remedies this situation by describing the nature of the text without designating any purported author. It also provides *Life Mart. Bapt.* with a concise label to distinguish it clearly from other "Lives" of John the Baptist, notably the *Life of John the Baptist* attributed to Serapion and the *Decapitation of John the Forerunner* purportedly written by his disciple Euriptus.[2]

Contents

In *Life Mart. Bapt.*, John is said to be born as part of a divinely orchestrated plan to serve as the forerunner of Jesus (1:1). For a "Life," the text surprisingly says nothing of its subject's youth and upbringing; instead, it promptly moves on to mention John's ascetic life in the Judean wilderness (1:2). There the archangel Gabriel appears to John and delivers God's instructions for him to preach repentance and baptize all who would come to him, including the Son of God (2). John then begins to baptize, issuing warnings to those who doubt him and attracting disciples to follow him (3). After learning about John's activity, King Herod sends for the Baptist but receives only public condemnation from him in

---

1. Since *Life Mart. Bapt.* was known by a variety of cumbersome titles in antiquity (see the note to the title below), modern scholars have provided their own designations. Initially, the text was given the German label, "Die dem Marcus zugeschriebene Erzählung" (Berendts, *Die handschriftliche Überlieferung*, 15). Then, it received a French alternative: "Histoire de saint Jean Baptiste attribuée à saint Marc l'Évangéliste" (see Nau, "Histoire de saint Jean Baptiste," 521). Finally, it was catalogued under the Latin appellation, "Vita et passio auctore Marco" (*CANT* 181; *BHG* 834).

2. For some introductory comments about the range of apocryphal texts that feature John the Baptist, see Burke, "Serapion's *Life of John the Baptist*," 285–91.

response (4). Thirty days later, Jesus comes to John and is baptized in the Jordan River, the Holy Spirit descending upon him in the form of a dove just as in the New Testament Gospel accounts (5). Then John goes to the city where Herod lives and rebukes him in person for committing adultery with the wife of his brother, Philip (6).

Herod becomes enraged and throws John into prison, where the Baptist gathers his disciples one last time in order to pray with them, warn them of his impending martyrdom, and exhort them to continue godly living after his death (7). Herod summons his top officials to his birthday celebration and sends one of them named Julian to question John in prison; after a tense exchange with John, Julian reports back that the Baptist obstinately refuses to stop condemning Herod's behavior (8). The birthday celebration commences and the daughter of Herodias—whose name is also Herodias—captivates a drunken Herod with her seductive dancing and persuades him to have John beheaded. So an executioner is sent to the prison, and he brings John's head back on a platter to Herod. Herod gives the Baptist's head to the daughter of Herodias, who in turn gives it to her mother (9). Acholius, one of Herod's guests and a disciple of John, retrieves the severed head from Herodias, seals it in a water jar, and gives it to six of the Baptist's disciples for burial in a cave near Emesa (modern-day Homs in western Syria). John's other disciples go to the prison to prepare the remainder of their teacher's body for burial (10:1–2).

Most of the narrative is told in the third person. However, the text momentarily switches to the first person at the start of John's interaction with his disciples in prison (7:5). The purported author is introduced near the end as an anonymous "sinful disciple of John who both followed him and was taught by him to believe in our Lord Jesus Christ" (10:3). The text then contains a first-person account about how the author's community commemorated the martyrdom of John at a specific time each year and concludes with a doxology (10:4).

Manuscripts and Versions

Life Mart. Bapt. was brought to the attention of modern scholars in 1904 by Alexander Berendts in his survey of apocryphal traditions about John the Baptist and his father Zechariah.[3] Berendts reported that different versions of the text were extant in Greek and Slavonic. All or most of the text has been preserved in the following seven Greek manuscripts (in order of composition):

P: Paris, Bibliothèque nationale de France, suppl. gr. 480, fol. 51v, 52r, 15, 10, 40, 33, 19, 22, 16, 9, 34, 39 (8th cent.); contains chapters 1–10:1 only

X: Jerusalem, Bibliotheke tou Patriarchou, Cod. 30, fol. 350–54 (10th/11th cent.)

V: Vienna, Österreichische Nationalbibliothek, Cod. hist. gr. 45, fol. 309r–310v (11th cent.); contains chapters 1–7:1 only

G: Genoa, Biblioteca Fanzoniana, Urbani 35, fol. 129–34 (11th cent.)

Q: Paris, Bibliothèque nationale de France, gr. 1608, fol. 156–63 (14th cent.)

R: Paris, Bibliothèque nationale de France, gr. 1021, fol. 270–282v (15th cent.)

Y: Jerusalem, Bibliotheke tou Patriarchou, Cod. 35 fol. 186v–189 (15th cent.)

In 1908, François Nau published the only modern edition of *Life Mart. Bapt.* Nau's edition includes a short introduction, the full Greek text of the palimpsest P with a critical

---

3. Berendts, *Die handschriftliche Überlieferung,* 15–17, 49–50, 61–63.

apparatus containing variant readings from the other manuscripts of the text available in Europe (G, Q, V, R) at the time, and an accompanying French translation.[4] Nau might be faulted for simply taking the oldest manuscript as his main text and ignoring X and Y rather than exhaustively studying all the manuscripts and working out the relationships between them. However, it is important to remember that *Life Mart. Bapt.* might still be generally inaccessible today without his work. Nau deserves considerable credit for making this little-known text available to the modern world, especially since the apparatus he prepared is so thorough.

X and Y have yet to be examined in detail by modern scholars; only the Greek titles and opening words of these manuscripts are available in the work of Berendts.[5] The situation is similar for the eight Slavonic manuscripts of the text that he catalogued (which date to the sixteenth and seventeenth centuries).[6] The need for a comprehensive critical edition incorporating all of the manuscript evidence remains to be fulfilled.

Although *Life Mart. Bapt.* has not survived from antiquity in its original form, the most nearly original version extant today is attested by G and Q. These two manuscripts, copied in the eleventh and fourteenth centuries, contain the entire writing in practically identical form. It seems quite probable that G actually served as the template for the scribe who copied Q. These manuscripts are the only extant witnesses that share the same title; they share also a number of notable readings (see, for example, the omission of "However, many were also offended" in 3:1), and their textual differences are so few and so minor that they are essentially negligible. The text of G and Q almost invariably includes shorter readings against at least one of the other extant versions, while the other versions repeatedly expand the text in *different* ways—that is, P adds certain supplemental details and V and R add others.[7] The persistent pattern observable throughout the entire text is that G and Q agree either with P against V and R or with V and R against P. For example, G and Q (with V and R) state simply that many "did not believe," but P clarifies that many "did not believe *in his preaching*" (see the note to 3:1); G and Q (with V and R) report that "John stood in (Herod's) presence," but P clarifies that "John stood in (Herod's) presence *and that of his nobles*" (see the note to 6:1); and G and Q (with V and R) have Herod's nobles warn him that his powers will "be reduced," but P clarifies that they will "be reduced *to nothingness*" (see the note to 8:5). Alternatively, G and Q (with P) claim that John was "filled with the Holy Spirit," but V and R clarify that he was "filled with the Holy Spirit *after thirty years*" (see the note to 1:2); G and Q (with P) indicate that "the Spirit" will descend on Jesus at his baptism, but V and R clarify that "the Spirit *of God*" will descend (see the note to 2:2); and G and Q (with P) frequently refer to the Baptist by only his first name "John," but V and R clarify that he is "*The Lord's Forerunner* John" (see the notes to 3:1, 4:6, 5:1, 8:8). A comparison of the three available versions makes it clear that the version preserved in G and Q contains the common core and most closely resembles the original text.

---

4. Nau, "Histoire de saint Jean Baptiste," 521–41.

5. Berendts, *Die handschriftliche Überlieferung*, 17.

6. Berendts, *Die handschriftliche Überlieferung*, 61–63.

7. G and Q seldom preserve shorter readings against P, V, and R, and when they do, it is only in minor and insignificant ways that can consistently be attributed to accidental (or at least nonsubstantive) scribal omissions usually involving no more than a word or two. For example, G and Q omit "sought and" from "Herod *sought and* wished to do away with John" (see the note to 4:10), "River" from "Jordan *River*" (see the note to 5:1), and "the poison and" from "you hide *the poison and* the worm in your wicked heart" (see the note to 6:2).

A minor revision of the text was prepared sometime before the eighth century to create the version preserved by P.[8] This revision seems to have been prepared by someone whose principal editorial aim was to clarify the meaning of the underlying text. Sometimes small portions of the text have been reworded, but more often the text has been emended through the addition of words, short phrases, and (on rare occasions) single sentences. For example, G and Q refer to Herod as "the most ungodly," but P clarifies with the addition of a single word that he is "the most ungodly *tyrant*" (see the note to 4:1); G and Q recount John condemning Herod because "you say, 'I am and there is no other,'" but P adds an adverbial phrase to clarify that John's condemnation of Herod is that "you say *in your depraved heart,* 'I am and there is no other'" (see the note to 4:8); and P simply adds an otherwise unattested sentence to clarify how Jesus departed from his baptism, "And as he went up out of the water, John released him" (see the note to 5:4). Still, the effect of these textual modifications should not be exaggerated: they do not alter the overall storyline or significantly change the meaning of any part of the text.[9] While the most nearly original version and the minor revision definitely can be distinguished from one another, they both contain essentially the same narrative.[10]

By the eleventh century, a much more significantly modified version of the text had entered circulation. This major revision of the text is attested by V and R, and it is clear that whoever prepared it intended not just to clarify the meaning of the underlying text but also to alter specific parts of it materially.[11] The text of the major revision repeatedly departs from that of G and Q in different ways than P does, and it has been reworked much more extensively. For example, John's prayer in prison and his exhortation to his disciples have been significantly expanded (see the notes to 7:6–7, 9–10). In addition, the roles played by Herodias and Satan in John's death have been increased. Herodias and her daughter intercept Herod's nobles on their way to his birthday celebration, intimating that John must be either silenced or beheaded (see the note to 8:2). Then, Satan instigates Herod to order the daughter of Herodias to dance, so that she can play her crucial role in the plot leading to the Baptist's execution (see the note to 9:1).

The major revision differs in three particularly noteworthy instances from the other surviving versions of the text. First, it states that Herod's residence was in Sebaste (ancient Samaria; see the notes to 4:4 and 6:1); the other versions locate the residence in Ake (an

---

8. This minor revision was nearly lost forever. After being copied onto P in the eighth century, the manuscript was reused in the fourteenth century. The main text of the palimpsest is a *Life of Pachomius,* but Nau and others were able to recover most of *Life Mart. Bapt.* and a number of the other underlying texts. See Nau, "Analyse des mss. Grecs palimpsestes," 515–20.

9. It is not difficult to see that many of the modifications made in P are merely the result of the scribe's wording preferences. For example, G and Q have "the origin of the world," but P has "the *creation* of the world" (see the note to 1:1); G and Q have "for repentance," but P has "*in* repentance" (see the note to 2:1); and G and Q have "six of his disciples," but P has "six of *the holy John's* disciples" (see the note to 10:1). Like these modifications, virtually all others retain the essential meaning of the underlying text.

10. Nau regarded the most nearly original version of G and Q and the minor revision of P as so similar that he casually classified all three manuscripts into a single group. See Nau, "Histoire de saint Jean Baptiste," 522.

11. Given that the first six chapters of *Life Mart. Bapt.* are virtually identical in V and R, it seems reasonable to assume that the same degree of similarity would be observable throughout the whole text if the final four chapters (everything after 7:1) had not been lost in V.

unknown place). Second, the major revision indicates that John was beheaded on the 29th of August (see the note to 10:4); the other versions give the date as the 29th of Dystros (a month in the Syro-Macedonian calendar). Third, it identifies the author of the text as Mark, who is said to have been a disciple of John before he later "accompanied the holy Peter, even the leader of the apostles" (see the note to 10:3);[12] the other versions ascribe the text to an anonymous disciple of John.

These textual emendations clearly are intended to improve the text's suitability for liturgical use. By locating Herod's residence in Sebaste, the major revision brings the text into agreement with the ancient tradition that John's body (if not his head) was buried there.[13] By changing the date of John's martyrdom to August 29, the major revision harmonizes the text with what had become broadly accepted as the date of the feast day commemorating John's beheading.[14] By attributing the text to Mark the Evangelist, the major revision transforms it into a considerably more authoritative writing.

The major revision of *Life Mart. Bapt.* seems to have enjoyed a significant measure of popularity in the East. It was translated into Slavonic, perhaps multiple times, in the sixteenth and seventeenth centuries. The title on each extant Slavonic manuscript includes both the date of John's death as August 29 and the attribution of the text to Mark.[15] While the use of the text in the West is more difficult to trace, the different versions did end up in manuscript collections in Paris, Vienna, and Genoa, Italy. Interestingly, a photographic reproduction of the most nearly original version as preserved in G was published for the golden sacerdotal jubilee of Pope Leo XIII in 1888.[16]

---

12. The major revision unmistakably implies that *Life. Mart. Bapt.* was written by Mark, the traditional author of the New Testament Gospel bearing his name. In the New Testament, Peter's brother Andrew is mentioned as a disciple of John the Baptist (John 1:40). The tradition that Mark wrote his Gospel based on the recollections of Peter can be traced back to Papias of Hierapolis in the early second century (quoted in Eusebius, *Hist. eccl.* 3.39.15).

13. Josephus states that John's execution took place at Machaerus (*Ant.* 18.5.2), and the New Testament gospels report that his disciples took and buried their teacher's body (Mark 6:29//Matt 14:12). The earliest known references to a location for the Baptist's tomb appear in fourth- and fifth-century sources, and they consistently place the tomb in Sebaste. Egeria apparently visited it there during her pilgrimage of 381–384 CE, according to excerpts of her writings preserved in Peter the Deacon's twelfth-century *Book on the Holy Places*. See John Wilkinson, *Egeria's Travels to the Holy Land* (rev. ed.; Jerusalem: Ariel Publishing House, 1981), 201. Jerome also visited the tomb with Paula in the late fourth century, as he recounts in *Epist.* 46.13 and 108.13 (cf. *Comm. Abd.* 1). Three fifth-century church histories report that the tomb was desecrated by pagans during the reign of the Emperor Julian (361–363 CE): Rufinus, *Hist.* 11.28; Philostorgius, *Hist. eccl.* 7.4; Theodoret, *Hist. eccl.* 3.3. *Life Bapt. Serap.* 13:10 reports that John's disciples took his body straight to Sebaste. Like the major revision of *Life Mart. Bapt.*, a few ancient authors suggest that John the Baptist was actually put to death in Sebaste (e.g., Theodosius and John Malalas in the sixth century, as well as Daniel the Higoumen in the twelfth). See John Wilkinson, *Jerusalem Pilgrims Before the Crusades* (Warminster, UK: Aris & Phillips, 2002), 344–45. However, this claim is historically problematic. Herod Antipas, who executed John the Baptist, established the city Tiberias and built a great palace for himself there (Josephus, *Ant.* 18.2.3; *Life* 12), but Sebaste was not even in the territory he ruled. It was a stronghold built up by his father, Herod the Great (Josephus, *Ant.* 15.8.5). It seems most likely that the confusion of Herod the Great and his son Herod Antipas gave rise to the erroneous tradition that John the Baptist was executed (rather than just buried) in Sebaste. See Kazan, "The Head of St John the Baptist," 4.

14. See David H. Farmer, *The Oxford Dictionary of Saints* (3rd ed.; Oxford: Oxford University Press, 1992), 259.

15. Berendts, *Die handschriftliche Überlieferung*, 49–50, 61–63.

16. Nau, "Histoire de saint Jean Baptiste," 521.

Literary Context

Life Mart. Bapt. addresses a challenge faced by all New Testament readers interested in John; namely, the brief canonical stories about him can seem scattered and out-of-sequence because they are found almost exclusively in the Gospels—writings about the life of Jesus, not the life of John. This apocryphal text provides a straightforward, cohesive narrative about John's life. It organizes the pertinent stories from the New Testament about the Baptist and carefully combines them with supplementary material to enhance the tale.

Although *Life Mart. Bapt.* does not alter the basic New Testament plot of John's life, it does significantly rework canonical material and substantially adds to the storyline. The text provides basic biographical details not included in the Gospels. For example, it indicates the time of John's birth (1:1) and his age at death (10:4); it numbers John's disciples (3:3) and names one of them (Acholius, 10:1), and it lists the names of the more than twenty high-ranking officials who attended Herod's birthday celebration (8:1). In addition, the text clarifies ambiguously brief passages from the Gospels. For example, it explains how "the word of God came to John" while he was in the wilderness (Luke 3:2; chap. 2), why John's disciples were allowed access to him in prison (7:3–4), and whether the disciples were able to retrieve John's decapitated head from Herodias for burial (10:1). Further, the text heightens the unfolding drama by giving certain characters more substantial roles. In particular, Herod's ruling officials spy on John (4:1) and urge Herod to keep him under control (8:4–5), while the devil himself initiates the sequence of events leading to the Baptist's death (8:2).

It is particularly noteworthy how *Life Mart. Bapt.* uses direct discourse and dialogue to flesh out John's character. The Baptist's harsh preaching about the need for genuine repentance, which is borrowed verbatim from the Gospels, reveals his firebrand personality (3:2; cf. Matt 3:7–9//Luke 3:7–8). His repeated denunciations of Herod for committing adultery, which go far beyond anything found in the Gospels, underscore his zeal (4:6–8; 6:2; 8:7–10). Still, not all of John's words are condemning. After embracing his distraught disciples when they visit him in prison, John offers up a prayer on their behalf that displays both humility and concern for their well-being (7:6–7). Further, he encourages them to act kindly and blamelessly towards others after his unjust murder, regardless of the personal sacrifice required (7:9–11). In this text, John the Baptist is not a one-dimensional character: he is a man of God who expresses both righteous indignation and goodwill toward others depending on the situation.

The one aspect in which *Life Mart. Bapt.* differs from the Gospels is its portrayal of the relationship between John and Jesus. In the text, these two key religious figures are not presented as potential rivals or leaders of rival movements (cf. John 3:26; 4:1). The Baptist has no need to make theatrical statements about his subordinate status to Jesus (cf. Mark 1:7–8 par.; John 1:26–27, 29–30; 3:27–30).[17] He never displays any uncertainty about the identity of Jesus (cf. Matt 11:2–6//Luke 7:18–23), and his instructions to his disciples about how to live and act are all but lifted from the lips of Jesus in the New Testament Gospels (7:9–11). In addition, the disciples of John and Jesus seem to be in perfect agreement about religious matters. No questions about differences in how the two groups of disciples fast or pray are raised (cf. Mark 2:18 par.), and none of John's disciples appear to have an in-

---

17. In this text, John's self-deprecation is limited to the statement taken from Matt 3:14 that he makes to Jesus before baptizing him: "I need to be baptized by you, and do you come to me?" (5:3).

complete understanding of Jesus' teachings (cf. Acts 18:24–25; 19:1–4). All canonical hints of disconnect or discord between John and Jesus or between their disciples have been omitted.

By the time *Life Mart. Bapt.* was written, concerns about the relationship between John and Jesus from the New Testament era evidently had long since been addressed. In the text, John has been thoroughly "Christianized." He is not merely the forerunner of Jesus or another prophet calling for repentance but a Christian teacher in his own right. He actively proclaims the need for faith in Christ (7:9–10).[18] And with his execution, he effectively becomes the first Christian martyr. In addition, Jesus has been fully exalted to the Godhead. As "our Lord Jesus Christ, the son of God" (1:1), he is almost certainly to be understood as the second member of the Trinity—the divine "Word" or *logos* mentioned in the Trinitarian invocation of God at the beginning of the Baptist's prayer (7:6). He is identified as "the judge of the living and the dead" (2:2), as he is in various Trinitarian creeds. The grammar of the closing doxology suggests that the text is informed by a basically orthodox Christology,[19] even if the text goes a bit beyond strictly orthodox christological understandings by bestowing on him a title usually reserved for God the Father, "the maker of all things, both seen and unseen" (7:7).[20]

Language, Date, and Provenance

Life Mart. Bapt. most likely was written in Greek in Syria in the late fifth century. The original language was almost certainly Greek, since this is the only ancient language in which the text has been preserved and it includes several verbatim quotations from the Greek New Testament.[21] A general Syrian provenance is suggested by the use of the Syro-Macedonian calendar to date John's beheading,[22] and it seems possible to identify when the text was written with a reasonable degree of precision because of its apparent association with a known historical event.

In 453 CE, a monk by the name of Marcellus declared that he had found the head of John the Baptist buried in a water jar in a cave near Emesa.[23] This abrupt unearthing of

---

18. In the canonical Gospels, John calls for repentance and announces that Jesus is coming to baptize with the Holy Spirit (Mark 1:8 par.; John 1:33), but his own teachings are at best vaguely described (cf. Matt 3:1–2//Luke 3:10–14). Only a single New Testament passage suggests that John taught people to "believe" in Jesus (Acts 19:4), and this is in a statement attributed to Paul, who knew neither John nor Jesus during their earthly ministries.

19. As in *Life Mart. Bapt.* 10:4, orthodox writers usually linked God and Christ in doxologies using a genitive referring to Christ after the Greek preposition *meta* (cf. Athanasius, *De inc.* 57.3). Arian authors preferred a grammatical construction in which *meta* was followed by an accusative for Christ, potentially suggesting a difference in time of origin between God and Christ. See section B under the entry for the Greek word *meta* in G. W. H. Lampe, *A Patristic Greek Lexicon* (Oxford: Clarendon, 1961), 848.

20. Most notably, the Nicene Creed (325 CE) uses language echoed in this text, affirming that Jesus "will come to judge the living and the dead" and that God the Father is "the maker of all things seen and unseen." See John H. Leith, *Creeds of the Churches: A Reader in Christian Doctrine, from the Bible to the Present* (3rd ed.; Louisville: John Knox, 1982), 30–31.

21. The author of the text seems to have adapted canonical traditions about John the Baptist from memory. Most of the stories have been paraphrased; however, short but memorable passages from the Greek New Testament are still quoted verbatim. See 1:2; 2:1; 3:2; 4:8; 5:2, 3.

22. John is said to have been beheaded on the 29th day of Dystros (10:4), a month in the Syro-Macedonian calendar corresponding to late February and March in the Julian calendar. See Jack Finegan, *Handbook of Biblical Chronology* (rev. ed.; Peabody, Mass.: Hendrickson, 1998), 58–59.

23. It has been suggested that John the Baptist's head was actually recovered in 452 CE. See Michael

John's head over 200 miles from the site of his death more than four centuries after his execution must have seemed quite astonishing, especially since the emperor Theodosius I had already used a head of the Baptist to consecrate a church built near Constantinople in 391 CE.[24] Contemporary writers evidently felt compelled to explain the circumstances surrounding the discovery. Notably, an anonymous fifth-century text known as the *Discovery of John the Baptist's Head (Disc. Head Bapt.)* records a fantastic tale about how the head had been brought recently from Palestine to Syria through a bizarre sequence of events involving various monks, an unnamed potter, a heretical priest, and multiple appearances of the deceased Baptist himself.[25]

Although a date of origin for *Life Mart. Bapt.* as late as the eighth century is theoretically possible,[26] the text seems best understood as the work of a late-fifth-century Syrian monk. As Theodoret reports, the monks of Syria in this period revered John the Baptist as a model of ascetic living and were especially enamored with relics associated with him.[27] *Life Mart. Bapt.* was almost certainly written in a monastic context by someone who believed the devil was "ever and always causing trouble through the weak vessels of girls" (8:2) and used the Syro-Macedonian calendar to mark time (10:4). The text obviously aims to present John as a paragon of Christian faith, unyielding in his commitment to righteousness even to the point of martyrdom. It also portrays the disciples who bury John's head much like monks devoting their lives to ascetic contemplation of a holy life (10:2). In addition, the text appears almost as intimately associated with the dramatic discovery of 453 CE as *Disc. Head Bapt.* does: both texts specifically explain how John's head ended up buried in a water jar in a cave near Emesa.[28] And *Disc. Head Bapt.* too appears to have been composed in a monastic context.[29]

It is difficult to imagine that *Life Mart. Bapt.*—with its mundane story about six of John's disciples burying his head shortly after his death—was written after the early sixth century. By this time, the more sensational story about the transportation of the head to

---

Whitby and Mary Whitby, *Chronicon Paschale: 284–629 AD* (Liverpool: Liverpool University Press, 1989), 82. However, a comprehensive analysis of the pertinent ancient sources suggests that the date of February 24, 453 CE for this event is quite secure. See Brian Croke, *The Chronicle of Marcellinus: A Translation and Commentary* (Byzantina Australiensa 7; Sydney: Australian Association for Byzantine Studies, 1995), 92.

24. See Sozomen, *Hist. eccl.* 7.21; *Chron. Pasch.* 391.

25. *De inventione capitis Johannis Baptistae* (PL 67:420C–430D), extant also in Greek, Coptic, and Armenian. Paul C. Dilley ("The Invention of Christian Tradition," esp. 597 n. 24) brings this text into his discussion of a subset of late antique apocrypha/hagiographa that he relates to relic invention. This group of texts includes the *Apocalypse of Paul,* the *Revelation of Stephen,* and the *Life of Joseph of Arimathea.*

26. The text obviously must have been written prior to the time it was copied onto the earliest extant manuscript (P) in the eighth century.

27. Theodoret, bishop of Cyrrhus (423–457 CE), interacted extensively with monks in the region and wrote about their intense fascination with John the Baptist in his *History of the Monks of Syria.* See Kazan, "The Head of St John the Baptist," 3–4.

28. It is remarkable that *Life Mart. Bapt.* and *Disc. Head Bapt.* agree even down to the detail that John's head was placed in a *hydria* ("water jar") before being buried. In contrast, other apocryphal texts that locate John's head in Emesa contain stories that are decidedly different than those circulating in Syria after the much-celebrated finding of the head in 453 CE. For example, *Life Bapt. Serap.* says nothing about John's head being buried in a cave where it could be dug up later. Instead, this text claims that the head flew to Emesa fifteen years after the Baptist's decapitation and that it was then collected and ceremoniously buried by the local residents in a place where a church could later be built on its sacred resting place (13:22–25).

29. The text details how the head was (eventually) recovered by the leader of a monastic community outside of Emesa. That monks were involved in the discovery of the head is supported also in the other sources on the discovery of John's head mentioned in n. 23.

Emesa contained in *Disc. Head Bapt.* had captured the popular imagination and been transformed into a kind of official account of the head's recovery; Dionysius Exiguus translated the entire text from Greek to Latin, and Marcellinus Comes abridged and incorporated it into his influential *Chronicle*.[30] The miraculous appearance of the relic was commemorated annually in Constantinople and other locations in the East on February 24, the date given in *Disc. Head Bapt.*[31] It seems unlikely that a sixth- or seventh-century Syrian author would have written a text contradicting broadly accepted tradition. Most probably, *Life Mart. Bapt.* and *Disc. Head Bapt.* are roughly contemporaneous writings.[32]

Translation

The following translation is based primarily on Nau's critical edition, which is essentially an edition of the minor revision found in P with an exhaustive apparatus of variant readings from G, Q, V, and R.[33] Supplementary information about X and Y has been obtained from Berendts.[34] The chapter divisions used by Nau have been retained; the verse divisions are my own.

It should be noted that the translation here presents the most nearly original version of the text as attested by G and Q, even though Nau's edition presents the text of the minor revision (P).[35] As a result, portions of the Greek text found in Nau's apparatus have been included as part of the translation's main text, and some of Nau's main text has been relegated to footnotes in the translation. While this creates a less than ideal relationship between Nau's Greek text and the following English translation, it has seemed necessary to present the earliest version in order to avoid obscuring the history of the text. It is hoped that a new critical edition based on G and employing all the other Greek manuscripts (including X and Y) can be prepared in the future.

Bibliography

EDITIONS AND TRANSLATIONS

Nau, François. "Histoire de saint Jean Baptiste attribuée à saint Marc l'Évangéliste." *PO* 4 (1908): 521–41. (*Editio princeps* of the text with French translation.)

---

30. Marcellinus released the first edition of his *Chronicle* shortly after 518 CE and later revised it to cover the time period up until 534 CE. His influential account of the discovery of the Baptist's head in 453 CE was then repeated as far away as England (Bede, *Commentary on Mark*) and at least until the thirteenth century (Jacob of Voragine, *Legenda Aurea; The Golden Legend: Readings on the Saints* [2 vols.; trans. William Granger Ryan; Princeton: Princeton University Press, 1993], 2:137–38). See Brian Croke, *Count Marcellinus and His Chronicle* (Oxford: Oxford University Press, 2001), 1, 205, 249.

31. The annual celebration of the head's discovery had clearly become a regular tradition in Constantinople well before the beginning of the sixth century. See Croke, *Count Marcellinus and His Chronicle*, 205. Similar celebrations also occurred at the same time each year in other locations, as indicated by an ancient Syriac martyrology. See Croke, *Count Marcellinus and His Chronicle*, 92.

32. Nau concurs that *Life Mart. Bapt.* was written, at least in part, to provide a backstory for the appearance of the relic in 453 CE. See Nau, "Histoire de saint Jean Baptiste," 522.

33. Nau, "Histoire de saint Jean Baptiste," 526–41.

34. Berendts (*Die handschriftliche Überlieferung*, 17) reproduces the Greek text of the titles of X and Y.

35. Nau's primary aim seems to have been to publish an edition based on the oldest manuscript (P), which was the most recently recovered version of the text. Consequently, he did not attempt to identify the earliest version of the text or perform a full text-critical analysis of the various manuscripts. See Nau, "Histoire de saint Jean Baptiste," 522.

STUDIES

Berendts, Alexander. *Die handschriftliche Überlieferung der Zacharias- und Johannes-Apokryphen.* TU, N.F. 11/3. Leipzig: Hinrichs, 1904. (Extensive discussion of the sources for the various Greek martyrdoms of John the Baptist.)

Burke, Tony. "The New Testament and Other Early Christian Traditions in Serapion's *Life of John the Baptist.*" Pages 281–99 in *Christian Apocrypha: Receptions of the New Testament in Ancient Christian Apocrypha.* Edited by Jean-Michel Roessli and Tobias Nicklas. Novum Testamentum Patristicum. Göttingen: Vandenhoeck & Ruprecht, 2014.

Dilley, Paul C. "The Invention of Christian Tradition: 'Apocrypha,' Imperial Policy, and Anti-Jewish Propaganda." *GRBS* 50 (2010): 586–615.

Kazan, Georges. "The Head of St John the Baptist—the Early Evidence." Paper presented at the "Saint John the Baptist and His Cults" colloquium. Oxford, June 24, 2011.

Nau, François. "Analyse des mss. Grecs palimpsestes: Paris, suppl. 480 et Chartres, 1753 et 1754." *PO* 4 (1908): 515–20.

The Life and Martyrdom of John the Baptist[a]

The birth and coming of John

1 [1]After 5500 years (except for six months[b]) had elapsed from the origin[c] of the world, the holy John the Baptist was born in accordance with a promise of the Holy Spirit as a fulfillment of the law and the prophets, to be both proclaimer and forerunner of our Lord Jesus Christ, the Son of God. [2]So, at once he was filled with the Holy Spirit,[d] and he traveled into the wilderness. He was brought up[e] in the wilderness, eating tips of plants[f] and the sap in the plants[g] *until the day*[h] *he appeared publicly to Israel.*

Luke 1:26

Luke 1:68–79

Mark 1:2 par.; John 1:6–8, 22–23

Luke 1:15; Mark 1:6// Matt 3:4

Luke 1:80

Gabriel delivers divine instructions to John

2 [1]Now the archangel[i] Gabriel appeared to him while he was staying in the wilderness[j] and said to him, "Thus says the Lord[k] God who formed you from the womb of your mother and marked you for salvation and knowledge of the people: 'Travel into the inhabited regions and baptize all who come to you for

Luke 3:2; *Life Bapt. Serap.* 8:3

Luke 1:77

---

a. G and Q have the title: "On the Beheading of John, the Holy Prophet, Forerunner, and Baptist." The other witnesses have: "A Testimony, that is to say, The Birth and Beheading of the Holy John, the Forerunner and Baptist" (P), "On This Very Day, The Life and Death of the Holy John, the Blessed Forerunner and Baptist" (V), "The Life and Conduct and Beheading of John, the Holy Prophet, Forerunner, and Baptist, Written Down by John, also known as Mark, his Disciple" (R), "The History and Perfection of the Holy John, the Prophet and Forerunner and Baptist" (X), and "The Beheading of John, the Holy Prophet, Forerunner, and Baptist" (Y).

b. According to this chronology, Jesus would have born precisely 5500 years after the creation of the world. In Luke 1:26, the angel Gabriel appears to Mary "in the sixth month" of her relative Elizabeth's pregnancy with John and informs her that she is about to become pregnant with Jesus.

c. P: "the creation."

d. V and R add "after thirty years."

e. R: "he turned about different ways"; V: "he lived."

f. P follows Mark and Matthew with "eating locusts and wild honey."

g. The Greek word *glykasma* is translated as "sap" because it usually means "sweetness" (e.g., Prov 16:24 LXX) and seems to be described as "in the plants." However, the term could be understood also as a different botanical liquid: V has "the sweetness on the plants, or the dew."

h. R lacks "the day."

i. R adds "of the Lord."

j. P: "appeared to him during the time while he was obtaining sustenance from the plant life."

k. P lacks "Lord."

Mark 1:4 par.

repentance.[a] And behold, I will send out my one and only Son so that he may deliver the people from all wrath.[b] So while you are baptizing,[c] say to them,

Matt 3:2; 10:7; Mark 1:15//Matt 4:17

"Repent,[d] for the kingdom of heaven has come near!" [2]Then my Son himself will come[e] and be baptized by you so that he may sanctify the waters, and then all who go down in them may be sanctified. This is the sign that will be provided for you so that you may know what sort of being he is:[f] upon whomever you see

John 1:32–33; Mark 1:10 par.

the Spirit[g] descend in the form of a dove and remain, this is he[h]—the judge of the

1 Pet 4:5; 2 Tim 4:1

living and the dead, the one who rescues the faithful[i] from all wrath.'"

John baptizes and preaches repentance

Mark 1:4 par.; John 1:28; 3:23

3 [1]So John went[j] to Elem[k] and baptized there.[l] And all the Jewish people came to him and were baptized.[m] However, many were also offended[n] by him and

Mark 1:5//Matt 3:5

did not believe.[o] [2]So he said to the Jewish people being baptized by him, *"You brood of vipers! Who warned you to flee from the wrath to come? Bear fruit*

Matt 3:7–9//Luke 3:7–8

worthy of repentance.[p] Do not presume to say to yourselves, 'We have Abraham as our ancestor.'"[q]

[3]Now John himself wore his clothing made out of camel hair and a leather

Mark 1:6 par.

belt around his waist. And word about him spread into the whole of Galilee and Judea, and many came to him. Forty disciples also gathered with him, and they

Ps.-Clem., *Hom.* 2.23.2

followed him.[r]

---

a. P: "in repentance."

b. P: "deliver the people from every deception of the devil."

c. P adds "the people."

d. R lacks "repent."

e. P and V add "to you."

f. P and R: "what sort of being my Son is."

g. V and R add "of God."

h. V and R: "this is the son of the living God."

i. P: "rescues those who believe in him."

j. V and R begin this sentence with "After hearing these things from the archangel Gabriel, the Lord's Forerunner John went."

k. The place name, "*Elēm,*" is evidently intended to refer to a location along the Jordan River. However, it is not clear what place (if any) might have been known by this name in antiquity. R has "Jerusalem," which is odd because Jerusalem is not located along the Jordan River.

l. V and R add "in the Jordan River."

m. V and R add "by him, confessing their sins."

n. G and Q lack "However, many were also offended." This reading, though absent in the best witnesses, is included in the translation because, as Nau notes, the omission is almost certainly the accidental result of a scribal error.

o. P adds "in his preaching."

p. For this sentence, P has "Bear fruit worthy of repentance, as it is written."

q. P lacks "Do not presume to say to yourselves, 'We have Abraham as our ancestor.'"

r. In the Pseudo-Clementine *Homilies,* John had thirty disciples corresponding to the lunar month.

Herod learns about John

4 ¹Now[a] Herod,[b] the most ungodly,[c] was ruling over Judea. So one of his ruling officials of distinction[d] went to John[e] and listened to his proclamations. Then he traveled back and reported[f] to Herod.

²After hearing about everything John did and the teaching he proclaimed, Herod said, "After many years, a prophet has arisen again[g]—a cause for offense to the people as always. By my power, I am delighted with this news! Now I also want him to stand before me in all my power."[h]

Mark 6:20

³Then Nilus said to him,[i] "O Divine One,[j] all of us who are loyal to you ask that you bring him to this city, and let us all learn about the things being done by him."[k]

⁴Now the residence of the king was in the city Ake.[l] So the king[m] sent for Berinus the lieutenant[n] and said to him, "Proceed to the region of the Jordan and bring John and his disciples to me."[o]

Mark 6:17

John refuses to appear before Herod

⁵So the lieutenant traveled and went to the place where John was baptizing. When he saw (John) and all who were with him and the glory covering him,[p] he was seized with fear and did not dare to speak anything to him.

⁶But[q] John,[r] knowing[s] why he had been sent, said to him, "Proceed and say to King Herod on my behalf, 'It is not now time for me to appear in your presence. But days will come when I will present myself before you and expose your impiety. And I will reveal in your presence the transgression of the law being

---

a. V and R add "in those days."

b. Herod Antipas, the son of Herod the Great and tetrarch of Galilee and Perea (ca. 4 BCE to 39 CE), is the Herod mentioned in this text. In the New Testament, he is known by the single name Herod and variously identified as "tetrarch" (Matt 14:1; Luke 3:1; 9:7) and "king" (Mark 6:14, 22, 25, 26; Matt 14:9). However, he was never actually a king; in fact, he was banished by the emperor Gaius while attempting to obtain this title (Josephus, *Ant.* 18.7.1–2).

c. P adds "tyrant."

d. P: "one of his ruling officials"; R: "one of his men of distinction by the name of Nilus"; and V: "one of his ruling officials of distinction by the name of Nilus."

e. P adds "where he was baptizing."

f. P adds "everything about him."

g. V and R add "in Israel."

h. P, V, and R add "for I have certain questions to ask him."

i. P begins this sentence with "Then Nilus, who was second to Herod, said to King Herod."

j. P: "O Master, Divine One"; R: "O Master, our Divine One."

k. P: "the things being said and done by him."

l. It is not clear what location (if any) might have been associated with the place name *Akē* in antiquity. V and R have "Sebaste." This textual emendation does clarify the identity of the location. However, the assertion that the Herod mentioned in this text resided in Sebaste is historically problematic because the city was not even in the territory he ruled.

m. P, V, and R have "So King Herod."

n. Literally, "commander of 50 men."

o. P: "bring both John and his 40 disciples here to me."

p. P, V, and R: "covering his face."

q. V and R add "the Lord's Forerunner."

r. P adds "seeing that he was afraid and."

s. V and R add "in the spirit."

committed by you, for your plotting is wicked and the inclination of your soul is bitter. [7]For not only have you been unsatisfied with the debaucheries drowning you, but you have also been disgustingly enthralled with them. And you are about to return to your brother's bed. [8]You refuse to recognize the God who sees from on high[a] and has given you a kingdom because you would be found a transgressor of this God. And abandoning the maker of all things, you say,[b] "I am and there is no other." But behold, *the one who is coming will come, and he will not delay.*'"

[9]Then the lieutenant returned and went to Herod, and he said to him everything that had been said by John. When Herod heard these things, he was astounded in his spirit and said to his court officials, "What is it that dwells in this deadly man? For[c] he is the first to report to me the plot that I have conceived, and nothing has been hidden from him. So I am altogether overwhelmed because of these things."

[10]From then on, Herod[d] wished to do away with John.

John baptizes Jesus

5 [1]Yet[e] John heard about our Lord[f] Jesus Christ.[g] So, he waited at the Jordan[h] because he[i] was about to come and be baptized by him there. After thirty days, Jesus[j] came to the Jordan.[k] [2]When John saw him coming, he extended his hands and spread out his cloak on the ground.[l] And he said to those standing there with him, *"Here is the Lamb of God who takes away the sin of the world!"*

[3]So Jesus came in order to be baptized by John. *But John would have prevented him, saying,*[m] *"I need to be baptized by you, and do you come to me?"* But Jesus said to him, "Let it be so now, for it is necessary to fulfill all righteousness in this way." [4]So John baptized him at once,[n] and he[o] saw the Holy Spirit[p] descend like a dove and remain on him.[q]

Mark 6:18//Matt 14:4

Isa 45:5–6, 18, 22
Heb 10:37 (Hab 2:3)

Matt 14:5

Mark 1:9–11 par.; John 1:29–34

John 1:29, 36

Matt 3:14

Matt 3:15

---

a. P and V: "the God who sees all."
b. P adds "in your depraved heart."
c. P adds "even though he is far away."
d. P, V, and R add "sought and."
e. V and R add "the Lord's Forerunner."
f. V: "our God."
g. P adds "that he was coming"; V and R add "that he was coming to him to be baptized."
h. P, V, and R add "River."
i. V and R: "because the Lord."
j. R: "the Lord."
k. P adds "River."
l. P: "the cloak he had on."
m. P begins this sentence with "But when John saw he was already going ahead to the deed, he said to him."
n. V and R add "in the Jordan River."
o. V and R: "and the Lord's Forerunner John."
p. P: "the Spirit of God."
q. P adds the sentence: "And as he went up out of the water, John released him."

John confronts Herod

6 [1]Then, after our Lord Jesus Christ was baptized, John went to the city Ake.[a] When Herod heard,[b] he had him brought in to him. As John stood in his presence,[c] he said to Herod, [2]"Why did you send for a servant not your own, especially when you are one who has such confidence in his own vanity? Why are you afraid that darkness is divided with light?[d] Why do you hide[e] the worm in your wicked heart, when you have wickedly defiled your brother's bed? Why do you appear strong[f] on the outside, when on the inside it is an illusion?[g] Do you put on the appearance of piety, even as you succumb to debauchery? You are not permitted to have the wife of Philip!"[h]

Mark 6:17//Matt 14:2

Mark 6:17–18//Matt 14:3–4

Herod throws John in prison

7 [1]Becoming filled with rage[i] because (John) had exposed him in front of all of his nobles,[j] Herod ordered that he be thrown in prison and secured with fetters. But all had heard John's words and had seen him gathered[k] at the prison. [2]When Herod saw that large crowds were gathering in the city and that there was great grumbling on John's behalf, he refrained from putting him to death quickly.[l]

Mark 1:14 par.; Mark 6:17//Matt 14:3; John 3:24

Matt 14:5

John's disciples visit him in prison

[3]John spoke to the prison keeper about his disciples coming into the prison to him, but the prison keeper did not want them to do this because he feared Herod. Nonetheless, John ordered his disciples to come to the prison. When they came, they were prevented by the prison keeper.[m] [4]Then John spoke to the

Life Bapt. Serap. 12

---

a. The MSS provide three distinct place names: "*Eisenakē*" (GQ), "*Akē*" (P), and "*Sebaste*" (V and R). "*Akē*" is the preferred reading here because John seems to be going to the city of Herod's residence (see 4:4). As Nau notes, "*Eisenakē*" seems to be a corruption. "*Sebaste*" is almost certainly an emendation (see p. 259 n. l above).

b. V and R add "about him."

c. P adds "and that of his nobles."

d. For this sentence, P has "Why are you afraid that light is divided by darkness?"

e. P, V, and R add "the poison and."

f. P: "appear manly and at peace." V and R have "appear manly and strong."

g. P: "when on the inside you have a depraved heart tormented because of your adultery?" V and R: "when on the inside you are more cowardly than frogs."

h. P: "the wife of your brother!" V and R: "the wife of your brother Philip!" Herod Philip, son of Herod the Great and half-brother of Herod Antipas, is the name frequently used by modern scholars to identify the Philip of this text. Although this dual name is not attested in any specific ancient writing, a Philip mentioned in the New Testament (Matt 14:3; Mark 6:17) and a Herod mentioned by Josephus (*Ant.* 18.5.1) appear to be the same person. So, it seems probable that Herod Philip had a dual name analogous to Herod Antipas.

i. P begins this sentence with "After hearing these things and becoming filled with great rage." V and R: "Then becoming filled with great rage and wrath."

j. P: "in front of everyone."

k. V and R add "for his sake." The remainder of the text has been lost in V.

l. Instead of this sentence, P has: "When Herod learned that large crowds were gathering at the prison and that there was great grumbling on John's behalf in the city, he contrived to put him to death quickly." R has: "As Herod saw that large crowds were gathering in the city because of him, there was great grumbling on John's behalf. He refrained from putting him to death quickly. However, he instructed the prison keeper not to let anybody come in to him."

m. For this sentence, P has "Then when his disciples came, they were prevented from com-

Matt 11:2//Luke 7:18 prison keeper,[a] and he brought them in.[b] As his disciples embraced him, they wept with great and powerful crying.[c] So the prison keeper had to go in and persuade them to be quiet.

Luke 5:33; 11:1 [5]Since evening was coming on by this time, we[d] all stood for prayer. After making a prayer, John embraced each one of us and prayed again in this manner:[e]

> [6]"O God, who is before the ages[f] with your Word (also our God),
> who filled us with the Holy Spirit,
> who established the heavens and laid a foundation for the earth
> and secretly implanted the beds of the clouds with the waters,
> who ordered the hosts of angels to rule[g] a well-ordered divine
>> government,[h]
> who fixed boundaries for the sea and does not permit it to be driven cha-
>> otically against us
> but even causes it to function in the service of the people,
> who ordered the waters to bring forth living creatures (and all things obey

Gen 1:1–25
>> your Word):
> [7]Give even these servants of yours, who have stood before you,
> the power to believe in your Christ,[i] the maker of all things, both seen and
>> unseen.
> Do not turn away.
> Do not stay away.
> Do not depart,[j] nor be angry with us.
> Rather save us, O Safe Haven, Good Guide,
> for yours is the glory forever.[k] Amen."[l]

---

ing in to him by the prison keeper." R has "Nonetheless, as he lingered in his prison cell, John ordered his disciples to come to him in the prison. But those who came were prevented by the prison keeper."

a. R: "Then John summoned the prison keeper and persuaded him."

b. R adds "So his disciples came into his prison cell."

c. For this sentence, R has "So his disciples came into his prison cell. Worshipping and embracing him, they wept with extremely great and powerful crying."

d. The abrupt change from third- to first-person narration here is striking.

e. For this sentence, P has "And he embraced each one of us and prayed again in this manner." R has "And after the prayer, John embraced each one of us and prayed again in this manner."

f. R adds "and in the beginning."

g. Or, "to begin."

h. R: "who made the hosts of angels a well-ordered divine government."

i. P: "who have stood with me, the power to believe before you in your Christ."

j. P: "Do not turn away. Do not depart. Do not stay away from us."

k. P adds "and ever."

l. For this verse, R has "O Benevolent Master, give even these servants of yours, who have stood before you, the power to believe always in your one and only son, our Lord Jesus Christ, and the maker of all things, both seen and unseen. Therefore, do not turn away. Do not stay away. Do not leave us alone, nor be angry with us. Rather save us all, O God our Savior, Safe Haven, Good Guide, Swift Guardian summoned in truth, for yours is the glory forever and ever. Amen."

John foretells his death

[8]After this prayer, he said, "My children, I want you to know[a] that at the sixth hour tomorrow, Herod will send out an executioner to cut off my head and escort it triumphantly on a platter to a banquet in the palace before his guests.[b] He will give it to a[c] girl, and the most abhorrent thing will happen.[d]

[9]"So I exhort you by both heaven and earth,[e] do not abandon my commandments. Do not display cowardice when I am put to death, nor ever display hatred toward them. Neither wander after disorderly men, nor speak evil of your brothers and sisters, nor let fear of people separate you from Christ. Accept death and do not deny Christ. [10]Go out of the cities and guard your faith in him. Renounce wealth and love this only. Allow yourself to be struck for his sake and do not strike back. Seek him and do not let your souls depart from him. Let theft be far from you. Turn your faces away from adultery. Spit in the face of the love of money.[f] Banish arrogance.[g]

[11]"Remember the things of Moses according to the Spirit. Turn your minds to things above. Let your souls ascend.[h] Let your lamps blaze. Let your torches shine. Let your mouths sing songs of praise. Love your enemies. Do not let your burnt offerings spoil. Let your words be seasoned."[i]

[12]He passed the peace again and embraced them a third time. And then he released them.[j]

Mark 6:26–28//Matt 14:9–11

Matt 10:28//Luke 12:4
Matt 10:32–33//Luke 12:8–9
Mark 10:17–22 par.

Matt 5:39//Luke 6:29
Mark 7:22//Matt 15:19;
Mark 10:12//Matt 19:9
1 Tim 6:10

Matt 5:16

Matt 5:44//Luke 6:27, 35

---

a. R begins this sentence with "My true children, I want us to know."

b. P: "to a banquet in the palace and to his feast in front of all his guests."

c. R adds "wicked."

d. For this sentence, P has "He will give it to a girl as a reward for her dancing, and she will give it to her mother because of wicked lust and the censure of Herod, whom I exposed."

e. P lacks "by both heaven and earth."

f. P: "Spit in the face of sexual immorality and love of money."

g. P adds "from yourselves." For verses 9–10, R has: "So I exhort us by both heaven and earth: do not abandon my commandments. Do not display cowardice when I am put to death, nor ever display hatred toward yourselves. Neither wander after disorderly men, nor speak evil of our brothers and sisters, nor let fear of people ever separate you from Christ. Accept death willingly and do not deny Christ. Go out of your cities and guard your faith in him. Renounce wealth and love the Lord only. Allow yourself to be struck for his sake and do not strike back. Seek him and do not let your souls depart from him. Let theft and all other evil and wickedness be far from you. Children, turn your faces away from fighting and sexual immorality and envy. Children, spit in the face of the love of money. Banish arrogance. Hate lying. Love friendship, freedom from fear, and genuineness."

h. P: "Remember the prophets of the Mosaic law. Keep your souls alert. Let your hearts ascend to God."

i. P adds "with salt." For verse 11, R has: "Remember the Mosaic law according to the Spirit. Set your minds always on things above. Both turn your souls to the highly esteemed commandment, and let your lamps blaze continually. Let your torches always shine. Let your mouths sing songs of praise continually to God. Do not harm anyone in return for harm. Do not let your burnt offerings and sacrifices spoil. But more importantly, let the very best of our first fruits be offered to God. Let your words be seasoned always with salt. And if you observe all these practices, children, let the grace of our Lord Jesus Christ be with you always, both now and forever. Amen."

j. R adds "to go in peace."

Herod summons guests to his birthday celebration

8 [1]So Herod's birthday celebration was held the next day, and he summoned all his nobles[a] and those summoned were: Nilus, second from Herod, Cyril third, Lucius fourth, Hygnus fifth, Acholius sixth, Gaius seventh, Felix eighth, Sosipater ninth, Antonius tenth, Acheilius eleventh, Alypius twelfth, Iras thirteenth, Alaphius fourteenth, Prochorus fifteenth, Himerius sixteenth, Africanus seventeenth, Julian eighteenth, Tranquillianus nineteenth, another Herod twentieth, another Julian twenty-first, and Aetius twenty-second.[b] These were the court officials of King Herod. They were summoned to his drinking party.

Mark 6:21//Matt 14:6

The devil plots John's death

[2]But one day before, Herod had gone mad in his desire for Herodias.[c] So the devil, who is ever and always causing trouble through the weak vessels of girls, reserved the girl to perform the lawless deed on that night.[d]

Life Bapt. Serap. 10:16; 11:6

Herod's nobles urge that John be released or beheaded

[3]Now, as his nobles came into the presence of the king, they began to praise him and say,[e] "The souls of all your servants long for the serenity of your piety.[f] Your enemies were quickly terrified and broken, and their end was destruction. Our military force, being supplied, flourishes because of the compassion that pours down from you on your subjects.

[4]"But nevertheless, O gloriously triumphant king, do not let your servants sit down at the feast until John is either released or beheaded. For this man has dismissed our hopes and done much damage and harm to us. [5]Although we place our hopes in your divinity, he brings another law himself and says that another is Christ, God, and king.[g] If such a law becomes followed, your decrees and powers[h] will be

---

a. P: "and Herod summoned everyone to the banquet."

b. The names here are taken from P, G, Q, and R differ somewhat with respect to the names of Herod's nobles. However, Nau's edition presents the name list of P most clearly, and the textual differences (many of which are related purely to spelling) are inconsequential because the individuals mentioned cannot be connected with any known historical figures.

c. Herodias, daughter of Aristobulus and Bernice, was a granddaughter of Herod the Great. She was first married to Herod Philip but later divorced him and married his brother, Herod Antipas (Josephus, *Ant.* 18.5.1). According to the New Testament Gospels, John the Baptist was imprisoned for his condemnation of the relationship between Herod Antipas and Herodias (Mark 6:17–18//Matt 14:3–4; Luke 3:19–20).

d. P: "to perform the lawless deed on the day of the birthday celebrations of Herod." R: "to perform that lawless deed on the same night. When morning came, Herod's nobles came to the feast from this and that place and were delayed. More specifically, they were called aside by the ignoble Herodias and the prizewinner (her daughter) about John, the great Forerunner and Baptist of Christ, whether he would stop the accusations against her or his head would be cut off in his prison cell."

e. R adds "since they were flatterers."

f. For this sentence, P has "The souls of all your servants desire to rejoice in the serenity of your piety"; R: "O good-loving King, the souls of all your servants desire to celebrate today in the greatest serenity of our piety."

g. P: "another is Christ and king"; R: "another is Christ, God, and eternal king."

h. P: "our decrees and our powers"; R: "all your decrees and powers."

reduced.[a] So send someone out[b] and make an inquiry of him, and if he stops this vain teaching, let him be released. However, if he does not, let him be beheaded."[c]

Julian interrogates John in prison

[6]So the king sent out Julian[d] and said to him, "Make an inquiry of John and learn what concerns him. And after you take his statements, let me know. Now hurry, before we recline at the hour of the feast.[e]"

[7]Then Julian went out[f] to the prison and said to John,[g] "Why were you thrown in prison?" John said, "Because I exposed the[h] impiety of your lord."

[8]Julian said to him, "It is not necessary[i] to proclaim these things[j] between just the two of us." John said,[k] "I proclaimed these things in the presence of your lord, and now you say that I should not proclaim them in your presence!"

[9]Julian said, "Stop, John! Stop this[l] most disruptive behavior! Do not seek zealously to expose kings, especially those considered deities!" John said to him, "I was sent for this reason."[m]

[10]Julian said, "We have no need for wordy spirits. Now refrain from making declarations."[n] The holy John said to him,[o] "Go out and say to your king, 'John opposes the things being proclaimed by you, and your palace is powerless.'"[p]

[11]After hearing these things, Julian went out and reported to King Herod.[q] But when Herod heard, he remained silent. For it was already the hour of the feast.

----

a. P adds "to nothingness."

b. R adds "to the prison."

c. R adds "quickly."

d. Like all of Herod's ruling officials named in this text, Julian cannot be connected with any known historical figure and most likely is a literary fiction created by the author.

e. For this verse, R has: "Hearing these things and at once sending out Julian, a certain one of his wicked ruling officials, Herod the king said to him, 'Go out quickly to the prison and make an inquiry of John and learn what concerns him. After you take his statements, let me know quickly and accurately about everything. Now hurry, so that it is (done) before we recline at the hour of the feast.'"

f. R adds "quickly."

g. R adds "the Baptist."

h. R adds "lawless."

i. R begins this sentence with "John, it is not necessary."

j. P adds "anew."

k. R: "The Lord's forerunner John said."

l. R adds "depraved and."

m. P adds "that I might expose lawless activity"; R adds "and I will never stop doing this until my final breath."

n. For this sentence, R has "From now on, stop making declarations of this kind since you are about to die miserably."

o. R: "The Lord's forerunner John said to him."

p. For this quotation, P has: "Proceed to your lord and say to him, 'John opposes the things being done by you, and your palace is powerless.'" R: "Go out quickly and say these things to your king, 'John the Baptist opposes the things being proclaimed by you, and your palace is powerless.'"

q. For this sentence, R has: "After hearing these things, Julian went out at great speed and reported everything to King Herod."

Mark 6:21–28//Matt
14:6–11

Herod's birthday celebration

9 [1]As they reclined and feasted, they became drunk and common sense departed from them. And Herod ordered the daughter of Herodias to come and dance in his presence.[a] When she came in, she refused. So the king said to her, "Ask me for up to half my kingdom or anything you want, and I will grant it for you." Then she danced.[b]

[2]Then she went out and said to her mother, "What should I ask of the king?" Her mother said to her, "The head of John the Baptist." So Herodias (daughter of Herodias)[c] went back in[d] and said to the king, "Give me[e] the head of John the Baptist on a platter and I will be paid in full."

Herod orders the execution of John

[3]Herod was grieved[f] because he had longed to speak face-to-face with him.[g] Nevertheless, because of the oaths and the guests, he did not refuse her.[h] So he summoned an executioner and said to him, "Go out to the prison and behead John. And put his head on a platter and bring it to me."

[4]So the executioner went out and cut off the head of the holy John.[i] He put it on a platter and brought it to Herod. Herod took it and gave it to Herodias, and Herodias gave it to her mother.[j]

The fate of John's mortal remains

10 [1]But Acholius,[k] one of Herod's guests, was a[l] disciple of the holy John, and he was also greatly liked by the mother, Herodias. So he arose[m] and asked for the head of John the Baptist.[n] When he received it, having an empty water jar[o] in

---

a. For this sentence, R has "Then, being instigated by Satan, Herod ordered the daughter of Herodias to the party and to dance in the presence of him and his guests."

b. P and R add "and pleased Herod and his (R: the) guests."

c. Mother and daughter in this text share the name Herodias. The girl who danced before Herod and convinced him to behead John the Baptist is often identified as Salome, the daughter of Herodias and her first husband (Herod Philip) mentioned by Josephus (*Ant.* 18.5.4). However, the girl is given different names in various apocryphal texts, such as Arcostriana/Uxatriana in *Life Bapt. Serap.* (10:4; 11:9). The New Testament Gospels are silent about the girl's name with one key exception: a well-attested (if problematic) variant reading of Mark 6:22 indicates that she had the name she does in this text: Herodias.

d. R adds "quickly."

e. P adds "here."

f. R begins this sentence with "When Herod heard this, he was greatly grieved."

g. P: "with the holy John."

h. P: "he did not wish to refuse her."

i. R: "the head of John, the holy Forerunner and Baptist."

j. For this sentence, P has: "Herod took it and gave it over to the girl. Then after taking it and dancing with it in the middle of the party, the girl gave it over to her mother, Herodias."

k. Like all of Herod's ruling officials named in this text, Acholius cannot be connected with any known historical figure and is most likely a literary fiction created by the author.

l. R adds "secret."

m. P adds "and went out from the feast"; R adds "from the party."

n. P: "asked for the head of the holy John from her"; R: "asked Herodias for the head of John the Baptist and she consented to his request."

o. P and R: "having a new water jar."

which nothing had ever been put[a] and securing it with a lead seal, he summoned six of his disciples[b] and said to them, "Take the head of our teacher,[c] travel far away from this city, and deposit it[d] just as it is in this water jar. And let others of you wrap up the[e] body[f] of the holy prophet."[g]

Luke 23:53; John 19:41

[2]So the six disciples of the holy John took the head and traveled to Emesa, a city that lies near the Saracens.[h] They found a cave and deposited the water jar that contained the[i] head of the holy John. And these six disciples of his remained there until the days of their deaths.

Mark 6:29//Matt 14:12

Life Bapt. Serap. 13:13

Author's note and John's feast day

[3]Now I have written these things, brothers and sisters, since I was a sinful disciple of John who both followed him and was taught by him to believe in our Lord Jesus Christ, who will rescue us from the coming wrath.[j]

1 Thess 1:10

[4]The holy John was thirty-three years old when he was beheaded. He was decapitated in the month of Dystros on the 29th. Therefore, we hold also his memorial at this time, so that we also may receive with him a part in the kingdom of heaven through our Lord Jesus Christ with whom be to the Father with the Holy Spirit glory, power, honor, and worship now and always and forever and ever. Amen.[k]

---

a. P adds "putting the venerable head into it"; R adds "he put it into it."

b. P: "he summoned six of the holy John's disciples."

c. R begins this sentence with "Brothers and sisters, take the head." P and R add: "of your teacher."

d. R adds "in a dignified place."

e. R adds "venerable."

f. P begins the sentence with "And let others of you take from the prison and wrap up the body." The rest of the text has been lost in P.

g. R adds "and our teacher."

h. For this sentence, R has: "So the six disciples of John, the holy Forerunner and Baptist, took the head and traveled quickly and went out to Emesa, a city that lies near the Saracens." Emesa, modern-day Homs, is a city located in western Syria. The Saracens are Arab tribes occasionally mentioned, but not clearly identified, in late Roman sources.

i. R adds "venerable and white."

j. For this verse, R has: "Now I, Mark, have written these things, Brothers and Sisters, since I was previously a disciple of John, the holy Forerunner and Baptist, who both followed him and was taught by him to believe in our Lord Jesus Christ, who will rescue us from the coming wrath. Then I accompanied the holy Peter, even the leader of the apostles."

k. For this verse, R has: "The holy John was thirty years and two months old when he was beheaded. He suffered in the month of August on the 29th. Therefore, we all also hold his holy and honorable memorial at this time, so that through his holy entreaties we also may receive with him a part in the kingdom of heaven in Christ Jesus our Lord, to whom be the glory and power now and always and forever and ever. Amen."

The Life of John the Baptist by Serapion
A new translation and introduction

by Slavomír Čéplö

The *Life of John the Baptist* (*Life Bapt. Serap.*; *CANT* 183) recounts the life of John the Baptist (Yūḥannā) from his annunciation to his death and concludes with the history of his remains and their transfer to Egypt. Purported to be composed by Serapion, a bishop in fourth/fifth-century Egypt, it combines various strands of tradition surrounding John the Baptist—both canonical and noncanonical—with accounts relating to the veneration of his remains. As such, it preserves apocryphal traditions not recorded elsewhere and sheds further light on the development of that tradition among Arabic-speaking Christians.

Contents
Life Bapt. Serap. can be divided into two major parts, each with distinct themes and style. The first part is the actual biography of John the Baptist (1–13) which begins with a faithful retelling of the account from Luke 1:5–80, interspersed with material from Matthew 1–2. The narrative then proceeds from the events surrounding the slaughter of the innocents and John's escape to the wilderness (3–4) through the death of Elizabeth and Jesus' miraculous flight to the wilderness to comfort John (7), to John's first encounter with Herod and Herodias (8). After baptizing Jesus (9), John once again runs afoul of Herod and Herodias (10) only to be arrested and executed at Herodias's behest (11). His head, however, continues to preach for fifteen years until it is buried (13). The second part of the text details the removal of the body of John the Baptist from his grave during the reign of Emperor Julian and its transfer to Egypt and veneration by the patriarchs of Alexandria (14). *Life Bapt. Serap.* concludes with the account of the consecration of a church dedicated to John's remains (15).

Unlike these two narrative sections which trace a more or less straight progression of events, chapters 5, 6, and partially 12 contain elements characteristic of homiletic style, such as exclamatory sentences addressed to the characters in the narrative (5:3–5) or the narrator speaking in the first person (6:2–3). Indeed, chapter 14 intimates that the entire work is a homily read on the day of the feast of John the Baptist. The text itself belies this—for example, the introduction offers no indication to that effect, nor does the majority of the text read as anything but a straightforward narrative. This discrepancy, combined with the sharp break in style and themes between the sections and a number of other telltale signs (such as repeating the same story twice with different focus and different details as in chaps. 8 and 10), suggests that *Life Bapt. Serap.* as we now have it is a composite work.

Manuscripts and editions
Life Bapt. Serap. is extant in Arabic only and survives in at least ten Garšūnī manuscript witnesses. In the majority of them, the text is followed by a collection of five miracles at-

tributed to John the Baptist. This work, which we will refer to as *Five Miracles of John the Baptist (Miracles Bapt.)*, also appears separately and its stylistic and linguistic features suggest that it was not originally a part of *Life Bapt. Serap.* The currently known witnesses are divided into two groups based primarily on the dominant form of Elizabeth's name used in the manuscript (Elīṣbāṭ or Elīṣābāṭ in Group A MSS; Elišbaʿ in Group B) and are as follows:

Group A:

A: Edgbaston, University of Birmingham, Mingana Syr. 22, fol. 29r–46r (dated 1527); complete with a few minor lacunae and one large one corresponding to *Life Bapt. Serap.* 13:14–14:9. *Miracles Bapt.* follows on fol. 46r–48v.

B: Edgbaston, University of Birmingham, Mingana Syr. 367, fol. 144v–173v (1550); complete with one lacuna corresponding to *Life Bapt. Serap.* 14:8–15:3. *Miracles Bapt.* follows on fol. 174r–177v.

C: Edgbaston, University of Birmingham, Mingana Syr. 369, fol. 142r–149v (1481); complete with minor lacunae. *Miracles Bapt.* follows on fol. 149v–150r.

D: Vatican, Biblioteca apostolica, Sbath 125, no foliation (1440); complete with minor lacunae at the beginning and one large one corresponding to *Life Bapt. Serap.* 10:2–11:4. The four following pages contain *Miracles Bapt.*

E: Mardin, Zaʿfaran Monastery, 207, fol. 20v–26r (19th/20th cent.); complete.

F: Mardin, Church of the Forty Martyrs 304, pp. 14–93[1] (16th cent.); complete with lacunae corresponding to 3:9–3:12 (pp. 29–30 are blank), 7:17–8:4 (pp. 49–52 are blank), 10:17–21 (pp. 65–66 are blank) and 14:3–5 (pp. 79–80 are blank). *Miracles Bapt.* continues on pp. 93–136 with pp. 97–100 and 109–28 blank.

G: Diyarbakir, Meryem Ana Syriac Orthodox Church, 134,[2] fol. 41r–55v (18th/19th cent.); incomplete, ends with *Life Bapt. Serap.* 10:16.

H: Aleppo, Syriac Catholic Archbishopric, 9/30, fol. 83r–107v (1825); complete. *Miracles Bapt.* continues on fol. 108r–111v.

Group B:

P: Edgbaston, University of Birmingham, Mingana Syr. 183, fol. 53v–72v (1746); complete with one lacuna corresponding to *Life Bapt. Serap.* 7:9–8:4.

Q: Diyarbakir, Meryem Ana Syriac Orthodox Church, 243, fol. ?–52r (1619/1620); incomplete at the beginning (the volume is heavily damaged at the beginning and the first thirty extant pages are torn in half), the first complete page starts with *Life Bapt. Serap.* 7:9. *Miracles Bapt.* continues on fol. 52r–56v.

Additionally, Addaï Scher's catalogue of the Syriac and Arabic manuscripts housed at the library of the Chaldean Archbishop in Diyarbakir lists a manuscript (designated Cod. 146) containing a work designated as *Histoire de saint Jean Baptiste.*[3] The fact that this work, like MSS A, B, C, D, F, H, and Q, is followed immediately by *Miracles Bapt.* (here titled *Miracles de saint Jean Baptiste*) indicates that this is indeed another copy of *Life Bapt. Serap.* Unfortunately, the current whereabouts of this manuscript are unknown.

---

1. The volume is paginated, not foliated.

2. In the HMML catalogue, this manuscript is assigned shelf mark 189; 3/23.

3. Addaï Scher, "Notice sur les manuscrits syriaques et arabes conservés à l'archevêché de Diarkbékir rédigée par Mgr Addaï Scher, archevêque chaldéen de Séert (Suite.)," *JA* 10 (1907): 385–431 at 420.

Manuscripts A and P were edited and translated into English by Alphonse Mingana.[4] He notes the existence of B and C in his catalogue of Arabic and Syriac manuscripts,[5] but neither these two nor the remaining six manuscripts have been used for a critical edition or translation to date. All ten manuscripts represent the same recension with only minor differences, some of which suggest they were translated independently, perhaps even from different manuscripts in the original language (likely Coptic). P contains a few idiosyncratic additions (e.g., *Life Bapt. Serap.* 6:5 and 13:7–8) drawn from other traditions.

One more manuscript ought to be mentioned in this context: Paris, Bibliothèque nationale de France, Fonds Arabe 258 (15th cent., sig. X). The manuscript is written in Arabic script *(nashī)* and contains a work (incomplete at the beginning) titled *A Report on Herod and John the Baptist*. Like *Life Bapt. Serap.*, the *Report* contains narrative elements within the framework of a sermon read on the saint's feast day. These narrative elements, however, only contain motifs from chapters 8, 10, and 13 of *Life Bapt. Serap.* and they differ from our text in several important aspects (such as what happened to John's head). The *Report* thus appears to be either an Arabic translation of one of the strands of tradition that were eventually combined into *Life Bapt. Serap.* as it has been handed down to us or a shorter version of *Life Bapt. Serap.* with omissions and some idiosyncratic additions.

Composition and transmission

The purpose of *Life Bapt. Serap.* is clear: to provide a comprehensive and entertaining biography of a major New Testament figure, including events taking place after his death involving his relics. To that end, an editor combined a wide range of sources at his disposal into a more-or-less coherent narrative, generally following the conventions of the genre known in Arabic literature as *sīra*. Treading somewhere between biography and historical novel, this genre was extremely popular in Arabic literature; while the earliest *siyar* focused on Muhammad and his life, the genre was soon extended to more-or-less fictionalized exploits of historical personalities and legendary figures (such as *Sīrat Banī Hilāl, Sīrat Sayf ibn Dī Yazān,* or *Sīrat Baybars*).[6] In what follows, we will briefly review the composition of *Life Bapt. Serap.* and highlight, whenever necessary, the changes its sources underwent in the editorial process.

As would be expected of a composite work recounting the life of a Christian saint,

---

4. Mingana, "New Life of John the Baptist."

5. Alphonse Mingana, *Catalogue of the Mingana Collection of Manuscripts* (3 vols.; Cambridge: W. Heffer & Sons Limited, 1933), 1:667–68 and 680.

6. Thomas Herzog, "Orality and the Tradition of Arabic Epic Storytelling," in *Medieval Oral Literature* (ed. Karl Reichl; Berlin: De Gruyter, 2012), 629–52 at 633–42. There are a number of Christian Arabic works that could be described as a *sīra*. One notable example, this time involving an Old Testament figure, is a work titled *Judgments of Solomon (JSol)* extant in at least five Arabic manuscripts from Egypt. Juan Pablo Monferrer-Sala published a critical edition and Spanish translation of *JSol* based on Paris and Vatican manuscripts titled *Testamentum Salomonis Arabicae* (Cordóba: Servicio de Publicaciones Universidade de Cordóba, 2006), arguing, as many had before, that *JSol* is an Arabic recension of the Greek pseudepigraphon known as *Testament of Solomon*. While *JSol* does contain motifs and narrative sections taken directly from *T. Sol.*, those make up only a small portion of the work. In fact, *JSol* is a composite work very similar in some aspects to *Life Bapt. Serap.* (see Slavomír Čéplö, "Testament of Solomon and Other Pseudepigraphical Material in *Aḥkām Sulaymān (Judgments of Solomon),*" in *The Canon of the Bible and the Apocrypha in the Churches of the East* [ed. Vahan S. Hovhanessian; New York: Peter Lang, 2012], 21–38). For example, both works appear out of nowhere as fully formed, self-contained narratives (*Life Bapt. Serap.* in the fourteenth century, *JSol* in the seventeenth), both begin with a canonical introduction and then combine various disparate strands of tradition, and both seem to be heavily dependent on Coptic sources.

the narration begins with the canonical account of John's birth taken from the gospels, sometimes nearly word-for-word, sometimes with substantial differences (like Zechariah's garbled tribal affiliation or the absence of the angel's greeting to Mary). In addition to starting off with the familiar, this compositional strategy also serves to lend an air of legitimacy to the strange and unusual that follows and thus to the entire compilation. The canonical narrative in chapters 1 and 2 is immediately followed by three chapters containing material that falls outside of the canon, but was definitely familiar to the audience. The story of Elizabeth's escape from Jerusalem (3) and the story of Zechariah's death (4 and 6) clearly echo similar motifs from the *Protevangelium of James* (22:3; 23), even if they differ from *Prot. Jas.*'s account in some important aspects. For example, *Life Bapt. Serap.* makes no mention of Elizabeth's hiding place in a mountain, Satan assumes a direct role in Zechariah's death (4:3), and the narrative ends with Zechariah's death and a reference to his blood boiling on the ground (6:5). MS P extends this story with the familiar motif of a foreign ruler finally putting a stop to it by slaughtering the priests as revenge for the prophet's death. This motif, traceable as far as the Talmud tractate *Gittin 57b*, is based on the conflation of Zechariah the father of John the Baptist and the minor prophet Zechariah son of Berechiah of the eponymous Old Testament book (see Matt 23:35). The ultimate source for the flashback to Elizabeth in chapter 5 is unknown, but the style of chapters 5 and 6 suggests that the narrative tradition involving the parents of John ended up in *Life Bapt. Serap.* via a homily or possibly a panegyric. References to monasteries and communities of monks in Elizabeth's speech (5:4, 8) indicate that this addition dates back no further than the rise of the monastic tradition in the fourth century CE.

Chapter 7 continues the chronological account of events with the death of Elizabeth and her burial, attended by Jesus, his mother, and Salome,[7] who are joined by the archangels Michael and Gabriel and the priests Zechariah and Simeon. The contents of this chapter are among those motifs in *Life Bapt. Serap.* that seem to be without parallel in the entire body of tradition surrounding John the Baptist or his parents. It is interesting to note that chronologically, the events described here take place during Jesus' childhood and would therefore fall within the infancy gospel genre. Some of the more miraculous elements, like Jesus' omniscience (7:3–5), his command of the elements (7:7–8), and his ability to retrieve any soul from the afterlife, albeit exercised through the archangels (7:11), are indeed reminiscent of other infancy narratives, but on the whole, these stories appear to be unique to *Life Bapt. Serap.* As for its connection to the rest of the narrative, chapter 7 provides an explanation for how the child John survived in the desert, attributing this explicitly to Jesus' care (7:17), Elizabeth's visits (7:17), and Gabriel's supervision (7:16).

In the next chapter, Gabriel turns from being John's protector to serving as his mentor. Gabriel takes on the same role in other apocryphal traditions, such as *Life Mart. Bapt.* 2,[8] but takes on a peculiar twist here: Gabriel instructs John the Baptist to not just make road for the Savior, but to specifically reproach Herod for taking the wife of his brother as his mistress (8:3). In the course of this mission, John's voice—magically amplified or perhaps even disembodied, thus becoming a literal voice in the wilderness—haunts Herodias during the night. Herodias convinces Herod to send soldiers to kill John and when this fails,

---

7. The presence of Salome at a burial, traditionally a family affair, suggests she is a relative of Mary's. Epiphanius (*Pan.* 78.8; *Ancor.* 60) gives Salome as the name of Mary's daughter and Jesus' sister (see Burke, "Serapion's *Life of John the Baptist*," 295).

8. A new translation of this text by Andrew Bernhard is included in this volume.

she entices Herod to ignore John and take her as his wife. Chapter 8 concludes with an editor's comment laying the blame for Herod's crimes against his brother at Herodias's feet (8:8), which sets the tone for the remainder of the work.

After being interrupted by chapter 9 (which offers a retelling of Luke's account of Jesus' baptism with some idiosyncratic additions), the narrative continues in chapter 10 with a restatement of the same events from chapter 8, but with a number of noticeable differences: in chapter 8, Herod has an affair with the wife of his brother (who remains unnamed) and the only reference to him marrying Herodias is inserted as an afterthought by the editor (8:8) in an apparent attempt to reconcile the text with the canonical account (Mark 6:17–18//Matt 14:3–4). In chapter 10, however, the events surrounding Herod's and Herodias's transgressions are described in great detail and partly in epistolary form: first Herod writes to the emperor to slander Philip (10:1), then, after Philip is deposed and ruined, Herodias writes a letter to Herod offering herself and her daughter to him, an offer Herod gladly accepts (10:6–8), and finally John writes to Herod to rebuke him (10:12). It is clear that these two chapters should be traced to two different strands of tradition.[9] The first, including the story of John's magically amplified voice, appears to be preserved only in *Life Bapt. Serap.* and the Arabic MS X. The second, however, is reminiscent of motifs found in a number of Coptic works of various genres devoted to John the Baptist, such as *Encom. Bapt.*[10] The most relevant of these for our understanding of *Life Bapt. Serap.* are two works titled *Panegyric on John the Baptist,* one anonymous in Bohairic[11] and one in Sahidic (*CANT* 185, *CPC* 0513), attributed to Patriarch Theodosius of Alexandria (d. 567).[12] While these works differ from each other in some parts, in others, they speak with one voice and it is those parts that offer a number of close parallels to the tradition represented in *Life Bapt. Serap.* 10. For example, both the *Panegyrics* and *Life Bapt. Serap.* describe in detail Herod's accusations against Philip, including Philip's purported refusal to pay tribute to Rome and his rejection of Rome's authority (10:1). Both then proceed to describe Philip's ruin and his appeal to John the Baptist, who is described as a widely respected moral authority (10:11). And in both works, John takes Philip's case to Herod, who is at first afraid of the prophet, but after talking to Herodias (10:13–16), he has John imprisoned (10:21). Considering these parallels and the relative dating, it is more than likely that the editor of *Life Bapt. Serap.* used a recension of one of the *Panegyrics* as a source for his biography.

The *Panegyric* tradition, however, has not survived the integration into *Life Bapt. Serap.* unscathed. Only the unique narrative parts of the *Panegyrics* have been included and then only those covering events taking place between Herod's betrayal of Philip and John's imprisonment. Also, some parts of the narration are compressed (such as Philip's appeal to John), some left out (the emperor's reaction to Herod's accusation, references to John's disciples as messengers), and, most importantly, Herodias's role in the unfolding of events is greatly expanded. The motif of Herodias as the driving force behind Herod's transgressions occurs already in chapter 8, but it comes to full fruition here in chapter 10.

---

9. Chapter 8 in general is an ill fit with the rest of the text. Compare, for example, the references to John's diet in 7:1 where both the Gospels and *Life Bapt. Serap.* have John eating locusts, whereas in 8:1 the locusts are replaced with wild grass.

10. A new translation of this text by Philip L. Tite is included in this volume.

11. De Vis, *Homélies coptes,* 1–51 with Sahidic fragments published in Rossi, *Trascrizione di tre manoscritti copti,* 101–10.

12. Kuhn, *Panegyric on John the Baptist,* 56–58. See also p. viii n. 27 for more on the complicated relationship between the two works.

Unlike the *Panegyric, Life Bapt. Serap.* has Herodias initiate the relationship with Herod, portrays Herodias and not Herod as offended at John's impudence (10:14), and once John appears before them (of his own will in the *Panegyrics,* already imprisoned in *Life Bapt. Serap.*), Herodias is the one who comes to negotiate with him, and failing, threatens him with execution. This pattern continues throughout chapter 11, which contains an account of the death of John the Baptist, and chapter 12, which describes what happened to his head afterwards. Whereas the Gospel narrative as well as the *Panegyrics* describe John's death as Herodias taking advantage of an unexpected opportunity (though they differ in the point in time at which this happens),[13] *Life Bapt. Serap.* 11 has Herodias orchestrate John's death from the beginning, suggesting the very idea of a birthday feast to Herod (11:3). And finally, in chapter 13, after being presented with John's head, Herodias launches a furious tirade against John, describing in great detail the way she plans to desecrate the saint's remains (13:3). Whether the editor of *Life Bapt. Serap.* simply rewrote the account of the *Panegyrics* to harmonize it with his own theology or intended moral lesson, or whether these discrepancies are the result of incorporation of the same account through another yet unidentified work, remains to be determined.

What follows after Herodias's tirade is perhaps the most fantastical part of the entire narrative, where John's head (still hearing and seeing) foils Herodias's plans by flying into the air and continuing to decry Herod's sin. While certainly striking, this narrative element is not without its parallels elsewhere in Arabic tradition. For example, the Coptic Arabic *Synaxarium* (a calendar with feasts of saints given for each day) includes the following in the entry for the 2nd of Tūt, the anniversary of the death of John the Baptist: "And the holy head flew from their hands and into the air, saying 'You must not take the wife of your brother.' It is said that the head is in the province of Homs."[14] Considering the disproportionate amount of detail provided by both accounts and the telling formula "it is said" employed in the *Synaxarium* (used to indicate a quotation from an unnamed source), it is unlikely that the *Synaxarium* is the ultimate source for this motif in *Life Bapt. Serap.* For example, a description of John's head preaching against Herod even after having been cut off is also a staple of Islamic *isrā'īliyāt*—stories of prophets and other notables taken from Jewish and Christian tradition—involving the prophet Yaḥyā bin Zakariyyā' (as John the Baptist is known in Islam). A typical example can be found in a collection of legends surrounding important figures of Islam titled *Lives of the Prophets* by Aḥmad al-Ṭa'labī (d. 1035). In his account, the king of the Israelites wishes to marry the daughter of one of his wives and seeks John's permission to do so. When John refuses, the mother of the girl tells the girl to get the king drunk and then ask for John's head, which she does. The king refuses at first and tells her to ask for something else, but she does not relent: "So when she had refused him, he sent for John and had his head brought. Now the head was still speaking when it was placed before him, and it said, 'She is not lawful for you.'"[15] Despite some changes to the narrative, al-Ṭa'labī makes it clear we are dealing here with the same cast of characters:

> Christian scholars have said that the king of the Israelites who killed John was called Hīradūs, because of his wife who was called Hiradawūya, and who had been the wife

---

13. In the Gospel narrative, Herodias is only involved once Herod asks her daughter to make a wish (cf. Mark 6:24). In the *Panegyric,* Herodias takes the initiative, but only once the feast has already started.

14. René Basset, trans., "Le synaxaire arabe jacobite," PO 1 (1907): 219–379; 3 (1909): 243–545; 11 (1915): 505–859; 16 (1922): 185–424; 17 (1923): 525–782; here 227–28, my translation.

15. Al-Ṭa'labī, *Lives of the Prophets,* 636.

of his brother named Fīlīqūs. He desired her and she agreed to fornication. John forbade her and told her that she was not permitted for the king. The woman asked Hīradūs to bring her the head of John, and when he did that it fell into his hands and he suffered great anxiety.[16]

Once John's head has made its escape, just punishment is visited upon all involved in John's death (13:5–8). Herodias, in keeping with the spirit of the work, goes first and meets the most horrible end: she is swallowed by the earth and her eyes are gouged out—fitting, perhaps, considering her plans for John's head—while Herod merely has a stroke. This account of the death of the adulterous couple appears to be without parallel, but the fate of Herodias's daughter (only given in P) closely resembles that described in the *Epistle of Herod to Pilate*[17] and an apocryphal text titled the *Decapitation of John the Forerunner,* attributed to John's disciple Euriptus (*CANT* 180.2).[18]

John's biography proper ends in chapter 13 with the description of his resting places. His body is taken by his disciples and buried in Sebaste. Rebuilt by Herod the Great on the site of ancient Samaria (in the vicinity of today's Nablus, which P makes specific), Sebaste is where, according to the geographical dictionary by Muslim geographer Yāqūt (d. 1229), John the Baptist and his father Zechariah are buried.[19] John's head finally comes to rest in the Syrian city of Homs, ancient Emesa, which is the place where, according to tradition,[20] it is found some time later.

In the final two chapters, *Life Bapt. Serap.* turns into a work of ecclesiastical history, describing the removal of John's body from Sebaste and its transfer to Alexandria. This account has parallels in many Arabic and Coptic works of similar nature, such as Severus ibn al-Muqaffaʻ's (d. 987) *History of the Patriarchs of Alexandria,*[21] a Coptic fragment of an encomium on John the Baptist preserved in a manuscript dated to the eleventh century,[22] and a Coptic fragment of a text on ecclesiastical history possibly written by Patriarch Theophilus himself.[23] The version of the events recorded in *Life Bapt. Serap.* closely follows the established account, from the destruction of relics in Sebaste through the journey

---

16. Al-Ṭaʻlabī, *Lives of the Prophets,* 636.

17. Available in *AG,* 523–27.

18. Athanasius Vassiliev, *Anecdota graeco-byzantina, pars prior* (Moscow: Imperial University, 1893), 1–4. The deaths of Herodias and her daughter are told also in Jacob of Voragine's *The Golden Legend* 125 (2 vols.; trans. William Granger Ryan; Princeton: Princeton University Press, 1993), 2:138–39 and several other sources (see Burke, "Serapion's *Life of John the Baptist,*" 291).

19. Yāqūt (al-Rūmī al-Ḥamawī, Yāqūt ibn ʻAbdullāh), *Muʻdžam al-buldān* (5 vols.; Beirut: Dar Sader, 1993), 3:184. See also Burke, "Serapion's *Life of John the Baptist,*" 296.

20. This tradition is preserved by a number of works describing the discovery of John's head *(Disc. John Bapt.)* extant in Latin (PL 67:420C–430D; see Paul C. Dilley, "The Invention of Christian Tradition: 'Apocrypha,' Imperial Policy and Anti-Jewish Propaganda," *GRBS* 50 [2010]: 586–615, esp. 597 n. 24), Greek (*BHG* 839 and 840), Armenian (Erevan, Matenadaran, 1524, fol. 82r–85v), and Coptic (a work titled *Invention of the Head of John the Baptist by Gesius and Isidorus* [*BHO* 485–86]; see Georg Steindorff, "Gesios und Isidoros: Drei sahidische Fragmente über die 'Auffindung der Gebeine Johannes des Täufers,'" *ZÄS* 21 [1883]: 137–58). For related traditions, see *Life Mart. Bapt.* 10:2 (a new translation of this text by Andrew Bernhard is included in this volume).

21. Severus Ibn al-Muqaffaʻ, *History of the Patriarchs of the Coptic Church of Alexandria (Saint Mark to Theonas)* (ed. and trans. Basil T. A. Evetts; PO 1.2; Paris: Firmin-Didot, 1948).

22. Van Lantschoot, "Fragments coptes," 237–38. Van Lantschoot himself notes the parallels between his fragment and *Life Bapt. Serap.*

23. Tito Orlandi, "Un frammento copto di Teofilo di Alessandria," *RSO* 44 (1970): 23–26.

to Egypt to the reception by Athanasius. This is followed by a historical excursus on the destruction of pagan temples, the actual construction of the church dedicated to John the Baptist, and Theophilus's recollection of the assignment given to him by Athanasius. The narration concludes with the finding of John's and Elisha's remains and the consecration of the church.[24]

Language, Date, and Provenance

Were one to take the text's claims regarding its author and date at their face value, one could be satisfied in noting that *Life Bapt. Serap.* was written by an Egyptian bishop named Serapion who was born in the second half of the fourth century CE (15:2) and was alive to report events taking place shortly after 391 CE (see 15:3 and the reference to the destruction of Alexandria's Serapeum). However, there are a few problems with this proposition. The fact that the identity of this Serapion cannot be satisfactorily established is not necessarily one of them—although any attempts to identify him with other famous figures of that name like Serapion of Thmuis (Serapion Scholasticus, d. 360) or Serapion of Antioch (d. 211) must fail on chronological grounds, it is not out of the realm of possibility that such a Serapion indeed existed. What is problematic is the fact that *Life Bapt. Serap.* as it has been handed down to us is only extant in late Arabic manuscripts, none of which predates 1400 CE. Assuming that a fourth-century Egyptian bishop wrote in Greek or Coptic and that the recension we have is a translation, the absence of any version or fragment of *Life Bapt. Serap.* in either of the presumed original languages is telling. Considering the composite nature of the work as described above, one could argue that any Greek or Coptic fragment of, say, a narrative of the annunciation or of John's death slightly different from existing recensions of the Gospels is a piece from an original recension of *Life Bapt. Serap.* rather than a new recension of Luke or Matthew. But combined with the apparent lack of any such original recension and supported by a firm slash of Occam's razor, the composite nature of *Life Bapt. Serap.* is the strongest argument against taking the claims of the text at their face value. And while there is no evidence to confirm or deny the existence of the good bishop Serapion and his authorship of some work on the transfer of John the Baptist's body to fourth-century Alexandria, *Life Bapt. Serap.* translated here is almost certainly a product of an anonymous editor who worked with a later copy (and possibly a translation) of such a work and a few others. This editor combined various narrative strands into a single text, and although some of these traditions ultimately may date as far back as the fifth century,[25] the final redaction of the Arabic text took its form at a much later date. Lacking any external information on the identity of this editor and the time and place of the composition of *Life Bapt. Serap.*, we must turn to the text itself in search of clues.

It is obvious that, although written in West Syriac script *(serṭā)*, the Arabic text of *Life Bapt. Serap.* originated somewhere far from any of the centers of Syriac Christianity. Use of the Coptic calendar (4:2, 7:14, 11:8, and 15:13, 17), Coptic loanwords (3:11), and dialectisms characteristic of Egyptian Arabic (e.g., 1:13) offer strong evidence that the Arabic text as it has been handed down to us was composed in Christian Egypt. Moreover, as Mingana points out,[26] a number of syntactic peculiarities suggest that at least some parts of the text

---

24. Orlandi, "Un frammento copto," 23.

25. Not including the Gospels nor *Prot. Jas.*, obviously.

26. Mingana, "New Life of John the Baptist," 249. However, Mingana considered Greek to be the most likely source language (ibid., 234–35).

were composed in a different language. The Egyptian focus of chapters 14 and 15, along with the linguistic evidence for Egyptian origin, make Coptic the most likely original language.

The use of the Coptic calendar is the strongest clue for establishing not only a place of origin but also a *terminus ante quem* for the composition of *Life Bapt. Serap.* Four dates are given in *Life Bapt. Serap.*: the 7th of Tūt (slaughter of the innocents), the 15th of Amšīr (death of Elizabeth), the 2nd of Tūt (beheading of John the Baptist), and the 2nd of Baʾūna (revelation of the body of John the Baptist and consecration of a church dedicated to him). Of these four dates, two correspond to the respective holidays in the Coptic Arabic Synaxarium: the 2nd of Tūt and the 2nd of Baʾūna (given as the date of the apparition of the corpse of John the Baptist with Elisha in Alexandria). In the Synaxarium, the 16th (not the 15th) of Amšīr is reserved for the commemoration of the death of Elizabeth. This discrepancy of one day may seem like an accidental error, but considering that in the Synaxarium the 7th of Tūt does not have any connection with the events described in *Life Bapt. Serap.*, while the 8th of Tūt commemorates the death of Zechariah (depicted in *Life Bapt. Serap.* as occurring simultaneously with the slaughter of the innocents), it may not be an error at all. One explanation for it could be that *Life Bapt. Serap.* was compiled before the Synaxarium took its present stable form, which is most likely to have taken place in the fourteenth century.[27]

None of what has been said here about the composite nature of *Life Bapt. Serap.* or its origins means that there are no traces of the themes unique to *Life Bapt. Serap.* before the fourteenth century—quite the contrary. Al-Ṯaʿlabī's eleventh-century account of John's death cited above gives Ismāʿīl as-Suddī (d. 745) as the source,[28] but the story of the head of John the Baptist preaching even after his death is known from earlier tradents such as Ibn Masʿūd (died ca. 652),[29] one of the earliest *Qurʾān* commentators. Who or what exactly al-Ṯaʿlabī refers to when he speaks of "Christian scholars" is unclear, but it is unlikely to be the Gospels since he refers to them by name, even though he does not cite from them. Considering his (or his sources') obvious familiarity with other Christian apocryphal works, it is not inconceivable that at least some of the unique episodes in the biography of John the Baptist that eventually ended up in *Life Bapt. Serap.* were known well enough to reach the scriptoria of early Muslim scholars in one form or another. In other words, the material unique to *Life Bapt. Serap.* most likely is not an invention of the editor or compiler of *Life Bapt. Serap.*, but continues an old tradition lost to the rest of the Christian world, fragments of which are preserved in early Islamic sources as well.

In summary, external as well as internal evidence regarding the authorship and origin of *Life Bapt. Serap.* supports the conclusion that it was compiled in its present form (i.e., as a full-fledged *sīra*) by an unknown editor somewhere in Egypt sometime in the fourteenth century from a number of older sources—some known from elsewhere, some not.

Translation

This translation is based primarily on MSS C and D, the oldest surviving manuscript witnesses. Where they differ from each other, C prevails. Where C, D, or both differ from the majority text, the majority reading is used, with the exception of Coptic dates. Readings

---

27. Oswald H. E. Burmester, "On the Date and Authorship of the Arabic Synaxarium of the Coptic Church," *JTS* 155 (1938): 249–54 at 253.

28. Al-Ṯaʿlabī, *Lives of the Prophets*, 636.

29. Brandon M. Wheeler, *Prophets in the Quran: An Introduction to the Quran and Muslim Exegesis* (London: Continuum, 2002), 295.

from other manuscripts are included as footnotes except for minor differences in wording or style, and passages from P that have no parallels in other manuscripts are integrated into the body text. I have introduced chapter and verse divisions.

The parts of the work that rely on the Gospel narrative have been adapted to the style of the New Revised Standard Version, as have names of persons and places throughout. In general, however, the translation strives to be a flowing and idiomatic one, using contemporary English while attempting to emulate the effects on the reader as the Arabic original would have on its readers. To that end, idiomatic expressions are rendered using their English equivalents (e.g., "in those days" is translated as "at that time"), grammatical but archaic-sounding structures are avoided whenever possible (e.g., the preposition "for" when "because" would serve just fine or the participle "saying" introducing reported speech) and elements not native to the language of the text are kept (such as the Coptic title "Anba" which would sound as foreign to a speaker of Syrian Arabic as it does to a speaker of English).

Bibliography

EDITIONS AND TRANSLATIONS

Mingana, Alphonse. "A New Life of John the Baptist." Pages 138–45, 234–87 in volume 1 of *Woodbrooke Studies: Christian Documents in Syriac, Arabic, and Garshūni. Edited and Translated with Critical Apparatus.* Edited by Alphonse Mingana. Cambridge: W. Heffer & Sons Limited, 1927. (*Editio princeps* based on two manuscripts in the Mingana collection.)

STUDIES

Abū Isḥāq Aḥmad ibn Muḥammad ibn Ibrāhīm Al-Ṭaʿlabī. *'Arā'is al-majālis fī qisas al-anbiyā'* or '*Lives of the Prophets*.' Translated by William M. Brinner. Leiden: Brill, 2002.

Burke, Tony. "The New Testament and Other Early Christian Traditions in Serapion's *Life of John the Baptist*." Pages 281–300 in *Christian Apocrypha: Receptions of the New Testament in Ancient Christian Apocrypha*. Edited by Jean-Michel Roessli and Tobias Nicklas. Göttingen: Vandenhoeck & Ruprecht, 2014.

De Vis, Henri. *Homélies coptes de la Vaticane.* Copenhagen: Gyldendalske Boghandel, 1922.

Kuhn, Karl H. *A Panegyric on John the Baptist attributed to Theodosius Archbishop of Alexandria.* CSCO 269, Copt. 34. Leuven: Secrétariat du CorpusSCO, 1966.

Lantschoot, Arnold van. "Fragments coptes d'un panégyrique de St. Jean-Baptiste." *Le Muséon* 44 (1931): 235–54.

Orlandi, Tito. "Un frammento copto di Teofilo di Alessandria." *RSO* 44 (1970): 23–26.

Rossi, Francesco. *Trascrizione di tre manoscritti copti del Museo Egizio di Torino con traduzione italian.* Turin: Ermanno Loescher, 1885.

The Life of John the Baptist by Serapion

Introduction

In the name of the Father, the Son and the Holy Spirit, one God. Asking for God's help and hopeful of his support for this endeavor, we write here the history of holy John the Baptist, the son of Zechariah, may he intercede on our behalf. Amen.

The birth of John the Baptist is foretold

1 ¹During the reign of king Herod of Judea, there was among the people of Israel a prophet, an old man named Zechariah, who was a Levite priest from the tribe of Judah.[a] He had a God-loving wife called Elizabeth who was a descendant of Aaron from the tribe of Levi. ²She had no children and both she and her husband were getting on in years. They were righteous before God, living blamelessly according to all the commandments and regulations of the Lord.

Luke 1:5–7
Prot. Jas. 26:1

³Zechariah was constantly officiating in the temple. When his turn came to offer incense to the Lord, he entered the temple at the time of the offering as usual. ⁴Suddenly an angel of the Lord appeared to him, standing on the right side of the altar. When Zechariah saw him, he was terrified and startled, but the angel said to him, "Rejoice and do not be afraid, Zechariah, because God has heard your prayers. ⁵Your wife Elizabeth will bear you a son who will be named John and he will cause you great joy and jubilation. ⁶He will be great in the sight of the Lord, he will not drink wine or strong drink and he will be filled with the Holy Spirit even in his mother's womb. He will turn many of the people of Israel to the Lord their God. With the spirit and strength of Elijah, he will go before

Luke 1:8–17

him to prepare the people for the Lord."

⁷When he heard these words, Zechariah was astonished and doubtful since he was old and did not have any children. He did not remember Abraham, the greatest among the patriarchs, to whom God gave Isaac, although he had already

Prot. Jas. 1:3

passed the age of one hundred. Nor did Zechariah remember Sarah, Abraham's wife, who was childless just like him.

⁸Zechariah said to the angel, "How will this happen? I am old and my wife is getting on in years." ⁹The angel replied, "I am Gabriel, the angel. I was sent to speak to you and bring you this good news. Because you did not believe

---

a. As Mingana ("New Life of John the Baptist," 235) points out, this does not make sense: a Levite priest is, by definition, a member of the tribe of Levi and therefore cannot be a member of the tribe of Judah.

my words, from now on you will be mute and unable to speak until the day these things occur, which will come in due course." [10]And with this, the angel disappeared.

Luke 1:18–20

[11]Meanwhile the people who were waiting outside for Zechariah were starting to wonder at his delay in the temple. When he finally came out, he could not speak to them and they realized he had seen a vision in the temple and could only gesture at them. When his time of service ended, he went home. [12]Elizabeth already knew of all that had transpired.[a]

Luke 1:21–23

[13]At that time, Elizabeth conceived and she remained in seclusion until the fifth month because she was ashamed. She was afraid to be seen as an old woman with her belly growing and milk dripping from her breasts. So she spent her days alone in a small room[b] in her house with everything she needed there with her. [14]Zechariah too lived like this and there was a locked door separating the two of them. For some time, both were completely cut off from the world.

Luke 1:24

The birth of Jesus is foretold

2 [1]When Elizabeth reached the sixth month, the angel Gabriel was sent by God to a town in Galilee called Nazareth, to the fiancée of a man named Joseph, of the house of David. This virgin's name was Mary. [2]When the angel came to her, he said, "Rejoice, Mary, *for you have found favor with God. You will conceive and bear a son and you will name him Jesus. He will be great and he will be called the son of the Most High.*" [3]*Mary said to the angel, "How can this be, since I am a virgin?" The angel replied, "The Holy Spirit will come upon you, and the power of the Most High will overshadow you; therefore the child to be born* of you *will be holy; he will be called Son of God.* [4]*And now, your relative Elizabeth has also conceived a son,* even though she is advanced in years. *This is the sixth month for her who was said to be barren. For nothing will be impossible with God.*" [5]Mary let go of all her doubts and said to the commander of angels, "*I am the servant of the Lord; let it be with me according to your word.*" The angel then said goodbye and departed from her.

Luke 1:26–38

[6]But Mary was still astonished at hearing about Elizabeth's pregnancy and said to herself, "Your deeds are truly great and wonderful, O omnipotent God, for you have brought forth offspring from an old barren woman. [7]I will now go and will not stop until I meet her and see the great miracle God has performed in our times: a virgin giving birth and an old woman breastfeeding."

[8]At that time, Mary set out and hurried to a Judean town in the hill country. [9]She entered the house of Zechariah and she greeted Elizabeth, who came out to meet her with joy and jubilation and greeted Mary with the words, "*Blessed are you among women, and blessed is the fruit of your womb.*"

Luke 1:39–42

[10]The pure holy Virgin kissed the Word's true turtle dove and the Word baptized John while he was still in his mother's womb. David appeared between

---

a. In the Sahidic *Panegyric on John the Baptist* (Kuhn, *Panegyric*, 18) after speaking to Zechariah, Gabriel visits Elizabeth as well.

b. *qaytūn*. An Egyptian dialectal word for a small room derived from Greek *koitōn* "bedroom" (Reinhart Dozy, *Supplément aux dictionnaires arabes* [2 vols.; 2nd ed.; Leiden: Brill, 1927], 2:378). Mingana ("New Life of John the Baptist," 237) translates as "secluded room" and traces it back to Syriac *qaytōna*, which ultimately derives from Arabic *qaytūn*.

Ps 85:10

them and said, "Mercy and justice have met and righteousness and peace have embraced." And John moved in his mother's womb as if he wanted to come out to see his Lord. ¹¹After they finished greeting each other, the Virgin stayed with Elizabeth for three months until Elizabeth was about to give birth, at which time she left and went home.

¹²When the chaste Elizabeth gave birth, there was great joy and jubilation in her house. ¹³After eight days they were going to circumcise him and name him Zechariah. *But his mother said, "No; he is to be called John." They said to her, "None of your relatives has this name."* She said to them, "Ask his father what his name should be." *He asked for a writing tablet and wrote, "His name is John."* ¹⁴Immediately after he finished writing, his mouth was opened and his tongue freed, praising God who gave him this great blessing. And he spoke prophecies concerning his son John the Baptist, since he was aware of the gift God bestowed upon him.

Luke 1:57–64

Luke 1:67

John and his mother escape from Herod

3 ¹John grew into a beautiful child and his mother breastfed him until he was two years old. The grace of God was in his face and he grew healthy and strong with the help of the Holy Spirit.

²When Jesus was born in Bethlehem of Judea, *wise men came from the East, saying, "Where is the child who has been born king of the Jews? For we observed his star* in the East *and have come to pay him homage."* ³When Herod heard this, he was frightened because of what he heard from the wise men about this king of the Jews and he immediately wanted to kill him. ⁴An angel of the Lord appeared to Joseph and said to him, *"Get up, take the* baby *and his mother, go to Egypt, and remain there until I tell you."* ⁵Herod did search for the Master[a] in order to kill him, but did not find him, so he started killing all children in Bethlehem.

Matt 2:1–3

Matt 2:13, 16

⁶Elizabeth feared that her son might be killed as well, so she took him and went to see Zechariah in the temple and she said to him, "My lord, come, let us go with our son John to some other land, lest Herod the unbeliever kills him because of Jesus the Messiah. Mary and Joseph already left for Egypt. Come, before they kill our son John and turn our joy into grief." ⁷Zechariah answered, "I cannot leave the service of the temple of the Lord and go to a foreign country where they worship idols." ⁸She said to him, "What should I do to save my little boy?" ⁹The old man replied, "Rise and go to the wilderness near ʿAyn Kārim[b] and if it pleases God, you will save your son. If they come looking for him, they will shed my blood instead of his."

¹⁰O how he cried when the time came for them to be separated from each other! Zechariah held the boy to his chest, kissed him and said, "Poor me, poor John, my son, the treasure of my old days, for they are keeping me from your face full of grace." ¹¹He then took him to the temple and blessed him, asking God to save him. Suddenly, Gabriel commander of the angels came down to him

---

a. I.e., Jesus.

b. A village in Palestine (now a neighborhood of Jerusalem), traditionally considered the birthplace of John the Baptist.

from heaven, holding a scapular[a] and a leather belt, and he said, "Zechariah, take these and put them on your son. God sent them from heaven, this scapular that belonged to Elijah and this belt worn by Elisha." [12]Holy Zechariah took them from the angel and prayed over them before putting them on his son, attaching them to his clothing, which was made of camel's hair.

Mark 1:6//Matt 3:4

[13]He brought him to his mother and said to her, "Take him and go with him to the wilderness, for the hand of the Lord is with him. I have learned from God that he will live in the wilderness until the day he shows himself to Israel." [14]The blessed Elizabeth took him with tears in her eyes and Zechariah was crying as well when he said, "I know I will never see the both of you again while we all live. So, go with God's peace and may he guide you." [15]And so Elizabeth walked away with her son; and they went to ʿAyn Kārim where she stayed with him.

Herod's soldiers come looking for John

4 [1]When King Herod sent his soldiers to Jerusalem to kill her children, they began killing them as soon as they arrived and did not stop until the evening. [2]This was on the seventh day of the month Tūt [b] (that is the month Elūl). [3]As they were about to return to their king, suddenly Satan came to them and said, "Why did you leave the son of Zechariah without killing him? He is hiding with his father in the temple. Do not let him get away; kill him, lest the king will be angry with you. Go to him, and if he tries to hide his son from you, kill him instead."

[4]The soldiers did as Satan instructed them and went to the temple early in the morning. They found Zechariah serving the Lord and they said to him, "Where is your son whom you have hidden from us?" He said to them, "There is no child here with me." They said, "But you do have a child and you have hidden him from the king's order." He replied, "You fools whose king drinks blood like lionesses, how long will you continue to shed the blood of innocents?" They said to him, "Bring out your son so that we can kill him, or we will kill you in his place." The prophet answered, "My son left for the wilderness and I do not know where he is."[c]

Prot. Jas. 23:1–2

Flashback to Elizabeth

5 [1]When Zechariah said goodbye to Elizabeth and his son John, he blessed him and made him a priest. Then he handed him to his mother and she said to him, "Pray over me, my holy father, so that my journey in the wilderness is easy." He said to her, "May he who gave us a child in our old age guide your path with him." [2]So she took him and went to the wilderness where no one else lived.

[3]O blessed Elizabeth, your story is truly wondrous and righteous, for you did not ask another adult to accompany you, although you did not know where to go or where to find shelter. You did not worry about having bread or little water

---

a. *skhēma* (a loanword from Coptic), a part of a monk's habit. Traditionally, it is an outer garment as wide as a person's shoulders, hanging down to the ground both front and back, but open on both sides. See Aziz S. Atiya, ed., *Coptic Encyclopedia* (8 vols.; New York: Macmillan, 1991), 2:650–55.

b. Only C, D, and F give the name of the month in Coptic with C and D adding the Syriac name in the margin.

c. Zechariah's answer is missing from F.

for the child to drink. You did not say to his father Zechariah, "To whom are you sending me in the wilderness?" [4]There were no monasteries in the wilderness at that time, nor any communities of monks, so you could not say "I will go and stay with them together with my son."

[5]Tell me, blessed Elizabeth, what did you rely on? For the evangelist testifies that you grew old without having children, yet now you have been breastfeeding this child for three years. [6]Listen to the answer the blessed Elizabeth gave.[a] She said, "Why are you astonished that I would go alone into the wilderness? I am not afraid of anything, because I have one of God's kin in my arms; and Gabriel travels with me and paves the way before me." [7]She said, "I rely on the kiss I received from Mary, mother of the Lord, because as I greeted her, the baby in my womb leaped with joy and jubilation and I heard both of them kissing each other in our wombs." [8]And Elizabeth said, "I went and dressed my son in a garment made of camel hair and a leather belt, so that the mountains in the holy wilderness may become inhabited, and that communities of monks grow and multiply and offerings are made in them in the name of the Lord. [9]So if God sustained Hagar and her son Ishmael, who were slaves, as they wandered through the desert, how can he not be bound by a rule he himself established?"

Luke 1:7

Mark 1:6//Matt 3:4

Gen 21:14–19

The death of Zechariah

6 [1]We have described to you virtues of holy Elizabeth, let us now return to holy Zechariah the holy martyr and explain to you his many virtues. [2]Me, I wish to recount your true story, but I am afraid that I will only hear your reproach, just as the happy Elizabeth did. [3]I am in awe of you, pious Zechariah! When Herod's soldiers came to you asking, "Where is your little boy, the son whom you had at an advanced age?" you did not deny him, nor did you say "I do not know him," you said "His mother took him to the wilderness."

[4]And when Zechariah said this about his son to the soldiers, they killed him inside the temple. The priests shrouded his body and they placed it next to the body of his father Berechiah in a hidden tomb out of fear of the wicked. [5]But his blood boiled on the ground and continued to do so for fifty years until Titus Vespasian, the king of Rome, destroyed Jerusalem and killed the Israelite priests for the blood of Zechariah as the Lord ordered him.[b]

Prot. Jas. 23:3

Matt 23:35

The death and burial of Elizabeth

7 [1]As for blessed John, he wandered in the wilderness together with his mother. God prepared locusts and wild honey for him to eat in accordance with the instructions Elizabeth received not to let anything unclean enter his mouth. [2]After five years, the blessed and pious venerable Elizabeth passed away. Holy John sat down to cry over her because he did not know how to shroud her or how to bury her, as he was only seven years and six months old. Herod also died the same day blessed Elizabeth passed away.

[3]Lord Jesus, whose eyes see heaven and earth, saw his relative John sitting

Luke 1:15

Matt 2:19

---

a. G omits "for the evangelist . . . Elizabeth gave."

b. The reference to Titus Vespasian and the execution of the Sanhedrin is unique to P, all other MSS (including Q which is partially defective at this location) end the chapter at "fifty years."

next to his mother, crying. He also started crying and cried for a long time, but no one knew why. ⁴When Jesus' mother saw him crying, she said to him, "My son, what happened? Why are you crying? Did Joseph or somebody else make you upset?" ⁵The mouth filled with life said to her, "No, mother, it is your relative, the venerable Elizabeth. She left my beloved John an orphan and he is now crying over her body, which is lying in the mountains."

⁶When the Virgin heard this, she started crying for her relative, but Jesus said, "Do not cry, my virgin mother, for you will see her with your own eyes this very hour." And as he was talking to his mother, suddenly a cloud filled with light appeared and landed between them. ⁷Jesus said, "Get Salome,ᵃ we will take her with us," and they mounted the cloud and it flew with them to the wilderness near 'Ayn Kārim, to the place where the body of blessed Elizabeth was together with holy John.

⁸The Savior said to the cloud, "Set us down here" and immediately the cloud stopped and descended to earth. The sound it made reached the ears of blessed John who became afraid, left the body of his mother, and ran. ⁹Immediately a voice reached him which said, "Do not be scared, John, my beloved. It is me, Jesus your Lord, Jesus your relative. I have come to you with my beloved mother to fulfill the commandᵇ of your happy mother Elizabeth because she is a relative of my mother." When he heard this, the blessed John turned back and the Messiah and his mother both kissed him. ¹⁰The Savior said to his virgin mother, "You and Salome, come and wash her body." So they washed the body of blessed Elizabeth in the spring from which she and her son used to draw water. The pure Virgin Mary held the Blessed One, cried with him and cursed Herod for the many evils he had committed.

¹¹Suddenly, Michael and Gabriel came down from heaven and dug a grave. The Savior said to them, "Go and bring the soul of Zechariah and the soul of Simeonᶜ the priest so that they will chant hymns while you bury her body." Michael brought the souls of Zechariah and Simeon and they buried Elizabeth's body and sang over it for a long time while Jesus' mother and Salome cried. ¹²The priests then made a sign of the cross and prayed over her three times before laying her to rest. Then they sealed the grave with the sign of the cross and went back to where they came from in peace. ¹³Jesus and his mother then sat down next to the blessed John and consoled him for seven days because of his mother. They also taught him how to get by in the desert. ¹⁴And the blessed Elizabeth passed away on the fifteenth day of the month Amšīrᵈ (Ševat).

¹⁵Jesus said to his mother, "Come, let us go to a place where I can complete my mission." But the Virgin cried because John was all alone and still a small child. And Mary said, "Son, let us take him with us, he is an orphan and has no one." Jesus said to her, "This is not the will of my Father in heaven. He

---

a. This is presumably the Salome who was present at Jesus' death (Mark 15:40) and who witnessed the empty tomb (Mark 16:1). For more on her identity, see Burke, "Serapion's *Life of John the Baptist*," 295.

b. Mingana erroneously translates "in order to attend to the business of the burial."

c. Presumably the Simeon present at Jesus' circumcision (Luke 2:25–35).

d. Only C and D give the Coptic name of the month, with the Syriac equivalent in the margin (C) or above the line (D).

will stay in the wilderness until the day he shows himself to Israel. [16]Instead of wild beasts, he will find a wilderness filled with multitudes of angels and prophets. I have ordered Gabriel the commander of angels to watch over him and give him the power of heaven. I will also make the water in this spring sweet as his mother's milk. [17]Who was it who watched over him since he was a small child? Was it not me, because I love him, O Mother, more than the world itself? Zechariah loved him as well, and I had him come and ask about him, for his body is buried in the ground, but his soul lives on. His mother Elizabeth will come see him regularly to take care of him and comfort him as if she had not died at all.

[18]"She truly is blessed, O mother, because she bore my beloved. Her mouth will never succumb to rot because she kissed the pure lips. Her tongue will not fall apart in the ground because she spoke a prophecy concerning you, which said, *'And blessed is she who believed that there would be a fulfillment of what was spoken to her by the Lord.'* Her insides will not putrefy in the ground, but her body will remain free of decay just like her soul. And my beloved John will persevere as he gazes upon her and he will be comforted." [19]This is what the Messiah said to his mother while John was in the desert.

Luke 1:45

[20]They mounted the cloud while John was looking at them crying. Mary cried with him and said, "O poor John, you will be all alone in the wilderness! Where is your father Zechariah? Where is your mother Elizabeth? Let them come and cry with me today." [21]Jesus said to her, "Do not cry for John, Mother, because I will not forget him." And as he said this, the cloud lifted them up and flew with them until they arrived in Nazareth where he lived to become fully human in all things except for sin.

John rebukes Herod and his voice haunts Herodias

8 [1]While holy John lived in the desert, God and his angels were with him. He led a strict ascetic life in great devoutness, did not eat anything but grass[a] and wild honey and prayed and fasted constantly, waiting for the salvation of Israel.

Mark 1:6//Matt 3:4

[2]In the second year of his reign, King Herod the Younger,[b] who ruled the province of Judea, took the wife of his brother for his own. He did not do so openly, but found opportunity to send for her and usher her into his private chambers filled with filth where the two of them perpetrated their perversions. [3]At that time in the desert, Gabriel the commander of angels taught John the son of Zechariah to say, "O king, you must not take the wife of your brother while he is alive." He kept repeating this in a loud voice as the angel taught him in the wilderness. [4]At night, people could hear his voice and Herodias would light a lamp and search her rooms believing there was somebody there with the two of them. But she could never find anyone and only heard the voice. [5]Both of them were distraught over this and she said to Herod, "Go and send your soldiers to

Life Mart. Bapt. 2:1

Mark 6:18//Matt 14:4

---

a. Mark 1:6 and Matt 3:4 speak of *akrides* i.e., "locusts," one of the species of insects belonging to the family Acrididae (compare also *Life Bapt. Serap.* 7:1). However, since asceticism and devoutness generally required abstaining from eating meat altogether (see also *Life Bapt. Serap.* 7:2), many traditions substitute a vegetarian meal of some sort. See James A. Kelhoffer, *The Diet of John the Baptist* (Tübingen: Mohr Siebeck, 2005) for more details.

b. I.e., Herod Antipas, son of Herod the Great.

the wilderness near ʿAyn Kārim to kill John because this is his voice." But God was with him and he delivered him from their hands. ⁶When she learned this, she could not find any rest in what she was doing. The wicked one then said to her, "If we hear this voice again, I will summon my magicians and order them to capture and kill him in secret." But the voice did not stop.

⁷The wicked Herodias said to Herod, "Who is this John who wanders around in the wilderness and the desert and whose body is not worthy of wearing the clothes of people, but has to dress in camel's hair? Who is he to chide the king of a province and the ruler of a region?" ⁸Herodias then pressed on and said to Herod, "Whatever you want to do, do it openly and do not think anyone in this province will blame you if you do it except for John. And if we find an opportunity, we will get rid of him." This is how this adulteress wooed the heart of Herod to commit this sin and seduced him until he sent his brother to his death and married her openly. ⁹And John remained in the desert and continued to rebuke Herod until he was thirty years old.

Jesus is baptized

9 ¹*As for Jesus, he grew in wisdom, stature, and grace with God and people.* He did not show any signs of his divine nature, but acted humbly towards all. ²When he reached the age of twelve, he began to rebuke the Jews and the teachers who led people astray.

Luke 2:52

Luke 2:42–50

³In the fifteenth year of the reign of Emperor Tiberius who ruled after Augustus, when Herod was the tetrarch of Galilee and Annas and Caiaphas were high priests, in that year, the word of God came down to John son of Zechariah in the wilderness. He came to the lands around the river Jordan, preaching, "*Repent, for the kingdom of heaven has come near.*" ⁴People from all over Judea and Jerusalem came to him and let themselves be baptized by him, confessing their sins.

Luke 3:1–3

Matt 3:2; cf. Mark 1:4

Mark 1:5//Matt 3:5–6

⁵At that time, the Savior came down from Galilee to the river Jordan to see him and said to him, "Baptize me." When John saw God standing before him asking to be baptized, he became very afraid and said to him, "He who led the children of Israel through the Red Sea and gave them sweet water to drink from solid rock, he is now standing before his servant who himself needs to be baptized by his divine hand and says to him, 'Baptize me.'" ⁶And with this, John began to turn away from him. But Jesus said to him, "Stay, this is how we must finish it now."

1 Cor 10:4

Matt 3:13–15

⁷The two of them went down into the water and holy John baptized him with these words, "I baptize the one who was sent by the Father to fulfill a great mystery." At that moment, the heavens opened and the Holy Spirit descended upon him in the form of a dove that came face to face with John. Then the voice of the Father rang, "This is my beloved son with whom I am well pleased. Obey him." ⁸The Savior climbed out of the water and went straight to the desert. Holy John stayed near the river Jordan and continued to baptize everyone who came to him.

Mark 1:10–11 par.

Mark 1:12 par.

John rebukes Herod and is imprisoned

10 ¹At that time, Herod rebelled against Philip his brother and slandered him with the king emperor saying to him, "My king, the one whom you appointed over the province of Trachonitis,[a] that is Philip, plundered your province and said, 'I will not pay tribute[b] to the king ever again because I am a king as well.'" [2]The emperor was filled with rage and ordered Herod to take Philip's province and all his property and his house from him without any pity, even for his soul. [3]Herod did as the king ordered and stole the province that belonged to his brother Philip, as well as his house and everything that he had, and assumed power over all that Philip had ruled.[c]

[4]Philip had a wife whose name was Herodias and she had a daughter with Philip whose name was Arcostariana.[d] Only the mother was more perverted than the daughter. [5]When Philip became poorer than anybody else, Herodias hated him very much and she said to him, "I will not stay with you anymore. I will be with Herod the king, your master who does not lack in security,[e] because he is better than you." [6]And she immediately wrote a letter to Herod: "Herodias writes to Herod. Now you rule over all of Syria and all the inhabited world, yet you still have not taken me for your wife, even though I am very beautiful and better than all the women of Judea. [7]I also have a daughter whose beauty and stature cannot be matched in all of the inhabited world. I wish to be your wife because I have come to hate your brother very much and because I am loyal to your kingdom."

[8]When these crafty words reached the ear of the wicked king, he liked what he had heard and arranged for her and her daughter to be taken from Philip's house. [9]When Philip saw his wife taken from him by force, he said to his daughter, "Stay with your father, even though your mother is taken from me." The little whore said to him, "I will not stay with you, but I will accompany my mother wherever she goes." [10]So they both were taken and brought to Herod who was greatly pleased with them because he was a whoremonger. And they performed deeds of Satanic trickery and the perverted Herod whored with both of them day after day.

[11]News of this reached holy John the Baptist from Philip her husband. People considered John a prophet and he was greatly respected by everyone because he preached to people proclaiming, "*Bear fruit worthy of repentance, for every tree that does not bear fruit will be cut down and thrown into the fire.*" [12]When John heard this from Philip, he was saddened by their damnation—that is, of Herod and Herodias—and he immediately wrote to them the following: "John the son of Zechariah, called the Baptist, says to you: Herod, you may not marry the wife of your brother while he is still alive."

[13]When Herod heard this, he was afraid and disturbed. He went to see Hero-

Matt 3:8,10; cf. Luke 3:8–9

Mark 6:18//Matt 14:4

---

a. All MSS have *Antarachonia* or a variation thereof.

b. The word here is *ḥarāǧ*, a term from Islamic law designating tax on land.

c. Josephus (*Ant.* 18.4.6) does not mention the conflict between the brothers and reports that Philip passed away peacefully still holding the office of the tetrarch. He does make a reference to his wife Herodias who divorced Philip (adding "while he was still alive") and married his brother Herod Antipas (*Ant.* 18.5.4).

d. This is the most likely reading of the name found in CEFHPQ. MSS ABG have Arcostiana or the like. Salome, the name most frequently associated with Herodias's daughter whom the gospels keep nameless, was adopted into Christian tradition from Josephus, *Ant.* 18.5.4.

e. Mingana erroneously translates this phrase as "your new lord Herod."

dias and said to her, "Herodias, what are we going to do? The news of our sin has reached John[a] and now he has rebuked us. We are doomed, because our sins have increased greatly and reached the ears of the prophets." [14]The wicked woman said to him, "Calm yourself, my king. Who is this John, who wears camel's hair, to contradict a mighty king like you? He surely deserves to have his tongue pulled out." [15]He said to her, "So what are we going to do? I cannot bear the rebuke of someone as mighty as him." [16]She answered, "Have him brought here and kill him, then we can continue to give pleasure to each other." And she did unspeakable things to him and performed acts of devious perversion. So Satan turned his heart against John and he had him arrested and thrown into a prison.

Life Mart. Bapt. 8:2

[17]Herodias then had him brought to her and she said to him, "What is your problem with me, you chaste man? Do you want to keep me and the king apart? I conjure you by the God of your fathers not to trouble me like this ever again. And I promise you, if you stop talking about me and stop making your accusations, I will release you from this prison right away and shower you with riches and honors." [18]Holy John said to her, "I am telling you, Herodias, you should not be with Herod while Philip is alive."

Mark 6:18//Matt 14:4

[19]When the wicked woman heard this, she became angry and said to him, "I will kill you dead. I will put the hair from your head into the pillow I lie on with Herod every night and I will bury your head where I wash myself every time I sleep with him." [20]John said to her, "You will kill me, since God wills it, but you will not lay eyes on my head. It will stay with me after my death and it will proclaim your humiliation and your shame to all the world. You will suffer for my unjust murder because your ruin is near." [21]She said to his guards, "Take him and throw him in prison in chains. And if he escapes, you will pay with your lives." The guards took him and put him in prison.

The death of John the Baptist

Mark 6:19–28//Matt 14:6–11

11 [1]Herodias tried to get Herod to kill him, but he said to her, "I cannot kill him just like that. The people will rise against me, chase me out and bring accusations against me with the king[b] who will then take my kingdom from me as he did with my brother Philip." And he said to her, "Show me a better way to kill him."[c] [2]She said to him, "I will tell you something and when you hear it, you will find a way to kill him." He said to her, "Tell me."[d]

[3]She said to him, "Well, the king's envoys are staying with you; so go and prepare a feast for them and invite all the high officials as well, since your birthday is near. Once everybody is happy and they all start getting drunk with wine, I will send in my daughter dressed in her best clothes to dance before you, my king, with her beautiful face. [4]When she does that, tell her 'Ask for whatever you wish' and you will swear to her by the king's life[e] 'Whatever you wish for, I will give it to you.' She will then ask for the head of John and you will have found a

---

a. Mingana erroneously translates as "It is the end of our sinful union."

b. I.e., the Roman emperor.

c. Herod's exhortation to Herodias is unique to P.

d. This exchange is missing from P.

e. Lit. "by king's redemption"—a very Christian turn of phrase and thus an obvious anachronism.

way to take his head." ⁵This is how Herod was tricked by the reasoning of the adulteress and he began to fulfill her wish because he loved her for her ruthless-nessᵃ and her devilish cunningness.

⁶That very day he prepared a feast and the king's envoys were sitting right next to him. When they started to get drunk, the cursed Uxatrianaᵇ entered the room wearing necklaces of gold and silver, perfumes and many jewels and she presented herself to all assembled. She danced in devilish ecstasy and Satan filled their hearts with evil and lust through her evil trickery, so they all were enthralled with her. ⁷Herod was proud of herᶜ and said to her, "If you ask for whatever you want, by the life of Emperor Tiberius, I will give it to you, even if it were half of my kingdom and my possessions." She said to him what her mother had taught her, "What I want here is the head of John the Baptist on a plate." ⁸He was greatly saddened because he swore on the king's life and it was clear to his dinner companions that he could not break the oath. And so he ordered the executioner to go to the prison and take his head on a plate—this was the second day of the month of Tūt (Elūl)ᵈ—and they brought it to Herod. Herod gave it to the girl and the girl gave it to her mother.

The last words of John the Baptist

12 ¹Before the king's menᵉ came with the executioner to take his head, John said to his disciples, "Look, the king has sent for my head. The king's men went out with unsheathed swords in their hands, carrying lanterns and torches and weap-ons. What is happening now will also happen on the night the Messiah will be betrayed. ²As for me, they will take my head and present it on a plate. As for the Messiah, he will be nailed to a cross so that he will purify all with his pure blood. ³As for me, I will go to where I am going; but woe to the king who ordered my head to be cut off, for many calamities will befall him and the people of Israel will be scattered because of him. ⁴As for you, do not be afraid, for no one will be able to harm you." ⁵He then opened his mouth and praised God and glorified him for his incomprehensible gifts, saying, "I bless you and praise you, invisible Father, visible Son and consoling Holy Spirit."

Life Mart. Bapt. 7:3–12

John 18:3

The head of John the Baptist

13 ¹Now let us return to the head of the blessed John. ²When his head was brought to Herodias, the eyes of holy John were open and his ears heard as well as they did when he was still alive. ³The whore then spoke before the

---

a. Mingana's translation has "beauty." It fits the context and could be obtained from the text by interpreting the existing word as a scribal error, but this is not supported by any of the manuscripts.

b. Alternatively, *Oxatriana*. P has *Arcostariana*. F and Q do not give her name and only call her "Herodias's daughter."

c. Alternatively, "came to his senses."

d. C and D give the Coptic name of the month with the Syriac name in the margin (C) or above the line (D). ABEFHQ give only the Syriac name while P converts the date to "the 29th of the month Ab." For more on the latter date, see Mingana, "New Life of John the Baptist," 251, note 1.

e. Somewhat confusingly, the same phrase is used here to refer to Herod's executioners and to the emperor's envoys in the previous verses.

head seething with anger, "Here is the eye[a] that was not ashamed to look into the eyes of the king and answer him. I will pluck you out with my own hand and put you on a plate. I will pull out the tongue that used to say to the king 'You are not permitted to take Herodias, the wife of your brother.' And I will take the hair from your head and your beard and sweep it under the feet of my bed." She said this without any shame or hesitation and with her outstretched hand she tried to grab John's head and do with it as she said. [4]Suddenly the head of the blessed John let the locks of its hair loose from the plate, spread them, and flew to the center of the room in front of the king and his high officials. At that very moment, the roof of the building opened and John's head flew high into the air.

Mark 6:18//Matt 14:4

[5]As for Herodias, her eyes were pulled out from her head and fell on the ground. Her room collapsed on top of her, the ground opened its mouth and its throat swallowed her, and then she sank to the depths of hell, still alive. [6]Herodias's daughter went mad and broke all the vessels that were there at the feast. [7]In her madness, she went to a frozen lake and danced on it. The Lord ordered the ice under her to break and the lake swallowed her. [8]Soldiers tried to pull her out and could not, because the Lord did not want her to be rescued. Finally, they cut off her head using the sword with which holy John was killed. At that very moment, a whale appeared and threw her out of the lake, dead. May God have no mercy on her![b] [9]Immediately after that, Herod suffered a stroke in front of his dinner companions.

Solomon of Basra, *Bk. Bee* 41

Ep. Herod Pil.; Solomon of Basra, *Bk. Bee* 41

[10]When his aide saw these great miracles, he quickly went to the prison, took the body of John and handed it over to his disciples. They took it and buried it in the city of Sebaste[c] next to the body of the prophet Elisha.

Mark 6:29//Matt 14:12

[11]His head, however, flew over Jerusalem and preached to the city for three years, saying, "Herod, you may not marry the wife of your brother while he is still alive." [12]Once three years of preaching over Jerusalem had passed, it left for the whole world to shout and announce Herod's scandalous actions, with the words "Herod, you may not marry the wife of your brother while he is still alive" until fifteen years since his murder had passed. [13]When fifteen years had passed, it stopped preaching and came to rest in the city of Homs.[d] The faithful in that city took it and buried it with great ceremony. [14]Some time after that, a church was built over it, which to this day is still standing in Homs. The head of holy John the Baptist was buried there fifteen years after the resurrection of our Lord and Savior and it is still there.

Mark 6:18//Matt 14:4

Life Mart. Bapt. 10:2

The body of John the Baptist is brought to Alexandria

14 [1]After four hundred years had passed, during which the body of the saint whose feast we are celebrating today (that is, John the Baptist) was buried in Sebaste,[e] at

---

a. Mingana erroneously translates as "accursed one."

b. Verses 7 and 8 are found only in P.

c. According to Islamic tradition, Sebastia is the resting place of John the Baptist and his father Zechariah (Yāqūt, *Mu'džam* 3:184).

d. A city in western Syria. See the introduction, p. 274.

e. P adds "which is Nablus of Samaria," referring to the ancient city of Samaria rebuilt and renamed as Sebaste during the reign of Herod Antipas, today's Sebastia in the West Bank.

that time there was an infidel king by the name of Julian[a] who reigned over Syria. [2]He was a Christian at the beginning of his reign, but after some time, Satan filled his heart and he abandoned the faith of our Lord and Savior and worshipped fire. At that time, he ordered that pagan temples and sanctuaries where idols would be worshipped should be built everywhere. [3]He also ordered that a pagan temple be built in Sebaste where the body of John was, but he could not build it or worship idols there because of the bodies. [4]They gathered and informed him that bodies of holy men were buried there and prevented them from building the pagan temple. He said to them, "Go burn them down and build the temple." So they set the place on fire, but the fire would not come near the coffins of the prophets. [5]Many treasures were found there, including a vessel above the coffins that contained a leather belt, a garment made of camel's hair, and a scapular with two leather belts.

[6]The faithful present there immediately understood that these coffins were those of John the Baptist and Elisha the prophet. They wanted to take them from that place, but they were not able to do so because they were afraid of the wicked king. [7]Then God brought him down with a death more wretched than anyone had ever endured. [8]After his death, righteous men gathered, took the coffins and went with them to the sea, planning to take them to Alexandria to the Holy Father Athanasius,[b] because they said that at that time, there was no one in the whole world who was worthy of taking possession of them except Anba[c] Athanasius, the patriarch in Alexandria.

[9]When they came to the seashore and found a ship sailing for Alexandria, they boarded and brought the coffins with them. They sailed the sea until they dropped anchor in the port of Alexandria and when they landed, they could not reveal their purpose to anyone, because time was pressing. [10]So they went to the patriarch and told him of everything that had happened and how they were moved by the Holy Spirit to bring the coffins to him. [11]The patriarch was overjoyed to have them and venerated them greatly. He went out to the ship with his brother at night and took the remains in a kerchief and brought them to his living quarters in the cathedral in secret. [12]This Holy Father wished to build a church for them, but could not because of the trouble at the time caused by the wicked.

A church is built to house the remains of John the Baptist

15 [1]The bodies remained hidden in the well where Anba Athanasius placed them until the day the Holy Father passed away. [2]After his death, he was succeeded by Anba Peter[d] who was followed on the patriarchal see by Anba Timothy[e] who appointed me, your unworthy father Serapion, to this office, even though I do not deserve it. When he passed away, he was succeeded by Anba Theophilus[f] who is now sitting on the patriarchal see. [3]During his time, God's grace and faith manifested themselves and were strengthened by the pi-

---

a. Roman Emperor Julian who ruled between 361 and 363.
b. Patriarch Athanasius of Alexandria (d. 373).
c. A title used for high officials in the Coptic church.
d. Patriarch Peter II of Alexandria (d. 380).
e. Patriarch Timothy I of Alexandria (d. 384).
f. Patriarch Theophilus of Alexandria (d. 412), assumed office in 385.

ous Theodosius,[a] and God through his love united the king and the patriarch. They opened the doors of pagan temples, which stored many treasures, notably the great pagan temple in Alexandria, which opened before them.[b] Inside, they found much gold and great amounts of silver. [4]The pious Theodosius honored the patriarch by appointing him to oversee all the treasures and he said to him, "Anba Theophilus, take this and use it to build churches from here to Aswan, for the greater glory of God and his saints." And indeed, the patriarch began to build churches.

[5]The first one to be built was a church dedicated to John the Baptist in Alexandria, which he adorned and made a beautiful church because he wished to place the body of John there. [6]When he completed it, he wanted to consecrate it and he wrote to all the bishops who were under his jurisdiction to gather and witness the consecration of the church he had built. I, the unworthy, also received the invitation and went with all the bishops to the Pope, Anba Theophilus. [7]When the news reached him that all the bishops had come to the city, Theophilus was pleased with us like someone who has found many riches. He went out to meet us together with many of those who were in the city and led us into the city where we stayed with him for some time. [8]After that, he began to consecrate the church and he took us to see it and we found it to be a wonderful building.

[9]And he said to us, "This is the place where Athanasius wanted to build it, but time was not in his favor." [10]Anba Theophilus then said, "I was walking with them when I was just an acolyte and I attended to him. When we came to this place, he said to me, 'My son Theophilus, when you find an opportunity, build here a church dedicated to John the Baptist and place his bones in it.' [11]After I had built this place, I remembered the words of this man of God, Anba Athanasius, especially when I remembered that my father Athanasius was like David the prophet who wanted to build a temple to the Lord, but he was not allowed to because of wars he fought. The Lord said to him, 'David, you will not be the one who builds my temple, but the one who comes out of your loins will' and this was Solomon. [12]Therefore, when I ceased waging wars on idolaters, I became worthy of building this church, which is dedicated to John the Baptist, the morning star." [c]

2 Sam 7:12–13

[13]When the second day of the month Ba'ūna (that is the month Ḥeziran)[d] came, he took us to the place where the body was hidden. We did not know exactly where it was, but after a prayer, God showed it to us. [14]When he brought it out, he called to him all the inhabitants of the town. They gathered around him with many lanterns and lamps so that the night shone like day. [15]He let bishops carry the coffins on their heads and the patriarch walked before them with deacons singing hymns until we came with them to the church with great ceremony. [16]The patriarch took the coffins, embraced them, and let all the people be blessed by the holy bodies. Then he put the coffins in the church on a chair

---

a. Roman Emperor Theodosius I (347–395).

b. This is a reference to the chain of incidents that culminated in the destruction of Alexandria's Serapeum ("the great pagan temple").

c. "Morning star" is missing from C.

d. So EFHQ. ABP have Ḥeziran only, C has Ba'ūna only, and D has Ḥeziran with Ba'ūna in the margin.

at the side of the altar and prepared the consecration for that very day. [17]He consecrated the church, we said mass, and all of us received communion from the patriarch.[a] This was the second day of the month Baʾūna.[b] [18]After this, the patriarch said goodbye to us and we left the city, each of us going to his own country in God's peace, amen.

[19]The body of holy John the Baptist performed miracles, proofs, and healings among the Christian people, as witnessed by many wondrous stories.[c]

[20]Praise and glory and power are due to you, Father, Son, and Holy Spirit, one in nature, now, always, and forever and ever, amen. Praise to God always, amen.

---

a. In C, the description of events in verses 6–17 is somewhat shortened.
b. So ABCDEFQ. H and P have Ḥeziran.
c. This refers to the work *Miracles Bapt.*, which in most manuscripts follows *Life Bapt. Serap.*

The Legend of the Thirty Pieces of Silver
A translation and introduction

by Tony Burke and Slavomír Čéplö

The *Legend of the Thirty Pieces of Silver (Leg. Sil.)* is a brief apocryphon ·detailing the voyages of the money paid to Judas to betray Jesus, beginning with the coins' origins in Mesopotamia and finishing with their use in the purchase of the potter's field (Matt 27:7–10). Along the way, the coins figure in several important events in Israelite history and the life of Jesus. Through it all, they remain together, guided providentially to their ultimate goal. Some versions of the text connect the coins to "Judas penny" relics circulating in the Middle Ages. A reader who owns one of these pennies thus becomes part of the story, joining the long list of biblical figures who played a role in safeguarding the silver pieces.

Contents
Leg. Sil. is found in two main forms: an Eastern text known in Syriac and Armenian, and a Western text in Latin with translations in a number of Romance languages. In the Eastern text, the coins were minted by Terah, who then passes them on to Abraham (1); after some time they come into the possession of Solomon (2) and then Nebuchadnezzar, when he plunders the temple (3). From there they pass into the hands of the Magi (4–5), who lose them in Edessa on their way to see the infant Jesus (6). Merchants find the coins and sell them to Abgar, the king of Edessa featured in *Ep. Chr. Abg.* and *Doctr. Addai* (7–10). Abgar sends them to Jesus, along with the Seamless Robe (John 19:23) purchased from a group of shepherds, as gifts for curing his illness (11). Jesus gives the coins to the treasury (12), and the priests use them to pay Judas to betray Jesus (13). After the betrayal, the coins return to the treasury and they are used to purchase the potter's field where Judas is buried (14). The story begins similarly in the Western text, but after the episode of Abraham, the two traditions begin to diverge. An episode is added in which the coins are used by the Ishmaelites to purchase Joseph from his brothers (3–4); the Queen of Sheba then brings them to Solomon (5). The episode involving Abgar is missing; so, instead the coins pass directly from the Magi to Mary (7), who subsequently loses them during the family's sojourn in Egypt (8). Eventually they come into the hands of a shepherd, who offers them to the adult Jesus but Jesus refuses the gifts so that the shepherd would himself deposit them in the temple treasury (9). Some of the Western witnesses add an explanation for how the silver pieces became the gold "Judas penny" relics (11) and finish with elaborate descriptions of the potter's field (12–13).

Manuscripts and Versions
The Eastern text of *Leg. Sil.* was available as early as the thirteenth century when Solomon of Basra incorporated *Leg. Sil.* into his *Book of the Bee,* a chronicle covering events and

figures from creation to the final day of judgment.[1] Solomon became bishop of Basra (in modern-day Iraq) around 1222. He includes the story of the silver pieces in a chapter (no. 44 in Budge's critical edition) that relates the origins of a variety of artifacts from the Passion of Christ, including the purple cloak, the cross, and the location of his tomb. Budge's edition of the *Book of the Bee* is based on three manuscripts:

London, Royal Asiatic Society, Syr. 1, fol. 26r–92v (1559)
London, British Library, Add. 25875, fol. 81v–157v (1709/1710)
Munich, Bayerische Staatsbibliothek, Syr. 7, fol. 1r–146v (end 17th/beginning 18th cent.)

Budge also consulted a Garšūnī manuscript (Oxford, Bodleian Library, 141 [formerly Poc. 79]; 1584) for comparison.[2] The same East Syriac recension of *Leg. Sil.* is found alone (i.e., not as part of *Bk. Bee*) in three other manuscripts:[3]

London, British Library, Syr. 9 (formerly India Office Syr. 9), fol. 242r–243r (1712/1713)
Berlin, Staatsbibliothek zu Berlin, Syr. 74 (formerly Sachau 9), fol. 20v–22r (1695)
Paris, Bibliothèque nationale de France, Syr. 309, fol. 51v–53v (1869)

Of these, only the first has been published to date.[4]

Leg. Sil. exists also as an independent text (again, not as part of *Bk. Bee*) in five manuscripts in West Syriac script:

Paris, Bibliothèque nationale de France, Syr. 197, fol. 93r–94v (16th cent.)
Paris, Bibliothèque nationale de France, Syr. 215, fol. 82v–83v (17th cent.), likely a copy of Syr. 197
Edgbaston, University of Birmingham, Mingana Syr. 71, fol. 134v–136v (ca. 1600)
Edgbaston, University of Birmingham, Mingana Syr. 369, fol. 130r–131r (ca. 1480), related to Syr. 71
Edgbaston, University of Birmingham, Mingana Syr. 480, fol. 241v–242r (1712)

Additionally, there are six Garšūnī manuscripts, reflecting three distinct translations from the Syriac, some showing affinities to the East Syriac text, some to the West Syriac:

Cambridge, University Library, Syriac Add. 2881, fol. 136v–139r (1484)
Edgbaston, University of Birmingham, Mingana Syr. 22, fol. 134v–136v (1527)
Edgbaston, University of Birmingham, Mingana Syr. 48, fol. 144r–145r (1906, but based in part on a MS from 1757)
Edgbaston, University of Birmingham, Mingana Syr. 479, fol. 123v–125r (1819)
Edgbaston, University of Birmingham, Mingana Syr. 514, fol. 140r–142r (1729 or 1750)
Mardin, Zaʿfaran Monastery, 240, fol. 95r–97v (19th/20th cent.)

---

1. Edition and translation: Budge, *Book of the Bee*. Budge's edition supersedes the earlier work of J. M. Schoenfelder, *Salomonis, episcope Bassorensis, liber apis, syriacum arabicumque textum latine* (Bamberg: O. Reindl, 1866), based on Munich, Bayerische Staatsbibliothek, Syr. 7.

2. Additional MSS of the *Book of the Bee* are known, at least twelve at last count. Budge (*Book of the Bee*, ix) mentions four of these.

3. Many of the East and West Syriac and Garšūnī MSS described below are listed, with some infelicities, in Jullien, "La légende," 209–10, 213.

4. Transliterated into Hebrew script in de Lagarde, ed., *Praetermissorum libri duo*, 94–96.

One more Arabic recension of *Leg. Sil.*, this time written in Arabic script proper, is preserved in the eighteenth-century Coptic Museum manuscript Serial No. 117 (Call No. Hist. 276). It comprises thirty-three folios and contains a work named in the explicit as "Mīmar on the 30 pieces of silver for which Judas betrayed the savior."[5] The manuscript is defective at the beginning, but it can be clearly established that folios 1a through 3a contain the second half of *Leg. Silv.*, starting with the first appearance of the Magi. This recension is essentially identical to the majority Garšūnī text, perhaps closest in wording to Mingana Syr. 22. The text then seamlessly continues with a sermon on the events just described.

Related to the Eastern text is an Armenian version appended to the Abgar Correspondence in two manuscripts: Yerevan, Matenadaran, 3854 (1471) and Matenadaran, 7993 (1692).[6] In this telling Abgar, seeking relief from his illness, instructs Addai to find a gift fitting for Jesus. The Seamless Robe is taken from a group of merchants and silver coins from some shepherds and these are carried, along with the letter requesting a cure, by Addai to Jesus. After Addai returns to Edessa with Jesus' response, Jesus asks the disciples if they know where the money given to him by Abgar came from. He then relates an abbreviated version of the remaining portions of *Leg. Sil.*

The Western tradition of *Leg. Sil.* is found incorporated in the works of four medieval writers, as well as in a number of related Latin manuscripts and translations into several European languages.[7] The earliest source is Godfrey of Viterbo's *Pantheon*, a world chronicle dedicated to Henry VI recording the history of the world from creation until 1185, the year of its completion.[8] The text, a mixture of Latin prose and poetry, adapts *Leg. Sil.* into twenty-three rhyming triplets. Godfrey claims to have taken the legend from a sermon in Hebrew presented by the apostle Bartholomew to the Armenians, but likely this information was fabricated to give the legend an exotic and authoritative origin.[9] Godfrey's version of the legend appears also in a number of Latin manuscripts in European libraries—at least seven at last count, ranging in date from the thirteenth to the sixteenth centuries. The second source for the Western *Leg. Sil.* is Ludolph of Suchem's *De Itinere Terrae Sanctae*, an account of Ludolph's journey to the Holy Land in 1336–1341 published between 1350 and 1361.[10] The chapter on the coins (chap. 39) is said to derive from a text called the "History of the Kings of the East." A third version of *Leg. Sil.* appears in chapters 28–29 of John of Hildesheim's *Historia trium Regum*,[11] written between 1364

5. For a description of the MS see Marcus Simaika Pasha and Yassa ʿAbd al Masiḥ, *Catalogue of the Coptic and Arabic manuscripts of the Coptic Museum, the Patriarchate, the principal churches of Cairo and Alexandria and the monasteries of Egypt* (3 vols.; Cairo: Government Press, 1939–1942), 1:61.

6. Outtier, "Une forme enrichie."

7. For extensive discussion of the Western versions see Hill, "Thirty Pieces of Silver"; see also Hook, "Legend of the Thirty Pieces," 207–8.

8. Hill provides a free translation in "Thirty Pieces of Silver," 91–93. For an accessible edition see PL 198:871–1044.

9. Paolo Cherchi, "A Legend from St Bartholomew's Gospel in the Twelfth Century," *RB* 91 (1984): 212–18 at 216, argues that the lost *Gospel of Bartholomew* may have incorporated the story of the coins, and that Godfrey perhaps used a Latin version of it. Hill thinks Godfrey instead may have drawn upon a Latin translation of some legend of Armenian origin ("Thirty Pieces of Silver," 93).

10. See Hill, "Thirty Pieces of Silver," 96–97, which includes a brief summary of the tale. For an edition of the text see Aubrey Stewart, trans., *Ludolph von Suchem's Description of the Holy Land, and of the Way Thither, Written in the Year AD 1350* (Palestine Pilgrims' Text Society 12; London: Palestine Pilgrims' Text Society, 1895).

11. See Hill, "Thirty Pieces of Silver," 97–99. The first modern edition was made by Ernst Köpke,

and 1375 to commemorate the translation of the bodies of the three Magi to Cologne in 1164. In chapter 4, John lists his sources as "books written in Hebrew and Chaldee of the life and deeds, and all matters of the 3 kings"; the source for the coins is given specifically as "books of the Indians." Likely this too is a fiction.

John's *Historia trium Regum* achieved a certain amount of popularity and seems to have led to the excerption and abbreviation of *Leg. Sil.* in at least one manuscript: British Library, Add. 34276, fol. 33v (15th cent.).[12] It may lie also behind a number of other manuscript witnesses to *Leg. Sil.*—British Library, Add. 34139 fol. 87r (1492 or early 16th cent.); British Library, 22553 fol. 144v (15th cent.);[13] Paris, Bibliothèque nationale de France, NAL 543, fol. 112v–113r (14th cent.); and Halle, Universitäts- und Landesbibliothek, Stolb.-Wernig. Za 69m, fol. 23v–24v (15th cent.)[14]—each of which reworks the tale considerably. Finally, *Leg. Sil.* is summarized by the pilgrim Felix Fabri of Nuremberg at the end of the fifteenth century in his account of travels in 1480–1483.[15] Fabri says he read the tale in a "certain long and wordy history"; this may be the same source known to Ludolph (the "History of the Kings of the East") or perhaps Fabri drew the story from Ludolph's own account. Fabri shares Ludolph's description of the potter's field,[16] and only Fabri and Ludolphe mention the king of Godolia and the kingdom of Nubia. The relationships between the other Latin versions are less certain. Hill speculates that Fabri, John, and Ludolph all used the same source.[17] Sylvia Harris says John took his account from Ludolph, and supplemented it with details from Godfrey,[18] but Hook thinks the differences between the two writers indicate that John's account relies on a text closer to a form of the legend shared by Godfrey and *Bk. Bee*.[19] Despite the exotic statements of origin for *Leg. Sil.* by Godfrey and John, the text likely became available to the writers in Latin, perhaps as a translation from a lost Greek original that lies also behind the Syriac tradition.

The Latin tradition spawned translations into several European languages including German, English, Italian, Spanish, Occitan, and Catalan.[20] Of the Hispanic versions, the

---

ed., *Mittheilungen aus den Handschriften der Ritter-Akademie zu Brandenburg A.H.*, vol. 1: *Johannes von Hildesheim* (Brandenburg: G. Matthes, 1878). The edition is reproduced, along with variants from other MSS, in Carl Horstmann, ed., *The Three Kings of Cologne: An Early English Translation of the 'Historia Trium Regum' by John of Hildesheim* (EETS, Old Series 85; London: Oxford University Press, 1886), 206–313. A new edition of the Middle English text has been produced by Frank Schaer, *The Three Kings of Cologne: Edited from London, Lambeth Palace MS 491* (Heidelberg: Universitätsverlag Winter, 2000).

12. Mentioned in Hill, "Thirty Pieces of Silver," 100.

13. Both discussed by Hill ("Thirty Pieces of Silver," 101) with a description of notable readings.

14. The latter two sources have not been discussed in previous scholarship.

15. Fabri's text is available in the edition of Conrad D. Hassler, ed., *Evagatorium in Terrae Sanctae, Arabia et Egypti peregrinationem, Fratris Felicis Fabri* (3 vols.; Stuttgart: Sumptibus Societatis Litterariae, 1843) and in the translation of Aubrey Stewart, *Book of the Wanderings of Brother Felix Fabri* (4 vols.; Palestine Pilgrims' Text Society 7–10; London: 24 Hanover Square W., 1893–1896); for the *Leg. Sil.* section see vol. 1.2, 537–38.

16. The description of the field appears prior to *Leg. Sil.* in Fabri's text. See Stewart, trans., *Book of the Wanderings*, 1.2:535–36.

17. Hill, "Thirty Pieces of Silver," 100–101.

18. Sylvia C. Harris, "The *Historia Trium Regum* and the Mediaeval Legend of the Magi in Germany," *Medium Aevum* 28 (1959): 23–30 at 29.

19. Hook, "Legend of the Thirty Pieces," 207–8.

20. The German and English texts are simply translations of John of Hildesheim (discussed in Hook, "Legend of the Thirty Pieces," 207–8). The other translations are surveyed *inter alia* by Hook.

Catalan poem is the most important as it contains traditions from both Godfrey and *Bk. Bee*, suggesting perhaps that the poem derives from an early form of the text.[21]

Leg. Sil. must be distinguished from another story of the silver pieces extant in Latin,[22] Greek,[23] Amharic,[24] and Arabic.[25] This particular version differs considerably from *Leg. Sil.* and ties the story of the silver pieces to the origin of the wood from which the True Cross was made. In the Latin version, Moses encounters three rods of cypress, cedar, and pine. The rods eventually come into the hands of David and he plants them in Jerusalem, where they grow together into one tree. Every year, for thirty years, David adds a silver ring to the tree; the rings expand as the tree grows. When Solomon builds the temple, a beam is needed, so the tree is cut down and the thirty silver rings are hung in the temple. Later the rings are given to Judas, and part of the tree is used for the cross of Jesus. Of interest also is a legend reported by an anonymous pilgrim in 1220 that the coins were minted at Capernaum, though the pilgrim erroneously conflates Capernaum with the coastal town Kefr Lam.[26] Another legend claims they were made in a tower at Acco named the Accursed.[27]

Date and Provenance

Leg. Sil. was available to Godfrey of Viterbo (in Italy) in 1185, the year he wrote *Pantheon*, and to Solomon of Basra after he became bishop around 1222. Given the great distance between these two writers, it is unlikely that one of them is the source for the other; instead, their shared features indicate that they drew upon common tradition.[28] Whatever that tradition was, it appears to have been unknown in Syriac lands before the ninth century, as it is not found incorporated in the eighth-century *Chronicle of Zuqnin* nor in the *Cave of*

---

21. See Hook, "Legend of the Thirty Pieces," 211–12.

22. See Hill, "Thirty Pieces of Silver," 102–3 for a summary of the Latin text reproduced in Arthur S. Napier, *History of the Holy Rood-tree* (EETS, Old Series 103; London: Oxford University Press, 1894), 69.

23. Jakob Gretser (*Hortus Sanctae Crucis* [Ingolstadt, 1610], 233) mentions the story from a cross legend found in two MSS of a twelfth-century Greek synaxarion. See the discussion in Wilhelm Meyer, "Die Geschichte des Kreuzholzes vor Christus," *Abhandlungen der philosophisch-philologischen Classe der Königlich Bayerischen Akademie der Wissenschaften* 16 (1882): 103–66 at 156.

24. Thomas L. Kane, "An Amharic Version of the Origin of the Cross," *BSAOS* 44, no. 2 (1981): 273–89.

25. See Carl Bezold, *Kebra Nagast, Die Herrlichkeit der Könige* (Munich: Verlag der Königlichen Bayerischen Akademie der Wissenschaften, 1909), xlii–lx. For the English translation, see Ernest A. W. Budge, *The Queen of Sheba and Her Only Son Menyelek* (London: Martin Hopkinson & Co., 1922), xxxix-xlv. This version of the story makes up part of a separate Arabic work (possibly with a Coptic Vorlage) preserved in Paris, Bibliothèque nationale de France, Chr. Ar. 264 detailing the transfer of the Israelite kingdom to Ethiopia. Bezold (p. xliii) describes this work as an extract from *Kebra Nagast* (a fourteenth-century account of the origins of the Solomonic line of the emperors of Ethiopia) with some original traits. Those original traits presumably include the story of the thirty silver pieces, since there is no trace of it in the rest of *Kebra Nagast* as edited by Bezold and translated by Budge. A version of this story is also preserved in an Arabic manuscript in Strasbourg, Bibliothèque nationale et universitaire, 4180 and Cairo, Coptic Museum, 645; see Georg Graf, *Geschichte der christlichen arabischen Literatur* (5 vols.; Vatican City: Biblioteca Apostolica Vaticana, 1944–1953), 1:210.

26. See Claude R. Conder, trans., *The City of Jerusalem* (Palestine Pilgrims' Text Society 6.2; London: 24 Hanover Square W., 1896), 31.

27. Hill, "Thirty Pieces of Silver," 103.

28. These shared features lead Jullien ("La légende," 217–18, 220) to conclude that there may be some truth to Godfrey of Viterbo's claim to have found *Leg. Sil.* in a sermon by the apostle Bartholomew to the Armenians. Indeed, the Armenian text does contain elements common to both Eastern and Western traditions.

Treasures (ca. 6th cent.), which was used by Solomon. The Western writers claim Eastern origins for their versions of *Leg. Sil.* but, again, these claims are likely fictitious.

Depending on the text's date of origin, it may derive ultimately from a Greek original, translated and expanded into Latin on the one hand, and Syriac on the other, with each branch of the tradition taking on regional coloring (e.g., the incorporation of the Abgar Correspondence in the Syriac and Armenian texts). Likely *Leg. Sil.* originated as early as the fifth century, when legends of relics associated with the Passion began to circulate.[29]

The original extent of the text is difficult to determine, given the amount of variation between and within the Eastern and Western traditions. Certain movements are common in all witnesses: the creation of the coins by Terah, their presence in Egypt, their donation to Solomon for his temple (either directly from Pharaoh or via the Queen of Sheba), their plunder by Nebuchadnezzar, and their transmission to the Magi. The sources differ, however, on how the coins are transferred from Abraham to the Pharaoh—either through the purchase of the field for Abraham's family tomb or a village for Isaac, with some witnesses adding an episode narrating the sale of Joseph to the Ishmaelites by his brothers—and from the Pharaoh to Solomon—some Latin sources say they went first from Pharaoh to Moses to the Queen of Sheba, who gave them to Solomon. All sources agree that Jesus arranged for the coins to be deposited in the temple treasury, from where they were taken to pay Judas, but the sources diverge dramatically before this episode. In the Eastern tradition, the Magi lose them in Edessa, where they are found by merchants, who sell them to King Abgar. Abgar then sends the coins, along with the Seamless Robe, to Jesus in gratitude for healing him. In the Western tradition, the coins are among the gifts given to Jesus by the Magi, and they are lost when Mary flees to Egypt. They are found either by a shepherd or an Armenian astrologer; or they are brought to the temple by the shepherds at Jesus' birth or even by Mary herself. Occasionally, agreements occur between individual Eastern and Western sources, indicating, perhaps, some early elements to the legend; for example, the Armenian translation agrees with John of Hildesheim in having Terah (Arm) or Abraham (John) use the coins to buy a tomb (from Gen 23), and with all the Western sources in including the sale of Joseph; and Godfrey (and, to a lesser extent, John of Hildesheim), like the Eastern sources, incorporates the Seamless Robe. However, some of these elements could have entered the legend independently of one another from a desire by redactors to integrate additional biblical stories and relics into the story.

Literary Context

Leg. Sil. draws upon an assortment of biblical and nonbiblical traditions to craft a history for a relic crucial to Christian understandings of the Passion of Christ. In the process of composition and transmission, the author and redactors of the legend often make egregious literary and historical errors—for example, history is dramatically shortened in the exchange of the coins from Isaac to the unnamed Pharaoh (East 2–3), Nebuchadnezzar is

---

29. The most widely known of these is the Legend of the True Cross, the earliest form of which (in Gelasius of Caesarea's *Historia ecclesiastica*) dates to ca. 390 CE, though the cross was being venerated already in Jerusalem as early as the 320s. See further Jan Willem Drijvers, *Helena Augusta: The Mother of Constantine the Great and the Legend of Her Finding of the True Cross* (Leiden/New York: Brill, 1992). Along with the True Cross, Helena is said to have found the nails of the crucifixion, the Holy Lance (John 19:34), and the *titulus* that was nailed above the cross (Mark 15:26 par.; John 19:19–22). The discovery of the Crown of Thorns, the Holy Sponge, and other relics followed in due course.

called the king of Persia (East 4 note d, f), Rehoboam (not Zedekiah) is named the king of Judah during the plunder of the temple (West 6), and Abgar is healed before (not after) Jesus' death (East 11). The Western text, in particular, takes great pains to connect the coins to biblical stories of other coins, though the amounts, and even the currency, in the original stories are usually altered in the retelling. The money paid for Abraham's field, for example, is not thirty silver pieces (West 2) but 400 shekels according to Gen 23; Joseph was sold to the Ishmaelites (West 3) for twenty pieces of silver in Gen 37:28; Sheba's gift to Solomon (West 5) was not silver but gold in 1 Kgs 10:10; and similar transmutation occurs with the Magi's gift of gold to the infant Jesus from Matt 2:11 (West 7). The Western text also incorporates the unspecified money paid to the guards at Jesus' tomb (West 11; Matt 28:11–15). Notably absent, however, is Zechariah's mention of the thirty shekels of silver that God instructs him to throw into the treasury (Zech 11:12–13)—the account that serves as the basis of the story of Judas's betrayal in the canonical Gospels. The problem of the change in currency from gold to silver is not ignored in the text; some Western sources explain this by stating that, in antiquity, all coins were called silver (West 11). Despite its many errors and inconsistencies, *Leg. Sil.* endeavors to be "orthodox" in its telling of the history of the coins by remaining essentially true to the biblical record of Judas's role in the arrest of Jesus.

Leg. Sil. is not the only text with an interest in documenting the history of a celebrated biblical artifact. According to medieval variations of the Legend of the True Cross, the cross was made from the Tree of Life,[30] an association common in typological readings of Jewish Scripture (e.g., *Ep. Barn.* 11–12; John of Damascus, *Orthodox Fidei* 4.12).[31] A particularly popular telling of the Legend incorporates the Jewish legend of the "Quest of Seth for the Oil of Mercy."[32] As the expanded tale goes, Adam is gravely ill and entreats his son Seth to journey to Paradise and return with the Oil of Mercy. Seth is refused entry but is given seeds from the Tree of Life, which he plants over Adam's grave. The seeds grow into three trees, from which Moses crafts his staff. The wood of the staff is eventually used by Solomon to build his forest house (1 Kgs 7:1–12), or the temple (depending on the source). It was then used as a bridge over a certain pond, and later it is revealed that this pond is the healing pool Bethzatha (John 5:2). When it came time to crucify Jesus, the wood floated to the surface and it was used to create the cross. The Staff of Moses, another artifact commonly read as a type of the cross, receives similar treatment in rabbinic texts.[33] The ninth-century *Midrash Yelamdenu* (Yalkhult on Ps. 110 § 869),

---

30. Jacob of Voragine, compiler of the *Legenda Aurea*, recounts some of these variants along with the following story of Seth (see *The Golden Legend: Readings on the Saints* [2 vols.; trans. William Granger Ryan; Princeton: Princeton University Press, 1993], 1:277–78).

31. See Esther C. Quinn, *The Quest of Seth for the Oil of Life* (Chicago: University of Chicago Press, 1962).

32. The initial portion of the "Quest for the Oil of Mercy" (Seth's efforts to retrieve the oil and the angel's refusal) is recounted in the *Life of Adam and Eve* 40–43 (with further elements added in later recensions of the text) and *Gos. Nic.* (Latin Recension B) 19. For its elaboration in medieval legends of the True Cross, see Meyer, "Geschichte des Kreuzholzes vor Christus." The story is also found in Godfrey of Viterbo's *Pantheon* and the *Rood-Tree Legend*, a text that incorporates another account of the thirty silver pieces (mentioned above, see n. 22). On the connection between the two texts see Napier, *History of the Holy Rood Tree*, xxxi–iii.

33. William Wood Seymour, *The Cross in Tradition, History and Art* (New York and London: G. P. Putnam's Sons, 1898), 50–52. The examples here are discussed in Louis Ginzberg, "Aaron's Rod," *JE* 1 (1901): 5–6.

for example, traces the history of the staff from Judah who gave it to Tamar (Gen 38:18), then God gave it to Moses (Exod 4:17), Moses passed it on to Aaron (Exod 7:10), and David used it to slay Goliath (1 Sam 17:40). The Davidic kings continued to use it as a scepter, but it was lost in the destruction of the temple. It is said, however, that it will be given to the Messiah when he comes. The fourteenth-century *Sarajevo Haggadah* goes further, stating that God gave the staff to Adam, and it was passed along until the time of Jethro, who planted it in a garden where it could not be uprooted until Moses' time. Solomon of Basra also details the providential transmission of the staff (*Bk. Bee* 30).[34] He says Phineas hid the staff in the desert until God showed it to Joseph, who used it on his journey to Egypt and the return to Nazareth. The staff was passed on to James and Judas stole it. It was then used for the crossbeam of the cross. Interestingly, the staff appears also in the West Syriac manuscripts of the Eastern text of *Leg. Sil.*; this version of the story concludes with the statement that the coins and the Staff of Moses were thrown into the temple fountain (East 14).

The Western text concludes differently, stating that the coins remained together after Judas's death thus allowing for their continued circulation as relics. John of Hildesheim even mentions having seen one of the coins in his own day (West 11 p. 308 n. d). Scholars have documented the existence of a number of "Judas-penny" relics.[35] More than thirty of these coins are recorded in various sources;[36] some of them are still extant, held in various abbeys and churches in Florence, Paris, and elsewhere. The references to the coins go back to as early as the fifteenth century and they seem to have been dispersed in France, Italy, Bologna, Rhodes, and Russia. However, not one of them was of the kind in circulation at the time of Jesus.[37] For owners of these coins, *Leg. Sil.* could function as a sort of guarantee of authenticity or a history of their treasure; they could feel that they were participating in the providential transmission of these sacred relics, created thousands of years ago by the father of Abraham.

Some versions of *Leg. Sil.* incorporate yet another famous relic: the Seamless Robe first mentioned in John 19:23–25. Of the robe's fate, the Gospels say only that, in fulfillment of Ps. 22:18, the soldiers cast lots for who would obtain Jesus' clothing. One tradition states that it exists today in Trier, bequeathed to the city by Helena, the mother of Constantine, who found it in 327 or 328 along with the True Cross.[38] Another tradition states that the Empress Irene made a gift of the robe to Charlemagne around 800. Charlemagne gave it to his daughter Theocrate, abbess of Argenteuil, where it remains today, though only in pieces. A third Seamless Robe resides in Mtskheta, Georgia. According to the Eastern text of *Leg. Sil.*, the Robe was given to the merchants of Edessa by shepherds who received it from an angel (East 8). King Abgar then passed the garment on to Jesus (East 10–11). In the Western tradition, the robe is mentioned by Godfrey, who says it was given to the infant

---

34. Note also the brief mention of the purple cloak placed upon Jesus in *Bk. Bee* 44 (found here just prior to the story from *Leg. Sil.*). The cloak is said to have been given to the Maccabees by the "emperors of the Greeks" and was given to the priests to dress the temple.

35. For a detailed discussion of the coins see de Mély, "Deniers de Judas"; summarized and updated in Hill, "Thirty Pieces of Silver," 103–16.

36. Felix Fabri, for one, mentions seeing one of the coins at Rhodes (see Stewart, trans., *Book of the Wanderings*, 1.2:538).

37. Hill, "Thirty Pieces of Silver," 103.

38. For a brief overview of the transmission of the Seamless Robe relic see Bernhard Schneider, "Holy Coat," in *Religion Past and Present* (12 vols.; ed. Hans Dieter Betz, Don S. Browning, Bernd Janowski, and Eberhard Jüngel; Leiden: Brill, 2006–2013), 6:218–19.

Jesus by an angel and it became longer as he grew older (West 7 n. e); John of Hildesheim also mentions the robe, though only cursorily (West 11 n. d). The *Leg. Sil.* tradition seems to attract stories of other relics just as effortlessly as it draws in biblical stories of other coins.

Translations

The two texts presented here summarize the evidence of the Eastern and Western traditions of *Leg. Sil.* The Eastern recension is based primarily on the best of the West Syriac manuscripts: Paris, Bibliothèque nationale, Syr. 197, chosen because it suffers from fewer errors and omissions than the other manuscripts. Variants are provided from the East Syriac tradition, the Garšūnī manuscripts, and the Armenian translation. The Western recension is based on Ludolph of Suchem's *De Itinere Terrae Sanctae*, selected because it is the earliest prose version of the text (Godfrey of Viterbo's *Pantheon* is earlier but it adapts the legend into verse). Noteworthy variants are provided from the other Latin traditions, including four of the unpublished Latin manuscripts noted in the introduction above (with the exception of Stolb.-Wernig. Za 69m as the condition of the MS makes it difficult to read).

Sigla

WSyr	West Syriac recension
ESyr	East Syriac recension (including Solomon of Basra's *Book of the Bee*)
Gar	Garšūnī translation
Arm	Armenian translation from Outtier, "Une forme enrichie," 140–43
Godfrey	Godfrey of Viterbo's *Pantheon*
JH	John of Hildesheim's *Historia trium regum* 28–29
La	London, British Library, Add. 34276
Lb	Paris, Bibliothèque nationale de France, NAL 543
Lc	London, British Library, 22553
Ld	London, British Library, Add. 34139

Bibliography

EDITIONS AND TRANSLATIONS

Budge, Ernest A. W., ed. *The Book of the Bee: The Syriac Text Edited from the Manuscripts in London, Oxford, Munich, with an English Translation.* Anecdota Oxoniensia, Semitic Series 1 part 2. Oxford: Clarendon, 1886. (Edition and translation of the East Syriac text incorporated as *Bk. Bee* 44.)

Burke, Tony, and Slavomír Čéplö. "The Syriac Tradition of the Legend of the Thirty Pieces of Silver." *Hugoye* 19.1 (2016): 35–121. (Critical editions of the East Syriac, West Syriac, and Garšūnī texts. With extensive overview of previous scholarship.)

Lagarde, Paul de, ed. *Praetermissorum libri duo.* Göttingen: Officina Academica Dieterichiana, 1879. (*Editio princeps* of the East Syriac text transliterated into Hebrew letters, pp. 94–96.)

Outtier, Bernard. "Une forme enrichie de la Légende d'Abgar en arménien." Pages 129–45 in *Apocryphes arméniens: transmission–traduction–création–iconographie; Acts du colloque international sur la littérature apocryphe en langue arménienne (Genève, 18–20 septembre 1997).* Edited by Valentina Calzolari Bouvier, Jean-Daniel Kaestli, and Bernard Outtier. Lausanne: Éditions du Zébre, 1999. (Edition and translation of the Armenian text.)

STUDIES

Creizenach, Wilhelm. *Judas Ischarioth in Legende und Sage des Mittelalters,* Separatabdruck aus den *Beiträgen zur Geschichte der Deutschen Sprache und Literatur,* Band II, Heft 2. Halle, Lippert'sche Buchhandlung, 1875.

Hill, George Francis. "The Thirty Pieces of Silver." *Archaeologica* 59 (1905): 235–54 (repr. in idem, *The Medallic Portraits of Christ, The False Shekels, The Thirty Pieces of Silver* [Oxford: Clarendon, 1920], 91–116). (Contains a broad discussion of the Western traditions.)

Hook, David. "The Legend of the Thirty Pieces of Silver." Pages 205–21 in *The Medieval Mind: Hispanic Studies in Honour of Alan Deyermond.* Edited by Ian R. MacPherson and Ralph J. Penny. London: Tamesis, 1997.

Jullien, Florence. "La légende des *Trente pièces d'argent de Judas* et le roi Abgar." *Apocrypha* 24 (2013): 207–20.

Mély, Fernand de. "Les Deniers de Judas dans la Tradition du Moyen Âge." *Revue Numismatique* 4, no. 3 (1899): 500–509.

The Legend of the Thirty Pieces of Silver
(Eastern Recension)[a]

The origin and early history of the coins

[1]These pieces were made by Terah, the father of Abraham. Abraham gave them to his son Isaac. And Isaac bought a village with them.[b] The master of (the village) brought them to Pharaoh. Gen 11:27

Gen 21:3; 26:6, 17

[2]Pharaoh sent them to Solomon, the son of David, for the temple he was building. And Solomon took the pieces and placed them around the door of the altar.[c] 1 Kgs 3:1; 6:20–21; 2 Chr 4:1

[3]When Nebuchadnezzar[d] came and took captive the children of Israel, he entered the temple of Solomon and saw that these pieces were beautiful, and he took and brought them to Babylon with the captive children of Israel. 2 Kgs 25:1–17; 2 Chr 36:6–7

[4]And there were some Persians there as hostages.[e] When Nebuchadnezzar came from Jerusalem, they[f] sent him everything fit for kings. And when King Nebuchadnezzar saw that all they had sent him was beautiful, he released their sons and gave them many presents. He gave them also those pieces. And the Persians brought them to their fathers.

The Magi bring the coins to Edessa

[5]When Christ was born and (the Magi) saw the star,[g] they rose and took those pieces and gold, myrrh, and frankincense. Matt 2:1–2

Matt 2:11

---

a. The titles in the Syriac MSS, with minor variations, are: "A demonstration of the origin of those pieces which Iscariot received as the price of Christ, those pieces which Judas received from the Jewish priests, where are they from and what is their story" (WSyr); "And so, with God's help, the tale of the pieces which Judas accepted for the price of our Lord, what is the history of their transmission? The thirty (pieces) of silver that Judas accepted and for which he sold his Lord, were thirty pieces according to the weight of the sanctuary. These were equal to 600 pieces according to the weight of our country" (ESyr).

b. In Arm, Terah uses the money to buy "the cave with the son of Amor." Presumably this is Abraham's burial cave from Gen 23, which was purchased from Ephron the Hittite for 400 shekels of silver. The burial cave appears also in the Western recension (see the note to v. 2). From here, like the Latin tradition, Arm moves right to the story of Joseph: "The Edessenians took the money and bought Joseph from his brothers. And the brothers of Joseph brought it as a gift to Joseph in Egypt."

c. Gar adds the detail that ten were placed on the upper frame and ten on each side.

d. Some WSyr MSS and Gar erroneously call Nebuchadnezzar the "king of Persia."

e. Some ESyr MSS add "according to the custom of the kings."

f. "They" likely refers here to the Persian rulers seeking to regain the hostages. This identification is made explicit in ESyr with its mention of the "king of the Persians" in this context.

g. ESyr (but not *Bk. Bee*) adds "as in the prophecy of Zarathustra" (though see *Bk. Bee* 37

[6]They brought those pieces and set forth on a journey until they reached the vicinity of Edessa. The day grew dark and they fell asleep on the side of the road. In the morning they arose to continue their journey. They forgot those pieces where they slept and did not know it.[a] Some merchants came and found the pieces.

John 19:23-25

[7]They came to the vicinity of Edessa by a certain well. And on that very day an angel came to the shepherds of that land and he gave them a robe without a seam on the upper end. And he said to them, "Take the robe in which there is salvation for humanity."

[8]The shepherds took the robe and came to a well. And they found the merchants who had found the pieces near the well. They said to the merchants, "Will you buy this beautiful robe without seam at the upper end?" The merchants said to them, "Bring it here." And when the merchants saw this robe, they marveled at it very much. The merchants said to the shepherds, "We have beautiful pieces fit for a king. Take them and give us this robe."[b]

King Abgar acquires the coins

[9]When the merchants had taken the robe, they arrived in the city and stopped at an inn.[c] Abgar the king sent for the merchants and said to them, "Have you anything worthy of a king that I could buy from you?" The merchants said to him, "Yes, we have a robe without a seam at the upper end."

[10]When King Abgar saw that robe of which there was no equal,[d] he said to them, "Where did you get this robe?" They said to him, "We came to a certain well by the gate of your city. And some shepherds said to us,[e] 'We have a robe without a seam at the upper end. Will you buy it?' And we looked at the robe and saw that there was no other like it in the world.[f] We had with us thirty pieces stamped with images of kings[g] which we gave to the shepherds and received this robe. And these pieces are worthy of kings such as yourself."

Ep. Chr. Abg.; Doctr. Addai 3-4

[11]When Abgar heard this, he sent for the shepherds and received the pieces from them. And Abgar sent the pieces and the robe to Christ for the good that he had done him with regard to the disease from which (Christ) had cured him.[h]

---

for a reference to this prophecy). One of the Gar MSS has a similar reading: "As was foretold by Balaam their grandfather," referring to Balaam ben Be'or (Num 23-24) whom some apocryphal traditions identify with Zoroaster and connect to the Magi. *Bk. Bee* 37 identifies Zoroaster, "this second Balaam," with Baruch the scribe.

a. In Gar, the Magi rest at a well and, unbeknownst to them, the coins fall into it.

b. Gar adds, "So they agreed on the price and the merchants took the robe while the shepherds took the coins."

c. ESyr lacks mention of an inn.

d. ESyr and some Gar MSS add "in the world." In *Cav. Tr.* 50:8, the robe gave whoever possessed it the ability to bring rain.

e. ESyr ends the verse here with, "We saw it with some shepherds. And we bought it for thirty pieces of stamped silver; these too are worthy of kings such as yourself."

f. In ESyr the merchants begin their reply, "'We came to a certain well of water by the gate of your city. And we saw it with some shepherds.'"

g. ESyr: "thirty pieces of stamped silver."

h. Arm summarizes verses 2-11 as, "When Nebuchadnezzar deported Jerusalem, he broke the door and carried it to Babylon. The Babylonians gave it to the Chaldeans. The Chaldeans gave it to the merchants, and the merchants gave it to the shepherds. And Abgar, having re-

The betrayal of Judas

[12]When Christ saw the robe and the pieces, he took the robe and sent the pieces to the Jewish treasury.[a] Our Lord knew their secrets. That is why he sent these pieces with which he would be bought.[b]

[13]And when the Jews came to Judas Iscariot they said to him, "Deliver to us Jesus, son of Joseph!" He said to them, "What will you give me if I deliver him to you?"[c] And they rose (and) brought those thirty pieces[d] and gave them to Judas Iscariot.

[14]And Iscariot[e] returned them to the Jews.[f] They bought with them a burial-place for strangers.[g] And then they brought the pieces to Solomon's temple and threw them into a fountain inside the temple—the pieces, as well as the Staff of Moses the prophet—and thus hid them.[h]

This completes the story of the pieces and the robe.[i]

Mark 14:10–11 par.;
John 13:2

Matt 27:3–10; Acts 1:19

Exod 4:2

---

ceived it from the shepherds gave it to us (i.e., Jesus and the apostles)." The merchants and shepherds are mentioned earlier in Arm (v. 5). In recounting Abgar's commissioning of Addai, the text details how the merchants appeared before Abgar in Edessa with the Seamless Robe and the purple cloak. The robe was purchased by the merchants from the shepherds who received it from angels. According to *Ep. Chr. Abg.*, Jesus does not directly cure the king; instead Thaddaeus/Addai is sent to heal Abgar after the death of Jesus.

a. ESyr ends the verse here.

b. In Arm, Jesus instructs his disciples to take the coins to the priests and say, "Jesus the Nazarean sent this to you."

c. ESyr and Gar report the exchange as, "And when Judas Iscariot came to the priests, he said to them, 'What will you give me if I deliver him to you?'"

d. Gar adds "which awakened his greed."

e. ESyr and Gar add that Judas "repented."

f. ESyr adds "and went and hanged himself."

g. ESyr and Gar explicitly identify this location as the potter's field. In Arm, like the Latin tradition (West v. 11), the priests give the money to the guards at the tomb, though in Arm the guards return it saying, "This money should not be kept, because it is the price of blood." So the priests buy the potter's field.

h. ESyr lacks this sentence, though the later history of the Staff of Moses receives much attention in *Bk. Bee* 30 (see above p. 300). Gar also lacks mention of the staff.

i. WSyr and some ESyr MSS lack this conclusion.

The Legend of the Thirty Pieces of Silver
(Western Recension)[a]

The origin and early history of the coins

Gen 11:27

Gen 10:8–11

[1]It is read in a certain account of the kings of the East who gave gifts to the Lord, that Terah, the father of Abraham, had made money, or coins,[b] by order of a certain king of Mesopotamia named Ninus.[c] He received thirty silver pieces for his pay.

[2]These silver pieces he gave to Abraham,[d] who spent them on journey in exile.[e]

Gen 37:27–28

[3]And these coins, passing through diverse hands, came into the hands of the Ishmaelites, and with them Joseph was bought from his brothers.[f]

Gen 42:2–3

[4]Afterwards, while Joseph was ruling in Egypt, these same coins were returned to the hands of Joseph from his brothers for grain. When they were restored to his brothers, the brothers gave these silver pieces to the treasurer of Joseph,[g] who sent them to Sheba for goods on behalf of Pharaoh.[h]

Gen 42:25

[5]In the time of Solomon, the queen of Sheba came from the east, hearing of his wisdom, and gave the thirty silver pieces to the temple.

1 Kgs 10:10; 2 Chr 9:9

---

a. Ludolphe does not provide a separate title for the Legend, nor do Godfrey and JH. The *Leg. Sil.* MSS related to JH bear the titles, "A report with respect to those thirty pieces of silver for which Christ was sold" (Lb, Ld), and "On the thirty silver pieces accepted by Judas when he sold Christ" (Lc). La has no title.

b. The JH related MSS explicitly state that Terah was the inventor of coins, making the thirty silver pieces the first coins made in the world.

c. Ninus is the legendary eponymous founder of Nineveh, though Gen 10:8–11 credits this accomplishment to Nimrod. La also calls the Mesopotamian king Ninus but JH does not mention his name. Lb, Lc, and Ld specify that the figure in the story is the king of Nineveh, though Lc goes on to say that his name was Naphtali (cf. Gen 35:25).

d. In Lb, Terah divides the coins between Lot and Abraham.

e. JH and La specify that Abraham went to Hebron and bought land for his tomb and for his wife and sons (cf. Gen 23); this tomb is mentioned also in Arm (see above, the note to East v. 1). According to Gen 23:15, the tomb was purchased for "400 shekels of silver." Lb, Lc, and Ld state that the double-caved tomb contained the bodies of Adam and Eve, a tradition found also in *Zohar Chadash*, Ruth 96. Godfrey says only that Abraham bought land from the men of Jericho.

f. The price for Joseph, according to Gen 37:28, is twenty pieces of silver; however, some early writers (e.g., Origen, *Hom. Exod.* 1:6; *Test. Gad* 2), in order to demonstrate that Joseph prefigured Christ, changed the figure to thirty. See further Erica Reiner, "Thirty Pieces of Silver," *JAOS* 88, no. 1 (1968): 186–90 at 188–89.

g. In Gen 42:25 Joseph refuses payment for the grain.

h. JH and La state that the coins were paid to the Queen of Sheba for spices at the tomb of Jacob and Joseph. Lb, Lc, and Ld introduce another stage in the journey of the coins. From the Egyptian treasury they came into the hands of Moses who gave them to the Queen of Sheba.

The coins and the Magi

[6]In the time of Rehoboam, Nebuchadnezzar plundered the temple and carried off the treasures.[a] He handed over the thirty coins with other treasures to the king of Godolia,[b] who was with him in the army. Thus they remained with other treasures of the king of Godolia until the birth of Christ.

[7]Then the kingdom of Godolia was transferred to the kingdom of Nubia. And so, when the Lord was born, Melchior, the king of Nubia,[c] seeing in the star Christ born of a virgin,[d] presented the thirty coins to Christ, because he could find no more ancient and noble gold in his treasures, according to the will of God.[e]

The coins are lost and found in Egypt

[8]Afterwards, the truly Blessed Virgin Mary, when fleeing to Egypt in fear of Herod, lost the thirty coins along with the other gifts of the Magi at the place where now there is the Garden of Balsam.[f] A certain shepherd found them and kept them in his hands for thirty years. And then, when the fame of Jesus grew, this same shepherd came to Jerusalem and Jesus freed him from his illnesses.[g]

[9]When Christ was preaching and teaching in the temple, (the shepherd) of-

2 Kgs 25:1–17; 2 Chr 36:6–7

Matt 2:1–12

Matt 2:19–21

(Arab.) Gos. Inf. 24

---

a. Rehoboam reigned ca. 931–930 BCE The king at the time of Nebuchadnezzar's plunder was Zedekiah.

b. Ludolph is the earliest-known writer to associate the Magi with Godolia, which seems to be located on the Arabian peninsula (see the discussion in Ugo Monneret de Villard, *Le leggendi orientali sui Magi evangelici* [Studi e Testi 163; Vatican City: Biblioteca Apostolica Vaticana, 1952], 216). Traditionally, Balthazar is said to be the king of Godolia. In JH (and Lb, Lc, and Ld), the coins are given to the "king of the Arabs," though JH identifies Balthazar's kingdom as Godolia earlier in his text (*Historia trium regum* 14). La lacks mention of how they came to Melchior but does identify Melchior as king of the Arabs and the Nubians, the locations typically associated with Melchior in Christian tradition. Godfrey says the coins were "given as pay for soldiers to the kings in Sheba"; the Magi, he says, are descendants of these kings.

c. Lb and Ld instead credit Balthazar with giving the money to Jesus. Neither Godfrey nor Lc names any of the Magi.

d. This concept of seeing Jesus in the star is found also in several other texts, including *Rev. Magi* (esp. 13), the related *Opus imperfectum in Matthaeum* (here the star contains a little boy and the image of a cross), and *Cav. Tr.* 45:3 (a girl holding a child with a crown being placed on her head).

e. Godfrey adds a verse on the Seamless Robe: "When, taught by angelic warnings, these kings returned home henceforth, a most-worthy robe was sent from heaven for the child; this (robe) without seam, was wonderfully colored. This (robe) the father sent from heaven, no woman spun; it became longer as the child grew in stature, woven of the thin thread of that time."

f. This garden, mentioned only by Ludolph, is the Garden of Matariyah in Egypt where, according to *(Arab.) Gos. Inf.* 24, the infant Jesus brought forth a fountain in which Mary washed his shirt. The sweat from the garment that was sprinkled on the ground produced balsam.

g. The sources differ on how the coins came to the temple treasury. According to Godfrey, shepherds came and carried away the gifts (including the robe) and then they came into the hands of an Armenian astrologer. When Jesus reached adulthood, an angel appeared to the astrologer instructing him to restore the gifts to Christ. Jesus put on the child-sized robe and it stretched to adult size; the coins were brought to the temple. In Lb and Lc, Mary gives the coins to the shepherds who attended Jesus' birth (Luke 2:8–20) because they were poor and the shepherds placed them in the temple. In Ld, the coins come to the temple as the price for which Mary redeemed her son according to the law (Luke 2:22–40).

fered him the thirty coins and the other gifts of the Magi, which Jesus refused to accept, anticipating that (the shepherd) might offer the coins to the temple and place the other gifts upon the altar,[a] which the shepherd did.

The betrayal of Judas

Mark 14:10–11 par.; John 13:2

[10]The Jews cast the thirty coins into the treasury, and afterwards they gave them to Judas for handing over Jesus.[b]

Matt 27:3–10; Acts 1:19

Matt 28:11–15

[11]When (the coins) were brought back by Judas,[c] they bought the potter's field with fifteen coins and handed over the remaining fifteen to the soldiers who guarded Jesus' tomb. And thus, when this had happened with the coins, which had been predestined, immediately they were divided and henceforth thereupon dispersed. But before this nothing happened that must happen with regard to them; as you have heard, they always remained together. But Scripture calls these coins silver, because in antiquity they called all (coins) silver; but no doubt in fact they were gold.[d]

The field of blood

[12]The actual field of blood is not large, as I said. It has an exceedingly deep pit dug in it, and a vaulted ceiling above, bored in round holes. Through those holes dead bodies are thrown down inside. And after three days nothing but the bones are found. Otherwise, a place so small would not suffice for so many dead bodies.[e]

[13]Near this field is a place very delightful and beautiful with trees, which the preaching brothers were trying to buy when I was leaving, but I do not know if they obtained it. It is near the very many hermitages of saints, cells, and oratories of grace, which are now deserted. Thus it is near the cave in which Peter continued denying Christ and hid himself and wept bitterly. Not far from this cave is

Matt 27:5

the place where Judas, despairing, hung himself.[f]

---

a. Compare East verse 12, which similarly portrays Jesus as being aware of and directing his fate.

b. JH says of the other gifts, that the priest "lit the frankincense on fire upon the altar" and later "a portion of the myrrh they mixed with wine and offered it to the mouth of the Lord, and the remaining portion Nicodemus brought with the other spices to the Lord's tomb." Lb ends here.

c. Godfrey adds details about the death of Judas: "Judas Iscariot brought them back; Christ was murdered, whom he rejected, because he repented after the death of his master, and hanging himself by the noose, his stomach burst asunder." Lc and Ld lack mention of the division of the coins between the soldiers and the purchase of the field, and nothing is said about the coins being gold.

d. JH places the explanation of the currency change after his description of the field. He adds also that the coins remained together, passed along by heredity, as did "the Seamless Robe of the Lord, very famous up to the present day." John (along with La) goes on to mention a specific coin perhaps known to him, with a head of a king on one side and an illegible Chaldean letter on the other.

e. Of the Western recension witnesses, only Ludolph and JH contain a description of the field, though a similar depiction is given by Felix Fabri (vol. 1.1, pp. 10–11 in Stewart's translation) and John Poloner in his 1421 account of his travels (Aubrey Stewart, trans., *John Poloner's Description of the Holy Land* [Palestine Pilgrims' Text Society 6.4; London: Palestine Pilgrims' Text Society, 1894], 12).

f. This final verse is found only in Ludolph.

The Death of Judas according to Papias
A new translation and introduction

by Geoffrey S. Smith

Papias was a church leader from Hierapolis in Asia Minor, who lived from approximately 60 to 140 CE.[1] Irenaeus reports that he was "a man from the early period," and a "hearer" of the disciple John and "companion" of Polycarp (*Haer.* 5.33.4).[2] Papias authored a popular five-volume work entitled *Exposition of the Sayings of the Lord*, which continued to circulate into the medieval period but has since disappeared.[3] It survives now only in excerpts quoted by later authors.

Papias discusses the death of Judas in the fourth book of his *Exposition*. We owe our knowledge of Papias's account to Apollinaris of Laodicea,[4] whose quotation of the passage survives in Greek catenae—i.e., collections of extracts from biblical commentators. We must agree with Kirsopp Lake, who suggested that further research into the manuscript tradition of the catenae would "enable these texts to be greatly improved."[5] In the absence of a critical text of Papias that takes into consideration all of the later testimonia, we will focus on the Greek text of Papias as printed in Cramer's catenae, where we find two versions of Papias's account: a shorter version in a catena on Matthew and a longer version in a catena on Acts.[6] Both versions begin by discussing Judas's enormous size but then diverge. In the shorter version a wagon strikes Judas and empties out his bowels, whereas in the longer version Judas apparently dies of disease. While the two accounts may be reconciled if we assume that the wagon incident in the shorter version was not fatal, they may also reflect separate traditions about Judas's death. Since it is difficult to decide which goes back to Papias, I have included translations of both versions below.

---

1. Eusebius reports that Papias was "the bishop" of Hierapolis (*Hist. eccl.* 2.15.2), yet it seems unlikely that there was a single office of "the bishop" in Hierapolis as early as the first decades of the second century. For more information on Papias, see Schoedel, "Papias."

2. Eusebius preserves the Greek of this passage in his quotation from Irenaeus (*Hist. eccl.* 3.39.1).

3. See Adolf von Harnack, *Geschichte der Altchristlichen Litteratur bis Eusebius* (2 vols.; Leipzig: Hinrichs, 1893–1897), 1:69. The most tantalizing reference to the work appears in Léon Ménard, who reports that an inventory of the holdings of the church in Nîmes from 1218 CE contained the following line: "Item: I discovered in a cloister a book of Papias, a book of the words of the Lord *(librum de verbis domini)*." This manuscript has not yet surfaced. See Léon Ménard, *Histoire civile, ecclésiastique et littéraire de la ville de Nismes* (7 vols.; Paris: Chaubert, 1750–1758), 1:67.

4. Theodor Zahn has argued that the Apollinaris who preserves the passage is not the Laodicean (ca. 310–ca. 390 CE), but Claudius Apollinaris of Hierapolis, the church leader and author who was active in the second half of the second century. For a summary of Zahn's argument and a critical response, see Lake, "Death of Judas," 23 n. 1.

5. Lake, "Death of Judas," 23 n. 2.

6. See Cramer, *Catenae*, 1:231 and 3:12–13. For Matthew he uses Paris, Bibliothèque nationale de France, Coislin gr. 23 and Oxford, Bodleian Library, Auctarium T.I.4; for Acts he uses Oxford, New College, 58. Lake conveniently places the Greek text of the two versions in parallel columns in "Death of Judas," 23–24.

These two versions are among a small number of early Christian reports concerning Judas's demise. Ancient authors did not agree upon the circumstances of the death of Judas Iscariot, the disciple who famously handed Jesus over to be crucified. While all four Gospels narrate Judas's betrayal of Jesus in the garden of Gethsemane (Mark 14:43–46 par.; John 18:1–9), only Matthew and Luke-Acts discuss his death. According to Matthew, Judas was so overcome with remorse following the arrest of Jesus that he tossed his payment of thirty pieces of silver into the temple and rushed off to hang himself (Matt 27:3–10); the priests then used his payment to purchase a field in which to bury foreigners, called the Field of Blood. The author of Luke-Acts reports that while standing in a field (again called the Field of Blood) that he had purchased with the money from the betrayal, Judas "fell headlong and burst open in the middle and all his bowels gushed out" (Acts 1:18–20). While many ancient and modern interpreters have attempted to harmonize these two accounts, we should appreciate their differences: the Judas of Matthew returns the money he received for the betrayal and then hangs himself, whereas the Judas of Luke-Acts falls down and bursts open in a field that he himself has purchased with the betrayal money. The mention of a field known as the Field of Blood in both accounts may reflect a historical reality underlying the two traditions.

The recently discovered *Gospel of Judas* might preserve yet another tradition concerning the death of Judas. In the text Judas tells Jesus about a vision that he received: "I saw myself in the vision as the twelve disciples threw stones at me and persecuted me zealously" (44.24–45.4; trans. *AG,* 389–411). This passage may indicate that some early Christians believed that Judas was stoned to death by the remaining disciples. Yet, since the author of the *Gospel of Judas* never confirms this belief, Judas's vision may simply represent in a general sense the hostility a recipient of secret teaching is likely to face.[7] The text ends with Judas receiving payment and delivering Jesus over to the authorities (58.24–26). Like the Gospels of Mark and John, the *Gospel of Judas* ultimately allows the fate of the betrayer to remain a mystery.

The relationship between Papias's account and those of Matthew and Acts is a matter of debate. J. R. Harris, for example, has suggested that Papias expanded the account in Acts.[8] He argues that the earliest text of Acts 1:18 did not read "falling headlong *(prēnēs genomenos)* he burst open in the middle and all his bowels gushed out" as it does now, but "becoming inflamed *(prēstheis genomenos)* he burst open . . ." Thus Papias sought to embellish the terse report in his version of Acts by supplying additional details. However, the manuscript evidence for such a variant in Acts 1:18 is late.[9] More recently, D. R. MacDonald has suggested that the literary influence went in the opposite direction. He argues that the accounts in Matthew, Papias, and Acts are all related: Papias "refutes" Matthew's account with his own, and Acts (assigned a late date by MacDonald) draws upon both Matthew and Papias. MacDonald has set forth this intriguing argument as

---

7. We find a similar scene in the *Gospel of Thomas.* After Thomas receives a private teaching from Jesus, Peter and Matthew ask about the teaching, to which Thomas responds: "If I tell you one of the sayings he said to me, you will take up stones and cast them at me, and fire will come out of the stones and burn you" (*Gos. Thom.* 13; trans. *AG,* 303–49).

8. See Harris, "Did Judas Really Commit Suicide?," esp. 497–500.

9. As evidence for the existence of an early variant in Acts 1:18 that read *prēstheis* in place of *prēnēs,* Harris calls attention to the presence of the variant in the Armenian and Georgian versions of Acts as well as in an Armenian catena of Acts. See Harris, "Did Judas Really Commit Suicide?" 498. However, the evidence marshaled by Harris is much too late to suggest the existence of the variant in the time of Papias.

part of a broader source-critical study of the Gospels.[10] It should be noted, however, that the most compelling evidence that Papias composed his account in response to Matthew's ("Judas did *not* die by hanging") comes not from Papias, but from Apollinaris's remarks prior to his quotation of Papias—he states "Judas did not die by hanging but lived on, having been cut down before he choked to death."[11] It is also important to point out that MacDonald's argument assumes the originality of the longer version of Papias's account of Judas's death, yet good arguments could be made in favor of the priority of the shorter version.

The vivid depiction of Judas's diseased and swollen body, especially in the longer version of Papias's account, calls to mind similar depictions of the dying days of other notorious villains. Josephus reports that God punished King Herod by cursing him with afflictions such as an insatiable appetite, ulcerated bowels, and putrefying and worm-emitting genitals (Josephus, *Ant.* 17.6.5).[12] Eusebius likewise describes the torturous final days of the emperor Galerius, whose ruthless treatment of Christians provoked divine punishment in the form of corpulence, abscessed genitals, and worm infestation (*Hist. eccl.* 8.16.3–5). The terrible death of Judas also recalls the story of Antiochus IV's death as recounted by the author of 2 Maccabees. The arrogant and antagonistic Seleucid king apparently fell out of his chariot and received an injury that caused his flesh to crawl with worms and eventually rot away, producing a putrid stench (9:5–29).[13] The author of the longer version of the account of Judas's death made use of a similar cluster of motifs in order to illustrate God's physical punishment of Judas for his act of betrayal.[14]

Translation

The two passages below are translated from the Greek text printed in Cramer's catenae on Matthew and Acts. The shorter version appears in Cramer's catena on Matthew 27 and the longer version appears in the catena on Acts 1. In both Matthew and Acts the death of Judas is presented as the typological fulfillment of biblical passages (see Matt 27:9–10 and Acts 1:20), and it appears as though the authors of both versions attributed to Papias, but especially the author of the longer version, shared this interest. Therefore, biblical allusions are noted in the translations below.[15]

Bibliography

EDITIONS AND TRANSLATIONS

Cramer, John Anthony. *Catenae Graecorum Patrum in Novum Testamentum*. 8 vols. Oxford: Academic Press, 1840–1844. (The short version is in vol. 1:231, the long version in vol. 3:12–13.)

---

10. For the details of the argument as well as his broader source-critical theory, see MacDonald, *Two Shipwrecked Gospels*, esp. 28–34, 43, 59–62, and 76–78. See also MacDonald, "Luke's Use of Papias."

11. Text and translation in Holmes, *Apostolic Fathers*, 582–85.

12. See a similar depiction of the dying Herod in Solomon of Basra, *Bk. Bee*, 88.

13. For additional examples see Zeichmann, "Papias as Rhetorician," 428 n. 3.

14. For more on Judas's death as a "punitive miracle," see Richard I. Pervo, *Acts: A Commentary* (Hermeneia; Minneapolis: Fortress, 2009), 52–53; and O. Wesley Allen, Jr., *The Death of Herod: The Narrative and Theological Function of Retribution in Luke-Acts* (Atlanta: Scholars, 1997).

15. For a detailed discussion of the death of Judas in Matthew, Acts, and Papias as the fulfillment of biblical prophecy, see Rick van de Water, "The Punishment of the Wicked Priest and the Death of Judas," *The Dead Sea Discoveries* 10, no. 3 (2003): 395–419 at 399–408.

Holmes, Michael W. *The Apostolic Fathers: Greek Texts and English Translations*. Rev. ed.; Grand Rapids, Mich.: Baker, 1999. (A reconstructed text of the long version with Apollinaris's introduction on pp. 582–85.)

STUDIES

Bartlett, J. Vernon. "Papias' 'Exposition': Its Date and Contents." Pages 15–44 in *Amicitiae Corolla. A Volume of Essays Presented to J. R. Harris*. Edited by Herbert G. Wood. London: University of London, 1933.

Beyschlag, Karlmann. "Herkunft und Eigenart der Papiasfragmente." Pages 268–80 in *Studia Patristica 4: Papers Presented to the 3rd International Conference on Patristic Studies at Christ Church, Oxford, 21–26 September 1959*. Edited by Frank L. Cross. TU 79. Berlin: Akademie-Verlag, 1961.

Harris, J. Rendel. "Did Judas Really Commit Suicide?" *AJT* 4 (1900): 490–513.

Herber, J. "La mort de Judas." *RHR* 129 (1945): 47–56.

Klauck, Hans-Josef. "Judas der 'Verräter'? Eine exegetische und wirkungsgeschichtliche Studie." *ANRW* II.26.1 (1992): 717–40.

Lake, Kirsopp. "The Death of Judas." Pages 22–30 in vol. 5 of *The Beginnings of Christianity, Part 1: The Acts of the Apostles*. Edited by Kirsopp Lake and Henry J. Cadbury. 5 vols. London: Macmillan, 1920–1933.

MacDonald, Dennis R. "Luke's Use of Papias for Narrating the Death of Judas." Pages 43–62 in *Reading Acts Today*. Edited by Steve Walton et al. London: T.&T. Clark, 2011.

———. *Two Shipwrecked Gospels: The Logoi of Jesus and Papias's Exposition of Logia about the Lord*. Atlanta: Society of Biblical Literature, 2012.

Schoedel, William R. "Papias." *ANRW* II.27.1 (1993): 235–70.

Schweizer, Eduard. "Zu Apg. 1:16–22." *TZ* 14 (1958): 46.

Zeichmann, Christopher B. "Papias as Rhetorician: Ekphrasis in the Bishop's Account of Judas' Death." *NTS* 56 (2010): 427–29.

The Death of Judas according to Papias

Short Version (*Catenae on Matthew,* ed. Cramer 1:231)

Judas walked about in this world as a weighty example of impiety. He was so inflamed in the flesh that he could not pass where a wagon could easily pass. When the wagon struck him, his bowels emptied out.

Gen 4:14; Ps 109:10

Num 5:21–22

Long Version (*Catenae on Acts,* ed. Cramer 3:12–13)

Judas walked about in this world as a weighty example of impiety. He was so inflamed in the flesh that he could not pass where a wagon could easily pass, in fact not even the bulk of his head alone could pass. For they say that the lids of his eyes were so swollen that neither could he see any light at all, nor could a doctor aided by instruments see his eyes. Such was their depth from the outer surface of his body. His genitals appeared to be more nauseating and enlarged than any other genitalia, and he passed through them pus and even worms that converged from throughout his body, causing an outrage on account of a simple necessity of life. After many tortures and punishments, they say, he died in his own land. His land remains until now desolate and uninhabited on account of the stench. Even to this day no one can travel through that place without holding their nose. So great was the judgment that spread through his flesh upon the earth.

Gen 4:14; Ps 109:10
Num 5:21–22

Ps 69:23

Ps 69:25

313

II. Apocryphal Acts and Related Traditions

The Acts of Barnabas

A new translation and introduction

by Glenn E. Snyder

The *Acts of Barnabas* (*Acts Barn.*; *CANT* 285), often titled "Travels and Martyrdom of Saint Barnabas the Apostle," is a collection of stories about Barnabas and John Mark. Some form of the martyrdom of Barnabas (*Acts Barn.* 8:1–3) was composed in the late fifth century, when the churches of Cyprus were establishing independence from the patriarchate of Antioch. The martyrdom was grouped together with traditions about John Mark to produce several forms of the *Acts of Barnabas*. These are distinct from the *Passion of Mark* (*CANT* 287),[1] which describes the subsequent teaching and martyrdom of John Mark in Alexandria; but some form of *Acts Barn.* may have been used in the *Acts of Mark* (*CANT* 288), just as the sixth-century *Encomium on Barnabas* by Alexander Monachus (*CANT* 286) functioned as an intertext for the later *Travels and Martyrdom of Saints Bartholomew and Barnabas* (*CANT* 264).

Contents

Acts Barn. presents a collection of *parerga*, "side-deeds," for characters who participated in the "first missionary journey" (Acts 13–15). The main character in the canonical Acts is Saul, who is also called Paul (Acts 13:9). But *Acts Barn.* uses Paul as a minor character to develop a cycle of stories about two other characters: Barnabas[2] and John Mark.[3] Alleg-

---

1. The *Passion of Mark* (*CANT* 287) has sometimes been called "Acts of Mark" in modern scholarship, for example in the translation ("The *Acts of Saint Mark*") and study ("The Acts of Mark") by Callahan. It is shorter and less heterodox than the *Acts of Mark* (*CANT* 288), which was published in François Halkin, "Actes inédits de Saint Marc," *AnBoll* 87 (1969): 343–71.

2. Barnabas was remembered diversely in other early Christian texts. In Gal 2:1–10, whose discrepancies with Acts 15 are well known, Barnabas and Paul (with Titus) visit Jerusalem, where Cephas, James, and John legitimate their gospel to the uncircumcised. Galatians 2:12 cites table fellowship as a source of division between Paul and Barnabas in Antioch. But Col 4:10, with its reference to Barnabas's cousin "Mark" (see next note), may imply that Paul continued relations with Barnabas. Continuing relations may also be assumed in 1 Cor 9:6, when Paul uses Barnabas to strengthen his rhetoric: "Or is it only Barnabas and I who have no right to refrain from working for a living?" Non-Pauline traditions about Barnabas have also been handed down. Sometimes he has been credited with writing Hebrews (e.g., Tertullian, *Pud.* 20); he has been associated with the *Epistle of Barnabas* (e.g., Clement of Alexandria, *Strom.* 5.10.63.1–6; Origen, *Cels.* 1.63); occasionally he is listed among the seventy(-two) (e.g., Clement of Alexandria, *Strom.* 2.20.116.3); the *Pseudo-Clementines* describe travels of Barnabas to Rome (*Rec.* 1.7–13) and Alexandria (*Hom.* 1.9–16); the *Decretum Gelasianum* lists a nonextant gospel written in his name; the medieval *Gospel of Barnabas* was ascribed to him; and so forth.

3. Some interpreters have understood the John Mark of Acts to be the "Mark" referenced in Phlm 24, a "co-worker" of Paul; the "Mark" described in Col 4:10 as a cousin of Barnabas, whom the Colossians have been instructed to receive; and/or the "Mark" of 2 Tim 4:11, whom Timothy is commanded to bring with him due to his usefulness in Paul's service. Other traditions associate "Mark" (sometimes "John Mark") with the tribe of Levi; the ministries of John the Baptist, Jesus, and Peter; the cities of Rome, Cyrene, and Alexandria;

edly written by John Mark, *Acts Barn.* is framed by references to the baptism and call of John to reveal its mysteries (1:1–2; 10:1–3), and the text begins with a backstory to explain his apostolic surname "Mark" (2:1–5; cf. Acts 12:12, 25; 15:37). Within this framework, the story describes three stages of travel: first, the travel of Paul, Barnabas, and John Mark through Seleucia, Cyprus, and Perga to Antioch (3:1–2; cf. Acts 13:4–5, 13–14a), where Paul parts ways with Barnabas and John Mark (4:1–5:13a; cf. Acts 15:36–41); second, the travel of Barnabas and John Mark through Cilicia to Cyprus (5:13b–6:8; cf. Acts 15:39; 27:2–4), where Barnabas is martyred by the Judeans[4] at Salamis (7:1–8:6; cf. Acts 13:5–12); and finally, the travel of John Mark and companions to Alexandria (9:1–2), where he continues to teach and to baptize as he had been instructed by "the apostles" (10:1–3).

Manuscripts and Versions

Acts Barn. was composed in Greek. Extant manuscripts attest to two Greek recensions, P and Σ, whose editions are discussed below. In the sixth century a Latin version was produced as the *Vita et passio Barnabae (Life and Passion of Barnabas)*, which has been preserved in at least two recensions: *Casinensis (c)* and *ad Nausea (n)*.[5] A Slavonic version is also attested in many manuscripts.[6]

The edited Greek manuscripts date from the ninth to the thirteen centuries. These manuscripts are listed below by siglum and in order of publication; each editor used the editions of *Acts Barn.* previously available.

V: Vatican, Biblioteca apostolica, gr. 1667 (11th cent.)[7]
P: Paris, Bibliothèque nationale de France, gr. 1470 (890 CE)[8]
B: Mount Athos, Vatopedi[9] (11th/12th cent.)
M: Messina, San Salvatore di Fitalia, gr. 29 (12th cent.)
Q: Paris, Bibliothèque nationale de France, gr. 1219 (11th cent.)
U: Vatican, Biblioteca apostolica, gr. 821 (13th cent.)[10]
Σ: siglum used by Bonnet to designate an archetype for the family V, B, M, Q, U

and the production of one or more gospels (1 Pet 5:13; Papias, according to Eusebius, *Hist. eccl.* 3.39.14–16; Ps.-Hippolytus, *On the Seventy Apostles; Acts of Mark; Pass. Mark*; etc.). A physiognomic description of John Mark (Callahan, "Acts of Mark," 73) occurs in *Pass. Mark* 13 (Vatican, Biblioteca apostolica, gr. 866).

4. Prior to 135 CE, the Greek term *Ioudaioi* referred to citizens of the Roman province *Ioudaia* ("Judea"), regardless of the citizens' ethnicity, religion, or residence. Normally (mis)translated as "Jews" (e.g., in the NRSV), the term has been rendered geopolitically as "Judeans" in this introduction and translation. See further p. 329 n. b below.

5. Mombrizio, *Sanctuarium seu Vitae sanctorum,* 130–35 (Latin version of *Vita et passio* = BHL 985, whose manuscript includes other reports of Barnabas's travels to Rome and Milan); Tosti, *Bibliotheca Casinensis,* 354–57 (Latin version of *Vita,* with Latin abridgment of *Acts of (Pseudo-)Mark* = BHL 983).

6. See the description by Aurelio de Santos Otero, *Die handschriftliche Überlieferung der altslavischen Apokryphen* (PTS 20; Berlin/New York: De Gruyter, 1978), 136–37; and the edition of the Old Slavonic edition of the fifteenth-century Bucharest manuscript by Kaluznjackij, "Sborniki." The Old Slavonic may be particularly related to the Greek text-type attested in V (see next note on Vat. gr. 1667), rather than more generally in Σ.

7. V was edited by Daniel Papebroek in Bolland, *Acta Sanctorum, Iunii,* 2:431–35 (3rd ed.: 2:425–29).

8. P was added in the edition by Tischendorf, *Acta Apostolorum Apocrypha,* xxvi–xxxi (introduction) and 64–74 (edition).

9. Bonnet did not provide precise manuscript identification (see Bonnet, "Acta Barnabae," xxvii, 292, 393).

10. B, M, Q, and U were added in the edition by Bonnet, "Acta Barnabae." In an appendix, Bonnet dates U's manuscript precisely to 1307 ("Acta Barnabae," 392).

According to Jacques Noret, six additional Greek manuscripts have been discovered: three at Mount Athos, one at Messina, a fragment at Paris, and a fragment at Cambridge.[11]

In the edition of Bonnet, the Greek recensions of *Acts Barn.* are represented by P and Σ. The Σ recension is a late, Western harmonization of *Acts Barn.* with the canonical Acts. Σ has introduced several emendations: for example, the replacement of Silas with Peter as a mentor of John Mark (1:2); the relocation of John Mark's baptism from Iconium to an anonymous site (1:2; 2:5); the relocation of Seleucia (3:1) and Antioch (3:2; 4:1) to Syria, in order to harmonize with Acts and allow a first mission to Cyprus to have occurred at 3:1 (esp. Acts 13:4–12; cf. also 12:12, 15; 13:1);[12] the omission of conflict with Paul in Pisidian Antioch (4:2–5:3) and other data (e.g., 6:2, 5, 8); harmonization with "orthodoxy" (e.g., baptismal formulae in 6:6 and 10:2, and doxology in 10:3); emendations that legitimate John Mark's role in the "second mission to Cyprus" (e.g., 6:8; 7:6, 8, 15; 8:1); and numerous grammatical improvements.

Conversely, the P recension of *Acts Barn.* identifies Silas rather than Peter as one of John's mentors (1:2); locates John Mark's baptism in Iconium, with probable reference to the house of Onesiphorus in the *Acts of Paul and Thecla* (1:2; 2:5); refers to Cilician "Seleucia," where Thecla was venerated (3:1), and to Pisidian "Antioch" (3:2; 4:1), without implying a mission to Cyprus (3:1; cf. Acts 13:4–12); and provides a backstory for Paul's "pain" over John Mark (4:2–5:3; cf. 2 Tim 4:11b–13) and other data (e.g., 6:2, 5, 8), while highlighting the role of Barnabas in Cyprus. Of the two extant Greek recensions, P is most proximate to the fifth-century politics of Cyprus.

Both recensions of the Latin include several significant omissions: *Acts Barn.* 1:2; 4:4; 5:2b, 4–10; 6:1–2, 7–8; and 7:11–17. The Latin *c* recension omits also 8:4–10:2. These omissions often are interpreted as excisions of material that was too detailed for hagiographic purposes. But some omissions may indicate an earlier Greek hypotext (e.g., 1:2; 5:2b; 6:1–2 and 7–8; 7:11–17), and others may denote sections that were considered theologically incompatible with certain ideologies of Paul, the apostles, and/or Acts (e.g., 4:4 and 5:4–10 are counternarratives for Acts 15:36–41). Particularly interesting is Latin *c*'s omission of 8:4–10:2, since these verses include the descriptions of Barnabas's remains (8:4: dust in linen and lead) and his burial with the Gospel of Matthew (8:5). Are these details a later addition to an earlier account of Barnabas's martyrdom (8:1–3), or a later deletion?

In any case, differences between the P and Σ recensions (esp. 4:2–5:3)—as well as certain section markers in the Greek (e.g., *toinun* at 3:1; 5:1, 8, 12), some of the Latin omissions, and syntactic and orthographic irregularities—indicate that *Acts Barn.* is the product of a complex compositional process that stitched together several blocks of material, with at least one stage occurring prior to the P and Σ recensions. Therefore, at least parts of *Acts Barn.* were produced prior to its late-fifth-century production for Cyprus, and certain traditions preserved in *Acts Barn.* may compete with the stories narrated in Acts 12–15, whose historicity has otherwise been questioned.[13]

Literary Context

Barnabas and John Mark are minor but important characters in the canonical Acts. There, the apostles in Jerusalem gave a certain Joseph the surname "*Bar-Nabas*," a Hebrew or

---

11. Van Deun and Noret, *Hagiographica Cypria*, 160 n. 5.

12. Compare *Acts Barn.* 7:8, which also "uploads" Acts 13:4–6.

13. See Schwartz, "End of the Line"; Read-Heimerdinger, "Barnabas in Acts"; *Acts of Mark* (*CANT* 288).

Aramaic phrase etymologized as "son of encouragement" (Acts 4:36; cp. 1:23 var.).[14] This "Barnabas" was a Levite and a Cypriot by birth (4:36), who sold his property and laid his possessions at the feet of the apostles (4:37). Later in Acts (9:26–30; 11:20–26), Barnabas introduces Saul to the apostles in Jerusalem (Judea), sends him to Tarsus (Cilicia), and recruits him to work at Antioch (Syria).

Once in Antioch, the church commissions Barnabas and Saul three times. The first commission is a trip to Jerusalem, where the two receive as counsel John "whose other name was Mark" (Acts 11:27–30; 12:12, 25).[15] The second commission, for which Barnabas and Saul are set apart by the Holy Spirit (13:1–3), is the so-called "first missionary journey" (13:1–14:28). From Antioch, the mission begins on the island of Cyprus (13:4–12), where a certain John assists in proclaiming the gospel to Judeans (see 13:5). The missionaries journey from the eastern port city of Salamis to the western port city of Paphos (13:4–6), where a Judean named "Bar-Jesus" (13:6)—identified as "Elymas" (13:8)—opposes their preaching to the Roman proconsul, Sergius Paulus. After sailing to Perga in Pamphylia, John separates and returns to Jerusalem (13:13; 15:38), as Barnabas and Saul—now called Paul (13:9)—preach throughout the regions of Pisidia and Lycaonia (13:14–14:25). After retracing their steps to Perga's port Attalia, Paul and Barnabas sail back to Antioch and report the completion of their work (14:26–28; cp. 13:1–3).

The third commission from Antioch occurs after some people come down from Jerusalem and teach that circumcision is necessary to be saved (Acts 15:1). This teaching may be similar to what Bar-Jesus had claimed at Paphos (13:6–12). In any case, Paul and Barnabas—"and some of the others"—go up to Jerusalem to discuss the matter with the apostles and elders (15:2), and then they return with two delegates from Jerusalem—Judas called "Bar-Sabbas" and Silas (15:22, 30)—to report what James had decided (15:19, 22). Whether John was a participant in any of these events is unclear. But after the delegate(s) from Jerusalem depart (see 15:33; cp. 15:40), Paul and Barnabas stay in Antioch, teaching and preaching "with many others" (15:35).

Later, Paul proposes traveling again to "oversee"[16] the brothers in the cities of the "first missionary journey" (Acts 15:36). Barnabas wants to take with them John "called" Mark (15:37), thus equating the "John whose other name was Mark" of Acts 12:12 and 25 with the "John" of Acts 13:5 and 13. But Paul reckons that someone who had not participated in all of the work should not be taken as counsel (15:38). Using a medical analogy, Acts says that an "irritation" (NRSV: "disagreement") required that they be separated from one other, so that Barnabas took "Mark" and sailed away to Cyprus (15:39). This reference to a "second mission to Cyprus" is the final mention of "John," "Mark," and/or "Barnabas" in Acts.

Barnabas and John Mark, therefore, play critical roles in Acts. John Mark, a Jerusalemite, assists in preaching to the Judeans on Cyprus, witnesses the first "conversion" of a non-Judean on Cyprus (Sergius Paulus), and occasions the separation of Barnabas and Paul. Barnabas, a Cypriot, unites Paul, the apostles in Jerusalem, and the church in Antioch,

---

14. For Barnabas in "D" or the "Western" text of Acts, see Read-Heimerdinger, "Barnabas in Acts." For Barnabas in *Acts Titus* 4, see Pervo, "Acts of Titus," esp. 464, 480–82.

15. Acts 11:27–30 refers to a famine in Judea (probably 46–48 CE), and Acts 12 refers to the rule of King Herod Agrippa I (41–44 CE). For source and redaction criticism of Acts 11–15, see for example Schwartz, "End of the Line."

16. The function of "overseeing" *(episkop-)* often included economic matters; so, in addition to other interpretive options (ideologies of *nomos*, filial piety, etc.), the "irritation" between Barnabas and Paul in Acts may be conflicting ideologies of compensation and/or financial management.

and then he separates, sailing back to his native Cyprus with John Mark. Dramatic and mysterious, Barnabas and John Mark are characters whose stories are related intimately to the churches in Jerusalem and Antioch, and who are foundational to the churches of Cyprus.

Acts Barn. collects *parerga*, "side deeds," about these characters, answering such questions as: When was John Mark baptized? On whose authority did he preach? Why was Paul so irritated with him? Were John Mark and Barnabas too Judean ("Jewish")? Why did Barnabas and Paul part ways? Was it John Mark who occasioned their separation, or was their division part of God's plan? Furthermore, what happened when Barnabas and John Mark returned to Cyprus (Acts 15:39)?—Where did they go? What did they preach? How effective was their work? Were they able to establish "overseers" (*episkopoi*, "bishops") over the churches? And, whatever happened with that Bar-Jesus character? *Acts Barn.* addresses these topics and more, including the martyrdom of Barnabas and the subsequent travel of John Mark to Alexandria.

The Formation of Acts of Barnabas

Acts Barn. collects traditions that originated separately and developed independently.[17] Consider first the framing material. The prescript (1:1–2), probably together with the postscript about Alexandria (9:1–10:3), describes an origin for John that differs from the story in Acts. In Acts, "John whose other name was Mark" is a resident of Jerusalem (or its environs) taken by Barnabas and Saul to provide counsel on Judean matters (Acts 12:12, 25; 13:5). But in *Acts Barn.* John, who is renamed "Mark," is a former *hypēretēs* ("assistant; officer") of Cyrus, "the chief-priest of Zeus" (cf. Acts 13:13). Because these origins are difficult to harmonize, the author of the prescript may not have known the story narrated in Acts 12 (and later developed by the *Acts of Mark*); the author of the framing materials may have only known oral tradition, some form of Acts 15:36–41 (where the character is "the John called Mark"), and/or other materials in *Acts Barn.* The author of the prescript ascribes John's baptism to Paul *and* Barnabas (with Σ and the Latin omitting "and Silas," and Σ prefixing "Peter the apostle"; see 1:2; cf. 10:2) and implies that the "mysteries" seen and heard by John are what is about to be explained (1:1). Neither the baptism nor the "mysteries" are in Acts, and it is unclear whether these narrative elements in the prescript are compatible with the story in the next section.

The next section (2:1–5), which provides a backstory for John being renamed "Mark" (cf. Acts 12:12, 25; 15:37), refers repeatedly to "the mysteries" revealed to John in a vision sometime after he was baptized. John's vision of the man wrapped in the white outfit (2:1) is related explicitly to the Lord's plan for Barnabas: the "mysteries" he saw and heard were provided to assist with Barnabas's "perfection" (2:2–3), presumably as post-mortem practices to facilitate the transfer and burial of his remains. Therefore, at least this part of *Acts Barn.* (2:1–5) was composed probably with some form of the martyrdom of Barnabas (8:1–3); this stage of the text probably also included some form of the burial of Barnabas (8:4–6), but the Latin *n* recension omits all such materials (8:4–10:2). Currently there is insufficient evidence to determine whether the prescript and postscript were composed with these materials or added later.

---

17. Czachesz (*Commission Narratives*, 173) describes *Acts Barn.* as an "itinerary style" collection, comparing Homer, *Od.* 14.244–58; Lucian, *Ver. hist.* 1.6; Pseudo-Lucian, *Asin.* 36–41; Achilles Tatius, *Leuc. Clit.* 3.1–5.

It is difficult also to determine where the story of John's vision ends (2:4/5). P's form of *Acts Barn.* 2:4–3:1 includes another reference to Iconium (and an allusion to a tradition handed down in the *Acts of Paul and Thecla*), interprets "Seleucia" as the one in Cilicia (where, e.g., Thecla was commemorated), and refers to the travelers as "passing by Cyprus." So also does the Latin. But Σ deletes the reference to Iconium in *Acts Barn.* 2:5 (cf. also 1:2), in order to harmonize *Acts Barn.* with Acts 12–13 by relocating John's renaming (2:1) to Syrian Antioch. Not surprisingly, Σ interprets the subsequent reference to "Seleucia" (3:1) as the Syrian port of Antioch, so that the travelers "sailed off in the Lord" to Cyprus (cf. Acts 13:4). Moreover, Σ's emendation to "going around all Cyprus" (3:1) is intended probably to harmonize with Acts 13:6's "going through the whole island," in order to "upload" Acts 13:4–6 into this part of *Acts Barn.*[18] Otherwise, as in P and the Latin, the travelers depart from Cilicia and travel to Pisidian Antioch, without referring to the events of Acts 13:4–12.[19]

Acts Barn. 3:1–5:13a explains John Mark's delay in Pamphylia and travel to Antioch. Only P's form of *Acts Barn.* includes all of the sections in this block of material: P's story— set in Pisidian Antioch—portrays John as a spiritual and faithful co-worker, whom a pathetic Paul was unable to forgive for petty reasons. But the Latin recensions, in addition to "omitting" a datum about Lucius (7:2b; see Acts 13:1), lack two critical references to John: John's "repentance" toward Paul (4:4), and Barnabas's "contention" with Paul about John Mark (5:4–10; cf. Acts 15:36–41). Whether these absences are intentional omissions in the Latin or indicate later additions in P and Σ is difficult to determine.[20] But in the Latin, the sequence from *Acts Barn.* 5:3 to 5:11 allows Paul (5:3) and Barnabas (5:11) to separate not over John Mark (as in Acts 15:37–39) but to fulfill God's separate plans for them. Σ's form of the story is yet different. Relocating the action to Syrian Antioch, Σ omits *Acts Barn.* 4:2–5:3, thereby excluding the references to John neglecting the parchments in Pamphylia (4:5; cf. 2 Tim 4:11b–13), causing a "pain" for Paul (4:2, 5), and repenting to Paul for his delay in Pamphylia (4:4), as well as the debate about "overseers" *(episkopoi)* in Cyprus (5:1–2) and Paul's vision that harmonizes with Acts (*Acts Barn.* 5:3). Like a narrative commentary on Acts 15:37–39, Σ has Paul and Barnabas debate the role of John Mark in subsequent travel plans; only, rather than parting because of an "irritation," they separate in order to divide and conquer what God has prepared for each (cf. Gal 2:9).

Thereafter, Barnabas and John travel to Cyprus via the Cilician coast (5:13b–6:8). As with the preceding unit, only P includes all of the sections. One of Σ's omissions is probably based on its ideology of baptism (6:5; cf. 6:3, 6; 10:1), and Σ's other variants in 6:8 function to emphasize John's participation in the ministry with Barnabas (cf. also 7:6). The Latin, which does not include *Acts Barn.* 6:1–2 and 6:7–8, is shorter and refers only to Anemurium. What the Latin "omits" is much of the travel narrative to Cyprus, just as it will "omit" much of the travel once there (7:11–17). Interestingly, such materials provide verisimilitude for the reader and often are used by scholars to associate *Acts Barn.* with the late-fifth-century history of Cyprus.[21]

---

18. Oddly, the scribes of the Σ MSS did not emend *Acts Barn.* 7:8, which also "uploads" Acts 13:4–6.

19. Acts 13:4–12 forms a unit, equating Bar-Jesus and Elymas. *Acts Barn.* apparently knew traditions related to Acts 13:4–6 and 13 (at least in part), but it is unclear that any of its compositional strata are familiar with Acts 13:7–12.

20. The Latin "omission" of *Acts Barn.* 4:4 functions to legitimate Paul's "pain" about John keeping the complete parchments in Pamphylia (cf. 2 Tim 4:11b–13).

21. The many geographical, historical, and cultural references that are narrated during the travels in

The travels on mainland Cyprus constitute the next part of *Acts Barn.* (7:1–17). Whatever its relation to other parts of *Acts Barn.*, this unit presupposes some form of the story in Acts 13:4–6, if not also parts of 13:7–12, as it narrates the travels of a "second mission to Cyprus" (cf. Acts 15:39). The theme of the mission is conquest of the "Greeks," including local residents of Cyprus who do not participate in idolatry. But throughout the island, Barnabas and John are opposed by a certain "Bar-Jesus" (7:8, 12, 14; cf. 8:2), who stirs up the local Judeans against the travelers (cf. Acts 13:5–6, referenced in *Acts Barn.* 7:8). With references to specific sites (wells, olive trees, houses, caverns, etc.) and to legendary figures (Timon, Ariston, Heracleides, Rhodon, Aristoclianus, an elderly widow, "Hypatius" the governor, and a "Jebusite" relative of Nero), many of the most important cities in Cyprus are mentioned explicitly in this unit: Crommyacita, Lapithus, Lampadistus, Tamasus, [Citium,] "snowy" Mt. Olympus, Old Paphos, (New) Paphos, Curium, Amathus, Citium, and "the islands" (probably beside modern Famagusta) near Salamis.[22] Practically all of these locations are associated with the fifth-century church districts of Cyprus and with earlier or contemporary "pagan" sites, especially temples to Aphrodite. But much of this material is not included in the Latin (7:11–17).

The martyrdom and translation of Barnabas are the final events on the island of Cyprus (*Acts Barn.* 8:1–5), apart from John Mark's apocryphal departure (8:6–9:2). Having rounded the island from the north to Paphos in the west and around the south, the "second mission to Cyprus" ends where "the first" reportedly began (cf. Acts 13:5): at the eastern port city of Salamis. There, perhaps for the first time in the narrative (cf. 4:3b), Barnabas begins to teach the Judeans alone, specifically in the synagogue of "the Chosen Scroll" with "the gospel taken from Matthew" (8:1; cf. Acts 13:5).[23] Two days into his instruction, Bar-Jesus arrives to gather the "entire multitude" of the Judeans against Barnabas (8:2),[24] who hastily drag him from the synagogue, encircle him (with wood), and burn him up with fire (8:3). The Latin *n* lacks all of the subsequent materials (8:4–10:2), stating only that "the witness" departed to the Lord to whom honor and glory are due. But P, Σ, and the Latin *c* continue by describing the preparation, theft, and interment of Barnabas's ashes (8:4–5). All are explicit that the interment occurred in a cavern that was previously inhabited by Jebusites (8:5), but it is unclear whether its location is related to a recently arrived "pious Jebusite," a relative of Nero (8:3). In any case, Σ and the Latin *c* clarify that the one who secured the remains of Barnabas was "John Mark" (8:5) and that Barnabas was laid to rest on the fourth hour of 11 June on a Roman calendar or 17 Pauni on a North African calendar (8:5).

In P, Σ, and the Latin *c*, the story continues with John Mark and his companions (8:6–10:2). After fleeing from the Judeans and hiding in another cave for three days, the travel-

---

Cyprus may represent later, and perhaps local, expansions to an earlier text type. These materials function similarly to the "we" materials in Acts (16:9–20; 20:5–21:18; 27:1–28:16), narrating specifics of travel.

22. Arriving at the north of Cyprus, the travelers go through the mountains to the west, down along the southern coastline, by boat to the east; later, the travelers must flee inland of Salamis and then depart from the unknown coastal location of "the village of Limnes."

23. Acts 13:5 refers to several "synagogues," as gatherings if not early architectural sites, but *Acts Barn.* 8:1 refers specifically to the synagogue of the "Chosen Scroll." It is difficult to determine, even within the historical narrative of *Acts Barn.*, whether the synagogue referenced was understood to have its name prior to the narrated event or whether it received its name later, perhaps in reference to the "scroll" Barnabas received from Matthew (cf. 7:2, with its variants between P and Σ). For, by reading *Acts Barn.* 7:2 and 8:1 together, it is normally inferred that the "scroll" (Σ) or "book" (P) in question is some form of the extant Gospel of Matthew. In any case, Matthew's gospel is "rolled out" by Barnabas like a scroll (8:1).

24. On "Bar-Jesus," see also Acts 13:6–12; *Acts Barn.* 7:8, 12, 14.

ers return to the site of the burial by night (8:6). Thereafter, they add to their group and board an Egyptian ship headed to Alexandria (9:1–2), where John Mark continues in the apostolic tradition of teaching and baptizing (10:1–2). Then all manuscripts (including Latin *n*) end with a short doxology (10:3), after which P includes the title: "The Travels and Martyrdom of the Holy Apostle Barnabas have been fulfilled through God."

The traditions collected in *Acts Barn.* thus developed in various forms. Prior to its extant forms in Greek (P and Σ) and Latin *(c* and *n)*, there was at least one earlier form of *Acts Barn.*,[25] whose constituent parts may represent distinct stages of composition. This proto-form comprised a collection of vignettes to develop the story of John Mark in Acts 15:37–39 (3:1–4:1; 5:11–12/13a; 6:3–6; 7:1, 5–10), as well as the framing materials that authorize John Mark as a successor of Barnabas (2:1–5; 8:1–3; 10:3). The proto-form may have included additional materials as well (1:1–2; 5:4; 7:2–3; 8:4–5; 10:2), but some materials in the extant forms are later additions (4:2–5:3; 5:5–10; 6:1–2, 7–8; 7:1, 11–17; 8:6–10:1).

Date and Provenance

Based on materials in *Acts Barn.* 6:1–9:2, the text's date and provenance are normally associated with the independence of the churches of Cyprus, declared at the Council of Ephesus and confirmed by emperor Zeno. Subsequent to the separation of the Latin Roman Empire and the Greek Byzantine Empire in 395, and during the theological debates occasioned by Arius and Nestorius, Cyprus was first authorized to consecrate its own bishops (*episkopoi*, "overseers") at the Council of Ephesus (431), and its status was confirmed by the Byzantine emperor Zeno early in his reign (474–491).[26] According to Enrico Norelli,[27] it was around this time that the entire martyrdom of Barnabas (*Acts Barn.* 8:1–6)—including the text's reference to a handwritten copy of the Gospel of Matthew (8:5; cp. 7:2)—was produced in order to authenticate Cyprus's claim to apostolicity. Some sixth-century documents (e.g., Theodorus Lector [Constantinople], *Hist. eccl.* 530; Alexander Monachus [Cyprus], *Encomium on Barnabas* 547–54) report that shortly before Zeno convened an assembly to debate the jurisdiction of Cyprus, a tomb was discovered outside of Salamis allegedly containing the body (rather than ashes[28]) of Barnabas and a handwritten copy of the Gospel of Matthew (see *Acts Barn.* 8:5; cp. 7:2).[29] The text and relics thus substantiated that Cyprus's churches had been sown by an apostle's words and watered with a martyr's blood. Other scholars, such as István Czachesz,[30] have emphasized discrepancies between *Acts Barn.* 8:4–6 and local Cyprian traditions.[31] But the martyrdom (8:1–3) may have been composed with an alternate description of the gathering and burial of Barnabas (8:4–6), and it is probable that at least the proto-form of *Acts Barn.* was completed by the late fifth century.

---

25. Czachesz (*Commission Narratives*, 182–83) has proposed that *Acts Barn.* and *Pass. Mark* (*CANT* 287) are based on an earlier, nonextant collection of "Acts of Mark," but that *Acts of Mark* (*CANT* 288) is based on *Acts Barn.* Many thematic parallels occur between *Pass. Mark* and the proto-form of *Acts Barn.* hypothesized above.

26. See Hackett, *History of the Orthodox Church in Cyprus*, 13–35.

27. Norelli, "Actes de Barnabé," 622–23; following Lipsius, *Die apokryphen Apostelgeschichten*, 2:291–93.

28. Lipsius (*Die apokryphen Apostelgeschichten*, 2:295) notes that Milan later claimed to have the ashes of Barnabas.

29. Dilley ("Invention of Christian Tradition," 601–3) provides a summary of the *Encomium on Barnabas*, in which many of the events of *Acts Barn.* are retold as a precursor to a tale of Barnabas appearing to Anthemius, bishop of Salamis, in 488 and revealing to him the location of his remains.

30. Czachesz, *Commission Narratives*, 180–82.

31. Lipsius, *Die apokryphen Apostelgeschichten*, 2:291–92.

Translation

A comprehensive edition and translation of *Acts Barn.* is a desideratum, but this translation follows the critical edition of Bonnet. As in Bonnet's edition, the translation normally favors the P recension of the Greek, since P is the most complete form of the text and often represents an earlier text-type than its parallel sections in Σ. But significant variants in Σ and in the Latin have been included in this introduction and the notes, and the sigla "Σ" and "Latin" are used as in Bonnet's edition. "Σ" refers collectively to the family of manuscripts separately designated as V, B, M, Q, and U; and "Latin" refers to all Latin manuscripts, with "Latin *c*" and "Latin *n*" specifying particular recensions. To facilitate comparison with Bonnet's edition, the original section markers have been set in parentheses within the translation. Other references, in the introduction and notes, are according to the chapter and verse divisions introduced in this translation.

Bibliography

EDITIONS AND TRANSLATIONS

Bolland, Jean et al., eds. *Acta Sanctorum, Iunii.* Vol. 2. Antwerp: P. Jacobs 1698; 3rd ed. Paris: V. Palmé, 1863. (*Editio princeps* by Daniel Papebroek, pp. 64–74.)

Bonnet, Maximilien. "Acta Barnabae." Pages xvii–xxviii and 292–302 in vol. 2.2 of *Acta Apostolorum Apocrypha.* Edited by Richard A. Lipsius and Maximilien Bonnet. 2 vols. in 3. Leipzig: H. Mendelssohn, 1903; repr. Hildesheim: Olms, 1972.

Erbetta, Mario. *Gli Apocrifi del Nuovo Testamento.* 3 vols. in 4. Turin: Marietti, 1966–1981. (Italian introduction and translation in vol. 2:595–600.)

Kaluznjackij, Emil. "Sborniki Njameckogo Monstyrja Nnr. 20 i 106 [164]." *Sbornik Otdelenija Russkago Jazyka i Slovesnosti Imp. Akademii Nauk* 83, no. 2 (1907): 50–57. (Critical edition of the Old Slavonic text.)

Mombrizio, Boninus. *Sanctuarium seu Vitae sanctorum. Novam editionem curaverunt duo monachi Solesmenses.* Paris: 1910; repr. New York: Hildesheim, 1978. (Critical edition of Latin traditions.)

Norelli, Enrico. "Actes de Barnabé." Pages 617–42 in *EAC* vol. 2.

Riddle, Matthew Brown, trans. "The Acts of Barnabas." Pages 493–96 in vol. 8 of *ANF.* (English translation of Tischendorf's edition.)

Tischendorf, Constantin. *Acta Apostolorum Apocrypha.* Leipzig: Avenarius et Mendelssohn, 1851.

Tosti, Luigi, ed., *Bibliotheca Casinensis seu codicum manuscriptorum qui in tabulario Casinensi asseruantur series* III: *Florilegeum.* Monte Cassino: Ex Typographia Casinensi, 1877. (Critical edition of Latin traditions.)

STUDIES

Callahan, Allen Dwight. "The Acts of Mark: Tradition, Transmission, and Translation of the Arabic Version." Pages 63–85 in *The Apocryphal Acts of the Apostles.* Edited by François Bovon, Ann Graham Brock, and Christopher R. Matthews. Harvard Divinity School Studies; Cambridge, Mass.: Harvard University Press, 1999.

———. "The *Acts of Saint Mark*: An Introduction and Translation." *Coptic Church Review* 14, no. 1 (1993): 3–10.

Czachesz, István. *Commission Narratives: A Comparative Study of the Canonical and Apocryphal Acts.* Leuven: Peeters, 2007. (See particularly pp. 184–207.)

Delehaye, Hippolyte. "Saints de Chypre." *AnBoll* 26 (1907): 161–301.

Deun, Peter van, and Jacques Noret, eds. *Hagiographica cypria. Sancti Barnabae laudatio auctore Alexandro monacho.* CCSG 26. Turnhout: Brepols; Leuven: University Press, 1993.

Dilley, Paul C. "The Invention of Christian Tradition: 'Apocrypha,' Imperial Policy, and Anti-Jewish Propaganda." *GRBS* 50 (2010): 586–615.

Hackett, John. *A History of the Orthodox Church of Cyprus.* London: Methuen & Co., 1901.

Lipsius, Richard A. *Die apokryphen Apostelgeschichten und Apostellegenden.* 2 vols. Braunschweig: Schwetschke, 1883–1887. (*Acts Barn.* is examined in 2:270–320.)

Pervo, Richard I. "The Acts of Titus: A Preliminary Translation, with an Introduction and Notes." Pages 455–82 in *Society of Biblical Literature 1996 Seminar Papers.* SBLSP 35. Atlanta: Scholars, 1996.

Read-Heimerdinger, Jenny. "Barnabas in Acts: A Study of His Role in the Text of Codex Bezae." *JSNT* 72 (1998): 22–66.

Schwartz, Daniel R. "The End of the Line: Paul in the Canonical Book of Acts." Pages 3–24 in *Paul and the Legacies of Paul.* Edited by William S. Babcock. Dallas: SMU Press, 1990.

Starowieyski, Marek. "Datation des *Actes (Voyages) de S. Barnabé* (*BHG* 225; *ClAp* 285) et du *Panégyrique de S. Barnabé par Alexandre le Moine* (*BHG* 226; *CPG* 7400; *ClAp* 286)." Pages 193–98 in *Philohistor. Miscellanea in honorem Caroli Laga septuagenarii.* Edited by A. Schoors and Peter Van Deun. OLA 60. Leuven: Peeters, 1994.

Young, Philip H. "The Cypriot Aphrodite Cult: Paphos, Rantidi, and Saint Barnabas." *JNES* 64, no. 1 (2005): 23–44.

The Acts of Barnabas[a]

Prescript

1 [1](1) From the descent of the presence of our Savior Jesus Christ—the confident, benevolent, and mighty one; the Shepherd, Teacher, and Healer—I gazed upon and saw the ineffable, sacred, blameless mystery of the Christians, who cling piously to hope and have been sealed. Since I myself beheld the mystery, to which I am willingly enslaved, I have considered it necessary to explain the mysteries that I heard and saw.

[2](2) I, John, was accompanying Barnabas and Paul, the holy apostles, as an assistant. Formerly, I was an assistant of Cyrus, the chief-priest of Zeus. But now I am assistant of the Holy Spirit,[b] after receiving grace through Paul and Barnabas and Silas,[c] who are worthy of the calling and who also baptized me in Iconium.[d]

The vision of John "Mark"

2 [1](3) Now, after I was baptized, I saw in a vision[e] a man standing over me, wrapped in a white outfit. He said to me, "Take heart, John. For indeed, your name will be changed to 'Mark,' and your glory will be proclaimed throughout the entire world. The darkness that was in you passed away from you, and comprehension has been given to you for knowing the mysteries of God."[f]

Acts 12:12, 25; 15:37

[2](4) When I saw the vision, trembling, I departed from the feet of Barnabas,[g] and I reported to him the mysteries I had seen and heard from that man. But Paul the apostle was not nearby when I communicated the mysteries. [3]Barnabas said to me, "You should not declare the power you saw to anyone. For, on this

---

a. In Bonnet's edition the title is "Travels and Martyrdom of Saint Barnabas the Apostle." M transposes the singulars "martyrdom and travel"; Σ modifies "of the holy apostle Barnabas"; and, at the desinit, P adds to Σ's title: "have been fulfilled through God."

b. *Pneuma hagion* ("spirit [that is] holy") is anarthrous in 1:2 and 7:6, referring to spirit/ Spirit received in baptism. Other references are articular (3:2; 5:9; 6:5) or occur in a baptismal formula where Father and Son are also anarthrous (6:6, 10:2; but the article is added in Σ).

c. Σ and Latin omit Silas from the end of the list; Σ also adds "Peter the apostle" to the beginning. A certain "Silas" is mentioned in Acts 15:22, 40; 17:10; 18:5. Compare "Silvanus" in 2 Cor 1:19; 1 Thess 1:1; 2 Thess 1:1; and 1 Pet 5:12.

d. For John Mark's origin at Cyrene of Pentapolis, see *Pass. Mark* 3 (Vatican, Biblioteca apostolica, gr. 866); compare Acts 12:12, 25. P and the Latin locate John Mark's baptism in Iconium, but Σ omits "in Iconium" (see note to 2:5 below).

e. P omits "in a vision." For John Mark's vision to depart for Alexandria, see *Pass. Mark* 4.

f. On Jesus as light in *Pass. Mark,* see Callahan, "Acts of Mark," 77–78.

g. To be "at the feet of" is to subordinate oneself as an apprentice (e.g., Acts 22:3).

very night the Lord also approached me, saying, 'Take heart. When you give your life for my name, to be murdered and exiled from your people, you will also be perfected. Moreover, the assistant who is with you,[a] collect him with you, for he has certain mysteries.' So now, child, guard for yourself the words that you saw and heard, for there is about to be an opportunity for you to reveal them."

[4](5) After I had been instructed by him about these things,[b] we remained for several days[c] [5]in Iconium, for in that place there was a pious and adherent man who welcomed us, whose very house Paul sanctified.[d]

Travel to Antioch[e]

3 [1]So then,[f] from there we arrived in Seleucia;[g] and after waiting for three days, we sailed to Cyprus.[h] Indeed, it was I who served them while we passed by Cyprus.[i] [2]Then after taking up anchor from Cyprus, we let down in Perga of Pamphylia. For about two months I stayed behind at that place, wishing to sail away to the western parts,[j] but the Holy Spirit did not permit me. After turning back, I searched for the apostles; and having learned that they were in Antioch, I traveled to them.

Acts 13:4–6
Acts 13:13–14
Acts 16:6
Acts 13:14–52; 15:2, 35

Antioch

4 [1](6) In Antioch I found Paul, resting from the labor of road travel.[k] [2]He was on the couch. When he saw me, he was violently pained because of my delay in

---

a. Apart from this plural "you," Barnabas's indirect discourse uses singular verbs and pronouns.

b. Σ has "Therefore, having been instructed through me by him. . . ."

c. Σ omits 2:5 and adds "in Jerusalem, and we entered Antioch," relocating the travelers to Syrian Antioch (cf. Acts 12:12, 25; 13:1).

d. Probably the Iconian house of Onesiphorus in *Acts Thecla* 3:3–4, 23–24; 4:42. But Σ does not include the reference (see preceding note).

e. Compare the itinerary in *Acts Titus* 3–4: Damascus, (perhaps somewhere else,) Jerusalem, Caesarea, (perhaps Jerusalem again,) Syrian Antioch, Seleucia, Cyprus including Salamis and Paphos, Perga, Pisidian Antioch, and Iconium. At Syrian Antioch (*Acts Titus* 4), Barnabas is described as "the son of Panchares whom Paul had raised." Pervo ("Acts of Titus," 464) understands the Greek reference to *Pancharēs* to be preserved in the Coptic *Ancharēs* of *Acts Paul* 2, which is also set in an Antioch.

f. *Toinun* is used to demark several subsections within 3:1–5:13 (see 3:1; 5:1, 8, 12).

g. In P and the Latin recensions, this is Seleucia on the Calycadnus—the Cilician site for Thecla's shrine, the famous "caves of heaven and hell," and a temple to Jupiter/Zeus that flourished in the second century. But in Σ, it is apparently understood as Seleucia Pieria, the Syrian port of Antioch mentioned in Acts 13:4.

h. Σ reads "we sailed off in the Lord," perhaps harmonizing with the verb in Acts 13:3.

i. *Acts Barn.* 3:1 narrates an initial visit to Cyprus, but the parallels with Acts 13:4–12 occur mainly in *Acts Barn.* 7:8, 12, 14–15; 8:2. *Acts Barn.* 3:1 uses *parerchomai* ("went by" Cyprus) rather than Acts 13:6's *dierchomai* ("went through" the whole island). But Σ harmonizes with *periēlthomen pasan* ("went around all" Cyprus), which occurs in the D-text of Acts 13:6, so that the reader may understand a "first mission to Cyprus" (cf. Acts 13:4–6, if not also 7–12) to have occurred during this part of *Acts Barn.*

j. Σ emends to the more general "*travel* to the limits of the west." Compare 5:1 on "eastern places," and consider 1 *Clem.* 5 on Paul coming to "the end of the west." Perhaps related is a Spain trip narrated, for example, in *Acts of Peter (Actus Vercellenses)* 1–3, 34–41 and *Life and Conduct of Xanthippe and Polyxena*; cf. Rom 15:23–24.

k. Beginning of Σ's omission from 4:2–5:3.

Pamphylia. [3]When Barnabas came, he exhorted Paul, and he offered bread; but little did he receive it. They preached the word of the Lord and they enlightened many of the Judeans and Greeks.[a]

Acts 20:11

Acts 14:1; 13:43-48

[4]I devoted myself only to them.[b] I was afraid to approach Paul, both because of the considerable time I spent in Pamphylia and because he was very upset by me. Moreover, with Paul I was offering repentance on my knees for the land, and he would not help me up.[c] After I had stayed for three Sabbaths, with exhortation and entreaty of kneelings, I was not able to change his opinion about me. [5]His great pain with me was due to my keeping the complete parchments in Pamphylia.

2 Tim 4:11-13

Division of Paul and Barnabas

5 [1](7) So then, after the completion of their teaching in Antioch,[d] on one of the Sabbaths, when seated together, they deliberated about traveling toward the eastern places and afterward coming to Cyprus and overseeing all the churches in which they spoke the word of God. [2]Barnabas exhorted that Paul who is foremost in Cyprus, and his household, might come to oversee his village.[e] Lucius also exhorted that he might receive oversight in his city Corina.[f] [3]Through sleep, a vision was seen by Paul that he should hasten toward Jerusalem on account of the brothers receiving him there.[g] [4]But Barnabas exhorted that those in Cyprus come[h] and spend the winter, and then they depart to Jerusalem during the feast.

Acts 15:30-35

Acts 15:36-41
Acts 4:36; 13:4-12
Acts 13:1

Acts 16:9; 18:21 (D); 21:17-26

[5](8) So then, a great contention occurred between them.[i] Barnabas exhorted that I also accompany them on account of my being their assistant[j] from the beginning. Indeed, in all of Cyprus I assisted them, until they ar-

Acts 15:36-41

Acts 13:5

---

a. Latin omits 4:4.

b. In Antioch John Mark was devoted to Greeks (the most proximate antecedent), perhaps also to Judeans, but not to Barnabas and Paul. In *Acts Barn.* "Greeks" denotes an ethnically and religiously distinct group (4:3; 6:3; 7:13–14), which may be dedicated particularly to Aphrodite and/or her local consort. Apart from this reference (4:3), "Judean(s)"—led by Bar-Jesus—are portrayed as opposing the gospel (7:8, 12, 14), to the extent of murdering Barnabas (8:1–3) and chasing after John Mark (8:6). Compare *Pass. Mark* 8, where "Greeks" (apparently, in contrast to native Copts) persecute John Mark in Alexandria.

c. Riddle (*ANF* 8:493) translates: "And I gave repentance on my knees upon the earth to Paul, and he would not endure it."

d. Note that the story in *Acts Barn.* concerns Pisidian Antioch. The "parallel" in Acts 15:36–41 is apparently situated in Syrian Antioch, from whence Barnabas and Saul had been sent (Acts 13:1–3 with 14:26–28, and 15:1–3 with 15:30–35). But note the editorial oddities about travel to/from Jerusalem in Acts 11:27–30 and 12:25, which probably indicate Lukan redaction of a tradition about a singular Jerusalem conference.

e. The preceding reference is probably to Sergius Paulus (cf. Acts 13:4–14a). In P and Σ, two Cyprians are delegating oversight to the Paulus in question, but the Latin omits the following sentence ("Lucius . . . Corina").

f. Tischendorf proposed an emendation of "Corina" to "Cyrene."

g. Or, "on account of him receiving the brothers there." End of Σ's omission from 4:2–5:3. Also beginning of Latin omission from 5:4–10.

h. Or, "that they come in Cyprus."

i. Given its absence in the Latin, 5:4–10 may be a separate authorial strand, even within 4:1–5:13. At stake is whether John "Mark" occasioned the division of Paul and Barnabas.

j. BQUV: "my assisting them."

rived[a] in Perga of Pamphylia; and there I remained behind for a considerable number of days. [6]But Paul shouted over Barnabas, saying, "This one is unable to come with us!" But even those who were with us there appealed that I also should accompany them on account of there being a vow for me to assist them until the end.[b] [7]So Paul said to Barnabas, "If you wish to take John—the one also renamed 'Mark'—with you, travel a different way, for he should not come with us."

[8]But Barnabas, having kept within himself, said, "From the one who once slaved for the gospel and who journeyed with us, the grace of God is not turning away. [9]So if this is indeed your pleasure, father Paul, now that I have received him, I am going." He said, "Travel in the grace of Christ, and we in the power of the Spirit."[c]

[10](9) So then, bowing their knees, they prayed to God. After rising up, Paul lamented and so did Barnabas, when they spoke to each other.[d] "Surely it was good for us, as in the beginning so also at the end, to do what is in humans commonly.[e] [11]Since it seemed so to you, father Paul, pray over me that my toil might be done for approval. For, you have seen how I slaved with you for the grace of Christ that was given to us. For, I am traveling in Cyprus, and I am eager to be perfected. For, I have seen that I will no longer behold your face, father Paul." Falling on the land at his feet, he lamented considerably.

[12](10) But Paul said to him, "And to me, on this very night the Lord approached, saying, 'Do not force Barnabas not to travel to Cyprus, for it has been prepared for him to enlighten many there. But you also, in the grace given to you, travel to Jerusalem to worship in the holy place. There indeed it will be shown to you where the spectacle has been prepared for you.'"

[13]So we bid each other farewell, and Barnabas welcomed me. (11) Having come down to Laodicea,[f] we requested to travel through to Cyprus.[g]

Travel to Cyprus: The Cilician Coast

6 [1]Having found a ship departing to Cyprus, we boarded. As we sailed, the wind was found to be contrary. But we entered Corasium.[h] When we deboarded, by

Marginal references:
- Acts 13:5, 13; Gal 5:2–4
- Acts 20:36; 21:5
- Acts 13:1–3
- Acts 21:16–23:31
- Acts 27:2–4

---

a. BMQV read "we arrived." The same verb is used also in Acts 16:1. The author-editor of this part of *Acts Barn.* may know and displace the story of Timothy's circumcision, attributing it to John Mark earlier (see Acts 16:2).

b. P omits the preceding rationale: "on account of . . ."; M omits only "to assist them." Concerning the "vow," in Acts the term *euchē* is used exclusively for a dedication similar to the Nazirite vow (Acts 18:18; 21:23), apparently in relation to an early Christian ideology of sacred time.

c. M omits 5:9; the remaining Σ manuscripts (BQUV) differ from P in Paul's response: "Travel in the grace of God, and we in the Holy Spirit."

d. Based partly on the Latin omission of 5:4–10, it is uncertain whether Paul or Barnabas speaks the first sentence of this reciprocal dialogue (5:10), but Barnabas certainly speaks thereafter (5:11).

e. End of Latin omission from 5:4–10.

f. Probably understood as Laodicea (ad Mare) in Syria. Extant in all manuscripts, the reference may indicate a distinct source or editorial "relocation" to Syrian Antioch.

g. Beginning of Latin omission from *Acts Barn.* 6:1–2.

h. "Corasium" may refer to Corycus (east of the next site, Old Isauria: so Riddle) or to Coracesium (at the far west of Cilicia: so Lipsius, Norelli).

the beach there was a stream.[a] We revived ourselves there, while showing ourselves to no one on account of not knowing anyone, since Barnabas was separated from Paul.

[2]After taking up from Corasium, we came into Old Isauria; and from there we came to a certain island called Pityusa.[b] When a winter storm occurred, we made preparations there[c] for three days. A certain pious man harbored us by the name of Euphemus,[d] for whom—with his whole household—Barnabas instructed many things for the faith. (12) From there we sailed by the Aconesiae.[e]

[3]We entered the city Anemurium; and when we had entered it, we acquired two Greeks.[f] When they came to us, they asked where we are from and who we are. Barnabas said to them, "If you wish to know where we are from and who we are, cast away the clothing that you have, and I will cover you with clothing that is never dirtied. There is not dirt in it; it is always white." [4]Entertained by the phrase, they asked us, "What outfit is going to give that?" Barnabas said to them, "If you confess your sins and align with our Lord Jesus Christ,[g] you obtain that outfit, which is imperishable forever." [5](13) Prodded by the Holy Spirit, they fell to his feet, exhorting and saying, "We value you, Father. Give us that outfit,[h] for we put our faith in the one whom you proclaim—the living and true God."

[6]After leading them down into the stream, (Barnabas) baptized them in the name of the Father, and of the Son, and of the Holy Spirit;[i] and they knew themselves,[j] since they were outfitted with power and sacred uniform.[k] Having seized one uniform from me, (Barnabas) outfitted one; and from his own uniform, he outfitted the other. They contributed goods to him, and straightaway Barnabas gave them to the poor.[l] [7]From these things the sailors also were able to profit much.

Matt 28:19; *Did.* 7.1

Acts 4:37; Gal 2:10

[8](14) When they came down onto the beach, (Barnabas) was speaking to them the word of God, blessing them.[m] We bid them farewell, and we went up on the ship. One among them, who is surnamed Stephen,[n] was wishing to accompany us, and Barnabas did not permit him.[o]

---

a. On "beach" and "stream," compare *Acts Barn.* 6:1, 8. Note the many omissions and variants between these references: 6:2–8 may have been added later, among other reasons to highlight particular understanding(s) of baptism.

b. Dana Island, northeast of Aphrodisias.

c. For "made preparations there," BQUV read "cast down" and M "remained."

d. Σ omits the preceding adjective "pious" (see 5:2; cf. 2:4) and the subsequent relative clause ("for whom . . . the faith").

e. End of Latin omission from 6:1–2.

f. Compare the acquisition of Timon and Ariston in Cyprus's Crommyacita (7:1).

g. The verbs are subjunctive, except for indicatives of "confess" in BMQU and "align" in MUV. As indicated by further variants below, Σ had a distinctive ideology of "conversion."

h. Σ ends the sentence here, so that God is addressed as "Father" rather than Barnabas.

i. The baptismal formulae in 6:6 and 10:2 are anarthrous except in Σ.

j. An indicative declaration of the Delphic maxim "know thyself."

k. All Σ manuscripts omit "power and"; BMQV also add an article ("the holy outfit").

l. Beginning of Latin omission from 6:7–8. Grammatical infelicities are abundant in this section of the Greek.

m. Σ emphasizes the group of travelers: "*we* greeted [them] and *we* said [to them] . . . and *we* blessed them." Not surprisingly, Σ therefore omits the following sentence ("We bid . . . ship.").

n. Σ states that the one "from among them" was "named" Stephen.

o. End of Latin omission from 6:7–8.

Cyprus

7 [1]After we had crossed over, we docked in Cyprus during the night. Having come to the so-called Crommyacita,[a] we acquired Timon[b] and Ariston[c] the temple-slaves, with whom we also were hosted. (15) But Timon was detained by a strong fever. Having laid our hands upon him, straightaway we removed his fever, calling on the name of the Lord Jesus.[d]

[2]Barnabas had taken lessons from Matthew—a scroll of God's language, and a writing of wonders and instructions.[e] This writing Barnabas would place upon the weak at the site opposing us, and straightaway it would bring about healing of the conditions. [3](16) But when we were in Lapithus and idol-mania was concluding in the theater, they did not permit us to enter into the city. Rather, at the gate we revived a little. [4]After his rising up out of the disease, Timon came with us.

[5]After coming out from Lapithus, we traveled through the mountains, and we came into the city[f] of Lampadistus, where Timon also had property. Having found that Heracleius[g] also was there with him, we were hosted by him.

[6](17) Heracleius was the one from Tamasus who had come to oversee his properties. Looking at him, Barnabas recognized him, having recently happened into him at the city of Citium with Paul.[h] To him also the Holy Spirit was given upon baptism, and he[i] renamed him "Heracleides." Having elected him as overseer for Cyprus and having confirmed the church in Tamasus,[j] we left him behind in a settlement of the brothers sojourning there.[k]

[7](18) But after we went through the mountain named "Snowy,"[l] we arrived in Old Paphos.[m] There we acquired Rhodon, a certain temple-slave who, once he

---

a. *Krommiou akris,* "peak of Krommion" (Norelli); Cape Krommyon is the northernmost point of central Cyprus, within the district of the city Lapithus.

b. Timon's healing is mentioned twice (7:1 and 7:4). The intervening verses may be later insertions (7:2–3; cp. 8:1, 5).

c. Ariston's martyrdom was celebrated in the West on 22 February. In *Acts Barn.* he is remembered as a former "temple-slave" (probably of Aphrodite), but sometimes he is numbered among the "72" and identified with an Aristion mentioned by Papias (Eusebius, *Hist. eccl.* 3.39.4). Temples to Aphrodite are attested on Cyprus at Lapithus, (Cyprian) Mt. Olympus, Old Paphos, Amathus, and Pidalion (Cape Greco).

d. P reads *oma* ("place") rather than *onoma* ("name"). Σ omits "Lord"; M substitutes "Christ" for "Jesus"; Q adds "Christ."

e. P calls it a "book" (*biblion* rather than *biblos*) and "writings" (plural); rather than "wonders and teachings," Σ labels its contents as "deeds" (*poiēmata*).

f. Σ has "village." The location is difficult to determine.

g. Σ has "Hercleon."

h. Rather than *Kitieōn,* P reads *Kētiaiōn.* Reference to Citium is unexpected, as it is not narrated earlier in *Acts Barn.* nor in Acts. Later, the travelers are not welcomed at Citium (7:16).

i. It is not clear whether it was Barnabas or Paul who baptized and renamed him.

j. After adding that the church was "in a cavern" in Tamasus, Σ ends the sentence differently: "and for the brothers who were instructed there with him, we provided to him the word of God." For appointing overseers (*presbyteroi*) and confirming a church, compare Acts 15:32; 19:1–7; 20:17–38; *Pass. Mark* 7.

k. See 7:17, where Heracleides rejoins the other travelers.

l. The Troodos mountains, such as Cyprian Mt. Olympus that housed a temple to Aphrodite (see n. c above), are especially snowy during the winter months. "Snowy" is also an epithet for Greek Olympus.

m. Probably modern Kouklia, which is immediately west of the Orites and Randi Forests and

also believed, accompanied us. [8]But we encountered a certain Judean with the name "Bar-Jesus"[a] who was coming away from Paphos. He is the one who indicated that Barnabas was recently with Paul. This one[b] did not permit us to enter into Paphos.[c] Rather, turning back, we went toward Curium.[d]

Acts 13:6–12

[9](19) We found that a race was being finished—a certain blood-polluted race on the road[e] near the city. There a multitude of females and males, both naked, were finishing the race. Much cheating and waywardness occurred in that place.[f] [10]Turning around, Barnabas rebuked this place.[g] The western part fell, so that many became wounded;[h] and many from among them also died. But those who remained fled to the temple of Apollo.[i] [11]That temple is nearby in the (wood) named Sacred.[j]

Acts Paul 5; *Acts Titus* 3, 7, 11; *Acts John* 37–47; *Acts Corn.* 2:11–12

[12]When we came close to Curium,[k] a great multitude of the Judeans who were there, having been subjected by Bar-Jesus, stood outside the city, and they did not permit us to enter into the city. Rather, under an olive tree that is[l] near the city, we made preparations for the day,[m] and we revived there.

[13](20) On the following day we entered a certain village where Aristoclianus[n] resided. This is the one who, when leprous, was purified in Antioch; whom Paul—and Barnabas—also sealed to be an overseer;[o] and whom they sent forth to his village in Cyprus on account of there being many Greeks

---

approximately 12 km southeast of modern Paphos. Kouklia housed the most famous temple of Aphrodite (see p. 332 n. c), for whom Rhodon must have been a temple-slave.

a. Bar-Jesus is introduced without the Lukan descriptors "magician" or "false prophet" (Acts 13:6), and its phrasing *(onomati Bariēsou)* is most similar to the forms extant in P45 *(onomati Bariēsous)* and D *(onomati kaloumenon Bariēsouan)*. For Bar-Jesus in *Acts Barn.*, see 7:8, 12, 14; 8:2 (twice in Σ).

b. Syntactically, is it Paul, Barnabas, or Bar-Jesus who does not permit entry to Paphos? Harmonization with Acts would favor the latter.

c. P has "did not want us to enter"; Σ "did not permit us in/to Paphos."

d. Immediately west of Curium *(Kourion)*, along modern highway B6, is the Sanctuary of Apollo Hylates, often etymologized as "woody." The temple was reconstructed in the first century CE (i.e., during the historicalized setting of *Acts Barn.*), and it was destroyed by an earthquake in the mid–360s. Nearby are also a large theater and Nymphaeum.

e. Σ has "a certain mountain" *(orei rather than odōi)*.

f. Young ("Cypriote Aphrodite Cult") argues that the site in question was on the hill of Lingrin tou Dhigeni, approximately 6 km east of Old Paphos. Called "Rantidi" after the forest in which it is located, the site has a temple that was apparently dedicated to the local consort of Aphrodite, known variously as Adonis or Apollo. Based on its location, Rantidi may have been part of a sacred processional between Old Paphos and Curium dedicated to ancient fertility rites (Strabo, *Geog.* 14.6.3).

g. Latin specifies *templum*.

h. Σ has "and he made many wounded."

i. Beginning of Latin omission from 7:11–17.

j. Σ has "in the temple that is Apollo's," omitting reference to the sacred wood.

k. P has "the temple."

l. Σ adds "on the mountain."

m. Σ has "the evening" *(hespera)* rather than "the day" *(hēmera)*.

n. Aristoclianus has been related to Aristocles of Tamasus, whose martyrdom (ca. 303–305 CE) is celebrated 23 June.

o. The verb is singular and the subject complex, probably indicating the later addition of Barnabas; BQUV emend with a plural. The story referenced is not included in *Acts Barn.*, but note John "Mark's" cooperation with the Judeans and Greeks at Antioch (*Acts Barn.* 6).

there. We were hosted in the cavern with him in the mountain, and there we remained one day.

[14]From there we entered Amathus.[a] A great multitude of Greeks, both indecent females and libation-offering males, were in the temple[b] on the mountain. In anticipation[c] Bar-Jesus had prepared the populace of the Judeans there also, and they did not permit us to enter into the city, [15]except for a woman—a certain widow of eighty years—who was outside the city.[d] She, not worshipping idols but harboring us,[e] received us into her house for a time. When we came out, we shook out[f] the dust from our feet opposite that temple where the libation of the priests[g] occurred.

[16](21) After departing from there, we went through the deserted places. Timon was also following with us. When we entered Citium, a mighty uproar also occurred there in their hippodrome.[h] Once we learned, we departed from the city, shaking out the dust from our feet altogether, for no one received us—except at the gate (where) we were revived for a time near the aqueduct.

Acts 17:16 [17](22) After we embarked on a ship from Citium, we went on to Salamis; and we disembarked on the so-called "islands,"[i] where the place was idol-ridden, for it was there also that festivals and libations occurred. There, having found Heracleides again, we taught him how to proclaim the gospel of God[j] and to station churches and (establish) officials in them.[k]

The martyrdom and translation of Barnabas

Acts 13:5 **8** [1]But when we entered into Salamis, we arrived at the nearby synagogue of the Chosen Scroll. There, after we entered and he rolled it out, Barnabas began to teach the Judeans the Gospel that was taken from Matthew, the co-worker.[l]

[2](23) But when Bar-Jesus arrived after two days—after the instruction of not a few Judeans[m]—he[n] angrily gathered the entire multitude of the Judeans.

---

a. Amathus, named after the mother of Adonis, had temples to Aphrodite (and Adonis) and to Hera; on Cyprian temples to Aphrodite, see p. 332 n. c.

b. P omits "in the temple."

c. The presence of Cypriots at the mountain's temple is an absence that allows Bar-Jesus and the Judeans (as "atheists") to guard the city's gates.

d. Σ omits "who was outside the city."

e. Σ omits "us."

f. Σ has "Barnabas shook out," specifying Barnabas and reconjugating the verb for the singular. Oddly, reference to "our feet" (plural) remains.

g. Σ has "of the blood-pollutions" (cf. 7:9).

h. Σ has "track" (*dromos* rather than *hippodromos*); P, in 7:16 and 8:3, uses *hippodromion* ("of the horserace") substantively, perhaps indicating that the structure was not a hippodrome proper.

i. Probably the islands beside modern Famagusta, but it is Cape Greco (Pidalion) that houses the final known temple of Aphrodite on Cyprus (see p. 332 n. c).

j. Σ has "of Christ."

k. End of Latin omission from 7:11–17.

l. Σ omits "the co-worker." For another reference to "lessons from Matthew," see 7:2.

m. Σ uses a passive infinitive and specifies the agent: "after not a few Judeans had been instructed by Barnabas."

n. Σ specifies "Bar-Jesus."

Having detained Barnabas, they wanted to hand him over[a] to Hypatius the governor[b] of Salamis. So they bound him for transfer to the governor. [3]But when they learned that a pious Jebusite—a relative of Nero—had arrived in Cyprus, the Judeans seized Barnabas during the night and bound him. With a rope over his neck, they dragged him[c] from the synagogue to the hippodrome[d] and passed outside of the gate. After encircling him, they burned him up with fire.[e]

[4]Therefore, even his bones became dust. Straightaway, on the same night, after taking his dust, they cast it in linen and in lead. Having secured themselves,[f] they were looking to hurl him down into the sea.

[5](24) But it was I[g] who found an opportunity during the night and, with Timon and Rhodon, was able to carry him away. We entered a certain place. Having discovered a cavern, we led him down there, where the populace of the Jebusites formerly settled. After finding a place that was hidden, we put him away in it—with the lessons that had been received from Matthew. It was the fourth hour during the second night from the Sabbath.[h]

[6](25) As we hid in the place, the Judeans made no small investigation for us. After nearly finding us, they chased after us to the village of Ledrai.[i] Having found a cavern[j] near the village there, we took refuge in it, and in this way we escaped from them.[k] We hid ourselves in the cave for three days. When the Judeans withdrew, we departed and arrived at the place during the night.[l]

---

a. Σ has "they wanted to detain Barnabas and to hand him over."

b. "Hypatius" (Gr. *hypatos*) is probably a name rather than a duplication of the title governor (*hēgemōn*). The Latin recensions read only *consul* and, rather than including subsequent reference to a "pious" Jebusite, add a relative clause explaining that the consul's name is "Eusebius." For the alleged "anti-Hypatius" (*anthypatos*, "proconsul") of Cyprus, see the story of Sergius Paulus (*Sergios Paulos*) in Paphos during the "first Cyprus mission" (Acts 13:4–12).

c. Callahan ("Acts of Mark," 76–77) has argued that the roping and dragging of John Mark at "Boukolou" (*Pass. Mark* 9 and 11) represents the practice of a Hellenized Egyptian cult: John Mark, like Serapis in the form of an Apis bull, was ceremonially led to his burial west of Memphis. Czachesz (*Commission Narratives*, 182–83) has argued that the martyrdom of Barnabas was based on the martyrdom of Mark. But in *Pass. Mark*, John Mark is dragged to death before he is burned; and his remains are miraculously preserved (*Pass. Mark* 12). Also, the burial in *Pass. Mark* 14 occurs during the reign of Gaius Caligula (37–41 CE).

d. Or "upon the horse-racing carriage."

e. Latin *n* omits 8:4–10:2 and substitutes a summary (*sicque beato fine Christi testis perrexit ad dominum*, "And so, with a blessed end, Christ's witness was guided to the Lord"), after which occurs its final doxology (10:3).

f. The protection may be from corpse impurity, spirit haunting, and/or resurrection.

g. Σ adds "John, who was renamed Mark"; Latin *c* adds "John who am also Mark."

h. Σ and Latin *c* provide the date of 11 June on a Roman calendar and 17 Pauni on a North African calendar.

i. Ledrai is in central Cyprus, near modern Nicosia. Particularly if Limnes (9:1) is near modern Paralimni (see p. 336 n. a), the travelers would have trodden most of the inhabitable parts of Cyprus.

j. Σ adds "on the mountain."

k. MU add "they stoned us" (cf. Acts 14:19–20).

l. Probably the burial site mentioned in 8:5.

Travel to Alexandria

9 ¹Adding Ariston and Rhodon, we entered the village of Limnes.ᵃ (26) Upon coming to the beach, we discovered an Egyptian ship; ²and after going up in it, we deboarded in Alexandria.ᵇ

Acts 28:11

Alexandria

10 ¹It was there that I remained, teaching the brothers who cameᶜ the word of the Lord, enlightening them, and announcing whatever I had been taught by the apostles of Christ—²they who had baptized me into the name of the Father and of the Son, and of the Holy Spirit,ᵈ and had renamed me "Mark" in the water of baptism. In baptism I hope to transfer many into the glory of Godᵉ through his grace,ᶠ ³sinceᵍ to him honor—and eternal glory—is fitting.ʰ Amen.

Matt 28:19; *Did.* 7.1

---

a. The first sentence of 9:1, which is omitted in P, duplicates 8:5's reference to Rhodon's inclusion. Czachesz (*Commission Narratives*, 187, 194) argues that the mission of four former temple slaves, probably dedicated to Aphrodite, may be modeled on the late-fifth-century conversion of the *philoponoi*, a group of Hellenistic rhetoricians. The location of Limnes is unknown, but it may be near modern Paralimni.

b. On John Mark in Egyptian Alexandria, see Eusebius, *Hist. eccl.* 2.16.1; *Chron.* 45. For his allotment, see *Pass. Mark* 1–2.

c. Σ has "the brothers who sought refuge."

d. See p. 331 n. a.

e. BQUV has "the Lord"; M "Christ."

f. End of Latin omission from 8:4–10:2.

g. BMUV omit "since."

h. Σ has "To him (be) the glory forever"; MQV add "and ever."

The Acts of Cornelius the Centurion
Introduction and translation

by Tony Burke and Witold Witakowski

The *Acts of Cornelius the Centurion* (*Acts Corn.*; *BHG* 370yz, 371) narrates the exploits of Cornelius, the centurion of the Italian Cohort and god-fearer of Acts 10:1–11:18, beginning with a retelling of his conversion by Peter through his evangelizing activity in the city of Skepsis, his death and burial, and his veneration as a saint. The text is available in Greek and Ethiopic, with summaries in synaxaria in Greek, Ethiopic, and Coptic; it has never before been translated into a modern language.

Contents

The longer form of the text, from Greek and Ethiopic sources, begins with the story of Cornelius's conversion and baptism by Peter as told in Acts 10–11 (chap. 1), sometimes reproduced verbatim. The one notable difference is the insertion in the Greek text (1:7) of a digression on the symbolism of the threefold refusal of Peter to eat the food (1:6; cf. Acts 10:14–16). With the dispersion of the Jerusalem church after the death of Stephen (as in Acts 11:19), Cornelius journeys with the other apostles and then accompanies Peter and Timothy in particular (2:1). The three learn of Skepsis, "a city subjected to idols," and Cornelius is selected by lot to preach to the city. Skepsis, located in Mysia (westernmost Asia Minor), is ruled by Demetrius, a worshipper of Apollo and Zeus and a persecutor of Christians (2:2). Cornelius is brought before Demetrius for interrogation, which ends with the ruler demanding Cornelius sacrifice to the gods (2:2–9). Cornelius asks to see these gods, so he is brought into the shrine of Zeus (2:10). There Cornelius prays to God to destroy the idols; he exits the shrine and it collapses, trapping Demetrius's wife and son in the rubble, though no one at the time is aware of their fate (2:11–12). Cornelius is imprisoned for his "sorcery" (2:13–14). When Demetrius learns of his family's demise, he sends orders to dig out their bodies from the ruins (3:1–2). But a voice is heard from the rubble praising God and calling for Demetrius to beg Cornelius to free them from their tomb (3:3–4). After baptizing Demetrius (3:5–6), Cornelius comes to the ruins, prays, and the earth opens to free those trapped within (3:7–8). The onlookers become believers and Cornelius remains in the city to teach and to baptize (3:9).

In time, Cornelius reaches the end of his life (4:1–2) and his body is placed in the coffin that was reserved for Demetrius's wife. The coffin is placed near the destroyed shrine of Zeus; then a great bush springs up and covers the coffin from view (4:3–4). Cornelius's resting place is lost to memory until the time of a certain Silvanus, bishop of Troas. Visiting the area, the bishop has a dream in which Cornelius reveals to him the location of his coffin and commands Silvanus to build him a sanctuary at a place called Pandochium (5:1–2). The bishop leads his clergy to the bush where, with divine assistance, they uncover the coffin (5:4–5). In the meantime, Cornelius appears in a vision to a wealthy man named

Eugenius and commands him to use his resources to build the sanctuary and to place the coffin inside the altar (5:6–7). Once the building is completed, Silvanus is summoned and he and Eugenius lead the congregation in a procession to the sanctuary; the coffin follows the supplicants into the shrine "as if alive" (5:8–10) and comes to rest beside the altar where "it remains until now unmovable" (5:11).

Time passes again until Philostorgius becomes bishop of Skepsis. The bishop commissions a painter named Encratius to decorate the shrine with an image of Cornelius (6:1). Encratius is distressed as he does not know what Cornelius looked like; frustrated, he sends "irreverent voices toward the holy one" and falls from the ladder to his death (6:2). After another brief interjection from the story's narrator (6:3 in the Greek only), Cornelius appears and heals the painter, thus providing an opportunity for Encratius to see Cornelius's features and complete his task (6:3–5).

Acts Corn. exists also in a shorter form, which essentially tells the same story except for an epilogue in which the hand of Cornelius is transferred from Skepsis to Caesarea Palaestina. Pamphilus, the metropolitan of the city, appoints his secretary Julian to the task (7:1 of the epitome). At Skepsis, Cornelius reveals himself to the local bishop, convincing him to give Julian the relic (7:2). Julian also has a vision, in which soldiers from Skepsis arrive at Cornelius's home with the hand (7:3). After a ceremonial opening of the coffin (7:4–5), the bishop gives Julian the hand of Cornelius and Julian takes it, along with a copy of the image of Cornelius painted by Encratius, and deposits them in the house of Cornelius in Caesarea (7:6–7).

Manuscripts and Versions

Acts Corn. made its first appearance in scholarship in 1725 in the first February volume of the *Acta Sanctorum*, in accordance with the date of the saint's festival in the Western church (February 12). The text was published in Latin translation on the basis of an unnamed manuscript from Paris.[1] Presumably this is the same manuscript—Paris, Bibliothèque nationale de France, gr. 1489 (fol. 96v–105v; 11th cent.; =A)—that was used as the basis for the 1864 publication of the Greek text in Jacques Paul Migne's *Patrologia Graeca* (114:1293–1312); here the earlier Latin translation appears in the facing columns. The Paris manuscript is a copy of the collection of saints' lives made in the late tenth century by Symeon Magister the Logothete, called Metaphrastes ("the compiler"), who edited over 150 hagiographical texts and arranged them in a menologion ("month-set") according to the commemoration dates of the saints. Symeon tended to shorten his sources to focus on the final events of his subjects' lives; it is possible, therefore, that there once existed an earlier, longer form of *Acts Corn.* and that other manuscripts of Symeon's menologion contain pre-metaphrastic material.[2] In Symeon's collection, Cornelius is placed among the saints for September since, in the Greek Orthodox Church, Cornelius's feast falls on September 13, which tradition states is the day of his death.[3]

---

1. Bolland et al., *Acta Sanctorum*, 4:281–87.

2. Albert Ehrhard, *Überlieferung und Bestand der hagiographischen und homiletischen Literatur der griechischen Kirche von den Anfängen bis zum Ende des 16. Jahrhunderts* (TU 50–52; Leipzig: Hinrichs, 1937–1952), 1:453, 3.2:800–801 speculated that Symeon's source for *Acts Corn.* could be found in Athos, Pantokratoros 53, though Halkin ("Une passion inédite"; cf. idem, "Un abrégé inédit," 32) has shown him to be incorrect. However, Halkin believed that the epitome of Athos, Philotheou 8 is based on a pre-metaphrastic text.

3. However, the three most well-known ancient synaxaria (abbreviated menologia read in public wor-

Aside from other copies of Symeon's collection,[4] *Acts Corn.* is available in different forms in three other Greek manuscripts. François Halkin assigned the designation *BHG* 370y to Mount Athos, Pantokratoros 53, fol. 209v–215v (12th cent.), initially believing the manuscript to be a witness to a distinctive form of *Acts Corn.* Subsequent investigation determined that the text is identical to Paris gr. 1489 except that the first three chapters are replaced with a short introduction that reads:

> The marvellous Luke fittingly drew up the excellence and piety and the calling of the blessed Cornelius when, likely, he was breathed upon by the divine spirit. And we shall interweave his activity with (his) calling and his death.

Pantokratoros 53 is now designated as *BHG* 371b.[5] Halkin called the third manuscript—Paris, Bibliothèque nationale de France, Coislin 286, fol. 185r–186r (14th cent.; *BHG* 371e; = C)—an "epitome," but more correctly it is an excerpt of the text, covering only chapters 1–4:2 though with many omissions. Coislin 286 remains unpublished. The fourth manuscript—Mount Athos, Philotheou 8, fol. 57–59 (11th cent.; *BHG* 370z), published by Halkin in 1964—is rightly considered an epitome: it summarizes the entire metaphrastic text, though perhaps from a pre-metaphrastic exemplar, plus it contains the epilogue recounting the exhumation of Cornelius's hand.[6] Noteworthy also in this manuscript is that Cornelius's feast day is given as June 9. Halkin considers the epitome to be particularly important as its text approaches that of a manuscript of the Jerusalem synaxary; unfortunately, he does not indicate the points of similarity.[7]

Acts Corn. is available also in Ethiopic, extant in a unique manuscript—EMML 1824, fol. 64r–75v—containing acts of saints and martyrs. It dates from the early fifteenth century,[8] and can thus be regarded as quite an old manuscript in the Ethiopian context. A colophon appended to the text reveals that the Ethiopic text was translated from Arabic. The name of the translator is not provided, but the person who commissioned the translation is named 'Aqabe Säʻat (lit. "the guardian of hours")[9] Yosef, probably the same Yosef who was archimandrite of the famous Däbrä Hayq 'Estifanos monastery, in the province of Wällo, north of Addis Ababa. This identification seems to be corroborated by the fact that the manuscript belongs to that monastery.[10] Yosef was archimandrite of Däbrä Hayq at the beginning of the fifteenth century (after 1403);[11] thus, the manuscript must have been a very early copy of the autograph of the translator. The Ethiopic text follows very closely the metaphrastic version of Paris gr. 1489, though with some significant departures: the omission of 1:3–7; 3:2; and the narrator's interjection at 6:4; lengthy additions at

---

ship) assign the feast to October 20, the same date adopted by the Ethiopic Church. See Halkin, "Un abrégé inédit," 32 n. 6.

4. Hippolyte Delehaye, "Synopsis metaphrastica," in *Biblioteca hagiographica graeca* (ed. Société des Bollandistes; Brussels: Société des Bollandistes, 1909), 269–92 at 275–77 lists thirty-eight Metaphrastes MSS for September.

5. See Halkin, "Une passion inédite."

6. Published by Halkin, "Un abrégé inédit."

7. Halkin, "Un abrégé inédit," 33.

8. Haile and Macomber, *Catalogue of Ethiopian Manuscripts,* 267.

9. The title of the high-ranking archimandrites of certain monasteries in Ethiopia, the most famous being Däbrä Hayq 'Estifanos, Wällo.

10. Haile and Macomber, *Catalogue of Ethiopian Manuscripts,* 267 n. 11.

11. Haile and Macomber, *Catalogue of Ethiopian Manuscripts,* 270.

4:1 and 5:8; the change of Cornelius's evangelizing activity from Skepsis to Ephesus, and from Stadium to Midan, Egypt (see 3:9); and the statement at the end of the text that the saint died October 20, which is his feast day in the Ethiopic church.[12]

No Arabic version of *Acts Corn.* is currently available, but that it existed is practically certain. First, there is nothing to suggest the Ethiopic text was translated from Greek. Given the time of composition of *Acts Corn.* (as late as the 9th/10th centuries), one has to accept that it was translated from Greek into Arabic and then into Ethiopic (Ge'ez), because in the era in question, direct translations from Greek were no longer made. Moreover, in the text there are mistakes or misreadings in rendering certain Greek names, apparently unknown to the translator, and which can best be understood on the basis of an Arabic *Vorlage* (see particularly the notes to 1:1 and 5:8). The actual copy from which the translator worked was most probably prepared in Egypt in a Syrian monastic context—the dates specified in the colophon include the names of months that, although misspelled, are clearly Syriac *(Elul, Teshrin).*

Traditions about Cornelius can be found also in various synaxaria. These briefer overviews of saints' lives, compiled in the ninth and tenth centuries, give few details from the larger story, though they reveal regional variations in practice for the veneration of the saint. However, the version in use today by the Greek Orthodox Church, influenced by efforts to enhance the biographies using the work of the Bollandists, is quite extensive, with a text approximating the length of the epitome but finishing before the tales of Cornelius's post-mortem appearances.[13] In addition, Demetrius and his family are given their own feast day (September 11) and it is revealed that they died of starvation, imprisoned by pagans. Cornelius is of less importance in the Latin church; the Western lives of the Saints contain only what is found in the canonical Acts, except for the detail that Cornelius went on to become bishop of Caesarea.[14] The Upper Egypt Coptic Synaxarium in use today[15] offers a summary of Cornelius's conversion from Acts and then adds that Cornelius was appointed by Peter as bishop of Caesarea, where he converted Demetrius the governor. His feast day is 23 Hatur (November 19). The earlier edition of the Coptic Synaxarium translated by Ferdinand Wüstenfeld and representing the Lower Egypt recension, states that Cornelius was bishop of Alexandria.[16] The Ethiopic Synaxarium is similar, with Cornelius again appointed bishop of Alexandria, though adding also the detail that he is numbered among the seventy disciples (as in the Ethiopic *Acts Corn.*; see the note to 1:1), and that his feast day is 10 Maskaram (September 20).[17]

---

12. Note, however, that the incipit (see the note to 1:1) gives the feast day as 23 Hatur (November 19) as in the Coptic Synaxarium.

13. Makarios of Simonos Petra, *The Synaxarion: The Lives of the Saints of the Orthodox Church* (7 vols.; trans. Christopher Hookway; Ormylia, Greece: Holy Convent of the Annunciation of Our Lady, 1998), 1:94–96. This particular edition departs from others by providing some details about the translation of Cornelius's relics: "Close by his tomb a plant sprang up that healed every sickness. When his relics were translated to the church built nearby in his honour, the shrine moved of its own accord to a position near the altar" (96).

14. See Halkin, "Un abrégé inédit," 31.

15. The edition appealed to here is published by the St. George Coptic Orthodox Church in Chicago and widely available in an online edition (e.g., https://oca.org/saints/lives/2011/09/13/102594-hieromartyr -cornelius-the-centurion).

16. Ferdinand Wüstenfeld, *Synaxarium das ist heiligen-kalender der Coptischen Christen* (2 vols.; Gotha: Friedrich Andreas Perthes, 1879), 1:134.

17. Ernest A. W. Budge, *The Book of the Saints of the Ethiopian Church: A Translation of the Ethiopic*

Literary Context

The Roman centurion Cornelius is known from Acts 10:1–11:18. His name, Latin for "of the horn," had been quite popular in the Roman Empire ever since the *dictator* Sulla (d. 78 BCE), himself of the Cornelii family, had manumitted around 10,000 slaves, all of whom took this name as *gentilicium*. From Acts, we learn that he was a centurion of a cohort belonging to the Italic Regiment (*speira Italikē*, Acts 10:1), which apparently in the late 30s CE was stationed at Caesarea Sebaste on the Mediterranean coast. However, this information is not completely trustworthy, or is, rather, anachronistic: it was probably projected into the apostolic period from a later period, as the presence of Roman troops at this place before the death of Herod Agrippa (44 CE) is rather unlikely.[18]

Cornelius seems to have belonged to the so-called *phoboumenoi ton theon,* or "god-fearing" people who obeyed the Decalogue commandments and sympathized with Judaism, without being circumcised or formally converted. In Acts, he is presented as a pious man who used to pray and give alms to the poor. Acts recounts that Cornelius was told in a vision by an angel to go to Joppa and contact Peter, who followed Cornelius back to Caesarea and baptized him and his family. Cornelius was thus the first polytheist (or "pagan") accepted by Peter directly into the hitherto purely Jewish-Christian community—that is, without becoming a Jew in advance, a procedure that was not uncontroversial. This acceptance had enormous importance as it opened the way for gentiles to join the church. Subsequently, gentile converts grew in number, a process that over time led to the marginalization of the Jewish-Christian communities within the Christian church. By the fourth century the various Jewish-Christian groups had come to be regarded as not only anomalies, but also as outright heretics (e.g., in the *Panarion* by Epiphanius of Cyprus, d. 403).

It may come as a surprise that outside the narrative of Acts, the figure who opened the way for a gentile-based Christian community was not the subject of more apocryphal stories than the one that is translated here. Outside of *Acts Corn.*, the only other appearance of Cornelius in an apocryphal text comes in the *Pseudo-Clementine Romance*. In one episode attested in both the *Homilies* and the *Recognitions* (*Hom.* 20.13//*Rec.* 10.54–55), a follower of Peter comes from Antioch to report on Simon Magus's activities. He mentions that Cornelius had arrived in the city, sent by Caesar on public business. The Christians there asked him to do something about Simon. Cornelius told them to pretend to be sympathetic to Simon and warn him that the centurion has orders to chase out sorcerers. They did so and Simon fled the city. There is one other reference to Cornelius in the fourth-century *Apostolic Constitutions* 7.46.3 (PG 1:1049). It states that Cornelius was the second bishop of Caesarea Palaestina after Zacchaeus; but neither Eusebius, a bishop of the same city, nor Origen, who had many contacts with it, confirm this information.[19] Nevertheless, Cornelius's association with Caesarea is reflected also in the story of the removal of the saint's hand to the house of Cornelius in Caesarea (epitome chap. 7); this house had become consecrated as a church by the time of Jerome (*Epist.* 108.8). To be sure, in a later period Cornelius was remembered in the liturgy, since each of the Catholic, Orthodox, Coptic, and the Ethiopian churches has feasts devoted to him, albeit on different days. It

---

Synaxarium: Made from the Manuscripts Oriental 660 and 661 in the British Museum (4 vols.; Cambridge: Cambridge University Press, 1928), 1:157–58.

18. Hans-Udo Rosenbaum, "Kornelios," in *Biographisch-Bibliographisches Kirchenlexikon* (33 vols.; ed. Friedrich Wilhelm Bautz and Traugott Bautz; Hamm-Herzberg-Nordhausen: Bautz, 1975–2012), 4:517; see also William M. Ramsay, "Cornelius and the Italic Cohort," *Expositor* 5, no. 4 (1896): 194–201.

19. T. Garcia de Orbiso, "Cornelio il Centurione, santo," *Bibliotheca Sanctorum* 4 (1964): 189–92 at 190.

is perhaps due to the needs of having something to be read on the day of Cornelius's feast that we have a commemorative text in the first place. This purpose is expressly stated in the colophon of the Ethiopic text, but is also clear from the character of the Greek text.

The opening chapter of *Acts Corn.* features a retelling of Cornelius's story from Acts, though with some noteworthy differences. First, the text reveals that Cornelius's emissaries (two slaves and a devout soldier) were delayed on their voyage to fetch Peter because Peter cannot consider meeting Cornelius until he receives his fateful vision. There is concern that, "because those from the circumcision were discriminating against those who were not circumcised," Peter would "send back again those who were sent by Cornelius empty-handed on the grounds that they were uncircumcised—since it is unlawful for Peter to associate with or visit a gentile" (1:4). The second departure from Acts comes in *Acts Corn.* 1:7 (MS A only), where the author pauses for some theological reflection on the typological meaning of Peter's vision. This kind of interjection is more common in homiletic literature and thus suggests that MS A's lengthier telling of Cornelius's conversion might be the result of the incorporation of a separate homily on the vision of Joppa. The story continues in Acts with Peter's recap of his vision to the church in Jerusalem (Acts 11:1–18); after this, Cornelius is not heard of again in the canonical account. But in *Acts Corn.*, the centurion departs Jerusalem with other Christians scattered to Phoenicia, Cyprus, and Antioch by the persecution after the death of Stephen (Acts 11:19; *Acts Corn.* 2:1). Then Cornelius heads off with Peter and Timothy (an unlikely pairing), and upon learning of the Skepsaeans, they cast lots for who should evangelize the city. This event breaks the narrative sequence of Acts, in which the broadening of the Christian mission from Jews to gentiles proceeds incrementally, beginning with Peter's vision, and moving through the stories of the Hellenized Jewish Christians' mission in Antioch (Acts 11:20) before culminating in the second Jerusalem council. Peter's vision allows for gentile inclusion, but despite initial acceptance of this development (11:18), the church does not approve of full gentile inclusion (that is, without the requirement of circumcision) until later. Indeed, Acts 11:19 states that those scattered from Jerusalem "spoke to no one except Jews." *Acts Corn.*, however, eliminates this detail (see 2:1), thus allowing for Cornelius's mission to the idol worshippers of Skepsis.

Acts Corn. follows the convention, found in both apocryphal acts and lives of saints, of the protagonist's encounter with hostile gentiles, who try to get the saint to sacrifice to pagan gods. Often this encounter results in the protagonist's death, and such a martyrdom makes her or him appropriate for celebration as a saint. Though *Acts Corn.* bears the title of *martyrium*, Cornelius does not die in defense of the faith. Consequently, in this case the word *martyrium* should be interpreted as "testimony." *Acts Corn.* increases the importance of the conflict between Christianity and gentile paganism with its depiction of the antagonist Demetrius; it is likely no accident that the governor of the city shares a name with Demetrius of Skepsis, who lived around 205–130 BCE and wrote a book on the geography in the area as it is depicted in Homer's *Iliad* (the *Marshalling of the Trojans*).[20] Demetrius is also called a "philosopher" in *Acts Corn.* (2:2); so, Cornelius not only converts a gentile governor, but, in a way, a famous transmitter of Hellenic tradition.

The story of the fall of the shrine in Skepsis recalls aspects of the story of Daniel and

---

20. The text no longer survives but fragments are preserved mainly by Strabo and Athenaeus. The citations have been collected and edited most recently in Richard Gaede, *Demetrii Scepsii quae supersunt* (diss. Greifswald, 1880).

Bel, which is mentioned explicitly in *Acts Corn.* 2:11. First, the interrogation of Cornelius by Demetrius (2:5–9) is similar to the dialogue between Daniel and Cyrus the Persian. Cyrus asks him, "Why do you not worship Bel?" Daniel responds, "Because I do not revere idols made with hands, but the living God, who created heaven and earth and has dominion over all living creatures" (Bel 4–5). Then Daniel, like Cornelius, goes into a temple to demonstrate the ineffectiveness of the pagan god—in Daniel's case to prove that Bel is not really eating the food put out for him (Bel 10–21). The story is reminiscent also of the destruction of the Ephesian temple of Artemis in *Acts John* 37–47. In this tale, John goes to the temple and challenges Artemis to kill him; if Artemis fails, then John threatens he will call upon God to kill everyone. The people plead for mercy but, at John's prayer, half the temple falls down and kills the priest of Artemis, thus recalling the entombment of Evanthia and little Demetrius. Everyone present converts and they pull down the rest of the temple. Then the body of the priest is brought to John, who revives him and the priest becomes a believer. Cornelius's rescue of Demetrius's wife and son similarly leads to the conversion of the Skepsaeans.

Following the peaceful death of Cornelius, *Acts Corn.* focuses on the invention (from the Latin *inventio*, "discovery") of the centurion's relics and the saint's afterlife appearances and intercessions. The text strays at this point from the genre of apocryphal literature and moves into hagiography, though hagiographical texts featuring early Christian figures naturally blur the lines between the two categories. Similar combinations of apocryphal tales and relic invention are found in the *Revelation of Stephen*, the *Discovery of John the Baptist's Head*, the *Life of John the Baptist* by Serapion, and others. Many themes in *Acts Corn.* are common in late antique apocrypha, with their emphasis on the liturgy, including the apostolic foundation of a church through the destruction of a temple; the narration of a liturgical procession; the miraculous appearance of a holy object (the bush) with its associated miracles; and the painting of Cornelius's icon by Encratius.[21]

Date and Provenance

There is no evidence for the existence of *Acts Corn.* before the late tenth century; it is assumed that Symeon Metaphrastes drew upon a source of some kind for his account, but it may not date much earlier than his day.[22] The text's references to certain fourth-/fifth-century ecclesiastical figures may help to narrow that date further. Silvanus, the bishop who discovers Cornelius's resting place (5:1–2), is likely the bishop of Philippopolis (modern-day Plovdiv in Bulgaria), who was later ordained bishop of Troas, in northeast Asia Minor (near Skepsis), by Atticus, archbishop of Constantinople from 406 to 425 (Socrates Scholasticus, *Eccl. hist.* 7.37). Little is known about subsequent bishops in Troas. The Athanasius mentioned in *Acts Corn.* 6:1 may be the same as a bishop of Skepsis mentioned at the Council of Ephesus in 431, though here he is transferred to Troas, thus allowing Philostorgius to take the seat.[23] A bishop Philostorgius of Skepsis was absent, but mentioned, at the Council of Chalcedon in 451;[24] at this time Pionius was bishop of Troas.

---

21. See Paul C. Dilley, "Christian Icon Practice in Apocryphal Literature: Consecration and the Conversion of Synagogues into Churches," *JRA* 23 (2010): 285–302 esp. 290–93.

22. Halkin, 'Un abrégé inédit," 31.

23. See the notes in PG 114:1309–10.

24. Diogenes, bishop of the metropolis of Cyzicus, signed session 16 on the behalf of several absent bishops, including Philostorgius. See Richard Price and Michael Gaddis, trans., *Acts of the Council of Chalcedon* (4 vols.; Liverpool: Liverpool University Press, 2005), 3:84. Note, however, session six, where

The final chapter of the epitome mentions a few other historical figures. Pamphilus, the metropolitan of Caesarea (see 7:1), is not known from the lists of bishops, but it is possible that this figure is meant to recall the late-third-century (d. 309) friend and teacher of Eusebius of Caesarea (see *Eccl. hist.* 7.32.25) and founder of the library at Caesarea Palaestina used by Jerome. Nothing is known of Pamphilus's "secretary" Julian of Constantinople (7:1) nor John of Mitylene (7:2). The story of Cornelius's hand, clearly a separate tradition grafted on to the *Acts Corn.* epitome, contradicts the ecclesiastical history of the remainder of the text—for if Silvanus, who found Cornelius's forgotten coffin, became bishop of Troas sometime in the reign of Atticus, then Pamphilus could not have been involved in the retrieval of the hand. Such lack of precision in detail about the lives and careers of the historical figures in *Acts Corn.* suggests a time of composition later than the fourth-century events it narrates.

Translation

Two texts are offered here. The first is a translation of *Acts Corn.* by Tony Burke (with assistance from John Horman) from Paris, Bibliothèque nationale de France, gr. 1489 (A) published by Migne, with the substantial errors in Migne's edition corrected from consultation of the manuscript. Readings from the excerpt (Paris, Bibliothèque nationale de France, Coislin 286 = C) and the Ethiopic, from a translation by Witold Witakowski, are provided in the notes. New chapter and verse divisions have been introduced. The second text is a translation by Tony Burke (again, with assistance from John Horman) of Halkin's edition of the epitome from Mount Athos, Philotheou 8. Halkin's chapter divisions have been retained, but the verse divisions are new.

Bibliography

Bolland, Jean, et al., eds. *Acta Sanctorum, Februarius.* Vol. 1 (= *Acta Sanctorum* vol. 4). Antwerp: P. Jacobs, 1658; 3rd ed. Paris: V. Palmé, 1863. (First publication of the text in a Latin translation, pp. 281–87.)

Haile, Getatchew, and William F. Macomber. *A Catalogue of Ethiopian manuscripts microfilmed for the Ethiopian Manuscript Microfilm Library, Addis Ababa, and for the Hill Monastic Manuscript Library, Collegeville,* vol. V: *Project Numbers 1501–2000.* Collegeville, Minn.: The Library, 1981.

Halkin, François. "Un abrégé inédit de la vie ancienne et disparue de Corneille le Centurion." *Rivista di Studi Bizantini e Neoellenici,* N.S. 1 (1964): 31–39. (*Editio princeps* of the *Acts Corn.* epitome.)

———. "Une passion inédite de Corneille le centurion? (*BHG3* 370y)." *AnBoll* 81 (1963): 28–30.

Migne, Jacques Paul. *Patrologiae cursus completus: Series graeca.* Vol. 114. Paris: Cerf, 1861. (*Editio princeps* of the text from Paris, gr. 1489 with Latin translation, cols. 1293–1312.)

Diogenes signs for "Eustorgius of Skepsis" (Price and Gaddis, *Acts,* 2:230). See further Halkin, "Un abrégé inédit," 37 n. 2.

The Acts and Consummation of the
Holy Cornelius the Centurion[a]

Cornelius is visited by an angel

1 [1]After the saving visitation of the Word upon the earth, and the voluntary cross and death for our sake, and the ascent into heaven, from where he came to build the fallen house of David, according to the prophets, there was the Amos 9:11 centurion Cornelius of the Italian Cohort, one of those who were seeking him and doing what was pleasing to him and abounding in good works—though not yet of his divine mercy, nor had he been deemed worthy of a call to him. This man was devout, and both he and his entire household were fearing God, and sharing from what he had with those in need. Furthermore, he prayed constantly to God.[b] Acts 10:1-2

[2]While he was living in Caesarea (as the divine Luke most clearly reports about him), an angel came at about three o'clock and said, "*Cornelius, your prayers and your alms have ascended as a memorial before God. Now, send men to Joppa and summon Simon, the one called Peter.* When he comes he will tell you Acts 10:3-5 words of life." After he had commanded these things, he was no longer visible.[c]

[3]So Cornelius at once called *two servants and one devout soldier from the ranks of those who served him. He revealed to them what he saw and sent (them) to Joppa.*[d] For that is where the angel said that Peter was staying and he revealed Acts 10:7-8 that he was lodging at the home of a certain Simon, a tanner. Thus Peter, going through every land and sea for proclamation, everywhere preached the truth to the saints living in Lydda—for truly he was appointed for a light to the gentiles and the salvation of all. After raising a certain Aeneas, who was bedridden for eight years, he crossed into Joppa, where he accomplished a miracle for Acts 9:32-35 Tabitha—who was named Dorcas—and then set himself down there with the tanner. Acts 9:36-43

---

a. MS M has the title: "Testimony of the holy and honoured great-witness Cornelius the centurion." The title used here is from C and is found also in many of the other metaphrastic MSS. It also better suits the genre of the text. The Ethiopic has: "A record of the life of the holy and pure Cornelius, one of the seventy disciples, the centurion who was in Caesarea, and of his death which took place on the 23rd of the month of Hatur (= Nov. 19), in the peace of God the Father; Amen."

b. Much of this introductory verse is lacking in Eth. It reads only: "The holy Cornelius was a centurion from Fartitalia." The peculiar "Fartitalia" seems to result from transmission through an intermediate (i.e., Arabic) translation.

c. This sentence is lacking in Eth. C breaks off here and resumes at 1:8.

d. Eth breaks off here and, like C, resumes at 1:8.

Peter's vision at Joppa and its meaning

Acts 10:9–16

⁴But God neglected him nothing about the things (promised to) the uninitiated Cornelius, nor, all the more, did he overlook the righteousness of Cornelius nor his prayers, but because those from the circumcision were discriminating against those who were not circumcised, lest (Peter) send back again those who were sent by Cornelius empty-handed on the grounds that they were uncircum-cised—since *it is unlawful* for Peter *to associate with or visit a gentile*—when they had already set off from Caesarea and were not far from Joppa, God demonstrated there the virtue and knowledge of Cornelius.

Acts 10:28

⁵There (Peter) went up on the roof to perform his noon prayers, and he had become in need of food and hungry. While the feasting for Peter was being prepared,ᵃ *he saw heaven had opened, and something like a large sheet coming (to) him, being lowered to the ground by its four corners.* The thing had on it both wild animals *and all kinds of four-footed creatures of the earth and reptiles and birds of the air.*

⁶And a voice seemed to go out from there to him, saying, "*Get up, Peter; kill and eat.*" And when he said to him, "*By no means, Lord,*" and continuing the reason, said, "*for, I never eat anything profane or unclean,*" the voice answered again, "*What God has made clean, you must not call profane.*" *After this happened three times, the thing was taken up again into heaven.*

⁷This, then, signified the conversion of Cornelius and those with him. As for Peter's need for food, this symbolized his goodwill concerning his godliness and zeal, and how he hungered for nothing so much, nor did he relent, as the enlightenment of the unbelievers and to bestow godliness and the proclamation of the Gospel at all times. The four-footed creatures and the reptiles and the birds were a sign of the multitude of those who were going to convert with Cornelius. The sending down of the object from heaven three times alludes to the threefold immersion in baptism. And these things cleansed by God indicate the righteousness and the compassion of Cornelius together with (his) entire house and how, then, they have all become holy to God.

The baptism of Cornelius

⁸Then, as Peter was pondering, able neither to understand nor interpret the vision, those sent by Cornelius came now to the doors. And at once the Spirit flew to him, revealed their arrival and commanded Peter to go to them making no discrimination. Then, when he came down to them, they reported to him everything Cornelius saw and heard from the angel.

Acts 10:17, 19

Acts 10:20–22

⁹The next day, they arrived in Caesarea.ᵇ When Cornelius advanced to meet (him), he fell at his feet. Peter raised him, saying, "I myself am only a mortal." Then he sowed the word of godliness in him and in the souls of those who had come with him, because he saw the mercy of the Spirit had flown to them

Acts 10:25–26

---

a. A garbled reading of Acts 10:10 perhaps due to a misreading of "trance" *(ekstasis)* as "feasting" *(estiasis)*.

b. Eth resumes, beginning the verse with: "When they arrived in Joppa, they met Peter and told him everything that had happened. He rose and went with them to Caesarea." Similarly, C reads: "Coming from Joppa to Caesarea, Simon Peter . . ."

and recommended baptism, to bring upon them the truth and perfect them by baptism.[a]

Acts 10:44–48

Cornelius is appointed to evangelize Skepsis

2 [1]After the dispersion of the apostles from Jerusalem after the grief over Stephen, Cornelius was present also,[b] and they went as far as Phoenicia and Cyprus and Antioch itself. He departed again with Peter and Timothy; and he had not been left behind <by> them in Ephesus.[c] Because, having learned of the Skepsaeans,[d] a city subjected to idols, they considered who might go to it. They let the matter go to lots. When the lot fell to Cornelius, immediately he went to the city.

Acts 11:19

[2]Serving as its governor was a certain Demetrius,[e] a philosopher and fearful in heathen matters,[f] who was breathing terror against the devout faith of the Christians and honoring other gods of the heathen, especially Apollo and Zeus.[g] When he learned of Cornelius's arrival, he sent for the man at once, and was enquiring why he had come, from where, and what was his business.

Cornelius is interrogated by Demetrius

[3]"I am the servant of the living God," he said. "And I was sent here to raise you up[h] from the deepest darkness of ignorance, to make you suitable for the light of the truth and to let the pure rays of enlightenment into your soul."[i]

[4]Understanding not even a little of these (words), (Demetrius) suddenly was filled with anger, and unexpectedly shouted madly and wildly, "I asked you some things; why do you answer me <about> other things? By all the gods, if you do not answer in good order and with speed, I will have no consideration for your old age, nor will I give concession to your years, nor respect your gray hair.[j] Now, speak: for what military service[k] and for what reason have you come?"

[5]And Cornelius (said), "If you wish to learn my rank, I am a centurion." At

---

a. The entire sentence in Eth reads: "Peter began to teach them. When he was teaching, the Holy Spirit descended upon them and Peter baptized them. The disciples rejoiced on hearing, 'Behold, pagans have accepted the word of God!'"

b. The parallel in Acts does not name any particular characters in this regard.

c. Based on Eth and the epitome (2:1), the meaning here seems to be that Cornelius accompanied them also to Ephesus.

d. Eth is corrupt here. It states instead that Cornelius remained in Ephesus because "the people of the city of Ephesus worshipped a graven idol." Thus all of the action with Cornelius in the text takes place in Ephesus, not Skepsis.

e. Another Demetrius is mentioned in Acts 19:23–41 and he is associated with Ephesus—he worked there as a silversmith making shrines to Artemis and opposed the mission of Paul in the city. A third Demetrius appears in 3 John 12; he may have been entrusted with delivering John's letter to its recipient Gaius.

f. Here and elsewhere, Greek (*hellēnikos*) is translated "heathen," reflecting Byzantine usage.

g. C lacks mention of Demetrius honoring these gods.

h. C: "to raise you up."

i. C lacks "and to let the pure rays of enlightenment into your soul." In Eth, Cornelius describes his mission as: "I am a servant of the living God, who can open the eyes of your heart that you may stop worshipping a worthless idol. Now, God has sent me to you that you may turn to the enlightenment of justice and venerate the Holy Trinity."

j. C finishes the verse here.

k. The text has "whom do you serve as a soldier?" but see Cornelius's reply in verse 5 below.

once he repeated more clearly the things he said before. "For learning," he said, "how both you and your wife and the whole province lying under you have fallen into great error, I came to break down the deception and guide you[a] to the way of truth and reconcile you to the only living God, who made heaven and earth[b] and by whom everything in them has been produced and by the will of whom they are led."[c]

Ps 146:6

[6]At these (words) Demetrius saw now (his) old age.[d] <He said>, "I have pity on account of your years, so I have allowed lengthy, empty greetings, but now I shall say little to you: approach the gods and make sacrifice." When asked again, "To which gods?" (Demetrius) said, "Who else but Zeus or Apollo? And if you refuse this, be certain that you will be handed over to harsh punishments and torture. There will be no god so powerful compared with these who will deliver you from my hands."

[7]And (Cornelius) said, "My God is able to preserve me not only by not suffering from evils nor from the abuse of more powerful men, but also (he is able) to destroy those you call gods and to topple their idols, break them into pieces and show them (to be) ashes and dust, (in order) to remove you of the empty hope in them and raise you up to himself through enlightenment."[e]

[8]Thus, when Cornelius answered, Demetrius said, "Now I have sworn by all the gods, that if you do not answer properly, if you do not offer sacrifice to the gods, harsh penalties and punishments will await you. Will you not believe me still?"

[9]Then straightaway the noble Cornelius nobly said, "Hear me correctly when I am speaking, O judge. I would never sacrifice to demons[f] and deaf and inanimate

Jer 10:11

idols. For it is written, '*Let gods who did not make sky and earth perish*,'[g] and again, '*You shall* prostrate yourself *before the Lord your God; him alone you shall wor-*

Deut 10:20

ship.' I came, therefore, that God may grant you repentance for the enlightenment of truth, and that at his wish, you may recover your senses from the snare of the devil.[h] But if it seems best <to you>, show me those whom you call gods."[i]

---

a. C: "I will show you."

b. C finishes the verse here.

c. Eth has: "I have come to guide you on to the path of justice, so that all of you may learn and begin to venerate the Living God who will be forever and ever, who made heavens, earth and sea, and everything that is in them."

d. Eth includes this as part of Demetrius's discourse, thus: "I see your old age." C has only, "At these (words) Demetrius saw his old age and had pity." C then resumes at 2:8.

e. Eth: "My God is able to do this, and to overthrow and destroy those who, according to you, are great gods, and turn your heart from them and soften your heart to learn truth."

f. "Demons" is uncertain. The Greek MSS (M and C) have the unattested form *daimosin*. Eth begins with "I will not return to the will of Satan."

g. After the citation of Jeremiah, Eth continues with: "Moreover, it is written that 'The wisdom of this world is foolishness with God' (1 Cor 3:19). As for me, I am now stronger than what you have said. I am a servant of God Most High who created heaven and earth, and he commanded me, saying, 'You shall fear the Lord your God, and him alone you shall worship' (Deut 10:20)."

h. C lacks this sentence. Eth has instead: "And you, O Prefect, why do you not turn away from the worship of gods that are worthless to you and turn to Christ, your God, to whom be glory? Now, you may save yourself and all who have the same faith as you."

i. C lacks "if it seems best <to you>." Eth has, "If you reject my words, show me those who say that these are gods, whereas I will show you the power of truth."

Cornelius destroys the shrine

[10]After he heard this, (Demetrius) rejoiced greatly with those who were with him.[a] They were filled with happy expectations, the fools thinking to themselves that soon they will see Cornelius make sacrifice.[b] So, the shrine of Zeus very quickly was opened to them, as if they thought that Cornelius would go in and sacrifice to the god.[c] Therefore, when the man went into the shrine, everyone flowed together there with speed—not only Demetrius, nor those who were around him, but also his wife Evanthia[d] and his son Demetrius, for so too was he named.

[11]Then, bowing his knee with his heart towards the east, Cornelius said, "God, the one who stirs up the earth and moves the mountains in the hearts of the seas,"[e] who destroyed Bel in the time of his servant Daniel, and who killed the dragon, and muzzled the lions, so that you may preserve your servant;[f] now, in the same way, destroy the idols,[g] these images both cast and carved, and offer your enlightenment to your people. Let them know that yours is the arm with power and you are the boast of our strength."[h]

Ps 46:2

Dan 6:19–24; Bel 23–40

[12]After offering these prayers, he went out of the shrine. Demetrius left with him, as did the multitude of the heathen who had come along. However, Evanthia and her son Demetrius still remained inside.[i] Suddenly, God shook the city greatly. At once, the shrine tumbled down and the idols broke into pieces and were reduced to dust and rubble, trapping Demetrius the son and the mother Evanthia inside.

Demetrius confronts Cornelius

[13]Then, when the father[j] Demetrius saw the destruction of the shrine, though not yet aware that his wife and son were left behind, the godly Cornelius was led into the courtroom[k] so that, thereupon, he could be compelled to reveal the

---

a. The entire sentence in C reads, "After the judge heard this, he rejoiced."

b. After "happy expectations," C finishes the sentence with "for the wretched act was not the goal of the holy one."

c. This sentence is absent in C.

d. In Eth, the wife's name is Atomia.

e. Eth has: "O heavenly Lord, who created the heaven, earth, sea and everything which is in them! You created man in your image and likeness, and by your command submitted to him the animals, birds and the fish of the seas! "

f. Eth adds: "You are the one who created the entire world! And you are the heavenly king, who sits on the (throne supported by) cherubs, and (you are) the performer of great miracles and wonders! You are the one who watches the earth and it shakes because of you, who touches the mountains and they smoke."

g. C finishes the verse here.

h. The final sentence in Eth reads: "You are the God of truth and thus you will be worshipped and your holy name praised. Praise and glory are due to you—to the Father, the Son, and the Holy Spirit—forever and ever, Amen."

i. C has only: "After praying, he went out of the shrine but Evanthia and her son were inside."

j. C: "the judge."

k. The verse finishes here in C. Eth also concludes the sentence at this point and then adds: "He said to those who came to him, 'Bring that treacherous magician who by his sorcery destroyed the house of the gods.' "

cause of the destruction. But he entered joyously, speaking softly to Jesus who strengthened him, and in high spirits over this incredible miracle, rather than the throne of Demetrius on its high and lofty platform.[a] Anticipating the question he said,[b] "Where are your great gods now, Demetrius?"

[14]Then (Demetrius) said, "Wretch! By what sorcery did you destroy the shrine and shatter the statues? Let all the gods know: I will subject you to the gravest penalties."[c] At once, he was deliberating what he might do to inflict the most terrible punishment on him.[d] Since evening had already come, he ordered the holy one to be hung up, his hands and feet bound together, and to continue hanging thus all night. He said these things and, at once, the prison held the holy one.[e]

Evanthia and her son are found

3 [1]Immediately, one of the members of the household named Telephon[f] ran quickly, saying, "O master, my mistress and your only son have been killed, when the shrine was brought down upon them." Then Demetrius, hearing, at once tore his clothes and was overcome by great grief. Meanwhile, he ordered those with him to dig out the rubble as soon as possible,[g] saying, "(dig) until you find for me the bones of my good and faithful wife and my very sweet only son and bring them into my hands."[h]

[2]He said these things to them with a voice flooded with tears and he was sighing most heavily and grieving. And he was accusing his gods, because he had been kept alive to this point, to hear such a terrible message.[i] The nobles of the city were sitting with him, on the one hand grieving with him[j] and on the other hand consoling him and hastening to quench his grief, insofar as it was possible, with how Cornelius's death had now become an interest to them. And a tomb was constructed where his wife would be buried with his son.

[3]A certain high priest of the heathen gods named Barbatos,[k] who had been entrusted with the clearing away of the shrine, quickly came to the attendants of Demetrius—for he was not allowed to appear before him on account of the grieving[l]—to report a voice from Evanthia and his son sent up from the ruins.[m]

---

a. Eth has only: "The holy man Cornelius came to him, glad, rejoicing and praising God."

b. C: "He said to the judge."

c. C: "And the judge asked, 'By what sorcery did you break asunder and destroy the shrine?'"

d. This sentence is lacking in Eth.

e. Eth: "And threw him into prison to sentence him the next morning."

f. In Eth, Telephon is Demetrius's brother; in the epitome Telephon is his "head-man" (2:6).

g. In Eth his orders are that thirty men should dig out the rubble; in the epitome, this number is 300 (see 2:6). Eth goes on to say: "For ten days those thirty men kept digging and removing whatever had fallen down from the house of gods, but they did not find the bodies of the prefect's wife or her son." Eth resumes again at 3:3.

h. C stipulates only: "until they find the bones."

i. C has only: "He was sighing and grieving and accusing his gods."

j. C finishes the verse here.

k. Both Eth and the epitome indicate that the voice came from the ruins ten days after the collapse (see above n. g). In Eth, the workers hear the voice and then inform the priest of Apollo. In the epitome, the priest is named Barbarus.

l. This detail is absent in C.

m. In Eth, the priests and others who heard the voices tell Demetrius: "Our lord! Your wife

The voice indicated,[a] "Great is the god of the Christians, who delivered us from this danger through his servant Cornelius, and who did not hand us over to complete destruction.[b] [4]Make haste then, Demetrius, and bring out from the prison this holy man. Fall at his feet with all those in our house and our next of kin and beg him to come to this ruin and save us and bring us out of this pit and out of this abyss, so that we may not completely perish. For we see here great miracles of God and angels crying out, '*Glory to God in the highest heaven, and on earth peace,* goodwill among people.'"[c]

Luke 2:14

Demetrius is baptized

[5]When the servants heard these things, they ran off at once, together with Barbatos the high priest, to Demetrius. They quickly reported everything to him. Hearing that his wife and son were still alive, (Demetrius) had a heart full of both joy and perplexity. Coming swiftly to the prison,[d] he found the divine Cornelius walking about with a book in his hand and praising God. For an angel had flown to him and loosed (him) from his bonds.

[6]Falling to his feet along with the multitude that had run together, (Demetrius) cried out, "Great is the God of Cornelius,[e] who protected[f] my wife Evanthia and my son Demetrius from the destruction of the shrine." At the same time, he begged the holy one, saying, "Servant of the highest God, we—myself and all those with me—will believe in the crucified one, whom you preach if you come and bring out from there alive my wife and son."[g] (Cornelius) said, "Receive first the seal in Christ and then I will come with you,[h] and your heart's desire will be given to you."[i] Then at once, Demetrius, together with all those with him, said again, "Great is the God of the Christians," as they received baptism.[j]

Cornelius rescues Evanthia and her son

[7]Then Cornelius took them and stood on the ruin. Raising his eyes toward the east into heaven, he said,[k] "Lord God of hosts, who looks upon the Earth and makes it tremble, who dissolves mountains with your gaze and dries up the bot-

---

and your son did not die but are alive! Behold! We ourselves have heard their voices from under the earth but we could not see them."

a. Eth expands with: "They went to the house of the destroyed statues, and (there could) hear the voices of a woman and her son, shouting."

b. C and Eth lack "And who did not hand us over to complete destruction."

c. Eth continues with: "Great is the god of the Christians! We thought that these (idols) were gods, worshipped them and relied on them, yet they perished like dust."

d. In Eth, Demetrius is present at the ruins to hear the voice. Thus, the verse begins instead with: "When the prefect and all who were with him heard these words." C has: "And Demetrius, hearing these things went swiftly with good cheer to the prison."

e. C: "of the Christians."

f. Eth has "rescued."

g. C: "bring out my wife and her son from the abyss."

h. C finishes the sentence here.

i. Eth: "If you and all who are with you have really accepted Christ, I will go with you and bring out the woman and then her son Demetrius."

j. Eth has no mention of a baptism; C has the baptism but no words from the baptized.

k. Before the prayer, both Eth and the epitome say Cornelius made the sign of the cross (see 3:4).

Neh 9:6 tomless depths with your presence; *you yourself are the Lord alone.* Hear the groaning of those who have been imprisoned, bring out Evanthia from the earth and do not turn away your face from her child, but take heed of their souls and set them free for the sake of your name."[a]

[8]Then, after Cornelius prayed, and the ones standing around shouted out[b] "Amen," immediately the earth was rent asunder, sending out the mother with the child safe and sound.[c] Those standing by cried out at once, "Great is the God of the Christians, who set us free from deception and this terrible death through your servant Cornelius, making known to us your power and your arm."[d] And at the same time, 207 people[e] were delivered to Christ.

[9]From that time, then, Cornelius stayed at a certain place called Stadium[f] teaching the believers. Demetrius and Evanthia frequently visited him with the child.[g] And the rest of the heathen were no longer heathen; cleansing the thorns of unbelief from their hearts, just like some good earth, they received the seed of godliness and were sealed in baptism.[h]

Cornelius dies and is buried

4 [1]So then, after he brought that entire city to Christ and drove away error, and sowed the word of godliness, becoming full of days of the Spirit, he was devoted to prayer and very fervent petition. It was entirely his way of life from that time, not raising his eyes to any of those things eagerly sought after in the present life. From that time he was initiated concerning his departure, to which he had looked with the entire eye of (his) soul and for which he had been prepared.[i] He

---

a. C omits the contents of the prayer. In Eth, the prayer is: "I praise you, my God, who have created heaven, earth and sea and everything that is in them! You Lord, show your power and your miracles to those who believe in you, and to your servant Demetrius, and bring out his wife Atomia and his son Demetrius from imprisonment beneath, that your name be praised! Glorious is the Father, the Son, and the Holy Spirit, forever and ever! Amen."

b. C: "cried out."

c. C finishes the verse here.

d. Eth: "Great is the God of the Christians, who revealed his power and glory by the hand of his servant Cornelius, and rescued us from the sin of the worship of idols!"

e. In Eth, the number is 10,007.

f. Eth says he stayed in Midan, not Stadium, for ten years. The epitome says Cornelius's career lasted three years (see 4:1).

g. Eth adds: "and he would admonish and teach them the word of God. They received his admonitions and teachings and they praised and extolled our Lord Jesus Christ."

h. Eth has instead: "Some of those who had remained pagans were drawn to the saint. He received them and made the sign of the cross of Christ over them, and baptized all of them in the name of the Father, the Son, and the Holy Spirit. He instructed them and commanded that they observe God's every commandment, and he prayed for them. When he finished his prayer all of them said 'Amen.'" For this verse, C says only: "He baptized them and everyone in that place was no longer heathen."

i. Eth lacks much of this verse, inserting in its place a typical Ethiopian addition called *kidan* ("covenant"), which enhances the importance of hagiographical and many other texts by providing promises of various rewards to people for venerating saints that had such a "covenant" with Christ. The addition reads: "(Then) the Savior, to whom be glory, descended upon him and said to Saint Cornelius: 'For every man who would write of your life, your testimony, and the affliction that you experienced on account of my name, and everybody who would call his son by your name, I will have Enoch, the scribe, erase the record of his sins, and will bless

heard[a] a voice from above saying, "Cornelius, come to me. For behold the crown of righteousness[b] has been prepared for you."

²The next day,[c] he summoned all of the Christians whom he had brought forward and taught them more perfectly what pertains to godliness and to hold safely to the teaching. Then, approaching more closely and gathering his whole self, he bent his knee finally in prayer, and said,[d] "Lord God our master, who has made me worthy to preserve the faith, to complete the struggle, and to conquer the adversary, I give you thanks. But also look down from heaven upon your servants, and help them from your holy heights and strengthen them by confessing you and your name, that always they may glorify your all-holy name, now and forever."[e] When everyone shouted out "Amen," immediately the spirit of the joyful one was given up to the one who was calling.[f]

³Demetrius, however, along with Evanthia and his son and all the Christians who were gathered together and the presbyter Eunomius,[g] wept suitable tears over the departure of the teacher. Then also they lit candles and sang departure hymns. Fulfilling Christian custom, they placed him in the new coffin, which was built earlier by Demetrius for his wife, near the destroyed shrine of Zeus.

⁴And immediately, the earth sent up a very great bush and it covered the coffin in a circle, so that no one afterwards knew that the coffin was inside, except for the ones at the time ministering with Demetrius for the burial.[h] Indeed, they visited the bush repeatedly and at each time sang sacred songs and the air above

---

all his possessions. Truly, I will bless him and his whole family, and I will save him from every calamity. And he who gives alms on account of your name, and feeds a hungry man, I will feed him with the fruits of the Garden and I will repay him in the kingdom of heaven. Also, I will bless the city in which your body will be put that will serve you sincerely in my name. If the (inhabitants) suffer illness, I will cure them. And my peace will be with it forever.' Having said this to Saint Cornelius, the Savior ascended into heaven in glory and peace. Amen."

a. C lacks the beginning of this verse, beginning here with "And after this he heard."

b. Eth: "crown of kingdom."

c. Perhaps "the next day" should be added to the previous sentence to read "(and) whoever is next."

d. Eth prefaces the prayer with only: "Cornelius lifted his eyes, looked to heaven and said."

e. The prayer is quite different in Eth: "O Lord, my God, you who have created the heaven, earth, sea and everything which is in them, you have created me. By your grace you helped me to complete my righteous struggle and to defeat Satan, the evil deceiver, who seduces your servants and maids! I give you thanks, good Lord, because you comforted my heart, woke up my troubled and tired soul, and enlightened my heart by (showing) the life of this transient world, so that I might turn to the enlightenment of truth. And you, O Lord, look from your heavens at your servants and maids and preserve their souls and bodies! Show to them favor out of the grace of your spiritual gifts and bequeath to them that they may not become old or decay, that they might praise your holy name. Praise is due to you—to the Father, the Son and the Holy Spirit, forever, Amen."

f. For this verse, C has only: "And at once gathering (?) he summoned the Christians. After clearly teaching and instructing the word of godliness and praying, (and) when everyone shouted out 'Amen,' immediately the spirit of the joyful one was given up to the one who was calling." The text then ends with a short doxology ("glory to him forever").

g. Instead of Eunomius, Eth has "Anumios, the priest." Also, Eth does not include Evanthia and her son here.

h. Eth continues after "inside" with: "so that nobody would see (it) until this very day has arrived."

it was made full of incense and sweet smells.[a] Miracles, however, were gushing forth from there for a long time, so that it seemed to the multitude, who did not know the disciple was lying inside, that even now the bush was hinting at something divine, just as happened previously also in the time of Moses.

Exod 3:1–22

Cornelius is rediscovered by Silvanus

5 [1]But not long after, Demetrius also died, and many of those perfected by divine baptism by Cornelius either departed from life or went away to other regions.[b] Then the godly Cornelius, appearing in a dream to a certain Silvanus, a man who both embraced virtue and was a friend of God, who served as bishop in Troas and who was once in Skepsis,[c] said, "I have dwelled here for a long time, and no one has visited me, except for those who were baptized by me."

[2]Then, after the bishop pondered the dream for a day, and not being able to interpret it,[d] the holy one appeared to him again the following night. "I am Cornelius the centurion," he said. "And my dwelling place is in the bush near the shrine of Zeus. But you, build another oratory[e] near the place of Demetrius, the servant of God. The place is called Pandochium, where also many bodies of the holy perfected brothers already lie."[f]

[3]Thus, in the morning, after the Pandochium had been dug through on all sides for tombs, the bishop considered building the shrine elsewhere. But the holy one would not cease. Then, gathering together the clergy[g] under him, (Silvanus) said, "A great treasure has been revealed to me, children. But come, let us retrieve it."

[4]When they heard this, they rushed willingly and gladly followed the bishop.[h] When they came upon the bush itself, at once the clergy said to the bishop, "A certain quite divine mercy flew here, O master, and we know a multitude has flowed together here and they have been freed from diseases and evil demons, and have written on the healing at the bush. But if the treasure is inside or under the bush," they said, "who would be able to cut it down and raise (the treasure), since it is impossible for it to be cut on account of its size? Besides, it is not easy to touch, since it is terrifying to the multitude because of the working of the miracles."[i]

---

a. Eth concludes the verse here.

b. Before Silvanus enters, Eth has: "Prefect Demetrius, his wife, his son and all the people of his family (later) died, whereas others who remained spread to (other) regions. Nobody who would have known Cornelius or the place where his body was laid was alive in this region. No one knew the reason for this, but people used to carry (there) the suffering, the sick and those whom demons had possessed. They used to come to the place of the brumble bush, burn incense, light torches and they would be cured of all their sicknesses." This anticipates some of the activity in verse 4 below.

c. In Eth, Silvanus is appointed bishop of the region. On Paul's activities in Troas, see 2 Cor 2:12; Acts 16:8–11.

d. Eth: "When Bishop Silvanus awoke he remembered what he had seen in his dream."

e. An *eukterion*.

f. Eth makes no mention of the other saints at Pandochium. This location is obscure. The name is a transliteration of the Greek word for "inn" or "dwelling-place." But it cannot be identified with any specific building in late antiquity.

g. The word here is "lot," meaning those under his administration.

h. This sentence is lacking in Eth.

i. In Eth, the clergy say: "O our Father! In this brumble bush many miracles have taken

[5]Then the bishop, praying to God and fastening the cross in the ground, laid his hand on the bush and cut it down by its very roots.[a] Inspired with confidence, the clergy at once were eager for the work and the bush was pulled up as if it was soft grass, and it was no longer a bush. But in a little while, at once the coffin was revealed, and the bishop pressed further, still urging on the digging.[b] Now, when evening had come, the bishop prayed again and straightaway gave orders to the clergy for all-night psalm-singing and hymns and torches and incense to honor the coffin.[c]

Cornelius recruits Eugenius to build the shrine

[6]Just as the bishop was perplexed about the expenses for the building of the shrine and his lack of means, the holy one resolved this (perplexity) and appeared to one of the wealthy men, a godly man named Eugenius.[d] He commanded him to build the shrine and delineated the shape and size of the building.[e]

[7]Then, in the morning, Eugenius came to the bishop, reported to him the vision, and at once set the builders to the work, first describing and indicating to them both the height of the structure and the length, and commanding them that the entrance of the altar be equal in width to the coffin;[f] for he had decided to lay the coffin inside the altar.[g]

The body of Cornelius is transferred to the shrine

[8]Since the shrine was completed quickly (on account of God working this wonder), builders coming to the place with triangles[h]—for Bishop Silvanus was there

---

place. Many people possessed by demons used to go there and have been cured and cleansed of unclean spirits, but we do not know by what force. Let us give thanks to God (as) he revealed to us in your days and through you this glorious treasure."

a. The reading in the Greek is unclear; Silvanus's prayer expects something miraculous to occur, spectacular enough to break the clergy out of their fear. Perhaps it should read "the roots pulled themselves up." Eth says only: "the bishop gathered the priests and all the faithful and they went to the place of the brumble bush."

b. Eth: "Then they quickly began to cut and tear out (the bush) like dry grass, and a casket appeared in which was the body of the saint. The bishop and all who were with him rejoiced."

c. Eth gives these instructions in direct speech and then adds: "and give thanks to (God), who gave us this glorious treasure that we may be blessed by it. And they stayed that night praying and praising God."

d. According to the epitome, Eugenius "was impelled by God through a revelation" to build the shrine (see 5:2).

e. The entire sentence in Eth is rendered as: "The bishop was eager to build a church for the saint. That same night the saint appeared to an honorable and believing man called Eugenius, and commanded him to construct for him a church from his means, and told (him) how to build it."

f. In Eth, these special instructions are given as: "He commanded them to make the middle door broader in order not to impede them in bringing the casket of the saint into the church."

g. This sentence is lacking in Eth. As will be seen, the coffin is not placed in the altar, but beside it.

h. The MS has *trigonois,* a word that refers to the use of triangles or triangular numbers. In Eth the city is called Terafses. The Bollandists' Latin translation has *in locum, qui dicitur Trigoni* ("to a place called Trigon"). The garbled Ethiopic form confirms an Arabic *Vorlage* of *Acts Corn.,* since the Greek *Gamma* must have been rendered in Arabic as *Qaf* (though not in Egypt), which is very similar to, and therefore easily confused with, *Fa.*

performing the festival of the blessed apostle Andrew[a]—revealed the completion of the building to him and said, "It is time now to transfer the coffin, for he would be more easily brought in this way."[b]

[9]Thus, at once, the bishop, together with the godly Eugenius, took up the sacred gospel book—since they had already prayed—and together they began to sing the Trisagion.[c] And everyone sang the hymn together with him and they went out praying.[d] Then the coffin—O your great mysteries, Master! Miraculous things!—followed as if alive, and no one moved it at all, nor held on to it, nor touched it.[e]

[10]And everyone, because of the great astonishment, did not think that they should believe the miracle even though it was seen.[f] Then, in ecstasy they cried, "Holy, holy, holy Lord Almighty, who through your servant Cornelius showed your miracles and your acts of power to us." Thereupon, all those who remained of the heathen believed. The procession[g] again went forth up to the shrine and the coffin followed.

[11]When they arrived at the shrine, they stood on this side and on that, so they could see where the coffin would proceed and where it would stand. And coming through the middle of them and through the side door on the right side, it stood near the altar.[h] Every machine was brought to transfer it inside the altar <but they were unable to move it>.[i] It remains until now unmovable, an unfailing treasure of miracles, an enjoyment of much spiritual benefit and mercy.[j]

Encratius paints a portrait of Cornelius

6 [1]After bishop Silvanus died, Athanasius was appointed to the episcopate of Troas and Philostorgius of Skepsis. And when also the life of piety-loving Euge-

---

a. Eth calls him Andrew the Wanderer.

b. Eth: "Give the order that the casket of the saint be brought before the central door is built; otherwise it will be difficult for us to bring the casket into the church." Eth then continues with a lengthy addition: "The bishop summoned all the priests and Eugenius. They took counsel among one another and decided to send someone to the region of Terwada (i.e., Troas) to bring the ropes needed to carry the casket to the church. Saint Cornelius, wishing to strengthen the faith of the bishop, said to him in a night dream: 'Assemble the priests and the faithful (in a procession) and pray (while) carrying a Gospel book and praising the Holy Trinity. Enter (the church) before me and I will follow you.' The bishop woke up and rejoiced greatly. He called Eugenius, and recounted to him what the saint had said. And behold, in the evening Eugenius sent (people) to Terwada to fetch the ropes. When he heard what the bishop had said, he commanded his servant to catch up to the men on their way (to Terwada) and turn them back."

c. Eth: "When the next day came, it was Saturday, the bishop gathered the priests and all the faithful. They went to the place where the casket (was), reciting prayers, (burning) incense, and carrying a gospel book. (The procession) moved reciting praises to the Holy Trinity."

d. Eth lacks this sentence.

e. In Eth, the body rises up and faces the people.

f. Eth lacks this sentence.

g. The MS has *litē* (prayer), but perhaps *litaneia* (procession) is meant.

h. Eth: "came through the entrance of the women's side of the shrine, moved further and stayed close to the altar." In the epitome it is the "narrow door" (5:5).

i. In both Eth and the epitome (see 5:5), the coffin was immovable. This situation is presupposed by the statement in the following sentence: "it remains there still," which is reflected also in Eth and the epitome.

j. Eth has only: "Thus it remained in its place until today, until now."

nius similarly came to an end,[a] Philostorgius exhorted a certain painter to paint the entire shrine and carefully craft an image of Cornelius himself, as much as possible dressed accurately so that he would be painted as an old man and entirely like himself.[b]

[2]Thus Encratius[c]—for this was the name of the painter—begged the holy one to reveal to him his own form, as he wished to depict it successfully and with precision. At the same time, he was annoyed at the command of the bishop, and he sent irreverent voices toward the holy one, completely at a loss and terribly distraught because of ignorance of his form and because he was unable to achieve the characteristics of the face. Then, when he fell from the ladder upon which he had stepped, he lay there not breathing. And worms crawled in and out of his mouth, and they seemed to be fruit of those slanderous words the distressed painter had spoken.[d]   Acts 12:23

[3]But you are surely the same Cornelius who, when he was breathing threateningly against you, gave Demetrius back his wife and son; nor from that point did you prolong the punishment appointed to the painter. For, appearing the next day,[e] (Cornelius) took his right (hand) and raised (him) as if he were sleeping.

[4]And these two great things he accomplished: he corrected his intemperate tongue, and healed the grief and despondency due to the perplexity concerning the painting, not <knowing him> in image, figure, and likeness; but he met with him also because he was showing him his form.[f] And so, straightaway, the painter was seen healthy and whole, set free entirely from the worms, and engaged in his craft again.

[5]Thereafter to be sure he painted him as he had seen, injecting much truth into the painting along with his craft,[g] through the prayers of the Holy One himself, through the mercy and benevolence of our Lord Jesus Christ, to whom, together with the Father and the Holy Spirit, be glory, power, honor, and worship forever. Amen.

---

a. Eth mentions only Silvanus's death and the succession of Philostorgius.

b. Eth: "He wanted to depict in the church Cornelius and his life. Then he asked Encratius, 'Paint for me an image of the saint that would truly present him as he looked.' But no one knew how he looked."

c. Eth names him Abqeratios.

d. The entire verse in Eth reads: "The painter was distressed and, while standing in the church's gallery, cried out in a loud voice: 'O Cornelius, the saint of God! Appear to me that I may know how you looked!' When the painter had finished these words, he fell down from the gallery and appeared to be dead."

e. In Eth and the epitome (see 6:3), the bishop finds the body of the painter and prays for him. Neither Eth nor the epitome records the substance of the prayer. Then Cornelius appears from the altar (epitome 6:3) or the shrine (Eth).

f. Eth lacks this entire sentence.

g. Hereafter Eth inserts a lengthy colophon, beginning "This saint worked many miracles. He was (present) when the church was consecrated on the first day of the month of *Elul* (September), which is *Ḥədar*. The martyr of Christ, Cornelius, died on the twentieth day of the month *First Täsrin* (October), which coincides with the Egyptians' [*Hātūr*] and with the (Ethiopian) month of *Ḥədar*." The colophon then says that the text was translated from Arabic.

A Life in Brief and Miracles of the Holy Cornelius the Centurion[a]

Cornelius is visited by an angel

Acts 10:1

1 [1]This blessed Cornelius was from Caesarea Palaestina, a centurion of the so-called Italian Cohort, having grown old in the time of the holy apostles, and the first of the gentiles who believed in Christ.

Acts 10:3–8

[2]For, coming to Caesarea Palaestina, he saw in a vision around three o'clock that an angel of the Lord came and said to him that his prayers and gifts had been received. He commanded also that a search be made for the apostle Peter, to hear from him the gospel of Christ, just as it is stated also in the Acts of the Holy Apostles.

Cornelius is appointed to evangelize Skepsis

2 [1]And when Peter, Timothy, and Cornelius had gone to Ephesus and were casting lots for the cities, the lot fell to Cornelius for him to go to the city of the Skepsaeans, lying near Abydos, full of idols.

[2]After going to Skepsis[b] and proclaiming the word of God, (Cornelius) was led away for interrogation before Demetrius, the ruler of the place and a heathen.

Cornelius is interrogated by Demetrius

[3](Demetrius) was raging in many words at the holy one, (but) so it seemed, this did not altogether disturb him. Rather, the holy Cornelius was urging him to turn away from the error of the idols and to believe in Christ. As he was raging, the holy Cornelius asked to go into the shrine of idols.

Cornelius destroys the shrine

[4]Cornelius went in together with the ruler and Evanthia his wife and Demetrius his son, who had the same name as him. Bending his knees, he prayed for a long time. And after this he went outside with the ruler.

[5]Then an earthquake occurred and the shrine, falling, took Evanthia, the wife of the ruler, and Demetrius his son. Then, after putting the holy Cornelius in chains, the ruler placed him under guard.

[6]And when Telephon, his head-man, made known to him that his wife was taken with his son in the ruins of the shrine, hearing these things, Demetrius the ruler tore his clothes. And every day he made groups of 300 men dig out the site.

---

a. The title is preceded by "on the ninth of the month (of June)."
b. Here "the city called of the Skepsaeans."

Evanthia and her son are found

3 ¹After \<they were\> clearing the site for ten days and were unable to find anything of them, a certain high priest of the idols named Barbarus said to Demetrius the ruler that he heard the voices of Evanthia and his son from the ruins saying,

²"Great is the god of the Christians who, through his servant Cornelius, delivered us from danger. But go and fall at the feet of the righteous Cornelius and bring (him) here, so that he may bring us out. For we hear angels speaking praises and saying, '*Glory to God in the highest heaven and on earth peace,* goodwill among people.'"

Luke 2:14

³And Demetrius the ruler, coming to the holy Cornelius and falling to his feet, begged him to bring out his wife and son from the ruins of the shrine. And (Cornelius) said, "If you believe in Christ, he fulfills your request."

Cornelius rescues Evanthia and her son

⁴And when the holy Cornelius had come to the site, had sealed them with the sign of the cross, and had performed a prayer upon the ruins, Evanthia and her son came out unharmed, crying out and saying, "Great is the god of the Christians." And 207 men, together with Demetrius, believed in Christ.

Cornelius dies and is buried

4 ¹When the holy Cornelius had instructed them and baptized them and had baptized for three years many others, a voice addressed him from heaven: "Come, Cornelius contender, you have struggled with yourself well." Giving thanks to God and praying for his flock, he fell into a beautiful sleep. ²And he was buried gloriously by Christians, both Demetrius and his wife Evanthia and the presbyter Eunomius, in the tomb which Demetrius the governor prepared at the report of his wife and son, when they were in the ruins of the shrine.

³At once, a bush, growing high, covered the tomb so that it could not be seen.

Cornelius is rediscovered by Silvanus

5 ¹When much time had gone by and the place had been neglected, the holy Cornelius revealed himself to Bishop Silvanus \<urging him\> to build a shrine and to find the coffin and place it there.

²Then, after clearing away the bush and performing a laudation all night long, he began the building of the shrine, since a certain Eugenius was impelled by God through a revelation to build the shrine from his own money.[a]

The body of Cornelius is transferred to the shrine

³Then, when Bishop Silvanus completed the work, he came together with Eunomius the presbyter[b] and Eugenius the friend of Christ, took the holy gospels and sang the Trisagion hymn according to the revelation of the holy one. His bier or coffin followed them, dragged without hand or chains.

---

a. Though unclear in the epitome, Silvanus is charged to have the shrine constructed, but Eugenius is the one who has the wealth and means to do so.

b. Eunomius is a contemporary of Demetrius in 4:2 (and in the longer text at 4:3).

⁴When everyone became greatly surprised, they cried out, "Holy, Holy, Holy One, who through your servant Cornelius performs great miracles."

⁵And they reached the shrine and wanted to bring the coffin in through the middleᵃ door. (But) not wanting to be confined, (the coffin) divided the crowd by divine power and without difficulty it went in through the narrow door sideways and stood near the altar. And when numerous machines were brought to guide it to the middle of the altar, the coffin did not give itself up, but it remained there firm and steadfast up to today.

Encratius paints a portrait of Cornelius

6 ¹And Bishop Philostorgiusᵇ ordered a certain Encratius, a painter, to depict the holy one according to (his) real form.

²And Encratius became distressed at this and reproachfully demanded the holy one to appear before him. Suddenly he fell down the stairs and at once remained there unable to speak for a long time, so that also worms spurted out of his mouth.

³And the bishop became very despondent at this and earnestly was praying for Encratius, when suddenly a noise happened in the altar. And the holy Cornelius came out and raised him immediately.

⁴And straightaway the worms disappeared from his mouth. And the holy one was no longer seen.

⁵And giving thanks to God, Encratius the painter depicted the holy Cornelius just as he saw him when he was raised by his prayer.

The hand of Cornelius is transferred to Caesarea

7 ¹Pamphilus, the metropolitan of Caesarea Palaestina, where also the house of the holy Cornelius is honored, after much time sent his secretary Julian, the deacon from Constantinople, and charged him to search the city where the precious relic of the holy Cornelius had been laid and take part of his relic in order to place it in the (previously) mentioned holy house. (Julian) found and consulted with a certain John, a deacon of Mitylene, who brought him to the bishop of Skepsis.ᶜ

²Then he sailed with him and came upon the same city. When all were together and begging to have revealed to them if it is pleasing to the holy one for (Julian) to take his precious relic, (Cornelius) revealed to the bishop in diverse visions that the great assembly eagerly awaited the patriarch since he was going to conduct the service.

³Likewise also the aforesaid Julian saw in a dream thirty soldiers arriving from Skepsis at the divine home of the holy Cornelius and another soldier concealing his face.ᵈ And when he inquired, "What are these?" They said, "These are the troops encamped in Skepsis and they came to supervise the removal of the relic of Cornelius." The soldier said to Julian, "Do you want a relic? I offer

---

a. Middle (*mesē*) may be a corruption of narrow (*stenē*) used later in this sentence.

b. Philostorgius became bishop of Skepsis during the episcopate of Silvanus's successor, Athanasius; see *Acts Corn.* 6:1.

c. Here and below, the text has "city of the Skepsaeans."

d. "Concealing his face" translates the hapax legomena *opsikeuthō*.

(one) to you." And opening the coffin, he offered the right hand of the holy one, saying, "Take, friend. It is the right hand of the holy Cornelius."

[4]When not only these but also many other visions happened, the bishop yielded. He put on the white robe and his *omophor*[a] and took hold of the holy gospel in his left hand, and an iron bar in the right. And Julian, putting on the deacon's *orarion*,[b] took a censer and a wax candle, and when they began to chisel the lid of the coffin, it opened immediately. The bishop lowered his hand into the coffin and, not grasping anything at first, he shook his head.

[5]Resuming their prayers with fear, he stooped over further, and the right hand of the holy Cornelius was given to him invisibly from the stump up to the fastening of the palm, so that he cried out and said, "My hand burns! Take what has been given to me, but see that it does not burn the vessel in which you put it."

[6]Thus Julian received the valuable and holy relic of the blessed Cornelius in a reliquary. And he went rejoicing and praising God.

[7]Bringing it away to Caesarea Palaestina, to the house of the holy Cornelius, he brought his image also, after copying it just as it is represented in the shrine of the holy Cornelius in Skepsis by Encratius the painter, where also the holy one has taken rest.

[8]From his intercessions, Lord, our God, may you grant us forgiveness for errors and deem us worthy of the eternal church, since you are good and benevolent; for to you is fitting all glory, honor, and worship now and always and forever and ever, amen.

---

a. The *omophor*, meaning "(something) borne on the shoulders," is the vestment of a bishop in the Byzantine (and modern Eastern Orthodox and Eastern Catholic) liturgical tradition.

b. The *orarion* is the distinctive deacon's vestment in Byzantine (and modern Eastern Orthodox and Eastern Catholic) liturgical tradition.

John and the Robber
A new translation and introduction

by Rick Brannan

Some teachings of Jesus in the canonical Gospels imply that it is either difficult or impossible for the rich to enter into the kingdom of God (Mark 10:17–25 par.; see also Luke 16:19–31). Some letters attributed to Paul appear to echo the difficulty (e.g., 1 Tim 6:6–19). Clement of Alexandria strives to settle the issue in his homily *Quis dives salvetur* ("Who Is the Rich One That Is Being Saved?"). At the end of the homily (§42.1–15) he provides an otherwise-unknown story of the apostle John commonly referred to as "St. John and the Robber." In the context of the homily, *John and the Robber* is the capstone, illustrating the degree to which the redemptive love of Christ reaches. If Christ, through John, can so completely redeem the robber in this story, surely the same Christ can redeem those who are rich, if they truly repent.

Contents
At the end of the homily *Quis dives salvetur,* Clement of Alexandria introduces the story of *John and the Robber* by emphasizing that it is not merely a story, but a true and genuine account of the apostle John. According to the account, John was released from his exile on Patmos after the death of Domitian and came to live in Ephesus (42.2). While in Ephesus, John would visit area churches to appoint bishops and resolve issues in each region. In one of these visits, perhaps to Smyrna,[1] John encountered a charismatic young man. After his business with the bishop, John entrusted this young man to the bishop (42.3). Then John departed Ephesus. The bishop did what John asked, ensuring the baptism of the young man (42.4). Considering the young man secure, the bishop put his attention elsewhere. The young man, now on his own, soon fell in with a band of robbers, was slowly corrupted, and renounced his faith. Due to his charisma and passion, he soon became the chief of the band of robbers (42.5–7). After a while, John returned to the bishop on regular business. After the business was conducted, John asked the bishop about the deposit he had left with him. The bishop was confused, thinking John was attempting to extort money from him. John clarified, and the bishop recounted the story of the young man's descent to thievery and subsequent alienation (42.8–9). John responded with action, mounting a horse and commandeering a guide to bring him to the young man (42.10–12). When he confronted the young man, John offered him salvation, heard his repentance, and restored him in the name of Christ (42.13–15).

Manuscripts and Versions
There are two primary manuscripts for *Quis div.*: El Escorial, Real Biblioteca de San Lorenzo, MS Ω III 19 (11th cent.); and Vatican, Biblioteca apostolica, gr. 623 (16th cent.), the

---

1. See "Date and Provenance" below.

latter most likely a copy of the former.[2] Each of these contains the account of *John and the Robber,* typically numbered in modern editions as section 42.

Eusebius also provides the account of *John and the Robber* in his *Ecclesiastical History* (3.23.1–19), acknowledging Clement of Alexandria as his source. The form of the story in Eusebius is clearly derived from Clement's account. Further, some manuscripts of Maximus the Confessor's scholia on the works of Dionysius the Areopagite contain the account in a form that is not likely based on Eusebius but derived from a manuscript of *Quis div.*[3] In his edition of *Quis div.,* Barnard lists the following additional manuscripts of the scholia that contain the account:[4]

> Florence, Biblioteca di San Marco 686, fol. 214r (12th cent.)
> Florence, Biblioteca Medicea Laurenziana, v. 32, fol. 217v (15th cent.)
> Florence, Biblioteca Medicea Laurenziana, Conv. Suppr. 202, fol. 190v (10th cent., with some supplied by a 15th-cent. hand)
> Jerusalem, Bibliotheke tou Patriarcheiou, 414 (16th cent.)
> London, British Library, Add. 18231, fol. 12r (972 CE)
> Milan, Biblioteca Ambrosiana, H 11 Sup. 2, fol. 212 (13th cent.)
> Moscow, Russian State Library, 36 (10th cent.)
> Oxford, Bodleian Library, Canon. 97, fol. 221r (14th cent.)
> Oxford, Corpus Christi College, 141, fol. 2v (12th cent.)
> Paris, Bibliothèque nationale de France, gr. 440, fol. 177r (12th cent.)
> Paris, Bibliothèque nationale de France, Coislin 86 (12th cent.)
> Vatican, Biblioteca apostolica, gr. 374, fol. 242 (13/14th cent.)
> Vatican, Biblioteca apostolica, gr. 404, fol. 76 (11/12th cent.)
> Vatican, Biblioteca apostolica, Ottob. 326, fol. 1 (16th cent.)
> Vatican, Biblioteca apostolica, Regin. 38, fol. 321 (11th cent.)
> Vienna, Österreichische Nationalbibliothek, Theol. gr. 65 (olim 49), fol. 117r (14th cent.?)
> Vienna, Österreichische Nationalbibliothek, Theol. gr. 110, fol. 197v (10th cent.)

The scholia of Maximus were translated into Latin around 860 CE.[5] Barnard mentions two Latin manuscripts of the scholia that he consulted:[6]

> Oxford, Bodleian Library, Ashmole 1526 (early 14th cent.)
> Cambridge, University Library, Ii-3-32 (13th cent.)

In addition to Eusebius and the scholia of Maximus, Antiochus of Palestine, writing in the seventh century, records the episode in his *Homily* 122, though he erroneously attributes it to Irenaeus. Anastasius of Sinai (also of the seventh century) correctly ascribes the story to Clement in his recording of the episode in his *Homilia in sextum Psalmum.*[7]

---

2. Barnard, *Quis Dives Salvetur,* xxiii–xxv; see also Barnard, *Homily,* 6–8.

3. Barnard, *Quis Dives Salvetur,* xxiii–xxiv.

4. Barnard, *Quis Dives Salvetur,* xxiv.

5. Barnard, *Homily,* xxiv.

6. Barnard, *Homily,* xxv.

7. See the discussion of these two sources in Joseph M. Cotterill, "The Epistle of Polycarp to the Philippians and the Homilies of Antiochus Palaestinensis," *Journal of Philology* 19 (1891): 241–85 at 279–82; Charles Taylor, "St. Polycarp to the Philippians," *Journal of Philology* 20 (1892): 65–110 at 106.

There is no large disagreement between the various sources; they can all be associated with the version given by Clement in *Quis div.* 42 either directly or through Eusebius. Barnard was the first to use the superior Escorial manuscript as the basis of his edition of *Quis div.*; subsequent editors have followed his lead.[8]

Date and Provenance

Given its place in *Quis div.*, the *terminus ad quem* for *John and the Robber* is within the lifetime of Clement (ca. 150–ca. 215)—the late second or early third century at the latest. As to Clement's source for the episode, little is known. Based on cues within Clement's version of the story, Butterworth supposes, "It was an oral tradition, then, which Clement heard and first put into writing."[9]

Clement of Alexandria displays hesitancy in stating the location of the story: "Therefore, having come also to a certain city not too far away, the name of which also is reported by some" (42.3). In doing so, he betrays knowledge of at least one tradition regarding the setting of the episode,[10] but may not consider it fully accurate or trustworthy. Fortunately, the *Chronicon Paschale,* dated to the first half of the seventh century,[11] preserves a note about *John and the Robber* in which Smyrna is mentioned as the location of the episode:

> John the apostle and evangelist remained alive until the time of Trajan, Irenaeus records. But even Clement of Alexandria himself approves of the same, and that he went around Asia and neighboring lands appointing bishops and clerics. During this time the youth was placed by the apostle John with the bishop of Smyrna. After this chief robber became new, his repentance through Saint John was made known.[12]

The *Chronicon Paschale* assigns a date of 101 CE to the account. As J. B. Lightfoot rightly points out, it is unknown whether the chronicler drew his information from a source also known but discounted by Clement, or whether Smyrna is conjecture on the chronicler's part.[13] It is possible also that tradition has associated Smyrna with the account in the interim between Clement's initial recording of the story and its mention in the *Chronicon.*

Further in Smyrna's favor is the placing of John in Smyrna in a similar timeframe by the *Acts of John.* In chapters 56–57 of their edition, Junod and Kaestli include an account of John in Smyrna casting out demons from the sons of Antipatros. This follows mention in chapter 55 of the Smyrnaeans sending messengers to John asking him to come to them.[14] Conceptually, then, the tradition surrounding John allows for the events described in *John and the Robber* to take place in Smyrna.

If the *Chronicon Paschale* is correct in placing the events in Smyrna prior to 101 CE,

---

8. See Stählin, *Clemens Alexandrinus,* 3:187–90; Butterworth, trans., *Clement of Alexandria: The Exhortation to the Greeks,* 357–65.

9. Butterworth, "Story of St John," 144.

10. Butterworth, "Story of St John," 144.

11. Frank Leslie Cross and Elizabeth A. Livingstone, eds., *The Oxford Dictionary of the Christian Church* (3rd rev. ed.; New York: Oxford University Press, 2005), 342.

12. Dindorf, ed., *Chronicon paschale,* 470 (author's translation).

13. Joseph Barber Lightfoot, *The Apostolic Fathers, Part II: S. Ignatius, S. Polycarp. Revised Texts with Introductions, Notes, Dissertations, and Translations* (2 vols.; London: Macmillan, 1885), 1:424–25.

14. English translation in *ANT,* 326–27; a more accessible version of Junod and Kaestli's French translation is available in *EAC* 1: 975–1037.

then perhaps it is possible to identify one of the participants in the episode as Polycarp. He is known to have been bishop of Smyrna (Ignatius, *Pol.* Salutation) and is identified as a disciple of John by Irenaeus (*Haer.* 5.33.4). Irenaeus records also that Polycarp was appointed bishop of Smyrna by apostles in Asia (*Haer.* 3.3.4); according to Tertullian (*Praescr.* 31) and Jerome (*Vir. ill.* 17.1) he was appointed specifically by John. Based on these commonalities, Pierre Halloix understood the bishop in *John and the Robber* to be Polycarp.[15] This is problematic, however, due to Clement's use of *presbyteros* ("elder," either a term for a liturgical office or simply an old man) in reference to the bishop. If "elder" is meant as a title, its usage reflects a conflation of terminology for "bishop" that is hard to reconcile. If meant as "old man," it is similarly troublesome. The *Martyrdom of Polycarp* has Polycarp claim "eighty-six years I have served him" (9.3). This statement is usually understood as Polycarp testifying to being eighty-six years old and having been a Christian from his birth. If this statement reflects Polycarp's actual age at his time of martyrdom (155–156 CE), his birth would have been around 70 CE, leaving little time for him to age enough to be referred to as *presbyteros* while John was still alive. If this information is anywhere near reflective of truth, Polycarp would be around thirty years old at John's death. Because of this discrepancy, Lightfoot posits Bucolus, a possible predecessor of Polycarp known from *Life of Polycarp* 3, as the bishop in the tale.[16]

The identity of the robber is not known. If Bucolus is identified as the bishop, then it is possible the robber could be identified as Polycarp. If the statement about Polycarp's actual age at his time of martyrdom has any validity, then there is time available for him to have a history as a youth and a robber prior to his conversion. However, that same statement of age qualifies itself as the length of time Polycarp confessed Christianity, leaving no room for a nefarious past on the part of Polycarp.

Relationship to the Acts of John

The *Acts of John,* dated as early as 150 CE,[17] contain a series of episodes supposedly from the life of the apostle John. No complete copy of the *Acts of John* is extant, but to date no manuscripts of the text have been found that contain the episode of *John and the Robber.*[18] Some manuscripts do place John in Smyrna as an evangelist and miracle worker (*Acts John* 56–57). But this material emphasizes John's role as healer and perhaps even as establishing the church in Smyrna. Such a description does not fit with the role of John or the

---

15. Pierre Halloix, *Illustrium Ecclesiae Orientalis Scriptorum, Vitae et Documenta* (2 vols.; Duaci: Bogard, 1633), 1:569.

16. Lightfoot, *Apostolic Fathers*, 1:425; for the text of *Life of Polycarp* see Lightfoot, *Apostolic Fathers*, 2:1096.

17. Schäferdiek, "Acts of John," at 166; Junod and Kaestli, *Acta Iohannis*, 1:694.

18. No reconstruction of the *Acts of John* has incorporated *John and the Robber,* including the *editio princeps:* Richard Adelbert Lipsius and Maximilien Bonnet, eds., *Acta Apostolorum Apocrypha* (2 vols. in 3; Leipzig: H. Mendelssohn, 1891–1903). Notably, Junod and Kaestli, *Acta Iohannis,* include the complete *Virtutes Iohannis* as related material in their second volume (799–834) and this text does include the story. The Latin text is also available in John Allen Giles, *Codex apocryphus Novi Testamenti. The uncanonical Gospels and other writings, referring to the first ages of Christianity; in the original languages: collected together from the editions of Fabricius, Thilo, and others* (London: D. Nutt, 1852), 336–69; more recently, Italian translations are available in Mario Erbetta, ed. and trans., *Gli apocrifi del Nuovo Testamento,* vol. 2: *Atti e legende* (Casale Monferrato, Italy: Marietti, 1975), 111–29; and Luigi Moraldi, ed. and trans., *Apocrifi del Nuovo Testamento,* vol. 2: *Atti degli Apostoli* (Classici delle Religioni 5; Casale Monferrato, Italy: Piemme, 1994), 583–609.

state of the church in Smyrna as described in *John and the Robber*. In *John and the Robber*, the apostle is portrayed primarily as an itinerant administrator who appoints bishops and corrects problems in established churches, and the church in Smyrna appears to be fairly well established.

The story of *John and the Robber* does appear in what is known as the *Virtutes Iohannis*, book five of Pseudo-Abdias's *Virtutes apostolorum*. A sixth-century work, the *Virtutes* includes Latin translations of some material also found in the *Acts of John*, as well as other ancient traditions of John. A related sixth-century work, the *Passio Iohannis* of Pseudo-Melito, shares some material with the *Virtutes*[19] but does not include *John and the Robber*.[20] Some consider the *Virtutes* to be an expansion of the *Passio*,[21] and others posit that *John and the Robber* came into the *Virtutes* through Rufinus's Latin translation of Eusebius.[22] Whatever the textual history, the sources all appear to derive ultimately from Clement. As Butterworth writes, "We know that Eusebius wrote it out in full, but Clement was his source; and all other copies or references came either from Clement direct or through Eusebius."[23]

Translation

The following translation is based on Otto Stählin's edition of *Quis dives salvetur* 42. The verse divisions were established by Stählin.

Bibliography

EDITIONS AND TRANSLATIONS

Barnard, Percy Mordaunt. *A Homily of Clement of Alexandria, Entitled: Who Is the Rich Man That Is Being Saved?* London: SPCK; New York: E. & J. B. Young & co., 1901.

————. *Clement of Alexandria: Quis Dives Salvetur.* TS 5.2. Cambridge: Cambridge University Press, 1897.

Butterworth, George William, trans. *Clement of Alexandria: The Exhortation to the Greeks, the Rich Man's Salvation, and the Fragment of an Address Entitled "To the Newly Baptized."* LCL 92. London: W. Heinemann; New York: G. P. Putnam's Sons, 1919.

Stählin, Otto. *Clemens Alexandrinus.* Vol. 3. GCS 17. Leipzig: J. C. Hinrichs, 1909.

STUDIES

Butterworth, George William. "The Story of St John and the Robber." *JTS* OS 18 (1917): 141–46.

Dindorf, Ludwig August, ed. *Chronicon paschale.* Bonn: E. Weber, 1832.

Junod, Eric, and Jean-Daniel Kaestli, eds. *Acta Iohannis.* Vol. 1: *Praefatio—Textus.* Vol. 2: *Textus alii—Commentarius—Indices.* CCSA 1–2. Turnhout: Brepols, 1983.

Lipsius, Richard A. *Die apokryphen Apostelgeschichten und Apostellegenden: Ein Beitrag zur altchristlichen Literaturgeschichte.* 3 parts in 2 vols. Braunschweig: C. A. Schwetschke und Sohn, 1883–1887.

---

19. For a discussion of the relationship between the two texts see Schäferdiek, "Die 'Passio Johannis'"; and Junod and Kaestli, *Acta Iohannis*, 2:750–98. Also see Lipsius, *Die apokryphen Apostelgeschichten*, 1:408–31.

20. Junod and Kaestli, *Acta Iohannis*, 2:771.

21. Schäferdiek, "The Acts of John," 160.

22. Junod and Kaestli, *Acta Iohannis*, 2:790.

23. Butterworth, "Story of St John," 144.

Schäferdiek, Knut. "The Acts of John." Pages 152–212 in *New Testament Apocrypha*. Vol. 2: *Writings Relating to the Apostles, Apocalypses and Related Subjects*. Edited by Wilhelm Schneemelcher. Translated by R. McLachlan Wilson. Louisville, Ky.: Westminster John Knox, 1992.

———. "Die 'Passio Johannis' des Melito von Laodikeia und die 'Virtutes Johannis.'" *AnBoll* 103 (1985): 367–82.

John and the Robber

John arrives in Ephesus

42 ¹Now so that you may have confidence when you have truly repented that a reliable hope of salvation remains for you, listen to a story (that is) not (actually) a story but a genuine account from John the apostle that was passed down and preserved in memory.

²For after the demise of the tyrant,ᵃ (John) came from the island of Patmos to Ephesus. He would go away upon request, even to the neighboring regions of the gentiles, appointing bishops in some places, reconciling whole churches in other places, and in other places appointing one of those indicated by the spirit.

Acts 1:17

John, the bishop, and the young man

³Therefore, having come also to a certain city not too far away, the name of which also is reported by some,ᵇ and having given resolution to the brethren in other things, in addition to everything else, he looked upon the newly appointed bishop. Upon seeing a young man, able in body, outwardly handsome and warm in spirit, he said, "I entrust this one to you with all eagerness before the church and the witness of Christ." And (the bishop) accepted (the trust) and made every promise and he committed himself and solemnly testified again to the same things.

⁴Then John left for Ephesus, and the elderᶜ took the young man entrusted to him to his house and brought him up, protected him, cherished him, and finally enlightened him (through baptism). And after this he relaxed his great care and watchfulness, as he had set the seal of the Lord over the young man as the perfect guard.

The degeneration of the young man

⁵But the young man received his liberty too soon and was joined together for mischief with certain idle, worthless (youths) of the same age (who were) accustomed to evil. First they strung him along with costly feasts, then sometimes at night they brought (him) along, going out to steal the clothes of bathers. Then they expected (him) to cooperate in something even greater.

---

a. Likely Domitian. See Barnard, *Homily,* 71.

b. Perhaps Smyrna; see the introduction p. 364.

c. This word could be translated either as "presbyter," referring to the same person named as a bishop earlier, or it could be translated as "old man." The translation "elder" has been preferred, leaving the intent ambiguous as it is in the Greek.

⁶Now in a short time he became accustomed (to this) and because of his great nature was utterly changed. Just as an unbroken and strong horse on the straight path also bites the bit, he rushed even more quickly down to ruin. ⁷Finally, renouncing salvation in God, he intended nothing small but instead to do some great thing because he was ruined once and for all, (and) he expected to suffer the same as the rest. So he took these very youths and organized them into a band of robbers with himself as zealous chief robber—the most violent, most murderous, most dangerous of them all.

John's return

⁸Time passed and something happened to make it necessary to summon John. Now John, after setting in order the matters that he came to address, said, "So come on bishop, return the deposit to us which both I and Christ[a] entrusted to you with the church, which you preside over, as witness."

⁹Now the bishop was amazed at first, supposing that money, which he had not received, was being extorted (from him), and neither could he believe (such a charge) concerning what he did not have nor could he disbelieve John. But when John said, "I demand the youth and the soul of our brother," the elder[b] groaned deeply and even cried. He said, "That one is dead." (John inquired,) "How, and what sort of death?" The bishop said, "He is dead to God. For he turned out wicked and utterly depraved, the chief robber, and now from the church he has taken to the hills with militants like himself."

John's reaction

¹⁰The apostle, ripping apart his clothes and striking his head with a loud groan, said, "Indeed, I left a fine guard over the soul of this brother, but even now, put a horse at my disposal and get me a guide (to show) the way." He rode just as he was, straight from the church.

¹¹Arriving at the place, he was captured by the guard of the robbers, neither fleeing nor imploring (for release), but shouting, "For this I have come, take me to your chief."

¹²The chief waited for a time, armed as he was, but upon approaching he recognized John and being shamed, he turned to fleè. John pursued with all his might, forgetting his own age, crying out, ¹³"Why do you flee me, child, your own father, unarmed[c] and old? Pity me, child, do not fear. You still have hope of life! I myself will give an account to Christ concerning you. If it is necessary, I will willingly endure your death, as the Lord did for us. For your life, I will give my own. Stand and believe; Christ has sent me."

The young man's repentance and redemption

¹⁴Upon hearing this, first the young man stood looking down, then he threw away his weapons; then, trembling, he wept bitterly. Going to the old man, he

Mark 14:72 par.

---

a. Some manuscripts have "the Savior."

b. See p. 368 n. c.

c. Literally "naked."

embraced (him). As he was able, he pleaded his case with groans and was baptized for the second time with tears, only hiding his right hand.[a]

¹⁵Now John, giving pledges (and) assurances that he had found pardon from his Savior, praying, kneeling, and kissing his right hand as having been purified by his repentance, brought (the youth) back to the church. Pleading with abundant prayers and joining together in continual fasting, and with various siren-like words, (John) calmed his mind. John did not leave his presence, as they say, before he had restored him to[b] the church, giving a great example of true repentance and great example of regeneration, a trophy of resurrection that can be seen.

a. Barnard, *Homily*, 75 n. 1 indicates "St. Chrysostom says his right hand was covered with blood," though Barnard provides no citation here and no mention in his Greek edition. In general, Chrysostom associates the notion of staining of the right hand with blood with taking responsibility for spilling the blood of others (*Diab.* 1.3; see also *Hom. Rom.* 7.22; *Hom. 2 Cor.* 3.7; *Hom. Heb.* 13.10). Such may be the thought here, that the robber is accepting responsibility for his actions and the blood he shed.

b. Or "he had set him over."

The History of Simon Cephas, the Chief of the Apostles
Translation and introduction

by F. Stanley Jones

The *History of Simon Cephas, the Chief of the Apostles* (*Hist. Sim. Ceph.*; CANT 200) is a Syriac text that, until now, had not been rendered and published in a modern language. This situation is surprising because *Hist. Sim. Ceph.* is known to be a witness to the lost Greek *Acts of Peter,* for which scholars rely largely on a single Latin manuscript (Vercelli, Biblioteca Capitolare, 158). The inaccessibility of Syriac for many modern scholars is the only explanation for the neglect of *Hist. Sim. Ceph.* in reconstructing the textual history of *Acts Pet.* The text is known in scholarship by a variety of names: "Acta Petri (syriace)," "Historia Petri (syriaca)," "Acts of Saint Peter," "Teachings of Simon Cephas," "Acts of Peter," and "Nestorian History of Peter"; because a history of Paul follows in the sole critical edition of the text and apparently also in the manuscript used for the edition, there are references to the writing also under such inclusive titles as "Acts of Saints Peter and Paul" and "Nestorian History of Peter and Paul."

Contents
As the author explains in his preface (1:1–9), *Hist. Sim. Ceph.* is largely an epitome of earlier accounts of Peter that the author compiled for the church's lectionary to be read at the yearly celebration of Peter's martyrdom. After remarks about the state of the world that brought on the incarnation (2:1–4:6), the author draws mainly on the canonical Acts of the Apostles to describe the early mission of the church, with unusual attention paid to God's role in bringing the disciples to missionize among the gentiles (5:1–9:3). The success of this mission causes the devil to raise up Simon Magus against the church (9:4–10:28). Detailed information on Simon Magus is supplied here from the Syriac version of the Pseudo-Clementine *Recognition* (see also 28:5–19).[1] After Peter refutes Simon several times, Simon heads to Rome, and Peter follows (11:1–12:3). For Peter's first days in Rome (12:4–14:8; see also 29:1; 33:1–3), the author apparently draws on another known Syriac account of Peter called the *Preaching of Simon Cephas in the City of Rome (Pre. Pet. Rome).* The author then adjoins other episodes about Peter and Simon in Rome from *Acts Pet.* 8–32 (14:9–28:42). The scenes demonstrate Peter's superiority over Simon, both in raising the dead as well as in causing Simon to fall after his flight over Rome. *Hist. Sim. Ceph.* ends with further chapters from *Acts Pet.* (33–40) documenting Peter's famous *Quo vadis* vision

---

1. I use here the title *Recognition* (rather than the more conventional *Recognitions*), as it appears to be the original title of the work. See F. Stanley Jones, "Photius's Witness to the *Pseudo-Clementines*," in *Nouvelles intrigues pseudo-clémentines: Plots in the Pseudo-Clementine Romance* (ed. Frédéric Amsler et al.; Publications de l'Institut romand des sciences bibliques 6; Lausanne: Éditions du Zèbre, 2008), 93–101 (repr. in F. Stanley Jones, *Pseudoclementina Elchasaiticaque inter Judaeochristiana: Collected Studies* [OLA 203; Leuven: Peeters, 2012], 345–55).

of Christ (Christ walks toward him with a cross on his way to suffer again because Peter is too weak), his crucifixion (upside down, as requested), and burial (29–35). Then follow a few closing remarks (36).

Manuscripts and Editions

The text translated here was published by Paul Bedjan[2] from a copy of an (unidentified) manuscript in Koj-Kerkuk in the possession of Ignazio Guidi. Guidi collated the edition against the copy of the manuscript and published a few corrections as well as the subscription.[3] No indication of the age of the original manuscript has ever been supplied.[4]

Literary and Theological Importance

Hist. Sim. Ceph. draws on three major nonbiblical sources:

1. The Syriac version of the Pseudo-Clementine *Recognition*.[5] The author of *Hist. Sim. Ceph.* was most interested in Simon's origins (*Rec.* 2.7–11 used in 9:5–23) and Simon's outrageous claims about his powers (*Rec.* 2.9.2–8; 2.14.2; and 3.47.1–2 used in 10:1–26; and *Rec.* 2.7.1; 2.9.3–5; 3.46.7–47.2; and 3.60.1 in 28:5–19).

2. *Preaching of Simon Cephas in the City of Rome* (*CANT* 199). This text was published and translated by William Cureton from two Nitrian Desert manuscripts in the British Library.[6] The text is also contained in four additional Syriac manuscripts: Edgbaston, University of Birmingham, Mingana Syr. 4 (19th cent.); Cambridge (Mass.), Harvard Houghton Library, Syr. 99 (19th cent.); St. Petersburg, National Library of Russia, Siriyskaya novaya seria 4 (6th cent.); and apparently Barcelona, Abbey of Montserrat 31 (dated 1915).[7] This writing seems to be loosely dependent on the (Syriac) *Acts Pet.* and also on the (Syriac) *Ps.-Clem.*

3. A lost Syriac translation of *Acts Pet.*, the martyrdom of which is preserved in London, British Library, Add. 12172, with fragments also in British Library, Add. 14732. This Syriac martyrdom has not been edited, but a translation of it was published by François Nau.[8]

---

2. Bedjan, *Acta Martyrum*, 1:1–33 (errata on p. 544).

3. Guidi, "Bemerkungen," 744–46.

4. Mosul, Chaldean Patriarchate, 90 contains a "History of Saint Peter, the Apostle," which may be the same text. See Addaï Scher, "Notice sur les manuscrits syriaques conservés dans la bibliothèque du Patriarcat Chaldéen de Mossoul," *Revue des bibliothèques* 17 (1907): 227–60 at 250. According to William F. Macomber ("New Finds of Syriac Manuscripts in the Middle East," *XVII. Deutscher Orientalistentag vom 21. bis 27. Juli 1968 in Würzburg* [ed. Wolfgang Voigt; 2 vols.; ZDMGSup 1; Wiesbaden: F. Steiner, 1969], 2:473–82 at 475) the manuscript was apparently transferred to Baghdad in 1960, but its whereabouts today are unknown.

5. The most recent edition is Frankenberg, *Die syrischen Clementinen*. I have prepared a new edition and translation for the Corpus Christianorum Series Apocryphorum. The translation is scheduled to appear ahead of time in the series Apocryphes: Collection de poche de l'AELAC.

6. Text and translation in Cureton, *Ancient Syriac Documents*, 35–41 (in Syriac page-numbering; text), 35–41 (translation), 173–77 (commentary).

7. The Montserrat manuscript is mentioned by Alain Desreumaux, "Les apocryphes apostoliques," in *Les apocryphes syriaques* (ed. Muriel Debié, Alain Desreumaux, Christelle Jullien, and Florence Jullien; Études syriaques 2; Paris: Geuthner, 2005), 71–95 at 87.

8. Nau, "La version syriaque inédite," 43–50. The existence of a Syriac *Acts. Pet.* has sometimes been doubted, but *Hist. Sim. Ceph.*'s manner of excerpting earlier texts renders such a lost Syriac version of *Acts Pet.* highly likely. The value of the Syriac for reconstructing the original Greek of *Acts Pet.* is yet to be

In terms of the importance of *Hist. Sim. Ceph.* as a textual witness to these earlier sources, there can be no doubt that *Hist. Sim. Ceph.* is most important as a witness to the text of *Acts Pet.*, the majority of which (chaps. 1–29) is preserved only in a fourth-century Latin translation found in one sixth- or seventh-century manuscript (Vercelli 158). Scholars have speculated about the degree to which the Latin accurately reflects the original Greek *Acts Pet.*[9] Apart from internal considerations, essentially only a single vellum Greek page from Oxyrhynchus in Egypt (P. Oxy. 849; late third or early fourth century; comprising portions of *Acts Pet.* 25–26) has been used for comparison with the Latin text of the Vercelli codex. *Hist. Sim. Ceph.* thus provides a little-utilized resource to regulate the debate since it contains an extensive sequential epitome of *Acts Pet.* 8–29, as well as the Martyrdom (chaps. 30–40). Notes to the translation will indicate some instances in which *Hist. Sim. Ceph.* has preserved a more original text than the Latin (particularly as evidenced by the Oxyrhynchus fragment), but also other instances in which the Syriac is obviously secondary in comparison.

Perhaps most significantly, *Hist. Sim. Ceph.* does not mention Paul and his mission in Rome prior to the arrival of Peter and thereby offers support for the supposition that these elements (found in the old Latin translation, chaps. 1–4) are later additions to *Acts Pet.* not found in the Syriac text's Greek source. By extension, whenever a passage or episode from *Acts Pet.* is absent in *Hist. Sim. Ceph.*, that passage or episode must be examined carefully as a possible later addition to the original *Acts Pet.* The christological discourse by Peter in the Latin *Acts Pet.* 24 but absent in *Hist. Sim. Ceph.*, for example, is unusual enough with its many proof texts from the Old Testament. Noteworthy also is the absence of the speeches of Peter in *Acts Pet.* 37–39. Thus, while *Hist. Sim. Ceph.* is epitomizing *Acts Pet.*, it also offers an invaluable underused tool for reconstruction of the original *Acts Pet.*

As the introduction to the text indicates, this work was compiled for reading in the church on the memorial of Peter's martyrdom. Those who listened to the text would have been treated to some notable lessons. First, its brief compendium of biblical history features a somewhat unique retelling of primeval history, as well as an account of the incarnation and mission of Jesus (2–4). Theologically, this distinctive summary is not without interest and provides a window into the realm of Syriac theology of the age. Also fascinating is the narrative about the primitive Jewish-Christian church in Jerusalem (5:13–6:6). The author explains that the disciples did not want to leave Jerusalem and mix with the gentiles (6:1), thus neglecting the Great Commission (Mark 16:15; Matt 28:19). This disobedience caused God to turn away, and the first persecution of the church ensued. Consequently, the apostles were scattered and the mission to the gentiles occurred. Through the following moving accounts of Peter's miracles and martyrdom, the text inspires allegiance to the faith. Simon is the villain who serves as the foil for God's triumph.

As indicated in several remarks in this text (8:3–5), the author continues his work with an account of Paul, but the break at the end of the account of Peter justifies its independent treatment here.

---

thoroughly evaluated. The Greek papyrus of *Acts Pet.* (P. Oxy. 849) contains at least one striking instance (where the prefect states that he wishes to test God; *Hist. Sim. Ceph.* 23:2) that demonstrates that the Syriac has preserved an original phrase bowdlerized in the Latin of the Vercelli manuscript.

9. See, e.g., Christine M. Thomas, *The Acts of Peter, Gospel Literature and the Ancient Novel: Rewriting the Past* (New York: Oxford University Press, 2003) and Matthew C. Baldwin, *Whose Acts of Peter? Text and Historical Context of the Actus Vercellenses* (WUNT 2/196; Tübingen: Mohr Siebeck, 2005).

Original Language, Date, and Provenance

The language of the text points to an origin in Syria. It is difficult to date the text exactly. It can be said to have originated after the church started regularly celebrating the liturgical calendar with memorial days for the saints. Comments toward the end of the account of Paul[10] indicate that "when peace came to the church," Peter's and Paul's relics were transferred to "the church" (Old St. Peter's Basilica, likely completed in the 320s CE), so this remark confirms a post-Constantinian date. Dependency on the Syriac translation of the Pseudo-Clementine *Recognition* (mid-fourth century) points further to the latter half of the fourth century. An indication of a date not much later may be the citation of Jesus' saying from John 21:15–17 (*Hist. Sim. Ceph.* 5:12) in a form likely witnessed only in the Syriac *Diatessaron*, the harmony of the Gospels that was current in the Syriac-speaking church before its replacement in the fifth century by the separate Gospels in the later Syriac New Testament, the Peshitta.[11] The same applies to the citation of Mark 16:15//Matt 28:19 (*Hist. Sim. Ceph.* 6:3).

Translation

The translation has been made from the edition of Bedjan, with consideration of the corrections provided by Guidi.[12] Chapter divisions largely follow the paragraphs in Bedjan's edition, with some adjustments to illustrate best the parallels in the text's source material; verses are numbered according to complete sentences. Clarifications of subjects, object, and the like are placed in parentheses. In Syriac, the difference in spelling between "Shemon" (Simon Peter) and "Simon" (Simon Magus) is marked and unambiguous; to reflect this difference and for the purpose of clarity, "Shemon" (for Simon Peter) has been adopted consistently in this translation.

Bibliography

Bedjan, Paul. *Acta Martyrum et Sanctorum.* 7 vols. Paris: Otto Harrassowitz, 1890–1897. (*Editio princeps* in vol. 1, pp. 1–33 with errata p. 544.)

Cureton, William. *Ancient Syriac Documents Relative to the Earliest Establishment of Christianity in Edessa and the Neighbouring Countries.* London: Williams & Norgate, 1864.

Frankenberg, Wilhelm. *Die syrischen Clementinen mit griechischem Paralleltext.* TU 48.3. Leipzig: J. C. Hinrichs, 1937.

Guidi, Ignazio. "Bemerkungen zum ersten Bande der syrischen Acta Martyrum et Sanctorum." *ZDMG* 46 (1892): 744–58.

Nau, François. "La version syriaque inédite des martyres de S. Pierre, S. Paul et S. Luc." *ROC* 3 (1898): 39–57, 151–67.

---

10. See Bedjan, *Acta Martyrum,* 1:42.

11. While the combination of the three terms into one statement ("Feed for me my lambs, my sheep, and my ewes") seems to derive from the Syriac *Diatessaron,* it is noteworthy that the three terms correspond in wording and order with the three commands in the Peshitta.

12. The vowel pointing in Bedjan's edition partially reflects modern usage. It is not clear how much of this pointing, if any, derives from the manuscript (Guidi's corrections and additions do not have vowel pointing). Accordingly, Bedjan's vowel pointing is not always followed.

The History of Simon Cephas, the Chief of the Apostles

Introduction

1 ¹The history of the friends of Christ we were required to tell. ²We do not have the strength to be able to fill some of the debt that was required of us because our anointing is small and our strength is too weak for the task. ³Even if we have not captured the fullness of the stories to show sufficiently the full heroism and the triumphs that they manifested in the world but if only here and there a few stories that are poor to show the glorious heroism of their fortitude—yet because the love of their compassion constrains us so that every year we celebrate these loving memories of them in the church—we have dared to try according to our strength and to avoid erring in the lines and in the broad places of the writings of our holy fathers. ⁴And all the fullness of their triumphs that are found in them may we gather, and may we lay on the censer of the love of their friends, and may we please with the fragrance of its smoke for the breath of the holy church. ⁵While we try, may we briefly make the story of their travails according to the demand of time of their readings (lections). ⁶First, we will make the beginning of our treatise the story of the great destruction and of the humiliation into which our nature was plunged. ⁷And we will tell about the divine compassion that overflowed on it in the coming of the Son of God. ⁸Then we will relate the trials of the holy apostles, these who were designated by him for the life-giving instruction. ⁹We are not relating everything that they did, but one or two (things) that previous fathers wrote concerning them.

The transgressions of primeval humanity

2 ¹For when the first man despised and transgressed the command of God, he was both deprived of the glorious good things and immediately cast out for the mortal life that is full of every misery. ²And the pleasure of trees was exchanged for him for this cursed earth. ³Again, those who were after him and filled the earth were even more evil than he in their disobedience that they showed toward their Creator.[a] ⁴And like beasts, they chose the life that was not life.

Gen 3:1–24

Gen 6:5

⁵When they were not shamed by the law of discernment that is planted in nature, they were also not persuaded by the divine admonitions that came in

---

a. Here and in the following, the author is not directly oriented on the biblical account but apparently on the (Syriac) tradition as received by the author, which cannot always be documented in the preserved sources.

revelations about the better things in them. [6]Rather, they were living like wild sleepers and the stubborn in the desert of ignorance. [7]They were destroying the thoughts that are right for the peaceful offspring of knowledge. [8]They were giving themselves entirely to every abomination. [9]While at times they were corrupting one another, sometimes they were killing each other, and sometimes they were eating humans. [10]And by the wars of those great men who are mentioned among the Greeks and among everyone, they were also planning to build a tower from earth to heaven. [11]In the madness of their thoughts, they were preparing to fight from their place with the one who is God over all. [12]And they brought forth gods and goddesses in the entire world.

Gen 11:1–9

3 [1]Because they were carried away in this manner, in a flood of water and fire he brought divine retribution upon them like thickets of animals that were spread throughout the entire earth. [2]In persistent famines, plagues, and wars and in the fire that he was sending down from the fire above, he was destroying them. [3]He was smiting (them) with malignant diseases of the souls in bitter punishment of retribution. [4]But when the evil was shed on nearly everyone, like a great drunkenness, it was also intoxicating the humans. [5]The effect was that the rational race arrived at the consummation of brutality, and they were defiled even in every type of corruption. [6]And for the honor appropriate to the One who lives eternally, they judged the impure race of demons. And henceforth they passed from the limit of every decency.

Gen 6:1–8:5; 19:24–25

The arrival of the Savior

4 [1]Then God the Word, the Savior of all, persuaded himself and came to the lower depth of death according to the will of himself and his Father. [2]And in the body with which he shrouded himself from the Virgin Mary, to every order of rational creatures from end to end he announced the greatness of himself and his Father. [3]He bound that deceiving demon of the world as a mighty one and he plundered his house. [4]Now, he appeared in the year 304 of the Macedonians, which is the year 43 of Augustus, the king of the Romans. [5]In the year 334 of Alexander, which is the year 15 of Tiberius Caesar, he was baptized by John the Forerunner. [6]After that, he began to proclaim the kingdom of God, which is the preparation of the new covenant, also because it was the time for the Savior generally to give correction to these human matters and again to recall their error after the demons and to return the glory of the creatures to the divine nature.

Matt 1:18; Luke 1:31, 35

Mark 3:27 par.

Luke 2:1

Mark 1:9–11 par.; John 1:29–34

The call of the disciples

5 [1]Since he was hastening to accomplish his course and to return from this world to his Father, he chose for himself therefore preachers of his heavenly teaching. [2]While he instructed them first in the knowledge of the proclamation, in the true teaching that was with them, he both confirmed them in himself by the signs that he performed before them and perfected them after his resurrection and ascent to heaven in the power of goodness of the Holy Spirit. [3]They would be empowered to heal ulcers without worldly knowledge, and they would repair the wounds and bruises that the peoples had received through the deception of the demons. [4]He first chose for himself the Twelve, who were disciples, and

Acts 1:8; 2:1–4

Mark 3:13–19 par.; Luke 10:1, 17

thereafter seventy-two.[a] [5]The ones after them preached the heavenly teaching to all.

Peter appointed chief of the apostles

[6]Now, he established the blessed Peter as captain, chief, and first of them all, as one who had looked into the eye of his divinity so that this one would be worthy to be the teacher of the world after him. [7]Therefore, he nicknamed him Cephas, because of the truth of his profession. [8]Because he was the first and displayed the true profession of the divinity and humanity of Christ through the revelation of the Father that was shown to him, he was also the first esteemed worthy of the blessing of the faith of the truth. [9]Our Savior professed that the faith of the church is built on the confession of his faith, and he first committed to him the keys of the kingdom of heaven.

Matt 16:15–19

[10]When for three years and a little more all the apostles had been instructed in the knowledge of the teaching, in the year 18 of Tiberius, our Lord suffered, died, and rose. [11]After his resurrection, he strengthened the disciples for forty days in various ways. [12]And he committed the flock of the church to Shemon: "Feed for me my lambs, my sheep, and my ewes."[b]

Acts 1:3

John 21:15–17

The church in Jerusalem

[13]Ten days after his ascension, when the Jews were assembled for the observance of the festival of Pentecost, the blessed apostles received the blessing of the Holy Spirit while they were assembled in the upper room. [14]And they narrated in various tongues the miracles of God that our Savior did. [15]Now the Jews came together and assembled near the upper room so that the likeness of fire enveloped them and the fragrant smell above was pouring out from there. [16]And they were hearing from the Galilean men, who were of one nation, that they were speaking in the tongues of all the nations. [17]Through the great powers that were working through them, they strengthened the miracle of the division of their tongues. [18]Thus they were making disciples of many powerful people of the Jews, who had assembled there from everywhere. [19]And the number of disciples was increasing day by day, including foreigners from the nations; a great assembly arose.

Acts 2

The martyrdom of Stephen

6 [1]Now the disciples did not want to leave Jerusalem, and they did not consent to be connected with the gentiles. [2]As such, they were holding to the Jewish doctrine that holds that only among the people of the Jews had God fixed his blessings. [3]For they had disregarded the life-giving Word that had admonished

---

a. A similar summarizing statement of the Gospel accounts is found in *Rec.* 1.40.4, which also numbers Luke's group of disciples as seventy-two, rather than seventy. *Hist. Sim. Ceph.* may well be dependent on *Rec.* 1.40.4 here because below, at *Hist. Sim. Ceph.* 9:1, the author speaks of seventy apostles.

b. This type of shortened form of John 21:15–17 (the three objects are contained in three separate commands in the original form of John's Gospel) is witnessed for the *Diatessaron;* thus, this citation apparently reflects the author's intimate acquaintance with the *Diatessaron* rather than with the later Peshitta version.

Mark 16:15; Matt 28:19   them, "Go to all the world and teach all the nations."[a] [4]Therefore, when they were diligent with teaching only the Jews, they were despising the rest of the nations as strangers and impure. [5]Then the common Creator turned away, and a persecution was stirred up against them in Jerusalem. [6]This is the one in which

Acts 7:54–60   the blessed Stephen was perfected with the crown of witness for the truth. [7]Because of this persecution, the holy apostles were scattered to Samaria and to all

Acts 8:1   the nations.

Acts of Philip

[8]And in this manner, the blessing of God managed that the Samaritans, too,

Acts 8:4–8   should receive the teaching of life through Philip, one of the Seven. [9]And through him the instruction of Ethiopia also began, when the blessing of God arranged that one believer, an emissary of Candace, queen of the Ethiopians, who are barbarians and foreigners, was instructed by Philip through a revelation

Acts 8:26–39   that came to him. He taught every place among the Ethiopians. [10]And he was the first born of all the believers from the gentiles. [11]And by him, what was said was

Ps 68:31   fulfilled: that Ethiopia will give the hand to God.

The conversion of Cornelius

7 [1]However, the twelve apostles were waiting in Jerusalem. [2]Therefore, as the Goodness willed that it should teach them to go for the teaching of the gentiles, through the chief of the apostles this was prepared so that it happened first: And the angel of the Lord appeared to Cornelius. [3]For this one was a man from the gentiles and a noble and a centurion in his rank. [4]He was righteous in his manner of life and in his thought and he very much desired to do the will of God in

Acts 10:1–2   the distinction of excellence of his soul. [5]To this one, thus, the angel of the Lord

Acts 10:3–5   appeared; it commanded him to send to summon Shemon Cephas, [6]and that he should speak with him the word of life.

[7]For also to the blessed Shemon a vision showed the form of a cloth being lowered down from heaven to the earth and the forms of every genus of living animal clean and unclean that were in it. [8]And it commanded him to slay from the unclean and eat. [9]When Shemon answered, "*I have never eaten anything that is profane and unclean,*" a voice came to him that was saying, "*What God has made clean, do not you yourself defile.*" [10]And when this happened three

Acts 10:11–16   times, the garment was raised to heaven. [11]Immediately, the Spirit taught him the interpretation of the vision: That he should rise and go with the men who

Acts 10:19–23   were sent to him from Cornelius. [12]Thus, he was persuaded and went to him. [13]As he was speaking with him concerning the good things that God was ready to give to humans through the providence that was in Christ, before he had finished his speech, the Spirit descended on Cornelius and the assembly that was with him, and they began to speak in tongues just as what happened with

Acts 10:44–46   the apostles.

---

a. This scriptural citation seems to reflect the *Diatessaron* rather than an *ad hoc* creation out of Mark 16:15 and Matt 28:19 because Ephrem, *Comm. Diat.* 8.1, similarly has the combination of the Markan "Go to all the world" and the Matthean "all the nations."

The call of Paul

8 [1]And so also until this time, the apostles were separated with the Jews because of the custom of their upbringing with them. [2]They were forbidding that they would proclaim openly to the gentiles. [3]Then the Goodness chose the great Paul—whose story we will narrate afterwards—so that in great joy he might labor in the teaching of the gentiles. [4]But first we will tell the heroic deeds that the Spirit effected through Peter. [5]Then we will approach the story of the blessed Paul.[a]

Acts 10:9–19

Simon Magus and Dositheus

9 [1]As the tiding of life was spread by the seventy apostles in all the world, it was also magnified by their industrious disciples in all the inhabitable regions. [2]They turned people away from the worship of Satan, and they yoked them in confession and in the worship of the one God, the Creator of all. [3]They were worshipping him in good ways and in goodliness of mind. [4]But the enemy of our nature was jealous, and he raised against the doctrine of the truth Simon, a Samaritan man, who through the guile of demons seduced many of the dwellers of Palestine to his error. [5]For this Simon was a Samaritan from the city Githnin.[b] [6]The name of his father was Anton, and his mother was Rachel. [7]He was a magician. And he instructed himself well in the discipline of the Greeks. [8]He was exalted and puffed up and announced concerning himself that he was the power that is greater than the Creator. [9]This one previously followed a certain man whose name was Dositheus. [10]Others were following him who were called "chiefs." [11]They were thirty in number with one woman who was called Selena,[c] which translates as "moon." [12]She, who previously stood in fornication in Caesarea of Phoenicia,[d] went around with him at that time. [13]For there were thirty licentious[e] accomplices with him so that they might be thirty like the course of the moon. [14]This Simon went and, in counterfeit love, asked Dositheus that he might follow him. [15]And Dositheus said to him, "We do not add to this number, until after one should fail from us."[f] [16]And he remained with him. [17]And when the number decreased, he brought in Simon.

Acts 8:9

Acts 8:10; *Rec.* 2.7.1

Rec. 2.8.1–3

---

a. The manuscript continues after Peter's martyrdom with an account of Paul.

b. The *Ps.-Clem.* parallels (*Rec.* 2.7.1–12.1; 2.14.1–2; 3.47.1–2, and 3.63) begin at this point and continue through *Hist. Sim. Ceph.* 9:26. *Hist. Sim. Ceph.* follows Syriac *Rec.* 2.7.1 in its representation of the name of Simon's hometown. The location and exact name of this village are disputed. The manuscript of Justin, *1 Apol.* 26.2, where the name is mentioned, is corrupt; Justin's reading is usually reconstructed from the excerpt of Justin in Eusebius, *Hist. eccl.* 2.13.3, as "Gitthon" or "Gittho," but there are many variants among the manuscripts of Eusebius. The manuscript of Hippolytus, *Haer.* 6.7.1, which also has the name, is usually considered corrupt.

c. Justin, *1 Apol.* 26.3, calls her "Helen," and so too does *Hom.* 2.23.3. In consistently using the Greek word for "moon" for the woman's name, *Hist. Sim. Ceph.* actually differs here and in the following also from the two main manuscripts of Syriac *Rec.* 2.8.1; 2.9.1; 2.12.1, which simply use the Syriac word for "moon."

d. This location is not found in *Ps.-Clem.*, nor is her previous lifestyle; Justin, *1 Apol.* 26.3, states that she had been placed in a brothel in Tyre of Phoenicia (this location is not actually mentioned in the manuscript of Justin, but it is found in writers dependent on Justin and thus sometimes it is conjectured to have been in Justin's original text).

e. This adjective does not appear in the parallel passage in *Rec.*

f. *Hist. Sim. Ceph.* apparently has enlivened the text by turning a narrative statement (so Syriac *Rec.* 2.8.2) into direct speech.

Rec. 2.9.1   [18]After a little while, (Simon) desired Selena, and he began to slander Dositheus, namely, "He is not imparting the doctrine to you purely. [19]And he is doing this not as if in jealousy but because he is ignorant." [20]When once Dositheus perceived in Simon's backbiting that this one wanted to destroy the opinion of the many and to show that he was the one who would abide forever, in rage he entered their school as was usual, found Simon, and struck him. [21]But Dositheus's hand seemed to pass through Simon like smoke when he struck him. [22]And Dositheus was amazed and said to him, "If you are the one who stands forever, I too will worship you."

[23]When Simon said, "I am," he fell and worshipped him and so also those twenty-eight chiefs who were with him. [24]And he commanded that they should

Rec. 2.11.1–4   obey him in all matters.

The preaching of Simon Magus

10 [1]When Dositheus died, Simon took Selena. [2]And he was preached in every place, and he proclaimed as he said, "To everyone who cleaves to me, I will grant

Rec. 2.9.2   that they be gods and great ones."[a] [3]And he was saying,

> "I am the great and first power,[b] and I am able to perform many signs.[c]
> [4]For if they wish to lay hold of me, I am able to not be seen.
> [5]And when I wish to be seen, I am seen.
> [6]If it is that I should escape, I will bore through the mountain as if it is soft mud and I will pass.
> [7]If I should hurl myself from the high mountain, I will descend to the earth as if things are supporting me.
> [8]I will free myself and will make those who bound me to be bound.
> [9]If I should be imprisoned, I will open the door.
> [10]And I will give souls to statues of stone so that those who see them will think that they are humans.
> [11]I will make young sprouts spring up.
> [12]I will instantly produce trees from the earth.
> [13]And if I should throw myself into fire, I will not burn.
> [14]I shall transform myself, and I will be seen with two faces by humans.
> [15]I will give a beard to a baby, and I will make (someone to be) the king, and I will amaze all.
> [16]I will effect that I will be worshipped and honored by everyone so that

Rec. 2.9.3–6   they will set up my image and will serve and worship me as God.

[17]In brief, everything that I wish to do I will be able to. [18]Behold, great things are done by me. [19]For once, when Rachel my mother commanded me to go to the

Rec. 2.9.8   harvest, I commanded the sickle that was placed flat to go. [20]And it is not, as is said, that I am the son of Anton. [21]Before my mother Rachel had intercourse

---

a. *Hist. Sim. Ceph.* is generalizing Syriac *Rec.* 2.9.2 (a promise made just to the twin brothers of Clement).

b. Syriac *Rec.* 3.47.1 has just "I am the first power." "Great" perhaps derives from Acts 8:10.

c. *Hist. Sim. Ceph.* leaves out "by magic" (Syriac *Rec.* 2.9.2).

with him, while she was a virgin, she conceived me. [22]Because I am able to become great and small as I wish. [23]For I did not receive a beginning so that at some time I should start to be. [24]But in the womb of Rachel I was begotten as a human in order that I might be seen by humans. [25]And I have flown, and I have been mingled with fire and air. [26]I have been led by the hands of angels, and I have made stones into bread."

Rec. 2.14.2; 3.47.1

Rec. 3.47.2

[27]He was saying some things greater than these in error,[a] and he was deceiving many of the Samaritans so that they thought concerning him that this one is the great power of God, because for a long time he amazed them with his enchantments. [28]And thus the blessing of the Spirit was abating wherever his fire consumed.

Acts 8:10–11

The apostles encounter Simon in Samaria

11 [1]But when Philip came and taught the crowds with signs and wonders, Simon too, being amazed, was baptized. [2]But he did not receive the grace of the Spirit, since he was not a vessel worthy for its reception. [3]When he offered money to the holy apostles to give him the power so that everyone upon whom he would lay hands would receive the Spirit of Holiness, he thought that everyone who gave money received (the Spirit), but that he did not receive (it) because he did not give. [4]Then, Shemon reproved him and rebuked him, "You are smitten with bitter wrath."

Acts 8:4–13

Acts 8:18–23

[5]And when he had been corrected by Peter many times first in the land of Judea,[b] then in Caesarea, (Peter) exposed him many times until everyone shrank from him. [6]And he was not accompanied except by one. [7]Thus he led him out at midnight and hurled his charms into the sea before him. [8]After these things, he too went and cleaved to Peter.

Rec. 3.63

Peter disputes with Simon in Rome

12 [1]And (Simon) decided to go to Rome. [2]As he went, the power of the demons was at work in him so much that even statues rose up for him as if to God. [3]When Peter heard, he departed from Antioch for Rome in the third year of Claudius the king[c] so that he might put an end to the deception of Simon. [4]As he was close to going up to Rome, many were hearing of his goodness and went out to meet him. [5]And he came and went to where the whole city was gathered. [6]Some of the chiefs of the city, who were clothed in the white garments[d] of the king, came out and went near him to hear him.

Pre. Pet. Rome pp. 35–38

---

a. It is at this point that the narrative rejoins Acts 8 for material that does not have a parallel in *Ps.-Clem.*

b. This phrase is possibly a reference to a supposedly lost part of *Acts Pet.* that recounted conflicts between Peter and Simon in Judea; the preserved Latin version of the *Acts Pet.* begins its report of Peter's activity with his departure for Rome (*Acts Pet.* 5), though God does say to Peter here: "Peter, Simon, whom you expelled from Judaea after having exposed him as a magician, has forestalled you at Rome" (trans. Elliott, *ANT*).

c. Here begins the parallel to *Pre. Pet. Rome*. However, Peter's actual preaching (pp. 36–38) is found here only in summary (at 12:7–9). The reading "third" year is preserved in Bedjan's manuscript. Cureton conjectured it, whereas his manuscript read "thirtieth."

d. Cureton translates this as "headbands" on the basis of a conjecture. See his notes in *Ancient Syriac Documents*, 156, 174.

[7]When the whole city was assembled to him, he rose to speak with them and to show them the proclamation of his teaching. [8]He began to speak with them about God and about the dispensation through Christ. [9]And he persuaded them to desist from what they were accustomed and to turn to the light of the truth preached by him, and they should not, as lacking reason, be persuaded by Simon to the form of error that he presents, "because all the apparitions that he displays are fantasy and are not the truth of real deeds." [10]And he said to them, "Choose for yourselves a sign that we should do before you. [11]And the one whom you see do that sign, it is yours to believe him."

Pre. Pet. Rome p. 39

Simon fails to revive the chief's son

13 [1]In that hour they sent and brought Simon to themselves. [2]And the people of his opinion said to him, "As the man in whom we trust to be powerful enough to do everything, do something before us and this Shemon the Galilean who preaches Christ will see." [3]While they were saying these things to him, it happened that a dead person was passing—a son of one of the chiefs and respected among them. [4]They said to those who were assembled, "The one of you who revives this dead person is the one who is true and trustworthy, and we will listen to him in everything that he should say to us."

[5]And they said to Simon, "Since you have the priority here over Shemon the Galilean and we were acquainted with you before Shemon, you will show the power that accompanies you." [6]Now Simon haltingly approached the dead person, and they placed the bier before him. [7]He was looking right and left and considering heaven while saying many words, some as shouts and some as chants, and he waited a long time, but he did not do anything. [8]And that dead person was prostrate on the bier.

[9]At that moment, Shemon Cephas approached confidently. [10]He called the attention of the crowds and said, "In the name of our Lord Jesus Christ, whom the Jews crucified in Jerusalem and whom we proclaim, rise from here!" [11]And with Shemon's word, that dead person revived. [12]They were all amazed and said to Shemon, "Christ, whom you proclaim, is true." [13]And many rose and said, "Let Simon the magician be stoned!" [14]But Simon, because all had run to see that dead person who had revived, was escaping from them, from one street to the next and from one courtyard to the next. [15]And he did not fall into their hands that day.

Pre. Pet. Rome p. 40

Peter establishes the church in Rome

14 [1]But the whole city held Shemon in great honor. [2]They were receiving him gladly and affectionately. [3]He did not cease doing signs and wonders in the name of Christ, and many were believing in him. [4]Cropinos, the father of the one who had come to life, led him into his house and received him in great honor. [5]There were many in Rome and in the villages and on the islands of the sea who were not yet believers in Shemon, for they were saying, "Simon, too, showed us many signs." [6]Now many of the Romans became disciples, from the Jews and pagans. [7]He made some of them presbyters and deacons. [8]And many assembled to see Shemon on Sunday, to hear from him the words of life, and to be strengthened in the faith.

Peter enquires about Simon Magus

[9]He was in the house of the presbyter Narcesos. [10]Many who had stumbled because of Simon also came to Shemon. [11]When he persuaded them and strengthened them in the faith, many rejoiced in his words. [12]They asked him to allow them to go after Simon and put him to death. [13]Shemon said to them, "Where is that magician, who, when I revived that dead person, was sought and was not found?" [14]And they were saying to him, "He is in the house of Marcellus, whom he has deceived. [15]And he said to him, 'I am the power of God.'"

[16](Shemon) said to them, "Who is this Marcellus?"[a] [17]They were saying to him, "That man is a senator and very rich. [18]And there is no one in all Rome who is greater in alms than he. [19]For he was nourishing all the widows, orphans, and poor so that even Caesar sent to him, 'Did I set you in authority in the city in order that you give your treasure to the poor?' [20]And he went to Caesar and said to him, 'I and the poor, we are your servants, O King. [21]And the possessions that I have are your own.' [22]Caesar said to him, 'If your treasure had been mine, I would have guarded it.' [23]But when Simon deceived him, he sat in great mourning and was repenting and said, 'Vainly have I wasted mounds of my money in the hope of God.' [24]Now he commands at the word of Simon[b] to drive away with the staff every poor person who approaches the gate of his house.[c] [25]And he said, 'I repent of what I have done to these people. [26]Now they are coming and staying at the gate of my house.' [27]And he is speaking evil words against the Christians, and he calls you a magician."

Peter at the home of Marcellus

15 [1]As Shemon said these things briefly,[d] many became disciples to the faith of Christ. [2]And he rose and went to the gate of Marcellus. [3]He called the gatekeeper and said to him, "Go and say to Simon the evil magician that Shemon Cephas is standing at the gate and is saying to you, 'Because of you, I have come to the city of Rome.'"

[4]The gatekeeper fell, did obeisance to him, and said, "My lord, from the day that you raised the dead, he came here and admonished me, 'If Shemon should come and ask you about me, say, He is not here.'"[e]

[5]There was a great crowd at the gate of Marcellus—the sick and ill who had come to be healed. [6]When he heard that Shemon Cephas was standing at his gate, he was alarmed and went out. [7]And when he saw the power and miracles that he did, he fell to his feet and said to him, "Have mercy on me, my lord Peter, and do not abandon me to perish in the error of Simon. [8]The magician deceived me such that I even put up a statue for him, and he persuaded me that I should

---

a. The parallel to *Acts Pet.* 8 starts here and ends at 35:4 in the midst of *Acts Pet.* 40.

b. This phrase is not paralleled in the Latin.

c. Impersonal Syriac usage. Notice the difference between this translation and the Latin ("when a pilgrim comes to the door of his house he beats him with a stick or has him driven off," trans. Elliott, *ANT*). The Syriac could well be more original.

d. The compiler seems to have omitted Peter's lengthy indictment of the devil that forms the latter half of the Latin *Acts Pet.* 8.

e. *Hist. Sim. Ceph.* does not have the account of the talking dog that is found in the Latin *Acts Pet.* 9 and 12, nor the account of the fish brought back to life in the Latin *Acts Pet.* 13.

write that Simon is the new, great, and holy god. [9]Therefore, I entreat you my lord Peter, have mercy on me since you serve God, forgiving sins." [10]Then Peter rejoiced greatly, and he presented a prayer to God for him. [11]Then he embraced Marcellus and kissed him.[a]

Acts Pet. 11

Peter instructs Marcellus to restore a broken statue

16 [1]Behold, a certain youth in whom there was an evil demon was ridiculing greatly. [2]Shemon looked and said to the crowd, "Who is it who is ridiculing? [3]Let him show himself!" [4]Then the demoniac ran to the house of Marcellus and was beating his head against the wall. [5]And Shemon rebuked him and said, "In the name of our Lord Jesus Christ, leave this young man and do not destroy anything in him!" [6]At that moment, that demon left him and overturned the statue of Caesar that was standing at the gate of Marcellus.

[7]When Marcellus was disturbed because of the statue, since he was fearful lest something bad would be done to him by Caesar, Shemon said to him, "Be still, man! I see that you are not yet truly in the faith of Christ. [8]Now you will perform a miracle by your hand. [9]Take in your hands waters that are flowing and sprinkle that statue and it will be whole as before."

[10]He approached with a peaceful heart and sprinkled some of that on the pieces of that statue and said, "I believe in you Jesùs Christ, my Lord!" [11]Immediately those pieces were reassembled, and that statue became as it was before. [12]Then Shemon was rejoicing greatly in Marcellus because he was found faithful in his petition, and many were amazed and fell to the feet of Peter. [13]Others, though they were doubting until then, were saying to Shemon, "Show us other signs, because Simon, too, has shown us many signs and then deceived us."

Acts Pet. 14

Marcellus expels Simon from his home

17 [1]Now Marcellus and that crowd were rejoicing in the faith of Christ, and Marcellus went to his house and found Simon sitting by himself in the court. [2]And he reviled him and said, "Satan and plunderer of humans, evil magician and destroyer of my soul: Leave my house!" [3]He raised his hand against him and hit him, and he cast out and reviled him. [4]He commanded his servants that they should expel him. [5]And some of them treated him shamefully, and others were beating him with rods and stones. [6]One of them ran and brought vessels full of dung and emptied them on his head because of the many times that Marcellus had enchained him because of him, who had said many words about him. [7]He had also accused them falsely in his assemblies before their lord. [8]And all were saying to Simon, "You are recompensed with this according to your deeds."

[9]Then Simon left Marcellus's house and went and stood at the gate of the presbyter Narcissus. [10]And he called out and said, "Shemon, Shemon, come outside! [11]I have a matter to discuss with you."

---

a. It has been suggested that the Latin translation of *Acts Pet.* reflects a secondary alteration of the original *Acts Pet.* when it presents Marcellus as a lapsed Christian and as someone who had been instructed by Paul (*Acts Pet.* 10). *Hist. Sim. Ceph.* does not mention Paul at this point and also seems to understand Marcellus as a pagan; *Hist. Sim. Ceph.* thus seems to support the opinion that, in these features, the Latin translation of *Acts Pet.* reflects a secondary alteration of the original *Acts Pet.*

Peter relates the story of Simon and Eubola

Acts Pet. 17

18 ¹Shemon came out and refuted him in many things,[a] and he spoke to the crowd about the vessels that Simon had stolen from a certain wealthy woman whose name was Eubola, who had received him as an apostle. ²When she was making a wedding for her son, he hired two youths for 200 dinars. ³And (the youths) went and stole her vessels. ⁴Shemon came and instructed Eubola. ⁵And on the day of their being sold, Shemon commanded her to send her servants to the gate of Napolis at the booth of Agropinos. (He said), "Capture the sellers." They handed them over to Papos the governor.[b] ⁶They revealed that Simon had hired them to steal those vessels, and they went to show where they were buried. ⁷When Eubola received her vessels, she provided for many poor with them. ⁸And she believed in our Lord Jesus until the end.[c]

Marcellus purifies his house and holds a feast

Acts Pet. 19–20

19 ¹When Marcellus heard these things and that Shemon Cephas had told such things as these, he brought a vessel of water to Shemon and said to him, "Rise, bless this water, and I will go sprinkle my house so that it might be cleansed of the traces of Simon the magician." ²Shemon blessed the water, and Marcellus sprinkled it in his entire house up to the latrine.[d] ³Marcellus held a feast for two hundred widows and two hundred poor; he persuaded Shemon also to come with them.

⁴As Narcissus the presbyter and all the brethren who were with Shemon were going to the house of Marcellus, (Shemon) saw a blind woman holding her companion with her hands and proceeding (together). ⁵Shemon placed (his) hand on her, and she saw the light. ⁶They were praising God for this miracle. ⁷For nine hours they prayed and sat down to eat, and Marcellus was serving them.[e]

Marcellus has a vision

Acts Pet. 22

20 ¹In that night, Marcellus saw a vision. ²First he told it to Shemon and said, "I saw you as you were sitting on a throne, and a great crowd was standing below you. ³And, behold, a woman was standing in the middle of that crowd. ⁴She was very black and foul in her appearance and clad in rags and tatters. ⁵A necklace of iron was around her neck, and iron fetters were on her hands and feet. ⁶And

---

a. The compiler does not reflect the material in the Latin *Acts Pet.* 15–16 in which Peter sends a woman and her baby to Simon. The baby rebukes Simon in a manly voice, and Simon flees Rome in fear until the next Sabbath. Then Peter has a vision in which Jesus tells him he will soon have a contest with Simon.

b. The governor is named "Pompey" in the Latin.

c. In the Latin *Acts Pet.*, the story of Simon and Eubola (dramatically shorter in *Hist. Sim. Ceph.*) is followed by Peter's command to his followers to pray for the power to oppose Simon (*Acts Pet.* 18).

d. In the Latin *Acts Pet.* Marcellus does not ask Peter for the holy water; instead, he tells Peter that he has purified and blessed the house himself.

e. The Latin of *Acts Pet.* 20 continues with a lengthy discourse of Peter featuring an expanded story of the Transfiguration (Mark 9:2–8 par.) in which he alludes to the polymorphy of Jesus. Then follows *Acts Pet.* 21–22a, the story of the healing of blind widows who, in recounting their healing, each say they saw Jesus in a different form. Perhaps the compiler omitted this material out of christological sensitivity.

she was dancing in the middle of that crowd. ⁷You called me and said to me, 'Marcellus, do you see this one dancing? ⁸It is the power of Simon the magician. Now cut off her head.'

⁹"And I said to you, 'No, my lord, because our Lord commanded not to kill.' ¹⁰Then you raised your voice and said, 'Let the sword of truth that is Christ come, and let it cut off not just her head but all her limbs.'"

¹¹When Shemon heard, he was happy and rejoicing because the Lord was with him in all things. ¹²And he was effecting great miracles in Rome and in its regions so that pagans and Jews without number were abandoning their own laws, holding to him, and accepting his teaching. ¹³Many magicians left their artifices and were taking refuge in the life-giving teaching. ¹⁴Everyone was regarding Simon as unclean, and they were honoring Shemon as the apostle of God.

Acts Pet. 23 ## Peter contends with Simon

21 ¹On a certain Saturday,[a] all Rome was gathered in the theater, along with Agerpus the governor and all the great ones of the city. ²Shemon came in the middle of that crowd, and all called out and were saying, "Shemon, show us the god in whose name you do these signs because all Rome is troubled and is saying, 'From you and from Simon we have seen signs, and we do not know which of you is legitimate and with whom God stands.' ³And there are some who say that Simon is legitimate."

⁴Shemon silenced them and said, "Men, Romans, I believe in the one true God who made the world and all in it, this one for whom the signs that came from me in his name witness to his truth. ⁵I banished Simon from Jerusalem[b] because of his evil deeds and because he stole vessels of a woman named Eubola. ⁶When Papos the governor saw him so that he might punish him, he fled and came to Rome. ⁷And he is trying to deceive you too, just as he deceived there." ⁸Shemon turned and said to Simon, "Thief and magician, did you not fall at the feet of myself and my fellow apostles in Judea?[c] ⁹And you brought us a great amount of money for us to give you the power of the Spirit so that you might work miracles. ¹⁰We rebuked you and drove you away. ¹¹How is it that you now stand before all Rome without shame and you seek to deceive it?"

Acts Pet. 25 ## Simon kills a boy with a word

22 ¹As Simon was reviling in many things and in many things was being outflanked by Shemon, the whole crowd called out and said to Shemon, "Cease with words, and in deeds show us that God is with you."[d] ²Shemon said to them, "The signs that I perform before you in his name witness that God is with you." ³They were saying to him, "Behold, before you came, many signs were performed also

---

a. This phrase is not found in the Latin.

b. The Latin speaks of only Judea here; so, the Syriac may well have preserved the original reading. The *Didascalia* 23 (6.7), which is likely also dependent on *Acts Pet.*, mentions Jerusalem as the location of the confrontation with Simon.

c. Contrast the Latin, which reads, "Did you not fall at my feet and those of Paul, when in Jerusalem?" (trans. Elliott, *ANT*).

d. The compiler does not reflect Simon's challenge to Peter's belief in Jesus as "the living and true God" nor Peter's response as found in the Latin of *Acts Pet.* 23–24.

by Simon." [4]Shemon said to them, "Let him do before me one of the deeds that he did before you, and I will reveal him to be false."[a]

[5]Simon said, "Let the governor order that I should kill one of these who stand before him, and Shemon will not be able to revive him." [6]And (the governor) commanded it. And (Simon) whispered to a youth who knew Caesar, and he fell and died. [7]Then the entire assembly was troubled, and they were saying, "There is no one like Simon!"

[8]Shemon said, "Pronounce a correct judgment! Humans, too, are able to kill; God alone is able to give life. [9]That Simon has killed does not show him to be legitimate. [10]But whether he gives life, the truth of God will demonstrate."

[11]While they were speaking, a certain woman came and cried out in mourning in the middle of the theater and said to Shemon, "I beseech you, my lord: I had an only son and he is dead!" [12]Shemon said to her, "My daughter, (I will attend to you) immediately after I raise this one whom Simon has killed."

[13]She fell to Shemon's feet and was saying, "Have mercy on me, my lord, for I have no son or daughter other than him." [14]Shemon said to her, "Go bring him here so that these might see and know that I raise him in the name of the true God."

[15]She said to him, "I have no one to bring him." [16]Shemon said to the governor, "Command the men to bring this (woman's) dead (son)." [17]And he commanded three young men to bring him.[b]

Peter revives the dead youth

Acts Pet. 26

23 [1]While they were going,[c] the governor said to Shemon, "Behold the young man dead and prostrate. Caesar knows him well. [2]And I wish to try your god[d] as to whether he is true or not."

[3]Shemon Cephas said to him, "God is not tested. But for the sake of your conversion and your life he will work signs and great deeds through my hands. [4]Rise, Governor, and try and grasp the youth by the right hand, and God will revive him."

[5]The governor rose and took the youth by the hand, and he rose and walked with him. [6]The entire crowd cried out and said, "One is the God of Shemon!"

Peter revives the widow's son

Acts Pet. 27

24 [1]And they brought in the son of that widow, and they placed him in the middle of the crowd. [2]Shemon prayed to God and raised his voice and said, "I say to you, young man, in the name of Jesus Christ the Nazarene, the one whom Simon has blasphemed, rise from your bier and go with your mother, honor her, and submit to the law of God!" [3]And immediately he rose.

---

a. These opening verses have no parallel in the Latin.

b. The text does not have the report of the young men confirming that the woman's son was really dead. The Greek fragment P. Oxy. 849, covering portions of *Acts Pet.* 25–26, contains the missing material and seems to confirm its presence in the original *Acts Pet.*

c. The Greek fragment shows this phrasing likely to be secondary. The Greek has the youths offering to bring the dead son and starts the next sentence with "While they were speaking . . ."

d. This is closer to the Greek ("I wished to try you and God through you," trans. mine) than is the Latin ("but I trusted in you and in your Lord whom you proclaim," trans. Elliott, *ANT*).

⁴The crowd praised God with joy, and they were saying, "You alone are God, and there is none besides you. ⁵You are not seen, and your works are seen. ⁶All who approach you in truth, you respond to them." ⁷And the fame of Shemon went out through all Rome.

Acts Pet. 28

Peter challenges Simon to revive a dead senator

25 ¹But again the son of another woman died, and she cried out, "Bury him!" ²Her servants said to her, "Do not let our mistress bury him! Rather, let us take him to Shemon, the apostle of God, and he will raise him." ³The name of that dead one was Nacisartertos,[a] and he was of senatorial rank.

⁴(His mother) came before the crowd and fell to the feet of Shemon Cephas and said to him, "My lord, I have heard from my servants and from many that you are the apostle of God. ⁵Now I ask of you: Have mercy on my son and raise him!" ⁶Shemon said to her, "If you are a believer in the true God and in Jesus his son, I will raise him." ⁷She cried out as she was weeping and said, "If he should live, I will believe in him."

⁸The entire crowd persuaded him and said to him, "By your god who made the world, raise also the son of this widow like the previous ones!" ⁹Shemon was angry, and he looked at the crowd and said, "Men, Romans, I am a passable human just like you. ¹⁰And it is not by my power that I do these things, but I request from Christ my Lord that he show us in his name, because he is lord of death and of life."

¹¹And he commanded, and they brought the dead person to the middle of the crowd, along with those five servants whom (Nacisartertos) had manumitted when he was dying, whose clothes were rent and on their heads dust had been raised, and they were mourning and going before the bier. ¹²They were coming with the great crowd and with all the great people of the Romans because he was a great man and renowned. ¹³When the crowds at the theater saw, they too were crying. ¹⁴And they brought him and placed him at the feet of Shemon; they brought with him his many clothes that they sought to burn with him.

¹⁵Shemon silenced them and raised his voice and said, "People, Romans, make now a correct judgment between myself and Simon, and examine and see who believes in the God of truth. ¹⁶For, behold, I have revived three dead people in front of you. Let him revive even one." ¹⁷All were saying to Simon, "Shemon has spoken well. Show your power, if your god is legitimate."

¹⁸When Simon saw that they stood against him, he said to them, "If I raise this dead person, will you chase Shemon from all of Rome?" ¹⁹They were saying to him, "Yes! And if you do not revive him, we will burn you in the fire."

²⁰Then Simon went and passed over to the dead person and bent himself over him. ²¹He captured the eyes of that entire crowd in his magic, and he showed them as if that dead person sat up and was shaking his head and his eyes were open. But he was not talking. ²²Now the crowd was amazed and cried out and said, "Simon, too, is God!"

²³Then Shemon silenced them at that moment and said to them, "Men, Ro-

---

a. The name varies in the Syriac edition (see below 25:42); the Latin Nicostratus doubtless better reflects the original.

mans, I see that you are being foolish. ²⁴Open the eyes of your minds and see that Simon has caused the dead person to sit, though not alive. ²⁵And does not the appearance of the dead person's face seem to you to be pale? Do you think that he has really revived him? ²⁶If he has truly revived him, let him rise from his bier and walk and go with his mother to his house. ²⁷And if you wish to see: the youth is still dead. ²⁸Let Simon rise from his side and you will see that he is dead."

²⁹The governor rose from his seat and grabbed Simon and removed him from the side of the dead person. ³⁰Immediately the dead person collapsed on his bier. ³¹And all the crowd was amazed at the magic of Simon and said, "Let him burn in the fire!" ³²Shemon said to them, "Even if he deserves to burn, our Savior Lord would not recompense evil with evil."

³³They were saying to him, "It is not only because he did not raise the dead that we wish to burn him, but because he took hold of our own eyes." ³⁴(Shemon) said to them, "Let him be. If he turns to God, he will have mercy on him. ³⁵And if he stays in his evil, it will be his ruin in this world, and in the world to come he will fall into eternal gehenna. ³⁶But do not raise your hands against him."

³⁷When he had said these things, he approached alongside the dead person and said to his mother, "I say to you, woman, these servants whom your son manumitted, when he revives he is not authorized to enslave them but they should be free in their standing. ³⁸And the sustenance that has gone out to them from your house will be given them."

³⁹She was saying to him, "All that you say to me I will do superabundantly. ⁴⁰Even the clothes that you mentioned that I brought with him I will give to them." ⁴¹He said to her, "Behold, before the governor and the great ones of the city I say to you, 'Do not change!'"

⁴²Shemon was filled with the Holy Spirit and poked that dead person and called him and said, "Nicstratos, in the name of Jesus Christ the Nazarene rise!" ⁴³Immediately that dead person jumped and rose. ⁴⁴He loosened the garment that was girding him, and he got down off his bier. ⁴⁵He asked for other clothes and dressed himself.

⁴⁶These things Shemon did on the day of Saturday. ⁴⁷And Shemon said, "People, Romans, the dead have laid aside their death and they have come to life. ⁴⁸You, too, lay aside your paganism like death, and believe in God the Creator of all, in his Son Jesus and in his Holy Spirit."

Peter brings many to the faith

Acts Pet. 29–30

26 ¹(Shemon) left the theater in the evening so that he might go to where he was lodged, and the entire crowd was coming after him, and they were kissing his feet. ²They were asking of him many times that he might go with them and heal their infirmities. ³The one who revived also followed Shemon. And (Shemon) did not wish for him to go with him. ⁴His mother brought 2,000 drachmas.

⁵On the day of Sunday, all the great men of the Romans were assembled, along with their wives and their children. ⁶Shemon was teaching them the word of God. And all were being strengthened in the faith. ⁷Shemon divided the drachmas among the poor and the widows and the needy free people. ⁸Also a certain woman whose name was Chryse brought to him a great amount of

drachmas. ⁹And he corrected her because she was an adulteress. He received (the money) from her and divided (it) for the poor.

Acts Pet. 31

Simon tries to win back followers with trickery

27 ¹Many sick were coming to him: the maimed and lame and lepers. He was healing them all. ²And many were believing in our Lord every day. ³Until then Simon was not desisting from his evil; ⁴instead, he was warning and threatening and saying, "I will show that Shemon is not a believer in the God of truth but rather an impostor." ⁵And he began showing phantoms and forms of falsehoods. ⁶Those who had been established in the faith were laughing at him, for they knew that he was an impostor, and they were not esteeming him in anything.

⁷Then Simon the magician got very angry. ⁸He went and rose in the middle of the city and called out and said, "You have thought that Shemon is good and superior to me, so that you have abandoned me and have gone after him. ⁹For behold, tomorrow I will leave you, and you will be without a god and you will die in your sins. ¹⁰In front of you I will ascend to that god whose power I am and from whom you have turned aside and you have believed in that one whom the Jews killed in Jerusalem."

Acts Pet. 32

Simon flies, falls, and is stoned to death

28 ¹Then all Rome assembled to see whether Simon would truly fly and ascend to heaven. Shemon Cephas was also going there so that he might reprove Simon the magician. ²Then Simon came and stood at a high place. ³When Shemon Cephas saw him, he said to him, "Evil magician, have you still not stopped with your magic? ⁴Did they not seek to burn you in the fire and I did not permit them?"

⁵Simon said to him,[a] "Simpleton, vainglorious one, and the disciple of a magician who was not able to free himself from the cross: Why do you call me a magician? ⁶I am the power of the exalted One above. ⁷Into the belly of Rachel,

Rec. 3.47.1

my mother, I crept and was born like a human so that I might save humans. ⁸I did many signs and will continue.

⁹For I will bore through the mountain and pass, and I will fly in the air.
¹⁰If I should fall from a mountain, I will not be injured.

Rec. 2.9.3

¹¹If they confine me to prison, I will open the gates and go out.
¹²I will effect it that those who confined me will be confined.
¹³I will give souls to statues and they will walk like humans.

Rec. 2.9.4
Rec. 3.60.1

¹⁴Sprouts and new trees I will cause to come out of the earth.
¹⁵I will order dogs of stone and they will bark.
¹⁶If it pleases me, I will be a sheep.
¹⁷If I wish, I will appear as a goat.
¹⁸I will cause an old man to come out of the womb.[b]

Rec. 2.9.5

¹⁹I will give babies beards.

---

a. The following again independently draws on passages from *Rec.* used also above in 10:3–16.

b. This particular statement is apparently unparalleled elsewhere.

[20]Everything that I wish I shall do. [21]Behold, today I will show you my own divinity so that you will fall and worship me when you see me ascending to heaven before this entire crowd. [22]And you will know that I am Christ."

[23]When he finished his words, he showed chains that were hitched in the form of a chariot of fire and were coming down for his honor. [24]They lifted him up from earth a great distance.[a] [25]He appeared to be flying, and he was lifted above all the high mountains. [26]That entire crowd was looking at Shemon.

[27]Now when Shemon saw that his image was about to be obscured from their eyes, he called out in a great voice in prayer to our Lord and said, "My Lord, do not allow this evil one to do what he wants! [28]If you turn away and allow him, all the ones who have believed in you will stumble. [29]And the signs that you did through my hands will be for naught. [30]But let your justice be revealed immediately, and let this evil one fall and not die, but let his limbs be broken!"

[31]As Shemon Cephas said these things, he called out in an exalted voice and said, "To you I say, evil magician, by that powerful word that confounded the magicians in the days of Moses: May your magic abandon you and may the strength of your evilness break!" [32]At that moment, that image of a chariot was undone and the chains released Simon and he fell. [33]His bones were broken in three places: his neck, his back, and his wrists. [34]And his power was extinguished and cut loose.

[35]Then all the crowds cried out in a great voice and said, "Great is the God of Shemon Cephas who has conquered Simon the magician!" [36]They ran hastily and pulled down that image that they had set up for him. [37]And all came to him that they might hear. [38]On that day, more than a great number of people believed and were baptized. [39]And many disciples of Simon received baptism on that day, besides those who had abandoned him while he was in Caesarea and Antioch and had been baptized.

[40]One man came whose name was Gemellus, and he was a friend of Simon. [41]When he saw him broken and loosened, he began to mock him and said, "Great Power of God, who is that one who has broken and dropped you? [42]Even if you have held the eyes of humans, are you also able to hold the eyes of God?" [43]Then the whole city was assembled and they stoned Simon the magician, and he died.[b] [44]And Gemellus was added to the believers.

Rec. 2.9.7

Rec. 3.46.7

Rec. 2.7.1

Peter is threatened by the governor Agrippa

29 [1]Many of the Jews and the gentiles were converted. [2]And (Shemon) built the churches in Rome and in all Italy. [3]The instruction increased in the district of Rome, and also many from the house of Caesar[c] believed in the teaching of our Lord.

Acts Pet. 33

Pre. Pet. Rome p. 40

---

a. This image of the chariot of fire is not found in the preserved *Acts Pet.*

b. The end of Simon here differs from the Greek martyrdom and Latin *Acts Pet.* 32, which recounts that, after Simon was stoned, he was taken away, was operated upon, and then died.

c. For the following compare the Syriac account of martyrdoms translated by Nau, "La version syriaque," 43–50. Nau's version has more material at the start. This material apparently was added to introduce the independent Syriac martyrdom; its absence here is doubtless an indication that *Hist. Sim. Ceph.* is drawing on a Syriac translation of the entire *Acts Pet.* (i.e., with the martyrdom) and not on the independent Syriac martyrdom.

⁴After these, two of the governor Agrippa's wives came (to Peter) and two of his concubines. ⁵These are their names: Agrippina and Crithna, and Aphja and Drosina.ᵃ ⁶They believed in our Lord Jesus, and he held them in holiness. ⁷He placed in their mind that they should not go again to the bed of the governor. ⁸(The governor) began to persecute them and to trouble them. ⁹He commanded his servants that they should watch where (the women) go and come. ¹⁰He knew that they were going to Shemon. ¹¹The governor warned them that they should not again go to that Christian: ¹²"For if I hear that you are going to him again, I will kill you and I will burn him in fire." ¹³But they were strengthened in our Lord, and he placed it in their heart that they should endure everything that would come on them and that they should not be with (the governor) again.

Acts Pet. 34

Albinus and the governor conspire against Peter

30 ¹Again, a woman by the name of Xanthippe,ᵇ the wife of Albinus the friend of Caesar, came to Shemon Cephas with other free women to hear the word of God from him. ²She, too, took a stand in holiness. ³Her husband was filled with rage, and he sought to kill Shemon because of his wife who had become a Christian. ⁴Many men with their wives had become holy away from copulation so that they might serve God. ⁵And Albinus took secret counsel with the governor so that they might speak to Caesar and kill Shemon: "Since he was making all of Rome Christian and has separated our wives from us."

Acts Pet. 35

Peter is comforted by Jesus

31 ¹Xanthippe heard and made known to Shemon, "If you do not depart, how will you preach the word of God?" ²Now the blessed Peter perceived that the time had come in which he should return to our Lord through death for him. ³He said to his disciples, "My brothers, it is not fitting for me to flee."ᶜ

⁴While they counseled, persuaded, and troubled him greatly, he stood and changed his clothes and went out alone. ⁵No one was aware of him because it was the depth of the night. ⁶He saw the form of our Savior in the flesh who was coming toward him. ⁷He was carrying a cross on his shoulder in that manner in which he was crucified by the Jews. ⁸Shemon was disturbed and fell on his face as he trembled and said to him, "What is the reason that while you are exalted at the right hand of God, you show this form of humiliation on earth?"

⁹Our Lord said to Shemon, "I endured death by the cross for the sake of the salvation of all, and by it I effected and gave you an example. ¹⁰Thus, while I was not guilty, I received the suffering of the cross so that you, too, should perfect yourselves with suffering for the truth of my teaching. ¹¹But now because I have seen that you still hold to the weakness of nature and you have not understood through sufferings that you will be perfected in sufferings for these divine

---

a. In the Greek *Acts Pet.* these last three are named Nicaria, Euphemia, and Doris.

b. Syr.: Cesnathepa.

c. Peter is not so decisive in *Acts Pet.*, so the following story of Christ's appearance with a cross, which, in *Acts Pet.* contains Peter's famous address of Christ with the words *quo vadis* ("where are you going?"), does not carry the same weight. Instead, the scene and speech of Christ is considerably more extensive in *Hist. Sim. Ceph.*

things, I have come to suffer for a second time. [12]In this way, you will perhaps be perfected and not be troubled by sufferings for me."

[13]When the great Peter heard these things, he was sorrowful, and he began entreating our Lord and said, "Because I have learned from you that this is your will, with gladness I will present myself for you. [14]And the debt of your great love that you show the world, as much as is possible, I will requite sufferings for you."

Peter is imprisoned

Acts Pet. 36

32 [1]Immediately, that form was lifted toward heaven, and Peter returned to the brothers. [2]He told them what he had seen and heard. [3]And it saddened the brothers very much. [4]He said to them, "Let it not sadden you, my brothers. Let the will of our Lord be. [5]But you, be strengthened in this faith that you have received and do not be slack."

[6]Then four men came and seized Shemon so that they might take him to Caesar. [7]And all the wealthy and the poor were running and crying out and saying, "What did Shemon the servant of God do wrong? And what evil has he done in this city?" [8]Then my lord Shemon pleasantly raised his hand and silenced them, and he sent each to his house. [9]Then they transported Shemon and confined him to prison.[a]

Peter appoints Linus bishop of Rome

Pre. Pet. Rome p. 40

33 [1]When he had served the dispensation of salvation in the city of Rome for twenty-five years and when he perceived that it was near for him to glorify God through a death on the cross, he sent and called for Linus the deacon, and he made him bishop in his place in Rome. [2]He admonished and commanded him to teach in the church everything that he had heard from him when he was teaching. [3]Then Nero the Caesar gave the sentence for him that he should die the death of the cross.

Peter is crucified upside down

Acts Pet. 37–39

34 [1]When they brought him out and prepared the wood to crucify him, he rejoiced and praised our Lord. [2]He was persuading his crucifiers and said, "I ask of you that they crucify me as I wish, not in that great manner of my Lord, for he was crucified right side up. [3]I am afraid that if I should be nailed up like him on the cross, I might acquire presumption from the similarity of form. [4]Rather, when I am crucified with my head downwards, I will recall the sufferings that were for me. [5]And let my mouth and eyes kiss the places that the nails were thrust into the feet of the body, the clothing the Word." [6]Now the crucifiers did to him as he had wished, rejoicing that thus he had determined his judgment to be double.[b]

---

a. In *Acts Pet.* the story continues with the people coming to Agrippa and calling for his release. Peter comforts his followers, telling them that his death must happen and that Agrippa is merely "a servant of the power of his father" (trans. Elliott, *ANT*).

b. The translator has dramatically shortened *Acts Pet.* here, eliminating, among other things, Peter's address to the cross in chapter 37.

Acts Pet. 40 **Marcellus buries Peter's body**

35 [1]As the soul of the holy one ascended, Marcellus drew near, though he had not taken counsel with anyone, and he took Shemon down from the cross and washed him. [2]He pulverized the spices of myrrh and aloe; he embalmed him. [3]He placed him in a large vessel of bright stone purchased with a large price. [4]And he placed him in his own mausoleum.[a]

Conclusion

36 [1]Thus was achieved the crowning of my blessed lord Shemon, the first-born of the apostles, through the goodness of Christ our Lord. [2]To whom be the glory and on us be his mercy forever and ever. Amen.[b]

[3]Now Clement was the disciple of Peter. And he disputed with Simon and overcame him. [4]He translated the letter of Hebrews, from Hebrew to Greek. And he wrote the tales of the twelve apostles and of the seventy-two.[c] [5]He laid down many writings, even if he stumbled in love of rulership. [6]His story of the glorious apostle Peter has ended. May his prayer be for the sinful scribe, the presbyter Abraham. Amen.

---

a. *Acts Pet.* continues with an appearance of Peter to Marcellus; the apostle admonishes him for wasting the preparation materials, saying "Marcellus, did you not hear the Lord say, 'Let the dead be buried by their own dead'?" (Matt 8:22//Luke 9:60; trans. Elliott, *ANT*).

b. The following words were not printed by Bedjan but were added from the manuscript by Guidi, "Bemerkungen," 745.

c. Anton Baumstark, *Die Petrus- und Paulusacten in der litterarischen Überlieferung der syrischen Kirche* (Leipzig: Otto Harrassowitz, 1902), 42–44, supposed that this was the Greek source of the writing translated here (apart from the sections taken from *Ps.-Clem.*, Acts, and *Pre. Pet. Rome*). I consider this very unlikely and think that the reference here is probably to *Ps.-Clem.* (e.g., *Rec.* 1.27–74). Bedjan (*Acta Martyrum*, 1:vi) originally suggested that this remark indicated perhaps that Clement was to be understood as the author of this story of Peter. For the tradition that Clement wrote Hebrews (an idea attributed to Origen) see Eusebius, *Eccl. hist.* 6.25.11–14.

The Acts of Timothy
A new translation and introduction

by Cavan W. Concannon

The *Acts of Timothy* (*Acts Tim.*; *CANT* 295) is a fifth-century account of Timothy's tenure as bishop of Ephesus, culminating in his martyrdom during the Katagogia, a festival in honor of Dionysus. Though Timothy is the focus of *Acts Tim.*, the text also narrates the arrival of the apostle John to the city, where he is instrumental in the production of the four canonical Gospels.

Contents
Timothy was a co-worker and close associate of the apostle Paul. He is listed as a co-author with Paul on a number of letters in the Pauline corpus (2 Corinthians, Philippians, Colossians, 1 and 2 Thessalonians, and Philemon) and frequently mediated between Paul and the communities to which he wrote (e.g., 1 Cor 4:17; 16:10; Phil 2:19). The canonical Acts offers some information about Timothy's early life and conversion (Acts 16:1–5) and details his work traveling with Paul and others in the eastern Mediterranean. While aware of material about Timothy in the canonical Acts and the Pauline letters, *Acts Tim.* focuses on Timothy's career as bishop of Ephesus under the tutelage of both Paul and John (vv. 3–4). After traveling with Paul, Timothy arrives in Ephesus and becomes the city's first bishop. Following Paul's martyrdom under Nero, the apostle John, who is here also equated with John of Patmos, arrives in Ephesus (v. 7). While in the city, John helps to organize loose sheets of paper containing traditions about Jesus into the four canonical Gospels (vv. 8–10). John is later exiled to the island of Patmos under Domitian (v. 11). Timothy, who is still ruling as bishop, publicly attacks a local pagan festival called the Katagogia (vv. 12–13). Incensed by his condemnations of their idolatry, the Ephesians martyr Timothy (v. 14). The local Christians take the bishop and bury him outside of the city in a place called Pion, where his martyrium remains, according to the author. Later, Nerva allows John to return from exile; John promptly takes up the position of bishop in Ephesus and holds the seat until the reign of Trajan (v. 15).

Manuscripts and Editions
Acts Tim. is extant in Latin and in Greek, both of which descend from an earlier Greek original.[1] The earliest manuscripts of the Greek recension (*BHG* 1487) come from the tenth century; however, the earliest citation of the story comes in the ninth century by Photius (*Bib. cod.* 254).[2] The Latin recension (*BHL* 8294) was published in 1485 in Leuven

---

1. For a useful summary of the history of both the Latin and Greek recensions, see Zamagni, "Passion (ou Actes) de Timothée," 343–45, 359–64.

2. Zamagni, "Passion (ou Actes) de Timothée," 351. Photius's summary of the story changes the order of

and then revised by the Bollandists in 1643.[3] In 1877 Hermann Usener published a bilingual edition of the Greek and Latin recensions; this remains the standard critical edition of *Acts Tim.* Usener updated the Bollandist edition of the Latin and paired it with a Greek version based on a single manuscript of the eleventh/twelfth century prepared for him by Maximilien Bonnet (Paris, Bibliothèque nationale de France, gr. 1219).[4] The major difference between the two recensions is that the Latin includes an introduction claiming that the text was authored by Polycrates of Ephesus (see below). While Usener produced the only critical edition of the Latin recension, Claudio Zamagni (2007) has produced the most recent critical edition of the Greek text, drawing upon seven manuscripts divided into two textual families:[5]

Family 1:
A: Mount Athos, Koutlumousiou, 37, fol. 276r–277v (10th cent.)
O: Vatican, Biblioteca apostolica, Ottob. gr. 54, fol. 11r–13r (11th cent.)
B: Berlin, Deutsche Bibliothek, 220, fol. 37v–40v (13th cent.)

Family 2:
P: Paris, Bibliothèque nationale de France, gr. 1219, fol. 64r–67r (11th cent.)
V: Vatican, Biblioteca apostolica, gr. 1595, fol. 56v–57v (11th cent.)
C: Vatican, Biblioteca apostolica, gr. 886, fol. 394r–395r (11th cent.)
M: Messina, Biblioteca Universitaria, 63, fol. 230v–232v (13th cent.)

Zamagni's two families are delineated by whether (Family 1) or not (Family 2) they include a concluding account of how the body of the martyred Timothy was transferred, along with those of Luke and Andrew, to the Church of the Holy Apostles in Constantinople (see page 404 n. e to the text below). These details are not found in the Latin recension of the text and were probably added later, since, as Zamagni argues, the transfer of Timothy's corpse to Constantinople is a common detail in later lives of Timothy.

Date and Provenance

Some details included in the text offer clues as to its date and provenance. In describing Timothy's home city (Lystra), the text calls the city the capital of the province of Lycaonia (v. 3). Since Lystra only became the capital of the province after 370 CE, this means that the text could not have been written before this date. Further evidence for the date of the text may be found in the addition of postscripts to several of the Greek manuscripts recounting the removal of Timothy's remains from Ephesus to Constantinople, which took place under the emperor Constantius in 356 CE (Jerome, *Chron.* 2.195).[6] Delehaye suggests

events slightly and adds what Zamagni notes is the anachronistic detail of the seven bishops who assisted the metropolitan bishop of Ephesus.

3. For details on the early publishing of the text see Usener, *Natalicia regis augustissimi Guilelmi*, 4–5; Zamagni, "Passion (ou Actes) de Timothée," 343–44.

4. Usener, *Natalicia regis augustissimi Guilelmi*, 5–6.

5. Zamagni, "Passion (ou Actes) de Timothée"; see also his earlier introduction and translation "Actes de Timothée" in *EAC*.

6. This is one interpretation offered for the illustration of Timothy's entry in the eleventh-century "imperial" menologion found in the library of the Greek Patriarchate of Alexandria and now owned by the Walters Museum (Baltimore, Walters Art Museum, w. 521, fol. 203v). Nancy Patterson Ševčenko ("The Walters 'Imperial' Menologion," *Journal of the Walters Art Gallery* 51 [1993]: 43–64) has shown that the

that it was the removal of Timothy's remains that prompted the writing of *Acts Tim.* as a way of explaining the saint's connection to the city and to the early apostles. All of this indicates that the text was not written before the late fourth century, though this date still may be too early. It is more probable that the text was written in the fifth century.[7]

The Latin recension includes an ascription of authorship claiming that the account was originally written by Polycrates, bishop of Ephesus in the 190s CE during the Quartodeciman controversy (Eusebius, *Hist. eccl.* 5.23–24). While early editions that were based on the Latin text argued that Polycrates was indeed the author, thus placing the production of the text in the late second or early third century, the attribution is spurious given the *terminus post quem* of Lystra's elevation to the capital of Lycaonia; however, Usener and Zamagni argue that the addition regarding Polycrates was added very early in the history of the text and may even have been included in the original, fifth-century version.[8]

That the author likely was familiar with Ephesus is indicated by his knowledge of local topography and cultic practice. For example, the text places Timothy's martyrium at a place called Pion, which was the name of a hill near the city. Also, Timothy's martyrdom occurs during the Katagogia (lit. "the coming down"), a local festival of which the author seems to have some reliable information (vv. 12–14). The text describes the worshippers as wearing masks and costumes and carrying clubs and images. They are also described as singing and otherwise behaving in an unseemly manner. These elements suggest that the festival was associated with the worship of Dionysus, an association supported by an inscription from Priene identifying a priest of the festival.[9] Some scholars have raised arguments against *Acts Tim.*'s direct knowledge of the Katagogia. Rick Strelan has noted that the text fundamentally misunderstands the festival, treating it as a wanton bloodbath in ways similar to how Christians often attacked what they deemed to be idolatrous practices.[10] Consider also that *Acts Tim.* may derive some details of its account from the story of John's destruction of the cult of the Ephesian temple of Artemis recorded in the *Acts of John* (37–47). Nevertheless, *Acts Tim.*'s intimacy with Ephesus suggests that the text was written in the city. This might also explain the addition of copious epithets for Ephesus in *Acts Tim.*, where the city is described as the "great" or "radiant" metropolis.[11] Often these epithets are modified by *hautē / ipsa* ("this"; vv. 4, 7, 14, 15), giving the impression that the author is writing in *this* city (i.e., Ephesus).

Walters menologion is dependent on the earlier Menologion of Basil II in the Vatican library (Biblioteca apostolica, gr. 1613, p. 341). The text accompanying the illustration used for Timothy's entry in the Menologion of Basil explicitly states that the burial scene refers to Timothy's burial in Ephesus, and not the removal of his remains to Constantinople.

7. So also Theodor Zahn, *Introduction to the New Testament* (trans. John Moore Trout et al.; 3 vols.; New York: Charles Scribner's Sons, 1909), 2:41 (trans. of *Einleitung in das neue Testament* [2nd ed.; Leipzig: Deichert, 1906–1907]); Hans-Josef Klauck, *The Apocryphal Acts of the Apostles: An Introduction* (trans. Brian McNeil; Waco, Tex.: Baylor University Press, 2008), 248–49; Delehaye, "Les actes de Saint Timothée," 77–84; and Timothy D. Barnes, *Early Christian Hagiography and Roman History* (Tübingen: Mohr Siebeck, 2010), 302.

8. Usener, *Natalicia regis augustissimi Guilelmi*, 4–5. On Polycrates' early association with the text, see Zamagni, "Passion (ou Actes) de Timothée," 347.

9. I. Priene 174.1.5, cited by Rick Strelan, *Paul, Artemis, and the Jews in Ephesus* (Berlin: Walter de Gruyter, 1996), 123. The inscription refers to someone who "also served as a priest of Dionysus of the Katagogia." Also relevant is the description of Marc Antony's arrival in Ephesus as part of a Dionysiac festival (Plutarch, *Ant.* 24.4–5).

10. Keil, "Zum Martyrium des heiligen Timotheus," 83; Strelan, *Paul, Artemis, and the Jews*, 122–24.

11. Delehaye, "Les actes de Saint Timothée," 79; Zamagni, "Passion (ou Actes) de Timothée," 349.

Literary Context

While the modern title associates *Acts Tim.* with the apocryphal acts, the narrative does not quite fit the genre. First, the text only really describes one "act" of Timothy in any detail—namely, his public condemnation of the idolatry of the Katagogia. Rather than following Timothy on a series of adventures, the story follows a simple arc from Timothy's first installation as bishop to his martyrdom. The author of the text recognizes his omission and directs the reader to the canonical Acts to find out more information on Timothy's adventures and miraculous deeds (v. 5). The focus of *Acts Tim.* is less on Timothy's evangelizing activities than on coordinating Timothy's bishopric with the movements of Paul and John in and out of Ephesus. Second, both the Greek and Latin recensions give the title of the text as the "martyrdom" (*martyrion* and *passio,* respectively) of Timothy. But even in this respect the text includes little description of the actual martyrdom, which is only briefly narrated (v. 14). Neither a standard "acts" nor martyrdom, *Acts Tim.* combines these genres as a way of organizing local Ephesian traditions around the person of Timothy, thereby augmenting the city's claim to a number of apostolic figures.

The events that the narrative purports to recount cover the period from Nero to Trajan. Each of the three major characters (Timothy, Paul, and John) arrives in Ephesus during Nero's reign. Under Domitian, John is banished to Patmos. Timothy is martyred under Nerva, after which John returns and rules until the time of Trajan. *Acts Tim.* also mentions the names of two proconsuls: Maximus (under Nero) and Peregrinus (under Nerva). Usener's confidence in the text's proconsular references allowed him to date the ordination and martyrdom of Timothy to 58 and 97 CE, respectively.[12] Theodor Zahn offered a decisive and early criticism of the text's historical reliability. He showed that these names cannot be linked with any extant proconsular lists and that other details of the text lack historical validity;[13] however, the text does seem to know details about the landscape of Ephesus and its Katagogia festival.

Acts Tim. makes use of a number of New Testament texts for details about Timothy and for the temporal framework within which it places its narrative. *Acts Tim.* cites the canonical Acts (16:1–3), from which the author takes information about Timothy's parents and his hometown of Lystra (v. 3). Timothy's ordination and ministry as bishop are drawn from the pseudo-Pauline 1 and 2 Timothy (v. 4). In 1 Timothy, Paul has left the young Timothy behind in Ephesus, where he charges him to continue instructing people in correct doctrine (1:3–5). First Timothy does not refer to Timothy as the bishop of the Ephesians, though the text discusses the qualifications of bishops (3:1–7). Eusebius claims Timothy was the first bishop (*Hist. eccl.* 3.4.5), but the *Apostolic Constitutions* says that Timothy and another John who was ordained by the apostle John were the first bishops of Ephesus (7.46.7). While 1 Timothy puts Timothy in Ephesus without Paul, there is little else upon which *Acts Tim.* seems dependent in the Pastorals. None of the characters or issues mentioned in 1 or 2 Timothy make an appearance in *Acts Tim.* Second Timothy locates Paul in Rome after leaving Ephesus (1:17), where he awaits trial and anticipates his coming death (4:6–8). *Acts Tim.* speaks of Paul's martyrdom under Nero (v. 7), but says nothing about

---

12. Usener, *Natalicia regis augustissimi Guilelmi,* 15–16, 28, and Keil, "Zum Martyrium des heiligen Timotheus," 82–84, put the range at 57/58 and 96/97 or 97/98.

13. Zahn, "Rezension Acta S. Timothei." Zahn's arguments are supported by Delehaye, "Les actes de Saint Timothée," along with Ronald Syme, *Roman Papers* (4 vols.; Oxford: Clarendon, 1988), 4:361, and Barnes, *Early Christian Hagiography,* 300–303. Usener's arguments are defended by Keil, "Zum Martyrium des heiligen Timotheus," 82–92.

it taking place in Rome, nor does it have room for Paul's command that Timothy leave Ephesus soon after the receipt of the letter and come meet him in Rome (2 Tim 4:9, 13, 21).

Aside from canonical materials related to Timothy, *Acts Tim.* is familiar with the four canonical Gospels and several other early Christian authors. *Acts Tim.* conflates the author of the Gospel of John and John of Patmos, as does *Acts John.* This is an interesting conflation, since the text does not give any hint that it is familiar with Revelation.[14] Following Irenaeus (*Haer.* 5.30.3; cf. Eusebius, *Hist. eccl.* 3.18.1–2), *Acts Tim.* says that John was banished to Patmos during the reign of Domitian (v. 11). Eusebius (*Hist. eccl.* 3.20.8–9) places the end of John's exile under Nerva, as does *Acts Tim.* (v. 15). Eusebius can cite no specific source for this information other than an ancient tradition; *Acts Tim.* offers no citation either. Similarly, Irenaeus places John in Ephesus until the reign of Trajan (*Haer.* 2.22.5; 3.3.4; cf. Eusebius, *Hist. eccl.* 3.23.3–4) just as in *Acts Tim.* While *Acts Tim.* does not relate the death of John, the *Acts of John* 111–15 narrates the apostle's conscious decision to go to sleep in a grave just outside the city. In a letter to bishop Victor of Rome, Polycrates (bishop of Ephesus in the late second century) claims that John's remains are still in Ephesus, though he refers to John as a martyr, which seems to contradict his peaceful passing in *Acts John* (Eusebius, *Hist. eccl.* 5.24.3).[15] Polycrates makes no mention of Timothy's burial site in Ephesus, which further confirms that his authorship of *Acts Tim.* is a fiction.

Acts Tim.'s knowledge about the activities of John could derive either from Irenaeus or Eusebius, though Eusebius is the more likely origin.[16] This possibility is strengthened when we look at the similarities between *Acts Tim.* and Eusebius in regard to the writing of John's Gospel. Both locate the writing of John's Gospel in Ephesus (*Hist. eccl.* 3.1.1 and *Acts Tim.* 10). Eusebius argues that John's Gospel was written after the three Synoptics (*Hist. eccl.* 3.24), a position he ascribes also to Clement of Alexandria (*Hist. eccl.* 6.14.7). According to Eusebius, at some point during his ministry, John was presented with the three Synoptics, of which he approved; however, John was moved to write his own account because the Synoptics only included information about the final year of Jesus' ministry. John set about narrating events and sayings from the first years of Jesus' ministry, prior to the arrest of John the Baptist. He also included information on Jesus' divine genealogy, since Luke and Matthew only wrote about Jesus' human genealogy. We can see a similar retelling of the production of John's Gospel in *Acts Tim.* 8–10. In this version, disciples of Jesus from various places have in their possession a disorganized collection of papers wherein are recorded sayings and deeds of Jesus.[17] Bringing these to John, the apostle organizes them together into the three Synoptics and names them. When he notices that they lack attention to Jesus' divine genealogy and that several miracles are missing, he adds what he learned while lying at Jesus' bosom (13:23–25; 21:24–25). The similarity of these stories is perhaps significant for understanding the sources behind *Acts Tim.*, though what is also striking is how the version in *Acts Tim.* seems to make John the primary agent in the production not just of his own Gospel, but of the Synoptics as well.

---

14. Helmut Koester, "Ephesus," 261–64 discusses in detail the various "Johns" that appear in literature related to Ephesian Christianity and offers an important study of all the different Christian texts, traditions, and groups in the city.

15. Both Papias (Eusebius, *Hist. eccl.* 3.39.4–5) and Eusebius (*Hist. eccl.* 3.39.6; 7.25.16) know of two Johns that were buried at Ephesus.

16. So also Zamagni, "Passion (ou Actes) de Timothée," 347.

17. A similar scene is evoked in the *Ap. Jas.* 2.8–16, where Jesus appears to the disciples after his resurrection while they are gathered together trying to recall the sayings of Jesus and write them down.

In addition to privileging John's role in the production of the Gospels, *Acts Tim.* synthesizes a number of apostolic traditions around the figure of Timothy, thereby increasing the prestige of the city of Ephesus as a whole. As Helmut Koester has argued, there were several strands of early Christian traditions in Ephesus in the first and second centuries.[18] He identifies groups, each associated with particular texts, connected to Paul (Acts, Ephesians, 1 and 2 Timothy, Ignatius), the apostle John (*Acts John*, Papias, Polycrates), John of Patmos (Rev 2:1–7), Apollos (Acts 18:24–28), and John the Baptist (Acts 19:1–7). Over time, the Apostle John and John of Patmos become conflated and "John" emerges as the primary saint for Christians in the city. *Acts Tim.* represents one way in which the diversity of early Christian hagiography could be synthesized to maximize its civic value. Timothy is made to anchor the diversity of local Ephesian traditions. He was a disciple of Paul and was appointed bishop by him over the Ephesians. He was also a disciple of John, who resided in the city for a time and there edited the Gospels. John's exile to Patmos resolves the awkwardness of putting John under the authority of Timothy as bishop. Timothy's martyrdom explains the existence of his cult in the city (and perhaps "proves" the authenticity of the remains that had been removed by Constantius to Constantinople). The martyrdom also clears Timothy out of the way so that John can return from exile and rule as bishop until the time of Trajan. Timothy's biography thus offers the author of *Acts Tim.* the opportunity to gather together local traditions and fuse them into a single narrative of early Christianity in Ephesus, despite the problems posed by 2 Timothy. The effect is to offer the "great city of the Ephesians" (v. 2) a similarly great apostolic tradition.

Translation

The following translation is based on Usener's critical edition of the Latin and Greek traditions, augmented by the Greek text of Zamagni's 2007 critical edition. Zamagni's critical edition is crucial because Usener's edition of the Greek relies on a single manuscript. This eleventh-/twelfth-century manuscript (Paris, Bibliothèque nationale de France, gr. 1219) remains the best witness to the earliest Greek version; however, its readings can now be compared with and contested by the other manuscripts collated by Zamagni, which range from the tenth to thirteenth centuries. Though the Latin and Greek recensions are of equal antiquity and vary little from each other, I have tended in the translation to favor the Greek because of Zamagni's critical edition. However, I have followed the Latin recension in including the introductory epithet claiming Polycrates as the author of the text (v. 1), though I have placed this in pointed brackets because it remains disputed as to whether it was part of the original version (see above). There remains a pressing need to update Usener's critical edition of the Latin, which is now well over a century old. I have followed the paragraph numbering introduced by Zamagni, rather than following the designation of lines in Usener's edition. For textual variants, I use Zamagni's sigla for the seven manuscripts of the Greek version.

Bibliography

EDITIONS AND TRANSLATIONS

Usener, Hermann. *Natalicia regis augustissimi Guilelmi imperatoris Germaniae ab Universitate Fridericia Guilelmia Rhenana [. . .] Insunt Acta S. Timothei.* Bonn: Programm der Univer-

---

18. Koester, "Ephesus," 251–65.

sität Bonn, 1877. (Critical edition of the Latin tradition and *editio princeps* of the Greek tradition based on one manuscript.)

Zamagni, Claudio. "Passion (ou Actes) de Timothée. Étude des traditions anciennes et édition de la forme *BHG* 1487." Pages 341–75 in *Poussières de christianisme et de judaïsme antiques. Études réunies en l'honneur de Jean-Daniel Kaestli et Éric Junod.* Edited by Albert Frey and Rémi Gounelle. Prahins: Publications de l'Institut Romand des Sciences Bibliques, 2007. (Critical edition of the Greek tradition based on seven manuscripts.)

———. "Actes de Timothée." Pages 587–601 in *EAC* 2.

STUDIES

Delehaye, Hippolyte. "Les actes de Saint Timothée." Pages 77–84 in *Anatolian Studies Presented to William Hepburn Buckler.* Edited by William Moir Calder and Josef Keil. Manchester: Manchester University Press, 1939.

Keil, Josef. "Zum Martyrium des heiligen Timotheus in Ephesus." *JÖAI* 29 (1935): 82–92.

Koester, Helmut. "Ephesus in Early Christian Literature." Pages 252–65 in *Paul and His World: Interpreting the New Testament in Its Context.* Minneapolis: Fortress, 2007. Originally published as pages 119–40 in *Ephesos, Metropolis of Asia: An Interdisciplinary Approach to Its Archaeology, Religion and Culture.* Edited by Helmut Koester. HTS 41. Valley Forge, Pa.; Trinity Int., 1995.

Zahn, Theodor. "Rezension Acta S. Timothei Edidit H. Usener (Programm der Universität Bonn zum 22. März 1877)." *Göttingische gelehrte Anzeigen* (1878): 97–114.

The Acts of Timothy

Introduction

¹The Martyrdom of the holy Timothy, who was a disciple of the holy apostle Paul and who was the first established as patriarch of the Ephesians, the metropolis of Asia. ²We know that many have put in writing the stories, lives, modes of life, public life, and deaths of men holy and beloved of God. From these writings these men became familiar to those living afterwards. Therefore, since we do not consider such a thing outside of propriety we were zealous to pass on the memory of the life, civic conduct, and death of the holy apostle Timothy, who was the first patriarch[a] of the great city of the Ephesians.

<To all my fellow presbyters of Asia and Phrygia, Pamphylia, Pontus and Galatia, and all living in peace among the orthodox: I, Polycrates, the least among you, considered it just to make known to you the things handed down to us that they saw themselves and which we regularly take up for edification. Peace and good health in Christ to my brothers.>[b]

Timothy's early life and travels with Paul

³For that thrice-blessed man, as we know from the historical work of the catholic Acts put in order by the most holy evangelist Luke, was born from a Greek father and a Judean mother who believed, but was originally from the city of the Lystrians, which is the capital[c] of the province of the Lycaonians.

Acts 16:1–3   ⁴He was instructed by Paul, divine among the apostles, and many things were witnessed by him. He was a fellow traveler with Paul and a fellow sufferer for the gospel of Christ and rendered himself useful to him. He settled in this radiant metropolis of the Ephesians at the same time as Paul and was the first to sit as bishop on the apostolic throne of this radiant metropolis,[d] at the time when Nero was ruling the state of the Romans and Maximus was proconsul of Asia.

⁵All that he had accomplished in teachings, wonders, healings, and civic

---

a. M and the Latin (patriarchae). O, P, and B have episkopou.

b. This attribution of authorship to Polycrates only appears in the Latin recension and not in the Greek. As noted above, there is some dispute as to whether this paragraph was part of the original version.

c. Lit. "first" (mia). The Latin recension calls Lystra one of the cities of the prefecture of the Lycaonians, not the capital.

d. P consistently lacks the epithet lampros in its descriptions of Ephesus and often demotes the metropolis to a mere city (polis), as in verses 4, 7, 12, 15.

conduct that exceeded human understanding, it is possible for anyone to learn from the things said in various ways concerning him in the acts of the holy apostles.[a]

The arrival of John in Ephesus

[6]It is right for us to show that this same Timothy, the most holy apostle and patriarch, was not only an eyewitness and direct hearer of the famous apostle Paul but also of the illustrious theologian[b] John who rested upon the breast of our great God and savior Jesus Christ.

John 13:23–25

[7]For when Nero was raging for the martyrdom of the chief apostles Peter and Paul, and with them their illustrious fellow disciples in different ways, John the great theologian happened to arrive in this radiant metropolis after being cast ashore from a shipwreck,[c] as it is possible to learn for those who wish from the things written about him by Irenaeus, bishop of Lugdunum.[d]

John's editing of the canonical Gospels

[8]At that time also those who had followed after the disciples of our Lord Jesus Christ did not know how to organize sheets of paper in their possession in various languages which had been sporadically organized and which concerned the miracles of our Lord Jesus Christ that happened at their time. When they were present in the city of the Ephesians, according to common consent, they brought them to the truly reverent John the theologian.

[9]He looked at them all and beginning from them[e] he put the things said by them in order in three Gospels and registered them as by Matthew, Mark, and Luke, assigning their names to the Gospels.

[10]But when he found that the Gospels recounted the genealogy of the matters relating to the economy of the incarnation, then he theologized about the things that were not mentioned, of which he had obtained an impression from the divine breast. Thus he supplemented the things that were left out by the others, in particular the divine miracles. Then he placed his own name on this ordering—namely, the Gospel.

Eusebius, *Hist. eccl.* 3.24; 6.14.7; *Ap. Jas.* 2.8–16

John's exile to Patmos

[11]But when a demon of mischief invaded the thoughts of Domitian, who reigned as king of the Roman state after Nero and those who ruled in between, and when slanders came forth against the saint, the oft-mentioned[f] apostle John the theologian, was exiled by Domitian from the city of the Ephesians and ordered to stay on the island of Patmos, which is one of the islands of the Cyclades.

Rev 1:9

---

a. Presumably this refers to the canonical Acts.

b. John is also named the "theologian" (*theologos*) in the fifth-century *Apocalypse of the Holy John the Theologian* (= *1 Apocr. Apoc. John*).

c. It is unclear where this tradition comes from but it may be that the author is conflating John's arrival in Ephesus with the shipwreck of Paul on Malta in Acts 27.

d. For a discussion of *Acts Tim.*'s use of Irenaeus, see the introduction, p. 399.

e. So A, B, P, M, and Usener's Latin. O, V, and C read *hormistheis*, which would give the sense of bringing the loose pages of documents to safe harbor through John's editing and collating.

f. B reads "oft-remembered" (*mnēmoneutheis*).

The martyrdom of Timothy during the Katagogia

[12]After these things happened among them, the bishopric was being managed piously and well by the oft-mentioned, most-holy Timothy. At that time the metropolis of the Ephesians held the remains of a bygone idolatry among those who lived there. At the festival of the Katagogia,[a] as they then called it, which was celebrated on certain days, they put around themselves unseemly costumes and they covered their faces with masks so that they might not be known. They carried around clubs and images of idols,[b] disparaged with songs, and set upon free men and respectable women in an uncivilized fashion. They performed slaughters in no ordinary manner and poured out an abundance of blood on the distinguished places of the city. They did not stop acting as if what they were doing was profitable for the soul.

[13]As a result, the most holy Timothy, who was at that time the archbishop, bewailed these things often, but his effort was not strong enough to repulse such madness of theirs through his petitions. On the day of their abominable festival, he put himself forth in the midst of the "Embolos" quarter[c] to exhort them saying, "Men of Ephesus,[d] do not be mad for idols, but acknowledge the one who truly is God."

Acts 19:35

[14]The agents of the devil were angry at his teaching and, making use of the clubs and stones that they carried with them, they killed the just one. But the servants of God took him while he was yet breathing and brought him to rest at the boundary of this splendid metropolis, which is situated on the opposite side of the harbor. There, when his spirit was returned in peace to God, they took his body and placed it in the place called Pion. It is there that his most holy martyrium is located.[e]

John's return to Ephesus

[15]When emperor Domitian's life came to an end, Nerva received imperial power and recalled the most-divine apostle and evangelist John from exile. He returned and took up his seat in this radiant metropolis of the Ephesians. And when he discovered that the most holy Timothy had completed his life in the manner previously mentioned, he took up the place of honor on the apostolic throne through those who were found at that time to be chief priests.[f] He endured and managed this office until the reign of Trajan.

---

a. This was a festival in honor of Dionysus.

b. B reads "some idols."

c. "Embolos" was the name for a quarter in the city near the Agora; see Zamagni, "Passion (ou Actes) de Timothée," 349–50. B makes the location of Timothy's speech more specific by adding that he put himself forth "in the middle of the main street *(hodoi)* of the Embolos."

d. Though a common form of address in civic speeches, this is the same opening as the speech of Alexander to the mob in the Ephesian theater in Acts 19:35.

e. Later witnesses in the Greek recension include the following here: "And he was transferred to the imperial city of Constantinople. He was placed in the most holy church of the holy apostles. From then up to the present his holy remains lie under the sacred altar, alongside the apostles Andrew and Luke."

f. This likely refers to a council of bishops or elders who voted on John's ordination. The text considers Timothy an archbishop *(archiepiskopos,* v. 13), which may mean that these chief priests are lower bishops or elders. It may also be that Ephesus is envisioned as the capital of

Conclusion

[16]The holy and illustrious Timothy, apostle, patriarch, and martyr of Christ, completed his life three days after the so-called Katagogia, which is the thirtieth day of the fourth month according to the Asians and, according to the Romans, the twenty-second of the month of January,[a] when Nerva, as already mentioned, was ruling the state of the Romans and Peregrinus was proconsul of Asia, but according to us when our Lord Jesus Christ was ruling, to whom be glory forever and ever. Amen.

---

a regional network of churches. Eusebius says that while he was living in Ephesus, John commanded *(diagoreuō)* the churches in Asia *(Hist. eccl.* 3.23.1). Irenaeus also speaks of elders that John conversed with during his time in Ephesus *(Haer.* 2.22.5).

a. Three of the manuscripts collated by Zamagni indicate the date for Timothy's martyrdom as January 21 (A, C, M). January 22 is the traditional date of Timothy's martyrdom in the ancient menologia (such as the "Imperial" Menologion in the Walters Museum and the Menologion of Basil II in the Vatican) and remains the date for his feast in Orthodox tradition. Roman Catholic and Protestant traditions celebrate Timothy's feast on either January 24 or 26.

The Acts of Titus
A new translation and introduction

by Richard I. Pervo

The *Acts of Titus* (*Acts Titus; CANT* 298) follows the life and career of Titus, the disciple of Paul and purported recipient of the New Testament epistle in his name. The "Life of Titus" would be a more accurate designation for the text; indeed, the title in one of the manuscripts is "The Life and Conduct of the Holy Apostle Titus, a Disciple of the Holy Apostle Paul, Who Became Bishop of Gortyna in Crete." In form, the text is a hagiographical biography with an ecclesiological interest, much like the *Acts of Barnabas,* which combines local ecclesiastical and biographical themes.[1] Modern research has mined the work for data about the structure and content of the *Acts of Paul.*

Contents
Acts Titus is a work in three parts: I. Titus's early life (chaps. 1–3); II. His time as a companion of Paul (chaps. 4–6); and III. as Bishop of Gortyna (chaps. 7–12). These sections roughly correspond to the three principal constituent genres of biography, acts, and ecclesiastical history. The subject of the text is Titus, who became the "metropolitan" (archbishop), as it were, of Crete. The alleged author is "Zenas the lawyer," mentioned in Titus 3:13.[2] Since the New Testament provides no information about Titus's background, he is logically assigned a Cretan origin (based on Titus 1:5) and a noble lineage at that. Commensurate with that heritage was a classical education. Troubling visions spoil Titus's love for Homer "and other philosophers." In response he turns to Isaiah (1). When the proconsul of Crete, who happens to be Titus's uncle, learns about Jesus' activity, he sends an investigative delegation to Jerusalem headed by Titus. They witness the miracles, death, and resurrection of Jesus (2).

One of the earliest believers, Titus receives ordination from the apostles and becomes Paul's forerunner and colleague (4). After founding the Corinthian church, the pair proceeds to Crete, now governed by Titus's brother-in law, Rustillus (5).[3] Ephesus is their next station. Titus, together with Luke and Timothy, remain with Paul until the apostle's execution under Nero. After depositing Luke in Greece and Timothy in Ephesus, Titus returns to Crete (6).[4]

Joyfully received in his homeland, Titus establishes churches—transforming some

---

1. On this text in relation to the *Acts of Titus* see Pervo, "Acts of Titus," 480–82.

2. Appropriation of characters from the Pastoral Epistles is characteristic also of *Acts Paul* (e.g., Demas and Hermogenes in 3:1–2). Chapter and verse divisions of *Acts Paul* reflect the translation in *ANT* 364–88.

3. This is a deviation from the itinerary of the canonical Acts. The text does not attempt to fit the Epistle to Titus into the story. Paul is with Titus on the first visit to Crete, dead during the second and final.

4. This picture conforms to traditions about Luke (e.g., the old Gospel prologues found in some manuscripts of Luke) and the Pastorals, which place Timothy in Ephesus and Titus in Crete.

temples, destroying others (7). He protects Jews during the First Revolt (8:2), and corresponds with such worthies as Dionysius the Areopagite, mentioned in Acts 17:34 (10:3). The good archbishop prepares and ordains eight bishops to head dioceses based upon cities (8:1). After a holy and active life he dies in peace at the age of ninety-four (10:4–10). The former polytheist temple in which he is laid to rest becomes a healing shrine (11). The text concludes with a chronology of Titus's life (12).

Manuscripts and Versions

Acts Titus exists in two recensions, each represented by two Greek manuscripts, none of which are earlier than the tenth century.[5] These are "menologia," stories of saints to be read on their feasts. The earlier recension is found in Paris, Bibliothèque nationale de France, gr. 548, fol. 192^v–196^r of the tenth century and Vatican, Biblioteca apostolica, Ottoboni gr. 411, fol. 476^v–480^r, copied in 1445. The other, inferior, recension, which exhibits numerous errors, is found in Vienna, Österreichische Nationalbibliothek, hist. gr. 45, fol. 260^v–263^r and Athens, Benaki Museum, 141, fol. 205^r–205^v (the latter containing only the last quarter of the text), both of the eleventh century. The only edition of *Acts Titus* to date is that of François Halkin.[6] No ancient versions exist, and there are no grounds for believing that the work in its present form ever existed other than in Greek. The sole known reception is its incorporation in the collections of liturgical hagiography, which substantially transform their sources. *Acts Titus* has appeared previously in a preliminary English translation by Richard Pervo and in French by Willy Rordorf.[7]

Genre, Structure, and Prosody

The overarching genre of *Acts Titus* is the ancient *bios* (biography). The account opens with Titus's ancestry (descended from the mythical king Minos), discusses his upbringing and education, the course of his career, his noble death, subsequent veneration, and finishes with a summary of his accomplishments. *Acts Titus* includes, as is appropriate to the life of a philosopher or saint, vocation and commission accounts.[8] Titus's career is described as a religious quest, like that of, and quite possibly modeled upon, the story of Clement in the *Pseudo-Clementines*. The quest narrative is rather skillfully integrated into another constituent genre: the story of the foundation of a cult.[9] Such foundations are often generated by an oracle or other revelation, as here.

The extant text is almost certainly a shortened form of a longer Life of Titus. In its present form, it survives as a text to be read in the monastic liturgy on the Feast of St. Titus (25 August in the Greek Church). The original Life too had a strong ecclesiological focus, both celebrating the patron of Christianity in Crete and making a bid for at least limited independence from Constantinople. The two editions of the menology presented by Halkin indicate that abbreviation continued, as the second is rather shorter in most segments.

The creation of a work celebrating Titus of Crete raised difficulties, as the information known about Titus and about the mission in Crete is somewhat bare and inconsistent. Titus first appears in Galatians, where Paul recounts his journey with Barnabas to Jerusa-

---

5. For descriptions and discussion of the manuscripts see Halkin, "Légende crétoise," 241–43.

6. Halkin, "Légende crétoise," 241–52 (Menology 1), 252–56 (Menology 2).

7. Pervo, "Acts of Titus"; Rordorf, "Actes de Tite."

8. See Czachesz, *Commission Narratives*, 210–15.

9. On this genre see Pervo, *Acts: A Commentary*, 389–90, with an example on 692–93.

lem to confer about requirements for gentiles (Gal 2:1–10). Titus was chosen as the model uncircumcised convert by Barnabas and Paul (2:3). Though Titus does not appear in Acts, perhaps his conversion can be fit into the period of Paul's first missionary journey sponsored by the community at Antioch (Acts 13–14). Crete is mentioned, however, as a stop on the voyage to Rome (27:7–12). When Paul split from Antioch, Titus went with him and became his co-worker (2 Cor 8:23). During the period of conflict reflected in 2 Corinthians, Titus became Paul's emissary to Corinth; it is in this context that Titus is mentioned repeatedly in the letter (2 Cor 2:13; 7:6, 13, 14; 8:6, 16, 23; 12:18). Since Acts suppresses Titus, he was probably a controversial figure. One reasonable conjecture was that he became so because of the Jerusalem conference.

In 2 Tim 4:10, Titus has "deserted" Paul and relocated to Dalmatia, though according to the Epistle to Titus, Paul has left Titus behind in Crete (Titus 1:5), but rather than characterize him as a Cretan native, the author deems it necessary to inform his assistant about the character of the locals, and his words are not flattering (Titus 1:10–13). The association between Titus and Crete is supported by Eusebius's claim that Titus eventually returned to the island and became its first bishop (*Hist. eccl.* 3.4.6), a detail mentioned also in a note at the end of the Epistle to Titus in Paris, Bibliothèque nationale, Coislin 202 (Nestle-Aland 015) and in the Byzantine textual tradition. In the *Acts of Paul*, Titus is credited with the description of Paul offered at the start of the story of Thecla (3:2–3) and he is featured at the end of the text when he returns from Dalmatia to meet Paul in Rome (11:1). He is portrayed also at Paul's grave alongside Luke (11:5, 7); there they baptize Longus the prefect and Cestus the centurion, who became disciples of Paul during his imprisonment.

The author of *Acts Titus* draws upon these traditions, and others, to create his text. The embassy to Judea (1–2) may depend upon the *Pseudo-Clementines*, which similarly portray Clement as an educated man dissatisfied with pagan learning,[10] with possible support from John 12:20–21 (Greeks desiring to see Jesus). Chapter 3, based upon Acts 1–7, lodges Titus among the "Cretans and Arabs" of Acts 2:11, as well as the 120 of Acts 1:15. The narrative knows but deviates from Acts 9 (3:9–11); in *Acts Titus*, Paul remains in Caesarea rather than journeying on to Tarsus (compare 3:11 with Acts 9:30). In chapter 4, the freshly ordained Titus is sent with Paul on mission by the Jerusalem leaders. Antioch is their first stop, where they encounter Barnabas. The influence of *Acts Paul* is not detectable here, but freedom from the canonical Acts is clear. The presumed author of the underlying Life of Titus evidently concocted a plot at variance with Acts in order to insert Titus into the Pauline story. Chapter 4 follows in general the outline of Acts 13–14, replacing Barnabas with Titus. This is justified by *Acts Paul* 3, where Titus functions as Paul's John the Baptizer, his precursor (*Acts Paul* 3:1–2; see also 11:1). Chapter 4 continues by following Acts 16–18, but the conclusion harmonizes Acts and *Acts Paul*, with Acts supplying the framework into which data from *Acts Paul* is inserted. The author treated the two as parallel rather than sequential narratives.

At the point of Acts 18:18 (or 19:1) the mission to Crete is introduced (chap. 5), an evident fabrication. In the next chapter the mission returns to Asia. The text prefers *Acts Paul* 9 to Acts 19 and introduces Timothy, who, with Titus, delivers 2 Corinthians. This is an intelligent coordination of Acts and the letters.

---

10. See the beginning of the Clement novel: *Rec.* 1.6//*Hom.* 1.6; *Rec.* 1.12//*Hom.* 1.15. Titus's devotion to Greek philosophy strengthens the possibility of dependence. The theme is not limited to this literature, however. See, e.g., Justin, *Dial.* 2–3.

The hypothetical Life of Titus probably offered no more than a brief summary of his work in Crete and a short account of his death. The biographical framework dominates chapters 7–12 as it does in 1–2.[11] Chapters 9–11 are a legend explaining how the site of a former pagan temple became a healing shrine of St. Titus. Cult-founding here becomes more important than the founder, and ecclesiological interests emerge. The story of Titus the missionary companion of Paul recedes before the story of the origins of the church in Crete as founded by Titus.

Unlike the earlier apocryphal acts, this text has not the faintest whiff of unorthodoxy and minimizes conflicts with lawful officials. Indeed both Titus and Paul receive support from Titus's ruling-class relatives (5:7–9). No lawful marriages are threatened with disruption. Titus is a severe ascetic, but he does not impose his views upon others. In these features, *Acts Titus* shows perhaps what medieval theologians found objectionable in the various earlier apocryphal acts. An unusual feature is the protection of Cretan Jews from reprisals connected with the Jewish War (or revolts) (8:2). Most early Christian writings are hostile to Jews.

Date and Provenance

Several factors establish Crete as the present text's place of composition—notably its promotion of Titus as a prominent native son and the detailed interest in the structure of the local church. Communities seeking to gain some autonomy found support in an apostolic foundation, a status greatly enhanced by possession of the apostle's remains. Titus belonged to the top tier of sub-apostolic personages. The canonical Epistle of Titus gave rise to the tradition that Titus was the first bishop of Crete. *Acts Titus*'s depiction of a metropolitan organization (local bishops under an archbishop) establishes a date for the text not prior to the early fifth century.[12] The reference to Dionysius the Areopagite (10:3) gives a fairly firm *terminus a quo* of ca. 500 CE,[13] while the Arab conquest of Crete ca. 824 provides a secure *terminus ad quem*. The text probably antedates the transfer of Crete from Roman to Constantinopolitan ecclesiastical jurisdiction (730), the iconoclastic controversy, and the ministry of Andrew of Crete (d. 740), who was well informed about the activity of Titus. If language and style were the sole criteria for dating, the late fifth century would be appropriate.[14] That would be a reasonable conjecture for the date of the hypothetical Life of Titus. The earliest form of the present *Acts Titus* can be dated with good probability to the early seventh century.

Translation

This translation follows the text established by Halkin for the earlier edition ("Menology 1"). He preferred manuscript P, which is clearly a more careful and intelligent text. The chapter divisions are Halkin's (followed also by Rordorf); the verse divisions are new to this translation.

---

11. See Czachesz, *Commission Narratives*, 212–13.

12. See Marina Falla Castelfranchi, "Crete," *EECh* 1:208–9.

13. So Halkin, "Légende crétoise," 242, who notes (251 n. 1) that ten letters in the Areopagitic corpus address Titus.

14. The practiced eye of James ("Acts of Titus," 555) found *Acts Titus* to be of about the same era as the *Acts of Barnabas*.

Sigla

Menology 1: the earlier edition, based upon P and O. The text translated is P, unless otherwise stated.

P   Paris, Bibliothèque nationale de France, gr. 548
O   Vatican, Biblioteca apostolica, Ottoboni gr. 411

Menology 2: the later edition, based on V and A
V   Vienna, Österreichische Nationalbibliothek, hist. gr. 45
A   Athens, Benaki Museum, 141

Bibliography

EDITIONS AND TRANSLATIONS

Halkin, François. "La légende crétoise de saint Tite." *AnBoll* 79 (1961): 241–56. (Critical editions of both menologia.)

Pervo, Richard I. "The Acts of Titus: A Preliminary Translation, with an Introduction and Notes." Pages 455–82 in *Society of Biblical Literature 1996 Seminar Papers*. SBLSP 35. Atlanta: Scholars, 1996 (with additional bibliography).

Rordorf, Willy. "Actes de Tite." Pages 605–15 in *EAC* vol. 2.

STUDIES

Czachesz, István, *Commission Narratives. A Comparative Study of the Canonical and Apocryphal Acts*. SECA 8. Leuven: Peeters, 2007.

James, Montague Rhodes. "The Acts of Titus and the Acts of Paul." *JTS* 6 (1905): 549–56.

Lipsius, Richard A. *Die apokryphen Apostelgeschichten und Apostellegenden: Ein Beitrag zur altchristlichen Literaturgeschichte und zu einer zusammenfassenden Darstellung der neutestamentlichen Apokryphen*. 2 vols. in 3 parts. Braunschweig, 1883–1890; repr., Amsterdam: Philo, 1976. (*Acts Titus* is examined in vol. 2.2:401–6.)

Niederwimmer, Kurt. "Zenas der Jurist (Tit 3,13)." Pages 267–79 in *Quaestiones Theologicae. Gesammelte Aufsätze*. Edited by Wilhelm Pratscher and Markus Öhler. BZNW 90. Berlin: De Gruyter, 1998.

Pervo, Richard I. *Acts: A Commentary*. Hermeneia. Edited by Harold W. Attridge. Minneapolis: Fortress, 2009.

The Acts of Titus[a]

The youth and education of Titus

1 [1]Zenas the Lawyer, whom the Holy Apostle Paul mentions, is the one who wrote (Titus's) life as set forth below:

Titus 3:13

[2]The most holy Titus stemmed from the lineage of Minos, king of Crete. [3]At age twenty, when he was quite devoted to the poems and dramas of Homer and the other philosophers, he heard a voice saying, "Titus, you must depart from here and save your soul, for this learning will be of no benefit to you." [4]He wanted to hear the same voice once more, for he was familiar with the deceptions issued vocally from statues.[b] [5]After remaining resistant for nine years, he was instructed in a vision to read the book of the Hebrews. Taking up the book of Isaiah, he came upon the following passage: "*Be dedicated to me, you many islands. Israel is being saved by the Lord with everlasting salvation,*" and so on.[c]

Isa 41:1; 45:17 LXX

The conversion of Titus

2 [1]Now when the proconsul of Crete, who was the uncle of St. Titus, heard of the salutary birth and baptism of Christ the Master and of the marvelous deeds he performed in Jerusalem and elsewhere, he took counsel with the leading people of Crete and then dispatched Titus with some others to Jerusalem so that he would be able to hear the message and speak and teach those things that he was going to see. [2]Titus arrived, saw, and worshipped Christ the Master. [3]He observed all of his marvelous deeds and also witnessed the Master's salutary sufferings, his burial, resurrection, and divine ascension, as well as the arrival of the all-holy Spirit upon the divine apostles. [4]He became a believer.

The church in Jerusalem

3 [1]He was numbered with the 120 and among the 3,000 who came to believe in Christ through Peter, the chief, as indeed it is written, "*Cretans and Arabs.*"

Acts 1:15

Acts 2:41; 2:11

---

a. The title in the MSS reads: "Of the Holy Apostle Titus, a Disciple of the Holy Apostle Paul, Who Became Bishop of Gortyna in Crete."

b. Cultic statues sometimes communicated by bleeding, sweating, trembling, falling, or speaking. This phenomenon still occurs in Christian churches today. See C. R. Phillips III, "Statues," *OCD*[3] 1439–40.

c. The citation may be a blend of two passages, but it is at least as likely that it suggests this entire section of the prophetic book.

Acts 18:25

Acts 4:4

Acts 3:1–10

Acts 5:35–39

Acts 7

[2]Titus was ardent and always zealous in the Spirit. [3]Three years later, 5,000 men had been added to the faith. [4]Two years later, after the cripple had been healed by Peter and John, the apostles were persecuted and charged not to speak in the name of the Lord Jesus. [5]When the priests were intent upon putting them to death, Gamaliel, the teacher of the law, deterred their plan. [6]After seven years had passed, Stephen was stoned.

Paul's early mission

Acts 9:1–25

Acts Paul 7

Acts Paul 6

Acts 9:26–30

[7]Thereafter occurred Paul's experiences in Damascus—that is, his blinding and recovery of sight. [8]Paul preached the message about Christ first in Damascus. [9]He healed Aphphia,[a] the wife of Chrysippus, who had been possessed by a demon. [10]After a fast of seven days he cast down the idol of Apollo. [11]Then he went to Jerusalem and in turn[b] to Caesarea.[c]

Titus becomes Paul's colleague

Acts 13:1; Acts Paul 2

Acts 12:1–2

Acts 13:4–12

Acts 13:13–52; 14:1–5

2 Tim 1:16–18; 4:19

4 [1]St. Titus was ordained by the apostles and sent with Paul to teach and to ordain whomever Paul might designate. [2]Arriving at Antioch, they found Barnabas, the son of Panchares[d] whom Paul had raised. [3]Herod the Tetrarch[e] killed James the brother of John with a sword. [4]After this they traveled to Seleucia, Cyprus, Salamis, and Paphos. [5]From there they went to Perga in Pamphylia and again[f] to Pisidian Antioch, then to Iconium, to the household of Onesiphorus, to whom Titus had previously reported the facts about Paul, since he was Paul's precursor in every city.[g]

Acts 16:25–40

[6]From there he (Titus?)[h] went to Lystra and Derbe. [7]The divinely inspired Titus both preached the word of God with Paul in every city and endured persecutions and whippings. [8]Both nonetheless enlightened the hearts of unbelievers by working signs and wonders just as (these) all are reported in the Acts of the Apostles.[i] [9]When Paul was in custody at Philippi, an earthquake occurred in the prison workshop[j] (and) he was freed.[k]

---

a. O reads "Amphia."

b. The Greek word *palin* is vexing. "Again" is possible.

c. *Acts Paul* 8 includes a trip to Jerusalem; Caesarea is not mentioned, but the material is quite fragmentary.

d. "Panchares" is the correct form. "Anchares," in *Acts Paul* 2 is the result of an error generated by construing the initial *p-* as the Coptic definite article. See Montague Rhodes James, *The Apocryphal New Testament* (Oxford: Clarendon, 1953), 271–72.

e. Acts 12:1 assigns responsibility for this deed to a "King Herod." The writer may have confounded this with Acts 13:1, which does refer to Herod the Tetrarch.

f. On this use of *palin* see Pervo, "Acts of Titus," 475 n. 130.

g. This is an evident generalization from *Acts Paul* 3:2; 11:1.

h. The variant reading "they" is almost certainly a secondary solution.

i. The plural *praxeis* evidently refers to Acts and *Acts Paul*, since Titus is absent from the former.

j. The reading "prison workshop" is difficult. For details see Pervo, "Acts of Titus," 468 n. 80.

k. At this point P contains a gloss: "Now some write 'Titus Justus,' but others 'Titus Pistos.'" This gloss is an attempt to identify the Titius Justus of Acts 18:7 with Titus. On the text of Acts see Pervo, *Acts: A Commentary*, 454. No manuscript of Acts contains "pistos" ("faithful"), which evidently derives from the Epistle to Titus.

Titus and Paul in Crete

5 [1]At that time Rustillus,[a] who was married to Titus's sister,[b] had completed a second period in the governorship of Crete. Paul and Titus arrived there. [2]When the ruler saw the divinely inspired Titus weighed down with tears, he attempted to compel him to live with him, but St. Titus did not obey him. [3]Rustillus advised him not to speak against the pagan gods. [4]St. Titus expounded the gospel of Christ to him, claiming "If you believe my message, you will be exalted on earth and in the city of Rome."

[5]Shortly thereafter his son died. He brought him to Paul at night. [6]Following prayer, Paul raised him. [7]After they had spent three months there, Rustillus sent them on with ample funds. [8]He went to Rome and was designated consul. [9]Thereafter, because Rustillus was a relative of Titus, those of the circumcision only engaged in verbal combat, not daring to do anything else to the proclaimers of God's word.

Titus 1:10

From Crete to Rome and the return to Crete

6 [1]Leaving Crete, they went to Asia. [2]In the course of Paul's teaching at Ephesus 12,000 persons came to believe. [3]There the apostle also fought with beasts, being cast to a lion. Titus, Timothy, and Erastus delivered the second epistle to the Corinthians.[c]

Acts 19:1–20
Acts Paul 9; 1 Cor 15:32

[4]Titus, Timothy, and Luke remained with the apostle until his consummation under Nero. [5]Thereupon they returned to Greece and established Luke there.[d] [6]Titus and Timothy then moved on to Colossae. [7]Timothy subsequently returned to Ephesus while Titus proceeded to Crete.

Acts Paul 11

1 Tim 1:3; Titus 1:5

Titus's ministry in Crete

7 [1]The Cretans greeted his arrival joyfully, like that of a relative, and decreed a holiday. [2]They adorned the temples of their idols, took in hand the sacred swords, and, clad in[e] their purple-trimmed ephebic tunics,[f] they went before him. [3]St. Titus addressed them graciously and urged them to be responsive to what he said. [4]He began by singing, in Hebrew, "*May God be gracious to us and bless us,*" and so on. [5]They responded that they did not know what he was saying. [6]Only the Hebrews present understood.

Ps 67:1

[7]Presently, as they drew near to the idol of Artemis, it cast itself down, breaking forth with a cry, "You (pl.) are acting insolently in ignorance!" [8]St. Titus said to them, "Since you are publicly carrying swords, condemnation therefore falls upon you." [9]Thereupon they threw down the swords and remained with-

Acts John 42

---

a. Menology 2 corrects (apparently) this otherwise-unattested name to the more familiar Rutillus.

b. Another sister, Euphemia, appears in chapter 10.

c. The author derived the mission of Timothy and Erastus from Acts 19:22, where they are sent to Macedonia. 2 Tim 4:20 deposits Erastus at Corinth. 2 Cor 2:13; 7:6; and chapter 8 relate Titus to Macedonia.

d. See the introduction p. 406 n. 4.

e. Or "carrying."

f. Or, less possibly, "tunics with diagonal purple stripes." The text is difficult. The subject is a procession. The writer of the present text may not have understood the ceremony.

out food until early morning, reciting the psalm in expectation that they would hear something from the idol. [10]Then, after numerous marvels, they began to exclaim, "There is one god, the one manifested to us this day!"[a] [11]Five hundred came to believe in Christ.

[12]The diet of the apostle consisted of garden vegetables. He took his rest upon goat's hair and sheepskin.[b]

Ministry in Crete continued; Jewish revolt

8 [1]Titus ordained bishops in Cnossus, Hierapytna, Cydonia, Chersonesus, Eleutherna,[c] Lampa, Cisamus, and Cantanus, so that there would be nine bishops with Gortyna as Metropolitan See. He taught them for four years.

[2]Now at that time the Roman Emperor Vespasian fell upon Jerusalem and took the Jews there and in every place captive. Yet, because of blessed Titus's relative, there was no persecution of the Jews in Crete.

A new healing shrine

9 [1]Now a certain Secundus, who had received funds from the Emperor Trajan to rebuild a temple of idols, did indeed begin the project. [2]St. Titus happened by, glimpsed the enormous undertaking, uttered a deep groan, and moved on. [3]The next morning it transpired that the entire foundation had collapsed and that the building-blocks were scattered about.

Acts Paul 5; Acts John 37–47; Acts Corn. 2:11–12; Xanth. 2:3

[4]Just as Secundus was on the verge of doing away with himself, someone advised him to hasten to Titus. [5]Once there, he knelt down and besought Titus to protect him from liability. [6]The saint replied, "If you should come to believe in my Christ, the building will be erected." [7]In response Secundus asked indulgence for himself and promised to give Titus a child he loved.[d] [8]The saint said, "Get to work on your task and, as you work, repeat together with the laborers, 'There is but one god, the god in heaven!'" [9]Thereafter this cry was repeated in the course of the work.[e]

[10]When the temple was completed, St. Titus said to the people, "Know well, brothers and sisters, that that place will become a proving-ground for holy relics."

Titus's death

10 [1]When Euphemia, the virgin sister of blessed Titus, died, he laid her remains in a place that he had built. [2]There he would often offer hymns and praise to God. [3]Subsequently, he wrote letters to Dionysius the Areopagite and to others.[f]

---

a. This text has evidently abbreviated a lengthy account of the humiliation of Artemis. Menology 2 represents an improvement, with substantial dialogue at the climax of which the idol is pulverized at Titus's invocation of Christ's name. It is possible that here this edition is closer to the original.

b. This is an abbreviation of a longer account. One expects an ascetic to wear uncomfortable fabrics.

c. "Eleutherna" so O; P has "Eleutherina."

d. Menology 2 states that he asked indulgence until the building was complete and notes, in the following sentence, that he had the child baptized.

e. "In the course of the work" renders a troublesome term that must have conveyed a meaning of this nature.

f. Abbreviation is apparent. See Pervo, "Acts of Titus," 472 n. 111.

[4]Then, after he had wrought many marvelous deeds, he saw the holy angels sent to take him. [5]Fragrant smoke and a cloud glowing more brightly than the sun filled the house. [6]Titus, with transfigured face, let forth a great, glad laugh. [7]Raising his hands toward heaven, he cried out, "Lord, I have kept your faith true and have preserved the people intact. [8]*Into your hands I commit my spirit.* [9]Of your own self strengthen your people." [10]After adding the "amen" he gave up his spirit joyfully and lives forever.

2 Tim 4:7

Acts 20:28; Luke 23:46
(Ps 31:5)

Titus's tomb becomes a healing shrine

11 [1]Then they anointed his remains with oils and aromatic spices, clothed them in a white garment, and carried them off for burial. [2]At that moment the temples of the idols collapsed, but the people within them came out unharmed and saw the remains of the saint.

Acts Paul 5; Acts John
37–47; Acts Corn.
2:11–12

[3]His precious tomb is in fact an altar, at which are the chains used to bind those afflicted by unclean spirits.[a] [4]In this place all who are deemed worthy to embrace the resting place of the saint experience healing.[b]

Chronology of Titus's life

12 [1]Now the holy apostle and hierarch of Christ was twenty years of age when he came to Jerusalem.[c] [2]One year passed until the ascension of the Lord. [3]He spent ten years before being ordained apostle and archbishop by the chief disciples of the Lord. [4]Titus contended for eighteen years in the proclamation of the gospel[d] and spent six years in Crete and the other islands.[e] [5]For thirty-nine years he dwelt in his native city, so that the total years of his earthly life were ninety-four.

[6]May we all receive mercy from his intercessions, we who give thanks to and believe in our Lord Jesus Christ, to whom belong all glory, honor, and reverence, with the Father and the Holy Spirit, now and always, to the end of the ages. Amen.

---

a. The text presumably means that healed demoniacs left their former chains as *ex-voto* offerings and attestations.

b. The relics of Titus were removed to St. Mark's Basilica in Venice following the Arab capture of Crete in 823 and were not restored to Crete until 1968, according to George D. Dragas, "Titus," *EEC* 904. That same page contains a photograph of the remains of a possibly sixth-century Church of St. Titus at Gortyna. For a more detailed description of this building see Marina Falla Castelfranchi, "Crete," *EECh* 1:209.

c. In this chronological summing up, it seems to have been appropriate to omit his delay of nine years between initial call and actual departure. It is difficult to reconcile the data in this chapter with the chronology given in chapter 2, which, if cumulative, yields twelve years before the death of Stephen, or seven, if counted from a single starting point. Seven may be correct if one presumes that Paul labored for three years before Titus was ordained to be his assistant.

d. This clause apparently refers to Titus's labor as a companion of Paul.

e. The narrator evidently means that Titus devoted these six years to erecting the hierarchy of Crete and adjacent islands.

The Life and Conduct of the Holy Women
Xanthippe, Polyxena, and Rebecca
A new translation and introduction

by David L. Eastman

This work (*Xanth.*; *BHG* 1877) is an ascetical treatise that incorporates elements of apocryphal acts, ancient romance novels, and hagiography. Written in Greek, it recounts the conversions and adventures of three fictional women: Xanthippe, a matron in Spain; Polyxena, her younger sister; and Rebecca, a Jewish slave girl who meets Polyxena in Greece. The text assumes Pauline missionary activity in Spain and features providential cameo appearances by several other apostles, but these apostles are only background players in this drama about the main female characters. The focus of the text is the glorification of sexual abstinence. *Xanth.* is sometimes referred to as the *Acts of Xanthippe and Polyxena*, but that title is misleading with respect to the genre and content of the work.

Contents
An unnamed servant of a Spanish aristocrat is in Rome and hears Paul's preaching, but he is forced by duty to return to Spain before he can hear the entire message. He falls deathly ill, leading his master, Probus, to ask how he might be cured. The servant speaks of a physician in Rome who alone can restore him (1). Xanthippe,[1] Probus's wife, overhears this conversation and is herself overcome by sickness and longing for this mysterious doctor and teacher. She embraces extreme asceticism and sexual abstinence and calls out to a god whose name she does not know. The pitiable Probus hears Xanthippe's groaning and does not know what to do (2–6). Some time later, Paul comes to Spain and Xanthippe immediately identifies him as the doctor from Rome. Probus compels Paul to stay with them, hoping that the apostle can heal his wife (the sick servant has disappeared from the story by this point), but soon those desiring to hear Paul overrun the house (7–10). Xanthippe realizes that Probus is about to expel Paul and begs for baptism, but the devil prompts Probus to throw out Paul and lock away Xanthippe before this can occur (11). Paul is invited to the house of another nobleman named Philotheus. While Probus sleeps, Xanthippe sneaks away to visit Paul by bribing the gatekeeper. Demons assail her on the way, but she is saved by a vision of Paul and Christ and is then baptized by Paul (12–16). Once awake, Probus summons two wise men to explain a disturbing dream, and they warn Probus that they must all seek baptism from Paul. Probus finally acquiesces, and Xanthippe is overjoyed (17–21).

Meanwhile, Xanthippe's younger sister, Polyxena, has a disturbing dream in which she is devoured by a serpent, and that very night a powerful enemy of her suitor kidnaps her (22–23). She is smuggled to the dock and put on board a ship headed for "Babylonia."

---

[1]. A character of the same name also appears in *Acts Pet.* 34, although there is no other clear connection between these stories.

At sea they nearly meet a ship bound for Rome carrying the apostle Peter, but demons intervene and divert Polyxena's ship (24). The ship lands in Greece, where the apostle Philip meets her and hands her over to an unnamed believer, and the kidnappers raise a large force to attack the man's house. The marauders are miraculously beaten back by the household servants, yet Polyxena sneaks out and begins wandering through the countryside (25). After spending the night in a lioness's den and convincing the beast not to eat her, she meets the apostle Andrew on the road. It comes to light that they both know Paul, and Polyxena begs for baptism (26–28). When they come to a spring, a Jewish slave girl named Rebecca, also still a virgin, is there and begs for help. Andrew baptizes both women and then departs (29–30). The two women then meet a kindly mule-driver, who offers to take them to the coast to find a ship. He advises Polyxena to disguise herself as a man, but she is kidnapped again due to her beauty, this time by a prefect (31–35). She is befriended by the prefect's son, who had heard Paul's preaching in Antioch and attempts to smuggle her to safety. Polyxena and the son are betrayed by an eavesdropping slave and condemned to death. The lioness in the arena refuses to attack them, and the prefect and everyone in the city come to believe (36–37).

At this point Onesimus, speaking in the first person, is introduced into the narrative. He stops in Greece on his way to carry letters to Paul in Spain. Obeying a direct command from God, he conducts Polyxena, Rebecca, and the prefect's son to Spain, despite another attack on them along the way (38–39). At last they arrive back in the unnamed Spanish city and are welcomed by Paul. Xanthippe rejoices at the safe return of her sister, whose virginity is intact. Even Polyxena's original kidnapper believes and is baptized. Everyone praises God, and thereafter Polyxena remains with Paul (40–42).

Manuscripts and Versions

There is little doubt that the original language of *Xanth.* is Greek. The presence of terms transliterated directly from Latin may be helpful for dating and locating the text (see below) but does nothing to undermine the clear stylistic indications of a Greek original. The text (or at least portions thereof) survives in only a few manuscripts,[2] all in Greek:

> Paris, Bibliothèque nationale de France, gr. 1458, fol. 5v–17 (11th cent.)
> Vatican, Biblioteca apostolica, gr. 803, fol. 66–79v (11th cent.)
> Moscow, State Historical Museum, gr. 161, fol. 259–72 (11th cent.)
> Moscow, Russian State Library, gr. 68 [521], fol. 86v–101v (15th cent.)

The standard edition, by M. R. James, is based on the Paris manuscript.[3] James's analysis of textual antecedents was hampered by the fact that he did not have access to the entire *Acts of Paul*. He subsequently published a list of corrections to the text.[4] To this list he added with approval some suggested alterations by Maximilien Bonnet.[5] The translation in this volume incorporates the corrections proposed by James and Bonnet. The only text-critical work performed on *Xanth.* after James is an article by A. N. Vesselovskij, who provided excerpts from Moscow gr. 161 and summaries in Russian of the other manuscripts.[6]

---

2. The four MSS are listed in Junod, "Vie et conduit des saintes," 84–85.
3. James, *Apocrypha Anecdota,* 43–57 (introduction), 58–85 (Greek text).
4. James, *Apocrypha Anecdota* 2, 139–40.
5. Bonnet, "Sur les actes de Xanthippe et Polyxène."
6. Vesselovskij, "Christian Transformation," 48–60.

Structure and Unity

The text has two clear divisions. Chapters 1–21 tell the story of Xanthippe. The Greek in this first section can be quite challenging, due to awkward turns of phrase and the occasional use of otherwise-unattested words. The events take place entirely within one city, and the focus is on the challenges of a chaste life within marriage. Xanthippe struggles to understand the strange sickness that comes over her and then to work out the implications of her new faith with her husband. She is presented as a tortured soul and repeatedly breaks into long, elaborate prayers decrying her fate. Her later prayers become profoundly theological, and for a new convert she displays a striking aptitude for dogmatic long-windedness. The devil or demons appear at several points, but their efforts are thwarted or, in one case, they are simply smashed in the face by an angry Xanthippe. Xanthippe's story is one of triumph, not only through her own baptism and acceptance of a life of chastity, but also through the conversion and baptism of her husband.

Chapters 22–42 recount the adventures of Polyxena and highlight threats to chastity for unmarried women, especially those who are mobile. Very little of this section takes place in Spain. Polyxena moves and is moved around frequently, alternating between meeting apostles and meeting men who want to kidnap and/or assault her. Her story is a white-knuckle tale of the dangers to virginity potentially encountered by any woman, even a woman who tries to hide her beauty by dressing like a man. Polyxena's story, therefore, can be linked to other Christian sources in late antiquity that reflect a substantial anxiety concerning female itinerancy. Women who moved around were women at risk. Some of this anxiety may have been based on actual instances of violence against women, yet there was also an element of social control in the propagation and encouragement of this anxiety.[7] Polyxena manages to escape kidnappers, lionesses, and a lustful prefect. Miraculously, her adventures end with a safe return home with her virginity intact, but other women of the time could not expect to be so fortunate.

Although the two parts of *Xanth.* are quite different from each other, scholars agree that these are not two distinct stories artificially joined together. The manuscript evidence shows no sign of separate transmission histories, and the style is overall similar enough to suggest a single author. The figure of Xanthippe holds the text together, from her illness at the outset to her eventual joy at the end after Polyxena's return. Moreover, the localized focus of Xanthippe complements the international tale of Polyxena, such that the two primary subplots balance each other. Eclectic though its various elements may be, *Xanth.* appears to be the integrated work of a single hand.

Genre

Xanth. represents a creative adaptation and combination of several literary genres: apocryphal acts of the apostles, ancient romance novels, and lives of saints. As the traditional name of the text *(Acts of Xanthippe . . .)* indicates, scholars have noted strong connections with the apocryphal acts. The authors of these acts recount the travels and adventures of the apostles, seeking, among other things, to elucidate which apostle brought the gospel to this or that region, to recount the mighty deeds performed as proof of the gospel, to list the trials experienced by the apostles, to identify early and important converts (especially those who became bishops), and to describe when, where, and how the apostles died. Al-

---

7. See David L. Eastman, "The Matriarch as Model: Sarah, the Cult of the Saints, and Social Control in a Syriac Homily of Pseudo-Ephrem," *JECS* 21, no. 2 (2013): 241–59.

lusions to canonical texts are meant to serve as markers of authenticity for the apocryphal acts' expanded narratives.

Several of these elements are incorporated into *Xanth.* Paul is the primary apostolic figure, and his missionary work in Rome and Spain provides the background for the entire narrative. The author ties in canonical traditions of Paul's journey to Rome and desired trip to Spain (see Rom 15:22–24), as well as other apocryphal accounts of Paul's activities. Peter also appears briefly. After Paul has left Rome, Peter journeys to the capital city on a ship to counter the destructive efforts of Simon Magus (24). This detail links *Xanth.* with several apocryphal foundation stories of the Roman church, which recount a Petrine visit to the capital to defeat Simon (*Acts Pet., Lin. Mart. Pet., Abd. Pass. Pet.,* etc.).[8] The other location identified in the text is Greece, where traditionally Philip[9] and Andrew had traveled. The author of *Xanth.* places Philip and Andrew in "their" territory, thus tying this text further to other apocryphal accounts (25–31). Narratives of new converts also appear prominently in *Xanth.*, for both Andrew and Paul baptize multiple people (14:1; 21:1–3; 30:3; 42:1), and Philip commits Polyxena to the care of a man he had converted (25:3). Finally, *Xanth.* is linked to other acts through the apostolic preaching of sexual renunciation. Xanthippe refuses to have relations with Probus, just as numerous aristocratic women in Rome withdraw from their husbands because of the preaching of Peter (e.g., *Acts Pet.* 34–35). And Xanthippe pines for Paul (3–6) just as Thecla does in *Acts Paul* (3:7–9).[10] The main concern surrounding Polyxena and Rebecca is not that they were kidnapped or enslaved, but that their virginity could be threatened. Indeed, perhaps the greatest triumph of the text is that Probus and the lustful kidnapper of Polyxena are eventually baptized and presumably accept a life of chastity (42:1). Thus, there are multiple narrative elements that have led scholars to note connections to the apocryphal acts when discussing the genre of *Xanth.*

Despite these similarities, there are also notable differences. The apostles suffer no misfortunes or even challenges in *Xanth.* Yes, Paul is evicted by Probus, but he is immediately invited into the home of one who is Probus's social equal (11). Peter, Philip, and Andrew all disappear before any trouble befalls them. So *Xanth.* is a story in which other people, not the apostles, suffer for their faith. Other distinctive aspects of *Xanth.* are that the apostles perform no miraculous deeds to prove their message, they fail to do any actual preaching, and they are not martyred at the end. The story of the servant at the beginning of the text is a specific case in which we see a clear distinction between *Xanth.* and other acts. The servant falls ill from Paul's preaching and returns to Spain, where he soon dies because the apostolic "doctor" is not there to help him. This makes him the antithesis of Eutychus in Acts (20:7–12) and Patroclus in *Acts Paul* (11:1–2), both of whom hear Paul preaching in Rome and fall asleep, tumbling to their deaths from a high window of the house in which Paul is preaching. Paul raises both servants from the dead as a sign of his power. The unnamed servant in *Xanth.* also dies as a result of hearing Paul's preaching, albeit by the slower, more excruciating means of wasting away through extreme asceti-

---

8. New translations of these texts can be found in David L. Eastman, *Ancient Martyrdom Accounts of Peter and Paul* (WGRW 39; Atlanta: Society of Biblical Literature, 2015).

9. This is Philip the apostle, not the evangelist/missionary in Acts, but from an early date Christians began conflating the two. See Christopher R. Matthews, *Philip: Apostle and Evangelist. Configurations of a Tradition* (NovTSup 105; Leiden: Brill, 2000), 15–34.

10. Chapter and verse divisions of *Acts Paul* reflect the translation in *ANT* 364–38.

cism. Paul does not bring him back. If the servant functions as a type of anti-Eutychus or anti-Patroclus, then this makes Paul in *Xanth.* a type of nonhealing anti-Paul.

Xanth. also shares some elements with ancient romance novels. The opening scenes (1–6) in which the servant and Xanthippe are pining for the nameless physician (Paul) are reminiscent of the descriptions of lovesick, frustrated protagonists in stories such as the *Ephesian Tale* of Xenophon of Ephesus. Struck by a mystery illness, Xanthippe gives up not only sex but also food and wastes away out of unfulfilled desire. For all his best efforts, poor Probus can do nothing to help her until Paul arrives and she seems to come back to life (7–8). She is no less melodramatic in the closing scene, when she proclaims that she can now die, because she has seen her sister returned with her virginity intact (41:2–4). The travails of her sister, Polyxena, also provide a connection to many of the narrative elements of romance novels. The main characters in such novels are typically star-crossed and separated from each other by circumstances beyond their control. Kidnapping (often by pirates) is a typical cause of this separation, and Polyxena herself is the victim of kidnapping twice. The first kidnappers immediately rush her to the dock and set sail for the distant shores of "Babylonia" (22–24, more on this below). Adventures and mishaps on the high seas are common in novels, and Polyxena survives a trying journey before landing in Greece (25:1). Once on land, she experiences yet more trials (26–37): pursued by brigands, lost in the wilderness, nearly eaten by a lion, kidnapped (again), betrayed by an eavesdropping servant, and nearly eaten by a lion (again). Along the way she meets famous people (apostles) and a traveling companion, the Jewish slave girl Rebecca (25, 28, 29). Even her sea voyage home is fraught with danger, for the warlike inhabitants of an unnamed island see her and, for no apparent reason, attack her retinue. Only the quick (and apparently long) arms of the ship's captain prevent her from killing herself at that point by leaping into the sea (39). Like other novelistic heroines, she has many adventures before finally arriving home. And like her sister Xanthippe, Polyxena adds to the tension in the story by her own impulsive responses and actions.

Yet, for all these thematic connections with novels, *Xanth.* is also noticeably different from those other texts. There is no frame story of love lost and re-found. The servant and Xanthippe are pining not for a lost lover, but for a preacher/physician whose identity they do not even know. Polyxena is separated from her beloved suitor by being kidnapped, but he is never otherwise mentioned in the text, and during her travels she fails to mention him even once. There is no sense that Polyxena is primarily concerned with being reunited with him, and after her homecoming, it is Paul, not a lover, to whom she attaches herself. Several scholars have attempted to sexualize the text by proposing a frame narrative dependent on an incestuous relationship between Xanthippe and Polyxena.[11] Because Xanthippe is described as loving her sister and expressing great joy at her safe return, including embracing and kissing her, these scholars have suggested that their relationship was other than just sisterly. Polyxena's traveling companion, Rebecca, is also brought into this discussion as a would-be lover. This reading is provocative but misses the consistent theme of *Xanth.*, which is the overt and total rejection of all sexuality (see further below). If there is any character in *Xanth.* that suffers from unrequited love, it is Probus, yet he too eventually surrenders his carnal desires in light of the message of renunciation. Elements

---

11. Gorman, "Reading and Theorizing Women's Sexualities"; idem, "Thinking with and about 'Same-Sex Desire'"; Burrus, "Desiring Women." Prof. Burrus graciously made this unpublished essay available to me.

of *Xanth.*, then, may echo some components of a Greek romance novel, but that genre is not a good fit overall.[12]

Another proposal has been to read *Xanth.* through the lens of hagiography (lives of saints).[13] This would account for the fact that the emphasis of the text is not on apostolic deeds or deaths, nor on lovers lost and reunited, but on the conduct of holy lives by the main characters. Despite various trials, multiple attacks by demons, and intense social pressure on her as a wife, Xanthippe perseveres in maintaining a chaste life after the message of Paul reaches her. Polyxena and Rebecca likewise preserve their virginity, even if not always through acts of particular bravery or sagacity. All three women ultimately serve as models of holy living, consistent with the genre of hagiography.

All told, *Xanth.* does not readily fit into any of these genres. It is an eclectic work, a mélange of narrative styles and themes stitched together into a patchwork quilt that is at points as frustrating as it is enticing. However, this evaluation should not be read as dismissive of the text or the skill of its author; on the contrary, the author at many points shows considerable finesse, and the peculiarities of the work do not mitigate its clear message of encouraging the idealized life of renunciation.

Date and Provenance

Early theories about the date of *Xanth.* took their cue primarily from allusions in the text to the apocryphal acts of Paul, Peter, Andrew, Thomas, and Philip. M. R. James believed that the latest of these *(Acts Phil.)* dated to the early decades of the third century and that *Xanth.* was produced soon after that, around 250 CE.[14] Stevan Davies, however, argued that the alleged dependence on *Acts Phil.* was dubious. In his mind, eliminating this early-third-century source as a *terminus a quo* yielded an even earlier date of 190–225.[15]

More recent scholarship has tended to push the date later. Eric Junod has argued that the unique vocabulary in *Xanth.* belongs in the fourth or fifth century at the earliest. In addition, there are two accounts in the text of people making or using crosses for protection: Xanthippe, when she goes to visit Paul after her baptism (23:1), and a small group of servants about to sally forth to defend Polyxena against a much larger military force (25:9). Such accounts, Junod suggests, belong to the post-Constantinian period, when the symbol of the cross took on greater importance. Junod offers a *terminus ad quem* of the eighth or ninth century, based on the textual corrections suggested by Bonnet. Bonnet explains several of his changes by appealing to scribal error in copying a text written in uncial (majuscule) script. Uncials were largely replaced by minuscule script around the year 800; so, if *Xanth.* had once existed in uncials, then it must have been composed prior to that date. Junod accepts Bonnet's argument on this point, thus leaving a broad range from the fourth to the ninth century.[16] Tibor Szepessy agrees with James that *Xanth.* shows dependence on *Acts Phil.*, but he dates *Acts Phil.* to the late fourth or early fifth century. Combining this with what he perceives as occasional signs of early Byzantine Greek,

---

12. The debate over the relevance of the ancient novel for the apocryphal acts is ongoing. For a summary of some of the central issues in this discussion with bibliography, see Christine M. Thomas, *The Acts of Peter, Gospel Literature, and the Ancient Novel: Rewriting the Past* (Oxford: Oxford University Press, 2003), 3–7.

13. Szepessy, "Narrative Model."

14. James, *Apocrypha Anecdota*, 52–54.

15. Davies, *Revolt of the Widows*, 8–10.

16. Junod, "Vie et conduit des saintes," 90–91; Bonnet, "Sur les actes de Xanthippe et Polyxène," 337.

he suggests a sixth-century date for *Xanth.*[17] Richard Pervo settles on a date between the fourth and sixth century. The author of *Xanth.* makes reference to the fact that Paul was baptizing in the name of the "life-giving Trinity," and Pervo states that the earliest known use of this term is credited to Gregory of Nyssa (died ca. 395). This suggests a *terminus a quo* of the late fourth century. In addition, Pervo proposes, the author's glorification of the military sortie by the slaves defending Polyxena reflects a departure from "that vigorous pacifism characteristic of ante-Nicene Christian thought." He sees this as further evidence that the text must post-date 325. In terms of how late to push the date, Pervo doubts that *Xanth.* was produced after the sixth century, when it would have been first translated into Latin.[18]

Pervo's range of dates seems the most judicious, although I would also eliminate the fourth century from consideration. It is indeed unlikely that the author of *Xanth.* is responsible for so theologically loaded an expression as the "life-giving Trinity," so we should date the text after the time of Gregory of Nyssa, as Pervo states. Yet, there is another indication that would place the text in the fifth century or later—namely, a possible reference to the works of Augustine. In one of her prayers, Xanthippe speaks of the God "who hates sins but gives mercy to sinners" (14:10). The notion that God hates sin but not sinners is not based on any specific biblical passage, and indeed several scriptural passages seem to suggest the opposite (e.g., Lev 20:22–23; Ps 5:5; 11:5; 15:4; Prov 6:16–19). The first known appearance of this idea is Augustine's *Ep.* 211.11 (423 CE), where he encourages a group of nuns to respond to the faults of others "with love for the people and hatred of the sins" *(cum dilectione hominum et odio vitiorum).*[19] This general concept appears implicitly throughout Augustine's anti-Pelagian works, where he attempts to explain how God is able to love humans, although they are all tainted by original sin. Xanthippe expresses the same idea here, and while direct dependence on Augustine cannot be proven, it is possible, particularly if the text is of Western provenance (see below). This would yield a date of the mid-fifth century or later for *Xanth.* The fifth and sixth centuries saw a proliferation of apocryphal texts, particularly related to the apostles Peter and Paul.[20] *Xanth.* seems very much at home in that context, although a seventh- or eighth-century date cannot be excluded.

Establishing the provenance of the text is no less challenging, but we can begin by narrowing down the possibilities. The two regions mentioned in the text—Spain and Greece—can be eliminated from consideration, because the author seems to know nothing about either one. Xanthippe's Spanish city is never identified, and there are no references to anything particular about Spanish geography or political institutions. E. N. Bennett has shown that the name Probus is attested multiple times in the area of Tarragona and provides an inscription for a local leader of this name, but he also grants that it could simply be a name easily used for any fictitious narrative.[21] If one were making up this

---

17. Szepessy, "Narrative Model," 318.

18. Pervo, "Dare and Back," 167. He suggests that a sixth-century text set in Spain could be explained by the reconquest of Spain by Justinian in 552. I am grateful to Dr. Pervo for making this essay available to me prior to its publication.

19. Latin text in Alfons Goldbacher, ed., *S. Aurelii Augustini Hipponiensis episcopi epistulae* (Vienna: Tempsky; Leipzig: Freytag, 1911), 365.

20. E.g., *Pass. Holy Pet. Paul, Acts Pet. Paul, Pass. Apost. Pet. Paul.* See Eastman, *Ancient Martyrdom Accounts.*

21. Bennett, "James' *Apocrypha Anecdota*," 103.

story, then Tarragona might be a likely place to set *Xanth.* It was a major port city and the first stop in Spain for ships coming from Rome via Marseille and Narbonne.[22] However, the author makes no effort to be specific about where in Spain the story occurs. This is in stark contrast to other acts, in which naming specific locations is meant to establish historical legitimacy and often justify the existence of cult sites. Greece is the primary setting for most of the Polyxena story, but here again we find only vague references. No city is named, and there is nothing particularly "Greek" about Greece in this story. The author seems unable even to name a specific port city, which we would not expect in a text produced in Greece.

Rome could be another possibility, and it has several factors in its favor. It was the location in which other apocryphal texts about Peter and Paul were produced, and the author of *Xanth.* is familiar with some of these, as the introduction below and the notes to the translation will demonstrate. In addition, while the text was written in Greek, there are several cases of direct transliterations into Greek from Latin.[23] This suggests a bilingual context, or at least a context in which both Greek and Latin were used. This was true of Rome during the likely period of production (fifth or sixth century). Greek was the language of the liturgy in Rome into the fourth century, and readings in Greek survive in certain Roman rites into the eighth century. A fifth- or sixth-century Roman author could not assume fluency in Greek for the entire audience, but Greek was still the language of choice for some apocryphal texts.[24] Finally, if the author is indeed citing Augustine in chapter 14 (or at least reflecting Augustinian thought), then the text was likely produced in a Latin-speaking region, because Augustine's writings were probably not available in Greek until the medieval period.[25] Given all these parameters, Rome could be a likely place of production.

On the other hand, there are indications that point away from Rome. The opening scene begins with a servant hearing Paul in the capital city; yet, the author displays nothing beyond general familiarity with the tradition that Paul had preached there. Similarly, the author is aware that Peter allegedly came to Rome to counter Simon Magus, but this story is well known through texts like the *Acts of Peter* and the *Pseudo-Clementines*. At no point do we find specialized local knowledge of Rome that would place the text there. Moreover, between Greece and Spain on the voyage home, war-mongering islanders attack Polyxena's ship, but the island is not identified. The route of a sea voyage from Greece to Spain would pass just below Italy, so we might expect a Roman author to provide details about which island was allegedly involved (Sicily? Sardinia?), even in a fictional narrative such as this. Overall, then, the author of *Xanth.* shows no specific knowledge of Greece nor any points west of that.

---

22. David L. Eastman, *Paul the Martyr: The Cult of the Apostle in the Latin West* (WGRWSup 4; Atlanta: Society of Biblical Literature; Leiden: Brill Academic Publishers, 2011), 127, fig. 3.3 and n. 19.

23. *Kouboukleiō* from *cubiculum* (11), *akoumbitou* from *accubitum* (13), *komēta* from *comes* (25), and probably the proper name *Lukios* from *Lucius* (38).

24. I have demonstrated elsewhere, for example, that the *Acts Pet. Paul* is a Greek text produced in Rome in the sixth century. An important factor in my argument is the author's use of transliterated Latin terms in the Greek text. See Eastman, *Paul the Martyr*, 62–66. On the survival of Greek in the Roman liturgy, see ibid., 72 n. 3; Louis Duchesne, *Christian Worship: Its Origin and Evolution. A Study of the Latin Liturgy up to the Time of Charlemagne* (trans. M. L. McClure; 3rd ed.; London: SPCK, 1903), 353–55.

25. See e.g. Michael Rackl, "Die griechischen Augustinus übersetzungen," in *Miscellanea in onore di Francesco Ehrle: Scritti di storia e paleografia* (5 vols. and 1 suppl.; ST 37–42; Rome: Vatican Library, 1924), 1:1–38; Eligius Dekkers, "Les traductions grecques des écrits patristiques latins," *SacEr* 5 (1953): 206–7; Berthold Altaner, "Augustinus in der griechischen Kirche bis auf Photius," *Historisches Jahrbuch* 71 (1952): 37–76.

Davies has suggested that a female monastic community in Asia Minor or Greece produced the text. I would eliminate Greece for the reasons stated just above, and Davies provides no compelling arguments in favor of Asia Minor. Junod proposes Constantinople, perhaps in a period when the apostle Andrew was taking on greater importance in that city. We cannot eliminate the eastern capital; yet, if a goal of the text is to highlight Andrew in a particular way, then the author has vastly undershot the mark. Andrew's role in this text is quite limited, and he does nothing to stand out above the other apostles mentioned. Junod also notes that the earliest external references to the text come from Constantinople (more below), but these are tenth-century references, so the Xanthippe tale certainly could have spread far from its origins by then. Pervo offers Constantinople or Asia Minor as reasonable speculations for the text's provenance.[26]

If we focus our attention on the eastern Mediterranean, then the reference to "Babylonia" may provide a further clue. The author states that Polyxena was put on a ship leaving from Spain for Babylonia, because the kidnapper had a brother there who was a *toparchēs*, or district governor. Babylon is, of course, on the Euphrates, not the Mediterranean, so finding a ship leaving Spain bound for Babylon would be most unusual. In the time of Paul, as at the time this story was written, there was no Babylonian Empire, and the city of Babylon was largely abandoned. We could read this as yet another example of the author's lack of familiarity with different regions—Babylonia here being "somewhere far to the east"—but Bennett has suggested that Babylonia should be read as a reference to Egypt. He argues that the term *toparchēs* enjoyed "special employment" in Edessa and Egypt. Like Babylon, Edessa is not directly on the sea; so Bennett concludes that the ship from Spain was bound for Egypt, where there were a port and a *toparchēs*. Strabo identifies a major garrison headquarters in Egypt as Babylon, and Bennett sees this as further evidence in his favor.[27] His argument is useful for our purposes, not in terms of where Polyxena's ship was trying to go in the story, but in terms of where *Xanth.* may have been produced. If Bennett is correct about the special use of *toparchēs*, then the author of this text likely was familiar with governmental structures and nomenclature in Egypt and/ or Syria. This may be an argument in favor of one of those regions as the provenance of *Xanth.* Bennett favors Egypt, but Everett Ferguson has argued that the baptism accounts in *Xanth.* "reflect Syrian baptismal practices,"[28] and this could point us back toward Syria.

Here we obviously venture into the realm of wide speculation across a sizable gap in the evidence. At the end of the day, the question of provenance remains very open. Each theory requires significant conjecture based on tenuous premises, and in each case there are drawbacks. We certainly seem to be on firmer ground saying where *Xanth.* was *not* produced (Spain or Greece) than saying where it was. Rome, Constantinople, Asia Minor, Egypt, and Syria all remain possibilities.

In terms of the original audience for the text, Davies suggests that *Xanth.* may have

---

26. Davies, *Revolt of the Widows*, 64–69; Junod, "Vie et conduit des saintes," 102–3; Pervo, "Dare and Back."

27. Strabo, *Geogr.* 17.30; Bennett, "James' *Apocrypha Anecdota*," 102. Medieval Spanish manuscripts also commonly refer to Cairo as Babylon. Bennett's argument becomes confused when he fails to distinguish between the ship's intended final destination (Babylonia/Egypt) and its actual destination in Greece. He makes much of the fact that Babylonia cannot refer to Greece, but the author of *Xanth.* never claims it does, for the unanticipated arrival in Greece results from demonic redirection of the ship.

28. Everett Ferguson, *Baptism in the Early Church: History, Theology, and Liturgy in the First Five Centuries* (Grand Rapids, Mich.: Eerdmans, 2009), 435–36.

been written for women, if not by a woman, attached to a monastic community, for the three main characters are presented as models of chastity and renunciation.[29] Pervo has questioned this view,[30] but Davies's proposal has considerable merit. In my view it is quite likely that the original audience was female monastic communities, for the text is deeply subversive in its attacks on any form of sexual attraction or desire, and the women in *Xanth.* lead the way in modeling the life of chastity. The marriage of Xanthippe and Probus is restored only when both, led by Xanthippe, embrace this new ethic of renunciation that replaces traditional social norms and expectations. The relationship between wife and husband (Xanthippe and Probus) on the surface may appear quite different from that between Polyxena and her kidnappers, but in the text they are presented as being much the same. Probus's carnal desires are no more righteous than those of the kidnappers, and only the gospel of renunciation can redeem these relationships. Eventually the relationships are redeemed, for Probus, Polyxena's original kidnapper, and the lecherous prefect are all baptized and end up at peace with the women they had formerly sought to conquer sexually.

Furthermore, while language typically associated with sexual desire in romance novels does appear, it is employed in a deeply ironic way that undermines its novelistic associations. Xanthippe longs for Paul, but not with sexual longing, for she expresses her desire by embracing severe asceticism. Even her joy at seeing him is focused not on Paul himself but on the air of graciousness and the odor of sanctity that surround holy people in general.[31] Polyxena may in some ways look like the heroine of a Greek novel; yet, her efforts are constantly focused not on being reunited with her lover, but on repelling or avoiding sexual desires and aggression toward her. Any sexual desire directed at Polyxena is thwarted; thus, attempts to caricature her as a sexual being of any sort miss the explicitly subversive, asexual nature of this character.[32] There is simply no positive view of sexual desire between any characters in this text; indeed, only after carnality is surrendered do the apostles administer baptism. Some early readers clearly understood that the encouragement of chastity was the goal of the text, because the longer ending to *Xanth.* in one of the Moscow manuscripts again praises the celibacy of each of the three women: "They shone brightly, one through her desire for Christ, asceticism, and chastity; the other through her constancy, faith, discipline, and virginity; the third through her exile, virginity, and hope in God."[33] The three heroes in *Xanth.* are all women defending their chastity, and for this reason Davies is likely correct in connecting this text to female monastic communities.

The author of *Xanth.* is unknown. Near the end of the text, the figure of Onesimus is introduced. He is traveling to Spain to see Paul and is told in a vision to look for two virgins and a young man, whom he should take with him to Spain. Onesimus speaks in the first person, suggesting that he is the author of at least the final sections of the text.

---

29. Davies, *Revolt of the Widows*, 64–69.

30. Pervo, "Dare and Back," 173. Pervo does note, however, that the names Polyxena and Rebecca are most likely taken from literary and scriptural models of sexual virtue and chastity.

31. Pervo, "Dare and Back": "Her pounding heart, her longing to touch even the hem of his clothes and to imbibe the aroma thereof are *not*, dear reader, to be confused with eroticism: the odor is that of sanctity, the hem of his robe heals, and her heart is strangely warmed by the advent of grace. These sentiments are not to be confused with eroticism."

32. Cf. Gorman, "Thinking"; Burrus, "Desiring Women." In "Dare and Back," particularly in the footnotes, Pervo notes many of the problems with Gorman's assumptions and arguments.

33. Junod, "Vie et conduite des saintes," 90.

In Paul's letter to Philemon, Onesimus is a runaway slave who is being sent back to his master with Paul's appeal for clemency. He is also mentioned in the closing greetings of Colossians (4:9). The author of *Xanth.* does not state explicitly that this is meant to be the same Onesimus, but it is a reasonable connection to make if we imagine the author trying to bolster this story about Paul with references to other known Pauline associates.[34] In any event, the biblical Onesimus obviously can be eliminated from consideration as the author, and there are no other indications of authorship.

Literary Context and Influence

The text of *Xanth.* contains a number of biblical allusions but few direct citations. In the opening sections of the Polyxena story, two specific passages are quoted. Both come from the Psalms and are presented as prophetic warnings about the trials that Polyxena is about to endure. Otherwise the author makes a number of references to biblical stories from both the Hebrew Bible and the New Testament. For example, we see hints of the meeting between Eliezer and Rebecca (Gen 24:15–32), the interpretations of dreams by Joseph (Gen 41:1–36) and Daniel (Dan 2:1–45), and the interactions of Jesus in the Gospels. The lament literature of the Hebrew Bible may provide inspiration for several of Xanthippe's prayers, and Paul's intended trip to Spain lies behind the narrative as a whole. The author is particularly indebted to the Lucan tradition, which we might expect given the traditional connection between Paul and Luke. Multiple narrative elements from both Luke's gospel and Acts are discernible, and in the tradition of Acts, the apostles in *Xanth.* are often guided to specific actions by heavenly visions or voices. The evangelist may even appear in *Xanth.*, if the Lucius of 38:4 is understood to be Luke himself.[35] The bipartite structure of *Xanth.* might be seen also as reminiscent of Luke's division of Acts into two sections on Peter and Paul.

As discussed above, the author also pulls themes and narrative elements from other apocryphal acts of the apostles and Greek romance novels. Pervo suggests that *Xanth.* is particularly dependent upon a collection of the "five major Acts" of the second and third century (Peter, Paul, Thomas, John, and Andrew).[36] *Acts John* is the only one of these texts not explicitly represented in *Xanth.*, while *Acts Paul* is by far the most often cited, particularly the section about Thecla. The influence of the story of Thecla on the author's construction of Xanthippe and Polyxena is undeniable, for Thecla represents the original model of a woman who hears Paul preach, shuns marriage, flees aggressive male assailants, is denied baptism by Paul, travels extensively, dresses like a man in a futile effort to protect herself, and survives an ordeal in the arena. Xanthippe and Polyxena are clear heirs to the legacy of Thecla.[37] With respect to the dependence on novels, emotionalism and a narrative of departure and return are typical elements of such stories, and the notes to the translation indicate apparent cases of reliance on specific novels. The author of *Xanth.* clearly feels free to draw on multiple sources in piecing together this entertaining and sometimes enigmatic text.

---

34. Pervo ("Dare and Back," 187) calls the connection "doubtless."

35. This connection is supported by Junod, "Vie et conduite des saintes," 100; Pervo, "Dare and Back," 187.

36. Pervo ("Dare and Back," 176) notes that this collection of the "big five" first appears in the fourth-century writings of Philaster of Brescia.

37. Cf. Léon Vouaux, *Les actes de Paul et ses lettres apocryphes* (Paris: Letouzey et Ané, 1913), who overstates the case by claiming that *Xanth.* is "nothing but the reproduction of our *Acts of Thecla*" (131).

Strangely, there is no evidence of a later cult for any of these women, not even in Spain. Therefore, Pervo describes Xanthippe and Polyxena as "literary saints" only, as they were never considered historical or honored with churches or shrines.[38] By the tenth century and the *Menologium* of Basil II, these women were associated with the date September 23 (their current feast day), although the Basilian account contains some variants from our text.[39] Parts of the *Xanth.* story are also retold in another tenth-century source: the *Menologium* of Simeon Metaphrastes. In his discussion of June 29, the joint festival day of Peter and Paul, Simeon summarizes the conversion of Xanthippe and Probus but completely leaves out Polyxena and Rebecca.[40] The Byzantine historian Michael Glycas then further epitomizes Simeon's version in his twelfth-century *Annales*. Reception in Spain is not confirmed until the late-sixteenth- or early-seventeenth-century *Adversaria* of Julianus Petri and *Chronicle* of Pseudo-Flavius Lucius Dexter.[41] Petri is the first to identify Patras as the place that Onesimus had met Polyxena (Rebecca is not mentioned), while Pseudo-Dexter provides some puzzling examples of reception of the *Xanth.* story. He suggests that the characters lived in Laminium and that Saint Eugenius in Toledo was visited many times by "Xantippe (sic) and *eius uxor* (his *or* her wife) Polyxena, a most holy virgin, and her companion Rebecca, also a virgin, and Saint Onesimus, the disciple of saint Paul."[42] Burrus proposes reading Pseudo-Dexter's comments through the lens of same-sex relations, stating that Pseudo-Dexter "seems to sum up very nicely the female love triangle that drives and animates" this text.[43] Pervo calls this peculiar entry by Pseudo-Dexter "an error that belongs in the hall of fame of Freudian slips."[44] The most likely explanation for this passage is quite simple, however. Pseudo-Dexter is working from a very corrupt version of *Xanth.*, if he even has a copy of the text at all; he simply may be repeating confused local traditions that attempt to link the figures from *Xanth.* with the more famous Eugenius. Note that Pseudo-Dexter does not seem to know about Probus, who is featured prominently in the first half of the text; so he concludes that Xanthippe is the husband. Pseudo-Dexter's general confusion about the story is confirmed soon after, when he pairs Polyxena with a woman named Sarah, although he had just correctly linked her with Rebecca. These errors are not easily explained if the author had access to even a mediocre edition of the text; so we might conjecture that he did not and should resist formulating any arguments about *Xanth.* based on this much later and problematic *Chronicle* account.

Translation

The following translation is based on M. R. James's edition of Paris, Bibliothèque nationale de France, gr. 1458. I have updated the text with corrections published subsequently by Maximilien Bonnet and James. Chapter divisions are those introduced by James, but here the text has been divided further into verses.

---

38. Pervo, "Dare and Back," 199.

39. James, *Apocrypha Anecdota*, 43–47, includes the relevant excerpts from all the later references discussed here. He notes that the Basilian summary is accompanied by a painting of Xanthippe and Polyxena standing in front of a building.

40. Pervo ("Dare and Back," 200) suggests that Xanthippe and Probus are included because they represent "a typical missionary triumph by Paul."

41. Flavius Lucius Dexter was a fourth-century historian and friend of Jerome whose name was attached to this medieval forgery.

42. Excerpt provided in James, *Apocrypha Anecdota*, 43–47 (see n. 39 above).

43. Burrus, "Desiring Women."

44. Pervo, "Dare and Back," 201.

Bibliography

EDITIONS AND TRANSLATIONS

Bonnet, Maximilien. "Sur les actes de Xanthippe et Polyxène." *Classical Review* 8, no. 8 (1894): 336–41. (Corrections to James's edition.)

Craigie, William A., trans. "The Acts of Xanthippe and Polyxena." Pages 205–17 in vol. 9 of *The Ante-Nicene Fathers*. Edited by Philip Schaff. 14 vols. 3rd ed. New York: Scribner's Sons, 1899.

James, Montague Rhodes. *Apocrypha Anecdota: A Collection of Thirteen Apocryphal Books and Fragments*. TS 2. Cambridge: Cambridge University Press, 1893. (Edition based on Paris gr. 1458, pp. 58–85.)

———. *Apocrypha Anecdota 2*. TS 5.1. Cambridge: Cambridge University Press, 1897. (Corrections to James's earlier edition, pp. 139–40.)

Vesselovskij, Alexander N. "The Christian Transformation of the Greek Romance: The Life of Xanthippe, Polyxena, and Rebecca" (in Russian). *Anthology of the Department of Russian Music and Literatures of the Imperial Academy of Sciences* 40, no. 2 (1886): 29–64. (Excerpts from Moscow gr. 161 and summaries of other *Xanth.* manuscripts.)

STUDIES

Bennett, E. N. "James' *Apocrypha Anecdota*." *Classical Review* 8, no. 3 (1894): 101–3.

Burrus, Virginia. "Desiring Women: Xanthippe, Polyxena, Rebecca." Unpublished manuscript.

Davies, Stevan L. *The Revolt of the Widows: The Social World of the Apocryphal Acts*. Carbondale, Ill.: Southern Illinois University Press, 1980.

Gorman, Jill. "Reading and Theorizing Women's Sexualities: The Representation of Women in the Acts of Xanthippe and Polyxena." (PhD diss., Temple University, 2003). From chapters in this dissertation Gorman published two articles: "Thinking with and about 'Same-Sex Desire': Producing and Policing Female Sexuality in the Acts of Xanthippe and Polyxena." *Journal of the History of Sexuality* 10, no. 3–4 (2001): 416–41; "Sexual Defense by Proxy: Interpreting Women's Fasting in the *Acts of Xanthippe and Polyxena*." Pages 206–15 in *A Feminist Companion to the New Testament Apocrypha*. Edited by Amy-Jill Levine. London: T.&T. Clark, 2006.

Junod, Eric. "Vie et conduit des saintes femmes Xanthippe, Polyxène et Rébecca." Pages 83–106 in *Oecumenica et patristica: Festschrift für Wilhelm Schneemelcher zum 75. Geburtstag*. Edited by Damaskinos Papandreou, Wolfgang A. Bienert, and Knut Schäferdiek. Stuttgart: Kohlhammer, 1989.

Pervo, Richard I. "Dare and Back: The Stories of Xanthippe and Polyxena." Pages 161–204 in *Early Christian and Jewish Narrative: The Role of Religion in Shaping Narrative Forms*. Edited by Ilaria Ramelli and Judith Perkins. Tübingen: Mohr Siebeck, 2015.

Szepessy, Tibor. "The Narrative Model of the Acta Xanthippae et Polyxenae." *Acta Antiqua Academiae Scientiarum Hungaricae* 44 (2004): 317–40.

The Life and Conduct of the Holy Women
Xanthippe, Polyxena, and Rebecca

The fame of Paul comes to Spain

1 ¹When the blessed Paul was in Rome for the sake of the word of the Lord, it happened that a certain servant of a royal man of Spain arrived in Rome with letters from his lord and heard the word of the Lord from Paul, the golden and beautiful nightingale. ²After that servant had been greatly moved—but was unable to remain and be filled by the divine word, because he was hurried along by the letters—with great grief he returned to Spain. ³He was not able to reveal his desire to anyone, because his master was an idolater, so he was always afflicted in spirit and groaned deeply. But this servant was honored and faithful to his master.

⁴After some time passed the servant fell ill and grew thin in his flesh. His master took notice and said to him, "What has happened to you that you have fallen thus in your countenance?" The servant said, "A great pain exists in my heart, and I am not at all able to find rest." ⁵His master said to him, "And what is the pain that is not able to obtain healing from my chief physician?" The servant said, "When I was still in Rome, this pain and its repeated distress came into my mind."

⁶His master said, "And do you not know any who have fallen into this disease and have received healing?" The servant said, "Yes, but I do not know where that physician is, for I left him in Rome. Those who have been treated by that physician and have gone through the water under him have received healing immediately."[a] ⁷But his master said, "I would not hesitate even to send you to Rome again, if somehow you might experience healing."

Xanthippe pines for the arrival of Paul

2 ¹As they were saying such things, behold his mistress by the name of Xanthippe overheard these words. After learning the teaching about Paul, she said, "What is the name of that teacher, or what is his treatment for warding off such a disease?" ²The servant said to her, "Calling upon a new name, and anointing with oil, and the washing of water.[b] By this treatment I have seen many with incurable pains receive healing." ³As he was saying these things, the images of idols that were standing in the house began to be shaken and fall down. ⁴His mistress

Acts Paul 5; Acts John 37–47; Acts Titus 9:3; Acts Corn. 2:11–12

---

a. In *Acts Pet.* 1, the Lord instructs Paul in a vision to leave Rome and go be a physician in Spain.

b. Anointing with oil prior to baptism follows the pattern of the Syriac version of *Acts Thom.* (26–27, 121, 132, and 157), which is likely the original. Everett Ferguson has agreed that the author of *Xanth.* "seems to reflect Syrian baptismal practice" and that elements of the text "could come directly from the *Acts of Thomas*" (*Baptism in the Early Church*, 435–36).

called to him, saying, "Do you see, brother, the images of the idols being shaken, and how they do not bear the power of the word?"

⁵But his master, named Probus, got up from a midday sleep very sad, for the devil troubled him violently, because the knowledge of God had come into his house. He asked the servant everything point by point. ⁶The servant, who by the providence of God had been overcome by sickness, gave up his human life, while Xanthippe had a soul that was quite incurable concerning this teaching. ⁷Probus was likewise distressed concerning Xanthippe, because from that time on she was causing herself to waste away with sleeplessness, self-discipline,ᵃ and other harsh training.

3 ¹Xanthippe went away to her bed and groaned, saying, "Woe is me, a pitiful one remaining in darkness, because I have not learned the name of the new teacher, so that I might beg for his prayer. I do not know what to say. ²Will I call upon him in the name of his God? But I do not know enough to say, 'O God that is preached by such a one as this.'ᵇ ³Nevertheless, I will say this by conjecture: O God who has enlightened those in Hades and has guided those in darkness, who is the lord of the free and of kings, who has been preached by worthy servants in the entire world,ᶜ who has been called upon by sinful men as a brother and quickly hears, to whom not even archangels are able to send up worthy hymns, who has shown even to me in my unworthiness and lowliness the seed that lives and abides forever—although my ignorance does not allow me to receive it: ⁴Turn quickly even to the things that concern me, O Master, because by your will you have made yourself hear me. In your compassion reveal to me the enlightenment of your herald, so that I may learn from him the things that are most pleasing to you. Truly I need you to look upon my ignorance, O God, and enlighten me by the light of your face, you who never neglect those who call upon you in truth."

⁵Her husband Probus said to her, "Why do you trouble yourself so much, lady, and do not turn your attention entirely toward resting?" Xanthippe said, "I am not able to rest, because an incurable pain has come upon me." ⁶Probus said to her, "What is your pain or condition, O lady, that I am insufficient to bring you relief? For whatever sorts of things you wanted up to today I have provided for you. Now what pain is it that you have and do not tell me?" ⁷Xanthippe said to him, "I beg only this one thing, my lord: Allow me for a little bit and today only to sleep apart from you." And Probus said to her, "Let it be, lady, as you wish. Only stop your groaning."

4 ¹Then she went alone into her bedchamber and said these things with tears, "In what ways I may inquire of you, my God, or what sort of insight I may receive, I do not know. ²Will I make known the thought that has come upon me?

1 Pet 3:18–20

Ps 4:6

---

a. This reference to "self-discipline" includes sexual abstinence, as the narrative soon makes clear. On sexual renunciation among women, see e.g. Elizabeth A. Clark, *Reading Renunciation: Asceticism and Scripture in Early Christianity* (Princeton: Princeton University Press, 1999), 24–27.

b. Xanthippe is not able to appeal to the God being preached, because she does not know even the name of the preacher.

c. Xanthippe knows nothing yet about Paul or Christianity, yet somehow she seems to know about the apostolic tradition.

But I fear the madness and instability of the city. ³Should I flee from this impious city? But I fear the plot of the devil through the seizing of the sheep. ⁴Should I wait for the compassion and swiftness of the Lord? But again I fear the untimely snatching away of life, for the death of sinners comes without warning. ⁵Should I leave and flee to Rome? But I fear the length of the journey, because I am unable to go on foot. ⁶When I say these things by guessing, compelled by my yearning—for I do not know how to speak with certainty—may I receive lenience from you, my God. ⁷Fill my longing with an overabundance of right words. Only hear me and deem me worthy of your herald. For if I say that I want to see his face, I am seeking after great things. ⁸Blessed is the one who is found in the choir of your heralds and is satisfied by their honored faces. ⁹Blessed are those who are yoked under the preaching of your commandments. Blessed are those who keep your commandments. ¹⁰Where now, O Lord, are your mercies that were given to our fathers, so that we may be their successors in love toward you and the descendants of faith?ᵃ ¹¹Look now, O Master. I do not find anyone who has affection toward you, so that I might spend even a little time with him and find rest for my soul. ¹²Hurry therefore, O Lord, to yoke me in my desire for you, and guard me under the shelter of your wings, for you alone are God, magnified forever, amen."

John 10:11–13

Acts Paul 3:5–6

Ruth 2:12; Ps 17:8; 36:7; 57:1; 61:4; 63:7; 91:4

Probus shows concern for Xanthippe

5 ¹Therefore, saying these things and other things like them, Xanthippe groaned continually through the whole night. Probus heard her and was greatly disheartened. ²Rising from his bed at daybreak, he went in to her and beheld her eyes that were swollen from tears, and he said, "Why, lady, do you disturb me thus but do not explain to me your pain? Tell me, so that I may do for you whatever is best, and do not burden me with your distress."

³Xanthippe said to him, "Rather be encouraged, my lord, and do not be disturbed, because my trouble will by no means harm you. But if I have found favor before you, then go forth now to the greeting and allow me to satisfy myself as I wish, for it is not possible for a man to remove this insatiable pain."

⁴After listening to her he went out immediately to receive the greetings of those in the city, for he was a great one among them and was known to the emperor Nero. After he sat down, great pain was showing on his face. ⁵When he was asked the reason for this pain by the chief men of the city, he said to them that he had fallen into many unavoidable misfortunes.

6 ¹Xanthippe went into the garden, so that after looking intently she might be raised up to certainty about her husband.ᵇ She saw the delight of the trees and the different twittering of birds, and after groaning she said,

²"O beauty of the world, for up to now we thought that it had come about
　　on its own, but we now know that all things were created beautifully
　　by the beautiful one.

---

a. Xanthippe speaks of "our fathers," as if she were part of the Jewish diaspora.

b. The text is unclear here, but Xanthippe apparently goes outside to observe her husband in the street and gauge his attitude toward her.

Gen 11:1–9

[3]O power and invention of Wisdom,[a] because not only did it put into men countless languages, but it also distinguished in birds many sounds, as if from their calls and responses it receives sweet-voiced and heart-pricking hymns from its own works.

[4]O pleasantness of the air, which points to the incomparable creator. Who will change my sorrow into gladness?"

[5]And again she said, "O God who is celebrated in song by all, give me rest and encouragement."

[6]After she said these things, Probus returned from the street for breakfast. As he saw her face altered by tears, he began to tear out the hair from his head, but he did not dare to say anything to her for a while, so that he would not add to her affliction more distress. [7]He went and fell on his couch, and groaning he said, "Woe is me, because I have not even had the consolation of a child from her, but I receive only grief upon grief. Less than two full years have passed since I was married to her, and already she is thinking about divorce."

Paul arrives in Spain

Rom 15:23–28

7 [1]Xanthippe was constantly looking out through the doors into the streets of the city. But blessed Paul, the herald and teacher and illuminator of the world, left Rome and came also to Spain through the providence of God. [2]Having approached the gates of the city, he stood and prayed. After sealing[b] himself he went into the city. [3]As Xanthippe saw the blessed Paul walking nobly and evenly and adorned with all virtue and sagacity, she was greatly delighted in him, and her heart leapt continually.

Acts Paul 3:3

[4]As if overcome by an unexpected joy, she said within herself, "Why does my heart leap so violently at the sight of that man? Why is his walk noble and even, like one who expects to take in his arms the one who is pursued? [5]Why is his face gracious, like one who cares for the sick? Why does he look around so beautifully here and there, like one who wishes to help those wanting to flee from the mouth of serpents? [6]Who will tell me if this one happens to be from the flock of heralds? If it were possible for me, I would want to touch the hem of his garments, so that I might perceive his pleasantness and acceptance and sweet smell"—for the servant had said to her that the hems of (the heralds') garments had the sweet smell of expensive perfumes.[c]

Mark 5:28; 6:56

Probus invites Paul into his home

8 [1]Probus heard her words and immediately leapt out into the street. He grabbed Paul by the hand and said to him, "Man, I do not know who you are, but deem it worthy to come into my house, and perhaps you may be for me the cause of salvation." [2]Paul said to him, "It will go well for you, child, at your request." They

---

a. On Wisdom's role in creation, see Prov 8:22–31.

b. This may be a reference to making the sign of the cross.

c. In late antique Christianity sweet smells were often associated with holy people, alive or dead. See e.g., Susan Ashbrook Harvey, *Scenting Salvation: Ancient Christianity and the Olfactory Imagination* (Berkeley: University of California Press, 2006), esp. 156–221; Eastman, "Matriarch as Model," 248–49.

went in together to Xanthippe. ³When Xanthippe saw the great Paul, the noetic eyes of her heart were opened, and she read these things on his forehead, as if it had golden seals on it: "Paul, the herald of God."

⁴Leaping and rejoicing, she threw herself at his feet. Twisting her hands together she cleaned the bottoms of his feet and said, "It is good that you have come, O man of God, to us lowly ones, who dwell with phantoms as phantoms. ⁵For you have numbered those who are running to Hades as something beautiful, those who address the crooked serpent and corrupter as provider and guardian, those who are running into dark Hades as if to their father, those who were formed with a rational nature but have become like irrational creatures. ⁶You have sought out lowly me, who have the sun of righteousness in my heart. Now the poison is stopped, because I see your honorable face. ⁷Now the one troubling me has been terrified, because your most excellent counsel has appeared to me. Now I will be considered worthy of repentance, because I also have received the seal of the herald of God. ⁸Up to now I have called blessed the many who have met with you, but now I dare to say that from this time on I will also be called blessed by others, because I have touched your hems, because I have profited from your prayers, because I have come into the enjoyment of your teaching that is pleasant and dripping with honey. ⁹You did not fail to come to us, you who, in your course, fish on dry land and gather together the fish that fall into the net of the heavenly kingdom."

Luke 7:38; John 11:2; 12:3

Mal 4:2

Luke 1:47–48

Mark 1:17

Xanthippe praises Paul for enduring trials

9 ¹The great Paul said to her, "Get up, child, and do not look at me, as if by my foreknowledge you have been sought out of your ignorance. ²For the supervisor of the world, Christ—the one who seeks out sinners and the lost, the one who not only has remembered those on the earth but has also ransomed those in Hades by his appearance—he had pity on you and sent me here, so that he may visit and show mercy to many others along with you. ³For this mercy and visitation are not from us, but are his command and order, even as we were shown mercy and saved by him."

Luke 19:10

1 Pet 3:18–20

⁴Probus heard and was astounded at their words, for he knew nothing at all about these things. By force Paul made Xanthippe get up from his feet, but she ran and set up a new golden chair so that Paul would sit upon it. ⁵The great Paul said to her, "My child Xanthippe, do not do this, for you have not yet agreed to faith in Christ. But wait a little while, until the Lord may set in order the things that are fitting."

⁶Xanthippe said to Paul, "Do you say these things to me as a test, O herald of God, or do you possess some foreknowledge?" ⁷Paul said, "No, child, but the one who hates the servants of God, the devil, puts wickedness in the mind of his servants as opposition to those working for the Lord by preaching, for his malice was in action against the apostles and even against the Lord himself. Therefore, it is necessary to bring the message to unbelievers nobly and graciously."

⁸Xanthippe said to Paul, "I beg you, if you feel affection for your servants, offer prayer on behalf of Probus, and let me see if the one who is hated by you will be able to be active in him. Let me see if he will even be able to stand against your prayer." ⁹Paul rejoiced greatly at the words of her faith and said to her, "Believe

2 Cor 11:23–25

me, child, that by his instigation and effort I have spent not a single hour without chains and blows." [10]Xanthippe said to him, "But you suffer these things by your own will, because you have not neglected your preaching even to the point of whippings. I say again that your chains are the undoing of the one who put them on you, and your humiliation is their destruction."

Many visit Paul at the house of Probus

10 [1]The word of his arrival spread quickly through the whole city and the countryside around it, for some people from that city had been in Rome and saw the wonders and signs done by the blessed Paul. [2]They came to see if that man was indeed he. Therefore, many people came into the house of Probus, and he began to be irritated and say, "I will not allow my house to become an inn." [3]But Xanthippe, knowing that the countenance of Probus had begun to change and that he had said such things, was utterly distressed and said, "Woe is me, the wretched one, because we were not considered altogether worthy to keep this man in our house. For when Paul has left here, the church also will be elsewhere."

[4]Then Xanthippe, thinking about these things, placed her hand on the foot of Paul. She took dust, and after calling Probus to her, she placed her hand on his breast and said, "O Lord my God, place in this heart the things that are fitting, O you who have sought out even me, though I was lowly and ignorant of you." [5]Paul heard her prayer and made the seal. For many days the people entered unhindered, and anyone who had those sick and troubled by unclean spirits brought them, and all of them were healed.

Paul moves to the house of Philotheus

11 [1]Xanthippe was saying to Paul, "Teacher, my heart burns intensely, because I have not yet been baptized."[a] After these things Probus was again provoked by the devil. He threw Paul out of the house and shut up Xanthippe in her bedchamber. [2]Then a certain one of the leading men of the city, named Philotheus,[b] earnestly asked the great Paul to come into his house. But the great Paul did not wish to do this, saying, "Do not let Probus trouble your house because of me."

[3]Philotheus said to him, "Not at all, father. In no way do I fall under him, for he is not above me in any way other than rank, and that is because the parents of Xanthippe are above me. If Probus comes to me, I happen to be above him in wealth and in military might." [4]Then Paul, the great apostle of the Lord, was persuaded and went into the house of Philotheus, who was one of the eparchs.[c] All this was done by the evil one, so that Xanthippe would receive holy baptism with affliction and would be indifferent concerning the commands of Christ.

Xanthippe refuses to sleep with Probus

12 [1]Then, with tears Xanthippe said to her servants, "Have you learned where Paul has gone?" [2]They said, "Yes, into the house of Philotheus, who is one of the

---

a. Thecla is also denied baptism by Paul in *Acts Paul* 3:25.

b. Philotheus means "lover of God" and is the transposition of the name Theophilus, the purported recipient of Luke's gospel and the Acts of the Apostles. Pervo also notes this connection in "Dare and Back," 181 n. 63.

c. An eparch was a high-ranking government administrator.

eparchs." ³Xanthippe rejoiced greatly that Philotheus believed, for he was able, she said, to persuade Probus also. Then Probus called Xanthippe to dinner. But when she did not come, Probus said, "Do not think that you will withdraw from me when it comes to sex."

⁴When he had reclined for dinner, Xanthippe fell to her knees and prayed to the Lord, saying,

> "Eternal and immortal God, who took dust from the ground and did not   Gen 2:7
>> value it according to the essence of its creation, but called it the son
>> of immortality;
> who came for our sake from the heart of the Father even to the heart of the
>> earth;   Phil 2:5–8
> at whom the cherubim do not dare to gaze;
> who for our sake was hidden in a womb, so that you might redeem the suf-
>> fering of Eve through dwelling in a womb.
> ⁵O you who drank gall and vinegar and were pierced in the rib with   Mark 15:36; John 19:29–30
>> a spear, so that you might heal for Adam the wound that came
>> from his rib. For being his rib, Eve caused a wound for Adam, and   John 19:34
>> through him for the whole world.   Gen 2:21–22
> ⁶O you who gave unperceived sleep to the serpent, so that he would not be
>> aware of your incarnation, remember also my groaning and tears,   Ignatius, *Eph* 19.1
>> and give fulfillment to my longing.
> ⁷Bring sleep upon Probus until I am considered worthy of the gift of holy
>> baptism, because I intensely desire to obtain this for the glory and
>> praise of your holy name."

Xanthippe seeks out Paul

13 ¹Probus was still dining and ordered the doors of their house to be secured by cruel and wicked soldiers. After he had ordered these things, immediately he fell asleep on his couch. ²Then the servants came to announce this to Xanthippe, so that he might be woken up, but she said, "Put out the lamps, my children, and leave him as he is." ³At the first watch of the night, she took three hundred gold coins and went to the doors, saying to herself, "Perhaps the gatekeeper will be persuaded by the quantity of money." But, being evil and having lost all sense, he was not persuaded to do this. ⁴But she took off her belt, which was set with precious stones equaling two hundred gold coins. She gave it to him and went out, saying, "Lord, I persuade my servants with money, so that your herald Paul may not be troubled by Probus."   *Acts Paul* 3:18

⁵Xanthippe went to the house of Philotheus, who was among the command-ers, as if she were doing a great and wonderful deed, running and praising God. When she went through a certain place, the demons ran after her with fiery torches and flashes of lightning. ⁶She turned around and saw that awful sight behind her, and overwhelmed with great fear she said, "What has become of you, wretched soul? You have been robbed of your desire. You were hurrying to salvation, hurrying to baptism, but you fell upon the serpent, his servants, and the things that your sins have prepared for you."

⁷After saying these things, she was giving up her soul out of great hopeless-

ness. But the great Paul had been forewarned by the Lord about this attack of the demons. Immediately he stood close to her, and a beautiful young man was standing in front of him.[a] [8]Just after the vision of the demons had disappeared, Paul said to her, "Get up, my child Xanthippe, and see the Lord who is desired by you. By his flame both the heavens are shaken and the great deep is dried up, but he is coming to you and pitying and saving you. [9]Look at the one who receives into his arms your prayers and immediately answers. Look at him coming in the shape of a man, and receive your freedom against the demons."

Job 9:6; Ps 18:7; Isa 13:13; 50:2; Hag 2:6; Nah 1:4

[10]She got up from the ground and said to him, "Teacher, why did you leave me alone? Hurry now to give me the seal, so that if death comes upon me, I may go encouraged to that one who is compassionate and humble."

Paul baptizes Xanthippe, who praises God

14 [1]Immediately the great Paul took her hand, and they went into the house of Philotheus. He baptized her in the name of the Father, and the Son, and the Holy Spirit. Then taking bread, he gave her the Eucharist, saying, "Let this be for you for the forgiveness of sins and the renewal of your soul."

[2]Then blessed Xanthippe received the divine grace of holy baptism and went back to her house rejoicing and praising God. But the gatekeeper saw her and complained bitterly in strong words, so that her departure would be thought to have been against his will, if Probus should come to know of it. [3]But the one who had enlightened her along with Paul kept the whole house in a deep sleep along with Probus, and they did not hear his words at all. [4]She ran and came into her bedchamber, saying, "What should I say about you, you who search out sinners, you who are fully present with us in our troubles? [5]Your goodness does these things, because for the sake of man, which you created, you lowered yourself even to death. For however many times man provokes you to anger, you repeatedly pour out your mercies upon him, O Master.

Ps 46:1

Phil 2:6–8

> [6]"O depth of pity and richness of mercy!
> O unmeasured goodness and immense benevolence!
> O treasure of good things, giver of mercy, and enricher of those who
>   believe in you!
> [7]If the one who loves you should say, 'Lord, be near me,' then you yourself
>   are already present with him beforehand.
> If he should say, 'I thank you, hear my words,' then even before these
>   things are said you yourself are paying attention.
> [8]Concerning those who are asking you, you give to each one according to
>   his request.
> Your goodness searches for those who do not know you, and you hurry to
>   sinners.
> [9]O cheerful glance that fills up the paths of sinners with mercy!
> O noble oversight and encouragement of the ignorant!
> [10]Who will report to my lord Paul the salvation that has now come to me,

Ps 139:4

---

a. Jesus also appears as a young man below in chapters 15 and 22:5–6. Cf. *Acts Thom.* 27, 154–55; *Acts John* 88–89; *Acts Andr. Mth.* 33; *Rev. Magi* 31:1–2; *Ap. John* 2.1–9.

so that he may come and give the words of thanksgiving[a] on my
behalf to that guardian of sinners?
Many of you, come, see, and know God, who hates sins but gives mercy to
sinners.[b]

[11]"Finally, come here, Paul, O herald of God, for with you I now am sitting
under instruction. Give the words of thanksgiving on my behalf, for I want to
be silent, because human reason makes me afraid, lest perhaps I do not have the
grace of eloquence. [12]I want to be silent but am forced to speak, for someone
kindles me within and gives me a sensation of sweetness. If I say, 'I will close my
mouth,' there is someone making music within me. [13]Should I say great things?
Or perhaps that is the teacher in Paul, the one who is humble, who fills the
heavens, who is speaking inside and waiting outside, who is seated on the throne
with his Father and stretched out upon the tree[c] by men. I do not know what I
will do. My paltry mind delights me and is not expanded to its limits. [14]O you
whose hands were fixed with nails and who was pierced in the side with a spear,
you who are the star out of Jacob, the lion from Judah, the rod from Jesse, man
and God from Mary,[d] the indivisible God in the bosom of the Father, the one
who cannot be looked upon by the cherubim,[e] who is insulted by Israel—glory
to you who appeared upon the earth, was seized by the people, was hung upon
the cross, was destroyed falsely by the word of lawless men, and has purchased
all of us together."

Phil 2:5–8

Rev 3:20

*Luke 22:69; Eph 1:20;
Col 3:11; Heb 1:3; 8:11;
10:12; 12:2*

*Num 24:17; Rev 5:5;
Isa 11:1; John 1:18*

Xanthippe has a vision of Christ

15 [1]When she was still saying these things, a cross appeared on the eastern wall.
Immediately a beautiful young man[f] entered through it. He had all around him
trembling rays, and from below him a light was spreading forth, and he was
walking on it. [2]When he had come inside, all the foundations of that house
shook and resounded with a great trembling. [3]Seeing him, Xanthippe cried out
and fell on the ground as if she were dead. But, being merciful and kind, he
changed immediately into the form of Paul[g] and raised her up, saying, "Get up,
Xanthippe, and do not fear, for the servants of God are glorified in this way."

[4]Standing up, Xanthippe gazed intently at him. Thinking that he was Paul,
she said, "How did you come here, O herald of God, when five hundred gold
pieces were given by me to the gatekeeper, who is also my servant, while you do
not possess any gold?" [5]But the Lord said to her, "My servant Paul is richer than
all wealth, for whatever treasure he acquires here, he sends it forth into the king-

---

a. Or "the words of the Eucharist," a phrase repeated a few lines later. Xanthippe's words here
are perplexing, given that Paul had just baptized her and served her the Eucharist.

b. For discussion of the possible relationship of this passage to the writings of Augustine,
particularly *Ep.* 211.11, see the introduction p. 422.

c. That is, the cross.

d. This is probably taken from the Niceno-Constantinopolitan Creed of 381, but it may also
reflect the fifth-century controversy surrounding Mary as the Theotokos.

e. This may be a reference to the cherubim in Isa 6:2 that cover their faces with their wings.

f. Here again Christ appears in the form of a youth.

g. In *Acts Paul* 3:21 Jesus appears to Thecla in the guise of Paul. Cf. *Acts Thom.* 11, where
Jesus appears in the likeness of Thomas.

Matt 6:19–20

dom of heaven, so that when he goes there he may enjoy a ceaseless and eternal rest. This is the treasure of Paul: you and those who are like you."

Matt 17:2; Rev 1:16

[6]And Xanthippe gazed intently at him, wanting to say something, and saw his face shining like the light. She was greatly astonished and put both hands over her face.[a] [7]She threw herself to the ground and said, "Hide, master, from my bodily eyes, and enlighten my understanding, for at last I know who you are. [8]You are that one who was preceded by the cross, who alone on high was the only-begotten Son from the only Father, and who alone below was the only-begotten son from the only virgin. You are that one who was nailed in the hands

Matt 27:51

and split the rocks. You are the one whom no one else is able to carry, except the bosom of the Father."

16 [1]As she was saying these things, the Lord was again hidden from her. Coming to herself, Xanthippe said, "Woe is me, altogether wretched one, because no one told me what is the response of servants to their master. [2]If Paul, the herald of God, were here, how would he sing? But perhaps in response to such graces and gifts even they would be silent, just being in tears, for it is not possible to sing praise to anyone in a worthy manner according to his grace." [3]Saying these things she was overcome by great faintness from lack of food, for being greatly focused on her desire for Christ, she had forgotten about food. Then being greatly worn out by self-denial, by the vision, by lack of sleep, and by other acts of asceticism, she was not able to get up from the ground.

A disturbing dream of Probus is interpreted

17 [1]Probus got up from the couch exceedingly sad, for while he was asleep he had a dream and was very downcast about it. Seeing him about to go out into the street, the gatekeeper greatly feared his having a face downcast in this way, "Lest perhaps," he said, "knowing what has happened he might destroy me wickedly." [2]But Probus, after going out and ordaining to those selling in the market the things fitting for the day and time, returned right away to his house and said to his servants, "Call for me quickly the wise men Barandus and Gnosteas."

[3]After they were called he said to them, "I have seen a very frightful dream, and the things that appeared in it are hard to understand according to our ability. Make known these things also to me, because you are the most excellent men in the entire world. Declare these things to me after I have recounted it."[b]

[4]Barandus said to him, "If the vision can be interpreted from our wisdom, then we will explain it to you. But if it is from the faith that is now being heard about, then we will be unable to declare it to you, for that is from another wisdom [. . .][c] and understanding. Nevertheless, let our lord and master relate the dream, and let us see if there is an explanation in it."

[5]Probus said to Gnosteas, "Why do you say nothing in response?" Gnosteas said, "I have not heard the dream, and what can I say about it except that it may

---

a. Perhaps Xanthippe fears that she will die for looking at the divine Christ (cf. Gen 32:30; Exod 33:20–23; Isa 6:5; 1 Tim 6:16).

b. This interpretation of a prophetic dream recalls the stories of Joseph (Gen 40:5–41:36) and Daniel (Dan 2:1–45), but such dreams are also prominent in Christian texts such as the *Martyrdom of Perpetua and Felicitas*.

c. There is a lacuna of five spaces in the text.

result from the preaching of Paul? Tell us now, and you will discover that it is so."[a]

[6]Probus said, "I believed that I was standing in some unseen and strange land, and there was seated a certain dark-faced[b] king, who held the entire earth and seemed never to have a successor. Multitudes of servants stood next to him, and they all were eagerly rushing to destruction and had authority over much. [7]When that dark-faced one seemed to have accomplished his purpose, a raven arose and, standing before him, cried out in a pitiful voice. [8]Immediately, from the eastern regions an eagle arose and snatched away the kingdom, and the king's strength was brought low.[c] Those standing by him fled to the eagle. That king struggled against those who fled to the eagle, but the eagle rose up into heaven. [9]Behold, a certain helper for those fleeing to the eagle came and left them his staff. Those who were holding it were not overcome by the strength of that king. [10]Whoever ran to those holding the staff, they washed them with pure water, and those who were washed ruled over the kingdom of that king. By that staff the enemies of the king were putting him to flight. Mighty men were holding the staff, and they turned to themselves many multitudes. [11]That king was struggling against them, but he was not able to do anything at all. He was hindering many from believing in the one who had sent out the men to bear witness in the world, and for this reason many were grieved. [12]However, this one (who had sent out the witnesses) was not compelling by force anyone as that king was, for he himself ruled over all light. That was the end."

18 [1]Then the wise Barandus said, "By the grace of God I will say the things sent into the world from the Lord. The king whom you see is the devil. The plethora of servants are the demons, and his multitudes are those who worship the gods. [2]He thought that he would not have a successor, because he was not expecting the coming of Christ. The raven revealed the weakness of his kingdom, for the raven was not obedient to the just Noah but loved despicable things.[d]   Gen 8:6–7
[3]But the eagle that rose up, seized his kingdom, rose up into heaven, came as a guardian of those fleeing to the eagle, and had the staff—this is the Lord Jesus Christ, who left for them his staff, that is, the honor of his cross. And that he washed those who fled to him, this signifies the unconquerable breastplate of baptism,[e] and because of it they were not overcome. [4]The mighty men who were sent into the world with the cross are the heralds of God, like Paul, who is now among us, and against them that king is able to do nothing. [5]This has been made known to you, because even on those who do not believe, God has compassion in some way. See, then, whether you are able to do harm to Paul, even if you

---

a. The Greek text here is corrupt, but Gnosteas is restating Barandus's point that they are unable to discern matters related to the other "wisdom . . . and understanding" taught by Paul.

b. The adjective *aithiopa* can also mean "Ethiopian," but there is no reason to think the author is seeking to associate Ethiopia with the devil.

c. Cf. the dream of Charisius in *Acts Thom.* 91, which also involves an eagle and a king.

d. Both Jewish and Christian commentators believed that the raven sent out by Noah did not return because it was feeding on human corpses. Philo and others, therefore, viewed the raven as a symbol of evil. See David Marcus, "The Mission of the Raven (Gen 8:7)," *Journal of Ancient Near Eastern Studies* 29 (2002): 71–80 esp. 75–77.

e. Cf. the "breastplate of righteousness" in Eph 6:14.

want to do so, for the strong power that shields him has been shown to you by the Lord. ⁶Understand, therefore, the things said to you by me, and do not serve that dark king. For just as you saw his kingdom disappear, so will all his servants be destroyed with him. ⁷Therefore, come, my lord, let us go to Paul and receive from him the washing,ᵃ so that Satan may not have mastery over us also."

⁸Probus said, "Let us first go forth to Xanthippe and see if she is still alive, for behold, it has been twenty-nine days since she ate anything. In the evening I saw her face, and it was like one preparing to die."

The song of Xanthippe

19 ¹After they went to her bedchamber, they heard her singing,

"Praise God, O sinners, because he accepts your prayers also. Alleluia.
Praise the Lord, you who like me have despaired, because his mercies are
    many. Alleluia.
²Praise him, you who are impious, because he was crucified for your sake.
    Alleluia.
Praise him, you who are struggling on behalf of the salvation of sinners,
    because God loves you. Alleluia.
³Praise him, you who rejoice at the calling of sinners, because you are fel-
    low citizens of the saints. Alleluia."

⁴After she had said these things and more things than these with tears, the wise Barandus and Gnosteas opened the door, went in, and fell down before her, saying, "Pray for us lowly ones, O servant of Christ, so that we may also be joined to your number." ⁵She said to them, "Brothers, I am not Paul, the one who forgives sins, but he is not far from you. Therefore, do not fall at my knees, but go to him, who is more able to do good on your behalf."

Probus and his "wise men" yield to the teaching of Paul

⁶They ran and came to the house of Philotheus to Paul, and they found him teaching a large crowd. Probus also came to hear Paul. Xanthippe also entered to greet him, and after coming near to Paul and bending her knees, she prostrated herself before him. ⁷Probus saw this and was amazed that such a haughty spirit as hers had lowered itself to such humility, for she sat on the ground next to the feet of Paul humbly and as one of the worthless. Probus was greatly vexed and was not yet paying attention to the hearing of the word, but was constantly looking intently and focusing his attention on Xanthippe.

20 ¹But the great Paul was teaching, "Let those burning in the flesh keep their lawful marriage, avoiding sexual impurities, especially with another's wife. And let those that are married keep to each other." ²Probus heard this teaching gladly and said, "O Paul, how beautifully and wisely you have proclaimed this teaching. Why, then, did Xanthippe separate from me?"

³Paul said, "My child Probus, those who see ahead that the works of men are tested by fire, and those who always have in their mind the inevitability of death,

1 Cor 7:1–6

---

a. That is, baptism.

they cast out every desire that is attached to the flesh. But woe when the desire judges the desirer! Then he will gnash his teeth in a useless and vain biting, for the correction of repentance is past."

[4]Hearing these things Probus went up to his house amazed and ate nothing that day, but went and fell upon his couch. At about nine o'clock that night he got up and said, "Woe is me. How bitter was the day on which I was married to Xanthippe. If only I had died and not seen her!" [5]Saying these things he got up and said, "I will pray to the God of Paul. Perhaps he will do also for me the things that are fitting, so that I, who have been neglected, may not become a matter of disgrace in the world on account of her."

[6]Immediately he fell to the earth and said, "O God of Paul, if, as I have heard from Xanthippe, you seek out the ignorant and turn around those who are wandering, then do also for me the things that are fitting. [7]For you are the king of life and death, as I have heard, and you rule over all things in heaven and on earth and under the earth, and over the thoughts and ideas of men. To you alone belongs the glory forever, amen." Phil 2:10

Probus is baptized

21 [1]Then, getting up from the ground, Probus fell again on his couch. Rising early in the morning, he went to Paul and found him baptizing many people in the name of the life-giving Trinity.[a] He said, "If I am worthy, my lord Paul, to receive baptism, then look, the hour is here." [2]Paul said to him, "Child, look, the water is ready for the cleansing of those coming to Christ." Immediately he quickly took off his garments. [3]After Paul had taken hold of him, he leapt into the water, saying, "Jesus Christ, Son of God and eternal God, let all my sin be kept[b] by this water." Paul said, "We baptize you in the name of the Father and the Son and the Holy Spirit." Then he made Probus receive the Eucharist of Christ.[c]

[4]Xanthippe became greatly overjoyed, and around evening in the house she began with her husband to bring good cheer to all those in the house and to complete preparations for a feast. When they had come, and after she had arranged that the meal would be magnificent, she went up to the dining room. [5]Behold, on the staircase was a demon, coming in the likeness of one of the mimes. Standing in a dark corner, he wanted to frighten and terrify Xanthippe. But she thought it was the mime she usually had and said angrily, "Many times I have said to him that I no longer put up with games, and he despises me as a woman." [6]Immediately she grabbed an iron vase pedestal[d] and threw it at his

---

a. See the introduction p. 422 on the possible importance of this expression for dating the text.

b. Probus expresses a strikingly literalistic understanding of baptism as "washing," for he believes that the water itself would hold on to *(katechō)* his sin.

c. As Gorman ("Reading and Theorizing," 28) has pointed out, Probus is converted by the faith of his wife in the style of 1 Cor 7:13. This story is reminiscent of the conversions of Candida and her husband Quartus in *Acts Pet.* 1 and the extended narrative of Charisius and Mygdonia in *Acts Thom.* 82–133. Pervo ("Dare and Back," 190) also compares it to *Jos. Asen.* 1–21 as "a story of conversion within the context of marriage," although the stories are otherwise quite distinct.

d. The term is difficult to render. According to Bonnet, *konchostatou* likely refers to the base upon which a hollow, shell-shaped vase called a *konchē* would be placed. See "Sur les actes de Xanthippe," 339.

face, shattering his entire image. Then the demon cried out, "O an act of violence by this vase pedestal![a] Even the women have received power to strike us!" But Xanthippe was very afraid.

The dream of Polyxena, Xanthippe's sister

22 [1]So then, after dinner Probus went to hear the word, but Xanthippe was sitting in her bedchamber reading aloud the prophets, with her sister Polyxena lying on the couch. Xanthippe loved Polyxena very much, because she was younger than her and beautiful in appearance. Probus also loved her very much. [2]While Polyxena was reclining on the couch, she saw this dream: a serpent[b] that was horrible in appearance came and beckoned her to come to it. When she did not listen and go, the serpent swallowed her. The child jumped up out of fear and was shaking. [3]Xanthippe ran to her and said, "What has happened to you, dearest one, that you have suddenly jumped up like this?" But for a long time she was not able to speak.

[4]Then she came back to herself and said, "Woe is me, my sister Xanthippe. What kind of danger or trouble stands before me, I do not know, for I saw in my dream that an ugly serpent is coming to beckon me to come to him. When I was unwilling to go, he ran and, grabbing me by the feet, devoured me. [5]After I had been thrown into confusion, suddenly into the light of the sun and from the air a certain attractive young man, whom I thought to be the brother of Paul,[c] spoke and said, 'Truly, you are able to do nothing.' [6]Taking me by the hand, he immediately drew me out of it, and right away the serpent disappeared. Behold, his hand was full of a sweet smell, as of balsam or some other kind of fragrance."

[7]Xanthippe said to her, "You have reason to be greatly troubled, my sister Polyxena, except that God holds you as his own, because he has shown you strange and wonderful things. Therefore, get up quickly early in the morning and receive holy baptism, and ask in baptism that you be drawn out of the traps of the serpent."

The abduction of Polyxena

23 [1]After saying these things to Polyxena and making a cross out of wood, Xanthippe went to Paul. Polyxena remained alone in the bedchamber, because her nurse had left at the same time as Xanthippe. [2]In the middle of the night, a certain man who had significant wealth and a strong military force found the doors open, having used a magical art. He went inside, wishing to snatch away Polyxena. She realized it and fled into the mill. The magicians found her, guided

---

a. James's first edition read *apo toutou chanotou.* Because the meaning of *chanotos* was unknown, W. A. Craigie rendered it "from this destroyer" in his *Ante-Nicene Fathers* translation (*ANF* 9:212). All scholars since have accepted this speculation. However, Bonnet ("Sur les actes de Xanthippe," 339) corrected this phrase to *apo toutou konchostatou* and James accepted this correction (*Apocrypha Anecdota* 2, 140). Craigie's translation, published nearly a decade later, failed to incorporate this update.

b. The term *drakōn* can refer to a dragon or a serpent. Given that this *drakōn* later devours Polyxena beginning with her feet, in the fashion of a large snake, I have chosen the latter option.

c. In *Acts Thom.* 11 Jesus looks like Thomas but identifies himself as Thomas's brother. In this text Jesus has already appeared as a young man in chapters 13 and 15.

by the demons.[a] [3]After not finding any doors through which she could get out, she said, "Woe is me, who have been handed over to this corrupter." She heard that he had a conflict with her suitor, and he did this to get back at him and cause him pain, for he was a cheating and very wild man.

[4]After taking her, they left the city, dragging her to the sea. She looked around here and there, but no one was coming to set her free. [5]Groaning she said, "Woe is me. My sister Xanthippe, you sent seven hundred gold pieces to Rome and got back for yourself books, so that you might prophesy things about me through them. For this evening you read aloud, 'I was looking to the right and watching, but there was no one who recognizes me. Escape is lost to me, and there is no one seeking out my soul.'"[b]

Ps 142:4

Peter diverts the ship carrying Polyxena

24 [1]While she was saying these things, those dragging her were going in a hurry. Then, after they came to the shore, they hired a ship for Babylonia, for the one who had taken her had a brother there who was a district governor.[c] But a contrary wind blew against them, so that they were not able to make progress because of her. [2]While they were rowing in the sea, behold, the great apostle of the Lord, Peter, was passing by in a ship, being urged by a vision to go to Rome. After Paul had left to go to Spain, a certain deceiver and sorcerer named Simon had come to Rome and destroyed the church that Paul had established. [3]Behold, as he was going he heard a voice from heaven saying to him, "Peter, tomorrow a ship coming from Spain will meet you. Stand up then and pray for the soul that is distressed within it."

Jonah 1:3

Acts Pet. 5

[4]As soon as Peter saw the ship, he remembered the vision and said,

> "O Jesus, you who have cared for the distressed,
> you who are moved to mercy by the trouble of those in a foreign land,
> you who were made to come by the weeping of those in captivity on earth,
> you who give to us at all times whatever we wish and never turn away from
>   our request,
> give mercy and support now to the soul that is being tossed about in that
>   ship, because you always have pity on those in pain, Lord."

[5]The demons heard the prayer and said to the sorcerers, "Turn away from the path of that ship, for if we meet it, we will not move."

Polyxena lands in Greece and meets Philip

25 [1]Because the loving God was making provision for Polyxena, the ship arrived in Greece. The blessed Philip was there.[d] Because of a vision he went to the

---

a. Apparently Polyxena's kidnapper has magicians in his retinue, and the demons aid them in finding her.

b. James corrected the text from *tychēn* in the manuscript to *psychēn*.

c. Bennett ("James' *Apocrypha Anecdota*," 102) argues that Babylonia is a reference to Egypt (see introduction p. 424). Here the author may be drawing upon Chariton's romance *Chaereas and Callirhoe*, in which the ill-fated Callirhoe is taken to Babylon (*Chaer.* 5.2).

d. *Acts Phil.* 2, 5–8 place Philip's activities in Greece.

shore, and large crowds being taught by him were following him. Behold, the ship in which Polyxena found herself appeared, being tossed about violently. [2]The blessed Philip said, "Behold, there is the ship for which we came down here, and in it there is a troubled soul." After the ship arrived and all of them came out onto dry land, they lay down as if half-dead because they had been tossed about on the sea. [3]The apostle Philip ordered Polyxena to be lifted up and carried to the place where he was staying as a guest, and the others to be taken care of. But the one who had kidnapped Polyxena recovered from the turmoil at sea and wanted to take her, for Philip had handed over Polyxena to one of those who had been taught by him and had set out on his way rejoicing.

Acts 8:39

[4]The one who had her said, "She was given to me by a holy man, and I am not able to give her to you." But he would not at all stand for this and discovered there a relative of his who was a government official.[a] He prepared for war, gathering 8,000 men. When Polyxena learned this, she left and fled by night.

[5]The one who had responsibility for Polyxena said, "I will take the robe of Philip and go out alone to meet them."[b] As he was saying these things, it was announced to him, "The virgin is not here." Leaving aside his thought about war, he ran into the bedchamber. [6]Not finding the virgin he threw himself to the ground, saying, "Woe is me, the wretched man who has become the enemy of Philip. How will I defend myself to him when he seeks the virgin from me?"

[7]His servants came and said to him, "Get up from the ground, our lord, because a military force has surrounded the house, and the virgin cannot be found." [8]He said, "Therefore, let me die for her sake. Perhaps in this the servant of Christ, Philip, may be satisfied, because I will be found as one who has ignored his command."[c]

[9]The servants, seeing that he did not listen to them, wanted to flee from the enemies. But again after a little bit, by the providence of God, they were stirred up and said, "It is not right that our master should die. Come on! Let us raise the sign of the cross and go out to meet them." [10]Then, raising the precious cross, about thirty men went out against the enemies and cut down 5,000. The remaining men fled.[d] They returned with victory to their master, singing praises to God and saying, "What god is as great as our God, who did not leave his servant to be killed by lawless men?" [11]They came to their master, who was still weeping, and said to him, "Get up, master, and do not weep, because it turns out not as we will, but as the Lord wills."

Polyxena escapes into the wilderness but encounters a lioness

26 [1]Polyxena went out of the city and did not know on which road she should travel. She found herself in the desolate places of the mountains, and sitting down with tears she said,

---

a. The ship was redirected to Greece from its original destination of "Babylonia," but the lucky kidnapper apparently has multiple relatives in high government positions.

b. Is Philip's robe meant to serve as a talisman?

c. The master of the house is a truly pathetic figure. He states a willingness to die for Polyxena's sake but then remains motionless on the ground until the fighting is over.

d. Pervo ("Dare and Back," 163) suggests a connection to the story of Gideon in Judg 7.

[2]"Woe is me, thrown out and taken prisoner, because I do not find even
  the cave of a wild beast in which to rest.

Woe is me, abandoned, because not even Hades, which no one escapes,
  has swallowed me.

[3]Woe is me, who at one time appeared not even to my servants but now am
  put to shame before demons.[a]

Woe is me, because I disdained to be seen by them, but now I am revealed
  to all of them.

[4]Woe to me, who was at one time dedicated to idols. For this reason now
  even the mercy of God has passed over me in silence.

[5]Upon whom, then, will I call for help? The God of Paul, whom I have continually provoked to anger? But who will help me now, because no one sees and
pays heed and hears my groaning? [6]Thus I will ask the one who sees the hidden
things, for who is more sympathetic and compassionate than the one who is
always watching over the oppressed? Because my mouth is unclean and defiled,
I do not dare to ask him for help. [7]If only I were like one of the wild beasts, so
that I would not know what captivity is. If only I had been thrown into the sea,
perhaps after receiving the divine bath I would go where no one is held captive.[b]
What, then, will I do? Because death tarries and night has come, but restoration
is nowhere to be found."

[8]After saying these things, she got up and began to walk along. After passing
through a narrow mountain pass, she came upon a very dense and large forest.
She found a hollow opening in a tree, which was the den of a lioness, and sat
down there, because the lioness had gone out to look for her food. [9]She sat down
and said, "O miserable birth. O grievous hour in which I, the wretched one, was
brought into the world. O mother who bore me, how did you see ahead of time
my troubles and travels abroad, because you named me Polyxena?[c] [10]Has anyone
else fallen into such troubles and misfortunes? Truly you read aloud about my
distress, my sister Xanthippe, when you said, 'I endured hardship and was bent
down completely.' These things you uttered while suffering pain, but I was lying   Ps 38:6
on the bed, not at all thinking about my evil deeds. [11]For this reason I have now
come to the depths of evil deeds and live in desert places like a wild beast.[d] But
the beasts live with others of their own kind, but I am alone, as if I were not of
the race of men."

27 [1]As she was saying these things and more like them, the dawn broke, and
the lioness came back from her hunt. Seeing the wild beast, Polyxena trembled
and said, "By the God of Paul, have mercy on me, wild beast, and do not tear
me apart until I receive baptism." [2]The beast was frightened by this oath and immediately went away. Standing far away it looked at her intently. She said, "Look,

---

a. Modesty had kept Polyxena out of the view of even some in her household, but in her
travels she is on display for all to see.

b. Polyxena regrets that she was not thrown overboard and "baptized" in the sea, then freed
by death.

c. The name Polyxena can be translated "much-traveled" or "often in foreign lands."

d. As Polyxena has stated just above, she believes that her plight is in part the result of her
own actions, including provoking the God of Paul to anger.

the wild beast obeyed me. I will give up this place for its house." ³Immediately she began to walk toward the east, but the beast was leading her until she left the forest. Polyxena said, "What will I give you in return for your kindness, O beast? The God of Paul will pay back this kindness to you." ⁴After hearing the prayer, the beast immediately returned to its place. Going down Polyxena found a public road, and standing on it she was weeping because she did not know where to go. ⁵Although many people passed by, she did not turn toward anyone but said, "Perhaps the God of Paul will remember me. Whoever has mercy on me, I will go to him."

Acts Paul 3:28, 33; ch. 7

Polyxena meets the apostle Andrew

28 ¹As she was saying these things, the apostle of the Lord, Andrew, passed by, because he was going to that place. As he approached Polyxena, he perceived in his heart some disturbance within himself. ²Stopping to pray, he formed his hands into the shape of a cross and said, "Lord Jesus Christ, partaker of light and knower of hidden things, from whom none of the things on earth is hidden, show me kindness and mercy. Reveal to me this disturbance, and bring peace to my reason, you who always make peace with those who love peace."

Heb 4:13

³Then Polyxena ran to him, and the apostle of the Lord, Andrew, said to her, "Do not approach me, child, but tell me who you are and where you come from." Polyxena said, "My lord, I am a foreigner among the people here, but I see that your face is full of grace. Your words are like the words of Paul, and I suspect that you are from the same God."

⁴Andrew perceived that she was speaking about the apostle Paul and said to her, "From where do you know Paul?" She said, "From my home country, for I left him in Spain." ⁵Andrew said to her, "How did you come to be here, so far away from your country?" She said, "Because this is how it was prescribed for me and came about. But I beg you and fall at your feet, seal me just as Paul seals

Titus 3:5

through the washing of regeneration, so that I also, the lowly one, may be known by our God. For seeing my distress and my suffering, the benevolent God sent you to have mercy on me."

⁶The great apostle of the Lord, Andrew, said to her, "Let us go, child, to where there is water."

Andrew baptizes Polyxena and Rebecca

29 ¹When they had gone not very far, they came upon a certain spring that was very clear and pure.ᵃ When the blessed Andrew was standing to pray over the spring, behold, a certain virgin named Rebecca from the tribe of Israel, who had been brought as a captive into that country, came to draw water at the spring.ᵇ ²She saw the blessed Andrew and recognized him by his appearance, for Re-

Gen 24:11–21

---

a. Cf. the roadside meeting and eventual baptism of the Ethiopian eunuch in Acts 8:26–39.

b. In Gen 24:11–21 Eliezer also prays just prior to meeting a woman named Rebecca at a water source. The MT and LXX describe the meeting place as a well (*beêr; phrear*) and a spring (*'ayin; pēgē*), language echoed in John 4:6–15. In this text, however, the meeting place is a spring (*pēgē*), and the fact that Andrew baptizes the women in running water is consistent with *Acts Thom.* 49,121. See Albertus F. J. Klijn, *The Acts of Thomas: Introduction, Text, Commentary* (NovTSup 5; Leiden: Brill, 1962), 13.

becca said, "This is the appearance of a prophet, and he is one of the apostles." ³She bowed down to him and said, "Have mercy on me, servant of the living God, a captive who has been sold three times, one who was once honored by prophets but is now mistreated by idolaters. Remember me, the lowly one, O you who were sent out to recall many sinners."

⁴The apostle of Christ, Andrew, said, "God will take care of the things concerning you, child, just as he will the things concerning this foreigner. Therefore, both of you receive baptism, and you will be as if of the same race,ᵃ giving praise to God always."

30 ¹Then the apostle stood and prayed, and behold the lioness came running and stood and looked intently at him. The apostle of the Lord, Andrew, said, "What does this wild beast want?" ²And the lioness opened its mouth and said in a human voice, "Apostle of Christ, Andrew, the prayer of the one standing on your right side overwhelmed me. Therefore, establish them, hold them fast, and admonish them in the right and true faith in Christ, because they greatly desire the name of the Lord. See the marvelous humility of God, because even on the irrational and untamed beasts he has poured out his mercy."ᵇ

³Weeping, the blessed Andrew said, "What should I say or proclaim about your mercy, O God? That thus you always cling to the lowly, and take thought for those in ignorance, because you are humble and very merciful?" After completing this prayer he baptized the virgins in the name of the Father, and the Son, and the Holy Spirit. ⁴The lioness immediately rushed off onto the mountain, and the apostle Andrew said to the virgins, "Be eager, children, to be esteemed before God by carrying yourselves well in a foreign land, and do not be separated from each other. But God, who is always present with those who call upon him, will protect you in holiness, driving away the evil one.ᶜ And pray also for me."

⁵Polyxena said, "We will follow you wherever you may go."ᵈ The apostle Andrew said, "This was not revealed to me by the Lord, children. Thus, remain at peace and hope in the Lord, and he will protect you to the end." *Acts Paul* 3:25; Ruth 1:16

Polyxena and Rebecca meet a mule driver, who tries to help them

31 ¹Andrew went on his way rejoicingᵉ and praising God. But Polyxena said, "Where will we go, sister?" Rebecca said, "Let us go wherever you wish, lest my mistress should send me away and separate us." ²And Polyxena said, "Come and let us go to the mountain to the lioness." Rebecca said, "Yes, it is better for us to live with the wild beasts and die from hunger than to be forced to fall into the mire of marriage by Greeks and idolaters."

³They began to go, and behold, according to the plan of God they met a man driving donkeys. Seeing them he said, "You are not from this country, and as I see it, you do not wear the local dress. Therefore, order your servant to eat bread

---

a. Pervo ("Dare and Back," 185) reads this as the fulfillment of Gal 3:28.

b. Talking animals are a common motif in the apocryphal acts. See e.g., Janet Spittler, *Animals in the Apocryphal Acts of the Apostles: The Wild Kingdom of Early Christian Literature* (Tübingen: Mohr Siebeck, 2008).

c. Or "evil."

d. Thecla makes the same promise to Paul in *Acts Paul* 3:25.

e. Here again an apostle goes away rejoicing in the style of Acts 8:39.

and take one silver coin, so that you remember your servant whenever you buy bread." [4]He hurried and took down the bags from the donkeys. After spreading them on the ground, he made the virgins rest upon them and said to them, "Because the wine that your servant is carrying was gathered from the Greeks, tell me of what sort of faith you are, so that we may enjoy it thus."[a]

[5]But Polyxena said, "Brother, we do not partake in wine, but we are of the god of Paul." The mule driver said, "Is this god upon the earth?" Polyxena said to him, "God is everywhere, both in heaven and on earth." [6]The mule driver wanted to learn more precisely and said, "Does Paul himself have this god that is preached by Philip?" And Polyxena, observing that he was a Christian, said, "Yes, brother. He is the god of all people, about whom Paul and Philip preach."

32 [1]After the mule driver heard these things, he wept continually. Polyxena said, "Did the providence of God overtake you that you wept this way?" [2]The mule driver said, "If you want to learn why I wept, hear the truth, for there is no need to shrink back from proclaiming things about Christ. [3]I was taught by Philip, the apostle of Christ, and seeing how all his care was for the poor, I took whatever I had and sold it. I took the proceeds, bought bread and wine, and was distributing them in the cities to those in need. [4]After I had been doing this for some time, in a neighboring city a certain maimed man cried out and said—yet he was not speaking but Satan through his mouth—'I wish for nothing. I am taking nothing from you, because you are a Christian.'[b] [5]The whole city arose against me and sought to seize me. They ran one this way and another that way,

Luke 4:30

while I walked in the midst of them and no one saw me. Having left the city I gave praise and glory to God, because I had been paid back in this way. [6]I prayed to my God that I would meet someone who knows his all-holy name, so that after describing these things I might find relief. For the men of this country do not at all want to hear things about Christ, because they are full of impiety and consumed by wickedness. I ask you, therefore, to take one coin from me, and if it seems good, then rest upon the mules."

[7]Polyxena said, "May you find mercy from God, brother. But if you wish to receive a full reward, then keep us safe as far as the sea, so that, God willing, we may sail off to Spain."

Polyxena and Rebecca are abducted by a local prefect

33 [1]The mule driver, as if commanded by the voice of God, after willingly receiving the virgins went on his way rejoicing in the Lord. And he said to Polyxena, "Change your appearance to that of a man, lest on account of your beauty someone

Acts Paul 3:26

should take you from me." [2]After reaching an inn, they remained there. They set out on the next day and were going forward, paying close attention to their route. Behold, a certain prefect came along who was going to Greece. Seeing the virgins he ordered Polyxena to be snatched away on his chariot. [3]But the mule driver followed, crying out and saying, "A prefect does no violence to anyone. Why are you doing these things?" Then they beat him and chased him away.

---

a. The man seems to have in mind to offer a libation to the relevant god(s), so he inquires about which god(s) the women worship.

b. Cf. the account of the devil speaking through a blind man in *Acts Andr.* 2.

34 [1]As he went he wept bitterly and said, "Woe is me, miserable and loathsome. Woe is me, who wanted to do good but now has done something evil. Woe is me, because my struggle and my race were unacceptable. [2]If only I had died before yesterday, so that I would not have met these women. But why do you accuse me, O miserable soul? [3]Let us go to Philip, the apostle of God. If there is no forgiveness for me, then it is better for me to choose death in whatever kind of way than to live with such an evil and bitter conscience." [4]He went and found the apostle of Christ, Philip, and said to him, "O disciple and herald of Christ, in this way and that it has happened to me and come to pass. Does my soul have salvation?"

[5]Philip, the apostle of Christ, said, "Do not be grieved about this, child, because it is impossible for them to be corrupted, for no one ever conquers God. [6]In the first few days after she had come from the sea, I entrusted this same Polyxena to a certain brother, who also was very greatly troubled because she secretly ran away from his house. I persuaded him not to be troubled, for through her distress and travel abroad many are learning to know God."

Rebecca escapes to the home of an old woman

35 [1]Then the prefect brought Polyxena to the city in which he was stationed and ordered her to be locked up in a bedchamber. A certain one of the soldiers seized Rebecca, but the virgin escaped and fled to the house of a certain old woman, who received the virgin graciously and treated her well. [2]Rebecca sat down and was weeping, saying, "Woe is me, my sister Polyxena. I, being wretched, did not think that anyone was as troubled as I am. Now I am persuaded and know that all my misfortunes and troubles do not compare with one day of yours. [3]The most painful thing of all is that, behold, I was separated from you and am again a captive. But search for me in the age that is to come, my sister Polyxena."

[4]The old woman said to her, "What happened to you, my child, that you lament so bitterly?" And Rebecca said, "Permit me, mother, to be troubled and to lament the incurable and great suffering of my heart." [5]The old woman felt great compassion for her and wept violently, for the virgin described everything that had happened to her and how she had believed in Christ through Polyxena.

Polyxena is aided by the prefect's son

[6]Likewise Polyxena, who was locked up in a bedchamber, said, "Woe is miserable me! Alas for wretched me! Now I understand clearly how the devil resents virginity. [7]But Lord Jesus Christ, God of all, because I do not dare to beg of you from myself,[a] I bring forth to you the prayers of your holy herald, Paul, lest you permit my virginity to be corrupted by anyone."

36 [1]While she was still praying, the attendants came to lead her away to the bed of the prefect. But Polyxena said to them, "Brothers, do not be eager for someone's destruction, for this time will quickly pass away, and those that work together with the destroyers will be destroyed with them. Instead, help strangers, so that you may not be found strangers of the angels of God." [2]The men were

---

a. That is, from my own standing.

put to shame by these words and went away to the prefect, saying, "Out of fear the virgin was overcome by a violent fever."[a]

Rev 19:9

³The prefect said, "Let her be." Behold, the son of the prefect came to Polyxena at night, and she saw him and was afraid. ⁴But the young man said to her, "Do not be afraid, girl, because I am not seeking to be married to you as a bridegroom of corruption, but I am seeking to be attached closely to you in the bridal chamber that is to come.[b] ⁴This is not the desire of corruption, for I know from your prayer that you are the bride of the heavenly God. I know this God that is never conquered by anyone, for a certain man highly esteemed for his appearance[c] was preaching about this God in Antioch some time ago. ⁵A certain virgin believed in God, followed the man, and experienced danger on account of her beauty. Her name was Thecla, and I have heard about her that she was sentenced to the wild beasts.

Acts Paul 3:7–45

⁶"Therefore, I was constantly gazing at the man, and he saw and said to me, 'May God take notice of you, child.' Since that time by the grace of Christ I have not returned to the sacrifices for idols, but sometimes I have faked illness, and other times I have given myself to some other affairs. My father said to me, 'Because you do not hurry to the sacrifices for the gods, you thus do not show strength, for you are not worthy of the gods.' ⁷But I was rejoicing when I heard that I was not worthy of the sacrifices for idols. By the grace of God you have come here as an act of providential care on my behalf."

⁸Polyxena said, "What is the name of that man?" And the young man said, "His name is Paul." Polyxena said, "He is in my city." ⁹And the young man said, "Come then, girl. After taking on my appearance, go down to the shore. Wait for me there, and after I take some money I will come quickly."

Polyxena and the prefect's son are thrown to the wild beasts

37 ¹A certain one of the servants overheard and reported these things to the prefect, who was filled with great anger and sentenced them to be thrown to the wild beasts. Then, when they were thrown into the arena, a fierce lioness was set loose upon them. Running up it wrapped around the feet of Polyxena and licked all over the soles of her feet. ²Then the prefect and the entire city saw this fearful and incredible marvel, and they gave praise and glory to the compassionate God,

Acts Paul 3:28, 33

---

a. Cf. Anthia's feigned illness to avoid prostitution in Xenophon's *Ephesian Tale* 5.7.

b. Cf. *Acts Thom.* 14–15, where the bride and bridegroom give thanks that they have avoided the shame of a temporary marriage based on sexual desire in favor of an eternal one.

c. To modern ears the physical description of Paul in *Acts Paul* 3:3 would not necessarily make his appearance "highly esteemed," but this is perhaps evidence of different ancient sensibilities based on physiognomy. See e.g. Robert M. Grant, "The Description of Paul in the Acts of Paul and Thecla," *VC* 36 (1982): 1–4; Abraham J. Malherbe, "A Physical Description of Paul," *HTR* 79 (1986): 170–75; János Bollók, "The Description of Paul in the Acta Pauli," in *The Apocryphal Acts of Paul and Thecla* (ed. Jan N. Bremmer; Kampen: Kok Pharos, 1996), 1–15; Heike Omerzu, "The Portrayal of Paul's Outer Appearance in the Acts of Paul and Thecla: Reconsidering the Correspondence Between the Body and Personality in Ancient Literature," *R&T* 15 (2008): 252–79. Cf. Monika Betz, "Die betörenden Worte des fremden Mannes: Zur Funktion der Paulusbeschreibung in den Theklaakten," *NTS* 53 (2007): 130–45, esp. 132–37, who argues that Paul is described in an intentionally unattractive way in order to emphasize that Thecla falls in love with the gospel, not him.

saying, "Truly you exist, and the only god is the one named by Polyxena. For the gods of the nations are the creations of the hands of men, and they are not able to save or help anyone. Therefore, let them perish, along with those who make them." [3]Immediately the prefect took his son and Polyxena into his palace and heard from them point by point about faith in Christ and piety with nothing left out. He and everyone in the city believed, and there was great joy and giving of glory to God.[a]

1 Sam 12:21; Ps 115:8; Jer 2:28

[4]Polyxena said to the prefect, "Do not despair, my lord, for soon the man of God will come to you. He will teach, admonish, instruct, and enlighten you perfectly in the knowledge of Christ." After putting everything in order, she was hurrying to leave for Spain.

Onesimus returns Polyxena safely to Spain

38 [1]When I, Onesimus,[b] was sailing to Spain to Paul, I received from the Lord a revelation that said to me, "Onesimus, the ship on which you are now is about to arrive in the region of the Greeks. You will find on the shore of the harbor two virgins with one young man. Help them and conduct them safely to Paul." [2]When we had come to the place according to the command of the Lord, we found the virgins with the young man looking for a ship. When the virgins saw us, they knew that we were of the hope in Christ. [3]Polyxena ran up and said, "Truly a man of God is not able to be hidden, for the gracefulness and kindness of his face makes him obvious."

[4]When we sought to sail off, by the providence of God the sea was stirred up. There was with me a disciple of Paul named Lucius,[c] who was able by speaking to teach the city. We remained, therefore, for seven days, and God opened for that place the great door of faith. Twenty thousand believed, and there was great joy and exultation in the entire city. [5]When the tide became favorable for us to sail away, the prefect again held us back, and we remained another seven days, until everyone believed and rejoiced in the Lord.

1 Cor 16:9 Acts 8:8

39 [1]Thus, by the providence of Christ, the prefect sent us forth with provisions and sent his son with us, also. After we had sailed for twenty days, Polyxena grew tired, and we directed our course to a certain island for the sake of rest. [2]Behold, certain savage and hardened men, having come down to us and seen Polyxena, prepared for war. By the grace of Christ our men fought for Polyxena and conquered them, although the foreign men were greater in number and stronger. [3]Polyxena, fearing that she might again become a captive, threw herself into the sea, but the captain grabbed her, and she suffered no harm. After embarking on the ship we fled, for the places were rugged and densely wooded, and we were afraid to stay there. In twelve days we arrived in Spain by the grace of God.

---

a. Cf. the conversion of king Misdaeus in *Acts Thom.* 170.

b. This Onesimus is likely meant to be the redeemed runaway slave of Philem and Col 4:9.

c. Or Luke (the evangelist, presumably), as supported by Junod, "Vie et conduit des saintes," 100; Pervo, "Dare and Back," 187. The names are similar—*Loukios* versus *Loukas*—but Lucius is also a well-attested Latin name, and the standard Latinized form of *Loukas* in the Vulgate is Lucas, not Lucius.

Polyxena and Xanthippe are reunited

40 [1]Seeing us, Paul rejoiced greatly and said, "Welcome, O you who have been troubled." But Polyxena grabbed his feet and said, "Perhaps this trouble came upon me because I might have blasphemed against you. Now I beg and plead that I not be handed over again to such troubles and misfortunes." [2]Paul wept and said, "It is necessary that we be troubled thus, child, so that we may know our protector, Jesus Christ."

41 [1]While we were giving the letters from the brothers to Paul, a certain man ran and announced to Xanthippe the arrival of Polyxena. She hurried and came to us, and seeing Polyxena, she was overtaken by unspeakable joy and fell on the ground.[a] But Polyxena embraced her, kissed her for a long time, and brought her to life again. [2]Then Xanthippe said to her, "My true sister Polyxena, I did not go out at all for forty days, but entreated the merciful God many times on your behalf, so that your virginity might not be stolen.

[3]"Paul, the herald of God said to me, 'Her virginity certainly will not be stolen, and she will come quickly.' [4]Probus said to me, 'It has been given to her by God to be troubled in this way. Do you see how through many means God saves many?' But now, my beloved sister, after unexpectedly seeing your face, I will die happily."

Polyxena's former abducter is baptized by Paul

42 [1]The one who had snatched away Polyxena came up and was looking for her again, but the great Paul convinced him to stay away from her. He believed and was baptized by Paul, and in the same way the suitor of Polyxena believed. [2]There was great joy in the entire city of Spain after the recovery of Polyxena. From then on, fearing temptations, she never left the blessed Paul.[b] [3]Because these things turned out in this way, everyone rejoiced in the Lord, glorifying the Father and the Son and the Holy Spirit, the one God to whom be glory and power now and always and forever and ever. Amen.

---

a. Strong emotional reactions at unlikely reunions are common in ancient novels. Cf. *Chaer.* 8.1, where Chaereas and Callirhoe are both overcome at their reunion and pass out.

b. Unlike Thecla, who undergoes severe trials after parting company with Paul, Polyxena wisely chooses to remain with the apostle.

III. Epistles

The Epistle of Christ from Heaven
A new translation and introduction

by Calogero A. Miceli

The *Epistle of Christ from Heaven* (*Ep. Chr. Heav.*; *CANT* 311)—also referred to as the *Letter(s) from Heaven, Sunday Letter(s), Leaflets from Heaven, Letter on the Observance of the Lord's Day,* and *Scrolls from Heaven*—is an ancient apocryphal letter purported to have been written by Jesus Christ and to have come down to earth from heaven. The work is comparable to a chain letter—a letter sent to a number of people, each of whom is requested to make and send copies of the letter to others who, in turn, will continue to do the same. The epistle is a fusion of several different literary genres (apocalyptic, prophetic, epistolary, sermonic, and legislative).[1] It exhorts its readers to observe the holy Day of the Lord (Sunday) and warns that those who fail in this observance or who do not own a copy of the letter will face terrible punishments as a consequence.

Contents

Ep. Chr. Heav. is a short letter attributed to Jesus, though at times the author fuses both Jesus and God into one speaker. Throughout the epistle, the author refers to having performed actions carried out by God in the Hebrew Bible (such as the creation of Adam and Eve, the giving of the commandments to Moses), as well as stating that he performed actions known to have been accomplished by Jesus in the New Testament (such as his resurrection, his baptism by John). This merging of characters is perhaps most evident when the author of the epistle deliberately refers to himself as God and then later as Christ (2:52; 2:56).

Over the centuries the letter has circulated widely and in numerous forms. As a result, copies of the text vary significantly from one place and language to another. The variations both within and between versions of the letters have made it difficult for scholars to establish an original version. The only constant between these many variations is that they instill an observance of Sunday, which is the primary purpose of the epistle.[2]

Most of the versions do not commence with the epistle directly; rather, they feature a framing narrative that offers a legendary account of the letter's delivery from heaven. In the American editions described by Edgar J. Goodspeed, for example, the author of the prescript writes anonymously in the first person and endorses the authorship of the letter from Jesus.[3] This endorsement also reveals that the epistle was found under an engraved stone by a child at the foot of Jesus' cross and was faithfully translated from its original Hebrew.[4] In other versions, the prescript claims that the letter fell down from heaven onto

---

1. Van Esbroeck, "Lettre sur le dimanche," 267.
2. Backus, "Lettre de Jésus-Christ," 1102; Delehaye, "Un exemplaire," 167.
3. Goodspeed, "Letter of Jesus Christ," 102–3.
4. Beskow, "Leaflets from Heaven," 26–27. Beskow notes that this variant coincides with the renowned legend of King Arthur.

the altar of a church (in some instances the church in question is located in Rome, while others use the setting of Jerusalem, Bethlehem, etc.), or that it was brought down to earth by the Archangel Michael or Gabriel. The version translated here begins with a story of the archbishop (or "high priest") of Rome who is visited by the apostle Peter in a dream and then witnesses the epistle miraculously appear before him, suspended in the air in the middle of the sanctuary—presumably St. Peter's Basilica (1:1–5). The bishop then reads the letter to his congregation and hereafter begin the contents of the letter itself. The letter ends with a return to the priest exhorting his community to keep the holy Day of the Lord. These frame stories work to promote the legend of the letter's divine acquisition and divine authority. In addition, since the letter vehemently urges its audience to read and copy the letter for others, there is no doubt that the story of the priest reading the epistle to his congregation provides a literary model for the proper conduct suggested by *Ep. Chr. Heav.*

The contents of the letter primarily concern the observation of Sunday. Jesus rebukes the audience for failing to have upheld the sacred day. *Ep. Chr. Heav.* explains why this day is so important by reminding the audience that it was on the Lord's Day that the heavens and the earth were first created, that the resurrection of Jesus took place, that God appeared to Moses on Mount Sinai, etc. (2:8–14). The author explains that continued noncompliance will result in stern consequences. The curses for violation are varied, but include burning in fire, divine judgment, inheriting the anathema, etc. (2:14–27). By the same token, the letter also provides rules for correct conduct, including the avoidance of superfluities, the keeping of the commandments, and continuous church attendance (2:34–38). Aside from keeping the holy Sunday, the letter also demands other types of observances, such as belief in the Scriptures, and condemnation of such sins as adultery and usury (2:39–46). In some versions of the epistle, the author writes that the reader needs to fast on Good Friday and the proceeding four Fridays as a commemoration of the five wounds Jesus received for all of humanity.[5] The person who honors the holy Sunday, however, will be blessed and will avoid judgment (2:55–56).

In order to ensure compliance with the letter's demands, the author threatens curses on priests who do not read the letter to their congregations (2:34, 47), and anathema on those who challenge the letter's authenticity (2:32). In some versions, the epistle offers reassurance for those who keep a copy of the letter in their home and makes the claim that goodness and prosperity accompany the house where this epistle is found.[6]

Manuscripts and Versions

Today, there exist numerous versions of *Ep. Chr. Heav.* in a dizzying number of ancient and modern languages, including Greek, Armenian, Syriac, Arabic, Coptic, Ethiopic, Latin, Russian, Modern Greek, French, English, German, Italian, Polish, Spanish, etc. It has been said that the letter's "countless forms defy any rigorously scientific classification, and the innumerable variants are in themselves a striking witness to its popularity."[7]

Concerning the original language of the epistle, it is generally assumed that the text was composed in Greek; however, certainty in the matter is elusive.[8] In his study of the

---

5. Goodspeed, "Letter of Jesus Christ," 111.

6. Goodspeed, "Letter of Jesus Christ," 113.

7. Norman H. Baynes, review of Robert Priebsch, *Letter from Heaven on the Observance of the Lord's Day*, *The Modern Language Review* 32, no. 4 (1937): 650.

8. Backus, "Lettre de Jésus-Christ," 1103–6; Erbetta, "Lettera della Domenica" (*Apocrifi del Nuovo Testamento*, 115–18), 114.

text, Maximilian Bittner published versions of the epistle in several ancient languages including Greek, Armenian, Syriac, Garšūnī, Arabic, and Ethiopic.[9] Of the twelve Greek witnesses used by Bittner, two of the oldest—Vatican, Biblioteca apostolica Vaticana, Barberinus gr. III 3, fol. 55–65 (dated 1497 CE)[10] and Paris, Bibliothèque nationale de France, gr. 929, pp. 548–61 (15th cent.)[11]—are believed to represent the earliest redaction of the text.[12]

Date and Provenance

The earliest mention of *Ep. Chr. Heav.* comes from the East at the end of the sixth century CE. It was at this time that bishop Vincent of Ibiza (an island off the eastern coast of Spain) had in his possession a document claiming to have fallen from heaven and to have been written by Jesus Christ. The bishop strongly believed in the legitimacy of this letter. As a result he made it known to his congregation and he sent a copy of it to bishop Licinian of Cartagena in Spain. Licinian's response, the *Epistola ad Licinianum Vincentium,* fervently condemns the text and calls for its destruction.[13] The epistle was later condemned as heretical at the Lateran Council in 745 CE.[14]

The question about the historical origin of *Ep. Chr. Heav.* is tied to the different textual traditions of the text: the Eastern tradition and the Western tradition.[15] The Eastern tradition boasts the most primitive version of the epistle, while the Western tradition includes a number of later redactions of the letter. Though the number of versions of the letter accessible to us today is abundant, an original date of the composition of *Ep. Chr. Heav.* is unknown. All that can be said for certain is that *Ep. Chr. Heav.* is at least as early as the sixth century CE based on its mention by Licinian.

Literary Context

Over the centuries of the epistle's existence, it has moved, morphed, and multiplied throughout the globe. It has been treasured in popular devotion, condemned by ecclesiastical authorities, utilized for protecting houses from fires, and worn as an amulet by the faithful to ward off disease and danger.[16] The letter's promise that one who copies it or proclaims its contents to others will not undergo the enumerated hardships has undoubtedly contributed to its popularity and widespread transmission. Like a chain letter, *Ep. Chr. Heav.* uses manipulative means to convince its recipients to make copies and pass them on to others. It exploits the superstitions of its recipients and threatens with commiserations or physical harm those who do not comply. These devices are what allowed for the long-term physical survival of the text throughout the centuries.

Ep. Chr. Heav. is one of only a handful of texts, all of them epistles, attributed directly to

---

9. Bittner, "Der vom Himmel gefallene Brief."

10. Transcribed in Bittner, "Der vom Himmel gefallene Brief," 11–16, reproduced from Vassiliev, *Anecdota greco-byzantina,* 23–28.

11. Transcribed in Bittner, "Der vom Himmel gefallene Brief," 16–21. Erroneously identified as gr. 925 in Backus, "Lettre de Jésus-Christ."

12. Erbetta, "Lettera della Domenica," in *Apocrifi del Nuovo Testamento,* 114.

13. For the Latin text of Licinian's letter see PL 72:689–700; an English translation is provided in Priebsch, *Letter from Heaven,* 1–3.

14. Beskow, "Leaflets from Heaven," 28.

15. For further information on dating the two traditions see van Esbroeck, "Lettre sur le dimanche," 270–81.

16. Stübe, *Der Himmelsbrief,* 1–4.

Jesus. The first of these is the letter to King Abgar of Edessa included in the Abgar Correspondence and incorporated later in the *Doctrina Addai*. The second is a letter mentioned in the *Narrative of Joseph of Arimathea* 3:4. Here Jesus, while hanging on the cross, writes a letter of introduction to the hosts of heaven for the good thief Demas, who will need it to precede Jesus into Paradise. And the third is the *Epistle to the Apostles* (or *Epistula Apostolorum*), which begins with a promise to offer the reader "what Jesus revealed to his disciples as a letter";[17] in reality, however, it is a letter by the apostles to all the churches and chiefly features a post-resurrection dialogue between the disciples and Jesus. Except for the Abgar Correspondence, all of these Jesus-penned epistles, *Ep. Chr. Heav.* included, are said to be composed by the risen or heavenly Jesus. The earthly Jesus, then, remains a figure of little literary accomplishment.

Translation

As pointed out by Backus, the great number of witnesses of *Ep. Chr. Heav.* and its wide transmission mean that a critical edition of the text is beyond reach.[18] Editors traditionally have chosen instead to publish translations of one or two particular manuscripts rather than endeavor to establish and translate something approximating an original text. Most often, Paris gr. 929 is chosen, since it is one of the earliest known sources.[19] The same strategy is employed here, with an English translation of Paris gr. 929 based on the transcription of Bittner.[20] The chapter and versification system is adopted from Backus; the subheadings are based on Erbetta's divisions of the text.

Bibliography

EDITIONS AND TRANSLATIONS

Backus, Irena. "Lettre de Jésus-Christ sur le dimanche." Pages 1101–19 in *EAC* 2.

Bittner, Maximilian. "Der vom Himmel gefallene Brief in seinen morgenländischen Versionen und Rezensionen." *Denkschriften der kaiserlichen Akademie der Wissenschaften: Philosophisch-historische Klasse* 51, no. 1 (1906): 1–240. (Comprehensive study of the tradition with versions published in numerous ancient languages, including the text of Paris gr. 929, pp. 16–21.)

Delehaye, Hippolyte. "Note sur la légende de la lettre du Christ tombée du ciel." Pages 171–213 in *Bulletin de l'Académie royale de Belgique: Classe de lettres*. Brussels: Hayez, 1899. [Repr. as pages 150–78 in Hippolyte Delehaye. *Mélanges d'hagiographie grecque et latine*. Subsidia Hagiographica 42. Brussels: Société des Bollandistes, 1966.] (Latin texts and a French version.)

———. "Un exemplaire de la lettre tombée du ciel." *RSR* 18 (1928): 164–68.

Erbetta, Mario. *Gli Apocrifi del Nuovo Testamento*. 3 vols. in 4. Turin: Marietti, 1966–1981. (The epistle is translated in vol. 3:113–18.)

---

17. English translation in *ANT* 555–88.

18. Backus, "Lettre de Jésus-Christ," 1107.

19. See Erbetta, "Lettera della Domenica"; De Santos Otero, "La Carta del Domingo" (*Evangelios Apócrifos*, 362–66); Stern, "La Salette et la légende des lettres tombées du ciel" (*La Salette*, 375–92). Backus ("Lettre de Jésus-Christ") translates Paris gr. 929 along with Munich, Bayerische Staatsbibliothek, lat. 9550. Goodspeed takes a different approach, printing three different English sources in parallel columns ("Letter of Jesus Christ," 102–3; reproduced in Beskow, "Leaflets from Heaven," 25–26).

20. Bittner, "Der vom Himmel gefallene Brief," 16–21.

Santos Otero, Aurelio de. *Los Evangelios Apócrifos.* 2nd ed. Madrid: Biblioteca de Autores Cristianos, 1963. (The epistle is translated on pp. 670–82.)

Vassiliev, Athanasius. *Anecdota graeco-byzantina, pars prior.* Moscow: Imperial University, 1893. (Greek text of Vatican, Barberinus gr. III 3.)

STUDIES

Beskow, Per. *Strange Tales about Jesus: A Survey of Unfamiliar Gospels.* Philadelphia: Fortress, 1983. (The epistle is discussed on pp. 25–30.)

Esbroeck, Michel van. "La Lettre sur le dimanche descendue du ciel." *AnBoll* 107 (1989): 267–84.

Goodspeed, Edgar J. *Strange New Gospels.* Chicago, Ill.: University of Chicago Press, 1931. (The epistle is discussed on pp. 96–107.)

Priebsch, Robert. *Letter from Heaven on the Observance of the Lord's Day.* Oxford: Basil Blackwell, 1936.

Stern, Jean. "La Salette et la légende des lettres tombées du ciel." Pages 375–92 in vol. 1 of *La Salette: Documents authentiques: Dossier chronologique intégral.* Collection Sanctuaires, Pèlerinages, Apparitions. 3 vols. Paris: Desclée de Brouwer, 1980–1991.

Stübe, Rudolf. *Der Himmelsbrief: Ein Beitrag zur allgemeinen Religionsgeschichte.* Tübingen: J. C. B. Mohr, 1918.

The Epistle of Christ from Heaven

Introduction

In the name of the Father, and of the Son, and of the Holy Spirit. Amen. Discourse concerning Sunday, the holiest of days, on which Jesus Christ, our Lord and God, rose from death. Praise, Lord.[a]

The epistle is sent to the altar

1 [1]Epistle of our Lord, God, and Savior Jesus Christ, sent to ancient Rome to the basilica[b] of the holy apostle and first leader Peter, to whom Christ said, "*You are Peter, and on this rock I will build my church, and the gates of Hades will not prevail against it. I will give you the keys of the kingdom of heaven, and whatever you bind on earth will be bound in heaven, and whatever you loose on earth will be loosed in heaven.*" [2]The epistle remained suspended in the middle of the basilica in the sanctuary. Peter, the great apostle, appeared to the bishop of Rome in a dream saying, "Get up, bishop, and see the undefiled epistle of our Lord Jesus Christ."

Matt 16:18–19

[3]The high priest got up trembling and went to the altar. Looking at the undefiled epistle in the middle of the basilica in the sanctuary, he cried out with tears, "You are great, Lord, and your works are wonderful, because you have made known to us the epistle for all the world." [4]Then he summoned all the people of the great church: the clerics, priests, monks, rulers, men, women, and children. For three days and three nights they said with tears, "Show us, Lord, the richness of your mercy, to the humble and unworthy people who pray for you."

Ps 86:10

Ps 84:8 LXX

[5]Then, at around nine o'clock in the morning, the undefiled epistle came down into the hands of the high priest and he welcomed and revered it with fear and trembling. Opening it, he found these things written. And it says:

2 Cor 7:15; Eph 6:5; Phil 2:12

Stubbornness and ingratitude

2 [1]"See now, humanity! Because I have given you the holy Sunday, but you have neither honored nor celebrated it, [2]I produced many afflictions and sent barbarian nations who shed your blood. But did you not repent nor hear the Gospel that says, '*Heaven and earth will pass away, but my words will not pass away*'? [3]I sent you storms, frosts, plagues, earthquakes, hail, locusts, grasshoppers, cat-

Mark 13:31 par.

---

a. This is a typical liturgical formula and evidence that the epistle was used in liturgical settings. See Backus, "Lettre de Jésus-Christ," 1109.

b. Lit.: temple.

erpillars, and many other afflictions for the sake of the holy Sunday, but none of you people repented. [4]I gave you grain, wine, oil, and other good things, but when you were filled, then again you did evil. [5]I was willing to destroy many humans for the sake of the holy Sunday, but again I had a change of heart because of the entreaty of my immaculate mother, the holy angels, apostles, martyrs, and even the Forerunner and Baptist. They turned my wrath away from you.

Num 18:12; Joel 2:19

Apoc. Virg. 34; *Liber Requiei* 100; *Apoc. Paul* 44

[6]"Widows, orphans, and beggars cry out in front of me, but you do not have mercy for them. The gentiles have mercy, but you Christians have no mercy. [7]Through Moses, I gave the law to the Hebrews and they did not break it. But to you I gave the holy Gospel, my law, and my baptism, but you did not keep these.

The history of Sunday

[8]"Do you not know, humanity, that I made the heavens and the earth on the first day and that I named it, 'the beginning of days and time', 'shining Sunday', 'great Passover', and 'resurrection'? On account of this all people who are baptized must honor, celebrate, and enter into God's holy church. [9]Do you not know that on the Friday I made Adam (the first-formed) and Eve, and again on the Friday I made the cross and endured the burial place, and on Sunday I made resurrection for the salvation of the world? [10]Because of this I gave you the commandments, so that on Wednesday and Friday all Christians fast from meat, cheese, and olive oil.

Gen 1:1–5

Gen 1:26–27

[11]"Do you not know that on the holy Sunday I lived in the house of Abraham because of his hospitality, when he sacrificed a young bull in hospitality of the holy Trinity? [12]Likewise on Sunday, I appeared to Moses on Mount Sinai and after he fasted forty days I gave him the tablets engraved by God (that is to say the Law). [13]On the holy Sunday my archangel Gabriel revealed the salutation (that is to say, the Annunciation). [14]Also on Sunday I received baptism by the Forerunner, so that I would provide an example to you, and you were not too arrogant to be baptized by poor priests (you were not arrogant; do not be arrogant with one who is poor). For John, the one who baptized me, wore nothing if he were not clothed with camel's hair, and he did not eat bread nor drink wine.

Gen 18:1–8

Exod 24:12; 31:18; 32:15–16

Luke 1:26–38

Mark 1:9–11 par.; John 1:29–34

Mark 1:6//Matt 3:4; Luke 1:15

[15]"Woe to the one who does not honor his godfather or his children! [16]Woe to the ones who trample the cross![a] [17]Do you not know that on the holy Sunday I shall judge the whole world and before me shall be standing kings and rulers; those who are rich and those who are poor; those who are naked and those who are ashamed? [18]I swear upon my exalted throne that if you do not observe the holy Sunday, the Wednesday, the Friday, as well as the distinguished holy festivals, I will send venomous wild beasts, so that they devour women's breasts (who then will be unable to breastfeed babies that do not have their mothers' milk), and savage wolves to snatch away your children. [19]Cursed is the one who does not honor the holy Sunday from three o'clock on Saturday until dawn on Monday, or the one who neither fasts nor eats dried foods on Wednesdays and Fridays! [20]Glorify my great name!

Heb 4:13

Apoc. Pet. 8:5

---

a. The term for "those who trample the cross" is not attested anywhere else, but twice in this epistle (here and in 2:28).

Woes and warnings

[21]"If you do not do these things I will not send another epistle. Instead I will open the heavens and I will make it rain fire, hail, and boiling water because humanity does not understand. [22]I will create terrible earthquakes, I will make it rain blood and ashes in April, I will wipe away all of the seeds, vineyards, and plants, I will destroy your sheep and animals, for the sake of the holy Sunday. [23]I will send winged wild beasts so they may consume your flesh in order that you may say, 'Open the tombs, those of you sleeping since the world began, and hide us from the punishment of the almighty Lord God!' [24]I will obscure the sun's light and spread dark clouds, as I did to the Egyptians through my servant Moses. [25]I will send the people of the Ishmaelites, so that by the sword they will enslave and kill you in a cruel death. [26]Then you will weep and you will regret, [27]but I will turn my face away not to hear you, on account of the holy Sunday.

[28]"O criminals, liars, adulterers, rebels, unbelievers, adversaries, enemies, traitors, schemers, blasphemers, hypocrites, abhorrers, false prophets, atheists, underminers,[a] eluders,[b] murderers, haters of your own children, tramplers of the cross, coveters of evil, disobeyers, slanderers, haters of the light and lovers of the darkness, those who say, 'We love Christ, but we despise our neighbor,' those who hate and consume the beggars, [. . .].[c] How much do those that do these things have to repent on the day of judgment? [29]How does the earth not split open and swallow you down alive? [30]Because they do the devil's works, they will inherit the curse along with Satan and, like dust, their children will disappear from the face of the earth.

[31]"By my immaculate mother, by the many-eyed cherubim, and John my Baptist, the epistle was not composed by a human, but it is written at full length by the unseen Father. [32]If there is a person who bears ill will and who is of low reputation, who comes upon this and says, 'The epistle is not from God,' then the person and their home will inherit the same curse as Sodom and Gomorrah; their soul will go into the outer fire, because they do not believe. [33]The things that are impossible for humans are possible for God.

[34]"Woe to the priest who does not receive and read this epistle in front of the people! [35]Woe also to that city and those people who do not listen to this with all of their heart! [36]Woe to the person who mistreats and dishonors the priest, [37]since the person does not mistreat the priest, but the church of God, their faith, and their baptism! For the priest prays on behalf of all of the people: on behalf of the ones who hate him and the ones that love him. [38]Woe to the ones who speak to one another during the divine service and who scandalize the priest who prays for their sins! For the priest and the deacon pray on behalf of the high priest and on behalf of the Christian people.

---

a. Emendation suggested by Bittner, "Der vom Himmel gefallene Brief," 19. The manuscript has *hydon nomiatai*.

b. The Greek word *parakampanistai* is not attested in lexicons. Backus believes the word is formed from the root verb *parakamptō*, which she takes to mean "to dodge" or "to rob." Consequently she translates the words as "robbers" ("Lettre de Jésus-Christ," 1113, fn). However, LSJ suggests "to bend aside," "to avoid," and "to shun" as possible translations of this verb. "Eluders" better captures the sense of the word.

c. The word *ptōchous* is repeated, followed by *tas kopas*.

Matt 27:52

Exod 10:21–23; 14:19–20

Ps 27:9; 30:7

Num 16:30

Ezek 10:12; Rev 4:6, 8

Gen 19:24–25

Mark 10:27 par.

³⁹"Woe to those who do not honor their godfather! He carried the cross of Christ into your home and through baptism he became a second father to you. ⁴⁰Woe to the ones who do not believe in the divine Scriptures! ⁴¹Woe to the ones who unite house with house and field with field so that the neighbor cannot spread out! ⁴²Woe to the ones who deprive their laborers of wages! ⁴³Woe to the ones who lend their money at interest, because they will be condemned with Judas! ⁴⁴Woe to the monk who does not remain with the monastery and the holy church of God! ⁴⁵Woe to the monk who commits fornication! ⁴⁶Woe to the one who abandons their spouse and is devoted to another! ⁴⁷Cursed is the priest that does not read this in front of the people, because he shuts the kingdom of God in front of them; he does not enter nor does he let in those that want to enter.

Isa 5:8

Jer 22:13; Jas 5:4

Matt 23:13

⁴⁸"Blessed is the priest who has and reads this epistle in front of the people and sends a written copy of it to another city and country. Truly I tell you, on the day of judgment he will find his reward and the pardon of his sins. ⁴⁹Woe to the master of the house who is not productive, because he will be burned in fire like an unproductive tree! ⁵⁰Woe to the one who brings gifts into the church, but has a conflict with their neighbors! ⁵¹Woe to the priest who celebrates the liturgy and lifts holy things while in conflict; for he is not celebrating alone, but the angels celebrate with him!

Matt 5:23

⁵²"I, God, am first; I am after all these things, and there is only me, no other. ⁵³Where will you escape from my presence? Where will you hide? ⁵⁴I examine hearts and minds,^a I know people's thoughts and I will make the secrets clear. ⁵⁵I command that all humans faithfully confess what they have done since their youth to the spiritual father, for he has been appointed by me and by my holy church to unfasten and retain the sins of the people. ⁵⁶Blessed is the one who honors the holy Sunday; I, Christ, blessed it and it will be blessed."

Ps 139:7

Ps 7:10 LXX; Jer 11:20; 17:10; 20:12; Rev 2:23

Ps 94:11; 1 Cor 3:20

Words of the archbishop

3 ¹Now the archbishop, the Pope of Rome, said to all, "Siblings and children of our humility, listen. O kings and lords, be wise and learn to do good. Judge and listen to what is righteous, O patriarchs, citizens, bishops, leaders, spiritual priests, monks, deacons, and all of the Christian people of the Lord! ²Keep what has been appointed by the Lord Christ because of the holy Sunday, in order that you have peace in the present world. ³Humans have nothing without pure love. Just as meats without salt are worthless and tasteless, thus humans without love are worthless. ⁴Because of this I implore you to keep and honor the holy Sunday and the resurrection—just as it is called—and the distinguished festivals, so that you may find compassion on the day of judgment and in Christ Jesus our Lord ⁵who is the glory and the power forever. Amen.

1 Cor 13:2–3

Mark 9:50 par.

---

a. The word *nephrous* literally means "kidneys," but is translated as "mind" since, in this case, the word is being used metaphorically as the site of human emotions, temperament, and wisdom.

The Epistle of Pseudo-Dionysius the Areopagite to Timothy concerning the Deaths of the Apostles Peter and Paul
A new translation and introduction

by David L. Eastman

The pseudepigraphical letter ostensibly from Dionysius the Areopagite (*Ep. Tim. Dion.*; *CANT* 197), one of the first Athenian converts of the apostle Paul (Acts 17:34), to Timothy, a protégé of Paul, is one of many texts produced in the late antique and early medieval periods that reflect later, often fanciful, traditions about the apostles' deaths.[1] This text stands out from the others, however, in that it is an epistle, rather than one of the apocryphal acts or a martyrdom, and includes lengthy passages of praise and mourning. The traditional title highlights Peter and Paul equally, but the emphasis is primarily on Paul and his legacy. This Pseudo-Dionysius must be distinguished from the Christian Neoplatonic theologian and philosopher of the fifth or sixth century CE.

Contents
The letter opens with praise for Timothy, who is credited with having endured many hardships and abuses alongside his master, Paul (1). In the New Testament Timothy is not known to have been, for example, shipwrecked with Paul, yet here he is presented as having done so. The author then turns to praise of Paul as the great teacher, destroyer of sin and demons, enemy of the Jews, builder of the church, etc. (2). Praise gives way to lament at the loss of so great a spiritual father, who will no longer send letters from abroad. Paul's disciples are destitute at the death of the last one who could open and explain the Scriptures, and Dionysius says they should weep like the prophets Amos and Jeremiah (3).

The author finally turns his attention to the martyrdoms to which he claims to have been an eyewitness (4–7). The two foundations of the church, he bemoans, were lost on a single day and have left the church orphans. Dionysius calls upon Timothy to hold a feast in honor of their sufferings and describes the chaotic scene as the apostles were led away to their deaths. When Peter and Paul were separated, he followed Paul and saw his bloody end. The author then shifts back into mourning and reports that he saw Peter and Paul ascending into heaven after their deaths. A woman named Lemobia also saw their ascent. She had given Paul a veil, which he had used to collect his own blood and then returned to her before his ascent (8). With yet more appeals to the Hebrew Bible, the author rejoices that Peter and Paul will never again be separated and renews his encouragement to Timothy to hold a vigil in honor of their deaths. The letter ends with a story about Paul's head, which was initially lost but later discovered by a shepherd. Miraculous signs drew the attention of the Roman bishop, and a further miracle confirmed that the true head had been restored to Paul's body (9).

---

1. For additional texts see Eastman, *Ancient Martyrdom Accounts.*

Manuscripts and Editions

The epistle survives in a number of manuscripts of various languages:[2]

1. Latin (*BHL* 6671; editions by Mombrizio and Martin)[3]

Admont, Stift Admont, 383 (14th cent.)

Bamberg, Staatliche Bibliothek, Q. III. 33 [Msc. Theol. 93] (15th cent.)

Brussels, Bibliothèque royale, 1900–1905[4] (15th cent.), 2415–18[5] (14th cent.)

Cesena, Istituzione Biblioteca Malatestiana, D.XI.7 (15th cent.)

Dijon, Bibliothèque Municipale, Ancien Fonds 640–41 (11th/12th cent.)

Klosterneuburg, Stift Klosterneuburg, 1112 (date undetermined)

Liège, Université, 57 (15th cent.), 134 (15th cent.)

Lilienfeld, Stift Lilienfeld, 96 (1263)

Melk, Stift Melk, 363 (15th cent.), 722 (15th cent.)

Milan, Biblioteca Ambrosiana, 3 supp. (date undetermined), 25 supp. (1231–1285), 139 supp. (date undetermined), 202 supp. (date undetermined), 216 supp. (1426–1475), 251 inf. (1376–1425)[6]

Munich, Universitätsbibliothek der LMU, lat. 18535 [Tegernsee 535a] (15th cent.)

Oxford, Bodleian Library, N–044 (1478)

Paris, Bibliothèque nationale de France, 3711[7] (14th cent.)

Prague, Státní Knihovan, XIII.E.14.c (1303)

Rostock, Kloster zum Heiligen-Kreuz, 56 (14th cent.)

Stams, Stift Stams, 5 (14th/15th cent.)

Vienna, Dominikanerkirche, 78 (15th cent.)

Vienna, Österreichische Nationalbibliothek, Lat. 3662 (15th cent.), 3926[8] (14th cent.), 4067 (15th cent.), 4248 (15th cent.), 4576 (15th cent.), 4936 (15th cent.), 4940 (15th cent.)

Vienna, Schottenstift, 29 (15th cent.)

Würzburg, Universitätsbibliothek, Mch. q. 156 (15th cent.)

2. Syriac (*BHO* 968; edition by Martin)[9]

London, British Library, Add. 17214 (7th cent.)

Paris, Bibliothèque nationale de France, Syr. 234 [143] (13th cent.), 235 [144] (13th cent.)

Vatican, Biblioteca apostolica, syr. Nitria 123 [19] (8th cent.?); syr. Ebedjesu 18 (14th cent. or earlier)

---

2. This the first comprehensive list of the manuscript evidence for *Ep. Tim. Dion.*

3. Mombrizio, "Epistola beati Dionisii Ariopagite"; Paulin Martin, "Dionysii Areopagitae," 261–71.

4. The Royal Library inventory number is 1900–05, but it is listed as 1063 in Joseph Van den Gheyn, *Catalogue des manuscrits de la Bibliothèque royale de Belgique* (Brussels: Lamertin, 1902), 2:114–15. See also Hagiographi Bollandiani, *Catalogus codicum hagiographicorum bibliothecae regiae Bruxellensis* (2 vols.; Brussels: Polleunis, Ceuterick and Lefébure, 1886 and 1889), 1:309–13.

5. Listed as 1423 in Gheyn, *Catalogue*, 2:338.

6. Martin ("Dionysii Areopagitae," 261) also notes the presence of the text in Biblioteca Ambrosiana 139, but the catalogue of the Ambrosian Library shows no record of this copy.

7. The number is incorrectly given as 3721 in Gabriel Théry, "Catalogue des manuscrits dionysiens des bibliothèques d'Autriche," *Archives d'histoire doctrinale et littéraire du Moyen Age* 10/11 (1935/1936): 163–264 at 174.

8. The number is incorrectly given as 3296 in Richard A. Lipsius, *Die apokryphen Apostelgeschichten und Legenden* (Braunschweig: Schwetschke, 1887), 2.1:227.

9. Martin, "Dionysii Areopagitae," 241–49.

3. Armenian (*BHO* 966–67; editions by Martin and Tsherakian)[10]
Jerusalem, Gulbenkian Library, 74 (1318)
Muş (Mush), Surb Karapet, 333 (date undetermined)[11]
Paris, Bibliothèque nationale de France, Arm. 118 [46/3] (1307), 120 [47] (14th cent.)
Venice, San Lazzaro degli Armeni, 17 (1224), 200, 201, 204, 301 (dates undetermined), 693 (13th cent.), 1014 (12th/13th cent.), 1252 (1695), 1553 (1215), 2154 (17th/18th cent.), 2724 [301] (18th cent.)
Yerevan, Matenadaran, 993 (date undetermined)

4. Georgian[12]
Mount Athos, Iviron, 57, 59 (dates undetermined)
Oxford, Bodleian Library, Georg.b.1 (1038–1040)
Tbilisi, National Centre of Manuscripts, A–382 (date undetermined)
Tbilisi, Tbeth, A–19 (8th/9th cent.)

5. Arabic (edition by Watson)[13]
Aleppo, Fondation Salem—Sbath, 1008 (1310)
Beirut, Université *Saint-Joseph,* 510 (18th cent.), 511 (1867), 512 (16th cent.)
Beirut, American University, 1194 (18th cent.)
Cairo, Coptic Museum, 296 (date undetermined), 311B (13th/14th cent.)
Edgbaston, University of Birmingham, Mingana ar. Christ. 92 [87b] (17th cent.); syr. 461 [Garšūnī] (19th cent.)
Göttingen, Universitätsbibliothek, ar. 104 (17th/18th cent.), 105 (1268)
Jerusalem, Holy Sepulcher, ar. 46 (13th cent.)
Jerusalem, Church of St. Anna, 38 (1874), 84 (1900)
Jerusalem, Church of St. Mark, 53 [Garšūnī] (1732/33)
Lebanon, Syro-Catholic Monastery of Charfet, ar. 2/4 (14th cent.)
Leiden, Universiteit Leiden, Or. 129 (14th/15th cent.)
Mount Sinai, St. Catherine's Monastery, ar. 268, 405, 448, 475, 482, 502, 539 (dates undetermined)[14]
Oxford, Bodleian Huntington, 383 (date undetermined)
Paris, Bibliothèque nationale de France, Syr. 4771 (19th cent.)
Vatican, Biblioteca apostolica, syr. 196 [Garšūnī; also listed as 77] (1551); ar. 43 (1313); Borg. ar. 200 (1670); Sbath 86 (16th cent.), 523 (17th cent.)
Watson, Syria (17th cent.)[15]

---

10. Martin, "Dionysii Areopagitae," 249–54; Tsherakian, *Libri apostolorum spurii*, 110–22. See also *Synaxarium armenium e recensione Ter-Israel* (Constantinople, 1834), Appendix 45–47; and the French translation of Tsherakian in Leloir, *Écrits apocryphes*, 173–88.

11. The manuscript was recorded in the late nineteenth century, but the monastery was destroyed in 1915 during the pogroms against Armenians in that region. This copy, therefore, may no longer survive.

12. There is, as yet, no critical edition of the Georgian tradition.

13. Watson, "Arabic Version."

14. In the introduction to her catalogue of the St. Catherine manuscripts, Margaret Dunlop Gibson notes with sadness that the title pages and final leaves of most of the manuscripts had been removed, rendering accurate dating impossible for any of these copies. See *Catalogue of the Arabic Mss. in the Convent of S. Catharine on Mount Sinai* (StSin 3; London: Clay, 1894), viii.

15. This manuscript is the basis of Watson's edition and translation. Of its origins, Watson states, "It

6. Ethiopic (*BHO* 970; edition by Budge)[16]

London, British Library, Orient. 677 (18th cent.), 678 (15th cent.), 679 (18th cent.), 680 (18th cent.), 681 (18th cent.), 682 (18th cent.), 683 (17th cent.), 684 (18th cent.), 685 (18th cent.)

Paris, Bibliothèque nationale de France, Abbadie 64 (date undetermined)[17]

Behind all these versions there appears to lie a Greek original. The Latin preserves several loanwords that suggest a Greek *Vorlage,* as does the inclusion of the story of the discovery of Paul's lost head, which another source suggests was originally written in Greek.[18] Johann Albert Fabricius reports the presence of Greek manuscripts in Florence and Vienna, but it appears that these alleged Greek copies do not exist.[19]

The relationship between the other versions has been the matter of some debate. At first reading, one can easily discern some similarities between the Syriac, Armenian, Georgian, Arabic, and Ethiopic versions over against the Latin, including the addition of theological commentary. These additions suggest a translation and editing history that is distinct from, and later than, the Latin. They also allow us to group these Eastern versions together, even if closer inspection reveals a number of minor variations among them. Which of these came first, then? The Syriac appears to be the oldest, based on details in the text and the manuscript history. However, W. Scott Watson claimed to have evidence that the Arabic may be older than all other translations and intended to demonstrate the point in a future publication, but there is no evidence that he ever did so.[20] Louis Leloir has shown that the Armenian does not follow the Syriac in every detail, but his work overall still suggests significant dependence on the Syriac.[21]

Genre, Structure, and Prosody

The frame of the text is structured as an epistle, with opening and closing salutations, but overall the text falls more into the genre of *consolation*. Consolations date back to classical Greece. By the Roman period this genre had gained a firm foothold among philosophers of the upper class, who seemed to assume that grief could be treated with a dose of philosophical argumentation. Cicero, for example, wrote numerous letters of consolation to

---

is from a manuscript obtained by me in Syria that, though without a date, is probably of the seventeenth century" ("Arabic Version," 225).

16. Budge, *Contendings of the Apostles,* 1:50–65 (Ethiopic), 2:51–69 (English).

17. This manuscript is listed in Antoine d'Abbadie, *Catalogue raisonné de manuscrits éthiopiens* (Paris: L'imprimerie impériale, 1859), 75. Abbadie's private collection of manuscripts went to the Bibliothèque nationale de France after his death.

18. The *Martyrdom of Paul the Apostle and the Discovery of His Severed Head (Mart. Head Paul),* translation in Eastman, *Ancient Martyrdom Accounts,* 203–17.

19. Johann Albert Fabricius, *Bibliothecae graecae* (14 vols.; Hamburg: C. Liebezeit, 1705–1728), 5:6–7. Fabricius cites Peter Lambeck as his source for the Vienna manuscripts. Scholars have continued to reproduce references to these manuscripts, but my correspondence with both libraries produced no evidence of their existence.

20. Watson, "Arabic Version," 225: "To the material for the critical study of this epistle I now add a hitherto unprinted Arabic translation that appears not only to have been made directly from the lost original, although already interpolated, Greek text, but also to show that an Arabic form lies back of three, if not of all, of the other versions." In a footnote Watson indicates that he will argue for the primacy of the Arabic version "at some future time." Princeton University holds Watson's unedited, collected papers, and the librarian there confirmed that no additional publications related to this text are known.

21. Leloir, *Écrits apocryphes,* 173–88.

friends who had lost loved ones. Slightly later the philosopher Seneca wrote three famous letters of consolation: one to Marcia after the death of her son, one to Polybius after the death of his brother, and one to his own mother, Helvia, who was grieving that Seneca himself was in exile. Thus, the epistolary form was sometimes part and parcel of the genre of consolation. In the early Christian period, authors such as Ambrose, Jerome, and Paulinus of Nola employed and modified the genre for their own purposes.[22]

In some, but not all consolations, the author eulogizes the dead at length, and this is a notable feature of this pseudo-Dionysian text. The death of Paul is particularly highlighted in this way, for his many sufferings and great deeds make his death all the more lamentable. Here, however, the author departs from the norms of the classical genre, for his goal is not so much to make Timothy feel better as to inspire him to establish a festival to commemorate the apostles (4, 9). In the case of this letter, we may also read the employment of the epistolary frame itself as homage to Paul, who was famous, as the author highlights, for writing letters to his disciples.

Notable in the latter portion of the text is the insertion of two miracle stories: Lemobia and her veil (8) and the discovery of Paul's head (9). The tale of Lemobia is clearly an adaptation of a story from other Pauline martyrdom accounts involving a woman who gives a scarf or veil to Paul and receives it back after his death. In the fourth-century Latin *Martyrdom of Paul* (*CANT* 211v), Paul sees a woman named Plautilla on his way to execution and asks for her scarf. He places it over his eyes at death and then comes back to return it to her, soaked with his blood. The Greek *Acts of the Apostles Peter and Paul* (*CANT* 193), probably produced in the sixth century, includes a very similar story involving a woman named Perpetua. In this version Perpetua is blind in one eye but is healed when she puts on the bloody scarf returned to her by Paul.[23] The pseudo-Dionysian version does not include a healing, but the posthumous—and in this case glorious—visitation by Paul is consistent with the tenor of these other accounts.

Scholars generally have not questioned the presence of this story in the original form of the letter, but there is reason to do so. The author is at pains to tell the story of the apostles' final moments together and their parting blessings to each other. He clearly states that they were separated from each other before their deaths and that he followed Paul and did not see Peter again until the apostles were ascending into heaven together (4–5, 8). In the Lemobia story, however, this pious woman asks where Paul's body is after his death. A soldier tells her that Paul lies "together with his friend there outside the city" (8). This information seems to contradict what the author had just said about their departure from each other before death. There is no suggestion that their bodies were carried back to the same place after execution, so this seam in the text indicates that the Lemobia story was inserted (a bit awkwardly) into the letter without any effort to resolve the discrepancy over

---

22. See e.g. Rudolf Kassel, *Untersuchungen zur griechischen und römischen Konsolationsliteratur* (Zetemata 18; Munich: Beck, 1958); Wilhelm Kierdorf, "Consolation as a Literary Genre," in *Brill's New Pauly* (Leiden: Brill, 2003), 2:704–6; J. H. D. Scourfield, *Consoling Heliodorus: A Commentary on Jerome, Letter 60* (OCM; Oxford: Oxford University Press, 1992); and the extensive bibliography in the footnotes in Paul A. Holloway, *Consolation in Philippians: Philosophical Sources and Rhetorical Strategy* (Cambridge: Cambridge University Press, 2001), 59–86.

23. *Mart. Paul* 14–17; *Acts Pet. Paul* 80. On the obvious parallels with the story of Veronica's Veil and the possible connection between this story and a relic in the Basilica of St. Paul on the Ostian Road, see David L. Eastman, *Paul the Martyr: The Cult of the Apostle in the Latin West* (SBLWGRWSup 4; Atlanta: Society of Biblical Literature; Leiden: Brill, 2011), 57–59.

whether Peter and Paul died separately or in the same place. Given the apparent popularity of the original Plautilla story, it is not surprising to find a modified form of it in a later epistle about Paul's death. Yet only in the Latin is the woman's name given as Lemobia. The story of the scarf does appear in the other versions (Syriac, Armenian, Ethiopic, Arabic, Georgian), but there the woman is unnamed and identified in some cases as a member of Nero's family. Some of the versions add the detail that Paul had previously baptized her. Thus, it appears that the scarf story was adapted from other texts and added to the epistle, where it was further adapted in the different translations. Here the Syriac and other Eastern versions could preserve a more original version of the text in which the woman is anonymous, for it is more likely that the name Lemobia would be added later by a Latin translator than omitted by Eastern scribes. On the other hand, details like membership in Nero's family could equally represent later expansions; so, again the precise history of the text defies easy explanation.

The narrative about the discovery of Paul's lost head is certainly a later addition to this letter. It is absent from some Syriac and nearly all the Armenian manuscripts, but even within manuscripts that include the account, it appears in different places. The Latin editor attaches it to the end of the letter with a clumsy transitional statement about Peter's head staying attached to his body. In the Syriac text used for Martin's edition, it is inserted earlier in the text, just after the author's initial description of the martyrdom itself (chap. 7 in this translation). The manuscript evidence alone, then, is enough to suggest that this was a freestanding piece inserted later. Further support for this theory comes from the fact that this story was also included in other manuscripts that did not replicate any other part of this epistle. It appears, for example, in a Syriac manuscript dated to around 500 CE. The editor includes the same story about Paul's head (*Mart. Head Paul*) and claims that his work represents the first translation of the text from Greek into Syriac. Therefore, the external and internal evidence concerning the history of transmission indicate that the miraculous story of Paul's head was not part of the original text of the letter.

Date and Provenance

No critical scholar gives credence to the ascription to Dionysius the Areopagite.[24] Beyond that point of agreement, the date and provenance of this text are difficult to discern, and scholarly opinion has varied. Paulin Martin (1883) argued for a fifth- or sixth-century date. Noting the existence of the seventh-century Syriac copy in the British Museum (Add. 17214), he took this as his *terminus ante quem*.[25] He then pushed the date back based on details in the miracle stories. He argued that the explicit reference to the ascent of the souls of Peter and Paul was a response to a controversy over the status of souls after death. This debate he placed at the very end of the fourth century, thus providing a potential *terminus post quem*. Furthermore, Martin claimed that in the story about the discovery of Paul's head, there are vestiges of debates about the moving of the apostles' bodies and the dates and relative chronology of their executions. He recognized that the head story itself is likely earlier than the rest of the text (see more on this below), but the perspective in this epistle on the aforementioned debates seemed to him to be at home in the fifth or sixth century. Martin offered no opinion on provenance, noting only that the text must have

---

24. This ascription might be due to the fact that Dionysius was traditionally a close follower of Paul (Acts 17:34) and could have stayed with his teacher to the end, but this is merely conjecture.

25. Martin, "Dionysii Areopagitae," iii-vii.

enjoyed wide acceptance in the East based on the manuscript evidence. Unfortunately, Martin's attempt to date the text based on the timing of particular theological controversies is problematic. The connections between this epistle and the controversies in question are not as clear as Martin would hope, and his arguments and conclusions simply ask too much of the evidence.

R. A. Lipsius initially offered a much later date for *Ep. Tim. Dion.*[26] He concluded that the head discovery story betrays a ninth-century date and Gallic provenance. In the ninth century, the church of Paris was actively promoting the conflation of Dionysius the Areopagite with Dionysius of Paris (St. Denis), a third-century Parisian bishop killed in the 250s during the Decian persecution. According to the legend told by Gregory of Tours (*Hist. Franc.* 1.30), this latter Dionysius was beheaded but then picked up his own head and carried it under his arm as he went about preaching. Lipsius concluded, therefore, that this epistle must be the work of the ninth-century Gallic church, here linking an association with Dionysius with a story about a beheaded saint who continues to move around after death—in Paul's case being functional enough to collect his own blood and deliver the scarf to Lemobia. The name Lemobia seemed to Lipsius to confirm his theory, for he read it as a variant of Lemovica, the ancient name for the city of Limoges in France—although the logic of a connection between this story and the city of Limoges is unclear. He did mention in a footnote that a feast in honor of the "discovery of the head of saint Paul the apostle" (February 25) is listed in a sixth-century Roman calendar known as the *Martyrology of Jerome*. However, this did not impact his dating, as he still placed the letter in the ninth century. Just three years later, Lipsius revised his theory based on Martin's work. He acknowledged a rhetorical style that could fit in either the fifth or the eighth/ninth century. He agreed with Martin that the head story pre-dates the rest of the letter and demonstrated that this story is missing from some of the earliest manuscripts in Syriac, Armenian, and Ethiopian. He also recognized the challenge to his previous dating posed by a seventh-century Syriac copy. Ultimately, he conceded that the letter in its original form may be earlier than he had thought but still argued that the Latin text, at least, took its final form in the ninth century. The subsequent work on the epistle by Théry and Leloir is notable, but they have not offered significant contributions on dating or provenance.

Based on details of the terminology in this text and the manuscript evidence cited above, the most likely date for this epistle is the late sixth or early seventh century. This dating is based on two factors: 1) In the reused story of Paul's lost and rediscovered head, the Latin text refers to the Roman bishop not as the bishop *(episcopus)* or pope *(papa)*, but as the patriarch *(patriarcha)*. The term patriarch was first used by the emperor Justinian I (527–565 CE) in *Novella* 131 as a title set aside for the heads of the five major episcopal sees in the Roman Empire (the Pentarchy): Rome, Constantinople, Alexandria, Antioch, and Jerusalem.[27] The presence of the term *patriarcha* in the Latin—a direct transliteration of the Greek term—strongly suggests that this was the title given in the original text, which therefore must date from the time of Justinian or later.[28] 2) The existence of a Syriac manuscript before the end of the seventh century provides the *terminus ante quem*. Some time must have elapsed between the production of the letter in Greek and the translation

---

26. Lipsius, *Die apokryphen Apostelgeschichten,* 227–31.

27. Adrian Fortescue, *The Orthodox Eastern Church* (repr. Piscataway, N.J.: Gorgias, 2001), 21–25. The Council in Trullo officially recognized and ranked these five sees in 692, but Justinian is the first to refer to their bishops as patriarchs.

28. The Syriac text also employs the direct transliteration *patriarca*.

into Syriac, so an early-seventh-century date for the original is to be preferred. Taken together, these details give us a likely range of about a century, between the middle of the sixth century and the middle of the seventh century.

The provenance is unclear. The author writes as if he were in Rome, for he claims to have witnessed firsthand the events of Paul's death in that city, but these eyewitness claims are spurious. Other details in the text, in fact, may suggest that the location of production was anywhere but Rome. First, when Lemobia asks a soldier where they have taken Paul, he states that Paul lies "outside the city in the valley of the fighters" (9). We cannot identify this location precisely, but a clue may come from the Syriac, Arabic, Armenian, and Ethiopic translations of this account. These versions employ terms that sound similar to each other but have no meaning in those languages: *Armeno* in Syriac, *Armanum* in Arabic, *Arerminon* in Armenian, and *Armaten or Armatul* in Ethiopic. It is possible that these forms are all taken from the Latin *Armamentaria*, a term used for the gladiatorial training facility (also known as the *Ludus Magnus*) located in a valley next to the Roman Colosseum. If this identification is correct, then the author of the epistle has made two mistakes. Domitian constructed the *Armamentaria* at the end of the first century CE in the valley between the Esquiline and Caelian hills, so it would not have existed at the time of Paul's death. In addition, the *Armamentaria* was built in a location that had been within the city walls since the construction of the Servian Wall in the fourth century BCE. Thus, Paul in fact would not have been lying "outside the city." The chronological and spatial problems could indicate a lack of familiarity with the layout of Rome. Even in an otherwise spurious text such as this, we might still expect an author familiar with Roman topography to get certain details right. Perhaps, then, the author knew only that the tombs of the apostles lay outside the city and assumed that all sites related to the apostles' deaths did as well.[29]

The second detail is found in the story about Paul's head, so it must be treated with caution. This text gives the Roman bishop's name as Fabellius, which is otherwise unattested. Why would an author in Rome, or at least familiar with the Roman church, make a mistake on the name of the bishop? The Syriac identifies the bishop as Sixtus (or Xystus), probably Sixtus II (257–258 CE). According to the *Burying of the Martyrs (Depositio martyrum)*, on 29 June 258, the Roman church celebrated the feast of "Peter in the Catacombs, of Paul on the Ostian Road." Scholars have interpreted the implications of this reference variously, but there is general agreement that a major celebration for Paul and Peter occurred in Rome during the time of Sixtus II.[30] Perhaps the original author of the missing head story knew about this date and included it in this account. The name Sixtus was taken into the Syriac version (that is, in those Syriac manuscripts that include the story) and influenced the other translations dependent upon it. As for the name Fabellius in the Latin, we are at a loss. It would be peculiar for any Roman author or editor to make such an error in assigning this story to a Roman bishop that had never existed.

Like Lipsius, I believe that we need to look outside Rome for the epistle's provenance, but Gaul is not compelling. I would instead suggest a location in the East, perhaps Constantinople. This would account for the production of the text in Greek, the relatively quick acceptance in the East and translation into Syriac and other languages, the seeming inaccuracies in Roman topography and episcopal history, and the adoption of the term

---

29. If the translators of certain versions (e.g., Syriac, etc.) attempted to connect this story to the *Armamentaria*, then this might be another example of only general, indirect knowledge of the city of Rome.

30. For a critique of previous scholarship and a new interpretation, see Eastman, *Paul the Martyr*, 95–97.

patriarch from the legal code of Justinian, whose capital was Constantinople. In the final analysis, however, the provenance of this text, like its authorship, remains a mystery.

Literary Context

The epistle draws heavily upon the Pauline corpus, as we might expect. Allusions to Paul's list of sufferings in 2 Corinthians open the letter, and the Pastoral Epistles are prominent, especially references to Paul's impending death that draw from 2 Timothy. The primary interest is biographical, rather than theological, so epistles such as Romans and Galatians are mined for titles that could be ascribed to Paul or for biographical details, rather than for reflections on doctrine. The text is also replete with allusions to the Hebrew Bible. Language used for God in the Psalms is ascribed to Paul: "a father of orphans, a zealous defender of widows, a comforter of the lame, the strength of the broken" (2:5). The author's angst at the death of the apostles is expressed through the words of Jacob and David, the Psalms, and the lamentations of the prophets Jeremiah, Amos, and Joel. Peter and Paul are compared to Saul and Jonathan, who are not separated in death, just as they were not in life. As for Timothy, the supposed recipient of this letter, he is to pick up the mantle handed to him by Paul, just as Elisha received the spirit of his master Elijah. The density of Hebrew Bible and New Testament references is a striking feature of the text, and the epistle can be read as a tableau of provocative words and images from Scripture.

As we have seen above, two of the important extrabiblical sources for the present form of the epistle are other martyrdom accounts and the story of Paul's head. The Lemobia story in chapter 8 undoubtedly depends on the Plautilla narrative from the Latin *Mart. Paul* and may have some connection to the Greek *Acts Pet. Paul.* In addition, the general story of Peter's crucifixion and Paul's beheading could come from any number of late-antique martyrdom narratives or patristic sources, although it is notable that the author makes no reference to Peter's inverted crucifixion, a colorful detail generally highlighted in later literary and artistic references to the event. The description of the abusive crowd probably comes from traditions concerning the treatment of Jesus on the way to his crucifixion, and in this way the author implicitly links the suffering of the apostles with that of their Lord. As for the story of the discovery of Paul's head, we have seen that this text was circulating independently prior to this epistle and was inserted by later editors at different places in the text.

Concerning the temporal relationship between the deaths, the author departs from the earliest martyrdom accounts and draws upon patristic commentators. The second-century *Acts of Peter* and *Acts of Paul* suggest no relationship whatsoever between the days on which the apostles died. However, as the two deaths became increasingly linked as proof of the unity of the apostles and the authority of the Roman church, a temporal connection was also introduced. *Ep. Tim. Dion.* follows the tradition that the apostles died on the same day. This viewed was espoused by Jerome (*Vir. ill.* 5; *Tract. Ps.* 96.10) and Maximus of Turin (*Serm.* 1.2; 2.1; 9.1), and implied by Dionysius of Corinth (Eusebius, *Hist. eccl.* 2.25.8).[31] Of a different opinion were Ambrose of Milan (*Virginit.* 19.124), Augustine (*Serm.* 295.7; 381.1), Prudentius (*Perist.* 12.5, 21–22), Gregory of Tours (*Glor. mart.* 28), and Arator (*Act. apost.* 2.1247–49), all of whom thought the apostles died on the same day but a year apart. In either case, linking the martyrdoms in time was a later

---

31. A similar passage credited to Damasus of Rome is spurious. See Cuthbert H. Turner, ed., *Ecclesiae occidentalis monumenta iuris antiquissima* (2 vols. in 9; Oxford: Clarendon, 1899–1939), 1.2:157.

development among patristic authors, and Pseudo-Dionysius shows dependence on these later traditions.

Other martyrdom accounts report the tearful greeting of Peter and Paul when Peter arrives in Rome, but in this text the author highlights their somber departure from each other. Eventually, Roman tradition fixed the site of this final farewell on the Ostian Road, just south of the Gate of St. Paul. This prompted the founding of a small church, identified in older pilgrimage guides as the Chapel of the Farewell, the Chapel of the Parting, or the Chapel of Saints Peter and Paul. A plaque on the church bore an inscription that incorporated the parting greetings from Pseudo-Dionysius:

> On this spot Peter and Paul parted, when they went to martyrdom. Then Paul said to Peter, "Peace to you, founder of the churches and shepherd of the sheep and lambs of Christ." Peter then said to Paul, "Go in peace, preacher of good tidings, mediator and chief of the salvation of the just."

Mussolini tore down the church, but the plaque can still be seen in the church of Santissima Trinita dei Pellegrini in the Piazza dei Pellegrini in Rome.[32]

Translation

The translation is based on the updated Latin edition of Mombrizio, which was completed by Albin Brunet and Henri Quentin, two Benedictine monks at the Abbeye Saint-Pierre in Solesmes and published in 1910.[33] This edition relies heavily upon Martin, who had based his text primarily on Paris, Bibliothèque nationale de France, 3711 and Milan, Biblioteca Ambrosiana, supp. 139 and supp. 216.[34] The other manuscripts used by the monks to update Mombrizio are not specified, and the section numbers assigned by Martin are omitted in this edition. I have restored Martin's chapter divisions here and divided the text further into verses.

Bibliography

EDITIONS AND TRANSLATIONS

Budge, Ernest A. W. *The Contendings of the Apostles, Being the Histories of the Lives and Martyrdoms and Deaths of the Twelve Apostles and Evangelists.* 2 vols. London: Henry Frowde, 1899. (Edition and translation of the Ethiopic text.)

Leloir, Louis. *Écrits apocryphes sur les apôtres. Traduction de l'édition arménienne de Venise.* CCSA 3. Turnhout: Brepols, 1986. (Translation based on the edition by Tsherakian, pp. 173–88. Leloir's introductory material provides significant details about the Armenian manuscript tradition.)

Malan, Solomon C. *The Conflicts of the Apostles: An Apocryphal Book of the Early Eastern Church.* London: Nutt, 1871. (The epistle appears in English translation pp. 230–43.)

Martin, Paulin. "Dionysii Areopagitae." Pages 241–71 in Joannes B. Pitra, *Analecta sacra spicile-*

---

32. Mariano Armellini, *Le chiese di Roma dal secolo IV al XIX* (2 vols.; 2nd ed.; Rome: R.O.R.E., 1942), 2:1148–49.

33. The edition does not give credit to Brunet and Quentin; this information was obtained through personal correspondence with the Abbey.

34. Mombrizio, "Epistola beati Dionisii ariopagite"; Martin, "Dionysii Areopagitae," 261–71.

gio solesmensi 4: *Patres antenicaeni*. Paris: Roger & Chernoviz, 1883. (Editions of the Latin, Syriac, and Armenian texts.)

Mombrizio, Bonino. "Epistola beati Dionisii ariopagite de morte apostolorum Petri et Pauli ad Timotheum." Pages 354–57, 709–10 in volume 2 of *Sanctuarium seu Vitae sanctorum*. New edition by Albin Brunet and Henri Quentin. 2 vols. Paris: Fontemoing, 1909. (Edition of the Latin text.)

Tsherakian (Tcherakhian), K. *Libri apostolorum spurii: Libri apostolici non canonici*. Thesaurus litterarum armeniarum antiquarum et recentium 3. Venice: 1904, 110–22. (Armenian edition is based primarily on manuscript Venice, San Lazzaro degli Armeni, 1014.)

Watson, W. Scott. "An Arabic Version of the Epistle of Dionysius the Areopagite to Timothy." *AJSL* 16, no. 4 (1900): 225–41.

STUDIES

Eastman, David L. *Ancient Martyrdom Accounts of Peter and Paul*. WGRW 39. Atlanta: Society of Biblical Literature, 2015.

Lipsius, Richard A. *Die apokryphen Apostelgeschichten und Apostellegenden*. 2nd ed. Braunschweig: Schwetschke, 1890.

Théry, Gabriel. "Catalogue des manuscrits dionysiens des bibliothèques d'Autriche." *Archives d'histoire doctrinale et littéraire du Moyen Age* 10 (1935): 174–76.

The Epistle of Pseudo-Dionysius the Areopagite to Timothy concerning the Deaths of the Apostles Peter and Paul

Greeting to Timothy, Paul's close companion

1 ¹I greet you, lord disciple and spiritual son of our true father and good friend, you who fulfilled the will of your master and underwent with him trials and all kinds of sufferings. And you bore steadfastly contests and floggings. ²You also accepted with him hunger and thirst, and you received all kinds of abuse and contempt and tortures and oppression. You also were sold with him, laboring at all times and in afflictions with pain and bitterness.

2 Cor 6:4–5; 11:23–27

Acts Tim. 1:4

³Amid perturbations and trials and with diligence you carried out your ministry, unconquered in self-denying vigils and prayers and acts of grace in strength and in struggle. On voyages with him you were scorned and flogged, held in contempt and cast out by enemies and friends. ⁴Never were you reluctant to be obedient or to yield to your spiritual master, afflicted and dragged through the streets, flogged and torn apart, broken to pieces and reviled in every place with him. ⁵You endured shipwreck on the sea, tossed about with him in ships. You were wounded in cities, in distress and in abuses, insults, and reproaches, in prisons day and night with him, in chains and in iron bars and shackles. ⁶In these trials you were his companion. You suffered not only these, but harsher and innumerable torments and struggles with him.

Mourning the loss of our spiritual father and teacher

2 ¹He was the father of fathers, the teacher of teachers, and the shepherd of shepherds. He was crucified to the world, and he bore the marks in his own body of our Lord Jesus Christ. ²I am speaking of Paul, the deep well of wisdom, the greatest pitch-pipe and tireless preacher of truth, the noblest apostle who brought light to the churches, who strengthened the Christians, and who destroyed the gates of sin, like a sword[a] twice-sharpened. ³He put to flight the unbelievers and threw down the temples of idols. He demolished altars. He broke into pieces the abominable idols and destroyed their altars. ⁴He threw down and humiliated the dwelling places of demons and caused their festivals and their worship to cease. He was truly an earthly angel and a heavenly man, the image and likeness of divinity,[b] the glory of believers.

Gal 6:14, 17

---

a. This is a Greek loanword: *rhomphaia*.

b. Cf. *Acts Paul* 3:3, where Paul is described as follows: "a man small in size, bald-headed, bandy-legged, of noble mien, with eyebrows meeting, rather hook-nosed, full of grace. *Sometimes he seemed like a man, and sometimes he had the face of an angel*" (my emphasis; trans. Elliott, *ANT*).

Rom 9:3

[5]He was a friend of the penitent, an advocate for his own race, esteemed and longed for by the peoples of the Diaspora. He was an enemy of the Jews, held in contempt by the Pharisees, the destroyer of their synagogue.[a] [6]He was a builder of the assembly of the saints and present to those in spiritual anxiety. He was a

Eph 6:16; Rom 15:16;
1 Cor 4:1; 2 Cor 11:23

shield of faith,[b] a servant of Christ, a herald of his gospel, a divine mouth, and a spiritual tongue. [7]He was an examiner of divine utterances, a seeker of the lost,

Luke 19:10; Ps 68:5;
145:14; 146:8

a father of orphans, a zealous defender of widows, a comforter of the lame, the strength of the broken. [8]He was an ornate ship with sails, attacking on the raging waves. He was a shipmaster diligent in spiritual wisdom, arranging all things well out of affection and longing for unwavering unity. [9]He was an enemy of heretics and those corrupt in mind, a diligent father and most excellent shepherd, a very great master and a pleasant and spiritual teacher. He was a holy craftsman,

1 Cor 9:26

a glorious architect, and an eager boxer. [10]He was holy and most worthy, and his divinely formed spirit has abandoned us all. [11]I say that we are poor and unworthy in this contemptible and wicked world, but he went forth to Christ his God and Lord and friend.

3 [1]O my brother, dear to my soul, where is your spiritual father, O good disciple and lover of his master? From what far-off place will he greet you? From the sea or from the desert? From Galatia or from Spain? From Asia or from Corinth? [2]Behold, you have indeed been made an orphan and have remained

2 Tim 4:6–7

alone. He has departed, and your course is complete, which you were making with your spiritual father, or because of which you were proceeding quickly to him. [3]And now by no means will he write to you with his most holy hand, saying

2 Tim 1:2

"*my beloved child.*" And he will not send to you from far away, calling, "*Do your*

2 Tim 4:9

best to come to me soon. I am waiting for you in such and such a city." [4]O dearest brother Timothy, you have finished your course, because you wrote and said to me: "If you have heard, where is my master? Tell me, so that I may hurry to him." [5]Today is fulfilled what the Lord said to his disciples, "Although you will desire

John 7:34

your master for one hour, you will not see him."

[6]Woe to me, brother Timothy, because this day of sadness and shadows and loss has befallen us, for we have been orphaned. Who will give water to our eyes

Jer 9:1

and fountains of tears to us orphans, so that we may weep day and night for the light of the churches, because it has been extinguished? [7]Brother, fold up the books of the prophets and place a seal upon them, because we have no interpreter of their parables and examples and pronouncements. We should therefore say, like Amos the prophet, "I am feeding in deserted places and in pastures where there is no food."[c] [8]Where are the lamentations of Jeremiah the prophet, who said, "My heart is overwhelmed by suffering and groans. There is no con-

Lam 1:20–21

solation or rest for me"?

Rom 1:1; Phil 1:1;
Titus 1:1

[9]Alas, my brother Timothy. Now his epistles will not come to you, in which it is written, "Paul, the humble servant of Jesus Christ." And no longer will he write

---

a. The author distinguishes between Paul's advocacy for "his own race" and his antagonism toward "the Jews" and "the Pharisees." It is not clear how these elements hold together, given that Paul trumpeted his credentials as both a Jew and a Pharisee, e.g., Rom 11:1; Phil 3:5. See also Acts 23:6; 26:5.

b. The Latin translator simply transliterates the Greek term (*skytos*).

c. This allusion does not correspond to any passage in Amos.

about you to the citizens, saying, "Receive my beloved son, Timothy." [10]Alas, my brother! Woe is me! Who will not put on wailing and groaning? Or who will not be clothed with garments of lamentation or astounded and confounded in their minds? [11]O dearest brother and spiritual priest, servant of Christ and the church, be clothed with sackcloth and weeping,[a] because in Ramah is heard a voice of wailing and shrieking—and not only of wailing and shrieking but of death and orphanage.

1 Cor 4:17; 16:10–11; Phil 2:19; 1 Thess 3:2

Joel 1:13

Matt 2:18 (Jer 31:15)

[12]These two terrible and bitter blows have come to us in one day.[b] Now is fulfilled in us what was said by Jacob the patriarch: "Joseph has already been lost, and Simeon has not returned." [13]Behold, indeed Peter, the foundation of the churches and the glory of the holy apostles, has departed from us and left us orphans. Paul also, the familiar comforter of the nations, has deprived us of a parent and is no more. [14]In you has been fulfilled the word of David, who said, "*They have given the bodies of your servants to the birds of the air for food, the flesh of your faithful to the wild animals of the earth.*" [15]Where are Paul's course and the labor of his holy feet? They have escaped chains, prisons, and the shackles of the stocks with their heavy bar. His diligent hands will no longer be given over to binding by iron chains. [16]Where is his mouth speaking? And where is his tongue giving counsel? And where is his spirit that is so pleasing to his God?

Gen 42:36

Ps 79:2

An account of the last moments of Peter and Paul

4 [1]O my brother Timothy, let us hold a feast for him who does not need to defend his speech. Who would not mourn and wail, for [Peter and Paul] have earned glory and honor before God, because they were handed over to death like evildoers? [2]O my brother Timothy, if you had seen the trials of their end, you certainly would have died from sadness and anguish. However, because you were not present, the struggle of their contest seems easy to you. [3]Who would not weep in that hour, when the order of the sentence was carried out against them, so that Peter of course was crucified, and Paul was decapitated? [4]You certainly would have seen then the uproar among the Jews and the crowds of unbelievers striking them, mocking them, and spitting in their faces. But they stood forth calm and tranquil, just like innocent and mild lambs. [5]When the terrible moment of their end had come, however, and they were separated from each other, then the soldiers bound the pillars of the world, and the brothers[c] left each other with groaning and weeping. [6]Then Paul said to Peter, "Peace to you, founder of the churches and shepherd of the sheep and lambs of Christ." [7]Peter then said to Paul, "Go in peace, preacher of good tidings, mediator and chief of the salvation of the just."

1 Pet 2:12

Matt 10:16; Isa 53:7

John 21:15–17

5 [1]When they separated them from each other, I followed my master Paul, because they did not kill them in the same part of the city. In that hour there was great sadness, my beloved brother, when the executioner told Paul to prepare

---

a. The Latin *cilicium* is taken from the Greek *kilikion* for "hair shirt." See e.g. Ps 34:13 LXX.

b. The author here reflects the tradition that Peter and Paul died on the same day. On this issue see the introduction to this text.

c. The image of Peter and Paul as brothers appears in several of these martyrdom texts, in order to reinforce their unity in life and death.

his neck. [2]Then the blessed apostle looked up into heaven and strengthened his forehead and chest with the sign of the cross. [3]He said, "My Lord Jesus Christ, *into your hands I commit my spirit.*" Then without sadness or compulsion he extended his neck and received his crown.

Luke 23:46 (Ps 31:5)

6 [1]Woe is me, because in that hour I gazed upon the holy body stained with innocent blood![a]

Paul's death a source of despair

7 [1]O my spiritual father and master and teacher. You were indeed not worthy of such a death. Now where will I go to look for you, O glory and praise of the Christians? [2]Who silenced your voice, O greatest pipe and plectrum of the ten-stringed lyre? Where may I seek you, O my teacher? Where may I seek and find you? [3]O true leader, what should I say to your disciples? Should I not say that you were arrested and enchained? Or who among them will be useful to you, and should I send him to you? [4]But from now on you have no need of us or of any others. You have gone to your God and Lord, whom you have sought and desired with all your heart. [4]Woe is me, because they bound in double chains those innocent hands, and in Rome they freed them. [5]David the prophet was bewailing his son Absalom, saying, "Woe is me on account of you, my son. Woe is me!" But I say, woe is me on account of you, master. Truly, woe is me!

2 Sam 19:4

[6]From now on your disciples will no longer come and look for you in Rome. [7]Now no one will say, "Let us go and see the teachers,[b] and let us ask them how we should oversee the churches that were commissioned to us. They will interpret for us the teachings of our Lord Jesus Christ and the oracles of the prophets." [8]Jerusalem and Rome are made equals in evil in a hideous friendship: Jerusalem crucified the Lord Jesus Christ, and Rome slew his apostles. Jerusalem serves the one it crucified. Rome celebrates with a feast the ones it slew.[c]

The miracle of Lemobia's veil

8 [1]O beloved brother, listen to a miracle and behold a sign that occurred on the day of their sacrifice. I was present at the time of their separation. [2]After their deaths I saw them one after the other entering the gates of the city hand in hand, and I saw them dressed in garments of light and adorned with bright and radiant crowns. [3]I was not the only one who saw this, but Lemobia, a handmaid in the service of the emperor and a disciple of Paul, also saw it. When Paul was being led to a martyr's death and was leaving the city, he met this handmaid, who was weeping with sorrow. [4]Then Paul said to her, "Do not weep, but give me the veil that is covering your head, and I will give it back to you immediately."[d]

[5]After the executioner had struck and cut off the head of Paul, the most blessed man spread out the veil on the wound and collected his own blood with the veil. He then tied the veil, wrapped it, and gave it back to that woman. [6]When the executioner was returning, holy Lemobia said to the soldier, "Where did you

---

a. The Syriac version of this letter inserts here the story of the discovery of Paul's head during the time of Xystus. An alternative version of this same story appears below in chapter 9.

b. The attention here shifts back to Paul and Peter together.

c. This is a reference to the June 29 joint feast of Peter and Paul.

d. The story of Paul's veil appears in several different forms as noted in the introduction.

send my master Paul?" [7]The soldier responded, "He lies together with his friend there outside the city in the valley of the fighters,[a] and his face is covered with your veil." [8]However, she responded and said, "Behold, Peter and Paul have already entered, dressed in radiant garments, and they had on their heads shining crowns radiating light." And she took out the veil stained with blood and showed it to them. [9]On account of this deed, very many believed in the Lord and became Christians.

Encouragement for Timothy

9 [1]And now, my brother Timothy, the ones whom you loved and longed for with all your heart are not separated in death, just as they were not separated in life— like King Saul and his son Jonathan. I also was not separated from my lord and master, except when evil and wicked men separated us. [2]The separation of this hour will not be forever. His spirit knows his beloved, even if those who were separated at that time do not speak. [3]On the day of the resurrection, however, it will be a great loss to be separated from them.[b] But truly, my brother, woe to these sons that were deprived of a spiritual father. This flock has been deprived. [4]Woe even unto us, brother, who have been deprived of our spiritual masters, those who gathered the understanding and knowledge of the old and new law and bound them up in their epistles. [5]One of them said, "If there is not in the assembly one who may interpret, then let the reader be silent."

[6]And now, my beloved brother and spiritual friend Timothy, make haste to seek the Lord with prayer and fasting, with vigils and great effort, so that he may give to you the grace of God that your master had, just as he gave the grace of Elijah to his disciple Elisha, when Elisha stayed with Elijah and did not depart until God took Elijah from him into heaven. [7]Elisha also endured the attacks of the impious and those who out of envy said to him, "Behold the disciple of a false prophet and transgressor of the law." [8]He heard these things but did not separate from his master. For this reason he obtained it, because he was seeking the same spirit.[c] [9]In the same way Paul had many disciples, yet on none of them did his spirit rest as much as it did on you. You endured with him trials and tribulations, which you endured with a joyful heart. [10]You alone are truly worthy to receive such charismatic gifts. May it be credited to you from above, since they hung glorious Peter on a cross,[d] and his head remained with his body.

2 Sam 1:23

2 Tim 2:19

1 Cor 14:27–28

2 Kgs 2:1–15

---

a. On the possible identification of this site, see the introduction and Eva Margareta Steinby, ed., *Lexicon topographicum urbis Romae* (Rome: Quasar, 1996), 1.126; 3.196–97. The much later author constructing this story may not have known or been concerned with such details, however.

b. The Latin text may be corrupt here. The argument seems to be that Peter and Paul will never be separated from each other or from their Lord. Therefore, if any are separated from the apostles on the day of resurrection, then they will necessarily be separated also from the Lord, which will be for them a great loss.

c. The source of the quotation about Elisha is unknown. There is no parallel in 2 Kgs, nor is there any reference to Elijah's being called a "false prophet and transgressor of law." The author of this text is most likely taking charges levied against Paul and retroactively applying them to Elijah in order to strengthen the comparison between Elisha and Timothy.

d. Literally, "from the wood."

The story of Paul's missing head

[11]When they decapitated Paul, however, they separated his head from his body and threw it into a valley separate from the body. It disappeared in front of the multitude of the dead who had been killed on that day, and the head of holy Paul was not found among the killed in that valley. However, all the Christians knew that the head of the holy Paul had not been found. [12]After a long time, the emperor ordered a trench to be dug. When it was dug, the head of holy Paul was thrown in with the other remains. [13]However, a certain shepherd making a journey near the place picked up the head on his staff and attached it next to the sheepfolds of his own sheep. On that same night he saw above that head a light and unspeakable glory, and he saw this three nights in a row. [14]Then he entered the city and told his master what he had seen. His master went out and saw the same thing the shepherd had seen. Quickly he announced it to the Roman patriarch Fabellius[a] and to all the presbyters and leaders of the people. [15]Many went out to see it, and they said the same thing, "Truly this is the head of Paul."

[16]The patriarch went out with a great multitude. They carried the head on a golden table and wanted to place it with the body of Paul, but the patriarch prohibited it, saying, "We know that many faithful people were killed in this city, and in that time their members were scattered by the unbelievers and not joined together. [17]Thus, I do not dare to join the head to the body of holy Paul. Let us set out the body of holy Paul and place the head at the feet of the body. Then let us pray and seek the mercy of God, so that if this head was torn off this body, then the body will turn and be joined to the head." [18]This idea, according to the judgment of the patriarch, was accepted, and there was no doubt or hesitation that the body would be able to go to meet the head. And they did as the patriarch had said. [19]While he was praying, the body turned and joined to the head. It was connected to the joint of the neck in its proper place, and all who saw it were amazed and gave glory to God. They knew that it was the body of the immaculate Paul, who was a servant and apostle of our Lord Jesus Christ.

[20]To him be glory, praise, and adoration, with the Father and the Holy Spirit, now and always and forever and ever.

---

a. This name is not among any list of Roman bishops. Sabellius was a third-century theologian in Rome, but he was condemned as a heretic and unlikely to be confused with a bishop.

IV. Apocalypses

The (Latin) Revelation of John about Antichrist
A translation and introduction

by Charles D. Wright

The *Revelation of John about Antichrist (Rev. John Ant.)* is a brief Latin apocalypse in which Christ responds to questions from John the Evangelist about the end of the world, focusing mainly on Antichrist. *Rev. John Ant.* is not a translation of any known Eastern apocalypse, and there is no concrete evidence that it was translated from Greek or another language. There are late-medieval to early-modern Irish translations or adaptations of *Rev. John Ant.* whose relation to it has gone unnoticed because *Rev. John Ant.* itself has remained almost completely unknown and unstudied, despite the fact that two versions appeared in print in the later nineteenth century.

Contents
Rev. John Ant. survives in a Longer Version and a Shorter Version. Both begin (without a specific narrative setting) with John asking the Lord about the end of the world. Christ responds with a list of portents that will occur at that time, and reveals that Antichrist will reign and perform signs and miracles. John then asks what Antichrist will look like (1). Christ answers by revealing details of Antichrist's birth and upbringing and by giving an extended description of Antichrist's grotesque physical appearance (2; this description is lacking in the Shorter Version). Christ continues with an account of Antichrist's branding of his followers and a list of his miracles (3). He then reveals a sign that will mark the day of Antichrist's birth and describes the social evils and cosmological disasters that will occur during his time (4). Christ next relates how Antichrist will slay his adversaries Enoch and Elijah and then in turn will be slain by the archangel Michael, after which three and a half years will remain until the end of the world. The Shorter Version ends here, while the Longer Version continues with very brief descriptions of a great silence in heaven and earth (6) and of the resurrection of the dead (7).

Manuscripts and Versions
The Longer Version of *Rev. John Ant.* survives in three late-medieval English manuscripts (two complete, one fragmentary), as well as in fragmentary form as brief quotations from a lost manuscript incorporated into one of three Irish translations (described below). The Latin manuscripts of the Longer Version are:

> London, British Library, Add. 33969, fol. 89v (early 14th cent.; from Lincoln) [contains only 1:1–4; 2:1–7; 3:1, 3; 2:8]
> London, British Library, Royal 17.B.xvii, fol. 97r–98v (late 14th cent.; Northern England)
> London, British Library, Add. 37787, fol. 23r–24v (late 14th or early 15th cent.; Bordesley, Worcestershire)

Dublin, Royal Irish Academy, 23 N 15 (490), pp. 53–58 (fragmentary Latin quotations in
Irish Text 2, written in 1740 with additions in 1810)

Carl Horstmann printed the text of the Royal manuscript, without commentary or discussion, in an appendix to his 1895–1896 study *Yorkshire Writers*, where it has remained
virtually unnoticed ever since.[1]

The Shorter Version was inserted by Roger of Howden (Hoveden) in his *Chronica*
under the year 1190–1191 as the last of three "views" *(opiniones)* about Antichrist (the first
consisting of an interview between Joachim of Fiore and Richard the Lionheart, the second of extracts from the popular ninth-century treatise *De ortu et tempore Antichristo* by
Adso). Roger claims to have found this third *opinio* "among the books of blessed Pope
Gregory," evidently referring to manuscripts containing works by Gregory the Great; but
no manuscript of the Shorter Version separate from Roger's chronicle has been identified.
Roger's *Chronica* was edited by William Stubbs in 1868–1871 from the autograph manuscript (Oxford, Bodleian Library, Laud Misc. 582; the other manuscripts of the *Chronica*
that include this addition therefore have no textual authority, since Laud Misc. 582 is their
archetype). Stubbs deemed the work a "curious document" but was not able to identify
it.[2] The text has occasionally been mentioned in passing by scholars more interested in
Joachim of Fiore's account of the Antichrist, but to my knowledge there has been no extended discussion since it was published by Stubbs,[3] nor has it previously been identified
as a variant version of the same apocryphon printed a few decades later by Horstmann,
who did not refer to the version in Roger's *Chronica*.

Noteworthy in its own right as a previously neglected apocryphal apocalypse of John,
Rev. John Ant. is also important as the hitherto unrecognized source of four vernacular
Irish Antichrist texts,[4] three of which (Irish Texts 1–3) represent fairly close and related
translations, though with substantial elaborations in Irish Texts 2 and 3. The fourth (*Geinimhuin Anntichrist* or "Birth of Antichrist") is a looser adaptation but nonetheless clearly
dependent on *Rev. John Ant.* In addition, chapter 7 of the Longer Version must share a
common source with certain Irish and Old English descriptions of the resurrection of
the dead. The relationship between *Rev. John Ant.* and its vernacular analogues will be
detailed in the forthcoming edition of the Irish texts together with the Latin texts of *Rev.
John Ant.* in the series *Apocrypha Hiberniae*.[5]

Literary and Theological Importance

As the summary above indicates, *Rev. John Ant.*'s account of Antichrist and the end times
is for the most part an amalgam of traditional motifs, both scriptural and apocryphal.[6]

1. Horstmann, *Yorkshire Writers*, 2:63–64. The work's existence has been briefly registered by catalogu-
ers of the three manuscripts, but without discussion and without reference to the Shorter Version in the
chronicle of Roger of Howden.

2. Roger of Howden, *Chronica Magistri*, 3:85–86.

3. Montague Rhodes James ("Man of Sin and Antichrist," in *A Dictionary of the Bible* [ed. James Hast-
ings; 5 vols.; New York: C. Scribner's Sons, 1898–1904], 3:228) mentions it as an addition to Bousset's dossier
of Antichrist texts (see n. 6).

4. See McNamara, "Irish Legend of Antichrist."

5. Irish texts ed. Caoimhín Breatnach and Martin McNamara; *Rev. John Ant.* ed. Charles D. Wright,
in *Apocrypha Hiberniae*, vol. 2.3: *Apocalyptica et Eschatologica* (ed. Martin McNamara; CCSA; Turnhout:
Brepols).

6. Bousset, *Antichrist Legend*, remains a valuable overview, but has been importantly supplemented by,

Within this conventional framework, however, there are a number of rare, archaic, or exotic details and embellishments. The most striking is the elaborate and grotesque physiognomy of Antichrist (2:2–8), a feature more characteristic of Eastern apocalyptic.[7] Antichrist's birth is, apparently uniquely, said to be manifested throughout the world by a sign—a corpse appearing in every house—that is supported by an otherwise unattested quotation from "Scripture" (4:1). The social evils that occur in his time include the immodesty of women who display their menstrual cloths (4:3). The list of Antichrist's miracles (3:4) includes raising the dead (though this is a sham) and turning trees upside down and making their roots flower. (The latter miracle—apparently unique to *Rev. John Ant.* in Latin apocalyptic tradition—found its way into the Middle English Chester play *The Coming of Antichrist* and several other late-medieval vernacular Antichrist texts, and was occasionally illustrated in manuscripts of these works.[8]) When Michael slays Antichrist, he cuts him in two with his sword (5:5). During the period of silence that follows, no creature in the world makes a sound or is heard (6:2). The angels do not blow trumpets but proclaim "Arise!" three times, awakening all those who had been burned by fire, submerged in the sea, or eaten by beasts (7:1–2).

It is also worth remarking how many traditional elements of the Antichrist legend the author of *Rev. John Ant.* ignores. He has no interest in relating Antichrist to any historical or end-time tyrants. There is no account of kings who will precede Antichrist—including the last Roman emperor—and no reference to Gog and Magog or the armies that precede Antichrist. There is no reference to Antichrist's number 666 or its mystical significance. There is no reference to Antichrist sitting in the temple of Jerusalem (though the Irish Texts 2 and 3 do include this episode), and his specific relation to the Jews is barely mentioned. In short, *Rev. John Ant.* is distinctive in its selection of traditional elements as well as in its transmission of several rare ones.

Rev. John Ant. belongs to the genre of the post-resurrection revelatory dialogue.[9] The work bears a very general resemblance to the much-longer Greek *First Apocryphal Apocalypse of John* (or *Apocalypse of John the Theologian*),[10] but specific parallels are few, and most are commonplaces. In chapters 6–9 of the Greek apocalypse, John asks Christ to reveal Antichrist's nature (6) and Christ responds with a physical description (7), but the details do not agree. Christ then tells John that he will send Enoch and Elijah, who will expose Antichrist but then be slain by him (8). Then Gabriel and Michael will sound

---

among others, Emmerson, *Antichrist in the Middle Ages*; Jenks, *Origins and Early Development*; McGinn, "Portraying Antichrist"; Geert W. Lorein, "The Antichrist in the Fathers and Their Exegetical Basis," *SacEr* 42 (2003): 5–60; Kevin L. Hughes, *Constructing Antichrist: Paul, Biblical Commentary, and the Development of Doctrine in the Early Middle Ages* (Washington, D.C.: Catholic University of America Press, 2005); and Cristian Badilita, *Métamorphoses de l'Antichrist chez les Pères de l'église*, Théologie Historique, 116 (Paris: Beauchesne, 2005). *Rev. John Ant.* is not referenced in any of these studies.

7. On physiognomies of Antichrist see esp. Berger, *Griechische Daniel-Diegese*, 115–18; McGinn, "Portraying Antichrist"; and Kaestli, "La figure de l'Antichrist," 277–90.

8. See, for example, Emmerson, *Antichrist*, fig. 4 and p. 198. For the Chester play see Linus Urban Lucken, *Antichrist and the Prophets in the Chester Cycle* (Washington, D.C.: Catholic University of America Press, 1940), 44 and 53.

9. On the genre see Richard Bauckham, *The Fate of the Dead: Studies on the Jewish and Christian Apocalypses* (NovTSup 93; Leiden: Brill, 1998), 171–74.

10. Ed. and trans. John M. Court, *The Book of Revelation and the Johannine Apocalyptic Tradition* (JSNTSup 190; Sheffield: Sheffield Academic, 2000), 23–63 (who refers to this text as the "Second Apocalypse of John"); French translation by Jean-Daniel Kaestli, in *EAC* 2:983–1018. See now also Kaestli, "La figure de l'Antichrist."

trumpets and the dead will arise in thirty-year-old bodies (9). There are also some similarities with a recently discovered Latin *Revelatio Iohannis,* particularly in the details of Antichrist's physiognomy.[11]

Original Language, Date, and Provenance

While the contents of *Rev. John Ant.* share many features with early Christian apocalyptic, in its surviving form the work is not earlier than the second half of the tenth century, since it appears to draw on Adso of Montier-en-Der's *De ortu et tempore Antichristi,* written about 950.[12] Roger's insertion of a text of the Shorter Version in his Chronicle for the year 1190–1191 proves that this version existed by the late twelfth century, and probably by the mid-twelfth century. Close parallels in Irish and Old English vernacular texts[13] for chapter 7 of the Longer Version suggest that this chapter is based on a source that existed already by the tenth century; but since chapters 6 and 7 are lacking in the Shorter Version and also in Irish translations of the Longer Version, both could be later additions to the original work. Lexical evidence common to both versions, moreover, favors a twelfth-century date of composition. The Latin word *menstruaciones* (at 4:3 in the Longer Version), meaning "menses," but in this context perhaps by extension "menstrual cloths," is exceedingly rare prior to the Renaissance and is not attested at all before 1255.[14] While it is possible that *menstruaciones* existed prior to the twelfth century, its occurrence in *Rev. John Ant.* is consistent with a twelfth-century date. Allowing for some prior circulation of the work before it was discovered by Roger of Howden, a mid-twelfth-century date for the composition of *Rev. John Ant.* is the most likely.

Though absent in Roger of Howden's *Chronica,* the physical description of Antichrist does occur in the three Irish translations, which also indirectly bear witness to a version of *Rev. John Ant.* lacking chapters 6–7. The fantastic and lurid quality of the Antichrist physiognomy may well have led Roger (or an earlier copyist) to censor it. Even if the description of Antichrist is a later addition to *Rev. John Ant.,* it certainly draws on much older sources, for some striking parallels to certain details exist in a fragmentary apocalypse copied in the tenth century,[15] and the inclusion of a physical description of Antichrist seems to have been a stock feature of such apocalypses from an early date.[16]

Aside from its length, the text of the Shorter Version does not differ greatly from the Longer Version in the passages transmitted by both; the notes to the translation draw attention to the more substantive differences in individual readings. Only select major differences in the Irish versions will be noted here, along with any individual readings that indirectly support an emendation of the base manuscript (British Library, Add. 37787).

The exclusively Irish and English transmission (on present evidence) of *Rev. John Ant.,*

---

11. The *Revelatio Iohannis,* recently discovered by Jean-Daniel Kaestli, has not yet been edited, but a description of its contents has been published: Kaestli, "Un nuovo apocrifo," with Italian translation of the text by Norelli, "Appendice."

12. Adso of Montier-en-Der, *Adso Dervensis. Rev. John Ant.* appears to draw on Adso for the information that Antichrist will be raised in Chorazin and dwell in Bethsaida (2:9).

13. The Old English passages have been discussed (without reference to *Rev. John Ant.*) in connection with the theme "the ways of bodily destruction and the resurrection" by James E. Cross, "On The Wanderer Lines 80–84: A Study of a Figure and Theme," *Vetenskaps-Societetens i Lund Årsbok* (1958–1959): 86–99.

14. The word may be a corruption of *menstruatae* in 4 Ezra 5:8 (see the note to 4:3 below). An attestation of Latin *menstruatio* from 1255 is cited by the *Oxford English Dictionary* in its etymology of "menstruation."

15. The Avranches apocalypse, edited by Bischoff, "Vom Ende der Welt."

16. See note 7 above.

as well as its survival in the vernacular Irish versions, raises the question of an Insular origin, though it may only be an Insular translation or adaptation of an older Continental (or perhaps Eastern) apocalypse. The English circulation of the work is localized in the North and Midlands. Roger was from Howden in the East Riding of Yorkshire, though he traveled widely in the service first of Henry II and then of Hugh of Puiset, bishop of Durham, so it is not possible to say where he encountered a copy of *Rev. John Ant.*; but all three manuscripts of the Longer Version are northern: one (British Library, Royal 17.B.xvii) is perhaps from Derbyshire, and contains works by the Yorkshire writer Richard Rolle, while the other two are from Worcestershire and Lincoln.

Translation

Because I believe that the description of Antichrist is an original part of the work, I have chosen to translate the Longer Version of the text instead of the Shorter Version. Manuscript L (British Library, Add. 33969), though a century older than A (British Library, Add. 37787) and R (British Library, Royal 17.B.xvii), transmits only the first half of the work, so it cannot serve as the base manuscript for a critical edition. The text of A preserves a more logical and presumably original sequence of verses in chapters 2–3, and therefore is the base manuscript for the critical text translated here, but I have emended A as necessary where A is corrupt, or when another manuscript offers a superior reading. The chapter and verse divisions are my own.

Only scriptural sources are cited here; for a full discussion of the sources and analogues of *Rev. John Ant.*, especially in other apocryphal texts and (for chap. 7) in Old English texts, see my forthcoming critical edition.

Sigla

Longer Version:

A   London, British Library, Add. 37787
R   London, British Library, Royal 17.B.xvii
L   London, British Library, Add. 33969
D   Dublin, Royal Irish Academy, 23 N 15 (490) = Latin quotations in Irish Text 2

Shorter Version:

C   Roger of Howden, *Chronica* (for the year 1190/1191) in Oxford, Bodleian Libr., Laud Misc. 582

Irish Versions:

Ir1   Irish Text 1
Ir2   Irish Text 2
Ir3   Irish Text 3
GA   *Geinimhuin Anntichrist* in the Irish *Life of John*

Bibliography

EDITIONS AND TRANSLATIONS

Horstmann, Carl. *Yorkshire Writers: Richard Rolle of Hampole and His Followers.* 2 vols. London: S. Sonnenschein, 1895–1896. (*Editio princeps* based on London, Royal 17.B.xvii.)
Roger of Howden (Hoveden). *Chronica Magistri Rogeri de Houedene.* Edited by William

Stubbs. Rolls Series 51. 4 vols. London: Longmans, Green, Reader & Dyer, 1868–1871. (The *Chronica* incorporates the Shorter Version of the text.)

STUDIES

Adso of Montier-en-Der. *Adso Dervensis, De ortu et tempore Antichristi necnon et tractatus qui ab eo dependunt.* Edited by Daniel Verhelst. CCCM 45. Turnhout: Brepols, 1976.

Berger, Klaus. *Die Griechische Daniel-Diegese: Eine altkirchliche Apokalypse.* StPB 27. Leiden: Brill, 1976.

Bischoff, Bernhard. "Vom Ende der Welt und vom Antichrist (I); Fragment einer Jenseitsvision (II) (Zehntes Jahrhundert)." Pages 80–84 in *Anecdota novissima: Texte des vierten bis sechzehnten Jahrhunderts.* Stuttgart: Hiersemann, 1984.

Bousset, Wilhelm. *The Antichrist Legend: A Chapter in Christian and Jewish Folklore.* Translated by A. H. Keane. London: Hutchinson & Co., 1896.

Emmerson, Richard K. *Antichrist in the Middle Ages: A Study of Medieval Apocalypticism, Art, and Literature.* Seattle: University of Washington Press, 1981.

Jenks, Gregory C. *The Origins and Early Development of the Antichrist Myth.* BZNW 59. Berlin: De Gruyter, 1991.

Kaestli, Jean-Daniel. "La figure de l'Antichrist dans 'l'Apocalypse de saint Jean le Théologien (Première apocalypse apocryphe de Jean)'." Pages 277–90 in *Les forces du Bien et du Mal dans les premiers siècles de l'Église. Actes du Colloque de Tours, septembre 2008.* Edited by Yves-Marie Blanchard, Bernard Pouderon, and Madeleine Scopello. ThH 118. Paris: Beauchesne, 2010.

————. "Un nuovo apocrifo da aggiungere al dossier dell'Anticristo: la *Revelatio Iohannis* recentemente scoperta in un manoscritto latino di Praga." Pages 47–69 in *L'ultimo nemico di Dio: Il ruolo dell'Anticristo nel cristianesimo antico e tardoantico.* Edited by Alberto D'Anna and Emanuela Valeriani. Bologna: Edizioni Dehoniane, 2013.

McGinn, Bernard. "Portraying Antichrist in the Middle Ages." Pages 1–48 in *The Use and Abuse of Eschatology in the Middle Ages.* Edited by Werner Verbeke, D. Verhelst, and A. Welkenhuysen. Leuven: Leuven University Press, 1988.

McNamara, Martin. "The Irish Legend of Antichrist." Pages 201–20 in *Jerusalem, Alexandria, Rome: Studies in Ancient Cultural Interaction in Honour of A. Hilhorst.* Edited by F. García Martinez and Gerard P. Luttikhuizen. Leiden: Brill, 2003.

Norelli, Enrico. "Appendice: [fol. 26v] *Apocalisse del beato Giovanni apostolo ed evangelista.* Traduzione e commento." Pages 71–83 in *L'ultimo nemico di Dio: Il ruolo dell'Anticristo nel cristianesimo antico e tardoantico.* Edited by Alberto D'Anna and Emanuela Valeriani. Bologna: Edizioni Dehoniane, 2013.

The (Latin) Revelation of John about Antichrist[a]

John asks Christ about the end of the world and about Antichrist

1 [1]John the Evangelist[b] asked the Lord about the end of the world. [2]The Lord replied to him: "*The sun shall be turned to darkness and the moon to blood,*[c] and *blood shall drip from trees, the stones shall utter voices; the peoples shall be troubled.* [3]Antichrist—that is, the devil—will reign and will perform great wonders and signs among the people."

[4]And John said to the Lord, "Lord, in what likeness will he be, so that those who see him will not believe in him?"[d]

Acts 2:20 (Joel 2:31)

4 Ezra 5:5

2 Thess 2:9; Rev 13:13; Mark 13:22//Matt 24:24

Antichrist's birth and upbringing, and his physical description

2 [1]Christ said,[e] "He will be born to a woman, a harlot from the tribe of Dan in Israel, [2]having 600 cubits in the length of his body and 400 in width. [3]And he will have one eye in his forehead, one ear in his head, (and his) lip hanging down to his chest. [4]He will have no upper teeth or knees; [5]the soles of his[f] feet (will be) round like the wheels of a cart. [6]One rib will be visible in his left side without others.[g] [7]The hairs of his head will be black and terrible.[h] [8]A threefold[i] fume will go out through his nose like[j] a sulfurous flame reaching up to heaven.[k] [9]He will be raised in Chorazin; after that he will dwell in the city of Bethsaida, but only for a few days.[l]

Matt 11:21//Luke 10:13

---

a. There is no title in A; R has the heading, "About Antichrist according to John the Evangelist"; L: "About the gospel." I have chosen the title "Revelation" instead of "Apocalypse" since there are several apocryphal Apocalypses of John in addition to the canonical one. The qualification "about Antichrist" (based on R's heading), accurately summarizes the main focus of the revelation and also serves to distinguish this apocryphal revelation of John from the recently discovered *Revelatio Iohannis*.

b. C identifies John as "apostle and evangelist, a virgin chosen by God and the more greatly loved among the others."

c. D: "The sun and the moon shall be turned to darkness."

d. C lacks John's question about Antichrist in 1:4 as well as Christ's description of him in 2:2–8.

e. C lacks "Christ said" and the verses it retains (see previous note) are in the order 3:1, 2:1, 3:3, 2:9, 3:2, 3:4.

f. A lacks "his."

g. R lacks "without others."

h. L moves 3:1 and 3:3 after 2:7.

i. D lacks "threefold" and lists the features in the order eye, nose, knees.

j. R and L: "and."

k. L breaks off with "hea[. . .]."

l. R has this and the following four verses in the order 3:1, 3:3, 2:9, 3:2, 3:4–5.

Antichrist's victims and followers, and his miracles ·

3 [1]"No one will be able to hide[a] himself from him. [2]All those whom he himself will kill and who will die[b] from hunger and thirst under his dominion will be God's elect. [3]And all who will believe[c] in him he will mark with a single letter[d] on their forehead, and no one[e] will be able to erase that device. [4]He will raise feigned dead,[f] he will make rivers reverse their course, he will uproot trees and turn the branches to the ground and their roots aloft, and he will make them flower by his diabolical wiles. [5]And he will seduce many.[g]

Rev 13:16

Matt 24:5, 11; Rev 13:14

The tribulations of the time of Antichrist

4 [1]"On the day he is born, all who inhabit the four parts of the world will realize he has been born, as the Scripture testifies that says, 'In every house the corpse of a dead man will be the sign.'[h] [2]Then in that time father will kill son, and son father, and brother brother, and in every dealing[i] there will be no faithful person.[j] [3]Women will reveal[k] their menstrual cloths[l] and will not conceal themselves from men.[m] [4]Churches will be destroyed, priests[n] will lament; people will have no thought for holy relics, nor for those places where the bodies of saints had lain at rest. [5]They will worship profane idols, like pagans and Jews.[o] [6]*Nation will rise against nation, and kingdom against kingdom; there will be great earthquakes in various places, plagues and famines, and stars will fall* to the earth, rivers and all waters that are below heaven will be turned to blood.

cf. Exod 12:30
Mark 13:12//Matt 10:21
Luke 21:10; cf. Mark 13:8//Matt 24:7
Matt 24:29; cf. Mark 13:25

---

a. C lacks "to hide."

b. R: "who have died."

c. RLC have the present tense.

d. So RC; A lacks "with a single" and adds "them" in the margin to read: "marks them with a brand" (an alternative meaning of *caracter*).

e. R lacks "no one."

f. The expression "feigned dead" seems to mean that Antichrist "raises" persons only pretending to be dead, as in the twelfth-century *Ludus de Antichristo*, ed. Gerhard Günther, *Der Antichrist: Der staufische Ludus de Antichristo* (Hamburg: Friedrich Witter Verlag, 1970), 140 (scene 69, stage direction).

g. Ir1–3 have nothing corresponding to this verse.

h. This alleged quotation of "Scripture" is not elsewhere attested.

i. So RC; A lacks "dealing" (Latin *re* might also be translated "circumstance," "matter").

j. C has the plural "faithful persons"; A adds "for you."

k. C has "will receive"; in the following clause A has present tense "conceal."

l. The rare word *menstruaciones* literally means "menses." This sign (*et mulieres menstruaciones suas aperient*) may have originated in a corruption of 4 Ezra 5:8, *et mulieres parient menstruatae monstra*, "and menstruous women shall bring forth monsters" (trans. Bruce M. Metzger, "The Fourth Book of Ezra," in *Old Testament Pseudeipigrapha* [ed. James H. Charlesworth; 2 vols.; ABRL; New York: Doubleday, 1983–1985], 1:517–59) with *aperient* "will reveal" instead of *parient* "will give birth to" (4 Ezra 5:5 is quoted in an otherwise unattested variant form in *Rev. John Ant.* 1:2).

m. R has "from everyone."

n. R lacks "Churches will be destroyed" and adds "faithful" before "priests."

o. C adds "and Saracens."

Antichrist slays Enoch and Elijah, and is slain by Michael

5 [1]"During his reign the two prophets Enoch and Elijah, who are now[a] sad[b] in Paradise because of the expectation of death, will wage war against him.[c] [2]And Antichrist will slay them. [3]They will lie dead in the streets for three days and three nights. [4]On the fourth day they will arise into eternal life. [5]On the next, that is on the last (day), almighty God,[d] *who desires everyone to be saved,*[e] will dispatch his[f] archangel Michael, holding in (his) hand his sharp sword—that is, the sword of the Holy Spirit—and he will slay him and split him in two from the top to the bottom; not so that the world should be destroyed, but so that it should be made anew in a better condition. [6]It will be thus for three years and six months until[g] the consummation of the world.[h]

Rev 11:3, 7–9

Rev 11:8–11

Rev 11:12

1 Tim 2:4

Rev 2:13

Eph 6:17; 2 Thess 2:8

Dan 7:25; 12:7; Rev 12:14; 13:5; Matt 28:20

Silence in heaven

6 [1]"After these tribulations there will be a great *silence in heaven* and earth for forty[i] days and nights. [2]No creature will make a sound or be heard.

Rev 8:1

The resurrection of the dead

7 [1]"And angels will come from the four parts of the earth and cry out, saying three times,[j] 'Arise! Arise! Arise!'[k] [2]And all who have died from Adam until that day will rise in the age of thirty[l] years, whatever fire had burned[m] on earth, animals devoured, or sea engulfed."[n]

Rev 7:1; Mark 13:27// Matt 24:31

1 Cor 15:52; 1 Thess 4:16

Rev 20:13

---

a. So RC; A lacks "now."

b. I adopt C's reading *tristantur,* an allusion to a common Insular motif that Enoch and Elijah are sad despite being in Paradise: see John Carey, ed., *In Tenga Bithnua / The Ever-new Tongue. Apocrypha Hiberniae*, vol. 1: *Apocalyptica 1* (CCSA 16; Turnhout: Brepols, 2009), 366. A reads "are ministered to" *(ministrantur)*; R "are settled in" *(collocantur).*

c. So C; AR read "war against war."

d. R has "God Christ" instead of "almighty God."

e. So RC; A lacks "who desires everyone to be saved."

f. R lacks "dispatch" and "his."

g. C: "in."

h. C ends here, as do Ir 1–3; GA translates chapter 6 and has a loose adaptation of chapter 7.

i. R: "thirty."

j. R lacks "three times."

k. A adds "ye dead, come to the true judgment," probably elaborating from memory of a popular dictum attributed to Jerome in the Middle Ages: "Whether I eat or drink, or whatever else I may do, I always seem to hear that trumpet resounding in my ears, 'Arise, ye dead, come to judgment!'" See William W. Heist, *The Fifteen Signs before Doomsday* (East Lansing: Michigan State College Press, 1952), 40–41 n. 21.

l. R has "33"; the perfect age at the resurrection was believed to be "the age of the fullness of Christ" (Eph. 4:13), which could be reckoned either as the age of one's baptism or death.

m. A ends here; the remaining words are only in R, but equivalent phrasing is found in the Irish and Old English analogues.

n. R alone adds "will worship," an abrupt concluding phrase not paralleled in the Irish and Old English analogues.

The Apocalypse of the Virgin
A new translation and introduction

by Stephen J. Shoemaker

The *Apocalypse of the Virgin* (*Apoc. Vir.*; *CANT* 327) or, as it is more traditionally known, the *Apocalypse of the Theotokos,* is an enormously popular apocryphon from the early Middle Ages that relates the Virgin Mary's visit to the places of punishment and her intercession on behalf of those afflicted there. It is a relatively more-recent exemplar of the well-established apocalyptic genre of cosmic tours, and more specifically of the subgenre, "tours of hell." This apocryphon shares close literary relations with the *Apocalypse of Paul* but also with the apocalypse of the Virgin that completes the earliest narrative of Mary's Dormition and Assumption: the *Obsequies of the Virgin* or the *Liber Requiei Mariae,* as the work is titled in the two main versions of this text.[1]

Contents

Apoc. Vir. begins as Mary goes to the Mount of Olives to pray. There she petitions the Archangel Michael to come to her, so that he may tell her "about the punishments and about the things in heaven and on the earth and below the earth" (1). When he arrives with angels from the heavenly host, they first greet one another and then, in response to Mary's request, Michael commands the "western" angels to open Hades for the Virgin (1–3). As a general rule, the sinners and the punishments that Mary beholds on her journey evidence a particular concern for "commonplace matters of parish morality."[2] Mary initially observes the torments that are inflicted on theological sinners—that is, those who failed to confess the Trinity, the Incarnation, and Mary's role therein (4–6). Next, at Mary's request they travel to the south, where she beholds a river of fire in which men and women are submerged to differing depths. These individuals, we learn, are guilty of various social and sexual transgressions (7–12). Then they come to the west where clerical sinners, those who behaved inappropriately in church, usurers, and others are tormented (13–24). Mary and her company next reach "the left parts of Paradise," where she sees what Michael calls

---

1. For a complete translation of the latter apocryphon, see Shoemaker, *Ancient Traditions,* 290–350. The Virgin Mary's apocalyptic tour can be found at pp. 341–50. The first title is generally used for the fragmentary Syriac version of this narrative, while the second is used for the complete Ethiopic version. They are, however, the same text. There is, one should note, an apocalypse of the Virgin that survives uniquely in Ethiopic that is in fact entirely derivative of the *Apocalypse of Paul,* simply replacing the figure of Paul with Mary. It should be clear, however, that this is an entirely different text from the one presented here, even though it belongs to the same family of apocalyptic tours of hell. In order to avoid confusion, this Ethiopic adaptation of the *Apocalypse of Paul* is specifically identified as the *Ethiopic Apocalypse of the Virgin.* See, e.g., Himmelfarb, *Tours of Hell,* 19–21; Mimouni, "Apocalypses de la Vierge," 103–4; Bauckham, "Four Apocalypses of the Virgin," 338–40.

2. Baun, *Tales from Another Byzantium,* 59 and 326–85, esp. 327, 331.

the "great punishments" (24–26): these torments are reserved for the Jews, murderers, and sorcerers, and those guilty of incest and infanticide.

Finally Mary sees the lake of fire where those Christians are punished who "did the works of the devil and lost the time of their repentance" (27). From this point on the apocalypse focuses on Mary's intercessions for these Christian sinners. At first she asks that she may also enter into the lake of fire to be punished along with these children of her son (28). Michael reminds her that this is impossible, to which she responds that they must pray to God for mercy on these sinners. Michael explains that he and the angels together petition God day and night for clemency, to no avail. Then at her request, the angels transport Mary to the presence of God the Father, whom she entreats for mercy (29). Following a brief dialogue between God and the Virgin, the Lord promises not to forsake anyone who calls upon the Virgin's name. Unsatisfied, Mary enlists Michael, Moses, John, and Paul to join her petitions, and she entreats God to have mercy on these foolish, simple people who were deceived by the wiles of the devil (30–31). When God still remains unswayed, Mary then commands all the angels, the righteous, the prophets, the apostles, the martyrs, and the elect to intercede with her (32). At last God succumbs to the supplications "of all those who were pleasing to him" (33), and because of their collective petitions, God allows a period of respite every year during Eastertide—the fifty days from the Resurrection to Pentecost (34).

Manuscripts and Editions

Despite its relative neglect and even outright disdain in much modern scholarship, *Apoc. Vir.* is undoubtedly one of the most popular and successful apocrypha in the history of the Christian tradition, particularly in the Eastern Christian tradition. One of its earliest editors, M. R. James could not conceal his contempt for the text, describing it as "extremely monotonous, quite contemptible as literature, and even positively repulsive in some parts," and further predicting that he will be criticized for "having spent pains on editing so late and so dismal a work."[3] More recently, Richard Bauckham has similarly assessed this apocalypse as "crude and unimaginative."[4] Nevertheless, readers with less "refined" tastes across the ages have enthusiastically embraced this vision of hell's torments and its promise of the intercessory powers of Mary and the saints. Feodor Dostoyevsky, for instance, famously provides a summary of this apocryphon at the beginning of the Grand Inquisitor scene from his *Brothers Karamazov* (2.5.5), where it is compared favorably with Dante. In fact, as Bauckham notes, *Apoc. Vir.* is "one of the two most influential of the extra-canonical Christian apocalypses," an honor it shares with the *Apocalypse of Paul,* which circulated primarily in the Christian West.[5] The result is an enormous manuscript tradition that probably knows few rivals among Christian apocrypha. According to James, "Hardly any collection of Greek MSS. is without one or more copies of it," and the as-yet-unknown number of Greek manuscripts must be in the hundreds.[6] In fact, handwritten copies of *Apoc. Vir.* continued to be produced as recently as the nineteenth century. This apocryphon even succeeded in making the transition to print, so that during the nineteenth and early twentieth centuries cheaply made pamphlets containing the

---

3. James, *Apocrypha Anecdota,* 1:110–11.
4. Bauckham, "Four Apocalypses of the Virgin," 337.
5. Bauckham, "Four Apocalypses of the Virgin," 332.
6. James, *Apocrypha Anecdota,* 1:109.

text in demotic Greek and Russian circulated widely.[7] Versions of this text also survive in the full range of Eastern Christian languages, including Old Church Slavonic, Romanian, Serbian, Armenian, Georgian, Syriac, Coptic, and Ethiopic, and possibly others as well.[8]

As one would imagine, this vast textual corpus contains an enormous amount of textual variety, such that this apocryphon defies the possibility of producing a traditional critical edition even more than most. The editorial principles of modern classical philology are essentially useless in the face of such diversity and continuous transformation, and any effort to recover the "original" version of this text seemingly would be futile. Moreover, as Jane Baun observes, the determination to produce such critical editions is often as much a hindrance as it is a help in coming to appreciate the true nature and significance of texts like *Apoc. Vir.* The strong prejudice of modern philology in favor of stable texts has largely contributed to the marginalization of *Apoc. Vir.* and other similarly complex textual traditions. The tendency is to regard any text that has been so frequently and deliberately modified as unworthy of being considered a "classic," and the interpolations, abbreviations, and other editorial rearrangements are instead seen as evidence of a lack of authority. Yet this sort of textual diversity and instability is often inherent in the nature of apocryphal texts and is a direct consequence of their use and value by medieval Christians. Indeed, as Baun notes, these frequent editorial transformations are, to the contrary, important indicators of how greatly these texts were esteemed by the medieval Christians who copied and used them; it was essential that they be updated continually to meet the needs and concerns of different historical communities.[9]

In light of this textual diversity and instability, scholarship on *Apoc. Vir.* understandably has tended to focus on individual manuscripts, and, not surprisingly, the earliest witnesses have attracted the most attention. In her important recent study of *Apoc. Vir.*, Baun provides a list of the earliest known manuscripts, twenty in total, the earliest of which date to the eleventh century and the latest of which were copied in the seventeenth century.[10] The most important of these has long been Oxford, Bodleian Library, Misc. gr. 77, an eleventh-century manuscript published by James in 1893 that has effectively become the canonical version of this apocryphon, particularly in English.[11] This Oxford manuscript and the only other eleventh-century manuscript, Vatican, Biblioteca apostolica, Ottoboni 1, uniquely preserve what Baun identifies as the "medieval mainstream recension" in a state prior to the introduction of a lengthy "sin-list" present in later medieval manuscripts.[12] The earliest manuscript preserving this "sin-list" recension, Vienna, Österreichischen Nationalbibliothek, Theol. gr. 333 (ca. 1300), was in fact the

---

7. Baun, *Tales from Another Byzantium*, 19–20, 40.

8. Bauckham, "Four Apocalypses of the Virgin," 335; Baun, *Tales from Another Byzantium*, 41.

9. Baun, *Tales from Another Byzantium*, 35–38. Baun's discussion here of the textual diversity and instability of Christian apocrypha and the significance of these qualities for their study is exemplary and offers considerable insight for how scholars might approach this relatively common and yet often overlooked feature of Christian apocrypha.

10. Baun, *Tales from Another Byzantium*, 41.

11. James, *Apocrypha Anecdota*, 1:109–26. This version was the basis for the English translation by Andrew Rutherfurd in *ANF* 9:167–74.

12. See the discussion of these versions and manuscripts in Baun, *Tales from Another Byzantium*, 39–59. One should note, however, that in her list of manuscripts Baun also notes the existence of an eleventh- or twelfth-century manuscript in Milan: Biblioteca Ambrosiana, gr. 405. Nevertheless, she does not appear to discuss or even mention this manuscript at any other point in her study, and it is not clear what its significance is nor why it was not included in her study.

first to be published in 1863, and other more recent exemplars of this version also have been published.[13] Among the most notable of these editions is Hubert Pernot's edition of three manuscripts in Paris from the fifteenth and sixteenth centuries, each of which he published in its entirety.[14] A similar approach can be found in Bogdan Petriceicu Hasdeu's groundbreaking study of Romanian folklore and apocrypha, where he published parallel versions of *Apoc. Vir.* in a sixteenth-century Romanian version, Old Church Slavonic, and Greek.[15] Finally, there is also a shorter, later medieval recension that has been published from two different manuscripts dating to the sixteenth and seventeenth centuries.[16]

Recently a new edition of *Apoc. Vir.* has been published by Olena Syrtsova (in 2000), which should now form the textual basis for all subsequent study of this apocryphon. As her base text, Syrtsova published the previously unedited Vatican, Biblioteca apostolica, Ottoboni 1, which together with the Oxford manuscript published by James is one of the two best witnesses to the earliest version of this apocalypse. In addition, Syrtsova has collated this eleventh-century version with all of the variants from the most important published editions, including especially the Oxford, Vienna, and Paris manuscripts.[17]

Literary Context

Scholars have long believed with relative certitude that *Apoc. Vir.* is derivative of *Apoc. Paul,* an early-fifth-century text with which it unquestionably shares literary relations.[18] In some instances this determination was apparently made in ignorance of the apocalyptic traditions that complete the earliest Dormition narratives, one of which, the *Obsequies of the Virgin* or the *Liber Requiei Mariae,* also shares literary relations with these two apocalypses.[19] James had already recognized the influence of these early Dormition apocrypha in preparing his edition, and in the introduction he names the Dormition apocrypha as one of *Apoc. Vir.*'s main sources, although he likewise notes that *Apoc. Paul*'s influence was "more wide-reaching."[20] In a more recent study, Simon Mimouni essentially merges the Dormition apocalypses and *Apoc. Vir.* into a single literary tradition, so that these

---

13. Sreznevskiy, *Drevnie pamyatniki russkago.*

14. Pernot, "Descente de la Vierge."

15. Hasdeu, *Cuvente den bătrâni,* 2:230–82.

16. Vasiliev, *Anecdota graeco-byzantina,* 125–34; Delatte, *Anecdota atheniensia,* 1:273–58.

17. Syrtsova, *Apokryfichna apokaliptyka.* I thank Leena Mari Peltomaa for drawing my attention to this recent edition and also for providing me with a copy of the text. Syrtsova also identifies two additional manuscripts in her edition, although these do not figure significantly at all in the apparatus: Venice, Museo Marciano, VII.43, from which excerpts were published in Constantin Tischendorf, *Apocalypses Apocryphae: Mosis, Esdrae, Pauli, Johannis, item Mariae dormito* (Leipzig: H. Mendelssohn, 1866), xxviii–xxix; and Vatican, Biblioteca apostolica, gr. 1190.

18. Concerning the date of *Apoc. Paul,* see Pierluigi Piovanelli, "Les Origines de l'*Apocalypse de Paul* reconsidérées," *Apocrypha* 4 (1993): 37–59.

19. E.g., Himmelfarb, *Tours of Hell,* esp. 23–24, 159–60. It is rather odd that this otherwise comprehensive survey of early Jewish and Christian tours of hell completely ignores the important tours of hell present in the early Dormition apocrypha, which unquestionably should have been included. The Syriac fragments of the *Obsequies of the Virgin* have been edited in William Wright, *Contributions to the Apocryphal Literature of the New Testament* (London: Williams & Norgate, 1865); the text of *Liber Requiei Mariae* was published in Victor Arras, *De transitu Mariae apocrypha aethiopice* (2 vols.; CSCO 342–43, 351–52; Leuven: Secrétariat du Corpus SCO, 1973), vol. 1. English translations of both texts can be found in Shoemaker, *Ancient Traditions,* 290–350.

20. James, *Apocrypha Anecdota,* 1:111.

different accounts of Mary's otherworldly journey are presented as versions of the same text—one as part of the Dormition tradition and the other circulating as an independent text. Nevertheless, Mimouni regards both versions as dependent on *Apoc. Paul,* inasmuch as he posits an improbably late date for the emergence of the Dormition apocrypha only sometime after the Council of Chalcedon (451).[21] Bauckham offers a much-needed correction to Mimouni, noting that in their current state the Dormition apocalypses and *Apoc. Vir.* are distinct works. Much less persuasive, however, is Bauckham's insistence that *Apoc. Vir.* in no way reflects a development of these earlier Dormition apocalypses, a position for which he does not provide a particularly good argument. Instead he seems to assume that *Apoc. Vir.* emerged primarily from *Apoc. Paul,* which it then replaced in the Christian East.[22]

Bauckham's conclusions regarding *Apoc. Vir.*'s sources are all the more surprising and questionable in light of the important new analysis that he brings to the Dormition apocalypses and their position within this broader literary tradition of tours of hell. Bauckham offers convincing arguments that date both the *Obsequies* apocalypse and the apocalypse from the related Syriac Six Books Dormition apocryphon earlier than *Apoc. Paul*—to at least the fourth century, if not perhaps even earlier.[23] Moreover, he also demonstrates a likelihood that *Apoc. Paul* depends on the traditions of the *Obsequies* apocalypse, and elsewhere I have added additional arguments that would seem to confirm this conclusion.[24] The fact that this Dormition apocalypse, which was originally written in Greek, survives in Syriac manuscripts from the later fifth century adds further indication that its traditions antedate those of *Apoc. Paul.*[25] Indeed, it would appear that this Dormition apocryphon was most likely composed during the third century or by the fourth century at the absolute latest.[26] Quite possibly some of its elements, including its final apocalypse of the Virgin, may be even older. Given, then, the priority of the *Obsequies* apocalypse of the Virgin and its apparent influence on *Apoc. Paul,* one would expect that more consideration would be given to its possible influence on *Apoc. Vir.,* even if the two traditions cannot be merged in the fashion that Mimouni has proposed. To be sure, there are a number of traditions common to *Apoc. Vir.* and *Apoc. Paul* that suggest some sort of literary relationship, but the former's direct dependence on *Apoc. Paul* is not the only or even the most likely explanation. Indeed, it is rather striking how little direct similarity there is between these two texts, a point conceded even by many scholars who identify *Apoc. Vir.* as an adaptation of *Apoc. Paul.* For instance, Himmelfarb notes some important structural differences, while Bauckham further observes that "there are few precise verbal echoes."[27]

---

21. Mimouni, "Apocalypses de la Vierge," 102–4, 107–9. Concerning the problems with Mimouni's late dating of the early Dormitions (as well as other issues with his presentation of this corpus), see Shoemaker, *Ancient Traditions,* esp. 142–289.

22. Bauckham, "Four Apocalypses of the Virgin," 337–38.

23. Bauckham, "Four Apocalypses of the Virgin," 345–46, 359–61.

24. Bauckham, "Four Apocalypses of the Virgin," 345–56; Shoemaker, *Ancient Traditions,* 42–46.

25. Concerning these manuscripts and the original language, see Shoemaker, *Ancient Traditions,* 33–34, 38–42; and idem, "New Syriac Dormition Fragments from Palimpsests in the Schøyen Collection and the British Library: Presentation, Edition and Translation," *Le Muséon* 124 (2011): 259–78 at 260–64, 267.

26. Regarding the date of the *Obsequies* apocryphon, see, e.g., Shoemaker, *Ancient Traditions,* 42–46, 253–56, 278–79, 284–86; idem, "Death and the Maiden: The Early History of the Dormition and Assumption Apocrypha," *SVTQ* 50 (2006): 59–97. See also the references to other scholarship reaching the same conclusion in Shoemaker, "New Syriac Dormition Fragments," 259–60 n. 1, 262.

27. Himmelfarb, *Tours of Hell,* 159–60; Bauckham, "Four Apocalypses of the Virgin," 335.

Baun similarly remarks that "the two texts are worlds apart in mood and attitude," and she notes a "conceptual disjunction" between the two texts that "pervades each text's presentation of how the Other World works."[28] Baun's analysis of the two texts is certainly the most thorough, and although she maintains that "the structure and contents of their punishments converge in place after place," her own study reveals a considerable number of dissimilarities that seem to invite other explanations. Particularly noteworthy are the five points of "common content" that she identifies as evidence of literary dependence.[29] Three of these—the hypocritical reader, the promise of beholding even-greater punishments, and Christ's reproaches—are all found in the *Obsequies* apocalypse, which is presumably the source from which *Apoc. Paul* has taken them. The fourth, that "It would be better for a person if he had not been born," is a seemingly appropriate quotation from the Synoptic sayings tradition (Mark 14:21//Matt 26:24). Only the punishments imagined for usurers do not have an obvious earlier common source, and yet here there are some important differences, including most notably that in *Apoc. Vir.* the usurers are women.

In light of these shared similarities with the *Obsequies* apocalypse, it would now appear that we must allow for the possibility that both *Apoc. Paul* and *Apoc. Vir.* may reflect more-or-less independent reworkings of this earlier tour of hell. Of course, it may well be the case that the *Obsequies* apocalypse influenced Paul's cosmic tour only to disappear shortly thereafter, so that the Virgin's apocalypse would later be reinvented solely on the basis of Paul's vision, as Bauckham's analysis seems to presume. Nevertheless, it perhaps makes more sense to understand *Apoc. Vir.* as having evolved directly from the apocalyptic finale of the *Obsequies* apocryphon, yet without simply collapsing the two traditions as Mimouni has done. This genealogy would of course not preclude the possibility of some parallel influence coming from *Apoc. Paul,* as in the case of the usurers, for instance. Yet it is equally conceivable that the punishments allotted to usurers and other similarities between the two texts also may have originated with the Dormition apocrypha, despite their absence from the few surviving manuscripts that preserve the *Obsequies* apocalypse.[30] Perhaps there was more to this early tradition of Mary's otherworldly journey than is visible in the current state of our evidence. From the sixth century onward these apocalyptic traditions were increasingly excised from the Dormition narratives that descend from the *Obsequies,* and so our knowledge of these traditions is potentially not as complete as it is for other elements of the early Dormition traditions. Moreover, this sundering of the Virgin's cosmic tour from the Dormition narratives during the sixth and seventh centuries could in itself largely explain the emergence of *Apoc. Vir.* as an independent apocryphon not long thereafter. Once removed from their original context, these traditions of Mary's visit to the places of torment likely were not simply discarded but instead began to take shape as a separate literary tradition.

Date and Provenance

There is much uncertainty regarding the date of this apocryphon, and scholars have proposed a range of possibilities, from as early as the fourth (or even the third) century to

---

28. Baun, *Tales from Another Byzantium,* 274–75.

29. Baun, *Tales from Another Byzantium,* 80–81.

30. For other witnesses to these traditions, see the table in Shoemaker, *Ancient Traditions,* 417–18. The same table also demonstrates effectively the tendency to eliminate these traditions in narratives redacted in the sixth and later centuries.

as late as the ninth, although a date before the sixth century does not seem very likely.[31] The Dormition apocalypses, to be sure, belong to the third or fourth centuries, but this independent *Apoc Vir.* seems to be a more recent development in the tradition of Mary's otherworldly journeys. The persistent use of liturgical titles for Mary (e.g., *Kecharitōmenē*, "Highly Favored One"; *Panagia*, "All-Holy One") and the presence of other liturgical qualities and ecclesiastical practices seem to indicate a date of the sixth century or later,[32] so that even if the text may have been composed at an earlier time, in its present state this recension appears to reflect the devotional practices of a later era. Primarily on the basis of this liturgical diction and other related features, Baun has proposed an even more recent date for the apocryphon's composition: sometime between the ninth and eleventh centuries.[33] In particular, Baun maintains that the Virgin's intercessory role in her apocalypse corresponds very closely with the Marian piety of the middle Byzantine period.[34]

Nevertheless, such a late dating seems rather unlikely, particularly in the light of certain new discoveries regarding the Marian piety of early Byzantium. Many of the elements that Baun considers distinctive of middle-Byzantine piety can now be located in the sixth and seventh centuries, in some cases even earlier. Belief in the special power of the Virgin's intercessions, for instance, is already attested in the ancient Dormition narratives. Likewise many of the specific qualities of Mary's intercessions that Baun links with the middle Byzantine period are now known to have emerged much earlier than previously thought, as evidenced especially by the long-overlooked *Life of the Virgin* attributed to Maximus the Confessor. This seventh-century biography of the Virgin laid much of the basis for later Byzantine devotion to Mary and served as the primary source for many of the most important and influential Marian writings of the middle Byzantine period. Of these works one might single out especially the tenth-century *Life of the Virgin* by John the Geometer, a text whose dependence on Maximus's *Life of the Virgin* is quite profound.[35] As Baun notes, John's *Life of the Virgin* and *Apoc. Vir.* "belong recognizably to the same Marian thought-world, one in which Mary is acclaimed as the mediatrix between God and man, the most powerful intercessor for sinners."[36] Yet it is now clear that the Marian thought-world of John's biography has been taken largely from the seventh-century Maximus *Life of the Virgin*. Therefore, Mary's intercessions in *Apoc. Vir.* not only are entirely consistent with an earlier dating, but their similarities to the earliest *Life of the Virgin* possibly even invite such a dating, according to Baun's own arguments.

Consequently, Bauckham's suggestion of a date sometime between the sixth and ninth

---

31. Syrtsova (*Apokryfichna apokaliptyka*, 45–46) suggests that we should not rule out the possibility of such an early date (I thank again Leena Mari Peltomaa for sharing with me Thomas Mark Németh's German translation of this key passage). James (*Apocrypha Anecdota*, 1:113) suggests the ninth century, while Richard Bauckham ("Virgin, Apocalypses of the," *ABD* 1:854) proposes sometime between the sixth and ninth centuries.

32. Baun frequently draws attention to these elements, although they do not necessarily date the text as late as she has proposed; see *Tales from Another Byzantium*, e.g., 12, 188, 193–96, 343–54.

33. Baun, *Tales from Another Byzantium*, 216, although one should note that Baun argues more extensively here, and perhaps more persuasively, for such a dating of the *Apocalypse of Anastasia*.

34. Baun, *Tales from Another Byzantium*, 91, 272–99.

35. Stephen J. Shoemaker, trans., *Maximus the Confessor, The Life of the Virgin: Translated, with an Introduction and Notes* (New Haven: Yale University Press, 2012), esp. 14–22.

36. Baun, *Tales from Another Byzantium*, 282–84. See also idem, "Discussing Mary's Humanity in Medieval Byzantium," in *The Church and Mary* (ed. Robert N. Swanson; Studies in Church History 39; Suffolk: Boydell & Brewer, 2004), 63–72.

century remains the most likely. Moreover, in light of *Apoc. Vir.*'s similarities to Maximus's *Life of the Virgin* and its apparent connections with the earliest Dormition apocrypha, one is further inclined to favor a date within the earlier end of this range, possibly in the seventh century. The only certainties are afforded by the earliest extant manuscripts from the eleventh century: the existence of two distinct recensions by this time would appear to indicate the apocryphon's composition by the tenth century at the latest. Nevertheless, even though this particular version of Mary's otherworldly journey is a relatively recent production, the fact that *Apoc. Paul* now seems to have made use of an even earlier and closely related apocalypse of the Virgin from the ancient Dormition traditions means that the status of this text within the broader tradition of "tours of hell" will need to be largely rethought.

Translation

The translation that follows is based on Syrtsova's recent edition, and accordingly it presents a translation of the eleventh-century Vatican manuscript that forms the basis of her edition. To my knowledge, this is the first translation of this important early version into any language other than Ukrainian. So, together with James's edition of the Oxford manuscript and the translations of it by Rutherfurd and Baun, this translation will now make both of the two earliest recensions available in English. The section numbers below follow Syrtsova's edition, while the numbers given in parentheses correspond with the section numbers in James's edition and the English translations by Rutherfurd and Baun. I have not provided the variants from the Oxford (or any other) manuscript in the notes to the translation, since they are fairly numerous and generally not of major significance. Readers interested in comparing the two earliest versions are accordingly advised to compare Baun's translation with the present one.

Bibliography

EDITIONS AND TRANSLATIONS

Baun, Jane. *Tales from Another Byzantium: Celestial Journey and Local Community in the Medieval Greek Apocrypha.* Cambridge: Cambridge University Press, 2006. (Comprehensive study with English translation of Oxford, Bodleian Library, Misc. gr. 77.)

Delatte, Armand. *Anecdota atheniensia.* 2 vols. Bibliothèque de la Faculté philosophie et lettres de l'Université de Liège 88. Liège: Faculté de Philosophie et Lettres, 1927. (Edition of the shorter medieval version in vol. 1:273–58.)

Hasdeu, Bogdan Petriceicu. *Cuvente den bătrâni: limba română vorbită între 1550–1600: studiu paleografico-linguistic.* 3 vols. Direcţia Generală a Arhivelor Statului. Publicatiuni istorico-filologice. Bucharest: Societatii Academice Romane, 1878–1881. (Synopsis of Romanian, Slavonic, and Greek versions.)

James, Montague Rhodes. *Apocrypha Anecdota: A Collection of Thirteen Apocryphal Books and Fragments Now First Edited from Manuscripts.* TS 2.3. Cambridge: Cambridge University Press, 1893. (Edition and translation of Oxford, Bodleian Library, Misc. gr. 77.)

Pernot, Hubert. "Descente de la Vierge aux Enfers, d'après les manuscrits de Paris." *Extrait de la revue des études grecques* 13 (1900): 233–57. (Editions of three Paris manuscripts.)

Rutherfurd, Andrew, trans. "The Apocalypse of the Virgin." *ANF* 9: 167–74.

Syrtsova, Olena Mykolaivna. *Apokryfična apokaliptyka: filosofs'ka ekzeheza i tekstolohiya z vydannyam hretskoho tekstu Apokalipsysa Bohorodytsi za rukopysom XI stolittya Ottobonia-*

nus, hr. 1, *Textologia antiquae et mediae aetatis.* Kiev: KM Academia, 2000. (Edition based on Vatican, Biblioteca apostolica, Ottoboni 1.)

Sreznevskiy, Izmail Ivanovič, ed. *Drevnie pamyatniki russkago pis'ma i yazyka X-XIV vekov.* Saint Petersburg: Tipografiya Imperatorskoy akademii nauk, 1863. (*Editio princeps* based on Vienna, Österreichische Nationalbibliothek, Theol. gr. 333.)

Vasiliev, Athanasius, ed. *Anecdota graeco-byzantina, pars prior.* Moscow: Imperial University, 1893. (Edition of the shorter medieval version, pp. 125–34.)

STUDIES

Bauckham, Richard. "The Four Apocalypses of the Virgin Mary." Pages 332–62 in *The Fate of the Dead: Studies on Jewish and Christian Apocalypses.* NovTSup 93. Leiden: Brill, 1998.

Himmelfarb, Martha. *Tours of Hell: An Apocalyptic Form in Jewish and Christian Literature.* Philadelphia: University of Pennsylvania Press, 1983.

Mimouni, Simon C. "Les Apocalypses de la Vierge: État de la question." *Apocrypha* 4 (1993): 101–12.

Shoemaker, Stephen J. *Ancient Traditions of the Virgin Mary's Dormition and Assumption.* OECS. Oxford: Oxford University Press, 2002.

The Apocalypse of the Virgin[a]

Michael appears to the Virgin Mary

1 (1) The All-Holy Theotokos was about to go to the Mount of Olives to pray. *Liber Requiei* 1–3 Praying to the Lord God she said, "In the name of the Father and the Son and the Holy Spirit; let the archangel Michael come, so that he may tell me about the punishments and about the things in heaven and on the earth and below the earth." As soon as she spoke, Michael, the commander-in-chief[b] came down with the angels of the east and the west and angels of the south and the north, and they saluted the Highly Favored One[c] and said to her:

> "Hail, radiance of the Father!
> Hail dwelling of the Son, hail overshadowing of the Holy Spirit! Luke 1:35
> Hail firmament of the seven heavens!
> Hail stronghold of the firmament!
> Hail worship of the angels, hail proclamation of the prophets!
> Hail loftier than all unto the throne of God!"

And the Highly Favored One said to the angel:

> "Hail to you as well Michael, commander-in-chief, the minister of the
>   invisible Father!
> Hail Michael, commander-in-chief, associate also of my Son!
> Hail Michael, commander-in-chief, who rules over all things and is worthy
>   to stand beside the throne of the Lord!
> Hail Michael, commander-in-chief, who is about to sound the trumpet
>   and awaken those who have been asleep for ages! Rev 11:15
> Hail Michael, commander-in-chief, first of all in the presence of God!"

2 (2) Having acclaimed all the angels in like manner, the Highly Favored One began to petition the commander-in-chief and to say, "Tell me of all things on the earth." The commander-in-chief said to her, "Whatever you ask me, Highly Favored One, I will tell you." The All-Holy One[d] said to him, "How many pun-

---

a. The title according to the manuscript is "The Apocalypse of the All-Holy Theotokos concerning the Punishments."
b. I.e., of the heavenly host.
c. *Kecharitōmenē*.
d. *Panagia*.

Liber Requiei 90;
Obseq. Virg. p. 47

ishments are there, by which the human race is punished?" And again the Highly Favored One said to him, "Tell me of the things in heaven and on the earth."

Mary and Michael travel to Hades

3 (3) Then the commander-in-chief Michael gave the order and it was revealed by the western angels. Hades opened, and she saw those who were being punished there. There lay a multitude of men and women who were wailing. The Highly Favored One asked the commander-in-chief, "Who are these and what are their sins?" The commander-in-chief said, "Mistress, these are those who did not believe in the Father and the Son and the Holy Spirit, and for this reason they are thus punished here."

Liber Requiei 90, 95;
Obseq. Virg. p. 47

4 (4) She saw in another place a great darkness, and there lay a multitude of men and women. And she said, "What is this darkness and who are those being punished in it?" The commander-in-chief said, "Lady, many souls lie in this darkness." The All-Holy One said, "Let the darkness be taken away so that I may see this punishment also." The commander-in-chief said to the Highly Favored One, "It is not possible that you should see this punishment." And those guarding them answered and said, "Mistress, we have a command from the invisible Father that they will not see the light until your blessed Son shines forth on the earth."

Overcome with grief, the All-Holy One lifted up her eyes to the undefiled throne of the Father and said, "In the name of the Father and the Son and the Holy Spirit, let the darkness be taken away, that I may see this punishment also." Immediately that darkness was lifted up so that it covered the seven heavens.

5 And there lay a multitude of men and women, and there was great lamentation and great wailing. Seeing them, the All-Holy One wept and said to them, "What are you doing, wretched ones? How is it that you are found there?" But there was no voice nor anything heard. The angels guarding them said, "Why do you not speak to the Highly Favored One?" Those being punished said to her, "Mistress, we have not seen light in ages, and we are not able to look up." Boiling pitch lay upon them, and seeing them the All-Holy One wept.

And again those being punished said to her, "How is it that you ask about us, holy Mistress? Your blessed Son came upon the earth and did not ask about us, neither did John the Baptist nor Moses the great prophet, and the apostle Paul did not appear to us. How is it that you, All-Holy One, the fortification of the Christians who intercedes exceedingly with the Master on behalf of Christians, would deem it worthy to ask about us, your servants?"

6 Then the All-Holy One said to Michael, the commander-in-chief, "What is their sin?" The commander-in-chief said, "These are they who did not honor the Father and the Son and the Holy Spirit and did not confess you as Theotokos, that from you our Lord Jesus Christ the Son of God was born and took

Apoc. Pet. (Eth.) 7

flesh, and for this reason they are punished here." Again weeping, the All-Holy One said to them, "Why did you commit such an error, wretched ones? Why did you not glorify the Father and the Son and the Holy Spirit? Why did you not worship the consubstantial Trinity? Why did you not confess that the Son and Word of God received flesh from me? Why did you not believe that Christ the Redeemer was born from me, his servant? Or did you not hear the voice of the prophet, '*Look the virgin shall be with child and bear a son, and you shall name him Emmanuel*'? The judgment of God is just."   Isa 7:14 (Matt 1:23)

When the All-Holy One said these things, the darkness again fell upon them as it was from the beginning.

The punishments in the southern places

7 (5) And the commander-in-chief said, "Where would you like us to go, Highly Favored One? To the west or to the south?" She said, "To the south." Immediately the cherubim and the seraphim appeared, and they led forth the Highly Favored One to the south, where the river of fire came forth. Therein lay a multitude of men and women, some up to the waist, some up to the chest, some up to the neck, and others up to the top of the head. Seeing them the Theotokos asked the commander-in-chief, saying, "Who are these, and what are their sins?" The commander-in-chief said, "These who lie in it up to their waist are those who inherited the curse of father and mother, and because of this they are thus punished here as accursed."   Apoc. Pet. (Eth.) 6 Apoc. Paul 31

8 (6) The All-Holy One said, "And who are these lying in the fire up to the chest?" The commander-in-chief said, "These are those who beat, outraged, and defiled their godparents in fornication, and because of this they are punished thus here."   Apoc. Pet. (Eth.) 7

9 (7) The Theotokos said to the commander-in-chief, "Who are these lying up to the neck in the flame of the fire?" He said, "These, All-Holy One, are those who ate human flesh." The Theotokos said, "And how is it possible for one person to eat of the flesh of another person?" The commander-in-chief (said), "Listen, Mistress, I will tell you about this. These are those who threw off their own unborn children from their wombs and cast them out as food for the dogs and those who betrayed their brothers before kings and rulers, and because of this they are punished thus."   Apoc. Pet. (Eth.) 8; Apoc. Paul 40

10 (8) The All-Holy One said, "Who are these lying in the fire up to the top of the head?" The commander-in-chief said, "These are those who take interest from their money and of their own free will go forth into the church of God. And because of this they are punished thus."   Apoc. Pet. (Eth.) 10; Apoc. Paul 37

11 (9) Then she saw in another place a person hanging by the feet, and worms were devouring him. She said to the commander-in-chief, "Who is this, and what is his sin?" He said, "This is one who laid hold of the precious and life-giving Cross and swore falsely. The angels tremble before it, but people lay hold of it and swear falsely. And because of this they are punished thus."

12 (10) Then she saw a woman hanging from her two ears, and (worms) were devouring her. And she asked, "Who is she, and what is her sin?" The commander-in-chief said, "This is one who eavesdropped in her neighbors' houses and made up wicked and contentious words. And because of this she is punished thus."

The punishments in the western places

13 (11) Seeing these things the All-Holy One wept and said to the angel, "*It would have been better for that one not to have been born.*" He said to her, "Truly, All-Holy One, you have not yet seen the great punishments and agonies of the sin-   Mark 14:21//Matt 26:24

ners." The All-Holy One said, "Come, Michael, the great commander, and lead me forth so that I may see all the punishments." The commander-in-chief said, "Where would you like for us to go?" The All-Holy One said, "To the west." And immediately a luminous cloud appeared and led her forth to the west.

14 (12) She saw a cloud of fire that was spread out, and a multitude of men and women lay therein. And the Theotokos said, "What was their sin?" He said, "These are they who on the morning of the holy Lord's Day lie like the dead and do not glorify God in the church. And because of this they are punished." The All-Holy One said, "If someone cannot go forth or cannot wake up early, what shall he do?" The commander-in-chief said, "Listen All-Holy One, if someone's house is set on fire on all four (sides), and fire surrounds him, and he cannot come out, he has a pardon, for it is not possible to flee from the fire because it surrounds him. Thus even sloth[a] is somehow able to have a pardon."

15 (13) Then she saw in another place fiery benches, and on them sat a multitude of men and women who were burning. The All-Holy One asked, "Who are these, and what are their sins?" The commander-in-chief said, "These, All-Holy One, are those who do not stand up for the priests when they enter into the temple of God, and similarly those who do not stand for their godparents. And because of this they are punished thus."

16 (14) Then the All-Holy One saw in another place an iron tree, and it had branches of iron, and a multitude of men and women were hanging on it by their tongues. Seeing them the All-Holy One wept, and asked, "Who are these and what are their sins?" The commander-in-chief said, "These are perjurers, blasphemers, slanderers, deniers of the faith of Christ, false accusers, the foul-mouthed, the quarrelsome, and those who divided brothers from brothers and wives from husbands, and those who did not keep the bed undefiled and separated faithful brothers from the faith of Christ, and were rousing strife and tension in them with their brothers."

Apoc. Pet. (Eth.) 7, 9, 12

17 (15) The All-Holy One saw in another place a man hanging from four (limbs), and from his nails blood poured forth violently, and his tongue was tied in a flame of fire, and he was unable to groan or say "Lord, have mercy on me." Seeing him the All-Holy One wept and said, "Lord, have mercy" thrice. After she said this, the angel who had authority over the scourge came and released the man's tongue for the glory and honor of the immaculate Lady.

The All-Holy One asked the commander-in-chief, "Who is this pitiful one who has such a punishment?" He said, "This, All-Holy One, is the steward who did not do the will of God but ate the things of the church, saying, 'The one who serves in the temple gets his food from the temple.' And because of this he is punished thus." The All-Holy One said, "Let it be unto him as he believed." And again he tied his tongue.

1 Cor 9:13

Liber Requiei 98

The punishments of the clergy

18 (16) Then the angel said, "Come, All-Holy One, and I will show unto you where the clergy are punished." The All-Holy One went forth and saw priests hanging from their twenty nails, and fire was coming out from their heads

---

a. Or possibly "hesitation" or "fear."

and flowing over them. Seeing them the All-Holy One wept and asked the commander-in-chief, saying, "Who are these and what are their sins?" The angel said, "These, All-Holy One, are those who were standing before the altar of God, and when they were breaking the body of our Lord Jesus Christ, the stars fell down, and the dreadful throne in heaven shook and the footstool of our Lord trembled, and they did not realize it, nor did they understand the mystery of God, but they were thinking little of his immaculate body and blood without fear of God. And because of this they are punished thus here."

Liber Requiei 95–96; Apoc. Paul 34, 36

19 (17) Then the All-Holy One saw a man and a winged beast having three heads like flames of fire; two heads were at the man's eyes and the third head was at his mouth. Seeing him the All-Holy One asked the angel, "Who is this, that he cannot free himself from the mouth of the dragon?" The angel said to her, "This, All-Holy One, is the reader who does not practice the commands of the holy Gospel."

Liber Requiei 95; Apoc. Paul 36

20 (18) And the angel said, "Come, All-Holy One, and I will show you where the angelic schema[a] is punished." She went forth and saw them where they were lying in the fire, and the sleepless worm gnawed them. The All-Holy One said, "Who are these, and what are their sins?" The angel said, "These, All-Holy One, are those who wore the angelic schema and on earth were called patriarchs and metropolitans and archbishops, but they were not worthy of their name, nor did they honor it. On earth they were asked, 'Bless, holy ones,'[b] but in heaven they are not called holy, because they did not act as those bearing the angelic schema, and because of this they are punished thus here."

Mark 9:48; Isa 66:24

Apoc. Paul 35

21 (19) Then she saw women hanging by their fingernails, and a flame of fire came out of their mouths and burned them. Many beasts devoured them, and they cried out, groaning, "Have mercy on us, for we are punished more severely than all those who are in the punishments!" Seeing them, the All-Holy One wept and asked the angel, "Who are these and what are their sins?" The angel said, "These are the wives of priests who did not honor the priests, but after their priests died they took husbands, and because of this they are punished thus here."

22 (20) The All-Holy One saw in the same manner also a deaconess hanging, and a two-headed beast was gnawing her breasts. The All-Holy One asked the angel, "What is her sin?" He said, "She is a deaconess who defiled her body in fornication, and because of this she is punished thus."

23 (21) She saw other women over the fire, and all the beasts devoured them. The All-Holy One asked, "Who are these and what is their sin?" He said, "These are those who did not do the will of God, being lovers of money, and being impious they took interest on accounts."

(22) Hearing these things, the All-Holy One wept and said, "Woe to the sinners!" And the angel said, "Why do you cry out, Lady? Truly you have not yet seen the great punishments."

---

a. A type of monastic habit indicating advanced rank. The text continues to indicate high-ranking bishops, who would have been celibate.

b. Or possibly "they were called blessed holy ones."

The punishments in the left parts of Paradise

24 The angel said, "Come, All-Holy One, and I will show you every punishment." And the Theotokos said, "Show me, great commander." He said to her, "Where would you like for us to go, Highly Favored One? To the eastern parts, or toward the left parts of Paradise?" She said, "To the left parts of Paradise."

(23) As soon as she spoke, he led forth the Highly Favored One to the left parts of Paradise. And behold, there was a great river of fire and great darkness. The appearance of the river was darker than pitch, and in it was lying a multitude of men and women, and it boiled like a cauldron and like a wild sea raging with waves, and the waves were upon the sinners. When the waves rose, they sank the sinners. And they were not able to look up and say, "Have mercy, just judge." But the sleepless worm was gnawing them, and there was no counting the number of the beasts that were gnawing them.

25 Seeing the All-Holy Theotokos, the angels who were punishing them all cried out with a great voice and said, "Holy is God who has compassion through the Theotokos! We give you thanks, O Son of God, since from eternity we have not seen light, and today we have seen it through the Theotokos." And again they all cried out with one voice, saying, "Hail, Highly Favored Theotokos! Hail, lamp of the light that never sets![a] Hail to you also, Michael, the commander-in-chief, the intercessor for all creation! For we, seeing the sinners being punished, are greatly grieved."

The All-Holy One, when she saw the angels humbled on account of the sinners, lamented and said, "Woe to sinners and their neighbors." And she said, "Let us see the sinners." When the All-Holy One went forth with the archangel and all the angels, they lifted up one voice saying, "Lord have mercy!"

26 After they made the fervent (prayer), the river's surge stopped, the fiery waves grew calm, and the sinners appeared as mustard seeds. Seeing them, the All-Holy One wept and said, "What is this river, and what are its waves?" The angel said, "This river is the outer fire, and those who are being tortured are the Jews, who crucified our Lord Jesus Christ the Son of God and who refused holy baptism, and those who commit fornication against the immaculate chrism of godparenthood, and he who fornicates against mother and daughter, and sorcerers and murderers, and women who strangle their babies."

The All-Holy One said, "According to their faith, let it be unto them." Immediately the waves were upon the sinners, and the darkness covered them. The commander-in-chief said, "If anyone should be cast into this darkness, there will be no remembrance of him in the presence of God." And the All-Holy One said, "Woe to sinners, for the flame of the fire is everlasting."

27 (24) The commander-in-chief said, "Come, All-Holy One, and I will show you the lake of fire, where the race of the Christians is punished." The All-Holy One went forth and saw the lake of fire and the sinners in it. Some she heard, but others she did not see.[b] She asked the angel, "What is their sin?" He said, "These, All-Holy One, are those who were baptized and swore allegiance to Christ the Word alone but did the works of the devil and lost the time of their repentance. And because of this they are punished thus."

---

a. Or "the inaccessible light."

b. Or possibly, "she saw easily."

Marginal references: Mark 9:48; Isa 66:24 · Apoc. Paul 41 · Rev 20:10, 14–15

Mary intercedes on behalf of the sinners in the torments

28 (25) The All-Holy One said, "I beg of you one request: I ask of you that I enter in and also be punished with the Christians, because they are the children of my son." The angel said to her, "May you rest in Paradise, Lady." The All-Holy One said, "I beg of you, let us pray for the sinners that the Lord our God will hear them and have mercy on them." The commander-in-chief said, "As the Lord God lives, seven times a day and seven times a night, when we offer up the hymn of the Master, we, the angels, intercede on behalf of them all, and the Lord God does not hear us."

Liber Requiei 93–94

29 (26) The All-Holy One said, "I beg of you, order the armies of the angels and raise me up to the height of heaven and make me to stand in the presence of the invisible Father." And she stretched forth her immaculate hands to the immaculate throne of the Father and said with a great voice, "Holy Trinity, Father, Son, and Holy Spirit, God, the invisible Lord who loves humankind, compassionate Master, have mercy on the sinners, for I have seen, Lord, their great afflictions and punishments, and I cannot bear their pain. Command your servant, Master, that I will also be punished with the Christians."

There came a voice saying, "How can I have mercy on them, who did not themselves have mercy? Let them receive what is due according to their deeds." The Theotokos said, "I do not beg, Master, on behalf of the unbelieving Jews, but for the piteous Christians I call upon your compassion." There came a voice for the second time, saying, "They did not have mercy on their own brothers, and how can I have mercy on them?"

Liber Requiei 100

The Theotokos said, "Long-suffering Lord, have mercy on the Christian sinners. Look upon their punishments, for every creature calls upon me, your servant, saying, 'Holy Mistress, help us!'" Then the Lord said to her, "Listen, Holy of Holies, All-Holy Virgin, if anyone calls upon your name, I will not forsake him, either in heaven or on earth."

Liber Requiei 99

30 (27) The Theotokos said, "Where is Moses? Where are all the prophets and fathers? Where are the holy apostles and martyrs and all the saints? Where are you, holy Paul, apostle of the Lord? Where are the four evangelists, the eyewitnesses of the Lord, who proclaimed him? Where is the power of the precious and life-giving Cross, which delivered Adam and Eve from the ancient curse? Where is the holy Lord's Day, the boast of Christians, the name of the Lord's third-day resurrection? Where are the orders of the angels? Come, and let us pray for the Christian sinners, that the Lord will hear them and have mercy on them."

31 Then Michael the archangel and all the angels raised one voice with the Lady, saying, "Have mercy, Master, on the Christians! Have mercy on those who confess you, the Father and the Son and the Holy Spirit, true immortal God, even if they have fallen into sin!" Then Moses also spoke, "Have mercy, Master, on those to whom I gave the Law!" And John said, "Have mercy, Master, on those to whom I gave your New Testament and the holy Gospel!" Then Paul cried out, saying, "Have mercy, Master, on those to whom I brought your epistles in the Church!"

Liber Requiei 92–93

And the Lord God said, "Listen, all of you: if they lived their lives according to the Law which Moses gave, and according to the Gospel which John gave, and according to the epistles which Paul brought, and according to the power of the precious and life-giving Cross, thus will they be judged." They had nothing to say except, "Have mercy, O just judge! Have mercy, Lord!"

(28) The Theotokos again said, "Have mercy, Master, on the sinners, because they kept your Law and heeded your Gospel, and believed in your Son, and were baptized with holy baptism, and honored your precious and life-giving Cross, and confessed you, the Father, and the Son, and the Holy Spirit on the earth, but they were foolish, simple people, and the devil envied them. And the Lord said, "Listen, All-Holy One: if anyone did evil to them, and they did not requite with evil, you speak rightly. But if some people did not do evil to them, and they requited with evil, how can I have mercy on them? But it will be given to them according to their deeds." Then they all, hearing the voice of the Master, had nothing to answer.

1 Thess 5:15; Rom 12:17; 1 Pet 3:9

32 When the All-Holy One saw that they were all at a loss, and the Master did not hear them, and his mercy was hidden from the sinners, she spoke thus, "Where is Gabriel, who declared to me 'Hail, for from before the ages you shall conceive him who is co-beginningless with the Father,' and now does not look upon the sinners? Come, all you righteous elect, whom God has justified, and let us fall down before the presence of the compassionate and merciful God, so that God will hear us and have mercy on them." Then Michael the archangel, and all the angels, and the righteous, and the prophets, and the apostles, and the martyrs, and all the elect fell down before God, saying, "Have mercy, have mercy, have mercy, Master, on the sinners according to your great mercy!"

The Lord grants a yearly respite to those in the torments

33 (29) Then the Master,[a] the merciful lover of humankind, seeing the supplication of all those who were pleasing to him, had compassion and said, "Go down, my beloved Son, and heed the supplication of my servants, and let your face shine on the sinners." Then when the Master, the Son and Word of God, came down from his immaculate throne and those who were in the punishments saw him, they all raised one voice saying, "Have mercy on us, Master!"

The Master said to them, "Listen, all of you: I made Paradise and formed humankind according to my own image. But humankind transgressed, and by its own sins it was handed over to death. But I would not suffer the works of my hands to be tyrannized by the serpent, on account of which I was born of the immaculate Virgin Mary. And having been baptized, I blessed the Jordan, on account of the nature that had grown old in sin. I was nailed to the cross, in order to free you from the ancient curse. I asked for water, and you gave me vinegar with gall. I was placed in the tomb by the Jews; I trampled down the enemy; I raised up my elect. And you would not listen to me, but you bound yourself to the present age, and falling into sins, you became playthings of the demons, and you have received what is due according to your deeds.

34 "But now, because of the supplication of my mother, and because of Michael my archangel and the multitude of the holy angels, and because of all the

---

a. The manuscript has here in addition "the Son," which is absent, however, from other early manuscripts, and so I have omitted this in light of the instructions given to the Son that follow.

saints of the ages who are pleasing to me, you will have rest for the days of the holy Resurrection, until the day of Pentecost to glorify the Father and the Son and the Holy Spirit."

Liber Requiei 100;
Apoc. Paul 44

(30) Then they all raised a voice, saying, "Glory to your Kingdom, Lord! Glory to your compassion, Master! Glory to your love of humankind, Holy One, for to you is due honor, majesty, and magnificence, to the Father, the Son, and the Holy Spirit, now and always, and forever. Amen."

The Tiburtine Sibyl
A new translation and introduction

by Stephen J. Shoemaker

Although the *Tiburtine Sibyl* (*Tib. Sib.*; *CANT* 320) is today largely obscure and forgotten, even among scholars of Christian apocrypha and late antiquity, it was once among the most popular and influential writings of Western Christendom. This text offers an apocalyptic vision of the Roman Empire's eschatological triumph, as related through the Sibyl's interpretation of a mysterious dream beheld simultaneously by one hundred Roman senators in a single night. Composed toward the end of the fourth century, seemingly between 378 and 390, *Tib. Sib.* presents one of the earliest articulations of the imperial eschatology that would dominate the apocalyptic imagination of both the Christian Roman Empire and its medieval imitators in the West.[1] Perhaps most notably, we meet here for the first time the legendary figure of the Last Emperor, who plays a starring role in this eschatological drama. Through his victory over the enemies of Christ, the Last Emperor will inaugurate the events of the *eschaton*, and then he will travel to Jerusalem to lay down his diadem and royal garments, thereby handing over rule to God. This myth of the Last Emperor's triumph and abdication prior to the Second Coming of Christ would become one of the cornerstones of medieval Christian eschatology.[2]

Contents
The story of *Tib. Sib.* begins at the dawn of Roman history, during the rule of a "Trojan" emperor, which would appear to be a reference to Rome's legendary foundation by Aeneas and other Trojan refugees (2:1).[3] When the Sibyl begins to preach in various places throughout the Mediterranean world, the leading citizens of Rome hear of her remarkable prophetic gifts and persuade the emperor to have her brought to Rome with great honor. We then learn that one hundred men from the Roman senate shared the same dream in a single night: a vision of nine different suns (2:1–4). These men approach the Sibyl and ask her for the meaning of their dream (2:5–6). She explains to them that "the nine suns that you saw prefigure all future generations. Truly the differences that you see among them will also be a different life for humankind." The Sibyl then begins to reveal the future,

---

1. See, e.g., Robert Konrad, *De ortu et tempore Antichristi: Antichristvorstellung und Geschichtsbild des Abtes Adso von Montier-en-Der* (Münchener historische Studien, Abteilung mittelalterliche Geschichte 1; Kallmünz, Opf.: Michael Lassleben, 1964); Podskalsky, *Byzantinische Reichseschatologie;* Paul J. Alexander, "The Diffusion of Byzantine Apocalypses in the Medieval West and the Beginnings of Joachimism," in *Prophecy and Millenarianism: Essays in Honour of Marjorie Reeves* (ed. Ann Williams; New York: Longman, 1980), 53–106.

2. For further discussion of this theme, see e.g., Alexander, *Byzantine Apocalyptic Tradition,* esp. 151–84; idem, "Byzantium"; idem, "Medieval Legend."

3. Sackur, *Sibyllinische Texte,* 172–73. See further note b to 2:1 of the translation.

describing the character of each of these nine generations to come. The first two ages will be idyllic; by the third age, however, things begin to take a turn for the worse: "nation will rise up against nation, and there will be many battles in Rome" (3:1). The fourth generation will witness the birth of Christ, and here the Sibyl relates a brief account of the birth, crucifixion, and resurrection of Christ that draws the ire of some of "the priests of the Hebrews," whom the Sibyl is quick to silence (3:3–8). The fifth generation will see the apostles spread the gospel throughout the world, and the sixth, seventh, and eighth generations will see mounting turmoil in the Roman Empire (3:11–13). In the ninth generation four kings will rule (i.e., the Tetrarchy), after which there "will arise another king, with the name C (i.e., Constantine), mighty in battle, who will reign for thirty years and will build a temple to God and will fulfill the law and establish justice on the earth for God's sake" (3:14–15).[4] The Sibyl then predicts that within sixty years the emperors will no longer rule from Constantinople (3:16). Next there is mention of an emperor who "will be burned with fire," seemingly a reference to the death of Valens, who died in 378 in the devastating Roman defeat by the Goths at Adrianople (3:16).[5]

At this point in the vision a lengthy medieval interpolation intrudes, updating the Sibyl's late ancient prophecies for a more recent audience by inserting a list of Lombard and German rulers from the sixth through the early eleventh centuries (chap. 4).[6] Eventually this inventory of medieval kings begins to break up, as material from the original late ancient text punctuates the notices concerning the most recent rulers. Here follows a forecast of war, famine, and natural disasters, as well as political corruption and religious persecution that correlates well with specific events from the reign of Constantius II (chap. 5).[7] Nevertheless, despite their historical basis, it is clear that these calamities are also introduced as portents of the impending end of the world. Then, after a second medieval interpolation (chap. 6), circumstances continue to degenerate, with "afflictions such as there have not been since the beginning of the world" (7:1) and the world is completely abandoned to the wicked and unjust. Then, the figure of the Last Emperor makes his dramatic appearance. His reign will witness great wealth and abundance, and this king will have before him a "Scripture" that says, "The king of the Romans will claim the entire kingdom of the Christians for himself" (7:5). Then he will destroy "the islands and cities of the pagans" together with their temples, forcing them to be baptized and to erect crosses in their temples, and the Jews will be forcibly converted (7:6). At this time the Antichrist will appear and begin to lead many astray, and the nations of Gog and Magog, which Alexander had enclosed, will come forth from the north (8:1–3). After the Last Emperor annihilates the peoples of Gog and Magog, he will travel to Jerusalem, and there "having laid down the diadem from his head and all his royal garb, he will hand over the kingdom of the Christians to God the Father and Jesus Christ his Son" (8:4). With the Roman Empire thus having come to an end, the Antichrist will be "openly revealed" for a time. The apocalypse then concludes with the Antichrist's defeat on the Mount of Olives by the Archangel Michael (8:5–6). *Tib. Sib.* comes to a close with a brief description of signs of the second coming and the judgment of the just and the impious (8:7–8).

---

4. Concerning the historical background, see esp. Sackur, *Sibyllinische Texte*, 156–57.

5. See Socrates, *Hist. eccl.* 4.38; Sozomen, *Hist. eccl.* 6.40.

6. For a discussion of dating the core of *Tib. Sib.* to the fourth century see Sackur, *Sibyllinische Texte*, 129–37, 181–84; Alexander, *Oracle of Baalbek*, 60–62.

7. As established by Sackur, *Sibyllinische Texte*, 157–62; see also Alexander, *Oracle of Baalbek*, 49–65.

Transmission History and Date of Composition

At present *Tib. Sib.* is best known from a Latin edition published by E. Sackur in 1898, which seems to preserve the earliest known version of the text. Working with only the small number of manuscripts known to him at the time, Sackur identified several different recensions and published the oldest of these on the basis of eight manuscripts. Except for the significant and obvious medieval interpolations noted above, this Latin version otherwise transmits this late ancient apocryphon with remarkable fidelity. Nevertheless, it is clear that a more comprehensive critical edition of the text is needed, particularly in light of the abundance of the manuscript tradition. The recent survey of *Tib. Sib.*'s transmission in the medieval Latin world by Anke Holdenried lays important groundwork for such an endeavor.[8] Moreover, it is also clear that the more recent Latin recensions do not depend on the version edited by Sackur, and so they may occasionally preserve some elements of the ancient text that were for some reason left out from this earliest redaction. The potential importance of the other Latin versions in this regard has been demonstrated particularly by the discovery and publication of a Greek version of *Tib. Sib.* This Greek version contains significant parallels to certain passages from the later Latin recensions that are absent from the version edited by Sackur, indicating that these passages once stood in their common Greek source.[9] Thus, a new edition would need to examine these later Latin versions in consultation with the Greek to determine the extent to which they may preserve ancient readings.

Even though the original language of *Tib. Sib.*'s composition was undoubtedly Greek, it is widely agreed that the Latin translation preserves an earlier version than the now extant Greek. Paul Alexander, who published the Greek version, convincingly demonstrated that it preserves a version of *Tib. Sib.* that was redacted at the very beginning of the sixth century, as is clearly indicated by the historical events and individuals to which it refers.[10] Like so many other similar apocalyptic texts, *Tib. Sib.*'s prophecies juxtapose a rehearsal of recent historical events with what amount to genuine predictions concerning events in the near future that will herald the *eschaton*'s arrival. Not surprisingly, as the text transitions from this historical section to its forecasts of the future, the seer's prognostic powers suddenly depart, and in this seam we can identify a fairly reliable date for the text's composition. As Alexander accordingly observes, "every apocalypse must have been written not long after the latest event to which it alludes," and so in the case of the Greek *Tib. Sib.*, this locates its production—or better still, redaction—sometime in the period between 502 and 506.[11]

These same principles convincingly place the Latin version of *Tib. Sib.* over a century earlier, and a broad scholarly consensus dates both the original Greek text and its Latin translation to the later fourth century.[12] Leaving aside the obvious medieval insertions,

---

8. Holdenried, *Sibyl and Her Scribes.*

9. See, e.g., Alexander, *Oracle of Baalbek*, 53–55 and 63–64 for examples that are also noted below. In addition to the translation that Alexander published with his edition of the Greek text, a second English translation has been published recently: Buitenwerf, "Tiburtine Sibyl (Greek)," in the More Old Testament Pseudepigrapha series. However, it is not clear, to me at least, how this text would fit within the category of Old Testament pseudepigrapha.

10. Alexander, *Oracle of Baalbek*, 41–47 and also 75–105. Concerning the original language, see Alexander, *Oracle of Baalbek*, 60–65.

11. Paul J. Alexander, "Medieval Apocalypses as Historical Sources," *AHR* 73 (1968): 997–1018 at 998–99, 1009.

12. See, e.g., Sackur, *Sibyllinische Texte*, 162–63; Konrad, *De ortu*, 43–53; Alexander, *Oracle of Baalbek*,

Sackur's painstaking analysis of the text demonstrates that the latest historical events to which the Latin *Tib. Sib.* refers belong to the end of the fourth century. Excluding the intrusive medieval kings, the latest figures to which Sackur's Latin version refers are Constantine and his sons, and the text reveals a rather detailed knowledge of events in the eastern provinces toward the end of Constantius II's reign, as noted already above. Alexander has also demonstrated on the basis of comparison with the Greek that references to the death of Valens and a prediction that Constantinople would no longer be the imperial capital after sixty years in the more recent Latin versions likely were present in the original text. Both of these restorations are consistent with composition at the end of the fourth century, and the forecast of Constantinople's demise in particular strongly indicates this date, since the prophecy would have been falsified by 390, which was the sixtieth year since the foundation of Constantinople. Likewise, as Alexander has demonstrated, structural comparison of the Greek version with the Latin reveals that the Greek has revised an earlier source that now largely survives in the Latin translation, further confirming its earlier date.[13]

However, there is some question as to whether the legend of the Last Emperor was already present in this earliest version of *Tib. Sib.*, inasmuch as this figure is largely absent from the early-sixth-century Greek version.[14] This is equally true of the much later Arabic, Garšūnī, and Ethiopic versions that have been published to date, although their significance for reconstructing the early tradition is not entirely clear, and it seems likely that they derive from the Greek. As other scholars have noted, there would appear to be some vestiges of the Last Emperor myth in these more recent versions, but the absence of many important elements is striking.[15] Nevertheless, it is quite clear that the myth of the Last Emperor belongs to the apocalyptic traditions of late antiquity, and elements of the legend itself indicate such a dating. Most notable is the complete absence of any mention of the Muslims or the Islamic conquests, which are defining features of more recent versions of this tradition. The concern instead with paganism would seem to reflect a fourth-century context, as does the Last Emperor's name: Constans.[16] Moreover, comparison of the Last Emperor's appearance in *Tib. Sib.* with his description in the mid-seventh-century *Apocalypse of Ps.-Methodius* also confirms the antiquity of this tradition: it is clear that *Apoc.*

49–65; idem, *Byzantine Apocalyptic Tradition*, 162–63, 171–72 esp. n. 74; Podskalsky, *Byzantinische Reichseschatologie*, 55 n. 333; Rangheri, "Epistola ad Gerbergam," 708–9 n. 79; John Wortley, "The Literature of Catastrophe," *Byzantine Studies/Études byzantines* 4 (1977): 16–17; Bernard McGinn, *Visions of the End: Apocalyptic Traditions in the Middle Ages* (Records of Civilization, Sources and Studies 96; New York: Columbia University Press, 1979), 43–44; idem, "*Teste David cum Sibylla*," 26–28; idem, "Oracular Transformations," 612–13; Möhring, *Weltkaiser der Endzeit*, 35–44, 49. Note that while some of these scholars have on occasion expressed some doubt as to whether the Last Emperor tradition was a part of this late-fourth-century *Tib. Sib.* (a point discussed in some detail below), there is unanimous agreement that the text—except, of course, for the lists of medieval kings—otherwise dates to this time.

13. Alexander, *Oracle of Baalbek*, 48–55, 63–64.

14. See Alexander, "Byzantium and the Migration," 67 n. 35; Wortley, "Literature of Catastrophe," 16–17; McGinn, *Visions of the End*, 44; idem, "*Teste David cum Sibylla*," 26–27; idem, "Oracular Transformations," 607, 609, 613. Nevertheless, despite the suggestion by some scholars that the Last Emperor traditions of *Tib. Sib.* may depend on *Apoc. Ps.-Meth.*, the differences in the two accounts are so significant that this does not seem possible: see, e.g., Alexander, "Diffusion," 58, 63–64, & esp. 93–94 n. 9; Sackur, *Sibyllinische Texte*, 170; and Rangheri, "Epistola ad Gerbergam," 708–9 n. 79.

15. E.g., Alexander, *Oracle of Baalbek*, 21, 29; Basset, *La sagesse*, 19.

16. Sackur, *Sibyllinische Texte*, 167–68. See also Konrad, *De ortu*, 46–47; Rangheri, "Epistola ad Gerbergam," 708–9 n. 79; and Möhring, *Weltkaiser der Endzeit*, 42; cf. McGinn, *Visions of the End*, 295 n. 9.

Ps.-Meth. has adapted this earlier account of the Last Emperor to match the contours of his Syriac cultural milieu and the circumstances of Islamic hegemony.[17]

It is uncertain why this prominent figure from the Latin version has seemingly disappeared from the Greek version. It is certainly possible that the Greek redactor has for some reason deliberately eliminated the tradition. Or perhaps for some reason it was lacking in the particular version of *Tib. Sib.* that formed the basis for his redaction. It is certainly not out of the question that this legend may have been added to the Latin version at the time of its translation from Greek during the later fourth century or perhaps not long thereafter.[18] In any case, this myth of the Last Emperor was clearly in circulation prior to the Islamic conquests, as confirmed by its adaptation in *Apoc. Ps.-Meth.* Equally important is the appearance of this mythic figure in *5 Baruch,* an Ethiopic apocalypse from the early seventh century,[19] and significant echoes of this myth in Jewish apocalyptic literature from the same era.[20] Moreover, the basic building blocks of this Last Emperor tradition already appear in the third-century *Apocalypse of Elijah* (see 2:46–3:1),[21] whose penultimate savior, a king from the City of the Sun, "no doubt forms," as David Frankfurter notes, "one of the major sources of the 'Last Emperor' tradition in Byzantine apocalypticism: a human ruler whose beneficent accession and dominion would paradoxically usher in the period of the Antichrist."[22] In concert with this idea of a final eschatological king was the

---

17. See, e.g., Sackur, *Sibyllinische Texte,* 44, 170–72. See also Konrad, *De ortu,* 47–48; Alexander, *Byzantine Apocalyptic Tradition,* 167–69; Gerrit J. Reinink, "Die syrischen Wurzeln der mittelalterlichen Legende vom römischen Endkaiser," in *Non Nova, Sed Nova: Mélanges de civilisation médiévale dédiés à Willem Noomen* (ed. Martin Gosman and Jaap van Os; Mediaevalia Groningana 5; Groningen: Bouma's Boekhuis, 1984), 201–2; Gerrit J. Reinink, "Ps.-Methodius: A Concept of History in Response to the Rise of Islam," in *The Byzantine and Early Islamic Near East: Papers of the First Workshop on Late Antiquity and Early Islam* (ed. Averil Cameron and Lawrence I. Conrad; Princeton: Darwin, 1992), 149–87, 170–74, 176–77. Although it is seemingly not Reinink's intent to demonstrate how *Apoc. Ps.-Meth.* has adapted the traditions of *Tib. Sib.,* comparison of his conclusions in particular with the traditions from *Tib. Sib.* in fact shows this to be the case. For more on this matter, see Stephen J. Shoemaker, "The Reign of God Has Come: Eschatology and Empire in Late Antiquity and Early Islam," *Arabica: Journal of Arabic and Islamic Studies* 61 (2014): 514–58.

18. Rangheri, "Epistola ad Gerbergam," 708–9 n. 79; Möhring, *Weltkaiser der Endzeit,* 43–44. Cf. Alexander, *Oracle of Baalbek,* 63–65.

19. Critical edition by Joseph Halévy, ed., *Tĕʾĕzâza sanbat (Commandements du sabbat), accompagné de six autres écrits pseudo-épigraphiques admis par les Falachas ou Juifs d'Abyssinie* (Bibliothèque de l'École des hautes études Sciences historiques et philologiques 137; Paris: É. Bouillon, 1902), 95–96; trans. in Wolf Leslau, *Falasha Anthology* (Yale Judaica Series 6; New Haven: Yale University Press, 1951), 75–76. Regarding the date of the text, Pierluigi Piovanelli presented his arguments in a paper entitled "The Visions of Baruch and Gorgorios: Two 'Moral' Apocalypses in Late Antique Ethiopia," at the 2012 Annual Meeting of the Society for Biblical Literature in Chicago (19 November 2012). The foundation of the argument is the text's failure to make any mention of the Islamic conquests or any other event beyond the end of the sixth century.

20. See, e.g., Wout J. van Bekkum, "Jewish Messianic Expectations in the Age of Heraclius," in *The Reign of Heraclius (610–41): Crisis and Confrontation* (ed. Gerrit J. Reinink and Bernard H. Stolte; Leuven: Peeters, 2002), 95–112 at 107–8.

21. Georg Steindorff, ed., *Die Apokalypse des Elias: Eine unbekannte Apokalypse und Bruchstücke der Sophonias-Apokalypse* (TUGAL N.F. 2.3a; Leipzig: J. C. Hinrichs, 1899), 84–87; trans. David Frankfurter, *Elijah in Upper Egypt: The Apocalypse of Elijah and Early Egyptian Christianity* (SAC; Minneapolis: Fortress, 1993), 311–13; also available in a translation by Orval S. Wintermute in *The Old Testament Pseudepigrapha:* Vol. 1: *Apocalyptic Literature and Testaments* (ed. James H. Charlesworth; ABRL; Garden City, N.Y.: Doubleday, 1983), 721–53.

22. Frankfurter, *Elijah in Upper Egypt,* 24, 202; see also Alexander, *Oracle of Baalbek,* 60, 137.

ideology of the Roman Empire as a divinely elected polity that, as the last of Daniel's four kingdoms, was destined to be the last world empire.[23] These two notions would rather easily combine to yield the myth of the Last Roman Emperor, and accordingly, despite its puzzling absence from the Greek version, it would appear that this tradition also belongs to the late-fourth-century text of *Tib. Sib.*

Influence in Christian History and Literature

Of course, one might wonder if a text such as *Tib. Sib.* in fact belongs among Christian apocrypha, particularly in light of its unmistakably "pagan" framework. After all, this apocalypse is set in the early years of Roman history, well before the birth of Christ and the beginnings of Christianity, both of which it predicts. Nevertheless, there is a long history of including a corpus of several earlier "Sibylline Oracles" among the apocryphal literature of both Judaism and Christianity,[24] and it is quite clear that *Tib. Sib.* is simply a late ancient continuation of this same tradition. Indeed, if these earlier Sibyllines are to be considered apocrypha, then there is no reason to exclude this related text simply because it is slightly more recent. Moreover, despite this vision's pagan context, its contents focus squarely on biblical events and characters. Not only does it offer a somewhat distinctive account of the life and teachings of Jesus and the ministry of the apostles,[25] but its predictions also concern key elements of biblical eschatology, including especially the peoples of Gog and Magog, the appearance of the Antichrist, and the Second Coming of Christ.

Perhaps no less important is the fact that in the medieval West, *Tib. Sib.*'s influence on Christian eschatology far outweighed that of the Apocalypse of John, and its broader impact on the medieval Christian tradition was surpassed only by the Bible and the writings of the church fathers.[26] This oracle was immensely popular, surviving in over 130 known Latin manuscripts, as well as in a Greek version and in an as-yet-unknown number of Arabic, Ethiopic, and Slavonic manuscripts.[27] Moreover, its prophecies often were invested with an authority parallel to the biblical traditions—as witnessed, for instance, in the opening stanza of the famous "Dies irae" hymn from the Latin Requiem Mass: "Dies irae! Dies illa! Solvet saeclum in favilla, teste David cum Sibylla!" ("Day of wrath, that day! It will dissolve the world into ashes, as foretold by David and the Sibyl").[28] The Sibyl's fore-

---

23. See, e.g, Podskalsky, *Byzantinische Reichseschatologie*, 11–12.

24. E.g., John J. Collins, "Sibylline Oracles" in Charlesworth, ed., *Old Testament Pseudepigrapha*, 1:317–472; Ursula Treu, "Christian Sibyllines," in *New Testament Apocrypha*, vol. 1: *Writings Relating to the Apostles, Apocalypses and Related Subjects* (ed. Wilhelm Schneemelcher; trans. R. McL. Wilson; 2 vols.; rev. ed.; Louisville, Ky.: Westminster John Knox, 1991–1992), 652–84.

25. Alexander, *Oracle of Baalbek*, 67–74. See also David Flusser, "An Early Jewish-Christian Document in the Tiburtine Sibyl," in *Paganisme, judaïsme, christianisme: influences et affrontements dans le monde antique: mélanges offerts à Marcel Simon* (ed. A. Benoit, M. Philonenko, and C. Vogel; Paris: E. de Boccard, 1978), 153–83.

26. McGinn, "Oracular Transformations," 603–5; Holdenried, *Sibyl and Her Scribes*.

27. Concerning the Latin tradition, see esp. Holdenried, *Sibyl and Her Scribes*, 173–221, which includes an inventory of the known manuscripts. The Greek version has been edited in Alexander, *Oracle of Baalbek*. Regarding the other traditions, see Basset, *La sagesse*; Schleifer, *Die Erzählung der Sibylle*; Rifaat Y. Ebied and Michael J. L. Young, "A Newly Discovered Version of the Arabic Sibylline Prophecy," *OrChr* 60 (1976): 83–94; eadem, "An Unrecorded Arabic Version of the Sibylline Prophecy," *OCP* 43 (1977): 279–307; and Moses Gaster, "The Sibyl and the Dream of One Hundred Suns: An Old Apocryphon," *JRASy* 42 (1910): 609–23. Concerning possible evidence of an Armenian tradition, see Basset, *La sagesse*, 8; and Schleifer, *Die Erzählung der Sibylle*, 75.

28. See, e.g., McGinn, "*Teste David cum Sibylla*," 19.

cast regarding the end times is here invoked alongside the biblical tradition, revealing *Tib. Sib.* as more than just a supplement to the canonical texts but as an authoritative source of Christian doctrine in its own right. Inasmuch as the Sibyl's extracanonical predictions concerning the Antichrist and the Second Coming of Christ were widely preferred to those of the canonical Apocalypse, which it largely displaced in this regard, it is seemingly obvious that this text belongs among the apocryphal writings of late ancient Christianity.

Translation

In the absence of any better alternative, Sackur's edition serves as the basis for the following translation. Nevertheless, I have supplemented his text occasionally by following certain restorations that Alexander determined on the basis of the Greek. These additions are identified as such in the translation. The italicized passages in the translation (italicized also in Sackur's edition) indicate medieval additions that have been introduced into the original fourth-century text; to avoid confusion, verbatim Scripture passages are set in normal type. With respect to the various kings who are mentioned in the text, in most instances the text gives only their first initials (the Last Emperor "Constans" forms an important exception). To aid with comprehension, I have added their names in parentheses following Sackur's determinations of their identities.[29] I have also altered on occasion Sackur's division of the text, since several of the paragraphs in the edition are quite long. Likewise I have added chapter and verse numbers for ease of reference, since these are not present in the editions by Sackur and Alexander.

Bibliography

EDITIONS AND TRANSLATIONS

Alexander, Paul J. *The Oracle of Baalbek: The Tiburtine Sibyl in Greek Dress*. Dumbarton Oaks Studies 10. Washington, D.C.: Dumbarton Oaks Center for Byzantine Studies, 1967.

Basset, René. *La sagesse de Sibylle*. Les Apocryphes Éthiopiens 10. Paris: Bibliothèque de la Haute Science, 1900.

Buitenwerf, Rieuwerd. "The Tiburtine Sibyl (Greek): A New Translation and Introduction." Pages 176–88 in *Old Testament Pseudepigrapha: More Noncanonical Scriptures*. Vol. 1. Edited by Richard Bauckham et al. Grand Rapids, Mich.: Eerdmans, 2013.

Sackur, Ernst. *Sibyllinische Texte und Forschungen: Pseudomethodius, Adso und die tiburtinische Sibylle*. Halle: M. Niemeyer, 1898. (*Editio princeps* of the Latin tradition.)

Schleifer, Joel. *Die Erzählung der Sibylle: Ein Apokryph. Nach den karschunischen, arabischen und äthiopischen Handschriften zu London, Oxford, Paris und Rom*. Denkschriften der kaiserlichen Akad. der Wissensch. in Wien, Phil.-hist. Klasse 53.1. Vienna: Alfred Hölder, 1910.

STUDIES

Alexander, Paul J. *The Byzantine Apocalyptic Tradition*. Berkeley: University of California Press, 1985.

———. "Byzantium and the Migration of Literary Works and Motifs: The Legend of the Last Emperor." *Medievalia et Humanistica* n. s. 2 (1971): 47–68.

———. "The Medieval Legend of the Last Roman Emperor and Its Messianic Origin." *Journal of the Warburg and Courtauld Institutes* 41 (1978): 1–15.

---

29. Sackur, *Sibyllinische Texte*, 129–37.

Holdenried, Anke. *The Sibyl and Her Scribes: Manuscripts and Interpretation of the Latin Sibylla Tiburtina c. 1050–1500. Church, Faith, and Culture in the Medieval West.* Aldershot, U.K.: Ashgate, 2006.

Kurfeß, Alfons, and Jörg-Dieter Gauger. *Sibyllinische Weissagungen: Griechisch-Deutsch.* Sammlung Tusculum. Düsseldorf: Artemis & Winkler, 1998.

McGinn, Bernard. "Oracular Transformations: The 'Sibylla Tiburtina' in the Middle Ages." Pages 603–44 in *Sibille e linguaggi oracolari: mito, storia, tradizione: atti del convegno, Macerata-Norcia, settembre 1994.* Edited by Ileana Chirassi Colombo and Tullio Seppilli. Pisa: Istituti editoriali e poligrafici internazionali, 1998.

———. *"Teste David cum Sibylla:* The Significance of the Sibylline Tradition in the Middle Ages." Pages 7–35 in *Women of the Medieval World: Essays in Honor of John H. Mundy.* Edited by Julius Kirshner and Susan F. Wemple. Oxford: Basil Blackwell, 1985.

Möhring, Hannes. *Der Weltkaiser der Endzeit: Entstehung, Wandel und Wirkung einer tausendjährigen Weissagung.* Mittelalter-Forschungen 3. Stuttgart: Thorbecke, 2000.

Podskalsky, Gerhard. *Byzantinische Reichseschatologie: die Periodisierung der Weltgeschichte in den vier Grossreichen (Daniel 2 und 7) und dem tausendjährigen Friedensreiche (Apok. 20) Eine motivgeschichtliche Untersuchung.* Munich: W. Fink, 1972.

Rangheri, Maurizio. "La 'Epistola ad Gerbergam reginam de ortu et tempore Antichristi' di Adsone di Montier-en-Der e le sue fonti." *Studi medievali* 14 (1973): 677–732.

Reinink, Gerrit J. "Ps.-Methodius: A Concept of History in Response to the Rise of Islam." Pages 149–87 in *The Byzantine and Early Islamic Near East: Papers of the First Workshop on Late Antiquity and Early Islam.* Edited by Averil Cameron and Lawrence I. Conrad. Studies in Late Antiquity and Early Islam 1. Princeton: Darwin, 1992.

The Tiburtine Sibyl

The Tiburtine Sibyl among the Sibyls

1 ¹*All female prophets in general are named Sibyl, these who were accustomed to give interpretations of the divine will to humankind and to foretell the future. In fact the most learned authorities relate that there were ten Sibyls: first the Persian, second the Libyan, third the Delphic, who prophesied before the Trojan War, fourth the Cimmerian in Italy, fifth the Erythraean in Babylonia (even though she is called Erythraean from the island where her oracles were first pronounced), sixth the Samian, so called from the island of Samos, seventh Amaltheia or the Cumaean,*[a] *eighth the Hellespontine, ninth the Phrygian, tenth the Tiburtine in Greek, called Abulnea in Latin, and in whose oracles many things are contained that were written about God and Christ.*

²Therefore, this Sibyl was the daughter of King Priam, born from a mother named Hecuba, called Tiburtine in Greek, but in Latin her name was Abulnea. Traveling around various parts of the world, she preached in Asia, Macedonia, Erostochia, Agaguldea, Cilicia, Pamphylia, and Galatia. When she had filled this part of the world with prophecies, from there she went to Egypt, Ethiopia, Bagada and Babylonia, Africa, Libya, the Pentapolis, Mauritania, and Palarinum. She preached in all of these lands, and being filled with the spirit of prophecy, she prophesied good things to the good and bad things to the wicked. For we know that in her proclamations she revealed the truth and predicted things that would come to pass in recent times.

The Sybil comes to Rome to interpret the senators' dream

2 ¹Then, when the leaders of Rome heard of her fame, they immediately brought it to the attention of the Trojan emperor.[b] Therefore, when the emperor sent legates to her, he had her led to Rome with great honor. ²Then one night, one

---

a. The edition reads here "Cimera," although some versions have "cumana, cumenia, or cumea."

b. The edition reads here "Troiani," although there is variation in the manuscript tradition, with some reading instead "Traiani." Of course, Trajan would make no sense in light of the fact that the Sibyl later says that the nine suns represent "all future generations," with the fourth generation witnessing the birth of Christ. Accordingly, some manuscripts read here instead "of their king Romulus" or "of the consul, whose name was Trojanus" or "of the senators." Sackur (*Sibyllinische Texte*, 172–73) explains, however, that "Troiani" is in fact the correct reading, and is a reflection of the traditions that the Romans were descended from the Trojans, and so their ancestral king here is Trojanus. So Basset (*La sagesse*, 64) also translates "l'empereur troyen," and Kurfeß and Gauger (*Sibyllinische Weissagungen*, 313) have "dem trojanischen Herrscher."

hundred men from the Roman senate had the same dream. Each one saw in a vision as if there were nine suns in the heaven, each of which had individually different qualities in themselves. ³The first sun was bright and shining over the whole earth. The second sun was brighter and great, having an ethereal clarity. The third sun was flaming with the color of blood—fiery and terrifying and also just bright enough. The fourth sun was red with blood, and four more were shining from it at midday. ⁴The fifth sun was dark, bloody, and shining as in a dark thunder. The sixth sun was exceedingly dark, having a sting like a scorpion's stinger. The seventh sun was truly terrifying and bloody, having a horrible sword in the middle. Nevertheless the eighth sun was expansive, having a bloody color in the middle. The ninth sun, however, was exceedingly dark, having just one shining ray.

⁵When the Sibyl was led into Rome, the citizens of Rome saw her and admired her excessive beauty, for she was lovely in countenance and elegant in appearance, eloquent with words and sufficiently arrayed with every beauty, and she offered delightful discourse to those who listened to her. ⁶Nevertheless, the men who had beheld the visions came to her and said, "Mistress and lady, since your bodily form is most exceedingly beautiful, such as we have never seen among women before you, we beseech you to reveal what the dream, which we all beheld on the same night, portends for the future." ⁷Answering them, the Sybil said, "It is not right to disclose the sacred mystery of this vision in a place full of excrement and polluted with every sort of defilement.ᵃ But come and let us go up to the Aventine Hill, and there I will make known the things that are to come upon the citizens of Rome." ⁸And they did as she said. When she asked them what was the vision that they had seen, they told her. And she said to them:

The Sibyl's interpretation of the dream and the "Sibylline gospel"

3 ¹"The nine suns that you saw prefigure all future generations. Truly the differences that you saw among them will also be a different life for humanity. Now the first sun is the first generation. People will be sincere and honorable, loving freedom, truthful, gentle, kind, loving consolation of the poor, and sufficiently wise. ²The second sun is the second generation. People will live nobly and increase greatly, revering God and dwelling on the earth without malice. The third sun is the third generation. Nation will rise up against nation, and there will be many battles in Rome. ³The fourth sun is the fourth generation. People will deny what is true, and in those days there will arise a woman from the race of the Hebrews named Mary, who has a betrothed named Joseph. From her will be born, without intercourse with a man, of the Holy Spirit, the Son of God named Jesus, and she herself will be a virgin before birth and a virgin after birth. ⁴Therefore, the one who is born from her will be true God and a true human being, as all the prophets prophesied, and he will fulfill the Law of the Hebrews. And at the same time he will add some things of his own, and his kingdom will remain unto forever. ⁵At his birth the hosts of angels will be at his right and left, saying, 'Glory to God in the

Mark 13:8 par.

Matt 1:18–25; Luke 1:26–35

a. According to Sackur (*Sibyllinische Texte*, 173), this is the Capitoline Hill, which would have been polluted and defiled by pagan temples, while the Aventine was the site of the earliest churches in Rome, built in commemoration of numerous martyrs.

Luke 2:14   highest heaven, and on earth peace among those whom he favors.' For a voice will

Mark 9:7 par.   come over him saying, 'This is my Son, the Beloved; listen to him.'"

[6]Now there were there some from the priests of the Hebrews, who, hearing these words became indignant and said to her, "These are horrible words; let this queen[a] be silent!" [7]Answering them the Sybil said, "Jews, it is necessary that

John 1:10-11   this will come about, as it has been said, but you will not believe in him." But they said, "We will not believe, because God gave his word and covenant to our fathers; and will he remove his hand from us?" [8]Again she responded to them,

Ps 2:7 (Acts 13:33; Heb 1:5; 5:5); Luke 2:52   "The God of Heaven will beget a Son, as it is written, who will be similar to[b] his Father. Then, as the infant will grow in age, the kings and rulers of the world will rise up against him. In those days Caesar Augustus will have a famous name, and

Luke 2:1   he will reign in Rome and will make the entire world subject to him. [9]Then the priests of the Hebrews will gather against Jesus, on account of the many signs

John 11:45-53   that he will do, and they will seize him. They will strike God with their defiled

Mark 15:16-20 par.; John 19:1-3   hands and will spit in his holy face with venomous spittle. Truly he will give his holy back freely to the whip, and receiving blows he will be silent. For food they

Mark 15:23; Matt 27:34; John 19:29   will give him gall, for his thirst, vinegar.[c] [10]And they will hang him on the wood and kill him, but it will be of no avail to them, for on the third day he will rise again and will appear to his disciples and will ascend into heaven with them

Luke 24:51; Acts 1:9   watching, and his reign will have no end."[d]

[11]And she said to the leaders of the Romans, "The fifth sun is the fifth genera-

Mark 1:16-20 par.; John 1:40-42   tion. And Jesus will choose for himself two fishermen from Galilee, and he will give them his own law, saying, 'Go and teach all the peoples the teaching that you have received from me, making subject all the nations through the seventy-

Matt 28:19   two languages.'[e] [12]The sixth sun is the sixth generation, and they will capture this

---

a. Sackur (*Sibyllinische Texte*, 174–75) convincingly explains this seemingly peculiar title for the Sibyl in light of the broader Sibylline tradition.

b. Although scholars regularly have assumed that the *Tib. Sib.* reflects a Nicene position, the use of the word "similis" here to describe the relation between the Father and the Son certainly seems noteworthy. In the fourth century, "similis" was often used to translate *homoiousias*, thus possibly indicating the "Arian" position that the Son's being was similar to the Father's. See, e.g., Richard P. C. Hanson, *The Search for the Christian Doctrine of God: The Arian Controversy 318–381* (Edinburgh: T.&T. Clark, 1988), 374; Maurice F. Wiles, *Archetypal Heresy: Arianism through the Centuries* (Oxford: Oxford University Press, 1996), 37; Peter Iver Kaufman, "Diehard Homoians and the Election of Ambrose," *JECS* 5 (1997): 421–40 at 422, 428. Nevertheless, just above the Sibyl says that he will be "true God," which clearly seems to reflect the Nicene position.

c. The passage is an interpolation of several verses from the *Sibylline Oracles* cited by Lactantius: see Sackur, *Sibyllinische Texte*, 175.

d. The language of this sentence echoes the Nicene Creed. See John H. Leith, *Creeds of the Churches: A Reader in Christian Doctrine, from the Bible to the Present* (3rd ed.; Louisville, Ky.: John Knox, 1982), 28.

e. "Per septuaginta et duas lignas": This is a peculiar expression, and one suspects that "lignas" is a mistake for "linguas." At the same time, one might expect here some sort of noun that would correlate with the seventy-two disciples sent out by Jesus according to Luke 10. Nevertheless, the Greek has here *kēruxate auton tois ethnesi tōn hebdomēkonta duo glōssōn*: "preach it to the peoples of the seventy-two languages" (in Alexander, *Oracle of Baalbek*, 12 and 24, cf. 14 and 25). Likewise the Newberry Library MS published by McGinn ("Oracular Transformations," 639) has here "per septuaginta duas linguas predicate." Kurfeß and Gauger (*Sibyllinische Weissagungen*, 317) translate instead "Schreibtafeln (writing tablets)."

city for three years and six months. The seventh sun will be the seventh generation, and two kings will rise up and will make many persecutions in the land of
the Hebrews on account of God.[a] [13]The eighth sun will be the eighth generation,
and Rome will be in desolation, and pregnant women will cry out in distress and
grief, saying, 'Do you think that we should give birth?'

Mark 13:17 par.

Constantine and the rise of Rome in the end times

[14]"The ninth sun is the ninth generation, and the leaders of Rome will rise up
in the ruin of many. Then two kings from Syria will rise up, and their army will
be as innumerable as the sands of the sea. And they will seize the cities and regions of the Romans as far as Chalcedon, and then there will be much shedding
of blood. When they remember all these things, city and nation will tremble at
them and destroy the eastern parts.[b] [15]And after that two kings will arise from
Egypt, and four kings[c] will conquer and kill them and all their army, and they
will reign for three years and six months. After them will arise another king,
with the name C (Constantine), mighty in battle, who will reign for thirty years
and will build a temple to God and will fulfill the law and establish justice on
the earth for God's sake. [16]<And there will be a great city, and many will dwell in
it, namely the seventy-two languages. Do not rejoice with joy: they will not rule
from Byzantium within sixty years.[d]> <Then other kings will arise, and one of
them will be burned with fire.[e]>

An insertion concerning medieval kings

4 [1]"*And after this another king will arise, who will reign for a little while, and they
will overcome him and kill him. After him there will be a king with the name B,
and from B will come forth king Audon (Audoin).[f] And from Audon will come
forth A (Alboin), and from A will come forth A (Autharic). [2]And from this A will
A (Aripert or Ariovald) be begotten. And this second A will be extremely warlike
and aggressive. And from this same A will be born a king with the name R (Ro-
thari). And from R will be born L (Liudprand), and he will have authority over
nineteen kings. [3]And after them will arise a Salian king of France with the name K
(Charlemagne). He will be great, most pious, powerful, merciful, and he will bring
justice to the poor. The grace of virtue will be so great in him that when he goes*

---

a. Seemingly a reference to Titus and Vespasian.

b. Or possibly "destroy those rising up," which also could be the subject: "et disperdunt
orientes." This sentence is particularly obscure.

c. I.e., the Tetrarchy.

d. Alexander (*Oracle of Baalbek*, 53–55) persuasively identifies this passage from some later
codices (versions W3, W4, and W5) as likely belonging to the earliest version of the text, on
the basis of comparison with the Greek version and the nature of the prophecy itself. For the
Latin text see Sackur, *Sibyllinische Texte*, 128 n. 4; and Alexander, *Oracle of Baalbek*, 14. See also
McGinn, "Oracular Transformations," 640.

e. Alexander (*Oracle of Baalbek*, 63–64) also persuasively identifies this passage from some
later codices (W3, W4, and W5)—a reference to the Emperor Valens—as belonging to the earliest version of the text, primarily on the basis of comparison with the Greek version. For the text
see Alexander, *Oracle of Baalbek*, 14; also McGinn, "Oracular Transformations," 640.

f. The names of the rulers in parentheses are not in the text but are supplied following
Sackur, *Sibyllinische Texte*, 129–37.

along the way, the tops of the trees will bow before him. In meeting him water will slow to the minimum. Never in the Roman Empire was there a king like him, and there will not be one after him. ⁴*And there will come after him a king by L (Louis or Lothar), and after him B (Berengar I) will reign. And after B go forth twenty-two Bs (Berengars).* ⁵*And from B (Berengar II) will come forth A (Adalbert), and he will be extremely warlike and mighty in battle, and he will pursue*[a] *many by sea and land. And he will not be given into the hands of his enemies, and he will die in exile outside of the kingdom, and his soul will be in the hand of God.*

⁶*"Then another king will arise with the name V (Hugh of Provence), on the one side a Salian and on the other a Lombard, and he will have power on earth against those opposing him and against all enemies. And in these days a king with the name O (Otto I) will come forth, and he will be most powerful and mighty and good, and he will bring justice to the poor and will judge fairly.* ⁷*And from this O will come forth another most powerful O (Otto II), and under him there will be battles between the pagans and the Christians, and the blood of the Greeks will be shed, and his heart will be in the hand of God, and he will reign for seven years.* ⁸*And from this woman will be born a king with the name O (Otto III). He will be bloodthirsty and criminal and without faithfulness and truth, and through him there will be much malice and shedding of blood.* And churches will be destroyed under his authority.

The wars, pestilence, and corruption of the end times

5 ¹*"*In other regions there will be many tribulations and battles. Then nation will rise against nation; they will take captive into Cappadocia and Pamphylia in that time by him, because he will not enter by the door into the sheep pen.[b] Now this king will reign for four years. ²*And after him will arise a king with the name A (Arduin), and in his time there will be many battles* <between the Hagarenes and Greeks. Even among the pagans there will be many battles and conflicts.>[c] They will capture Syria and take captive the Pentapolis. *This king (Arduin) will be from the nation of the Lombards.* ³*Then a Salian king will arise with the name E (Henry II), and he will subdue the Lombards, and there will be battles and conflicts. Moreover this Salian king will be mighty and powerful, and his reign will*

Mark 13:8 par.

---

a. Or possibly "persecute": *persecuturus.*

b. This is an especially obscure sentence.

c. This passage is absent from several of the manuscripts that Sackur edited, and it is placed in brackets in the edition. It is equally absent from the version published by Usinger and Waitz (W2) and the Newberry version (W4): see G. Waitz, "Vaticinium Sibyllae," in *Monumenta Germaniae historica inde ab anno Christi quingentesimo usque ad annum millesimum et quingentesimum* (ed. G. H. Pertz; Hannover: Impensis Bibliopolii Avlici Hahniani, 1872), Scriptorum 22, 375–76; and McGinn, "Oracular Transformations," 641. In his introduction, Sackur understands this passage as regarding Arduin (Sackur, *Sibyllinische Texte,* 157); Arduin's reign, 1002–1015, was in fact a period of increased conflict between the Byzantines and the "Hagarenes," when, under Basil II (976–1025), the empire was resurgent and around the turn of the millennium fought a successful campaign against the Arabs in Syria and elsewhere on the eastern frontier. This was the culmination of a broader campaign of reconquest that began in the later ninth century and resulted in the reestablishment of Roman sovereignty over much of northern and coastal Syria at this time. See, e.g., Mark Whittow, *The Making of Orthodox Byzantium, 600–1025* (New Studies in Medieval History; London: Macmillan, 1996), 310–90. The reference here to conflicts and battles among the pagans, however, is a bit more puzzling.

be for only a short time. Then the Hagarenes and tyrants will arise, and they will capture Taranto and Bari and will pillage many cities.

4"When they want to come to Rome, there will be no one who can oppose them, except for the God of Gods and Lord of Lords. Then the Armenians will destroy the Persians, so that the cities that they pillage will not recover. And the Persians will take care,[a] and they will set up fortified encampments near the east. They will conquer the Romans and establish peace for some time. 5And a warrior king of the Greeks will enter Hierapolis and destroy the temples of idols. And locusts and grasshoppers will come and eat all the trees and fruit of Cappadocia and Cilicia, and they will be tormented with hunger, and then there will be plenty. 6Another *Salian* king will arise, a mighty man and a warrior, and many neighbors and relatives will become indignant with him.[b] And in those days brother will hand over brother to death and father, son, and brother will have intercourse with sister. 7There will be many abominable crimes of humankind on the earth, and old men will lie down with virgins and wicked priests with deceived young girls. There will be bishops of maleficent followers,[c] and there will be an effusion of blood on the earth. And they will defile the churches of the saints.[d]

Mark 13:12//Matt 10:21

Sib. Or. 7:44–45

8"There will be fornication with impurity among the people and the crime of Sodom, so that their own appearance will seem outrageous to them. And people will be robbers and abusers, hating justice and loving falsehood. And the Roman judges will change. If today they confer a judgment, on another day they will change on account of bribery, and they will not decide what is right but what is wrong. 9And in those days the people will be rapacious and greedy and perjurers and loving the benefits of falsehood. Law and the truth will be destroyed, and there will be earthquakes in various places. The cities of the islands will be submerged by sinking, and in places there will be plagues affecting human beings and cattle and a carnage of human beings. And the earth will be afflicted by the enemies, and the nothingness of the gods will not be able to console them.

Mark 13:8 par.

A second medieval insertion

6 1"*After this a king will arise by the name of B (Bernhard or Berengar), and there will be wars under him, and he will reign for two years.* 2*And after him a king will arise by the name of A (Arnulf), and when he comes he will have dominion for some time, and he will come to Rome and capture it. And his soul will not be destroyed by the hand of his enemies in the days of his life. He will be good and great and will bring justice to the poor, and he will live for a long time.* 3*After him*

---

a. Or possibly "will hasten," but then one would expect *accurrentes*.

b. Sackur suggests Conrad II was likely intended by the interpolator, but the original passage—without the interpolated "Salian"—is quite possibly a reference to Julian the Apostate, particularly in light of the fact that Alexander has persuasively argued (against Sackur's earlier dating) that the text should be dated to after Julian's reign.

c. Or possibly, "of followers of sorcerers," which is a little closer to the Greek version here (see Alexander, *Oracle of Baalbek*, 16). The precise meaning of the passage is not entirely clear.

d. Reading the passage here in light of the close parallel from the *Oracle of Baalbek*: "bands of soldiers will defile the churches of the saints" (Alexander, *Oracle of Baalbek*, 16). The Latin is a bit irregular and could also be interpreted as "they will defile the holy churches" or even "the lawgivers will defile the churches."

another king will arise with the name B,[a] *and from this B come forth twelve Bs. And he will be from the nation of the Lombards, and he will reign for one hundred years. Then after him will arise a Salian from France with the name B.*

The final conflict and the Last Emperor's appearance

7 [1]"Then will be the beginning of afflictions such as there have not been since the beginning of the world. In his days there will be many battles and tribulations of many and an effusion of blood and earthquakes in cities and the countryside, and many lands will be taken captive. [2]And there will not be anyone who could resist the enemies, because then the Lord will be enraged with the earth. Rome will be subdued by persecution and the sword, and it will be seized by the hand of the king himself. [3]And people will be greedy, tyrannical, hating the poor, oppressing the innocent, and saving the guilty. And they will be unjust and worthless, and the condemners of destruction[b] will be captured. There will be no one on earth who can resist them or cast them out on account of their wickedness and greed.

[4]"Then will arise a king of the Greeks, whose name is Constans, and he will be king of the Romans and the Greeks. He will be tall in stature, handsome in appearance, shining in countenance, and well-put-together in all of his bodily features. And his reign will end after 112 years. Therefore, in those days there will be great riches, and the earth will bring forth fruit abundantly, so that a measure of wheat will be sold for one denarius, a measure of wine for one denarius, and a measure of oil for one denarius. [5]And the king will have before his eyes a Scripture that says, 'The king of the Romans will claim the entire kingdom of the Christians for himself.'[c] Therefore, he will devastate all the islands and cities of the pagans and destroy all the temples of idols. [6]He will call all the pagans to baptism, and the cross of Jesus Christ will be erected in all the temples. Then 'Egypt and Ethiopia will hasten to offer their hand to God.'[d] Whoever will not worship the cross of Jesus Christ will be punished by the sword. And when 120 years have been completed, the Jews will be converted to the Lord, and 'his sepulcher will be glorified by all.' 'In these days Judah will be saved and Israel will encamp in confidence.'

Ps 68:31

Isa 11:10
Jer 23:6

The Last Emperor's triumph and the final victory

1 John 2:18, 22; 4:2;
2 John 7
John 17:12; 2 Thess 2:3

8 [1]"At that time the prince of iniquity, who will be called the Antichrist, will arise from the tribe of Dan.[e] He will be the Son of Perdition, the head of pride, the master of error, and the fullness of malice, who will overturn the world and work wonders and great signs through false deceits. [2]Moreover, he will delude many by magical art, so that fire will seem to descend from heaven. And the years will

---

a. Sackur (*Sibyllinische Texte*, 136) remarks that the following "Bs" seem to be "pure fantasy."

b. "Damnatores exterminii" is a peculiar expression; Kurfeß and Gauger (*Sibyllinische Weissagungen*, 325) translate as "auswärtigen Schädlinge" (foreign pests).

c. The source of this "Scripture," likely fictional, is unknown.

d. Literally: "Egypt and Ethiopia will outstrip to give its hand to God."

e. See Gregory C. Jenks, *The Origins and Early Development of the Antichrist Myth* (Beihefte zur Zeitschrift für die neutestamentliche Wissenschaft und die Kunde der älteren Kirche 59; Berlin: W. de Gruyter, 1991), 78–80.

be shortened like months, and the months like weeks, and the weeks like days, and the days like hours, and the hours like moments. ³And the most unclean nations that Alexander, the Indian king, enclosed, Gog and Magog, will arise from the north. These are the twenty-two kingdoms, whose number is like the sand of the sea.ᵃ Nevertheless, when the king of the Romans hears of this, he will assemble his army and will vanquish and destroy them in a massacre.

Rev 20:8

4"Then he will come to Jerusalem, and there having laid down the diadem of his head and all his royal garb, he will hand over the kingdom of the Christians to God the Father and Jesus Christ his Son. And when the Roman Empire will have come to an end, then the Antichrist will be openly revealed, and he will sit in the House of the Lord in Jerusalem. ⁵Nevertheless, while he is reigning, two most distinguished men, Elijah and Enoch, will go forth to announce the coming of the Lord, and the Antichrist will kill them. After three days they will be resurrected by the Lord.ᵇ ⁶Then there will be a great persecution, such as there was not before nor as will follow thereafter. Nevertheless, the Lord will shorten those days for the sake of the elect, and the Antichrist will be slain by the power of the Lord by the Archangel Michael on the Mount of Olives."

1 Cor 15:24

Rev 11:1–13

Matt 24:21–22

The signs of the coming of the Lord

⁷When the Sibyl had predicted these and many other future events for the Romans, she also spoke by prophesying the signs with which the Lord will come to judge, saying, ...ᶜ Then the Lord will judge according to the deeds of each person, and the impious will go into the gehenna of eternal fire, but the just will receive the reward of eternal life. ⁸And there will be a new heaven and a new earth, and both will remain forever, and the sea will be no more. And the Lord will reign among the saints, and they will reign with him unto forever, Amen.

Mark 9:43 par.

Rev 21:1

---

a. For earlier references concerning Alexander's enclosure of the twenty-two peoples of Gog and Magog, see Josephus, *J.W.* 7.7.4; *Ant.* 1.6.1; Wilhelm Kroll, *Historia Alexandri Magni (Pseudo-Callisthenes)*, vol. 1: *Recensio vetusta* (Berlin: Weidmannsche Buchhandlung, 1926), 146; Richard Stoneman, trans., *The Greek Alexander Romance* (Penguin Classics; New York: Penguin Books, 1991), 159; and Jerome, *Epist.* 77.8.

b. According to early Christian tradition, the two witnesses of Rev 11:1–13 are identified with Enoch and Elijah, since they did not die because God took them up to heaven.

c. Several lines of verse follow, which Sackur does not fully reproduce here. These are a later insertion from a Latin translation of an acrostic from *Sibylline Oracle 8*: see Sackur, *Sibyllinische Texte*, 154, 187; Kurfeß and Gauger, *Sibyllinische Weissagungen*, 184, 326–27, 463.

The Investiture of Abbaton, the Angel of Death
A new translation and introduction

by Alin Suciu with Ibrahim Saweros

The *Investiture of Abbaton* (*Invest. Abbat.*; CANT 334; CPC 0405; CPG 2530), also known in scholarship as the *Enthronement of Abbaton,* is an apocryphal writing extant in Coptic concerning the transformation of the angel Muriel into Abbaton, the Angel of Death. The text purports to be a revelation of Christ written down by the apostles and deposited in the library of Jerusalem. The apostolic book was allegedly found later by Timothy of Alexandria (likely intended to be Timothy Aelurus), who incorporated it in a sermon delivered during the feast of Abbaton (Hathor 13). With few exceptions, the text has been ignored by all major collections of Christian apocrypha.[1] *Invest. Abbat.* is mentioned as well in the *Kitāb al-īḍāḥ*, a catechetical writing that has survived under the name of Severus ibn al-Muqaffaʿ, but which was composed perhaps in the eleventh century, after the death of Severus.[2] In *Kitāb al-īḍāḥ, Invest. Abbat.* is attributed to Theophilus of Alexandria.

Contents
The Sahidic version of *Invest. Abbat.* opens with a lengthy title summarizing the content of the work; likely, this elaborate title is a later addition. The title introduces the text as an encomium pronounced by Timothy of Alexandria for the feast of Abbaton on Hathor 13 (November 24 of the Gregorian calendar). The text begins with a *proemium* in which Ps.-Timothy develops homiletically a series of biblical passages concerning those who seek after spiritual matters (chap. 1). Unfortunately, the *proemium* is followed by a long lacuna of six pages (designated chap. 2). Among the material lost in this lacuna is Timothy's account of his journey to Jerusalem to celebrate the feast of the Cross, a journey mentioned in the title to the text. After the lacuna, the text resumes with Timothy recounting his arrival in Jerusalem, where he visited the church of the Virgin in the Valley of Jehoshaphat (3:1). On this occasion, he was invited to the house of an old priest named John and found there a mysterious book, in which the apostles had written a revelation of Christ concerning the

---

1. See Erbetta, *Gli apocrifi del Nuovo Testamento,* 471–81 (Italian translation); a résumé of the text features in Moraldi, *Apocrifi del Nuovo Testamento,* 427–30. A Dutch translation is available in Oussoren and Dekker, *Buiten de vesting,* 461–72.

2. On the *Kitāb al-īḍāḥ* in general, see Mark Swanson, "*Kitāb al-īḍāḥ,*" in *Christian-Muslim Relations: A Bibliographical History,* vol. 3 (ed. David Thomas and Alex Mallett; The History of Christian-Muslim Relations 15; Leiden: Brill, 2011), 265–69. On the refutation of *Invest. Abbat.* in the *Kitāb al-īḍāḥ,* see idem, "The Specifically Egyptian Context of a Coptic Arabic Text: Chapter Nine of the *Kitab al-Idah* of Sawîrus ibn al-Muqaffaʿ," *Medieval Encounters* 2 (1996): 214–27 at 218–20. Cf. also Arnold van Lantschoot, "Fragments coptes d'une homélie de Jean de Parallos contre les livres hérétiques," in *Miscellanea Giovanni Mercati,* vol. 1: *Bibbia. Letteratura cristiana antica* (Studi e testi 121; Vatican: Biblioteca apostolica, 1946), 296–326 at 297 n. 7; Georg Graf, *Geschichte der christlichen arabischen Literatur* (5 vols.; Studi e testi 118, 133, 146, 147, 172; Vatican: Biblioteca Apostolica, 1944), 1:467.

investiture of Abbaton, the Angel of Death (3:4). What follows is presented as simply a transcription of this apostolic writing (chaps. 4–11).

The book Timothy discovered begins just before the Ascension, with the apostles gathered around Jesus on the Mount of Olives where they are to be blessed before going to preach in the world (4:1–3). Peter has one last question to address: when was Abbaton enthroned, the psychopomp angel who carries away the souls of the departed? (4:7). What follows is a long *exposé* of Christ concerning the investiture of the angel Muriel as Abbaton, the Angel of Death, a topic that appears to be linked with the creation of the first human couple, the Fall, and the incarnation of Christ in order to redeem Adam (4:8–8:2).

Jesus reveals that after the creation of the world, God sent seven angels to bring him clay from Eden in order to create the first man. However, each time the angels approach the clay, it swears oaths on the name of God so that the angels are not able to retrieve it (5:1–8). Seeing that all angels have failed to bring him the clay, God decides to send to Eden the angel Muriel. This angel is the only one who is not afraid when he hears the name of God. Consequently, he manages to bring the clay from Eden (5:9–11). God molds Adam out of it, but not before Christ promises that he will incarnate in order to save human beings from the sins for which the descendants of Adam will be responsible (5:12–13). After the creation of Adam, God enthrones him in heaven and gathers all the angels to worship him (5:16). However, the First-Creature *(Archeplasma)* refuses to prostrate before Adam because of his pride (6:1–3). Although the text is laconic at this point, it seems that the First-Creature possesses a roll on which are written the names of all the angels. This gives him special powers over them—apparently through the magical function of names—so that when God orders the angels to expel the First-Creature from heaven because of his arrogance, they are not able to approach him. However, a powerful Cherub manages to defeat the malevolent angel and to throw him down to earth (6:4–5).

After this prologue in heaven, God puts Adam in the earthly Paradise. One hundred years later, he creates Eve as Adam's companion (7:1–3). However, the fallen angel, who became the devil, seeks revenge. He enters into the snake and tricks the couple into eating from the forbidden tree (7:4–10). For doing so, Adam and Eve are expelled from Paradise to live mortal lives (7:11–13; 9:1). After his death, Adam is kept captive in hell because of his sins until Christ descends into a virgin womb, dies on the cross, and liberates the first human being through his sacrifice (chap. 8). Hearing that Adam and his descendants have been saved by Christ, the devil tries again to ensnare humankind (9:2). In humanity's defense, God appoints the angel Muriel, who brought him the clay *in illo tempore,* as Abbaton, the Angel of Death, on Hathor 13, the same day when he brought the clay from Eden. The Angel of Death saves the souls of the righteous from the hands of the devil. However, to sinners Abbaton's appearance is terrifying (9:3–11).

The story of the investiture of Abbaton ends here, but the apostle John has one more question for Jesus: How will the righteous survive the Final Judgment if Abbaton will come in his disturbing disguise? Will they not die of fear? (10:1). What follows is a revelation of Christ concerning the Final Judgment, which will take place in the Valley of Jehoshaphat (10:2–4). The apostles will sit on their thrones and they will judge the world. According to an interesting interpretation of 1 Cor 6:3, the first judged will be the angels and the saints. Because of his purity, the apostle John will play this important judging role. Therefore, he will be the first who will die and resurrect after three and a half hours in order to pass judgment on his fellow apostles and all the saints (10:5–6). Then follows the judgment of human beings, after which the sinners will go to hell and the righteous to heaven (10:6–10). The binding of Satan is also mentioned as the final act of the Parousia (10:11). The revelation closes here, with Christ ascending to heaven and the apostles spreading throughout the whole world to proclaim not only the gospel, but also the story of the investiture of Abbaton (chap. 11). Ps.-Timothy's homily continues with an exhortation to commemorate properly the angel Abbaton in order to obtain eternal salvation (chap. 12).

Manuscripts and Editions

Invest. Abbat. is known in a single manuscript written in the Sahidic dialect of Coptic: London, British Library, Or. 7025. The codex is dated Thoout 12, 698 Era of the Martyrs (= September 9, 981) and belonged to the Monastery of St. Mercurius, situated near Edfu in Upper Egypt.[3] *Invest. Abbat.* is the only writing in the manuscript, covering pages 1–70. Although the codex is legible and generally well preserved,[4] three folios of the first quire (= pages 7–12) have disappeared. In 1914, E. A. W. Budge edited the text and translated it into English.[5]

Invest. Abbat. is refuted as heretical in chapter 9 of the *Kitāb al-īḍāḥ*, an Arabic work attributed to Severus ibn al-Muqaffaʿ. Ps.-Severus gives a detailed account of the content of this apocryphon, so we have included a translation of the relevant section of his text. For the translation provided here, three nearly identical manuscripts were consulted: Paris, Bibliothèque nationale de France, Ar. 170 (fol. 135v–146v; 13th cent.); Cairo, Coptic Orthodox Patriarchate, Theol. 92 (fol. 199v–221r; dated March 22, 1681); and Wādī al-Natrūn, Monastery of St. Macarius, Theol. 28 (fol. 142r–156r; 18th cent.).[6]

Authorship

The authorship of *Invest. Abbat.* is a complicated issue. The author of *Kitāb al-īḍāḥ* attributes *Invest. Abbat.* to Theophilus of Alexandria. It is likely that this confusion occurred during the transmission of the text in Arabic, due to the resemblance of the names Timothy (تيموثاوس) and Theophilus (ثيوفيلوس) in this language. The only surviving manuscript of *Invest. Abbat.* introduces the text as "an encomium delivered by . . . Apa Timothy the archbishop of Alexandria," but it does not mention which of the three Alexandrian patriarchs named Timothy is intended. Budge stated, without any further argument, that the author is Timothy I, who was patriarch between 380 and 385. Budge's attribution was taken over by the Clavis Patrum Graecorum, which lists *Invest. Abbat.* under the name of the same author. For his part, Caspar Detlef Müller left the question of authorship open.[7]

However, it is likely that the Timothy referred to in the title is actually Timothy II Aelurus, who occupied the throne of Mark the Evangelist between 457–460 and 475–477.[8] Our text belongs to a period when the Egyptian church was struggling to define itself after the

---

3. For the colophon of the manuscript see Arnold van Lantschoot, *Recueil des colophons des manuscrits chrétiens d'Égypte* (Bibliothèque du *Muséon* 1; Leuven: J.-B. Istas, 1929), 187–89 (= no. 110).

4. Description of the manuscript in Bentley Layton, *Catalogue of Coptic Literary Manuscripts in the British Library Acquired Since the Year 1906* (London: British Library, 1987), 135–36 (= no. 121).

5. Budge, *Coptic Martyrdoms*, 225–48 (Sahidic text), 474–96 (English translation).

6. A critical edition will appear in Saweros, "How Does the Copt Die?"

7. Caspar Detlef G. Müller, *Die alte koptische Predigt: Versuch eins Überblicks* (PhD diss., Heidelberg, 1953; printed Berlin, 1954), 180–89 and esp. 98–99; idem, *Die Engellehre der koptischen Kirche. Untersuchungen zur Geschichte der christlichen Frömmigkeit in Ägypten* (Wiesbaden: Harrassowitz, 1959), 273–75.

8. See Layton, *Catalogue*, 135; Hagen, "Diaries of the Apostles," 359 n. 51. Cf. also Suciu, *Apocryphon Berolinense/Argentoratense*, 89.

Council of Chalcedon. Therefore, in this period were composed numerous texts attributed to the major figures of Miaphysite orthodoxy, in an attempt to establish the orthodox fundaments of post-Chalcedonian Egyptian Christianity. Thus, the one who is laconically named "Timothy, the archbishop of Alexandria" in the title of several works preserved in the Coptic-Arabic-Ethiopic literary continuum, must be Timothy Aelurus,[9] one of the champions of Miaphysite orthodoxy and successor of the great archbishop Dioscorus. Timothy Aelurus's figure overshadows those of his other two homonyms.[10] He is known in the Coptic church not only for his strong position against the Chalcedonians, but also for his literary heritage, of which unfortunately only few authentic writings have survived, especially in Syriac and Armenian.[11]

Nevertheless, the encomium on Abbaton does not bear any of the theological imprint of Timothy's authentic writings; very likely it is pseudonymous. As a result, it is virtually impossible to date *Invest. Abbat.* within narrow limits. However, as Timothy Aelurus died in 477 CE, the text is probably posterior to this date. If *Invest. Abbat.* depends indeed upon a Muslim source concerning the Angel of Death (see further below), which is a very unlikely hypothesis, this would place the text after the Arabic conquest of Egypt (641 CE).

Literary Context

Invest. Abbat. belongs to a little-studied genre of Coptic literature that originated, likely, after the Council of Chalcedon. The texts related to Ps.-Timothy's sermon on Abbaton have survived exclusively in Coptic, Arabic, and Ethiopic versions, with occasional attestations in Old Nubian. Although some of these writings are lost (or not yet identified) in Coptic and came to us only in Arabic or Ethiopic, they arguably go back to Coptic originals.

According to these documents, the apostles received from Jesus a series of revelations concerning his life and the commemoration of various saints and angelic beings. The apostles wrote down Jesus' words in books and deposited them in a library in Jerusalem. In light of this motif, I conventionally call the texts in question "Coptic pseudo-apostolic memoirs." There are two types of such memoirs. The most numerous are the books allegedly written by the apostles and their disciples, which a notable father of the Coptic Church finds during a pilgrimage to the Holy Land. These writings include: several homilies attributed to Cyril of Jerusalem (e.g., *On the Life and Passion of Christ* [CPG 3604; CPC 0113]; *On Mary Magdalene* [CANT 73; CPC 0118]; etc.), Archelaos of Neapolis (*On Gabriel* [CPC 0045]), John Chrysostom (*On the Four Bodiless Creatures* [CPG 5150.11; CPC 0177]; and *On John the Baptist* [CPG 5150.3; CANT 184; CPC 0170]),[12] Theodosius of Alexandria (*On the Dormition of the Virgin* [CPG 7153; CPC 0385]), and others.[13] *Invest. Abbat.* falls into this category. The second group is formed of pseudo-apostolic writings that are not included in patristic sermons. To this category belong, e.g., the *History of Joseph the*

---

9. Beside *Invest. Abbat.*, the Coptic literary tradition attributes to Timothy Aelurus a homily on the archangel Michael (CPG 2529 [attributed to Timothy I]; CPC 0404); *On the Consecration of the Church of Pachomius* (CPG 5491); *On the Church of the Rock* (no clavis number); and *On the Death of the Children* (CPG 5490). The latter writing, previously known only in Gǝʿǝz, has recently been identified in Coptic as well; see Catherine Louis, "Une version copte de l'Epistula de morte puerorum de Timothée Ælure (CPG 5490)," *Journal of Coptic Studies* 13 (2011): 89–98.

10. It seems that Timothy III, patriarch between 520 and 537, has not left any trace in Coptic literature.

11. See CPG 5475–89.

12. Translated by Philip L. Tite in the present volume.

13. For a more complete inventory, see Suciu, *Apocryphon Berolinense/Argentoratense*, 4–5 and 75–91. See also the important contribution of Hagen, "Ein anderer Kontext," 349–53.

Carpenter (*BHO* 532–33; *CANT* 60; *CPC* 0037), the *Investiture of Michael* (*CPC* 0488), the *Book of Bartholomew* (*CANT* 80; *CPC* 0027), the *Dance of the Savior* (no clavis number),[14] and the books attributed to Evodius, the disciple of the apostle Peter.[15]

The writings in the two categories outlined above share not only the same genre, but also specific literary motifs and peculiar expressions. One such expression that features only in the Coptic corpus of pseudo-apostolic memoirs is the vocative "O my holy members," with which Jesus addresses his apostles several times in *Invest. Abbat.*[16]

Within the category of pseudo-apostolic memoirs, *Invest. Abbat.* belongs to a narrower group that comprises investitures *(taho eratef)* of angelic beings.[17] This subgroup includes also a book written by the apostle John concerning the investiture of the archangel Michael on Hathor 12; a book about the investiture of the archangel Gabriel on Koiak 22, attributed to Stephen the Protomartyr; a homily by Ps.-Chrysostom that includes a book of the apostles on the investiture of the Four Bodiless Creatures on Hathor 8. It is possible that the *Investiture of the Archangel Raphael* (*CPC* 0347) attributed to Severus of Antioch contained a similar revelation about this angelic being; unfortunately, only two folios written in the Sahidic dialect of Coptic have survived of this text, and these contain only the title and the beginning of the work.[18]

Some aspects of the roles of the angels in *Invest. Abbat.* indicate connections with Jewish and Muslim sources. According to *Invest. Abbat.*'s anthropogonic scenario, in which God seven times sends a different angel to bring him clay in order to fashion Adam, the clay says to the angels, "I swear to you on the one who sent you to me, if you take me to him he shall mold me to become a man with a living soul and great sins will come to existence because of me . . . Let me go to rest and ease" (5:4–6). As all the angels are afraid of God's name, they are not able to fulfill their task. Finally, God sends the angel Muriel, who does not show pity for the laments and menaces of the clay, and he carries it to God, who creates Adam out of it. A similar narrative is found in a late Jewish text incorporated into the *Chronicles of Jerahmeel*:

> When at last the assent of the angels to the creation of man was given, God said to Gabriel: "Go and fetch Me dust from the four corners of the earth, and I will create man therewith." Gabriel went forth to do the bidding of the Lord, but the earth drove him away, and refused to let him gather up dust from it. Gabriel remonstrated: "Why, Oh Earth, dost thou not hearken unto the voice of the Lord, who founded thee upon the waters without props or pillars?" The earth replied, and said: "I am destined to become a curse, and to be cursed through man, and if God Himself does not take the dust from me, no one else shall ever do it." When God heard this, He stretched out His hand, took of the dust of the ground, and created the first man therewith.[19]

---

14. Translated by Paul C. Dilley in the present volume.

15. For other texts included in this category, see Suciu, *Apocryphon Berolinense/Argentoratense*, 5 and 91–101.

16. This expression is analyzed in detail in Suciu, *Apocryphon Berolinense/Argentoratense*, 103–15.

17. See Hagen, "Diaries of the Apostles."

18. This is London, British Library, Or. 7028, fol. 25–26; cf. Layton, *Catalogue*, 160; Ernest A. W. Budge, *Miscellaneous Coptic Texts in the Dialect of Upper Egypt* (London: British Museum, 1915), li and plate XXI (photographic reproduction of fol. 25r).

19. Moses Gaster, *The Chronicles of Jerahmeel, or, the Hebrew Bible Historiale* (London: Royal Asiatic Society, 1899), 15.

The Muslim exegesis of the biblical anthropogonic narrative provides the closest parallel to the story in *Invest. Abbat.* For example, in his *Annals*, Muhammad ibn Jarir al-Tabari (838–923) tries to trace the history of the world from the beginning to his own day. Al-Tabari says that when God wanted to create man, he sent the archangel Gabriel for a handful of clay of different colors. However, the earth refused to give clay to the archangel because of the many sins that will come out of it. God sends after this the archangel Michael but the result is identical: the angel is not able to fulfill God's request. Finally, God commissions the Angel of Death, ʿIzrāʾīl, to bring him the clay. ʿIzrāʾīl has greater hardness of heart than his fellow-angels and the oaths of the clay do not impress him. Thus, he manages to bring it to God, who fashions Adam out of it.[20] Remarkably, after the anthropogony, al-Tabari relates the episode of the veneration of Adam by the angels. Just as in *Invest. Abbat.*, the devil is expelled from heaven because of his arrogant refusal to worship the first human being.[21] Several versions of this story circulated in Muslim sources, but the core is the same: God created Adam with the help of the Angel of Death (ʿIzrāʾīl). Although the details vary, the Muslim accounts are so similar to the story of the investiture of Abbaton as the Angel of Death that one may suspect that the two stories are somehow related. Haim Schwarzbaum has suggested a Muslim origin of the story.[22] However, the possibility that *Invest. Abbat.* depends on Muslim sources is difficult to assess. Although it should not be dismissed *a priori,* it is more likely that both Ps.-Timothy and the Muslim exegetes depend on similar sources.

The Angel Abbaton in Christian Tradition

The only biblical reference to Abbaton appears in the Apocalypse of John: "They have as king over them the angel of the bottomless pit; his name in Hebrew is Abaddon (i.e., Destruction), and in Greek he is called Apollyon (i.e., Destroyer)" (Rev 9:11). For the Copts, Abbaton is the Angel of Death. Although *Invest. Abbat.* is the only text exclusively dedicated to this angel, he features in several other Coptic texts. Remarkably, except for an unidentified manuscript fragment that is difficult to assess, all of these texts are pseudo-apostolic memoirs.

In *Bk. Bart.* 7–26, Christ has a long dialogue with Abbaton during the descent into hell

---

20. See the summary in Arent Jan Wensinck, "ʿIzrāʾīl," in *The Encyclopaedia of Islam. A Dictionary of the Geography, Ethnography and Biography of the Muhammadan Peoples* (ed. Martijn T. Houtsma et al.; 4 vols. and Suppl.; Leiden: Brill, 1913–1938), 4:570a–571a, at 570a.

21. Hermann Zotenberg, *Cronique de Abou-Djafar-Moʿhammed-ben-Djarir-ben-Yezid Tabari* (4 vols.; Paris: Imprimerie Impériale, 1867–1874), 1:72–73, 77–78. The theme of the veneration of Adam by the angels and the subsequent fall of the devil from heaven is common both in Coptic and in apocryphal literature in general. See Jean-Marc Rosenstiehl, "La chute de l'ange: origines et développement d'une légende. Ses attestations dans la littérature copte," in *Écritures et traditions dans la littérature copte. Journée d'études coptes. Strasbourg, 28 mai 1982* (Cahiers de la bibliothèque copte 1; Leuven: Peeters, 1983), 37–60; and e.g., Jean-Daniel Kaestli, "Le mythe de la chute de Satan et la question du milieu d'origine de la *Vie d'Adam et Ève*," in *Early Christian Voices in Texts, Traditions and Symbols. Essays in Honor of François Bovon* (ed. David H. Warren, Ann Graham Brock, and David W. Pao; Leiden and Boston: Brill, 2003), 341–54.

22. Haim Schwarzbaum, "Jewish and Moslem Sources of a Falasha Creation Myth," in *Studies in Biblical and Jewish Folklore* (ed. Raphael Patai, Francis Lee Utley, and Dov Noy; American Folklore Society Memoir 51; Bloomington: Indiana University Press, 1960), 41–56. Cf. also Menaham J. Kister, "Ādam: A Study of Some Legends in Tafsīr and Ḥadīt Literature," *Israel Oriental Studies* 13 (1993): 113–74. On the Angel of Death in Muslim literature, see Stephen R. Burge, *Angels in Islam: A Commentary with Selected Translations of Jalāl al-Dīn al-Suyūtīʾs Al-Ḥabāʾik fi akhbār al-malāʾik (The Arrangement of the Traditions about the Angels)* (PhD diss.; University of Edinburgh, 2009), 136–46.

between the crucifixion and resurrection.[23] In one of the Sahidic manuscripts of *Hist. Jos. Carp.*, the dying Joseph looks frightened as Abbaton and his helpers come to take away his soul (21:1–5).[24] And, in a book on the Dormition of the Virgin attributed to Prochorus (*CANT* 147; 153) allegedly discovered by an Egyptian bishop named Cyriacus of Behnesa during a pilgrimage to Jerusalem, the myth of the creation of Adam featured in *Invest. Abbat.* is further developed. After the Dormition of the Virgin, Christ orders the apostles to gather in the earthly Paradise where her body is buried, in order to witness her assumption to heaven. The apostles watch as the seven archangels ask for Mary's body from the earth where she is buried, in very much the same way the angels ask for clay in Ps.-Timothy's homily. However, the earth refuses each time to give away the body of the Virgin, saying that by holding her, it compensates for the loss of Adam, who was molded out of it. This is obviously a continuation of the anthropogonic account in *Invest. Abbat.* When Abbaton, who is called Aflāṭon in the Arabic version of the Dormition text,[25] takes his turn to request the body of Mary, Christ appears in Paradise and the earth finally gives up the body. The literary connections between this story and the account of the creation of Adam in *Invest. Abbat.* show once more the close relationships between the Coptic pseudo-apostolic memoirs. Abbaton features in another text on the Dormition of the Virgin found in the ruins of the Monastery of the Archangel Gabriel in Naqlun, Fayyum (Naqlun N. 76/93).[26] This text seems to be an extract from a larger unidentified literary work. Here the dying Mary is afraid of Abbaton and his helpers, just like Joseph in *Hist. Jos. Carp.*

The title of the only surviving manuscript of *Invest. Abbat.* seems to imply that Abbaton was venerated in the Monastery of St. Mercurius in Edfu, from where the text came. Similarly, one of the frescos discovered at a Coptic monastery in Tebtunis, in the Fayyum oasis, depicts Abbaton as a frightful angel.[27] Interestingly, Abbaton is not mentioned in the surviving recensions of the Coptic synaxary. Therefore, if Abbaton was indeed worshipped by Coptic Christians, probably his cult was restricted to certain areas and periods.

Translation

The following translation of *Invest. Abbat.* is based upon photographic reproductions of the manuscript.[28] Chapter and verse divisions are our own. The missing material from the lacuna pp. 7–12 has been designated as chapter 2. Quotations of Scripture, in most cases,

---

23. I follow here the separation of the text into paragraphs made by Matthias Westerhoff, *Auferstehung und Jenseits im koptischen "Buch der Auferstehung Jesu Christi, unseres Herrn"* (Orientalia biblica et christiana 11; Wiesbaden: Harrassowitz, 1999), 60–93.

24. Louis Théophile Lefort, "À propos de 'L'Histoire de Joseph le Charpentier,'" *Le Muséon* 66 (1953): 201–23 at 211.

25. Vatican, Biblioteca apostolica, arab. 170, fol. 331v (unpublished). The Ethiopic version simply transcribes the Arabic form of the name; see Victor Arras, *De transitu Mariae apocrypha aethiopice* II (2 vols.; CSCO 351–52, Aeth. 68–69; Leuven: Secrétariat du CSCO, 1974), 1:47 (Ethiopic text), 2:36 (Latin translation).

26. Cf. Jacques van der Vliet, "Literature, Liturgy, Magic: A Dynamic Continuum," in *Christianity in Egypt: Literary Production and Intellectual Trends. Studies in Honor of Tito Orlandi* (ed. Paolo Buzi and Alberto Camplani; SEAug 125; Rome: Institutum Patristicum Augustinianum, 2011), 555–74 at 568–69.

27. Colin C. Walters, "Christian Paintings from Tebtunis," *JEA* 75 (1989): 191–208 at 200–204. The painting identifies him as "Lord Abbaton, the unbribed Angel of Death." For the dating and more details see Ramez W. Boutros, "The Christian Monuments of Tebtunis," in *Christianity and Monasticism in the Fayoum Oasis* (ed. Gawdat Gabra; Cairo: American University in Cairo Press, 2005), 126–27.

28. The photos are available in the collection of the *Corpus dei Manoscritti Copti Letterari* project (Hiob Ludolf Zentrum, Hamburg).

have not been harmonized with the NRSV in an effort to best preserve the particular readings of the Coptic text. The excerpt from the *Kitāb al-īḍāḥ* concerning *Invest. Abbat.* is published here for the first time in a modern translation by Ibrahim Saweros based primarily on Paris, Bibliothèque nationale de France, Arab. 170.

Bibliography

EDITIONS AND TRANSLATIONS

Budge, Ernest A. W. *Coptic Martyrdoms in the Dialect of Upper Egypt.* London: British Museum, 1914. (*Editio princeps* of *Invest. Abbat.*, pp. 225–48, 474–96.)

Erbetta, Mario. *Gli apocrifi del Nuovo Testamento.* 3 vols. in 4. Turin: Marietti, 1966–1981. (Italian translation in vol. 3:471–81.)

Moraldi, Luigi. *Apocrifi del Nuovo Testamento.* 3 vols. 2nd ed. Turin: UTET, 1994. (A summary of the text appears in vol. 3:427–30.)

Oussoren, Pieter, and Renate Dekker. *Buiten de vesting. Een woord-voor-woord vertaling van alle deuterocanonieke en vele apocriefe bijbelboeken.* Vught, The Netherlands: Skandalon & Plantijn, 2008. (Dutch translation pp. 461–72.)

Saweros, Ibrahim. "How Does the Copt Die? A Study of the Angel of Death in the Coptic Tradition together with a Critical Edition of the Ninth Chapter of *Kitāb al-īḍāḥ* attributed to Severus ibn al-Muqaffaʿ." In *Proceedings of the First International Conference on Christian Egypt: Thought and Culture in Egypt 284–641 A.D. Cairo 1st–3rd April 2014.* Edited by Tarek M. Muhammad (forthcoming).

STUDIES

Hagen, Joost L. "Ein anderer Kontext für die Berliner und Straßburger 'Evangelienfragmente'. Das 'Evangelium des Erlösers' und andere 'Apostelevangelien' in der koptischen Literatur." Pages 339–71 in *Jesus in apokryphen Evangelienüberlieferungen. Beiträge zu außerkanonischen Jesusüberlieferungen aus verschiedenen Sprach- und Kulturtraditionen.* Edited by Jörg Frey and Jens Schröter. WUNT 254. Tübingen: Mohr Siebeck, 2010.

———. "The Diaries of the Apostles: 'Manuscript Find' and 'Manuscript Fiction' in Coptic Homilies and Other Literary Texts." Pages 349–67 in *Coptic Studies on the Threshold of a New Millennium. Proceedings of the Seventh International Congress of Coptic Studies, Leiden, 27 August–2 September 2000.* Edited by Mat Immerzeel and Jacques van der Vliet. OLA 133. Leuven: Peeters, 2004.

Suciu, Alin. *Apocryphon Berolinense/Argentoratense (Previously Known as the Gospel of the Savior). Reedition of P. Berol. 22220, Strasbourg Copte 5–7 and Qasr el-Wizz Codex ff. 12v–17r with Introduction and Commentary.* PhD diss., Université Laval, 2013.

The Investiture of Abbaton, the Angel of Death

Introduction

An encomium delivered by our holy father, blessed in every respect, Apa Timothy the archbishop of Alexandria. He delivered it for the investiture of Abbaton, the Angel of Death. When our fathers, the apostles, were enquiring the Savior about him in order to proclaim him to all humanity, knowing that they will be asked about everything, the Savior, not wanting to disappoint them about anything they asked, informed them, "The day on which my Father enthroned him is the thirteenth of the month of Hathor. He appointed him king over the entire creation that he made because of the transgression of Adam and Eve." The archbishop wished to know how God made him frightful and disturbing and to come after each being that gives its spirit in misery. While he was going to Jerusalem to worship the cross of our Savior and his life-giving tomb, on the seventeenth of the month Thoout, he examined the books that were in the library of Jerusalem, these that our fathers the apostles instituted and put in it, until he found his Investiture with the help of an old Jerusalemite priest. He was questioning him about the topic of the discourse because it interested him. He also spoke about the holy apostle Saint John the Theologian and Virgin, that he will not taste death until the thrones will be prepared in the Valley of Jehoshaphat, where the last combat of the world shall take place. In the peace of God, Amen. Bless us.

Proemium

1 ¹I hear the one with a sweet mouth and filled with every gladness, my Lord and my God, speaking to us every day in the holy Gospels, "Everyone who asks will receive, the one who searches will find and to the one that knocks it will be opened." And also, "Everything that you will ask my Father in my name will happen to you." ²David, the holy songwriter, also says,

Matt 7:8//Luke 11:9
John 15:16

> "Blessed are the blameless in the way and those who walk in the law of the Lord.
> Blessed are the blameless and those who seek after them.
> Blessed are those who search out his testimonies, those who seek for him with their whole heart."

Ps 119:1–2

Ps 34:10 And again, "Those who seek after the Lord will not lack any good."

³Who are those who seek after the Lord, O my beloved? Listen carefully, O (you) who love to hear. Those who seek after the Lord is every man who takes

care day and night of his Law, commandments, and prescriptions, as it is written, "the Law of God shall not leave your mouth." And again, "It is fitting for every Christian man to satiate with the fruits of his lips as if it were corporeal food." Josh 1:8
cf. Prov 18:20

> [4]Those who seek the Lord is anyone who inquires about the investiture of
>   the angels of God, revealing their holy remembrance.
> Those who seek the Lord is anyone who inquires about his saints, takes
>   care of the sufferings that they endured and puts them in the
>   churches.[a]
> Those who seek the Lord is anyone who gives alms and oblation to God at
>   their holy remembrance, each one according to his power.
> Those who seek the Lord is anyone who loves the strangers and the poor
>   and clothes the naked at the feasts of the saints, each one according
>   to his power.

[5]Therefore then, my brothers and my beloved, let us give for the day of the saints, each one according to his power. Therefore then, my brothers and my beloved, let us give with a straight heart and a perfect faith so that they could find us in the day of our visitation. Our Savior informs us in the holy Gospel, "Whoever shall give to drink even a cup of cold water to one of these little ones in the name of a disciple, Amen I say [to you] [. . .]" Matt 10:42; Mark 9:41

three folios missing

Timothy discovers a book written by the apostles

3 [1][. . .] a week before the feast came. Thus, we entered into the sanctuary of the holy Theotokos Mary, the one that has been built for her in the Valley of Jehoshaphat. We received the blessing, and we prayed with those who came for the feast. And thus we prepared for the oblation and we assembled with the entire people that day. (Afterwards,) each one went to his house, waiting for the feast. But as for me, I remained in the church.

[2]Yet as we were sitting, an old priest named John approached me. He begged me saying, "If your servant has found favor before you, let my lord father come to the house of your servant so we could enjoy your blessing." When I saw his great benevolence and courtesy, which were like those of an angel of God, I and those who were with me rose up and went with him. [3]As he took us into an upper room of his house, we prayed and we sat down, according to the commandment of our Savior. And he made for us a great meal that day because he was generous like the patriarch Abraham, especially towards strangers and everyone who visited the church.

[4]When morning came, we were still talking with each other about the deeds and the miracles that our Lord has done and about how the godless Jews crucified him because of their envy toward him. And thus I said to the old priest, "My blessed son, did not the book of the Investiture of Abbaton, the Angel of Death,

---

a. Here the author refers to the process of copying or commissioning a scribe to copy the acts of the martyrs and to donate the books to church libraries.

come to your hand among all these books? For I want it in order to know how God made him king over all humanity and creation that he made, and how God made him to be frightful and disturbing when he comes and goes after every being that dies." [5]The old priest told me immediately with a face filled with grace, "Christ, the master of us all, has said well in the holy gospel, 'the one who seeks will find, (for) the one who knocks it will be opened, and to the one who asks it will be given.' You, O my holy father, have sought and found, you knocked and it was opened, you asked and received. The Lord will fulfill the demand that you asked."

Matt 7:7–8//Luke 11:9–10

[6]When I heard these things from the old priest, I thanked God because he did not vex me in anything that I asked from him. And thus he brought it to me. When it came into my hand, I rejoiced over it more than over a great many treasures. I proclaimed together with David, the psalmist and righteous king, "I shall rejoice over your word like the one who has found much loot." I read it and found written in it thus:

Ps 119:162

Peter asks the Savior about the investiture of Abbaton

4 [1]It came to pass that as our Savior, the entire root of Goodness, was finishing everything, that the day[a] of his ascension had been completed for him to go up to his Father, he raised his hand over each one of his holy apostles. He prayed over them in order to send them out to the whole world to preach his holy resurrection to all nations. [2]He filled them with power and the Holy Spirit, saying to them, "The miracles and wonders which I did, you will do in your turn. You will raise your hand over the sick and they will be relieved. You will trample upon serpents and scorpions. You will take serpents with your hands to drink a deadly poison and it will not harm you. [3]Those who will believe in me, my good Father, and the Holy Spirit, baptize them in the name of the Father, Son, and Holy Spirit and I will forgive them in my turn. Those who will not believe will be condemned to a second death. Go in peace. May my peace be with you. I will not cease to walk with you until the end of this age."

Matt. 28:19–20; Mark 16:15–18; Luke 10:19

[4]Then Saint Peter, the great apostle, the column of the church and the steward of the kingdom of heaven, replied saying, "The one that you want to take inside, take him, and the one that you want to throw out, throw him out." [5]He said again, "My Lord and my God, behold, you have informed us about everything that we asked from you and you have not hidden anything from us. Now then, my Lord and my God, behold, you are sending us to the whole world to proclaim your holy resurrection to all nations, the miracles and wonders that you have done, (those that) we saw with our eyes and that we heard. [6]You revealed all of them to us, even about your Virgin mother and your holy birth. And you know, my Lord, that as there are many quarrelers in the world and unbelievers who will enquire us about everything, we want to find out how to answer them.[b] [7]Now then, my Lord, we would like you to inform us about the day when you invested Abbaton, the Angel of Death, and how you made him to be frightful and disturbing when he comes after all beings that give up their spirit. (Inform us), so

Matt 16:18–19

John 20:28

John 20:28

---

a. MS reads, "days."
b. The MS adds "about everything."

that we may proclaim him to all humanity, even as you informed us about the day of the investiture of all his fellow-angels that you created,[a] and also because if they hear about the day of his investiture, people will become afraid, repent and give charities and alms on the day of his remembrance, just as they do for Michael and Gabriel, and their souls will find mercy and rest in the day of your holy resurrection."

[8]The Savior, the treasury filled with every mercy and compassion, the one who loves what is good for his creature, did not want to vex us in anything that we asked. He said to us,[b] "O those that I have chosen out of the entire world, I will not hide anything from you, but I will inform you about how my Father enthroned him over the entire creation which he made, because I and my Father are one. [9]As Philip told me, 'Lord, instruct us about your Father and it is enough for us,' I told him, 'The whole time you were with me you did not know me, O Philip? The one who has seen me has seen my Father. Believe that I am in my Father and my Father in me. If not, believe in his deeds.' Now then, O my holy members, those that I have chosen out of the entire world, I will not hide anything from you.

John 10:30

John 14:8

John 14:9–11

The angel Muriel brings clay to create Adam

5 [1]"And it came to pass after my Father made the heaven, the earth and all those that are in them, he spoke and all came into existence—whether angel, or archangel, Cherubs and Seraphs, Thrones, Rulers and Powers, all the Dominions that are in heaven and the entire heavenly host. He also made the earth for the beasts, reptiles, cattle, birds and all those that move upon it, and he planted the Paradise in the eastern part. [2]My Father saw that the whole earth was deserted because no one worked it. My Father said, 'Let us make man according to our image and likeness in order to praise us continuously day and night and to be known that the hand of the Lord made all these, for I was before all these came into being.'

Gen 1:1–25

Gen 1:26

[3]"My Father commanded an angel, 'Go at my wish and my command to the land of Eden to bring me virgin earth so that I may make man according to our image and likeness to praise us continuously day and night.' And the angel went to the land of Eden according to the command of my Father. He stood upon the clay and stretched out his hand to take it to my Father. [4]Immediately the clay cried out saying with a great voice, 'I swear to you on the one who sent you to me, if you take me to him he shall mold me to become a man with a living soul and great sins will come to existence because of me. [5]There are many fornications, denunciations, envies, hates, and quarrels (that) will come to existence because of him. There are many murders and bloodshedding (that) will come to existence from him. [6]I will be thrown before my time to the dogs and pigs, in the wells, pits, and waters. Finally, after all these things, I will be thrown to punishments and I will be punished day and night. Let me go to rest and ease.'

---

a. This may be a reference to the *Investiture of Michael* (CPC 0488) and the *Investiture of Gabriel* (CPC 0378).

b. MS: "them."

[7]"When the angel of the Lord heard these things, he became afraid of my Father's name. He turned away and came to my Father. He said, 'My Lord, when I heard your frightful name I was not able to bring (the clay) to you.' [8]Immediately, he commanded the second angel and sent him to it, (then) the third until the seventh angel. They were not able to approach (the clay) because it swore to them with great frightening oaths.

[9]"When my Father saw that they were not able to bring it to him, he sent the angel Muriel to him, saying, 'Go at my command to the land of Eden and bring me virgin clay to mold from it a man according to my image and my likeness in order to praise us day and night.' [10]When the angel of the Lord went after it, he stood upon it with great power and assurance, at the command of the Lord. He stretched out his hand to take it. Immediately, the clay cried out with a great voice, 'I swear to you upon the one who created the heaven, the earth, and all those that are in them that you shall not approach me to take me to God.' [11]But the angel Muriel did not become afraid of the name of my Father when he heard it, nor did he have compassion for (the clay), but he approached it and grabbed it with firmness and cruelty. He brought it to my Father and he rejoiced over it.

Gen 1:26; 2:7

[12]"He took the clay from the hand of the angel and he made Adam according to our image and likeness. He left him lying for forty days and forty nights without giving him spirit and moaning over him every day, 'He will endure many sufferings if I give him spirit.' I said to my Father, 'Give him spirit, I pledge for him.' [13]My Father told me, 'If I give him spirit, my beloved Son, you will have to descend to the world and you will endure great sufferings for him until you save him and turn him to his initial state again.' I said to my Father, 'Give him spirit, I shall pledge for him and I shall descend to the world to fulfill your command.'

Rev 13:8

[14]"Wishing to give him spirit, he took the book and he wrote down his descendants who will enter the kingdom of heaven, as it is written, 'These are those whose names are written in the book of life from the foundation of the world.' And he gave him the spirit of life in this way: he blew three times into his face a breath of life saying, 'Live, live, live according to the type of my divinity!' [15]And in that moment he received life and became a living spirit according to the image and likeness of God. When Adam rose up, he threw himself down before the Father saying, 'My Lord and my God, you made me be out of nothing.'

Gen 2:7

John 20:28

[16]"Thus my Father installed him upon a great throne and put upon him a glorious crown and a kingly scepter. My Father ordered every heavenly host to come and worship him. Whether angel or archangel, the entire heavenly host came and worshipped, first God and then Adam saying, 'Greetings, image and likeness of God.'

The fall of the First-Creature

6 [1]"The order of the First-Creature arrived in its turn to worship him. My Father told him, 'You too, come to worship my image and likeness.' But a great pride and effrontery came upon him. He said, 'It is fitting for him to come and worship me because I existed before him.' [2]When my Father saw his great pride, that his malfeasance and entire mischief had become full, he ordered the entire heavenly hosts saying to them, 'Come and take the roll from the hand of the proud one, strip off his armor and throw him down to earth, for his time has

come.' ³Since he was the greatest of them all, being chief over them like a king that orders an army of soldiers and like a general, their names were written on his hand. Thus is this deceiver.

⁴"The (names of the) angels being written on his hand, all the angels surrounded him but could not take the roll from him. My Father ordered to bring a sharp knife and to cut him this side and that. (However,) what he had in the palm of his hand could not be taken away from him. ⁵Immediately, my Father ordered a great Cherub and he struck him and threw him down from heaven to earth because of his pride. He broke his wings and his rib and weakened him. He and those that he took with him became devils.

Adam and Eve in the garden

7 ¹"My Father made a throng of angels to take Adam to Paradise while singing before him. And they put him there and he remained to praise God. Adam was alone in Paradise for a hundred years. When the hundred years that Adam was in the Paradise of Delight were completed—he was staying there alone with the angels visiting him every day—, my Father said, 'It is not good that the man remains alone, but let us make for him a helper like him.' ²He brought a sleep over Adam and he slept. He took one of his ribs, filled it with flesh and made a woman according to Adam's model. When Adam woke up from his sleep, he saw her. He said, 'This is now bone of my bones and flesh (of my flesh). She will be called "woman" for she was taken out of her man.' ³For it was Adam who gave name to all cattle, beasts, birds, and all animals that move upon earth and even to those that are in waters. Adam was the one who named them all according to the command of my good Father.

⁴"During the two hundred years that Adam was with his wife Eve in the Paradise of Delight, they were virgins, being like the angels of God. But at the end of the two hundred years that they spent in the Paradise of Delight, Eve came walking near the hedge of the northern part of the Paradise to pick up fruits for the cattle and all the other animals. Because my Father asked them to feed (the animals), according to his command, they received their food from the hand of Adam and Eve.

⁵"The serpent also came, as usual, at the evening hour to feed himself. Because the serpent was like all beasts, he was walking on his legs. But the devil lived near the Paradise, lying in wait for them day and night. ⁶When he saw (Eve) alone, he entered into the serpent and said to himself, 'Behold, I found the opportunity. I will speak to her ear and I will see that I make her eat from the tree so that they will be thrown out from the Paradise for I was also thrown out because of them.' ⁷He said to her with the mouth of the serpent, 'Why do you not eat from the tree in the midst of Paradise like from all the trees, for its fruits are good?' But she said,ᵃ 'When eating, the Lord told us, eat from every tree of Paradise except the tree of knowledge of good and evil. In the day when you will eat from it, by dying you shall die.' ⁸The serpent told her, 'You will not die but you will be like gods and you will know good and evil and you will distinguish sweet from bitter. God spoke to you like this so that you should not eat and

Gen 2:18

Gen 2:21–23

Gen 2:20

Gen 3:3

---

a. MS: "he said."

Gen 3:4–5 become like gods.' And he did not cease to talk to her until he deceived her and she ate from the tree.

⁹"And immediately she became naked and she was aware that she was naked. She took fig leaves and covered her nakedness. Eve went to Adam but when Adam saw her naked, he was very sad. He was in a great affliction and cried abundantly. He said to her, 'Why did you become like this? Behold, from today we are mortal and the Lord will be angry at us and throw us out of Paradise.' ¹⁰But she told him, 'Come and eat. If God admonishes you, you will put everything upon me in front of him.' And thus Adam took and ate. He became naked and he knew immediately that he was naked. He covered his nakedness with fig

Gen 3:1–7 leaves.

¹¹"Straightaway, the voice of my Father reached him in Paradise, 'Adam, where are you?' He said, 'My Lord, when I heard your voice I became afraid and I hid myself, for I am naked.' My Father said to him, 'Who told you to eat from the tree so that you became naked?' He said, 'My Lord, the woman that you gave me as helper made me eat and I became naked.' My Father said to her, 'Why did you

Gen 3:8–13 do this?' She said, 'My Lord, the serpent deceived me. I ate to become like gods.'

¹²"My Father said to the serpent, 'Because you did this, cursed are you among all the beasts of the earth! You shall walk on your belly all the days of your life, you and your entire seed until all generations of the earth. You and all your descendants shall eat earth and ashes your entire lives.' And this is why he walks on his belly, as my Father decided for him. He said again to the woman, 'Because you did this, you shall beget your children in sorrow and moaning and you will return to your husband.'

¹³"And thus he turned to Adam and said to him, 'Cursed is the earth because of your deeds! You and all your descendants shall eat your bread with the sweat of your face. Behold, you are mortal from today because you are earth and you

Gen 5:5
Gen 3:14–19
Ps 107:10
will return to earth. You will live an earthly life for 930 years, then death will come upon you and you will return to the earth again. Your soul will be in hell and you will sit in gloomy darkness for 4,500 years.

The promise of salvation

8 ¹" 'In the 5,500th year, I will send my beloved Son to the world and he will dwell nine months in a virgin womb—this being Mary, the holy Virgin. She will bring

Matt 1:18–25; Luke 2:1–6
him forth to the world like a poor person and she will remain virgin as she was (before). He will be thirty-three-and-a-half years in the world and will experi-

Heb 4:15
ence everything human except sin. ²He will perform an innumerable multitude of miracles and wonders: he will raise the dead, throw out demons, cure the paralytics, make the lame walk, make the deaf hear, the dumb speak, clean the lepers and the withered hands, and open the eyes of the blind by the word of his

Matt 11:5//Luke 7:22
power. Briefly, innumerable are the wonders that he will make but despite all of these (miracles), they will not believe in him.

³" 'After all these things, they will rise against him, hand him over to death

Mark 15:1–14 par.; John 18:33–19:22
and give him to a governor, Pilate, to judge him because of you. He will be in the

Phil 2:7
form of a slave because of you. They will slap his face because of you, they will smite and disgrace him because of you, they will judge him like the temple robbers, they will lift him up on the wood of the cross between two thieves because

of you, they will put a crown of thorns upon his head, they will give him vinegar and gall to drink because of you, they will nail his hands and feet because of you. [4]He will give up his spirit on the cross and they will pierce his side with a spear so that water and blood will come out from it, which will cleanse the sins of the world. They will put him in a new tomb, he will rise from the dead on the third day and will descend to hell, crush the gates of copper, break the bolts of iron, and bring you up from the entire imprisonment in which you are.[a] [5]Because of you, O Adam, the Son of God will endure all these until he will save you and return you to Paradise once more, to the place that you left first, for he guaranteed for you while you were still clay, before he gave you spirit.'

Mark 15:15–41 par.; John 19:23–37

John 1:29; Matt 27:59

1 Pet 3:19–20; Acts Pil. B 21–24; Quest. Bart. 1:6–20; Bk. Bart 6:1–3

Muriel becomes Abbaton, the Angel of Death

9 [1]"I am the Son of God and I endured all these until I saved the human being from the hand of the devil, and you saw all these with your own eyes, O my holy apostles. And thus my Father threw out Adam and Eve from Paradise. He shut the gate and assigned a power of fire to guard the gate of Paradise so that no one could enter it until all the things that I told you would happen to Adam.

Gen 3:24

[2]"But the devil approached Adam outside Paradise. He said to him, 'Behold, O Adam, I was thrown out from my glory because of you. Behold, I caused you to be thrown out from the Paradise of Delight because you estranged me from my heavenly dwelling-place. Know that I will not cease to strive with you and all your descendants until I take them all down to hell with me.' When Adam heard these words, he was very afflicted and cried abundantly day and night.

[3]"My Father said to the angel Muriel, 'Behold, the man that I made according to my image has transgressed the command that I gave him. He ate from the tree and brought great damage upon all humanity. Therefore, I appoint you king over him, for you are the one who brought him to me on this day, the thirteenth of Hathor.

[4]" 'Your name will be frightful in the mouth of everyone, you shall be called Abbaton, the Angel of Death. Your likeness and your image will be dark, angry, and threatening for every being that dies.[b] Your eyes and your face will be like fiery wheels, which will continuously throw waves in front of you.[c] The sound of your nose will be like the sound of the fiery lake that burns with fire and sulfur. The roaring sound of your lips will be like the sound of seven thunders speaking in their tongues. Your head will be like the great pillars of fire from the top to the bottom. Your teeth will come out of your mouth half a cubit long. The fingers of your hands and the toes of your feet will be like sharp knives. [5]Seven heads will be on top of your head, changing their aspect and form. Their teeth will come out from their mouths two palms long, pointing towards the four parts of the world. You shall hang in the middle of the sky, sitting on your throne of fire. Your eyes will look at those upon the earth and even at those in the waters. Nothing will be hidden to you from the sky to the earth, from north to south

Rev 21:8

Rev 10:3–4

Exod 13:21

Rev 12:3; 13:1; 17:7

---

a. Chapter and verses divisions for the Bartholomew literature reflect the translations of Jean-Daniel Kaestli and Pierre Cherix in *EAC* 1:257–356.

b. Literally, "gives up his spirit."

c. MS: "me."

and east to west, in all the creation that I made. ⁶Not a single person shall die until they see you. You will not be compassionate towards the small or the great, but you shall carry them all away without mercy. The powers will submit to you so that you can send them after every soul, and they will frighten (people) by changing their forms. When their life will end, you will appear so that they can see you. When they see your face, their souls will not stay inside them for a single moment but they will die. You will remain thus to reign over them until the time that I appointed for the world to end.'

⁷"When the angels saw him, they were agitated against each other saying, 'Woe, woe to the sons of men who will be born in the world! For behold, even we, who are incorporeal, were destroyed by fear.' ⁸Then, Abbaton, the Angel of Death, bowed down before my Father saying, 'My Lord, behold, you made me more fearful than all the angels. Now then, my Lord, I beseech you and I demand from your goodness that if the sons of men who will be born in the world will listen about the way that you made me fearful and disturbing, they will become afraid and give charities and alms in my name, copy the book concerning the day on which you invested me, showing forth my memorial and looking after mercy and rest for their souls. ⁹Now then, my Lord, let your mercy befall them and give me power over them to take them to the places of rest, the dwelling-place of all those who rejoice, for they celebrate my memorial upon earth as they do to all my fellow-angels. Verily, my Lord, let your mercy fall upon them.'

¹⁰"My Father said, 'I tell you, O angel Abbaton, that all those who fear you, who give charities and alms in your name, repent and copy the book of your investiture, this being on the thirteenth of Hathor, the day when I invested you over Adam because of his disobedience, I will write their names in the book of

Rev 3:5

life and I will grant them to you in my kingdom and they will not experience any torture. And you will not visit them in this frightful form, but you shall visit them being tender towards them until you bring them out of the body. ¹¹I will give you power over them to take them to the places of rest, the dwelling-place of

Ps 86:7 LXX

all those who rejoice, for I am a good God, compassionate towards my creature.' Then the angel Abbaton bowed down before my Father saying, 'I will cleanse them, O Lord, my God and my King, for all the things that you have done for me.'

¹²"Now then, O my holy apostles, behold, I informed you how my Father made Abbaton frightful and disturbing to the entire creation that he made because of the transgression of Adam and Eve. Proclaim him to all humanity."

The final judgment

John 20:28

10 ¹Saint John the Virgin replied saying, "My Lord and my God, the one who has purified me to him and set all my thoughts to gather to him, the one who kept

Acts John 113

me from marriage: in the day of your resurrection, you will gather your entire creation to the Valley of Jehoshaphat so that each one may receive according to

Joel 3:2

what he did, either good or bad, while Abbaton, the Angel of Death, will also come that day in such (terrifying) forms. If so, my Lord, no single soul will be able to stand by your frightful tribunal. Behold, even we have been destroyed by fear hearing these things from you."

²But the Savior smiled, laughing in John's face. He said to him, "O my be-

loved John, the one who threw himself upon my breast because of the purity of his heart, the purity of his holy body and his virginity. Do you not know that, because the old things have passed away, on the day of my holy resurrection they neither marry, nor are given in marriage, nor will there be death, save the second death for those who will arrive at it? ³In the day of my holy resurrection, I will come on the clouds of the sky so that every eye can see me. And all the tribes and languages will lament, for hundreds of hundreds and thousands of thousands of angels will precede me while my cross will walk before me like the ensigns before their king, just as I told you, 'The Son of Man will come in his glory and in his Father's and all his holy angels will be with him.'

⁴"I will command my great holy archangel Michael to blow the trumpet in the Valley of Jehoshaphat so that the dead will rise incorruptible. No soul will remain upon earth without resurrection from Adam, the first man, until the last man that will be born in the world. They will all come to the Valley of Jehoshaphat, so that everyone may receive for the deeds done in his body, according to what he has done, whether good or bad, standing in fear and trembling and looking for the mercy of my Father.

⁵"But you, O my beloved John, you will not die until the thrones are prepared on the day of my holy resurrection. For the thrones of glory will descend from heaven and you will sit upon them while I will sit in your midst. All the saints will see the honor that I shall give you, O my beloved John. I will command the angel Abbaton and he will come to you in that day without any frightful form; rather he shall come to you with a gentle face like Michael to take your soul and bring it to me. Your body will never stay in a tomb nor will the earth ever be upon it. All the saints will be amazed at you because they will not be able to judge before you judge them. ⁶For three and a half hours you will be dead, sleeping on your throne while the entire creation will be looking at you. I will return again your soul to your body and you shall rise, wrapped in a robe of glory[a] like someone who has risen in the bridal chamber. You will judge the entire world as I covenanted with you that, 'you will sit upon the thrones and judge the twelve tribes of Israel.' ⁷And I said with the mouth of Paul, 'We will judge angels' before arriving to those of the world. For on that day, the entire creation will stand in fear and trembling. I will command them to separate from each other like a shepherd that separates the sheep from the goat, the righteous to the right, the sinners to the left, and no one will speak until the Ancient of His Days orders him. ⁸I will look upon my entire creation and, when I see that it is going to destruction, I will cry up to my Father, 'My Father, what is the profit of my blood if it goes to destruction?' Immediately, the voice of my Father will reach me from the seventh heaven and no one will hear it except me alone because I and my Father are one, 'The power belongs to you, my Son, to do whatever pleases you with your creation.' And that day I will say rejoicing, 'You tore off my sackcloth, you girded me with gladness so that my right hand will bless you because I am not sorrowed.'

⁹"That day I shall tell you, O my holy apostles and all my saints, whether

Margin references:
John 13:23; 21:20

2 Cor 5:17
Mark 12:25 par.

Mark 8:38 par.

2 Cor 5:10

John 21:22–23
Matt 19:28//Luke 22:30

Isa 61:10; *1 En.* 62:15–16

Matt 19:28//Luke 22:30
1 Cor 6:3

Matt 25:32–33
Dan 7:9

John 10:30

Ps 30:11

---

a. See further Sebastian Brock, "The Robe of Glory: A Biblical Image in the Syriac Tradition," *The Way* 39 (1999): 247–59.

angels, or archangels, or prophets, or the righteous, but especially my Virgin mother and my great archangels Michael and Gabriel, I shall tell them, 'No one who celebrated your memorial upon the earth, giving bread in your name, will be left to go to destruction.' And immediately all the saints will approach them and each one will seize his own. Everyone who has done your will upon earth will be returned next to the others who are on the right.

10"Then the others, being afflicted, will cry out with a loud, weeping voice saying, 'Merciful Lord, the Son of the Merciful one, forgive us too!' In that moment, the Son of God will weep over them and say to them, 'Wait until I talk to my Father.' In that instant, my Father will close the gate of heaven and he will withdraw. Then I will tell them, 'My Father did not want to forgive you.' And they will cry out even more, 'Forgive us, for the devil did not let us repent. Had we known that these things would happen, we would have repented even unto shedding (our own) blood.'

11"And I will curse Satan that day and I will have him seized and bound with unbreakable bonds. And the false prophet who deceives all the nations, and the Antichrist, the son of perdition, and all those who followed them will be thrown in the world into the fiery lake that burns with fire and sulfur. And they will never rest, day and night, nor will their worm die and their fire be quenched.

margin: Rev 20:1–3
John 17:12; 2 Thess 2:3; 1 John 2:18, 22; 4:2; 2 John 7
Rev 20:10; 21:8; Isa 66:24; Mark 9:44, 48

The commissioning of the apostles

11 ¹"Now then, O my holy apostles, behold: I informed you about everything that you asked from me, about the way Adam transgressed, so that death came into the world, and how the angel Abbaton became king over the entire creation. Now proclaim the day of his memorial so that the sons of men will be afraid and repent. Tell all humanity, saying, 'the one who will do good, for a resurrection of life, the one who will do evil, for a resurrection of judgment.'"

margin: John 5:29

²Then the apostles worshipped the Savior saying, "Our Lord and our God, you filled us with every blessing for you did not vex us in anything we asked from you." The Savior greeted them and the angels carried him to heaven as (the apostles) were looking after him. The apostles also greeted him and each one went to proclaim as he commanded them.

Exhortation

12 ¹Behold, we told you these things, O my beloved, as we found them in the library of Jerusalem, these things that our holy fathers, the apostles, instituted and placed there for the believers and for the salvation of the unbelievers. Now then, my beloved, let us be zealous in giving charities and alms on the day of the memorial of Abbaton, the Angel of Death, each one according to his power. ²Remember that it is written in the Gospel that our Savior blessed the poor woman who threw in two mites rather than those who threw all of them in the treasury. These, he said, threw all of them out of their abundance, but she, for her part, gave her entire poverty. ³May God, the one who made us worthy to gather today in this place to commemorate Abbaton, the Angel of Death, the one whom God appointed king over us, make us worthy to gather to his heavenly kingdom. O my beloved, we all need the mercy of God, as a wise man said, "the way I want to live, I wish to make everybody live." ⁴And O my beloved, may he make us wor-

margin: Mark 12:41–44//Luke 21:1–4

thy to listen to the blessed voice filled with every gladness, "Come, you that are blessed by my Father, inherit the kingdom prepared for you from the foundation of the world." Through the grace and philanthropy of our Lord Jesus Christ, the one through whom is the glory, to him and his good Father and Holy Spirit, forever and ever, Amen!

Matt 25:34

Appendix: *Kitāb al-īḍāḥ* 9

Introduction

In the name of the Father, the Son, and the Holy Spirit; One God. Amen. An article in which (he) determines what is the death that the Lord trampled on the cross, and refutes what was compiled by the one who said that it is a holy appointed angel of God that causes people to die. In peace of God. Amen.

Invest. Abbat. 1–4

The sermon of Theophilus and the book he discovered

[1]You mentioned, O beloved, that people alleged that the reason for death is a holy angel. God assigned him to put people to death. And you mentioned that people arranged a feast for that angel and wrote a *maimar*[a] for his sake and attributed it to Theophilus,[b] Patriarch of Alexandria. They included in it that Apa Theophilus found an ancient book about the holy apostles. They narrate in it that, "when we assembled with the Lord after his resurrection, we asked him to tell us about the Angel of Death, and why did he give him power over humans?"

Invest. Abbat. 5:1–6:3

God sends angels to bring clay to create Adam

The Lord told them that he created the heavens, the earth, the seas, the plants, the sun, the moon, the planets, the sea creatures, the beasts, the livestock, and the creepers, and then, when he wanted to create man, he sent one of the archangels to the earth to bring him a lump of clay in order to create man out of it. The clay swore an oath in the name of God saying, "Do not take me to God to create out of me a man, who would commit sins: fornicate, steal, kill, and make God angry." The angel was frightened of the oath. He left the clay and came back to God and told him what happened. God sent another angel. The clay did the same with him.

[2]Six angels were sent and the clay swore to them and they were frightened of the oath and left it (alone). When the seventh angel—he is called Muriyal, as they alleged—was sent to take the lump of clay, the clay swore to him by God. The angel did not care about the oath, and took the lump of clay to God. God said to him, "Because you obeyed me and did not consider the oath of the lump

---

a. *Maimar* is a Syriac word that means speech, discourse, and sermon. When used in Arabic, *maimar* is usually translated as homily, but it is also used to describe many kinds of literary texts, especially hagiographic texts. See Georg Graf, *Verzeichnis arabischer kirchlicher Termini* (CSCO 147; Leuven: Durbecq, 1954), 110.

b. A corruption of Timothy due to the similar renderings of the names in Arabic. See the introduction, p. 528.

of clay, I give you power over it forever, to put it to death." Immediately, God changed the glorious, beautiful appearance of that angel into an ugly, terrifying one. Then he made the human body from the clay and said, "Who ensures that man and guarantees all sins he will commit, so that I (may) create a soul in him?" Man stayed like this, as clay without soul, for forty days until his guarantor came. The soul was created. When he created him, he ordered all the angels to prostrate to him.

The fall of Satan

All of them prostrated but one disobeyed and did not prostrate to Adam. He ordered him to be dropped. He is Satan. ³Adam was left in Paradise for around a hundred years, and then he created Eve out of him. Adam and Eve spent another hundred years (in Paradise), and then they transgressed and fell down.

Invest. Abbat. 6:4–7:13

Refutation of the sermon

⁴You mentioned this *maimar,* which tells about that angel, his investiture, and that he is able to put people to death. The refutation of this *maimar,* O beloved, is clear to everybody who knows the Bible and who is mindful. Its falsehood is clear to the ignorant, let alone to the mindful. Anyone who believes it has neither mind nor knowledge. Its refutation and falsehood start with its saying that (God) sent his angels, one by one, to bring him a lump of clay in order to create man. He restricted God in a certain place and he impounded him about it! And God needed to send someone to bring him a lump of clay! (If) it is saying that the clay spoke and adjured the angels not to take it to God to create out of it man, who would kill, fornicate, and make God angry, then the clay is more experienced than God and the angels, and aware of the unseen! It speaks and foretells!

⁵It is known that the clay is inanimate, mindless, and motionless. Even if this is so, then the author of the *maimar* should mention along with it who brought the clay (which is one of the four natures from which man was created) to God (who brought to him the other three natures: fire, water and air) and how these were brought, just as he mentioned the coming of the clay. It is most clear that this is impossible, because the Book of Creation, which was written by Moses, testifies that God took the clay from the ground. It does not say that he sent someone to bring it, and then created man. The word "man" refers to the whole man: flesh, bones, blood, soul, mind, and utterance. It is not as the *maimar* recounts, that he was created as soulless clay and in such way he stayed many days; rather, he was created complete since the beginning. Then he breathed into his nostrils the breath of life that is the grace of the Holy Spirit, by which he is connected with God, and his soul became alive by God. This grace left him at the transgression. Also, the Bible witnesses that on the same day, God caused a deep sleep to fall upon him and formed Eve out of him.

Gen 2:7

Gen 2:21–22

⁶They transgressed and he caused them to fall down before the evening of that day, not as the author of the book deceives that he lived a hundred years in Paradise before the creation of Eve, and after her creation, they lived another hundred years before Adam's transgression. As for his saying that the angels prostrated to Adam, this is not satisfactory to the believers at all to mention because it is a blasphemy upon God and the angels (to say), he made them prostrate

to the created but not to the creator. And his saying that the devil transgressed and (his refusal) to prostrate to Adam made him fall down, by this the author of that *maimar* invalidates both the Old and New Testaments, because both testaments agreed that the devil fell down on Sunday, on which he was created, six days before the formation of Adam. The reason for his falling down is his not sharing with the other angels in praising God and he was arrogant and (wished to) imitate God. The prophet Isaiah witnesses saying, "How you are fallen, O Day Star, who was above all the stars!" But he became arrogant and said, "I will ascend to my throne above the clouds and make myself like the Most High."

Isa 14:12

[7]The prophet declared that the reason for his fall is his arrogance but not what is told by the author of this *maimar* due to his inability. If Adam was created before the falling of Satan, as that author stated, then God need not have created Adam. On the contrary, the truth is what all the holy books of God declare, that when Satan fell down from his rank as an archangel—together with all his host to whom he was a leader, due to their obedience to him in stopping God's praise, just like him—God created Adam in order to create offspring (in place) of the host who fell down with the devil, and to raise them to the rank of archangels from which the devil and his host fell down. For this reason, the devil envied them: for their rank. He deceived them until they became arrogant like him and asked for divinity. As a result, God cast them down like him, and put on them the same punishment forever because their sins were the same.

[8]The Son of God gave himself for them, and endured the punishment that is obligatory to them. He released them through his blood to the state for which they were created. If what the author of that book said is correct, then Adam was created and fell down for no reason. Thus the incarnation of the Son of God, his crucifixion, and all that he did are nonsense and needless. The author of that *maimar* said that God gave the one he called Muriyal the power to kill man because he dared to bring him the clay. He changed his beautiful, delightful appearance into an ugly, terrifying one that kills humans. So, why did God need to create the one for whom he created death even before he created man?

Thus the books that witness that God had created man to stay eternally are refuted! Why would he create (man) to stay eternally yet also create the one who will put him to death and finish him? All these, O beloved, declare the falsehood and refutation of that *maimar*. It is a pseudo writing in (the name of) the holy man and father. Many pseudo *maimars* were refuted by the holy man Apa John, bishop of Paralos.[a] He took them out of the holy places and burnt them.

The true nature of death

[9]It is wrong to say that one single angel put all people to death, for people do not die in one single place or in one single home. Instead it happens that in one hour, many people die all over the earth. If he who put all of them to death is one single angel, then he is a god and not an angel, because he is stretched over the whole earth. No one is able to fill the whole earth except for God alone, who

---

a. See Arnold van Lantschoot, "Fragments coptes d'une homélie de Jean de Parallos contre les livres hérétiques," in *Miscellanea Giovanni Mercati* vol. 1: *Bibbia. Letteratura cristiana antica* (Studi e testi 121; Vatican: Biblioteca Apostolica, 1946), 297 n. 7.

is everywhere and nowhere is empty of him. All the angels are limited and restricted. They move from one place to another. When one of them comes to one place, the other place is free of him. It is strange that a dark angel with a black face can be seen all over the countries of the world! If he is enlightened, perhaps that might happen because of the spread of his light like the sun and the moon.

How bad is it to say that the holy angel of God is an angel of death? How an angel of life puts (someone) to death? Death does not belong to God. Death came by sin, not by God's will. Sin came from the serpent. The serpent is the devil. Thus death is from the devil but not from God. From the devil, death came because of sin. By death came hell. There are two deaths: death of the body and death in hell, and the reason for both is sin. The reason of sin is the devil, who is the serpent.

Paul's views of death and sin

[10]The apostle Paul said, "*Sin came into the world through one man, and death came through sin.*" Death has reigned. Sin is death. And both came through Satan. Our Lord Jesus Christ said to the Jews in the Gospel of John, "You desire to kill me just like your father, the devil. *He was a murderer from the beginning.*" Our Lord Jesus Christ testified that Satan is still killing people. Here, he means not only killing the souls in hell but also killing bodies, for he said, "You desire to kill me just as your father kills people." It is known that the Jews killed Christ, our Lord, by killing the body only. It is clear from the Lord's speech that the death of bodies comes through the devil and his wicked host but not through God and his pure angels.

Rom 5:12

John 8:44

[11]The apostle Paul said too, "*Sin exercised dominion in death.*" Sin is the death of the soul in hell. The death that reigned through it is the death of the body, for the death of the body is the reason for the descending of the soul into hell. If death reigned through sin, then sin, no doubt, came through Satan. Now, Satan is the authority of death and sin, for both are in his hand and came through him.

Rom 5:21

The words of Basil of Caesarea

Apa Basil says in the prayer of peace in his liturgy, "O God, the Great and the Eternal, who formed man in incorruption, when death entered into the world by the envy of the devil, you destroyed it by the life-giving manifestation of your Only-Begotten Son, our Lord and God, Jesus Christ."[a]

[12]O beloved, look to the speech of this saint; God created man in incorruption. On the contrary, the author of that *maimar* said that God, before creating Adam, gave authority to the one who will put him to death and corruption. The saint declared that when he formed him in incorruption, death came upon him not through the devil but through God. The saint said in the liturgical prayers, "Our Lord, Jesus Christ, incarnated and became man. He gave himself up for our salvation to the death that reigned over us through sin."[b]

Did our Lord Jesus Christ give himself up for us to his angel? The one that is

---

a. See Khalil Samir, "La version arabe du Basile alexandrin (Codex Kacmarcik)," *OCP* 44 (1978): 342–90 at 368.

b. Samir, "La version arabe," 372–73.

obedient to his orders? Did he save us from his angel? Did his angel reign over us through sin? It is proved that the one who reigned over us through sin is the devil. He reigned over us through our obedience to him. The Son of God gave himself for us to save us, for he demanded back from (the devil) the indemnity of his killing, when he gave himself to him and saved us from his hands by his death; he redeemed us by his blood and he took us in his indemnity.

Death is the enemy of God

[13]Thus death is from the devil and his impure host and not from God nor any of his pure angels. If death is a holy angel and obedient to God, then Christ's crucifixion and his death are ineffectual, for he is able to save us from his angel who obeys his order without putting himself to death for us and redeeming us by himself. The prophet witnesses that death fought Christ, and Christ won over it. He said, "Death is swallowed up in victory." "O Death, where is your sting? O Hell, where is your power?" Is death an obedient angel to God while fighting the Son of God? Does the prophet say that an obedient angel is swallowed up in victory? Will a prophet of God gloat about an angel of God saying, "Death, where is your sting?"

Isa 25:8
Hos 13:14

It is clear now that the death of the body and the death (that is in) hell are enemies of God. So when the prophet of God gloated saying, "O Death, where is your sting? O Hell, where is your power?" with its sting, he[a] means the ugliness of his appearance, by which he attacks the hearts of the bodies like stings of thorns. It frightens them until their blood dries and they die due to the death of their blood because the soul of every living creature (is in) his blood, as God told Noah in the Book of Creation.

Gen 9:5

Body and soul at death

[14]When their blood dries, their reasoning mindful souls have no place in their bodies, for bodies are rough, but souls are subtle. God, the Creator, connects the rough bodies with the subtle souls by blood, which is between them, because blood has both subtleness that suits soul and roughness that suits body. When man fears of the ugly appearance of the angels of death—I mean Satan's soldiers, who appear to him on the day of his death—his thirst increases. Then, due to his great fear, his blood dries in his body. When his blood dries, the soul has no place in the rough body. When the soul leaves the body, its angel, who is appointed over it during its life, either from God or Satan, receives it.

Because when God created the angels, as foremost of what he created in heaven and earth, Satan was the leader of the first and highest rank. He became arrogant and fell down together with all the host that was with him. Therefore, God created Adam and Eve to compete by them, and by those who were created out of them, the high rank from which Satan fell down.

[15]Satan knew this. He worked against (Adam and Eve) until they committed sin like him. They fell under his power. They were cast down from Paradise to the earth, upon which he fell down. At this moment (Satan) was appointed over (Adam) together with two of his soldiers, the impure spirits, the angels of death,

Gen 3:23–24

---

a. MS: I.

who fell down with him. When they (Adam and Eve) have sex like animals and give birth to children, he appointed an impure spirit over every one of their children. For if the parents are his slaves, then their children are the same. This impure spirit, which is appointed over man, stays with him until the day of his death. When the ugly appearance of the impure spirit, which is appointed over him, is revealed, immediately his fear goes up, his thirst increases, his blood dries, and his soul leaves his body. Then the impure spirit takes it down into hell, which is below.

Satan at the birth of Christ

Humans stayed like this for 5,500 years until Christ, the Son of God, was born from the pure Virgin Mary without a human relation. When he was born, no one of the impure spirits, who used to be appointed over the newly born, was able to approach the door of the cave where he was born, due to the great number of the heavenly host that were around it.

[16]They hurried back to their leader, the anti(Christ), the liar, and told him. He fears the prophecies, with which the prophets announced that the Son of God will come and save Adam and his offspring out of him. When his soldiers told him about the great number of angels that were around the cave where he was born, he became afraid. He knew that the newborn was the one whose name the angels announced. He hurried to the cave. God, who came to set the secret for our salvation, intended to hide himself from him in order that he not know that he is the Son of God. He indicated to all the angels to leave heaven. He moved the heart of his mother to wrap him in rags and to put him in a manger. When the Impure reached the cave, he did not see any of the angels, whom his soldiers saw. (Satan) saw the Lord in this poor state. He immediately doubted. He thought that he is not God but a weak man. He left him.

[17]He moved King Herod to kill him in order to be relieved of his fear. When Joseph and the Virgin Mary fled to Egypt, his fear was removed. (God) made sure that (Jesus) was a weak man; if he were God, he would have had no need to flee. God dealt with him in the same way for the thirty years that he lived on earth. He neither showed him his ability, nor revealed his power in order not to be recognized.

The temptation in the wilderness

He was baptized in the Jordan by John. John testified that he is the Son of God, he saw the Holy Spirit descending like a dove on him, and he heard the Father saying, "You are my beloved son, with him I am well pleased." Satan recognized that he is the Son of God and was frightened of him. When God knew this, he left to the desert where he fasted for forty days and forty nights. Satan saw him fasting and praying, and doubted in him. He said: If he is God, he would not need to fast nor pray. God called him son just as when he called Israel his son, though he is not his natural son.

[18]During the three years in which God revealed his glory after his baptism, God hid his likeness. He did not perform any miracle indicating his power without also showing weakness in order to conceal himself from Satan. For Satan doubted very much and was unsettled about him. He moved the hearts of the

Luke 2:13–14

Luke 2:11

Matt 2:13–18

John 1:34

Mark 1:10–11 par.

Jewish high priests to kill him, so that he could take him down into hell just as he did with all the sons of Adam, and to be relieved.

The crucifixion

When he was struck, hung on the cross, and his hands and legs were nailed, Satan watched him while he was in this weakness. He became sure that he was merely a weak man. As (Satan) was aware that none of his soldiers was able to kill (Jesus), because they were not able to be appointed to him on the day of his birth, as they used to be appointed to the newly born sons of Adam, he came by himself, namely the evil one, to show his ugly terrifying appearance to him, to make him afraid, to dry his blood due to the fear and thirst, and to put him to death.

He came and stood up in front of the cross of God at the ninth hour of Friday just as God told his disciples on Thursday's eve: "*The ruler of this world is*
John 14:30
coming. He has no power over me"—he means he is not able to kill him[a]—"*So*
John 14:31
that the world may see that I love my Father, and that I am doing as I am ordered by the Father." He means he gives his soul by his own free will for the sake of his[b] Father, who desired to give him for the salvation of the world from out of (Satan's) hands.

[19]When the evil one revealed his ugly appearance to God, God looked at him without fear, and his blood did not dry. He realized that he is the Son of God and fled. Jesus Christ, the almighty God, he who set the providence, looked at him while fleeing, and then decided to continue his deception that he prepared for the salvation of the world. He cried out with a loud voice saying, "*My God, my*
Mark 15:34//Matt
27:46
God, why have you forsaken me?" Satan heard him saying these words, and again he doubted, thinking that he is a weak man. Though he was hesitating, he came back to him bravely. God desired to remove his hesitation, to make him doubt-
John 19:28
less and fearless when he came to him. He said, "*I am thirsty.*" When the evil one heard this, he became sure that he was a weak man and that he was afraid of him. The evidence of his fear is his thirst. Immediately, he approached him boldly and doubtless. When he reached him, God let his human soul leave his body by his own free will without the dryness of his blood.

The Harrowing of Hell

[20]As he said in his holy Gospel, "*I lay down my life in order to take it up again. No one takes it from me, but I lay it down of my own accord. I have power to lay it*
John 10:17–18
down, and I have power to take it up again," he laid his soul down by his power without the dryness of his blood in order to fulfill the deception on the evil one that he had killed him. Then (Jesus) demanded his indemnity out of him. He bound (Satan), took him down to the depths of hell, and tied him with the bonds that are not to be detached. He freed Adam together with his offspring, whom
1 Pet 3:19–20; *Acts Pil.*
B 21–24; *Quest. Bart.*
1:6–20; *Bk. Bart.* 6:1–3
Satan ruled through their obedience to him, took them up out of his prison, and released them out of his hands justly as indemnity for his murder. The proof of his death without the dryness of his blood is that, when he was wounded in his

---

a. MS: me.
b. MS: my.

side, an hour and a half after his death, water and blood flowed out. Then his John 19:34
blood returned to his body. His soul returned to his body on the third day. He
resurrected from death. He appeared to his disciples. He taught them how to
practice baptism, with which they save whoever is under the power of the impure spirits, the angels of death, who are assigned to all the newly born of earth.

Teaching on the Holy Spirit and the impure spirit

[21]He taught them to invite whoever wants to be a believer to the holy church,
and ask the Father through the Son to cast out the impure spirit that is appointed
upon him since the day of his birth. Then they should turn his face towards the
west to repudiate Satan and all his soldiers. By this, the impure spirit assigned to
him from Satan, leaves. They should turn (the new believer's) face back to the
east to accept Christ and to believe in him. Then they ask the Father through the
Son to let the Holy Spirit come on the water, in which they baptize him in the
name of the Father, the Son, and the Holy Spirit, which was breathed in Adam's
face by God at the time of his creation, and left him when he transgressed. Jesus Gen 2:7
Christ brings (the Holy Spirit) back into the believers in baptism.

He makes it dwell in them to save them from the impure spirits, which work
against them because they were cast out of them. As long as the baptized confesses that Christ is the Son of God, the Holy Spirit does not leave him, (he remains) together with a heavenly angel of Christ that was appointed to him at the
time of his baptism, to protect him. This angel stays protecting the believer until
God wants him to die. His blood decreases, he sees the ugly appearance of the
impure spirits, of which the atmosphere is filled, he fears, his blood dries, and
then his soul leaves his body. This heavenly angel, who was with (the soul) since
the day of baptism, receives it, and takes it to the place that it deserves.

[22]If the baptized repudiates the Son of God, the Holy Spirit, and the heavenly
angel that protect him, they leave him. The impure spirit, which was cast out of
him, is not satisfied to go back to him alone, but it goes to collect seven other
spirits more evil than itself, and they enter and dwell in this disbeliever. Therefore, the last state of this person is worse than his first, as mentioned in the holy
Gospel. He should believe this and not believe in the sayings of the liar author Matt 12:45//Luke 11:26
of that *maimar.*

These are the testimonies, O beloved, from the prophets and the holy gospel.
He who has a mind, who has knowledge of the Scriptures, should not believe
that the holy angels of God are those who put people to death. Because death is
terror, as the prophet David said in his Psalms, "Death's terrors fell upon me." Ps 55:5
The holy angels of God have no terror. Our father, Antony,[a] the one who clothed
the Spirit, witnesses saying, "The angels do not fear anybody to whom they appear; on the contrary they remove his fear just like the angel who appeared to
Zechariah and called him saying, 'O Zechariah, do not be afraid.' The same was Luke 1:13
said to the Virgin Mary: 'Do not be afraid, O Mary'; to the shepherds: 'Fear not, Luke 1:30
for I bring you good news of great joy'; and to the women who came to the sep- Luke 2:10
ulcher of our Lord Jesus Christ: 'Do not be afraid.'" Matt 28:5

---

a. See Albert Haase, trans., *Athanasius: The Life of Antony* (Classics in Spiritual Formation;
Downers Grove, Ill.: InterVarsity, 2012), 53.

²³Saint Antony says that all kinds of fear come from the impure spirits.[a] He made it clear that the angels of God cause no fear. David said that death is terror. As the angels cause no fear, then fear is not a killer, but both death and fear are from the impure spirits, which are the enemies (of humans), and from them the Son of God saved us when he came, was crucified, died in place of us, asked them for the indemnity of his death, and took us in his indemnity away from them.

Paul in his letter to the Hebrews explains that Satan has power over death, and Christ saved us through his death. He says about Christ, "*Through death he might destroy the one who has the power of death, that is,* Satan, *and free those* Heb 2:14–15 *who all their lives were held in slavery by the fear of death.*" By this Paul makes it clear that Satan is the one who has the power of death, and God stopped it through his death. By his power he redeemed those who believe in him. (Paul explains) that death is fear; consequently, it is clear now that whoever says that death comes from a pure angel is a liar.

²⁴Paul testifies that death is Christ's enemy in his letter to the Corinthians, in which he proves the resurrection of the dead. He says, "Christ is the first to resurrect, *then at his coming those who belong to Christ. Then comes the end, when he hands over the kingdom to God the Father, after he has destroyed every ruler, and every authority, and power. For he must reign until he has put all his* 1 Cor 15:23–26 *enemies under his feet. The last enemy to be destroyed is death.*" By saying that, "*Then comes the end, when he delivers the kingdom to God the Father, after he has destroyed every ruler, and every authority, and power,*" who are the soldiers of Satan, I mean that they are the ones who kill people. When he raises the ones who killed him and destroys their power, the kingship becomes in the hands of God, the Father, he who raises the ones who killed him, his enemies, as (Paul) says: "*the last enemy to be destroyed is death.*" If Paul says that death is Christ's enemy, how does he who has no mind say that it comes from the holy angels?

Satan speaks through the *Investiture of Abbaton*

²⁵It is proved that Satan, who has many frauds, is the one who speaks (in the tongue of) the author of that *maimar*. It is his trick to make people arrange a feast for him and to let them present sacrifices to him. For who will celebrate and sacrifice to the name of the angel of death, when the angel of death is no one but Satan? Satan did this. It is his fraud. He cheated people in some parts of the land of Egypt, but neither in the entire land of Egypt, nor the whole lands of Christianity, is there one who makes it or says it. No one of all languages and tongues knows this. It is a mere tradition in all the churches of believers to draw his painting with his terrifying appearance and hideous manifestation together with his impure soldiers (standing) around him, ready to torture, in order that the believers fear them, care about performing good deeds in order to be saved from their hands, and praise the Son of God who redeemed them in his blood.

Glory, praise, and dignity are to him, and to his Father, the merciful, and to his Holy Spirit, the life-giving, and the consubstantial. Now, in every time, forever and ever. Amen.

---

a. Haase, trans., *Athanasius*, 53.

Index of Modern Authors

Citations to footnotes are represented by superscript letters and numbers.

Index of Scripture and Other Ancient Texts